# *Traditions in*
# LITERATURE

**AMERICA READS**                    **CLASSIC EDITION**

AMERICA READS

CLASSIC EDITION

**BEGINNINGS** IN LITERATURE
Alan L. Madsen
Sarah Durand Wood
Philip M. Connors

**DISCOVERIES** IN LITERATURE
L. Jane Christensen
Edmund J. Farrell

**EXPLORATIONS** IN LITERATURE
Nancy C. Millett
Raymond J. Rodrigues

**PATTERNS** IN LITERATURE
Edmund J. Farrell
Ouida H. Clapp
Karen J. Kuehner

**TRADITIONS** IN LITERATURE
Helen McDonnell
James E. Miller, Jr.
Russell J. Hogan

**THE UNITED STATES** IN LITERATURE
*The Red Badge of Courage* edition
*Three Long Stories* edition
James E. Miller, Jr.
Kerry M. Wood
Carlota Cárdenas de Dwyer

**ENGLAND** IN LITERATURE
*Macbeth* edition
*Hamlet* edition
John Pfordresher
Gladys V. Veidemanis
Helen McDonnell

**CLASSICS** IN WORLD LITERATURE
Kerry M. Wood
Helen McDonnell
John Pfordresher
Mary Alice Fite
Paul Lankford

The authors and editors wish to thank the following consultants for reading and teaching editorial material and proposed selections for America Reads.
■ Barbara E. Anderson, Junior Level Coordinator and Teacher, James B. Conant High School, Hoffman Estates, Illinois
■ Anita Arnold, Chairman, English Department, Thomas Jefferson High School, San Antonio, Texas
■ Pat Dudley, Principal, Jane Long Elementary School, Abilene ISD, Abilene, Texas
■ Dr. V. Pauline Hodges-McLain, Coordinator, Language Arts, Jefferson County Public Schools, Golden, Colorado
■ Rance Howe, English/Language Arts Consultant K-12, Anoka-Hennepin ISD 11, Coon Rapids, Minnesota
■ Lisbeth Johnson, English Teacher, Capital High School, Olympia, Washington
■ Daniel Lane, Supervisor of Humanities, Holmdel Twp. Public Schools, Holmdel, New Jersey
■ May Lee, English Teacher, Baldwin Senior High School, Baldwin, New York
■ Richard T. Martin, English Department Chairman, Burrillville Junior-Senior High School, Harrisville, Rhode Island
■ Barbara McCormick, Systemwide Chairman of English, Greenville Public Schools, Greenville, Mississippi
■ James McCullough, English Teacher, Carmel High School, Mundelein, Illinois
■ Cathy Nufer, Teacher, Grade 6, Elm School, Hinsdale, Illinois
■ Marlyn Payne, Teacher, Grade 7, Nichols Middle School, Evanston, Illinois
■ Sally P. Pfeifer, English Department Chair, Lewis and Clark High School, Spokane, Washington
■ James B. Phillips, Instructor in English and Reading, Norwood Senior High School, Norwood, Massachusetts
■ John Pratt, Language Arts Chairperson, Edison High School, Stockton, California
■ Cora Wolfe, English Department Chairperson, Antelope Union High School, Wellton, Arizona

# Traditions in
# LITERATURE

**AMERICA READS**   **CLASSIC EDITION**

Helen McDonnell
James E. Miller, Jr.
Russell J. Hogan

S C O T T ,   F O R E S M A N

Scott, Foresman and Company   Editorial Offices: Glenview, Illinois
Regional Offices:
Sunnyvale, California   Tucker, Georgia   Glenview, Illinois   Oakland, New Jersey   Dallas, Texas

**Helen McDonnell**

Professor of English (adjunct faculty) at Manatee Community College, South Campus, Venice, Florida. Formerly: English Supervisor of the Ocean Township Junior and Senior High Schools, Oakhurst, New Jersey. Formerly: Member of the Commission on Literature, National Council of Teachers of English. Member and former chairman of the Committee on Comparative and World Literature, NCTE. Coeditor, *Teacher's Guide to World Short Stories*, NCTE.

**James E. Miller, Jr.**

Helen A. Regenstein Professor of Literature and former Department Chairman, University of Chicago. Visiting professor at the Sorbonne, Paris, 1984–1985 and 1986. Fulbright Lecturer in Naples and Rome, Italy, 1958–1959, and in Kyoto, Japan, 1968. Chairman, Commission on Literature, National Council of Teachers of English, 1967–1969. Guggenheim Fellow, 1969–1970. President, NCTE, 1970. Author of *Quests Surd and Absurd; Word, Self, and Reality; T.S. Eliot's Personal Waste Land;* and *The American Quest for a Supreme Fiction.*

**Russell J. Hogan**

Chairman of the English Department, Clayton High School, Missouri. Formerly: Chairman of the Committee on Comparative and World Literature of the National Council of Teachers of English. Foreign Expert, Foreign Language School, Beijing, China, 1983–1984. Contributor of an article on the poetry of François Villon to *Teachers' Guide to World Literature* (NCTE).

Cover art: German artist Caspar David Friedrich, *On a Sailboat* (detail), 1818, The Hermitage State Museum, Leningrad

Pronunciation key and dictionary entries are from *Scott, Foresman Advanced Dictionary* by E. L. Thorndike and Clarence L. Barnhart. Copyright © 1988 Scott, Foresman and Company.

ISBN: 0-673-29380-7

Copyright © 1991, 1989
Scott, Foresman and Company, Glenview, Illinois
All Rights Reserved. Printed in the United States of America.

9101112131415-RRC-020199989796

# CONTENTS

## UNIT 1    TRADITIONS IN THE SHORT STORY

## RHYME, RHYTHM, AND PATTERNS

# UNIT 4    LEGENDS OF ARTHUR

# UNIT 5    EXPERIENCE IN SHORT FICTION

# UNIT 6     SHAKESPEAREAN DRAMA

# UNIT 7     NONFICTION

ESSAYS

## THINKING CRITICALLY ABOUT LITERATURE

# UNIT 8    NOVELS

## THINKING CRITICALLY ABOUT LITERATURE

# READING LITERATURE

# COMMENT ARTICLES

# WRITER'S CRAFT

# HANDBOOK OF LITERARY TERMS     787

## WRITER'S HANDBOOK    *833*

## GLOSSARY OF LITERARY TERMS    *870*

# PREVIEW

★ *Traditions in Literature* has four units containing short stories, poems, and nonfiction selections. Two units contain plays, one having three modern dramas and the other *Julius Caesar* by Shakespeare. Another unit is made up of Arthurian legends, and the eighth unit consists of two novels, *The Pearl* and *Master and Man*.

## UNIT ORGANIZATION

Units begin with an illustration and a unit preview to quickly show you what each unit contains. Many literary selections are preceded by a wide yellow bar at the top of the page. This bar directs you to the Handbook of Literary Terms at the back of the text, where you will learn about an essential literary term before you read the selection.

**Think and Discuss** questions that follow each selection or group of selections are divided into three levels of thinking: Understanding, Analyzing, and Extending. Reading these questions before you read the selection will help guide your reading.

**Applying/Reviewing** questions about the literary term you have studied also appear after literary works. These questions help you understand how an author has developed such elements as plot, figurative language, and theme.

**Reading Literature Skillfully** lessons appear from time to time. These are short exercises on topics such as cause/effect relationships, predicting outcomes, and summarizing.

**Vocabulary** exercises throughout the book will help you understand words or meanings that are new to you. They will also show you how to determine the meanings of words from context or word structure. You may be tested on the words in these exercises.

**Thinking Skills** lessons will help you learn to think about literature in new ways by practicing *classifying, generalizing, synthesizing* (putting together parts or elements to form new ideas), and *evaluating*.

**Composition** assignments and ideas follow most selections. You will find it useful to refer to the Writer's Handbook at the back of this text for help with some of these assignments.

**Enrichment** selections are included to provide ideas for class projects and speaking and listening activities.

**Author biographies** follow each selection or group of short selections. In the Gallery features in Unit 3, however, a biography precedes each grouping of a major poet's works.

## OTHER FEATURES

Three types of articles can be found throughout this anthology. Comment articles provide interesting sidelights on a work, an author, or a related subject. (See, for example, "The Story Behind the Play," page 149.)

Eight "Writer's Craft" articles focus on how writers achieve their effects and help you strive for similar success in your writing. Finally, there are eleven articles such as "Reading a Legendary Tale," page 327, that will give you helpful hints on reading various types of literature. These are followed by the **Reading Literature Skillfully** lessons already noted.

*Julius Caesar,* in Unit 6, contains two types of sidenotes to help you interpret this play.

## UNIT REVIEWS

Each unit ends with a three-part review entitled "Thinking Critically About Literature." Here you will be asked to read a new, short work and answer questions to apply what you have learned. You will also review the selection or selections in the unit and complete writing assignments related to the unit material.

## END-OF-BOOK MATERIAL

At the back of this text on page 787 is a Handbook of Literary Terms, followed by a Writer's Handbook. You will be referred to the Handbook of Literary Terms and the Writer's Handbook from time to time throughout the text. A Glossary of Literary Terms, page 870, covers additional terms you may encounter in your study of literature. It is followed by a dictionary-type Glossary containing all vocabulary words, plus other words you will encounter in your reading.

The stories, plays, poems, and nonfiction material in this book were written by a wide variety of authors from many countries. Many of these works are "classics"—popular and time-tested selections written by many of the most respected and important writers of all time. Their works in this book prove that great literature offers timeless insights into human behavior.

# TRADITIONS IN THE SHORT STORY

Gustave Caillebotte, *Paris, A Rainy Day* (detail), 1877, The Art Institute of Chicago

# PREVIEW

## UNIT 1   TRADITIONS IN THE SHORT STORY

**The Conjurer's Revenge** / Stephen Leacock
**The Monkey's Paw** / W. W. Jacobs
**The Adventure of the Blue Carbuncle** /
   Sir Arthur Conan Doyle
**The Parachutist** / D'Arcy Niland
**The Secret Life of Walter Mitty** /
   James Thurber
**A Visit to Grandmother** /
   William Melvin Kelley
**The Other Wife** / Colette

**The Boar Hunt** / José Vasconcelos
**Life Is Sweet at Kumansenu** / Abioseh
   Nicol
**Home** / Gwendolyn Brooks
**Forgiveness in Families** / Alice Munro
**Lamb to the Slaughter** / Roald Dahl
**Through the Tunnel** / Doris Lessing
**The Story of the Widow's Son** / Mary Lavin
**The Chameleon** / Anton Chekhov
**Shaving** / Leslie Norris

**Features**
Reading a Short Story
Comment: The Plot-Centered,
   Suspenseful Story
Writer's Craft: Be Specific
Comment: The Oldest Ghost Story?

**Application of Literary Terms**
plot               point of view
characterization    theme
setting

**Reading Literature Skillfully**
cause and effect

**Vocabulary Skills**
etymology
dictionary
context
root words
Latin and Greek word parts

**Thinking Skills**
classifying
generalizing
synthesizing
evaluating

**Composition Assignments Include**
Explaining a Character's Goals
Writing About Plot Devices
Writing a Vivid Description
Writing a Dramatic Monologue
Reading/Writing Log
Defending Your Judgment of a Character
Explaining the Causes of a Conflict
Writing a Narrative
Describing a Setting
Commenting on Author's Purpose
Contrasting Two Related Ideas
Writing About Point of View
Analyzing a Character's Reactions
Considering an Alternative Ending
Writing Satire

**Enrichment**
Reporting an Unusual Occurrence
Creating a "Portrait" of Sherlock Holmes
Exploring the Food in Fiction
Finding a Setting on a Map
Interpretive Reading

**Thinking Critically About Literature**
Concept Review
Content Review
Composition Review

# The Conjurer's Revenge

**Stephen Leacock**  Canada

---

**All around the hall people were saying, "Oh, how wonderful! How does he do it?"**

---

ow, ladies and gentlemen," said the conjurer,[1] "having shown you that the cloth is absolutely empty, I will proceed to take from it a bowl of goldfish. Presto!"

All around the hall people were saying, "Oh, how wonderful! How does he do it?"

But the Quick Man on the front seat said in a big whisper to the people near him, "He — had — it — up — his — sleeve."

Then the people nodded brightly at the Quick Man and said, "Oh, of course"; and everybody whispered round the hall, "He — had — it — up — his — sleeve."

"My next trick," said the conjurer, "is the famous Hindostanee[2] rings. You will notice that the rings are apparently separate; at a blow they all join (clang, clang, clang) — Presto!"

There was a general buzz of stupefaction till the Quick Man was heard to whisper, "He — must — have — had — another — lot — up — his — sleeve."

Again everybody nodded and whispered, "The — rings — were — up — his — sleeve."

The brow of the conjurer was clouded with a gathering frown.

"I will now," he continued, "show you a most amusing trick by which I am enabled to take any number of eggs from a hat. Will some gentleman kindly lend me his hat? Ah, thank you— Presto!"

Paul Klee, *Conjuring Trick*, 1927, Philadelphia Museum of Art: The Louise and Walter Arensberg Collection

---

1. *conjurer*, person who performs tricks with quick, deceiving hand movements; magician.
2. *Hindostanee*, Hindustani. The conjurer is saying that his next trick originated in India.

"The Conjurer's Revenge" by Stephen Leacock. Used by permission of the Canadian Publishers, McClelland and Stewart, Toronto.

He extracted seventeen eggs, and for thirty-five seconds the audience began to think that he was wonderful. Then the Quick Man whispered along the front bench, "He — has — a — hen — up — his — sleeve," and all the people whispered it on. "He — has — a — lot — of — hens — up — his — sleeve."

The egg trick was ruined.

It went on like that all through. It transpired from the whispers of the Quick Man that the conjurer must have concealed up his sleeve, in addition to the rings, hens, and fish, several packs of cards, a loaf of bread, a doll's cradle, a live guinea-pig, a fifty-cent piece, and a rocking-chair.

The reputation of the conjurer was rapidly sinking below zero. At the close of the evening he rallied for a final effort.

"Ladies and gentlemen," he said, "I will present to you, in conclusion, the famous Japanese trick recently invented by the natives of Tipperary. Will you, sir," he continued, turning toward the Quick Man, "will you kindly hand me your gold watch?"

It was passed to him.

"Have I your permission to put it into this mortar and pound it to pieces?" he asked savagely.

The Quick Man nodded and smiled.

The conjurer threw the watch into the mortar and grasped a sledge hammer from the table. There was a sound of violent smashing. "He's — slipped — it — up — his — sleeve," whispered the Quick Man.

"Now, sir," continued the conjurer, "will you allow me to take your handkerchief and punch holes in it? Thank you. You see, ladies and gentlemen, there is no deception, the holes are visible to the eye."

The face of the Quick Man beamed. This time the real mystery of the thing fascinated him.

"And now, sir, will you kindly pass me your silk hat and allow me to dance on it? Thank you."

The conjurer made a few rapid passes with his feet and exhibited the hat crushed beyond recognition.

"And will you now, sir, take off your Celluloid collar and permit me to burn it in the candle? Thank you, sir. And will you allow me to smash your spectacles for you with my hammer? Thank you."

By this time the features of the Quick Man were assuming a puzzled expression. "This thing beats me," he whispered, "I don't see through it a bit."

There was a great hush upon the audience. Then the conjurer drew himself up to his full height and, with a withering look at the Quick Man, he concluded:

"Ladies and gentlemen, you will observe that I have, with this gentleman's permission, broken his watch, burnt his collar, smashed his spectacles, and danced on his hat. If he will give me the further permission to paint green stripes on his overcoat, or to tie his suspenders in a knot, I shall be delighted to entertain you. If not, the performance is at an end."

And amid a glorious burst of music from the orchestra the curtain fell, and the audience dispersed, convinced that there are some tricks, at any rate, that are not done up the conjurer's sleeve.

## THINK AND DISCUSS

### Understanding

1. How does the Quick Man explain the first several tricks performed by the conjurer?
2. How do the Quick Man's comments ruin the egg trick and other parts of the performance?
3. Does the conjurer win the audience back to his side of the conflict by the end of the performance? How do you know?

### Analyzing

4. What does the Quick Man expect will happen to the items that he voluntarily hands to the conjurer to be handled so roughly?

5. When the Quick Man whispers, "This thing beats me . . . I don't see through it a bit," what is it that he really fails to see?
6. What details does the author include to poke fun at the audience and the Quick Man?

### Extending

7. The Quick Man has threatened the conjurer's show much the way a heckler interrupts a speech by making loud or annoying remarks. Does the conjurer's reprisal, or revenge, provide a satisfying resolution to the conflict, in your opinion? Why or why not?

 **BIOGRAPHY**

## Stephen Leacock
## 1869–1944

Born in Hampshire, England, Stephen Butler Leacock moved to rural Ontario, Canada, with his family at the age of six. He would become one of Canada's best-known writers and humorists. His family experienced hard times as farmers, and Leacock and his brothers saw education as a means to escape these hard times. He attended Upper Canada College and the University of Toronto, where he studied languages. Later he taught at Upper Canada College before entering graduate studies at the University of Chicago, where he received a Ph.D. degree in 1903. He taught at McGill University in Montreal, Canada, for many years, and he wrote several serious books on economics and history. His true talent, however, was exhibited in his humorous writings.

Leacock wrote a series of comical literary sketches and fantasies published in a collection entitled *Literary Lapses* (1910). Another collection, *Nonsense Novels* (1911), strengthened his reputation as a writer of lively works. When friends wondered whether his intellectual brain might be "too tired" to create serious literature, Leacock dismissed their doubts. "My own experience is exactly the other way," he mused. "Personally I would rather have written *Alice in Wonderland* than the whole *Encyclopaedia Britannica*."

When you read a story, you participate in your entertainment more than most of the spectators in the story "The Conjurer's Revenge" do. You may get to know fictional characters as they find themselves involved in thought-provoking conflicts, suspense, humor, or adventure. Through your involvement in a story, you can be enlightened as well as entertained.

A short story concisely presents events. Edgar Allan Poe, a master of short fiction, believed that stories should not contain a word or sentence that does not point to one effect, be it suspense, horror, comedy, or any other impression. He felt writers could create interesting characters, a rich setting, and a strong plot with economy and brevity. This does not mean that short stories must avoid complex events or characters. It *does* mean that you will want to read attentively.

In fiction **plot** is a pattern of events that present and then resolve a story's **conflict.** The conflict is a struggle between the main character or characters and an adverse character, group, or force. The conjurer and the Quick Man in "The Conjurer's Revenge" represent a classic pair of characters in conflict. A story's conflict intensifies until it reaches a **climax,** a turning point at which the conflict is confronted head-on. The story then can end with the **resolution** of the struggle.

In any pattern of action, events are related to one another in time and place, as well as in terms of **cause and effect.** In tightly woven stories, most events can be traced to other events that have caused them. For example, characters say and do things in direct response to what happens around them. Sometimes reactions are not immediate or clearly related to causes. Do not be concerned if clue words such as *because, if, then, since, therefore,* and *consequently* do not appear in a story to spell out certain cause and effect relationships. You can understand causes by asking yourself why an event happened or effects by considering what is likely to occur as a result of an event.

Also central to a short story is **characterization.** The author may depict a character directly by stating the character's appearance and thoughts. At times, writers choose to suggest certain character traits, demanding that the reader make inferences based on what is done or said by other characters.

The **setting** of a story serves as a background for characters and events.

Stories are told by narrators. A narrator may be a character or an observer not appearing in the story. If the narrator is a character telling his or her own story, the **point of view** is subjective, because one character's opinions dominate. Be aware that this subjective viewpoint will influence the way you perceive the action.

Appreciating the **theme,** the underlying idea or meaning of a story, will enrich your experience as you read. Be aware of any clues the author provides to help you recognize the theme. In "The Conjurer's Revenge" what happens to the Quick Man's belongings strikes most readers as a fitting upshot to the performance. The story deals humorously with the theme of retaliation. Many stories convey their themes much more seriously.

Each part of this unit contains stories that illustrate one of the elements of fiction—plot, characterization, setting, point of view, and theme. Any short story, however, combines these elements in a way meant to entertain readers.

**See PLOT in the Handbook of Literary Terms, page 813.**

# The Monkey's Paw

**W. W. Jacobs**  Great Britain

---

**"If I could have three wishes . . ."** —the start of many a daydream.
**But the fulfillment of wishes may lead to nightmarish consequences.**

---

ithout, the night was cold and wet, but in the small parlor of Lakesnam Villa the blinds were drawn and the fire burned brightly. Father and son were at chess, the former, who possessed ideas about the game involving radical changes, putting his king into such sharp and unnecessary perils that it even provoked comment from the white-haired old lady knitting placidly by the fire.

"Hark at the wind," said Mr. White, who, having seen a fatal mistake after it was too late, was amiably desirous of preventing his son from seeing it.

"I'm listening," said the latter, grimly surveying the board as he stretched out his hand. "Check."[1]

"I should hardly think that he'd come tonight," said his father, with his hand poised over the board.

"Mate," replied the son.

"That's the worst of living so far out," bawled Mr. White, with sudden and unlooked-for violence; "of all the beastly, slushy, out-of-the-way places to live in, this is the worst. Pathway's a bog, and the road's a torrent. I don't know what people are thinking about. I suppose because only two houses on the road are let, they think it doesn't matter."

"Never mind, dear," said his wife soothingly; "perhaps you'll win the next one."

Mr. White looked up sharply, just in time to intercept a knowing glance between mother and son. The words died away on his lips, and he had a guilty grin in his thin gray beard.

"There he is," said Herbert White, as the gate banged to loudly and heavy footsteps came toward the door.

The old man rose with hospitable haste, and

---

1. *Check,* a call made by a chess player to warn an opponent that the opponent's king piece is in danger and must be moved. When a chess player makes the winning move that will capture the opponent's king, he or she calls "Checkmate" or "Mate."

From *The Lady of the Barge* by W. W. Jacobs. Reprinted by permission of The Society of Authors as the literary representative of the Estate of W. W. Jacobs. Slightly abridged.

Thomas Hicks, *There's No Place Like Home* (detail), 1877, Schweitzer Gallery, New York

opening the door, was heard condoling with the new arrival. The new arrival also condoled with himself, so that Mrs. White said "Tut, tut!" and coughed gently as her husband entered the room, followed by a tall burly man, beady of eye and rubicund of visage.

"Sergeant-Major Morris," he said, introducing him.

The sergeant-major shook hands, and, taking the proffered seat by the fire, watched contentedly while his host got out whiskey and tumblers and stood a small copper kettle on the fire.

At the third glass his eyes got brighter, and he began to talk, the little family circle regarding with eager interest this visitor from distant parts, as he squared his broad shoulders in the chair and spoke of strange scenes and doughty deeds, of wars and plagues and strange peoples.

"Twenty-one years of it," said Mr. White, nodding at his wife and son. "When he went away he was a slip of a youth in the warehouse. Now look at him."

"He don't look to have taken much harm," said Mrs. White politely.

"I'd like to go to India myself," said the old man, "just to look round a bit, you know."

"Better where you are," said the sergeant-major, shaking his head. He put down the empty glass and, sighing softly, shook it again.

"I should like to see those old temples and fakirs and jugglers," said the old man. "What was that you started telling me the other day about a monkey's paw or something, Morris?"

"Nothing," said the soldier hastily. "Leastways, nothing worth hearing."

"Monkey's paw?" said Mrs. White curiously.

"Well, it's just a bit of what you might call magic, perhaps," said the sergeant-major offhandedly.

His three listeners leaned forward eagerly. The visitor absent-mindedly put his empty glass to his lips and then set it down again. His host filled it for him.

"To look at," said the sergeant-major, fumbling in his pocket, "it's just an ordinary little paw, dried to a mummy."

He took something out of his pocket and proffered it. Mrs. White drew back with a grimace, but her son, taking it, examined it curiously.

"And what is there special about it?" inquired Mr. White, as he took it from his son and, having examined it, placed it upon the table.

"It had a spell put on it by an old fakir," said the sergeant-major, "a very holy man. He wanted to show that fate ruled people's lives, and that those who interfered with it did so to their sorrow. He put a spell on it so that three separate men could each have three wishes from it."

His manner was so impressive that his hearers were conscious that their light laughter jarred somewhat.

"Well, why don't you have three, sir?" said Herbert White cleverly.

The soldier regarded him in the way that middle age is wont to regard presumptuous youth. "I have," he said quietly, and his blotchy face whitened.

"And did you really have the three wishes granted?" asked Mrs. White.

"I did," said the sergeant-major, and his glass tapped against his strong teeth.

"And has anybody else wished?" inquired the old lady.

"The first man had his three wishes, yes," was the reply. "I don't know what the first two were, but the third was for death. That's how I got the paw."

His tones were so grave that a hush fell upon the group.

"If you've had your three wishes, it's no good to you now, then, Morris," said the old man at last. "What do you keep it for?"

The soldier shook his head. "Fancy, I suppose," he said slowly. "I did have some idea of selling it, but I don't think I will. It has caused enough mischief already. Besides, people won't buy. They think it's a fairy tale, some of them, and those who do think anything of it want to try it first and pay me afterward."

"If you could have another three wishes," said the old man, eying him keenly, "would you have them?"

"I don't know," said the other. "I don't know."

He took the paw, and dangling it between his front finger and thumb, suddenly threw it upon the fire. White, with a slight cry, stooped down and snatched it off.

"Better let it burn," said the soldier solemnly.

"If you don't want it, Morris," said the old man, "give it to me."

"I won't," said his friend doggedly. "I threw it on the fire. If you keep it, don't blame me for what happens. Pitch it on the fire again, like a sensible man."

The other shook his head and examined his new possession closely. "How do you do it?" he inquired.

"Hold it up in your right hand and wish aloud," said the sergeant-major, "but I warn you of the consequences."

"Sounds like the *Arabian Nights*,"[2] said Mrs. White, as she rose and began to set the supper.

---

2. *Arabian Nights*, a collection of old tales from Arabia, Persia, and India, dating from the tenth century.

"Don't you think you might wish for four pairs of hands for me?"

Her husband drew the talisman from his pocket and then all three burst into laughter as the sergeant-major, with a look of alarm on his face, caught him by the arm.

"If you must wish," he said gruffly, "wish for something sensible."

Mr. White dropped it back into his pocket, and placing chairs, motioned his friend to the table. In the business of supper the talisman was partly forgotten, and afterward the three sat listening in an enthralled fashion to a second installment of the soldier's adventures in India.

"If the tale about the monkey's paw is not more truthful than those he has been telling us," said Herbert, as the door closed behind their guest, just in time for him to catch the last train, "we shan't make much out of it."

"Did you give him anything for it, Father?" inquired Mrs. White, regarding her husband closely.

"A trifle," said he, coloring slightly. "He didn't want it, but I made him take it. And he pressed me again to throw it away."

"Likely," said Herbert, with pretended horror. "Why, we're going to be rich, and famous, and happy. Wish to be an emperor, Father, to begin with; then you can't be henpecked."

He darted round the table, pursued by the maligned Mrs. White armed with an antimacassar.[3]

Mr. White took the paw from his pocket and eyed it dubiously. "I don't know what to wish for, and that's a fact," he said slowly. "It seems to me I've got all I want."

"If you only cleared the house,[4] you'd be quite happy, wouldn't you?" said Herbert, with his hand on his shoulder. "Well, wish for two hundred pounds,[5] then; that'll just do it."

His father, smiling shamefacedly at his own credulity, held up the talisman, as his son, with a solemn face somewhat marred by a wink at his mother, sat down at the piano and struck a few impressive chords.

"I wish for two hundred pounds," said the old man distinctly.

A fine crash from the piano greeted the words, interrupted by a shuddering cry from the old man. His wife and son ran toward him.

"It moved," he cried; with a glance of disgust at the object as it lay on the floor. "As I wished, it twisted in my hands like a snake."

"Well, I don't see the money," said his son, as he picked it up and placed it on the table, "and I bet I never shall."

"It must have been your fancy, Father," said his wife, regarding him anxiously.

He shook his head. "Never mind, though; there's no harm done, but it gave me a shock all the same."

They sat down by the fire again while the two men finished their pipes. Outside, the wind was higher than ever, and the old man started nervously at the sound of a door banging upstairs. A silence unusual and depressing settled upon all three, which lasted until the old couple rose to retire for the night.

"I expect you'll find the cash tied up in a big bag in the middle of your bed," said Herbert, as he bade them good night, "and something horrible squatting up on top of the wardrobe watching you as you pocket your ill-gotten gains."

In the brightness of the wintry sun next morning as it streamed over the breakfast table, Herbert laughed at his fears. There was an air of prosaic wholesomeness about the room which it

---

3. *antimacassar* (an′ti mə kas′ər), small covering to protect the back or arms of a chair or sofa from soiling.
4. *cleared the house*, paid the debt that was still owed on the purchase of a house.
5. *two hundred pounds*. At the time of the story, this amount in British money was worth about one thousand American dollars.

had lacked on the previous night, and the dirty, shriveled little paw was pitched on the sideboard with a carelessness which betokened no great belief in its virtues.

"I suppose all old soldiers are the same," said Mrs. White. "The idea of our listening to such nonsense! How could wishes be granted in these days? And if they could, how could two hundred pounds hurt you, Father?"

"Might drop on his head from the sky," said the frivolous Herbert.

"Morris said the things happened so naturally," said his father, "that you might if you wished attribute it to coincidence."

"Well, don't break into the money before I come back," said Herbert, as he rose from the table. "I'm afraid it'll turn you into a mean, avaricious man, and we shall have to disown you."

His mother laughed, and following him to the door, watched him down the road, and returning to the breakfast table, was very happy at the expense of her husband's credulity. All of which did not prevent her from scurrying to the door at the postman's knock, nor prevent her from referring somewhat shortly to retired sergeant-majors of bibulous habits when she found that the post brought a tailor's bill.

"Herbert will have some more of his funny remarks, I expect, when he comes home," she said as they sat at dinner.

"I dare say," said Mr. White, pouring himself out some beer; "but for all that, the thing moved in my hand; that I'll swear to."

"You thought it did," said the old lady soothingly.

"I say it did," replied the other. "There was no thought about it; I had just—What's the matter?"

His wife made no reply. She was watching the mysterious movements of a man outside, who, peering in an undecided fashion at the house, appeared to be trying to make up his mind to enter. In mental connection with the two hundred pounds, she noticed that the stranger was well dressed and wore a silk hat of glossy newness. Three times he paused at the gate and then walked on again. The fourth time he stood with his hand upon it, and then with sudden resolution flung it open and walked up the path. Mrs. White at the same moment placed her hands behind her and hurriedly unfastening the strings of her apron, put that useful article of apparel beneath the cushion of her chair.

She brought the stranger, who seemed ill at ease, into the room. He gazed furtively at Mrs. White, and listened in a preoccupied fashion as the old lady apologized for the appearance of the room, and her husband's coat, a garment which he usually reserved for the garden. She then waited as patiently as her sex would permit for him to broach his business, but he was at first strangely silent.

"I—was asked to call," he said at last, and stooped and picked a piece of cotton from his trousers. "I come from Maw and Meggins."

The old lady started. "Is anything the matter?" she asked breathlessly. "Has anything happened to Herbert? What is it? What is it?"

Her husband interposed. "There, there, Mother," he said hastily. "Sit down, and don't jump to conclusions. You've not brought bad news, I'm sure, sir," and he eyed the other wistfully.

"I'm sorry—" began the visitor.

"Is he hurt?" demanded the mother.

The visitor bowed in assent. "Badly hurt," he said quietly, "but he is not in any pain."

"Oh, thank God!" said the old woman, clasping her hands. "Thank God for that! Thank—"

She broke off suddenly as the sinister meaning of the assurance dawned upon her and she saw the awful confirmation of her fears in the other's averted face. She caught her breath, and turning to her slower-witted husband, laid her trembling old hand upon his. There was a long silence.

"He was caught in the machinery," said the visitor at length, in a low voice.

"Caught in the machinery," repeated Mr. White, in a dazed fashion, "yes."

He sat staring blankly out of the window, and taking his wife's hand between his own, pressed it as he had been wont to do in their old courting days nearly forty years before.

"He was the only one left to us," he said, turning gently to the visitor. "It is hard."

The other coughed, and rising, walked slowly to the window. "The firm wished me to convey their sincere sympathy with you in your great loss," he said, without looking round. "I beg that you will understand I am only their servant and merely obeying orders."

There was no reply; the old woman's face was white, her eyes staring, and her breath inaudible; on the husband's face was a look such as his friend the sergeant might have carried into his first action.

"I was to say that Maw and Meggins disclaim all responsibility," continued the other. "They admit no liability at all, but in consideration of your son's services they wish to present you with a certain sum as compensation."

Mr. White dropped his wife's hand, and rising to his feet, gazed with a look of horror at his visitor. His dry lips shaped the words, "How much?"

"Two hundred pounds," was the answer.

Unconscious of his wife's shriek, the old man smiled faintly, put out his hands like a sightless man, and dropped, a senseless heap, to the floor.

In the huge new cemetery, some two miles distant, the old people buried their dead, and came back to a house steeped in shadow and silence. It was all over so quickly that at first they could hardly realize it and remained in a state of expectation as though of something else to happen—something else which was to lighten this load, too heavy for old hearts to bear. But the days passed, and expectation gave place to resignation—the hopeless resignation of the old, sometimes miscalled apathy. Sometimes they hardly exchanged a word, for now they had nothing to talk about, and their days were long to weariness.

It was about a week after that that the old man, waking suddenly in the night, stretched out his hand and found himself alone. The room was in darkness, and the sound of subdued weeping came from the window. He raised himself in bed and listened.

"Come back," he said tenderly. "You will be cold."

"It is colder for my son," said the old woman and wept afresh.

The sound of her sobs died away on his ears. The bed was warm, and his eyes heavy with sleep. He dozed fitfully, and then slept until a sudden wild cry from his wife awoke him with a start.

"The monkey's paw!" she cried wildly. "The monkey's paw!"

He started up in alarm. "Where? Where is it? What's the matter?"

She came stumbling across the room toward him. "I want it," she said quietly. "You've not destroyed it?"

"It's in the parlor, on the bracket," he replied, marveling. "Why?"

She cried and laughed together, and bending over, kissed his cheek.

"I only just thought of it," she said hysterically. "Why didn't I think of it before? Why didn't you think of it?"

"Think of what?" he questioned.

"The other two wishes," she replied rapidly. "We've only had one."

"Was not that enough?" he demanded fiercely.

"No," she cried triumphantly; "we'll have one more. Go down and get it quickly, and wish our boy alive again."

The man sat up in bed and flung the bedclothes

from his quaking limbs. "You are mad!" he cried, aghast.

"Get it," she panted; "get it quickly, and wish—Oh, my boy, my boy!"

Her husband struck a match and lit the candle. "Get back to bed," he said unsteadily. "You don't know what you are saying."

"We had the first wish granted," said the old woman feverishly; "why not the second?"

"A coincidence," stammered the old man.

"Go and get it and wish," cried the old woman, and dragged him toward the door.

He went down in the darkness, and felt his way to the parlor, and then to the mantelpiece. The talisman was in its place, and a horrible fear that the unspoken wish might bring his mutilated son before him ere he could escape from the room seized upon him, and he caught his breath as he found that he had lost the direction of the door. His brow cold with sweat, he felt his way round the table, and groped along the wall until he found himself in the small passage with the unwholesome thing in his hand.

Even his wife's face seemed changed as he entered the room. It was white and expectant, and to his fears seemed to have an unnatural look upon it. He was afraid of her.

"Wish!" she cried, in a strong voice.

"It is foolish and wicked," he faltered.

"Wish!" repeated his wife.

He raised his hand. "I wish my son alive again."

The talisman fell to the floor, and he regarded it shudderingly. Then he sank trembling into a chair as the old woman, with burning eyes, walked to the window and raised the blind.

He sat until he was chilled with the cold, glancing occasionally at the figure of the old woman peering through the window. The candle end, which had burned below the rim of the china candlestick, was throwing pulsating shadows on the ceiling and walls, until, with a flicker larger than the rest, it expired. The old man, with an unspeakable sense of relief at the failure of the talisman, crept back to his bed, and a minute or two afterward the old woman came silently and apathetically beside him.

Neither spoke, but both lay silently listening to the ticking of the clock. A stair creaked, and a squeaky mouse scurried noisily through the wall. The darkness was oppressive, and after lying for some time screwing up his courage, the husband took the box of matches and striking one went downstairs for a candle.

At the foot of the stairs the match went out, and he paused to strike another, and at the same moment a knock, so quiet and stealthy as to be scarcely audible, sounded on the front door.

The matches fell from his hand. He stood motionless, his breath suspended until the knock was repeated. Then he turned and fled swiftly back to his room and closed the door behind him. A third knock sounded through the house.

"*What's that?*" cried the old woman, starting up.

"A rat," said the old man, in shaking tones— "a rat. It passed me on the stairs."

His wife sat up in bed listening. A loud knock resounded through the house.

"It's Herbert!" she screamed. "It's Herbert!"

She ran to the door, but her husband was before her, and catching her by the arm, held her tightly.

"What are you going to do?" he whispered hoarsely.

"It's my boy; it's Herbert!" she cried, struggling mechanically. "I forgot it was two miles away. What are you holding me for? Let go. I must open the door."

"For heaven's sake don't let it in," cried the old man, trembling.

"You're afraid of your own son," she cried, struggling. "Let me go. I'm coming, Herbert; I'm coming."

There was another knock, and another. The old woman with a sudden wrench broke free and ran from the room. Her husband followed to the landing, and called after her appealingly as she hurried downstairs. He heard the chain rattle back and the bottom bolt drawn slowly and stiffly from the socket. Then the old woman's voice, strained and panting.

"The bolt," she cried loudly. "Come down. I can't reach it."

But her husband was on his hands and knees groping wildly on the floor in search of the paw. If he could only find it before the thing outside got in. A perfect fusillade of knocks reverberated through the house, and he heard the scraping of a chair as his wife put it down in the passage against the door. He heard the creaking of the bolt as it came slowly back, and at the same moment he found the monkey's paw and frantically breathed his third and last wish.

The knocking ceased suddenly, although the echoes of it were still in the house. He heard the chair drawn back and the door opened. A cold wind rushed up the staircase, and a long loud wail of disappointment and misery from his wife gave him courage to run down to her side, and then to the gate beyond. The street lamp flickering opposite shone on a quiet and deserted road.

## THINK AND DISCUSS
### Understanding
1. How does Mr. White acquire the monkey's paw?
2. What happens to Herbert White, the son?
3. When does Mr. White make his final wish?

### Analyzing
4. Contrast the scene outside the Whites' home with the scene in the living room as the Whites await the sergeant-major's arrival. What does the author intend the reader's attitude toward the White family to be?
5. Explain the Whites' conflicting attitudes toward the monkey's paw.
6. How do Herbert's words, "Well, I don't see the money, and I bet I never shall," come to have a significance that he did not intend?
7. What is Mr. White's third wish? Why do you think he makes it?

### Extending
8. Do you think the author should have described who or what was outside the door? Would such a description increase or reduce the effectiveness of the story for readers?
9. Are the Whites partly responsible for the tragedy that occurs, or are they innocent victims of an evil curse? Explain.

## APPLYING: Plot HZ
**See Handbook of Literary Terms, p. 813**

You have learned that a good short story features a tightly woven **plot**, a series of related events that present and resolve a conflict. The usual pattern of plot includes conflict, climax, and resolution. Some stories, however, have two or even three conflicts. Sometimes one can be the cause of another.

1. At what point does the conflict between Mr. White and the paw actually begin? Explain.
2. When Mr. White begins to deal with the

monkey's paw, what internal conflict is initiated in his mind?

3. What is the climax of the story?

## READING LITERATURE SKILLFULLY
### Cause / Effect Relationships

In fiction as in real life, people's acts have consequences, and events in general have both causes and effects. Plots unfold as one action leads to another and as characters react to what happens to them and around them. Events can be considered in their relationships of natural causes and effects. Yet authors of fiction sometimes develop the action through other plot devices such as coincidence—events happening together by chance—and unnatural causes including fantastical or magical forces. Explain the following related events as either coincidence or cause and effect relationships. Identify the causes and effects as either natural or unnatural.

1. The movement of the paw during each wish
2. The wish for 200 pounds and the son's death
3. The third wish and nobody being at the door

## VOCABULARY
### Etymology, Dictionary

At the end of most dictionary entries, after the entry word's definition, is the word's etymology. An etymology is an explanation of a word's origin and history. It generally tells the language from which a word has come and the original word or words from which the entry word is derived. Knowing the meaning of such original words helps you understand the meaning of the modern word more completely. If an original word or a meaning is not given, you can assume that that element is the same as in the English entry word.

Check the Glossary for the etymologies of the following words. For each, list the language from which the word is derived and the meaning of the original word.

1. bog; 2. rubicund; 3. wont; 4. fakir; 5. fusillade.

## COMPOSITION
### Explaining a Character's Goals

Often the plot of a story progresses as a main character makes decisions that affect the ensuing action. Such a character's goals or aims may change as the action continues. Review the story to determine how Mr. White's goals change from scene to scene in "The Monkey's Paw." Compile a list of his successive goals from the point at which he recovers the paw from the fire to the last wish. Write an essay of at least three paragraphs, describing how this character's goals change and how they affect the action and outcome of the story. You will want to comment on his conflicts in the plot and whether he feels satisfied when he achieves certain goals. For help in developing your paper, see "The Writing Process" in the Writer's Handbook.

### Writing About Fantasy

Consider how convincingly the author has depicted supernatural events in "The Monkey's Paw." Review the story to analyze the details of plot that present questions about how or why something unusual has happened. You may want to list the most convincing (and the least convincing) points or descriptions of magic or unexplained happenings in the story, for your own reference. Write a three-paragraph essay to express your opinion about how effectively W. W. Jacobs built his plot around supernatural events and mysterious circumstances. Consider your audience to be your teacher and classmates. See "The Writing Process" in the Writer's Handbook.

### ENRICHMENT
### Reporting an Unusual Occurrence

You and a few classmates may want to stage a

radio or television-style news report about the tragic accident that claimed the life of Herbert White, a young worker at the Maw and Meggins factory. Assume that you are a reporter preparing a broadcast about the incident and you have just learned about the monkey's paw and the first wish by Mr. White. Review the short story to determine which facts could be known by a reporter, and then decide whether you would attach any importance to the strange rumors about the paw. Then prepare and deliver a report, with your class as the audience. Invent interviews with fellow workers or managers at Maw and Meggins, Herbert's employer. Make sure your account agrees with details in the story.

# BIOGRAPHY

## W. W. Jacobs
## 1863–1943

W. W. (William Wymark) Jacobs was born in Wapping, near Tower Bridge, in the ship-docking section of London, England. There his father was employed as a wharf manager, and there Jacobs gathered the raw material for many of his stories. Educated privately, Jacobs became a clerk in the Civil Service in 1883, and during the next sixteen years he served in a department of the General Post Office. In 1896 his first book, *Many Cargoes,* was published, followed by one-act plays, novels, and short stories. When Jacobs was certain he could support himself by his writing, he left the Civil Service.

The influence of Jacobs's early life around the London docks is reflected in many of his book titles, such as *Light Freights, The Lady of the Barge* (in which "The Monkey's Paw" appears), and *Deep Waters,* and in the plots of a number of his short stories. In addition to stories about mariners, Jacobs wrote macabre tales and stories dealing with country village life. "The Monkey's Paw" is a good example.

Review PLOT in the Handbook of Literary Terms, page 813.

# The Adventure of the Blue Carbuncle

**Sir Arthur Conan Doyle**   Great Britain

**Sherlock Holmes sat up with a whistle when he saw the blue carbuncle. "It's more than a precious stone. It is *the* precious stone."**

I had called upon my friend Sherlock Holmes upon the second morning after Christmas, with the intention of wishing him the compliments of the season. He was lounging upon the sofa in a purple dressing-gown, a pipe-rack within his reach upon the right, and a pile of crumpled morning papers, evidently newly studied, near at hand. Beside the couch was a wooden chair, and on the angle of the back hung a very seedy and disreputable hard-felt hat, much the worse for wear, and cracked in several places. A lens and a forceps lying upon the seat of the chair suggested that the hat had been suspended in this manner for the purpose of examination.

"You are engaged," said I; "perhaps I interrupt you."

"Not at all. I am glad to have a friend with whom I can discuss my results. The matter is a perfectly trivial one"—he jerked his thumb in the direction of the old hat—"but there are points in connection with it which are not entirely devoid of interest and even of instruction."

I seated myself in his armchair and warmed my hands before his crackling fire, for a sharp frost had set in, and the windows were thick with the ice crystals. "I suppose," I remarked, "that, homely as it looks, this thing has some deadly story linked on to it—that it is the clue which will guide you in the solution of some mystery and the punishment of some crime."

"No, no. No crime," said Sherlock Holmes, laughing. "Only one of those whimsical little incidents which will happen when you have four million human beings all jostling each other within the space of a few square miles. Amid the action and reaction of so dense a swarm of humanity, every possible combination of events may be ex-

Sir Arthur Conan Doyle, "The Adventure of the Blue Carbuncle," from *Adventures of Sherlock Holmes*, Harper and Bros., 1892. Slightly abridged.

pected to take place, and many a little problem will be presented which may be striking and bizarre without being criminal. We have already had experience of such."

"So much so," I remarked, "that of the last six cases which I have added to my notes, three have been entirely free of any legal crime."

"Precisely. You allude to my attempt to recover the Irene Adler papers, to the singular case of Miss Mary Sutherland, and to the adventure of the man with the twisted lip.[1] Well, I have no doubt that this small matter will fall into the same innocent category. You know Peterson, the commissionaire?"

"Yes."

"It is to him that this trophy belongs."

"It is his hat."

"No, no; he found it. Its owner is unknown. I beg that you will look upon it not as a battered billycock[2] but as an intellectual problem. And, first, as to how it came here. It arrived upon Christmas morning, in company with a good fat goose, which is, I have no doubt, roasting at this moment in front of Peterson's fire. The facts are these: about four o'clock on Christmas morning, Peterson, who, as you know, is a very honest fellow, was returning from some small jollification and was making his way homeward down Tottenham Court Road. In front of him he saw, in the gaslight, a tallish man, walking with a slight stagger, and carrying a white goose slung over his shoulder. As he reached the corner of Goodge Street, a row[3] broke out between this stranger and a little knot of roughs. One of the latter knocked off the man's hat, on which he raised his stick to defend himself and, swinging it over his head, smashed the shop window behind him. Peterson had rushed forward to protect the stranger from his assailants; but the man, shocked at having broken the window, and seeing an official-looking person in uniform rushing towards him, dropped his goose, took to his heels, and vanished amid the labyrinth of small streets which lie at the back of Tottenham Court Road. The roughs had also fled at the appearance of Peterson, so that he was left in possession of the field of battle, and also of the spoils of victory in the shape of this battered hat and a most unimpeachable Christmas goose."

"Which surely he restored to their owner?"

"My dear fellow, there lies the problem. It is true that 'For Mrs. Henry Baker' was printed upon a small card which was tied to the bird's left leg, and it is also true that the initials 'H. B.' are legible upon the lining of this hat; but as there are some thousands of Bakers, and some hundreds of Henry Bakers in this city of ours, it is not easy to restore lost property to any one of them."

"What, then, did Peterson do?"

"He brought round both hat and goose to me on Christmas morning, knowing that even the smallest problems are of interest to me. The goose we retained until this morning, when there were signs that, in spite of the slight frost, it would be well that it should be eaten without unnecessary delay. Its finder has carried it off, therefore, to fulfil the ultimate destiny of a goose, while I continue to retain the hat of the unknown gentleman who lost his Christmas dinner."

"Did he not advertise?"

"No."

"Then, what clue could you have as to his identity?"

"Only as much as we can deduce."

"From his hat?"

"Precisely."

"But you are joking. What can you gather from this old battered felt?"

"Here is my lens. You know my methods.

---

1. *Irene Adler . . . Mary Sutherland . . . man with the twisted lip.* Holmes is referring to his work on other cases recounted by Dr. Watson in *The Adventures of Sherlock Holmes* by Sir Arthur Conan Doyle.
2. *billycock,* British term for a derby hat.
3. *row* (rou), a noisy quarrel or disturbance.

Actors Jeremy Brett as Sherlock Holmes and David Burke as Dr. Watson in *The Adventures of Sherlock Holmes*, a television production based on stories by Sir Arthur Conan Doyle.

What can you gather yourself as to the individuality of the man who has worn this article?"

I took the tattered object in my hands and turned it over rather ruefully. It was a very ordinary black hat of the usual round shape, hard and much the worse for wear. The lining had been of red silk, but was a good deal discoloured. There was no maker's name; but, as Holmes had remarked, the initials "H. B." were scrawled upon one side. It was pierced in the brim for a hat-securer, but the elastic was missing. For the rest, it was cracked, exceedingly dusty, and spotted in several places, although there seemed to have been some attempt to hide the discoloured patches by smearing them with ink.

"I can see nothing," said I, handing it back to my friend.

"On the contrary, Watson, you can see everything. You fail, however, to reason from what you see. You are too timid in drawing your inferences."

"Then, pray tell me what it is that you can infer from this hat?"

He picked it up and gazed at it in the peculiar introspective fashion which was characteristic of him. "It is perhaps less suggestive than it might have been," he remarked, "and yet there are a few inferences which are very distinct, and a few others which represent at least a strong balance of probability. That the man was highly intellectual is of course obvious upon the face of it, and also that he was fairly well-to-do within the last three years, although he has now fallen upon evil days. He had foresight, but has less now than formerly, pointing to a moral retrogression, which, when taken with the decline of his fortunes, seems to indicate some evil influence, probably drink, at work upon him. This may account also for the obvious fact that his wife has ceased to love him."

"My dear Holmes!"

"He has, however, retained some degree of self-respect," he continued, disregarding my remonstrance. "He is a man who leads a sedentary life, goes out little, is out of training entirely, is middle-aged, has grizzled hair which he has had cut within the last few days, and which he anoints with lime-cream. These are the more patent facts which are to be deduced from his hat. Also, by the way, that it is extremely improbable that he has gas laid on in his house."

"You are certainly joking, Holmes."

"Not in the least. Is it possible that even now, when I give you these results, you are unable to see how they are attained?"

"I have no doubt that I am very stupid, but I must confess that I am unable to follow you. For example, how did you deduce that this man was intellectual?"

For answer Holmes clapped the hat upon his head. It came right over the forehead and settled upon the bridge of his nose. "It is a question of cubic capacity," said he; "a man with so large a brain must have something in it."

"The decline of his fortunes, then?"

"This hat is three years old. These flat brims curled at the edge came in then. It is a hat of the very best quality. Look at the band of ribbed silk and the excellent lining. If this man could afford to buy so expensive a hat three years ago, and has had no hat since, then he has assuredly gone down in the world."

"Well, that is clear enough, certainly. But how about the foresight and the moral retrogression?"

Sherlock Holmes laughed. "Here is the foresight," said he, putting his finger upon the little disc and loop of the hat-securer. "They are never sold upon hats. If this man ordered one, it is a sign of a certain amount of foresight, since he went out of his way to take this precaution against the wind. But since we see that he has broken the elastic and has not troubled to replace it, it is obvious that he has less foresight now than formerly, which is a distinct proof of a weakening nature. On the other hand, he has endeavoured to conceal some of these stains upon the felt by daubing them with ink, which is a sign that he has not entirely lost his self-respect."

"Your reasoning is certainly plausible."

"The further points, that he is middle-aged, that his hair is grizzled, that it has been recently cut, and that he uses lime-cream, are all to be gathered from a close examination of the lower part of the lining. The lens discloses a large number of hair-ends, clean cut by the scissors of the barber. They all appear to be adhesive, and there is a distinct odour of lime-cream. This dust, you will observe, is not the gritty, gray dust of the street but the fluffy brown dust of the house, showing that it has been hung up indoors most of the time; while the marks of moisture upon the inside are proof positive that the wearer perspired very freely, and could, therefore, hardly be in the best of training."

"But his wife—you said that she had ceased to love him."

"This hat has not been brushed for weeks. When I see you, my dear Watson, with a week's accumulation of dust upon your hat, and when your wife allows you to go out in such a state, I shall fear that you also have been unfortunate enough to lose your wife's affection."

"But he might be a bachelor."

"Nay, he was bringing home the goose as a peace-offering to his wife. Remember the card upon the bird's leg."

"You have an answer to everything. But how on earth do you deduce that the gas is not laid on in his house?"

"One tallow stain, or even two, might come by chance; but when I see no less than five, I think that there can be little doubt that the individual must be brought into frequent contact with burning tallow—walks upstairs at night probably with his hat in one hand and a guttering candle in the other. Anyhow, he never got tallow-stains from a gas-jet. Are you satisfied?"

"Well, it is very ingenious," said I, laughing; "but since, as you said just now, there has been no crime committed, and no harm done save the loss of a goose, all this seems to be rather a waste of energy."

Sherlock Holmes had opened his mouth to reply, when the door flew open, and Peterson, the commissionaire, rushed into the apartment with flushed cheeks and the face of a man who is dazed with astonishment.

"The goose, Mr. Holmes! The goose, sir!" he gasped.

"Eh? What of it, then? Has it returned to life and flapped off through the kitchen window?" Holmes twisted himself round upon the sofa to get a fairer view of the man's excited face.

"See here, sir! See what my wife found in its crop!" He held out his hand and displayed upon the centre of the palm a brilliantly scintillating blue stone, rather smaller than a bean in size, but of such purity and radiance that it twinkled like an electric point in the dark hollow of his hand.

Sherlock Holmes sat up with a whistle. "By Jove, Peterson!" said he, "this is treasure trove indeed. I suppose you know what you have got?"

"A diamond, sir? A precious stone. It cuts into glass as though it were putty."

"It's more than a precious stone. It is *the* precious stone."

"Not the Countess of Morcar's blue carbuncle!" I ejaculated.

"Precisely so. I ought to know its size and shape, seeing that I have read the advertisement about it in *The Times* every day lately. It is absolutely unique, and its value can only be conjectured, but the reward offered of £1000[4] is certainly not within a twentieth part of the market price."

"A thousand pounds! Great Lord of mercy!" The commissionaire plumped down into a chair and stared from one to the other of us.

"That is the reward, and I have reason to know that there are sentimental considerations in the background which would induce the Countess to part with half her fortune if she could but recover the gem."

"It was lost, if I remember aright, at the Hotel Cosmopolitan," I remarked.

"Precisely so, on December 22d, just five days ago. John Horner, a plumber, was accused of having abstracted it from the lady's jewel-case. The evidence against him was so strong that the case has been referred to the Assizes. I have some account of the matter here, I believe." He rummaged amid his newspapers, glancing over the dates, until at last he smoothed one out, doubled it over, and read the following paragraph:

Hotel Cosmopolitan Jewel Robbery. John Horner, 26, plumber, was brought up upon the charge of having upon the 22nd inst.[5] abstracted

---

4. *£1000*, one thousand pounds in British money, worth several thousand dollars at the time of this story. £ is the symbol for the pound sterling, the basic unit of money in Great Britain.

5. *inst.*, instant, meaning "of the present month."

from the jewel-case of the Countess of Morcar the valuable gem known as the blue carbuncle. James Ryder, upper-attendant at the hotel, gave his evidence to the effect that he had shown Horner up to the dressing-room of the Countess of Morcar upon the day of the robbery in order that he might solder the second bar of the grate, which was loose. He had remained with Horner some little time, but had finally been called away. On returning, he found that Horner had disappeared, that the bureau had been forced open, and that the small morocco casket in which, as it afterwards transpired, the Countess was accustomed to keep her jewel, was lying empty upon the dressing-table. Ryder instantly gave the alarm, and Horner was arrested the same evening; but the stone could not be found either upon his person or in his rooms. Catherine Cusack, maid to the Countess, deposed to having heard Ryder's cry of dismay on discovering the robbery, and to having rushed into the room, where she found matters as described by the last witness. Inspector Bradstreet, B division, gave evidence as to the arrest of Horner, who struggled frantically, and protested his innocence in the strongest terms. Evidence of a previous conviction for robbery having been given against the prisoner, the magistrate refused to deal summarily with the offence, but referred it to the Assizes. Horner, who had shown signs of intense emotion during the proceedings, fainted away at the conclusion and was carried out of court.

"Hum! So much for the police-court," said Holmes thoughtfully, tossing aside the paper. "The question for us now to solve is the sequence of events leading from a rifled jewel-case at one end to the crop of a goose in Tottenham Court Road at the other. You see, Watson, our little deductions have suddenly assumed a much more important and less innocent aspect. Here is the stone; the stone came from the goose, and the goose came from Mr. Henry Baker, the gentleman with the bad hat and all the other characteristics with which I have bored you. So now we must set ourselves very seriously to finding this gentleman and ascertaining what part he has played in this little mystery. To do this, we must try the simplest means first, and these lie undoubtedly in an advertisement in all the evening papers. If this fail, I shall have recourse to other methods."

"What will you say?"

"Give me a pencil and that slip of paper. Now, then:

Found at the corner of Goodge Street, a goose and a black felt hat. Mr. Henry Baker can have the same by applying at 6:30 this evening at 221B, Baker Street.

That is clear and concise."

"Very. But will he see it?"

"Well, he is sure to keep an eye on the papers, since, to a poor man, the loss was a heavy one. He was clearly so scared by his mischance in breaking the window and by the approach of Peterson that he thought of nothing but flight, but since then he must have bitterly regretted the impulse which caused him to drop his bird. Then, again, the introduction of his name will cause him to see it, for everyone who knows him will direct his attention to it. Here you are, Peterson, run down to the advertising agency and have this put in the evening papers."

"In which, sir?"

"Oh, in the *Globe, Star, Pall Mall, St. James's, Evening News Standard, Echo,* and any others that occur to you."

"Very well, sir. And this stone?"

"Ah, yes, I shall keep the stone. Thank you. And, I say, Peterson, just buy a goose on your way back and leave it here with me, for we must have one to give to this gentleman in place of the one which your family is now devouring."

When the commissionaire had gone, Holmes took up the stone and held it against the light. "It's a bonny thing," said he. "Just see how it glints and sparkles. Of course it is a nucleus and focus of crime. Every good stone is. They are the devil's pet baits. In the larger and older jewels every facet may stand for a bloody deed. This stone is not yet twenty years old. It was found in the banks of the Amoy River in southern China and is remarkable in having every characteristic of the carbuncle, save that it is blue in shade instead of ruby red. In spite of its youth, it has already a sinister history. There have been two murders, a vitriol-throwing, a suicide, and several robberies brought about for the sake of this forty-grain weight of crystallized charcoal. Who would think that so pretty a toy would be a purveyor to the gallows and the prison? I'll lock it up in my strong box now and drop a line to the Countess to say that we have it."

"Do you think that this man Horner is innocent?"

"I cannot tell."

"Well, then, do you imagine that this other one, Henry Baker, had anything to do with the matter?"

"It is, I think, much more likely that Henry Baker is an absolutely innocent man, who had no idea that the bird which he was carrying was of considerably more value than if it were made of solid gold. That, however, I shall determine by a very simple test if we have an answer to our advertisement."

"And you can do nothing until then?"

"Nothing."

"In that case I shall continue my professional round. But I shall come back in the evening at the hour you have mentioned, for I should like to see the solution of so tangled a business."

"Very glad to see you. I dine at seven. There is a woodcock,[6] I believe. By the way, in view of recent occurrences, perhaps I ought to ask Mrs. Hudson to examine its crop."

I had been delayed at a case, and it was a little after half-past six when I found myself in Baker Street once more. As I approached the house I saw a tall man in a Scotch bonnet with a coat which was buttoned up to his chin waiting outside in the bright semicircle which was thrown from the fanlight. Just as I arrived the door was opened, and we were shown up together to Holmes's room.

"Mr. Henry Baker, I believe," said he, rising from his armchair and greeting his visitor with the easy air of geniality which he could so readily assume. "Pray take this chair by the fire, Mr. Baker. It is a cold night, and I observe that your circulation is more adapted for summer than for winter. Ah, Watson, you have just come at the right time. Is that your hat, Mr. Baker?"

"Yes, sir, that is undoubtedly my hat."

He was a large man with rounded shoulders, a massive head, and a broad, intelligent face, sloping down to a pointed beard of grizzled brown. A touch of red in nose and cheeks, with a slight tremor of his extended hand, recalled Holmes's surmise as to his habits. His rusty black frock-coat was buttoned right up in front, with the collar turned up, and his lank wrists protruded from his sleeves without a sign of cuff or shirt. He spoke in a slow staccato fashion, choosing his words with care, and gave the impression generally of a man of learning and letters who had had ill-usage at the hands of fortune.

"We have retained these things for some days," said Holmes, "because we expected to see an advertisement from you giving your address. I am at a loss to know now why you did not advertise."

Our visitor gave a rather shamefaced laugh.

---

6. *woodcock*, a small game bird, in this case the main course to be served at Holmes's dinner by his servant, Mrs. Hudson.

"Shillings have not been so plentiful with me as they once were," he remarked. "I had no doubt that the gang of roughs who assaulted me had carried off both my hat and the bird. I did not care to spend more money in a hopeless attempt at recovering them."

"Very naturally. By the way, about the bird, we were compelled to eat it."

"To eat it!" Our visitor half rose from his chair in his excitement.

"Yes, it would have been of no use to anyone had we not done so. But I presume that this other goose upon the sideboard, which is about the same weight and perfectly fresh, will answer your purpose equally well?"

"Oh, certainly, certainly," answered Mr. Baker with a sigh of relief.

"Of course, we still have the feathers, legs, crop, and so on of your own bird, so if you wish——"

The man burst into a hearty laugh. "They might be useful to me as relics of my adventure," said he, "but beyond that I can hardly see what use the *disjecta membra*[7] of my late acquaintance are going to be to me. No, sir, I think that, with your permission, I will confine my attentions to the excellent bird which I perceive upon the sideboard."

Sherlock Holmes glanced sharply across at me with a slight shrug of his shoulders.

"There is your hat, then, and there your bird," said he. "By the way, would it bore you to tell me where you got the other one from? I am somewhat of a fowl fancier, and I have seldom seen a better-grown goose."

"Certainly, sir," said Baker, who had risen and tucked his newly gained property under his arm. "There are a few of us who frequent the Alpha Inn, near the Museum—we are to be found in the Museum itself during the day, you understand. This year our good host, Windigate by name, instituted a goose club, by which, on considera-tion of some few pence every week, we were each to receive a bird at Christmas. My pence were duly paid, and the rest is familiar to you. I am much indebted to you, sir, for a Scotch bonnet is fitted neither to my years nor my gravity." With a comical pomposity of manner he bowed solemnly to both of us and strode off upon his way.

"So much for Mr. Henry Baker," said Holmes when he had closed the door behind him. "It is quite certain that he knows nothing whatever about the matter. Are you hungry, Watson?"

"Not particularly."

"Then I suggest that we turn our dinner into a supper and follow up this clue while it is still hot."

"By all means."

It was a bitter night, so we drew on our ulsters and wrapped cravats about our throats. Outside, the stars were shining coldly in a cloudless sky, and the breath of the passers-by blew out into smoke like so many pistol shots. Our footfalls rang out crisply and loudly as we swung through the doctors' quarter, Wimpole Street, Harley Street, and so through Wigmore Street into Oxford street. In a quarter of an hour we were in Bloomsbury at the Alpha Inn, which is a small public-house at the corner of one of the streets which runs down into Holborn. Holmes pushed open the door of the private bar and ordered two glasses of beer from the ruddy-faced, white-aproned landlord.

"Your beer should be excellent if it is as good as your geese," said he.

"My geese!" The man seemed surprised.

"Yes. I was speaking only half an hour ago to Mr. Henry Baker, who was a member of your goose club."

"Ah! yes, I see. But you see, sir, them's not *our* geese."

---

7. *disjecta membra,* cast-off members, or parts [*Latin*]; in this case, the unused parts of the goose.

"Indeed! Whose, then?"

"Well, I got the two dozen from a salesman in Covent Garden."

"Indeed? I know some of them. Which was it?"

"Breckinridge is his name."

"Ah! I don't know him. Well, here's your good health, landlord, and prosperity to your house. Good-night.

"Now for Mr. Breckinridge," he continued, buttoning up his coat as we came out into the frosty air. "Remember, Watson, that though we have so homely a thing as a goose at one end of this chain, we have at the other a man who will certainly get seven years' penal servitude unless we can establish his innocence. It is possible that our inquiry may but confirm his guilt; but, in any case, we have a line of investigation which has been missed by the police, and which a singular chance has placed in our hands. Let us follow it out to the bitter end. Faces to the south, then, and quick march!"

We passed across Holborn, down Endell Street, and so through a zigzag of slums to Covent Garden Market. One of the largest stalls bore the name of Breckinridge upon it, and the proprietor, a horsy-looking man, with a sharp face and trim side-whiskers, was helping a boy to put up the shutters.

"Good-evening. It's a cold night," said Holmes.

The salesman nodded and shot a questioning glance at my companion.

"Sold out of geese, I see," continued Holmes, pointing at the bare slabs of marble.

"Let you have five hundred tomorrow morning."

"That's no good."

"Well, there are some on the stall with the gas-flare."

"Ah, but I was recommended to you."

"Who by?"

"The landlord of the Alpha."

"Oh, yes; I sent him a couple of dozen."

"Fine birds they were, too. Now where did you get them from?"

To my surprise the question provoked a burst of anger from the salesman.

"Now, then, mister," said he, with his head cocked and his arms akimbo, "what are you driving at? Let's have it straight, now."

"It is straight enough. I should like to know who sold you the geese which you supplied to the Alpha."

"Well, then, I shan't tell you. So now!"

"Oh, it is a matter of no importance; but I don't know why you should be so warm over such a trifle."

"Warm! You'd be as warm, maybe, if you were as pestered as I am. When I pay good money for a good article there should be an end of the business; but it's 'Where are the geese?' and 'Who did you sell the geese to?' and 'What will you take for the geese?' One would think they were the only geese in the world, to hear the fuss that is made over them."

"Well, I have no connection with any other people who have been making inquiries," said Holmes carelessly. "If you won't tell us the bet is off, that is all. But I'm always ready to back my opinion on a matter of fowls, and I have a fiver on it that the bird I ate is country bred."

"Well, then, you've lost your fiver, for it's town bred," snapped the salesman.

"It's nothing of the kind."

"I say it is."

"I don't believe it."

"D'you think you know more about fowls than I, who have handled them ever since I was a nipper? I tell you, all those birds that went to the Alpha were town bred."

"You'll never persuade me to believe that."

"Will you bet, then?"

"It's merely taking your money, for I know that I am right. But I'll have a sovereign on with you, just to teach you not to be obstinate."

The salesman chuckled grimly. "Bring me the books, Bill," said he.

The small boy brought round a small thin volume and a great greasy-backed one, laying them out together beneath the hanging lamp.

"Now then, Mr. Cocksure," said the salesman, "I thought that I was out of geese, but before I finish you'll find that there is still one left in my shop. You see this little book?"

"Well?"

"That's the list of the folk from whom I buy. D'you see? Well, then, here on this page are the country folk, and the numbers after their names are where their accounts are in the big ledger. Now, then! You see this other page in red ink? Well, that is a list of my town suppliers. Now, look at that third name. Just read it out to me."

"'Mrs. Oakshott, 117, Brixton Road—249,'" read Holmes.

"Quite so. Now turn that up in the ledger."

Holmes turned to the page indicated. "Here you are, 'Mrs. Oakshott, 117, Brixton Road, egg and poultry supplier.'"

"Now, then, what's the last entry?"

"'December 22d. Twenty-four geese at 7s. 6d.'"[8]

"Quite so. There you are. And underneath?"

"'Sold to Mr. Windigate of the Alpha, at 12s.'"

"What have you to say now?"

Sherlock Holmes looked deeply chagrined. He drew a sovereign from his pocket and threw it down upon the slab, turning away with the air of a man whose disgust is too deep for words. A few yards off he stopped under a lamp-post and laughed in the hearty, noiseless fashion which was peculiar to him.

"When you see a man with whiskers of that cut and the 'pink 'un'[9] protruding out of his pocket, you can always draw him by a bet," said he. "I daresay that if I had put £100 down in front of

him, that man would not have given me such complete information as was drawn from him by the idea that he was doing me on a wager. Well, Watson, we are, I fancy, nearing the end of our quest, and the only point which remains to be determined is whether we should go on to this Mrs. Oakshott tonight, or whether we should reserve it for tomorrow. It is clear from what that surly fellow said that there are others besides ourselves who are anxious about the matter, and I should——"

His remarks were suddenly cut short by a loud hubbub which broke out from the stall which we had just left. Turning round we saw a little rat-faced fellow standing in the centre of the circle of yellow light which was thrown by the swinging lamp, while Breckinridge the salesman, framed in the door of his stall, was shaking his fists fiercely at the cringing figure.

"I've had enough of you and your geese," he shouted. "I wish you were all at the devil together. If you come pestering me any more with your silly talk I'll set the dog at you. You bring Mrs. Oakshott here and I'll answer her, but what have you to do with it? Did I buy the geese off you?"

"No; but one of them was mine all the same," whined the little man.

"Well, then, ask Mrs. Oakshott for it."

"She told me to ask you."

"Well, you can ask the King of Proosia, for all I care. I've had enough of it. Get out of this!" He rushed fiercely forward, and the inquirer flitted away into the darkness.

---

8. *7s. 6d.,* seven shillings and six pence, or pennies, in British money. A shilling was worth one-twentieth of a pound, and a penny was worth one-twelfth of a shilling.
9. *the "pink 'un,"* the "pink one," a popular name for *The Sporting Times,* a British publication about racehorses, printed on pink paper.

"Ha! this may save us a visit to Brixton Road," whispered Holmes. "Come with me, and we will see what is to be made of this fellow." Striding through the scattered knots of people who lounged round the flaring stalls, my companion speedily overtook the little man and touched him upon the shoulder. He sprang round, and I could see in the gas-light that every vestige of colour had been driven from his face.

"Who are you, then? What do you mean?" he asked in a quavering voice.

"You will excuse me," said Holmes blandly, "but I could not help overhearing the questions which you put to the salesman just now. I think that I could be of assistance to you."

"You? Who are you? How could you know anything of the matter?"

"My name is Sherlock Holmes. It is my business to know what other people don't know."

"But you can know nothing of this?"

"Excuse me, I know everything of it. You are endeavouring to trace some geese which were sold by Mrs. Oakshott, of Brixton Road, to a salesman named Breckinridge, by him in turn to Mr. Windigate, of the Alpha, and by him to his club, of which Mr. Henry Baker is a member."

"Oh, sir, you are the very man whom I have longed to meet," cried the little fellow with outstretched hands and quivering fingers. "I can hardly explain to you how interested I am in this matter."

Sherlock Holmes hailed a four-wheeler which was passing. "In that case we had better discuss it in a cosy room rather than in this wind-swept market-place," said he. "But pray tell me, before we go farther, who it is that I have the pleasure of assisting."

The man hesitated for an instant. "My name is John Robinson," he answered with a sidelong glance.

"No, no; the real name," said Holmes sweetly.

"It is always awkward doing business with an alias."

A flush sprang to the white cheeks of the stranger. "Well, then," said he, "my real name is James Ryder."

"Precisely so. Head attendant at the Hotel Cosmopolitan. Pray step into the cab, and I shall soon be able to tell you something which you would wish to know."

The little man stood glancing from one to the other of us with half-frightened, half-hopeful eyes, as one who is not sure whether he is on the verge of a windfall or of a catastrophe. Then he stepped into the cab, and in half an hour we were back in the sitting-room at Baker Street. Nothing had been said during our drive, but the high, thin breathing of our new companion, and the claspings and unclaspings of his hands, spoke of the nervous tension within him.

"Here we are!" said Holmes cheerily as we filed into the room. "The fire looks very seasonable in this weather. You look cold, Mr. Ryder. Pray take the basket-chair. I will just put on my slippers before we settle this little matter of yours. Now, then! You want to know what became of those geese?"

"Yes, sir."

"Or rather, I fancy, of that goose. It was one bird, I imagine, in which you were interested—white, with a black bar across the tail."

Ryder quivered with emotion. "Oh, sir," he cried, "can you tell me where it went to?"

"It came here."

"Here?"

"Yes, and a most remarkable bird it proved. I don't wonder that you should take an interest in it. It laid an egg after it was dead—the bonniest, brightest little blue egg that ever was seen. I have it here in my museum."

Our visitor staggered to his feet and clutched the mantel-piece with his right hand. Holmes unlocked his strong-box and held up the blue car-buncle, which shone out like a star, with a cold, brilliant, many-pointed radiance. Ryder stood glaring with a drawn face, uncertain whether to claim or to disown it.

"The game's up, Ryder," said Holmes quietly. "Hold up, man, or you'll be into the fire! Give him an arm back into his chair, Watson. He's not got blood enough to go in for felony with impunity. Give him a dash of brandy. So! Now he looks a little more human. What a shrimp it is, to be sure!"

For a moment he had staggered and nearly fallen, but the brandy brought a tinge of colour into his cheeks, and he sat staring with frightened eyes at his accuser.

"I have almost every link in my hands, and all the proofs which I could possibly need, so there is little which you need tell me. Still, that little may as well be cleared up to make the case complete. You had heard, Ryder, of this blue stone of the Countess of Morcar's?"

"It was Catherine Cusack who told me of it," said he in a crackling voice.

"I see— her ladyship's waiting-maid. Well, the temptation of sudden wealth so easily acquired was too much for you, as it has been for better men before you; but you were not very scrupulous in the means you used. It seems to me, Ryder, that there is the making of a very pretty villain in you. You knew that this man Horner, the plumber, had been concerned in some such matter before, and that suspicion would rest the more readily upon him. What did you do, then? You made some small job in my lady's room—you and your confederate Cusack—and you managed that he should be the man sent for. Then, when he had left, you rifled the jewel-case, raised the alarm, and had this unfortunate man arrested. You then——"

Ryder threw himself down suddenly upon the rug and clutched at my companion's knees. "For God's sake, have mercy!" he shrieked. "Think of my father! of my mother! It would break their hearts. I never went wrong before! I never will again. I swear it. I'll swear it on a Bible. Oh don't bring it into court! Don't!"

"Get back into your chair!" said Holmes sternly. "It is very well to cringe and crawl now, but you thought little enough of this poor Horner in the dock for a crime of which he knew nothing."

"I will fly, Mr. Holmes. I will leave the country, sir. Then the charge against him will break down."

"Hum! We will talk about that. And now let us hear a true account of the next act. How came the stone into the goose, and how came the goose into the open market? Tell us the truth, for there lies your only hope of safety."

Ryder passed his tongue over his parched lips. "I will tell you it just as it happened, sir," said he. "When Horner had been arrested, it seemed to me that it would be best for me to get away with the stone at once, for I did not know at what moment the police might not take it into their heads to search me and my room. There was no place about the hotel where it would be safe. I went out, as if on some commission, and I made for my sister's house. She had married a man named Oakshott, and lived in Brixton Road, where she fattened fowls for the market. All the way there every man I met seemed to me to be a policeman or a detective; and, for all that it was a cold night, the sweat was pouring down my face before I came to the Brixton Road. My sister asked me what was the matter, and why I was so pale; but I told her that I had been upset by the jewel robbery at the hotel. Then I went into the back yard and smoked a pipe, and wondered what it would be best to do.

"I had a friend once called Maudsley, who went to the bad, and has just been serving his time in Pentonville. One day he had met me, and fell into

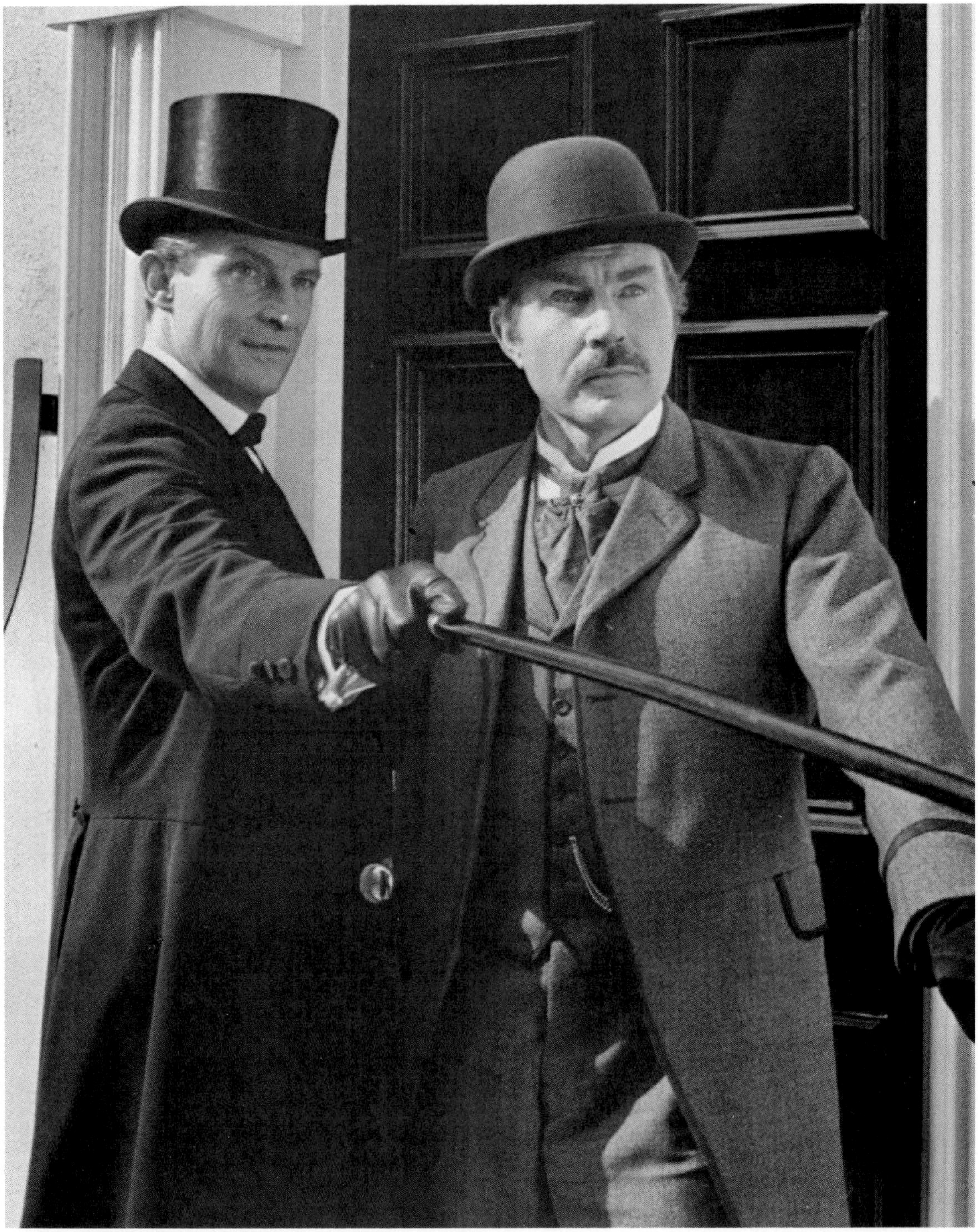

Holmes and Watson stand in the doorway of 221B Baker Street.

talk about the ways of thieves, and how they could get rid of what they stole. I knew that he would be true to me, for I knew one or two things about him; so I made up my mind to go right on to Kilburn, where he lived, and take him into my confidence. He would show me how to turn the stone into money. But how to get to him in safety? I thought of the agonies I had gone through in coming from the hotel. I might at any moment be seized and searched, and there would be the stone in my waistcoat pocket. I was leaning against the wall at the time and looking at the geese which were waddling about round my feet, and suddenly an idea came into my head which showed me how I could beat the best detective that ever lived.

"My sister had told me some weeks before that I might have the pick of her geese for a Christmas present, and I knew that she was always as good as her word. I would take my goose now, and in it I would carry my stone to Kilburn. There was a little shed in the yard, and behind this I drove one of the birds—a fine big one, white, with a barred tail. I caught it, and, prying its bill open, I thrust the stone down its throat as far as my finger could reach. The bird gave a gulp, and I felt the stone pass along its gullet and down into its crop. But the creature flapped and struggled, and out came my sister to know what was the matter. As I turned to speak to her the brute broke loose and fluttered off among the others.

"'Whatever were you doing with that bird, Jem?' says she.

"'Well,' said I, 'you said you'd give me one for Christmas, and I was feeling which was the fattest.'

"'Oh,' says she, 'we've set yours aside for you—Jem's bird, we call it. It's the big white one over yonder. There's twenty-six of them, which makes one for you, and one for us, and two dozen for the market.'

"'Thank you, Maggie', says I; 'but if it is all the same to you, I'd rather have that one I was handling just now.'

"'The other is a good three pound heavier,' said she, 'and we fattened it expressly for you.'

"'Never mind. I'll have the other, and I'll take it now,' said I.

"'Oh, just as you like,' said she, a little huffed. 'Which is it you want, then?'

"'That white one with the barred tail, right in the middle of the flock.'

"'Oh, very well. Kill it and take it with you.'

"Well, I did what she said, Mr. Holmes, and I carried the bird all the way to Kilburn. I told my pal what I had done, for he was a man that it was easy to tell a thing like that to. He laughed until he choked, and we got a knife and opened the goose. My heart turned to water, for there was no sign of the stone, and I knew that some terrible mistake had occurred. I left the bird, rushed back to my sister's, and hurried into the back yard. There was not a bird to be seen there.

"'Where are they all, Maggie?' I cried.

"'Gone to the dealer's, Jem.'

"'Which dealer's?'

"'Breckinridge, of Covent Garden.'

"'But was there another with a barred tail?' I asked, 'the same as the one I chose?'

"'Yes, Jem; there were two barred-tailed ones, and I could never tell them apart.'

"Well, then, of course I saw it all, and I ran off as hard as my feet would carry me to this man Breckinridge; but he had sold the lot at once, and not one word would he tell me as to where they had gone. You heard him yourselves tonight. Well, he has always answered me like that. My sister thinks that I am going mad. Sometimes I think that I am myself. And now—and now I am myself a branded thief, without ever having touched the wealth for which I sold my character. God help me! God help me!" He burst into convulsive sobbing, with his face buried in his hands.

There was a long silence, broken only by his heavy breathing, and by the measured tapping of Sherlock Holmes's finger-tips upon the edge of the table. Then my friend rose and threw open the door.

"Get out!" said he.

"What, sir! Oh, Heaven bless you!"

"No more words. Get out!"

And no more words were needed. There was a rush, a clatter upon the stairs, the bang of a door, and the crisp rattle of running footfalls from the street.

"After all, Watson," said Holmes, reaching up his hand for his clay pipe, "I am not retained by the police to supply their deficiencies. If Horner were in danger it would be another thing; but this fellow will not appear against him, and the case must collapse. I suppose that I am commuting a felony, but it is just possible that I am saving a soul. This fellow will not go wrong again; he is too terribly frightened. Send him to jail now, and you make him a jail-bird for life. Besides, it is the season of forgiveness. Chance has put in our way a most singular and whimsical problem, and its solution is its own reward. If you will have the goodness to touch the bell, Doctor, we will begin another investigation, in which, also, a bird will be the chief feature."

## THINK AND DISCUSS

### Understanding

1. Arrange the following names according to the order in which each person had possession of the Blue Carbuncle: Sherlock Holmes, the Countess of Morcar, James Ryder, Henry Baker, and Peterson.
2. Why did Mr. Baker, the owner of the hat, abandon the goose in the street?
3. Why had Ryder forced the gem into the goose's throat?

### Analyzing

4. Give two examples where chance plays an important role in the story.
5. In a mystery story, the climax is almost always very near the end. Why?
6. Identify the climax in this story.

### Extending

7. Do you think Holmes's decision to let Ryder go is right or wrong? Explain your decision.

## REVIEWING: Plot    H☑

### See Handbook of Literary Terms, p. 813

While the conflict in some plots features physical struggles between characters, mystery stories often highlight the mental conflict between detectives and criminals. A climax may come about when a criminal is identified or captured. The events that make the action go forward may be discoveries in the mind of the detective. When a significant discovery is made, you may think of the old saying, "the plot thickens." This expression refers to a point when the action in a story no longer seems simple and straightforward, because a character learns that unforeseen forces are at work or new problems have developed.

1. When does Holmes discover that the "problem" of the battered hat, which he had dismissed as whimsical, involves a crime?
2. What trick does Holmes use to discover the source of the goose that Mr. Breckinridge, the salesman, had sold to the Alpha Inn?

## COMPOSITION
### Writing About Plot Devices

In this Sherlock Holmes adventure Dr. Watson marvels at Holmes's ability to draw conclusions based on what seem to be trivial details about a hat. The author invented these details, of course, as he planned the story. Arthur Conan Doyle conceived the crime and built the plot that allows Holmes to trace the goose from Peterson to Baker, to the Alpha Inn, and so on, as we, the readers, observe Holmes's progress. Review the story to note the events that bring Holmes closer to the truth. Write an essay of about four paragraphs, identifying these events and telling which depend on detection that only a master such as Holmes could accomplish. If you feel that any judgment by Holmes is weak, explain why you doubt his point. Revise your paper as if you are preparing a report to be read by a mystery story readers' club. See "Writing About Plot and Plot Devices" in the Writer's Handbook.

### Describing Examples About Crime

Holmes condemns Ryder's motives for theft when he says, "Well, the temptation of sudden wealth so easily acquired was too much for you, as it has been for better men before you." Can you think of famous people or fictional characters whom you would condemn for yielding to such temptation, at the expense of victims similar to the Countess of Morcar or the unfortunate plumber, Horner? Write a four-paragraph paper offering examples of people or characters whose crimes prove Holmes's point. You may include examples from recent times or from before Ryder's attempt.

## ENRICHMENT
### Creating a "Portrait" of Sherlock Holmes

Some mystery fans are not even aware that Holmes is not a real person, since they know from books, movies, and other sources exactly what he looked like and where he lived (221B Baker Street, London). Based on this story and any other contact you can make with the stories and character of Sherlock Holmes, choose one of the following ways to depict the famous detective or his friend Dr. John Watson: a painting or sketch, a clay figure or other small sculpture, a picture or model of his famous parlor room.

## BIOGRAPHY

## Sir Arthur Conan Doyle
## 1859–1930

Born in Edinburgh, Scotland, Arthur Conan Doyle was the son of a civil servant in the Government Office of Works. As a medical student at Edinburgh University, he encountered Professor Joseph Bell—a thin, wiry, angular man whose strong point was the diagnosis of his patients' occupations and character traits as well as diseases. Bell became the model for Sherlock Holmes. After graduation in 1881 Conan Doyle served for a time as a ship's doctor, then tried to start a private practice. During this time he began writing, and in 1887 he introduced Sherlock Holmes in the novel *A Study in Scarlet*. His immediate success led Conan Doyle to further detective stories and a career not as a doctor but as an author.

# The Parachutist

**D'Arcy Niland**  Australia

"The kitten knew that it had no place here in the heart of space, and its terrified instincts told it that its only contact with solidity and safety was the thing that held it."

The hurricane came down from Capricorn,[1] and for two days and a night it rained.

In the darkness of the second night, softening away to dawn, there was silence. There was only the gurgle and drip of the wet world, and the creatures that lived on the earth began to appear, freed from the tyranny of the elements.

The hawk, ruffled in misery, brooding in ferocity, came forth in hunger and hate. It struck off into the abyss of space, scouring the earth for some booty of the storm—the sheep lying like a heap of wet kapok in the sodden paddocks, the bullock like a dark bladder carried down on the swollen stream and washing against a tree on the river flats, the rabbit, driven from its flooded warren and squeezed dead against a log.

With practiced eye it scrutinized the floating islands of rubble and the wracks of twigs lying askew on the banks for sign of lizard or snake, dead or alive. But there was nothing. Once, in the time before, there had been a rooster, draggled, forlorn, derelict, riding a raft of flotsam: too weak to fight and too sick to care about dying or the way it died.

The hawk rested on a crag of the gorge and conned the terrain with a fierce and frowning eye.

The lice worried its body with the sting of nettles. Savagely it plucked with its beak under the fold of its wings, first on one side, then on the other. It rasped its bill on the jagged stone, and dropped over the lip. It climbed in a gliding circle, widening its field of vision.

The earth was yellow and green. On the flats were chains of lagoons as if the sky had broken and fallen in sheets of blue glass. The sun was hot and the air heavy and humid.

Swinging south, the hawk dropped over a vast graveyard of dead timber. The hurricane had ravaged the gaunt trees, splitting them, felling them, tearing off their naked arms and strewing the ground with pieces, like a battlefield of bones, gray with exposure and decay.

A rabbit sprang twenty yards like a bobbing wheel, and the sight drew the hawk like a plummet, but the rabbit vanished in a hollow log,

***D'Arcy Niland*** (där′sē nī′lənd).

1. ***Capricorn***, that is, the Tropic of Capricorn, an imaginary circle around the earth south of the equator, representing the point farthest south at which the sun shines directly overhead. The hurricane came "down" from there because this story is set in the Southern Hemisphere.

*The Parachutist*  **33**

Glen Loates, *Cooper's Hawk* (detail), 1981,
Private Collection

and stayed there, and there was no other life.

Desperate, weak, the hawk alighted on a bleak limb and glared in hate. The sun was a fire on its famished body. Logs smoked with steam and the brightness of water on the earth reflected like mirrors. The telescopic eye inched over the ground—crawled infallibly over the ground, and stopped. And then suddenly the hawk swooped to the ground and tore at the body of a dead field mouse—its belly bloated and a thin vapor drifting from the gray, plastered pelt.

The hawk did not sup as it supped on the hot running blood of the rabbit in the trap—squealing in eyeless terror; it did not feast in stealthy leisure as it did on the sheep paralyzed in the drought, tearing out bit by bit its steaming entrails. Voraciously it ripped at the mouse, swallowing fast and finishing the meal in a few seconds.

But the food was only a tantalization, serving to make the hawk's appetite more fierce, more lusty. It flew into a tree, rapaciously scanning the countryside. It swerved into space and climbed higher and higher in a vigilant circle, searching the vast expanse below, even to its uttermost limits.

Hard to the west something moved on the earth, a speck: and the hawk watched it: and the speck came up to a walnut, and up to a plum, and up to a ball striped with white and gray.

The hawk did not strike at once. Obedient to instinct, it continued to circle, peering down at the farmhouse and the outbuildings, suspicious; seeing the draught horses in the yard and the fowls in the hen coop, the pigs in the sty, and the windmill twirling, and watching for human life in their precincts.

Away from them all, a hundred yards or more, down on the margin of the fallowed field, the kitten played, leaping and running and tumbling, pawing at a feather and rolling on its back biting at the feather between its forepaws.

Frenzied with hunger, yet ever cautious, the hawk came down in a spiral, set itself, and swooped. The kitten propped and froze with its head cocked on one side, unaware of danger but startled by this new and untried sport. It was no more than if a piece of paper had blown past it in a giant brustle of sound. But in the next moment the hawk fastened its talons in the fur and the fat belly of the kitten, and the kitten spat and twisted, struggling against the power that was lifting it.

Its great wings beating, paddling with the rhythm of oars, the hawk went up a slope of space with its cargo, and the kitten, airborne for the first time in its life, the earth running under it in a blur, wailed in shrill terror. It squirmed frantically as the world fell away in the distance, but the hawk's talons were like the grabs of an iceman.

The air poured like water into the kitten's eyes and broke against its triangular face, streaming back against its rippling furry sides. It howled in infinite fear, and gave a sudden desperate twist, so that the hawk was jolted in its course and dropped to another level, a few feet below the first.

Riding higher and higher on the wind, the hawk went west by the dam like a button of silver far below. The kitten cried now with a new note. Its stomach was wambling. The air gushing into its mouth and nostrils set up a humming in its ears and an aching dizziness in its head. As the hawk turned on its soundless orbit, the sun blazed like flame in the kitten's eyes, leaving its sight to emerge from a blinding grayness.

The kitten knew that it had no place here in the heart of space, and its terrified instincts told it that its only contact with solidity and safety was the thing that held it.

Then the hawk was ready to drop its prey. It was well practiced. Down had gone the rabbit, a whistle in space, to crash in a quiver of death on the ruthless earth. And the hawk had followed to its gluttonous repast.

Now there at two thousand feet the bird hovered. The kitten was alarmingly aware of the change, blinking at the pulsations of beaten air as the wings flapped, hearing only that sound. Unexpectedly, it stopped, and the wings were still— outstretched, but rigid, tilting slightly with the poised body, only the fanned tail lifting and lowering with the flow of the currents.

The kitten felt the talons relax slightly, and that was its warning. The talons opened, but in the first flashing shock of the movement the kitten completed its twist and slashed at the hawk's legs and buried its claws in the flesh like fishhooks. In the next fraction of a second the kitten had consolidated its position, securing its hold, jabbing in every claw except those on one foot which thrust out in space, pushing against insupportable air. And then the claws on this foot were dug in the breast of the hawk.

With a cry of pain and alarm the bird swooped crazily, losing a hundred feet like a dropping stone. And then it righted itself, flying in a drunken sway that diminished as it circled.

Blood from its breast beaded and trickled down the paw of the kitten and spilled into one eye. The kitten blinked, but the blood came and congealed, warm and sticky. The kitten could not turn its head. It was frightened to risk a change of position. The blood slowly built over its eye a blinding pellicle.[2]

The hawk felt a spasm of weakness, and out of it came an accentuation of its hunger and a lust to kill at all costs the victim it had claimed and carried to this place of execution. Lent an excess of power by its ferocity, it started to climb again, desperately trying to dislodge the kitten. But the weight was too much and it could not ascend. A great tiredness came in its dragging body, an ache all along the frames of its wings. The kitten clung tenaciously, staring down at the winding earth and mewling in terror.

2. *pellicle* (pel'ə kəl), a very thin skin; membrane.

For ten minutes the hawk gyrated on a level, defeated and bewildered. All it wanted to do now was to get rid of the burden fastened to its legs and body. It craved respite, a spell on the tallest trees, but it only flew high over these trees, knowing it was unable to perch. Its beak gaped under the harsh ruptures of its breath. It descended three hundred feet. The kitten, with the wisdom of instinct, never altered its position, but rode down like some fantastic parachutist.

In one mighty burst the hawk with striking beak and a terrible flapping of its wings tried finally to cast off its passenger—and nearly succeeded. The kitten miauled[3] in a frenzy of fear at the violence of the sound and the agitation. Its back legs dangled in space, treading air, and like that it went around on the curves of the flight for two minutes. Then it secured a foothold again, even firmer than the first.

In a hysterical rage, the hawk tried once more to lift itself, and almost instantly began to sweep down in great, slow, gliding eddies that became narrower and narrower.

The kitten was the pilot now and the hawk no longer the assassin of the void, the lord of the sky, and the master of the wind. The ache coiled and throbbed in its breast. It fought against the erratic disposition of its wings and the terror of its waning strength. Its heart bursting with the strain, its eyes dilated wild and yellow, it came down until the earth skimmed under it; and the kitten cried at the silver glare of the roofs not far off, and the expanding earth, and the brush of the grass.

The hawk lobbed and flung over, and the kitten rolled with it. And the hawk lay spraddled in exhaustion, its eyes fiercely, cravenly aware of the danger of its forced and alien position.

The kitten staggered giddily, unhurt, toward the silver roofs, wailing loudly as if in answer to the voice of a child.

---

3. *miauled,* meowed.

## THINK AND DISCUSS
### Understanding
1. What is the cause of the hawk's desperate hunger?
2. How does the hawk plan to kill the kitten?
3. What makes the kitten aware of the hawk's intentions?

### Analyzing
4. Why do the hawk and kitten struggle against each other?
5. In this story's **plot,** the hawk is in conflict with something else besides the kitten. Is this a struggle between the hawk and another character or with nature? Where in the story is this conflict described?

### Extending
6. In your opinion, is the climax when the kitten learns how to hold on, or when the hawk finally returns to earth? Give reasons for your answer.
7. Some readers have commented that the title adds much to this story. Do you agree or disagree? Why?

## THINKING SKILLS
### Classifying
To **classify** things is to arrange them into classes or groups according to some system. Details of imagery in "The Parachutist" can be classified either as places and things that are part of nature or as places and things made or

kept by humans. Review the story to find five items for each of these lists: *Things showing the presence of humans* (such as the silver roofs) and *Things that are part of the world of nature.*

## COMPOSITION
### Writing a Vivid Description

"The Parachutist" is a particularly vivid story in which the author uses strong action verbs that appeal to the reader's senses. The darkness softens, the hawk broods and scours the earth, the air pours into the kitten's eyes and gushes into its mouth and nostrils. The hawk is described with other verbs such as *plucked, rasped, supped, ripped, fastened, gyrated,* and *lobbed.* The kitten *leaped, pawed, propped itself, froze, spat, squirmed, howled, slashed, blinked, clung, "miauled," rolled,* and *staggered.* Think of an animal whose actions you can imagine and then describe. Write a composition describing a struggle or playful activity of the animal. Use

any of the verbs mentioned here and other vivid verbs of your choice. Try to help your readers, such as your friends or family members, see and hear the scene you describe.

### Writing a Dramatic Monologue

The characters in "The Parachutist" are animals that do not act in a human manner, yet the author figuratively personifies the kitten as a parachutist and describes the hawk's motivation in terms understandable to human readers. Imagine that either character can think in the English language. Decide what you imagine the hawk or the kitten would be thinking in the moments just after the end of the story. Write a dramatic monologue—words capturing what the character might be thinking—at this time. Try to keep the character you choose true to the portrayal in the story. As you revise, you may want to read your monologue aloud, privately, to hear how it sounds and to improve it.

## BIOGRAPHY

## D'Arcy Niland
## 1920–1967

A native of New South Wales, a state in Australia, D'Arcy Niland produced an amazing number of short stories—over five hundred of them. Before becoming a full-time writer, Niland worked as a magazine editor and as a journalist. In addition to short stories, he also wrote novels and television scripts. His first novel, *The Shiralee* (1955), was translated into twelve languages and then made into a successful motion picture. He and his wife, Ruth Park, who is also an author, collaborated on an autobiographical work, *The Drums Go Bang* (1956), and Niland himself wrote several other novels. A short story like "The Parachutist" shows his universality: except for a few terms native to Australia, the story could have taken place almost anywhere else in the world.

### The Plot-Centered, Suspenseful Story

A most popular form of short story among all readers is the plot-centered, suspenseful account that quickly establishes a conflict, carries the reader along breathlessly, and ends with a sudden, sometimes totally unexpected climax. In dramatic form these are the stories that shape some of the most exciting and famous films of our time.

Though they may deal with death or violence, these stories generally leave little or no sympathetic feelings in the reader. This is because the author carefully underplays characterization and concentrates instead either exclusively on plot, or on plot and setting insofar as they help heighten the mood of the plot. Of the stories you have read, two—"The Parachutist" and "The Monkey's Paw"— definitely fit into the plot-centered, suspense-filled category. "The Parachutist," though ultimately a survival-of-the-fittest animal tale, focuses on characters that need no individuality. Any hawk and any kitten might act as these two animals do in the circumstances offered by the plot.

"The Adventure of the Blue Carbuncle" features suspense and a strong plot, but the characterization of Sherlock Holmes, the conversations filled with long explanations, and the recounting of action that has taken place outside the story give it a different pace than the plot-centered short story has.

The first thing plot-centered stories have in common is their abbreviated length: it is impossible to maintain edge-of-the-chair suspense for any extended length of time. Necessary setting and background are quickly painted in, and the conflict is established as soon as possible. The author's next step is to arouse suspense and keep the reader hanging on every word, then speedily bring the story to its climax and tie up any loose ends.

Analyze the selections mentioned in this Comment article to see how well they fit into this category, or subgenre, of short story. How long does it take to establish the main conflict in each? Do any give a hint of the ending before or while the conflict is presented? What sort of background and setting does each use, and how important are these elements in the development of plot? Which has the most unexpected ending? Which, if any, leave you wanting to know more about what happens later to the characters?

If you are like most readers, you probably enjoy reading what might be called "action-packed" stories. While you may not want to read a steady diet of nothing besides plot-centered, suspenseful stories, they offer light reading that races the blood not only of the characters, but of the readers as well.

## Be Specific

Good writing does not simply flow from a writer's poised pen. The writing of literature is an art, just as the creation of sculpture or the painting of masterpieces is. Even personal writing is a craft, because a writer is devising a work just as creative jewelers, carpenters, and potters work at jewelry, carpentry, and pottery. Artisans use precise, time-honored techniques to produce crafted objects, and writers employ recognized techniques to create literary works.

One of a writer's techniques is using specific details. Enticing pieces of information not only interest the reader, but clarify ideas better than generalities. W. W. Jacobs does not begin "The Monkey's Paw," for example, with a vague statement about a storm outside while a family awaits a visitor. Instead, the author includes details about the storm's effects on the pathway and the road. He describes a father and son playing chess in a specific fashion, as the mother knits. As we read about Mr. White's "hand poised over the board," we can imagine the characters, not as vague figures, but as individuals of certain ages and manners.

Good writers also use details to describe settings and convey action. We tend to become more concerned about particular people, places, and events than about generalities.

Arthur Conan Doyle's portrayal of Sherlock Holmes as a successful detective focuses on this character's close attention to details.

> Sherlock Holmes laughed. "Here is the foresight," said he, putting his finger upon the little disc and loop of the hat-securer. "They are never sold upon hats. If this man ordered one, it is a sign of a certain amount of foresight, since he went out of his way to take this precaution against the wind. But since we see that he has broken the elastic and has not troubled to replace it, it is obvious that he has less foresight now than formerly. . . ."

Had the author omitted such illustrations of Holmes's method of inductive thought, we might develop little appreciation for his genius.

In "The Parachutist" author D'Arcy Niland combines details that make the action between the hawk and the kitten vivid and memorable.

> Its great wings beating, paddling with the rhythm of oars, the hawk went up a slope of space with its cargo, and the kitten, airborne for the first time in its life, the earth running under it in a blur, wailed in shrill terror.

Through such verbal "snapshots," the writer compels the reader to visualize the story's central struggle between predator and prey.

An article called "Writer's Craft" appears in each unit of this book. Each article discusses one writing technique. To make these techniques useful, you might keep a reading/writing log, a notebook to record samples of the writing techniques discussed in "Writer's Craft." This log will also give you a place to copy effective samples of writing from your outside reading and to try your hand at using the techniques. Reviewing your log before you write will help you master these techniques in your own compositions. Instructions for using a reading/writing log are found after some selections in each unit.

---

When you read, note specific details.
When you write, convey specific information about people, places, events, or ideas.

---

See CHARACTERIZATION in the Handbook of Literary Terms, page 792.

# The Secret Life of Walter Mitty

**James Thurber**   USA

Can Mitty make it through one tense situation after another? Or is he just having "one of his days"?

e're going through!" The Commander's voice was like thin ice breaking. He wore his full-dress uniform, with the heavily braided white cap pulled down rakishly over one cold gray eye. "We can't make it, sir. It's spoiling for a hurricane, if you ask me." "I'm not asking you, Lieutenant Berg," said the Commander. "Throw on the power light! Rev her up to 8500! We're going through!" The pounding of the cylinders increased: ta-pocketa-pocketa-pocketa-*pocketa-pocketa*. The Commander stared at the ice forming on the pilot window. He walked over and twisted a row of complicated dials. "Switch on No. 8 auxiliary!" he shouted. "Switch on No. 8 auxiliary!" repeated Lieutenant Berg. "Full strength in No. 3 turret!" shouted the Commander. "Full strength in No. 3 turret!" The crew, bending to their various tasks in the huge, hurtling eight-engined Navy hydroplane, looked at each other and grinned. "The Old Man'll get us through," they said to one another. "The Old Man ain't afraid of Hell!"

"Not so fast! You're driving too fast!" said Mrs. Mitty. "What are you driving so fast for?"

"Hmm?" said Walter Mitty. He looked at his wife, in the seat beside him, with shocked astonishment. She seemed grossly unfamiliar, like a strange woman who had yelled at him in a crowd: "You were up to fifty-five," she said. "You know I don't like to go more than forty. You were up to fifty-five." Walter Mitty drove on toward Waterbury in silence, the roaring of the SN202 through the worst storm in twenty years of Navy flying fading in the remote, intimate airways of his mind. "You're tensed up again," said Mrs. Mitty. "It's one of your days. I wish you'd let Dr. Renshaw look you over."

Walter Mitty stopped the car in front of the building where his wife went to have her hair done. "Remember to get those overshoes while I'm having my hair done," she said. "I don't need

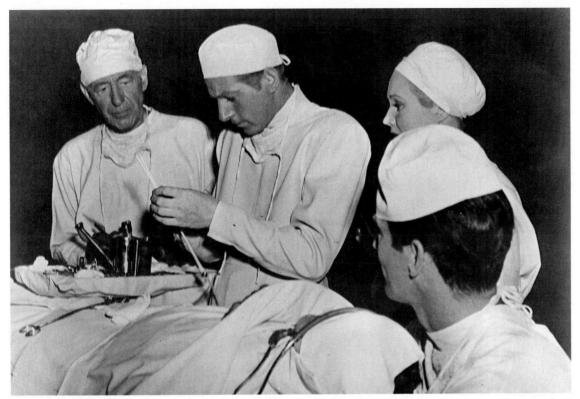

Actor Danny Kaye (center) appears in the 1947 film adaptation of "The Secret Life of Walter Mitty."

overshoes," said Mitty. She put her mirror back into her bag. "We've been all through that," she said, getting out of the car. "You're not a young man any longer." He raced the engine a little. "Why don't you wear your gloves? Have you lost your gloves?" Walter Mitty reached in a pocket and brought out the gloves. He put them on, but after she had turned and gone into the building and he had driven on to a red light, he took them off again. "Pick it up, brother!" snapped a cop as the light changed, and Mitty hastily pulled on his gloves and lurched ahead. He drove around the streets aimlessly for a time, and then he drove past the hospital on his way to the parking lot.

. . . "It's the millionaire banker, Wellington McMillan," said the pretty nurse. "Yes?" said Walter Mitty, removing his gloves slowly. "Who has the case?" "Dr. Renshaw and Dr. Benbow, but there are two specialists here, Dr. Remington from New York and Mr. Pritchard-Mitford from London. He flew over." A door opened down a long, cool corridor and Dr. Renshaw came out. He looked distraught and haggard. "Hello, Mitty," he said, "We're having the devil's own time with McMillan, the millionaire banker and close personal friend of Roosevelt. Obstreosis of the ductal tract. Tertiary.[1] Wish you'd take a look at him." "Glad to," said Mitty.

In the operating room there were whispered introductions: "Dr. Remington, Dr. Mitty. Mr. Pritchard-Mitford, Dr. Mitty." "I've read

---

1. *Obstreosis of the ductal tract. Tertiary.* The diagnosis that the imaginary Dr. Renshaw is giving to Walter Mitty is complete nonsense.

your book on streptothricosis," said Pritchard-Mitford, shaking hands. "A brilliant performance, sir." "Thank you," said Walter Mitty. "Didn't know you were in the States, Mitty," grumbled Remington. "Coals to Newcastle, bringing Mitford and me up here for a tertiary." "You are very kind," said Mitty. A huge, complicated machine, connected to the operating table, with many tubes and wires, began at this moment to go pocketa-pocketa-pocketa. "The new anesthetizer is giving way!" shouted an intern. "There is no one in the East who knows how to fix it!" "Quiet, man!" said Mitty, in a low, cool voice. He sprang to the machine, which was now going pocketa-pocketa-queep-pocketa-queep. He began fingering delicately a row of glistening dials. "Give me a fountain pen!" he snapped. Someone handed him a fountain pen. He pulled a faulty piston out of the machine and inserted the pen in its place. "That will hold for ten minutes," he said. "Get on with the operation." A nurse hurried over and whispered to Renshaw, and Mitty saw the man turn pale. "Coreopsis has set in," said Renshaw nervously. "If you would take over, Mitty?" Mitty looked at him and at the craven figure of Benbow, who drank, and at the grave, uncertain faces of the two great specialists. "If you wish," he said. They slipped a white gown on him; he adjusted a mask and drew on thin gloves; nurses handed him shining . . .

"Back it up, Mac! Look out for that Buick!" Walter Mitty jammed on the brakes. "Wrong lane, Mac," said the parking-lot attendant, looking at Mitty closely. "Gee. Yeh," muttered Mitty. He began cautiously to back out of the lane marked "Exit Only." "Leave her sit there," said the attendant. "I'll put her away." Mitty got out of the car. "Hey, better leave the key." "Oh," said Mitty, handing the man the ignition key. The attendant vaulted into the car, backed it up with insolent skill, and put it where it belonged.

They're so damn cocky, thought Walter Mitty, walking along Main Street; they think they know everything. Once he had tried to take his chains off, outside New Milford, and he had got them wound around the axles. A man had had to come out in a wrecking car and unwind them, a young, grinning garageman. Since then Mrs. Mitty always made him drive to a garage to have the chains taken off. The next time, he thought, I'll wear my right arm in a sling; they won't grin at me then. I'll have my right arm in a sling and they'll see I couldn't possibly take the chains off myself. He kicked at the slush on the sidewalk. "Overshoes," he said to himself, and he began looking for a shoe store.

When he came out into the street again, with the overshoes in a box under his arm, Walter Mitty began to wonder what the other thing was his wife had told him to get. She had told him twice, before they set out from their house for Waterbury. In a way he hated these weekly trips to town—he was always getting something wrong. Kleenex, he thought, Squibb's, razor blades? No. Toothpaste, toothbrush, bicarbonate, carborundum, initiative and referendum? He gave it up. But she would remember it. "Where's the what's-its-name?" she would ask. "Don't tell me you forgot the what's-its-name." A newsboy went by shouting something about the Waterbury trial.

. . . "Perhaps this will refresh your memory." The District Attorney suddenly thrust a heavy automatic at the quiet figure on the witness stand. "Have you ever seen this before?" Walter Mitty took the gun and examined it expertly. "This is my Webley-Vickers 50.80," he said calmly. An excited buzz ran around the courtroom. The judge rapped for order. "You are a crack shot with any sort of firearms, I believe?" said the District Attorney, insinuatingly. "Objection!" shouted Mitty's attorney. "We have shown that the defendant could not have fired the shot. We have shown that he wore his right arm in a sling on the night of the fourteenth of July." Walter Mitty raised his hand briefly and the bickering attorneys were stilled. "With any known make of gun," he said evenly, "I could have killed Gregory Fitzhurst at three hundred feet *with my left hand.*" Pandemonium broke loose in the courtroom. A woman's scream rose above the bedlam and suddenly a lovely, dark-haired girl was in Walter Mitty's arms. The District Attorney struck at her savagely. Without rising from his chair, Mitty let the man have it on the point of the chin. "You miserable cur!"

"Puppy biscuit," said Walter Mitty. He stopped walking and the buildings of Waterbury rose up out of the misty courtroom and surrounded him again. A woman who was passing laughed. "He said 'Puppy biscuit,'" she said to her companion. "That man said 'Puppy biscuit' to himself." Walter Mitty hurried on. He went into an A. & P., not the first one he came to but a smaller one farther up the street. "I want some biscuit for small, young dogs," he said to the clerk. "Any special brand, sir?" The greatest pistol shot in the world thought a moment. "It says 'Puppies Bark for It' on the box," said Walter Mitty.

His wife would be through at the hairdresser's in fifteen minutes, Mitty saw in looking at his watch, unless they had trouble drying it; sometimes they had trouble drying it. She didn't like to get to the hotel first; she would want him to be there waiting for her as usual. He found a big leather chair in the lobby, facing a window, and he put the overshoes and the puppy biscuit on the floor beside it. He picked up an old copy of *Liberty* and sank down into the chair. "Can Germany Conquer the World Through the Air?" Walter Mitty looked at the pictures of bombing planes and of ruined streets.

. . . "The cannonading has got the wind up in young Raleigh, sir," said the sergeant. Captain Mitty looked up at him through tousled hair.

"Get him to bed," he said wearily. "With the others. I'll fly alone." "But you can't, sir," said the sergeant anxiously. "It takes two men to handle that bomber and the Archies are pounding hell out of the air. Von Richtman's circus is between here and Saulier." "Somebody's got to get that ammunition dump," said Mitty. "I'm going over. Spot of brandy?" He poured a drink for the sergeant and one for himself. War thundered and whined around the dugout and battered at the door. There was a rending of wood and splinters flew through the room. "A bit of a near thing," said Captain Mitty carelessly. "The box barrage is closing in," said the sergeant. "We only live once, Sergeant," said Mitty, with his faint fleeting smile. "Or do we?" He poured another brandy and tossed it off. "I never see a man could hold his brandy like you, sir," said the sergeant. "Begging your pardon, sir." Captain Mitty stood up and strapped on his huge Webley-Vickers automatic. "It's forty kilometers through hell, sir," said the sergeant. Mitty finished one last brandy. "After all," he said softly, "what isn't?" The pounding of the cannon increased; there was the rat-tat-tatting of machine guns, and from somewhere came the menacing pocketa-pocketa-pocketa of the new flame throwers. Walter Mitty walked to the door of the dugout humming "Auprès de Ma Blonde."[2] He turned and waved to the sergeant. "Cheerio!" he said. . . .

Something struck his shoulder. "I've been looking all over this hotel for you," said Mrs. Mitty. "Why do you have to hide in this old chair? How did you expect me to find you?" "Things close in," said Walter Mitty vaguely. "What?" Mrs. Mitty said. "Did you get the what's-its-name? The puppy biscuit? What's in that box?" "Overshoes," said Mitty. "Couldn't you have put them on in the store?" "I was think-

---

2. **Auprés de Ma Blonde** (ō prä′ də mà blôn′də), the title of a French song, "Near My Blonde."

Walter Mitty (played by Danny Kaye) in a moment of glory.

ing," said Walter Mitty. "Does it ever occur to you that I am sometimes thinking?" She looked at him. "I'm going to take your temperature when I get you home," she said.

They went out through the revolving doors that made a faintly derisive whistling sound when you pushed them. It was two blocks to the parking lot. At the drugstore on the corner she said, "Wait here for me. I forgot something. I won't be a minute." She was more than a minute. Walter Mitty lighted a cigarette. It began to rain, rain with sleet in it. He stood up against the wall of the drugstore, smoking. . . . He put his shoulders back and his heels together. "To hell with the handkerchief," said Walter Mitty scornfully. He took one last drag on his cigarette and snapped it away. Then, with that faint, fleeting smile playing about his lips, he faced the firing squad; erect and motionless, proud and disdainful, Walter Mitty the Undefeated, inscrutable to the last.

## THINK AND DISCUSS

### Understanding

1. Identify the various roles Walter Mitty plays in his imagination.
2. Identify the people who interrupt Mitty's imaginary adventures.

### Analyzing

3. Contrast the two Walter Mittys.
4. Cite some examples of the transitional devices the author uses to connect incidents in reality to Mitty's imaginary adventures.

### Extending

5. Why do you think Walter Mitty daydreams?
6. Do you think daydreaming is good or bad? Explain your answer.

### APPLYING: Characterization HℤT
See Handbook of Literary Terms, p. 792

Author James Thurber presents the title character, Walter Mitty, through various methods of **characterization**. The secret life that we see represents the inner thoughts and feelings of the character. We also hear what Mitty says in the story's dialogue, as well as how other characters react to him.

1. How do the comments of Mrs. Mitty, the parking lot attendant, and a woman on the street help to reveal Mitty's character?
2. What details in the fantasy scenes and in Mitty's attempts to deal with the real people and circumstances in his everyday life heighten the comical aspect of his character?

## THINKING SKILLS

### Synthesizing

One thinking skill that helps a person make intelligent decisions and solve problems when thinking about literature is synthesizing. To

**synthesize** is to combine bits of knowledge and thought into a complex, sensible, whole picture. You can combine new knowledge—for example, what you have learned about Walter Mitty—with your old knowledge of people, and then express a thought that reflects both. Think about Mitty's tendency to drift into heroic fantasies. Consider that Mrs. Mitty has urged him to see a doctor and that Mitty is aware of how passers-by make comments about him.

1. Would you predict that Mitty will become more serious and abandon his dreamy state?
2. If he did stop daydreaming, do you think he would be a pleasant human being to know?

Make a list of things Mitty might do or say if he were suddenly to become a serious, alert man who never daydreamed. Exchange lists with a classmate and discuss which items on the lists might make the new Mitty a person you would like to know and which items might make him someone you'd like to avoid.

## COMPOSITION ◄━

### Reading/Writing Log

One reader has expressed amusement and surprise after observing that the narrator of "The Secret Life of Walter Mitty" never makes any general statements that Walter Mitty daydreams or that Mrs. Mitty nags him. Instead, the narrator depicts specific daydreams in great detail and recounts particular encounters between the Mittys. Review the story to note any detail illustrating that his heroic exploits are fantastic figments of the main character's imagination. If you think that Mrs. Mitty is an amusing character—or if you feel that this character does not enrich the story— jot down information that supports your judgment of her characterization. Write lists or prepare a chart of your evidence in your reading/writing log or on another paper or notebook page.

### Explaining a Character's Personality

Write an essay describing the personality of Walter Mitty to someone who has not read the story. Use details to show how Mitty's mind works and to illustrate what you find amusing or admirable or, if you prefer, pitiful or negative about him. If you found the story interesting, point out how Mitty's personality or behavior makes the story worth reading. See "Writing About Characters" in the Writer's Handbook.

### Defending Your Judgment of a Character

A critic has commented that, although James Thurber draws Mrs. Mitty merely as a two-dimensional character to add humor to the story, he provides her with a distinct personality and some genuinely funny dialogue. What do you think? Does she represent an unfair stereotype of a nagging wife, or is she a funny character whose presence helps the humor in the story work? Write an essay in which you express your opinion about Thurber's characterization of Mrs. Mitty.

**BIOGRAPHY**

**James Thurber**
**1894–1961**

James Thurber grew up in Columbus, Ohio, to become one of the foremost American humorists of his time. After working for a short time in the U.S. Embassy in France during World War I, he worked as a journalist in Paris and in New York. He became associated with *The New Yorker* magazine shortly after it was founded and contributed stories and cartoon drawings to it throughout his career. One source of Thurber's literary humor was his childhood in Ohio, and he shared his family's strange experiences with delighted readers in books such as *My Life and Hard Times* (1933). Other pieces were published in such books as *The Seal in the Bedroom and Other Predicaments* (1932) and *My World and Welcome to It* (1942). He was a talented cartoonist who often illustrated his own stories. Among the Thurber works that have been successfully dramatized, the most popular is "The Secret Life of Walter Mitty," which served as the basis for a well-known 1947 movie starring comic actor Danny Kaye.

Review CHARACTERIZATION in the Handbook of Literary Terms, page 792.

# A Visit to Grandmother

**William Melvin Kelley**   USA

**Three generations—grandmother, son, and grandson—discover a long-unspoken misunderstanding that has in some way touched each one.**

hig knew something was wrong the instant his father kissed her. He had always known his father to be the warmest of men, a man so kind that when people ventured timidly into his office, it took only a few words from him to make them relax, and even laugh. Doctor Charles Dunford cared about people.

But when he had bent to kiss the old lady's black face, something new and almost ugly had come into his eyes: fear, uncertainty, sadness, and perhaps even hatred.

Ten days before in New York, Chig's father had decided suddenly he wanted to go to Nashville to attend his college class reunion, twenty years out. Both Chig's brother and sister, Peter and Connie, were packing for camp and besides were too young for such an affair. But Chig was seventeen, had nothing to do that summer, and his father asked if he would like to go along. His father had given him additional reasons: "All my running buddies got their diplomas and were snapped up by them crafty young gals, and had kids within a year—now all those kids, some of them gals, are your age."

The reunion had lasted a week. As they packed for home, his father, in a far too offhand way, had suggested they visit Chig's grandmother. "We're this close. We might as well drop in on her and my brothers."

So, instead of going north, they had gone farther south, had just entered her house. And Chig had a suspicion now that the reunion had been only an excuse to drive south, that his father had been heading to this house all the time.

His father had never talked much about his family, with the exception of his brother, GL, who seemed part con man, part practical joker, and part Don Juan; he had spoken of GL with the kind of indulgence he would have shown a cute, but ill-behaved and potentially dangerous five-year-old.

Chig's father had left home when he was fifteen. When asked why, he would answer: "I wanted to go to school. They didn't have a Negro high school at home, so I went up to Knoxville and lived with a cousin and went to school."

They had been met at the door by Aunt Rose, GL's wife, and ushered into the living room. The old lady had looked up from her seat by the window. Aunt Rose stood between the visitors.

The old lady eyed his father. "Rose, who that? Rose?" She squinted. She looked like a doll made of black straw, the wrinkles in her face running in one direction like the head of a broom. Her hair was white and coarse and grew out straight from her head. Her eyes were brown—the whites, too, seemed light brown—and were hidden behind thick glasses, which remained somehow on a tiny nose. "That Hiram?" That was another of his father's brothers. "No, it ain't Hiram; too big for Hiram." She turned then to Chig. "Now that man, he look like Eleanor, Charles's wife, but Charles wouldn't never send my grandson to see me. I never even hear from Charles." She stopped again.

"It Charles, Mama. That who it is." Aunt Rose, between them, led them closer. "It Charles come all the way from New York to see you, and brung little Charles with him."

The old lady stared up at them. "Charles? Rose, that really Charles?" She turned away, and reached for a handkerchief in the pocket of her clean, ironed, flowered housecoat, and wiped her eyes. "God have mercy, Charles." She spread her arms up to him, and he bent down and kissed her cheek. That was when Chig saw his face, grimacing. She hugged him; Chig watched the muscles in her arms as they tightened around his father's neck. She half rose out of her chair. "How are you, son?"

Chig could not hear his father's answer.

She let him go, and fell back into her chair, grabbing the arms. Her hands were as dark as the wood, and seemed to become part of it. "Now, who that standing there? Who that man?"

"That's one of your grandsons, Mama." His father's voice cracked. "Charles Dunford, junior. You saw him once, when he was a baby, in Chicago. He's grown now."

"I can see that, boy!" She looked at Chig squarely. "Come here, son, and kiss me once." He did. "What they call you? Charles too?"

"No, ma'am, they call me Chig."

She smiled. She had all her teeth, but they were too perfect to be her own. "That's good. Can't have two boys answering to Charles in the same house. Won't nobody at all come. So you that little boy. You don't remember me, do you. I used to take you to church in Chicago, and you'd get up and hop in time to the music. You studying to be a preacher?"

"No, ma'am. I don't think so. I might be a lawyer."

"You'll be an honest one, won't you?"

"I'll try."

"Trying ain't enough! You be honest, you hear? Promise me. You be honest like your daddy."

"All right. I promise."

"Good. Rose, where's GL at? Where's that thief? He gone again?"

"I don't know, Mama." Aunt Rose looked embarrassed. "He say he was going by his liquor store. He'll be back."

"Well, then where's Hiram? You call up those boys, and get them over here—now! You got enough to eat? Let me go see." She started to get up. Chig reached out his hand. She shook him off. "What they tell you about me, Chig? They tell you I'm all laid up? Don't believe it. They don't know nothing about old ladies. When I want help, I'll let you know. Only time I'll need help getting anywheres is when I dies and they lift me into the ground."

She was standing now, her back and shoulders

straight. She came only to Chig's chest. She squinted up at him. "You eat much? Your daddy ate like two men."

"Yes, ma'am."

"That's good. That means you ain't nervous. Your mama, she ain't nervous. I remember that. In Chicago, she'd sit down by a window all afternoon and never say nothing, just knit." She smiled. "Let me see what we got to eat."

"I'll do that, Mama." Aunt Rose spoke softly. "You haven't seen Charles in a long time. You sit and talk."

The old lady squinted at her. "You can do the cooking if you promise it ain't because you think I can't."

Aunt Rose chuckled. "I know you can do it, Mama."

"All right. I'll just sit and talk a spell." She sat again and arranged her skirt around her short legs.

Chig did most of the talking, told all about himself before she asked. His father only spoke when he was spoken to, and then only one word at a time, as if by coming back home, he had become a small boy again, sitting in the parlor while his mother spoke with her guests.

When Uncle Hiram and Mae, his wife, came, they sat down to eat. Chig did not have to ask about Uncle GL's absence; Aunt Rose volunteered an explanation: "Can't never tell where the man is at. One Thursday morning he left here and next thing we knew, he was calling from Chicago, saying he went up to see Joe Louis fight. He'll be here though; he ain't as young and footloose as he used to be." Chig's father had mentioned driving down that GL was about five years older than he was, nearly fifty.

Uncle Hiram was somewhat smaller than Chig's father; his short-cropped kinky hair was half gray, half black. One spot, just off his forehead, was totally white. Later, Chig found out it had been that way since he was twenty. Mae (Chig could

Charles White, *Take My Mother Home*, 1950, Private Collection

not bring himself to call her Aunt) was a good deal younger than Hiram, pretty enough so that Chig would have looked at her twice on the street. She was a honey-colored woman, with long eyelashes. She was wearing a white sheath.

At dinner, Chig and his father sat on one side, opposite Uncle Hiram and Mae; his grandmother and Aunt Rose sat at the ends. The food was good; there was a lot and Chig ate a lot. All through the meal, they talked about the family as it had been thirty years before, and particularly about the young GL. Mae and Chig asked questions; the old lady answered; Aunt Rose directed the discussion, steering the old lady onto the best stories; Chig's father laughed from time to time. Uncle Hiram ate.

"Why don't you tell them about the horse, Mama?" Aunt Rose, over Chig's weak protest, was spooning mashed potatoes onto his plate. "There now, Chig."

"I'm trying to think." The old lady was holding her fork halfway to her mouth, looking at them over her glasses. "Oh, you talking about that crazy horse GL brung home that time."

"That's right, Mama." Aunt Rose nodded and slid another slice of white meat on Chig's plate.

Mae started to giggle. "Oh, I've heard this. This is funny, Chig."

The old lady put down her fork and began: Well, GL went out of the house one day with an old, no-good chair I wanted him to take over to the church for a bazaar, and he met up with this man who'd just brung in some horses from out West. Now, I reckon you can expect one swindler to be in every town, but you don't rightly think there'll be two, and heaven forbid they should ever meet—but they did, GL and his chair, this man and his horses. Well, I wished I'd-a been there; there must-a been some mighty high-powered talking going on. That man with his horses, he told GL them horses was half Arab, half Indian, and GL told that man the chair was an antique he'd stole from some rich white folks. So they swapped. Well, I was a-looking out the window and seen GL dragging this animal to the house. It looked pretty gentle and its eyes was most closed and its feet was shuffling.

"GL, where'd you get that thing?" I says.

"I swapped him for that old chair, Mama," he says. "And made myself a bargain. This is even better than Papa's horse."

Well, I'm a-looking at this horse and noticing how he be looking more and more wide-awake every minute, sort of warming up like a teakettle until, I swears to you, that horse is blowing steam out its nose.

"Come on, Mama," GL says, "come on and I'll take you for a ride." Now George, my husband, God rest his tired soul, he'd brung home this white folks' buggy which had a busted wheel and fixed it and was to take it back that day and GL says: "Come on, Mama, we'll use this fine buggy and take us a ride."

"GL," I says, "no, we ain't. Them white folks'll burn us alive if we use their buggy. You just take that horse right on back." You see, I was sure that boy'd come by that animal ungainly.

"Mama, I can't take him back," GL says.

"Why not?" I says.

"Because I don't rightly know where that man is at," GL says.

"Oh," I says. "Well, then I reckon we stuck with it." And I turned to go back into the house because it was getting late, near dinner time, and I was cooking for ten.

"Mama," GL says to my back. "Mama, ain't you coming for a ride with me?"

"Go on, boy. You ain't getting me inside kicking range of that animal." I was eying that beast and it was boiling hotter all the time. I reckon maybe that man had drugged it. "That horse is wild, GL," I says.

"No, he ain't. He ain't. That man say he is buggy and saddle broke and as sweet as the inside of an apple."

My oldest girl, Essie, had-a come out on the porch and she says: "Go on, Mama. I'll cook. You ain't been out the house in weeks."

"Sure, come on, Mama," GL says. "There ain't nothing to be fidgety about. This horse is gentle as a rose petal." And just then that animal snorts so hard it sets up a little dust storm around its feet.

"Yes, Mama," Essie says, "you can see he gentle." Well, I looked at Essie and then at that horse because I didn't think we could be looking at the same animal. I should-a figure how Essie's eyes ain't never been so good.

"Come on, Mama," GL says.

"All right," I says. So I stood on the porch and watched GL hitching that horse up to the white folks' buggy. For a while there, the animal was pretty quiet, pawing a little, but not much. And I was feeling a little better about riding with GL behind that crazy-looking horse. I could see how GL was happy I was going with him. He was scurrying around that animal buckling buckles and strapping straps, all the time smiling, and that made me feel good.

Then he was finished, and I must say, that horse looked mighty fine hitched to that buggy and I knew anybody what climbed up there would look pretty good, too. GL came around and stood at the bottom of the steps, and took off his hat and bowed and said: "Madam," and reached out his hand to me and I was feeling real elegant like a fine lady. He helped me up to the seat and then got up beside me and we moved out down our alley. And I remember how black folks came out on their porches and shook their heads, saying: "Will you *look* at Eva Dunford, the fine lady! Don't she look good sitting up there!" And I pretended not to hear and sat up straight and proud.

We rode on through the center of town, up Market Street, and all the way out where Hiram is living now, which in them days was all woods, there not being even a farm in sight, and that's when that horse must-a first realized he weren't at all broke or tame or maybe thought he was back out West again, and started to gallop.

"GL," I says, "now you ain't joking with your mama, is you? Because if you is, I'll strap you purple if I live through this."

Well, GL was pulling on the reins with all his meager strength, and yelling, "Whoa, you. Say now, whoa!" He turned to me just long enough to say, "I ain't fooling with you, Mama. Honest!"

I reckon that animal weren't too satisfied with the road, because it made a sharp right turn just then, down into a gulley and struck out across a hilly meadow. "Mama," GL yells. "Mama, do something!"

I didn't know what to do, but I figured I had to do something so I stood up, hopped down onto the horse's back, and pulled it to a stop. Don't ask me how I did that; I reckon it was that I was a mother and my baby asked me to do something, is all.

"Well, we walked that animal all the way home; sometimes I had to club it over the nose with my fist to make it come, but we made it, GL and me. You remember how tired we was, Charles?"

"I wasn't here at the time." Chig turned to his father and found his face completely blank, without even a trace of a smile or a laugh.

"Well, of course you was, son. That happened in . . . in . . . it was a hot summer that year and—"

"I left here in June of that year. You wrote me about it."

The old lady stared past Chig at him. They all turned to him; Uncle Hiram looked up from his plate.

"Then you don't remember how we all laughed?"

"No, I don't, Mama. And I probably wouldn't have laughed. I don't think it was funny." They were staring into each other's eyes.

"Why not, Charles?"

"Because in the first place, the horse was gained by fraud. And in the second place, both of you might have been seriously injured or even killed." He broke off their stare and spoke to himself more than to any of them: "And if I'd done it, you would've beaten me good for it."

"Pardon?" The old lady had not heard him; only Chig had heard.

Chig's father sat up straight as if preparing to debate. "I said that if I had done it, if I had done just exactly what GL did, you would have beaten me good for it, Mama." He was looking at her again.

"Why you say that, son?" She was leaning toward him.

"Don't you know? Tell the truth. It can't hurt me now." His voice cracked, but only once. "If GL and I did something wrong, you'd beat me first and then be too tired to beat him. At dinner, he'd always get seconds and I wouldn't. You'd do things with him, like ride in that buggy, but if I wanted you to do something with me, you were always too busy." He paused and considered whether to say what he finally did say: "I cried when I left here. Nobody loved me, Mama. I cried all the way up to Knoxville. That was the last time I ever cried in my life."

"Oh, Charles." She started to get up, to come around the table to him.

He stopped her. "It's too late."

"But you don't understand."

"What don't I understand? I understood then; I understand now."

Tears now traveled down the lines in her face, but when she spoke, her voice was clear. "I thought you knew. I had ten children. I had to give all of them what they needed most." She nodded. "I paid more mind to GL. I had to. GL could-a ended up swinging if I hadn't. But you was smarter. You was more growed up than GL when you was five and he was ten, and I tried to show you that by letting you do what you wanted to do."

"That's not true, Mama. You know it. GL was light-skinned and had good hair and looked almost white and you loved him for that."

"Charles, no. No, son. I didn't love any one of you more than any other."

"That can't be true." His father was standing now, his fists clenched tight. "Admit it, Mama . . . please!" Chig looked at him, shocked; the man was actually crying.

"It may not-a been right what I done, but I ain't no liar." Chig knew she did not really understand what had happened, what he wanted of her. "I'm not lying to you, Charles."

Chig's father had gone pale. He spoke very softly. "You're about thirty years too late, Mama." He bolted from the table. Silverware and dishes rang and jumped. Chig heard him hurrying up to their room.

They sat in silence for a while and then heard a key in the front door. A man with a new, lacquered straw hat came in. He was wearing brown and white two-tone shoes with very pointed toes and a white summer suit. "Say now! Man! I heard my brother was in town. Where he at? Where that rascal?"

He stood in the doorway, smiling broadly, an engaging, open, friendly smile, the innocent smile of a five-year-old.

## THINK AND DISCUSS
### Understanding
1. Is it merely coincidental that Dr. Dunford and Chig visit Chig's grandmother? Explain.
2. How does Dr. Dunford react to his mother's greeting? Why does this surprise Chig?
3. Dr. Dunford and others describe GL as they talk to Chig. What character traits does GL seem to have?

### Analyzing
4. Unlike the rest of his family, Dr. Dunford left home when he was fifteen. In what other ways is he different from the others?

5. At one point Chig's grandmother says, "I had ten children. I had to give all of them what they needed most." What did she feel she was giving to GL?

**Extending**

6. One student has commented that this story is about a misunderstanding based on love. Do you agree? Explain.

**REVIEWING: Characterization**
**See Handbook of Literary Terms, p. 792**

As you know, a writer may characterize a person in a story by describing a character's appearance, revealing the character's thoughts, and showing reactions of other characters. An author sometimes clearly develops a character before that character actually appears. GL is not introduced until the end of "A Visit to Grandmother," but the reader knows him well.

1. Explain what method the author has used to characterize GL.
2. Does the information the author presents about GL in the last sentence of the story change your opinion of GL? of Dr. Dunford? Explain.
3. Who would you say is the most important character in the story? Defend your answer.

**COMPOSITION**
**Writing a Character Sketch**

Just as the account of the frantic buggy ride revealed GL's personal characteristics in the story, a particular incident can sometimes make clear the qualities of a person in real life. Reconstruct from your memory an incident that showed something admirable or significant about a person you know. Jot down details about the incident and why they were important. Write a three- or four-paragraph character sketch built around the incident.

**Explaining the Causes of a Conflict**

You have read about conflicts in stories and probably have learned about conflicts in the news and perhaps witnessed them in your own community. Think about a conflict between individual people or groups that you think was due to a failure to communicate clearly. It may be a real or a fictional disagreement or struggle that could have been avoided. Write a three-paragraph essay explaining who opposed one another and how the conflict developed. In the first two paragraphs you may wish to identify the parties and indicate what caused the misunderstanding to begin or to grow more serious. In the third paragraph, note the outcome of the conflict and the effects it may have had on both parties.

## BIOGRAPHY

### William Melvin Kelley
### 1937–

Although many of his stories have southern settings, Kelley was born and raised in New York City. His novels include *A Different Drummer* and *Dunfords Travels Everywhere*. Kelley often is exasperated by reviewers who put all black writers into one category under the assumption that they speak for American blacks in general. As he has written, "I am not a sociologist or a politician or a spokesman. Such people try to give answers. A writer, I think, should ask questions. He should depict people, not symbols or ideas disguised as people."

# The Other Wife

**Colette**   France

---

**"Why didn't you ever tell me that she had blue eyes too?"**

---

or two? This way, *monsieur* and *madame*, there's still a table by the bay window, if *madame* and *monsieur* would like to enjoy the view."

Alice followed the *maître d'hôtel*.[1]

"Oh yes, come on, Marc, we'll feel we're having lunch on a boat at sea. . . ."

Her husband restrained her, passing his arm through hers.

"We'll be more comfortable there."

"There? In the middle of all those people? I'd much prefer . . ."

"Please, Alice."

He tightened his grip in so emphatic a way that she turned round.

"What's the matter with you?"

He said "shh" very quietly, looking at her intently, and drew her towards the table in the middle.

"What is it, Marc?"

"I'll tell you, darling. Let me order lunch. Would you like shrimps? Or eggs in aspic?"

"Whatever *you* like, as you know."

They smiled at each other, wasting the precious moments of an overworked, perspiring *maître d'hôtel* who stood near to them, suffering from a kind of St. Vitus' dance.[2]

"Shrimps," ordered Marc. "And then eggs and bacon. And cold chicken with cos lettuce salad. Cream cheese? *Spécialité de la maison*?[3] We'll settle for the *spécialité*. Two very strong coffees. Please give lunch to my chauffeur; we'll be leaving again at two o'clock. Cider? I don't trust it. . . . Dry champagne."

He sighed as though he had been moving a wardrobe, gazed at the pale noonday sea, the nearly white sky, then at his wife, finding her pretty in her little Mercury-type hat[4] with its long hanging veil.

---

**1.** *maître d'hôtel* (mă'trə dō tel'), headwaiter. [*French*]
**2.** *St. Vitus'* (sănt vī'təs) *dance*, a nervous disease characterized by involuntary twitching of the muscles.
**3.** *Spécialité de la maison* (spă syal ē tā' də la mă zōn'), specialty of the house. [*French*]
**4.** *Mercury-type hat.* The god Mercury is characteristically pictured wearing a rounded hat with small wings.

Reprinted with permission of Macmillan Publishing Company and Peter Owen Ltd. from *The Other Woman* by Colette, translated by Margaret Crosland. Copyright © 1971, 1972 by Peter Owen Ltd.

"You're looking well, darling. And all this sea-blue color gives you green eyes, just imagine! And you put on weight when you travel. . . . It's nice, up to a point, but only up to a point!"

Her rounded bosom swelled proudly as she leaned over the table.

"Why did you stop me taking that place by the bay window?"

It did not occur to Marc Séguy[5] to tell a lie.

"Because you'd have sat next to someone I know."

"And whom I don't know?"

"My ex-wife."

She could not find a word to say and opened her blue eyes wider.

"What of it, darling? It'll happen again. It's not important."

Alice found her tongue again and asked the inevitable questions in their logical sequence.

"Did she see you? Did she know that you'd seen her? Point her out to me."

"Don't turn round at once, I beg you; she must be looking at us. A lady with dark hair, without a hat; she must be staying at this hotel. . . . On her own, behind those children in red. . . ."

"Yes, I see."

Sheltered behind broad-brimmed seaside hats, Alice was able to look at the woman who fifteen months earlier had still been her husband's wife. "Incompatibility," Marc told her. "Oh, it was total incompatibility! We divorced like well-brought-up people, almost like friends, quietly and quickly. And I began to love you, and you were able to be happy with me. How lucky we are that in our happiness there haven't been any guilty parties or victims!"

The woman in white, with her smooth, lustrous hair over which the seaside light played in blue patches, was smoking a cigarette, her eyes half closed. Alice turned back to her husband, took some shrimps and butter, and ate composedly.

"Why didn't you ever tell me," she said after a moment's silence, "that she had blue eyes too?"

"But I'd never thought about it!"

He kissed the hand that she stretched out to the bread basket and she blushed with pleasure. Dark-skinned and plump, she might have seemed slightly earthy, but the changing blue of her eyes, and her wavy golden hair, disguised her as a fragile and soulful blond. She showed overwhelming gratitude to her husband. She was immodest without knowing it and her entire person revealed overconspicuous signs of extreme happiness.

They ate and drank with good appetite and each thought that the other had forgotten the woman in white. However, Alice sometimes laughed too loudly and Marc was careful of his posture, putting his shoulders back and holding his head up. They waited some time for coffee, in silence. An incandescent stream, a narrow reflection of the high and invisible sun, moved slowly over the sea and shone with unbearable brilliance.

"She's still there, you know," Alice whispered suddenly.

"Does she embarrass you? Would you like to have coffee somewhere else?"

"Not at all! It's she who ought to be embarrassed! And she doesn't look as though she's having a madly gay time; if you could see her. . . ."

"It's not necessary. I know that look of hers."

"Oh, was she like that?"

He breathed smoke through his nostrils and wrinkled his brows.

"Was she like that? No. To be frank, she wasn't happy with me."

"Well, my goodness!"

"You're delightfully generous, darling, madly generous. . . . You're an angel, you're . . . You love me. . . . I'm so proud, when I see that look in your eyes . . . yes, the look you have

---

5. *Séguy* (sā gē′).

Howard Chandler Christy, *The Cunning of Lord Felixstone*, 1920, Private Collection

now. . . . She . . . No doubt I didn't succeed in making her happy. That's all there is to it, I didn't succeed."

"She's hard to please!"

Alice fanned herself irritably, and cast brief glances at the woman in white, her head leaning against the back of the cane chair, her eyes closed with an expression of satisfied lassitude.

Marc shrugged his shoulders modestly.

"That's it," he admitted. "What can one do? We have to be sorry for people who are never happy. As for us, we're so happy. . . . Aren't we, darling?"

She didn't reply. She was looking with furtive attention at her husband's face, with its good color and regular shape, at his thick hair, with its occasional thread of white silk, at his small, well-cared-for hands. She felt dubious for the first time, and asked herself: "What more did she want, then?"

And until they left, while Marc was paying the bill, asking about the chauffeur and the route, she continued to watch, with envious curiosity, the lady in white, that discontented, hard-to-please, superior woman. . . .

## THINK AND DISCUSS

### Understanding

1. Why did Marc resist sitting by the bay window?
2. What physical description is given for Marc's first wife?
3. How long has it been since Marc divorced his first wife?

### Analyzing

4. Why might Marc have married Alice, who seems so different from his first wife?
5. Although a character's statements and conversational manners often are important parts of **characterization,** it is possible to have a character remain silent throughout a story. What is achieved by having the first wife say nothing and merely be part of the environment?
6. At the end of the story, Alice "continued to watch, with envious curiosity, the lady in white, that discontented, hard-to-please, superior woman . . ." How might the things she has learned during this lunch make Alice feel "dubious for the first time"?

### Extending

7. To which of the two wives do you think the title of the story applies? Explain.

## THINKING SKILLS

### Evaluating

To **evaluate** is to make a judgment based on some sort of standard. Just as a movie critic judges how well a movie is directed, you may judge how well the author portrays Alice, Marc, and the "other wife" in this story. Write a paragraph telling whether you feel that their actions under the circumstances are believable and why you feel as you do.

## COMPOSITION

### Explaining a Change in Attitude

It seems apparent that Alice's attitude toward her life has undergone a subtle change during the lunch depicted in "The Other Wife." You may recall a moment when your attitude toward a place, an event, or any topic underwent a change. Call to mind your feelings about the subject both before and after the change. Write a three-paragraph paper describing your experience. In the first paragraph, explain how you felt at the beginning. In the second paragraph, recount the incident or period of time when you changed your opinion, telling how it came about. In the final paragraph, express the new attitude you adopted at that time.

### Describing a Person

Just as the first wife makes a strong impression on Alice in "The Other Wife," certain people may have made an impression on you when you saw or met them for the first time. Recall an experience when you have noticed a person and remembered that first impression. Think of all the ways we sense details about a person, including sight, sound, and the other senses. In a contact sport, the first impression may impact the sense of touch; in an elevator, the sense of smell may be affected by a perfume. Write a detailed description telling about a strong impression someone once made on you. It may have been a new acquaintance, a relative being introduced, or even a person you never saw again. Use specific details that appeal to the reader's senses and imagination. Indicate why meeting or seeing the person was memorable. If you wish, write about a favorite pet instead of a person.

## Exploring the Food in Fiction

One interesting way to appreciate the imagery and details in a story set during a meal is to learn more about the food mentioned in the work. "The Other Wife" takes place in an elegant restaurant in an exotic place: France. The main characters are wealthy (they have a chauffeur), and so their lunch promises to include delicacies prepared by chefs who specialize in dainty meals. By doing library research on French restaurants, or by consulting experts such as cooks, teachers of foreign languages and home economics, and relatives who know about food preparation, you may be able to learn about foods named in the story. They include eggs in aspic, cos lettuce, and dishes that might be the *spécialité de la maison* at a restaurant like the one in the story. Report to the class about any or all of the foods, and bring photographs or artwork to illustrate your report. If possible, prepare any of the foods for your own enjoyment or to share with classmates.

# BIOGRAPHY

## Colette
### 1873–1954

Thoroughly French in every respect, Colette (full name: Sidonie Gabrielle Claudine Colette) was born in France's Burgundy region and died in Paris. She enjoyed a happy and creative childhood in her small village, growing extremely close to her mother. Memories of her childhood are preserved in the book *My Mother's House* (1923).

Married to Henri Gauthier-Villars, a man considerably older than herself, Colette collaborated with him on the *Claudine* series of novels. Later she established herself independently as a major novelist with the publication of such works as *Chéri* (1920) and *Gigi* (1944). Concentrating on characterization rather than plot, Colette often places her protagonist in a crisis situation, delicately showing the changes in mood and the emotional subtleties as the character confronts the situation and reacts to it. This is what happens in "The Other Wife," when Alice first views her predecessor in Marc's affections.

See SETTING in the Handbook of Literary Terms, page 824.

# The Boar Hunt

José Vasconcelos   Mexico

---

**The promise of adventure attracts hunters to unexplored jungles of the Amazon. There they discover where greed and recklessness lead.**

---

e were four companions, and we went by the names of our respective nationalities: the Colombian, the Peruvian, the Mexican; the fourth, a native of Ecuador, was called Quito[1] for short. Unforeseen chance had joined us together a few years ago on a large sugar plantation on the Peruvian coast. We worked at different occupations during the day and met during the evening in our off time. Not being Englishmen, we did not play cards. Instead, our constant discussions led to disputes. These didn't stop us from wanting to see each other the next night, however, to continue the interrupted debates and support them with new arguments. Nor did the rough sentences of the preceding wrangles indicate a lessening of our affection, of which we assured ourselves reciprocally with the clasping of hands and a look. On Sundays we used to go on hunting parties. We roamed the fertile glens, stalking, generally with poor results, the game of the warm region around the coast, or we entertained ourselves killing birds that flew in the sunlight during the siesta hour.

We came to be tireless wanderers and excellent marksmen. Whenever we climbed a hill and gazed at the imposing range of mountains in the interior, its attractiveness stirred us and we wanted to climb it. What attracted us more was the trans-Andean region:[2] fertile plateaus extending on the other side of the range in the direction of the Atlantic toward the immense land of Brazil. It was as if primitive nature called us to her breast. The vigor of the fertile, untouched jungles promised to rejuvenate our minds, the same vigor which rejuvenates the strength and the thickness of the trees each year. At times we devised crazy plans. As with all things that are given a lot of thought,

---

*José Vasconcelos* (hō zā′ väs kōn sä′ lōs)

**1. *Ecuador*** (ek′ wə dôr) . . . ***Quito*** (kē′ tō). Ecuador is located in northwestern South America. Quito is its capital.

**2. *trans-Andean region,*** the area across—that is, to the east of—the Andes Mountains. The Andes run in a generally north-south direction through the length of South America.

"The Boar Hunt" by José Vasconcelos, translated by Paul Waldorf, from *The Muse in Mexico: A Mid-Century Miscellany, Supplement to the Texas Quarterly*, Volume II, Number 1, Spring 1959, pp. 64–69. Reprinted by permission of The University of Texas Press.

these schemes generally materialized. Ultimately nature and events are largely what our imaginations make them out to be. And so we went ahead planning and acting. At the end of the year, with arranged vacations, accumulated money, good rifles, abundant munitions, stone- and mud-proof boots, four hammocks, and a half dozen faithful Indians, our caravan descended the Andean slopes, leading to the endless green ocean.

At last we came upon a village at the edge of the Marañón River.[3] Here we changed our safari. The region we were going to penetrate had no roads. It was unexplored underbrush into which we could enter only by going down the river in a canoe. In time we came to the area where we proposed to carry out the purpose of our journey, the hunting of wild boars.

We had been informed that boars travel in herds of several thousands, occupying a region, eating grass and staying together, exploiting the grazing areas, organized just like an army. They are very easy to kill if one attacks them when they are scattered out satisfying their appetites—an army given over to the delights of victory. When they march about hungry, on the other hand, they are usually vicious. In our search we glided down river between imposing jungles with our provisions and the company of three faithful Indian oarsmen.

One morning we stopped at some huts near the river. Thanks to the information gathered there, we decided to disembark a little farther on in order to spend the night on land and continue the hunt for the boars in the thicket the following day.

Sheltered in a backwater, we came ashore, and after a short exploration found a clearing in which to make camp. We unloaded the provisions and the rifles, tied the boat securely, then with the help of the Indians set up our camp one-half kilometer from the riverbank. In marking the path to the landing, we were careful not to lose ourselves in the thicket. The Indians withdrew toward their huts, promising to return two days later. At dawn we would set out in search of the prey.

Though night had scarcely come and the heat was great, we gathered at the fire to see each other's faces, to look instinctively for protection. We talked a little, confessed to being tired, and decided to go to bed. Each hammock had been tied by one end to a single tree, firm though not very thick in the trunk. Stretching out from this axis in different directions, the hammocks were supported by the other end on other trunks. Each of us carried his rifle, cartridges, and some provisions which couldn't remain exposed on the ground. The sight of the weapons made us consider the place where we were, surrounded by the unknown. A slight feeling of terror made us laugh, cough, and talk. But fatigue overcame us, that heavy fatigue which compels the soldier to scorn danger, to put down his rifle, and to fall asleep though the most persistent enemy pursues him. We scarcely noticed the supreme grandeur of that remote tropical night.

I don't know whether it was the light of the magnificent dawn or the strange noises which awakened me and made me sit up in my hammock and look carefully at my surroundings. I saw nothing but the awakening of that life which at night falls into the lethargy of the jungle. I called my sleeping companions and, alert and seated in our hanging beds, we dressed ourselves. We were preparing to jump to the ground when we clearly heard a somewhat distant, sudden sound of rustling branches. Since it did not continue, however, we descended confidently, washed our faces with water from our canteens, and slowly prepared and

---

3. *Marañón* (mä′rä nyôn′) *River,* a river in Peru, flowing north and then east into the Amazon.

George Catlin, *A Fight with Peccaries, Rio Trombutas, Brazil* (detail), The American Museum of Natural History.

enjoyed breakfast. By about 11:00 in the morning we were armed and bold and preparing to make our way through the jungle.

But then the sound again. Its persistence and proximity in the thicket made us change our minds. An instinct made us take refuge in our hammocks. We cautiously moved our cartridges and rifles into them again, and without consulting each other we agreed on the idea of putting our provisions safely away. We passed them up into the hammocks, and we ourselves finally climbed in. Stretched out face down, comfortably suspended with rifles in hand, we did not have to

wait long. Black, agile boars quickly appeared from all directions. We welcomed them with shouts of joy and well-aimed shots. Some fell immediately, giving comical snorts, but many more came out of the jungle. We shot again, spending all the cartridges in the magazine. Then we stopped to reload. Finding ourselves safe in the height of our hammocks, we continued after a pause.

We counted dozens of them. At a glance we made rapid calculations of the magnitude of the destruction, while the boars continued to come out of the jungle in uncountable numbers. Instead of going on their way or fleeing, they seemed confused. All of them emerged from the jungle where it was easy for us to shoot them. Occasionally we had to stop firing because the frequent shooting heated the barrels of our rifles. While they were cooling we were able to joke, celebrating our good fortune. The impotent anger of the boars amazed us. They raised their tusks in our direction, uselessly threatening us. We laughed at their snorts, quietly aimed at those who were near, and Bang! a dead boar. We carefully studied the angle of the shoulder blade so that the bullet would cross the heart. The slaughter lasted for hours.

At 4:00 P.M. we noticed an alarming shortage of our ammunition. We had been well supplied and had shot at will. Though the slaughter was gratifying, the boars must have numbered, as we had been informed previously, several thousands, because their hordes didn't diminish. On the contrary, they gathered directly beneath our hammocks in increasing groups. They slashed furiously at the trunk of the tree which held the four points of the hammocks. The marks of the tusks remained on the hard bark. Not without a certain fear we watched them gather compactly, tenaciously, in tight masses against the resisting trunk. We wondered what would happen to a man who fell within their reach. Our shots were now sporadic, well aimed, carefully husbanded. They did not drive away the aggressive beasts, but only redoubled their fury. One of us ironically noted that from being the attackers we had gone on the defensive. We did not laugh very long at the joke. Now we hardly shot at all. We needed to save our cartridges.

The afternoon waned and evening came upon us. After consulting each other, we decided to eat in our hammocks. We applauded ourselves for taking the food up—meat, bread, and bottles of water. Stretching ourselves on our hammocks, we passed things to each other, sharing what we needed. The boars deafened us with their angry snorts.

After eating, we began to feel calm. We lit cigars. Surely the boars would go. Their numbers were great, but they would finally leave peacefully. As we said so, however, we looked with greedy eyes at the few unused cartridges that remained. Our enemies, like enormous angry ants, stirred beneath us, encouraged by the ceasing of our fire. From time to time we carefully aimed and killed one or two of them, driving off the huge group of uselessly enraged boars at the base of the trunk which served as a prop for our hammocks.

Night enveloped us almost without our noticing the change from twilight. Anxiety also overtook us. When would the cursed boars leave? Already there were enough dead to serve as trophies to several dozen hunters. Our feat would be talked about; we had to show ourselves worthy of such fame. Since there was nothing else to do, it was necessary to sleep. Even if we had had enough bullets it would have been impossible to continue the fight in the darkness. It occurred to us to start a fire to drive the herd off with flames, but apart from the fact that we couldn't leave the place in which we were suspended, there were no dry branches in the lush forest. Finally, we slept.

We woke up a little after midnight. The darkness was profound, but the well-known noise made us aware that our enemies were still there. We imagined they must be the last ones which were leaving, however. If a good army needs several hours to break camp and march off, what can be expected of a vile army of boars but disorder and delay? The following morning we would fire upon the stragglers, but this painful thought bothered us: they were in large and apparently active numbers. What were they up to? Why didn't they leave? We thus spent long hours of worry. Dawn finally came, splendid in the sky but noisy in the jungle still enveloped inwardly in shadows. We eagerly waited for the sun to penetrate the foliage in order to survey the appearance of the field of battle of the day before.

What we finally saw made us gasp. It terrified us. The boars were painstakingly continuing the work which they had engaged in throughout the entire night. Guided by some extraordinary instinct, with their tusks they were digging out the ground underneath the tree from which our hammocks hung; they gnawed the roots and continued to undermine them like large, industrious rats. Presently the tree was bound to fall and we with it, among the beasts. From that moment we neither thought nor talked. In desperation we used up our last shots, killing more ferocious beasts. Still, the rest renewed their activity. They seemed to be endowed with intelligence. However much we concentrated our fire against them, they did not stop their attack against the tree.

Soon our shots stopped. We emptied our pistols, and then silently listened to the tusks gnawing beneath the soft, wet, pleasant-smelling earth. From time to time the boars pressed against the tree, pushing it and making it creak, eager to smash it quickly. We looked on, hypnotized by their devilish activity. It was impossible to flee because the black monsters covered every inch in sight. It seemed to us that, by a sudden inspiration, they were preparing to take revenge on us for the ruthless nature of man, the unpunished destroyer of animals since the beginning of time. Our imagination, distorted by fear, showed us our fate as an atonement for the unpardonable crimes implicit in the struggle of biological selection. Before my eyes passed the vision of sacred India, where the believer refuses to eat meat in order to prevent the methodical killing of beasts and in order to atone for man's evil, bloody, treacherous slaughter, such as ours, for mere vicious pleasure. I felt that the multitude of boars was raising its accusing voice against me. I now understood the infamy of the hunter, but what was repentance worth if I was going to die with my companions, hopelessly devoured by that horde of brutes with demonlike eyes?

Stirred by terror and without realizing what I was doing, I hung from the upper end of my hammock, I balanced myself in the air, I swung in a long leap, I grasped a branch of a tree facing the one on which the boars were digging. From there I leaped to other branches and to others, reviving in myself habits which the species had forgotten.

The next moment a terrifying sound and unforgettable cries told me of the fall of the tree and the end of my companions. I clung to a trunk, trembling and listening to the chattering of my jaws. Later, the desire to flee gave me back my strength. Leaning out over the foliage, I looked for a path, and I saw the boars in the distance, marching in compressed ranks and holding their insolent snouts in the air. I knew that they were now withdrawing, and I got down from the tree. Horror overwhelmed me as I approached the site of our encampment, but some idea of duty made me return there. Perhaps one of my friends had managed to save himself. I approached hesitantly. Each dead boar made me tremble with fear.

But what I saw next was so frightful that I could not fix it clearly in my mind: remains of clothing—and footwear. There was no doubt; the boars had devoured them. Then I ran toward the river, following the tracks we had made two days before. I fled with great haste, limbs stiff from panic.

Running with long strides, I came upon the boat. With a great effort, I managed to row to the huts. There I went to bed with a high fever which lasted many days.

I will participate in no more hunts. I will contribute, if I have to, to the extermination of harmful beasts. But I will not kill for pleasure. I will not amuse myself with the ignoble pleasure of the hunt.

## THINK AND DISCUSS
### Understanding
1. When the four men get to know one another at the sugar plantation, how do they spend their time together?
2. Where and how do the men go about setting up their camp during the boar hunting expedition?
3. When the hunters first see the boars, how do they react?
4. What is the fate of the narrator's three companions?

### Analyzing
5. In what way is the hunters' decision to tie all four hammocks to the same tree significant to the plot?
6. Trace the narrator's attitude toward killing animals from the beginning of the story through the very end.

### Extending
7. "The Boar Hunt" might be understood as a tale of the triumph of hunted animals over people who have killed them for pleasure. Why is it important to this meaning that the hunters be of different nationalities?
8. Review the descriptive details the author uses to emphasize the extent of the slaughter of the boars. Why, in your opinion, does the narrator describe the slaughter so vividly? Do you think the vivid description makes the story more compelling or simply more troubling to readers?

### APPLYING: Setting HF
### See Handbook of Literary Terms, p. 824
   **Setting,** the time and place in which the action of a narrative occurs, often does more than merely provide a background for a story's action. Sometimes the setting makes the action believable. The place where this story is set is fairly specific—near the Marañón River, east of the Andes Mountains in Peru. However, what the area looks like becomes clear only gradually; details are presented throughout the story.

1. Using these details, describe the setting in your own words.
2. How important is the setting to what happens in the story—that is, would the story work as well if set elsewhere? Defend your answer.
3. What aspect of setting is never made clear? Why do you think it is not mentioned?

## VOCABULARY
### Context
   One aid in understanding a word you don't know is context, the words and sentences around the word that may provide clues to the word's meaning. Context also helps you determine the proper meaning of a word having more than one definition.
   Read each of the following quotations from "The Boar Hunt." If there is enough information to determine the meaning of the italicized word, write what you think it means on a separate sheet of paper. If there is not enough information in the sentence, write *No.* Then, if necessary, check the Glossary for the meanings and pronunciations of all the italicized words. Complete the exercise by using each of the words in an original sentence that provides a new context and shows you understand its meaning.

1. "The afternoon *waned* and evening came upon us."
2. "The *impotent* anger of the boars amazed us."

3. "I saw nothing but the awakening of that life which at night falls into the *lethargy* of the jungle."
4. "We shot again, spending all the cartridges in the *magazine*."
5. "They were digging out the ground underneath the tree from which our hammocks hung; they gnawed the roots and continued to *undermine* them."

## COMPOSITION

### Writing a Narrative

In "The Boar Hunt" the men act with supreme self-confidence in their power over nature, perhaps because they have guns. The reader senses that unlimited confidence may be rewarded with disaster. You undoubtedly can either remember from experience or imagine a person acting with great confidence, only to be disappointed. Create a narrative with an outcome that is the opposite of the overconfident expectations that motivated an act or an undertaking. You may want to present a conflict that allows the reader chances to foresee the dangers early in the narrative.

### Describing a Setting

Think of a favorite place that makes you feel good, or imagine a setting that may induce a feeling of foreboding, irritation, or boredom. Describe the place in a composition, using details of imagery that appeal to the reader's senses and create the appropriate mood.

## ENRICHMENT

### Finding a Setting on a Map

It takes only a short time to locate the main geographical setting of "The Boar Hunt," if you have access to a good world atlas. Using a home, classroom, or library atlas, find Peru on a map of South America or of the Amazon River region. Then, on a map of Peru, find the Andes Mountains and the Marañón River in northern Peru. The setting of the story is east of the Andes, in a jungle near the river. The precise location is never mentioned.

## BIOGRAPHY

### José Vasconcelos
### 1882–1959

A thinker and a politician as well as an author, José Vasconcelos did much to improve the level of living in his native land of Mexico. Not long after the revolution of 1910, Vasconcelos was appointed Minister of Public Education by the new government. During this period (1920–1924) he instituted important reforms in the educational system and was responsible for the opening of many rural schools. Extending his activities to cultural matters, he commissioned the first murals for public buildings, assisted orchestras and musicians, and invited other Latin American intellectual leaders to Mexico. In 1929 he even made an unsuccessful run for the presidency but was later forced into exile by his successful opponent.

Vasconcelos's most important literary work is undoubtedly his autobiography, one of the best studies of culture and life in twentieth-century Mexico ever written.

**Review SETTING in the Handbook of Literary Terms, page 824.**

# Life Is Sweet at Kumansenu

**Abioseh Nicol**   Sierra Leone

---

**Bola could not overcome suspicions about her son's visit. Perhaps it was because mystery had marked his life from the beginning.**

---

he sea and the wet sand to one side of it; green tropical forest on the other; above it the slow tumbling clouds. The clean round blinding disc of sun and the blue sky covered and surrounded the small African village, Kumansenu.[1]

A few square mud houses with roofs like helmets, here thatched and there covered with corrugated zinc where the prosperity of cocoa and trading had touched the head of the family.

The widow Bola stirred her palm-oil stew and thought of nothing in particular. She chewed a kola nut[2] rhythmically with her strong toothless jaws and soon unconsciously she was chewing in rhythm with the skipping of Asi, her granddaughter. She looked idly at Asi as the seven-year-old brought the twisted palm-leaf rope smartly over her head and jumped over it, counting in English each time the rope struck the ground and churned up a little red dust. Bola herself did not understand English well, but she could count easily up to twenty in English for market purposes. Asi shouted six and then said nine, ten.

Bola called out that after six came seven. And I should know, she sighed. Although now she was old, there was a time when she bore children regularly every two years. Six times she had borne a boy child and six times they had died. Some had swollen up and with weak plaintive cries had faded away. Others had shuddered in sudden convulsions, with burning skins, and had rolled up their eyes and died. They had all died. Or rather he had died, Bola thought, because she knew it was one child all the time whose spirit had crept up restlessly into her womb to be born and to mock her.[3] The sixth time Musa, the village ma-

---

*Abioseh Nicol* (ä'bē ōs'ə nik ōl').

1. *Kumansenu* (kü män sā'nü).

2. *kola nut,* the bitter seed of an African evergreen tree, used in making medicines and soft drinks.

3. *one child . . . to mock her,* a reference to a West African belief in a spirit-child who does not live to maturity but returns in a series of rebirths.

From *The Truly Married Woman* by Abioseh Nicol, 1965, published by Oxford University Press. Reprinted by permission of David Higham Associates Limited. Slightly abridged.

gician whom time had transformed into a respectable Muslim, had advised her and her husband to break the bones of the quiet little corpse and mangle it so that it couldn't come back to torment them alive again. But she held on to the child, and refused to let them handle it. Secretly she had marked it with a sharp pointed stick at the left buttock before it was wrapped in a mat and they had taken it away. When, the seventh time she had borne a son, and the purification ceremonies had taken place, she had turned it slyly to see whether the mark was there. It was. She showed it to the old woman who was the midwife and asked her what that was, and she had forced herself to believe the other who said it was an accidental scratch made whilst the child was being scrubbed. But this child had stayed. Meji,[4] he had been called. And he was now thirty years of age and a second-class clerk in government offices in a town ninety miles away. Asi, his daughter, had been left with her to do the things an old woman wanted a small child for, to run and take messages to the neighbors, to fetch a cup of water from the earthenware pot in the kitchen, to sleep with her and be fondled.

She threw the washed and squeezed cassava[5] leaves into the red boiling stew, putting in a finger's pinch of salt, and then went indoors, carefully stepping over the threshold to look for the dried red pepper. She found it, and then dropped it, leaning against the wall with a little cry. He turned round from the window and looked at her with a twisted half smile of love and sadness. In his short-sleeved, open-necked white shirt and gray gabardine trousers, a gold wristwatch and brown suede shoes, he looked like the pictures in African magazines of a handsome clerk who would get to the top because he ate the correct food, or regularly took the correct laxative, which was being advertised. His skin was grayish brown and he had a large handkerchief tied round his neck.

"Meji, God be praised," Bola cried. "You gave me quite a turn. My heart is weak and I can no longer take surprises. When did you come? How did you come? By lorry,[6] by fishing boat? And how did you come into the house? The front door was locked. There are so many thieves nowadays. I'm so glad to see you, so glad," she mumbled and wept, leaning against his breast.

Meji's voice was hoarse, and he said: "I am glad to see you too, Mother," beating her back affectionately.

Asi ran in and cried, "Papa, Papa," and was rewarded with a lift and a hug.

"Never mind how I came, Mother," Meji said, laughing. "I'm here, and that's all that matters."

"We must make a feast, we must have a big feast. I must tell the neighbors at once. Asi, run this very minute to Mr. Addai,[7] the catechist, and tell him your papa is home. Then to Mami Gbera to ask her for extra provisions, and to Pa Babole[8] for drummers and musicians . . ."

"Stop," said Meji raising his hand. "This is all quite unnecessary. I don't want to see *anyone*, no one at all; I wish to rest quietly and completely. No one is to know I'm here."

Bola looked very crestfallen. She was proud of Meji, and wanted to show him off. The village would never forgive her for concealing such an important visitor. Meji must have sensed this because he held her shoulder comfortingly and said: "They will know soon enough. Let us enjoy each other, all three of us, this time. Life is too short."

Bola turned to Asi, picked up the packet of pepper, and told her to go and drop a little into the boiling pot outside, taking care not to go too near the fire or play with it. After the child had

---

4. *Meji* (mä′jē).

5. *cassava* (kə sä′və), a tropical plant with starchy roots.

6. *lorry,* truck. [*British*]

7. *Addai* (ä dī′).

8. *Mami Gbera* (mä′mē gə be′rä) . . . *Pa Babole* (pä bä-bō′lē).

gone, Bola said to her son, "Are you in trouble? Is it the police?"

He shook his head. "No," he said, "it's just that I like returning to you. There will always be this bond of love and affection between us, and I don't wish to share it. It is our private affair and that is why I've left my daughter with you," he ended up irrelevantly; "girls somehow seem to stay with relations longer."

"And don't I know it," said Bola. "But you look pale," she continued, "and you keep scraping your throat. Are you ill?" She laid her hand on his brow. "And you're cold, too."

"It's the cold wet wind," he said, a little harshly. "I'll go and rest now if you can open and dust my room for me. I'm feeling very tired. Very tired indeed. I've traveled very far today and it has not been an easy journey."

"Of course, my son, of course," Bola replied, bustling away hurriedly but happily.

Meji slept all afternoon till evening, and his mother brought his food to his room, later took the empty basins away. Then he slept again till morning.

The next day, Saturday, was a busy one, and after further promising Meji that she would tell no one he was about, Bola went off to market. Meji took Asi for a long walk through a deserted path and up into the hills. She was delighted. They climbed high until they could see the village below in front of them, and the sea in the distance, and the boats with their wide white sails. Soon the sun had passed its zenith and was halfway towards the west. Asi had eaten all the food, the dried fish and the flat tapioca pancakes and the oranges. Her father said he wasn't hungry, and this had made the day perfect for Asi, who had chattered, eaten, and then played with her father's fountain pen and other things from his pocket. They soon left for home because he had promised they would be back before dark; he had carried her down some steep boulders and she had

held on to his shoulders because he had said his neck hurt so and she must not touch it. She had said: "Papa, I can see behind you and you haven't got a shadow. Why?"

He had then turned her round to face the sun. Since she was getting drowsy, she had started asking questions, and her father had joked with her and humored her. "Papa, why has your watch stopped at twelve o'clock?" "Because the world ends at noon." Asi had chuckled at that. "Papa, why do you wear a scarf always round your neck?" "Because my head would fall off if I didn't." She had laughed out loud at that. But soon she had fallen asleep as he bore her homewards.

Just before nightfall, with his mother dressed in her best, they had all three, at her urgent request, gone to his father's grave, taking a secret route and avoiding the main village. It was a small cemetery, not more than twenty years or so old, started when the Rural Health Department had insisted that no more burials take place in the backyards of households. Bola took a bottle of wine and a glass and four split halves of kola, each a half sphere, two red and two white. They reached the graveside and she poured some wine into the glass. Then she spoke to the dead man softly and caressingly. She had brought his son to see him, she said. This son whom God had given success, to the confusion and discomfiture of their enemies. Here he was, a man with a pensionable clerk's job and not a farmer, fisherman, or a mechanic. All the years of their married life people had said she was a witch because her children had died young. But this boy of theirs had shown that she was a good woman. Let her husband answer her now, to show that he was listening. She threw the four kola nuts up into the air and they fell on the grave. Three fell with the flat face upwards and one with its flat face downwards. She picked them up again and conversed with him once more and threw the kola nuts up again. But

Charles White, *Man*, 1959.
Collection of Harry Belafonte.

still there was an odd one or sometimes two.

They did not fall with all four faces up, or with all four faces down, to show that he was listening and was pleased. She spoke endearingly, she cajoled, she spoke sternly. But all to no avail. Then she asked Meji to perform. He crouched by the graveside and whispered. Then he threw the kola nuts and they rolled a little, Bola following them eagerly with her sharp old eyes. They all ended up face downwards. Meji emptied the glass of wine on the grave and then said that he felt nearer his father at that moment than he had ever done before in his life.

It was sundown, and they all three went back silently home in the short twilight. That night, going outside the house near her son's room window, she found, to her sick disappointment, that he had been throwing away all the cooked food out there. She did not mention this when she went to say goodnight, but she did sniff and say that there was a smell of decay in the room. Meji said he thought there was a dead rat up in the rafters, and he would clear it away after she had gone to bed.

That night it rained heavily, and sheet lightning turned the darkness into brief silver daylight for one or two seconds at a time. Then the darkness again and the rain. Bola woke soon after midnight and thought she could hear knocking. She went to Meji's room to ask him to open the door, but he wasn't there. She thought he might have gone out for a while and been locked out by mistake. She opened the door quickly, holding an oil lamp upwards. He stood on the veranda, curiously unwet, and refused to come in.

"I have to go away," he said hoarsely, coughing.

"Do come in," she said.

"No," he said, "I have to go, but I wanted to thank you for giving me a chance."

"What nonsense is this?" she said. "Come in out of the rain."

"I did not think I should leave without thanking you."

The rain fell hard, the door creaked, and the wind whistled.

"Life is sweet, Mother dear, good-by, and thank you."

He turned round and started running.

There was a sudden diffuse flash of lightning and she saw that the yard was empty. She went back heavily, and fell into a restless sleep. Before she slept she said to herself that she must see Mr. Addai next morning, Sunday, or, better still, Monday, and tell him about this in case Meji was in trouble. She hoped Meji would not be annoyed. He was such a good son.

But it was Mr. Addai who came instead, on Sunday afternoon, quiet and grave, and saw Bola sitting on an old stool in the veranda, dressing Asi's hair in tight thin plaits.

Mr. Addai sat down and, looking away, he said: "The Lord giveth and the Lord taketh away." And soon half the village were sitting round the veranda and in the yard.

"But I tell you, he was here on Friday and left Sunday morning," Bola said. "He couldn't have died on Friday."

Bola had just recovered from a fainting fit after being told of her son's death in town. His wife, Asi's mother, had come with the news, bringing some of his property. She said Meji had died instantly at noon on Friday and had been buried on Saturday at sundown. They would have brought him to Kumansenu for the burial. He had always wished that. But they could not do so in time as bodies did not last much after a day.

"He was here, he was here," Bola said, rubbing her forehead and weeping.

Asi sat by quietly. Mr. Addai said comfortingly, "Hush, hush, he couldn't have been, because no one in the village saw him."

"He said we were to tell no one," Bola said.

The crowd smiled above Bola's head, and shook their heads. "Poor woman," someone said, "she is beside herself with grief."

"He died on Friday," Mrs. Meji repeated, crying. "He was in the office and he pulled up the window to look out and call the messenger. Then the sash broke. The window fell, broke his neck, and the sharp edge almost cut his head off; they say he died at once."

"My papa had a scarf around his neck," Asi shouted suddenly.

"Hush," said the crowd.

Mrs. Meji dipped her hand into her bosom and produced a small gold locket and put it round Asi's neck, to quieten her. "Your papa had this made last week for your Christmas present. You may as well have it now."

Asi played with it and pulled it this way and that.

"Be careful, child," Mr. Addai said, "it was your father's last gift."

"I was trying to remember how he showed me yesterday to open it," Asi said.

"You have never seen it before," Mrs. Meji said, sharply, trembling with fear mingled with anger.

She took the locket and tried to open it.

"Let me have it," said the village goldsmith, and he tried whispering magic words of incantation. Then he said, defeated, "It must be poor-quality gold; it has rusted. I need tools to open it."

"I remember now," Asi said in the flat complacent voice of childhood.

The crowd gathered round quietly and the setting sun glinted on the soft red African gold of the dangling trinket. The goldsmith handed the locket over to Asi and asked in a loud whisper: "How did he open it?"

"Like so," Asi said and pressed a secret catch. It flew open and she spelled out gravely the word inside: "ASI."

The silence continued.

"His neck, poor boy," Bola said a little wildly, "that is why he could not eat the lovely meals I cooked for him."

Mr. Addai announced a service of intercession after vespers that evening. The crowd began to leave quietly.

Musa, the magician, was one of the last to leave. He was now very old and bent. In times of grave calamity, it was known that even Mr. Addai did not raise objection to Musa being consulted.

He bent over further and whispered in Bola's ear: "You should have had his bones broken and mangled thirty-one years ago when he went for the sixth time and then he would not have come back to mock you all those years by pretending to be alive. I told you so. But you women are naughty and stubborn."

Bola stood up, her black face held high, her eyes terrible with maternal rage and pride.

"I am glad I did not," she said, "and that is why he came back specially to thank me before he went for good."

She clutched Asi to her. "I am glad I gave him the opportunity to come back, for life is sweet. I do not expect you to understand why I did so. After all, you are only a man."

## THINK AND DISCUSS
### Understanding
1. How many of Bola's baby boys died?
2. What advice did Musa, the village magician, give Bola and her husband to prevent the dead child from tormenting them?
3. According to Meji's wife, what were the circumstances of Meji's death?
4. According to Bola, why did Meji return to see her?

### Analyzing
5. List at least three details concerning Meji that suggest there is something extraordinary going on in the story.

### Extending
6. At the conclusion, Musa gloats over Bola's not following his advice thirty years earlier. Bola responds, "I do not expect you to understand why I did so. After all, you are only a man." Explain in your own words what you suppose she means.
7. Can the appearance of Meji in the village be rationally explained, or must the reader accept, willingly or not, the supernatural explanation?

## REVIEWING: Setting  HΣ
### See Handbook of Literary Terms, p. 824
Action that would seem implausible or impossible in one setting, such as a North American city today, may appear believable in another setting, such as a remote African village. For instance, it is not surprising that the villagers in Bola's home village, Kumansenu, gather around the veranda to hear the news brought by Mr. Addai or that he presents very personal news quite publicly. In what other ways does the setting in a primitive village contribute to this story?

## COMPOSITION

### Commenting on Author's Purpose

Any story that contains elements of fantasy—that is, unreal or otherworldly characters or occurrences—often raises a question in the reader's mind: can a story that features the fantastic convey a believable message? Review "Life Is Sweet at Kumansenu" to determine what the author's basic message is. For example, do you think the author is illustrating the worth of Bola's belief in giving her child life, no matter what? Do you think the theme is more generally a mother's love? Then decide whether you think the author's use of supernatural elements adds to or detracts from it, and why.

Write a three-paragraph composition identifying the message you think the story conveys and discussing reasons why the supernatural elements help or hurt in conveying it.

### Explaining the Appropriateness of Setting

Review the story to find details in the plot and characterization that are believable particularly because of the setting. Write a three-paragraph essay explaining how the setting is appropriate to this ghostly story featuring characters such as Bola, Meji, Asi, Musa, Mr. Addai, and the others. See "Writing About Setting" in the Writer's Handbook.

## BIOGRAPHY

### Abioseh Nicol

### 1924–

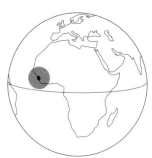

Abioseh Nicol is the pen name of Davidson Sylvester Hector Willoughby Nicol, who has had a varied career as administrator, teacher, and doctor as well as writer. As a child he was educated both in his native Sierra Leone and in Nigeria; he later received a medical degree from Cambridge University, England. He has worked as a physician in both England and Africa and as a school administrator in Sierra Leone; he has also held various executive posts in the United Nations.

Although he had published many articles on medical subjects, education, and politics, it was largely through the efforts of the late American writer Langston Hughes that his creative writing began to appear in print. Nicol has written poetry as well as short stories; his story collections include *The Truly Married Woman and Other Stories* and *Two African Tales*. Many of his stories involve a mixture of the old and new in Africa—tribal life is shown side by side with the more European style of living in the cities.

# Comment

### The Oldest Ghost Story?

Stories in which the dead walk the earth in some form may be as old as the human race itself. Certainly the ancient Egyptians and Greeks believed that spirits could return to the world of the living. The tale that follows was included in a letter from the Roman writer Pliny (plin′ē) the Younger, A.D. 62?–A.D. 113, and may be one of the earliest written ghost stories. Even this translation of it is old, having been done by the Englishman John Henley in 1724:

"There was a house at Athens large and capacious, but forsaken and of a very ill name. In the depth of night, a noise was heard in it, and if you listened closer the rattling of chains, first at a distance, then very near you. Presently appeared a spectre in the shape of an old man, worn out with age, meagre, and dejected, with a long beard and bristled hair; he wore fetters on his legs and chains on his hands, and shook them. On this, the inhabitants of the house passed several uneasy and melancholy nights; want of sleep brought a distemper upon them, and this, redoubling their terror, was followed by death. For in the day time, though the phantasm was absent, the memory of the appearance was still before their eyes, and their past fear produced a longer.

"Upon that, the house was quitted, and left entire to the phantasm. Yet an advertisement was put upon it, for the selling or letting it, if any stranger was inclined to the bargain.

"Athenodorus (a thē′nō dôr′əs) the philosopher came to Athens, he read the inscription; hearing the price and suspecting the lowness of the terms, he enquires, and is informed of every circumstance, and yet takes it, indeed the more readily upon that account.

"About evening he orders a bed in the fore-part of the house, calls for his writing-tables, his pencil, and a light. He dismisses all his family to the inner part of it, then he applies himself closely to writing, that his mind should not be vacant and form to itself imaginary fears and appearances. At first a profound silence reigned throughout the house as at other times; then the shaking of irons and the clink of chains began. He did not raise his eyes or lay down his pencil, but confirmed his resolution and was content only to listen.

"Then the noise increased and approached nearer, and sometimes was heard as at the entrance of the door, and sometimes within it. He looks back, sees it, and owns the shape as it was described to him. It stood still and beckoned with the finger as if it called him. He made a sign with his hand that it should stay a little and again set himself to his writing. The spectre renewed the noise of his chains and rattled them about the ears of the philosopher. He looked back, it beckoned again as before. So, without more delay, he takes up the light and follows it. It stalked along with a slow pace as if it were over laden with the chains, turned into a court belonging to the house, and vanished.

"When he was left alone Athenodorus laid some weeds and leaves, which he pulled off for the purpose, for a mark upon the place. The next day he went to the magistrates and advised them to give an order for digging up the spot. Several bones were found in it, bound up and entangled with chains which the body, putrefied by the length of time and lying in the ground, had left behind it, bare: for the flesh had been eaten off by the irons.

"They were gathered up and buried publicly, and the house afterwards was free from the apparition, after this last duty was paid to it by a solemn interment."

Pliny, *Epistles*, Book VII, number xxvi. Translated by John Henley, 1724.

# Home

**Gwendolyn Brooks**   USA

**There was little hope. The Home Owners' Loan was hard.**

What had been wanted was this always, this always to last, the talking softly on this porch, with the snake plant in the jardiniere in the southwest corner, and the obstinate slip from Aunt Eppie's magnificent Michigan fern at the left side of the friendly door. Mama, Maud Martha and Helen rocked slowly in their rocking chairs, and looked at the late afternoon light on the lawn, and at the emphatic iron of the fence and at the poplar tree. These things might soon be theirs no longer. Those shafts and pools of light, the tree, the graceful iron, might soon be viewed possessively by different eyes.

Papa was to have gone that noon, during his lunch hour, to the office of the Home Owners' Loan. If he had not succeeded in getting another extension, they would be leaving this house in which they had lived for more than fourteen years. There was little hope. The Home Owners' Loan was hard. They sat, making their plans.

"We'll be moving into a nice flat somewhere," said Mama. "Somewhere on South Park,[1] or Michigan, or in Washington Park Court." Those flats, as the girls and Mama knew well, were burdens on wages twice the size of Papa's. This was not mentioned now.

"They're much prettier than this old house," said Helen. "I have friends I'd just as soon not bring here. And I have other friends that wouldn't come down this far for anything, unless they were in a taxi."

Yesterday, Maud Martha would have attacked her. Tomorrow she might. Today she said nothing. She merely gazed at a little hopping robin in the tree, her tree, and tried to keep the fronts of her eyes dry.

"Well, I do know," said Mama, turning her hands over and over, "that I've been getting tireder and tireder of doing that firing. From October to April, there's firing to be done."

"But lately we've been helping, Harry and I," said Maud Martha. "And sometimes in March and April and in October, and even in November, we could build a little fire in the fireplace. Sometimes the weather was just right for that."

She knew, from the way they looked at her, that this had been a mistake. They did not want to cry.

But she felt that the little line of white, somewhat ridged with smoked purple, and all that cream-shot saffron, would never drift across any western sky except that in back of this house. The rain would drum with as sweet a dullness nowhere but here. The birds on South Park were mechan-

---

1. *South Park,* the former name of Dr. Martin Luther King, Jr. Drive, an avenue in Chicago.

"Home" from *The World of Gwendolyn Brooks* (New York: Harper & Row, 1971). Reprinted by permission of the author.

ical birds, no better than the poor caught canaries in those "rich" women's sun parlors.

"It's just going to kill Papa!" burst out Maud Martha. "He loves this house! He *lives* for this house!"

"He lives for us," said Helen. "It's us he loves. He wouldn't want the house, except for us."

"And he'll have us," added Mama, "wherever."

"You know," Helen sighed, "if you want to know the truth, this is a relief. If this hadn't come up, we would have gone on, just dragged on, hanging out here forever."

"It might," allowed Mama, "be an act of God. God may just have reached down, and picked up the reins."

"Yes," Maud Martha cracked in, "that's what you always say—that God knows best."

Her mother looked at her quickly, decided the statement was not suspect, looked away.

Helen saw Papa coming. "There's Papa," said Helen.

They could not tell a thing from the way Papa was walking. It was that same dear little staccato walk, one shoulder down, then the other, then repeat, and repeat. They watched his progress. He passed the Kennedys', he passed the vacant lot, he passed Mrs. Blakemore's. They wanted to hurl themselves over the fence, into the street, and shake the truth out of his collar. He opened his gate—the gate—and still his stride and face told them nothing.

"Hello," he said.

Mama got up and followed him through the front door. The girls knew better than to go in too.

Presently Mama's head emerged. Her eyes were lamps turned on.

"It's all right," she exclaimed. "He got it. It's all over. Everything is all right."

The door slammed shut. Mama's footsteps hurried away.

"I think," said Helen, rocking rapidly, "I think I'll give a party. I haven't given a party since I was eleven. I'd like some of my friends to just casually see that we're homeowners."

## THINK AND DISCUSS
### Understanding
1. How long has the family lived in the home?
2. For what purpose has Papa gone to the office of the Home Owners' Loan?

### Analyzing
3. Which two characters appear to speak more casually or negatively about the house than they really feel? Support your answer with details from the story.

4. At what point in the story does the reader experience the most suspense, and when does it end?

### Extending
5. The title, "Home," focuses our attention on the importance of **setting** in this story of the interplay among family members. The setting is not merely a house; it is the family's home, and that setting (like the word *home*) has sentimental value to every reader. Imagine that this story had taken place away from the home. How do you

think the mood—the atmosphere and feeling of the story—would be affected if the three characters waiting for Papa's news had gathered to meet him on a nearby park bench? in a library lobby? in their car outside the Home Owners' Loan office?

## COMPOSITION
### Describing a Home

In "Home" we see a family with pride and a strong sense of identity as they gather at home. Home doesn't have to be a house or an apartment; it can be any place that gives a sense of comfort, security, and belonging. Describe a place called home—yours or another home you have seen or heard of—that makes its residents happy or proud to live there. Illustrate why they feel that way. If you prefer, recount an event that reminds you of a place you like, or tell about an accomplishment that has made you feel "at home" in a particular place.

## Contrasting Two Related Ideas

This story could have been entitled "The House" rather than "Home." The given title, however, has connotations—rich interpretations added to the word's dictionary definition—that make "Home" seem the proper word. Write a two-paragraph composition in which you explain the differences between the words *house* and *home* and tell why you think this story is called "Home" rather than "The House."

## ENRICHMENT
### Interpretive Reading

This short story features emotional dialogue among a small group of characters. It is a good literary work for reading aloud to an audience of class members. You and a few classmates may want to rehearse a reading, interpreting the conversation of Mama, Helen, and Maud Martha. One person can read the part of the narrator, omitting words such as "said Helen" and "added Mama." Members of the audience can listen actively, to hear whether the dramatic reading interprets the conversations as the audience remembers them from silent reading.

## BIOGRAPHY

### Gwendolyn Brooks
### 1917–

Gwendolyn Brooks is one of America's best-known poets. "Home," however, represents her fiction, which is also highly esteemed by readers. Born in Topeka, Kansas, Brooks was soon brought to Chicago, where she grew up and has lived ever since. In her own words, she "began to put rhymes together at about seven." Her first poem was published at the age of thirteen. Both her poetry and her prose draw heavily on her personal experience, yet her works transcend the specifics of one life and achieve a meaning that people throughout this country and around the world appreciate. Her novel *Maud Martha* was published in 1953.

See POINT OF VIEW in the Handbook of Literary Terms, page 816.

# Forgiveness in Families

**Alice Munro**   Canada

---

**Mother had a way of viewing my brother's faults as virtues.
I, however, found his list of shortcomings too long.**

---

've often thought, suppose I had to go to a psychiatrist, and he would want to know about my family background, naturally, so I would have to start telling him about my brother, and he wouldn't even wait till I was finished, would he, the psychiatrist, he'd commit me.

I said that to Mother; she laughed. "You're hard on that boy, Val."

"Boy," I said. "*Man.*"

She laughed, she admitted it. "But remember," she said, "the Lord loves a lunatic."

"How do you know," I said, "seeing you're an atheist?"

Some things he couldn't help. Being born, for instance. He was born the week I started school, and how's that for timing? I was scared, it wasn't like now when the kids have been going to play-school and kindergarten for years. I was going to school for the first time and all the other kids had their mothers with them and where was mine? In the hospital having a baby. The embarrassment to

me. There was a lot of shame about those things then. . . .

I will skip over what he did between getting born and throwing up at my wedding except to say that he had asthma and got to stay home from school weeks on end, listening to soap operas. Sometimes there was a truce between us, and I would get him to tell me what happened every day on "Big Sister" and "Road of Life" and the one with Gee-Gee and Papa David. He was very good at remembering all the characters and getting all the complications straight, I'll say that, and he did read a lot in *Gateways to Bookland*, that lovely set Mother bought for us and that he later sneaked out of the house and sold, for ten dollars, to a secondhand-book dealer. Mother said he could have been brilliant at school if he wanted to be. That's a deep one, your brother, she used to say,

---

he's got some surprises in store for us. She was right, he had.

He started staying home permanently in Grade Ten after a little problem of being caught in a cheating ring that was getting math tests from some teacher's desk. One of the janitors was letting him back in the classroom after school because he said he was working on a special project. So he was, in his own way. Mother said he did it to make himself popular, because he had asthma and couldn't take part in sports.

Now. Jobs. The question comes up, what is such a person as my brother—and I ought to give him a name at least, his name is Cam, for Cameron, Mother thought that would be a suitable name for a university president or honest tycoon (which was the sort of thing she planned for him to be)—what is he going to do, how is he going to make a living? Until recently the country did not pay you to sit on your uppers and announce that you had adopted a creative lifestyle. He got a job first as a movie usher. Mother got it for him, she knew the manager, it was the old International Theater over on Blake Street. He had to quit, though, because he got this darkness phobia. All the people sitting in the dark he said gave him a crawly feeling, very peculiar. It only interfered with him working as an usher, it didn't interfere with him going to the movies on his own. He got very fond of movies. In fact, he spent whole days sitting in movie houses, sitting through every show twice, then going to another theater and sitting through what was there. He had to do something with his time, because Mother and all of us believed he was working then in the office of the Greyhound Bus Depot. He went off to work at the right time every morning and came home at the right time every night, and he told all about the cranky old man in charge of the office and the woman with curvature of the spine who had been there since 1919 and how mad she got at the young girls chewing gum, oh, a lively story, it

would have worked up to something as good as the soap operas if Mother hadn't phoned up to complain about the way they were withholding his paycheck—due to a technical error in the spelling of his name, he said—and found out he'd quit in the middle of his second day.

Well. Sitting in movies was better than sitting in beer parlors, Mother said. At least he wasn't on the street getting in with criminal gangs. She asked him what his favorite movie was and he said *Seven Brides for Seven Brothers*. See, she said, he is interested in an outdoor life,[1] he is not suited to office work. So she sent him to work for some cousins of hers who have a farm in the Fraser Valley. I should explain that my father, Cam's and mine, was dead by this time, he died away back when Cam was having asthma and listening to soap operas. It didn't make much difference, his dying, because he worked as a conductor on the P.G.E. when it started at Squamish, and he lived part of the time in Lillooet.[2] Nothing changed. Mother went on working at Eaton's as she always had, going across on the ferry and then on the bus; I got supper, she came trudging up the hill in the winter dark.

Cam took off from the farm, he complained that the cousins were religious and always after his soul. Mother could see his problem, she had after all brought him up to be a freethinker. He hitchhiked east. From time to time a letter came. A request for funds. He had been offered a job in northern Quebec if he could get the money together to get up there. Mother sent it. He sent word the job had folded, but he didn't send back the money. He and two friends were going to start a turkey farm. They sent us plans, estimates. They were supposed to be working on contract for

---

1. *Seven Brides . . . outdoor life.* The movie, a 1954 musical, celebrated outdoor life in that it was set in the Oregon backwoods.
2. *P.G.E. . . . Lillooet* (lil′ü ət). The P.G.E. is the Pacific Grand Eastern Railway Company; Squamish and Lillooet are towns in the Canadian province of British Columbia.

the Purina Company, nothing could go wrong. The turkeys were drowned in a flood, after Mother had sent him money and we had too against our better judgment. Everywhere that boy hits turns into a disaster area, Mother said. If you read it in a book you wouldn't believe it, she said. It's so terrible it's funny.

She knew. I used to go over to see her on Wednesday afternoon—her day off—pushing the stroller with Karen in it, and later Tommy in it and Karen walking beside, up Lonsdale and down King's Road, and what would we always end up talking about? That boy and I, we are getting a divorce, she said. I am definitely going to write him off. What good will he ever be until he stops relying on me, she asked. I kept my mouth shut, more or less. She knew my opinion. But she ended up every time saying, "He was a nice fellow to have around the house, though. Good company. That boy could always make me laugh."

Or, "He had a lot to contend with, his asthma and no dad. He never did intentionally hurt a soul."

"One good thing he did," she said, "you could really call it a good turn. That girl."

Referring to the girl who came and told us she had been engaged to him, in Hamilton, Ontario, until he told her he could never get married because he had just found out there was hereditary fatal kidney disease in the family. He wrote her a letter. And she came looking for him to tell him it didn't matter. Not at all a bad-looking girl. She worked for the Bell Telephone. Mother said it was a lie told out of kindness, to spare her feelings when he didn't want to marry her. I said it was a kindness, anyway, because she would have been supporting him for the rest of his life.

Though it might have eased things up a bit on the rest of us.

But that was then and now is now and as we all know times have changed. Cam is finding it easier. He lives at home, off and on, has for a year

and a half. His hair is thin in front, not surprising in a man thirty-four years of age, but shoulder-length behind, straggly, graying. He wears a sort of rough brown robe that looks as if it might be made out of a sack (is that what sackcloth is supposed to be, I said to my husband Haro, I wouldn't mind supplying the ashes),[3] and hanging down on his chest he has all sorts of chains, medallions, crosses, elk's teeth, or whatnot. Rope sandals on his feet. Some friend of his makes them. He collects welfare. Nobody asks him to work. Who could be so crude? If he has to write down his occupation he writes priest.

It's true. There is a whole school of them, calling themselves priests, and they have a house over in Kitsilano,[4] Cam stays there too sometimes. They're in competition with the Hare Krishna bunch,[5] only these ones don't chant, they just walk around smiling. He has developed this voice I can't stand, a very thin, sweet voice, all on one level. It makes me want to stand in front of him and say, "There's an earthquake in Chile, two hundred thousand people just died, they've burned up another village in Vietnam, famine as usual in India." Just to see if he'd keep saying, "Ve-ery ni-ice, ve-ery ni-ice," that sweet way. He won't eat meat, of course, he eats whole-grain cereals and leafy vegetables. He came into the kitchen where I was slicing beets—beets being forbidden, a root vegetable—and, "I hope you understand that you're committing murder," he said.

"No," I said, "but I'll give you sixty seconds to get out of here or I may be."

So as I say he's home part of the time now and he was there on the Monday night when Mother

---

3. *sackcloth . . . ashes.* Wearing sackcloth and ashes (that is, putting ashes on one's head) is a sign of mourning or penitence.
4. *Kitsilano* (kit′si lä′nō).
5. *Hare Krishna* (hä′re krish′nä) *bunch.* Hare Krishna is the popular name of a religious sect founded in India in 1954 that has attracted young members worldwide.

got sick. She was vomiting. A couple of days before this he had started her on a vegetarian diet—she was always promising him she'd try it—and he told her she was vomiting up all the old poisons stored up in her body from eating meat and sugar and so on. He said it was a good sign, and when she had it all vomited out she'd feel better. She kept vomiting, and she didn't feel better, but he had to go out. Monday nights is when they have the weekly meeting at the priests' house, where they chant and burn incense or celebrate the black mass, for all I know. He stayed out most of the night, and when he got home he found Mother unconscious on the bathroom floor. He got on the phone and phoned *me*.

"I think you better come over here and see if you can help Mom, Val."

"What's the matter with her?"

"She's not feeling very well."

"What's the matter with her? Put her on the phone."

"I can't."

"Why can't you?"

I swear he tittered. "Well, I am afraid she's passed out."

I called the ambulance and sent them for her, that was how she got to the hospital, five o'clock in the morning. I called her family doctor, he got over there, and he got Dr. Ellis Bell, one of the best-known heart men in the city, because that was what they had decided it was, her heart. I got dressed and woke Haro and told him and then I drove myself over to the Lions Gate Hospital. They wouldn't let me in till ten o'clock. They had her in Intensive Care. I sat outside Intensive Care in their slick little awful waiting room. They had red slippery chairs, cheap covering, and a stand full of pebbles with green plastic leaves growing up. I sat there hour after hour and read *The Reader's Digest*. The jokes. Thinking this is how it is, this is it, really, she's dying. Now, this moment, behind those doors, dying. Nothing stops

or holds off for it the way you somehow and against all your sense believe it will. I thought about Mother's life, the part of it I knew. Going to work every day, first on the ferry, then on the bus. Shopping at the old Red-and-White, then at the new Safeway—new, fifteen years old! Going down to the Library one night a week, taking me with her, and we would come home on the bus with our load of books and a bag of grapes we bought at the Chinese place, for a treat. Wednesday afternoons too when my kids were small and I went over there to drink coffee. And I thought, all these things don't seem that much like life, when you're doing them, they're just what you do, how you fill up your days, and you think all the time something is going to crack open, and you'll find yourself, *then* you'll find yourself, in life. It's not even that you particularly want this to happen, this cracking open, you're comfortable enough the way things are, but you do expect it. Then you're dying, Mother is dying, and it's just the same plastic chairs and plastic plants and ordinary day outside with people getting groceries and what you've had is all there is, and going to the Library, just a thing like that, coming back up the hill on the bus with books and a bag of grapes seems now worth wanting, oh doesn't it, you'd break your heart wanting back there.

When they let me in to see her she was bluish-gray in the face and her eyes were not all-the-way closed, but they had rolled up, the slit that was open showed the whites. She always looked terrible with her teeth out, anyway, wouldn't let us see her. Cam teased her vanity. They were out now. So all the time, I thought, all the time even when she was young it was in her that she was going to look like this.

They didn't hold out hope. Haro came and took a look at her and put his arm around my shoulders and said, "Val, you'll have to be prepared." He meant well but I couldn't talk to him. It wasn't his mother and he couldn't remember anything. That

Peter Berg, *Interior, The Unmailed Letter* (detail),
1984, Private Collection

wasn't his fault but I didn't want to talk to him, I didn't want to listen to him telling me I better be prepared. We went and ate something in the hospital cafeteria.

"You better phone Cam," Haro said.

"Why?"

"He'll want to know."

"Why do you think he'll want to know? He left her alone last night and he didn't know enough to get an ambulance when he came in and found her this morning."

"Just the same. He has a right. Maybe you ought to tell him to get over here."

"He is probably busy this moment preparing to give her a hippie funeral."

But Haro persuaded me as he always can and I went and phoned. No answer. I felt better because I had phoned, and justified in what I had said because of Cam not being in. I went back and waited, by myself.

About seven o'clock that night Cam turned up. He was not alone. He had brought along a tribe of co-priests, I suppose they were, from that house. They all wore the same kind of outfit he did, the brown sacking nightgown and the chains and crosses and holy hardware, they all had long hair, they were all a good many years younger than Cam, except for one old man, really old, with a curly gray beard and bare feet—in March, bare feet—and no teeth. I swear this old man didn't have a clue what was going on. I think they picked him up down by the Salvation Army and put that outfit on him because they needed an old man for a kind of mascot, or extra holiness, or something.

Cam said, "This is my sister Valerie. This is Brother Michael. This is Brother John, this is Brother Louis." Etc., etc.

"They haven't said anything to give me hope, Cam. She is dying."

"We hope not," said Cam with his secret smile. "We spent the day working for her."

"Do you mean praying?" I said.

"Work is a better word to describe it than praying, if you don't understand what it is."

Well of course, I never understand.

"Real praying is work, believe me," says Cam and they all smile at me, his way. They can't keep still, like children who have to go to the bathroom they're weaving and jiggling and doing little steps.

"Now where's her room?" says Cam in a practical tone of voice.

I thought of Mother dying and through that slit between her lids—who knows, maybe she can see from time to time—seeing this crowd of dervishes celebrating around her bed. Mother who lost her religion when she was thirteen and went to the Unitarian Church and quit when they had the split about crossing God out of the hymns, Mother having to spend her last conscious minutes wondering what had happened, if she was transported back in history to where loonies cavorted around in their crazy ceremonies, trying to sort her last reasonable thoughts out in the middle of their business.

Thank God the nurse said no. The intern was brought and he said no. Cam didn't insist, he smiled and nodded at them as if they were granting permission and then he brought the troupe back into the waiting room and there, right before my eyes, they started. They put the old man in the center, sitting down with his head bowed and his eyes shut—they had to tap him and remind him how to do that—and they squatted in a rough sort of circle round him, facing in and out, in and out, alternately. Then, eyes closed, they started swaying back and forth moaning some words very softly, only not the same words, it sounded as if each one of them had got different words, and not in English of course but Swahili or Sanskrit[6] or something. It got louder, gradually it got louder, a pounding singsong, and as it did they rose to their

---

**6. Swahili** (swä hē′lē) . . . **Sanskrit** (san′skrit). Swahili is spoken in much of eastern Africa; Sanskrit, the ancient and sacred literary language of India, is now extinct.

feet, all except the old man who stayed where he was and looked as if he might have gone to sleep, sitting, and they began a shuffling kind of dance where they stood, clapping, not very well in time. They did this for a long while, and the noise they were making, though it was not terribly loud, attracted the nurses from their station and nurses' aides and orderlies and a few people like me who were waiting, and nobody seemed to know what to do, because it was so unbelievable, so crazy in that ordinary little waiting room. Everybody just stared as if they were asleep and dreaming and expecting to wake up. Then a nurse came out of Intensive Care and said, "We can't have this disturbance. What do you think you're doing here?"

She took hold of one of the young ones and shook him by the shoulder, else she couldn't have got anybody to stop and pay attention.

"We're working to help a woman who's very sick," he told her.

"I don't know what you call working, but you're not helping anybody. Now I'm asking you to clear out of here. Excuse me. I'm not asking. I'm telling."

"You're very mistaken if you think the tones of our voices are hurting or disturbing any sick person. This whole ceremony is pitched at a level which will reach and comfort the unconscious mind and draw the demonic influences out of the body. It's a ceremony that goes back five thousand years."

"Good lord," said the nurse, looking stupefied as well she might. "Who are these people?"

I had to go and enlighten her, telling her that it was my brother and what you might call his friends, and I was not in on their ceremony. I asked about Mother, was there any change.

"No change," she said. "What do we have to do to get them out of here?"

"Turn the hose on them," one of the orderlies said, and all this time, the dance, or ceremony, never stopped, and the one who had stopped and done the explaining went back to dancing too, and I said to the nurse, "I'll phone in to see how she is, I'm going home for a little while." I walked out of the hospital and found to my surprise that it was dark. The whole day in there, dark to dark. In the parking lot I started to cry. Cam has turned this into a circus for his own benefit, I said to myself, and said it out loud when I got home.

Haro made me a drink.

"It'll probably get into the papers," I said. "Cam's chance for fame."

Haro phoned the hospital to see if there was any news and they said there wasn't. "Did they have—was there any difficulty with some young people in the waiting room this evening? Did they leave quietly?" Haro is ten years older than I am, a cautious man, too patient with everybody. I used to think he was sometimes giving Cam money I didn't know about.

"They left quietly," he said. "Don't worry about the papers. Get some sleep."

I didn't mean to but I fell asleep on the couch, after the long day. I woke up with the phone ringing and day lightening the room. I stumbled into the kitchen dragging the blanket Haro had put over me and saw by the clock on the wall it was a quarter to six. She's gone, I thought.

It was her own doctor.

He said he had encouraging news. He said she was much better this morning.

I dragged over a chair and collapsed in it, both arms and my head too down on the kitchen counter. I came back on the phone to hear him saying she was still in a critical phase and the next forty-eight hours would tell the story, but without raising my hopes too high he wanted me to know she was responding to treatment. He said that this was especially surprising in view of the fact that she had been late getting to hospital and the things they did to her at first did not seem to have much effect, though of course the fact that she survived the first few hours at all was a good sign.

Nobody had made much of this good sign to me yesterday, I thought.

I sat there for an hour at least after I had hung up the phone. I made a cup of instant coffee and my hands were shaking so I could hardly get the water into the cup, then couldn't get the cup to my mouth. I let it go cold. Haro came out in his pajamas at last. He gave me one look and said, "Easy, Val. Has she gone?"

"She's some better. She's responding to treatment."

"The look of you I thought the other."

"I'm so amazed."

"I wouldn't've given five cents for her chances yesterday noon."

"I know. I can't believe it."

"It's the tension," Haro said. "I know. You build yourself up ready for something bad to happen and then when it doesn't, it's a queer feeling, you can't feel good right away, it's almost like a disappointment."

Disappointment. That was the word that stayed with me. I was so glad, really, grateful, but underneath I was thinking, so Cam didn't kill her after all, with his carelessness and craziness and going out and neglecting her he didn't kill her, and I was, yes, I was, sorry in some part of me to find out that was true. And I knew Haro knew this but wouldn't speak of it to me, ever. That was the real shock to me, why I kept shaking. Not whether Mother lived or died. It was what was so plain about myself.

Mother got well, she pulled through beautifully. After she rallied she never sank back. She was in the hospital three weeks and then she came home, and rested another three weeks, and after that went back to work, cutting down a bit and working ten to four instead of full days, what they call the housewives' shift. She told everybody about Cam and his friends coming to the hospital. She began to say things like, "Well, that boy of mine may not be much of a success at anything else but you have to admit he has a knack of saving lives." Or, "Maybe Cam should go into the miracle business, he certainly pulled it off with me." By this time Cam was saying, he is saying now, that he's not sure about that religion, he's getting tired of the other priests and all that not eating meat or root vegetables. It's a stage, he says now, he's glad he went through it, self-discovery. One day I went over there and found he was trying on an old suit and tie. He says he might take advantage of some of the adult education courses, he is thinking of becoming an accountant.

I was thinking myself about changing into a different sort of person from the one I am. I do think about that. I read a book called *The Art of Loving*.[7] A lot of things seemed clear while I was reading it but afterwards I went back to being more or less the same. What has Cam ever done that actually hurt me, anyway, as Haro once said. And how am I better than he is after the way I felt the night Mother lived instead of died? I made a promise to myself I would try. I went over there one day taking them a bakery cake—which Cam eats now as happily as anybody else—and I heard their voices out in the yard—now it's summer, they love to sit in the sun—Mother saying to some visitor, "Oh yes I was, I was all set to take off into the wild blue yonder, and Cam here, this *idiot*, came and danced outside my door with a bunch of his hippie friends—"

"My lord, woman," roared Cam, but you could tell he didn't care now, "members of an ancient holy discipline."

I had a strange feeling, like I was walking on coals and trying a spell so I wouldn't get burned.

Forgiveness in families is a mystery to me, how it comes or how it lasts.

---

7. *The Art of Loving*, a philosophical work arguing that love is a feeling of universal brotherhood as much as anything else, by psychoanalyst Erich Fromm.

## THINK AND DISCUSS
### Understanding
1. How does Val feel about Cam as the story opens?
2. Give examples of things Cam has done that make Val feel as she does about him.
3. Describe the religious group Cam joins.
4. What crisis sends Val's mother to the hospital?

### Analyzing
5. Compare Val's and her mother's judgments about Cam's behavior throughout the story.
6. Why does Val feel a bit disappointed to find out that Cam's behavior hasn't really caused the outcome that she feared? Later, what does she think of herself for feeling this sense of disappointment?

### Extending
7. Outside her mother's hospital room, Val remembers the ordinary, satisfying life her mother has led and concludes that her mother is dying. Do you think her frame of mind at this point influences her reaction to Cam's and his friends' "ceremony"? Explain your answer.
8. The title of the story is "Forgiveness in Families." Who do you think needs to be forgiven? By the end of the story has that person experienced forgiveness? Explain.

### APPLYING: Point of View HT
#### See Handbook of Literary Terms, p. 816
A story's **point of view** is the relationship between the narrator and the story's characters and action. If the narrator is a character, the story is told in a first-person point of view. Authors generally use minor characters as first-person narrators when they want someone to stand slightly apart from the action and comment on it. However, when authors decide to have a major character tell the story, they often choose the most important character. Since the story is primarily about this character, it is helpful to know directly what he or she is thinking, feeling, and so on.

1. Why do you think the author made Val, rather than Cam, the narrator? Isn't the story more about him than about her? Explain.
2. How would you expect Cam to describe himself if he were telling the story? How might he characterize his sister?
3. What advantage, if any, has the author gained by making Val the narrator?

## VOCABULARY
### Dictionary and Etymology
Dictionaries and glossaries help you learn word meaning and usage by providing definitions and features such as etymologies, or histories of entry words. Using the Glossary, determine if the following statements about the italicized words are true or false. On a separate paper write "T" or "F" after the number of each statement. Be sure you can spell each italicized word.

1. *Tycoon* comes from Chinese words meaning "great lord."
2. A synonym for *stupefy* is "astound."
3. A *freethinker* is a person who solves problems for others without charging for his or her services.
4. A *dervish* would be unlikely to *cavort*.
5. The words *phobia* and *atheist* come originally from Greek.

## THINKING SKILLS
### Generalizing
To **generalize** is to draw a general rule or conclusion from particular information. Having

read "Forgiveness in Families" and read about or witnessed other family ordeals, you may be able to generalize about how family members should or do forgive one another for faults. Write a general "rule" or statement expressing your conclusion about how family members show forgiveness. Your class may want to gather the various generalizations in a folder.

## COMPOSITION
### Describing a Hospital Scene

This story contains an episode that takes place in a hospital. Hospitals and medical facilities, such as clinics and doctors' offices, often serve as the settings for memorable incidents. Recall an event in such a place that you have experienced, heard about, or seen depicted by actors. If you prefer, make up a dramatic story set in part of a hospital. List your characters and jot down details about what happened. Then write a narrative account of the event, showing how it looks, sounds, and feels to the observer or participant who is narrating

or who is the focus of the narrator's attention. Whether your composition is based on a memory or is fictional, try to capture the atmosphere and mood of the setting. You may write the narrative using a first-person or third-person point of view.

### Writing About Point of View

In this story Val describes her feelings in a depth available to a perceptive first-person narrator. Review the story to find points in which Val focuses on her judgments of her mother, Cam, and her husband. Look at points in which she questions herself or seems to change her opinions. Consider how a third-person narrator would sound when describing these sentiments. Write a three-paragraph essay to prove that this is a story about Val that could only be told as effectively by Val herself. (If you disagree with this conclusion, write to support your view.) Use examples from the narration to illustrate your thesis. See "Writing About Point of View" in the Writer's Handbook.

## BIOGRAPHY

### Alice Munro
### 1931–

Recognized for her refreshing portrayals of the Canadian small-town experience, Alice Munro was born and educated in Ontario. While working in the Vancouver, British Columbia, Public Library in the early 1950s, she began to have her short stories published by small magazines. Her first collection, *Dance of the Happy Shades* (1968), received the Governor General's Award for Literature. Her keen eye for detail and the murkier depths of the human personality is evidenced in many of her works, including the novel *Lives of Girls and Women* (1971); the story collections *Something I've Been Meaning to Tell You* (1974), *The Beggar Maid* (1982), and *The Progress of Love* (1986); and the short stories that frequently appear in such prominent magazines as *The New Yorker* and *The Atlantic*. She resides in Ontario.

Review POINT OF VIEW in the Handbook of Literary Terms, page 816.

# Lamb to the Slaughter

**Roald Dahl**   Great Britain

"It's the old story. Get the weapon, and you've got the man."

he room was warm and clean, the curtains drawn, the two table lamps alight—hers and the one by the empty chair opposite. On the sideboard behind her, two tall glasses, soda water, whiskey. Fresh ice cubes in the Thermos bucket.

Mary Maloney was waiting for her husband to come home from work.

Now and again she would glance up at the clock, but without anxiety, merely to please herself with the thought that each minute gone by made it nearer the time when he would come. There was a slow smiling air about her, and about everything she did. The drop of the head as she bent over her sewing was curiously tranquil. Her skin—for this was her sixth month with child—had acquired a wonderful translucent quality, the mouth was soft, and the eyes, with their new placid look, seemed larger, darker than before.

When the clock said ten minutes to five, she began to listen, and a few moments later, punctually as always, she heard the tires on the gravel outside, and the car door slamming, the footsteps passing the window, the key turning in the lock.

She laid aside her sewing, stood up, and went forward to kiss him as he came in.

"Hullo, darling," she said.

"Hullo," he answered.

She took his coat and hung it in the closet. Then she walked over and made the drinks, a strongish one for him, a weak one for herself; and soon she was back again in her chair with the sewing, and he in the other, opposite, holding the tall glass with both his hands, rocking it so the ice cubes tinkled against the side.

For her, this was always a blissful time of day. She knew he didn't want to speak much until the first drink was finished, and she, on her side, was content to sit quietly, enjoying his company after the long hours alone in the house. She loved to luxuriate in the presence of this man, and to feel—almost as a sunbather feels the sun—that

*Roald Dahl* (rō′əl däl)

*Lamb to the Slaughter* **87**

warm male glow that came out of him to her when they were alone together. She loved him for the way he sat loosely in a chair, for the way he came in a door, or moved slowly across the room with long strides. She loved the intent, far look in his eyes when they rested on her, the funny shape of the mouth, and especially the way he remained silent about his tiredness, sitting still with himself until the whiskey had taken some of it away.

"Tired, darling?"

"Yes," he said. "I'm tired." And as he spoke, he did an unusual thing. He lifted his glass and drained it in one swallow although there was still half of it, at least half of it left. She wasn't really watching him, but she knew what he had done because she heard the ice cubes falling back against the bottom of the empty glass when he lowered his arm. He paused a moment, leaning forward in the chair, then he got up and went slowly over to fetch himself another.

"I'll get it!" she cried, jumping up.

"Sit down," he said.

When he came back, she noticed that the new drink was dark amber with the quantity of whiskey in it.

"Darling, shall I get your slippers?"

"No."

She watched him as he began to sip the dark yellow drink, and she could see little oily swirls in the liquid because it was so strong.

"I think it's a shame," she said, "that when a policeman gets to be as senior as you, they keep him walking about on his feet all day long."

He didn't answer, so she bent her head again and went on with her sewing; but each time he lifted the drink to his lips, she heard the ice cubes clinking against the side of the glass.

"Darling," she said. "Would you like me to get you some cheese? I haven't made any supper because it's Thursday."

"No," he said.

"If you're too tired to eat out," she went on,

"it's still not too late. There's plenty of meat and stuff in the freezer, and you can have it right here and not even move out of the chair."

Her eyes waited on him for an answer, a smile, a little nod, but he made no sign.

"Anyway," she went on, "I'll get you some cheese and crackers first."

"I don't want it," he said.

She moved uneasily in her chair, the large eyes still watching his face. "But you *must* have supper. I can easily do it here. I'd like to do it. We can have lamb chops. Or pork. Anything you want. Everything's in the freezer."

"Forget it," he said.

"But darling, you *must* eat! I'll fix it anyway, and then you can have it or not, as you like."

She stood up and placed her sewing on the table by the lamp.

"Sit down," he said. "Just for a minute, sit down."

It wasn't till then that she began to get frightened.

"Go on," he said. "Sit down."

She lowered herself back slowly into the chair, watching him all the time with those large, bewildered eyes. He had finished the second drink and was staring down into the glass, frowning.

"Listen," he said. "I've got something to tell you."

"What is it, darling? What's the matter?"

He had now become absolutely motionless, and kept his head down so that the light from the lamp beside him fell across the upper part of his face, leaving the chin and mouth in shadow. She noticed there was a little muscle moving near the corner of his left eye.

"This is going to be a bit of a shock to you, I'm afraid," he said. "But I've thought about it a good deal and I've decided the only thing to do is tell you right away. I hope you won't blame me too much."

And he told her. It didn't take long, four or five

minutes at most, and she sat very still through it all, watching him with a kind of dazed horror as he went further and further away from her with each word.

"So there it is," he added. "And I know it's kind of a bad time to be telling you, but there simply wasn't any other way. Of course I'll give you money and see you're looked after. But there needn't really be any fuss. I hope not anyway. It wouldn't be very good for my job."

Her first instinct was not to believe any of it, to reject it all. It occurred to her that perhaps he hadn't even spoken, that she herself had imagined the whole thing. Maybe, if she went about her business and acted as though she hadn't been listening, then later, when she sort of woke up again, she might find none of it had ever happened.

"I'll get the supper," she managed to whisper, and this time he didn't stop her.

When she walked across the room she couldn't feel her feet touching the floor. She couldn't feel anything at all—except a slight nausea and a desire to vomit. Everything was automatic now—down the steps to the cellar, the light switch, the deep freeze, the hand inside the cabinet taking hold of the first object it met. She lifted it out, and looked at it. It was wrapped in paper, so she took off the paper and looked at it again.

A leg of lamb.

All right then, they would have lamb for supper. She carried it upstairs, holding the thin bone-end of it with both her hands, and as she went through the living room, she saw him standing over by the window with his back to her, and she stopped.

"For heaven's sake," he said, hearing her, but not turning round. "Don't make supper for me. I'm going out."

At that point, Mary Maloney simply walked up

Georges Braque, *Le Salon*, 1944, Hugo Gallery, New York

behind him and without any pause she swung the big frozen leg of lamb high in the air and brought it down as hard as she could on the back of his head.

She might just as well have hit him with a steel club.

She stepped back a pace, waiting, and the funny thing was that he remained standing there for at least four or five seconds, gently swaying. Then he crashed to the carpet.

The violence of the crash, the noise, the small table overturning, helped bring her out of the shock. She came out slowly, feeling cold and surprised, and she stood for a while blinking at the body, still holding the ridiculous piece of meat tight with both hands.

All right, she told herself. So I've killed him.

It was extraordinary, now, how clear her mind became all of a sudden. She began thinking very fast. As the wife of a detective, she knew quite well what the penalty would be. That was fine. It made no difference to her. In fact, it would be a relief. On the other hand, what about the child? What were the laws about murderers with unborn children? Did they kill them both—mother and child? Or did they wait until the tenth month? What did they do?

Mary Maloney didn't know. And she certainly wasn't prepared to take a chance.

She carried the meat into the kitchen, placed it in a pan, turned the oven on high, and shoved it inside. Then she washed her hands and ran upstairs to the bedroom. She sat down before the mirror, tidied her hair, touched up her lips and face. She tried a smile. It came out rather peculiar. She tried again.

"Hullo, Sam," she said brightly, aloud.

The voice sounded peculiar too.

"I want some potatoes please, Sam. Yes, and I think a can of peas."

That was better. Both the smile and the voice were coming out better now. She rehearsed it several times more. Then she ran downstairs, took her coat, went out the back door, down the garden, into the street.

It wasn't six o'clock yet and the lights were still on in the grocery shop.

"Hullo, Sam," she said brightly, smiling at the man behind the counter.

"Why, good evening, Mrs. Maloney. How're *you?*"

"I want some potatoes please, Sam. Yes, and I think a can of peas."

The man turned and reached up behind him on the shelf for the peas.

"Patrick's decided he's tired and doesn't want to eat out tonight," she told him. "We usually go out Thursdays, you know, and now he's caught me without any vegetables in the house."

"Then how about meat, Mrs. Maloney?"

"No, I've got meat, thanks. I got a nice leg of lamb from the freezer."

"Oh."

"I don't much like cooking it frozen, Sam, but I'm taking a chance on it this time. You think it'll be all right?"

"Personally," the grocer said, "I don't believe it makes any difference. You want these Idaho potatoes?"

"Oh, yes, that'll be fine. Two of those."

"Anything else?" The grocer cocked his head on one side, looking at her pleasantly. "How about afterwards? What you going to give him for afterwards?"

"Well—what would you suggest, Sam?"

The man glanced around his shop. "How about a nice big slice of cheesecake? I know he likes that."

"Perfect," she said. "He loves it."

And when it was all wrapped and she had paid, she put on her brightest smile and said, "Thank you, Sam. Goodnight."

"Goodnight, Mrs. Maloney. And thank *you.*"

And now, she told herself as she hurried back,

all she was doing now, she was returning home to her husband and he was waiting for his supper; and she must cook it good, and make it as tasty as possible because the poor man was tired, and if, when she entered the house, she happened to find anything unusual, or tragic, or terrible, then naturally it would be a shock and she'd become frantic with grief and horror. Mind you, she wasn't *expecting* to find anything. She was just going home with the vegetables. Mrs. Patrick Maloney going with the vegetables on Thursday evening to cook supper for her husband.

That's the way, she told herself. Do everything right and natural. Keep things absolutely natural and there'll be no need for any acting at all.

Therefore, when she entered the kitchen by the back door, she was humming a little tune to herself and smiling.

"Patrick!" she called. "How are you, darling?"

She put the parcel down on the table and went through into the living room; and when she saw him lying there on the floor with his legs doubled up and one arm twisted back underneath his body, it really was rather a shock. All the old love and longing for him welled up inside her, and she ran over to him, knelt down beside him, and began to cry her heart out. It was easy. No acting was necessary.

A few minutes later she got up and went to the phone. She knew the number of the police station, and when the man at the other end answered, she cried to him. "Quick! Come quick! Patrick's dead!"

"Who's speaking?"

"Mrs. Maloney. Mrs. Patrick Maloney."

"You mean Patrick Maloney's dead?"

"I think so," she sobbed. "He's lying on the floor and I think he's dead."

"Be right over," the man said.

The car came very quickly, and when she opened the front door, two policemen walked in. She knew them both—she knew nearly all the men at that precinct—and she fell right into Jack Noonan's arms, weeping hysterically. He put her gently into a chair, then went over to join the other one, who was called O'Malley, kneeling by the body.

"Is he dead?" she cried.

"I'm afraid he is. What happened?"

Briefly, she told her story about going out to the grocer and coming back to find him on the floor. While she was talking, crying and talking, Noonan discovered a small patch of congealed blood on the dead man's head. He showed it to O'Malley, who got up at once and hurried to the phone.

Soon, other men began to come into the house. First a doctor, then two detectives, one of whom she knew by name. Later, a police photographer arrived and took pictures, and a man who knew about fingerprints. There was a great deal of whispering and muttering beside the corpse, and the detectives kept asking her a lot of questions. But they always treated her kindly. She told her story again, this time right from the beginning, when Patrick had come in, and she was sewing, and he was tired, so tired he hadn't wanted to go out for supper. She told how she'd put the meat in the oven—"it's there now, cooking"—and how she'd slipped out to the grocer for vegetables, and come back to find him lying on the floor.

"Which grocer?" one of the detectives asked.

She told him, and he turned and whispered something to the other detective, who immediately went outside into the street.

In fifteen minutes he was back with a page of notes, and there was more whispering, and through her sobbing she heard a few of the whispered phrases—" . . . acted quite normal . . . very cheerful . . . wanted to give him a good supper . . . peas . . . cheesecake . . . impossible that she . . ."

After a while, the photographer and the doctor departed and two other men came in and took the corpse away on a stretcher. Then the fingerprint man went away. The two detectives remained, and so did the two policemen. They were exceptionally nice to her, and Jack Noonan asked if she wouldn't rather go somewhere else, to her sister's house perhaps, or to his own wife, who would take care of her and put her up for the night.

No, she said. She didn't feel she could move even a yard at the moment. Would they mind awfully if she stayed just where she was until she felt better. She didn't feel too good at the moment, she really didn't.

Then hadn't she better lie down on the bed? Jack Noonan asked.

No, she said. She'd like to stay right where she was, in this chair. A little later perhaps, when she felt better, she would move.

So they left her while they went about their business, searching the house. Occasionally one of the detectives asked her another question. Sometimes Jack Noonan spoke to her gently as he passed by. Her husband, he told her, had been killed by a blow on the back of the head administered with a heavy blunt instrument, almost certainly a large piece of metal. They were looking for the weapon. The murderer may have taken it with him, but on the other hand he may've thrown it away or hidden it somewhere on the premises.

"It's the old story," he said. "Get the weapon, and you've got the man."

Later, one of the detectives came up and sat beside her. Did she know, he asked, of anything in the house that could've been used as the weapon? Would she mind having a look around to see if anything was missing—a very big spanner,[1] for example, or a heavy metal vase.

They didn't have any heavy metal vases, she said.

"Or a big spanner?"

She didn't think they had a big spanner. But there might be some things like that in the garage.

The search went on. She knew that there were other policemen in the garden all around the house. She could hear their footsteps on the gravel outside, and sometimes she saw the flash of a torch through a chink in the curtains. It began to get late, nearly nine she noticed by the clock on the mantel. The four men searching the rooms seemed to be growing weary, a trifle exasperated.

"Jack," she said, the next time Sergeant Noonan went by. "Would you mind giving me a drink?"

"Sure I'll give you a drink. You mean this whiskey?"

"Yes, please. But just a small one. It might make me feel better."

He handed her the glass.

"Why don't you have one yourself," she said. "You must be awfully tired. Please do. You've been very good to me."

"Well," he answered. "It's not strictly allowed, but I might take just a drop to keep me going."

One by one the others came in and were persuaded to take a little nip of whiskey. They stood around rather awkwardly with the drinks in their hands, uncomfortable in her presence, trying to say consoling things to her. Sergeant Noonan wandered into the kitchen, came out quickly and said, "Look, Mrs. Maloney. You know that oven of yours is still on, and the meat still inside."

"Oh, *dear* me!" she cried. "So it is!"

"I better turn it off for you, hadn't I?"

"Will you do that, Jack. Thank you so much."

When the sergeant returned the second time, she looked at him with her large, dark, tearful eyes. "Jack Noonan," she said.

"Yes?"

"Would you do me a small favor—you and these others?"

"We can try, Mrs. Maloney."

"Well," she said. "Here you all are, and good

---

1. **spanner**, wrench. [*British*]

friends of dear Patrick's too, and helping to catch the man who killed him. You must be terrible hungry by now because it's long past your supper-time, and I know Patrick would never forgive me, God bless his soul, if I allowed you to remain in his house without offering you decent hospitality. Why don't you eat up that lamb that's in the oven. It'll be cooked just right by now."

"Wouldn't dream of it," Sergeant Noonan said.

"Please," she begged. "Please eat it. Personally I couldn't touch a thing, certainly not what's been in the house when he was here. But it's all right for you. It'd be a favor to me if you'd eat it up. Then you can go on with your work again after-wards."

There was a good deal of hesitating among the four policemen, but they were clearly hungry, and in the end they were persuaded to go into the kitchen and help themselves. The woman stayed where she was, listening to them through the open door, and she could hear them speaking among themselves, their voices thick and sloppy because their mouths were full of meat.

"Have some more, Charlie?"

"No. Better not finish it."

"She *wants* us to finish it. She said so. Be doing her a favor."

"Okay then. Give me some more."

"That's a big club the guy must've used to hit poor Patrick," one of them was saying. "The doc says his skull was smashed all to pieces just like from a sledgehammer."

"That's why it ought to be easy to find."

"Exactly what I say."

"Whoever done it, they're not going to be carrying a thing like that around with them longer than they need."

One of them belched.

"Personally, I think it's right here on the premises."

"Probably right under our very noses. What you think, Jack?"

And in the other room Mary Maloney began to giggle.

---

## THINK AND DISCUSS

### Understanding

1. What preparations had Mary Maloney made for her husband's return from work?
2. What is Mr. Maloney's occupation?
3. What do the police search for in the story?
4. What "small favor" does Mary ask of Jack Noonan and the others?

### Analyzing

5. What indications are provided early in the story that Mary loves her husband?
6. What do you think Patrick Maloney tells Mary that is so terribly shocking to her?
7. Explain the ironic ending to the story, beginning with Mary inviting the police to eat. Give details to support your answer.

### Extending

8. Do you find Mary's calmness and care in working out her alibi after the crime believable? Why or why not?

### REVIEWING: Point of View   H▮
See Handbook of Literary Terms, p. 816

To achieve an ironically humorous effect in "Lamb to the Slaughter," author Roald Dahl had to decide who would narrate the story. The point of view he chose allows certain crucial information to be withheld from each character and even from the reader. Yet the reader has to know one character's thoughts without that character—Mary—knowing enough to tell the whole story in a detached, objective manner.

1. Is the story told in the first-person or the third-person point of view?
2. Does the narrator describe only what can be seen happening, both what can be seen happening and what all the major characters are thinking, or what can be seen happening and the thoughts of one character?
3. What is this point of view called?

## COMPOSITION
### Analyzing a Character's Reactions

The last sentence of the story has surprised many readers. Think about whether the last sentence reveals something new about Mary, or whether the same wearying, disturbing events that have caused most of the action may have prompted her giggling at the end. Review the characterization of Mary throughout the story to determine whether the last sentence reveals a more sinister Mary or if it shows the same character merely affected by exhaustion, possible hysteria, or some other feeling. Write an essay stating your belief about the story's last sentence and supporting your opinion with evidence from the story. See "Writing About Characters" in the Writer's Handbook.

### Using a Different Point of View

Imagine that you are one of the following characters in "Lamb to the Slaughter": Mary, Patrick, or Jack Noonan. Find a part of the story at which you (as a reader) are most curious about what that character is thinking. Write a monologue expressing the inner thoughts of the character at that point in the action. Since you will write your composition in the first-person point of view, you may invent the thoughts that you feel fit the character. Make sure your monologue is consistent with what happens before, during, and after that moment or period of time in the story.

## BIOGRAPHY

### Roald Dahl
### 1916–

Born in Llandaff, South Wales, Roald Dahl spent his early career, from 1932 to 1939, with an oil company in East Africa. After Hitler invaded Poland in 1939, Dahl joined the Royal Air Force of Britain.

The short-story collections *Over to You* (1946) and *Someone Like You* (1953), plus stories published in *The New Yorker*, acquainted American readers with Dahl's growing talents. *Kiss, Kiss* (1960), *The Best of Roald Dahl* (1983), and other story collections have added to his reputation. He has twice received the Edgar Allan Poe Award of the Mystery Writers of America.

**See THEME in the Handbook of Literary Terms, page 829.**

# Through the Tunnel

**Doris Lessing**  Zimbabwe (Rhodesia)

"He looked down into the blue well of water. He knew he must find his way through that cave, or hole, or tunnel, and out the other side."

oing to the shore on the first morning of the vacation, the young English boy stopped at a turning of the path and looked down at a wild and rocky bay, and then over to the crowded beach he knew so well from other years. His mother walked on in front of him, carrying a bright striped bag in one hand. Her other arm, swinging loose, was very white in the sun. The boy watched that white, naked arm, and turned his eyes, which had a frown behind them, toward the bay and back again to his mother. When she felt he was not with her, she swung around. "Oh, there you are, Jerry!" she said. She looked impatient, then smiled. "Why, darling, would you rather not come with me? Would you rather—" She frowned, conscientiously worrying over what amusements he might secretly be longing for, which she had been too busy or too careless to imagine. He was very familiar with that anxious, apologetic smile. Contrition sent him running after her. And yet, as he ran, he looked back over his shoulder at the wild bay; and all morning, as

he played on the safe beach, he was thinking of it.

Next morning, when it was time for the routine of swimming and sunbathing, his mother said, "Are you tired of the usual beach, Jerry? Would you like to go somewhere else?"

"Oh, no!" he said quickly, smiling at her out of that unfailing impulse of contrition—a sort of chivalry. Yet, walking down the path with her, he blurted out, "I'd like to go and have a look at those rocks down there."

She gave the idea her attention. It was a wild-looking place, and there was no one there; but she said, "Of course, Jerry. When you've had enough, come to the big beach. Or just go straight back to the villa, if you like." She walked away, that bare arm, now slightly reddened from yesterday's sun, swinging. And he almost ran after her again, feeling it unbearable that she could go by herself, but he did not.

She was thinking. Of course he's old enough to be safe without me. Have I been keeping him too close? He mustn't feel he ought to be with me. I must be careful.

He was an only child, eleven years old. She was a widow. She was determined to be neither possessive nor lacking in devotion. She went worrying off to her beach.

As for Jerry, once he saw that his mother had gained her beach, he began the steep descent to the bay. From where he was, high up among red-brown rocks, it was a scoop of moving bluish green fringed with white. As he went lower, he saw that it spread among small promontories and inlets of rough, sharp rock, and the crisping, lapping surface showed stains of purple and darker blue. Finally, as he ran sliding and scraping down the last few yards, he saw an edge of white surf and the shallow, luminous movement of water over white sand, and, beyond that, a solid, heavy blue.

He ran straight into the water and began swimming. He was a good swimmer. He went out fast over the gleaming sand, over a middle region where rocks lay like discolored monsters under the surface, and then he was in the real sea—a warm sea where irregular cold currents from the deep water shocked his limbs.

When he was so far out that he could look back not only on the little bay but past the promontory that was between it and the big beach, he floated on the buoyant surface and looked for his mother. There she was, a speck of yellow under an umbrella that looked like a slice of orange peel. He swam back to shore, relieved at being sure she was there, but all at once very lonely.

On the edge of a small cape that marked the side of the bay away from the promontory was a loose scatter of rocks. Above them, some boys were stripping off their clothes. They came running, naked, down to the rocks. The English boy swam toward them, but kept his distance at a stone's throw. They were of that coast; all of them were burned smooth dark brown and speaking a language he did not understand. To be with them, of them, was a craving that filled his whole body. He swam a little closer; they turned and watched him with narrowed, alert dark eyes. Then one smiled and waved. It was enough. In a minute, he had swum in and was on the rocks beside them, smiling with a desperate, nervous supplication. They shouted cheerful greetings at him; and then, as he preserved his nervous, uncomprehending smile, they understood that he was a foreigner strayed from his own beach, and they proceeded to forget him. But he was happy. He was with them.

They began diving again and again from a high point into a well of blue sea between rough, pointed rocks. After they had dived and come up, they swam around, hauled themselves up, and waited their turn to dive again. They were big boys—men, to Jerry. He dived, and they watched him; and when he swam around to take his place, they made away for him. He felt he was accepted and he dived again, carefully, proud of himself.

Soon the biggest of the boys poised himself, shot down into the water, and did not come up. The others stood about, watching. Jerry, after waiting for the sleek brown head to appear, let out a yell of warning; they looked at him idly and turned their eyes back toward the water. After a long time, the boy came up on the other side of a big dark rock, letting the air out of his lungs in a sputtering gasp and a shout of triumph. Immediately the rest of them dived in. One moment, the morning seemed full of chattering boys; the next, the air and the surface of the water were empty. But through the heavy blue, dark shapes could be seen moving and groping.

Jerry dived, shot past the school of underwater swimmers, saw a black wall of rock looming at him, touched it, and bobbed up at once to the surface, where the wall was a low barrier he could see across. There was no one visible; under him, in the water, the dim shapes of the swimmers had disappeared. Then one, and then another of the boys came up on the far side of the barrier of rock, and he understood that they had swum through some gap or hole in it. He plunged down again. He could see nothing through the stinging salt water but the blank rock. When he came up the boys were all on the diving rock, preparing to attempt the feat again. And now, in a panic of failure, he yelled up, in English, "Look at me! Look!" and he began splashing and kicking in the water like a foolish dog.

They looked down gravely, frowning. He knew

David Ligare, *Untitled Study, Symi Island, Greece* (detail), 1982, Private Collection

the frown. At moments of failure, when he clowned to claim his mother's attention, it was with just this grave, embarrassed inspection that she rewarded him. Through his hot shame, feeling the pleading grin on his face like a scar that he could never remove, he looked up at the group of big brown boys on the rock and shouted, *"Bonjour! Merci! Au revoir! Monsieur, monsieur!"*[1] while he hooked his fingers round his ears and waggled them.

Water surged into his mouth; he choked, sank, came up. The rock, lately weighted with boys, seemed to rear up out of the water as their weight was removed. They were flying down past him, now, into the water; the air was full of falling bodies. Then the rock was empty in the hot sunlight. He counted one, two, three. . . .

At fifty, he was terrified. They must all be drowning beneath him, in the watery caves of the rock! At a hundred, he stared around him at the empty hillside, wondering if he should yell for help. He counted faster, faster, to hurry them up, to bring them to the surface quickly, to drown them quickly—anything rather than the terror of counting on and on into the blue emptiness of the morning. And then, at a hundred and sixty, the water beyond the rock was full of boys blowing like brown whales. They swam back to the shore without a look at him.

He climbed back to the diving rock and sat down, feeling the hot roughness of it under his thighs. The boys were gathering up their bits of clothing and running off along the shore to another promontory. They were leaving to get away from him. He cried openly, fists in his eyes. There was no one to see him, and he cried himself out.

It seemed to him that a long time had passed, and he swam out to where he could see his mother. Yes, she was still there, a yellow spot under an orange umbrella. He swam back to the big rock, climbed up, and dived into the blue pool among the fanged and angry boulders. Down he went, until he touched the wall of rock again. But the salt was so painful in his eyes that he could not see.

He came to the surface, swam to shore, and went back to the villa to wait for his mother. Soon she walked slowly up the path, swinging her striped bag, the flushed, naked arm dangling beside her. "I want some swimming goggles," he panted, defiant and beseeching.

She gave him a patient inquisitive look as she said casually, "Well, of course, darling."

But now, now, now! He must have them this minute, and no other time. He nagged and pestered until she went with him to a shop. As soon as she had bought the goggles, he grabbed them from her hand as if she were going to claim them for herself, and was off, running down the steep path to the bay.

Jerry swam out to the big barrier rock, adjusted the goggles, and dived. The impact of the water broke the rubber-enclosed vacuum, and the goggles came loose. He understood that he must swim down to the base of the rock from the surface of the water. He fixed the goggles tight and firm, filled his lungs, and floated, face down, on the water. Now, he could see. It was as if he had eyes of a different kind—fish eyes that showed everything clear and delicate and wavering in the bright water.

Under him, six or seven feet down, was a floor of perfectly clean, shining white sand, rippled firm and hard by the tides. Two grayish shapes steered there, like long, rounded pieces of wood or slate. They were fish. He saw them nose toward each other, poise motionless, make a dart forward, swerve off, and come around again. It was like a water dance. A few inches above them

---

1. *"Bonjour!"* (bôn zhür′) *Merci!* (mer sē′) *Au revoir!* (ō rə-vwär′) *Monsieur . . ."* (mə syèr′), French terms meaning "good morning," "thank you," "good-by," and "mister" or "sir."

the water sparkled as if sequins were dropping through it. Fish again—myriads of minute fish, the length of his fingernail, were drifting through the water, and in a moment he could feel the innumerable tiny touches of them against his limbs. It was like swimming in flaked silver. The great rock the big boys had swum through rose sheer out of the white sand—black, tufted lightly with greenish weed. He could see no gap in it. He swam down to its base.

Again and again he rose, took a big chestful of air, and went down. Again and again he groped over the surface of the rock, feeling it, almost hugging it in the desperate need to find the entrance. And then, once, while he was clinging to the black wall, his knees came up and he shot his feet out forward and they met no obstacle. He had found the hole.

He gained the surface, clambered about the stones that littered the barrier rock until he found a big one, and, with this in his arms, let himself down over the side of the rock. He dropped, with the weight, straight to the sandy floor. Clinging tight to the anchor of stone, he lay on his side and looked in under the dark shelf at the place where his feet had gone. He could see the hole. It was an irregular, dark gap; but he could not see deep into it. He let go of his anchor, clung with his hands to the edges of the hole, and tried to push himself in.

He got his head in, found his shoulders jammed, moved them in sidewise, and was inside as far as his waist. He could see nothing ahead. Something soft and clammy touched his mouth; he saw a dark frond moving against the grayish rock and panic filled him. He thought of octopuses, of clinging weed. He pushed himself out backward and caught a glimpse, as he retreated, of a harmless tentacle of seaweed drifting in the mouth of the tunnel. But it was enough. He reached the sunlight, swam to shore, and lay on the diving rock. He looked down into the blue well of water. He knew he must find his way through that cave, or hole, or tunnel, and out the other side.

First, he thought, he must learn to control his breathing. He let himself down into the water with another big stone in his arms, so that he could lie effortlessly on the bottom of the sea. He counted. One, two, three. He counted steadily. He could hear the movement of blood in his chest. Fifty-one, fifty-two . . . His chest was hurting. He let go of the rock and went up into the air. He saw that the sun was low. He rushed to the villa and found his mother at her supper. She said only "Did you enjoy yourself?" and he said "Yes."

All night the boy dreamed of the water-filled cave in the rock, and as soon as breakfast was over he went to the bay.

That night, his nose bled badly. For hours he had been underwater, learning to hold his breath, and now he felt weak and dizzy. His mother said, "I shouldn't overdo things, darling, if I were you."

That day and the next, Jerry exercised his lungs as if everything, the whole of his life, all that he would become, depended upon it. Again his nose bled at night, and his mother insisted on his coming with her the next day. It was a torment to him to waste a day of his careful self-training, but he stayed with her on that other beach, which now seemed a place for small children, a place where his mother might lie safe in the sun. It was not his beach.

He did not ask for permission, on the following day, to go to his beach. He went, before his mother could consider the complicated rights and wrongs of the matter. A day's rest, he discovered, had improved his count by ten. The big boys had made the passage while he counted a hundred and sixty. He had been counting fast, in his fright. Probably now, if he tried, he could get through that long tunnel, but he was not going to try yet. A curious, most unchildlike persistence, a controlled impatience, made him wait. In the meantime, he lay underwater on the white sand, littered now by stones he had brought down from the upper air, and studied the entrance to the tunnel. He knew every jut and corner of it, as far as it was possible to see. It was as if he already felt its sharpness about his shoulders.

He sat by the clock in the villa, when his mother was not near, and checked his time. He was incredulous and then proud to find he could hold his breath without strain for two minutes. The words "two minutes," authorized by the clock, brought close the adventure that was so necessary to him.

In another four days, his mother said casually one morning, they must go home. On the day before they left, he would do it. He would do it if it killed him, he said defiantly to himself. But two days before they were to leave—a day of triumph when he increased his count by fifteen—his nose bled so badly that he turned dizzy and had to lie limply over the big rock like a bit of seaweed, watching the thick red blood flow on the rock and trickle slowly down to the sea. He was frightened. Supposing he turned dizzy in the tunnel? Supposing he died there, trapped? Supposing—his head went around, in the hot sun, and he almost gave up. He thought he would return to the house and lie down, and next summer, perhaps, when he had another year's growth in him —*then* he would go through the hole.

But even after he had made the decision, or thought he had, he found himself sitting up on the rock and looking down into the water; and he knew that now, this moment, when his nose had only just stopped bleeding, when his head was still sore and throbbing—this was the moment when he would try. If he did not do it now, he never would. He was trembling with fear that he would not go; and he was trembling with horror at that long, long tunnel under the rock, under the sea. Even in the open sunlight, the barrier rock seemed very wide and very heavy; tons of rock pressed down on where he would go. If he died there, he would lie until one day—perhaps not before next year—those big boys would swim into it and find it blocked.

He put on his goggles, fitted them tight, tested the vacuum. His hands were shaking. Then he chose the biggest stone he could carry and slipped over the edge of the rock until half of him was in the cool, enclosing water and half in the hot sun. He looked up once at the empty sky, filled his lungs once, twice, and then sank fast to the bottom with the stone. He let it go and began to count. He took the edges of the hole in his hands and drew himself into it, wriggling his shoulders in sidewise as he remembered he must, kicking himself along with his feet.

Soon he was clear inside. He was in a small rock-bound hole filled with yellowish-gray water. The water was pushing him up against the roof. The roof was sharp and pained his back. He pulled himself along with his hands—fast, fast— and used his legs as levers. His head knocked against something; a sharp pain dizzied him. Fifty, fifty-one, fifty-two . . . He was without light, and the water seemed to press upon him with the weight of rock. Seventy-one, seventy-two . . . There was no strain on his lungs. He felt like an inflated balloon, his lungs were so light and easy, but his head was pulsing.

He was being continually pressed against the sharp roof, which felt slimy as well as sharp. Again he thought of octopuses, and wondered if the tunnel might be filled with weed that could tangle him. He gave himself a panicky, convulsive kick forward, ducked his head, and swam. His feet and hands moved freely, as if in open water. The hole must have widened out. He thought he must be swimming fast, and he was frightened of banging his head if the tunnel narrowed.

A hundred, a hundred and one . . . The water paled. Victory filled him. His lungs were beginning to hurt. A few more strokes and he would be out. He was counting wildly; he said a hundred and fifteen, and then, a long time later, a hundred and fifteen again. The water was a clear jewel-green all around him. Then he saw, above his head, a crack running up through the rock. Sunlight was falling through it, showing the clean, dark rock of the tunnel, a single mussel shell, and darkness ahead.

He was at the end of what he could do. He looked up at the crack as if it were filled with air and not water, as if he could put his mouth to it to draw in air. A hundred and fifteen, he heard himself say inside his head—but he had said that long ago. He must go on into the blackness ahead, or he would drown. His head was swelling, his lungs cracking. A hundred and fifteen, a hundred and fifteen pounded through his head, and he feebly clutched at rocks in the dark, pulling himself forward, leaving the brief space of sunlit water behind. He felt he was dying. He was no longer quite conscious. He struggled on in the darkness between lapses into unconsciousness. An immense, swelling pain filled his head, and then the darkness cracked with an explosion of green light. His hands, groping forward, met nothing; and his feet, kicking back, propelled him out into the open sea.

He drifted to the surface, his face turned up to the air. He was gasping like a fish. He felt he would sink now and drown; he could not swim the few feet back to the rock. Then he was clutching it and pulling himself up onto it. He lay face down, gasping. He could see nothing but a red-veined, clotted dark. His eyes must have burst, he thought; they were full of blood. He tore off his goggles and a gout of blood went into the sea. His nose was bleeding, and the blood had filled the goggles.

He scooped up handfuls of water from the cool, salty sea, to splash on his face, and did not know whether it was blood or salt water he tasted. After a time, his heart quieted, his eyes cleared, and he sat up. He could see the local boys diving and playing half a mile away. He did not want them. He wanted nothing but to get back home and lie down.

In a short while, Jerry swam to shore and climbed slowly up the path to the villa. He flung himself on his bed and slept, waking at the sound of feet on the path outside. His mother was coming back. He rushed to the bathroom, thinking she must not see his face with bloodstains, or tearstains, on it. He came out of the bathroom and met her as she walked into the villa, smiling, his eyes lighting up.

"Have a nice morning?" she asked, laying her hand on his warm brown shoulder a moment.

"Oh, yes, thank you," he said.

"You look a bit pale." And then, sharp and anxious, "How did you bang your head?"

"Oh, just banged it," he told her.

She looked at him closely. He was strained; his eyes were glazed looking. She was worried. And then she said to herself, Oh, don't fuss! Nothing can happen. He can swim like a fish.

They sat down to lunch together.

"Mummy," he said, "I can stay underwater for two minutes—three minutes, at least." It came bursting out of him.

"Can you, darling?" she said. "Well, I shouldn't overdo it. I don't think you ought to swim anymore today."

She was ready for a battle of wills, but he gave in at once. It was no longer of the least importance to go to the bay.

## THINK AND DISCUSS

### Understanding

1. What makes Jerry feel a sense of failure when he watches the older boys dive and swim?
2. Why does Jerry insist his mother buy him goggles?
3. What skill does Jerry decide he must master first if he is to swim through the tunnel?
4. What physical problems does Jerry experience in preparing to swim through the tunnel?

### Analyzing

5. Explain how the older boys' attitude toward Jerry changes during the time he is with them.
6. Describe the changing relationship between Jerry and his mother throughout the story.
7. Why does Jerry choose to swim through the tunnel when he really has doubts about succeeding?
8. Describe Jerry's external and internal conflicts while swimming through the tunnel.
9. Identify the climax of the story.
10. After swimming through the tunnel, Jerry sees the older boys and thinks that he does not want to be with them, that he wants nothing more but to go home and lie down. How is this a change in attitude?

### Extending

11. Imagine that Jerry's mother knows what he is planning and doing throughout the story. Do you think she would stop him? Would her response, as you have imagined it, be right or wrong?
12. Describe some other challenges that young people might face and overcome, thus making them more mature.

## APPLYING: Theme  H

See Handbook of Literary Terms, p. 829

The **theme**, the underlying main idea of a literary work, may be stated directly in a story or implied. For example, a theme may be conveyed through the significance of the action in characters' lives. One approach to understanding theme is to think through the events of the plot and decide what effect they've had on the characters. Another is to keep in mind all the things that theme is *not*. A theme is not a moral. It is not a statement of the subject of the story, such as "the adventure of swimming." It is not a plot summary.

Choose the best theme statement from the following, and explain what is wrong with the others. Remember that the statement you choose will not be the only possible way to express the theme of the story.

1. To be treated like an adult, act like one!
2. A young boy puts himself through strict training to swim successfully through a perilously long underwater tunnel.
3. The accomplishment of a difficult task through one's own will and effort can be an important step in growing up.

## VOCABULARY

### Root Words, Latin and Greek Word Parts

Certain Latin and Greek words, or parts of them, form the roots of dozens of English words. An example is the Latin word *lucere*, "to shine," and its related noun *lumen*, "light." The italicized words in the following sentences are derived from one or the other of these roots. Keeping the meaning of the Latin words in mind, and using context clues as well, write the meaning of each italicized word.

1. A spotlight under the water made the whole pool *luminous*.

2. How can you expect two candles to *illuminate* a big room like this?
3. *Luminaries* from the worlds of sports and theater made the banquet the place to be.
4. Since no one could understand the poem, I offered to *elucidate* it.
5. As she got over her morning grogginess, her remarks became more *lucid*.

## COMPOSITION
### Explaining a Relationship

In "Through the Tunnel" Jerry is a boy who encounters a challenge and decides to master it on his own, independent of his mother's watchful care. Yet the early part of the story focuses on the way Jerry and his mother get along and react to one another. Review the story to recall the attitudes of both characters toward their child-parent relationship. Note how Jerry's feelings change due to his experiences. Write a three-paragraph essay describing their relationship and explaining how it changes during the story. Base your analysis on evidence from the text, such as the thoughts of the characters. Feel free to reflect your judgments about the characters' decisions and emotions, but base any evaluation on a solid understanding of their concerns and motives as well as their actions.

### Considering an Alternate Ending

Readers are free to appreciate a theme that concerns growth and change in life as dealt with in "Through the Tunnel," because Jerry succeeds in his endeavor. Yet he considers the possibility that he will fail and even die in his quest. Review the parts of the story in which he trains himself, decides to make his attempt, envisions failure, and struggles to swim through the tunnel. Decide whether and how the theme would be different if Jerry had been forced to turn back in order to survive. What idea might be conveyed by that story? Would the theme resemble the existing theme? Write a three-paragraph essay in which you pose the alternate ending and comment on the theme that you suppose it would carry. See "Writing About Theme" in the Writer's Handbook.

## BIOGRAPHY

### Doris Lessing
### 1919–

The daughter of a British army captain, Doris Lessing was born in Persia, now called Iran; soon afterwards, however, her family moved to a country then called Rhodesia, now known as Zimbabwe. At age thirty, she left Southern Rhodesia for England, but Africa remained a dominant influence on her writing. *African Stories* (1964) contains some of her best portrayals of the problems of southern Africa. In addition to several science fiction works, Lessing has written many stories and novels, such as *The Golden Notebook* (1962) and the ironically titled *The Good Terrorist* (1985), dealing with the problems people encounter trying to deal with the political and social upheavals of this century.

**Review THEME in the Handbook of Literary Terms, page 829.**

# The Story of the Widow's Son

**Mary Lavin**   Ireland

---

**Which is more painful: the death of love or the death of a loved one?**

---

This is the story of a widow's son, but it is a story that has two endings.

There was once a widow, living in a small neglected village at the foot of a steep hill. She had only one son, but he was the meaning of her life. She lived for his sake. She wore herself out working for him. Every day she made a hundred sacrifices in order to keep him at a good school in the town, four miles away, because there was a better teacher there than the village dullard that had taught herself.

She made great plans for Packy, but she did not tell him about her plans. Instead she threatened him, day and night, that if he didn't turn out well, she would put him to work on the roads, or in the quarry under the hill.

But as the years went by, everyone in the village, and even Packy himself, could tell by the way she watched him out of sight in the morning, and watched to see him come into sight in the evening, that he was the beat of her heart, and that her gruff words were only a cover for her pride and her joy in him.

It was for Packy's sake that she walked for hours along the road, letting her cow graze the long acre of the wayside grass, in order to spare the few poor blades that pushed up through the stones in her own field. It was for his sake she walked back and forth to the town to sell a few cabbages as soon as ever they were fit. It was for his sake that she got up in the cold dawning hours to gather mushrooms that would take the place of foods that had to be bought with money. She bent her back daily to make every penny she could, and as often happens, she made more by industry, out of her few bald acres, than many of the farmers around her made out of their great bearded meadows. Out of the money she made by selling eggs alone, she paid for Packy's clothes and for the greater number of his books.

When Packy was fourteen, he was in the last class in the school, and the master had great hopes of his winning a scholarship to a big college in the city. He was getting to be a tall lad, and his

---

"The Story of the Widow's Son" by Mary Lavin, from *Irish Harvest*. Reprinted by permission of the author.

features were beginning to take a strong cast. His character was strengthening too, under his mother's sharp tongue. The people of the village were beginning to give him the same respect they gave to the sons of the farmers who came from their fine colleges in the summer, with blue suits and bright ties. And whenever they spoke to the widow they praised him up to the skies.

One day in June, when the air was so heavy the scent that rose up from the grass was imprisoned under the low clouds and hung in the air, the widow was waiting at the gate for Packy. There had been no rain for some days and the hens and chickens were pecking irritably at the dry ground and wandering up and down the road in bewilderment.

A neighbor passed.

"Waiting for Packy?" said the neighbor, pleasantly, and he stood for a minute to take off his hat and wipe the sweat of the day from his face. He was an old man.

"It's a hot day!" he said. "It will be a hard push for Packy on that battered old bike of his. I wouldn't like to have to face into four miles on a day like this!"

"Packy would travel three times that distance if there was a book at the other end of the road!" said the widow, with the pride of those who cannot read more than a line or two without wearying.

The minutes went by slowly. The widow kept looking up at the sun.

"I suppose the heat is better than the rain!" she said, at last.

"The heat can do a lot of harm too, though," said the neighbor, absent-mindedly, as he pulled a long blade of grass from between the stones of the wall and began to chew the end of it. "You could get sunstroke on a day like this!" He looked up at the sun. "The sun is a terror," he said. "It could cause you to drop down dead like a stone!"

The widow strained out further over the gate.

She looked up the hill in the direction of the town.

"He will have a good cool breeze on his face coming down the hill, at any rate," she said.

The man looked up the hill. "That's true. On the hottest day of the year you would get a cool breeze coming down that hill on a bicycle. You would feel the air streaming past your cheeks like silk. And in the winter it's like two knives flashing to either side of you, and peeling off your skin like you'd peel the bark off a sally-rod."[1] He chewed the grass meditatively. "That must be one of the steepest hills in Ireland," he said. "That hill is a hill worthy of the name of a hill." He took the grass out of his mouth. "It's my belief," he said, earnestly looking at the widow—"it's my belief that that hill is to be found marked with a name in the Ordnance Survey map!"[2]

"If that's the case," said the widow, "Packy will be able to tell you all about it. When it isn't a book he has in his hand it's a map."

"Is that so?" said the man. "That's interesting. A map is a great thing. A map is not an ordinary thing. It isn't everyone can make out a map."

The widow wasn't listening.

"I think I see Packy!" she said, and she opened the wooden gate and stepped out into the roadway.

At the top of the hill there was a glitter of spokes as a bicycle came into sight. Then there was a flash of blue jersey as Packy came flying downward, gripping the handlebars of the bike, with his bright hair blown back from his forehead. The hill was so steep, and he came down so fast, that it seemed to the man and woman at the bottom of the hill that he was not moving at all, but that it was the bright trees and bushes, the bright ditches and wayside grasses that were

---

1. *sally-rod*, a willow twig.
2. *Ordnance Survey map*, a very complete and detailed map of a limited area, prepared by the British Royal Engineers. (Britain at one time controlled Ireland.)

streaming away to either side of him.

The hens and chickens clucked and squawked and ran along the road looking for a safe place in the ditches. They ran to either side with feminine fuss and chatter. Packy waved to his mother. He came nearer and nearer. They could see the freckles on his face.

"Shoo!" cried Packy at the squawking hens that had not yet left the roadway. They ran with their long necks straining forward.

"Shoo!" said Packy's mother, lifting her apron and flapping it in the air to frighten them out of his way.

It was only afterwards, when the harm was done, that the widow began to think that it might, perhaps, have been the flapping of her own apron that frightened the old clucking hen and sent her flying out over the garden wall into the middle of the road.

The old hen appeared suddenly on top of the grassy ditch and looked with a distraught eye at the hens and chickens as they ran to right and left. Her own feathers began to stand out from her. She craned her neck forward and gave a distracted squawk, and fluttered down into the middle of the hot dusty road.

Packy jammed on the brakes. The widow screamed. There was a flurry of white feathers and a spurt of blood. The bicycle swerved and fell. Packy was thrown over the handlebars.

It was such a simple accident that, although the widow screamed, and although the old man looked around to see if there was help near, neither of them thought that Packy was very badly hurt, but when they ran over and lifted his head, and saw that he could not speak, they wiped the blood from his face and looked around, desperately, to measure the distance they would have to carry him.

It was only a few yards to the door of the cottage, but Packy was dead before they got him across the threshold.

"He's only in a weakness!" screamed the widow, and she urged the crowd that had gathered outside the door to do something for him. "Get a doctor!" she cried, pushing a young laborer towards the door. "Hurry! Hurry! The doctor will bring him around."

But the neighbors that kept coming in the door, quickly, from all sides, were crossing themselves, one after another, and falling on their knees, as soon as they laid eyes on the boy, stretched out flat on the bed, with the dust and dirt and the sweat marks of life on his dead face.

Martin Gale, *Bus Stop*,
Private Collection

When at last the widow was convinced that her son was dead, the other women had to hold her down. She waved her arms and cried out aloud, and wrestled to get free. She wanted to wring the neck of every hen in the yard.

"I'll kill every one of them. What good are they to me, now? All the hens in the world aren't worth one drop of human blood. That old clucking hen wasn't worth more than six shillings,[3] at the very most. What is six shillings? Is it worth poor Packy's life?"

But after a time she stopped raving, and looked from one face to another.

"Why didn't he ride over the old hen?" she asked. "Why did he try to save an old hen that wasn't worth more than six shillings? Didn't he know he was worth more to his mother than an old hen that would be going into the pot one of these days? Why did he do it? Why did he put on the brakes going down one of the worst hills in the country? Why? Why?"

The neighbors patted her arm.

"There now!" they said. "There now!" and that was all they could think of saying, and they said it over and over again. "There now! There now!"

And years afterwards, whenever the widow spoke of her son Packy to the neighbors who dropped in to keep her company for an hour or two, she always had the same question to ask, the same tireless question.

"Why did he put the price of an old clucking hen above the price of his own life?"

And the people always gave the same answer.

"There now!" they said, "there now!" And they sat as silently as the widow herself, looking into the fire.

But surely some of those neighbors must have been stirred to wonder what would have happened had Packy not yielded to his impulse of fear, and had, instead, ridden boldly over the old clucking hen? And surely some of them must have stared into the flames and pictured the scene of the accident again, altering a detail here and there as they did so, and giving the story a different end. For these people knew the widow, and they knew Packy, and when you know people well it is as easy to guess what they would say and do in certain circumstances as it is to remember what they actually did say and do in other circumstances. In fact it is sometimes easier to invent than to remember accurately, and were this not so two great branches of creative art would wither in an hour: the art of the storyteller and the art of the gossip. So, perhaps, if I try to tell you what I myself think might have happened had Packy killed that cackling old hen, you will not accuse me of abusing my privileges as a writer. After all, what I am about to tell you is no more of a fiction than what I have already told, and I lean no heavier now upon your credulity than, with your full consent, I did in the first instance.

And moreover, in many respects the new story is the same as the old.

It begins in the same way too. There is the widow grazing her cow by the wayside, and walking the long roads to the town, weighted down with sacks of cabbages that will pay for Packy's schooling. There she is, fussing over Packy in the mornings in case he would be late for school. There she is in the evening watching the battered clock on the dresser for the hour when he will appear on the top of the hill at his return. And there too, on a hot day in June, is the old laboring man coming up the road, and pausing to talk to her, as she stood at the door. There he is dragging a blade of grass from between the stones of the wall, and putting it between his teeth to chew, before he opens his mouth.

And when he opens his mouth at last it is to utter the same remark.

---

3. *six shillings*. At the time of this story, this amount was worth about $1.20.

"Waiting for Packy?" said the old man, and then he took off his hat and wiped the sweat from his forehead. It will be remembered that he was an old man. "It's a hot day," he said.

"It's very hot," said the widow, looking anxiously up the hill. "It's a hot day to push a bicycle four miles along a bad road with the dust rising to choke you, and sun striking spikes off the handlebars!"

"The heat is better than the rain, all the same," said the old man.

"I suppose it is," said the widow. "All the same, there were days when Packy came home with the rain dried into his clothes so bad they stood up stiff like boards when he took them off. They stood up stiff like boards against the wall, for all the world as if he was still standing in them!"

"Is that so?" said the old man. "You may be sure he got a good petting on those days. There is no son like a widow's son. A ewe lamb!"

"Is it Packy?" said the widow, in disgust. "Packy never got a day's petting since the day he was born. I made up my mind from the first that I'd never make a soft one out of him."

The widow looked up the hill again, and set herself to raking the gravel outside the gate as if she were in the road for no other purpose. Then she gave another look up the hill.

"Here he is now!" she said, and she rose such a cloud of dust with the rake that they could hardly see the glitter of the bicycle spokes, and the flash of blue jersey as Packy came down the hill at a breakneck speed.

Nearer and nearer he came, faster and faster, waving his hand to the widow, shouting at the hens to leave the way!

The hens ran for the ditches, stretching their necks in gawky terror. And then, as the last hen squawked into the ditch, the way was clear for a moment before the whirling silver spokes.

Then, unexpectedly, up from nowhere it seemed, came an old clucking hen and, clucking despairingly, it stood for a moment on the top of the wall and then rose into the air with the clumsy flight of a ground fowl.

Packy stopped whistling. The widow screamed. Packy yelled and the widow flapped her apron. Then Packy swerved the bicycle, and a cloud of dust rose from the braked wheel.

For a minute it could not be seen what exactly had happened, but Packy put his foot down and dragged it along the ground in the dust till he brought the bicycle to a sharp stop. He threw the bicycle down with a clatter on the hard road and ran back. The widow could not bear to look. She threw her apron over her head.

"He's killed the clucking hen!" she said. "He's killed her! He's killed her!" and then she let the apron fall back into place, and began to run up the hill herself. The old man spat out the blade of grass that he had been chewing and ran after the woman.

"Did you kill it?" screamed the widow, and as she got near enough to see the blood and feathers she raised her arm over her head, and her fist was clenched till the knuckles shone white. Packy cowered down over the carcass of the fowl and hunched up his shoulders as if to shield himself from a blow. His legs were spattered with blood, and the brown and white feathers of the dead hen were stuck to his hands, and stuck to his clothes, and they were strewn all over the road. Some of the short white inner feathers were still swirling with the dust in the air.

"I couldn't help it, Mother. I couldn't help it. I didn't see her till it was too late!"

The widow caught up the hen and examined it all over, holding it by the bone of the breast, and letting the long neck dangle. Then, catching it by the leg, she raised it suddenly above her head, and brought down the bleeding body on the boy's back, in blow after blow, spattering the blood all over his face and his hands, over his clothes and over the white dust of the road around him.

"How dare you lie to me!" she screamed, gasping, between the blows. "You saw the hen. I know you saw it. You stopped whistling! You called out! We were watching you. We saw." She turned upon the old man. "Isn't that right?" she demanded. "He saw the hen, didn't he? He saw it?"

"It looked that way," said the old man, uncertainly, his eye on the dangling fowl in the widow's hand.

"There you are!" said the widow. She threw the hen down on the road. "You saw the hen in front of you on the road, as plain as you see it now," she accused, "but you wouldn't stop to save it because you were in too big a hurry home to fill your belly! Isn't that so?"

"No, Mother. No! I saw her all right but it was too late to do anything."

"He admits now that he saw it," said the widow, turning and nodding triumphantly at the onlookers who had gathered at the sound of the shouting.

"I never denied seeing it!" said the boy, appealing to the onlookers as to his judges.

"He doesn't deny it!" screamed the widow. "He stands there as brazen as you like, and admits for all the world to hear that he saw the hen as plain as the nose on his face, and he rode over it without a thought!"

"But what else could I do?" said the boy, throwing out his hand; appealing to the crowd now, and now appealing to the widow. "If I'd put on the brakes going down the hill at such a speed I would have been put over the handlebars!"

"And what harm would that have done you?" screamed the widow. "I often saw you taking a toss when you were wrestling with Jimmy Mack and I heard no complaints afterwards, although your elbows and knees would be running blood, and your face scraped like a gridiron!" She turned to the crowd. "That's as true as God. I often saw

him come in with his nose spouting blood like a pump, and one eye closed as tight as the eye of a corpse. My hand was often stiff for a week from sopping out wet cloths to put poultices on him and try to bring his face back to rights again." She swung back to Packy again. "You're not afraid of a fall when you go climbing trees, are you? You're not afraid to go up on the roof after a cat, are you? Oh, there's more in this than you want me to know. I can see that. You killed that hen on purpose—that's what I believe! You're tired of going to school. You want to get out of going away to college. That's it! You think if you kill the few poor hens we have there will be no money in the box when the time comes to pay for books and classes. That's it!" Packy began to redden.

"It's late in the day for me to be thinking of things like that," he said. "It's long ago I should have started those tricks if that was the way I felt. But it's not true. I want to go to college. The reason I was coming down the hill so fast was to tell you that I got the scholarship. The teacher told me as I was leaving the schoolhouse. That's why I was pedaling so hard. That's why I was whistling. That's why I was waving my hand. Didn't you see me waving my hand from once I came in sight at the top of the hill?"

The widow's hands fell to her sides. The wind of words died down within her and left her flat and limp. She didn't know what to say. She could feel the neighbors staring at her. She wished that they were gone away about their business. She wanted to throw out her arms to the boy, to drag him against her heart and hug him like a small child. But she thought of how the crowd would look at each other and nod and snigger. A ewe lamb! She didn't want to satisfy them. If she gave in to her feelings now they would know how much she had been counting on his getting the scholarship. She wouldn't please them! She wouldn't satisfy them!

She looked at Packy, and when she saw him

standing there before her, spattered with the furious feathers and crude blood of the dead hen, she felt a fierce disappoinment for the boy's own disappointment, and a fierce resentment against him for killing the hen on this day of all days, and spoiling the great news of his success.

Her mind was in confusion. She started at the blood on his face, and all at once it seemed as if the blood was a bad omen of the future that was for him. Disappointment, fear, resentment, and above all defiance raised themselves within her like screeching animals. She looked from Packy to the onlookers.

"Scholarship! Scholarship!" she sneered, putting as much derision as she could into her voice and expression.

"I suppose you think you are a great fellow now? I suppose you think you are independent now? I suppose you think you can go off with yourself now, and look down on your poor slave of a mother who scraped and sweated for you with her cabbages and her hens? I suppose you think to yourself that it doesn't matter now whether the hens are alive or dead? Is that the way? Well, let me tell you this! You're not as independent as you think. The scholarship may pay for your books and your teacher's fees but who will pay for your clothes? Ah-ha, you forgot that, didn't you?" She put her hands on her hips. Packy hung his head. He no longer appealed to the gawking neighbors. They might have been able to save him from blows but he knew enough about life to know that no one could save him from shame.

The widow's heart burned at sight of his shamed face, as her heart burned with grief, but her temper too burned fiercer and fiercer, and she came to a point at which nothing could quell the blaze till it had burned itself out. "Who'll buy your suits?" she yelled. "Who'll buy your boots?" She paused to think of more humiliating accusations. "Who'll buy your breeches?" She paused again and her teeth bit against each other. What

would wound deepest? What shame could she drag upon him? "Who'll buy your nightshirts or will you sleep in your skin?"

The neighbors laughed at that, and the tension was broken. The widow herself laughed. She held her sides and laughed, and as she laughed everything seemed to take on a newer and simpler significance. Things were not so bad as they seemed a moment before. She wanted Packy to laugh too. She looked at him. But as she looked at Packy her heart turned cold with a strange new fear.

"Get into the house!" she said, giving him a push ahead of her. She wanted him safe under her own roof. She wanted to get him away from the gaping neighbors. She hated them, man, woman, and child. She felt that if they had not been there things would have been different. And she wanted to get away from the sight of the blood on the road. She wanted to mash a few potatoes and make a bit of potato cake for Packy. That would comfort him. He loved that.

Packy hardly touched the food. And even after he had washed and scrubbed himself there were stains of blood turning up in the most unexpected places: behind his ears, under his fingernails, inside the cuff of his sleeve.

"Put on your good clothes," said the widow, making a great effort to be gentle, but her manners had become as twisted and as hard as the branches of the trees across the road from her, and even the kindly offers she made sounded harsh. The boy sat on the chair in a slumped position that kept her nerves on edge, and set up a further conflict of irritation and love in her heart. She hated to see him slumping there in the chair, not asking to go outside the door, but still she was uneasy whenever he as much as looked in the direction of the door. She felt safe while he was under the roof; inside the lintel; under her eyes.

Next day she went in to wake him for school, but his room was empty; his bed had not been slept in, and when she ran out in the yard and called him everywhere there was no answer. She ran up and down. She called at the houses of the neighbors but he was not in any house. And she thought she could hear sniggering behind her in each house that she left, as she ran to another one. He wasn't in the village. He wasn't in the town. The master of the school said that she should let the police have a description of him. He said he never met a boy as sensitive as Packy. A boy like that took strange notions into his head from time to time.

The police did their best but there was no news of Packy that night. A few days later there was a letter saying that he was well. He asked his mother to notify the master that he would not be coming back, so that some other boy could claim the scholarship. He said that he would send the price of the hen as soon as he made some money.

Another letter in a few weeks said that he had got a job on a trawler, and that he would not be able to write very often but that he would put aside some of his pay every week and send it to his mother whenever he got into port. He said that he wanted to pay her back for all she had done for him. He gave no address. He kept his promise about the money but he never gave any address when he wrote.

. . . And so the people may have let their thoughts run on, as they sat by the fire with the widow, many a night, listening to her complaining voice saying the same thing over and over. "Why did he put the price of an old hen above the price of his own life?" And it is possible that their version of the story has a certain element of truth about it too. Perhaps all our actions have this double quality about them; this possibility of alternative, and that it is only by careful watching and absolute sincerity that we follow the path that is destined for us, and, no matter how tragic that may be, it is better than the tragedy we bring upon ourselves.

## THINK AND DISCUSS
### Understanding
1. How did the widow pay for Packy's clothes and most of his school books?
2. According to the narrator, what two great branches of creative art are the result of invention rather than recalling facts?
3. In the second version of the story, what excuse does Packy offer his mother for running over the hen?
4. What news is Packy rushing home to tell his mother?

### Analyzing
5. The setting for the accident is the same in both versions. Describe this setting, explaining in what way it is a cause of what happens.
6. Through what methods of characterization does the author reveal Packy's character in each version? In which version do we learn more about him? Explain.
7. In which version of the story is the widow more responsible for the outcome? Explain.

### Extending
8. Would you say the widow has done a good job molding Packy's character? Why or why not?
9. When you read a short story, you normally develop a certain trust in the narrator, expecting a reliable account of the action. In "The Story of the Widow's Son," however, the narrator leaves the reader with doubts. Did your opinion of the narrator change when the narrator began discussing the possibility of more than one outcome? Explain your reaction.

## REVIEWING: Theme
**See Handbook of Literary Terms, p. 829**
In "The Story of the Widow's Son," the narrator discusses the theme, or underlying

idea, directly in the final paragraph. Yet the comments are quite philosophical and make sense only by considering them with both halves of the story in mind. Reread the final paragraph and answer the following questions.

1. How would you state the theme?
2. The theme deals with possible alternatives in all our actions and proposes a choice of the "destined" outcome. How do the two endings illustrate this theme?

## COMPOSITION

### Writing About New Possibilities

One point made by the two endings to this story is that people tend to look for new possibilities in past, unchangeable events. Imagine that someone objects to the second ending on the basis that it does not really support this point. Reread the second version, noting the ways the author shows that it does offer "new possibilities." In a three-paragraph composition argue in favor of the use of the second ending, citing evidence that shows how the author uses it to accomplish her purpose. If you disagree with this view, write to support your judgment that the second version does not convincingly express the point. Use evidence from the story to back up your view.

### Altering the Ending of a Story

You may have read or heard a story and been dissatisfied with the outcome or just curious about how an alternate ending might work. Choose a story that you have read in this unit or heard earlier in your life. Write a summary of the story and follow it with a new ending that you invent and narrate. For example, you may want to have Sherlock Holmes turn the criminal over to the police in "The Adventure of the Blue Carbuncle." You will have to devise an interesting new climax and resolution, or decide what details you wish to change, before you write your new conclusion. As you revise your work, try to make the writing style and the story elements consistent with the story as you have read or heard it.

## BIOGRAPHY

### Mary Lavin
### 1912–

Although she was born in Walpole, Massachusetts, Mary Lavin must be considered an Irish author, for she was born of Irish parents and as a child moved to Ireland, where she has lived since. At first she looked forward to a career in literary research—she received her master's degree from the National University of Ireland for a thesis on novelist Jane Austen—but the publication of one of her short stories changed the direction of her work. The detour into fiction writing has resulted in works in which she combines the gifts of a born storyteller with a penetrating insight into the human heart. They include *A Memory and Other Stories* (1972) and *The Stories of Mary Lavin, Volume III* (1985), as well as her critically acclaimed novels *The House in Clewe Street* (1945) and *Mary O'Grady* (1950). Lavin lives on a farm in Bective, County Meath, Ireland.

# The Chameleon

**Anton Chekhov**  Russia

**It's not only lizards that can change to blend in with the surroundings. . . .**

cross the market square comes Police Inspector Moronoff. He is wearing a new greatcoat and carrying a small package. Behind him strides a ginger-headed constable bearing a sieve filled to the brim with confiscated gooseberries. There is silence all around . . . Not a soul in the square . . . The wide-open doors of the shops and taverns look out dolefully on the world, like hungry jaws; even their beggars have vanished.

"Bite me, would you, you little devil?" Moronoff suddenly hears. "Catch him, lads, catch him! Biting's against the law now! Grab him! Ouch!"

A dog squeals. Moronoff looks round—and sees a dog run out of merchant Spatchkin's woodyard, hopping along on three legs and glancing backwards. A man in a starched calico shirt and unbuttoned waistcoat comes chasing out after it. He runs behind, bends down right over it, and tumbles to the ground catching the dog by the hind legs. There is another squeal and a shout: "Hold him, lads!" Sleepy countenances thrust themselves out of the shop windows and soon a crowd has sprung up from nowhere by the woodyard.

"Looks like trouble, your honor!" says the constable.

Moronoff executes a half-turn to his left and marches towards the throng. He sees the afore-mentioned man in the unbuttoned shirt is standing at the yard gates and with his right hand raised high in the air is showing the crowd a blood-stained finger. His half-sozzled face seems to be saying "You'll pay for this, you scoundrel!" and his very finger has the air of a victory banner. Moronoff recognizes the man as Grunkin the goldsmith. On the ground in the midst of the crowd, its front legs splayed out and its whole body trembling, sits the actual cause of the commotion; a white borzoi[1] puppy with a pointed muzzle and a yellow patch on its back. The expression in its watering eyes is one of terror and despair.

"What's all this about?" asks Moronoff, cutting through the crowd. "Why are you lot here? What's your finger—? Who shouted just now?"

"I was walking along, your honor, minding me own business . . ." Grunkin begins, giving a slight cough, "on my way to see Mitry Mitrich about some firewood—when all of a sudden, for no reason, this little tyke goes for my finger . . .

---

1. *borzoi* (bôr′zoi), a breed of dogs that are tall, slender, and swift and have silky hair; also called Russian wolfhounds.

Beg pardon, sir, but I'm a man what's working . . . My work's delicate work. I want compensation for this—after all, I may not be able to lift this finger for a week now . . . There's nothing in the law even that says we have to put up with that from beasts, is there your honor? If we all went round biting, we might as well be dead . . ."

"Hm! All right . . ." says Moronoff sternly, clearing his throat and knitting his brows, "Right . . . Who owns this dog? I shall not let this matter rest. I'll teach you to let dogs run loose! It's time we took a closer look at these people who won't obey regulations! A good fat fine'll teach the blighter what I think of dogs and suchlike vagrant cattle! I'll take him down a peg! Dildin," says the inspector, turning to the constable, "find out who owns this dog, and take a statement! And the dog must be put down. Forthwith! It's probably mad anyway . . . Come on then, who's the owner?"

"Looks like General Tartaroff's!" says a voice from the crowd.

"General Tartaroff's? Hm . . . Dildin, remove my coat for me, will you? . . . Phew it's hot! We must be in for rain . . . What I don't understand, though, is this: how did it manage to bite you?" says Moronoff, turning to Grunkin. "How could it reach up to your finger? A little dog like that, and a hulking great bloke like you! I expect what happened was, you skinned your finger on a nail, then had the bright idea of making some money out of it. I know your lot! You devils don't fool me!"

"He shoved a fag in its mug for a lark, your honor, but she weren't having any and went for him . . . He's always stirring up trouble, your honor!"

"Don't lie, Boss-Eye! You couldn't see, so why tell lies? His honor here's a clever gent, he knows who's lying and who's telling the gospel truth . . . And if he thinks I'm lying, then let the justice decide. He's got it all written down there

in the law . . . We're all equal now . . . I've got a brother myself who's in the po-lice . . . you may like to know—"

"Stop arguing!"

"No, it's not the General's . . ." the constable observes profoundly. "The General ain't got any like this. His are more setters . . ."

"Are you sure of that?"

"Quite sure, your honor—"

"Well of course I know that, too. The General has dogs that are worth something, thoroughbreds, but this is goodness knows what! It's got no coat, it's nothing to look at—just a load of rubbish . . . Do you seriously think he'd keep a dog like that? Use your brains. You know what'd happen if a dog like that turned up in Petersburg or Moscow? They wouldn't bother looking in the law books, they'd dispatch him—double quick! You've got a grievance, Grunkin, and you mustn't let the matter rest . . . Teach 'em a lesson! It's high time . . ."

"Could be the General's, though . . ." muses the constable aloud. "It ain't written on its snout . . . I did see one like that in his yard the other day."

"Course it's the General's!" says a voice from the crowd.

"Hm . . . Help me on with my coat, Dildin old chap . . . There's a bit of a breeze got up . . . It's quite chilly . . . Right, take this dog to the General's and ask them there. Say I found it and am sending it back. And tell them not to let it out on the street in future. It may be worth a lot, and if every swine is going to poke cigarettes up its nose, it won't be for much longer. A dog's a delicate creature . . . And you put your hand down, you oaf! Stop showing your stupid finger off! It was all your own fault!"

"Here comes the General's cook, let's ask him . . . Hey, Prokhor! Come over here a moment, will you? Take a look at this dog . . . One of yours, is it?"

Rien Poortvliet, *Borzoi, A Dog from Russia*,
Private Collection

"You must be joking! We've never had none like that!"

"Right, we can stop making enquiries," says Moronoff. "It's a stray! We can cut the chat . . . If everyone says it's a stray, it is a stray . . . So that's that, it must be put down."

"No, it's not one of ours," Prokhor continues. "It belongs to the General's brother what come down the other day. Our General don't go much on borzois. His brother does, though—"

"You mean to say his Excellency's brother's arrived? Vladimir Ivanych?"[2] asks Moronoff, his face breaking into an ecstatic smile. "Well blow me down! And I didn't know! Come for a little stay, has he?"

"He's on a visit . . ."

"Well I never . . . So he felt like seeing his dear old brother again . . . And fancy me not know-ing! So it's his little dog, is it? Jolly good . . . Take him away with you, then . . . He's a good little doggie . . . Pretty quick off the mark, too . . . Took a bite out of this bloke's finger— ha, ha, ha! No need to shiver, little chap! 'Grr-rrr' . . . He's angry, the rascal . . . the little scamp . . ."

Prokhor calls the dog over and it follows him out of the woodyard . . . The crowd roars with laughter at Grunkin.

"I'll deal with you later!" Moronoff threatens him, and wrapping his greatcoat tightly round him, resumes his progress across the market square.

---

2. **Vladimir Ivanych** (vlad'ə mir ē von'ich), a Russian name meaning "Vladimir, son of Ivan."

## THINK AND DISCUSS
### Understanding
1. What is the puppy accused of doing?
2. It is suggested by a few characters that the dog belongs to someone important. Who is this important person?
3. When Moronoff thinks the dog is not owned by anyone important, what does he suggest?
4. To whom does the dog actually belong?

### Analyzing
5. How do Moronoff's activities with his coat comically reflect his major decisions that reveal his character?
6. How does Prokhor, the General's cook, make Moronoff change his mind about the dog twice?

7. This story uses satire, a way of poking fun at individuals or society to expose weakness or evils, to comment on a type of public official. What aspects of character is the author satirizing? Why is the story called "The Chameleon"?
8. "The Chameleon" uses humor to convey its **theme.** How would you state the theme?

### Extending
9. When do you think it would be wrong to ridicule authority? Explain your answer, giving examples.

## COMPOSITION  ◄━►
### Commenting on Humor
Anton Chekhov planted a number of comical details in this story, beginning with the main

character's name and ending with the blustery threat at the end. *Moronoff* is a translation of the Russian name *Ochumelov*, the name that Chekhov made up using a Russian word for "crazy." The author then refers to the red-headed constable as "ginger-headed" and characterizes the events in the story as silly attempts to victimize a puppy or otherwise manipulate what happens. Review the story and list every funny detail that you can find. Discuss your list with a classmate or a friend. Then write a two-paragraph paper discussing the kind of humor Chekhov has planted in his story and telling which details you find most humorous. (If you find the humor dry or weak, explain your reaction and tell how you might change the story to improve the humor.)

**Writing Satire**

Decide what you consider to be a type of person, group, or activity in society that could be deservedly criticized using humor. Remember that sometimes petty practices or customs lend themselves to humor more easily than tragic issues, because audiences can be offended by comic approaches to certain tragedies, deadly evils, and grave problems. Consider how you might use exaggeration and sarcasm to poke fun at your target. Write a story in which you mildly or spiritedly ridicule a social custom or corrupt practice. Use characterization, descriptive details, and plot devices to lend humor to your brief story. See "Developing Your Style" in the Writer's Handbook.

## BIOGRAPHY

### Anton Chekhov
### 1860–1904

Dramatist, short-story writer, and journalist, Anton Chekhov was one of six children in a family living in Taganrog, Russia, in the era of the Russian czars, or emperors. His father operated a grocery store, but bankruptcy forced the family to move to Moscow. In 1879 Chekhov enrolled in the medical school of Moscow University and supported his family by writing for various humor magazines and periodicals. He received his medical degree in 1884, and from 1887 to 1892 he traveled throughout Russia, Europe, the Far East, and the Middle East. Chekhov married in 1901, and he and his wife lived in Badenweiler, Germany, until he died of tuberculosis. He is buried in Moscow.

Chekhov is hailed as a modern master of the short story and an important modern playwright whose dramas are produced today throughout the world. His plays include such modern classics as *The Cherry Orchard*, *Uncle Vanya*, and *The Three Sisters*. While he wrote light and humorous fiction, most of his stories deal with serious themes and characters caught up in universal problems such as the struggle to improve one's life, poverty, love, old-world class distinctions, and family relationships.

# THINKING CRITICALLY
# ABOUT LITERATURE

## UNIT 1   TRADITIONS IN THE SHORT STORY

### ■ CONCEPT REVIEW

At the end of each unit in *Traditions in Literature* is a selection that illustrates many of the important literary elements and ideas that you have just studied. It also is accompanied by notes designed to help you think critically about your reading. Page numbers in the notes refer to applications of literary terms. A more extensive discussion of these terms appears in the Handbook of Literary Terms.

In "Shaving" Leslie Norris portrays the care and love a teenage son shows to his desperately ill father. Read the story and then answer the questions that follow.

# Shaving

**Leslie Norris**   Great Britain

Earlier, when Barry had left the house to go to the game, an overnight frost had still been thick on the roads, but the brisk April sun had soon dispersed it, and now he could feel the spring warmth on his back through the thick tweed of his coat. His left arm was beginning to stiffen up where he'd jarred it in a tackle, but it was nothing serious. He flexed his shoulders against the tightness of his jacket and was surprised again by the unexpected weight of his muscles, the thickening strength of his body. A few years back, he thought, he had been a small, unimportant boy, one of a swarming gang laughing and jostling to school, hardly aware that he possessed an identity. But time had transformed him. He walked solidly now, and often alone. He was tall, strongly made, his hands and feet were adult and heavy, the rooms in which all his life he'd moved had grown too small for him. Sometimes a devouring restlessness drove him from the house to walk long distances in the dark. He hardly understood how it had happened. Amused and quiet, he walked the High Street among the morning shoppers.

■ **Setting** (page 64): Note the emphasis on the time and conditions rather than place.

■ **Point of view** (page 85): Narrator apparently is not a character. Story focuses on Barry; narrator reveals his thoughts and feelings.

■ **Characterization** (page 45): Note the physical description and implied indication of Barry's age.

Slight abridgment of "Shaving" by Leslie Norris from *Atlantic*, April 1977. Copyright © 1977 by Leslie Norris. Reprinted by permission of Brandt & Brandt Literary Agents, Inc.

He saw Jackie Bevan across the road and remembered how, when they were both six years old, Jackie had swallowed a pin. The flustered teachers had clucked about Jackie as he stood there, bawling, cheeks awash with tears, his nose wet. But now Jackie was tall and suave, his thick, pale hair sleekly tailored, his gray suit enviable. He was talking to a girl as golden as a daffodil.

"Hey, hey!" called Jackie. "How's the athlete, how's Barry boy?"

He waved a graceful hand at Barry.

"Come and talk to Sue," he said.

Barry shifted his bag to his left hand and walked over, forming in his mind the answers he'd make to Jackie's questions.

"Did we win?" Jackie asked. "Was the old Barry Stanford magic in glittering evidence yet once more this morning? Were the invaders sent hunched and silent back to their hovels in the hills? What was the score? Give us an epic account, Barry, without modesty or delay. This is Sue, by the way."

"I've seen you about," the girl said.

"You could hardly miss him," said Jackie. "Four men, roped together, spent a week climbing him—they thought he was Everest. He ought to carry a warning beacon, he's a danger to aircraft."

"Silly," said the girl, smiling at Jackie. "He's not much taller than you are."

She had a nice voice too.

"We won," Barry said. "Seventeen points to three, and it was a good game. The ground was hard, though."

He could think of nothing else to say.

"Let's all go for a frivolous cup of coffee," Jackie said. "Let's celebrate your safe return from the rough fields of victory. We could pour libations all over the floor for you."

"I don't think so," Barry said. "Thanks. I'll go straight home."

"Okay," said Jackie, rocking on his heels so that the sun could shine on his smile. "How's your father?"

"No better," Barry said. "He's not going to get better."

"Yes, well," said Jackie, serious and uncomfortable, "tell him my mother and father ask about him."

"I will," Barry promised. "He'll be pleased."

Barry dropped the bag in the front hall and moved into the room which had been the dining room until his father's illness. His father lay in the white bed, his long body gaunt, his still head scarcely denting the pillow. He seemed asleep, thin blue lids covering his eyes, but when Barry turned away he spoke.

"Hullo, son," he said. "Did you win?"

His voice was a dry, light rustling, hardly louder than the breath which

■ Barry has a vivid memory.

■ suave (swäv): polite and gracious in manners

■ Jackie exaggerates Barry's size for humorous effect.

■ Note the contrast between the speaking styles of the two boys.

■ Plot (page 14): The introduction of Barry's problem suggests a source of conflict.

■ Characterization: Details reveal father's condition.

carried it. Its sound moved Barry to a compassion that almost unmanned him, but he stepped close to the bed and looked down at the dying man.

"Yes," he said. "We won fairly easily. It was a good game."

His father lay with his eyes closed, inert, his breath irregular and shallow. "Did you score?" he asked.

"Twice," Barry said. "I had a try in each half."

He thought of the easy certainty with which he'd caught the ball before his second try; casually, almost arrogantly he had taken it on the tips of his fingers, on his full burst for the line, breaking the fullback's tackle. Nobody could have stopped him. But watching his father's weakness he felt humble and ashamed, as if the morning game, its urgency and effort, was not worth talking about. His father's face, fine-skinned and pallid, carried a dark stubble of beard, almost a week's growth, and his obstinate, strong hair stuck out over his brow.

■ Note the contrast between Barry and his father.

"Good," said his father, after a long pause. "I'm glad it was a good game."

Barry's mother bustled about the kitchen, a tempest of orderly energy.

"Your father's not well," she said. "He's down today, feels depressed. He's a particular man, your father. He feels dirty with all that beard on him."

She slammed shut the stove door.

"Mr. Cleaver was supposed to come up and shave him," she said, "and that was three days ago. Little things have always worried your father, every detail must be perfect for him."

■ Details about all three family members are given or suggested here.

Barry filled a glass with milk from the refrigerator. He was very thirsty.

"I'll shave him," he said.

His mother stopped, her head on one side.

"Do you think you can?" she asked. "He'd like it if you can."

"I can do it," Barry said.

He washed his hands as carefully as a surgeon. His father's razor was in a blue leather case, hinged at the broad edge and with one hinge broken. Barry unfastened the clasp and took out the razor. It had not been properly cleaned after its last use and lather had stiffened into hard yellow rectangles between the teeth of the guard. There were water-shaped rust stains, brown as chocolate, on the surface of the blade. Barry removed it, throwing it in the wastebin. He washed the razor until it glistened, and dried it on a soft towel, polishing the thin handle, rubbing its metal head to a glittering shine. He took a new blade from its waxed envelope, the paper clinging to the thin metal. The blade was smooth and flexible to the touch, the little angles of its cutting clearly defined. Barry slotted it into the grip of the razor, making it snug and tight in the head.

■ Note how Barry's care and preparation illustrate his motivation and concern.

The shaving soap, hard, white, richly aromatic, was kept in a wooden bowl. Its scent was immediately evocative and Barry could almost see his father in the days of his health, standing before his mirror, thick white lather on his face and neck. As a little boy Barry had loved the generous perfume of the soap, had waited for his father to lift the razor to his face, for one careful stroke to take away the white suds in a clean revelation of the skin. Then his father would renew the lather with a few sweeps of his brush, one with an ivory handle and the bristles worn, which he still used.

His father's shaving mug was a thick cup, plain and serviceable. A gold line ran outside the rim of the cup, another inside, just below the lip. Its handle was large and sturdy, and the face of the mug carried a portrait of the young Queen Elizabeth II, circled by a wreath of leaves, oak perhaps, or laurel. A lion and unicorn balanced precariously on a scroll above her crowned head, and the Union Jack, the Royal Standard, and other flags were furled each side of the portrait. And beneath it all, in small black letters, ran the legend: "Coronation June 2nd 1953." The cup was much older than Barry. A pattern of faint translucent cracks, fine as a web, had worked itself haphazardly, invisibly almost, through the white glaze. Inside, on the bottom, a few dark bristles were lying, loose and dry. Barry shook them out, then held the cup in his hand, feeling its solidness. Then he washed it ferociously, until it was clinically clean.  *(Continued)*

■ Barry's memory reveals much about his relationship with his father.

■ **lion and unicorn:** British royal symbols

■ **Union Jack:** a name for the British flag

■ **Setting:** Many details indicate the country where action takes place.

René Magritte, *Personal Values*, 1952, Private Collection

Methodically he set everything on a tray, razor, soap, brush, towels. Testing the hot water with a finger, he filled the mug and put that, too, on the tray. His care was absorbed, ritualistic. Satisfied that his preparations were complete, he went downstairs, carrying the tray with one hand.

His father was waiting for him. Barry set the tray on a bedside table and bent over his father, sliding an arm under the man's thin shoulders, lifting him without effort so that he sat against the high pillows.

"You're strong. . . ." his father said. He was as breathless as if he'd been running.

"So are you," said Barry.

"I was," his father said. "I used to be strong once."

He sat exhausted against the pillows.

"We'll wait a bit," Barry said.

"You could have used your electric razor," his father said. "I expected that."

"You wouldn't like it," Barry said. "You'll get a closer shave this way."

He placed the large towel about his father's shoulders.

"Now," he said, smiling down.

The water was hot in the thick cup. Barry wet the brush and worked up the lather. Gently he built up a covering of soft foam on the man's chin, on his cheeks and his stark cheekbones.

"You're using a lot of soap," his father said.

"Not too much," Barry said. "You've got a lot of beard."

His father lay there quietly, his wasted arms at his sides.

"It's comforting," he said. "You'd be surprised how comforting it is."

Barry took up the razor, weighing it in his hand, rehearsing the angle at which he'd use it. He felt confident.

"If you have prayers to say, . . ." he said.

"I've said a lot of prayers," his father answered.

Barry leaned over and placed the razor delicately against his father's face, setting the head accurately on the clean line near the ear where the long hair ended. He held the razor in the tips of his fingers and drew the blade sweetly through the lather. The new edge moved light as a touch over the hardness of the upper jaw and down to the angle of the chin, sliding away the bristles so easily that Barry could not feel their release. He sighed as he shook the razor in the hot water, washing away the soap.

"How's it going?" his father asked.

"No problem," Barry said. "You needn't worry."

It was as if he had never known what his father really looked like. He was discovering under his hands the clear bones of the face and head; they became sharp and recognizable under his fingers. When he moved his

■ **Plot, characterization:** Note how the normal roles of parent and child are becoming reversed. This rising action could lead to tension.

■ **Point of view:** The father's thoughts are revealed by what he says.

■ **Setting:** Details have revealed the place (the room) and established the scene's mood.

■ Imagine Barry's tone of voice as he makes this joke.

father's face a gentle inch to one side, he touched with his fingers the frail temples, the blue veins of his father's life. With infinite and meticulous care he took away the hair from his father's face.

"Now for your neck," he said. "We might as well do the job properly."

"You've got good hands," his father said. "You can trust those hands, they won't let you down."

Barry cradled his father's head in the crook of his left arm, so that the man could tilt back his head, exposing the throat. He brushed fresh lather under the chin and into the hollows alongside the stretched tendons. His father's throat was fleshless and vulnerable, his head was a hard weight on the boy's arm. Barry was filled with unreasoning protective love. He lifted the razor and began to shave.

■ Barry has accepted his new role. But he may wonder how his father accepts it.

"You don't have to worry," he said. "Not at all. Not about anything."

He held his father in the bend of his strong arm and they looked at each other. Their heads were very close.

"How old are you?" his father said.

"Seventeen," Barry said. "Near enough seventeen."

"You're young," his father said, "to have this happen."

"Not too young," Barry said. "I'm bigger than most men."

"I think you are," his father said.

■ Note how both characters mean more than they say directly.

He leaned his head tiredly against the boy's shoulder. He was without strength, his face was cold and smooth. He had let go all his authority, handed it over. He lay back on his pillow, knowing his weakness and his mortality, and looked at his son with wonder, with a curious humble pride.

"I won't worry then," he said. "About anything."

"There's no need," Barry said. "Why should you worry?"

■ Plot: Father's acceptance is a turning point.

He wiped his father's face clean of all soap with a damp towel. The smell of illness was everywhere, overpowering even the perfumed lather. Barry settled his father down and took away the shaving tools, putting them by with the same ceremonial precision with which he'd prepared them: the cleaned and glittering razor in its broken case; the soap, its bowl wiped and dried, on the shelf between the brush and the coronation mug; all free of taint. He washed his hands and scrubbed his nails. His hands were firm and broad, pink after their scrubbing. The fingers were short and strong, the little fingers slightly crooked, and soft dark hair grew on the backs of his hands and his fingers just above the knuckles. Not long ago they had been small bare hands, not very long ago.

■ **Theme** (page 102): Barry's problem will not disappear, but he has faced it and matured enough to feel a sense of control.

Barry opened wide the bathroom window. Already, although it was not yet two o'clock, the sun was retreating and people were moving briskly, wrapped in their heavy coats against the cold that was to come. But now the window was full in the beam of the dying sunlight, and Barry stood there, illuminated in its golden warmth for a whole minute, knowing it would soon be gone.

■ The sun is not only part of the setting. It also serves as a symbol.

## THINK AND DISCUSS

### Understanding

1. In what country and in what month does the story take place?
2. Barry has vivid memories of his early childhood. What memory of his father is evoked by something Barry smells?

### Analyzing

3. In the morning Barry has played in a game of rugby, a sport similar to football. Which of Barry's characteristics are emphasized by the details of how he played?
4. After Jackie Bevan carries on spirited, witty conversation about Barry and the ball game, how does his talk change when he asks about Barry's father?
5. Barry's preparations to shave his father are called *ritualistic*, or ceremonial. Why does he prepare so carefully?
6. Identify one example of the several contrasts in the story.
7. In the last sentence Barry stands in dying sunlight, "knowing it would soon be gone." What does the sun seem to stand for here?

### Extending

8. This story involves a reversal of roles between a father and son. From your own experience or imagination, describe a situation that would involve a person (or perhaps a pet) taking care of or taking responsibility for a person who had earlier been the care giver.

## REVIEWING LITERARY TERMS

### Point of View

1. "Shaving" is told in a third-person limited point of view. Explain what this means.
2. How is this point of view appropriate to the story?

### Setting

3. When Barry gets home, he goes to his father in "the room which had been the dining room until his father's illness." What does

this detail about setting suggest about how serious the illness is?

4. More important than the country in which this story takes place is the time in the main character's life. How does his father point out that Barry is facing an unusual event for someone his age?

### Characterization

5. How do the details about Barry's size and athletic power help to highlight the characterization of Barry's father?
6. Why does Barry say, "If you have prayers to say . . ."?

### Plot

7. What is the most important message that Barry communicates to his father during the shaving ritual?
8. What climactic statement does his father make to indicate he accepts the message?

### Theme

9. If someone were to ask you what "Shaving" is about, you could answer that the story concerns a boy carefully shaving his dying father's beard or that it concerns a show of love for a father by a maturing son. Which answer deals with the theme? Explain.

## ■ CONTENT REVIEW

### THINKING SKILLS

### Classifying

1. Supernatural elements in stories may be presented by authors either as "magic show" tricks and other illusions based on characters pretending or as magical events and ghostly appearances presented as if they are really happening in the plot. Classify the following stories into the two categories suggested by that distinction: "The Conjurer's Revenge," "Life Is Sweet at Kumansenu," and "The Monkey's Paw." Explain your decisions.
2. Both "The Adventure of the Blue Carbuncle" and "The Chameleon" involve

investigations of legal matters and laws being broken. Using evidence from each story, explain why Sherlock Holmes can be classified among successful or serious detectives, while Moronoff must be classified among unsuccessful, bumbling investigators.

### Generalizing

3. In both "Lamb to the Slaughter" and "The Monkey's Paw," a nonliving object is used to develop an unusual or unexpected ending. Explain how both objects advance the plot due to the way they are manipulated or used by major characters.
4. In both "A Visit to Grandmother" and "Forgiveness in Families," an important character is a brother who is a source of family disagreement. How do the main characters, Dr. Dunford and Val, judge their mothers' treatment of GL and Cam?

### Synthesizing

5. In many stories, the climax is a turning point that changes characters' lives. Some stories, however, leave readers assured that the characters' lives will not suffer abrupt changes. Explain how the lives of the family in "Home" and the couple in "The Secret Life of Walter Mitty" are likely to change or remain the same after each story ends.

### Evaluating

6. Both "The Boar Hunt" and "The Parachutist" deal with survival in the world of nature. Compare and contrast the two in regard to the main conflict and the way it is resolved. Which story do you find more believable? Why?
7. "The Story of the Widow's Son" and "Through the Tunnel" both deal with the attitudes of widows toward their sons. Compare and contrast these attitudes. Which woman behaves more unselfishly toward her son, in your judgment? Explain.

# ■ COMPOSITION REVIEW

From the assignments that follow choose one and write the composition.

### Explaining a Selection of Stories

Suppose you have been asked to choose four stories from this unit to make up a "mini-unit" for other students to use. You are looking for four stories featuring topics or themes that work well together. Review the unit and select the four stories that you think would best interest your audience and form a reasonable thematic unit. Jot down reasons for your choices. Write a brief description of your unit as an introduction for the students. Begin by identifying the four stories and describing them enough to get students interested in reading them. Then explain how they fit well together.

### Writing About Character Believability

Choose the character in Unit 1 who you feel is the most believable or the most unbelievable character in the unit. Review that character's actions and consider how they help make him or her a likely or unlikely figure. Write a short essay discussing the character and explaining why you find him or her believable or unbelievable. If you are writing about an unbelievable character, explain also whether the lack of believability interferes with or increases your enjoyment of the story.

### Reviewing Writer's Craft: Be Specific

Select a story from the unit that gives a clear picture of what life in the place it is set is like. Review the story, noting details that make life in that location or country particularly interesting and different from life in your community or in the United States. Write an essay explaining in detail what insights you have gained into life in that setting or that area of the world.

# ODERN DRAMA

Richard Estes, *Broadway and 64th, Spring '84* (detail), 1984, Private Collection

# UNIT 2

(Lincoln Center theater complex is shown at left.)

# PREVIEW

## UNIT 2    MODERN DRAMA

**Twelve Angry Men** / Reginald Rose
**The Romancers** / Edmond Rostand
**Our Town** / Thornton Wilder
from **A Doll's House** / Henrik Ibsen

**Features**
Reading Modern Drama
Comment: The Story Behind the Play
Writer's Craft: Use a Voice That Suits the
    Purpose
Comment: The Romantic Comedy
Comment: Thornton Wilder on *Our Town*

**Application of Literary Terms**
protagonist/antagonist
inference
flashback

**Reading Literature Skillfully**
predicting outcomes
sequence

**Vocabulary**
dictionary and glossary
pronunciation
synonyms and antonyms
word structure

**Thinking Skills**
generalizing
synthesizing
evaluating

**Composition Assignments Include**
Predicting Characters' Actions
Writing from Personal Experience
Explaining Your Decisions
Analyzing Suspense in a Drama
Reading/Writing Log
Creating a Comical Voice
Analyzing a Comic Scene
Analyzing Dramatic Technique
Writing About Your Community
Writing a Note of Congratulations
Describing a Character
Responding to a Speech in a Play

**Enrichment**
Performing Scenes
Speaking and Listening
Dramatic Reading

**Thinking Critically About Literature**
Concept Review
Content Review
Composition Review

The word *drama* derives from a Greek verb that means "to do." A drama, a play written to be enacted, is waiting to be "done." Just as musical notes on a page come into our lives as art when they are played by musicians, the drama exerts its power when it is performed. That power develops as actors portray characters who speak, quarrel, love, and occasionally die in our presence.

The script of a drama, written by an author known as a playwright or dramatist, may survive as a work of literature to be read. When you read a play, keep images of a stage (or film) performance in mind.

"Staging the play" in your imagination will allow you to understand **stage directions** and **dialogue.** For example, a stage direction describing how two characters carry on conversation over a garden wall helps you picture the relationship between the characters and imagine their appearance and movements. When a stage direction indicates that a character's speech is an *aside*—words spoken so that the audience can hear but other characters cannot—you learn how the character is thinking or feeling. Similarly, directions in a film script or a television play tell how characters move and talk, how the setting looks, and what props appear. Camera directions, such as "fade in" and "fade out" for the beginning and end of a scene, indicate how characters and settings appear on screen.

If you consider the play as a script for a performance, you may be able to read every line as the character would speak it. You will vividly picture the movements and expressions of every character, even without the help of a narrator.

## Modern Drama Develops

You can appreciate modern drama better if you know something about the recent history of the theater. The stage in the nineteenth and early twentieth century was defined by a *proscenium* arch, a border which framed the space on which a play's action took place. The stage was conceived as a room with one wall removed. (Most stages in schools are proscenium stages.) Acting, costumes, sets, and dialogue became more realistic than in previous ages; characters no longer moved downstage to deliver a speech, costumes were designed for a specific role rather than a type, and verse plays almost disappeared. Traveling troupes of performers took drama to eager audiences everywhere.

With the development of motion pictures and television, touring companies gradually disappeared. Instead, regional theaters sprang up and live theater became more experimental and innovative than film or television drama. In new theaters, the arena stage or theater-in-the-round replaced the proscenium stage, thus breaking the barrier between actor and audience.

## Drama as Literature

Dramas written for various media—stage, movies, and television—share many elements, including characters, settings, dialogue, and action. The dialogue, conversational talk in the play, is an essential part of the action, because through it the plot unfolds.

Characters create or heighten or resolve **conflict** by arguing, expressing emotions, announcing plans and decisions, asking questions, and demanding responses. The movement of characters and the physical actions they perform fill out the play.

When you read a play, you will want to note the **sequence** of events in the story and how events in each scene affect the ensuing action. As you read *Twelve Angry Men* in this unit, for example, note how the order in which courtroom jurors make statements reveals the direction that arguments take and the effectiveness of characters' attempts to persuade one another.

Sometimes statements are made or actions are taken at the same time on stage, as in real life. Simultaneous events are part of sequence, too. In Act One of *Our Town*, another play in this unit, you will witness the concurrent activities and conversations of two families in their houses, which appear side by side on the stage.

In plays and other literary works, all events are not necessarily presented in sequential order. Scenes called **flashbacks** may show episodes of earlier times, and future occurrences may be revealed. In *Our Town* one character speaks directly to the audience to comment on the order of events and the other characters' past and future.

At any point in a play you may be able to **predict the outcome** of a conversation, a scene, or the entire drama. You will develop opinions and feelings about what may happen, based on what you know of the characters and what has occurred so far. A willingness to think ahead and form reasonable predictions makes your appreciation of literature more active and complete. Your skillful reading of drama can begin as soon as you see the title and read the cast of characters, the list naming and often describing or identifying the people in the play.

The description of the characters at the beginning of *Twelve Angry Men* is especially useful. Most of the characters are identified throughout the play by juror number rather than by name. As you read, you may want to refer to the character descriptions to refresh your memory about the identity or characteristics of any juror as he speaks.

## Types of Drama

Of the three modern dramas in this unit, the most traditional is *The Romancers*, a romantic comedy often performed on the conventional proscenium stage. The least traditional is *Our Town*, which its author, Thornton Wilder, has characterized as a celebration of "the smallest events in our daily life." When first produced it was considered revolutionary in its dramatic technique, with its use of one character (the "Stage Manager") presiding over other characters and a barren stage, furnishing a minimum of props as the audience watched. This play could easily be staged in a theater-in-the-round production, projected into the space of a participating audience.

*Twelve Angry Men*, the suspenseful TV drama depicting a jury's deliberations at a murder trial, is the most recent of these dramas. Television provides dramatic techniques unavailable in the theater. The camera controls what the audience sees, how closely it is seen, and how long it remains within the audience's sight and hearing.

Drama produced on stage, on television, or in motion pictures can provide powerful aesthetic experiences. For the attentive and imaginative reader, the written version of a play can reflect a dramatic performance.

**H̶L̶T̶** See PROTAGONIST/ANTAGONIST in the Handbook of Literary Terms, page 817.

# Twelve Angry Men

**Reginald Rose**   USA

## DESCRIPTIONS OF JURORS

**FOREMAN.** *A small, petty man who is impressed with the authority he has and handles himself quite formally. Not overly bright, but dogged.*

**JUROR NUMBER TWO.** *A meek, hesitant man who finds it difficult to maintain any opinions of his own. Easily swayed and usually adopts the opinion of the last person to whom he has spoken.*

**JUROR NUMBER THREE.** *A very strong, very forceful, extremely opinionated man within whom can be detected a streak of sadism. A humorless man who is intolerant of opinions other than his own and accustomed to forcing his wishes and views upon others.*

**JUROR NUMBER FOUR.** *Seems to be a man of wealth and position. A practiced speaker who presents himself well at all times. Seems to feel a little bit above the rest of the jurors. His only concern is with the facts in this case, and he is appalled at the behavior of the others.*

**JUROR NUMBER FIVE.** *A naïve, very frightened young man who takes his obligations in this case very seriously, but who finds it difficult to speak up when his elders have the floor.*

**JUROR NUMBER SIX.** *An honest but dull-witted man who comes upon his decisions slowly and carefully.*

*A man who finds it difficult to create positive opinions, but who must listen to and digest and accept those opinions offered by others which appeal to him most.*

**JUROR NUMBER SEVEN.** *A loud, flashy, glad-handed salesman type who has more important things to do than to sit on a jury. He is quick to show temper, quick to form opinions on things about which he knows nothing. Is a bully and, of course, a coward.*

**JUROR NUMBER EIGHT.** *A quiet, thoughtful, gentle man. A man who sees all sides of every question and constantly seeks the truth. A man of strength tempered with compassion. Above all, a man who wants justice to be done and will fight to see that it is.*

**JUROR NUMBER NINE.** *A mild, gentle old man, long since defeated by life and now merely waiting to die. A man who recognizes himself for what he is and mourns the days when it would have been possible to be courageous without shielding himself behind his many years.*

**JUROR NUMBER TEN.** *An angry, bitter man. A man who antagonizes almost at sight. A bigot who places no values on any human life save his own. A* man who has been nowhere and is going nowhere and knows it deep within him.

**JUROR NUMBER ELEVEN.** *A refugee from Europe who had come to this country in 1941. A man who speaks with an accent and who is ashamed, humble, almost subservient to the people around him,* but who will honestly seek justice because he has suffered through so much injustice.

**JUROR NUMBER TWELVE.** *A slick, bright advertising man who thinks of human beings in terms of percentages, graphs, and polls and has no real understanding of people. A superficial snob, but trying to be a good fellow.*

---

# ACT ONE

*Fade in[1] on a jury box. Twelve men are seated in it, listening intently to the voice of the* JUDGE *as he charges them.[2] We do not see the* JUDGE. *He speaks in slow, measured tones and his voice is grave. The camera drifts over the faces of the* JURYMEN *as the* JUDGE *speaks and we see that most of their heads are turned to camera's left.* SEVEN *looks down at his hands.* THREE *looks off in another direction, the direction in which the defendant would be sitting.* TEN *keeps moving his head back and forth nervously. The* JUDGE *drones on.*

**JUDGE.** Murder in the first degree—premeditated homicide—is the most serious charge tried in our criminal courts. You've heard a long and complex case, gentlemen, and it is now your duty to sit down to try and separate the facts from the fancy. One man is dead. The life of another is at stake. If there is a reasonable doubt in your minds as to the guilt of the accused . . . then you must declare him not guilty. If, however, there is no reasonable doubt, then he must be found guilty. Whichever way you decide, the verdict must be unanimous. I urge you to deliberate honestly and thoughtfully. You are faced with a grave responsibility. Thank you, gentlemen.

*(There is a long pause.)*

**CLERK** *(droning).* The jury will retire.

*(And now, slowly, almost hesitantly, the members of the jury begin to rise. Awkwardly, they file out of the jury box and off camera to the left. Camera holds on jury box, then fades out.*

*Fade in on a large, bare, unpleasant-looking room. This is the jury room in the county criminal court of a large Eastern city. It is about 4:00* P.M. *The room is furnished with a long conference table and a dozen chairs. The walls are bare, drab, and badly in need of a fresh coat of paint. Along one wall is a row of windows which look out on the skyline of the city's financial district. High on another wall is an electric clock. A washroom opens off the jury room. In one corner of the room is a water fountain. On the table are pads, pencils, ashtrays. One of the windows is open. Papers blow across the table and onto the floor as the door opens. Lettered on the outside of the door are the words "Jury Room." A uniformed* GUARD *holds the door open. Slowly, almost self-consciously, the twelve* JURORS *file in. The* GUARD *counts them as they enter the door, his lips moving, but no sound coming forth. Four or five of the* JURORS *light cigarettes as they enter the room.* FIVE *lights his pipe, which he smokes constantly throughout the play.* TWO *and* TWELVE *go to the water fountain,* NINE *goes into the washroom, the door of which is lettered "Men." Several of the* JURORS *take seats*

---

1. *Fade in,* term used in television to indicate that the picture or scene is slowly brought into focus. When the camera "fades out," the picture gradually disappears.
2. *he charges them,* he tells them what their duties are as jurors.

*at the table. Others stand awkwardly around the room. Several look out the windows. These are men who are ill at ease, who do not really know each other to talk to, and who wish they were anywhere but here.* SEVEN, *standing at window, takes out a pack of gum, takes a piece, and offers it around. There are no takers. He mops his brow.*)

SEVEN (*to* SIX). Y'know something? It's hot. (SIX *nods.*) You'd think they'd at least air-condition the place. I almost dropped dead in court.

(SEVEN *opens the window a bit wider. The* GUARD *looks them over and checks his count. Then, satisfied, he makes ready to leave.*)

GUARD. Okay, gentlemen. Everybody's here. If there's anything you want, I'm right outside. Just knock.

(*He exits, closing the door. Silently they all look at the door. We hear the lock clicking.*)

FIVE. I never knew they locked the door.

TEN (*blowing nose*). Sure, they lock the door. What did you think?

FIVE. I don't know. It just never occurred to me.

(*Some of the* JURORS *are taking off their jackets. Others are sitting down at the table. They still are reluctant to talk to each other.* FOREMAN *is at head of table, tearing slips of paper for ballots. Now we get a close shot of* EIGHT. *He looks out the window. We hear* THREE *talking to* TWO.)

THREE. Six days. They should have finished it in two. Talk, talk, talk. Did you ever hear so much talk about nothing?

TWO (*nervously laughing*). Well . . . I guess . . . they're entitled.

THREE. Everybody gets a fair trial. (*He shakes his head.*) That's the system. Well, I suppose you can't say anything against it.

(TWO *looks at him nervously, nods, and goes over to water cooler. Cut[3] to shot of* EIGHT *staring out window. Cut to table.* SEVEN *stands at the table, putting out a cigarette.*)

SEVEN (*to* TEN). How did you like that business

about the knife? Did you ever hear a phonier story?

TEN (*wisely*). Well, look, you've gotta expect that. You know what you're dealing with.

SEVEN. Yeah, I suppose. What's the matter, you got a cold?

TEN (*blowing*). A lulu. These hot-weather colds can kill you.

(SEVEN *nods sympathetically.*)

FOREMAN (*briskly*). All right, gentlemen. Let's take seats.

SEVEN. Right. This better be fast, I've got tickets to *The Seven Year Itch*[4] tonight. I must be the only guy in the whole world who hasn't seen it yet. (*He laughs and sits down.*) Okay, your honor, start the show.

(*They all begin to sit down. The* FOREMAN *is seated at the head of the table.* EIGHT *continues to look out the window.*)

FOREMAN (*to* EIGHT). How about sitting down? (EIGHT *doesn't hear him.*) The gentleman at the window.

(EIGHT *turns, startled.*)

FOREMAN. How about sitting down?

EIGHT. Oh, I'm sorry. (*He heads for a seat.*)

TEN (*to* SIX). It's tough to figure, isn't it? A kid kills his father. Bing! Just like that. Well, it's the element. They let the kids run wild. Maybe it serves 'em right.

FOREMAN. Is everybody here?

TWELVE. The old man's inside.

(*The* FOREMAN *turns to the washroom just as the door opens.* NINE *comes out, embarrassed.*)

FOREMAN. We'd like to get started.

NINE. Forgive me, gentlemen. I didn't mean to keep you waiting.

FOREMAN. It's all right. Find a seat.

---

3. **Cut,** indicates an immediate switch from one camera to another to show what is happening on another part of the television stage.

4. **The Seven Year Itch,** a comedy that opened on Broadway in 1952.

(NINE *heads for a seat and sits down. They look at the* FOREMAN *expectantly.*)

FOREMAN. All right. Now, you gentlemen can handle this any way you want to. I mean, I'm not going to make any rules. If we want to discuss it first and then vote, that's one way. Or we can vote right now to see how we stand.

SEVEN. Let's vote now. Who knows, maybe we can all go home.

TEN. Yeah. Let's see who's where.

THREE. Right. Let's vote now.

FOREMAN. Anybody doesn't want to vote? (*He looks around the table. There is no answer.*) Okay, all those voting guilty raise your hands. (*Seven or eight hands go up immediately. Several others go up more slowly. Everyone looks around the table. There are two hands not raised,* NINE's *and* EIGHT's. NINE's *hand goes up slowly now as the* FOREMAN *counts.*)

FOREMAN. . . . Nine . . . ten . . . eleven . . . That's eleven for guilty. Okay. Not guilty? (EIGHT's *hand is raised.*) One. Right. Okay. Eleven to one, guilty. Now we know where we are.

THREE. Somebody's in left field. (*To* EIGHT) You think he's not guilty?

EIGHT (*quietly*). I don't know.

THREE. I never saw a guiltier man in my life. You sat right in court and heard the same thing I did. The man's a dangerous killer. You could see it.

EIGHT. He's nineteen years old.

THREE. That's old enough. He knifed his own father. Four inches into the chest. An innocent little nineteen-year-old kid. They proved it a dozen different ways. Do you want me to list them?

EIGHT. No.

TEN (*to* EIGHT). Well, do you believe his story?

EIGHT. I don't know whether I believe it or not. Maybe I don't.

SEVEN. So what'd you vote not guilty for?

EIGHT. There were eleven votes for guilty. It's not so easy for me to raise my hand and send a boy off to die without talking about it first.

SEVEN. Who says it's easy for me?

EIGHT. No one.

SEVEN. What, just because I voted fast? I think the guy's guilty. You couldn't change my mind if you talked for a hundred years.

EIGHT. I don't want to change your mind. I just want to talk for a while. Look, this boy's been kicked around all his life. You know, living in a slum, his mother dead since he was nine. That's not a very good head start. He's a tough, angry kid. You know why slum kids get that way? Because we knock 'em on the head once a day, every day. I think maybe we owe him a few words. That's all.

(*He looks around the table. Some of them look back coldly. Some cannot look at him. Only* NINE *nods slowly.* TWELVE *doodles steadily.* FOUR *begins to comb his hair.*)

TEN. I don't mind telling you this, mister. We don't owe him a thing. He got a fair trial, didn't he? You know what that trial cost? He's lucky he got it. Look, we're all grownups here. You're not going to tell us that we're supposed to believe him, knowing what he is. I've lived among 'em all my life. You can't believe a word they say. You know that.

NINE (*to* TEN *very slowly*). I don't know that. What a terrible thing for a man to believe! Since when is dishonesty a group characteristic? You have no monopoly on the truth—

THREE (*interrupting*). All right. It's not Sunday. We don't need a sermon.

NINE. What this man says is very dangerous— (EIGHT *puts his hand on* NINE's *arm and stops him. Somehow his touch and his gentle expression calm the old man. He draws a deep breath and relaxes.*)

Juror THREE, played by actor Lee J. Cobb (with hand raised), confronts juror EIGHT, played by Henry Fonda, in the 1957 film *Twelve Angry Men*, directed by Sidney Lumet.

**FOUR.** I don't see any need for arguing like this. I think we ought to be able to behave like gentlemen.

**SEVEN.** Right!

**FOUR.** If we're going to discuss this case, let's discuss the facts.

**FOREMAN.** I think that's a good point. We have a job to do. Let's do it.

**ELEVEN** (*with accent*). If you gentlemen don't mind, I'm going to close the window. (*He gets up and does so.*) (*Apologetically*) It was blowing on my neck. (TEN *blows his nose fiercely.*)

**TWELVE.** I may have an idea here. I'm just thinking out loud now, but it seems to me that it's up to us to convince this gentleman—(*Indicating* EIGHT)—that we're right and he's wrong. Maybe if we each took a minute or two, you know, if we sort of try it on for size—

**FOREMAN.** That sounds fair enough. Supposing we go once around the table.

**SEVEN.** Okay, let's start it off.

**FOREMAN.** Right. (*To* TWO) I guess you're first.

**TWO** (*timidly*). Oh. Well . . . (*Long pause*) I just think he's guilty. I thought it was obvious. I mean nobody proved otherwise.

**EIGHT** (*quietly*). Nobody has to prove otherwise. The burden of proof is on the prosecution. The defendant doesn't have to open his mouth. That's in the Constitution. The Fifth Amendment.[5] You've heard of it.

**TWO** (*flustered*). Well, sure, I've heard of it. I know what it is. I . . . what I meant . . . well, anyway, I think he was guilty.

**THREE.** Okay, let's get to the facts. Number one, let's take the old man who lived on the second floor right underneath the room where the murder took place. At ten minutes after twelve on the night of the killing he heard loud noises in the upstairs apartment. He said it sounded like a fight. Then he heard the kid say to his father, "I'm gonna kill you." A second later he heard a body falling, and he ran to the door of his apartment, looked out, and saw the kid running down the stairs and out of the house. Then he called the police. They found the father with a knife in his chest.

**FOREMAN.** And the coroner fixed the time of death at around midnight.

**THREE.** Right. Now what else do you want?

**FOUR.** The boy's entire story is flimsy. He claimed he was at the movies. That's a little ridiculous, isn't it? He couldn't even remember what pictures he saw.

**THREE.** That's right. Did you hear that? (*To* FOUR) You're absolutely right.

**TEN.** Look, what about the woman across the street? If her testimony don't prove it, then nothing does.

**TWELVE.** That's right. She saw the killing, didn't she?

**FOREMAN.** Let's go in order.

**TEN** (*loud*). Just a minute. Here's a woman who's lying in bed and can't sleep. It's hot, you know. (*He gets up and begins to walk around, blowing his nose and talking.*) Anyway, she looks out the window, and right across the street she sees the kid stick the knife into his father. She's known the kid all his life. His window is right opposite hers, across the el tracks, and she swore she saw him do it.

**EIGHT.** Through the windows of a passing elevated train.

**TEN.** Okay. And they proved in court that you can look through the windows of a passing el train at night and see what's happening on the other side. They proved it.

**EIGHT.** I'd like to ask you something. How come you believed her? She's one of "them," too, isn't she?

(TEN *walks over to* EIGHT.)

---

5. **The Fifth Amendment,** the amendment to the United States Constitution that guarantees a person on trial for a criminal offense cannot be forced to testify against himself or herself.

**TEN.** You're a pretty smart fellow, aren't you?

**FOREMAN** (*rising*). Now take it easy.

(THREE *gets up and goes to* TEN.)

**THREE.** Come on. Sit down. (*He leads* TEN *back to his seat.*) What're you letting him get you all upset for? Relax.

(TEN *and* THREE *sit down.*)

**FOREMAN.** Let's calm down now. (*To* FIVE) It's your turn.

**FIVE.** I'll pass it.

**FOREMAN.** That's your privilege. (*To* SIX) How about you?

**SIX** (*slowly*). I don't know. I started to be convinced, you know, with the testimony from those people across the hall. Didn't they say something about an argument between the father and the boy around seven o'clock that night? I mean, I can be wrong.

**ELEVEN.** I think it was eight o'clock. Not seven.

**EIGHT.** That's right. Eight o'clock. They heard the father hit the boy twice and then saw the boy walk angrily out of the house. What does that prove?

**SIX.** Well, it doesn't exactly prove anything. It's just part of the picture. I didn't say it proved anything.

**FOREMAN.** Anything else?

**SIX.** No.

(SIX *goes to the water fountain.*)

**FOREMAN** (*to* SEVEN). All right. How about you?

**SEVEN.** I don't know, most of it's been said already. We can talk all day about this thing, but I think we're wasting our time. Look at the kid's record. At fifteen he was in reform school. He stole a car. He's been arrested for mugging. He was picked up for knife-fighting. I think they said he stabbed somebody in the arm. This is a very fine boy.

**EIGHT.** Ever since he was five years old his father beat him up regularly. He used his fists.

**SEVEN.** So would I! A kid like that.

**THREE.** You're right. It's the kids. The way they are—you know? They don't listen. (*Bitter*) I've got a kid. When he was eight years old he ran away from a fight. I saw him. I was so ashamed, I told him right out, "I'm gonna make a man out of you or I'm gonna bust you up into little pieces trying." When he was fifteen he hit me in the face. He's big, you know. I haven't seen him in three years. Rotten kid! You work your heart out. . . . (*Pause*) All right. Let's get on with it. (*Looks away embarrassed*)

**FOUR.** We're missing the point here. This boy—let's say he's a product of a filthy neighborhood and a broken home. We can't help that. We're not here to go into reasons why slums are breeding grounds for criminals. They are. I know it. So do you. The children who come out of slum backgrounds are potential menaces to society.

**TEN.** You said it there. I don't want any part of them, believe me.

(*There is a dead silence for a moment, and then* FIVE *speaks haltingly.*)

**FIVE.** I've lived in a slum all my life—

**TEN.** Oh, now wait a second!

**FIVE.** I used to play in a backyard that was filled with garbage. Maybe it still smells on me.

**FOREMAN.** Now let's be reasonable. There's nothing personal—(FIVE *stands up.*)

**FIVE.** There is something personal!

(*Then he catches himself and, seeing everyone looking at him, sits down, fists clenched.*)

**THREE** (*persuasively*). Come on, now. He didn't mean you, feller. Let's not be so sensitive. . . .

(*There is a long pause.*)

**ELEVEN.** I can understand this sensitivity.

**FOREMAN.** Now let's stop the bickering. We're wasting time. (*To* EIGHT) It's your turn.

**EIGHT.** All right. I had a peculiar feeling about this trial. Somehow I felt that the defense counsel never really conducted a thorough cross-examination. I mean, he was appointed by the court to defend the boy. He hardly seemed interested. Too many questions were left un-asked.

THREE (*annoyed*). What about the ones that were asked? For instance, let's talk about that cute little switch-knife.[6] You know, the one that fine upright kid admitted buying.

EIGHT. All right. Let's talk about it. Let's get it in here and look at it. I'd like to see it again, Mr. Foreman.

(*The* FOREMAN *looks at him questioningly and then gets up and goes to the door. During the following dialogue the* FOREMAN *knocks, the* GUARD *comes in, the* FOREMAN *whispers to him, the* GUARD *nods and leaves, locking the door.*)

THREE. We all know what it looks like. I don't see why we have to look at it again. (*To* FOUR) What do you think?

FOUR. The gentleman has a right to see exhibits in evidence.

THREE (*shrugging*). Okay with me.

FOUR (*to* EIGHT). This knife is a pretty strong piece of evidence, don't you agree?

EIGHT. I do.

FOUR. The boy admits going out of his house at eight o'clock after being slapped by his father.

EIGHT. Or punched.

FOUR. Or punched. He went to a neighborhood store and bought a switch-knife. The store-keeper was arrested the following day when he admitted selling it to the boy. It's a very un-usual knife. The storekeeper identified it and said it was the only one of its kind he had in stock. Why did the boy get it? (*Sarcastically*) As a present for a friend of his, he says. Am I right so far?

EIGHT. Right.

THREE. You bet he's right. (*To all*) Now listen to this man. He knows what he's talking about.

FOUR. Next, the boy claims that on the way home the knife must have fallen through a hole in his coat pocket, that he never saw it again. Now there's a story, gentlemen. You know what ac-

tually happened. The boy took the knife home and a few hours later stabbed his father with it and even remembered to wipe off the fin-gerprints.

(*The door opens and the* GUARD *walks in with an oddly designed knife with a tag on it.* FOUR *gets up and takes it from him. The* GUARD *exits.*)

FOUR. Everyone connected with the case identi-fied this knife. Now are you trying to tell me that someone picked it up off the street and went up to the boy's house and stabbed his father with it just to be amusing?

EIGHT. No, I'm saying that it's possible that the boy lost the knife and that someone else stabbed his father with a similar knife. It's possible.

(FOUR *flips open the knife and jams it into the table.*)

FOUR. Take a look at that knife. It's a very strange knife. I've never seen one like it before in my life. Neither had the storekeeper who sold it to him.

(EIGHT *reaches casually into his pocket and with-draws an object. No one notices this. He stands up quietly.*)

FOUR. Aren't you trying to make us accept a pretty incredible coincidence?

EIGHT. I'm not trying to make anyone accept it. I'm just saying it's possible.

THREE (*shouting*). And I'm saying it's not possi-ble.

(EIGHT *swiftly flicks open the blade of a switch-knife and jams it into the table next to the first one. They are exactly alike. There are several gasps and everyone stares at the knife. There is a long si-lence.*)

THREE (*slowly, amazed*). What are you trying to do?

TEN (*loud*). Yeah, what is this? Who do you think you are?

---

6. *switch-knife,* switchblade knife.

FIVE. Look at it! It's the same knife!

FOREMAN. Quiet! Let's be quiet.

(They quiet down.)

FOUR. Where did you get it?

EIGHT. I got it last night in a little junk shop around the corner from the boy's house. It cost two dollars.

THREE. Now listen to me! You pulled a real smart trick here, but you proved absolutely zero. Maybe there are ten knives like that, so what?

EIGHT. Maybe there are.

THREE. The boy lied and you know it.

EIGHT. He may have lied. (To TEN) Do you think he lied?

TEN (violently). Now that's a stupid question. Sure he lied!

EIGHT (to FOUR). Do you?

FOUR. You don't have to ask me that. You know my answer. He lied.

EIGHT (to FIVE). Do you think he lied?

(FIVE can't answer immediately. He looks around nervously.)

FIVE. I . . . I don't know.

SEVEN. Now wait a second. What are you, the guy's lawyer? Listen, there are still eleven of us who think he's guilty. You're alone. What do you think you're gonna accomplish? If you want to be stubborn and hang this jury,[7] he'll be tried again and found guilty, sure as he's born.

EIGHT. You're probably right.

SEVEN. So what are you gonna do about it? We can be here all night.

NINE. It's only one night. A man may die.

(SEVEN glares at NINE for a long while, but has no answer. EIGHT looks closely at NINE and we can begin to sense a rapport between them. There is a long silence. Then suddenly everyone begins to talk at once.)

THREE. Well, whose fault is that?

SIX. Do you think maybe if we went over it again? What I mean is—

TEN. Did anyone force him to kill his father? (To THREE) How do you like him? Like someone forced him!

ELEVEN. Perhaps this is not the point.

FIVE. No one forced anyone. But listen—

TWELVE. Look, gentlemen, we can spitball all night here.

TWO. Well, I was going to say—

SEVEN. Just a minute. Some of us've got better things to do than sit around a jury room.

FOUR. I can't understand a word in here. Why do we all have to talk at once?

FOREMAN. He's right. I think we ought to get on with it.

(EIGHT has been listening to this exchange closely.)

THREE (to EIGHT). Well, what do you say? You're the one holding up the show.

EIGHT (standing). I've got a proposition to make.

(We catch a close shot of FIVE looking steadily at him as he talks. FIVE, seemingly puzzled, listens closely.)

EIGHT. I want to call for a vote. I want you eleven men to vote by secret ballot. I'll abstain. If there are still eleven votes for guilty, I won't stand alone. We'll take in a guilty verdict right now.

SEVEN. Okay. Let's do it.

FOREMAN. That sounds fair. Is everyone agreed?

(They all nod their heads. EIGHT walks over to the window, looks out for a moment, and then faces them.)

FOREMAN. Pass these along.

(The FOREMAN passes ballot slips to all of them, and now EIGHT watches them tensely as they begin to write.)

(Fade out)

---

7. **hang this jury,** keep this jury from reaching a verdict. A jury that fails to reach a verdict is called a "hung" jury.

## THINK AND DISCUSS
### Understanding
1. The first speech in *Twelve Angry Men* is the judge's charge to the jury. What key words must the jury ponder in deciding between an innocent and a guilty verdict? Why are these words important?
2. What do we learn from the judge's charge to the jury about the crime and the possible sentence?
3. Which juror is particularly anxious to make a quick decision? Why?
4. What is the result of the first vote?
5. What reasons does Juror Eight give for his vote?
6. How do the others react to Eight's statement?
7. What testimony from witnesses is mentioned by Three? by Ten? by Six?

### Analyzing
8. How do the comments made by Seven, Three, and Four about the defendant's past have a bearing on the case? Discuss these comments and Five's reaction.
9. How has testimony about the switchblade knife—the murder weapon—figured in the trial, both for the prosecution and the defense?
10. How does the knife figure in the climax of Act One?
11. Why might some of the jurors begin to have doubts after this point?

### Extending
12. As the jury files into the jury room early in the play, we learn something about the time of day, the weather, and the nature of the room. How do you think these circumstances might affect the jury's deliberations?

## READING LITERATURE SKILLFULLY
### Predicting Outcomes
As you read this play, you become aware of arguments for and against a verdict of guilty and the reactions of various jurors to the persuasive statements of others. This allows you to make reasonable predictions about the outcome of votes. How do you think Four, Three, Five, and Nine will vote on the second ballot? Give reasons for each answer.

## VOCABULARY
### Dictionary and Glossary, Synonyms
If you were a juror deciding the guilt or innocence of the accused, you would need to understand the meanings of many words as used in a court of law—and understand them with absolute precision. You can use a dictionary or glossary as a reference source, just as the jurors may hear definitions from a judge. Use the Glossary to help you write answers to the following questions.

1. What is the difference between *homicide* and *premeditated homicide*?
2. A defendant must be found not guilty if a "reasonable doubt" of his or her guilt exists in the minds of the jurors. What is significant about the meaning of *reasonable* in this phrase?
3. *Evidence, testimony,* and *proof* have fairly similar meanings in a trial setting. Use the synonym study following *testimony* in the Glossary to explain the difference between the words.

**Predicting Characters' Actions**

When we see a play and begin to feel that we know the outcome, we often attribute the feeling to intuition, an understanding without reasoning. But it probably more closely reflects insight or understanding of characters. With this understanding in mind, write two paragraphs for your classmates, giving your notions about what is likely to happen in this TV drama and why you think so.

Before you write, look back at Act One to review each character's developing attitudes and the jury's responsibility. Base your prediction on reasonable evidence, but do not become too concerned about choosing the "wrong" outcome. Your composition can be judged on how reasonable your arguments are, rather than how precise or certain they turn out to be.

**Writing from Personal Experience**

A familiar form of external conflict is the kind that pits one person against a group, as Juror Eight is pitted against his fellow jurors in Act One. Think about the problems of the individual versus the group as demonstrated in a real-life situation you have seen or experienced, or in the play thus far. Consider these questions: Why is it easier to join the group than to stand alone? Do personal feelings sometimes overshadow the real issues? What might an individual do to get the opposition at least to consider his or her side of the conflict?

Write a three- to four-paragraph letter to a newspaper, first describing the specifics of the individual-versus-group conflict you've considered. Then present your views on at least one of the questions mentioned in the preceding paragraph.

# ACT TWO

*Fade in on same scene, no time lapse.* EIGHT *stands tensely watching as the* JURORS *write on their ballots. He stays perfectly still as one by one they fold the ballots and pass them along to the* FOREMAN. *The* FOREMAN *takes them, riffles through the folded ballots, counts eleven, and now begins to open them. He reads each one out loud and lays it aside. They watch him quietly, and all we hear is his voice and the sound of* TWO *sucking on a cough drop.*

FOREMAN. Guilty. Guilty. Guilty. Guilty. Guilty. Guilty. Guilty. Guilty. Guilty. (*He pauses at the tenth ballot and then reads it.*) Not Guilty. (THREE *slams down hard on the table. The* FOREMAN *opens the last ballot.*) Guilty.

TEN (*angry*). How do you like that!

SEVEN. Who was it? I think we have a right to know.

ELEVEN. Excuse me. This was a secret ballot. We agreed on this point, no? If the gentleman wants it to remain secret—

THREE (*standing up angrily*). What do you mean? There are no secrets in here! I know who it was. (*He turns to* FIVE.) What's the matter with you? You come in here and you vote guilty and then this slick preacher starts to tear your heart out with stories about a poor little kid who just couldn't help becoming a murderer. So you change your vote. If that isn't the most sickening—

(FIVE *stares at* THREE, *frightened at this outburst.*)

FOREMAN. Now hold it.

THREE. Hold it? We're trying to put a guilty man into the chair where he belongs—and all of a sudden we're paying attention to fairy tales.

FIVE. Now just a minute—

ELEVEN. Please. I would like to say something here. I have always thought that a man was entitled to have unpopular opinions in this country. This is the reason I came here. I wanted to have the right to disagree. In my own country, I am ashamed to say—

**TEN.** What do we have to listen to now—the whole history of your country?

**SEVEN.** Yeah, let's stick to the subject. (*To* FIVE) I want to ask you what made you change your vote.

(*There is a long pause as* SEVEN *and* FIVE *eye each other angrily.*)

**NINE** (*quietly*). There's nothing for him to tell you. He didn't change his vote. I did. (*There is a pause.*) Maybe you'd like to know why.

**THREE.** No, we wouldn't like to know why.

**FOREMAN.** The man wants to talk.

**NINE.** Thank you. (*Pointing at* EIGHT) This gentleman chose to stand alone against us. That's his right. It takes a great deal of courage to stand alone even if you believe in something very strongly. He left the verdict up to us. He gambled for support and I gave it to him. I want to hear more. The vote is ten to two.

**TEN.** That's fine. If the speech is over, let's go on.

(FOREMAN *gets up, goes to door, knocks, hands* GUARD *the tagged switch-knife and sits down again.*)

**THREE** (*to* FIVE). Look, buddy, I was a little excited. Well, you know how it is. I . . . I didn't mean to get nasty. Nothing personal. (FIVE *looks at him.*)

**SEVEN** (*to* EIGHT). Look, supposing you answer me this. If the kid didn't kill him, who did?

**EIGHT.** As far as I know, we're supposed to decide whether or not the boy on trial is guilty. We're not concerned with anyone else's motives here.

**NINE.** Guilty beyond a reasonable doubt. This is an important thing to remember.

**THREE** (*to* TEN). Everyone's a lawyer. (*To* NINE) Supposing you explain what your reasonable doubts are.

**NINE.** This is not easy. So far, it's only a feeling I have. A feeling. Perhaps you don't understand.

**TEN.** A feeling! What are we gonna do, spend the night talking about your feelings? What about the facts?

**THREE.** You said a mouthful. (*To* NINE) Look, the old man heard the kid yell, "I'm gonna kill you." A second later he heard the father's body falling, and he saw the boy running out of the house fifteen seconds after that.

**TWELVE.** That's right. And let's not forget the woman across the street. She looked into the open window and saw the boy stab his father. She saw it. Now if that's not enough for you . . .

**EIGHT.** It's not enough for me.

**SEVEN.** How do you like him? It's like talking into a dead phone.

**FOUR.** The woman saw the killing through the windows of a moving elevated train. The train had five cars, and she saw it through the windows of the last two. She remembers the most insignificant details.

(*Cut to close shot of* TWELVE, *who doodles a picture of an el train on a scrap of paper.*)

**THREE.** Well, what have you got to say about that?

**EIGHT.** I don't know. It doesn't sound right to me.

**THREE.** Well, supposing you think about it. (*To* TWELVE) Lend me your pencil.

(TWELVE *gives it to him. He draws a tick-tack-toe square on the same sheet of paper on which* TWELVE *has drawn the train. He fills in an X, hands the pencil to* TWELVE.)

**THREE.** Your turn. We might as well pass the time.

(TWELVE *takes the pencil.* EIGHT *stands up and snatches the paper away.* THREE *leaps up.*)

**THREE.** Wait a minute!

**EIGHT** (*hard*). This isn't a game.

**THREE** (*angry*). Who do you think you are?

**SEVEN** (*rising*). All right, let's take it easy.

**THREE.** I've got a good mind to walk around this table and belt him one!

FOREMAN. Now, please. I don't want any fights in here.

THREE. Did ya see him? The nerve! The absolute nerve!

TEN. All right. Forget it. It don't mean anything.

SIX. How about sitting down.

THREE. This isn't a game. Who does he think he is?

*(He lets them sit him down.* EIGHT *remains standing, holding the scrap of paper. He looks at it closely now and seems to be suddenly interested in it. Then he throws it back toward* THREE. *It lands in center of table.* THREE *is angered again at this, but* FOUR *puts his hand on his arm.* EIGHT *speaks now and his voice is more intense.)*

EIGHT *(to* FOUR*).* Take a look at that sketch. How long does it take an elevated train going at top speed to pass a given point?

FOUR. What has that got to do with anything?

EIGHT. How long? Guess.

FOUR. I wouldn't have the slightest idea.

EIGHT *(to* FIVE*).* What do you think?

FIVE. About ten or twelve seconds, maybe.

EIGHT. I'd say that was a fair guess. Anyone else?

ELEVEN. I would think about ten seconds, perhaps.

TWO. About ten seconds.

FOUR. All right. Say ten seconds. What are you getting at?

EIGHT. This. An el train passes a given point in ten seconds. That given point is the window of the room in which the killing took place. You can almost reach out of the window of that room and touch the el. Right? *(Several of them nod.)* All right. Now let me ask you this. Did anyone here ever live right next to the el tracks? I have. When your window is open and the train goes by, the noise is almost unbearable. You can't hear yourself think.

TEN. Okay. You can't hear yourself think. Will you get to the point?

EIGHT. The old man heard the boy say, "I'm going to kill you," and one second later he heard a body fall. One second. That's the testimony, right?

TWO. Right.

EIGHT. The woman across the street looked through the windows of the last two cars of the el and saw the body fall. Right? The *last two* cars.

TEN. What are you giving us here?

EIGHT. An el takes ten seconds to pass a given point or two seconds per car. That el had been going by the old man's window for at least six seconds, and maybe more, before the body fell, according to the woman. The old man would have had to hear the boy say, "I'm going to kill you," while the front of the el was roaring past his nose. It's not possible that he could have heard it.

THREE. What d'ya mean! Sure he could have heard it.

EIGHT. Could he?

THREE. He said the boy yelled it out. That's enough for me.

NINE. I don't think he could have heard it.

TWO. Maybe he didn't hear it. I mean with the el noise—

THREE. What are you people talking about? Are you calling the old man a liar?

FIVE. Well, it stands to reason.

THREE. You're crazy. Why would he lie? What's he got to gain?

NINE. Attention, maybe.

THREE. You keep coming up with these bright sayings. Why don't you send one in to a newspaper? They pay two dollars.

*(EIGHT looks hard at THREE and then turns to NINE.)*

EIGHT *(softly).* Why might the old man have lied? You have a right to be heard.

NINE. It's just that I looked at him for a very long time. The seam of his jacket was split under the arm. Did you notice that? He was a very old man with a torn jacket, and he carried two canes. I think I know him better than anyone here. This is a quiet, frightened, insignificant man who has been nothing all his life, who has never had recognition—his name in the newspapers. Nobody knows him after seventy-five years. That's a very sad thing. A man like this needs to be recognized. To be questioned, and listened to, and quoted just once. This is very important.

TWELVE. And you're trying to tell us he lied about a thing like this just so that he could be important?

NINE. No, he wouldn't really lie. But perhaps he'd make himself believe that he heard those words and recognized the boy's face.

THREE (*loud*). Well, that's the most fantastic story I've ever heard. How can you make up a thing like that? What do you know about it?

NINE (*low*). I speak from experience.

(*There is a long pause. Then the* FOREMAN *clears his throat.*)

FOREMAN (*to* EIGHT). All right. Is there anything else?

(EIGHT *is looking at* NINE. TWO *offers the* FOREMAN *a box of cough drops. The* FOREMAN *pushes it away.*)

TWO (*hesitantly*). Anybody . . . want a cough . . . drop?

FOREMAN (*sharply*). Come on. Let's get on with it.

EIGHT. I'll take one. (TWO *almost gratefully slides him one along the table.*) Thanks. (TWO *nods and* EIGHT *puts the cough drop into his mouth.*)

EIGHT. Now. There's something else I'd like to point out here. I think we proved that the old man couldn't have heard the boy say, "I'm going to kill you," but supposing he really did hear it? This phrase: how many times has each of you used it? Probably hundreds. "If you do that once more, Junior, I'm going to murder you." "Come on, Rocky, kill him!" We say it

every day. This doesn't mean that we're going to kill someone.

THREE. Wait a minute. The phrase was "I'm going to kill you," and the kid screamed it out at the top of his lungs. Don't try and tell me he didn't mean it. Anybody says a thing like that the way he said it—they mean it.

TEN. And how they mean it!

EIGHT. Well, let me ask you this. Do you really think the boy would shout out a thing like that so the whole neighborhood would hear it? I don't think so. He's much too bright for that.

TEN (*exploding*). Bright! He's a common, ignorant slob. He don't even speak good English!

ELEVEN (*slowly*). He *doesn't* even speak good English.

(TEN *stares angrily at* ELEVEN, *and there is silence for a moment. Then* FIVE *looks around the table nervously.*)

FIVE. I'd like to change my vote to not guilty.

(THREE *gets up and walks to the window, furious, but trying to control himself.*)

FOREMAN. Are you sure?

FIVE. Yes. I'm sure.

FOREMAN. The vote is nine to three in favor of guilty.

SEVEN. Well, if that isn't the end. (*To* FIVE) What are you basing it on? Stories this guy—(*Indicating* EIGHT)—made up! He oughta write for *Amazing Detective Monthly*. He'd make a fortune. Listen, the kid had a lawyer, didn't he? Why didn't his lawyer bring up all these points?

FIVE. Lawyers can't think of everything.

SEVEN. Oh, brother! (*To* EIGHT) You sit in here and pull stories out of thin air. Now we're supposed to believe that the old man didn't get up out of bed, run to the door, and see the kid beat it downstairs fifteen seconds after the killing. He's only saying he did to be important.

FIVE. Did the old man say he ran to the door?

SEVEN. Ran. Walked. What's the difference? He got there.

Jurors TWELVE (played by Robert Webber), ONE (Martin Balsam), TWO (John Fielder), and THREE (Lee J. Cobb) gather at the jury room table.

FIVE. I don't remember what he said. But I don't see how he could run.

FOUR. He said he went from his bedroom to the front door. That's enough, isn't it?

EIGHT. Where was his bedroom again?

TEN. Down the hall somewhere. I thought you remembered everything. Don't you remember that?

EIGHT. No. Mr. Foreman, I'd like to take a look at the diagram of the apartment.

SEVEN. Why don't we have them run the trial over just so you can get everything straight?

EIGHT. Mr. Foreman—

FOREMAN (rising). I heard you.

(The FOREMAN gets up, goes to door during following dialogue. He knocks on door, GUARD opens it, he whispers to GUARD, GUARD nods and closes door.)

THREE (to EIGHT). All right. What's this for? How come you're the only one in the room who wants to see exhibits all the time?

FIVE. I want to see this one, too.

THREE. And I want to stop wasting time.

FOUR. If we're going to start wading through all that nonsense about where the body was found . . .

EIGHT. We're not. We're going to find out how a man who's had two strokes in the past three years, and who walks with a pair of canes, could get to his front door in fifteen seconds.

THREE. He said twenty seconds.

TWO. He said fifteen.

THREE. How does he know how long fifteen seconds is? You can't judge that kind of a thing.

NINE. He said fifteen. He was positive about it.

THREE (angry). He's an old man. You saw him. Half the time he was confused. How could he be positive about . . . anything?

(THREE looks around sheepishly, unable to cover up his blunder. The door opens and the GUARD walks in, carrying a large pen-and-ink diagram of the apartment. It is a railroad flat.[1] A bedroom faces the el tracks. Behind it is a series of rooms off

---

1. railroad flat, long, narrow apartment with rooms joined in a line.

*a long hall. In the front bedroom is a diagram of the spot where the body was found. At the back of the apartment we see the entrance into the apartment hall from the building hall. We see a flight of stairs in the building hall. The diagram is clearly labeled and included in the information on it are the dimensions of the various rooms. The* GUARD *gives the diagram to the* FOREMAN.)

GUARD. This what you wanted?

FOREMAN. That's right. Thank you.

*(The* GUARD *nods and exits.* EIGHT *goes to* FOREMAN *and reaches for it.)*

EIGHT. May I?

*(The* FOREMAN *nods.* EIGHT *takes the diagram and sets it up on a chair so that all can see it.* EIGHT *looks it over. Several of the* JURORS *get up to see it better.* THREE, TEN, *and* SEVEN, *however, barely bother to look at it.)*

SEVEN *(to* TEN). Do me a favor. Wake me up when this is over.

EIGHT *(ignoring him).* All right. This is the apartment in which the killing took place. The old man's apartment is directly beneath it and exactly the same. *(Pointing)* Here are the el tracks. The bedroom. Another bedroom. Living room. Bathroom. Kitchen. And this is the hall. Here's the front door to the apartment. And here are the steps. *(Pointing to front bedroom and then front door)* Now the old man was in bed in this room. He says he got up, went out into the hall, down the hall to the front door, opened it, and looked out just in time to see the boy racing down the stairs. Am I right?

THREE. That's the story.

EIGHT. Fifteen seconds after he heard the body fall.

ELEVEN. Correct.

EIGHT. His bed was at the window. It's—*(Looking closer)*—twelve feet from his bed to the bedroom door. The length of the hall is forty-three feet, six inches. He had to get up out of bed, get his canes, walk twelve feet, open the

bedroom door, walk forty-three feet, and open the front door—all in fifteen seconds. Do you think this possible?

TEN. You know it's possible.

ELEVEN. He can only walk very slowly. They had to help him into the witness chair.

THREE. You make it sound like a long walk. It's not.

*(EIGHT gets up, goes to the end of the room, and takes two chairs. He puts them together to indicate a bed.)*

NINE. For an old man who uses canes, it's a long walk.

THREE *(to* EIGHT). What are you doing?

EIGHT. I want to try this thing. Let's see how long it took him. I'm going to pace off twelve feet—the length of the bedroom. *(He begins to do so.)*

THREE. You're crazy. You can't re-create a thing like that.

ELEVEN. Perhaps if we could see it . . . this is an important point.

THREE *(mad).* It's a ridiculous waste of time.

SIX. Let him do it.

EIGHT. Hand me a chair. *(Someone pushes a chair to him.)* All right. This is the bedroom door. Now how far would you say it is from here to the door of this room?

SIX. I'd say it was twenty feet.

TWO. Just about.

EIGHT. Twenty feet is close enough. All right, from here to the door and back is about forty feet. It's shorter than the length of the hall, wouldn't you say that?

NINE. A few feet, maybe.

TEN. Look, this is absolutely insane. What makes you think you can—

EIGHT. Do you mind if I try it? According to you, it'll only take fifteen seconds. We can spare that. *(He walks over to the two chairs now and lies down on them.)* Who's got a watch with a second hand?

**TWO.** I have.

**EIGHT.** When you want me to start, stamp your foot. That'll be the body falling. Time me from there. (*He lies down on the chairs.*) Let's say he keeps his canes right at his bedside. Right?

**TWO.** Right!

**EIGHT.** Okay. I'm ready.

(*They all watch carefully.* TWO *stares at his watch, waiting for the second hand to reach sixty. Then, as it does, he stamps his foot loudly.* EIGHT *begins to get up. Slowly he swings his legs over the edges of the chairs, reaches for imaginary canes, and struggles to his feet.* TWO *stares at the watch.* EIGHT *walks as a crippled old man would walk, toward the chair which is serving as the bedroom door. He gets to it and pretends to open it.*)

**TEN** (*shouting*). Speed it up. He walked twice as fast as that.

(EIGHT, *not having stopped for this outburst, begins to walk the simulated forty-foot hallway.*)

**ELEVEN.** This is, I think, even more quickly than the old man walked in the courtroom.

**EIGHT.** If you think I should go faster, I will.

(*He speeds up his pace slightly. He reaches the door and turns now, heading back, hobbling as an old man would hobble, bent over his imaginary canes. They watch him tensely. He hobbles back to the chair, which also serves as the front door. He stops there and pretends to unlock the door. Then he pretends to push it open.*)

**EIGHT** (*loud*). Stop.

**TWO.** Right.

**EIGHT.** What's the time?

**TWO.** Fifteen . . . twenty . . . thirty . . . thirty-one seconds exactly.

**ELEVEN.** Thirty-one seconds.

(*Some of the* JURORS *adlib[2] their surprise to each other.*)

**EIGHT.** It's my guess that the old man was trying to get to the door, heard someone racing down the stairs, and assumed that it was the boy.

**SIX.** I think that's possible.

**THREE** (*infuriated*). Assumed? Now, listen to me, you people. I've seen all kinds of dishonesty in my day . . . but this little display takes the cake. (*To* FOUR) Tell him, will you?

(FOUR *sits silently.* THREE *looks at him and then he strides over to* EIGHT.)

**THREE.** You come in here with your heart bleeding all over the floor about slum kids and injustice and you make up these wild stories, and you've got some soft-hearted old ladies listening to you. Well I'm not. I'm getting real sick of it. (*To all*) What's the matter with you people? This kid is guilty! He's got to burn! We're letting him slip through our fingers here.

**EIGHT** (*calmly*). Our fingers. Are you his executioner?

**THREE** (*raging*). I'm one of 'em.

**EIGHT.** Perhaps you'd like to pull the switch.

**THREE** (*shouting*). For this kid? You bet I'd like to pull the switch!

**EIGHT.** I'm sorry for you.

**THREE** (*shouting*). Don't start with me.

**EIGHT.** What it must feel like to want to pull the switch!

**THREE.** Shut up!

**EIGHT.** You're a sadist.

**THREE** (*louder*). Shut up!

**EIGHT** (*strong*). You want to see this boy die because you personally want it—not because of the facts.

**THREE** (*shouting*). Shut up!

(*He lunges at* EIGHT, *but is caught by two of the* JURORS *and held. He struggles as* EIGHT *watches calmly.*)

**THREE** (*screaming*). Let me go! I'll kill him. I'll kill him!

**EIGHT** (*softly*). You don't really mean you'll kill me, do you?

(THREE *stops struggling now and stares at* EIGHT. *All the* JURORS *watch in silence as we fade out.*)

---

2. **adlib,** make up words that are not in the script.

## THINK AND DISCUSS

### Understanding

1. Which juror begins the discussion of who changed his ballot on the second vote?
2. Which juror immediately jumps into the conversation in an angry manner?
3. Why do Five, Eleven, and Nine take offense at this juror's anger?
4. What evidence does Eight first offer to discount the testimony of an old man at the trial?
5. What is the connection between the el train's noise and the old man's testimony?

### Analyzing

6. Reread the comments Nine makes about the old man, beginning on page 143. Are these comments based on fact or do they reflect Nine's personal feelings? Explain.
7. What is the significance of Ten's comment that the defendant "don't even speak good English"?
8. How do Eleven and Five react to Ten's comment?
9. Is the comment consistent with Ten's previous behavior? Explain.
10. How does Eight interpret the result of his timed experiment? Discuss the effect of the experiment on the other jurors.

### Extending

11. If you were one of the jurors, what would your vote be at the end of this act? Explain your reasons.

### APPLYING: Protagonist/Antagonist HT
See Handbook of Literary Terms, p. 817

In a longer work like *Twelve Angry Men*, it may take some time to get a clear idea of just who is at odds with whom. For instance, it was fairly obvious even in Act One that Juror Eight is the **protagonist,** the leading character who faces conflict in the play. But at that point you may have felt that *all* the other jurors were **antagonists,** adversaries or opponents of the protagonist. Now, however, having read further, you probably have begun to reassess this opinion.

1. Which juror has emerged as the main antagonist by the end of Act Two?
2. Contrast the attitudes of this juror with those of Juror Eight.

### THINKING SKILLS
#### Evaluating

To **evaluate** is to make a judgment based on some standard. For example, a judge in court must decide whether evidence and arguments are relevant, or significant to the case. Listed below are some arguments which have been presented in the play. Decide whether each is relevant or irrelevant in determining the boy's guilt or innocence.

1. The boy was raised in a slum.
2. The old man says he heard the crime.
3. The boy says he was at the movies.
4. The lady across the street "saw" the crime through the windows of the passing train.
5. The boy was seen storming out of the house.
6. The boy has a violent police record.
7. The boy admitted buying the knife.
8. The old man may have lied to get attention.
9. The boy speaks poor English.

# Comment

### The Story Behind the Play

Reginald Rose has said the following about his thoughts and motivations as he set about writing *Twelve Angry Men:*

*Twelve Angry Men* is the only play I've written which has any relation at all to actual personal experience. A month or so before I began the play I sat on the jury of a manslaughter case in New York's General Sessions Court. This was my first experience on a jury, and it left quite an impression on me. The receipt of my jury notice activated many grumblings and mutterings, most of which began with lines like "Eight million people in New York and they have to call me!" All the prospective jurors I met in the waiting room the first day I appeared had the same grim, horribly persecuted attitude. But, strangely, the moment I walked into the courtroom to be empaneled and found myself facing a strange man whose fate was suddenly more or less in my hands, my entire attitude changed. I was hugely impressed with the almost frightening stillness of the courtroom, the impassive, masklike face of the judge, the brisk, purposeful scurrying of the various officials in the room, and the absolute finality of the decision I and my fellow jurors would have to make at the end of the trial. I doubt whether I have ever been so impressed in my life with a role I had to play, and I suddenly became so earnest that, in thinking about it later, I probably was unbearable to the eleven other jurors.

It occurred to me during the trial that no one anywhere ever knows what goes on inside a jury room but the jurors, and I thought then that a play taking place entirely within a jury room might be an exciting and possibly moving experience for an audience.

Actually, the outline of *Twelve Angry Men*, which I began shortly after the trial ended, took longer to write than the script itself. The movements in the play were so intricate that I wanted to have them down on paper to the last detail before I began the construction of the dialogue. I worked on the idea and outline for a week and was stunned by the time I was finished to discover that the outline was twenty-seven typewritten pages long. The average outline is perhaps five pages long, and many are as short as one or two pages. This detailed setting down of the moves of the play paid off, however. The script was written in five days and could have been done in four had I not written it approximately fifteen pages too long.

In writing *Twelve Angry Men* I attempted to blend four elements which I had seen at work in the jury room during my jury service. These elements are: (a) the evidence as remembered and interpreted by each individual juror (the disparities here were incredible); (b) the relationship of juror to juror in the life-and-death situation; (c) the emotional pattern of each individual juror; and (d) physical problems such as the weather, the time, the uncomfortable room, etc. All of these elements are of vital importance in any jury room and all of them presented excellent dramatic possibilities.

# ACT THREE

*Fade in on same scene. No time lapse.* THREE *glares angrily at* EIGHT. *He is still held by two* JURORS. *After a long pause, he shakes himself loose and turns away. He walks to the windows. The other* JURORS *stand around the room now, shocked by this display of anger. There is silence. Then the door opens and the* GUARD *enters. He looks around the room.*

**GUARD.** Is there anything wrong, gentlemen? I heard some noise.

**FOREMAN.** No. There's nothing wrong. (*He points to the large diagram of the apartment.*) You can take that back. We're finished with it.
(*The* GUARD *nods and takes the diagram. He looks curiously at some of the* JURORS *and exits. The* JURORS *still are silent. Some of them slowly begin to sit down.* THREE *still stands at the window. He turns around now. The* JURORS *look at him.*)

**THREE** (*loud*). Well, what are you looking at?
(*They turn away. He goes back to his seat now. Silently the rest of the* JURORS *take their seats.* TWELVE *begins to doodle.* TEN *blows his nose, but no one speaks. Then, finally—*)

**FOUR.** I don't see why we have to behave like children here.

**ELEVEN.** Nor do I. We have a responsibility. This is a remarkable thing about democracy. That we are . . . what is the word? . . . Ah, notified! That we are notified by mail to come down to this place and decide on the guilt or innocence of a man we have not known before. We have nothing to gain or lose by our verdict. This is one of the reasons why we are strong. We should not make it a personal thing.
(*There is a long, awkward pause.*)

**TWELVE.** Well—we're still nowhere. Who's got an idea?

**SIX.** I think maybe we should try another vote. Mr. Foreman?

**FOREMAN.** It's all right with me. Anybody doesn't want to vote? (*He looks around the table.*)

**SEVEN.** All right, let's do it.

**THREE.** I want an open ballot. Let's call out our votes. I want to know who stands where.

**FOREMAN.** That sounds fair. Anyone object? (*No one does.*) All right. I'll call off your jury numbers.
(*He takes a pencil and paper and makes marks now in one of two columns after each vote.*)

**FOREMAN.** I vote guilty. Number Two?

**TWO.** Not guilty.

**FOREMAN.** Number Three?

**THREE.** Guilty.

**FOREMAN.** Number Four?

**FOUR.** Guilty.

**FOREMAN.** Number Five?

**FIVE.** Not guilty.

**FOREMAN.** Number Six?

**SIX.** Not guilty.

**FOREMAN.** Number Seven?

**SEVEN.** Guilty.

**FOREMAN.** Number Eight?

**EIGHT.** Not guilty.

**FOREMAN.** Number Nine?

**NINE.** Not guilty.

**FOREMAN.** Number Ten?

**TEN.** Guilty.

**FOREMAN.** Number Eleven?

**ELEVEN.** Not guilty.

**FOREMAN.** Number Twelve?

**TWELVE.** Guilty.

**FOUR.** Six to six.

**TEN** (*mad*). I'll tell you something. The crime is being committed right in this room.

**FOREMAN.** The vote is six to six.

**THREE.** I'm ready to walk into court right now and declare a hung jury. There's no point in this going on anymore.

**SEVEN.** I go for that, too. Let's take it in to the judge and let the kid take his chances with twelve other guys.

FIVE (to SEVEN). You mean you still don't think there's room for reasonable doubt?

SEVEN. No, I don't.

ELEVEN. I beg your pardon. Maybe you don't understand the term "reasonable doubt."

SEVEN (angry). What do you mean I don't understand it? Who do you think you are to talk to me like that? (To all) How do you like this guy? He comes over here running for his life, and before he can even take a big breath he's telling us how to run the show. The arrogance of him!

FIVE (to SEVEN). Wait a second. Nobody around here's asking where you came from.

SEVEN. I was born right here.

FIVE. Or where your father came from. . . . (He looks at SEVEN, who doesn't answer but looks away.) Maybe it wouldn't hurt us to take a few tips from people who come running here! Maybe they learned something we don't know. We're not so perfect!

ELEVEN. Please—I am used to this. It's all right. Thank you.

FIVE. It's not all right!

SEVEN. Okay, okay, I apologize. Is that what you want?

FIVE. That's what I want.

FOREMAN. All right. Let's stop the arguing. Who's got something constructive to say?

TWO (hesitantly). Well, something's been bothering me a little . . . this whole business about the stab wound and how it was made, the downward angle of it, you know?

THREE. Don't tell me we're gonna start that. They went over it and over it in court.

TWO. I know they did—but I don't go along with it. The boy is five feet eight inches tall. His father was six two. That's a difference of six inches. It's a very awkward thing to stab *down* into the chest of someone who's half a foot taller than you are.

(THREE jumps up, holding the knife.)

THREE. Look, you're not going to be satisfied till you see it again. I'm going to give you a demonstration. Somebody get up.

(He looks around the table. EIGHT stands up and walks toward him. THREE closes the knife and puts it in his pocket. They stand face to face and look at each other for a moment.)

THREE. Okay. (To TWO) Now watch this. I don't want to have to do it again. (He crouches down now until he is quite a bit shorter than EIGHT.) Is that six inches?

TWELVE. That's more than six inches.

THREE. Okay, let it be more.

(He reaches into his pocket and takes out the knife. He flicks it open, changes its position in his hand, and holds the knife aloft, ready to stab. He and EIGHT look steadily into each other's eyes. Then he stabs downward, hard.)

TWO (shouting). Look out!

(He stops short just as the blade reaches EIGHT's chest. THREE laughs.)

SIX. That's not funny.

FIVE. What's the matter with you?

THREE. Now just calm down. Nobody's hurt, are they?

EIGHT (low). No. Nobody's hurt.

THREE. All right. There's your angle. Take a look at it. Down and in. That's how I'd stab a taller man in the chest, and that's how it was done. Take a look at it and tell me I'm wrong.

(TWO doesn't answer. THREE looks at him for a moment, then jams the knife into the table, and sits down. They all look at the knife.)

SIX. Down and in. I guess there's no argument.

(EIGHT picks the knife out of the table and closes it. He flicks it open and, changing its position in his hand, stabs downward with it.)

EIGHT (to SIX). Did you ever stab a man?

SIX. Of course not.

EIGHT (to THREE). Did you?

THREE. All right, let's not be silly.

EIGHT. Did you?

THREE (loud). No, I didn't!

EIGHT. Where do you get all your information about how it's done?

THREE. What do you mean? It's just common sense.

EIGHT. Have you ever seen a man stabbed?

THREE (*pauses and looks around the room nervously*). No.

EIGHT. All right. I want to ask you something. The boy was an experienced knife fighter. He was even sent to reform school for knifing someone, isn't that so?

TWELVE. That's right.

EIGHT. Look at this. (EIGHT *closes the knife, flicks it open, and changes the position of the knife so that he can stab overhanded.*) Doesn't it seem like an awkward way to handle a knife?

THREE. What are you asking me for?

(EIGHT *closes the blade and flicks it open, holds it ready to slash underhanded.*)

FIVE. Wait a minute! What's the matter with me? Give me that. (*He reaches out for the knife.*)

EIGHT. Have you ever seen a knife fight?

FIVE. Yes, I have.

EIGHT. In the movies?

FIVE. In my backyard. On my stoop. In the vacant lot across the street. Too many of them. Switch-knives came with the neighborhood where I lived. Funny I didn't think of it before. I guess you try to forget those things. (*Flicking the knife open*) Anyone who's ever used a switch-knife would never have stabbed downward. You don't handle a switch-knife that way. You use it underhanded.

EIGHT. Then he couldn't have made the kind of wound which killed his father.

FIVE. No. He couldn't have. Not if he'd ever had any experience with switch-knives.

THREE. I don't believe it.

TEN. Neither do I. You're giving us a lot of mumbo jumbo.

EIGHT (*to* TWELVE). What do you think?

TWELVE (*hesitantly*). Well . . . I don't know.

EIGHT (back to camera, at left) faces THREE. Other jurors are played by Ed Begley, Robert Webber, Jack Klugman, E. G. Marshall, Jack Warden, John Fielder, and Edward Binns.

EIGHT (to SEVEN). What about you?

SEVEN. Listen, I'll tell you something. I'm a little sick of this whole thing already. We're getting nowhere fast. Let's break it up and go home. I'm changing my vote to not guilty.

THREE. You're what?

SEVEN. You heard me. I've had enough.

THREE. What do you mean, you've had enough? That's no answer.

ELEVEN (angry). I think perhaps you're right. This is not an answer. (To SEVEN) What kind of a man are you? You have sat here and voted guilty with everyone else because there are some theater tickets burning a hole in your pocket. Now you have changed your vote for the same reason. I do not think you have the right to play like this with a man's life. This is an ugly and terrible thing to do.

SEVEN. Now wait a minute . . . you can't talk like that to me.

ELEVEN (strong). I can talk like that to you! If you want to vote not guilty, then do it because you are convinced the man is not guilty. If you believe he is guilty, then vote that way. Or don't you have the . . . the . . . guts—the guts to do what you think is right?

SEVEN. Now listen . . .

ELEVEN. Is it guilty or not guilty?

SEVEN (hesitantly). I told you. Not . . . guilty.

ELEVEN (hard). Why?

SEVEN. I don't have to—

ELEVEN. You have to! Say it! Why?

(They stare at each other for a long while.)

SEVEN (low). I . . . don't think . . . he's guilty.

EIGHT (fast). I want another vote.

FOREMAN. Okay, there's another vote called for. I guess the quickest way is a show of hands. Anybody object? (No one does.) All right. All those voting not guilty, raise your hands.

(TWO, FIVE, SIX, SEVEN, EIGHT, NINE, and ELEVEN raise their hands immediately. Then, slowly, TWELVE raises his hand. The FOREMAN looks around the table carefully and then he too raises his hand. He looks around the table, counting silently.)

FOREMAN. Nine. (The hands go down.) All those voting guilty.

(THREE, FOUR, and TEN raise their hands.)

FOREMAN. Three. (They lower their hands.) The vote is nine to three in favor of acquittal.

TEN. I don't understand you people. How can you believe this kid is innocent? Look, you know how those people lie. I don't have to tell you. They don't know what the truth is. And lemme tell you, they—(FIVE gets up from table, turns his back to it, and goes to window.)—don't need any real big reason to kill someone either. You know, they get drunk, and bang, someone's lying in the gutter. Nobody's blaming them. That's how they are. You know what I mean? Violent! (NINE gets up and does the same. He is followed by ELEVEN.)

TEN. Human life don't mean as much to them as it does to us. Hey, where are you going? Look, these people are drinking and fighting all the time, and if somebody gets killed, so somebody gets killed. They don't care. Oh, sure, there are some good things about them, too. Look, I'm the first to say that. (EIGHT gets up, and then TWO and SIX follow him to the window.)

TEN. I've known a few who were pretty decent, but that's the exception. Most of them, it's like they have no feelings. They can do anything. What's going on here?

(The FOREMAN gets up and goes to the window, followed by SEVEN and TWELVE.)

TEN. I'm speaking my piece, and you—Listen to me! They're no good. There's not a one of 'em who's any good. We better watch out. Take it from me. This kid on trial . . .

(THREE sits at table toying with the knife and FOUR gets up and starts for the window. All have their backs to TEN.)

TEN. Well, don't you know about them? Listen to

me! What are you doing? I'm trying to tell you something. . . .

(FOUR *stands over him as he trails off. There is a dead silence. Then* FOUR *speaks softly.*)

**FOUR.** I've had enough. If you open your mouth again, I'm going to split your skull. (FOUR *stands there and looks at him. No one moves or speaks.* TEN *looks at him, then looks down at the table.*)

**TEN** (*softly*). I'm only trying to tell you. . . .

(*There is a long pause as* FOUR *stares down at* TEN.)

**FOUR** (*to all*). All right. Sit down, everybody. (*They all move back to their seats. When they are all seated,* FOUR *then sits down.*)

**FOUR** (*quietly*). I still believe the boy is guilty of murder. I'll tell you why. To me, the most damning evidence was given by the woman across the street who claimed she actually saw the murder committed.

**THREE.** That's right. As far as I'm concerned, that's the most important testimony.

**EIGHT.** All right. Let's go over her testimony. What exactly did she say?

**FOUR.** I believe I can recount it accurately. She said that she went to bed at about eleven o'clock that night. Her bed was next to the open window, and she could look out of the window while lying down and see directly into the window across the street. She tossed and turned for over an hour, unable to fall asleep. Finally she turned toward the window at about twelve-ten and, as she looked out, she saw the boy stab his father. As far as I can see, this is unshakable testimony.

**THREE.** That's what I mean. That's the whole case.

(FOUR *takes off his eyeglasses and begins to polish them, as they all sit silently watching him.*)

**FOUR** (*to the* JURY). Frankly, I don't see how you can vote for acquittal. (*To* TWELVE) What do you think about it?

**TWELVE.** Well . . . maybe . . . there's so much evidence to sift.

**THREE.** What do you mean, maybe? He's absolutely right. You can throw out all the other evidence.

**FOUR.** That was my feeling. (TWO, *polishing his glasses, squints at clock, can't see it.* SIX *watches him closely.*)

**TWO.** What time is it?

**ELEVEN.** Ten minutes of six.

**TWO.** It's late. You don't suppose they'd let us go home and finish it in the morning. I've got a kid with mumps.

**FIVE.** Not a chance.

**SIX** (*to* TWO). Pardon me. Can't you see the clock without your glasses?

**TWO.** Not clearly. Why?

**SIX.** Oh, I don't know. Look, this may be a dumb thought, but what do you do when you wake up at night and want to know what time it is?

**TWO.** What do you mean? I put on my glasses and look at the clock.

**SIX.** You don't wear them to bed.

**TWO.** Of course not. No one wears eyeglasses to bed.

**TWELVE.** What's all this for?

**SIX.** Well, I was thinking. You know the woman who testified that she saw the killing wears glasses.

**THREE.** So does my grandmother. So what?

**EIGHT.** Your grandmother isn't a murder witness.

**SIX.** Look, stop me if I'm wrong. This woman wouldn't wear her eyeglasses to bed, would she?

**FOREMAN.** Wait a minute! Did she wear glasses at all? I don't remember.

**ELEVEN** (*excited*). Of course she did. The woman wore bifocals. I remember this very clearly. They looked quite strong.

**NINE.** That's right. Bifocals. She never took them off.

FOUR. She did wear glasses. Funny. I never thought of it.

EIGHT. Listen, she wasn't wearing them in bed. That's for sure. She testified that in the midst of her tossing and turning she rolled over and looked casually out the window. The murder was taking place as she looked out, and the lights went out a split second later. She couldn't have had time to put on her glasses. Now maybe she honestly thought she saw the boy kill his father. I say that she saw only a blur.

THREE. How do you know what she saw? Maybe she's farsighted. (*He looks around. No one answers.*)

THREE (*loud*). How does he know all these things? (*There is silence.*)

EIGHT. Does anyone think there still is not a reasonable doubt?

(*He looks around the room, then squarely at* TEN. TEN *looks down and shakes his head no.*)

THREE (*loud*). I think he's guilty.

EIGHT (*calmly*). Does anyone else?

FOUR (*quietly*). No. I'm convinced.

EIGHT (*to* THREE). You're alone.

THREE. I don't care whether I'm alone or not! I have a right.

EIGHT. You have a right.

(*There is a pause. They all look at* THREE.)

THREE. Well, I told you I think the kid's guilty. What else do you want?

EIGHT. Your arguments. (*They all look at* THREE.)

THREE. I gave you my arguments.

EIGHT. We're not convinced. We're waiting to hear them again. We have time.

(THREE *runs to* FOUR *and grabs his arm.*)

THREE (*pleading*). Listen. What's the matter with you? You're the guy. You made all the arguments. You can't turn now. A guilty man's gonna be walking the streets. A murderer. He's got to die! Stay with me.

FOUR. I'm sorry. There's a reasonable doubt in my mind.

EIGHT. We're waiting.

(THREE *turns violently on him.*)

THREE (*shouting*). Well, you're not going to intimidate me! (*They all look at* THREE.) I'm entitled to my opinion! (*No one answers him.*) It's gonna be a hung jury! That's it!

EIGHT. There's nothing we can do about that, except hope that some night, maybe in a few months, you'll get some sleep.

FIVE. You're all alone.

NINE. It takes a great deal of courage to stand alone.

(THREE *looks around at all of them for a long time. They sit silently, waiting for him to speak, and all of them despise him for his stubbornness. Then, suddenly, his face contorts as if he is about to cry, and he slams his fist down on the table.*)

THREE (*thundering*). All right!

(THREE *turns his back on them. There is silence for a moment and then the* FOREMAN *goes to the door and knocks on it. It opens. The* GUARD *looks in and sees them all standing. The* GUARD *holds the door for them as they begin slowly to file out.* EIGHT *waits at the door as the others file past him. Finally he and* THREE *are the only ones left.* THREE *turns around and sees that they are alone. Slowly he moves toward the door. Then he stops at the table. He pulls the switch-knife out of the table and walks over to* EIGHT *with it. He holds it in the approved knife-fighter fashion and looks long and hard at* EIGHT, *pointing the knife at his belly.* EIGHT *stares back. Then* THREE *turns the knife around.* EIGHT *takes it by the handle.* THREE *exits.* EIGHT *closes the knife, puts it away, and, taking a last look around the room, exits, closing the door. The camera moves in close on the littered table in the empty room, and we clearly see a slip of crumpled paper on which are scribbled the words "Not guilty."*)

(*Fade out*)

## THINK AND DISCUSS

### Understanding

1. At the beginning of Act Three, the jurors vote for the third time. What is the result of this vote?
2. Which jurors have changed their votes?
3. What information does Five provide that discounts an important piece of testimony?
4. Is Five qualified to speak as an expert about the switchblade knife?

### Analyzing

5. In what way is Seven's willingness to change his vote consistent with his earlier behavior?
6. Why does Eleven question Seven so closely? Discuss the results of Eleven's questioning.
7. Explain the behavior of the other jurors when Ten begins to rant and rave about the way "those people" (meaning people like the accused) behave.
8. In the fourth vote, Four is one of the three jurors still voting guilty. Is he voting out of prejudice or conviction? Explain.
9. How is the evidence provided by a woman from beyond the el tracks cast into doubt? Discuss.

### Extending

10. At the end of the play, has the jury *proven* the defendant not guilty? Explain.
11. Do you think Three was unfairly pressured into agreeing with the majority? Why or why not?
12. In some court cases, people can choose to have a jury trial or a *bench* trial, in which the case is decided by the judge. Having read this play, would you prefer a bench trial or a jury trial? Explain your choice.

## VOCABULARY

### Pronunciation, Dictionary

**A.** Dictionaries and glossaries illustrate the pronunciation of words by representing sounds with symbols. Look at the pronunciation symbols in the following items, and write the letter of the correct pronunciation for each of the following words. The pronunciation key of the Glossary includes samples of the sounds represented by each symbol in the answer choices. You may consult the Glossary entry for any word to check its pronunciation or definition. Then use each word in a sentence that shows you understand its meaning.

1. sadism: (**a**) si dish′ən (**b**) sā′diz′əm
2. bigot: (**a**) big′ət (**b**) bi get′
3. appall: (**a**) ə pôl′ (**b**) ə pēl′
4. rapport: (**a**) ra pôr′ (**b**) ri pôrt′
5. prosecution: (**a**) pėr′sə kyü′shən (**b**) pros′ə kyü′shən

**B.** Copy the following words; then divide them into syllables and put the stress marks after each accented syllable. You may want to look at entry words in the Glossary or in a dictionary to see how syllable breaks and accent marks are shown. Finally, use each word in a meaningful sentence.

1. simulate; 2. unanimous; 3. superficial; 4. subservient; 5. insignificant

## COMPOSITION

### Explaining Your Decisions

Assume you are on the jury in *Twelve Angry Men*. Review the play to examine the discussion leading up to each of the four votes. Jot down words or brief notes identifying what you, as a juror, would regard as key points of evidence. In a four-paragraph composition written for your fellow jurors, tell how you would vote in each instance and the reasons for your decision. Do not let later discussions influence your earlier votes. See "Writing to Persuade an Audience" in the Writer's Handbook.

### Analyzing Suspense in a Drama

Playwrights face special challenges in ending the acts of their plays. They must find the means to arouse and intensify interest so as to hold the audience's attention during the breaks between the acts. Otherwise the audience might tune out or walk out. Write a three- to four-paragraph essay for your fellow students assessing the endings of Acts One and Two of *Twelve Angry Men*. How has the playwright built suspense or intensified interest in each case? See "Writing About Plot and Plot Devices" in the Writer's Handbook.

### ENRICHMENT
### Playing a Scene

Because so much of the "action" of this play depends upon the actor's tone of voice, this is an ideal play to read aloud in class. You and other interested students may want to memorize and present a scene to the class. Scenes for such presentation might be: the introduction of the second knife, the re-creation of the old man going to the hall, and Ten's outburst. Authentic props such as knives and apartment diagrams are not needed. Props can be represented by carefully prepared cardboard substitutes, or handling of props may be pantomimed.

## BIOGRAPHY

### Reginald Rose
### 1920–

A native New Yorker, Rose was a publicity writer and advertising copywriter during the early 1950s. He sold his first television script, which he had written in his spare time, in 1951. He wrote *Twelve Angry Men* in 1954 for television; later he wrote the script for the motion-picture version and then another script for the stage version. Among his numerous awards are three Emmys, one for *Twelve Angry Men* and two for the television series *The Defenders,* another work that dealt with the American legal system. Rose has written feature films as well as television plays and is a television producer.

## *Writer's Craft*

### Use a Voice That Suits the Purpose

Good writing, be it in the form of a play, a story, a poem, an essay, or a letter, has a distinctive voice. The writer expresses ideas using a tone and style to suit a specific purpose and to affect readers in particular ways. Consider how Reginald Rose speaks directly to the reader when giving stage directions in *Twelve Angry Men*. His purpose is to convey information to people directing, producing, and performing the play, or reading it for other reasons. The directions are written in a voice that is clear and to the point. The voice is not emotional.

*Fade in on a jury box. Twelve men are seated in it, listening intently to the voice of the* JUDGE. . . . *He speaks in slow, measured tones and his voice is grave. The camera drifts over the faces of the* JURYMEN *as the* JUDGE *speaks and we see that most of their heads are turned to the camera's left.*

The voice expressing this description is clear, but it does not seem cold or distant. Rose has written that "we see" the heads of the characters. It is as if he were sitting with the readers or television viewers.

Notice that the voice of the Judge is described. In *Twelve Angry Men* and other plays and stories, writers speak indirectly to readers through the voices of characters. A playwright creates and must maintain a recognizable voice for each character, and these voices are purposefully used, too.

Rose saw Juror Eight as thoughtful, truth-seeking, and determined that justice be upheld in this case. The writer created a voice—a style of speaking—for this character that suits Eight's personality and purpose. Observe the way Eight speaks on behalf of justice and the defendant in response to the nervous voice of Two.

TWO. . . . I just think he's guilty. I thought it was obvious. I mean nobody proved otherwise.
EIGHT (*quietly*). Nobody has to prove otherwise. The burden of proof is on the prosecution. The defendant doesn't have to open his mouth. That's in the Constitution. The Fifth Amendment. You've heard of it.

In contrast, the voice of Juror Three expresses this character's intolerant and sadistic attitude. Three flies off the handle when a second juror joins Eight in voting "Not guilty." Notice the aggressive, accusatory voice the writer gives to Three.

THREE (*standing up angrily*). What do you mean? There are no secrets in here! (*He turns to* FIVE.) What's the matter with you? You come in here and you vote guilty and then this slick preacher starts to tear your heart out with stories about a poor little kid who just couldn't help becoming a murderer. So you change your vote. Isn't that the most sickening—

A writer chooses a certain voice to portray the personality and express the purpose of each character. These voices also achieve the purpose of the dramatist who is dealing with ideas in an entertaining way.

Writers speaking in their own voices—as you might write a letter, an essay, or another composition—express themselves in voices used to achieve purposes in writing. A voice might be particularly courteous, boldly defiant, witty, or marked by any sincere feeling or intention.

When you read, note the writer's voice. When you write, use a voice to achieve a purpose. Keep your audience in mind.

See INFERENCE in the Handbook of Literary Terms, page 803.

# The Romancers

**Edmond Rostand**   France

## CHARACTERS

SYLVETTE (sēl vet′)
PERCINET (per sē nā′)
STRAFOREL (strȧ fô rel′)
BERGAMIN (ber gä maN′), *Percinet's father*

PASQUINOT (pȧ skē nō′), *Sylvette's father*
A WALL, *silent figurant*
SWORDSMEN, MUSICIANS, MOORS, TORCH-BEARERS

*The action can take place anywhere, as long as the costumes are attractive.*

*The stage is cut in half by an old moss-grown wall completely covered with lush vines, creepers, and flowers. At the right, a corner of the* BERGAMIN *park, at the left a corner of the* PASQUINOT *park. A bench is placed on each side of the wall. As the curtain goes up,* PERCINET *is sitting atop the wall. He has a book in his lap and is reading to* SYL- VETTE, *who listens attentively. She is standing on the bench on the other side and leaning against the wall.*

SYLVETTE. Oh! *Monsieur* Percinet, how beautiful!

PERCINET. Yes, isn't it? Listen to Romeo's reply. (*He reads.*)

It was the lark, the herald of the morn;

No nightingale. Look, love, what envious streaks
Do lace the severing clouds in yonder East.
Night's candles are burnt out, and jocund day
Stands tiptoe on the misty mountaintops.[1]

SYLVETTE (*suddenly straining her ear*). Hush!

PERCINET (*listening for a moment, then*). There's no one coming, *Mademoiselle.* You mustn't take fright like the sparrow that flutters from a

---

*Edmond Rostand* (ed môN′ rôs täN′).

1. *It was the lark . . . misty mountaintops,* lines from Act Three, Scene 5 of William Shakespeare's tragic play, *Romeo and Juliet.* The title characters, members of two feuding families in Verona, Italy, die for their love.

branch at the slightest sound. . . . Listen to the Immortal Lovers speak:

JULIET.
Yond light is not daylight; I know it, I;
It is some meteor that the sun exhales,
To be to thee this night a torchbearer
And light thee on thy way to Mantua.
Therefore stay yet; thou need'st not to be gone.
ROMEO.
Let me be ta'en, let me be put to death;
I am content, so thou wilt have it so. . . .
Come, death, and welcome!

SYLVETTE. Oh no! I don't want him to talk about that! If he does, I'll start crying. . . .

PERCINET. All right, then let's stop there: we'll close our book until tomorrow, and for your sake we'll let gentle Romeo live on. (*He shuts the book and looks around.*) What a wonderful spot. I think it's the perfect place to indulge in the beautiful verses of the Great Bard.[2]

SYLVETTE. Yes, those lines are so beautiful, and the divine murmur of the leaves and the boughs is really a fine accompaniment, and the setting of this green shade is just right. Yes, indeed, *Monsieur* Percinet, those verses *are* lovely. But what makes their beauty even more poignant is the way you recite them in your melodious voice.

PERCINET. You terrible flatterer, you!

SYLVETTE (*sighing*). Ah! The poor lovers! How cruel their destiny, how wretched the world was to them! (*With a sigh*) Ah! . . .

PERCINET. What are you thinking about?

SYLVETTE (*sharply*). Nothing!

PERCINET. But all at once, something made you turn crimson.

SYLVETTE (*sharply*). Nothing!

PERCINET. You little liar. . . . Your eyes are too transparent! I can see what you're thinking about! (*Lowering his voice*) Our parents!

SYLVETTE. Perhaps . . .

PERCINET. Your father and mine, and the hatred that divides them!

SYLVETTE. Well, yes, that's what distresses me and often makes me weep in secret. Last month, when I came home from the convent my father showed me your father's park and said, "My dear child, there you see the lair of my old mortal enemy Bergamin. Keep away from that wretch and that son of his; and I'll disown you unless you promise me to regard those people as your everlasting enemies, for since time immemorial their family has execrated ours." I gave him my word. . . . And you see, *Monsieur*, how I keep it.

PERCINET. And didn't I also promise my father to hate you forever, Sylvette?—And I love you!

SYLVETTE. Oh, goodness me!

PERCINET. And I love you, my darling.

SYLVETTE. How sinful.

PERCINET. Very sinful . . . but who can blame us? The more you're kept from loving someone, the more you *want* to love. Sylvette, kiss me!

SYLVETTE. Never! (*She jumps off the bench and moves away from the wall.*)

PERCINET. But you *do* love me!

SYLVETTE. What did he say?

PERCINET. My darling, I said something that your heart is still struggling against, but it would be foolish to deny it any longer. I said . . . the very same thing you said. Yes, you, Sylvette, when you compared us to the Lovers of Verona.

SYLVETTE. I never compared—

PERCINET. You did so! You likened my father and yours to those of Romeo and Juliet, my darling! That's why *we* are Romeo and Juliet, and that's why we're so madly in love! And despite all their intense hatred, I'll defy both

---

2. *the Great Bard,* Shakespeare. *Bard* here means "poet."

Pasquinot-Capulet and Bergamin-Montague![3]

SYLVETTE (*drawing a bit closer to the wall*). So then we're in love? But *Monsieur* Percinet, how did it happen so quickly?

PERCINET. Love comes when it has to, and no one can say how or why. I would often see you passing by my window. . . .

SYLVETTE. And I saw you passing, too. . . .

PERCINET. And our eyes conversed in code.

SYLVETTE. One day, I was here, gathering nuts near the wall, and by chance . . .

PERCINET. I happened to be reading Shakespeare; and see how all things conspired to unite two hearts. . . .

SYLVETTE. Whoosh! The wind blew my ribbon over to you!

PERCINET. I climbed up on the bench to retrieve it. . . .

SYLVETTE (*climbing*). I climbed up on the bench. . . .

PERCINET. And ever since then, my darling, I've been waiting for you every day, and every day my heart beats faster when—oh, blessed signal—your gentle fledgling laughter rises from behind the wall, and it doesn't stop until your head emerges from the trembling tangle of vines and ivy.

SYLVETTE. Since we're in love, we ought to be engaged.

PERCINET. I was just thinking the very same thing.

SYLVETTE (*solemnly*). I, the last of the Pasquinots, do pledge myself to you, the last of the Bergamins.

PERCINET. What noble folly!

SYLVETTE. They'll speak of us in future ages!

PERCINET. Oh! Tenderhearted children of two callous fathers!

SYLVETTE. But, darling, who knows? Perhaps the time's at hand when Heaven will use us to wipe out their hatred.

PERCINET. I don't think so.

SYLVETTE. Well, I have faith. I can foresee five or six highly possible solutions.

PERCINET. Really? Tell me.

SYLVETTE. Just suppose—I've read of similar things in lots of old romances—just suppose the Reigning Prince were to ride by one day. . . . I would hurry over to him, throw myself at his feet, tell him about our love and the old feud dividing our fathers. . . . After all, a king married Don Rodrigo and Ximene[4]— The Prince will summon our fathers and reconcile them.

PERCINET. And he'll give me your hand!

SYLVETTE. Or else it will happen the same way as in *The Donkey's Skin*.[5] You'll be at the point of death, a stupid doctor will despair of your life. . . .

PERCINET. My father, panic-stricken, will ask me, "What do you want?"

SYLVETTE. You'll say, "I want Sylvette!"

PERCINET. And his stubborn pride will be forced to yield!

SYLVETTE. Or else, here's another possibility: an old duke, seeing my portrait, falls in love with me, sends a magnificent equerry to me in his name, and offers to make me a duchess. . . .

PERCINET. And you answer "No!"

SYLVETTE. This infuriates him. One lovely evening, as I wander, lost in dreams, down a dark garden path, strange men seize me! . . . I scream! . . .

PERCINET. And I'm at your side immediately. Trusting in my sword, I fight like a lion, slice up—

SYLVETTE. Three or four men. My father runs

---

3. *Pasquinot-Capulet and Bergamin-Montague.* The family names of Sylvette and Percinet are paired respectively with the family names of Juliet and Romeo.

4. *Don Rodrigo and Ximene* (ksē mān′), characters in Pierre Corneille's play *The Cid* (1636). Their dutifulness to their fathers presents an obstacle to their love; however, they overcome it.

5. *The Donkey's Skin*, a French fairy tale in which the heroine hides her beauty in the skin of a donkey.

up, flings his arms about you. You tell him your name. His heart softens. He gives me to my rescuer. And your father is so proud of your valor that he consents!

PERCINET. And we live happily ever after!

SYLVETTE. And none of this seems the least bit unlikely.

PERCINET (*hearing a noise*). Someone's coming!

SYLVETTE (*losing her head*). Kiss me good-by!

PERCINET (*kisses her*). And tonight, when the bell rings for Mass, will you be here? Tell me.

SYLVETTE. No.

PERCINET. Yes.

SYLVETTE (*vanishing behind the wall*). Your father!

(PERCINET *leaps down from the wall.* SYLVETTE, *having stepped down, can't be seen by* BERGA-MIN.)

BERGAMIN. Ah! So I've caught you daydreaming again, all alone in this corner of the park?

PERCINET. Father, I love . . . this part of the park! I love sitting on this bench, sheltered by the overhanging vines on the wall! . . . Isn't the vine graceful? Look at those arabesque festoons.[6] It's so good to breathe pure air in this spot.

BERGAMIN. In front of that wall?

PERCINET. I love this wall.

BERGAMIN. I don't see anything lovable about it.

SYLVETTE (*aside*). How can he?

PERCINET. Why, it's a wonderful old wall. Look at its grassy top; look at the scarlet creeper, and the green ivy, and the long flossy clusters of the mauve wisteria, and the honeysuckle and the woodbine over there. This ancient, crumbling wall is studded with tiny flowers and filled with cracks that hang strange red hair into the sunshine. And the moss is so thick and rich that like a velvet backdrop it turns the humble bench into a royal throne!

BERGAMIN. Now, now, you young pup, do you really expect me to believe that you come here just to feast your eyes on the wall?

PERCINET. To feast my eyes on the eyes of the wall! . . . (*Facing the wall*) Such lovely eyes, fresh azure smiles, gentle blue crannies, deep flowers, limpid eyes, to feast my eyes upon. And if ever any tears dim your hue, I'll kiss them away at once.

BERGAMIN. But the wall hasn't got any eyes.

PERCINET. It's got these morning glories. (*And quickly breaking one off, he gracefully presents it to* BERGAMIN.)

SYLVETTE. Oh, he's so clever!

BERGAMIN. What a dunce! But I know why you're all wrought up. (PERCINET *and* SYLVETTE *start.*) You come here to read on the sly! (*He takes the book jutting out of* PERCINET's *pocket and glances at the title.*) Plays! (*He opens it and, horrified, drops it.*) In verse! Verse. That's why your brain's in a whirl. No wonder you roam about dreaming, avoiding other people. No wonder you carry on about wisteria; no wonder you see blue eyes in the wall! Walls don't need to be attractive; they have to be sturdy! I'm going to have all that green junk removed; it may be concealing some open gaps. And for better protection against that insolent neighbor, I'm going to remortar the whole surface and build a fine white wall. Very white, very smooth, and very clean. And there'll be no wisteria. I'll cut notches into the plaster on top for broken bottle ends, a sharp and jagged battalion of them in serried ranks.

PERCINET. Have pity, Father!

BERGAMIN. Never! I hereby issue a decree: up and down and all along the top.

SYLVETTE *and* PERCINET (*aghast*). Ohh!

BERGAMIN (*sitting down on the bench*). Now then, it's time you and I had a chat! (*He gets up again*

---

6. *arabesque* (ar′ə besk′) *festoons*, a reference to the vine. It is an elaborate design of leaves and flowers (arabesque) hung in curves (festoons).

Jean Honoré Fragonard (zhän ô nô rä′ frä gô när′), 1732–1806, *The Meeting* (detail), 1773, The Frick Collection

*and, as if suspecting something, steps back from the wall.)* Hmmm! . . . Walls may not have eyes, but they do have ears! *(He is about to mount the bench.* PERCINET *is terror stricken.* SYLVETTE, *hearing the noise, crouches against the wall. However,* BERGAMIN, *grimacing because of some chronic pain, changes his mind and motions to his son to climb up instead and have a look.)* Just see if anyone's eavesdropping. . . .

*(*PERCINET *hops lithely onto the bench and leans over the wall.* SYLVETTE *stands up and he murmurs to her.)*

PERCINET. Till tonight!

SYLVETTE *(letting him kiss her hand, whispers back).* I'll come before the hour strikes.

PERCINET *(whispering).* I'll be here.

SYLVETTE *(whispering).* I love you.

BERGAMIN *(to* PERCINET*).* Well?

PERCINET *(jumping back down, says aloud).* Well, nobody there!

BERGAMIN *(feeling reassured, sits down again).* Fine, then let's have our little talk. . . . Percinet, I want you to get married.

SYLVETTE. Ohh!

BERGAMIN. What was that?

PERCINET. Nothing.

BERGAMIN. I heard a feeble cry.

PERCINET *(looking up).* Some fledgling must have hurt itself—(SYLVETTE *sighs.)*—in the branches.

BERGAMIN. At any rate, my boy, after careful consideration, I've settled on a wife for you. *(*PERCINET *walks upstage, whistling.)*

BERGAMIN *(after choking for an instant, follows him).* I'm a stubborn man, sir, and I'll force you to—

*(*PERCINET *returns, whistling.)*

BERGAMIN. Will you stop that whistling, you magpie! . . . The woman I've chosen is still young and she's very rich—a gem of a girl.

**PERCINET.** Who cares about your gem!

**BERGAMIN.** Just you wait! I'll show you, you scamp. . . .

**PERCINET** (*pushing back his father's raised cane*). Spring has filled the bushes with the fluttering of wings, Father, and near the forest brooks tiny birds swoop down as loving couples. . . .

**BERGAMIN.** You're indecent!

**PERCINET.** All creatures are blithely welcoming April. The butterflies—

**BERGAMIN.** You rascal!

**PERCINET.** —are flocking through the countryside to marry all the flowers that they love! . . . Love—

**BERGAMIN.** You villain!

**PERCINET.** —is making all hearts blossom. . . . And you expect me to marry for money!

**BERGAMIN.** Of course, you little cur!

**PERCINET** (*in a vibrant voice*). Well, then, no, Father, no! I swear—by this wall—I hope it can hear me—that my marriage will be more romantic than the wildest romance in any of the old romances. (*He dashes away.*)

**BERGAMIN** (*running after him*). Oh, when I catch him!

(*Exeunt.*)

**SYLVETTE** (*alone*). Honestly, now I understand why Daddy hates that nasty old—

**PASQUINOT** (*entering left*). Well, what are you doing here, young lady?

**SYLVETTE.** Nothing. Just strolling about.

**PASQUINOT.** Here! All by yourself? Why, you silly thing! . . . Aren't you afraid?

**SYLVETTE.** I'm not the nervous kind.

**PASQUINOT.** All by yourself near that wall! . . . Didn't I order you never to go near it? You foolhardy child, just take a good look at that park: it's the lair of my old mortal enemy—

**SYLVETTE.** I know, Father.

**PASQUINOT.** And yet you deliberately expose yourself to insults, or even . . . ? There's no telling what those people are capable of! If that wretched neighbor of mine or his son knew that my daughter comes all alone to this arbor to daydream—Oh! It makes me shiver just to think of it. Why, I'll cover that wall with armor, I'll bard it, I'll caparison it.[7] I'll put a row of spikes on top to impale any invader, to disembowel anyone trying to climb over it, to slash anyone who even comes near it!

**SYLVETTE.** He'll never do it; it would cost too much. Daddy's a bit stingy.

**PASQUINOT.** Get back in the house—and quickly!

(*She exits; he stares after her angrily.*)

**BERGAMIN** (*in the wings*). Take this letter to *Monsieur* Straforel immediately.

**PASQUINOT** (*dashes over to the wall and climbs up*). Bergamin!

**BERGAMIN** (*following suit*). Pasquinot!

(*They embrace.*)

**PASQUINOT.** How *are* you?

**BERGAMIN.** Not bad.

**PASQUINOT.** How's your gout?

**BERGAMIN.** Better. And how's your head cold?

**PASQUINOT.** The thing won't go away.

**BERGAMIN.** Well, the marriage is settled!

**PASQUINOT.** What?

**BERGAMIN.** I was hidden in the foliage and I heard everything. They're madly in love.

**PASQUINOT.** Wonderful!

**BERGAMIN.** Now, we've got to bring matters to a head! (*Rubbing his hands*) Ha! Ha! Both of us widowers, and fathers to boot. My son had a slightly overromantic mother who named him Percinet.

**PASQUINOT.** Yes, it does sound grotesque.

**BERGAMIN.** And your daughter Sylvette is a daydreaming little maid from school, with an ethereal soul. What was our sole aim?

**PASQUINOT.** To tear down the wall.

---

7. *bard it . . . caparison it,* drape it with leather armor and other ornamental trappings, as one would cover a horse before riding into battle.

BERGAMIN. To live together—

PASQUINOT. And merge our two estates into one.

BERGAMIN. A scheme of old friends—

PASQUINOT. And landowners.

BERGAMIN. How could we do it?

PASQUINOT. If our children married each other.

BERGAMIN. Exactly! But could we have succeeded if they had so much as suspected our wishes and our agreement? A prearranged marriage is not very enticing for two young poetic canaries. Which is why, taking advantage of their living far away, we hushed up our matrimonial plans. But then, his boarding school and her convent came to an end this year. I thought that if we prevented them from meeting they'd be sure to seek one another out and fall in love surreptitiously and sinfully. And so I concocted this marvelous hatred! . . . Remember, you were worried that such an extraordinary plan might not succeed? Well, now all we have to do is give our consent.

PASQUINOT. Fine! But how? How can we be foxy to say "Yes" without arousing their suspicions? After all, I called you a wretch, an idiot—

BERGAMIN. An idiot? "Wretch" would have been enough. Don't say any more than you have to.

PASQUINOT. Yes, but what pretext can we use? . . .

BERGAMIN. Listen! Your daughter herself gave me the idea. As she spoke, my plan for a final stratagem took shape. They're meeting here tonight. Percinet is coming first. The moment Sylvette appears, men in black will burst out of hiding and seize her. She'll scream, and my young hero will leap upon the kidnappers and attack them with his sword. They'll pretend to flee, you turn up suddenly, so do I, your daughter and her honor will be safe and sound, you're overjoyed, you shed a few tears and bless the rescuing hero, I relent: tableau and curtain!

PASQUINOT. Why, that's brilliant! . . . That's absolutely brilliant. . . .

BERGAMIN (modestly). Well, yes . . . if I do say so myself. Hush! Look who's coming! It's Straforel, the famous bravo. I just dropped him a line about my project. He's the one who's going to stage our kidnapping.

(STRAFOREL, gorgeously bedizened as a bravo, appears upstage and moves forward majestically.)

BERGAMIN (descending from the wall and bowing). Ahem! First of all, may I introduce my friend Pasquinot. . . .

STRAFOREL (bowing). Monsieur . . .

(Upon straightening up, he is astonished not to see PASQUINOT.)

BERGAMIN (pointing to PASQUINOT astride the wall). There he is, on the wall.

STRAFOREL (aside). An amazing exercise for a man of his years!

BERGAMIN. What do you think of my plan, Straforel?

STRAFOREL. There'll be no problems.

BERGAMIN. Good; you know how to grasp things quickly and act swiftly—

STRAFOREL. And hold my tongue.

BERGAMIN. A make-believe abduction and a sham swordfight, have you got that?

STRAFOREL. It's all clear.

BERGAMIN. Use skillful swordsmen who won't wound my little boy. I love him. He's my only child.

STRAFOREL. I'll attend to the operation personally.

BERGAMIN. Excellent. In that case, I needn't worry. . . .

PASQUINOT (in a low voice to BERGAMIN). Listen, ask him how much it's going to cost us.

BERGAMIN. How much do you charge for an abduction, Monsieur Straforel?

STRAFOREL. It all depends on what's involved, Monsieur. And the prices vary accordingly. But I gather that you don't care about the expense. So if I were you, Monsieur, I'd take a—first-class abduction!

BERGAMIN. Oh! You've got more than one class?

STRAFOREL. Why of course, *Monsieur!* We offer an abduction with two men in black; a commonplace abduction by carriage—it's one of our least popular items. A midnight abduction. A daytime abduction. A pomp-and-circumstance abduction, by royal coach, with powdered and bewigged lackeys—there's an extra charge for the wigs—and with mutes, Moors, sbirri, brigands, musketeers[8]—all included in the price! Then we offer an abduction by post chaise, two horses, or three, four, five—as many as you like. A discreet abduction in a berlin coach—it's a bit somber. Then a humorous abduction, in a sack. A romantic abduction by boat—except we'd need a lake! A Venetian abduction by gondola—but we'd have to have a canal! An abduction by the dark of the moon—moonlight is so much in demand nowadays that the cost is slightly higher! A sinister abduction with flashes of lightning, stamping of feet, screams and shouts, dueling, clash of swords, wide-brimmed hats, and gray cloaks. A brutal abduction. A polite abduction. A torchlight abduction—it's very lovely! A so-called classical abduction in masks. A gallant abduction, to a musical accompaniment. An abduction by sedan chair,[9] the gayest, the most modern, *Monsieur*, and by far the most distinguished!

BERGAMIN (*scratching his head*, to PASQUINOT). Well, what do you think?

PASQUINOT. Uh . . . I don't know, what do you think?

BERGAMIN. I think we've got to overwhelm their imagination! Money can be no object! . . . We need a bit of everything! . . . Let's have—

STRAFOREL. Everything! Why not?

BERGAMIN. Give us something memorable for our young romancers. A sedan chair, cloaks, torches, music, masks!

STRAFOREL (*jotting down notes in a memo book*).

To combine these diverse elements, we'll have a first-class abduction—with all the trimmings.

BERGAMIN. Wonderful!

STRAFOREL. I'll be back soon. (*Pointing to* PASQUINOT) But he'll have to leave the gate to his park ajar. . . .

BERGAMIN. He will, don't worry.

STRAFOREL (*bowing*). Gentlemen, I wish you the very best! (*Before exiting*) A first-class abduction with all the paraphernalia. (*Exit.*)

PASQUINOT. Off he goes, a gentleman and a scholar, with his high-and-mighty manner . . . and he didn't even set the price.

BERGAMIN. Never mind, the whole thing's settled! We're going to knock down the wall and have only one home.

PASQUINOT. And during the winter, only one rent to pay in town.

BERGAMIN. We'll do entrancing things in the park!

PASQUINOT. We'll trim the yew trees!

BERGAMIN. We'll gravel the paths.

PASQUINOT. In the middle of each flower bed, we'll intertwine our monograms in floral calligraphy!

BERGAMIN. And since this greenery is a bit too severe—

PASQUINOT. We'll brighten it up with decorations!

BERGAMIN. We'll have fish in a brand-new pond!

PASQUINOT. We'll have a fountain with a stone egg dancing on the peak of the spray! We'll have a mass of rock! What do you think of that!

BERGAMIN. All our wishes are coming true.

PASQUINOT. We'll grow old together.

BERGAMIN. And your daughter's provided for.

---

8. *mutes, Moors, sbirri* (sbē′rē), *brigands, musketeers*, all mentioned here as attendants and helpers. Moors are Moslems from northwestern Africa; sbirri are police officers from Italy; brigands are highway robbers; musketeers are soldiers armed with muskets.
9. *sedan chair*, a covered chair for one person, carried on poles by two bearers.

PASQUINOT. And so is your son.

BERGAMIN. Ah, good old Pasquinot!

PASQUINOT. Ah, good old Bergamin!

(SYLVETTE and PERCINET suddenly enter on their respective sides.)

SYLVETTE (seeing her father holding BERGAMIN). Oh!

BERGAMIN (to PASQUINOT, upon noticing SYLVETTE). Your daughter.

PERCINET (seeing his father holding PASQUINOT). Oh!

PASQUINOT (to BERGAMIN, upon noticing PERCINET). Your son!

BERGAMIN (sotto voce[10] to PASQUINOT). Let's fight. (They turn their hug into a scuffle.) You blackguard!

PASQUINOT. You wretch!

SYLVETTE (pulling at her father's coattails). Daddy! . . .

PERCINET (pulling at his father's coattails). Dad! . . .

BERGAMIN. Leave us alone, you little brats.

PASQUINOT. He started it; he insulted me!

BERGAMIN. He hit me!

PASQUINOT. Coward!

SYLVETTE. Daddy!

BERGAMIN. Swindler!

PERCINET. Dad!!

PASQUINOT. Robber!

SYLVETTE. Daddy!!

(The children manage to separate them.)

PERCINET (dragging his father off). Let's go home; it's getting late.

BERGAMIN (trying to come back). I'm in a towering rage!

(PERCINET takes him away.)

PASQUINOT (likewise with SYLVETTE). I'm boiling!

SYLVETTE. It's getting cool out. Think of your rheumatism!

(All exeunt.)

(Twilight is beginning to set in. The stage is empty for a moment. Then STRAFOREL and his SWORDSMEN, MUSICIANS, et al., enter the park.)

STRAFOREL. There's already one star out in the clear sky; the day is dying. . . . (He places his men in their positions.) You stay there. . . . And you, here. . . . And you, over there. Evening Mass will be starting any moment. She'll appear as soon as the bell rings, and then I'll whistle. . . . (He looks at the moon.) The moon? . . . Wonderful! We won't omit a single effect tonight! (Looking at the extravagant cloaks of his bravos) The cloaks are excellent! . . . Let them ride a bit more on the rapiers: bear down on the hilts. (A sedan chair is brought in.) Put the chair over here, in the shade. (Staring at the chairmen) Ah! The Moors! Not bad at all! (Speaking into the wings) Don't forget to bring out the torches when I signal. (The back of the stage is tinged with the dim pink reflections of the torches from behind the trees. The MUSICIANS enter.) The musicians? There, against a background of rosy light. (He positions them upstage.) Grace, tenderness! Vary your poses! Will the mandolinist please stand up, and the violinist sit down! Just as in Watteau's Rustic Concert![11] (In a severe tone, to a bravo) Masked man, number one: stop slouching! Is that what you call bearing?—Fine.—Instruments, con sordini![12] Please tune up. . . . Very good! Sol, mi, sol. (He puts on his mask.)

PERCINET (enters slowly. As he declaims the following lines, the night grows darker and the stars emerge). My father's calmed down. . . . I've managed to come here. . . . The twilight is settling. . . . The air is redolent with the heady fragrance of the elder trees. . . . The gray shadows are making the flowers close.

10. *sotto voce* (sot′ō vō′chē), in a low tone.
11. *Watteau's Rustic Concert*, a painting by French artist Jean Antoine Watteau, 1684–1721.
12. *con sordini*, (kon sôr dē′nē), (in music) used to indicate a softening or muffling of sound. [*Italian*]

STRAFOREL (*sotto voce to the violins*). Music! (*The* MUSICIANS *play softly until the end of the act.*)

PERCINET. I'm trembling like a reed. What's wrong with me? . . . She'll be here soon!

STRAFOREL (*to the* MUSICIANS). Amoroso![13] . . .

PERCINET. This is my first evening rendezvous. . . . Oh! I feel faint! . . . The breeze is rustling like a silken gown. . . . I can't see the flowers anymore . . . there are tears in my eyes. . . . I can't see the flowers . . . but I can smell their fragrance! Oh! That tall tree with a star on top! . . . But who's playing here? The night has come—

Now old desire doth in his deathbed lie,
And young affection gapes to be his heir;
That fair for which love groaned for and would
  die,
With tender Juliet matched, is now not fair.
Now Romeo is beloved and loves again,
Alike bewitched by the charm of looks;
But to his foe supposed he must complain,
And she steal love's sweet bait from fearful hooks.
Being held a foe, he may not have access
To breathe such vows as lovers use to swear,
And she as much in love, her means much less
To meet her new belovèd anywhere;
But passion lends them power, time means, to meet,
Temp'ring extremities with extreme sweet.

(*A bell peals in the distance.*)

SYLVETTE (*appearing at the sound of the bell*). The bell! He must be waiting. (*A whistle.* STRAFOREL *looms up before her; the torches appear.*) Oh! (*The bravos seize her and thrust her into the sedan chair.*) Help!

PERCINET. Good lord!

SYLVETTE. Percinet, I'm being abducted!

PERCINET. I'm coming. (*He leaps over the wall, draws his sword, and fences with a few of the bravos.*) Take that . . . and that . . . and that.

STRAFOREL (*to the* MUSICIANS). Tremolo![14] (*The violins surge up in a dramatic tremolo. The bravos dash off.* STRAFOREL, *in a theatrical voice*)

Zounds! That lad's a devil! (*Duel between* STRAFOREL *and* PERCINET. STRAFOREL *clutches his chest.*) That blow . . . is mortal. (*He falls.*)

PERCINET (*running over to* SYLVETTE). Sylvette! (*Tableau. She is in the sedan chair, he is kneeling beside her.*)

SYLVETTE. My hero!

PASQUINOT (*appearing*). Bergamin's son a hero? Your rescuer? . . . Let me shake his hand.

SYLVETTE *and* PERCINET. Oh joy!

(BERGAMIN *enters on his side, followed by torch-bearing servants.*)

PASQUINOT (*to* BERGAMIN, *who appears on top of the wall*). Bergamin, your son is a hero! . . . Let's put an end to our feud and make our children happy!

BERGAMIN (*solemnly*). My hatred is allayed.

PERCINET. Sylvette, we must be dreaming. Sylvette, speak low, or else the sound of our voices will awaken us! . . .

BERGAMIN. Hatred always ends in a wedding. Peace is upon us. (*Pointing to the wall*) Down with the Pyrenees![15]

PERCINET. Who would have dreamed that my father could change?

SYLVETTE (*naïvely*). Didn't I tell you it would all work out in the end?

(*As the lovers go upstage with* PASQUINOT, STRAFOREL *rises and hands* BERGAMIN *a slip of paper.*)

BERGAMIN (*in a low voice*). What? What's this piece of paper with your signature on it?

STRAFOREL (*bowing*). Monsieur, this is my bill. (*He drops back to the ground.*)

---

13. *Amoroso* (ä mə rō′sō), loving, fond; (in music) perform lyrically and romantically. [*Italian*]
14. *Tremolo* (trem′əlō), a rapid repetition of musical notes, causing a trembling or vibrating effect.
15. *Pyrenees* (pir′ə nēz′), the wall is compared to the Pyrenees, a mountain range between France and Spain.

## THINK AND DISCUSS
### Understanding
1. What is happening as *The Romancers* begins?
2. What do we quickly discover about the relationship of Percinet and Sylvette?
3. At what point in the play does the audience know that the fathers are not sworn enemies? Do the son and daughter also know at this point?

### Analyzing
4. Early in the play, Sylvette and Percinet speak in an elevated, poetic style similar to the lines from *Romeo and Juliet*. For example, Sylvette refers to the quarreling fathers by saying, "Perhaps the time's at hand when Heaven will use us to wipe out their hatred." What does their style of speaking reveal about their relationship?
5. As Sylvette and Percinet ponder their situation Sylvette can see "five or six highly possible solutions." Describe the three solutions she actually proposes.
6. Do Sylvette's solutions seem realistic? Why or why not?
7. In what way does Sylvette's final solution become different from the others?
8. Who sees the wall as more of a barrier to the progress of the love relationship—Sylvette and Percinet themselves, or their fathers? Explain.
9. Which elements of the abductions that Straforel proposes may be difficult or impossible for him to furnish?
10. What effect is achieved by closing the play with Straforel giving Bergamin the bill?

### Extending
11. Is Straforel best described as a practical realist, an idealistic romantic, or a combination of the two? Defend your answer.
12. In your opinion, who are "the romancers" of the title? Discuss.

## APPLYING: Inference H⃥⃥
### See Handbook of Literary Terms, p. 803
When we read a literary work, we know much more than we are told directly. In addition to facts that we take in directly, we deduce or **infer** others through clues, suggestions, or hints. Such inferences are important in the reading process. In *The Romancers*, we seem to learn by inference about Sylvette and Percinet's feelings before they reveal them to each other.

1. *The Romancers* opens with Sylvette listening to Percinet read *Romeo and Juliet;* what might we infer from her opening speech: "Oh! *Monsieur* Percinet, how beautiful!"
2. What might we infer when Sylvette cuts Percinet off from reading about Romeo's death by exclaiming (in her third speech): "Oh no! I don't want him to talk about that! If he does, I'll start crying. . . ."?

## VOCABULARY
### Synonyms, Antonyms
Check the meaning of each numbered word below in the Glossary. Then from the lists that follow, choose first a synonym (a word that means the same) and then an antonym (a word that means the opposite) for each italicized word. Write each set of three words. You will not use all the words.

1. *insolent;* 2. *poignant;* 3. *diverse;* 4. *lithe;* 5. *redolent.*

| | | | |
|---|---|---|---|
| varied | jealous | rude | unfelt |
| fragrant | supple | similar | stiff |
| intense | odorless | courteous | attractive |

## THINKING SKILLS
### Generalizing

To **generalize** is to draw general conclusions from particular examples. *The Romancers* presents fathers who contrive to promote their children's romance. The parents of Romeo and Juliet try to keep their children apart. How do you think plays, stories, songs, and narratives generally portray parents' involvement in the lives of their adolescent children? Help your class prepare a list of literary works, popular entertainments such as movies, and songs about young people whose parents are involved in their decisions, for good or ill.

## COMPOSITION ◁━▪
### Reading/Writing Log

There are many comic elements in *The Romancers,* and the "voices" used by Edmond Rostand and his characters enhance the humor. Rostand's first stage direction, for example, does not employ the normally straightforward tone of a note describing a play's setting. Instead, Rostand uses the direction to poke gentle fun at his own play. Refer to the play to answer the following questions. If you are keeping a reading/writing log, write your answers under the heading, "Writer's Craft: Use a Voice That Suits the Purpose."

1. What does Rostand say about setting in the stage direction following the cast of characters at the beginning of the play?
2. This stage direction is seen only by readers such as the director and performers, not by a theater audience. How might this humorous stage direction affect the attitudes of these readers as they prepare a production?
3. Often the characters in the play are speaking quite seriously, yet their speeches are funny to the audience that knows secrets not shared by the characters. What two speeches can you find that illustrate the comic effect of

dialogue involving characters speaking in serious voices? (You might look at the scene in which the fathers pretend to fight when the young lovers arrive unexpectedly and the scene in which the abduction is planned.)

### Creating a Comical Voice

Make up a character and a setting designed to add humor to a monologue by your character. Write both a stage direction that sets the scene and the monologue, a speech by one character alone. Your setting may contain another person, beast, or hazard unseen by the character. See "Developing Your Style" in the Writer's Handbook.

### Analyzing a Comic Scene

Write a two-paragraph essay in which you analyze the comedy in any scene from *The Romancers.* Remember that the dramatist used serious and cheerful character voices, secrets unkown to some characters, and other techniques to achieve or intensify a humorous effect. Your writing should use a serious voice as you point out comic elements. See "Writing About Drama" in the Writer's Handbook.

## ENRICHMENT
### Performing a Scene

With other students, plan a read-aloud performance of the episode early in the play in which Bergamin surprises his son Percinet as he is talking over the wall in the garden with Sylvette. There are *asides* in which a character speaks directly to the audience and whispered conversations that can be quite funny but challenging for actors. Conclude the scene with the exit of Bergamin.

Cast the three parts and rehearse the scene, deciding jointly with the actors how it is to be read to the class so as to highlight the comedy. Before the reading, explain to the class what it must imagine in the way of stage set and props. You might use two stepladders facing each other, one on either side of the imaginary wall.

## BIOGRAPHY

### Edmond Rostand

### 1868–1918

When Edmond Rostand began writing for the theater in the 1890s, most dramatists were producing somber works about the realities and difficulties of modern life. Rostand's romantic liveliness and vague optimism offered a refreshing alternative.

Born in Marseilles, France, Rostand studied to be a lawyer, but abandoned that career in 1890 when he published a small volume of poems. In that same year he wrote *The Romancers*, which was immediately successful. Later he tried to add more acts to the play, but the expanded form never achieved popularity. It was the original version that served as the inspiration for the popular musical *The Fantasticks*, a comedy that set records as one of New York's longest-running plays.

Rostand's best-known work is *Cyrano de Bergerac* (sir′ə nō′ də bèr′zhə-rak′), a comedy set in the seventeenth century about a young man with an enormous nose. Though Rostand wrote poetry and other plays, he never equaled the success of *Cyrano* and *The Romancers*.

# Comment

## The Romantic Comedy

A romantic comedy may be defined as a play that features love as the central motivating force and that ends happily once the lovers have overcome all the obstacles to their love. Such a play is *The Romancers*.

Shakespeare's *Romeo and Juliet* is a tragedy in which the two lovers die. Had the play ended happily, however, it would have been a romantic comedy. Clearly *The Romancers* has been patterned after Shakespeare's play, but the plot is reversed. Instead of the families of the lovers scheming to keep the two apart, they scheme to bring them together by pretending to want to keep them apart. And the lovers finally "live happily ever after"—as they must in romantic comedy.

*The Romancers*, however, must be considered a romantic comedy with a difference. The flowery language and ridiculous plot complications, compared as they are with more serious works involving lovers like *Romeo and Juliet* and Don Rodrigo and Ximene of the play *The Cid*, make clear that the writer not only knows the romantic comedy form; he also is poking gentle fun at it. Early in the play, a trite abduction plot is described by Sylvette; then it is painstakingly enacted with showy display. As a result, the action of the play seems to mock the conventional action of the traditional romantic comedy. We laugh as much at a play that makes fun of itself—or of its genre—as at the comic characters and events.

**HT** See FLASHBACK in the Handbook of Literary Terms, page 798.

# Our Town

**Thornton Wilder**   USA

---

## CHARACTERS *(in the order of their appearance)*

| | | |
|---|---|---|
| STAGE MANAGER | WALLY WEBB | MRS. SOAMES |
| DR. GIBBS | EMILY WEBB | CONSTABLE WARREN |
| JOE CROWELL, JR. | PROFESSOR WILLARD | SI CROWELL |
| HOWIE NEWSOME | MR. WEBB | THREE BASEBALL PLAYERS |
| MRS. GIBBS | WOMAN IN THE BALCONY | SAM CRAIG |
| MRS. WEBB | MAN IN THE AUDITORIUM | JOE STODDARD |
| GEORGE GIBBS | LADY IN THE BOX | |
| REBECCA GIBBS | SIMON STIMSON | |

*The entire play takes place in Grover's Corners, New Hampshire.*

---

# ACT ONE

*No curtain.*

*No scenery.*

*The audience, arriving, sees an empty stage in half-light.*

*Presently the* STAGE MANAGER, *hat on and pipe in mouth, enters and begins placing a table and three chairs downstage left, and a table and three chairs downstage right. He also places a low bench at the corner of what will be the Webb house, left.*

*"Left" and "right" are from the point of view of the actor facing the audience. "Up" is toward the back wall.*

*As the house lights go down he has finished setting the stage and leaning against the right proscenium pillar watches the late arrivals in the audience.*

---

*When the auditorium is in complete darkness he speaks:*

STAGE MANAGER. This play is called *Our Town*. It was written by Thornton Wilder; produced and directed by A. . . . (or: produced by A. . . . ; directed by B. . . .). In it you will see Miss C. . . ; Miss D. . . . ; Miss E. . . . ; and Mr. F. . . . ; Mr. G. . . . ; Mr. H. . . . ; and many others. The name of the town is Grover's Corners, New Hampshire—just across the Massachusetts line: latitude 42 degrees 40 minutes; longitude 70 degrees 37 minutes. The First Act shows a day in our town. The day is May 7, 1901. The time is just before dawn. (*A rooster crows.*) The sky is beginning to show some streaks of light over in the East there, behind our mount'in. The morning star always gets wonderful bright the minute before it has to go—doesn't it? (*He stares at it for a moment, then goes upstage.*)

Well, I'd better show you how our town lies. Up here—(*That is: parallel with the back wall*) is Main Street. Way back there is the railway station; tracks go that way. Polish Town's across the tracks, and some Canuck[1] families. (*Toward the left*) Over there is the Congregational Church; across the street's the Presbyterian. Methodist and Unitarian are over there. Baptist is down in the holla' by the river. Catholic Church is over beyond the tracks. Here's the Town Hall and Post Office combined; jail's in the basement. Bryan[2] once made a speech from these very steps here. Along here's a row of stores. Hitching posts and horse blocks in front of them. First automobile's going to come along in about five years—belonged to Banker Cartwright, our richest citizen . . . lives in the big white house up on the hill. Here's the grocery store and here's Mr. Morgan's drugstore. Most everybody in town manages to look into those two stores once a day. Public School's over yonder. High

The STAGE MANAGER, played by Tom Jones, in the musical *Grover's Corners*, based on *Our Town*.

School's still farther over. Quarter of nine mornings, noontimes, and three o'clock afternoons, the hull town can hear the yelling and screaming from those schoolyards. (*He approaches the table and chairs downstage right.*) This our doctor's house—Doc Gibbs's. This is the back door. (*Two arched trellises, covered with vines and flowers, are pushed out, one by each proscenium pillar.*) There's some scenery for those who think they have to have scenery. This is Mrs. Gibbs's garden. Corn . . . peas . . . beans . . . hollyhocks . . . heliotrope . . . and a lot of burdock. (*Crosses the stage*) In those days our newspaper come out twice a week— the Grover's Corners *Sentinel*—and this is Editor Webb's house. And this is Mrs. Webb's garden. Just like Mrs. Gibbs's, only it's got a

---

1. *Polish Town's . . . Canuck families,* references to a neighborhood populated by Polish-Americans and Canadian families. *Canuck* (kə nuk′) means "Canadian." [Slang]
2. *Bryan,* William Jennings Bryan, 1860–1925, American political leader and orator.

lot of sunflowers, too. (*He looks upward, center stage.*) Right here . . . 's a big butternut tree. (*He returns to his place by the right proscenium pillar and looks at the audience for a minute.*)

Nice town, y'know what I mean? Nobody very remarkable ever come out of it, s'far as we know. The earliest tombstones in the cemetery up there on the mountain say 1670–1680—they're Grovers and Cartwrights and Gibbses and Herseys—same names as are around here now. Well, as I said: it's about dawn. The only lights on in town are in a cottage over by the tracks where a Polish mother's just had twins. And in the Joe Crowell house, where Joe Junior's getting up so as to deliver the paper. And in the depot, where Shorty Hawkins is gettin' ready to flag the 5:45 for Boston. (*A train whistle is heard. The* STAGE MANAGER *takes out his watch and nods.*) Naturally, out in the country—all around—there've been lights on for some time, what with milkin's and so on. But town people sleep late.

So—another day's begun. There's Doc Gibbs comin' down Main Street now, comin' back from that baby case. And here's his wife comin' downstairs to get breakfast.

(MRS. GIBBS, *a plump, pleasant woman in the middle thirties, comes "downstairs" right. She pulls up an imaginary window shade in her kitchen and starts to make a fire in her stove.*)

Doc Gibbs died in 1930. The new hospital's named after him. Mrs. Gibbs died first—long time ago, in fact. She went out to visit her daughter, Rebecca, who married an insurance man in Canton, Ohio, and died there—pneumonia—but her body was brought back here. She's up in the cemetery there now—in with a whole mess of Gibbses and Herseys—she was Julia Hersey 'fore she married Doc Gibbs in the Congregational Church over there. In our town we like to know the facts about everybody. There's Mrs. Webb, coming downstairs to get

her breakfast, too.—That's Doc Gibbs. Got that call at half-past one this morning. And there comes Joe Crowell, Jr., delivering Mr. Webb's *Sentinel*.

(DR. GIBBS *has been coming along Main Street from the left. At the point where he would turn to approach his house, he stops, sets down his—imaginary—black bag, takes off his hat, and rubs his face with fatigue, using an enormous handkerchief.*

MRS. WEBB, *a thin, serious, crisp woman, has entered her kitchen, left, tying on an apron. She goes through the motions of putting wood into a stove, lighting it, and preparing breakfast.*

*Suddenly,* JOE CROWELL, JR., *eleven, starts down Main Street from the right, hurling imaginary newspapers into doorways.*)

JOE CROWELL, JR. Morning, Doc Gibbs.

DR. GIBBS. Morning, Joe.

JOE CROWELL, JR. Somebody been sick, Doc?

DR. GIBBS. No. Just some twins born over in Polish Town.

JOE CROWELL, JR. Do you want your paper now?

DR. GIBBS. Yes, I'll take it.—Anything serious goin' on in the world since Wednesday?

JOE CROWELL, JR. Yessir. My schoolteacher, Miss Foster, 's getting married to a fella over in Concord.

DR. GIBBS. I declare.—How do you boys feel about that?

JOE CROWELL, JR. Well, of course, it's none of my business—but I think if a person starts out to be a teacher, she ought to stay one.

DR. GIBBS. How's your knee, Joe?

JOE CROWELL, JR. Fine, Doc, I never think about it at all. Only like you said, it always tells me when it's going to rain.

DR. GIBBS. What's it telling you today? Goin' to rain?

JOE CROWELL, JR. No, sir.

DR. GIBBS. Sure?

JOE CROWELL, JR. Yessir.

DR. GIBBS. Knee ever make a mistake?

JOE CROWELL, JR. No, sir. (JOE *goes off.* DR. GIBBS *stands reading his paper.*)

STAGE MANAGER. Want to tell you something about that boy Joe Crowell there. Joe was awful bright—graduated from high school here, head of his class. So he got a scholarship to Massachusetts Tech. Graduated head of his class there, too. It was all wrote up in the Boston paper at the time. Goin' to be a great engineer, Joe was. But the war broke out and he died in France.—All that education for nothing.

HOWIE NEWSOME (*off left*). Giddap, Bessie! What's the matter with you today?

STAGE MANAGER. Here comes Howie Newsome, deliverin' the milk.

(HOWIE NEWSOME, *about thirty, in overalls, comes along Main Street from the left, walking beside an invisible horse and wagon and carrying an imaginary rack with milk bottles. The sound of clinking milk bottles is heard. He leaves some bottles at* MRS. WEBB's *trellis, then, crossing the stage to* MRS. GIBBS's, *he stops center to talk to* DR. GIBBS.)

HOWIE NEWSOME. Morning, Doc.

DR. GIBBS. Morning, Howie.

HOWIE NEWSOME. Somebody sick?

DR. GIBBS. Pair of twins over to Mrs. Goruslawski's.

HOWIE NEWSOME. Twins, eh? This town's gettin' bigger every year.

DR. GIBBS. Goin' to rain, Howie?

HOWIE NEWSOME. No, no. Fine day—that'll burn through. Come on, Bessie.

DR. GIBBS. Hello, Bessie. (*He strokes the horse, which has remained up center.*) How old is she, Howie?

HOWIE NEWSOME. Going on seventeen. Bessie's all mixed up about the route ever since the Lockharts stopped takin' their quart of milk every day. She wants to leave 'em a quart just the same—keeps scolding me the hull trip.

(*He reaches* MRS. GIBBS's *back door. She is waiting for him.*)

MRS. GIBBS. Good morning, Howie.

HOWIE NEWSOME. Morning, Mrs. Gibbs. Doc's just comin' down the street.

MRS. GIBBS. Is he? Seems like you're late today.

HOWIE NEWSOME. Yes. Somep'n went wrong with the separator. Don't know what 'twas. (*He passes* DR. GIBBS *up center.*) Doc!

DR. GIBBS. Howie!

MRS. GIBBS (*calling upstairs*). Children! Children! Time to get up.

HOWIE NEWSOME. Come on, Bessie! (*He goes off right.*)

MRS. GIBBS. George! Rebecca!

(DR. GIBBS *arrives at his back door and passes through the trellis into his house.*)

MRS. GIBBS. Everything all right, Frank?

DR. GIBBS. Yes. I declare—easy as kittens.

MRS. GIBBS. Bacon'll be ready in a minute. Set down and drink your coffee. You can catch a couple hours' sleep this morning, can't you?

DR. GIBBS. Hm! . . . Mrs. Wentworth's coming at eleven. Guess I know what it's about, too. Her stummick ain't what it ought to be.

MRS. GIBBS. All told, you won't get more'n three hours' sleep. Frank Gibbs, I don't know what's goin' to become of you. I do wish I could get you to go away someplace and take a rest. I think it would do you good.

MRS. WEBB. Emileeee! Time to get up! Wally! Seven o'clock!

MRS. GIBBS. I declare, you got to speak to George. Seems like something's come over him lately. He's no help to me at all. I can't even get him to cut me some wood.

DR. GIBBS (*washing and drying his hands at the sink.* MRS. GIBBS *is busy at the stove*). Is he sassy to you?

MRS. GIBBS. No. He just whines! All he thinks about is that baseball—George! Rebecca! You'll be late for school.

DR. GIBBS. M-m-m . . .

MRS. GIBBS. George!

DR. GIBBS. George, look sharp!

GEORGE'S VOICE. Yes, Pa!

DR. GIBBS (*as he goes off the stage*). Don't you hear your mother calling you? I guess I'll go upstairs and get forty winks.

MRS. WEBB. Walleee! Emileee! You'll be late for school! Walleee! You wash yourself good or I'll come up and do it myself.

REBECCA GIBBS'S VOICE. Ma! What dress shall I wear?

MRS. GIBBS. Don't make a noise. Your father's been out all night and needs his sleep. I washed and ironed the blue gingham for you special.

REBECCA. Ma, I hate that dress.

MRS. GIBBS. Oh, hush-up-with-you.

REBECCA. Every day I go to school dressed like a sick turkey.

MRS. GIBBS. Now, Rebecca, you always look *very* nice.

REBECCA. Mama, George's throwing soap at me.

MRS. GIBBS. I'll come and slap the both of you— that's what I'll do.

(*A factory whistle sounds. The* CHILDREN *dash in and take their places at the tables. Right,* GEORGE, *about sixteen, and* REBECCA, *eleven. Left,* EMILY *and* WALLY, *same ages. They carry strapped schoolbooks.*)

STAGE MANAGER. We've got a factory in our town too—hear it? Makes blankets. Cartwrights own it and it brung 'em a fortune.

MRS. WEBB. Children! Now I won't have it. Breakfast is just as good as any other meal and I won't have you gobbling like wolves. It'll stunt your growth—that's a fact. Put away your book, Wally.

WALLY. Aw, Ma! By ten o'clock I got to know all about Canada.

MRS. WEBB. You know the rule's well as I do—no books at table. As for me, I'd rather have my children healthy than bright.

EMILY. I'm both, Mama: you know I am. I'm the brightest girl in school for my age. I have a wonderful memory.

MRS. WEBB. Eat your breakfast.

WALLY. I'm bright, too, when I'm looking at my stamp collection.

MRS. GIBBS. I'll speak to your father about it when he's rested. Seems to me twenty-five cents a week's enough for a boy your age. I declare I don't know how you spend it all.

GEORGE. Aw, Ma—I gotta lotta things to buy.

MRS. GIBBS. Strawberry phosphates—that's what you spend it on.

GEORGE. I don't see how Rebecca comes to have so much money. She has more'n a dollar.

REBECCA (*spoon in mouth, dreamily*). I've been saving it up gradual.

MRS. GIBBS. Well, dear, I think it's a good thing to spend some every now and then.

REBECCA. Mama, do you know what I love most in the world—do you?—Money.

MRS. GIBBS. Eat your breakfast.

THE CHILDREN. Mama, there's first bell.—I gotta hurry.—I don't want any more.—I gotta hurry.

(*The* CHILDREN *rise, seize their books, and dash out through the trellises. They meet, down center, and chattering, walk to Main Street, then turn left. The* STAGE MANAGER *goes off, unobtrusively, right.*)

MRS. WEBB. Walk fast, but you don't have to run. Wally, pull up your pants at the knee. Stand up straight, Emily.

MRS. GIBBS. Tell Miss Foster I send her my best congratulations—can you remember that?

REBECCA. Yes, Ma.

MRS. GIBBS. You look real nice, Rebecca. Pick up your feet.

ALL. Good-by.

(MRS. GIBBS *fills her apron with food for the chickens and comes down to the footlights.*)

MRS. GIBBS. Here, chick, chick, chick. No, go away, you. Go away. Here, chick, chick, chick.

What's the matter with *you?* Fight, fight, fight—that's all you do. Hm . . . *you* don't belong to me. Where'd you come from? *(She shakes her apron.)* Oh, don't be so scared. Nobody's going to hurt you. (MRS. WEBB *is sitting on the bench by her trellis, stringing beans.)* Good morning, Myrtle. How's your cold?

MRS. WEBB. Well, I still get that tickling feeling in my throat. I told Charles I didn't know as I'd go to choir practice tonight. Wouldn't be any use.

MRS. GIBBS. Have you tried singing over your voice?

MRS. WEBB. Yes, but somehow I can't do that and stay on the key. While I'm resting myself I thought I'd string some of these beans.

MRS. GIBBS *(rolling up her sleeves as she crosses the stage for a chat).* Let me help you. Beans have been good this year.

MRS. WEBB. I've decided to put up forty quarts if it kills me. The children say they hate 'em, but I notice they're able to get 'em down all winter. *(Pause. Brief sound of chickens cackling)*

MRS. GIBBS. Now, Myrtle. I've got to tell you something, because if I don't tell somebody I'll burst.

MRS. WEBB. Why, Julia Gibbs!

MRS. GIBBS. Here, give me some more of those beans. Myrtle, did one of those secondhand-furniture men from Boston come to see you last Friday?

MRS. WEBB. No-o.

MRS. GIBBS. Well, he called on me. First I thought he was a patient wantin' to see Dr. Gibbs. 'N he wormed his way into my parlor, and, Myrtle Webb, he offered me three hundred and fifty dollars for Grandmother Wentworth's highboy, as I'm sitting here!

MRS. WEBB. Why, Julia Gibbs!

MRS. GIBBS. He did! That old thing! Why, it was so big I didn't know where to put it and I almost give it to Cousin Hester Wilcox.

MRS. WEBB. Well, you're going to take it, aren't you?

MRS. GIBBS. I don't know.

MRS. WEBB. You don't know—three hundred and fifty dollars! What's come over you?

MRS. GIBBS. Well, if I could get the Doctor to take the money and go away someplace on a real trip, I'd sell it like that.—Y'know, Myrtle, it's been the dream of my life to see Paris, France.—Oh, I don't know. It sounds crazy, I suppose, but for years I've been promising myself that if we ever had the chance—

MRS. WEBB. How does the Doctor feel about it?

MRS. GIBBS. Well, I did beat about the bush a little and said that if I got a legacy—that's the way I put it—I'd make him take me somewhere.

MRS. WEBB. M-m-m . . . What did he say?

MRS. GIBBS. You know how he is. I haven't heard a serious word out of him since I've known him. No, he said, it might make him discontented with Grover's Corners to go traipsin' about Europe; better let well enough alone, he says. Every two years he makes a trip to the battlefields of the Civil War and that's enough treat for anybody, he says.

MRS. WEBB. Well, Mr. Webb just *admires* the way Dr. Gibbs knows everything about the Civil War. Mr. Webb's a good mind to give up Napoleon and move over to the Civil War, only Dr. Gibbs being one of the greatest experts in the country just makes him despair.

MRS. GIBBS. It's a fact! Dr. Gibbs is never so happy as when he's at Antietam or Gettysburg. The times I've walked over those hills, Myrtle, stopping at every bush and pacing it all out, like we were going to buy it.

MRS. WEBB. Well, if that secondhand man's really serious about buyin' it, Julia, you sell it. And then you'll get to see Paris, all right. Just keep droppin' hints from time to time—that's how I got to see the Atlantic Ocean, y'know.

MRS. GIBBS. Oh, I'm sorry I mentioned it. Only it seems to me that once in your life before you die you ought to see a country where they don't talk in English and don't even want to.

(*The* STAGE MANAGER *enters briskly from the right. He tips his hat to the ladies, who nod their heads.*)

STAGE MANAGER. Thank you, ladies. Thank you very much. (MRS. GIBBS *and* MRS. WEBB *gather up their things, return into their homes, and disappear.*) Now we're going to skip a few hours. But first we want a little more information about the town, kind of a scientific account, you might say. So I've asked Professor Willard of our State University to sketch in a few details of our past history here. Is Professor Willard here? (PROFESSOR WILLARD, *a rural savant, pince-nez on a wide satin ribbon, enters from the right with some notes in his hand.*) May I introduce Professor Willard of our State University. A few brief notes, thank you, Professor—unfortunately our time is limited.

PROFESSOR WILLARD. Grover's Corners . . . let me see. . . . Grover's Corners lies on the old Pleistocene granite of the Appalachian range. I may say it's some of the oldest land in the world. We're very proud of that. A shelf of Devonian basalt crosses it with vestiges of Mesozoic[3] shale, and some sandstone outcroppings; but that's all more recent: two hundred, three hundred million years old. Some highly interesting fossils have been found . . . I may say: unique fossils . . . two miles out of town, in Silas Peckham's cow pasture. They can be seen at the museum in our University at any time—that is, at any reasonable time. Shall I read some of Professor Gruber's notes on the meteorological situation—mean precipitation, et cetera?

STAGE MANAGER. Afraid we won't have time for that, Professor. We might have a few words on the history of man here.

PROFESSOR WILLARD. Yes . . . anthropological data: Early Amerindian stock. Cotahatchee[4] tribes . . . no evidence before the tenth century of this era . . . hm . . . now entirely disappeared . . . possible traces in three families. Migration toward the end of the seventeenth century of English brachiocephalic blue-eyed stock . . . for the most part. Since then some Slav and Mediterranean—

STAGE MANAGER. And the population, Professor Willard?

PROFESSOR WILLARD. Within the town limits: 2,640.

STAGE MANAGER. Just a moment, Professor. (*He whispers into the* PROFESSOR'S *ear.*)

PROFESSOR WILLARD. Oh, yes, indeed?—The population, *at the moment*, is 2,642. The Postal District brings in 507 more, making a total of 3,149.—Mortality and birth rates: constant.—By MacPherson's gauge: 6.032.

STAGE MANAGER. Thank you very much, Professor. We're all very much obliged to you, I'm sure.

PROFESSOR WILLARD. Not at all, sir; not at all.

STAGE MANAGER. This way, Professor, and thank you again. (*Exit* PROFESSOR WILLARD.) Now the political and social report: Editor Webb.—Oh, Mr. Webb?

(MRS. WEBB *appears at her back door.*)

MRS. WEBB. He'll be here in a minute. . . . He just cut his hand while he was eatin' an apple.

STAGE MANAGER. Thank you, Mrs. Webb.

MRS. WEBB. Charles! Everybody's waitin'. (*Exit* MRS. WEBB.)

STAGE MANAGER. Mr. Webb is Publisher and Editor of the Grover's Corners *Sentinel*. That's our local paper, y'know.

---

3. *Pleistocene* (plī′stə sēn′) . . . *Devonian* (də vō′nē-ən) . . . *Mesozoic* (mes′ə zō′ik), geological time periods, all predating the emergence of civilized human beings, when granite, basalt, and shale, respectively, were formed.
4. *Amerindian* (am′ə rin′dē ən) . . . *Cotahatchee* (kō′ta-ha′chē). *Amerindian* here refers to American Indians.

(MR. WEBB *enters from his house, pulling on his coat. His finger is bound in a handkerchief.*)

**MR. WEBB.** Well . . . I don't have to tell you that we're run here by a Board of Selectmen.—All males vote at the age of twenty-one. Women vote indirect. We're lower middle class: sprinkling of professional men . . . ten percent illiterate laborers. Politically, we're eighty-six percent Republicans; six percent Democrats; four percent Socialists; rest, indifferent. Religiously, we're eighty-five percent Protestants; twelve percent Catholics; rest, indifferent.

**STAGE MANAGER.** Have you any comments, Mr. Webb?

**MR. WEBB.** Very ordinary town, if you ask me. Little better behaved than most. Probably a lot duller. But our young people here seem to like it well enough. Ninety percent of 'em graduating from high school settle down right here to live—even when they've been away to college.

**STAGE MANAGER.** Now, is there anyone in the audience who would like to ask Editor Webb anything about the town?

**WOMAN IN THE BALCONY.** Is there much drinking in Grover's Corners?

**MR. WEBB.** Well, ma'am, I wouldn't know what you'd call *much*. Satiddy nights the farmhands meet down in Ellery Greenough's[5] stable and holler some. We've got one or two town drunks, but they're always having remorses every time an evangelist comes to town. No, ma'am, I'd say likker ain't a regular thing in the home here, except in the medicine chest. Right good for snake bite, y'know—always was.

**BELLIGERENT MAN AT BACK OF AUDITORIUM.** Is there no one in town aware of—

**STAGE MANAGER.** Come forward, will you, where we can all hear you.—What were you saying?

**BELLIGERENT MAN.** Is there no one in town aware of social injustice and industrial inequality?

**MR. WEBB.** Oh, yes, everybody is—somethin' terrible. Seems like they spend most of their time talking about who's rich and who's poor.

**BELLIGERENT MAN.** Then why don't they do something about it? (*He withdraws without waiting for an answer.*)

**MR. WEBB.** Well, I dunno. . . . I guess we're all hunting like everybody else for a way the diligent and sensible can rise to the top and the lazy and quarrelsome can sink to the bottom. But it ain't easy to find. Meanwhile, we do all we can to help those that can't help themselves and those that can we leave alone.—Are there any other questions?

**LADY IN A BOX.** Oh, Mr. Webb? Mr. Webb, is there any culture or love of beauty in Grover's Corners?

**MR. WEBB.** Well, ma'am, there ain't much—not in the sense you mean. Come to think of it, there's some girls that play the piano at High School Commencement; but they ain't happy about it. No, ma'am, there isn't much culture; but maybe this is the place to tell you that we've got a lot of pleasures of a kind here: we like the sun comin' up over the mountain in the morning, and we all notice a good deal about the birds. We pay a lot of attention to them. And we watch the change of the seasons; yes, everybody knows about them. But those other things—you're right, ma'am—there ain't much.—*Robinson Crusoe* and the Bible; and Handel's "Largo," we all know that; and Whistler's "Mother"[6]—those are just about as far as we go.

---

5. *Greenough's* (grē′nōz).
6. *Robinson Crusoe . . . Whistler's "Mother,"* familiar works of art. *Robinson Crusoe* is an English novel by Daniel Defoe about a man surviving on a desert island. Handel's "Largo" is a slow, stately musical composition by German-English composer George Frederic Handel that is often played on solemn occasions like weddings (see Act Three). Whistler's "Mother" is the common name for a painting by American artist James Abbott McNeill Whistler that is actually entitled *Arrangement in Grey and Black No. 1: Portrait of the Artist's Mother.*

**LADY IN A BOX.** So I thought. Thank you, Mr. Webb.

**STAGE MANAGER.** Thank you, Mr. Webb. (MR. WEBB *retires.*) Now, we'll go back to the town. It's early afternoon. All 2,642 have had their dinners and all the dishes have been washed. (MR. WEBB, *having removed his coat, returns and starts pushing a lawn mower to and fro beside his house.*) There's an early-afternoon calm in our town: a buzzin' and a hummin' from the school buildings; only a few buggies on Main Street— the horses dozing at the hitching posts; you all remember what it's like. Doc Gibbs is in his office, tapping people and making them say "ah." Mr. Webb's cuttin' his lawn over there; one man in ten thinks it's a privilege to push his own lawn mower. No, sir. It's later than I thought. There are the children coming home from school already.

(*Shrill girls' voices are heard, off left.* EMILY *comes along Main Street, carrying some books. There are some signs that she is imagining herself to be a lady of startling elegance.*)

**EMILY.** I *can't*, Lois. I've got to go home and help my mother. I *promised.*

**MR. WEBB.** Emily, walk simply. Who do you think you are today?

**EMILY.** Papa, you're terrible. One minute you tell me to stand up straight and the next minute you call me names. I just don't listen to you. (*She gives him an abrupt kiss.*)

**MR. WEBB.** Golly, I never got a kiss from such a great lady before. (*He goes out of sight.* EMILY *leans over and picks some flowers by the gate of her house.*)

(GEORGE GIBBS *comes careening down Main Street. He is throwing a ball up to dizzying heights, and waiting to catch it again. This sometimes requires his taking six steps backward. He bumps into an* OLD LADY *invisible to us.*)

**GEORGE.** Excuse me, Mrs. Forrest.

**STAGE MANAGER** (*as* MRS. FORREST). Go out and play in the fields, young man. You got no business playing baseball on Main Street.

**GEORGE.** Awfully sorry, Mrs. Forrest.—Hello, Emily.

**EMILY.** H'lo.

**GEORGE.** You made a fine speech in class.

**EMILY.** Well . . . I was really ready to make a speech about the Monroe Doctrine, but at the last minute Miss Corcoran made me talk about the Louisiana Purchase instead. I worked an awful long time on both of them.

**GEORGE.** Gee, it's funny, Emily. From my window up there I can just see your head nights when you're doing your homework over in your room.

**EMILY.** Why, can you?

**GEORGE.** You certainly do stick to it, Emily. I don't see how you can sit still that long. I guess you like school.

**EMILY.** Well, I always feel it's something you have to go through.

**GEORGE.** Yeah.

**EMILY.** I don't mind it really. It passes the time.

**GEORGE.** Yeah.—Emily, what do you think? We might work out a kinda telegraph from your window to mine; and once in a while you could give me a kinda hint or two about one of those algebra problems. I don't mean the answers, Emily, of course not . . . just some little hint. . . .

**EMILY.** Oh, I think *hints* are allowed.—So—ah— if you get stuck, George, you whistle to me; and I'll give you some hints.

**GEORGE.** Emily, you're just naturally bright, I guess.

**EMILY.** I figure that it's just the way a person's born.

**GEORGE.** Yeah. But, you see, I want to be a farmer, and my Uncle Luke says whenever I'm ready I can come over and work on his farm and if I'm any good I can just gradually have it.

**EMILY.** You mean the house and everything?

GEORGE and EMILY in *Grover's Corners*, based on *Our Town*

(*Enter* MRS. WEBB *with a large bowl and sits on the bench by her trellis.*)

GEORGE. Yeah. Well, thanks . . . I better be getting out to the baseball field. Thanks for the talk, Emily.—Good afternoon, Mrs. Webb.

MRS. WEBB. Good afternoon, George.

GEORGE. So long, Emily.

EMILY. So long, George.

MRS. WEBB. Emily, come and help me string these beans for winter. George Gibbs let himself have a real conversation, didn't he? Why, he's growing up. How old would George be?

EMILY. I don't know.

MRS. WEBB. Let's see. He must be almost sixteen.

EMILY. Mama, I made a speech in class today and I was very good.

MRS. WEBB. You must recite it to your father at supper. What was it about?

EMILY. The Louisiana Purchase. It was like silk off a spool. I'm going to make speeches all my life.—Mama, are these big enough?

MRS. WEBB. Try and get them a little bigger if you can.

EMILY. Mama, will you answer me a question, serious?

MRS. WEBB. Seriously, dear—not serious.

EMILY. Seriously—will you?

MRS. WEBB. Of course, I will.

EMILY. Mama, am I good-looking?

MRS. WEBB. Yes, of course you are. All my children have got good features; I'd be ashamed if they hadn't.

EMILY. Oh, Mama, that's not what I mean. What I mean is: am I *pretty*?

MRS. WEBB. I've already told you, yes. Now that's enough of that. You have a nice young pretty face. I never heard of such foolishness.

EMILY. Oh, Mama, you never tell us the truth about anything.

MRS. WEBB. I *am* telling you the truth.

EMILY. Mama, were *you* pretty?

MRS. WEBB. Yes, I was, if I do say it. I was the prettiest girl in town next to Mamie Cartwright.

EMILY. But, Mama, you've got to say *something* about me. Am I pretty enough . . . to get anybody . . . to get people interested in me?

MRS. WEBB. Emily, you make me tired. Now stop it. You're pretty enough for all normal purposes.—Come along now and bring that bowl with you.

EMILY. Oh, Mama, you're no help at all.

STAGE MANAGER. Thank you. Thank you! That'll do. We'll have to interrupt again here. Thank you, Mrs. Webb; thank you, Emily. (MRS. WEBB *and* EMILY *withdraw.*) There are some more things we want to explore about this town. (*He comes to the center of the stage. During the following speech the lights gradually dim to darkness, leaving only a spot on him.*) I think this is a good time to tell you that the Cartwright interests have just begun building a new bank in Grover's Corners—had to go to Vermont for the marble, sorry to say. And they've asked a friend of mine what they should put in the cornerstone for people to dig up . . . a thousand years from now. . . . Of course, they've put in a copy of the *New York Times* and a copy of Mr. Webb's *Sentinel.* . . . We're kind of interested in this because some scientific fellas have found a way of painting all that reading matter with a glue—a silicate glue—that'll make it keep a thousand—two thousand years. We're putting in a Bible . . . and the Constitution of the United States—and a copy of

William Shakespeare's plays. What do you say, folks? What do you think? Y'know—Babylon once had two million people in it, and all we know about 'em is the names of the kings and some copies of wheat contracts . . . and contracts for the sale of slaves. Yet every night all those families sat down to supper, and the father came home from his work, and the smoke went up the chimney—same as here. And even in Greece and Rome, all we know about the *real* life of the people is what we can piece together out of the joking poems and the comedies they wrote for the theater back then. So I'm going to have a copy of this play put in the cornerstone and the people a thousand years from now'll know a few simple facts about us—more than the Treaty of Versailles and the Lindbergh flight.[7] See what I mean? So—people a thousand years from now—this is the way we were in the provinces north of New York at the beginning of the twentieth century.—This is the way we were: in our growing up and in our marrying and in our living and in our dying. (*A choir partially concealed in the orchestra pit has begun singing "Blessed Be the Tie That Binds."* SIMON STIMSON *stands directing them. Two ladders have been pushed onto the stage; they serve as indication of the second story in the* GIBBS *and* WEBB *houses.* GEORGE *and* EMILY *mount them, and apply themselves to their schoolwork.* DR. GIBBS *has entered and is seated in his kitchen reading.*) Well!—good deal of time's gone by. It's evening. You can hear choir practice going on in the Congregational Church. The children are at home doing their schoolwork. The day's running down like a tired clock.

SIMON STIMSON. Now look here, everybody. Music come into the world to give pleasure.—

---

7. *Treaty of Versailles* (ver sī′) . . . *Lindbergh Flight.* The Treaty of Versailles (1919) ended World War I; the (Charles) Lindbergh flight (1927) was the first solo flight across the Atlantic.

Softer! Softer! Get it out of your heads that music's only good when it's loud. You leave loudness to the Methodists. You couldn't beat 'em, even if you wanted to. Now again. Tenors!

GEORGE. Hssst! Emily!

EMILY. Hello.

GEORGE. Hello.

EMILY. I can't work at all. The moonlight's so *terrible.*

GEORGE. Emily, did you get the third problem?

EMILY. Which?

GEORGE. The *third?*

EMILY. Why, yes, George—that's the easiest of them all.

GEORGE. I don't see it. Emily, can you give me a hint?

EMILY. I'll tell you one thing: the answer's in yards.

GEORGE. ! ! ! In yards? How do you mean?

EMILY. In *square* yards.

GEORGE. Oh . . . in square yards.

EMILY. Yes, George, don't you see?

GEORGE. Yeah.

EMILY. In square yards of *wallpaper.*

GEORGE. Wallpaper—oh, I see. Thanks a lot, Emily.

EMILY. You're welcome. My, isn't the moonlight *terrible?* And choir practice going on.—I think if you hold your breath you can hear the train all the way to Contoocook. Hear it?

GEORGE. M-m-m—What do you know!

EMILY. Well, I guess I better go back and try to work.

GEORGE. Good night, Emily. And thanks.

EMILY. Good night, George.

SIMON STIMSON. Before I forget it: how many of you will be able to come in Tuesday afternoon and sing at Fred Hersey's wedding?—show your hands. That'll be fine; that'll be right nice. We'll do the same music we did for Jane Trowbridge's last month.—Now we'll do: "Art Thou Weary; Art Thou Languid?" It's a ques-

tion, ladies and gentlemen, make it talk. Ready.

DR. GIBBS. Oh, George, can you come down a minute?

GEORGE. Yes, Pa. *(He descends the ladder.)*

DR. GIBBS. Make yourself comfortable, George; I'll only keep you a minute. George, how old are you?

GEORGE. I? I'm sixteen, almost seventeen.

DR. GIBBS. What do you want to do after school's over?

GEORGE. Why, you know, Pa. I want to be a farmer on Uncle Luke's farm.

DR. GIBBS. You'll be willing, will you, to get up early and milk and feed the stock . . . and you'll be able to hoe and hay all day?

GEORGE. Sure, I will. What are you . . . what do you mean, Pa?

DR. GIBBS. Well, George, while I was in my office today I heard a funny sound . . . and what do you think it was? It was your mother chopping wood. There you see your mother—getting up early; cooking meals all day long; washing and ironing—and still she has to go out in the back-yard and chop wood. I suppose she just got tired of asking you. She just gave up and decided it was easier to do it herself. And you eat her meals, and put on the clothes she keeps nice for you, and you run off and play baseball—like she's some hired girl we keep around the house but that we don't like very much. Well, I knew all I had to do was call your attention to it. Here's a handkerchief, son. George, I've decided to raise your spending money twenty-five cents a week. Not, of course, for chopping wood for your mother, because that's a present you give her, but because you're getting older—and I imagine there are lots of things you must find to do with it.

GEORGE. Thanks, Pa.

DR. GIBBS. Let's see—tomorrow's your payday. You can count on it.——Hmm. Probably

Rebecca'll feel she ought to have some more, too. Wonder what could have happened to your mother. Choir practice never was as late as this before.

**GEORGE.** It's only half-past eight, Pa.

**DR. GIBBS.** I don't know why she's in that old choir. She hasn't any more voice than an old crow. . . . Traipsin' around the streets at this hour of the night. . . . Just about time you retired, don't you think?

**GEORGE.** Yes, Pa. (GEORGE *mounts to his place on the ladder.*)

(*Laughter and good nights can be heard on stage left and presently* MRS. GIBBS, MRS. SOAMES, *and* MRS. WEBB *come down Main Street. When they arrive at the corner of the stage they stop.*)

**MRS. SOAMES.** Good night, Martha. Good night, Mr. Foster.

**MRS. WEBB.** I'll tell Mr. Webb; I *know* he'll want to put it in the paper.

**MRS. GIBBS.** My, it's late!

**MRS. SOAMES.** Good night, Irma.

**MRS. GIBBS.** Real nice choir practice, wa'n't it? Myrtle Webb! Look at that moon, will you! Tsk-tsk-tsk. Potato weather, for sure. (*They are silent a moment, gazing up at the moon.*)

**MRS. SOAMES.** Naturally I didn't want to say a word about it in front of those others, but now we're alone—really, it's the worst scandal that ever was in this town!

**MRS. GIBBS.** What?

**MRS. SOAMES.** Simon Stimson!

**MRS. GIBBS.** Now, Louella!

**MRS. SOAMES.** But, Julia! To have the organist of a church *drink* and *drunk* year after year. You know he was drunk tonight.

**MRS. GIBBS.** Now, Louella! We all know about Mr. Stimson, and we all know about the troubles he's been through, and Dr. Ferguson knows too, and if Dr. Ferguson keeps him on there in his job the only thing the rest of us can do is just not to notice it.

**MRS. SOAMES.** *Not to notice it!* But it's getting worse.

**MRS. WEBB.** No, it isn't, Louella. It's getting better. I've been in that choir twice as long as you have. It doesn't happen anywhere near so often. . . . My, I hate to go to bed on a night like this.—I better hurry. Those children'll be sitting up till all hours. Good night, Louella. (*They all exchange good nights. She hurries downstage, enters her house, and disappears.*)

**MRS. GIBBS.** Can you get home safe, Louella?

**MRS. SOAMES.** It's as bright as day. I can see Mr. Soames scowling at the window now. You'd think we'd been to a dance the way the menfolk carry on.

(*More good nights.* MRS. GIBBS *arrives at her home and passes through the trellis into the kitchen.*)

**MRS. GIBBS.** Well, we had a real good time.

**DR. GIBBS.** You're late enough.

**MRS. GIBBS.** Why, Frank, it ain't any later 'n usual.

**DR. GIBBS.** And you stopping at the corner to gossip with a lot of hens.

**MRS. GIBBS.** Now, Frank, don't be grouchy. Come out and smell the heliotrope in the moonlight. (*They stroll out arm in arm along the footlights.*) Isn't that wonderful? What did you do all the time I was away?

**DR. GIBBS.** Oh, I read—as usual. What were the girls gossiping about tonight?

**MRS. GIBBS.** Well, believe me, Frank—there is something to gossip about.

**DR. GIBBS.** Hmm! Simon Stimson far gone, was he?

**MRS. GIBBS.** Worst I've ever seen him. How'll that end, Frank? Dr. Ferguson can't forgive him forever.

**DR. GIBBS.** I guess I know more about Simon Stimson's affairs than anybody in this town. Some people ain't made for small-town life. I don't know how that'll end; but there's nothing we can do but just leave it alone. Come, get in.

MRS. GIBBS. No, not yet. . . . Frank, I'm worried about you.

DR. GIBBS. What are you worried about?

MRS. GIBBS. I think it's my duty to make plans for you to get a real rest and change. And if I get that legacy, well, I'm going to insist on it.

DR. GIBBS. Now, Julia, there's no sense in going over that again.

MRS. GIBBS. Frank, you're just *unreasonable!*

DR. GIBBS (*starting into the house*). Come on, Julia, it's getting late. First thing you know you'll catch cold. I gave George a piece of my mind tonight. I reckon you'll have your wood chopped for a while anyway. No, no, start getting upstairs.

MRS. GIBBS. Oh, dear. There's always so many things to pick up, seems like. You know, Frank, Mrs. Fairchild always locks her front door every night. All those people up that part of town do.

DR. GIBBS (*blowing out the lamp*). They're all getting citified, that's the trouble with them. They haven't got nothing fit to burgle and everybody knows it. (*They disappear.*)

(REBECCA *climbs up the ladder beside* GEORGE.)

GEORGE. Get out, Rebecca. There's only room for one at this window. You're always spoiling everything.

REBECCA. Well, let me look just a minute.

GEORGE. Use your own window.

REBECCA. I did, but there's no moon there. . . . George, do you know what I think, do you? I think maybe the moon's getting nearer and nearer and there'll be a big 'splosion.

GEORGE. Rebecca, you don't know anything. If the moon were getting nearer, the guys that sit up all night with telescopes would see it first and they'd tell about it, and it'd be in all the newspapers.

REBECCA. George, is the moon shining on South America, Canada, and half the whole world?

GEORGE. Well—prob'ly is.

(*The* STAGE MANAGER *strolls on. Pause. The sound of crickets is heard.*)

STAGE MANAGER. Nine thirty. Most of the lights are out. No, there's Constable Warren trying a few doors on Main Street. And here comes Editor Webb, after putting his newspaper to bed.

(MR. WARREN, *an elderly policeman, comes along Main Street from the right,* MR. WEBB *from the left.*)

MR. WEBB. Good evening, Bill.

CONSTABLE WARREN. Evenin', Mr. Webb.

MR. WEBB. Quite a moon!

CONSTABLE WARREN. Yepp.

MR. WEBB. All quiet tonight?

CONSTABLE WARREN. Simon Stimson is rollin' around a little. Just saw his wife movin' out to hunt for him so I looked the other way—there he is now.

(SIMON STIMSON *comes down Main Street from the left, only a trace of unsteadiness in his walk.*)

MR. WEBB. Good evening, Simon. . . . Town seems to have settled down for the night pretty well. . . . (SIMON STIMSON *comes up to him and pauses a moment and stares at him, swaying slightly.*) Good evening. . . . Yes, most of the town's settled down for the night, Simon. . . . I guess we better do the same. Can I walk along a ways with you? (SIMON STIMSON *continues on his way without a word and disappears at the right.*) Good night.

CONSTABLE WARREN. I don't know how that's goin' to end, Mr. Webb.

MR. WEBB. Well, he's seen a peck of trouble, one thing after another. . . . Oh, Bill . . . if you see my boy smoking cigarettes, just give him a word, will you? He thinks a lot of you, Bill.

CONSTABLE WARREN. I don't think he smokes no cigarettes, Mr. Webb. Leastways, not more 'n two or three a year.

MR. WEBB. Hm . . . I hope not.—Well, good night, Bill.

CONSTABLE WARREN. Good night, Mr. Webb. (*Exit.*)

MR. WEBB. Who's that up there? Is that you, Myrtle?

EMILY. No, it's me, Papa.

MR. WEBB. Why aren't you in bed?

EMILY. I don't know. I just can't sleep yet, Papa. The moonlight's so *won*-derful. And the smell of Mrs. Gibbs's heliotrope. Can you smell it?

MR. WEBB. Hm . . . Yes. Haven't any troubles on your mind, have you, Emily?

EMILY. *Troubles*, Papa? *No.*

MR. WEBB. Well, enjoy yourself, but don't let your mother catch you. Good night, Emily.

EMILY. Good night, Papa.

(MR. WEBB *crosses into the house, whistling "Blessed Be the Tie That Binds," and disappears.*)

REBECCA. I never told you about that letter Jane Crofut got from her minister when she was sick. He wrote Jane a letter and on the envelope the address was like this: It said: Jane Crofut; The Crofut Farm; Grover's Corners; Sutton County; New Hampshire; United States of America.

GEORGE. What's funny about that?

REBECCA. But listen, it's not finished: the United States of America; Continent of North America; Western Hemisphere; the Earth; the Solar System; the Universe; the Mind of God—that's what it said on the envelope.

GEORGE. What do you know!

REBECCA. And the postman brought it just the same.

GEORGE. What do you know!

STAGE MANAGER. That's the end of the First Act, friends. You can go and smoke now, those that smoke.

## THINK AND DISCUSS
### Understanding
1. What is the Stage Manager doing at the beginning of the play, as the audience arrives?
2. What does the audience learn from the long opening speech of the Stage Manager? Give a summary of the information.
3. Cite examples from the play in which the Stage Manager becomes a mover or manipulator of the action.
4. Cite an example from the play's first act in which the Stage Manager becomes a player of minor parts.

### Analyzing
5. Rather early in the first act it becomes clear that the playwright wishes to focus on the Gibbs and Webb households. Point out the differences of the two families (particularly their professions and family members) and their similarities.
6. Give possible reasons for the playwright's intermingling the family scenes, shifting focus from one side of the stage to another as the families engage in similar activities.
7. By the end of Act One Emily and George are established as major characters. Find evidence in the following two scenes that their relationship will be of concern throughout the play: the scene in which George suggests they "work out a kinda telegraph" to communicate between their windows; and the scene in which Emily helps George with an arithmetic problem.
8. In the scene where the town is discussed,

what kind of information does Professor Willard present and what is its relevance to the play? Discuss.

9. What do Mr. Webb's replies to the questions of the "audience" tell about the town, and how do his comments square with what has been shown about the town up to this point in the play?

10. What, according to the Stage Manager, are the items to be placed in the new bank's cornerstone, to be opened in a thousand years, and what would they reveal to the future about the town and country?

11. Why does the Stage Manager include a copy of *Our Town* among the cornerstone items, and what will it reveal?

12. Describe the following minor **characters** and the function of each in Act One: Joe Crowell, Jr.; Howie Newsome; Simon Stimson; Mrs. Soames.

## Extending

13. At the end of Act One, Rebecca Gibbs tells George about the peculiar address the minister used in his letter to Jane Crofut. How does that story suggest the play is about more than just Grover's Corners? In what other ways has the playwright called attention to the universal quality of the play?

## READING LITERATURE SKILLFULLY
### Sequence

In *Our Town* the Stage Manager often mentions important events out of sequence, but normally he informs the audience when each event has happened or will happen. He tells the date (that is, the time setting) of each act and sometimes refers to past or future dates.

1. In the Stage Manager's long introductory speech at the beginning of Act One, he makes these statements: "There's Doc Gibbs comin' down Main Street now. . . . And here's his wife comin' downstairs to get breakfast" and "Doc Gibbs died in 1930. . . . Mrs. Gibbs died first—long time

ago, in fact." How can both pairs of statements be true?

2. What light does the revelation of the Gibbses' deaths cast on the importance of the everyday breakfast scene to the audience?

3. To better appreciate the conversations in the simultaneous breakfast scenes in the Gibbs and Webb homes, join other volunteers in reading the roles of the two families, on opposite sides of the classroom. (The Stage Manager may stand in the middle.) The reading can begin with Mrs. Gibbs's line, "George! Rebecca!" (page 175) and end with the children leaving for school.

## THINKING SKILLS
### Synthesizing

To **synthesize** is to combine parts, such as details and facts, into a new structure. Mr. Webb tells a great deal about the people of Grover's Corners when he says their culture is limited to such art as *Whistler's Mother*, shown here. Prepare an advertisement showing how you would sell framed prints of this painting to shoppers in Grover's Corners.

James Abbott McNeill Whistler, *Arrangement in Grey and Black No. 1: Portrait of the Artist's Mother*, 1872, The Louvre, Paris

## COMPOSITION

### Writing About Your Community

Assume that people in your community are suggesting items to go into the cornerstone of a new public building. Choose three items you think would convey to future generations what everyday life in your area is like. Write a three- to four-paragraph essay for the local newspaper describing the items, explaining why you included them, and predicting what conclusions someone in the future might draw from each.

### Analyzing Dramatic Technique

Write a five-paragraph essay analyzing Thornton Wilder's use of the Stage Manager in Act One. Assume that Wilder's purpose in the first act is to portray one day in the life of Grover's Corners from dawn to nightfall, getting in as many aspects of the town as possible, from dry statistics to the pulsating life of ordinary people performing daily tasks. At the same time the dramatist intends to launch the central action of the play, the love developing between George and Emily. Consider advantages you see in Wilder's use of the Stage Manager and weigh them against any possible disadvantages (as, for example, the possible breaking of the dramatic illusion). In a final paragraph, indicate your view of Wilder's success or failure in getting the first act to work well dramatically through the use of the Stage Manager. See "Writing About Drama" in the Writer's Handbook.

## ENRICHMENT

### Speaking and Listening

Organize a group to read scenes of the play aloud as dramatic readings. Possibilities include Mrs. Gibbs and Mrs. Webb's conversation over the string beans, George and Emily's conversation in Main Street when he is on his way to baseball practice, and the Stage Manager's speech about the cornerstone. After rehearsing the scenes and improving the presentation, volunteer to give the readings in front of the class.

# ACT TWO

*The tables and chairs of the two kitchens are still on the stage.*

*The ladders and the small bench have been withdrawn. The* STAGE MANAGER *has been at his accustomed place watching the audience return to its seats.*

STAGE MANAGER. Three years have gone by. Yes, the sun's come up over a thousand times. Summers and winters have cracked the mountains a little bit more and the rains have brought down some of the dirt. Some babies that weren't even born before have begun talking regular sentences already; and a number of people who thought they were right young and spry have noticed that they can't bound up a flight of stairs like they used to, without their heart fluttering a little. All that can happen in a thousand days. Nature's been pushing and contriving in other ways, too: a number of young people fell in love and got married. Yes, the mountain got bit away a few fractions of an inch; millions of gallons of water went by the mill; and here and there a new home was set up under a roof. Almost everybody in the world gets married—you know what I mean? In our town there aren't hardly any exceptions. Most everybody in the world climbs into their graves married.

The First Act was called the Daily Life. This act is called Love and Marriage. There's another act coming after this: I reckon you can guess what that's about.

So: It's three years later. It's 1904. It's July 7th, just after High School Commencement. That's the time most of our young people jump up and get married. Soon as they've passed their last examinations in solid geometry and Cicero's Orations,[1] looks like they suddenly

---

1. *Cicero's Orations,* speeches of ancient Roman orator Marcus Tullius Cicero that students translate from Latin to English.

feel themselves fit to be married. It's early morning. Only this time it's been raining. It's been pouring and thundering. Mrs. Gibbs's garden, and Mrs. Webb's here: drenched. All those bean poles and pea vines: drenched. All yesterday over there on Main Street, the rain looked like curtains being blown along. Hm . . . it may begin again any minute. There! You can hear the 5:45 for Boston.

(MRS. GIBBS *and* MRS. WEBB *enter their kitchens and start the day as in the First Act.*)

And there's Mrs. Gibbs and Mrs. Webb come down to make breakfast, just as though it were an ordinary day. I don't have to point out to the women in my audience that those ladies they see before them, both of those ladies cooked three meals a day—one of 'em for twenty years, the other for forty—and no summer vacation. They brought up two children apiece, washed, cleaned the house—and *never a nervous breakdown.*

It's like what one of those Middle West poets said: You've got to love life to have life, and you've got to have life to love life.[2] . . . It's what they call a vicious circle.

HOWIE NEWSOME (*off stage left*). Giddap, Bessie!

STAGE MANAGER. Here comes Howie Newsome delivering the milk. And there's Si Crowell delivering the papers like his brother before him.

(SI CROWELL *has entered hurling imaginary newspapers into doorways;* HOWIE NEWSOME *has come along Main Street with Bessie.*)

SI CROWELL. Morning, Howie.

HOWIE NEWSOME. Morning, Si.—Anything in the papers I ought to know?

SI CROWELL. Nothing much, except we're losing about the best baseball pitcher Grover's Corners ever had—George Gibbs.

HOWIE NEWSOME. Reckon he is.

SI CROWELL. He could hit and run bases, too.

HOWIE NEWSOME. Yep. Mighty fine ballplayer.—Whoa! Bessie! I guess I can stop and talk if I've a mind to!

SI CROWELL. I don't see how he could give up a thing like that just to get married. Would you, Howie?

HOWIE NEWSOME. Can't tell, Si. Never had no talent that way. (CONSTABLE WARREN *enters. They exchange good mornings.*) You're up early, Bill.

CONSTABLE WARREN. Seein' if there's anything I can do to prevent a flood. River's been risin' all night.

HOWIE NEWSOME. Si Crowell's all worked up here about George Gibbs's retiring from baseball.

CONSTABLE WARREN. Yes, sir; that's the way it goes. Back in '84 we had a player, Si—even George Gibbs couldn't touch him. Name of Hank Todd. Went down to Maine and become a parson. Wonderful ballplayer.—Howie, how does the weather look to you?

HOWIE NEWSOME. Oh, 'tain't bad. Think maybe it'll clear up for good. (CONSTABLE WARREN *and* SI CROWELL *continue on their way.* HOWIE NEWSOME *brings the milk first to* MRS. GIBBS's *house. She meets him by the trellis.*)

MRS. GIBBS. Good morning, Howie. Do you think it's going to rain?

HOWIE NEWSOME. Morning, Mrs. Gibbs. It rained so heavy, I think maybe it'll clear up.

MRS. GIBBS. Certainly hope it will.

HOWIE NEWSOME. How much did you want today?

MRS. GIBBS. I'm going to have a houseful of relations, Howie. Looks to me like I'll need three-a-milk and two-a-cream.

HOWIE NEWSOME. My wife says to tell you we both hope they'll be very happy, Mrs. Gibbs. Know they *will.*

MRS. GIBBS. Thanks a lot, Howie. Tell your wife I hope she gits there to the wedding.

2. *you've got to have life to love life.* The Stage Manager is paraphrasing Edgar Lee Masters, whose *Spoon River Anthology* depicts life in the Middle-Western United States. The last line of the poem "Lucinda Matlock" by Masters is "It takes life to love Life."

HOWIE NEWSOME. Yes, she'll be there; she'll be there if she kin. (HOWIE NEWSOME *crosses to* MRS. WEBB's *house.*) Morning, Mrs. Webb.

MRS. WEBB. Oh, good morning, Mr. Newsome. I told you four quarts of milk, but I hope you can spare me another.

HOWIE NEWSOME. Yes'm . . . and the two of cream.

MRS. WEBB. Will it start raining again, Mr. Newsome?

HOWIE NEWSOME. Well. Just sayin' to Mrs. Gibbs as how it may lighten up. Mrs. Newsome told me to tell you as how we hope they'll both be very happy, Mrs. Webb. Know they *will*.

MRS. WEBB. Thank you, and thank Mrs. Newsome and we're counting on seeing you at the wedding.

HOWIE NEWSOME. Yes, Mrs. Webb. We hope to git there. Couldn't miss that. Come on, Bessie. (*Exit* HOWIE NEWSOME.)

(DR. GIBBS *descends in shirtsleeves, and sits down at his breakfast table.*)

DR. GIBBS. Well, Ma, the day has come. You're losin' one of your chicks.

MRS. GIBBS. Frank Gibbs, don't you say another word. I feel like crying every minute. Sit down and drink your coffee.

DR. GIBBS. The groom's up shaving himself—only there ain't an awful lot to shave. Whistling and singing, like he's glad to leave us.—Every now and then he says "I do" to the mirror, but it don't sound convincing to me.

MRS. GIBBS. I declare, Frank, I don't know how he'll get along. I've arranged his clothes and seen to it he's put warm things on—Frank! they're too *young*. Emily won't think of such things. He'll catch his death of cold within a week.

DR. GIBBS. I was remembering my wedding morning, Julia.

MRS. GIBBS. Now don't start that, Frank Gibbs.

DR. GIBBS. I was the scaredest young fella in the State of New Hampshire. I thought I'd make a mistake for sure. And when I saw you comin' down that aisle I thought you were the prettiest girl I'd ever seen, but the only trouble was that I'd never seen you before. There I was in the Congregational Church marryin' a total stranger.

MRS. GIBBS. And how do you think I felt!—Frank, weddings are perfectly awful things. Farces—that's what they are! (*She puts a plate before him.*) Here, I've made something for you.

DR. GIBBS. Why, Julia Hersey—French toast!

MRS. GIBBS. 'Tain't hard to make and I had to do *some*thing. (*Pause.* DR. GIBBS *pours on the syrup.*)

DR. GIBBS. How'd you sleep last night, Julia?

MRS. GIBBS. Well, I heard a lot of the hours struck off.

DR. GIBBS. Ye-e-s! I get a shock every time I think of George setting out to be a family man—that great gangling thing!—I tell you, Julia, there's nothing so terrifying in the world as a *son*. The relation of father and son is the darndest, awkwardest—

MRS. GIBBS. Well, mother and daughter's no picnic, let me tell you.

DR. GIBBS. They'll have a lot of troubles, I suppose, but that's none of our business. Everybody has a right to their own troubles.

MRS. GIBBS (*at the table, drinking her coffee, meditatively*). Yes . . . people are meant to go through life two by two. 'Tain't natural to be lonesome. (*Pause.* DR. GIBBS *starts laughing.*)

DR. GIBBS. Julia, do you know one of the things I was scared of when I married you?

MRS. GIBBS. Oh, go along with you!

DR. GIBBS. I was afraid we wouldn't have material for conversation more'n'd last us a few weeks. (*Both laugh.*) I was afraid we'd run out and eat our meals in silence, that's a fact.—Well, you and I been conversing for twenty years now without any noticeable barren spells.

**MRS. GIBBS.** Well—good weather, bad weather—'tain't very choice, but I always find something to say. (*She goes to the foot of the stairs.*) Did you hear Rebecca stirring around upstairs?

**DR. GIBBS.** No. Only day of the year Rebecca hasn't been managing everybody's business up there. She's hiding in her room.—I got the impression she's crying.

**MRS. GIBBS.** Lord's sakes!—This has got to stop.—Rebecca! Rebecca! Come and get your breakfast.

(GEORGE *comes rattling down the stairs, very brisk.*)

**GEORGE.** Good morning, everybody. Only five more hours to live. (*Makes the gesture of cutting his throat, and a loud "k-k-k," and starts through the trellis.*)

**MRS. GIBBS.** George Gibbs, where are you going?

**GEORGE.** Just stepping across the grass to see my girl.

**MRS. GIBBS.** Now, George! You put on your overshoes. It's raining torrents. You don't go out of this house without you're prepared for it.

**GEORGE.** Aw, Ma. It's just a *step!*

**MRS. GIBBS.** George! You'll catch your death of cold and cough all through the service.

**DR. GIBBS.** George, do as your mother tells you! (DR. GIBBS *goes upstairs.*)

(GEORGE *returns reluctantly to the kitchen and pantomimes putting on overshoes.*)

**MRS. GIBBS.** From tomorrow on you can kill yourself in all weathers, but while you're in my house you'll live wisely, thank you.—Maybe Mrs. Webb isn't used to callers at seven in the morning.—Here, take a cup of coffee first.

**GEORGE.** Be back in a minute. (*He crosses the stage, leaping over the puddles.*) Good morning, Mother Webb.

**MRS. WEBB.** Goodness! You frightened me!—Now, George, you can come in a minute out of the wet, but you know I can't ask you in.

**GEORGE.** Why not—?

**MRS. WEBB.** George, you know's well as I do: the groom can't see his bride on his wedding day, not until he sees her in church.

**GEORGE.** Aw!—that's just a superstition.—Good morning, Mr. Webb.

(*Enter* MR. WEBB.)

**MR. WEBB.** Good morning, George.

**GEORGE.** Mr. Webb, you don't believe in that superstition, do you?

**MR. WEBB.** There's a lot of common sense in some superstitions, George. (*He sits at the table, facing right.*)

**MRS. WEBB.** Millions have folla'd it, George, and you don't want to be the first to fly in the face of custom.

**GEORGE.** How is Emily?

**MRS. WEBB.** She hasn't waked up yet. I haven't heard a sound out of her.

**GEORGE.** Emily's *asleep!!!*

**MRS. WEBB.** No wonder! We were up 'til all hours, sewing and packing. Now I'll tell you what I'll do; you set down here a minute with Mr. Webb and drink this cup of coffee; and I'll go upstairs and see she doesn't come down and surprise you. There's some bacon, too; but don't be long about it. (*Exit* MRS. WEBB.)

(*Embarrassed silence.* MR. WEBB *dunks doughnuts in his coffee. More silence*)

**MR. WEBB** (*suddenly and loudly*). Well, George, how are you?

**GEORGE** (*startled, choking over his coffee*). Oh, fine, I'm fine. (*Pause*) Mr. Webb, what sense could there be in a superstition like that?

**MR. WEBB.** Well, you see—on her wedding morning a girl's head's apt to be full of . . . clothes and one thing and another. Don't you think that's probably it?

**GEORGE.** Ye-e-s. I never thought of that.

**MR. WEBB.** A girl's apt to be a mite nervous on her wedding day. (*Pause*)

**GEORGE.** I wish a fellow could get married without all that marching up and down.

**MR. WEBB.** Every man that's ever lived has felt that way about it, George; but it hasn't been any use. It's the womenfolk who've built up weddings, my boy. For a while now the women have it all their own. A man looks pretty small at a wedding, George. All those good women standing shoulder to shoulder making sure that the knot's tied in a mighty public way.

**GEORGE.** But . . . you *believe* in it, don't you, Mr. Webb?

**MR. WEBB** (*with alacrity*). Oh, yes; *oh, yes*. Don't you misunderstand me, my boy. Marriage is a wonderful thing—wonderful thing. And don't you forget that, George.

**GEORGE.** No, sir.—Mr. Webb, how old were you when you got married?

**MR. WEBB.** Well, you see: I'd been to college and I'd taken a little time to get settled. But Mrs. Webb—she wasn't much older than what Emily is. Oh, age hasn't much to do with it, George—not compared with . . . uh . . . other things.

**GEORGE.** What were you going to say, Mr. Webb?

**MR. WEBB.** Oh, I don't know.—Was I going to say something? (*Pause*) George, I was thinking the other night of some advice my father gave me when I got married. Charles, he said, Charles, start out early showing who's boss, he said. Best thing to do is to give an order, even if it don't make sense; just so she'll learn to obey. And he said: if anything about your wife irritates you—her conversation, or anything—just get up and leave the house. That'll make it clear to her, he said. And, oh, yes! he said never, *never* let your wife know how much money you have, never.

**GEORGE.** Well, Mr. Webb . . . I don't think I could . . .

**MR. WEBB.** So I took the opposite of my father's advice and I've been happy ever since. And let that be a lesson to you, George, never to ask advice on personal matters.—George, are you going to raise chickens on your farm?

**GEORGE.** What?

**MR. WEBB.** Are you going to raise chickens on your farm?

**GEORGE.** Uncle Luke's never been much interested, but I thought—

**MR. WEBB.** A book came into my office the other day, George, on the Philo System of raising chickens. I want you to read it. I'm thinking of beginning in a small way in the backyard, and I'm going to put an incubator in the cellar— (*Enter* MRS. WEBB.)

**MRS. WEBB.** Charles, are you talking about that old incubator again? I thought you two'd be talking about things worthwhile.

**MR. WEBB** (*bitingly*). Well, Myrtle, if you want to give the boy some good advice, I'll go upstairs and leave you alone with him.

**MRS. WEBB** (*pulling* GEORGE *up*). George, Emily's got to come downstairs and eat her breakfast. She sends you her love but she doesn't want to lay eyes on you. Good-by.

**GEORGE.** Good-by.

(GEORGE *crosses the stage to his own home, bewildered and crestfallen. He slowly dodges a puddle and disappears into his house.*)

**MR. WEBB.** Myrtle, I guess you don't know about that older superstition.

**MRS. WEBB.** What do you mean, Charles?

**MR. WEBB.** Since the cavemen: no bridegroom should see his father-in-law on the day of the wedding, or near it. Now remember that.

(*Both leave the stage.*)

**STAGE MANAGER.** Thank you very much, Mr. and Mrs. Webb.—Now I have to interrupt again here. You see, we want to know how all this began—this wedding, this plan to spend a lifetime together. I'm awfully interested in how big things like that begin. You know how it is: you're twenty-one or twenty-two and you make some decisions; then whisssh! you're seventy:

you've been a lawyer for fifty years, and that white-haired lady at your side has eaten over fifty thousand meals with you. How do such things begin? George and Emily are going to show you now the conversation they had when they first knew that . . . that . . . as the saying goes . . . they were meant for one another. But before they do it I want you to try and remember what it was like to have been very young. And particularly the days when you were first in love; when you were like a person sleepwalking, and you didn't quite see the street you were in, and didn't quite hear everything that was said to you. You're just a little bit crazy. Will you remember that, please? Now they'll be coming out of high school at three o'clock. George has just been elected President of the Junior Class, and as it's June, that means he'll be President of the Senior Class all next year. And Emily's just been elected Secretary and Treasurer. I don't have to tell you how important that is. (*He places a board across the backs of two chairs, which he takes from those at the* GIBBS *family's table. He brings two high stools from the wings and places them behind the board. Persons sitting on the stools will be facing the audience. This is the counter of* MR. MORGAN's *drugstore. The sounds of young people's voices are heard off left.*) Yepp—there they are coming down Main Street now.

(EMILY, *carrying an armful of—imaginary— schoolbooks, comes along Main Street from the left.*)

EMILY. I can't, Louise. I've got to go home. Good-by. Oh, Ernestine! Ernestine! Can you come over tonight and do Latin? Isn't that Cicero the worst thing—! Tell your mother you *have* to. G'by. G'by, Helen. G'by, Fred.

(GEORGE, *also carrying books, catches up with her.*)

GEORGE. Can I carry your books home for you, Emily?

EMILY (*coolly*). Why . . . uh . . . Thank you. It isn't far. (*She gives them to him.*)

GEORGE. Excuse me a minute, Emily.—Say, Bob, if I'm a little late, start practice anyway. And give Herb some long high ones.

EMILY. Good-by, Lizzy.

GEORGE. Good-by, Lizzy.—I'm awfully glad you were elected, too, Emily.

EMILY. Thank you.

(*They have been standing on Main Street, almost against the back wall. They take the first steps toward the audience when* GEORGE *stops and says:*)

GEORGE. Emily, why are you mad at me?

EMILY. I'm not mad at you.

GEORGE. You've been treating me so funny lately.

EMILY. Well, since you ask me, I might as well say it right out, George—(*She catches sight of a teacher passing.*) Good-by, Miss Corcoran.

GEORGE. Good-by, Miss Corcoran.—Wha— what is it?

EMILY (*not scoldingly; finding it difficult to say*). I don't like the whole change that's come over you in the last year. I'm sorry if that hurts your feelings, but I've got to—tell the truth and shame the devil.

GEORGE. A *change?*—Wha—what do you mean?

EMILY. Well, up to a year ago I used to like you a lot. And I used to watch you as you did everything . . . because we'd been friends so long . . . and then you began spending all your time at *baseball* . . . and you never stopped to speak to anybody anymore. Not even to your own family you didn't . . . and, George, it's a fact, you've got awful conceited and stuck-up, and all the girls say so. They may not say so to your face, but that's what they say about you behind your back, and it hurts me to hear them say it, but I've got to agree with them a little. I'm sorry if it hurts your feelings . . . but I can't be sorry I said it.

GEORGE. I . . . I'm glad you said it, Emily. I never thought that such a thing was happening to me. I guess it's hard for a fella not to have faults creep into his character.

(*They take a step or two in silence, then stand still in misery.*)

EMILY. I always expect a man to be perfect and I think he should be.

GEORGE. Oh . . . I don't think it's possible to be perfect, Emily.

EMILY. Well, my *father* is, and as far as I can see *your* father is. There's no reason on earth why you shouldn't be, too.

GEORGE. Well, I feel it's the other way round. That men aren't naturally good; but girls are.

EMILY. Well, you might as well know right now that I'm not perfect. It's not as easy for a girl to be perfect as a man, because we girls are more—more—nervous.—Now I'm sorry I said all that about you. I don't know what made me say it.

GEORGE. Emily—

EMILY. Now I can see it's not the truth at all. And I suddenly feel that it isn't important, anyway.

GEORGE. Emily . . . would you like an ice-cream soda, or something, before you go home?

EMILY. Well, thank you. . . . I would.

(*They advance toward the audience and make an abrupt right turn, opening the door of* MORGAN'S *drugstore. Under strong emotion,* EMILY *keeps her face down.* GEORGE *speaks to some passers-by.*)

GEORGE. Hello, Stew—how are you?—Good afternoon, Mrs. Slocum.

(*The* STAGE MANAGER, *wearing spectacles and assuming the role of* MR. MORGAN, *enters abruptly from the right and stands between the audience and the counter of his soda fountain.*)

STAGE MANAGER. Hello, George. Hello, Emily.—What'll you have?—Why, Emily Webb—what you been crying about?

GEORGE (*he gropes for an explanation*). She . . . she just got an awful scare, Mr. Mor-

gan. She almost got run over by that hardware-store wagon. Everybody says that Tom Huckins drives like a crazy man.

STAGE MANAGER (*drawing a drink of water*). Well, now! You take a drink of water, Emily. You look all shook up. I tell you, you've got to look both ways before you cross Main Street these days. Gets worse every year.—What'll you have?

EMILY. I'll have a strawberry phosphate, thank you, Mr. Morgan.

GEORGE. No, no, Emily. Have an ice-cream soda with me. Two strawberry ice-cream sodas, Mr. Morgan.

STAGE MANAGER (*working the faucets*). Two strawberry ice-cream sodas, yes sir. Yes, sir. There are a hundred and twenty-five horses in Grover's Corners this minute I'm talking to you. State Inspector was in here yesterday. And now they're bringing in these automobiles, the best thing to do is to just stay home. Why, I can remember when a dog could go to sleep all day in the middle of Main Street and nothing come along to disturb him. (*He sets the imaginary glasses before them.*) There they are. Enjoy 'em. (*He sees a customer, right.*) Yes, Mrs. Ellis. What can I do for you? (*He goes out right.*)

EMILY. They're so expensive.

GEORGE. No, no—don't you think of that. We're celebrating our election. And then do you know what else I'm celebrating?

EMILY. N-no.

GEORGE. I'm celebrating because I've got a friend who tells me all the things that ought to be told me.

EMILY. George, *please* don't think of that. I don't know why I said it. It's not true. You're—

GEORGE. No, Emily, you stick to it. I'm glad you spoke to me like you did. But you'll *see*: I'm going to change so quick—you bet I'm going to change. And, Emily, I want to ask you a favor.

EMILY. What?

GEORGE. Emily, if I go away to State Agriculture College next year, will you write me a letter once in a while?

EMILY. I certainly will. I certainly will, George. . . . (*Pause. They start sipping the sodas through the straws.*) It certainly seems like being away three years you'd get out of touch with things. Maybe letters from Grover's Corners wouldn't be so interesting after a while. Grover's Corners isn't a very important place when you think of all—New Hampshire; but I think it's a very nice town.

GEORGE. The day wouldn't come when I wouldn't want to know everything that's happening here. I know *that's* true, Emily.

EMILY. Well, I'll try to make my letters interesting. (*Pause*)

GEORGE. Y'know, Emily, whenever I meet a farmer I ask him if he thinks it's important to go to Agriculture School to be a good farmer.

EMILY. Why, George—

GEORGE. Yeah, and some of them say that it's even a waste of time. You can get all those things, anyway, out of the pamphlets the government sends out. And Uncle Luke's getting old—he's about ready for me to start in taking over his farm tomorrow, if I could.

EMILY. My!

GEORGE. And, like you say, being gone all that time . . . in other places and meeting other people . . . Gosh, if anything like that can happen I don't want to go away. I guess new people aren't any better than old ones. I'll bet they almost never are. Emily . . . I feel that you're as good a friend as I've got. I don't need to go and meet the people in other towns.

EMILY. But, George, maybe it's very important for you to go and learn all that about—cattle judging and soils and those things. . . . Of course, I don't know.

GEORGE (*after a pause, very seriously*). Emily, I'm going to make up my mind right now. I won't

go. I'll tell Pa about it tonight.

EMILY. Why, George, I don't see why you have to decide right now. It's a whole year away.

GEORGE. Emily, I'm glad you spoke to me about that . . . that fault in my character. What you said was right; but there was *one* thing wrong in it, and that was when you said that for a year I wasn't noticing people, and . . . you, for instance. Why, you say you were watching me when I did everything. . . . I was doing the same about you all the time. Why, sure—I always thought about you as one of the chief people I thought about. I always made sure where you were sitting on the bleachers, and who you were with, and for three days now I've been trying to walk home with you; but something's always got in the way. Yesterday I was standing over against the wall waiting for you, and you walked home with *Miss Corcoran*.

EMILY. George! . . . Life's awful funny! How could I have known that? Why, I thought—

GEORGE. Listen, Emily, I'm going to tell you why I'm not going to Agriculture School. I think that once you've found a person that you're very fond of . . . I mean a person who's fond of you, too, and likes you enough to be interested in your character . . . Well, I think that's just as important as college is, and even more so. That's what I think.

EMILY. I think it's awfully important, too.

GEORGE. Emily.

EMILY. Y-yes, George.

GEORGE. Emily, if I *do* improve and make a big change . . . would you be . . . I mean: *could* you be . . .

EMILY. I . . . I am now; I always have been.

GEORGE (*pause*). So I guess this is an important talk we've been having.

EMILY. Yes . . . yes.

GEORGE (*takes a deep breath and straightens his back*). Wait just a minute and I'll walk you home. (*With mounting alarm he digs into his pockets for the money. The* STAGE MANAGER *enters, right.* GEORGE, *deeply embarrassed, but direct, says to him)* Mr. Morgan, I'll have to go home and get the money to pay you for this. It'll only take a minute.

STAGE MANAGER (*pretending to be affronted*). What's that? George Gibbs, do you mean to tell me—!

GEORGE. Yes, but I had reasons, Mr. Morgan.— Look, here's my gold watch to keep until I come back with the money.

STAGE MANAGER. That's all right. Keep your watch. I'll trust you.

GEORGE. I'll be back in five minutes.

STAGE MANAGER. I'll trust you ten years, George—not a day over.—Got all over your shock, Emily?

EMILY. Yes, thank you, Mr. Morgan. It was nothing.

GEORGE (*taking up the books from the counter*). I'm ready.

(*They walk in grave silence across the stage and pass through the trellis at the* WEBBS' *back door and disappear. The* STAGE MANAGER *watches them go out, then turns to the audience, removing his spectacles.*)

STAGE MANAGER. Well—(*He claps his hands as a signal.*) Now we're ready to get on with the wedding. (*He stands waiting while the set is prepared for the next scene.* STAGEHANDS *remove the chairs, tables, and trellises from the* GIBBS *and* WEBB *houses. They arrange the pews for the church in the center of the stage. The congregation will sit facing the back wall. The aisle of the church starts at the center of the back wall and comes toward the audience. A small platform is placed against the back wall on which the* STAGE MANAGER *will stand later, playing the minister. The image of a stained-glass window is cast from a lantern slide upon the back wall. When all is ready the* STAGE MANAGER *strolls to the center of the stage, down front, and musingly, addresses the audience.*) There are a lot of things to be said about a wedding; there are a lot of thoughts that go on during a wedding. We can't get them all into one wedding, naturally, and especially not into a wedding at Grover's Corners, where they're awfully plain and short. In this wedding I play the minister. That gives me the right to say a few more things about it. For a while now, the play gets pretty serious. Y'see, some churches say that marriage is a sacrament. I don't quite know what that means, but I can guess. Like Mrs. Gibbs said a few minutes ago: People were made to live two-by-two. This is a good wedding, but people are so put together that even at a good wedding there's a lot of confusion way down deep in people's minds and we thought that that ought to be in our play, too.

The real hero of this scene isn't on the stage at all, and you know who that is. It's like what one of those European fellas said: every child born into the world is nature's attempt to make a perfect human being. Well, we've seen nature pushing and contriving for some time now. We all know that nature's interested in quantity; but I think she's interested in quality, too— that's why I'm in the ministry. And don't forget all the other witnesses at this wedding—the ancestors. Millions of them. Most of them set out to live two-by-two, also. Millions of them.

Well, that's all my sermon. 'Twan't very long, anyway.

(*The organ starts playing Handel's "Largo." The congregation streams into the church and sits in silence. Church bells are heard.* MRS. GIBBS *sits in the front row, the first seat on the aisle, the right section; next to her are* REBECCA *and* DR. GIBBS. *Across the aisle* MRS. WEBB, WALLY, *and* MR. WEBB. *A small choir takes its place, facing the audience under the stained-glass window.* MRS. WEBB, *on the way to her place, turns back and speaks to the audience.*)

MRS. WEBB. I don't know why on earth I should be crying. I suppose there's nothing to cry about. It came over me at breakfast this morning; there was Emily eating her breakfast as she's done for seventeen years and now she's going off to eat it in someone else's house. I suppose that's it. And Emily! She suddenly said: I can't eat another mouthful, and she put her head down on the table and *she* cried. (*She starts toward her seat in the church, but turns back and adds*) Oh, I've got to say it: you know, there's something downright cruel about sending our girls out into marriage this way. I hope some of her girlfriends have told her a thing or two. It's cruel, I know, but I couldn't bring myself to say anything. I went into it blind as a bat myself. (*In half-amused exasperation*) The whole world's wrong, that's what's the matter. There they come. (*She hurries to her place in the pew.*)

(GEORGE *starts to come down the right aisle of the theater, through the audience. Suddenly* THREE MEMBERS *of his baseball team appear by the right proscenium pillar and start whistling and catcalling to him. They are dressed for the ball field.*)

THE BASEBALL PLAYERS. Eh, George, George! Hsst—yaow! Look at him, fellas—he looks scared to death. Yaow! George, don't look so innocent, you old geezer. We know what you're thinking. Don't disgrace the team, big boy. Whoo-oo-oo.

STAGE MANAGER. All right! All right! That'll do. That's enough of that. (*Smiling, he pushes them off the stage. They lean back to shout a few more catcalls.*) There used to be an awful lot to that kind of thing at weddings in the old days—Rome, and later. We're more civilized now—so they say.

(*The choir starts singing "Love Divine, All Love Excelling—"* GEORGE *has reached the stage. He stares at the congregation a moment, then takes a few steps of withdrawal, toward the right proscenium pillar. His mother, from the front row, seems to have felt his confusion. She leaves her seat and comes down the aisle quickly to him.*)

MRS. GIBBS. George! George! What's the matter?

GEORGE. Ma, I don't want to grow old. Why's everybody pushing me so?

MRS. GIBBS. Why, George . . . you wanted it.

GEORGE. No, Ma, listen to me—

MRS. GIBBS. No, no, George—you're a man now.

GEORGE. Listen, Ma—for the last time I ask you . . . All I want to do is to be a fella—

MRS. GIBBS. George! If anyone should hear you! Now stop. Why, I'm ashamed of you!

GEORGE (*he comes to himself and looks over the scene*). What? Where's Emily?

MRS. GIBBS (*relieved*). George! You gave me such a turn.

GEORGE. Cheer up, Ma. I'm getting married.

MRS. GIBBS. Let me catch my breath a minute.

GEORGE (*comforting her*). Now, Ma, you save Thursday nights. Emily and I are coming over to dinner every Thursday night . . . you'll see. Ma, what are you crying for? Come on; we've got to get ready for this.

(MRS. GIBBS, *mastering her emotion, fixes his tie and whispers to him. In the meantime,* EMILY, *in white and wearing her wedding veil, has come through the audience and mounted onto the stage. She too draws back, frightened, when she sees the congregation in the church. The choir begins: "Blessed Be the Tie That Binds."*)

EMILY. I never felt so alone in my whole life. And George over there, looking so . . . ! I *hate* him. I wish I were dead. Papa! Papa!

MR. WEBB (*leaves his seat in the pews and comes toward her anxiously*). Emily! Emily! Now don't get upset. . . .

EMILY. But, Papa—I don't want to get married. . . .

MR. WEBB. Sh—sh—Emily. Everything's all right.

EMILY. Why can't I stay for a while just as I am? Let's go away—

MR. WEBB. No, no, Emily. Now stop and think a minute.

EMILY. Don't you remember that you used to say—all the time you used to say—all the time: that I was *your* girl! There must be lots of places we can go to. I'll work for you. I could keep house.

MR. WEBB. Sh . . . You mustn't think of such things. You're just nervous, Emily. (*He turns and calls:*) George! George! Will you come here a minute? (*He leads her toward* GEORGE.) Why, you're marrying the best young fellow in the world. George is a fine fellow.

EMILY. But Papa—

(MRS. GIBBS *returns unobtrusively to her seat.* MR. WEBB *has one arm around his daughter. He places his hand on* GEORGE's *shoulder.*)

MR. WEBB. I'm giving away my daughter, George. Do you think you can take care of her?

GEORGE. Mr. Webb, I want to . . . I want to try. Emily, I'm going to do my best. I love you, Emily. I need you.

EMILY. Well, if you love me, help me. All I want is someone to love me.

GEORGE. I will, Emily. Emily, I'll try.

EMILY. And I mean for*ever*. Do you hear? Forever and ever.

(*They fall into each other's arms. The "March" from* Lohengrin *is heard. The* STAGE MANAGER, *as* CLERGYMAN, *stands on the box, up center.*)

MR. WEBB. Come, they're waiting for us. Now you know it'll be all right. Come, quick.

(GEORGE *slips away and takes his place beside the* STAGE MANAGER-CLERGYMAN. EMILY *proceeds up the aisle on her father's arm.*)

STAGE MANAGER. Do you, George, take this

EMILY and GEORGE get married.

woman, Emily, to be your wedded wife, to have . . .

(MRS. SOAMES *has been sitting in the last row of the congregation. She now turns to her neighbors and speaks in a shrill voice. Her chatter drowns out the rest of the* CLERGYMAN'S *words.*)

**MRS. SOAMES.** Perfectly lovely wedding! Loveliest wedding I ever saw. Oh, I do love a good wedding, don't you? Doesn't she make a lovely bride?

**GEORGE.** I do.

**STAGE MANAGER.** Do you, Emily, take this man, George, to be your wedded husband—

(*Again his further words are covered by those of* MRS. SOAMES.)

**MRS. SOAMES.** Don't know *when* I've seen such a lovely wedding. But I always cry. Don't know why it is, but I always cry. I just like to see young people happy, don't you? Oh, I think it's lovely.

(*The ring. The kiss. The stage is suddenly arrested into silent tableau. The* STAGE MANAGER, *his eyes on the distance, as though to himself:*)

**STAGE MANAGER.** I've married over two hundred couples in my day. Do I believe in it? I don't know. M. . . . marries N. . . . millions of them. The cottage, the go-cart, the Sunday-afternoon drives in the Ford, the first rheumatism, the grandchildren, the second rheumatism, the deathbed, the reading of the will— (*He now looks at the audience for the first time, with a warm smile that removes any sense of cynicism from the next line.*) Once in a thousand times it's interesting.

—Well, let's have Mendelssohn's "Wedding March"!

(*The organ picks up the "March." The* BRIDE *and* GROOM *come down the aisle, radiant, but trying to be very dignified.*)

**MRS. SOAMES.** Aren't they a lovely couple? Oh, I've never been to such a nice wedding. I'm sure they'll be happy. I always say: *happiness,* that's the great thing! The important thing is to be happy.

(*The* BRIDE *and* GROOM *reach the steps leading into the audience. A bright light is thrown upon them. They descend into the auditorium and run up the aisle joyously.*)

**STAGE MANAGER** That's all the Second Act, folks. Ten minutes' intermission.

---

## THINK AND DISCUSS
### Understanding
1. What is the time—year, day, and hour—at the beginning of Act Two?
2. What do we learn is about to happen from Howie Newsome's conversations with various characters at the opening of the act?
3. When were George and Emily elected to high-school class offices, and what offices did they hold?
4. Why, according to the Stage Manager, does he present the scene that takes place just after the high-school election?

### Analyzing
5. Compare and contrast the brief appearances of the paperboy and milkman with their similar roles in Act One. Discuss the effect of having them in both acts.
6. Describe the nature of the advice that Mr.

Webb gives to George, his future son-in-law, on the morning of the wedding.

7. In the scene showing how their love began, what does Emily's frank criticism of George reveal about each of them?

8. Why does George decide soon after Emily's long speech that he does not want to go to college? Is his decision the right one, in your opinion? Discuss.

9. Just before the wedding, neither Emily nor George seems to want to go through with it. Why are they suddenly reluctant and how do they overcome these feelings?

10. What is the nature of Mrs. Soames's comments during the wedding, and what effect do they have on the solemnity of the scene?

### Extending

11. In his opening speech for Act Two, the Stage Manager describes the passing of three years in terms of a thousand sunrises and the erosion of mountainsides. How would *you* describe the passage of three years? What changes or activities can you imagine during this period?

### APPLYING: Flashback   H𝒯
See Handbook of Literary Terms, p. 798

A **flashback** is an interruption of a narrative for the portrayal of an earlier incident or sequence of events. Flashbacks are common in novels and short stories, where the story is told rather than acted out. They do not occur often in stage plays, however, where it is more difficult to show movement backward in time. The scene showing Emily and George discovering their affection for one another following the high-school election is a flashback.

1. Why does the flashback not seem unexpected or out of place in this play?

2. Could the information in the flashback have been communicated as effectively if it had just been explained by one of the characters? Why or why not?

### COMPOSITION   ◄━━━
#### Writing a Note of Congratulations

Assume you are in the same class as George and Emily and you are fond of them both. As a boy you may have had a crush on Emily; as a girl, on George. Write a two-paragraph note to them after the wedding congratulating them on their marriage and wishing them happiness on the farm. Before writing, decide whether you attended and heard the ceremony or perhaps sat behind Mrs. Soames and heard about it from her. Try to write the note with a light touch, avoiding clichés.

#### Describing a Character

From the little we see of Mrs. Soames in the play, imagine her background. Write a three-paragraph letter to a friend who could not attend the wedding (and who doesn't know Mrs. Soames), giving a brief account of what happened and a thumbnail sketch of Mrs. Soames—her background and appearance. Include details that you think will make her vivid to your friend. See "Writing About Characters" in the Writer's Handbook.

# ACT THREE

*During the intermission the audience has seen the* STAGEHANDS *arranging the stage. On the right-hand side, a little right of the center, ten or twelve ordinary chairs have been placed in three openly spaced rows facing the audience.*

*These are graves in the cemetery.*

*Toward the end of the intermission the* ACTORS *enter and take their places. The front row contains: toward the center of the stage, an empty chair; then* MRS. GIBBS; SIMON STIMSON.

*The second row contains, among others,* MRS. SOAMES. *The third row has* WALLY WEBB.

*The dead do not turn their heads or their eyes to right or left, but they sit in a quiet without stiffness. When they speak their tone is matter-of-fact, without sentimentality and, above all, without lugubriousness.*

*The* STAGE MANAGER *takes his accustomed place and waits for the house lights to go down.*

**STAGE MANAGER.** This time nine years have gone by, friends—summer, 1913. Gradual changes in Grover's Corners. Horses are getting rarer. Farmers coming into town in Fords. Everybody locks their house doors now at night. Ain't been any burglars in town yet, but everybody's heard about 'em. You'd be surprised, though—on the whole, things don't change much around here.

This is certainly an important part of Grover's Corners. It's on a hilltop—a windy hilltop—lots of sky, lots of clouds—often lots of sun and moon and stars. You come up here on a fine afternoon and you can see range on range of hills—awful blue they are—up there by Lake Sunapee and Lake Winnipesaukee . . . and way up, if you've got a glass, you can see the White Mountains and Mt. Washington—where North Conway and Conway is. And, of course, our favorite mountain, Mt. Monadnock,[1] 's right here—and all these towns that lie around it: Jaffrey, 'n East Jaffrey, 'n Peterborough, 'n Dublin; and *(Then pointing down in the audience)* there, quite a ways down, is Grover's Corners. Yes, beautiful spot up here. Mountain laurel and li-lacks. I often wonder why people like to be buried in Woodlawn and Brooklyn when they might pass the same time up here in New Hampshire. Over there— *(Pointing to stage left)* are the old stones—1670, 1680. Strong-minded people that come a long way to be independent. Summer people walk around there laughing at the funny words on the tombstones . . . it don't do any harm. And genealogists come up from Boston—get paid by city people for looking up their ancestors. They want to make sure they're Daughters of the American Revolution and of the *Mayflower*. . . . Well, I guess that don't do any harm, either. Wherever you come near the human race, there's layers and layers of nonsense. . . .

Over there are some Civil War veterans. Iron flags on their graves . . . New Hampshire boys . . . had a notion that the Union ought to be kept together, though they'd never seen more than fifty miles of it themselves. All they knew was the name, friends—the United States of America. The United States of America. And they went and died about it.

This here is the new part of the cemetery. Here's your friend Mrs. Gibbs. 'N let me see—here's Mr. Stimson, organist at the Congregational Church. And Mrs. Soames who enjoyed the wedding so—you remember? Oh, and a lot of others. And Editor Webb's boy, Wallace, whose appendix burst while he was on a Boy Scout trip to Crawford Notch. Yes, an awful lot of sorrow has sort of quieted down up here. People just wild with grief have brought their relatives up to this hill. We all know how it

---

1. *Monadnock* (mə näd′nok).

is . . . and then time . . . and sunny days . . . and rainy days . . . 'n snow . . . We're all glad they're in a beautiful place and we're coming up here ourselves when our fit's over.

Now there are some things we all know, but we don't take'm out and look at'm very often. We all know that *something* is eternal. And it ain't houses and it ain't names, and it ain't earth, and it ain't even the stars . . . everybody knows in their bones that *something* is eternal, and that something has to do with human beings. All the greatest people ever lived have been telling us that for five thousand years and yet you'd be surprised how people are always losing hold of it. There's something way down deep that's eternal about every human being. (*Pause*)

You know as well as I do that the dead don't stay interested in us living people for very long. Gradually, gradually, they lose hold of the earth . . . and the ambitions they had . . . and the pleasures they had . . . and the things they suffered . . . and the people they loved. They get weaned away from earth—that's the way I put it—weaned away. And they stay here while the earth part of 'em burns away, burns out; and all that time they slowly get indifferent to what's goin' on in Grover's Corners. They're waitin' for something that they feel is comin'. Something important, and great. Aren't they waitin' for the eternal part in them to come out clear? Some of the things they're going to say maybe'll hurt your feelings—but that's the way it is: mother 'n daughter . . . husband 'n wife . . . enemy 'n enemy . . . money 'n miser . . . all those terribly important things kind of grow pale around here. And what's left when memory's gone, and your identity, Mrs. Smith? (*He looks at the audience a minute, then turns to the stage.*) Well! There are some *living* people. There's Joe Stoddard, our undertaker, supervising a new-made grave. And here comes a Grover's Corners boy, that left town to go out West.

(JOE STODDARD *has hovered about in the background.* SAM CRAIG *enters left, wiping his forehead from the exertion. He carries an umbrella and strolls front.*)

SAM CRAIG. Good afternoon, Joe Stoddard.

JOE STODDARD. Good afternoon, good afternoon. Let me see now: do I know you?

SAM CRAIG. I'm Sam Craig.

JOE STODDARD. Gracious sakes' alive! Of all people! I should'a knowed you'd be back for the funeral. You've been away a long time, Sam.

SAM CRAIG. Yes, I've been away over twelve years. I'm in business out in Buffalo now, Joe. But I was in the East when I got news of my cousin's death, so I thought I'd combine things a little and come and see the old home. You look well.

JOE STODDARD. Yes, yes, can't complain. Very sad, our journey today, Samuel.

SAM CRAIG. Yes.

JOE STODDARD. Yes, yes. I always say I hate to supervise when a young person is taken. They'll be here in a few minutes now. I had to come here early today—my son's supervisin' at the home.

SAM CRAIG (*reading stones*). Old Farmer McCarty, I used to do chores for him—after school. He had the lumbago.

JOE STODDARD. Yes, we brought Farmer McCarty here a number of years ago now.

SAM CRAIG (*staring at* MRS. GIBBS's *knees*). Why, this is my Aunt Julia. . . . I'd forgotten that she'd . . . of course, of course.

JOE STODDARD. Yes, Doc Gibbs lost his wife two-three years ago . . . about this time. And today's another pretty bad blow for him, too.

MRS. GIBBS (*to* SIMON STIMSON, *in an even voice*). That's my sister Carey's boy, Sam . . . Sam Craig.

SIMON STIMSON. I'm always uncomfortable

when *they're* around.

**MRS. GIBBS.** Simon.

**SAM CRAIG.** Do they choose their own verses much, Joe?

**JOE STODDARD.** No . . . not usual. Mostly the bereaved pick a verse.

**SAM CRAIG.** Doesn't sound like Aunt Julia. There aren't many of those Hersey sisters left now. Let me see: where are . . . I wanted to look at my father's and mother's . . .

**JOE STODDARD.** Over there with the Craigs . . . Avenue F.

**SAM CRAIG** (*reading* SIMON STIMSON's *epitaph*). He was organist at church, wasn't he?—Hm, drank a lot, we used to say.

**JOE STODDARD.** Nobody was supposed to know about it. He'd seen a peck of trouble. (*Behind his hand*) Took his own life, y'know?

**SAM CRAIG.** Oh, did he?

**JOE STODDARD.** Hung himself in the attic. They tried to hush it up, but of course it got around. He chose his own epy-taph. You can see it there. It ain't a verse exactly.

**SAM CRAIG.** Why, it's just some notes of music—what is it?

**JOE STODDARD.** Oh, I wouldn't know. It was wrote up in the Boston papers at the time.

**SAM CRAIG.** Joe, what did she die of?

**JOE STODDARD.** Who?

**SAM CRAIG.** My cousin.

**JOE STODDARD.** Oh, didn't you know? Had some trouble bringing a baby into the world. 'Twas her second, though. There's a little boy 'bout four years old.

**SAM CRAIG** (*opening his umbrella*). The grave's going to be over there?

**JOE STODDARD.** Yes, there ain't much more room over here among the Gibbses, so they're opening a whole new Gibbs section over by Avenue B. You'll excuse me now. I see they're comin'.

(*From left to center, at the back of the stage, comes a procession. Four Men carry a casket, invisible to us. All the rest are under umbrellas. One can vaguely see:* DR. GIBBS, GEORGE, *the* WEBBS, *etc. They gather about a grave in the back center of the stage, a little to the left of center.*)

**MRS. SOAMES.** Who is it, Julia?

**MRS. GIBBS** (*without raising her eyes*). My daughter-in-law, Emily Webb.

**MRS. SOAMES** (*a little surprised, but no emotion*). Well, I declare! The road up here must have been awful muddy. What did she die of, Julia?

**MRS. GIBBS.** In childbirth.

**MRS. SOAMES.** Childbirth. (*Almost with a laugh*) I'd forgotten all about that. My, wasn't life awful—(*With a sigh*) and wonderful.

**SIMON STIMSON** (*with a sideways glance*). Wonderful, was it?

**MRS. GIBBS.** Simon! Now, remember!

**MRS. SOAMES.** I remember Emily's wedding. Wasn't it a lovely wedding! And I remember her reading the class poem at Graduation Exercises. Emily was one of the brightest girls ever graduated from High School. I've heard Principal Wilkins say so time after time. I called on them at their new farm, just before I died. Perfectly beautiful farm.

**A WOMAN FROM AMONG THE DEAD.** It's on the same road we lived on.

**A MAN AMONG THE DEAD.** Yepp, right smart farm.

(*They subside. The group by the grave starts singing "Blessed Be the Tie That Binds."*)

**A WOMAN AMONG THE DEAD.** I always liked that hymn. I was hopin' they'd sing a hymn.

(*Pause. Suddenly* EMILY *appears from among the umbrellas. She is wearing a white dress. Her hair is down her back and tied by a white ribbon like a little girl. She comes slowly, gazing wonderingly at the dead, a little dazed. She stops halfway and smiles faintly. After looking at the mourners for a moment, she walks slowly to the vacant chair beside* MRS. GIBBS *and sits down.*)

EMILY (*to them all, quietly, smiling*). Hello.

MRS. SOAMES. Hello, Emily.

A MAN AMONG THE DEAD. Hello, M's Gibbs.

EMILY (*warmly*). Hello, Mother Gibbs.

MRS. GIBBS. Emily.

EMILY. Hello. (*With surprise*) It's raining. (*Her eyes drift back to the funeral company.*)

MRS. GIBBS. Yes . . . They'll be gone soon, dear. Just rest yourself.

EMILY. It seems thousands and thousands of years since I . . . Papa remembered that that was my favorite hymn. Oh, I wish I'd been here a long time. I don't like being new here.—How do you do, Mr. Stimson?

SIMON STIMSON. How do you do, Emily.

(EMILY *continues to look about her with a wondering smile; as though to shut out from her mind the thought of the funeral company she starts speaking to* MRS. GIBBS *with a touch of nervousness.*)

EMILY. Mother Gibbs, George and I have made that farm into just the best place you ever saw. We thought of you all the time. We wanted to show you the new barn and a great long cement drinking fountain for the stock. We bought that out of the money you left us.

MRS. GIBBS. I did?

EMILY. Don't you remember, Mother Gibbs— the legacy you left us? Why, it was over three hundred and fifty dollars.

MRS. GIBBS. Yes, yes, Emily.

EMILY. Well, there's a patent device on the drinking fountain so that it never overflows, Mother Gibbs, and it never sinks below a certain mark they have there. It's fine. (*Her voice trails off and her eyes return to the funeral group.*) It won't be the same to George without me, but it's a lovely farm. (*Suddenly she looks directly at* MRS. GIBBS.) Live people don't understand, do they?

MRS. GIBBS. No, dear—not very much.

EMILY. They're sort of shut up in little boxes, aren't they? I feel as though I knew them last a thousand years ago. . . . My boy is spending the day at Mrs. Carter's. (*She sees* MR. CARTER *among the dead.*) Oh, Mr. Carter, my little boy is spending the day at your house.

MR. CARTER. Is he?

EMILY. Yes, he loves it there—Mother Gibbs, we have a Ford, too. Never gives any trouble. I don't drive, though. Mother Gibbs, when does this feeling go away?—Of being . . . one of *them*? How long does it . . . ?

MRS. GIBBS. Sh! dear. Just wait and be patient.

EMILY (*with a sigh*). I know.—Look, they're finished. They're going.

MRS. GIBBS. Sh—

(*The umbrellas leave the stage.* DR. GIBBS *has come over to his wife's grave and stands before it a moment.* EMILY *looks up at his face.* MRS. GIBBS *does not raise her eyes.*)

EMILY. Look! Father Gibbs is bringing some of my flowers to you. He looks just like George, doesn't he? Oh, Mother Gibbs, I never realized before how troubled and how . . . how in the dark live persons are. Look at him. I loved him so. From morning till night, that's all they are—troubled. (DR. GIBBS *goes off.*)

THE DEAD. Little cooler than it was.—Yes, that rain's cooled it off a little. Those northeast winds always do the same thing, don't they? If it isn't a rain, it's a three-day blow.

(*A patient calm falls on the stage. The* STAGE MANAGER *appears at his proscenium pillar, smoking.* EMILY *sits up abruptly with an idea.*)

EMILY. But, Mother Gibbs, one can go back; one can go back there again . . . into living. I feel it. I know it. Why just then for a moment I was thinking about . . . about the farm . . . and for a minute I *was* there, and my baby was on my lap as plain as day.

MRS. GIBBS. Yes, of course you can.

EMILY. I can go back there and live all those days over again . . . why not?

MRS. GIBBS. All I can say is, Emily, don't.

EMILY (*she appeals urgently to the* STAGE MAN-

Characters sit in the cemetery in Grover's Corners. In this production, crates are used in place of chairs.

AGER). But it's true, isn't it? I can go and live . . . back there . . . again.

STAGE MANAGER. Yes, some have tried—but they soon come back here.

MRS. GIBBS. Don't do it, Emily.

MRS. SOAMES. Emily, don't. It's not what you think it'd be.

EMILY. But I won't live over a sad day. I'll choose a happy one—I'll choose the day I first knew I loved George. Why should that be painful?

(*They are silent. Her question turns to the* STAGE MANAGER.)

STAGE MANAGER. You not only live it; but you watch yourself living it.

EMILY. Yes?

STAGE MANAGER. And as you watch it, you see the thing that they—down there—never know. You see the future. You know what's going to happen afterwards.

EMILY. But is that—painful? Why?

MRS. GIBBS. That's not the only reason why you shouldn't do it, Emily. When you've been here longer you'll see that our life here is to forget all that, and think only of what's ahead, and be ready for what's ahead. When you've been here longer you'll understand.

EMILY (*softly*). But, Mother Gibbs, how can I *ever* forget that life? It's all I know. It's all I had.

MRS. SOAMES. Oh, Emily. It isn't wise. Really, it isn't.

EMILY. But it's a thing I must know for myself. I'll choose a happy day, anyway.

MRS. GIBBS. *No!*—At least, choose an unimportant day. Choose the least important day in your life. It will be important enough.

EMILY (*to herself*). Then it can't be since I was married; or since the baby was born. (*To the* STAGE MANAGER, *eagerly*) I can choose a birthday at least, can't I?—I choose my twelfth birthday.

STAGE MANAGER. All right. February 11th, 1899. A Tuesday. ——Do you want any special time of day?

EMILY. Oh, I want the whole day.

STAGE MANAGER. We'll begin at dawn. You remember it had been snowing for several days; but it had stopped the night before, and they had begun clearing the roads. The sun's coming up.

EMILY (*with a cry; rising*). There's Main Street . . . why, that's Mr. Morgan's drugstore before he changed it! . . . And there's the livery stable.

(*The stage at no time in this act has been very dark; but now the left half of the stage gradually becomes very bright—the brightness of a crisp winter morning.* EMILY *walks toward Main Street.*)

STAGE MANAGER. Yes, it's 1899. This is fourteen years ago.

EMILY. Oh, that's the town I knew as a little girl. And, *look*, there's the old white fence that used to be around our house. Oh, I'd forgotten that! Oh, I love it so! Are they inside?

STAGE MANAGER. Yes, your mother'll be coming downstairs in a minute to make breakfast.

EMILY (*softly*). Will she?

STAGE MANAGER. And you remember: your father had been away for several days; he came back on the early-morning train.

EMILY. No . . . ?

STAGE MANAGER. He'd been back to his college to make a speech—in western New York, at Clinton.

EMILY. Look! There's Howie Newsome. There's our policeman. But he's *dead*; he *died.*

(*The voices of* HOWIE NEWSOME, CONSTABLE WARREN, *and* JOE CROWELL, JR., *are heard at the left of the stage.* EMILY *listens in delight.*)

HOWIE NEWSOME. Whoa, Bessie!—Bessie! 'Morning, Bill.

CONSTABLE WARREN. Morning, Howie.

HOWIE NEWSOME. You're up early.

CONSTABLE WARREN. Been rescuin' a party; darn near froze to death, down by Polish Town thar.

Got drunk and lay out in the snowdrifts. Thought he was in bed when I shook'm.

EMILY. Why, there's Joe Crowell. . . .

JOE CROWELL. Good morning, Mr. Warren. 'Morning, Howie.

(MRS. WEBB *has appeared in her kitchen, but* EMILY *does not see her until she calls.*)

MRS. WEBB. Chil-*dren!* Wally! Emily! . . . Time to get up.

EMILY. Mama, I'm here! Oh! how young Mama looks! I didn't know Mama was ever that young.

MRS. WEBB. You can come and dress by the kitchen fire, if you like; but hurry. (HOWIE NEWSOME *has entered along Main Street and brings the milk to* MRS. WEBB'S *door.*) Good morning, Mr. Newsome. Whhhh—it's cold.

HOWIE NEWSOME. Ten below by my barn, Mrs. Webb.

MRS. WEBB. Think of it! Keep yourself wrapped up. (*She takes her bottles in, shuddering.*)

EMILY (*with an effort*). Mama, I can't find my blue hair ribbon anywhere.

MRS. WEBB. Just open your eyes, dear, that's all. I laid it out for you special—on the dresser, there. If it were a snake it would bite you.

EMILY. Yes, yes . . .

(*She puts her hand on her heart.* MR. WEBB *comes along Main Street, where he meets* CONSTABLE WARREN. *Their movements and voices are increasingly lively in the sharp air.*)

MR. WEBB. Good morning, Bill.

CONSTABLE WARREN. Good morning, Mr. Webb. You're up early.

MR. WEBB. Yes, just been back to my old college in New York State. Been any trouble here?

CONSTABLE WARREN. Well, I was called up this mornin' to rescue a Polish fella—darn near froze to death he was.

MR. WEBB. We must get it in the paper.

CONSTABLE WARREN. 'Twan't much.

EMILY (*whispers*). Papa.

(MR. WEBB *shakes the snow off his feet and enters his house.* CONSTABLE WARREN *goes off, right.*)

**MR. WEBB.** Good morning, Mother.

**MRS. WEBB.** How did it go, Charles?

**MR. WEBB.** Oh, fine, I guess, I told'm a few things.—Everything all right here?

**MRS. WEBB.** Yes—can't think of anything that's happened, special. Been right cold. Howie Newsome says it's ten below over to his barn.

**MR. WEBB.** Yes, well, it's colder than that at Hamilton College. Students' ears are falling off. It ain't Christian.—Paper have any mistakes in it?

**MRS. WEBB.** None that I noticed. Coffee's ready when you want it. (*He starts upstairs.*) Charles! Don't forget; it's Emily's birthday. Did you remember to get her something?

**MR. WEBB** (*patting his pocket*). Yes, I've got something here. (*Calling up the stairs*) Where's my girl? Where's my birthday girl? (*He goes off left.*)

**MRS. WEBB.** Don't interrupt her now, Charles. You can see her at breakfast. She's slow enough as it is. Hurry up, children! It's seven o'clock. Now, I don't want to call you again.

**EMILY** (*softly, more in wonder than in grief*). I can't bear it. They're so young and beautiful. Why did they ever have to get old? Mama, I'm here. I'm grown up. I love you all, everything.—I can't look at everything hard enough.

(*She looks questioningly at the* STAGE MANAGER, *saying or suggesting: "Can I go in?" He nods briefly. She crosses to the inner door to the kitchen, left of her mother, and as though entering the room, says, suggesting the voice of a girl of twelve*) Good morning, Mama.

**MRS. WEBB** (*crossing to embrace and kiss her; in her characteristic matter-of-fact manner*). Well, now, dear, a very happy birthday to my girl and many happy returns. There are some surprises waiting for you on the kitchen table.

**EMILY.** Oh, Mama, you *shouldn't* have. (*She* throws an anguished glance at the STAGE MANAGER.) I can't—I can't.

**MRS. WEBB** (*facing the audience, over her stove*). But birthday or no birthday, I want you to eat your breakfast good and slow. I want you to grow up and be a good strong girl. That in the blue paper is from your Aunt Carrie; and I reckon you can guess who brought the postcard album. I found it on the doorstep when I brought in the milk—George Gibbs . . . must have come over in the cold pretty early . . . right nice of him.

**EMILY** (*to herself*). Oh, George! I'd forgotten that. . . .

**MRS. WEBB.** Chew that bacon good and slow. It'll help keep you warm on a cold day.

**EMILY** (*with mounting urgency*). Oh, Mama, just look at me one minute as though you really saw me. Mama, fourteen years have gone by. I'm dead. You're a grandmother, Mama. I married George Gibbs, Mama. Wally's dead, too. Mama, his appendix burst on a camping trip to North Conway. We felt just terrible about it—don't you remember? But, just for a moment now we're all together. Mama, just for a moment we're happy. *Let's look at one another.*

**MRS. WEBB.** That in the yellow paper is something I found in the attic among your grandmother's things. You're old enough to wear it now, and I thought you'd like it.

**EMILY.** And this is from you. Why, Mama, it's just lovely and it's just what I wanted. It's beautiful!

(*She flings her arms around her mother's neck. Her mother goes on with her cooking, but is pleased.*)

**MRS. WEBB.** Well, I hoped you'd like it. Hunted all over. Your Aunt Norah couldn't find one in Concord, so I had to send all the way to Boston. (*Laughing*) Wally has something for you, too. He made it at manual-training class and he's very proud of it. Be sure you make a big fuss about it.—Your father has a surprise for you, too; don't know what it is myself. Sh—here he comes.

MR. WEBB (*offstage*). Where's my girl? Where's my birthday girl?

EMILY (*in a loud voice to the* STAGE MANAGER). I can't. I can't go on. It goes so fast. We don't have time to look at one another. (*She breaks down sobbing. The lights dim on the left half of the stage.* MRS. WEBB *disappears.*) I didn't realize. So all that was going on and we never noticed. Take me back—up the hill—to my grave. But first: Wait! One more look. Good-by. Good-by, world. Good-by, Grover's Corners . . . Mama and Papa. Good-by to clocks ticking . . . and Mama's sunflowers. And food and coffee. And new-ironed dresses and hot baths . . . and sleeping and waking up. Oh, earth, you're too wonderful for anybody to realize you. (*She looks toward the* STAGE MANAGER *and asks abruptly, through her tears*) Do any human beings ever realize life while they live it?—every, every minute?

STAGE MANAGER. No. (*Pause*) The saints and poets, maybe—they do some.

EMILY. I'm ready to go back.

(*She returns to her chair beside* MRS. GIBBS. *Pause*)

MRS. GIBBS. Were you happy?

EMILY. No . . . I should have listened to you. That's all human beings are! Just blind people.

MRS. GIBBS. Look, it's clearing up. The stars are coming out.

EMILY. Oh, Mr. Stimson, I should have listened to them.

SIMON STIMSON (*with mounting violence; bitingly*). Yes, now you know. Now you know! That's what it was to be alive. To move about in a cloud of ignorance; to go up and down trampling on the feelings of those . . . of those about you. To spend and waste time as though you had a million years. To be always at the mercy of one self-centered passion, or another.

Now you know—that's the happy existence you wanted to go back to. Ignorance and blindness.

MRS. GIBBS (*spiritedly*). Simon Stimson, that ain't the whole truth and you know it. Emily, look at that star. I forget its name.

A MAN AMONG THE DEAD. My boy Joel was a sailor—knew 'em all. He'd set on the porch evenings and tell 'em all by name. Yes, sir, wonderful!

ANOTHER MAN AMONG THE DEAD. A star's mighty good company.

A WOMAN AMONG THE DEAD. Yes. Yes, 'tis.

SIMON STIMSON. Here's one of *them* coming.

THE DEAD. That's funny. 'Tain't no time for one of them to be here.—Goodness sakes.

EMILY. Mother Gibbs, it's George.

MRS. GIBBS. Sh, dear. Just rest yourself.

EMILY. It's George.

(GEORGE *enters from the left, and slowly comes toward them.*)

A MAN FROM AMONG THE DEAD. And my boy, Joel, who knew the stars—he used to say it took millions of years for that speck o' light to git to the earth. Don't seem like a body could believe it, but that's what he used to say—millions of years.

(GEORGE *sinks to his knees, then falls full length at* EMILY's *feet.*)

A WOMAN AMONG THE DEAD. Goodness! That ain't no way to behave!

MRS. SOAMES. He ought to be home.

EMILY. Mother Gibbs?

MRS. GIBBS. Yes, Emily?

EMILY. They don't understand, do they?

MRS. GIBBS. No, dear. They don't understand.

(*The* STAGE MANAGER *appears at the right, one hand on a dark curtain which he slowly draws across the scene. In the distance a clock is heard striking the hour very faintly.*)

STAGE MANAGER. Most everybody's asleep in Grover's Corners. There are a few lights on:

Shorty Hawkins, down at the depot, has just watched the Albany train go by. And at the livery stable somebody's setting up late and talking.—Yes, it's clearing up. There are the stars—doing their old, old crisscross journeys in the sky. Scholars haven't settled the matter yet, but they seem to think there are no living beings up there. Just chalk . . . or fire. Only this one is straining away, straining away all the time to make something of itself. The strain's so bad that every sixteen hours everybody lies down and gets a rest. (*He winds his watch.*) Hm. . . . Eleven o'clock in Grover's Corners.—You get a good rest, too. Good night.

THE END

## THINK AND DISCUSS
### Understanding
1. As indicated in the opening stage directions, how are the cemetery and the dead represented on stage as Act Three begins?
2. What is the year when Act Three opens?
3. In his introductory remarks the Stage Manager describes how the living, after a wild grief, tend gradually to forget the dead. Then he describes how one might imagine the dead being gradually "weaned away from earth." Explain the parallels the Stage Manager draws between the response of the dead to the living and that of the living to the dead.
4. The first living characters appearing in Act Three are new—Sam Craig and Joe Stoddard. What do we learn about Mrs. Gibbs and Simon Stimson from their conversation?
5. At the beginning of the conversation between Craig and Stoddard we learn that Sam Craig is back for his cousin's funeral. At the end of the conversation what do we learn about his cousin that advances the dramatic action of the play?

### Analyzing
6. One hymn, "Blessed Be the Tie That Binds," is heard over and over again in the play. What are the scenes in which it is heard, and what is the effect of the repetition? Discuss.
7. When the dead Emily appears in the cemetery, she says, "Live people don't understand, do they?" and she adds, "They're sort of shut up in little boxes." What does she mean?
8. Against the advice of her mother-in-law Emily decides to relive one day of her life. Why does she choose her twelfth birthday, and how is George involved in her return?
9. Would you call the scene portraying Emily reliving her twelfth birthday a **flashback?** Why or why not?
10. On her day of return Emily exclaims to her mother, "Oh, Mama, just look at me one minute as though you really saw me. Mama, fourteen years have gone by. I'm dead. You're a grandmother, Mama. I married George Gibbs, Mama. Wally's dead, too." What is Mrs. Webb's reaction? In what way is the speech the turning point of Emily's day of return?

### Extending
11. When Emily returns to the dead, Simon Stimson blurts out, "Now you know—

that's the happy existence you wanted to go back to. Ignorance and blindness." Mrs. Gibbs chimes in, "Simon Stimson, that ain't the whole truth and you know it." Who do you think is right? Discuss.

12. Does the appearance of George, falling at Emily's feet at the close of the play, tend to support Simon Stimson's view or Mrs. Gibbs's? Discuss.

13. Thornton Wilder has said that his play is not a "picture of life in a New Hampshire village" nor an explanation of the "conditions of life after death," but rather an "attempt to find a value above all price for the smallest events in our daily life." Review the entire action of the play. In your opinion, has Wilder succeeded in this attempt? Explain.

## VOCABULARY
### Dictionary, Word Structure

| | | | |
|---|---|---|---|
| tableau | traipse | exertion | bereave |
| epitaph | diligent | torrent | cynicism |

Check your Glossary for the meanings of the words listed above; then use the words to complete the following sentences. In each case, however, the form of the word must be changed by the addition (or subtraction) of a prefix, suffix, or plural ending, or by a change of tense. Do not use the words as they appear above without altering their form to fit the meaning of the sentences. You will not use all the words.

1. Everyone ＿＿＿ the utmost effort at the last drive, but the fund is still too low.
2. Although they worked ＿＿＿, they were unable to finish the dissection before the end of class.
3. Her hobby is searching out unusual ＿＿＿ in old burial grounds.
4. While ＿＿＿ around in southwestern Idaho, we discovered many unusual and fascinating rock formations.
5. People usually experience a period of ＿＿＿ following the death of a loved one.

## COMPOSITION
### Responding to a Speech in a Play

Reread the speech made by Emily near the end of the play, concluding, "Do any human beings ever realize life while they live it?—every, every minute?" Write a five-paragraph letter to your best friend in which you attempt to answer Emily's question. If you say it is possible, tell how. If you say it is impossible, tell why. If you believe it is an ideal never to be achieved, but still worth striving for, explain. Draw freely on personal experience or contemplation. See "Writing About Theme" in the Writer's Handbook.

### Analyzing the Speeches of a Play

Reread all the monologues of the Stage Manager in the play. In Act One we find him commenting on life, in Act Two on love, and in Act Three on death. In a five-paragraph essay written for your classmates, summarize his significant generalizations about life, love, and death, and give your opinion of his views. In a closing paragraph characterize the Stage Manager by an overall evaluation of his vision of life—and death. See "Writing About Theme" in the Writer's Handbook.

## ENRICHMENT
### Dramatic Reading

The Stage Manager's monologues introducing the three acts of the play make great dramatic readings. Hold a try-out for those who would like to read them aloud, giving attention to the pace, posture, dress, and general air of those reading to fill the role of the Stage Manager. Reach a consensus on the best readings and offer them to the class for presentation. Ask the class to listen to all three monologues and then make comparisons and contrasts, not only among the readers but also among the monologues. Which is the most humorous? Which the most melancholy? Which filled with the most wisdom? Which makes the best dramatic reading?

# Comment

**Thornton Wilder on *Our Town***

*Our Town* is not offered as a picture of life in a New Hampshire village; or as a speculation about the conditions of life after death (that element I merely took from Dante's *Purgatory*[1]). It is an attempt to find a value above all price for the smallest events in our daily life. I have made the claim as preposterous as possible, for I have set the village against the largest dimensions of time and place. The recurrent words in this play (few have noticed it) are "hundreds," "thousands," and "millions." Emily's joys and griefs, her algebra lessons and her birthday presents—what are they when we consider all the billions of girls who have lived, who are living, and who will live? Each individual's assertion to an absolute reality can only be inner, very inner. And here the method of staging finds its justification—in the first two acts there are at least a few chairs and tables; but when she revisits the earth and the kitchen to which she descended on her twelfth birthday, the very chairs and table are gone. Our claim, our hope, our despair are in the mind—not in things, not in "scenery." Molière[2] said that for the theatre all he needed was a platform and a passion or two. The climax of this play needs only five square feet of boarding and the passion to know what life means to us.

---

**1. *Dante's* Purgatory,** one of three parts of the epic poem *The Divine Comedy* by Dante (dän′tā), Italian poet (1265–1321).
**2. *Molière*** (mō lyer′), French playwright (1622–1673).

# BIOGRAPHY

## Thornton Wilder
## 1897–1975

The works of Thornton Wilder present insights in ways that were, in his lifetime, unconventional and innovative. Born in Madison, Wisconsin, Wilder attended schools in China, the United States (where he took degrees at Yale and Princeton), and Rome. Beginning his writing career as a novelist, he published his first book, *The Cabala*, in 1926. His next book, *The Bridge of San Luis Rey*, a story weaving the complex relationships of a group of people who die in a bridge collapse, brought him worldwide attention and a Pulitzer Prize in 1928.

*Our Town* established Wilder as an important playwright. When it was first tried out in Boston in 1938, its reception was so cool that the play moved to New York. There it received rave reviews, winning the Pulitzer Prize in drama for the year. In 1943, Wilder won his third Pulitzer Prize for his play *The Skin of Our Teeth*. His following success, *The Matchmaker* (1954), is remembered primarily as the basis for the highly popular musical comedy *Hello, Dolly!*

# THINKING CRITICALLY
# ABOUT LITERATURE

## UNIT 2   MODERN DRAMA

### ■ CONCEPT REVIEW

The following dramatic scene illustrates literary elements that you have studied. It is accompanied by notes designed to help you think critically about your reading. Page numbers in the notes refer to applications of literary terms. These terms are also discussed in the Handbook of Literary Terms.

# *from* A Doll's House

**Henrik Ibsen**   Norway

*A Doll's House* takes place in a town in Norway in the nineteenth century. Nora and Torvald Helmer have been married several years, but Torvald, a newly appointed bank manager, has always treated Nora like a child, a doll-wife. Some years back, when Torvald was desperately ill and told by his doctor to go abroad, Nora had secretly borrowed money for him by forging her ill father's name to a document. She worked and saved to pay this money back, but had not been able to do so completely. The man who had lent Nora the money, finding himself about to be fired by Torvald Helmer from his job at the bank, threatens to expose Nora's forgery and ruin both her and her husband. When Torvald reads the letter from the lender about his wife's forgery and imagines himself ruined, he accuses Nora of having betrayed her family and her religion, of being a criminal and a liar and unfit to bring up their children. Shocked by these accusations, Nora sees for the first time the shallowness of Torvald's love. Although his attitude changes when he receives another letter from the lender promising not to expose the forgery, it is too late. Torvald has shown himself to Nora as hypocritical and self-centered,

---

From *A Doll's House* by Henrik Ibsen, translated by R. Farquharson Sharp, Everyman's Library Series. Reprinted by permission of J. M. Dent & Sons Ltd.

concerned more for his own fate than for hers. It is a wiser Nora who, in the following scene, insists that she and her husband have a serious talk.

NORA (*looking at her watch*). It is not so very late. Sit down here, Torvald. You and I have much to say to one another. (*She sits down at one side of the table.*)

HELMER. Nora—what is this?—this cold, set face?

NORA. Sit down. It will take some time; I have a lot to talk over with you.

HELMER (*sits down at the opposite side of the table*). You alarm me, Nora!—and I don't understand you.

NORA. No, that is just it. You don't understand me, and I have never understood you either—before tonight. No, you mustn't interrupt me. You must simply listen to what I say. Torvald, this is a settling of accounts.

HELMER. What do you mean by that?

NORA (*after a short silence*). Isn't there one thing that strikes you as strange in our sitting here like this?

HELMER. What is that?

NORA. We have been married now eight years. Does it not occur to you that this is the first time we two, you and I, husband and wife, have had a serious conversation?

HELMER. What do you mean by serious?

NORA. In all these eight years—longer than that—from the very beginning of our acquaintance, we have never exchanged a word on any serious subject.

HELMER. Was it likely that I would be continually and forever telling you about worries that you could not help me to bear?

NORA. I am not speaking about business matters. I say that we have never sat down in earnest together to try and get at the bottom of anything.

HELMER. But, dearest Nora, would it have been any good to you?

NORA. That is just it; you have never understood me. I have been greatly wronged, Torvald—first by Papa and then by you.

HELMER. What! By us two—by us two, who have loved you better than anyone else in the world?

NORA (*shaking her head*). You have never loved me. You have only thought it pleasant to be in love with me.

HELMER. Nora, what do I hear you saying?

NORA. It is perfectly true, Torvald. When I was at home with Papa, he told me his opinion about everything, and so I had the same opinions; and if I differed from him I concealed the fact, because he would not have liked it. He called me his doll-child; and he played with me just as I used to play with my dolls. And when I came to live with you—

HELMER. What sort of an expression is that to use about our marriage?

NORA (*undisturbed*). I mean that I was simply transferred from Papa's hands

■ Note Nora's "take-charge" attitude.

■ Note Torvald's concern and bafflement.

■ **Protagonist** (page 148): Nora becomes central as she takes control of her life (and the scene).

■ Note how Torvald's misunderstanding of Nora reveals his lack of sensitivity.

■ Note how Nora's speech reveals her motivation by exposing her past, much like a **flashback** (page 200) might do in another narrative.
■ The reference to a "doll-child" (and "doll-wife" later) clarifies the play's title.

into yours. You arranged everything according to your own taste, and so I got the same tastes as you—or else I pretended to, I am really not quite sure which—I think sometimes the one and sometimes the other. When I look back on it, it seems to me as if I had been living here like a poor woman—just from hand to mouth. I have existed merely to perform tricks for you, Torvald. But you would have it so. You and Papa have committed a great sin against me. It is your fault that I have made nothing of my life.

HELMER. How unreasonable and how ungrateful you are, Nora! Have you not been happy here?

■ Nora's extension of the accusation against her father to her husband encourages the audience to see the play's theme reaching toward a general questioning of male-female relationships.

NORA. No, I have never been happy. I thought I was, but it has never really been so.

HELMER. Not—not happy!

NORA. No, only merry. And you have always been so kind to me. But our home has been nothing but a playroom. I have been your doll-wife, just as at home I was Papa's doll-child; and here the children have been my dolls. I thought it great fun when you played with me, just as they thought it great fun when I played with them. That is what our marriage has been, Torvald.

HELMER. There is some truth in what you say—exaggerated and strained as your view of it is. But for the future it shall be different. Playtime shall be over, and lesson-time shall begin.

■ **Antagonist** (page 148): Torvald remains an adversary in his inability or unwillingness to acknowledge Nora as more than a child.

NORA. Whose lessons? Mine, or the children's?

HELMER. Both yours and the children's, my darling Nora.

NORA. Alas, Torvald, you are not the man to educate me into being a proper wife for you.

HELMER. And you can say that!

NORA. And I—how am I fitted to bring up the children?

HELMER. Nora!

NORA. Didn't you say so yourself a little while ago—that you dare not trust me to bring them up?

HELMER. In a moment of anger! Why do you pay any heed to that?

NORA. Indeed, you were perfectly right. I am not fit for the task. There is another task I must undertake first. I must try and educate myself—you are not the man to help me in that. I must do that for myself. And that is why I am going to leave you now.

HELMER (*springing up*). What do you say?

■ Note that Nora's decision revealed here was reached before the scene began, giving her a firmness of purpose.

NORA. I must stand quite alone, if I am to understand myself and everything about me. It is for that reason that I cannot remain with you any longer.

HELMER. Nora! Nora!

NORA. I am going away from here now, at once. I am sure my friend Christine will take me in for the night—

HELMER. You are out of your mind! I won't allow it! I forbid you!

■ Note that Torvald still foolishly thinks he controls Nora as his "doll-wife."

NORA. It is no use forbidding me anything any longer. I will take with me what belongs to myself. I will take nothing from you, either now or later.

HELMER. What sort of madness is this!

NORA. Tomorrow I shall go home—I mean, to my old home. It will be easiest for me to find something to do there.

HELMER. You blind, foolish woman!

NORA. I must try and get some sense, Torvald.

HELMER. To desert your home, your husband, and your children! And you don't consider what people will say!

NORA. I cannot consider that at all. I only know that it is necessary for me.

HELMER. It's shocking. This is how you would neglect your most sacred duties.

NORA. What do you consider my most sacred duties?

HELMER. Do I need to tell you that? Are they not your duties to your husband and your children?

NORA. I have other duties just as sacred.

HELMER. That you have not. What duties could those be?

NORA. Duties to myself.

HELMER. Before all else, you are a wife and a mother.

NORA. I don't believe that any longer. I believe that before all else I am a reasonable human being, just as you are—or, at all events, that I must try and become one. I know quite well, Torvald, that most people would think you right, and that views of that kind are to be found in books; but I can no longer content myself with what most people say, or with what is found in books. I must think over things for myself and get to understand them.

HELMER. Can you not understand your place in your own home? Let me try and awaken your conscience. I suppose you have some moral sense? Or—answer me—am I to think you have none?

NORA. I assure you, Torvald, that is not an easy question to answer. I really don't know. The thing perplexes me altogether. I only know that you and I look at it in quite a different light. I am learning, too, that the law is quite another thing from what I supposed; but I find it impossible to convince myself that the law is right. According to it a woman has no right to spare her old dying father, or to save her husband's life. I can't believe that.

HELMER. You talk like a child. You don't understand the conditions of the world in which you live.

NORA. No, I don't. But now I am going to try. I am going to see if I can make out who is right, the world or I.

■ Notice Torvald's concern for his reputation rather than for Nora.

■ Observe signs of Nora's new maturity, as she questions the views of books and the community.

■ Note that Nora's challenge reveals how a protagonist's role is not free of conflict.

■ **Inference** (page 169): An observant reader must conclude that Torvald has learned nothing; he still thinks of Nora as a doll-wife.

■ The last line indicates that Nora, obviously in conflict with Helmer, also feels that she has involved herself in a larger struggle.

## THINK AND DISCUSS

### Understanding

**1.** How long has Nora been married?

**2.** When Nora complains that they have never had a serious conversation, what does Torvald think she is referring to?

**3.** Who else besides Torvald does Nora blame for the state her mind is in?

### Analyzing

**4.** Characterize Nora as she appears in her first three speeches.

**5.** Characterize Torvald as he appears in his first few responses to her.

**6.** When Nora tells Torvald that he has never loved her, but has "only thought it pleasant to be in love" with her, what do you think she means?

**7.** When Nora announces her intention to leave, Torvald exclaims, ". . . you don't consider what people will say!" What may we infer from this remark about his feelings for Nora?

### Extending

**8.** Nora says that her father called her his "doll-child" and that Torvald made her into his "doll-wife," terms that relate to the title of the play. Discuss both Nora's meaning in using these terms and the play's title.

**9.** In this scene, Nora first levels accusations at her husband, then accuses her father, and finally calls into question the "rightness" of the law. How does this progression appear to expand the **theme** of the play? Discuss.

## REVIEWING LITERARY TERMS

### Inference

**1.** What inference do we draw about the characters' future when Torvald promises things will be different and says, "Playtime shall be over, and lesson-time shall begin"?

**2.** What inference do we draw about Torvald when, at the end of the scene, he exclaims to Nora: "You talk like a child"?

### Protagonist/Antagonist

**3.** What are the main clues we pick up in this scene that Nora is the protagonist and Torvald the antagonist?

### Flashback

**4.** Nora's comments about her childhood and her father reveal a good deal about her. Do these comments about her past constitute a flashback, or is this some other sort of revelation by the dramatist?

## ■ CONTENT REVIEW

### THINKING SKILLS

#### Classifying

**1.** You probably have noticed that the camera directions and stage directions in *Twelve Angry Men* differ from the directions in *The Romancers* and *Our Town*. It was written as a television script, not as a stage play. Review the directions for all three plays. Make a list of five directions that are applicable only to stage plays, five that can apply only to a television drama, and five that fit either form.

#### Generalizing

**2.** Thornton Wilder limited the action of *Our Town* to a few small settings, such as the immediate area of two houses and the cemetery. Both can be depicted within the space of a theater stage. How do dramatists Reginald Rose and Edmond Rostand limit the settings of their plays in this unit? How do the settings make stage or film production more manageable?

#### Synthesizing

**3.** Choose a scene from *The Romancers* or *Our Town* and rewrite the stage directions as though you were planning a film or television production. Be ready to explain how your directions would help make an effective production.

**4.** Consider the following alternate titles for the dramas in this unit. Compare and contrast the strengths or weaknesses of each with the real title of each drama.

*The Jury System Exposed*   (*Twelve Angry Men*)
*Fluff and Nonsense*   (*The Romancers*)
*Grover's Corners*   (*Our Town*)

### Evaluating

5. The action of *Twelve Angry Men* unfolds in a realistic setting and style, with real props for the audience to see and scenes performed in the same time the action would take in real life. The action of *Our Town* flows between scenes on a bare stage without realistic props, scenery, or passage of time. How effective is each play in using its realistic or nonrealistic style? How would *Our Town* be affected by a more realistic presentation, and *Twelve Angry Men* by a less realistic style?

6. In *Our Town* and *The Romancers*, simple items such as chairs, ladders, and a wall are used to suggest settings. Imagine that you are in an audience at stage productions of the two plays. Name four props or scenery pieces and explain how each might suggest the setting or action of a scene.

## ■ COMPOSITION REVIEW

From the assignments that follow choose one and write the composition.

### Writing a Letter

Emily of *Our Town* is enabled to relive one day of her life on earth. If the same privilege were granted to you, what day would you choose? Recollect the day in your mind and decide on specific reasons you would want to relive it. Then write a letter to a friend explaining your choice of that particular day.

### Choosing a Setting

*Our Town* and *The Romancers* portray two different worlds. The world of *Our Town* is that of a small town, offering a simple life and simple pleasures. *The Romancers* portrays a world of more sophistication and gaiety, not only in the basic action but particularly in the dialogue, such as the long speech by Straforel listing his various kinds of mock-abductions. Which of these two worlds would you prefer to inhabit? Think of specific details to illustrate what living in that world would be like. Then write an essay setting forth your preference and describing the life you imagine you might live in such a world.

### Expressing and Supporting Opinions

The jury system has sometimes been assailed as a burdensome system that does not always result in justice being done. Some critics argue that the number of jurors should be fewer (perhaps six, the number used in some American court cases), that individuals should be required to have a certain level of education to qualify as jurors, or that all cases should be decided by judges alone. What is your view on these questions? You may form your opinions based on *Twelve Angry Men* as well as on anything else you know about the jury system. In an essay argue your opinion on one or more of the issues mentioned above. Use examples and reasons to back up the points you make.

### Reviewing Writer's Craft: Use a Voice That Suits the Purpose

Nora of *A Doll's House*, Sylvette of *The Romancers*, and Emily of *Our Town* display such qualities as determination, imagination, and perceptiveness. Which of these characters is most admirable? Think about reasons for which you admire her, and review the play, if necessary, for evidence to support your view. Then write an essay identifying the character and discussing reasons for your admiration. Write in a voice that suits your purpose—to convince readers that the character is worthy of your respect.

# POETRY

Drossos P. Skyllas, *The Blue Kiosk* (detail), 1953, Private Collection

# UNIT 3

# PREVIEW

## UNIT 3  POETRY

**Poets in This Unit Include**

| | | |
|---|---|---|
| Naomi Shihab Nye | Matsuo Bashō | Walt Whitman |
| William Blake | Langston Hughes | Edgar Lee Masters |
| William Wordsworth | Jorge Luis Borges | A. E. Housman |
| Gwendolyn Brooks | T. S. Eliot | Emily Dickinson |
| Gabriela Mistral | William Butler Yeats | Robert Frost |
| Carl Sandburg | John Keats | Federico García Lorca |
| May Swenson | Nguyen Trai | Edna St. Vincent Millay |

**Features**
Reading Narrative and Lyric Poetry
Comment: The Art of Translation
Writer's Craft: Use Comparisons
Comment: The Speaker and the Poet
Comment: On "The Street"
Comment: Images in Haiku Poetry
Comment: The Psalms
Reading a Poem for Sound and Sense
Comment: Sonnets
Comment: Spoon River Anthology
Comment: On "What Mystery Pervades
   a Well!"
Comment: Surrealistic Imagery

**Application of Literary Terms**

| | | |
|---|---|---|
| lyric | metaphor | alliteration |
| tone | personification | assonance |
| imagery | hyperbole | consonance |
| figurative | rhythm | onomatopoeia |
|    language | rhyme | free verse |
| simile | | |

**Vocabulary Skills**
context
etymology

**Reading Literature Skillfully**
conclusions
generalizations
author's purpose

**Thinking Skills**
classifying
generalizing
synthesizing

**Composition Assignments Include**
Analyzing a Poem's Structure
Reading/Writing Log
Recollecting a Vivid Experience
Taking Sides in a Debate
Writing About Tone
Describing a Landscape or Cityscape
Writing About an Animal
Comparing Two Poems
Writing a Free Verse Poem
Analyzing Imagery
Considering Career Decisions

**Enrichment**
Performing Poetry
Readers Theater
Memorizing a Poem

**Thinking Critically About Literature**
Concept Review
Content Review
Composition Review

Words in poems speak more gracefully and wildly than they do in prose, it has been said. Sometimes the words are playful, and sometimes they are somber. When we read poems we must listen to the words with great care. Often they convey more than they directly tell us; occasionally they even overflow with meaning, filling the surrounding silences.

Poetry, like prose, can tell a story or express deep emotion. Thus two basic kinds of poetry are **narrative** and **lyric**.

## Narrative Poetry

Here are some pointers for reading narrative poems:

**Focus on the action.** Narrative poems have plots in which conflicts arise between characters. In "Phoebus and Boreas," for example, the sun and the north wind hold a contest to see which can force a traveler to remove his cloak. The action rises to its climax, and the conflict is resolved.

**Keep an eye on the characters.** Characters determine action; the blustery boasts of the north wind forebode his loss of the contest. The sun is more modest and levelheaded.

**Consider generalizations and conclusions that may be drawn from your reading.** In "Phoebus and Boreas" the sun quietly wins without using power harshly. One **conclusion** we might draw is that power need not be wielded with full force to be effective. The truth of this idea transcends this narrative. A **generalization** that we might formulate for ourselves is handed to us by the poem because it is a fable: "Clemency [gentleness in the use of force] may be our best resource." This generalization in the poem tells us what the narrative has dramatized concretely. Many

poems directly state ideas for alert readers to appreciate. Other poems invite readers to draw reasonable conclusions for themselves.

## Lyric Poetry

Here are some pointers for reading lyric poems:

**Focus on the emotion.** In William Wordsworth's "I Wandered Lonely as a Cloud" the poet's loneliness is overpowered by a suffusing sense of joy on coming suddenly upon a field of "dancing daffodils."

**Listen for the poet's voice.** Many humans experience gladness; some write poems of joy. Yet only Wordsworth wrote "I Wandered Lonely as a Cloud." What makes his poem distinctive? His *images, comparisons,* and *word choice,* as well as his *rhythmic* and *musical language* all come together to express the sound of his deepest being.

**Consider conclusions and generalizations.** If we remember only Wordsworth's original experience, we miss the point of his poem. It invites the reader to draw a conclusion about the single experience. The poet reveals the "wealth" the experience has bestowed in its returning in moments of solitude through his "inward eye." His emotion, encountered by chance, turns out to be a renewable and perhaps inexhaustible joy! We can also emerge from the poem with our own generalization: Wordsworth's inspiration can be experienced in some form by anyone.

These pointers should ease your entry into the selection of excellent poems in this unit. But remember, the best advice is to open yourself to the experience of each poem. To experience deeply is the fullest kind of understanding.

**Review PLOT in the Handbook of Literary Terms, page 813.**

# Phoebus and Boreas[1]

**La Fontaine**   France

*Translated by* Marianne Moore

The sun and the north wind observed a traveler
       Who was cloaked with particular care
Because fall had returned; for when autumn has come,
What we wear must be warm or we dare not leave home.
5 Both rain and rainbow as the sun shines fitfully,
       Warn one to dress warily
In these months when we don't know for what to prepare,
An uncertain time in the Roman calendar.
Though our traveler was fortified for a gale,
10 With interlined cloak which the rain could not penetrate,
The wind said, "This man thinks himself impregnable
And his cloak is well sewn, but my force can prevail
       As he'll find in the blast I create,
No button has held. Indeed before I am through,
15        I may waft the whole mantle away.
The battle could afford us amusement, I'd say.
Do you fancy a contest?" The sun said, "I do.
       Mere words are unprofitable,
Let us see which can first unfasten the mantle
20        Protecting the pedestrian.
Begin: I shall hide; you uncloak him if you can."
Then our blower swelled, swallowed what wind he could,

---

*La Fontaine* (là fôɴ tän′).

**1.** *Phoebus* (fē′bəs), *Boreas* (bôr′ē əs), in Greek myths, the
sun and the north wind, respectively.

To form a balloon, and with the wager to win,
        Made demoniacal din.
25 Puffed, snorted, and sighed till the blast that he brewed
Left ships without a sail and homes without a roof
        Because a mantle proved stormproof.
It was a triumph for the man to have withstood
        The onslaught of wind that had rushed in,
30 As he somehow stood firm. The wind roared his chagrin—
A defeated boaster since his gusts had been borne.
Controlling clasp and skirt required dexterity,
        But the wind found nothing torn
        And must stop punctually.
35        The cloud had made it cool
Till the sun's genial influence caused the traveler to give way,
        And perspiring because wearing wool,
        He cast off a wrap too warm for the day
Though the sun had not yet shone with maximum force.


40        Clemency may be our best resource.


## THINK AND DISCUSS
### Understanding
1. What at first draws the attention of Phoebus and Boreas to the traveler?
2. What is the time of year and the nature of the weather?
3. What is the object of the contest that Phoebus and Boreas engage in?

### Analyzing
4. What does Phoebus do as Boreas tries to force the traveler to uncloak? Why do you suppose he does what he does?
5. Who wins the contest? How does he win?
6. Both Phoebus and Boreas are **characterized** in the poem by their speeches and actions. Describe their personalities.

### Extending
7. The narrative in this poem is really a fable— a tale involving animals or things as characters—told to convey a lesson or moral. What is the moral and how is it related to the action of the tale?
8. Notice the cautious way the moral is phrased ("may be"). Why do you suppose it is stated in this way?

### REVIEWING: Plot  H𝓣
See Handbook of Literary Terms, p. 813
    A plot is a series of related events in a pattern of conflict, climax, and conclusion.

1. In this poem what is the conflict?
2. What is the climax in the narrative?

**Review INFERENCE in the Handbook of Literary Terms, page 803.**

# The Stone

**Wilfrid Wilson Gibson**   Great Britain

"And will you cut a stone for him,
To set above his head?
And will you cut a stone for him—
A stone for him?" she said.

5 Three days before, a splintered rock
Had struck her lover dead—
Had struck him in the quarry dead,
Where, careless of the warning call,
He loitered, while the shot was fired—
10 A lively stripling, brave and tall,
And sure of all his heart desired . . .
A flash, a shock,
A rumbling fall . . .
And, broken 'neath the broken rock,
15 A lifeless heap, with face of clay,
And still as any stone he lay,
With eyes that saw the end of all.

I went to break the news to her:
And I could hear my own heart beat
20 With dread of what my lips might say;
But some poor fool had sped before;
And, flinging wide her father's door,
Had blurted out the news to her,
Had struck her lover dead for her,
25 Had struck the girl's heart dead in her,
Had struck life, lifeless, at a word,
And dropped it at her feet:
Then hurried on his witless way,
Scarce knowing she had heard.

30 And when I came, she stood alone—
A woman, turned to stone:
And, though no word at all she said,
I knew that all was known.

Because her heart was dead,
35 She did not sigh nor moan.
His mother wept:
She could not weep.
Her lover slept:
She could not sleep.
40 Three days, three nights,
She did not stir:
Three days, three nights,
Were one to her,
Who never closed her eyes
45 From sunset to sunrise,
From dawn to evenfall—
Her tearless, staring eyes,
That, seeing naught, saw all.

The fourth night when I came from work,
50 I found her at my door.
"And will you cut a stone for him?"
She said: and spoke no more:
But followed me, as I went in,
And sank upon a chair;

*(Continued)*

"The Stone" from *Collected Poems* by W. W. Gibson. Reprinted by permission of Mr. Michael Gibson and Macmillan, London and Basingstoke.

55 And fixed her grey eyes on my face,
With still, unseeing stare.
And, as she waited patiently,
I could not bear to feel
Those still, grey eyes that followed me,
60 Those eyes that plucked the heart from me,
Those eyes that sucked the breath from me
And curdled the warm blood in me,
Those eyes that cut me to the bone,
And pierced my marrow like cold steel.

65 And so I rose, and sought a stone;
And cut it, smooth and square:
And, as I worked, she sat and watched,
Beside me, in her chair.
Night after night, by candlelight,
70 I cut her lover's name:
Night after night, so still and white,
And like a ghost she came;
And sat beside me, in her chair,
And watched with eyes aflame.

75 She eyed each stroke,
And hardly stirred:

She never spoke
A single word:
And not a sound or murmur broke
80 The quiet, save the mallet-stroke.

With still eyes ever on my hands,
With eyes that seemed to burn my hands,
My wincing, overwearied hands,
She watched, with bloodless lips apart,
85 And silent, indrawn breath:
And every stroke my chisel cut,
Death cut still deeper in her heart:
The two of us were chiselling,
Together, I and death.

90 And when at length the job was done,
And I had laid the mallet by,
As if, at last, her peace were won,
She breathed his name; and, with a sigh,
Passed slowly through the open door;
95 And never crossed my threshold more.

Next night I labored late, alone,
To cut her name upon the stone.

## THINK AND DISCUSS
### Understanding
1. Who is the narrator in this poem?
2. Does the narrator seem to have any special feelings for the woman? Explain.
3. What caused the death of the man for whom the woman orders a stone?
4. What is indicated by the last three lines?

### Analyzing
5. Does the main body of the poem prepare for the ending? Discuss any hints in the poem.

6. What do we learn about the woman through her characterization in the narrative?
7. What are some of the various things to which the title of the poem might refer?

## REVIEWING: Inference
See Handbook of Literary Terms, p. 803
An inference is a reasonable conclusion about the behavior of a character or meaning of an event drawn from limited details supplied by the author. In "The Stone," what may we infer has happened to the woman, from what we are told in the last two lines?

# My Father & The Figtree

## Naomi Shihab Nye   USA

For other fruits my father was indifferent.
He'd point at the cherry trees and say,
"See those? I wish they were figs."
In the evenings he sat by my bed
5 weaving folktales like vivid little scarves.
They always involved a figtree.
Even when it didn't fit, he'd stick it in.
Once Joha was walking down the road & he saw a figtree.
Or, he tied his camel to a figtree & went to sleep.
10 Or, later when they caught & arrested him,
his pockets were full of figs.

At age six I ate a dried fig & shrugged.
"That's not what I'm talking about!" he said,
"I'm talking about a fig straight from the earth,

*(Continued)*

---

*Naomi Shihab* (shĕ′hab) *Nye.*

"My Father & The Figtree" by Naomi Shihab Nye published in *A Geography of Poets* edited by Edward Field (*Bantam Books*, 1978) and *Different Ways to Pray* by Naomi Shihab Nye (Breitenbush Books, 1980). Reprinted by permission of the author.

Juan vander Hamen y Leon, *Still Life with Flowers and Fruit* (detail), 1629, Private Collection

15 gift of Allah![1]—on a branch so heavy it touches the ground."
"I'm talking about picking the largest fattest sweetest fig
in the world & putting it in my mouth."
(Here he'd stop and close his eyes.)

Years passed, we lived in many houses, none had figtrees.
20 We had lima beans, zucchini, parsley, beets.
Plant one! my mother said, but my father never did.
He tended garden halfheartedly, forgot to water,
let the okra get too big.
"What a dreamer he is. Look how many things he starts
25 and doesn't finish."

The last time he moved, I got a phonecall.
My father, in Arabic, chanting a song I'd never heard.
"What's that?" I said.
"Wait till you see."

30 He took me out back to the new yard.
There, in the middle of Dallas, Texas,
a tree with the largest, fattest, sweetest figs in the world.
"It's a figtree song!" he said.
plucking his fruits like ripe tokens,
35 emblems, assurance
of a world that was always his own.

---

1. *Allah* (al′ə), the Moslem name for God.

**THINK AND DISCUSS**
**Understanding**
1. What is the constant element in all the folk tales told by the father?
2. What is the reaction of the speaker on first eating a dried fig? How does her father respond?
3. Why does the father neglect his gardens, forgetting to water the okra, for example?

**Analyzing**
4. What part of the world is the speaker's father from? How do you know?

5. When the father finally gets his figtree, what do you think it reminds him of?
6. How do his actions show that the tree is a dream fulfilled?

**Extending**
7. Does the father's dream of having a figtree seem to you eccentric or understandable? Have you experienced or observed in others a similar yearning for something out of the past? Discuss.

# The Fox and the Woodcutter

**Aesop**  Greece

*Translated by* Denison B. Hull

A fox was fleeing. As she fled
A hunter fast behind her sped.
But being wearied, when she spied
An old man cutting wood, she cried,
5 "By all the gods that keep you well,
Hide me among these trees you fell,
And don't reveal the place, I pray."
He swore that he would not betray
The wily vixen; so she hid,
10 And then the hunter came to bid
The old man tell him if she'd fled,
Or if she'd hidden there. He said,
"I did not see her," but he showed
The place the cunning beast was stowed
15 By pointing at it with his finger.
But still the hunter did not linger.
He put no faith in leering eye,
But trusting in the words, went by.
Escaped from danger for a while
20 The fox peeked out with coaxing smile.
The old man said to her, "You owe
Me thanks for saving you, you know."
"Most certainly; for I was there
As witness of your expert care.
25 But now farewell. And don't forget,
The god of oaths will catch you yet
For saving with your voice and lips
While slaying with your finger tips."

---

*Aesop* (ē′səp).

Reprinted from *Aesop's Fables* told by Valerius Babrius, translated by Denison B. Hull. Copyright © 1960 by the University of Chicago Press. Reprinted by permission.

**THINK AND DISCUSS**
**Understanding**
1. How does the man try to betray the fox?
2. Why does the woodcutter fail in his attempt to betray the fox?

**Analyzing**
3. What might the moral of the fable be?

**Extending**
4. How do you think the effect and meaning of the fable would change if "wily vixen" in line 9 became "innocent lamb" instead?
5. What difference do you think it would make if instead of an "old man cutting wood" we had "a young man whittling wood"?

**READING LITERATURE SKILLFULLY**
**Conclusions and Generalizations**
   Poets who tell stories often have more in mind than entertaining the reader. A poet may intend to express a truth about life. A poem may state such an idea explicitly or convey the idea more subtly. The poet may invite the reader to draw conclusions about the action and perhaps make a generalization, applying the idea beyond the narrative poem itself.

1. What principle of behavior might we recognize in the statement in lines 26–28?
2. Can a reader apply the principle you have recognized to situations in life that go beyond this poem's circumstances? Explain.

### The Art of Translation

There are some who believe poetry cannot be successfully translated from one language to another. Poet Robert Frost once said that poetry was what got *lost* in translation. It is true that certain elements of poetry may cause problems for a less-than-skillful translator.

A good many poems contain figurative language; to translate it literally often would render the poem ridiculous. Beyond this, however, there is the question of what even literally used words mean. People who share a language as a mother tongue in a particular period of history share more than simple definitions of words. They also share feelings that words arouse because of the aura of emotion that builds up around them. This aura of emotion is likely to fade away in translation—unless it can be captured in new ways by the imaginative translator.

A literal translation, then, may give us what the poet said, but not necessarily what he or she really meant. In fact, the literal translation is the one most likely to lose the rhythm, the harmony of sounds, and the imagery.

Thus, an imaginative translator of poetry is in effect a poet. Such a translator can re-create the poem in the new language so that it approximates (not duplicates) the effect of the poem in its original words. This process may leave a literal translation far behind—in order to reproduce something in the nature of, but not exactly like, the original in sound and sense.

The following are two English translations of the opening lines of *"Mi Prima Agueda"* ("My Cousin Agueda") by Mexican poet Ramon Lopez Velarde, one by Willis Knapp Jones, the other by Cheli Duran. By comparing the versions, you can see how differently two translators interpret the same poetic lines.

### My Cousin Agueda

My godmother often invited my cousin Agueda
To come and spend the day,
My cousin used to arrive
Appearing in a mixed-up way,
5 Suggesting starch and fearful
Mourning of a funeral day.

Agueda would appear rustling
With starch and with her eyes green.

And her rosy cheeks
10 Protecting me against the mourning
That I'd seen.

I was a kid
And knew nothing at all,
And Agueda, who was moving
15 Tamely and persistently in the hall,
With her rustling brought excitement
About which I knew nothing at all.

(I even think she is responsible
For my mad habit of talking to myself.)

"My Cousin Agueda" by Ramón López Velarde from *Spanish-American Literature in Translation*, translated by Willis Knapp Jones. Copyright © 1963 by Frederick Ungar Publishing Company, Inc. Reprinted by permission of the publisher.

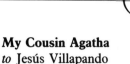

**My Cousin Agatha**
*to* Jesús Villapando

My godmother used to ask my cousin Agatha
to spend the day with us,
and my cousin used to arrive
wrapped in a contradictory magic
5 of starch and odious ritual
mourning.

Agatha entered, rustling
starch, and her green eyes
and warm red cheeks
10 protected me from the dreadful
black . . .
        I was only a child
who knew the O by its roundness,
and Agatha, who knitted
mildly, persistently, in the echoing
     corridor,
15 sent little unknown shivers
up my spine.

(I think I owe her, too, my crazy
but heroic habit of talking alone.)

---

From "My Cousin Agatha" by Ramón López Velarde in *The Yellow Canary Whose Eye Is So Black*, edited and translated by Cheli Duran. Copyright © 1977 by Cheli Duran Ryan. Reprinted with permission of Macmillan Publishing Company.

# A Poison Tree

**William Blake**   Great Britain

I was angry with my friend:
I told my wrath, my wrath did end.
I was angry with my foe:
I told it not, my wrath did grow.

5 And I water'd it in fears,
Night & morning with my tears;
And I sunnèd it with smiles,
And with soft deceitful wiles.

And it grew both day and night,
10 Till it bore an apple bright.
And my foe beheld it shine,
And he knew that it was mine,

And into my garden stole,
When the night had veil'd the pole;[1]
15 In the morning glad I see
My foe outstretch'd beneath the tree.

---

1. *night had veil'd the pole,* night had covered one half of the earth, including the North Pole.

William Blake, "A Poison Tree," from *Songs of Experience,* 1794.

**THINK AND DISCUSS**
**Understanding**
1. According to the first stanza, what happens to unexpressed anger?
2. What is the "it" referred to in the second and third stanzas?

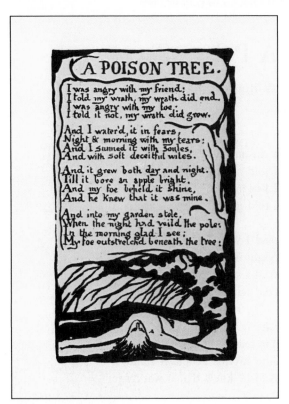

**A POISON TREE.**

I was angry with my friend:
I told my wrath, my wrath did end.
I was angry with my foe:
I told it not, my wrath did grow.

And I water'd it in fears,
Night & morning with my tears:
And I sunned it with smiles,
And with soft deceitful wiles.

And it grew both day and night.
Till it bore an apple bright.
And my foe beheld it shine.
And he knew that it was mine.

And into my garden stole,
When the night had veild the pole:
In the morning glad I see;
My foe outstretchd beneath the tree.

William Blake's illustration, *The Poison Tree*, 1794, from the book *Songs of Experience*. The poet was an artist who created pictures for many of his own poems.

### Analyzing

3. How does this "it" tie in with the title of the poem?
4. What is the connection between the apple and the speaker's foe?
5. What seems to be the attitude of the speaker toward his own behavior?

### Extending

6. The implication in the first stanza is that if we tell our anger, it ceases; but if we hold it in, it grows. Do you believe this is true? Why or why not?

### VOCABULARY
#### Context

The sentences in the following paragraph contain italicized words that don't make sense in context. The appropriate word for each sentence appears in italic type in another sentence. Check the Glossary for the meanings of the words; then rewrite each sentence using the word that best fits the context of each sentence.

**1.** An air of excited anticipation seemed to *wrath* over the spectators. **2.** The opposing players still were angry about their bitter loss to our hockey team in last season's championship game, but we felt prepared to deal with their *naught*. **3.** Our star goalie, whose ability to catch flying pucks is amazing, was said to have more *chagrin* than theirs. **4.** He blocked countless shots throughout the game, but his valiant efforts were all for *waft*. **5.** Much to the *dexterity* of the home crowd, the opposing left wing slapped the winning goal past him.

### COMPOSITION
#### Commenting on a Moral

Write a three- to four-paragraph essay for a class bulletin-board display giving your view as to the truth, falsity, or importance of the moral of "Phoebus and Boreas": *Clemency may be our best resource.* Review the poem and, if necessary, a definition of *clemency*. Draw on your own experience, observation, and reading in examining this moral.

#### Analyzing a Poem's Structure

Write a four- to five-paragraph essay for class discussion analyzing the structure of "The Stone." Lines 1–4 and 49–95 present a narrative episode in chronological order, but this episode is interrupted by lines 5–48 to portray previous episodes. Lines 96–97 move beyond the other episodes in time and only by implication indicate an important concluding event. Consider whether another structure may have been better (straight chronological sequence, for example). Consider the possible virtues of the present structure. See "Writing About Poetry and Poetic Devices" in the Writer's Handbook.

# BIOGRAPHIES

## La Fontaine   1621–1695

La Fontaine grew up in the French countryside but spent most of his adult life in Paris. A learned man, he did translations as well as wrote poetry and fiction. His fame rests on his *Fables,* tales adapted from the Greek stories of Aesop and from later collections in other cultures. Volumes of his fables appeared in 1668, 1678, and 1694.

## Wilfrid Wilson Gibson   1878–1962

Gibson was a prolific poet who began as a romantic verse-writer and turned, in midstream, to become a poet of the people. His origins in Hexham, in the north of England, gave him the background to write about nature and country people; yet he first wrote about knights and historical characters. In 1910, his book *Daily Bread* turned to everyday life, and thereafter he concerned himself with that subject.

## Naomi Shihab Nye   1952–

Naomi Shihab Nye was born in St. Louis and now lives in San Antonio. She participates there in the "poets-in-the-schools" program. She has published several books of poetry, including *Eye-to-Eye* (1978), *Different Ways to Pray* (1980), and *Hugging the Jukebox* (1982).

## Aesop   620?–560? B.C.

It is not known for certain whether the man Aesop ever really lived, although references to him do exist in the works of Plutarch and Aristotle. The most prevalent theory is that he was a Phrygian slave who was freed and who traveled about the country telling his fables. A statue, supposedly of Aesop, in the Villa Albani in Paris, depicts him as an ugly dwarf, but this too is a matter of controversy. The fables themselves are drawn from folk tales, many of them centuries old. As we know them, they were related by the Greek writer Valerius Babrius, who probably lived during the second century B.C.

## William Blake   1757–1827

Blake's only formal education was in art. He studied in London, his birthplace, and at fourteen was apprenticed as an engraver. At this time he also began writing verse. He is best known for his poetry collections *Songs of Innocence* (1789) and *Songs of Experience* (1794), which he illustrated with watercolor-painted engravings. His illustration for "A Poison Tree" appears with the poem in this unit. Virtually unknown in his lifetime, Blake was recognized as a poetic genius only in the twentieth century.

## Use Comparisons

The effective use of comparisons enriches writing. Poets often compare people, places, and things in descriptive lines. Consider the comparison you have read in lines 71–72 of "The Stone."

> Night after night, so still and white,
> And like a ghost she came. . . .

This description takes the form of a simile, a comparison using a word such as *like* to add vividness and impact to the image. The woman is compared to a ghost in the way she moves, coming to the stonecutter's door. This comparison reveals the sad, almost frightening, silence that characterizes her arrival.

In "Phoebus and Boreas" the wind compares his own strength to the protective strength of a man's cloak, claiming that, although the cloak is sewn well, his force can prevail.

Unlike the direct comparison that the wind makes, some comparisons are more subtle, such as the description of the dead man in "The Stone," who is said to have a "face of clay." The comparison of the lifeless face to clay is a **metaphor,** an implied comparison. It not only enriches the picture but also emphasizes the theme of death.

A philosophical kind of parallel is pointed out in an **analogy,** a comparison drawn between different things that have certain points in common, often to explain a difficult idea in terms of a simple one. Read this poem to understand its analogy.

## Our Little Kinsmen

Our little Kinsmen—after Rain
In plenty may be seen,
A Pink and Pulpy multitude
The tepid Ground upon.

A needless life, it seemed to me
Until a little Bird
As to a Hospitality
Advanced and breakfasted.

As I of He, so God of Me
I pondered, may have judged,
And left the little Angle Worm
With Modesties enlarged.

*Emily Dickinson*

After the speaker begins to dismiss the worms as worthless, she is humbled by thinking of an analogy. Perhaps the worms are to a person as a person is to God, she supposes. This comparison expresses a complex belief simply.

Comparisons provide the key images and figures of speech in many kinds of writing. Look for vivid comparisons as you read the selections in this book. Be aware of them in your outside reading, and use comparisons such as similes, metaphors, and analogies to express your ideas when you write.

When you read, notice comparisons.
When you write, use comparisons to enrich language and to help your readers grasp ideas quickly.

**See LYRIC in the Handbook of Literary Terms, page 806.**

# I Wandered Lonely as a Cloud

**William Wordsworth**   Great Britain

I wandered lonely as a cloud
That floats on high o'er vales and hills,
When all at once I saw a crowd,
A host, of golden daffodils;
5 Beside the lake, beneath the trees,
Fluttering and dancing in the breeze.

Continuous as the stars that shine
And twinkle on the milky way,
They stretched in never-ending line
10 Along the margin of a bay:
Ten thousand saw I at a glance,
Tossing their heads in sprightly dance.

The waves beside them danced; but they
Outdid the sparkling waves in glee:
15 A poet could not but be gay,
In such a jocund company:
I gazed,—and gazed,—but little thought
What wealth the show to me had brought:

For oft, when on my couch I lie
20 In vacant or in pensive mood,
They flash upon that inward eye
Which is the bliss of solitude;
And then my heart with pleasure fills,
And dances with the daffodils.

---

"I Wandered Lonely as a Cloud" by William Wordsworth, 1807.

## THINK AND DISCUSS
### Understanding
1. In the first stanza, what attracts the attention of the speaker as he wanders?
2. What is emphasized in the second stanza?

### Analyzing
3. In the third stanza, how does the immediacy of the scene affect the poet?
4. What is the "wealth" cited in line 18?

### Extending
5. In lines 21–22, the speaker refers to the "inward eye / Which is the bliss of solitude." What in your view is such an "inward eye"?

## APPLYING: Lyric
**See Handbook of Literary Terms, p. 806**
   A **lyric** is a short poem expressing the feelings of a poet—joy, sorrow, exuberance, melancholy, elation, or regret. The emotions may be evoked by different kinds of experiences, such as encounters with nature, falling in love, or meditating in solitude.
1. What has precipitated the feelings of the poet in "I Wandered Lonely as a Cloud"?
2. Is there a difference in the emotion he feels the first time and the feeling he has later when it comes upon him alone through his "inward eye?" Discuss.

# The Crazy Woman

**Gwendolyn Brooks**   USA

I shall not sing a May song.
A May song should be gay.
I'll wait until November
And sing a song of gray.

5 I'll wait until November.
That is the time for me.
I'll go out in the frosty dark
And sing most terribly.

And all the little people
10 Will stare at me and say,
"That is the Crazy Woman
Who would not sing in May."

## THINK AND DISCUSS
### Understanding
1. Why does the speaker say she will sing not a May song but a song of November?
2. Why does the speaker assume that others will say, when she sings her November song, that she is a "crazy woman"?

### Analyzing
3. Why do you suppose the speaker refers to these people as "little"?

4. Does the view of the others (that the speaker is a "crazy woman") necessarily mean that she is crazy? Why or why not?

### Extending
5. Do you think "November Song" would be a better title for this poem than "The Crazy Woman"? Why or why not?
6. What do you suppose might be the nature of the November song that the speaker would "sing most terribly" in the "frosty dark"?

# Gift

**Czeslaw Milosz**   Poland

A day so happy.
Fog lifted early, I worked in the garden.
Hummingbirds were stopping over
    honeysuckle flowers.
There was no thing on earth I wanted to possess.
5 I knew no one worth my envying him.
Whatever evil I had suffered, I forgot.
To think that once I was the same man
    did not embarrass me.
In my body I felt no pain.
When straightening up, I saw the
    blue sea and sails.

James J. Audubon, *Columbian Hummingbird*,
The Newberry Library, Chicago

*Czeslaw Milosz* (ches′wäf mē′wôsh).

## THINK AND DISCUSS
### Understanding
1. What ideas or attitudes does the speaker mention that might have kept him from being happy in the past?
2. What about this day makes him happy?

### Analyzing
3. What is the meaning of the poem's title?
4. What is the effect of placing "A day so happy" as the first line of the poem?

### Extending
5. Would you agree that happiness can be the absence of negative things as well as the presence of positive things? Discuss.

# Hope

## Lisel Mueller    USA

It hovers in dark corners
before the lights are turned on,
   it shakes sleep from its eyes
   and drops from mushroom gills,
5      it explodes in the starry heads
      of dandelions turned sages,
         it sticks to the wings of green angels
         that sail from the tops of maples.

It sprouts in each occluded eye
10 of the many-eyed potato,
   it lives in each earthworm segment,
   surviving cruelty,
      it is the motion that runs
      from the eyes to the tail of a dog,
15         it is the mouth that inflates the lungs
         of the child that has just been born.

It is the singular gift
we cannot destroy in ourselves,
the argument that refutes death,
20 the genius that invents the future,
all we know of God.

It is the serum which makes us swear
not to betray one another;
it is in this poem, trying to speak.

---

Reprinted by permission of Louisiana State University Press from *The Private Life* by Lisel Mueller, copyright © 1976.

## THINK AND DISCUSS
### Understanding
1. In line 1, what "hovers in dark corners"?
2. What does "it" invariably mean and where does "it" invariably appear in the poem?

### Analyzing
3. In Lines 4–10, the mushroom, dandelions, maples, and potato all appear as dynamic images at critical moments of their growth. What do these moments have in common? Explain the role of hope.

4. How does hope live "in each earthworm segment"?
5. How is hope a unique or "singular" gift (line 17) to human beings?

### Extending
6. What do you think the last line means?

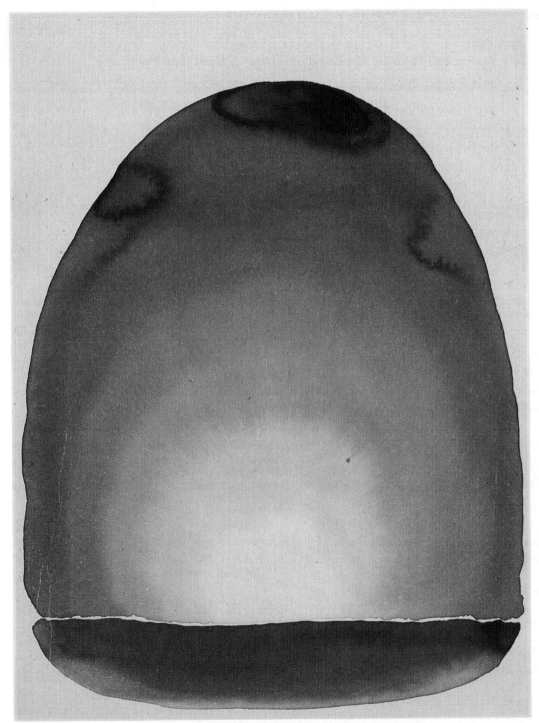

Georgia O'Keeffe, *Light Coming on the Plains III*, 1917. Amon Carter Museum, Fort Worth.

**Review LYRIC in the Handbook of Literary Terms, page 806.**

# New Face

### Alice Walker   USA

I have learned not to worry about love;
but to honor its coming
with all my heart.
To examine the dark mysteries
5 of the blood
with headless heed and
swirl,
to know the rush of feelings
swift and flowing
10 as water.

The source appears to be
some inexhaustible
spring
within our twin and triple
15 selves;
the new face I turn up
to you
no one else on earth
has ever
20 seen.

## THINK AND DISCUSS
### Understanding
1. In line 1 the speaker states that she has "learned not to worry about love." How do lines 2–3 help explain her meaning?
2. Lines 4–10 appear incomplete. What words from the foregoing lines may be attached to them for completion?

### Analyzing
3. Explain the "dark mysteries / of the blood" (lines 4–5).
4. What does "source" refer to in line 11?
5. What might the poet mean by "twin and triple / selves" in lines 14–15?

### Extending
6. What do you believe is the "new face" referred to in line 16?
7. What do you think would be the effect if the title were changed to "About Love"?

### REVIEWING: Lyric   H𝒵
**Handbook of Literary Terms, p. 806**
A lyric is a relatively short poem expressing the poet's emotions or feelings.

1. In Alice Walker's "New Face," what has caused the emotion being expressed?
2. Describe the nature and effect of the emotion as expressed in the poem.

## THINKING SKILLS
### Classifying

To **classify** things is to arrange them into categories or groups according to some system. The speaker in "The Crazy Woman" by Gwendolyn Brooks apparently classifies May as a happy month and November as a month that is not so happy. This classification may reflect the widespread feeling that months of pleasant weather—also classified as spring and summer months—are cheery, while months of darkness or cold—classified as fall and winter—are also "dark" emotionally. You may or may not endorse, or believe in, this classification.

Make a chart or circular calendar of the year, with space under the name of each month. Fill the space with as many labels as you can to show ways that *you* classify months. For example, categories can include school and vacation months; sports seasons; seasons of weather, astronomy, and farming; social, religious, or political seasons; and so on.

## COMPOSITION ◄━━━
### Reading/Writing Log

In "I Wandered Lonely as a Cloud," Wordsworth makes vivid his sudden sight of a scene in nature by using remarkable and striking comparisons to describe it. Copy the heading at the top of the next column in your reading/writing log or another notebook. Then find at least two examples from the poem of other comparisons or extensions of this one.

*Examples of Comparisons to Describe Nature*
[A host of golden daffodils appeared]
Continuous as the stars that shine
And twinkle on the milky way.

### Recollecting a Vivid Experience

Wordsworth enables readers to experience with him the astonishing field of "dancing daffodils" by using vivid comparisons. Now you can use comparisons to describe (in two or three paragraphs) an experience that made such a deep impression on you that you have relived it in your imagination. It is a common human experience to recall through the imagination such moments of great joy or sorrow—sometimes even in dreams. In your account of an intensely felt moment, set side by side the original and recollected experiences. Be sure to use several apt comparisons to make your experiences come alive. See "Developing Your Style" in the Writer's Handbook.

### Describing an Emotion

Reread Lisel Mueller's "Hope" and note the concrete comparisons she has used to make the abstraction *Hope* something palpable and real. Now select an emotion—such as Love, Hate, Joy, Envy, Discouragement—and write a three- to four-paragraph essay in which you make at least three original comparisons to render your abstraction concrete. Before you write, list the comparisons you plan to use and place them in the order you think most effective.

 **BIOGRAPHIES**

## William Wordsworth 1770–1850

Wordsworth and Samuel Taylor Coleridge published a small volume of poems entitled *Lyrical Ballads* in 1789. The poems that Wordsworth contributed to this volume differed greatly from the kind of poems usually written in his day. In the famous *Preface*, he explained that he would use simple language, "language really used by men," and would select incidents from "common life." "Poetry," he said, "is the spontaneous overflow of powerful feelings," originating from "emotion recollected in tranquility." In the ordinary aspects of nature, he found abundant means of interpreting the basic values of life. Wordsworth lived a large portion of his life amid the natural grandeur of the mountainous Lake District of northwestern England. The beauty of this locality inspired many of his poems. Although his early work met with hostility, he gradually gained critical acceptance and was appointed Poet Laureate of England in 1843.

## Czeslaw Milosz   1911–

Born in Lithuania, Milosz became one of the leaders of the new poetry movement in Poland during the 1930s and then fought in the Resistance against the Nazis in World War II. After serving in the diplomatic service for Poland during the post-war years, he came to the United States to teach at the University of California, Berkeley. He continued to write throughout his various careers. One critic has described Milosz's poetry as offering a "sober version of stoicism which does not ignore reality, however absurd and horrendous." He was awarded the Nobel Prize for Literature in 1980.

## Gwendolyn Brooks   1917–

Although she was born in Topeka, Kansas, Brooks grew up in Chicago and identifies closely with the city in her poetry. She published her first book of poems, *A Street in Bronzeville*, 1945, and in 1950 won a Pulitzer Prize for *Annie Allen*. In 1968, she was named Poet Laureate of Illinois. Her poetry is vivid in both diction and image, often evoking a slum apartment or street scene in a few short lines. A collection of her work appeared in 1971, entitled *The World of Gwendolyn Brooks*. More biographical information about Brooks appears on page 76.

## Lisel Mueller   1924–

Born in Hamburg, Germany, Mueller fled from the country with her family in 1939 and settled in Indiana. After graduating from college, she married, raised a family, and still lives in the Great Lakes region, in Illinois. Writing poetry has grown to be a major interest in her life. Her book, *The Private Life*, won the Lamont Poetry Prize in 1976.

## Alice Walker   1944–

Walker was born in Eatonton, Georgia, and attended Sarah Lawrence College, graduating in 1966. By the age of twenty-nine she had written five books. Also a novelist and teacher, Walker has taught creative writing and black literature at several colleges nationwide. Her volumes of poetry include *Once* (1968) and *Revolutionary Petunias and Other Poems* (1973), which was nominated for the National Book Award. In 1983, she won an American Book Award for her widely acclaimed novel *The Color Purple*.

# To Julia de Burgos

**Julia de Burgos**  Puerto Rico

The word is out that I am your enemy
   that in my poetry I am giving you away.

   They lie, Julia de Burgos. They lie, Julia de Burgos.
That voice that rises in my poems is not yours: it is my voice;
5 you are the covering and I the essence;
and between us lies the deepest chasm.

   You are the frigid doll of social falsehood,
and I, the virile sparkle of human truth.

   You are honey of courtly hypocrisy, not I;
10 I bare my heart in all my poems.

   You are selfish, like your world, not I;
I gamble everything to be what I am.

   You are but the grave lady, ladylike;
not I; I am life, and strength, and I am woman.

15   You belong to your husband, your master, not I;
I belong to no one or to everyone, because to all, to all
I give myself in pure feelings and in my thoughts.

   You curl your hair, and paint your face, not I;
I am curled by the wind, painted by the sun.

20   You are lady of the house, resigned and meek,
tied to the prejudices of men, not I;
smelling the horizons of the justice of God.
I am Rocinante,[1] running headlong.

---

1. *Rocinante* (rō sē nän′tā), the broken-down but spirited horse of Don Quixote (dōn kē hō′tā)
in Miguel de Cervantes' classic Spanish novel, *Don Quixote de la Mancha.*

"To Julia de Burgos" by Julia de Burgos, translated by Maria Arrillaga, 1971. Reprinted by permission of
Maria Consuelo Saez Burgos.

Will Barnet, *Hera*, 1980, Private Collection

## THINK AND DISCUSS

### Understanding
1. Who is the "I" of the poem?
2. Who is the "you" to whom the "I" speaks?
3. Who are "they" introduced in line 3 and what is their lie?

### Analyzing
4. The speaker says to the living Julia, "You are the covering and I the essence." Explain how this statement relates to the rest of the poem and its meaning.

### Extending
5. The speaker seems angry with the living Julia. Do you judge her attitude to be fair? Why or why not?

### The Speaker and the Poet

Poems often portray someone speaking in the first person—"I"—and readers often wonder whether the "I" is really the poet speaking. The answer is complicated, as is evident in "To Julia de Burgos."

A close reading of the poem reveals that Julia de Burgos is thinking of herself as double. The speaker in the poem, the "I," is separated from the living Julia de Burgos by the "deepest chasm." The latter is possessed by the social world, her husband, and the demands of everyday life; the former is free to deal in truth and bare her heart. Thus the poem demonstrates a truth about all poetry—that the speaker in the poem, even when mentioned by name as the same person as the writer, is different from the living author in many subtle ways.

In many poems there is little reason to confuse the speaker and the writer. A work like Wilfrid Wilson Gibson's "The Stone," for example, has a speaker—the stonecutter—who has clearly been created by the writer for a dramatic role in the poem. But in poems like Naomi Shihab Nye's "My Father & The Figtree," the author may seem to be speaking in her own voice. Yet if she is doing so, she presents only one aspect of herself—her role in relation to her father—and is shaping and somehow inventing that aspect of herself.

When reading collections of poems by the same poet, as you will do later in this unit, a reader often detects a "voice" that runs through many poems, giving them the poet's personal stamp. There may be characteristic patterns of speech, thought, and style that help the reader identify the writer even when no by-line is provided. It is still best not to assume that the "I" in any poem is the same "I" speaking in the writer's other poems or that this "I" can be matched with the poet's biography. The poet Emily Dickinson once said to a critic, "When I state myself, as the representative of the verse, it does not mean me, but a supposed person." It is, of course, all right to refer to this "I," when it seems to be the author's voice, by the author's name—as long as you understand that it encompasses only the author's identity as portrayed in this poem. To avoid confusion, it may be better to identify "I" as "the speaker."

# Don't Ask Me What to Wear

**Sappho**  Greece

Don't ask me what to wear

I have no embroidered
headband from Sardis[1] to
give you, Cleis,[2] such as
5  I wore
       and my mother
always said that in her
day a purple ribbon
looped in the hair was thought
to be high style indeed

10 but we were dark:
                   a girl
whose hair is yellower than
torchlight should wear no
headdress but fresh flowers

Sandro Botticelli, *La Primavera* (detail), c. 1475-1478
Uffizi Gallery, Florence, Italy

---

1. *Sardis,* capital of Lydia, chief kingdom of Asia Minor.
2. *Cleis* (klē′is), Sappho's daughter.

"Don't Ask Me What to Wear" from *Sappho, A New Translation* by
Mary Barnard. Copyright © 1958 by the Regents of the University
of California. Reprinted by permission of the University of California
Press.

## THINK AND DISCUSS
### Understanding
1. To whom is this poem addressed and what is
   the relationship of **speaker** and listener?
2. What are the three hair adornments
   mentioned in the poem and with whom are
   they associated?
3. Why does the speaker suggest flowers for her
   daughter?

### Analyzing
4. What do you imagine has preceded this
   statement from the mother to the daughter?
5. The mother implies in line 1 that she won't
   advise her daughter on what to wear. Does
   she advise her? Explain.

### Extending
6. Do the mother's comments sound to you like
   those of a modern mother? Why or why not?
7. This poem concerns fashion and appearance.
   Do you think this is a subject of greater
   interest to women than to men? Discuss.

See TONE in the Handbook of Literary Terms, page 831.

# One Perfect Rose

**Dorothy Parker**   USA

A single flow'r he sent me, since we met.
  All tenderly his messenger he chose;
Deep-hearted, pure, with scented dew still wet—
  One perfect rose.

5 I knew the language of the floweret;
  "My fragile leaves," it said, "his heart enclose."
Love long has taken for his amulet
  One perfect rose.

Why is it no one ever sent me yet
10  One perfect limousine, do you suppose?
Ah no, it's always just my luck to get
  One perfect rose.

Ansel Adams, *Rose and Driftwood*, c. 1932. Photograph courtesy of the Ansel Adams Publishing Rights Trust. All Rights Reserved.

# If You'll Just Go to Sleep

**Gabriela Mistral** Chile
*Translated by* Langston Hughes

The blood red rose
I gathered yesterday,
and the fire and cinnamon
of the carnation,

5 Bread baked with
anise seed and honey,
and a fish in a bowl
that makes a glow:

All this is yours,
10 baby born of woman,
if you'll *just*
go to sleep.

A rose, I say!
I say a carnation!
15 Fruit, I say!
And I say honey!

A fish that glitters!
And more, I say—
if you will *only*
20 sleep till day.

---

*Gabriela Mistral* (gä brē ā′lä mē sträl′)

"If You'll Just Go to Sleep" from *Selected Poems of Gabriela Mistral*, translated by Langston Hughes. Copyright © 1957 by Indiana University Press. Reprinted by permission of Joan Daves.

## THINK AND DISCUSS

**Understanding**
1. What is the messenger in stanza 1?
2. What is the meaning of the observation in lines 7–8?

**Analyzing**
3. In line 6, the speaker quotes the rose. Characterize the nature of the rose's remark.
4. Each of the three stanzas ends with the words *one perfect rose*. How might we imagine the speaker varying her delivery as she sounds the phrase the three times?

**Extending**
5. What do you think would be the effect if in line 10 the word *limousine* were replaced with *diamond*?

## APPLYING: Tone HⱫ
### See Handbook of Literary Terms, p. 831

**Tone** is the attitude of the author toward the subject, such as awe, anger, fear, humor, or cynicism. Almost every element in the poem can reveal tone, including diction, or style of expression (elevated or common); imagery (pleasant or unpleasant); syntax, or arrangement of words in sentences; and rhythm (lilting, running, or slow).

1. Where and how does the author adopt a clear tone in "One Perfect Rose"? What is the tone?
2. How does this tone affect the romantic feeling created in the first two stanzas?

Mary Cassatt, *Mother and Child*, The Louvre, Paris

## THINK AND DISCUSS

**Understanding**

1. What does the speaker promise the baby at the beginning of the poem?
2. How might these gifts appeal to the baby?

**Analyzing**

3. Why is *just* emphasized by italic type in line 11?
4. The list of the gifts is repeated in the last two stanzas. How is the language made more intense and what is added?

5. What in the end does the speaker want in return from the baby? How does it differ from the previous request?

**Extending**

6. In your opinion, is this poem a plea, a bribe, or a threat? Discuss.

---

TONE

 **Review TONE in the Handbook of Literary Terms, page 831.**

# The Zoo

**Stevie Smith**   Great Britain

The lion sits within his cage,
Weeping tears of ruby rage,
He licks his snout, the tears fall down
And water dusty London town.

5 He does not like you, little boy,
It's no use making up to him,
He does not like you any more
Than he likes Nurse, or Baby Jim.

Nor would you do if you were he,
10 And he were you, for dont you see
God gave him lovely teeth and claws
So that he might eat little boys.

---

So that he might
In anger slay
15 The little lambs
That skip and play
Pounce down upon their placid dams[1]
And make dams flesh to pad his hams.

So that he might
20 Appal the night
With crunching bones
And awful groans
Of antelope and buffalo,

And the unwary hunter whose "Hallo"
25 Tells us his life is over here below.
There's none to help him, fear inspired,
Who shouts because his gun misfired.

All this the lion sees, and pants
Because he knows the hot sun slants
30 Between the rancid jungle-grass,
Which never more shall part to let him pass
Down to the jungle drinking-hole,
Whither the zebra comes with her sleek foal.

The sun is hot by day and has his swink,[2]
35 And sops up sleepy lions' and tigers' stink,
But not this lion's stink, poor carnivore,
He's on the shady shelf for ever more.

His claws are blunt, his teeth fall out,
No victim's flesh consoles his snout,
40 And that is why his eyes are red
Considering his talents are misusèd.

---

1. *dams*, the female parents of the sheep.
2. *swink*, an archaic term for labor or toil. [*British*]

## THINK AND DISCUSS
### Understanding
1. In the first stanza, does the lion appear gentle, menacing, or angry? Discuss.
2. To whom is the speaker talking and what has he probably been doing?

### Analyzing
3. What does the speaker say that might frighten the little boy?
4. In lines 28–33, the speaker imagines the lion as remembering the past. How does that past contrast with the lion's present condition?
5. Why does the speaker call the lion "poor carnivore" in line 36?
6. What do we learn about the lion in the last stanza?
7. How are we to take the explanation in the last line as to why the lion's eyes are red (with tears)?

### Extending
8. Why do you suppose the speaker saved the most revealing details about the lion—his powerlessness—for the last stanza?

### REVIEWING: Tone  H 
See Handbook of Literary Terms, p. 831
A poem's tone is the poet's attitude toward its subject, as revealed through the language of the poem.

1. How does the dramatic situation in "The Zoo"—the speaker addressing a little boy—help to shape the poem's tone?
2. Does the speaker appear to want to frighten the little boy, entertain him, delight him, instruct him—or some combination of these?

# The Street

**Octavio Paz**   Mexico

The street is very long and filled with silence.
I walk in shadow and I trip and fall,
And then get up and walk with unseeing feet
Over the silent stones and the dry leaves,
5 And someone close behind, tramples them, too.
If I slow down and stop, he also stops.
If I run, so does he. I look. No one!
The whole street seems so dark, with no way out,
And though I turn and turn, I can't escape.

10 I always find myself on the same street
Where no one waits for me and none pursues.
Where I pursue, a man who trips and falls
Gets up and seeing me, keeps saying: "No one!"

"The Street" by Octavio Paz from *Spanish-American Literature in Translation*, translated by Willis Knapp Jones. Copyright © 1963 by Frederick Ungar Publishing Company, Inc. Reprinted by permission of the publisher.

Giorgio de Chirico, *The Melancholy and Mystery of a Street*, 1914, Private Collection

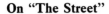 

# *Comment*

## On "The Street"

"The Street" may easily be read as a dream, with the speaker encountering the kind of unreal world we all encounter in our dreams—especially dreams that frighten us. The place is without geographical location—simply a street, long and without sound of any kind. There seem to be no buildings or houses along the street—at least the speaker does not refer to them. And there seems to be little or no light, the darkness thus deepening the mystery and increasing the fear. The speaker trips and falls, gets up and goes on, and then hears someone behind him trampling the same "stones and . . . dry leaves" he has passed over. If the speaker runs, so does the pursuer; if he stops, so does the pursuer. The speaker looks—and sees no one. The street turns but offers no way out. And, perplexingly, the speaker always finds himself on the same street, with no one waiting for him, and no one pursuing. At the end of the poem the incident involving pursued and

pursuer is repeated, but this time, the speaker becomes the pursuer, a change not unusual in dreams. He is running after a man who trips and falls; who, on getting up and looking back, says "No one!"

As with all dreams, the content of this dream-poem stands for something, and we may guess at what. The speaker is really both the pursued and the pursuer. The maze of streets, without escape, represents an unbearable situation, mental entanglement, or emotional strain from which the speaker can find no exit. In first being pursued by himself, and then later becoming the pursuer pursuing himself, the speaker appears to be divided or torn within. He is uncertain of his identity, his direction, and his purpose. In this state of uncertainty, the speaker may be seen to stand for modern humanity, filled with fear and anxiety as to the nature of the self and the meaning of life.

## THINK AND DISCUSS
### Understanding
1. What is the **setting** of the poem? Discuss.
2. Describe the behavior of "someone" introduced in lines 5–7.

### Analyzing
3. What new aspect do we learn about the speaker's plight in lines 9–10?

4. What does the use of "always" in line 10 suggest about the speaker's plight?

### Extending
5. Do any situations or events in this poem resemble circumstances you have ever encountered in a dream? If so, explain.
6. How is the poem relevant to the fears and concerns of people in today's world?

# Ordinance on Lining Up

**Naomi Lazard**  USA

A line will form to the right
and one to the left. You must join
one of them. After careful consideration
choose the line you are most attracted to;
5 stand at the end of it.
Both lines are serpentine. However,
if you look closely
you will see subtle differences.
The one to the right moves more quickly,
10 the left line at a more leisurely pace
which may prove beneficial
to certain dispositions.

Try to see where the lines go;
this is your option.
15 Everything possible is being done

to protect your privileges.
A factor to keep in mind:
in joining the line to the right
you will end life as a beggar.
20 If you decide on the line to the left
everything you believe will become nonsense.
You will be spending
a great deal of time on whichever one
you choose. Choose wisely.
25 No changing from one line to the other
once you have joined.
     Common sense
will tell you that you will become
an indispensable link
in the line of your choice.
     Good luck to you.

## THINK AND DISCUSS
### Understanding
1. What choice are you given at the beginning of the poem, and what are its limits?
2. What are the differences between the two lines?

### Analyzing
3. An ordinance is a rule or law issued by an authority. What manner of speaking, or tone of voice, in the poem reveals that it sets forth an ordinance?
4. In line 24 you are told to "choose wisely." Have you been given enough information to do so? Explain.
5. Are you given a reason as to why you can't change lines once you've chosen? Explain.

## Extending

6. Do you think the choices between the lines can be related to choices faced in life in some way? Discuss.

## VOCABULARY
### Etymology

Some words have come into English through several different languages, others through several forms in one language. In the etymology of a dictionary entry the symbol <, meaning "derived from," is placed before each source of the word. The most recent source is listed first and the earliest source last.

Check the Glossary for the etymologies of the italicized words that follow to determine if the statements in which they appear are true or false. On your paper write "T" after the number of each true statement. Correct each false one.

1. *Virile* may be traced back to its Latin origins in *vir*, the word for "man."
2. The earliest source for *chasm* is Latin.
3. The earliest source for *essence* is Latin *esse*, "to be."
4. *Foal* comes from an Old English word.
5. *Appal* derives from Greek.

## THINKING SKILLS
### Synthesizing

To **synthesize** is to put together elements, such as ideas, to form a pattern or structure. You have read poems in which Julia de Burgos creates an inner dialogue, Octavio Paz depicts a dreamy setting, and Naomi Lazard portrays life as an arbitrary choice. Imagine your own dreamlike incident or a dialogue between a character and his or her self. Write a poem or paragraph presenting your synthesized setting or dialogue. You may want to give it unity by using a strong tone such as hope or optimism.

## COMPOSITION
### Taking Sides in a Debate

Write a three- to four-paragraph essay in which you argue that either men or women are more concerned than the other about their clothes and appearance. Reread "Don't Ask Me What to Wear," and discuss the poem and the question with your friends. Draw from your own experience and observation examples you wish to cite. See "Writing to Persuade an Audience" in the Writer's Handbook.

### Writing About Tone

Write a three- to four-paragraph essay analyzing the tone of "Ordinance for Lining Up." What do you believe is the attitude of the author toward the orders given in the ordinance? Is her attitude explicit or implicit? If you believe the latter, you'll need to speculate from whatever hints you find in the poem as to her attitude toward such arbitrary orders, such limited choices, and such inflexible rules. See "Writing About Mood or Tone" in the Writer's Handbook.

## ENRICHMENT
### Performing Poetry

The poems in "Poet, Speaker, and Tone" all lend themselves quite well to reading aloud—as do also those in the "Lyric Poetry" cluster. Assemble a group of students who enjoy reading aloud in a group. Select a number of poems and practice reading them to each other. Try to capture the tone of the poem by your voice. Reflect the shift in tone by your voice when reading Dorothy Parker's "One Perfect Rose"; sound the fear felt in Octavio Paz's "The Street"; emphasize the bossiness that is evident when you read Naomi Lazard's "Ordinance on Lining Up." Offer your group performance to the class.

# BIOGRAPHIES

## Julia de Burgos   1914–1953

The oldest of thirteen children, de Burgos was born in Carolina, Puerto Rico, and educated at the University of Puerto Rico. She published her first book in 1938 and taught briefly at the University of Havana. In 1940 she came to the United States, where she suffered from bouts of illness and poverty and died virtually unknown as a poet. Since her death, her poetic force has been recognized, and her *Collected Works* appeared in 1961.

## Sappho   600 B.C.–? B.C.

Although stories about Sappho have been passed on through the ages, little is known for certain about her life. Her poems are said to have filled nine books, but only fragments have survived; these indicate that her family was aristocratic. Her poems are noted for their simplicity and perfection of form. The ancients ranked Sappho with such honored writers as Homer, and called her the "Tenth Muse." Even today she is probably the most famous Greek woman poet.

## Dorothy Parker   1893–1967

Parker delighted the reading public with her witty, often cynical verse for many years. Early in her career as a critic in New York she became friendly with humorist Robert Benchley and playwright Robert Sherwood, and together they formed the nucleus of a witty and influential group of writers and critics known as the Algonquin Round Table. The titles of some of Parker's books of poetry suggest the wry humor that she favored: *Enough Rope* (1926), *Death and Taxes* (1931), and *Collected Poems: Not So Deep as a Well* (1936). She also wrote stories.

## Gabriela Mistral   1889–1957

Gabriela Mistral, a pen name for Lucila Godoy, won the Nobel Prize for Literature in 1945. One of Chile's most distinguished poets, she spent many years teaching in rural and secondary schools. Her social commitment and love of humanity brought her recognition. She served in several international posts, including the League of Nations.

### Stevie Smith   1902–1971

Her real name was Florence Margaret Smith, but she adopted her nickname "Stevie" for her poetry. Born in Yorkshire, England, she began working at a publishing house soon after high school and lived all her life with an aunt. Her first book of poems, *A Good Time Was Had by All*, appeared in 1937, and others followed, including what is probably her best known, *Not Waving But Drowning*, in 1957. Hers is a warm and witty, sometimes sharp and incisive, poetic voice.

### Octavio Paz   1914–

One of the Latin American poets best known outside that region, Paz was a precocious youth who published his first volume of poems before he was twenty. He served in a number of diplomatic posts for Mexico, and while in Europe was influenced by the surrealists, writers who used dream-imagery techniques. One of his best-known collections is *La estación violenta* (1958), which contains his ambitious poem "The Sun Stone," based on the engraved stone calendar of the Aztec Indians. Paz won the T. S. Eliot Award for Creative Writing in 1987.

### Naomi Lazard   1936–

Born in Philadelphia, Lazard attended the City College of New York, where she took a Master of Arts degree in 1964. Prior to the 1967 publication of her first collection, *Cry of the Peacocks*, Lazard's poems had appeared in many magazines. Her works include *Ordinances* (1977), *The Moonlit Upper Deckerina* (1977), and the children's story *What Amanda Saw* (1981). She has served as president of the Poetry Society of America.

**See IMAGERY in the Handbook of Literary Terms, page 802.**

# Improved Farm Land

**Carl Sandburg**   USA


Tall timber stood here once, here on a corn belt farm along the Monon.[1]
Here the roots of a half mile of trees dug their runners deep
    in the loam for a grip and a hold against wind storms.
Then the axmen came and the chips flew to the zing of steel and handle—
    the lank railsplitters cut the big ones first, the beeches and
    the oaks, then the brush.
Dynamite, wagons and horses took the stumps—the plows sunk their
      teeth in—
    now it is first class corn land—improved property—and the hogs
    grunt over the fodder crops.
5 It would come hard now for this half mile of improved farm land along
    the Monon corn belt, on a piece of Grand Prairie, to remember
    once it had a great singing family of trees.

---

1. **Monon,** The Monon Railroad ran in a generally north-south direction through western Indiana.

Grant Wood, *Spring Turning*, 1936, James Maroney, New York

## THINK AND DISCUSS
### Understanding
1. The poem describes land that has changed over a period of many years. Which lines describe it as it originally was?
2. What stage does line 3 represent in the changing land?
3. Where does the poem begin the description of the land as it is now?

### Analyzing
4. How would you describe the actions of the men, dynamite, wagons, horses, and plows?
5. In the few words describing the "improved property," the speaker focuses on hogs grunting over "the fodder crops." Given the descriptions that have gone before, how is this detail suggestive?

### Extending
6. Why might Sandburg have entitled the poem "Improved Farm Land" instead of "Great Singing Family of Trees"?

## APPLYING: Imagery H⅄
### See Handbook of Literary Terms, p. 802
**Images** are concrete details that engage the reader's imagination. **Imagery** appeals to one or more of the five senses—sight, sound, touch, smell, and taste.

1. In "Improved Farm Land," to what senses do the images appeal? Which most frequently, and which least?
2. In the last line the poet presents an image of what the land once had, "a great singing family of trees." How does this final image constitute a comment on what was done to the land?

**Review IMAGERY in the Handbook of Literary Terms, page 802.**

# Water Picture

**May Swenson**   USA

In the pond in the park
all things are doubled:
Long buildings hang and
wriggle gently. Chimneys
5 are bent legs bouncing
on clouds below. A flag
wags like a fishhook
down there in the sky.

The arched stone bridge
10 is an eye, with underlid
in the water. In its lens
dip crinkled heads with hats
that don't fall off. Dogs go by,
barking on their backs.
15 A baby, taken to feed the
ducks, dangles upside-down,
a pink balloon for a buoy.

Treetops deploy a haze of
cherry bloom for roots,
20 where birds coast belly-up
in the glass bowl of a hill;
from its bottom a bunch
of peanut-munching children
is suspended by their
25 sneakers, waveringly.

A swan, with twin necks
forming the figure three,
steers between two dimpled
towers doubled. Fondly
30 hissing, she kisses herself,
and all the scene is troubled:
water-windows splinter,
tree-limbs tangle, the bridge
folds like a fan.

Tom Heflin, *Sinnissippi Swan* (detail), 1986, Private Collection

## THINK AND DISCUSS
### Understanding
1. Where are all things "doubled"?
2. List at least two unusual pictures the mirror effect causes.

### Analyzing
3. What makes the mirror effect disappear?
4. At the end of the poem, "the bridge folds like a fan." Explain.

### Extending
5. The still water of the pond reflects an upside-down world, often adding a dash of distortion. What in your view is the effect of seeing the bridge become an eye, dogs "barking on their backs," children "suspended by their sneakers" munching peanuts, and so forth?

## REVIEWING: Imagery HT
### See Handbook of Literary Terms, p. 802
"Water Picture" is rich in images that appeal to the senses, with the sense of sight primary (as the title implies it will be).

1. What senses other than sight are appealed to in the poem?
2. Explain the distortions of the image of the chimneys in the first stanza.

# The Red Wheelbarrow

**William Carlos Williams**   USA

so much depends
upon

a red wheel
barrow

5 glazed with rain
water

beside the white
chickens.

## THINK AND DISCUSS
### Understanding
1. "The Red Wheelbarrow" may be considered "minimalist poetry"—poetry made out of a minimal number of words and images. Out of sixteen words, the poet has created a picture or still life which comments on itself. How does the first pair of lines differ from the other pairs in the poem?
2. What is the most visually compelling word in each of the three last pairs of lines?

### Analyzing
3. What, according to the poem's suggestion, are not enough by themselves, but "depend" on something additional?

4. What is the meaning of "depends upon" in lines 1–2? Discuss.

### Extending
5. What would happen to the poem if the words were printed (or read aloud) continuously in a line of prose? Discuss.

# Six Haiku

## Matsuo Bashō   Japan

Spring:
A hill without a name
Veiled in morning mist.


On a bare branch
A rook roosts:
Autumn dusk.


Clouds now and then
Giving men relief
From moon-viewing.

## Yosa Buson   Japan

Spring rain:
In our sedan
Your soft whispers.


Mosquito-buzz
Whenever honeysuckle
Petals fall.


Sudden shower:
Grasping the grass-blades
A shoal of sparrows.

From *The Penguin Book of Japanese Verse* translated by Geoffrey Bownas and Anthony Thwaite (Penguin Books, 1964). Copyright © Geoffrey Bownas and Anthony Thwaite, 1964, pp. 111–112, 119–120. Reprinted by permission of Penguin Books Ltd.

## THINK AND DISCUSS
### Understanding
1. Which of the haiku poems use images from nature? Identify at least two images that represent natural things.

### Analyzing
2. It is customary in English to use complete sentences to describe things, even if they are not active: *The blue car had a rusty fender.*
Are the haiku poems written in complete sentences? Explain.
3. Compare and contrast the first and second Bashō haiku.
4. Given the context in the first Buson haiku (which mentions a sedan chair, an enclosed seat carried by servants), what does the image "soft whispers" suggest?
5. Compare and contrast the third haiku by Buson with the first by the same poet.

### Extending

**6.** Each of the haiku associates two images or ideas: spring and a hill in mist, the sound of mosquitoes and flower petals falling, and so on. Which pair of images do you find most clear and natural? Which do you find most surprising? Explain.

## COMPOSITION
### Describing a Landscape or Cityscape

Write a three-paragraph description of a familiar landscape or cityscape for your journal and to share with friends. Don't rely entirely on memory, but take a fresh look and set down in a notebook the images that might prove telling or suggestive in a description. Decide on an overall impression or feeling you want to evoke and place the elements of your description in the order that seems most likely to develop it. See "Developing Your Style" in the Writer's Handbook.

### Writing Haiku

Read the Comment article, "Images in Haiku Poetry," and then try your hand at writing three haiku to share with the class. Carve out a period of time in which you are able to quietly observe and meditate on a variety of scenes, indoors and outdoors. Let an image you yourself experience set each poem in motion, and at the same time try to capture the emotion you have felt in the images you pack into the small space of a haiku.

# Comment

## Images in Haiku Poetry

Haiku (hī′kü) is the shortest form in Japanese poetry. A haiku poem consists of seventeen syllables in three lines of 5, 7, and 5 syllables each. In translation, the number of syllables may change, since the meaning is conveyed in English words.

Haiku characteristically juxtaposes, or presents together, two elements often linked by implication, not by specific connecting words or phrases. The haiku focuses on images and pares language down to its leanest state. In the Bashō haiku about a rook (a large bird) roosting on a branch, the bird suggests or symbolizes the feeling of dusk during autumn. The poet depends on your imagination to link the two.

The emotions of the poet are seldom expressed directly in haiku but appear indirectly through the selection and arrangement of images. In the haiku about the rook, the autumn images embody and give rise to a feeling of melancholy, or a somber mood.

Early in the twentieth century, Japanese literature became popular with American poets. The structure of Japanese haiku could not be reproduced exactly in English, but a close approximation captured its spirit.

The two poets appearing here, Bashō and Buson, are considered by the Japanese as their classic haiku poets.

The concentration on images that characterizes haiku has influenced the imagistic movement in America, represented by poets such as William Carlos Williams. The publication, beginning in 1915, of a series of volumes entitled *Some Imagist Poets* had a strong impact on Willliams in the writing of such poems as "The Red Wheelbarrow," with their sharp focus on vivid, clear, and emotionally charged images.

# BIOGRAPHIES

---

## Carl Sandburg   1878–1967

Born of Swedish immigrants in Galesburg, Illinois, Sandburg left school at thirteen for a series of jobs out west, then returned to attend Lombard College. He worked as a newspaperman in Chicago and there began to publish his poems in *Poetry* magazine, receiving wide attention. His many books include *Chicago Poems* (1916) and *The American Songbag* (1927). He often gave public poetry readings, accompanying himself on guitar.

## May Swenson   1919–1989

A noted modern American poet, Swenson was born in Logan, Utah, and took a degree from the University of Utah. Her first book of poems was *Another Animal: Poems* (1954); in this and in subsequent collections, such as *Half Sun Half Sleep* (1967) and *More Poems to Solve* (1971), she showed a tendency to play with language, combining words in original and unusual ways.

## William Carlos Williams   1883–1963

Williams advised any poet to write on "things with which he is familiar, simple things—at the same time to detach them from ordinary experience to the imagination." He also adopted as a kind of poetic credo, "no idea but in things." Williams spent his life as a doctor in Rutherford, New Jersey, writing poetry in his free moments. In addition to producing several volumes of short poems, he spent many of his later years writing his long masterpiece, *Paterson*.

## Matsuo Bashō   1644–1694

Bashō, the greatest of all writers of haiku, was born into a family of samurai—men of the warrior class—at a time of great peace and stability in Japan. At eight years of age, he was taken into the service of a nobleman's son. His young master taught Bashō much and by the time he was nine he had written his first verses. Though he wrote for most of his life, he did not reach the peak of his ability until his last ten years. Though some of Bashō's poems are infused with a religious mysticism, most are simple descriptions of real scenes and real events.

## Yosa Buson   1715–1783

Buson, considered second only to Bashō as a writer of haiku, is equally famous as a painter, and many of his poems are in themselves lovely pictures. His subject matter displays a great appreciation of the ever-changing world. Born Taniguchi Buson, he later took the name Yosa in honor of a region near Kyoto known for its scenic beauty.

**See FIGURATIVE LANGUAGE in the Handbook of Literary Terms, page 796.**

# Those Winter Sundays

**Robert Hayden** USA

Sundays too my father got up early
and put his clothes on in the blueblack cold,
then with cracked hands that ached
from labor in the weekday weather made
5 banked fires blaze. No one ever thanked him.

I'd wake and hear the cold splintering, breaking.
When the rooms were warm, he'd call,
and slowly I would rise and dress,
fearing the chronic angers of that house,

10 Speaking indifferently to him,
who had driven out the cold
and polished my good shoes as well.
What did I know, what did I know
of love's austere and lonely offices?

## THINK AND DISCUSS
### Understanding
1. What does the word *too* in line 1 tell you?
2. What are some of the possible reasons "no one ever thanked him"?

### Analyzing
3. What do phrases like "fearing the chronic angers" and "speaking indifferently to him" tell about the speaker's attitude toward his father?
4. How do the last two lines suggest that his attitude has changed?

### Extending
5. This poem is a portrait of the speaker's father, but it tells something about a son as well. What impression do you get of each character? Discuss.

## APPLYING: Figurative Language
See Handbook of Literary Terms, p. 796

**Figurative language** is language used in a non-literal way, to add beauty, vitality, or conciseness to literary works. It is fairly easy to spot figures of speech that make or suggest clear comparisons between unlike things. Less obvious, however, are figurative expressions containing only nouns and modifiers that subtly blend unlike qualities.

1. How can "cold" be *blueblack*, as described in line 2 of "Those Winter Sundays"? Does the time of day mentioned help you understand the figurative language? Explain.
2. What subtle comparison is suggested by the figurative description of cold in line 6?

See SIMILE in the Handbook of Literary Terms, page 826.

# Harlem

**Langston Hughes**   USA

What happens to a dream deferred?

Does it dry up.
like a raisin in the sun?
Or fester like a sore—
5 And then run?
Does it stink like rotten meat?
Or crust and sugar over—
like a syrupy sweet?

Maybe it just sags
10 like a heavy load.

*Or does it explode?*

**THINK AND DISCUSS**
**Understanding**
1. Check the meaning of *deferred* in the Glossary; then explain the kind of dream the speaker is talking about in line 1.
2. Is there a clear answer to the questions posed in lines 2–8? Explain.

**Analyzing**
3. What is the significance of the title?
4. What is the speaker's tone throughout the poem?

**Extending**
5. What do you think the dream of people in Harlem might be? What choices are implied for all Americans in the last 3 lines?

**APPLYING: Simile** HＺ
**See Handbook of Literary Terms, p. 826**
   A **simile** is a figure of speech involving a comparison of two basically different things, using such words as *like* or *as*.

1. Identify the four similes in lines 2–8 of "Harlem."
2. How does the simile of the festering sore differ from the other three?
3. What is the effect of these four similes?

**See METAPHOR in the Handbook of Literary Terms, page 807.**

# Afterglow

**Jorge Luis Borges**   Argentina

Sunset is always disturbing
whether theatrical or muted,
but still more disturbing
is that last desperate glow
5  that turns the plain to rust
when on the horizon nothing is left
of the pomp and clamor of the setting sun.
How hard holding on to that light, so tautly drawn and different,
that hallucination which the human fear of the dark
10  imposes on space
and which ceases at once
the moment we realize its falsity,
the way a dream is broken
the moment the sleeper knows he is dreaming.

*Jorge Luis Borges* (hôr′hā lwēs bôr′hes)

Excerpted from the book *Jorge Luis Borges: Selected Poems 1923-1967*, edited, with an Introduction and Notes, by Norman Thomas Di Giovanni. Copyright © 1968, 1969, 1970, 1971, 1972 by Jorge Luis Borges, Emece Editores S.A. and Norman Thomas Di Giovanni. Reprinted by permission of Delacorte Press/Seymour Lawrence and Emece Editores S.A.

## THINK AND DISCUSS
### Understanding
1. What is the afterglow of a sunset?
2. The afterglow of the sunset is described as "tautly drawn and different" from the "pomp and clamor" of the sunset. Explain.

### Analyzing
3. Why is the sunset "always disturbing"?
4. To what do the words *its falsity* in line 12 refer?

## APPLYING: Metaphor   H𝒵
### See Handbook of Literary Terms, p. 807

A **metaphor** is a figure of speech involving an implied comparison between two basically different things.

1. Locate and explain a metaphor in the first five lines of "Afterglow."
2. What is the implied comparison in line 7, "the pomp and clamor of the setting sun"?
3. In line 9, how might the afterglow be comparable to a hallucination?

Review METAPHOR in the Handbook of Literary Terms, page 807.

# Sunset

**Oswald Mbuyiseni Mtshali** South Africa

The sun spun like
a tossed coin.
It whirled on the azure sky,
it clattered into the horizon,
5 it clicked in the slot,
and neon-lights popped
and blinked "Time expired,"
as on a parking meter.

*Oswald Mbuyiseni Mtshali* (əm bü yē sä nē   əm chä lē)

"Sunset" from *Sounds of a Cowhide Drum* by Oswald Mbuyiseni Mtshali. Copyright © 1971 by Oswald Mbuyiseni Mtshali. Reprinted by permission of Oxford University Press.

## THINK AND DISCUSS

### Understanding

1. What does a "tossed coin" (line 2) usually imply? Discuss.

### Analyzing

2. Explain the meaning of "Time expired" in line 7.

### Extending

3. Do you think that by describing the sunset as he does the poet has made it a less mysterious occurrence? Why or why not?

### REVIEWING: Metaphor HⱫ
See Handbook of Literary Terms, p. 807
A metaphor is an implied comparison, differing from a simile in that the latter makes the comparison explicit with such words as *like* or *as*. In some poems, metaphors and similes become so intermixed it is difficult to disentangle them. Such a poem is "Sunset." It begins with a simile, is extended by a sequence of metaphors, and closes with a simile. Since a central comparison is used throughout the poem, the figure of speech may be called an "extended metaphor."

1. What is the central comparison running through the whole of "Sunset?"
2. Which of the metaphors in lines 3–6 appear to stretch or go beyond this basic comparison? Discuss.
3. What might the "neon-lights" be in the description of the sunset?

See PERSONIFICATION in the Handbook of Literary Terms, page 812.

# The Naming of Cats

**T. S. Eliot**   Great Britain

The Naming of Cats is a difficult matter,
  It isn't just one of your holiday games;
You may think at first I'm as mad as a hatter
When I tell you, a cat must have THREE DIFFERENT NAMES.
5 First of all, there's the name that the family use daily,
  Such as Peter, Augustus, Alonzo or James,
Such as Victor or Jonathan, George or Bill Bailey—
  All of them sensible everyday names.
There are fancier names if you think they sound sweeter,
10   Some for the gentlemen, some for the dames:
Such as Plato, Admetus, Electra, Demeter[1]—
  But all of them sensible everyday names.
But I tell you, a cat needs a name that's particular,
  A name that's peculiar, and more dignified,
15 Else how can he keep up his tail perpendicular,
  Or spread out his whiskers, or cherish his pride?
Of names of this kind, I can give you a quorum,
  Such as Munkustrap, Quaxo, or Coricopat,
Such as Bombalurina, or else Jellylorum[2]—
20   Names that never belong to more than one cat.
But above and beyond there's still one name left over,
  And that is the name that you never will guess;
The name that no human research can discover—
  But THE CAT HIMSELF KNOWS, and will never confess.
25 When you notice a cat in profound meditation,
  The reason, I tell you, is always the same:
His mind is engaged in a rapt contemplation
  Of the thought, of the thought, of the thought of his name:
    His ineffable effable
30     Effanineffable[3]
Deep and inscrutable singular Name.

1. *Plato . . . Demeter*, names from Greek history or mythology.
2. *Munkustrap . . . Jellylorum*, names made up by the poet.
3. *effanineffable*, a made-up word combining *effable* and *ineffable*.

"The Naming of Cats" from *Old Possum's Book of Practical Cats* by T. S. Eliot. Copyright 1939 by T. S. Eliot; renewed 1967 by Esme Valerie Eliot. Reprinted by permission of Harcourt Brace Jovanovich, Inc., and Faber and Faber Ltd.

Edward Gorey, *The Naming of Cats* (detail), 1982, from the artist's illustrations for *Old Possum's Book of Practical Cats*

---

## THINK AND DISCUSS
### Understanding
1. What is the nature of the first name the speaker says a cat needs?
2. How does the second necessary name differ from the first?

### Analyzing
3. What is unusual about the third name a cat needs? Discuss.
4. Describe the effect of the last five lines of the poem. How is the effect achieved?

### Extending
5. Does the description of how cats react to their secret names correspond with what you know about cats' habits? Explain.

## APPLYING: Personification  HT
### See Handbook of Literary Terms, p. 812
**Personification** is a a figure of speech in which human characteristics and capabilities are attributed to non-human things or events.

1. What are the clues in the first 16 lines of the poem that the speaker is portraying cats as having human characteristics?
2. What are the human traits attributed to the cat in lines 21–31? What behavior of the cat may be the basis for this attribution? Discuss.

See HYPERBOLE in the Handbook of Literary Terms, page 801.

# For Anne Gregory

**William Butler Yeats**   Ireland

"Never shall a young man,
Thrown into despair
By those great honey-coloured
Ramparts at your ear,
5 Love you for yourself alone
And not your yellow hair."

"But I can get a hair-dye
And set such colour there,
Brown, or black, or carrot,
10 That young men in despair
May love me for myself alone
And not my yellow hair."

"I heard an old religious man
But yesternight declare
15 That he had found a text to prove
That only God, my dear,
Could love you for yourself alone
And not your yellow hair."

---

*William Butler Yeats* (yāts)

Reprinted with permission of Macmillan Publishing Company and A. P. Watt Ltd. on behalf of Michael B. Yeats and Macmillan London Ltd. from *Collected Poems* by W. B. Yeats. Copyright 1933 by Macmillan Publishing Company, renewed 1961 by Bertha Georgie Yeats.

## THINK AND DISCUSS
### Understanding
1. This poem is a dialogue. Who seems to be speaking in stanza 1? in stanza 2?
2. Who is the speaker in the last stanza?

### Analyzing
3. Look up *ramparts* in the Glossary. In what way might the young woman's hair look like "honey-colored ramparts"?
4. Summarize the opinion expressed by the man in stanza 1.
5. Would what the young woman proposes she could do in stanza 2 alter her lot? Discuss.

### Extending
6. Do you believe the speaker in the third stanza when he says he heard an "old religious man" citing a text that proves what the speaker believes? Why or why not?

## APPLYING: Hyperbole
### See Handbook of Literary Terms, p. 801
   **Hyperbole** is a figure of speech involving great exaggeration, used sometimes to reinforce a strong belief and sometimes for comic effect.

1. What is the hyperbole in "For Anne Gregory"? What is the effect?
2. What might be the motive for the speaker exaggerating as he does in the last stanza?

**Review SIMILE in the Handbook of Literary Terms, page 826.**

# Psalm 1

**The Bible**  Israel

Blessed is the man that walketh not in the counsel of the ungodly,
Nor standeth in the way of sinners,
Nor sitteth in the seat of the scornful.
But his delight is in the law of the Lord;
5 And in his law doth he meditate day and night.
And he shall be like a tree planted by the rivers of water,
That bringeth forth his fruit in his season;
His leaf also shall not wither;
And whatsoever he doeth shall prosper.
10 The ungodly are not so;
But are like the chaff which the wind driveth away.
Therefore the ungodly shall not stand in the judgment,
Nor sinners in the congregation of the righteous.
For the Lord knoweth the way of the righteous;
15 But the way of the ungodly shall perish.

Psalm 1 from the King James Translation, 1611.

**THINK AND DISCUSS**
**Understanding**
1. Which lines, among 1–5, describe the way of the ungodly and which the way of the godly?
2. The good man is compared to a tree. What details indicate that he is like a healthy tree?

**Analyzing**
3. The godly and ungodly are sorted in lines 1–5 in accord with the ways they follow. What is the source of the way for the ungodly and the source for the godly?
4. Who is the "he" of line 9? Does "prosper" mean gain in material goods? Explain.

5. What is the **tone** of Psalm 1? How is the tone related to the language?

**REVIEWING: Simile**
**See Handbook of Literary Terms, p. 826**
   A simile is a figure of speech comparing two things, using words such as *like* and *as*.

1. Find the first simile in Psalm 1 and explain its meaning.
2. What will happen to the ungodly according to the simile describing their fate?

# Comment

### The Psalms

The Book of Psalms is the nineteenth book of the Bible. The Psalms constituted the Jewish hymnbook, a collection of sacred songs written over a period of many centuries. Some psalms have been ascribed to David, king of the ancient Hebrews.

The word *psalm* derives from the Greek *psalmos*, a song sung to a harp. Psalms have been used as hymns in religious ceremonies for thousands of years.

The first book published in America, in 1640, was *The Bay Psalm Book*, a translation of the psalms into meter and rhyme that the pilgrim settlers could sing. Lines 6–8 of Psalm 1 were rendered:

> And he shall be like to a tree
>  planted by water-rivers;
> that in his season yields his fruit,
>  and his leaf never withers.

Some people are distracted by the singsong sound of the lines and prefer the King James version of the Psalms, another translation.

The Psalms consist of prayers, reflections on the wonders of creation, lamentations, celebrations of divine power, and other verses. Psalm 1, beginning with "Blessed is the man . . . ," is considered a *beatitude*, or an invocation of a blessing.

Psalms often are read aloud at solemn ceremonies. One of the most familiar lines of the Bible comes from Psalm 23: "The Lord is my shepherd; I shall not want." Psalms are popular in part because they have the immediate appeal of timeless poetry. As one critic has written, "Certainly no other western hymnbook even distantly approaches the collection of Psalms in literary value."

---

## COMPOSITION

### Reading/Writing Log

In "The Naming of Cats," T. S. Eliot uses personification by comparing the cats to human beings, actually describing them in human terms. Copy the following heading and example in your reading/writing log or another notebook. Then find at least two additional such comparisons in the poem and add them to your log.

*Specific Example of Comparison: Personification (Referring to cats)*

> There are fancier names if you think they
>  sound sweeter,
> Some for the gentlemen, some for the dames

### Writing About an Animal

You have encountered personification in "The Naming of Cats," in which cats are compared to humans. Now use comparisons such as personification in a three-paragraph essay about an animal you know or have known. What human traits can you attribute to the animal? For example, do you carry on conversations with it, pretending it understands? Do you tell it secrets? Perhaps you have imagined a pet that is willing to sit to have its portrait painted, or you may have a friend that happens to be a neighbor's cat.

### Comparing Two Poems

Write a four-paragraph essay for your class comparing and contrasting "Afterglow" and "Sunset." Explore what they have in common and how they differ. Describe how they engage your imagination. If you prefer, explain your preference for one poem. See "Writing to Compare and Contrast" in the Writer's Handbook.

# BIOGRAPHIES

## Robert Hayden   1913–1980

Born and raised in the Detroit area, Hayden later taught at both the University of Michigan and Fisk University in Nashville. He received little early recognition for his poetry, but beginning in the 1960s he won several awards, including a National Book Award in 1971 for his collection *Words in the Mourning Time*. Though Hayden's writing frequently reflects his black heritage, it often extends far beyond it, revealing his love and compassion for all humanity.

## Langston Hughes   1902–1967

Although Hughes is best known as a poet, his novels, short stories, plays, and translations, as well as his poems, have given voice to the concerns of minorities. Born in Joplin, Missouri, Hughes became known to the literary world during the 1920s. Works such as *The Weary Blues* (1926), *The Dream Keeper* (1932), and *The Panther and the Lash* (1967) reflected the changing role of blacks in American society. Toward the end of his career, he devoted his energies to helping young writers.

## Jorge Luis Borges   1899–1986

Borges is perhaps the best known of modern South American writers. He was born in Buenos Aires into a well-educated family and learned English as a youth. He received his college education in Switzerland. His first book of poetry, *Fervor de Buenos Aires*, was published in 1923; it was followed by several others, and by many collections of uniquely conceived short stories and parables, often set in a fantasy world of his own creation. After gradually losing sight over a period of years, Borges wrote most imaginatively despite his blindness.

## Oswald Mbuyiseni Mtshali   1940–

Mtshali was born in South Africa and lives in Johannesburg, where he has been under house arrest for opposition to the apartheid system of racial segregation. His first book of poetry, *Sounds of a Cowhide Drum* (1972), won prizes including a fellowship to study at the University of Iowa. His second book, *Fireflames* (1980), reportedly was banned by the South African government because he dedicated it to the schoolchildren of Soweto, a black township in that country. The novelist Nadine Gordimer has compared some of his poetry to that of William Blake.

## T. S. Eliot   1888–1965

Eliot was born in St. Louis, but he went to England when World War I broke out and lived there for the rest of his life, becoming a British citizen in 1927. He had begun to write poetry while a student at Harvard, including the famous "The Love Song of J. Alfred Prufrock." His great poem *The Waste Land,* expressing the acute modern feeling of futility, appeared in 1922. Though Eliot's poetry was generally serious, there were always comic or absurd elements in it. In 1939 he published an entire volume of light verse about cats, which was the basis of the Broadway musical *Cats* and from which "The Naming of Cats" is taken. In 1948 he received the Nobel Prize for Literature.

## William Butler Yeats   1865–1939

Yeats was born of Anglo-Irish parents in Dublin, and at an early age he began to write poetry. Moving frequently between London and Dublin in the 1890s, he published a number of volumes during that time, including many poems influenced by his study of Irish folklore. He helped found the famous Abbey Theatre in Dublin in 1904 and for a time concentrated on writing plays. He turned again to poetry as he grew older, writing much about the frustrations of aging. In 1923, at the height of his poetic powers, he was awarded the Nobel Prize for Literature.

'Tis not enough no harshness gives offense,
The sound must seem an echo to the sense.

Thus Alexander Pope formulated the ideal for poetry as the harmonious marriage of sound and meaning. Here are some pointers for reading poetry to appreciate sound and sense.

**Determine the poet's purpose.** Read until you know what the poet is up to. In Robert Graves's "The Traveler's Curse After Misdirection" the speaker is getting rid of pent-up rage by formulating a devastating curse. In Alexander Pope's "The Fool and the Poet" the speaker is creating a barbed insult sharpened by wit. Both poems are comical; the **author's purpose** in each is to entertain.

**Read the poem aloud.** By listening as you read, you begin to hear complex connections between a poem's sounds and its meanings.

**Hear the beat of the rhythm.** As we feel the pulsing of our blood or hear the ticking of a clock, we know we live our life at some of its deepest levels by sensing **rhythm.** No wonder that poetry taps this primal music. In the second line of Pope's couplet above, "The sound must seem an echo to the sense," note how the accent falls on all the important words and syllables.

**Hear the chiming of the rhyming.** Repeated sounds, especially in patterns, produce harmony. Pope's couplet is bound together by two end words: *offense* and *sense.* The lines convey two "rules" of poetry, the first negative, as expressed by *offense,* and the second positive, in that a poem should make *sense.* Pope has taken his own advice by making his lines follow the rules they state.

**Hear the heady harmony of alliteration.** Repetitions of sounds inside a poem can add music at surprising moments. **Alliteration** is the repetition of consonant sounds, as in the words *sound, seem,* and *sense* in Pope's line.

**Hear the quieter harmony of assonance and consonance. Assonance** is the repetition of vowel sounds, usually in stressed syllables; **consonance** is the repetition of consonant sounds preceded by different vowel sounds. A line of warning from Nguyen Trai's "A Round Shape Water Takes Inside the Gourd" uses both assonance and consonance: "Fall *in* w*i*th thieves—you'll rue *it* and ea*t* stick."

**Hear sound echo sense in onomatopoeia.** Things *bang,* snakes *hiss,* flies *buzz,* and bells *clang* in poems. Edgar Allan Poe once tried, in his poem "The Bells," to make his words ring like bells, as in the line "From the jingling and the tinkling of the bells."

**Understand the sentences in poems.** Despite the rhymes, rhythms, and capital letters at the beginning of the lines in many poems, the poems may be read as sentences that are as sensible as those in prose. You can read the sentences as statements, questions, exclamations, and imperative commands, just as you would in a letter, essay, or story. In some poems, certain sentences are inverted; the subject, verb, and other sentence parts may appear in an unusual order. A poet may use **inversion** to emphasize certain words or to maintain a poem's rhythm. The title of a poem in this unit, "White in the Moon the Long Road Lies," is an inverted sentence describing the color of a road in moonlight. It, like most lines in poems you will study, uses language to express meaning vividly.

**See RHYTHM in the Handbook of Literary Terms, page 819.**

# The Traveler's Curse
# After Misdirection

**Robert Graves**   Great Britain

May they stumble, stage by stage
On an endless pilgrimage,
Dawn and dusk, mile after mile,
At each and every step, a stile;
5 At each and every step withal
May they catch their feet and fall;
At each and every fall they take
May a bone within them break;
And may the bone that breaks within
10 Not be, for variation's sake,
Now rib, now thigh, now arm, now shin,
But always, without fail THE NECK.

---

Paul Klee, *Mural from the Temple of Longing Thither*, 1922, The Metropolitan Museum of Art, The Berggruen Klee Collection, 1984

## THINK AND DISCUSS
### Understanding
1. Who are "they" that the traveler curses?
2. How is the curse suitable as revenge?

### Analyzing
3. Notice that the words *step, fall, bone,* and *break* are repeated. How does the curse change with each repetition?
4. What is the effect of the last line, and especially the last word? Discuss.

### Extending
5. What is the tone of this poem? Do you consider this a serious curse? Explain.

## APPLYING: Rhythm HT
### See Handbook of Literary Terms, p. 819
**Rhythm** (or meter) is the arrangement of stressed and unstressed syllables in speech or writing. In poetry the four most common metrical feet are *iamb* ($\smile$ ′), *trochee* (′ $\smile$), *anapest* ($\smile$ $\smile$ ′), and *dactyl* (′ $\smile$ $\smile$).

1. Scan the first line of this poem and identify its metrical pattern.
2. In line 3 we encounter an interruption of this pattern. Explain.
3. What is the metrical pattern of line 4? Which lines follow this pattern and which follow the pattern of line 1?

See RHYME in the Handbook of Literary Terms, page 818.

# The Fool and the Poet

**Alexander Pope**   Great Britain

Sir, I admit your general rule,
That every poet is a fool,
But you yourself may serve to show it,
That every fool is not a poet.

"Epigram from the French" by Alexander Pope, 1732.

## THINK AND DISCUSS

**Understanding**
1. Who is the "Sir" addressed in the first line?
2. Who is the speaker of the poem?

**Analyzing**
3. What is it the speaker says he admits? Should we take him at his word?
4. What may we infer from the last two lines about the person to whom the poem is addressed?

**Extending**
5. Do you judge the tone of this poem to be angry or witty? Explain.

## APPLYING: Rhyme  H⧸T

**See Handbook of Literary Terms, p. 818**

**Rhyme** is the repetition of similar or identical sounds in at least the final accented syllable of two or more words. It adds to the musical pleasure of a poem, provides a means for emphasis of particular words, and in patterns (as end rhymes) helps structure a poem.

1. What is the rhyme scheme of "The Fool and the Poet"?
2. How does the title figure in the rhyme scheme of the poem?
3. How does the second rhyme (*show it* and *poet*) differ from the first (*rule* and *fool*)? Discuss the effect.

See ALLITERATION in the Handbook of Literary Terms, page 788.

# Sonnet 65

**William Shakespeare**   Great Britain

Since brass, nor stone, nor earth, nor boundless sea,
But sad mortality o'er-sways their power,
How with this rage shall beauty hold a plea,
Whose action[1] is no stronger than a flower?
5 O how shall summer's honey breath hold out
Against the wrackful[2] siege of batt'ring days,
When rocks impregnable[3] are not so stout,
Nor gates of steel so strong, but Time decays?
O fearful meditation! where, alack,
10 Shall Time's best jewel from Time's chest lie hid?
Or what strong hand can hold his swift foot back,
Or who his spoil[4] of beauty can forbid?
    O none, unless this miracle have might,
    That in black ink my love may still shine bright.

1. *action,* vigor.
2. *wrackful,* destructive.
3. *impregnable,* incapable of being reduced by force.
4. *spoil,* goods seized by conquest.

"Sonnet 65" by William Shakespeare, 1609.

## THINK AND DISCUSS
### Understanding
1. According to lines 1 and 2, what does "sad mortality" (death) overcome?
2. According to lines 3 and 4, how strong is the "action" (vigor) of beauty?
3. The speaker asks how beauty can hold out against death when such powerful things as brass, stone, earth, and sea cannot. He poses a similar question in lines 5–8; what is threatened and by whom?
4. What is the "fearful meditation" (line 9)?
5. What is provided in the last two lines?

### Analyzing
6. In lines 5–12, what **metaphor** is used to portray time?
7. What words in the poem apply to "my love" in the last line?
8. What if the poet had substituted "my love" for the words *beauty* (line 3), *summer's honey breath* (line 5), and *Time's best jewel* (line 10)? Would the poem have been as effective? Explain.
9. What "miracle" might overcome Time?

**Alliteration** is the repetition of consonant sounds at the beginnings of words or within words, particularly in accented syllables. It gives force to thought, emphasizes words, and may produce musical effects.

1. Cite all the examples you can find of alliteration in line 1 of "Sonnet 65."
2. Find the alliteration in line 5 and discuss its effect.

## READING LITERATURE SKILLFULLY
### Author's Purpose

Understanding traditional poetry becomes easier if the reader recognizes the poet's purpose—what the poet means to communicate. Shakespeare presents a problem in "Sonnet 65," and it is a problem that could be recognized by anyone who has loved another person. If even stone and earth are wracked by the passage of Time, he asks, how can his love, a fragile beauty, withstand the ruins of Time?

1. How does the idea offered in the final couplet solve the poet's stated problem?
2. How is this poem an expression of love?

## RHYME, RHYTHM, AND PATTERNS

**HZ**     See ASSONANCE in the Handbook of Literary Terms, page 790.

# On the Grasshopper and Cricket

**John Keats**    Great Britain

The poetry of earth is never dead:
    When all the birds are faint with the hot sun,
    And hide in cooling trees, a voice will run
From hedge to hedge about the new-mown mead;
5 That is the Grasshopper's—he takes the lead
    In summer luxury,—he has never done
    With his delights; for when tired out with fun
He rests at ease beneath some pleasant weed.
The poetry of earth is ceasing never:
10    On a lone winter evening, when the frost
    Has wrought a silence, from the stove there shrills
The Cricket's song, in warmth increasing ever,
    And seems to one in drowsiness half lost,
     The Grasshopper's among some grassy hills.

"On the Grasshopper and Cricket" by John Keats, 1817.

Kitagawa Utamaro, illustration from *Picture Book of Selected Insects*, 1788

## THINK AND DISCUSS
### Understanding
1. What details in the first eight lines of the poem tell you the season of the year?
2. What detail suggests that the birds are not singing?
3. What voice is heard after the birds hide and where does it come from?
4. What is the season in the second part of the poem, and what song is heard?

### Analyzing
5. What three sounds does the speaker imply can be called "the poetry of earth?"
6. What idea is repeated in the poem and why?
7. How is the cricket's song like the grasshopper's? How does it differ?
8. Someone lost in drowsiness (perhaps the speaker) is introduced in line 13. What causes the drowsiness and how does it affect perception of the cricket's song?

### Extending
9. Think about the seasons named in the poem. What is the effect of the blending of the cricket's song with the grasshopper's in the last three lines?

### APPLYING: Assonance H▨
**See Handbook of Literary Terms, p. 790**

**Assonance** is the repetition of similar vowel sounds followed by different consonant sounds, usually in stressed syllables. Assonance can enhance the musical quality of the work and contribute to meaning and unity.

1. Find the assonance in line 1 that carries over into line 2.
2. Find the assonance in line 8 and discuss its effect.

## Comment

### Sonnets

Sometimes poets like to write within the constraints of an imposed form just to see how deep they might reach, how high they might soar, and yet remain anchored in a familiar or traditional form.

Such a form is the sonnet, represented here by Shakespeare's "Sonnet 65" and John Keats's "On the Grasshopper and Cricket." Both are fourteen lines long, and the lines are made up of iambic pentameter (five feet of unaccented/accented syllables).

There are two basic kinds of sonnets. The most ancient is the Petrarchan, so-called after the Italian master Petrarch (1304–1374) and represented here by Keats's sonnet. The main feature of the Petrarchan sonnet is that it consists of two parts, the first eight lines forming the *octet*, the last six lines forming the *sestet*. The sense of the sonnet follows this division, with a problem usually posed in the octet and a resolution of the problem presented in the sestet.

Notice the rhyme scheme of Keats's sonnet divides it into these two parts:

*abbc abbc // def def*

The octet focuses on the "poetry" of the grasshopper in summer, while the sestet focuses on the "poetry" of the cricket in winter. Thus the proposition of the poem stated in the first line—that the "poetry of earth is never dead"—seems conclusively demonstrated by the end of the sonnet.

"Sonnet 65" is a Shakespearean sonnet—so-called because Shakespeare used and perfected its form. Its structure may be thought of as breaking down into two major parts of 12 lines and 2 lines. But the first 12 lines break down into three interrelated parts of four lines each, called *quatrains*.

Note the rhyme scheme of Shakespeare's sonnet supports these divisions:

*abab cdcd efef // gg*

Usually the quatrains present variations on a problem or argument and the final *couplet* (two rhyming lines) presents the solution, answer, or summary.

Shakespeare's three quatrains pose varied questions on how the speaker's love can possibly escape the ravages of time; the couplet provides the answer—in the speaker's poetry: ". . . in black ink my love may still shine bright."

See CONSONANCE in the Handbook of Literary Terms, page 795.

# A Round Shape Water Takes Inside the Gourd

**Nguyen Trai**   Vietnam

*Translated by* **Huynh Sanh**

A round shape water takes inside the gourd.
For good or ill, all fit some frame or mold.
Live near the rich—you'll munch on crackly rice.
Fall in with thieves—you'll rue it and eat stick.
5 Befriend a fool—you'll join the pack of fools.
Meet clever men—you'll learn some clever tricks.
Mix with low folk—you'll stoop to their low plane.
Get black near ink, get red near cinnabar.

*Nguyen Trai* (nə win′ trī).

"A round shape water takes inside the gourd" by Nguyen Trai from *The Heritage of Vietnamese Poetry*, edited and translated by Huynh Sanh Thong. Copyright © 1979 by Yale University. All rights reserved. Reprinted by permission of Yale University Press.

## THINK AND DISCUSS
### Understanding
1. State the idea in line 1 in your own words.

### Analyzing
2. How does line 1 relate to the rest of the poem?

### Extending
3. Do you think the message of the poem is true? Discuss.
4. If it is true, what choice does it seem to leave people with?

## APPLYING: Consonance   HLT
**See Handbook of Literary Terms, p. 795**
   **Consonance** is the repetition of similar or identical consonant sounds preceded by different vowel sounds. It is often used to reinforce mood or meaning.

1. Identify examples of consonance in line 2 of the poem. Discuss its effect.
2. Identify the consonance in line 4 and discuss the effect.

**See ONOMATOPOEIA in the Handbook of Literary Terms, page 810.**

# In an Iridescent Time

**Ruth Stone**   USA

My mother, when young, scrubbed laundry in a tub,
She and her sisters on an old brick walk
Under the apple trees, sweet rub-a-dub.
The bees came round their heads, the wrens made talk.
5 Four young ladies each with a rainbow board
Honed their knuckles, wrung their wrists to red,
Tossed back their braids and wiped their aprons wet.
The Jersey calf beyond the back fence roared;
And all the soft day, swarms about their pet
10 Buzzed at his big brown eyes and bullish head.
Four times they rinsed, they said. Some things they starched,
Then shook them from the baskets two by two,
And pinned the fluttering intimacies of life
Between the lilac bushes and the yew:
15 Brown gingham, pink, and skirts of Alice blue.[1]

1. *Alice blue,* a light blue, named after Alice Roosevelt, daughter of President Theodore Roosevelt.

"In an Iridescent Time" from *Second-Hand Coat* by Ruth Stone. Copyright © 1987 by Ruth Stone. Reprinted by permission of David R. Godine, Publisher.

## THINK AND DISCUSS
### Understanding
1. How are the women described in the poem related to the speaker?
2. Where is the washing being done?

### Analyzing
3. What is the "time" referred to in the title? Explain "iridescent."

### Extending
4. What do you judge the poem's tone to be?

## APPLYING: Onomatopoeia   H𝓣
### See Handbook of Literary Terms, p. 810
**Onomatopoeia** is the use of words that imitate or suggest the sound of the thing being described.

1. Find an example of onomatopoeia in line 3 and discuss its effect.
2. Identify another example of onomatopoeia in lines 9–10, and discuss its effect.

See FREE VERSE in the Handbook of Literary Terms, page 800.

# By the Bivouac's Fitful Flame

## Walt Whitman   USA

By the bivouac's fitful flame,
A procession winding around me, solemn and sweet and slow—but first I
    note,
The tents of the sleeping army, the fields' and woods' dim outline,
The darkness lit by spots of kindled fire, the silence,
5 Like a phantom far or near an occasional figure moving,
The shrubs and trees, (as I lift my eyes they seem to be stealthily
    watching me,)
While wind in procession thoughts, O tender and wondrous thoughts,
Of life and death, of home and the past and loved, and of those that are
    far away;
A solemn and slow procession there as I sit on the ground,
10 By the bivouac's fitful flame.

"By the Bivouac's Fitful Flame" from *Drum-Taps* by Walt Whitman, 1865.

Civil War photograph of a camp at Johnsonville, Tennessee, 1864, from the collection of the Library of Congress. Countryside around this encampment of black Union soldiers may have resembled the fields Whitman described.

## THINK AND DISCUSS
### Understanding
The poem presents a scene from the American Civil War (1861–1865); the speaker is with the army at its temporary encampment, with its campfire flickering in the night.

1. Where in the encampment is the speaker situated and what time of day is it?
2. Where is the "procession" mentioned in line 2 finally described?

### Analyzing
3. What does the speaker emphasize in describing the actual scene of the encampment in lines 3–6?
4. What is the relationship between the description of the encampment and the "procession" described in lines 7–9?
5. What might we have expected the *procession* to be at first? What in fact is it?

### Extending
6. The poem portrays a Civil War scene. Would you call it a war poem? Why or why not?

### APPLYING: Free Verse  HT
See Handbook of Literary Terms, p. 800
   **Free verse** is poetry that follows no set patterns of rhyme, meter, or line length, but uses a variety of poetic devices in their stead. Some of the devices used frequently by Walt Whitman are alliteration and assonance; repetition of words, phrases, and clauses; and parallel or balanced structures.

1. What is the main poetic sound device used in the first line of the poem?
2. Compare and contrast the first two and the last two lines of the poem. Discuss the effect of poetic devices you find.

## COMPOSITION ◄━●
### Writing a Free Verse Poem
   Using Whitman's poetic style as a model, write a poem of twelve to fourteen lines in free verse, using poetic devices to replace the traditional metrical and rhyming patterns you'll avoid. Write about a meditative moment, a feeling of strong passion (such as awe, anger, or interest), or a scene deeply imprinted on your imagination.

### Comparing Two Sonnets
   Reread the two sonnets by Shakespeare and Keats and use them as the basis for comparing and contrasting the effects achieved in the two different forms. Read the Comment article, "Sonnets," for general information. Write a three- to four-paragraph essay comparing and contrasting the two. See "Writing About Poetry and Poetic Devices" in the Writer's Handbook.

# BIOGRAPHIES

## Robert Graves    1895–1985

Poet, novelist, and scholar, Graves fought in World War I and began to publish poetry at the same time. Reported dead in battle, he read his own obituary in the London *Times*. After the war he taught for a time in Egypt, but then decided to devote himself entirely to writing. He has published several historical novels, such as *I, Claudius* (1934), and many volumes of poems characterized by wit, melancholy, and robust bravado alternating with lyric tenderness. Church bells tolled on the Spanish island of Majorca when he died there in 1985.

## Alexander Pope    1688–1744

Pope was considered the literary dictator of his day. Anyone who crossed him came to regret the deed because Pope's stinging criticism and malicious wit could deflate a reputation with one blow of the pen. He was left hunchbacked and disabled from an illness at the age of 12, and he was only four feet six inches tall. His physical condition may have intensified the mordancy of his humor. He was the acknowledged master of the dominant verse form of the eighteenth century, the heroic couplet— rhymed couplets of iambic pentameter. Among his important works are *An Essay on Criticism* and *The Rape of the Lock*.

## William Shakespeare    1564–1616

Shakespeare, probably the most renowned dramatist in history, might have achieved lasting fame as a poet even if he hadn't written plays. He is often called "the Bard," which means "the Poet," in honor of his sonnets and other verse. He wrote 154 sonnets, most likely during the last decade of the 1500s. A more complete biography appears on page 586.

## John Keats    1795–1821

John Keats died at 25, but in that brief span he arose from humble origins to take his place among the great English Romantic poets. Born the eldest of four children to the manager of a livery stable in Cockney London, Keats lost his father when he was eight and his mother when he was fourteen. At fifteen he was apprenticed to a surgeon with whom he studied for five years. By the time he was licensed to practice, poetry had become the main interest of his life. His first book published in 1817 was largely ignored, but his second, *Endymion* (1818), was viciously attacked. After dealing with the death of one younger brother from tuberculosis and the departure for America of the other, Keats almost abandoned

poetry. Poor and ill with tuberculosis, and knowing he would never be able to marry his true love Fanny Brawne, Keats left England for Italy in an attempt to regain his health. He died there and was buried under the epitaph he had composed for himself: "Here lies one whose name was writ in water."

## Nguyen Trai 1380–1442

Nguyen Trai was born in the capital of Vietnam, now called Hanoi, and in the year 1400 won a doctoral degree. Caught up in the wars between Vietnam and China, Trai was imprisoned for a time, but escaped to fight with fellow Vietnamese for national independence. When the Chinese were driven out, he wrote an acclaimed poem for the victory celebration. He is looked upon by the Vietnamese as an important figure in their history and literature.

## Ruth Stone 1915–

Ruth Stone was born in Roanoke, Virginia, and brought up in Indiana and Illinois. She was educated at the University of Illinois. When her husband died in 1958, leaving her a widow with three daughters, she turned to university teaching for support and has held posts at Wellesley, Brandeis, and other universities. She published her first book of poems, *In an Iridescent Time,* in 1959. She has said about her work, "I found that poems came with this mysterious feeling, and it was a kind of peculiar ecstasy." She has held two Guggenheim Fellowships, granted to support artists and writers, and has won the Shelley Award of the Poetry Society of America.

## Walt Whitman 1819–1892

Whitman pioneered new forms, new rhythms, and new subject matter in American poetry. Born and reared on Long Island, New York, Whitman began his writing career as a journalist. In 1848 he traveled to New Orleans by way of the Ohio and Mississippi Rivers, a journey that broadened his knowledge and strengthened his love of America and its people. During the Civil War, he served as a nurse in military hospitals in Virginia and Washington, D.C. Whitman's early verse was conventional and sentimental. Soon, however, he developed his free-verse technique. In 1855 his first book of free verse, *Leaves of Grass,* appeared. While it was hailed with enthusiasm by many readers, it was condemned by others for its formlessness and coarse language. Now translated into every major language, *Leaves of Grass* has proven to be a major influence in twentieth-century poetry—in America and throughout the world.

**BIOGRAPHY**

**Edgar Lee Masters**
**1869–1950**

Edgar Lee Masters became famous overnight with the publication of *Spoon River Anthology* in 1915. He was in his forties and had written many books of poems and essays, but was virtually unknown as an author. He had practiced law in Chicago for many years. In 1920 he gave up his law practice and devoted himself to writing. During his career he published over fifty volumes, including *The New Spoon River* (1924), but he never again captured the public imagination as he had in *Spoon River Anthology*. That book has been translated into many languages, including Arabic, Korean, and Chinese. It has affinities with Thornton Wilder's *Our Town* and with many other works that deal with small-town life.

# Comment

### Spoon River Anthology

The characters speaking in the following poems—their names serve as the titles of the poems—are speaking from beyond the grave. They are all buried in the same graveyard of a community in rural Illinois called Spoon River (not a real town, but one incorporating features of two towns Edgar Lee Masters had known as a youth). The characters lived in Spoon River in the late 1800s and early 1900s.

These characters are but five examples from a total of 244 portrayed in Masters's book *Spoon River Anthology*, published in 1915. Taken together, the poems give readers candid glimpses into the life of a small town at the turn of the century. There is enough variety in the characters, diversity in their occupations and interests, and range in their social status to give the impression of an entire community—a universal portrait of Small Town, USA. In reading *Spoon River Anthology*, readers recognize themselves and their own villages.

The inhabitants of the Spoon River graveyard speak the truth, confessing their own sins or weaknesses. For example, Mrs. Kessler admits that she learned people's secrets by doing their laundry, while Cooney Potter states that the real cause of his death was bolting down his food as he drove himself with his ambitions. These and similar revelations created a sensation when *Spoon River Anthology* was published, because many portraits were based on real people who had been involved in one scandal or another.

Though there are portraits of happy, fulfilled people in *Spoon River Anthology*, there are probably more that convey sadness and melancholy—for wasted or twisted lives, for unfulfilled dreams, or for dreams turned bitter even when fulfilled. And yet the overall effect of the collection is not morbid. The reader feels sad at misfortunes and happy or amused with successes, but tends to forget after a while that all these people are supposed to be dead. The poems become, in essence, fascinating character sketches of the various individuals in a town.

# Mrs. Kessler

Mr. Kessler, you know, was in the army,
And he drew six dollars a month as a pension,
And stood on the corner talking politics,
Or sat at home reading Grant's Memoirs;[1]
5 And I supported the family by washing,
Learning the secrets of all the people
From their curtains, counterpanes,
        shirts and skirts.
For things that are new grow old at length,
They're replaced with better or none at all:
10 People are prospering or falling back.
And rents and patches widen with time;
No thread or needle can pace decay,
And there are stains that baffle soap,
And there are colors that run in spite of you,
15 Blamed though you are for spoiling a dress.

Handkerchiefs, napery, have their secrets—
The laundress, Life, knows all about it.
And I, who went to all the funerals
Held in Spoon River, swear I never
20 Saw a dead face without thinking it looked
Like something washed and ironed.

---

**1. Grant's Memoirs,** the book of memories and recollections written by Ulysses S. Grant, U.S. President from 1869 to 1877.

"Mrs. Kessler," "Hortense Robbins," "Dow Kritt," "Samuel Gardner," and "Cooney Potter" from *Spoon River Anthology* by Edgar Lee Masters. Copyright 1915, 1916, 1942, 1949 by Edgar Lee Masters. Reprinted by permission of Ellen C. Masters.

Tom Heflin, *Lover's Lane,* 1973, Private Collection

# Hortense Robbins

My name used to be in the papers daily
As having dined somewhere,
Or traveled somewhere,
Or rented a house in Paris,
5 Where I entertained the nobility.
I was forever eating or traveling,
Or taking the cure at Baden-Baden.[1]
Now I am here to do honor
To Spoon River, here beside the family whence I sprang.
10 No one cares now where I dined,
Or lived, or whom I entertained,
Or how often I took the cure at Baden-Baden!

---

1. *Baden-Baden* (bäd′n bäd′n), a famous health resort with curative waters, in southwestern Germany.

## THINK AND DISCUSS
### Understanding
1. What did Mrs. Kessler's husband do and why does she describe his activities?
2. Hortense Robbins begins telling what "used to be" and ends with how it is now. Explain.

### Analyzing
3. Describe and contrast the main interests in life of Mrs. Kessler and Hortense Robbins.

4. How do the two women differ in attitudes as they recall their lives and their fates?

### Extending
5. Are Mrs. Kessler and Hortense Robbins exaggerated as characters or are they types that one might encounter in today's world? Explain your choice.

# Samuel Gardner

I who kept the greenhouse,
Lover of trees and flowers,
Oft in life saw this umbrageous elm,
Measuring its generous branches with my eye,
5 And listened to its rejoicing leaves
Lovingly patting each other
With sweet æolian whispers.
And well they might:
For the roots had grown so wide and deep
10 That the soil of the hill could not withhold
Aught of its virtue, enriched by rain,
And warmed by the sun;
But yielded it all to the thrifty roots,
Through which it was drawn and whirled to the trunk,
15 And thence to the branches, and into the leaves,
Wherefrom the breeze took life and sang.
Now I, an under-tenant of the earth, can see
That the branches of a tree
Spread no wider than its roots.
20 And how shall the soul of a man
Be larger than the life he has lived?

Tom Heflin, *Hard Day's Work*,
Private Collection

# Dow Kritt

Samuel is forever talking of his elm—
But I did not need to die to learn about roots:
I, who dug all the ditches about Spoon River.
Look at my elm!
5 Sprung from as good a seed as his,
Sown at the same time,
It is dying at the top:
Not from lack of life, nor fungus,
Nor destroying insect, as the sexton thinks.
10 Look, Samuel, where the roots have struck rock,
And can no further spread.
And all the while the top of the tree
Is tiring itself out, and dying,
Trying to grow.

## THINK AND DISCUSS
### Understanding
1. What kind of work did each of these men do?
2. How did their occupations acquaint them with certain parts of trees?

### Analyzing
3. How do the elms that the two men are buried under differ?

4. How are the personalities of the two men, as revealed in the poems, suggested by their respective trees? Discuss.

### Extending
5. What do the last four lines of "Samuel Gardner" mean? In your view does the observation contain a truth about life?

# Cooney Potter

I inherited forty acres from my Father
And, by working my wife, my two sons and two daughters
From dawn to dusk, I acquired
A thousand acres. But not content,
5 Wishing to own two thousand acres,
I bustled through the years with axe and plow,
Toiling, denying myself, my wife, my sons, my daughters.
Squire Higbee wrongs me to say
That I died from smoking Red Eagle cigars.
10 Eating hot pie and gulping coffee
During the scorching hours of harvest time
Brought me here ere I had reached my sixtieth year.

Tom Heflin, *The Widow Woman's Place*, Private Collection

## THINK AND DISCUSS
### Understanding
1. Why did Potter continue to work so hard?
2. How did his family fare during his life?
3. Why does he mention the cause of his own death? What does he say was the cause?

### Analyzing
4. Does Cooney Potter sound happy about the sort of life he has led? Discuss.
5. Is Potter persuasive in describing the real cause of his early death? Discuss.

### Extending
6. Does Cooney Potter seem, in your opinion, to have any remorse for his treatment of his family? Discuss.

## VOCABULARY
### Precise Words
Edgar Lee Masters uses precise words in his poems to communicate the importance each character feels about his or her job or life experience. When you write, you can use precise words to provide a clear picture too. Use one of the following words from the poems to complete each sentence. You will not use one word. The words appear in the Glossary.

| | | |
|---|---|---|
| rent | sexton | counterpane |
| napery | aught | umbrageous |

1. The _____ completely covered the bed.
2. We used blue _____ on the dinner table.
3. The _____ in the trousers was near the cuff.
4. Often during the summer, Grandma and I shared lunch under the _____ willows.
5. The _____ used great care to clean the ancient floor tiles in the church.

## COMPOSITION
### Writing as a Character
Write a three- to four-paragraph account in diary form of what you, as the washwoman Mrs. Kessler, think of the socialite Hortense Robbins. Imagine that you have just picked up some laundry from Hortense Robbins, who has recently returned from a trip. Consider what your conversation with Robbins must have been like, the kind of clothing she has given you to launder, and what you might deduce about her life from the garments. After you have finished writing, exchange your diary entry with a classmate so that you can evaluate one another's compositions.

### Answering as a Relative
Write a four-paragraph letter in the character of Mrs. Cooney Potter (or a son or daughter) to Cooney Potter, describing in detail the kind of life you have lived, how hard you have worked, and what you have wanted but had to do without. Perhaps after his death, your life has changed—or was it too late? Explain how you have lived your life since his death. You may want to write it from wherever "you" are living—a big city, a foreign land, or Spoon River.

## ENRICHMENT
### Readers Theater
Find a copy of the complete *Spoon River Anthology* and assemble a cast of students who want to take part in a production. Spend some time as a group finding favorite poems to read aloud. Many of them are interconnected (husband and wife, two neighbors, and so on) and constitute little dramas of their own when read in sequence. After rehearsing, offer your production to the class, using stools as tombstones on which to sit.

**BIOGRAPHY**

## A. E. Housman
## 1859–1936

A. E. Housman is widely recognized as a poet who wrote a small number of deeply moving poems about certain melancholy themes—unfulfilled love, dashed hopes, thwarted ambitions, death at a young age before a life is lived, or the longing for a land of no return. His poems often bring a lump to the throat, but they are not sentimental. Their very brevity and brilliantly turned phrases guard against gush.

Housman was born in the British county of Worcestershire (wŭs′tər shər) —not in Shropshire, the locale made famous by his poems. He had two ambitions, to become a poet and a classical scholar; he succeeded in both. He taught at University College, London, and later at Cambridge University, dedicating most of his scholarly life to editing the poetry of the Latin writer Manilius. In 1896 his poetic career was launched with publication of *A Shropshire Lad*, which made him famous. He published more poems later in life, including a volume in 1922, but his total poetic output was just over one hundred works, most of them written in the early 1890s. All were written in the conviction that poetry should be "more physical than intellectual" and should "entangle the reader in a net of thoughtless delight."

# Oh, When I Was in Love with You

Oh, when I was in love with you,
  Then I was clean and brave,
And miles around the wonder grew
  How well did I behave.

5 And now the fancy passes by,
  And nothing will remain,
And miles around they'll say that I
  Am quite myself again.

John Constable, *Haystacks*, Private Collection

## THINK AND DISCUSS
### Understanding
1. What has happened between stanzas 1 and 2 to cause a change in the speaker?

### Analyzing
2. How has the speaker changed because of the happening?

3. What is the **tone** of this poem?

### Extending
4. In stanza 1 the speaker attributes his improved behavior to his being in love. Do you believe love can so affect an individual? Discuss.

## A. E. Housman

# White in the Moon the Long Road Lies

White in the moon the long road lies,
    The moon stands blank above;
White in the moon the long road lies
    That leads me from my love.

5 Still hangs the hedge without a gust,
    Still, still the shadows stay:
My feet upon the moonlit dust
    Pursue the ceaseless way.

The world is round, so travellers tell,
10     And straight though reach the track,
Trudge on, trudge on, 'twill all be well,
    The way will guide one back.

But ere the circle homeward hies
    Far, far must it remove:
15 White in the moon the long road lies
    That leads me from my love.

From "A Shropshire Lad"—Authorized Edition—from *The Collected Poems of A. E. Housman*. Copyright 1939, 1940, © 1965 by Holt, Rinehart and Winston. Copyright © 1967, 1968 by Robert E. Symons. Reprinted by permission of Henry Holt and Company, Inc.

## THINK AND DISCUSS
### Understanding
1. What image dominates the first stanza?
2. What do "travelers tell" the speaker about the road? Explain.

### Analyzing
3. Why might the speaker be going on the road leading him from his love?

4. **Inversion** shifts the normal word order of sentences. What words are emphasized by the inversion in line 1? How would the line fit the poem if it were not inverted?

### Extending
5. In your view, what difference would it make if the poem did not have stanza 4?

# When First My Way to Fair I Took

When first my way to fair I took
   Few pence in purse had I,
And long I used to stand and look
   At things I could not buy.

5 Now times are altered: if I care
   To buy a thing, I can;
The pence are here and here's the fair,
   But where's the lost young man?

—To think that two and two are four
10    And neither five nor three
The heart of man has long been sore
   And long 'tis like to be.

---

"When first my way to fair I took" from *The Collected Poems of A. E. Housman.* Copyright 1950 by Barclays Bank Ltd. Reprinted by permission of Henry Holt and Company, Inc.

## THINK AND DISCUSS

### Understanding

1. What has the speaker gained since he first went to fair?
2. What has the speaker lost since first going to fair?

### Analyzing

3. How is the simple mathematical truth stated in lines 9–10 related to the statements made in lines 11–12?

### Extending

4. The last lines of this poem present the melancholy view that man's heart "has long been sore" and "long 'tis like to be." How do you interpret these lines? Do you agree or disagree? Discuss.

# An Epitaph

Stay, if you list, O passer by the way;
Yet night approaches: better not to stay.
   I never sigh, nor flush, nor knit the brow,
    Nor grieve to think how ill God made me, now.
5 Here, with one balm for many fevers found,
   Whole of an ancient evil, I sleep sound.

A. E. Housman, "An Epitaph," in *My Brother, A. E. Housman: Personal Recollections together with Thirty hitherto Unpublished Poems*, by Laurence Housman. Copyright 1938 Laurence Housman; copyright renewed © 1966 Lloyds Bank Limited. Reprinted with the permission of Charles Scribner's Sons, an imprint of Macmillan Publishing Co. and the Society of Authors.

## THINK AND DISCUSS

### Understanding

An *epitaph* is a statement in memory of a dead person, often inscribed on a gravestone.

1. Who is the speaker of this epitaph?
2. What is the "one balm" found "for many fevers" in line 5?

### Analyzing

3. What might we infer from lines 3–4 about the nature of the "many fevers" now over?

### Extending

4. What kind of person do you think would have such an epitaph as this?

## COMPOSITION

### Writing About Then and Now

Reread "When First My Way to Fair I Took." Then write a three- to four-paragraph essay for a school literary journal about something you yearned to do years ago (but couldn't) and which now you can do but no longer wish to. Perhaps you wanted to shoot marbles or skip rope all day long, or go to four movies in a row, or watch TV all day long, or eat a quart of chocolate ice cream at one sitting. Describe your feelings then, and tell how they've changed now.

### Analyzing Imagery

Write a three- to four-paragraph essay to serve as a basis for class discussion analyzing the imagery in "White in the Moon the Long Road Lies." Most readers finish the poem with a sense of melancholy or sadness. How do the images of the poem contribute to this overall effect? First write down your own responses to the images and then revise your essay, putting it into proper form for an audience of your classmates. See "Writing to Analyze Author's Style" in the Writer's Handbook.

# BIOGRAPHY

## Emily Dickinson
### 1830–1886

Rarely has a poet of such genius as Emily Dickinson remained so nearly unknown among her contemporaries. She wrote over 1,750 poems, but only ten were published in her lifetime—some without her knowledge. She never sought fame. Perhaps she knew she was ahead of her time; when the poems were published, editors regularized her grammar and punctuation, eliminating the breathlike dashes she used as a controlling device. Not until 1955, over seventy years after her death, did her complete poetic works appear in print the way she wrote them. She has been called "an American artist of words as inexhaustible as Shakespeare."

Dickinson grew up in Amherst, Massachusetts, the daughter of a well-known lawyer. For college education she had one year at Mount Holyoke Female Seminary. To all outward appearance, little of interest happened to her. She lived at the family home in Amherst, traveled very little, and never married. In the latter part of her life she dressed in white. And she was so acutely sensitive that she would often talk with visitors from behind a door. But obviously much happened in her inner life, the source of her poetry. Through her imagination she lived through the full range of emotional and spiritual experiences recorded in her poems. She found more in her private garden to inspire her wonder and passion than many people find wandering all over the world.

*Emily Dickinson*
*American Poet*
U.S. 8c

**Emily Dickinson**

# Hope Is the Thing with Feathers

"Hope" is the thing with feathers—
That perches in the soul—
And sings the tune without the words—
And never stops—at all—

5  And sweetest—in the Gale—is heard—
And sore must be the storm—
That could abash the little Bird
That kept so many warm—

I've heard it in the chillest land—
10 And on the strangest Sea—
Yet, never, in Extremity,
It asked a crumb—of Me.

## THINK AND DISCUSS
### Understanding
1. What is the **metaphor** for "hope" introduced at the beginning of the poem, and what significant details do we learn about it in the first stanza?

### Analyzing
2. How is this metaphor extended in the second stanza?
3. Is the metaphor extended through stanza 3? Explain.

### Extending
4. Does the poet feel hope can be easily lost? Do you agree with her? Discuss.

Review RHYTHM in the Handbook of Literary Terms, page 819.

# The Grass So Little Has to Do

The Grass so little has to do—
A Sphere of simple Green—
With only Butterflies to brood
And Bees to entertain—

5 And stir all day to pretty Tunes
The Breezes fetch along—
And hold the Sunshine in its lap
And bow to everything—

And thread the Dews, all night, like Pearls—
10 And make itself so fine
A Duchess were too common
For such a noticing—

And even when it dies—to pass
In Odors so divine—
15 Like Lowly spices, lain to sleep—
Or Spikenards,[1] perishing—

And then, in Sovereign Barns to dwell—
And dream the Days away,
The Grass so little has to do
20 I wish I were a Hay—

---

1. **Spikenards**, sweet-smelling herbs, with green flowers and fragrant roots.

**THINK AND DISCUSS**
**Understanding**
1. The speaker says the Grass has little to do but goes on to describe several of its activities. What are they?
2. Do the activities of the grass in the poem appear pleasant or unpleasant?

**Analyzing**
3. What appears to be the meaning of "only Butterflies to brood" in line 3?
4. Explain line 9: "And thread the Dews, all night, like Pearls."
5. Explain line 17: "in Sovereign Barns to dwell."

**Extending**
6. How would you characterize the poet's attitude toward the grass throughout the poem? Discuss.

**REVIEWING: Rhythm**
**See Handbook of Literary Terms, p. 819.**
A poet may employ a regular rhythm in a poem yet vary line length. The title of "The Grass So Little Has to Do" has four iambic feet.

What pattern of varying line lengths has Emily Dickinson established in the poem?

## Emily Dickinson

# What Mystery
# Pervades a Well!

What mystery pervades a well!
That water lives so far—
A neighbor from another world
Residing in a jar

5   Whose limit none have ever seen,
But just his lid of glass—
Like looking every time you please
In an abyss's face!

The grass does not appear afraid,
10  I often wonder he
Can stand so close and look so bold
At what is awe to me.

Related somehow they may be,
The sedge stands next the sea—
15  Where he is floorless
And does no timidity betray

But nature is a stranger yet;
The ones that cite her most
Have never passed her haunted house,
20  Nor simplified her ghost.

To pity those that know her not
Is helped by the regret
That those who know her, know her less
The nearest her they get.

Camille Pissarro, *Woman and Child at the Well*, 1882, The Art
Institute of Chicago

# *Comment*

### On "What Mystery Pervades a Well!"

Imagine a well in the nineteenth century, in the backyard of a farmhouse, with a bucket suspended over it for pulling up water from the cool depths below. The surface of the water gleams, reflecting what little light that may find its way so far down.

Such a well must be what Emily Dickinson is describing. The water "lives so far" down that it is as mysterious as an alien living in similar remoteness in a huge jar. The grass, which grows boldly close to the edge of the well, is not afraid of this distant water that inspires the speaker's "awe."

In stanza 4, Dickinson speculates that the bold grass may be related in some mysterious way to the well. In a similar way, sedge (grassy plants growing in marshy places) springs up next to the sea, in places where it is watery ("floorless"), yet shows no fear of the ocean.

In stanza 5, Dickinson drops reference to the well and, moving from the particular to the general, speaks of "nature" (thus the well stands for nature). Nature remains a stranger, with all the mystery of a stranger. Yet, ironically, those who speak of her most have never experienced her mystery directly ("Have never passed her haunted house") nor analyzed the essence of that mystery ("simplified her ghost").

Stanza 6 leaves us with a **paradox,** an expression that seems contradictory but still is true. Since we feel "pity" for those who do not know nature at all (like those who "cite her most" in stanza 5), we might expect the opposite of pity, perhaps pleasure, for those who do know her. But no—for them we feel "regret" (close to pity!) because those who do know nature "know her less the nearer her they get." In other words, they have a knowledge that is even more baffling—because of nature's mysteries—than the total ignorance of those who "know her not" at all.

---

## THINK AND DISCUSS
### Understanding
1. Describe the **personification** of the water in the well in the first two stanzas.
2. Explain the personification in stanza 3.

### Analyzing
3. Explain the metaphor introduced in lines 7–8 and discuss its effect.
4. How has the poet prepared us for the generalization made in line 17?
5. What is the nature of a well's "mystery" that emerges from the poem? Discuss.

### Extending
6. What is the tone of this poem? Do you share the poet's attitude toward nature? Discuss.

# A Thought Went Up
# My Mind To-day

A Thought went up my mind today—
That I have had before—
But did not finish—some way back—
I could not fix the Year—

5 Nor where it went—nor why it came
The second time to me—
Nor definitely, what it was—
Have I the Art to say—

But somewhere—in my Soul—I know—
10 I've met the Thing before—
It just reminded me—'twas all—
And came my way no more—

## THINK AND DISCUSS
### Understanding
1. How long ago was it that the speaker had the thought before?
2. What puzzles the speaker about the thought?

### Analyzing
3. How would the meaning be changed if "soul" in line 9 were changed to "mind"?

### Extending
4. Do you think the experience described in the poem is unique or common? Discuss.

## COMPOSITION
### Describing an Aspect of Nature
Write a three- to four-paragraph essay for your journal or diary about some aspects of nature which you find baffling, humorous, awesome, symbolic, or interesting in some way. Choose bolts of lightning, summer sun, autumn clouds, an ant, dog, or horse, a particular tree, a field of wild grass, a snowfall, or another face of nature. Write from observation and meditation.

### Comparing Poems on Hope
Write a four-paragraph essay for your class comparing and contrasting Lisel Mueller's "Hope" and Emily Dickinson's "Hope Is the Thing with Feathers." How do the poems differ? What do they have in common? Which is more successful? Explain. See "Writing About Poetry and Poetic Devices" in the Writer's Handbook.

## ENRICHMENT
### Memorizing a Poem
Many poems, like songs, lend themselves to memorization because they have a regular rhythm. Choose a poem from this unit that you like, and memorize it for your own enjoyment or for sharing it with your friends, family, or class.

## BIOGRAPHY

## Robert Frost

## 1874–1963

Although we seem to hear a shrewd Yankee or New England voice in Frost's poetry, he was actually born in San Francisco. However, he moved to Massachusetts at the age of eleven, and his poems tend to be set in New England, especially on the farm or in the rural areas.

Frost married at twenty, studied at Harvard, and supported himself at a number of odd jobs before settling down on a New Hampshire farm. After eleven years of farming and writing poetry, Frost had little success to show: his farm was a failure and only the local newspaper would accept his poems for publication. In a discouraged mood he moved to England and offered his collected work to a publisher. The book came out as *A Boy's Will* in 1913 and was immediately recognized for its fresh, original poetry. Frost followed this with *North of Boston* (1914).

Now famous, Frost returned home in 1915. He was to become one of the most popular poets in America. In 1924 he won the first of several Pulitzer Prizes for his poetry. In 1961 he was invited to read a poem at the inauguration ceremonies of President John F. Kennedy.

Robert Frost speaks at the inauguration of President John F. Kennedy, 1961

# The Road Not Taken

Two roads diverged in a yellow wood,
And sorry I could not travel both
And be one traveler, long I stood
And looked down one as far as I could
5 To where it bent in the undergrowth;

Then took the other, as just as fair,
And having perhaps the better claim,
Because it was grassy and wanted wear;
Though as for that, the passing there
10 Had worn them really about the same,

And both that morning equally lay
In leaves no step had trodden black.
Oh! I kept the first for another day!
Yet knowing how way leads on to way,
15 I doubted if I should ever come back.

I shall be telling this with a sigh
Somewhere ages and ages hence:
Two roads diverged in a wood, and I—
I took the one less traveled by,
20 And that has made all the difference.

## THINK AND DISCUSS

### Understanding

1. At the beginning of the poem, what is the speaker's feeling about the two roads?
2. How are the roads different and how alike?
3. How does the speaker decide which of the two roads to take?

### Analyzing

4. Explain lines 13–15.

5. Is there any way of telling how long the speaker has been traveling the "less traveled" road? Explain.

### Extending

6. What might the two roads stand for in the speaker's mind? Discuss.
7. The last line of the poem is suggestive. What might it mean? Discuss.

# The Exposed Nest

You were forever finding some new play.
So when I saw you down on hands and knees
In the meadow, busy with the new-cut hay,
Trying, I thought, to set it up on end,
5 I went to show you how to make it stay,
If that was your idea, against the breeze,
And, if you asked me, even help pretend
To make it root again and grow afresh.
But 'twas no make-believe with you today,
10 Nor was the grass itself your real concern,
Though I found your hand full of wilted fern,
Steel-bright June-grass, and blackening
    heads of clover.
'Twas a nest full of young birds on
    the ground
The cutter-bar had just gone champing over
15 (Miraculously without tasting flesh)
And left defenseless to the heat and light.
You wanted to restore them to their right
Of something interposed between their sight

And too much world at once—could means
    be found.
20 The way the nest-full every time we stirred
Stood up to us as to a mother-bird
Whose coming home has been too long deferred,
Made me ask would the mother-bird return
And care for them in such a change of scene
25 And might our meddling make her more afraid.
That was a thing we could not wait to learn.
We saw the risk we took in doing good,
But dared not spare to do the best we could
Though harm should come of it; so built
    the screen
30 You had begun, and gave them back their shade.
All this to prove we cared. Why is there then
No more to tell? We turned to other things.
I haven't any memory—have you?—
Of ever coming to the place again
35 To see if the birds lived the first night through,
And so at last to learn to use their wings.

---

**THINK AND DISCUSS**
**Understanding**
1. What does the speaker first think his friend is busy doing?
2. What is the friend actually doing?

**Analyzing**
3. How do the birds react to the movements of the two humans?

4. Explain how line 27 relates to the action in the latter part of the poem.

**Extending**
5. Why do you suppose the story is left with the birds' fate uncertain?

# Neither Out Far Nor In Deep

The people along the sand
All turn and look one way.
They turn their back on the land.
They look at the sea all day.

5 As long as it takes to pass
A ship keeps raising its hull;
The wetter ground like glass
Reflects a standing gull.

The land may vary more;
10 But wherever the truth may be—
The water comes ashore,
And the people look at the sea.

They cannot look out far.
They cannot look in deep.
15 But when was that ever a bar
To any watch they keep?

Maurice Brazil Prendergast, *Viewing the Ships*, 1896, Daniel Terra Collection, Terra Museum of American Art, Chicago

## THINK AND DISCUSS
### Understanding
1. According to the poem, what are some things people see when gazing out to sea?

### Analyzing
2. Which offers more variety for the observer, the sea or the land? Does this make a difference to people? Discuss.

3. Explain the meaning of the title as it relates to stanzas 3 and 4.

### Extending
4. From your own experience or observations, do people tend to gaze at the ocean (or at the water of a large lake) when at the shoreline? What do you suppose sea-gazers think about? Discuss.

# Desert Places

Snow falling and night falling fast, oh, fast
In a field I looked into going past,
And the ground almost covered smooth in snow,
But a few weeds and stubble showing last.

5  The woods around it have it—it is theirs.
All animals are smothered in their lairs.
I am too absent-spirited to count;
The loneliness includes me unawares.

And lonely as it is that loneliness
10 Will be more lonely ere it will be less—
A blanker whiteness of benighted snow
With no expression, nothing to express.

They cannot scare me with their empty spaces
Between stars—on stars where no human race is.
15 I have it in me so much nearer home
To scare myself with my own desert places.

**THINK AND DISCUSS**
**Understanding**
1. What, precisely, is described in stanza 1?
2. What does "it" refer to in line 5 (repeated three times)?

**Analyzing**
3. In stanza 2, what is the speaker referring to when he says, "The loneliness includes me unawares"?

4. What does the speaker foresee in stanza 3, particularly in the last line?
5. What are the "desert places" referred to in the last line of the poem?

**Extending**
6. Do you think the recognition of such "desert places" within a person is peculiar to the poet or is it a part of general human experience? Discuss.

# The Secret Sits

We dance round in a ring and suppose,
But the Secret sits in the middle and knows.

## THINK AND DISCUSS

### Understanding

1. Who are the "we" mentioned in line 1?

### Analyzing

2. Describe the personification in line 2.

### Extending

3. How might the poem be a description of life? Discuss.

## THINKING SKILLS

### Generalizing

To generalize is to draw a general conclusion from particular information. From his observation of people looking at the sea, Robert Frost generalizes that wherever people encounter a shore they all watch the water. Think of places where large groups of people tend to act somewhat alike: schools, bus stops, airports, sports stadiums, buses, or other gathering points. With a classmate, compare your generalizations about how all or most people act in at least ten public places.

## COMPOSITION

### Considering Career Decisions

Reread "The Road Not Taken" in the light of your own plans for a career, however vague they may be. Then write a three- or four-paragraph essay for your journal or diary, considering the following questions. Do you think it wise to take a road "less traveled"? Why or why not? What consideration do you think should go into a career decision besides earnings? What kinds of non-monetary rewards do you want from a career?

### Describing Contrasting Images

Reread "Desert Places," studying its images closely. Then write a three-paragraph essay for the class describing a mood opposite to that of the poem. You might begin: "There are times when I experience my own 'desert places,' but there are other times when I feel I have found a 'green retreat' or a 'shady haven.'" Go on to describe a scene that reflects your upbeat, euphoric, self-possessed mood, in contrast with that in the poem.

**BIOGRAPHY**

**Federico García Lorca**

**1898–1936**

When the Spanish Civil War broke out in 1936, Federico García Lorca, the leading young poet of Spain, fled from the capital city of Madrid to the place where he grew up, the city of Granada in Andalusia. There he was arrested and executed without trial by Fascist supporters of General Francisco Franco. He was no doubt judged guilty because of his sympathy for the poor and his support of the common people. His death was a loss to world literature.

García Lorca was, at his death, a widely read and popular poet in Spain. By the time he was twenty he had published his first book—*Landscape Impressions,* a work in prose. His first volume of poems appeared in 1921, followed by *Canciones (Songs)* in 1927. But the work that brought him international fame was *Gypsy Ballads* (1928), eighteen poems that combined the folk ballads so popular in his native Andalusia with the startling imagery he had developed in his association with surrealism. (See the Comment on page 317.)

García Lorca continued to write poetry; a trip to the United States resulted in *Poet in New York,* a collection not published until 1940. His interest turned more and more toward drama; he founded a group of wandering players who brought classical theater to the working people, and he wrote several plays of his own. Among the most popular are *Blood Wedding* and *The House of Bernarda Alba,* both frequently produced in the United States. These plays blend humor and melancholy in actions that are starkly tragic.

# Half Moon

The moon goes over the water.
How tranquil the sky is!
She goes scything slowly
the old shimmer from the river;
5  meanwhile a young frog
takes her for a little mirror.

"Half Moon," translated by W. S. Merwin, "The Moon Rising," translated by Lysander Kemp, "Pause of the Clock," translated by Stanley Read, and "The Guitar," translated by J. L. Gili and Stephen Spender, from *Selected Poems of Federico García Lorca.* Copyright 1955 by New Directions Publishing Corporation. Reprinted by permission of the publisher.

**THINK AND DISCUSS**
**Understanding**
1. Describe in your own words the picture created in this poem.
2. Describe the metaphor in lines 3–4.

**Analyzing**
3. Describe the personification introduced in lines 5–6.

**Extending**
4. What do you suppose might be the poet's reason for including the image of the frog contemplating the moon as a mirror?

# The Moon Rising

When the moon rises,
the bells hang silent,
and impenetrable footpaths
appear.

5 When the moon rises,
the sea covers the land,
and the heart feels
like an island in infinity.

Nobody eats oranges
10 under the full moon.
One must eat fruit
that is green and cold.

When the moon rises,
moon of a hundred equal faces,
15 the silver coinage
sobs in the pocket.

## THINK AND DISCUSS

### Understanding

1. Each stanza of the poem indicates what happens "when the moon rises." Describe the effect of the rising moon according to the first three stanzas.

### Analyzing

2. What are the possible reasons for the speaker prescribing the color and temperature of fruit to be eaten under a full moon?

3. How can the moon have "a hundred equal faces" as described in the last stanza?

### Extending

4. The image of silver coins sobbing in the pocket mystifies many readers. Why do you imagine "silver coinage" might sob in the pocket at the rise of the moon?

### Surrealistic Imagery

García Lorca's poetry, as you have seen, contains startling and unexpected images, and many critics see a direct connection between these and the paintings of Salvador Dalí, a famous Spanish artist with whom García Lorca was friendly. Dalí was a surrealist, a painter who believed that art should try to show what takes place in the subconscious mind. His paintings represent the startling juxtapositions found in dreams—a gigantic ear standing upright in a desert, an oversized watch melting on a rocky plain. The influence of surrealism on García Lorca seems unmistakable.

In "Half Moon," for instance, the moon is presented as a scythe—not cutting grass as scythes usually do, but moving over the "shimmer from the river." In "The Moon Rising," the startling imagery involves not only sight, but sound and touch as well, ending with "silver coinage" sobbing "in the pocket," perhaps in ecstatic appreciation of the moon's rising or perhaps in despair over the moon's power, which eclipses the coins' material influence.

The remaining García Lorca poems that you will read contain similar imagery. In "Pause of the Clock," we find a "white silence"—a color given to a sound (or its absence)—and stars colliding with the black numerals of a clock, a surrealistic picture highly suggestive of dreams.

In "The Guitar," the "lament" of the instrument evokes a succession of surrealistic images. The "glasses of the dawn are broken" by lament (perhaps dawn's light streaking the sky, suggesting cracked glasses). The "sands of the warm South" seek "white camellias." The "first bird" is "dead upon the branch." And the heart is "pierced through with five swords." In calling forth these images the lament of the guitar apparently reaches into the same unconscious that is the source of dreams.

Such strange and exotic combinations of images tend to make us uneasy, even uncomfortable. They jar us out of our easy ways of thinking. Perhaps they even startle us into a new awareness of things and their possible relationships, into new ways of seeing the reality around us.

Federico García Lorca

# Pause of the Clock

I sat down
in a space of time.
It was a backwater
of silence,
5 a white silence,
a formidable ring
wherein the stars
collided with the twelve floating
black numerals.

Robert Amft, Untitled, Private
Collection

## THINK AND DISCUSS
### Understanding
1. How does the phrase "a space of time" catch the reader's attention or curiosity?

### Analyzing
2. What possibly has happened to the speaker, causing him to sit in a "backwater" of "white silence"?
3. How do space and time come together in the last four lines of the poem?

### Extending
4. What kind of effect on the world can you imagine if the stars of the heavens were to collide with the twelve "black numerals" of the clock floating in space?

## REVIEWING: Figurative Language  H𝕋
### See Handbook of Literary Terms, p. 796

Figurative language calls upon readers to accept descriptions and images that are not literal. Time is a dimension that cannot be divided into spaces, yet the speaker refers to a "space of time."

How could a moment of solitude between busy, noisy times, for example, be likened to a place?

# The Guitar

The lament
of the guitar begins.
The glasses of the dawn
are broken.
5 The lament
of the guitar begins.
It is useless
to hush it.
It is impossible
10 to hush it.
Monotonously weeping
as the water weeps,
as the wind weeps
over the snowfall.
15 It is impossible
to hush it.
Weeping for things
far away.
Sands of the warm South
20 seeking white camellias.
It weeps, like an arrow without a target,
evening without morning,
and the first bird dead
upon the branch.
25 Oh guitar!
Heart pierced through
with five swords.

## THINK AND DISCUSS

### Understanding

1. How would the effect of the first line be changed if it were to read "The melody" or "The tune"?

### Analyzing

2. What is the effect of the repetition of lines 1–2 as lines 5–6?
3. What other pair of lines is repeated with a minor variation? What is the effect of its repetition?
4. Discuss the effect of the closing image in the poem.

### Extending

5. Choose one other unusual image and explain the picture or idea it brings to your mind.
6. How would you describe the mood created by the lament of the guitar?

## COMPOSITION

### Comparing Two "Moon" Poems

Reread A. E. Housman's "White in the Moon the Long Road Lies" and García Lorca's "The Moon Rising." Write a two- to four-paragraph essay for class discussion, comparing and contrasting the way the moon is used as an image in the two poems. How do the moods of the two poems differ, and how does the use of the moon in each contribute to that difference?

### Analyzing the Imagery of a Poem

Write a three- to four-paragraph essay for class discussion in which you analyze each of the images appearing in "The Guitar," showing how they contribute to the poem's overall effect. You may want to discuss the line-breaks, resulting in the short lines that emphasize certain words; and the repetitions, not only of pairs of lines, but of phrases and words.

# THINKING CRITICALLY
# ABOUT LITERATURE

## UNIT 3    POETRY

### ■ CONCEPT REVIEW

At the end of each unit in *Traditions in Literature* is a selection that illustrates many of the important literary elements that you have studied. It is accompanied by notes designed to help you think critically about your reading. Page numbers in the notes refer to applications of literary terms. A more extensive discussion of these terms appears in the Handbook of Literary Terms.

In "The Rabbit," American poet Edna St. Vincent Millay reveals an encounter with a rabbit—and a hawk. Read the poem and then answer the questions that follow to review your understanding of the concepts and literary terms presented in this unit.

# The Rabbit

## Edna St. Vincent Millay    USA

Hearing the hawk squeal in the high sky
I and the rabbit trembled.
Only the dark small rabbits newly kittled in their neatly dissembled
Hollowed nest in the thicket thatched with straw
5 Did not respect his cry.
At least, not that I saw.

But I have said to the rabbit with rage and a hundred times, "Hop!
Streak it for the bushes! Why do you sit so still?
You are bigger than a house, I tell you, you are bigger than a hill, you are
    a beacon for air-planes!

■ **Alliteration** (page 282): Note the *h* sounds, line 1.

■ **newly kittled:** just born
■ Note the young rabbits are well hidden.

■ **Hyperbole** (page 272): "a hundred times."
■ **Hyperbole:** description of rabbit's visibility.
■ **Metaphor** (page 268): the rabbit as a beacon, or airport signal tower.

Painting by Dutch artist Rien
Poortvliet

10 O indiscreet!
  And the hawk and all my friends are out to kill!
  Get under cover!" But the rabbit never stirred; she never will.

  And I shall see again and again the large eye blaze
  With death, and gently glaze;
15 The leap into the air I shall see again and again, and the kicking feet;
  And the sudden quiet everlasting, and the blade of grass green in the
      strange mouth of the interrupted grazer.

■ **friends:** probably the
speaker's friends who hunt

■ **Rhyme:** (page 280): end
rhyme in many lines.

■ **Imagery** (page 259):
Color of grass in mouth is a
haunting detail.

## THINK AND DISCUSS
### Understanding
1. On hearing the hawk squeal in the sky, who trembles?
2. When the speaker refers in line 5 to respecting the hawk's cry, what does she mean?
3. What is the "interrupted grazer" in line 16? Explain.

### Analyzing
4. What does the speaker notice about the rabbit's size that attracts the hawk to attack?
5. What seems to be the speaker's greatest concern as revealed in stanza 3?

## REVIEWING LITERARY TERMS
### Alliteration, Tone, Imagery
1. What words alliterate in line 1?
2. What is the speaker's tone in stanza 2?
3. What changing image of the rabbit's eye does the speaker notice and remember?

### Figurative Language, Metaphor, Simile

4. The speaker suggests that she will see again and again something figuratively called "the sudden quiet everlasting." What is this eternal silence?

5. The speaker calls the rabbit a "beacon for air-planes." What similarity is there between the rabbit and an airport signal tower? Why is this comparison called a metaphor, not a simile?

### Hyperbole, Personification

6. Find an example of hyperbole in the poem.

7. Although the rabbit is never said to act like a person, how do some of the speaker's pleas imply personification?

### Lyric, Free Verse, Rhythm, Rhyme

8. Is this poem a lyric or a narrative? Give reasons for your answer.

9. Reread "The Rabbit" to notice its rhythm, rhyme, and other sound devices. Explain how this poem, despite its rhyme, resembles free verse.

## ■ CONTENT REVIEW
### THINKING SKILLS
#### Classifying

1. Some poems in the "Narrative Poetry" section that begins this unit present traditional narratives with regular plot and character development, while others have less developed stories or stories that stand for something else. Group the poems according to these two types and explain what elements in each poem led you to place it in the group you did.

2. T. S. Eliot's "The Naming of Cats" and Dorothy Parker's "One Perfect Rose" are humorous poems. Compare and contrast their comic effects and then indicate how they achieved such effects. How do their comic methods differ?

#### Generalizing

3. Both Edgar Lee Masters and A. E. Housman have been described as generally creating sad and melancholy characters in their poems. Compare and contrast the overall impressions created by the speakers in the Masters poems with those of the speakers in the Housman poems.

#### Synthesizing

4. Lyric poems express emotions or feelings. Although these emotions are often complex and unique, they tend to fit within a range from extreme joy to extreme unhappiness. Place the poems in the "Lyric Poetry" section along such a line, and explain what elements of each poem determined the placement.

5. Select any poem written in traditional metrical and rhyming patterns and another that does not use such patterns but still conveys a sense of rhythm and the sound of music. Compare and contrast the two, exploring in each poem the relation of rhythm or rhyme—or any other poetic device—to sense. Some possible pairs: "The Traveler's Curse After Misdirection" and "By the Bivouac's Fitful Flame"; "A Poison Tree" and "My Father & The Figtree"; "I Wandered Lonely as a Cloud" and "Gift"; "For Anne Gregory" and "Improved Farm Land."

#### Evaluating

6. The authors of the poems in the unit's "Tone" section represent a wide range of attitudes toward their subjects. Select two poems from the section that appeal to you and that represent different or contrasting tones. Identify the tone of each, and explain why you believe the tone you have defined for each poem is the right one. If you wish, you may indicate your preference.

7. Select a poem from "Imagery" or "Figurative Language" that you believe

especially successful in its use of images or figurative language. Analyze the imagery or the figurative language, showing how it contributes to the effect of the poem. (A poem especially rich in images is May Swenson's "Water Picture"; one especially rich in simile is Langston Hughes's "Harlem." But choose any poem from the section that interests you.)

8. Review the "Gallery" sections of poems by five well-known poets. Choose one poet whose works, in your judgment, demonstrate the poet's perceptiveness, mastery of poetic language, or ability to entertain a reader. Explain your choice, using evidence from the poems.

# ■ COMPOSITION REVIEW

Choose one of the following assignments.

## Writing About Your Preference in Poetry

Review the poems in the two sections "Narrative Poetry" and "Lyric Poetry." Then write a three- to four-paragraph essay saying why you prefer to read one kind of poetry more than the other. You may if you wish decide that you like or dislike them equally. In any case, make your case by setting forth your reasons and citing specific examples in poems. See "Writing About Poetry and Poetic Devices" in the Writer's Handbook.

## Comparing Tone in Poems

Write a three- to four-paragraph essay on two poems of similar or contrasting tones selected from the "Poet, Speaker, and Tone" and the "Imagery and Figurative Language" sections. Select poems that you like and examine the poems closely for the techniques used in establishing the tones you have found. Indicate which poem you regard as the greater achievement and why.

## Evaluating Poems

Suppose all the poems in the "Rhyme, Rhythm, and Patterns" section were submitted to a poetry contest for which you are the judge. Review the poems, analyzing them for such things as originality of thought, effective use of language, and appropriate imagery. In a four-paragraph essay explain your reasons for awarding first and second prizes. See "Writing About Poetry and Poetic Devices" in the Writer's Handbook.

## Explaining Your Preference in Poets

You have read a number of the poems of Masters, Housman, Dickinson, Frost, and García Lorca. Select the poet from this group that most appeals to you; reread his or her poems and the biographical note, attempting to get a feel for this poet's "voice." Write a letter to a friend recommending the poet and trying to persuade him or her to read the poet's works. Set forth your reasons for liking the poet, including such things as technique and subject matter, and quoting favorite lines to make your points.

## Reviewing Writer's Craft: Use Comparisons

You have read poems in this unit in which many comparisons have been introduced to make an object, scene, or person more vivid and striking. Now try your hand at using comparisons in a four-paragraph essay describing the work-space where you study. Avoid such clichés as "neat as a pin" or "it looks like a cyclone has struck"; rather, seek out fresh and unusual comparisons to describe what you are surrounded by when you do your homework and especially when you write. (Is the television glaring at you? Is the radio squawking for your attention? Is there a picture staring sternly at you when you look up?) List the comparisons you want to make, and then arrange them in the order you think most effective. If you wish, write your composition in verse and entitle it as a poem. See "Developing Your Style" in the Writer's Handbook.

# EGENDS OF ARTHUR

**Fourteenth-century illustration showing Gwynevere watching Launcelot jousting (detail), artist unknown**

Pierpont Morgan Library, New York

# PREVIEW

## UNIT 4 LEGENDS OF ARTHUR

**The Coronation of Arthur** / Sir Thomas Malory
from **The Hollow Hills** / Mary Stewart
**The Lady of the Lake and Excalibur** / Sir Thomas Malory
**Arthur Marries Gwynevere** / Sir Thomas Malory
**The Tale of Sir Launcelot du Lake** / Sir Thomas Malory
from **The Once and Future King** / T. H. White
**The Death of King Arthur** / Sir Thomas Malory
from **Idylls of the King** / Alfred, Lord Tennyson
**Gawain and Launcelot in Combat** / Sir Thomas Malory

**Features**
Reading a Legendary Tale
Background
Comment: Why Was the Table Round?
Writer's Craft: Build
    Sentences for Emphasis and Interest
Comment: Malory and Middle English
Comment: Was Arthur Buried at
    Glastonbury?

**Application of Literary Terms**
paradox
allusion

**Reading Literature Skillfully**
summarizing

**Vocabulary Skills**
word analogies
root words and suffixes
synonyms

**Thinking Skills**
generalizing
synthesizing

**Composition**
Writing a Letter
Comparing Two Versions of an Event
Writing About a Character
Expressing an Opinion
Reading/Writing Log
Retelling a Launcelot Adventure
Writing a Character Sketch
Writing Arthur's Last Letter
Analyzing a Poem

**Enrichment**
Researching Medieval Weapons
Recruiting for the Round Table
Discovering Arthur in Other Media

**Thinking Critically About Literature**
Concept Review
Content Review
Composition Review

# Reading A LEGENDARY TALE

When you read a legendary tale, it is useful to remember that you are reading neither pure history nor pure fiction, but a narrative that includes elements of both. Legends are told not only to entertain, but to celebrate folk or national heroes, and to pass on the cultural values of a people.

Here are some points to keep in mind as you read.

**Different versions of the tale exist.** There is seldom one "correct" version of a legend. Usually legends are told orally for generations before being written down, a process that assures variety. Sir Thomas Malory based his stories of King Arthur on several sources. Arthur's story continues to be told today in a variety of ways, including the presentations in such films as *Camelot, Excalibur,* and *The Sword in the Stone.*

**Extraordinary events are commonplace.** A hand holding a sword appears in the middle of a lake. Spells and enchantments are everyday risks. Arthur's adviser is a magician who sees into the future. Knights duel for hours with seemingly unlimited energy and blood supply. Instead of dismissing these unrealistic plot elements, set aside your skepticism and enjoy the wonder and mystery they add to the story.

**Heroes and villains are clearly defined.** King Arthur is presented as the hero of all heroes, a model of character and fighting skill for all knights to follow. By contrast, the wicked Sir Modred displays the dark side of human nature. The clear difference between good and bad helps Malory teach virtue and honor.

Good does not mean perfect, however. You will find that even the best knights have human weaknesses; even Arthur makes mistakes.

**The action is episodic.** The legend of King Arthur is made up of many stories that focus not only on Arthur, but also on the actions of his knights of the Round Table. Usually when a knight sets out looking for adventure, his story soon breaks up into a series of independent episodes—like beads on a string—each with its own setting, characters, and conflict. Malory sometimes starts a new adventure before the old one is quite finished. It can be easy to get tangled in the plots of Arthurian legend.

**Summarizing makes for clear reading.** To keep various episodes clear in your mind, you will find it helpful to write summaries as you read. Keep in mind that a **summary** should be brief, accurate, and focused on the major actions of the story. Below is a summary of the first part of Arthur's story as told by Malory. It will be useful as an example for your own summaries and as a frame for understanding the first three Malory passages you will be reading.

Arthur, son of the King of Britain, grows to manhood ignorant of his royal birth. When his right to the throne is miraculously revealed, Arthur is crowned king. With the help of the magician Merlin, Arthur begins a series of campaigns that bring unity and peace to his kingdom. He marries Gwynevere and establishes the fellowship of the Round Table.

# BACKGROUND

Among the popular tales to gain a permanent place in world literature are the romances of chivalry that originated in western Europe during the twelfth century. These stories are romantic narratives of high adventure glorifying the hero-knight and such illustrious kings as Arthur of Britain.

The vibrant pageantry of medieval romance derives from the concept of chivalry—the rules and customs of knights in the Middle Ages. A knight first swore supreme allegiance to God, becoming a special defender of the Christian faith. Second, he affirmed his loyalty to his liege lord, promising to uphold the laws of the realm and to bring honor to himself and his liege through courage and fair play in battle. And third, he vowed to protect the weak and helpless—widows, orphans, serfs (slaves bound to the land), and all ladies in distress. The main themes of medieval fiction were set up by the chivalric code, and the action of the stories deals with knights who attempt to live by this code.

In addition to their highly idealized accounts of knightly adventure, the medieval tales often reveal some realistic aspects of life in the Middle Ages—a life that was crude, barbaric, and even cruel. Fair play often is forgotten as knights quarrel among themselves and engage in struggles for power. Loyalty to the liege lord frequently is put aside in favor of gainful plots against the realm. Knightly protection is more often reserved for ladies of high rank and wealth than for poor serfs, widows, and orphans.

The romances of chivalry gave medieval readers a splendid vision of a new world—a world in which the dull routines of everyday existence would be replaced by adventure and excitement; a world in which the grim and sordid would be cleansed with glittering fancy; a world in which good would triumphantly conquer evil. Perhaps it is these same visions that appeal so much to the modern reader of medieval fiction.

## Origins of the King Arthur Legend

The medieval tales that were written about King Arthur in the twelfth century were based upon an oral legend that was already centuries old. The legend of Arthur originated in Wales. There, as early as the sixth century, storytellers were celebrating his heroic deeds. It seems likely that their stories were inspired by Arturius (or Arthur), a British chieftain who helped to defend Britain against the Saxon invaders. During five centuries of telling and retelling, the Welsh embroidered Arthur's courageous exploits with fiction and fantasy and pagan belief. They endowed him with superhuman qualities and surrounded him with supernatural beings. The Welsh may have been the first to tell how Arthur, healed of his fatal wounds, would return to rule Britain one day.

By the twelfth century, Arthur's fame had spread from Wales to a province of France called Brittany, and from Brittany throughout France and western Europe. The Norman Conquest of 1066, which imposed the French culture and language on England, made it natural for a British legend to migrate quickly to France during this period. Seeing the legendary Arthur as a perfect feudal and Christian king, the French endowed him with the principles of chivalry, attached to his court a number of colorful knights, and made him the hero of their metrical romances.

## Sir Thomas Malory

In the fifteenth century, Sir Thomas Malory brought together the first complete English collection of King Arthur stories in his *Le Morte d'Arthur (The Death of Arthur)*.

Malory drew together the many strands of French romance and wove them into eight prose tales that present a unified account of the life and adventures of the legendary king and his knights of the Round Table. He finished his work in 1469 or 1470, a time of great instability in England. The right of Edward IV to the throne was contested in the War of the Roses. The king himself was devoted to a life of pleasure in a corrupt court. Malory's portrayal of King Arthur as the ideal of knighthood presented a stark contrast to the reigning monarch.

## Retelling Arthur's Story

The eight prose romances that make up Malory's *Morte d'Arthur* have inspired innumerable poets, novelists, and playwrights—among them Alfred, Lord Tennyson, the Victorian poet laureate, who was fascinated with the pageantry and adventure that he found in Malory's tales of King Arthur and undertook to write his own version. The result was twelve long poems published in 1891 as *The Idylls of the King*.

Several twentieth-century writers have tried their hand at retelling Arthur's story. British author T. H. White published one of the most popular versions, *The Once and Future King*, in 1958. This work has been adapted into a musical for stage and screen under the title *Camelot*.

Drawing from many sources, the British novelist Mary Stewart told the story through the narrative voice of Merlin in a series of novels known as the "Merlin Trilogy," published in the 1970s.

Passages from these writers are included in this unit in order that you might compare modern versions with Malory's.

## Notable Names in the Arthurian World

**UTHER PENDRAGON,** King of Britain and father of Arthur. He gives his son to Merlin for secret upbringing and dies two years later.

**IGRAINE,** mother of Arthur.

**MERLIN,** prophet and magician. He arranges for Arthur to be raised by Sir Ector and serves as Arthur's adviser during childhood and the early years of Arthur's reign.

**GWYNEVERE,** Arthur's queen. The Round Table is her dowry. She later falls in love with Sir Launcelot. Many writers spell her name Guinevere.

**CAMELOT,** where Arthur holds his court.

**EXCALIBUR,** Arthur's magical sword.

**LADY OF THE LAKE,** a supernatural being who gives Excalibur to Arthur. She is one of the queens who carry the mortally wounded Arthur to Avalon where he may be healed.

**MORGAN LE FAY,** a sorceress who often plots against Arthur. She is Arthur's half-sister.

**SIR LAUNCELOT,** the bravest of Arthur's knights. His love for Queen Gwynevere eventually destroys the fellowship of the Round Table. His name is often rendered as Sir Launcelot du Lake or Sir Lancelot.

**SIR KAY,** the son of Sir Ector. He and Arthur are reared as brothers. When Arthur becomes king, the churlish Kay is appointed Royal Seneschal and becomes a knight.

**SIR GAWAIN,** nephew of Arthur and knight of the Round Table. His strength—like that of the sun—grows each morning and then wanes during the afternoon.

**SIR MODRED,** a knight of the Round Table, often identified as Arthur's nephew or illegitimate son. He tries to usurp the throne during Arthur's absence abroad. Arthur slays Modred but receives a fatal wound. Some writers spell the name Mordred.

**SIR BEDIVERE,** surviving companion of Arthur who returns Excalibur to the Lady of the Lake at the dying king's request.

**H₮**  See PARADOX in the Handbook of Literary Terms, page 811.

# The Coronation of Arthur

**Sir Thomas Malory**  Great Britain

*Translated by* Keith Baines

---

**This episode begins with the marriage of Arthur's parents, King Uther and Queen Igraine, and a plan for the secret rearing of their first-born child, who is destined to become a renowned knight and ruler. The magician Merlin, who can foresee King Uther's early death, arranges for Arthur to be taken to Sir Ector, who will educate him along with his own son, Sir Kay. Later, Arthur will demonstrate to all the warring nobles that he is the rightful heir to the throne.**

---

he marriage of King Uther and Igraine was celebrated joyously, and then, at the king's request, Igraine's sisters were also married: Margawse, who later bore Sir Gawain, to King Lot of Lowthean and Orkney; Elayne, to King Nentres of Garlot. Igraine's daughter, Morgan le Fay, was put to school in a nunnery; in after years she was to become a witch, and to be married to King Uryens of Gore, and give birth to Sir Uwayne of the Fair Hands.[1]

A few months later it was seen that Igraine was with child. . . .

Sometime later Merlin appeared before the king. "Sire," he said, "you know that you must provide for the upbringing of your child?"

"I will do as you advise," the king replied.

"That is good," said Merlin. . . . "Your child is destined for glory, and I want him brought to me for his baptism. I shall then give him into the care of foster parents who can be trusted not to reveal his identity before the proper time. Sir Ector would be suitable: he is extremely loyal,

---

1. *Margawse . . . Sir Uwayne of the Fair Hands.* The royal relatives and descendants are named here because they figure later in the tales of King Arthur. Sir Gawain, for example, becomes one of the most celebrated knights at the Round Table; and Morgan le Fay appears as an enchantress in "The Tale of Sir Launcelot du Lake."

This image of Arthur as one of nine exemplary rulers of the past appears in a tapestry attributed to Nicolas Bataille. *The Nine Worthies* (detail), completed circa 1385, The Metropolitan Museum of Art, The Cloisters Collection

owns good estates, and his wife has just borne him a child. She could give her child into the care of another woman, and herself look after yours."

Sir Ector was summoned, and gladly agreed to the king's request, who then rewarded him handsomely. When the child was born he was at once wrapped in a gold cloth and taken by two knights and two ladies to Merlin, who stood waiting at the rear entrance to the castle in his beggar's disguise. Merlin took the child to a priest, who baptized him with the name of Arthur, and thence to Sir Ector, whose wife fed him at her breast.

Two years later King Uther fell sick, and his enemies once more overran his kingdom, inflicting heavy losses on him as they advanced. Merlin prophesied that they could be checked only by the presence of the king himself on the battlefield, and suggested that he should be conveyed there on a horse litter. King Uther's army met the invader on the plain at St. Albans, and the king duly appeared on the horse litter. Inspired by his presence, and by the lively leadership of Sir Brastius and Sir Jordanus, his army quickly defeated the enemy and the battle finished in a rout. The king returned to London to celebrate the victory.

But his sickness grew worse, and after he had lain speechless for three days and three nights Merlin summoned the nobles to attend the king in his chamber on the following morning. "By the grace of God," he said, "I hope to make him speak."

In the morning, when all the nobles were assembled, Merlin addressed the king: "Sire, is it your will that Arthur shall succeed to the throne, together with all its prerogatives?"

The king stirred in his bed, and then spoke so that all could hear: "I bestow on Arthur God's blessing and my own, and Arthur shall succeed to the throne on pain of forfeiting my blessing." Then King Uther gave up the ghost. He was buried and mourned the next day, as befitted his rank, by Igraine and the nobility of Britain.

During the years that followed the death of King Uther, while Arthur was still a child, the ambitious barons fought one another for the throne, and the whole of Britain stood in jeopardy. Finally the day came when the Archbishop of Canterbury,[2] on the advice of Merlin, summoned the nobility to London for Christmas morning. In his message the Archbishop promised that the true succession to the British throne would be miraculously revealed. Many of the nobles purified themselves during their journey, in the hope that it would be to them that the succession would fall.

The Archbishop held his service in the city's greatest church (St. Paul's), and when matins[3] were done the congregation filed out to the yard. They were confronted by a marble block into which had been thrust a beautiful sword. The block was four feet square, and the sword passed through a steel anvil which had been struck in the stone, and which projected a foot from it. The anvil had been inscribed with letters of gold:

WHOSO PULLETH OUTE THIS SWERD OF THIS STONE AND ANVYLD IS RIGHTWYS KYNGE BORNE OF ALL BRYTAYGNE[4]

The congregation was awed by this miraculous sight, but the Archbishop forbade anyone to touch the sword before mass had been heard. After mass, many of the nobles tried to pull the sword out of the stone, but none was able to, so a watch of ten knights was set over the sword, and a tournament proclaimed for New Year's Day, to provide men of noble blood with the opportunity of proving their right to the succession.

Sir Ector, who had been living on an estate near London, rode to the tournament with Arthur and

---

2. *Archbishop of Canterbury,* head of the Church of England.
3. *matins,* morning prayers.
4. *WHOSO . . . BRYTAYGNE,* "Whoever pulls this sword out of this stone and anvil is rightwise king born of all Britain."

his own son Sir Kay, who had been recently knighted. When they arrived at the tournament, Sir Kay found to his annoyance that his sword was missing from its sheath, so he begged Arthur to ride back and fetch it from their lodging.

Arthur found the door of the lodging locked and bolted, the landlord and his wife having left for the tournament. In order not to disappoint his brother, he rode on to St. Paul's, determined to get for him the sword which was lodged in the stone. The yard was empty, the guard also having slipped off to see the tournament, so Arthur strode up to the sword, and, without troubling to read the inscription, tugged it free. He then rode straight back to Sir Kay and presented him with it.

Sir Kay recognized the sword, and taking it to Sir Ector, said, "Father, the succession falls to me, for I have here the sword that was lodged in the stone." But Sir Ector insisted that they should all ride to the churchyard, and once there bound Sir Kay by oath to tell how he had come by the sword. Sir Kay then admitted that Arthur had given it to him. Sir Ector turned to Arthur and said, "Was the sword not guarded?"

"It was not," Arthur replied.

"Would you please thrust it into the stone again?" said Sir Ector. Arthur did so, and first Sir Ector and then Sir Kay tried to remove it, but both were unable to. Then Arthur, for the second time, pulled it out. Sir Ector and Sir Kay both knelt before him.

"Why," said Arthur, "do you both kneel before me?"

"My lord," Sir Ector replied, "there is only one man living who can draw the sword from the stone, and he is the true-born King of Britain." Sir Ector then told Arthur the story of his birth and upbringing.

"My dear father," said Arthur, "for so I shall always think of you—if, as you say, I am to be king, please know that any request you have to make is already granted."

Sir Ector asked that Sir Kay should be made Royal Seneschal,[5] and Arthur declared that while they both lived it should be so. Then the three of them visited the Archbishop and told him what had taken place.

All those dukes and barons with ambitions to rule were present at the tournament on New Year's Day. But when all of them had failed, and Arthur alone had succeeded in drawing the sword from the stone, they protested against one so young, and of ignoble blood, succeeding to the throne.

The secret of Arthur's birth was known only to a few of the nobles surviving from the days of King Uther. The Archbishop urged them to make Arthur's cause their own; but their support proved ineffective. The tournament was repeated at Candlemas[6] and at Easter, and with the same outcome as before.

Finally at Pentecost,[7] when once more Arthur alone had been able to remove the sword, the commoners arose with a tumultuous cry and demanded that Arthur should at once be made king. The nobles, knowing in their hearts that the commoners were right, all knelt before Arthur and begged forgiveness for having delayed his succession for so long. Arthur forgave them, and then, offering his sword at the high altar, was dubbed first knight of the realm. The coronation took place a few days later, when Arthur swore to rule justly, and the nobles swore him their allegiance.

King Arthur's first task was to re-establish those nobles who had been robbed of their lands during the troubled years since the reign of King Uther. Next, to establish peace and order in the counties near London. . . .

---

5. **Royal Seneschal,** the steward (or manager) in charge of the royal household.
6. **Candlemas,** a church festival held on February 2, celebrated with lighted candles.
7. **Pentecost,** a church festival celebrated the seventh Sunday after Easter.

# *from* The Hollow Hills

**Mary Stewart**  Great Britain

**In this modern novelist's account of Arthur drawing the sword from the stone, Merlin is the narrator. The author changes some details of the plot to heighten the dramatic impact. The sword is in a small forest chapel rather than the yard of London's finest church. Merlin presides over the ceremony and uses the old sword of a Roman ruler of ancient Britain. The gathered nobles are hushed, in a mysterious setting that blends opposites such as cold and fire, darkness and glittering light, as Arthur steps forth to become king.**

he place was small, the throng of men great. But the awe of the occasion prevailed; orders were given, but subdued; soft commands which might have come from priests in ritual rather than warriors recently in battle. There were no rites to follow, but somehow men kept their places; kings and nobles and kings' guards within the chapel, the press of lesser men outside in the silent clearing and overflowing into the gloom of the forest itself. There, they still had lights; the clearing was ringed with light and sound where the horses waited and men stood with torches ready; but forward under the open sky men came lightless and weaponless, as beseemed them in the presence of God and their King. And still, this one night of all the great nights, there was no priest present; the only intermediary was myself, who had been used by the driving god for thirty years, and brought at last to this place.

At length all were assembled, according to order and precedence. It was as if they had divided by arrangement, or more likely by instinct. Outside, crowding the steps, waited the little men from the hills; they do not willingly come under a roof. Inside the chapel, to my right, stood Lot, King of Lothian, with his group of friends and followers; to the left Cador, and those who went with him. There were a hundred others, perhaps more, crowded into that small and echoing space, but these two, the white Boar of Cornwall, and the red Leopard of Lothian,[1] seemed to face one another balefully from either side of the altar, with Ector four-square and watchful at the door between them. Then Ector, with Cei[2] behind him, brought Arthur forward, and after that I saw no one but the boy.

---

**1.** *white Boar . . . Lothian.* Two kings, Cador of Cornwall and Lot of Lothian, use the symbols of a white boar and a red leopard, respectively, on their standards.
**2.** *Cei* (kā), variant spelling of Kay, Ector's son.

The chapel swam with color and the glint of jewels and gold. The air smelled cold and fragrant, of pines and water and scented smoke. The rustle and murmuring of the throng filled the air and sounded like the rustle of flames licking through a pile of fuel, taking hold. . . .

Flames from the nine lamps, flaring and then dying; flames licking up the stone of the altar; flames running along the blade of the sword until it glowed white hot. I stretched my hands out over it, palms flat. The fire licked my robe, blazing white from sleeve and finger, but where it touched, it did not even singe. It was the ice-cold fire, the fire called by a word out of the dark, with the searing heat at its heart, where the sword lay. The sword lay in its flames as a jewel lies embedded in white wool. *Whoso taketh this sword . . .*[3] The runes[4] danced along the metal: the emeralds burned. The chapel was a dark globe with a center of fire. The blaze from the altar threw my shadow upwards, gigantic, into the vaulted roof. I heard my own voice, ringing hollow from the vault like a voice in a dream.

"Take up the sword, he who dares."

Movement, and men's voices, full of dread. Then Cador: "That is the sword. I would know it anywhere. I saw it in his hand, full of light.[5] It is his, God witness it. I would not touch it if Merlin himself bade me."

There were cries of, "Nor I, nor I," and then, "Let the King take it up, let the High King show us Macsen's[6] sword."

Then finally, alone, Lot's voice, gruffly: "Yes. Let him take it. I have seen, by God's death, I have seen. If it is his indeed, then God is with him, and it is not for me."

Arthur came slowly forward. Behind him the place was dim, the crowd shrunk back into darkness, the shuffle and murmur of their presence no more than the breeze in the forest trees outside. Here between us, the white light blazed

Arthur drawing the sword from the stone, from a Flemish illuminated manuscript, circa 1290. Bibliotheque Nationale, Paris

and the blade shivered. The darkness flashed and sparkled, a crystal cave of vision, crowded and whirling with bright images.[7] A white stag, collared with gold. A shooting star, dragon-shaped, and trailing fire. A king, restless and desirous, with a dragon of red gold shimmering on the wall behind him. A woman, white-robed and queenly, and behind her in the shadows a sword standing in an altar like a cross. A circle of vast linked stones standing on a windy plain with a king's grave at its center. A child, handed into my arms on a winter night. A grail, shrouded in mouldering cloth, hidden in a dark vault. A young king, crowned.

He looked at me through the pulse and flash of vision. For him, they were flames only, flames

3. *Whoso . . . sword.* The words "Whoso taketh [takes] this sword from under this stone is rightwise King born of all Britain" appear in their entirety earlier in this novel.
4. *runes,* inscriptions or letters.
5. *I saw . . . light.* Cador had seen Arthur with the same sword earlier, when it was found in a cavern.
6. *Macsen's,* Maximus's. *Macsen* is the British name for the Roman ruler Magnus Maximus, who lived in the fourth century in Britain. Mary Stewart has introduced the idea that the sword once belonged to another ruler of Great Britain, a new twist on the Arthurian legend.
7. *bright images.* Merlin proceeds to identify images of a stag, a shooting star, and other omens and scenes from Arthur's life up to this point.

which might burn, or not; that was for me. He waited, not doubtful, nor blindly trusting; waiting only.

"Come," I said gently. "It is yours."

He put his hand through the white blaze of fire and the hilt slid cool into the grip for which, a hundred and a hundred years before, it had been made.

## THINK AND DISCUSS
### THE CORONATION OF ARTHUR
### Understanding

1. What advice does Merlin give to King Uther about his child's upbringing? What does Uther proclaim from his deathbed?
2. What miraculous sign will reveal the true king of England?
3. Explain how Arthur gets a sword for Sir Kay.
4. What are Arthur's first tasks as king?

### Analyzing

5. What is the cause of unrest in England during Arthur's childhood?
6. Why do you think the barons are so slow to accept Arthur? What finally causes them to honor Arthur as king?
7. List at least three personal qualities Arthur displays in this passage. Describe the actions that reveal those characteristics.

### Extending

8. Arthur had been chosen for the throne long ago by his father. Would this story have been as effective if the Archbishop had simply proclaimed Arthur the true heir to the throne? Why or why not?
9. Pulling the sword from the stone is a legendary test of leadership. Do leaders today undergo public "tests" to prove their ability to lead people? Explain.

### FROM THE HOLLOW HILLS
### Understanding

1. Who is describing the ceremony?
2. Whose sword is lying on the altar?

### Analyzing

3. Compare this scene with Malory's account of the coronation of Arthur. What differences do you find in **point of view, setting,** and **tone?**
4. In what sense is Stewart's version less "magical" than Malory's? In what sense is it more magical?

### Extending

5. In both versions of the event, all the potential leaders are given the chance to take up the sword. Do you think this openness contributed to Arthur's acceptance as king? Explain.

### APPLYING: Paradox HⱫ
### See Handbook of Literary Terms, p. 811

A **paradox** is an apparently self-contradictory statement that still has validity; for example, the statement "The more things change, the more they remain the same" is a paradox. Writers use such "collisions of opposites" to make readers stop and think and to create symbolic or metaphoric emphasis.

1. What paradox do you find in the fourth paragraph of the excerpt from *The Hollow Hills?*
2. How does this paradox affect the description?

## THINKING SKILLS
### Synthesizing

To **synthesize** is to put together elements to form a whole, a new pattern or structure not evident before. Synthesis can involve personal experience and imagination.

Consider the appropriateness of Arthur's test of leadership. Freeing the sword suggests Arthur's strength and skill with weapons, important leadership qualities in his time.

1. What skills and personal qualities does a national leader need today? List as many as you can.
2. Devise a test of leadership that you think will reveal important qualities that you value in a leader. (You may wish to work with several classmates, then compare your test with those of other groups.)

## COMPOSITION
### Writing a Letter

Malory's account does not reflect the personal shock Arthur must have felt upon learning that Sir Ector was not his real father, that his destiny was to be king. Imagine that you are Arthur writing a letter to a friend after you first pulled the sword from the stone. In your letter try to accurately explain what happened and how you feel about the sudden changes in your life.

### Comparing Two Versions of an Event

Review Malory's and Stewart's descriptions of Arthur taking up the sword of kingship. Write a four- or five-paragraph analysis of the similarities and differences you find. Use your final paragraph to explain why you prefer one version over the other. See "Writing to Compare and Contrast" in the Writer's Handbook.

## BIOGRAPHY

### Mary Stewart
### 1916–

For most of her career English novelist Florence Elinor, writing as Mary Stewart, specialized in romantic thrillers with modern international settings. In 1970 Stewart surprised many of her readers with the publication of *The Crystal Cave*, her first work of historical fiction. Taking a new approach to the well-worn Arthurian material, Stewart placed her story in fifth-century Britain (some seven centuries earlier than Malory's setting), and she told events from the viewpoint of Merlin. *The Hollow Hills* (1973) and *The Last Enchantment* (1979) develop and conclude her interpretation of the legend of King Arthur.

(A biography of Sir Thomas Malory appears on page 346.)

# The Lady of the Lake and Excalibur

**Sir Thomas Malory** Great Britain

*Translated by* Keith Baines

---

**King Arthur spends the early part of his reign subduing the rebellious
rulers who do not acknowledge him as rightful king. Throughout this
time he is closely aided and advised by Merlin. In the following episode
Arthur attempts to avenge the wounding of one of his knights.**

---

hen Arthur was armed and
mounted, he instructed the chamberlain to await his return, and then
galloped off toward the well. He
had not gone far when he saw Merlin being chased
by three ruffians; he galloped up to them and the
ruffians fled in terror.

"Your magic did not save you that time," said
Arthur.

"It could have," Merlin replied, "had I so
wished, whereas your anger will certainly not save
you from the superior strength of King Pellinore,
whom you are about to challenge."

Merlin accompanied Arthur to the well, and
when they arrived they found King Pellinore
seated outside his pavilion.[1] "Sir," said Arthur,
"it would seem that no knight can pass this well
without your challenging him."

"That is so," said King Pellinore.

"I have come to force you to change this custom
of yours, so defend yourself!"

They jousted three times, each time breaking
their spears, until the third time, when Arthur
was flung from his horse. "Very well," said
Arthur, "you have won the advantage jousting;
now let us see what you can do on foot." King
Pellinore was reluctant to dismount and lose the
advantage he had won; however, when Arthur
rushed at him boldly with drawn sword, he grew
ashamed and did dismount.

They fought until both collapsed from pain and
exhaustion; their armor was splintered and the
blood flowed from their wounds. They fought
again, until Arthur's sword broke in his hand.
"Now," said King Pellinore, "you shall yield to
me, or die."

"Not so!" Arthur shouted as he sprang at him,
and grabbing him around the waist, threw him to
the ground. Arthur was unlacing his helmet

---

1. *pavilion,* a large tent.

Charles Ernest Butler,
*King Arthur*, 1903,
Private Collection

when, with a sudden fearful effort, King Pellinore overturned Arthur and clambered on top of him. King Pellinore had loosened Arthur's helmet and raised his sword to strike off his head when Merlin spoke.

"Hold your hand!" he said; "you will endanger the whole realm. You do not realize who it is you are about to kill."

"Who is it, then?"

"King Arthur."

Hearing this, King Pellinore feared that he would receive little mercy from Arthur if he spared him—so he raised his sword once more. Merlin adroitly put him to sleep with a magic spell.

"You have killed him with your magic," said Arthur hotly. "I would rather that my whole realm were lost, and myself killed; he was a magnificent fighter."

"He is more whole than you are," Merlin replied. "He will not only live, but serve you excellently: It is to him that you will give your sister in marriage, and she will bear two sons—Sir Percivale and Sir Lamerok—who will be two of the most famous of the Knights of the Round Table."

They mounted, and Merlin led the way to a hermit, who treated Arthur's wounds, and in whose dwelling they rested for three days. They resumed their journey, which was to the Lake of Avalon,[2] and as they were approaching the lake, Arthur said, "How sad that I broke my magic sword!"

"You shall have another one," Merlin replied.

Just then Arthur saw that in the center of the lake the surface was broken by an arm, clothed in white samite,[3] and that the hand grasped a finely jeweled sword and scabbard.

"That is the magic sword Excalibur," said Merlin, "and it will be given to you by the Lady of the Lake, who is now crossing the water in her bark. She comes from her castle, which is hewn in the rock, and more beautiful than any earthly dwelling. You must address her courteously, and do as she directs you."

The Lady of the Lake appeared before them. "My lady," said Arthur, "I beg you to make me a gift of the sword Excalibur."

"King Arthur," she replied, "Excalibur shall be yours, if you consent now to granting me whatever gift I shall ask of you in my own time."

"I swear," said Arthur, "whatever gift is in my power to grant."

"Even so," said the Lady of the Lake. "Now use my bark and row yourself to the sword, and take it, together with the scabbard."

Arthur and Merlin tethered their horses to two trees, and boarded the bark. When Arthur had taken the sword and scabbard the arm disappeared into the water.

On the homeward journey they repassed King Pellinore's pavilion, and Arthur asked Merlin why King Pellinore was not there. "He has been fighting Sir Egglame, and has chased him nearly all the way into Caerleon,"[4] Merlin replied.

"What a pity!" said Arthur. "Because now that I have this beautiful sword I should like to fight him again, and perhaps this time have my revenge."

"That you shall not do," said Merlin. "King Pellinore is already tired from his fight with Sir Egglame. To win would bring you no honor, to lose would be to increase your shame. And lose you might, because he is still stronger than you are."

"I will do as you advise," said Arthur, as he examined his sword once more, admiring its beauty and temper. "Tell me," said Merlin, "do you prefer the sword or the scabbard?"

"The sword," said Arthur.

---

2. **Avalon,** an island believed to be an earthly paradise; it was to become the final resting place of King Arthur.
3. **samite,** a heavy silk fabric interwoven with gold.
4. **Caerleon,** site of Roman ruins in present-day Wales, southwest Great Britain; long associated with the Arthur legend.

"You are a fool," said Merlin. "The scabbard is worth ten of the sword, because while you wear it, regardless of how seriously you are wounded, you will lose no blood."

They were drawing close to Caerleon when they passed King Pellinore; he appeared not to see them. "Why," asked Arthur, "did King Pellinore not speak to us?"

"Because he did not see us," Merlin replied. "I cast a spell over him; had he done so, you would not have escaped so lightly."

When Arthur and Merlin arrived at the court, they were questioned eagerly on all that had happened; and when the story was told, Arthur's knights rejoiced in the boldness of their king.

## THINK AND DISCUSS
### Understanding
1. How does Merlin affect the outcome of the fight between Arthur and Pellinore?
2. How does Arthur react to Merlin's help?
3. How does Arthur obtain the sword Excalibur?
4. Why is the scabbard more valuable than the sword itself?

### Analyzing
5. Though he knows that Pellinore is stronger, Arthur challenges him anyway. What does this fact tell you about Arthur?
6. What details in this passage show that Arthur is still immature and needs Merlin's guidance?

### Extending
7. Merlin advises and magically protects Arthur in this passage. How does Merlin's aid affect your opinion of Arthur as a heroic **protagonist**?

## ENRICHMENT
### Researching Medieval Weapons
Swords have played a major part in Arthur's life thus far. Use library reference books on ancient weapons to discover what a medieval sword looked like. Combine these details with your imagination to create a drawing or a model of either the sword in the stone or Excalibur.

# Arthur Marries Gwynevere

**Sir Thomas Malory**   Great Britain

*Translated by* Keith Baines

---

**After securing his sovereignty, King Arthur settles at Camelot and marries the beautiful Gwynevere. He receives as dowry the fabled Round Table, which had belonged to his father. Sworn to the famous Round Table oath, King Arthur and his knights are bound in a fellowship that is an important means of maintaining order in the kingdom.**

---

It was natural that King Arthur, having sought Merlin's advice during the early years of his reign, while enforcing his sovereignty over the petty kings of the north and west of Britain who had challenged his right to the succession, should again seek Merlin's advice in the matter of marriage, which his loyal barons were urging upon him now that peace had been established.

"Certainly a king should marry," said Merlin. "But tell me, is there already a lady who has captured your heart?"

"There is," Arthur replied. "The daughter of my friend King Lodegreaunce[1] of Camylarde. I mean, of course, the incomparably innocent and beautiful Gwynevere."

"She is certainly as beautiful as one could wish, and if indeed you are set on making her your queen, I suppose that you must do so, although many more as beautiful, and more happily destined, could be found."

"Why do you say that?"

"Because Gwynevere is destined to love Sir Launcelot, and he her, and many disasters will result from their love. However, provide me with a royal escort and I will go to King Lodegreaunce and tell him that you are in love with Gwynevere and would like to marry her."

King Lodegreaunce was overjoyed when Merlin disclosed the purpose of his visit. "What greater honor could I receive," he said, "than that so illustrious a king as Arthur should choose my daughter for his queen?"

Instead of the usual lands or riches for a wedding gift, King Lodegreaunce decided to give King Arthur the Round Table which he had received from King Uther, and to place under Arthur's command the hundred knights who served him. This would leave empty at the table fifty seats, which had belonged to knights who had been killed or captured in King Lo-

---

1. *Lodegreaunce* (lō′də grôns)

An illustration of the wedding of Gwynevere and Arthur (detail), from an illuminated manuscript by Guillaume Vrelant (gē yōm′  vrə làɴ′), circa 1468. Bibliotheque Royale Albert Ier, Brussels, Belgium.

degreaunce' service in the course of the years.

When Merlin and his escort, with the Round Table, and accompanied by Gwynevere and the hundred knights, returned to Camelot, he was received by Arthur with unabashed delight; and orders were given to prepare for the royal wedding and the coronation of Gwynevere.

Merlin then scoured the country for suitable knights to occupy the empty seats at the table, and found twenty-eight, who were sworn in to Arthur's service by the Archbishop of Canterbury. When the ceremony was over it was seen that each place at the table was now marked in gold letters with the name of the knight to which it belonged; but two places were left blank, and the one between them was marked: SIEGE PERELOUS.[2]

King Arthur had issued a proclamation that on the day of the feast all reasonable petitions would be granted, and the first to take advantage of this was Gawain, King Lot's son, who begged to be knighted. Gawain was Arthur's nephew, and he readily assented. . . .

At last the day of the feast arrived, and the royal wedding and the coronation of Gwynevere took place in the church of St. Stephens, and were conducted with befitting solemnity by the Archbishop of Canterbury. When it was over, King Arthur with his queen and their suite repaired to the Round Table for the banquet.

"Tell me, Merlin," said Arthur, "why those two seats are blank, and why the one between them is marked: SIEGE PERELOUS."

"Sire, because it would be death for any but the appointed knight to sit at the Siege Perelous, and only a little less disastrous at the unmarked seats on either side. The knight who shall sit at the Siege Perelous has not yet been born; the names of the knights who shall sit at the other two seats will appear when they arrive at the court. . . ."

King Arthur . . . established each of the knights of the Round Table with sufficient lands and wealth to maintain the dignity of the fellowship; and every time the feast of Pentecost came round, the oath was renewed, which was: only to fight in just causes, at all times to be merciful, at all times to put the service of ladies foremost.

---

2. *SIEGE PERELOUS*, dangerous seat. The knight who later sits here is Sir Galahad, who becomes famous for an adventure known as the Quest of the Holy Grail.

## THINK AND DISCUSS
### Understanding
1. What does Arthur accomplish before he thinks of marriage?
2. What prophecy does Merlin make about Arthur's marriage to Gwynevere?
3. Describe the Round Table.
4. What is the oath of the Round Table?

### Analyzing
5. How do you explain the fact that Merlin makes no effort to prevent Arthur's marriage to Gwynevere?

6. Discuss the **paradox** that Arthur's marriage brings promise of greatness and promise of disaster.
7. How does Malory create suspense in his description of the Round Table?

### Extending
8. In your opinion, would the Round Table oath be a valuable guide in today's society? What changes, if any, would you make to modernize the oath?

## READING LITERATURE SKILLFULLY
### Summarizing

An episodic work like Malory's may be easier to keep in mind if you summarize events as you read along. A good summary is brief, concise, and accurate. It usually is written in the present tense.

1. Evaluate this summary of "The Lady of the Lake and Excalibur": "Arthur is taken to a lake where a mysterious Lady of the Lake arranges to replace his broken sword with one held by an arm reaching out of the lake. Thus Arthur obtains Excalibur, the sword that will prevent him from bleeding in battle."
2. Write a brief summary of the important details of "Arthur Marries Gwynevere."

## VOCABULARY
### Word Analogies

Word analogy tests require you to understand the relationship between a pair of words and then to choose another pair of words that have that same relationship. For example, *hilt* is to *sword* as *handle* is to *hammer*. Such word analogies usually are expressed in a formula as follows. HILT : SWORD :: HANDLE : HAMMER. Study the relationship of the following pairs of words in capital letters; then choose another pair that has the same relationship.

1. ILLUSTRIOUS : GLORIOUS :: (a) king : monarch; (b) anvil : hammer
2. JEOPARDY : SAFETY :: (a) realm : kingdom; (b) unabashed : embarrassed
3. RESUME : CONTINUE :: (a) stand : kneel; (b) assent : agree
4. SWORD : SCABBARD :: (a) pavilion : tent; (b) coat : closet
5. RUFFIAN : BULLY :: (a) ritual : ceremony; (b) throng : individual

### Root Words and Suffixes

Combine each root word below with an appropriate suffix. The spelling of some roots may change. Use each new word in a sentence to show you understand its meaning.

| | |
|---|---|
| nun | -er |
| adroit | -ity |
| sovereign | -ly |
| solemn | -ty |
| common | -ery |

## COMPOSITION
### Writing About a Character

Write a three-paragraph character sketch of Arthur based on the first three excerpts from Malory that you have read. What strengths do you see? What weaknesses do you detect? In a closing paragraph, give your overall appraisal of Arthur at this point in his life. See "Writing About Characters" in the Writer's Handbook.

### Expressing an Opinion

Malory's story of Arthur presents both a hero and a code of conduct, a model and a guide to right actions. Do these ideas still have influence today? Do we still in some way measure heroism by the standard set by Arthur and his knights? Are our standards of fairness and decent behavior influenced at all by the oath of the Round Table? Write a paper of three to five paragraphs expressing your opinion. Be sure to support that opinion with reasons and examples.

## ENRICHMENT
### Recruiting for the Round Table

Imagine that you have been asked to prepare an advertising campaign to encourage brave and honorable knights to join the fellowship of the Round Table. Working with a group of classmates, create a slogan, a poster ad, and a sixty-second commercial (to be performed "live" before the class). Be sure your ads clearly state the knightly requirements the candidates must meet.

Very little is known about Malory's life; the clearest details concern his prison record. The charges included breaking and entering, plundering, extortion, and escape from prison. Whether these represented Malory's actual crimes or only the plots of his enemies may never be known. But we might conclude that Malory was fully involved in the conflicts of his time, when a prolonged War of the Roses was fought between the House of Lancaster (whose emblem was the red rose) and the House of York (with the emblem of the white rose) for the throne of Great Britain.

It is known that Malory was in prison when he wrote the work for which he is remembered, *Le Morte d'Arthur*. He referred several times to "the French book" as his source, but the specific work has not been identified. He finished his work in 1469–1470, shortly before he died. It was one of the first books published by William Caxton on the newly invented printing press, appearing in 1485.

*Comment*

**Why Was the Table Round?**

Malory speaks of the Round Table in two senses. First, he refers to it when he means the *fellowship* that bound King Arthur and his knights. Secondly, he refers to the Round Table when he means the *actual table,* seating one hundred and fifty knights, that could be transported from Camelot to another of Arthur's courts.

Why was the actual table round instead of rectangular? At Arthur's court, each knight was considered to be the equal of his fellows. Thus, Arthur could not seat the highest-ranking knights at the head of a rectangular table and the knights of lowest rank at the foot. Only at a circular table—one that had no head or foot— could Arthur seat his knights equally.

The idea of a Round Table may have come into the Arthurian legend from a custom of early British chieftains. In order to avoid giving one warrior precedence over another, these chieftains sat at the center of a circle formed by their warriors.

During the long history of the Arthurian legend, the Round Table also acquired many Christian associations. The Siege Perelous, for example, was reserved for the knight who was destined to accomplish the quest of the Holy Grail, the discovery and retrieval of the cup used by Jesus at the Last Supper.

Once Malory has established the valor and prestige of King Arthur in *Morte d'Arthur,* he then takes up the lives and adventures of the chivalrous knights who sat at the "Table Round."

An Italian manuscript illustration, circa 1370, of Sir Galahad being introduced at King Arthur's Round Table. Bibliotheque Nationale, Paris

## Build Sentences for Emphasis and Interest

Good writing doesn't dully drone. It has a lilt or rhythm that results from the skilled crafting of each individual sentence and careful composition of every paragraph. Skilled writers vary their sentences for interest and emphasis. Read the following passage from Malory's *Morte d'Arthur*, as modernized by Keith Baines.

> In order not to disappoint his brother, he [Arthur] rode on to St. Paul's, determined to get for him the sword which was lodged in the stone. The yard was empty, the guard also having slipped off to see the tournament, so Arthur strode up to the sword, and without troubling to read the inscription, tugged it free. He then rode straight back to Sir Kay and presented him with it.

Notice that two long sentences are followed by a short one. This variation makes the writing more lively and helps establish a rhythm.

Good writers also take care to vary the pattern within sentences. While most sentences follow a basic subject-predicate order, a series of sentences beginning with subjects can be monotonous. Notice in the passage above that the first sentence begins with an introductory phrase.

Key ideas or details can be emphasized by placing them at the beginning or end of sentences. In the passage below the writer saves the most important detail for the end of the sentence.

> Just then Arthur saw that in the center of the lake the surface was broken by an arm, clothed in white samite, and that the hand grasped a finely jeweled sword and scabbard.

Parallel construction can be used to add emphasis and build momentum in a passage. As you read the following passage from Mary Stewart's *The Hollow Hills*, notice how Stewart uses parallel construction to describe the lighting in the cave. The repetition heightens the tension and captures the mystical aura surrounding the sword.

> Flames from the nine lamps, flaring and then dying; flames licking up the stone of the altar; flames running along the blade of the sword until it glowed white hot.

Finally, good writers use the very sounds of words to create emphasis, variety, and other effects.

In the following passage the repetition of the "l" sound mimics the murmur of the crowd described in the passage.

> The rustle and murmuring of the throng filled the air and sounded like the rustle of flames licking through a pile of fuel, taking hold.

Careful crafting of sentences adds to the reader's enjoyment of a piece of writing.

---

When you read, notice the writer's craft in sentence building.

When you write, construct sentences that make an impact; vary sentences to create interest.

---

See ALLUSION in the Handbook of Literary Terms, page 789.

# The Tale of Sir Launcelot du Lake

**Sir Thomas Malory**   Great Britain

*Translated by* Keith Baines

The Arthurian legend incorporates the tales of many brave knights of
the Round Table. The most renowned was Sir Launcelot du Lake (Sir
Launcelot of the Lake). He was so called because, according to legend,
he was stolen as a baby from his home in Brittany (a province of
France) and brought up by the Lady of the Lake.

**W**hen King Arthur returned from Rome he settled his court at Camelot, and there gathered about him his knights of the Round Table, who diverted themselves with jousting and tournaments. Of all his knights one was supreme, both in prowess at arms and in nobility of bearing, and this was Sir Launcelot, who was also the favorite of Queen Gwynevere, to whom he had sworn oaths of fidelity.

One day Sir Launcelot, feeling weary of his life at the court, and of only playing at arms, decided to set forth in search of adventure. He asked his nephew Sir Lyonel to accompany him, and when both were suitably armed and mounted, they rode off together through the forest.

At noon they started across a plain, but the intensity of the sun made Sir Launcelot feel sleepy, so Sir Lyonel suggested that they should rest beneath the shade of an apple tree that grew by a hedge not far from the road. They dismounted, tethered their horses, and settled down.

"Not for seven years have I felt so sleepy," said Sir Launcelot, and with that fell fast asleep, while Sir Lyonel watched over him.

Soon three knights came galloping past, and Sir Lyonel noticed that they were being pursued by a fourth knight, who was one of the most powerful he had yet seen. The pursuing knight overtook each of the others in turn, and as he did so, knocked each off his horse with a thrust of his spear. When all three lay stunned he dismounted,

From *Le Morte D'Arthur* by Sir Thomas Malory, translated into the English language by Keith Baines. Copyright © 1962 by Keith Baines. Reprinted by arrangement with NAL Penguin Inc., New York, New York. Abridged.

*The Tale of Sir Launcelot du Lake*   **349**

bound them securely to their horses with the reins, and led them away.

Without waking Sir Launcelot, Sir Lyonel mounted his horse and rode after the knight, and as soon as he had drawn close enough, shouted his challenge. The knight turned about and they charged at each other, with the result that Sir Lyonel was likewise flung from his horse, bound, and led away a prisoner.

The victorious knight, whose name was Sir Tarquine, led his prisoners to his castle, and there threw them on the ground, stripped them naked, and beat them with thorn twigs. After that he locked them in the dungeon where many other prisoners, who had received like treatment, were complaining dismally.

Meanwhile, Sir Ector de Marys,[1] who liked to accompany Sir Launcelot on his adventures, and finding him gone, decided to ride after him. Before long he came upon a forester.

"My good fellow, if you know the forest hereabouts, could you tell me in which direction I am most likely to meet with adventure?"

"Sir, I can tell you: Less than a mile from here stands a well-moated castle. On the left of the entrance you will find a ford where you can water your horse, and across from the ford a large tree from which hang the shields of many famous knights. Below the shields hangs a caldron, of copper and brass: strike it three times with your spear, and then surely you will meet with adventure—such, indeed, that if you survive it, you will prove yourself the foremost knight in these parts for many years."

"May God reward you!" Sir Ector replied.

The castle was exactly as the forester had described it, and among the shields Sir Ector recognized several as belonging to knights of the Round Table. After watering his horse, he knocked on the caldron and Sir Tarquine, who castle it was, appeared.

They jousted, and at the first encounter Sir

Ector sent his opponent's horse spinning twice about before he could recover.

"That was a fine stroke; now let us try again," said Sir Tarquine.

This time Sir Tarquine caught Sir Ector just below the right arm and, having impaled him on his spear, lifted him clean out of the saddle, and rode with him into the castle, where he threw him on the ground.

"Sir," said Sir Tarquine, "you have fought better than any knight I have encountered in the last twelve years; therefore, if you wish, I will demand no more of you than your parole[2] as my prisoner."

"Sir, that I will never give."

"Then I am sorry for you," said Sir Tarquine, and with that he stripped and beat him and locked him in the dungeon with the other prisoners. There Sir Ector saw Sir Lyonel.

"Alas, Sir Lyonel, we are in a sorry plight. But tell me, what has happened to Sir Launcelot? for he surely is the one knight who could save us."

"I left him sleeping beneath an apple tree, and what has befallen him since I do not know," Sir Lyonel replied; and then all the unhappy prisoners once more bewailed their lot.

While Sir Launcelot still slept beneath the apple tree, four queens started across the plain. They were riding white mules and accompanied by four knights who held above them, at the tips of their spears, a green silk canopy, to protect them from the sun. The party was startled by the neighing of Sir Launcelot's horse and, changing direction, rode up to the apple tree, where they discovered the sleeping knight. And as each of the queens gazed at the handsome Sir Launcelot, so each wanted him for her own.

"Let us not quarrel," said Morgan le Fay.[3]

1. *Sir Ector de Marys*, Sir Launcelot's half-brother.
2. *parole*, word [*French*]; here, word of honor not to escape.
3. *Morgan le Fay*, a sorceress, half-sister of King Arthur.

Sir Launcelot is discovered, asleep, by the four queens, in a fourteenth-century manuscript illustration. The Bodleian Library, University of Oxford, England

"Instead, I will cast a spell over him so that he remains asleep while we take him to my castle and make him our prisoner. We can then oblige him to choose one of us for his paramour."

Sir Launcelot was laid on his shield and borne by two of the knights to the Castle Charyot, which was Morgan le Fay's stronghold. He awoke to find himself in a cold cell, where a young noblewoman was serving him supper.

"What cheer?" she asked.

"My lady, I hardly know, except that I must have been brought here by means of an enchantment."

"Sir, if you are the knight you appear to be, you will learn your fate at dawn tomorrow." And with that the young noblewoman left him. Sir Launcelot spent an uncomfortable night but at dawn the four queens presented themselves and Morgan le Fay spoke to him:

"Sir Launcelot, I know that Queen Gwynevere loves you, and you her. But now you are my prisoner, and you will have to choose: either to take one of us for your paramour, or to die miserably in this cell—just as you please. Now I will tell you who we are: I am Morgan le Fay, Queen of Gore; my companions are the Queens of North Galys, of Estelonde, and of the Outer Isles. So make your choice."

"A hard choice! Understand that I choose none of you, lewd sorceresses that you are; rather will I die in this cell. But were I free, I would take pleasure in proving it against any who would champion you that Queen Gwynevere is the finest lady of this land."

"So, you refuse us?" asked Morgan le Fay.

"On my life, I do," Sir Launcelot said finally, and so the queens departed.

Sometime later, the young noblewoman who had served Sir Launcelot's supper reappeared.

"What news?" she asked.

"It is the end," Sir Launcelot replied.

"Sir Launcelot, I know that you have refused the four queens, and that they wish to kill you out of spite. But if you will be ruled by me, I can save you. I ask that you will champion my father at a tournament next Tuesday, when he has to combat the King of North Galys, and three knights of the Round Table, who last Tuesday defeated him ignominiously."

"My lady, pray tell me, what is your father's name?"

"King Bagdemagus."

"Excellent, my lady, I know him for a good king and a true knight, so I shall be happy to serve him."

"May God reward you! And tomorrow at dawn I will release you, and direct you to an abbey which is ten miles from here, and where the good monks will care for you while I fetch my father."

"I am at your service, my lady."

As promised, the young noblewoman released Sir Launcelot at dawn. When she had led him through the twelve doors to the castle entrance, she gave him his horse and armor, and directions for finding the abbey.

"God bless you, my lady; and when the time comes I promise I shall not fail you."

Sir Launcelot rode through the forest in search of the abbey, but at dusk had still failed to find it, and coming upon a red silk pavilion, apparently unoccupied, decided to rest there overnight, and continue his search in the morning. . . .

As soon as it was daylight, Sir Launcelot armed, mounted, and rode away in search of the abbey, which he found in less than two hours. King Bagdemagus' daughter was waiting for him, and as soon as she heard his horse's footsteps in the yard, ran to the window, and, seeing that it was Sir Launcelot, herself ordered the servants to stable his horse. She then led him to her chamber, disarmed him, and gave him a long gown to wear, welcoming him warmly as she did so.

King Bagdemagus' castle was twelve miles away, and his daughter sent for him as soon as she had settled Sir Launcelot. The king arrived with his retinue[4] and embraced Sir Launcelot, who then described his recent enchantment, and the great obligation he was under to his daughter for releasing him.

"Sir, you will fight for me on Tuesday next?"

"Sire, I shall not fail you; but please tell me the names of the three Round Table knights whom I shall be fighting."

"Sir Modred, Sir Madore de la Porte, and Sir Gahalantyne. I must admit that last Tuesday they defeated me and my knights completely."

"Sire, I hear that the tournament is to be fought within three miles of the abbey. Could you send me three of your most trustworthy knights, clad in plain armor, and with no device,[5] and a fourth suit of armor which I myself shall wear? We will take up our position just outside the tournament field and watch while you and the King of North Galys enter into combat with your followers; and then, as soon as you are in difficulties, we will come to your rescue, and show your opponents what kind of knights you command."

This was arranged on Sunday, and on the following Tuesday Sir Launcelot and the three knights of King Bagdemagus waited in a copse,[6] not far from the pavilion which had been erected for the lords and ladies who were to judge the tournament and award the prizes.

The King of North Galys was the first on the field, with a company of ninescore[7] knights; he was followed by King Bagdemagus with fourscore[8] knights, and then by the three knights of the Round Table, who remained apart from both companies. At the first encounter King Bagdemagus lost twelve knights, all killed, and the King of North Galys six.

With that, Sir Launcelot galloped on to the

---

4. *retinue,* followers, including friends, companions, and servants.
5. *device,* heraldic emblem of identification.
6. *copse,* clump of trees.
7. *ninescore,* nine times twenty, or 180.
8. *fourscore,* four times twenty, or 80.

field, and with his first spear unhorsed five of the King of North Galys' knights, breaking the backs of four of them. With his next spear he charged the king, and wounded him deeply in the thigh.

"That was a shrewd blow," commented Sir Madore, and galloped onto the field to challenge Sir Launcelot. But he too was tumbled from his horse, and with such violence that his shoulder was broken.

Sir Modred was the next to challenge Sir Launcelot, and he was sent spinning over his horse's tail. He landed head first, his helmet became buried in the soil, and he nearly broke his neck, and for a long time lay stunned.

Finally Sir Gahalantyne tried; at the first encounter both he and Sir Launcelot broke their spears, so both drew their swords and hacked vehemently at each other. But Sir Launcelot, with mounting wrath, soon struck his opponent a blow on the helmet which brought the blood streaming from eyes, ears, and mouth. Sir Gahalantyne slumped forward in the saddle, his horse panicked, and he was thrown to the ground, useless for further combat.

Sir Launcelot took another spear, and unhorsed sixteen more of the King of North Galys' knights, and with his next, unhorsed another twelve; and in each case with such violence that none of the knights ever fully recovered. The King of North Galys was forced to admit defeat, and the prize was awarded to King Bagdemagus.

That night Sir Launcelot was entertained as the guest of honor by King Bagdemagus and his daughter at their castle, and before leaving was loaded with gifts.

"My lady, please, if ever again you should need my services, remember that I shall not fail you."

The next day Sir Launcelot rode once more through the forest, and by chance came to the apple tree where he had previously slept. This time he met a young noblewoman riding a white palfrey.

"My lady, I am riding in search of adventure; pray tell me if you know of any I might find hereabouts."

"Sir, there are adventures hereabouts if you believe that you are equal to them; but please tell me, what is your name?"

"Sir Launcelot du Lake."

"Very well, Sir Launcelot, you appear to be a sturdy enough knight, so I will tell you. Not far away stands the castle of Sir Tarquine, a knight who in fair combat has overcome more than sixty opponents whom he now holds prisoner. Many are from the court of King Arthur, and if you can rescue them, I will then ask you to deliver me and my companions from a knight who distresses us daily, either by robbery or by other kinds of outrage."

"My lady, please first lead me to Sir Tarquine, then I will most happily challenge this miscreant knight of yours."

When they arrived at the castle, Sir Launcelot watered his horse at the ford, and then beat the caldron until the bottom fell out. However, none came to answer the challenge, so they waited by the castle gate for half an hour or so. Then Sir Tarquine appeared, riding toward the castle with a wounded prisoner slung over his horse, whom Sir Launcelot recognized as Sir Gaheris, Sir Gawain's brother and a knight of the Round Table.

"Good knight," said Sir Launcelot, "it is known to me that you have put to shame many of the knights of the Round Table. Pray allow your prisoner, who I see is wounded, to recover, while I vindicate the honor of the knights whom you have defeated."

"I defy you, and all your fellowship of the Round Table," Sir Tarquine replied.

"You boast!" said Sir Launcelot.

At the first charge the backs of the horses were broken and both knights stunned. But they soon recovered and set to with their swords, and both struck so lustily[9] that neither shield nor armor could resist, and within two hours they were cutting each other's flesh, from which the blood flowed liberally. Finally they paused for a moment, resting on their shields.

"Worthy knight," said Sir Tarquine, "pray hold your hand for a while, and if you will, answer my question."

"Sir, speak on."

"You are the most powerful knight I have fought yet, but I fear you may be the one whom in the whole world I most hate. If you are not, for the love of you I will release all my prisoners and swear eternal friendship."

"What is the name of the knight you hate above all others?"

"Sir Launcelot du Lake; for it was he who slew my brother, Sir Carados of the Dolorous Tower, and it is because of him that I have killed a hundred knights, and maimed as many more, apart from the sixty-four I still hold prisoner. And so, if you are Sir Launcelot, speak up, for we must then fight to the death."

"Sir, I see now that I might go in peace and good fellowship, or otherwise fight to the death; but being the knight I am, I must tell you: I am Sir Launcelot du Lake, son of King Ban of Benwick, of Arthur's court, and a knight of the Round Table. So defend yourself!"

"Ah! this is most welcome."

Now the two knights hurled themselves at each other like two wild bulls; swords and shields clashed together, and often their swords drove into the flesh. Then sometimes one, sometimes the other, would stagger and fall, only to recover immediately and resume the contest. At last, however, Sir Tarquine grew faint, and unwittingly lowered his shield. Sir Launcelot was swift to follow up his advantage, and dragging the other down to his knees, unlaced his helmet and beheaded him.

Sir Launcelot then strode over to the young noblewoman: "My lady, now I am at your service, but first I must find a horse."

Then the wounded Sir Gaheris spoke up: "Sir, please take my horse. Today you have overcome the most formidable knight, excepting only yourself, and by so doing have saved us all. But before leaving, please tell me your name."

"Sir Launcelot du Lake. Today I have fought to vindicate the honor of the knights of the Round Table, and I know that among Sir Tarquine's prisoners are two of my brethren, Sir Lyonel and Sir Ector, also your own brother, Sir Gawain. According to the shields there are also: Sir Brandiles, Sir Galyhuddis, Sir Kay, Sir Alydukis, Sir Marhaus, and many others. Please release the prisoners and ask them to help themselves to the castle treasure. Give them all my greetings and say I will see them at the next Pentecost. And please request Sir Ector and Sir Lyonel to go straight to the court and await me there."

When Sir Launcelot had ridden away with the young noblewoman, Sir Gaheris entered the castle, and finding the porter[10] in the hall, threw him on the ground and took the castle keys. He then released the prisoners, who, seeing his wounds, thanked him for their deliverance.

"Do not thank me for this work, but Sir Launcelot. He sends his greetings to you all, and asks you to help yourselves to the castle treasure. He has ridden away on another quest, but said that he will see you at the next Pentecost." . . .

Sir Launcelot returned to Camelot two days before the feast of Pentecost, and at the court was acclaimed by many of the knights he had met on his adventures.

Sir Gaheris described to the court the terrible battle Sir Launcelot had fought with Sir Tarquine, and how sixty-four prisoners had been freed as a result of his victory.

---

9. *lustily,* vigorously.
10. *porter,* gatekeeper.

Sir Launcelot relates his adventures to Arthur and Gwynevere at the Whitsuntide, or Pentecost, feast, in a French manuscript illustration, circa 1316. The British Library, London

Sir Kay related how Sir Launcelot had twice saved his life, and then exchanged armor with him, so that he should ride unchallenged.

Sir Gawtere, Sir Gylmere, and Sir Raynolde described how he had defeated them at the bridge, and forced them to yield as prisoners of Sir Kay; and they were overjoyed to discover that it had been Sir Launcelot nevertheless.

Sir Modred, Sir Mador, and Sir Gahalantyne described his tremendous feats in the battle against the King of North Galys; and Sir Launcelot himself described his enchantment by the four queens, and his rescue at the hands of the daughter of King Bagdemagus. . . .

And thus it was, at this time, that Sir Launcelot became the most famous knight at King Arthur's court.

# *from* The Once and Future King

**T. H. White**   Great Britain

---

**This modern retelling of the Arthurian legends, often in popular, irreverent prose, has become a classic work of the imagination, taking the stiffness out of the legend and bringing the characters to rollicking life. This episode is from "The Ill-made Knight," the tale of Sir Lancelot.[1] By rejecting the attentions of the four queens who have kidnapped him, the knight has insulted them all. He is about to receive help from the daughter of King Bagdemagus.**

---

hen the fair damsel came in with the next meal, she showed signs of wanting to talk to him. Lancelot noticed that she was a bold creature, who was probably fond of getting her own way.

"You said you might be able to help me?"

The girl looked suspiciously at him and said: "I can help you if you are who you are supposed to be. Are you really Sir Lancelot?"

"I am afraid I am."

"I will help you," she said, "if you will help me."

Then she burst into tears.

While the damsel is weeping, which she did in a charming and determined way, we had better explain about the tournaments which used to take place in Gramarye in the early days. A real tournament was distinct from a joust. In a joust the knights tilted or fenced with each other singly, for a prize. But a tournament was more like a free fight. A body of knights would pick sides, so that there were twenty or thirty on either side, and then they would rush together harum-scarum. These mass battles were considered to be impor-tant—for instance, once you had paid your green fee for the tournament, you were admitted on the same ticket to fight in the jousts—but if you had only paid the jousting fee, you were not allowed to fight in the tourney. People were liable to be dangerously injured in the mêlées. They were not bad things altogether, provided they were properly controlled. Unfortunately, in the early days, they were seldom controlled at all.

Merry England in Pendragon's time was a little like Poor Ould Ireland in O'Connell's.[2] There were factions. The knights of one county, or the inhabitants of one district, or the retainers of one nobleman, might get themselves into a state in which they felt a hatred for the faction which lived

---

1. *Lancelot,* modern spelling of Launcelot. This episode is White's version of an incident in Malory's "Tale of Sir Launcelot du Lake."
2. *Pendragon's time . . . O'Connell's.* Pendragon is Uther Pendragon, Arthur's father. "Poor, old Ireland" in the time of Daniel O'Connell (1775–1847), Irish leader known as the "Liberator," was wracked by battles for the freedom of Ireland from Great Britain.

next door. This hatred would become a feud, and then the king or leader of the one place would challenge the leader of the other one to a tourney—and both factions would go to the meeting with full intent to do each other mischief. It was the same in the days of Papist and Protestant, or Stuart and Orangeman,[3] who would meet together with shillelaghs[4] in their hands and murder in their hearts.

"Why are you crying?" asked Sir Lancelot.

"Oh dear," sobbed the damsel. "That horrid King of Northgalis has challenged my father to a tournament next Tuesday, and he has got three knights of King Arthur's on his side, and my poor father is bound to lose. I am afraid he will get hurt."

"I see. And what is your father's name?"

"He is King Bagdemagus."

Sir Lancelot got up and kissed her politely on the forehead. He saw at once what he was expected to do.

"Very well," he said. "If you can rescue me out of this prison, I will fight in the faction of King Bagdemagus next Tuesday."

"Oh, thank you," said the maiden, wringing

---

**3. Papist and Protestant, or Stuart and Orangeman,** references to religious disputes and wars in British history between Roman Catholics (sometimes called Papists by opponents) and Protestants. The royal Stuart family included James II, who reigned 1685–1688 and had Catholic sympathies. He was forcibly replaced by the Protestant William of Orange, whose reign lasted 1689–1702.
**4. shillelaghs** (shə lā′ lēz), clubs used in fights.

This tapestry by Edward Burne-Jones and William Morris, *The Arming of the Knights* (detail), was woven during the Victorian era in nineteenth-century England. City Museums and Art Gallery, Birmingham, England.

out her handkerchief. "Now I must go, I am afraid, or they will miss me downstairs."

Naturally she was not going to help the magic Queen of Northgalis to keep Lancelot in prison— when it was the King of Northgalis himself who was going to fight her father. . . .

There is no need to give a long description of the tourney. Malory gives it. Lancelot picked three knights who were recommended by the young damsel to go with him, and he arranged that all four of them should bear the vergescu. This was the white shield carried by unfledged knights, and Lancelot insisted on this arrangement because he knew that three of his own brethren of the Round Table were going to fight on the other side. He did not want them to recognize him, because it might cause ill-feeling at court. On the other hand, he felt that it was his duty to fight against them because of the promise which he had given to the damsel. The King of Northgalis, who was the leader of the opposite side, had one hundred and sixty knights in his faction, and King Bagdemagus only had eighty. Lancelot went for the first knight of the Round Table, and put his shoulder out of joint. He went for the second one so hard that the unlucky fellow was carried over his horse's tail and buried his helm several inches in the ground. He hit the third knight on the head so hard that his nose bled, and his horse ran away with him. By the time he had broken the thigh of the King of Northgalis, everybody could see that to all intents and purposes the tournament was over.

---

## THINK AND DISCUSS
### THE TALE OF SIR LAUNCELOT DU LAKE
### Understanding
1. How does Launcelot become imprisoned?
2. Who helps him escape? Why?
3. What choice does Tarquine give Launcelot during their combat? How does Launcelot respond?
4. What is Launcelot's reputation as a result of these adventures?

### Analyzing
5. How does the episode with Sir Tarquine show Launcelot living up to the oath of the Round Table? What other qualities does he display?
6. Launcelot reveals his true identity to Tarquine, but keeps his name secret from the three Round Table knights that he fights. How do you account for this difference?

### Extending
7. What similarities do you see between the adventures of Launcelot and the exploits of television and movie heroes (such as western pioneers, doctors, nurses, detectives, secret agents, and space explorers)?
8. Are there any real-life persons that you would consider modern-day knights? Explain.

### FROM THE ONCE AND FUTURE KING
### Understanding
1. What is Lancelot's first impression of King Bagdemagus's daughter?

2. According to the narrator, why is there "no need" for a long description of the tourney?

**Analyzing**

3. Compare White's description of a typical tourney with Malory's description of the tourney Launcelot won. What different **tone** do you sense in each?

4. According to the narrator, why were early tournaments violent and uncontrolled?

**Extending**

5. Consider the informal tone that White uses in his version. Does this informality tend to make events more realistic, in your opinion, or does it make the story less effective? Explain.

**APPLYING: Allusion** H𝓣

**See Handbook of Literary Terms, p. 789**

An **allusion** is a reference to a fictitious, mythical, or real event, person, or place—or to a work of literature or art. Such references can help a reader understand more clearly; they also create richer emotional impressions.

1. What allusions do you find in the eighth paragraph of the T. H. White excerpt?

2. To what do the allusions refer?

3. What associations do the allusions have in common? How are they relevant to the time of Pendragon?

**THINKING SKILLS**

**Generalizing**

To **generalize** is to draw a general conclusion from particular information. Generalizations often include words such as *all, most, none, usually,* and *always.* You can state thoughtful generalizations as you answer these questions by drawing conclusions from the Arthurian legends you have read so far.

1. Considering the number and reputations of the knights of the Round Table, do you think most people in Arthur's realm were knights? Give reasons for your answer.

2. Did knights usually or always travel armed? Again, explain your answer.

**COMPOSITION**  ◄━━

**Reading/Writing Log**

In "The Tale of Sir Launcelot du Lake," Malory provides several examples of sentences built for emphasis in combat scenes. Copy the following heading and example in your reading/ writing log or on another paper. Then find at least one more example in the story and add your examples to the log.

*Sentences Built for Emphasis*

"Sir Launcelot took another spear, and unhorsed sixteen more of the King of North Galys' knights, and with his next, unhorsed another twelve; and in each case with such violence that none of the knights ever fully recovered."

**Retelling a Launcelot Adventure**

Choose one episode from Launcelot's story and retell it in a modern setting. Suppose, for example, that King Bagdemagus were the owner of a professional football team. How would "Lance Lake" be able to assist him? Or imagine Bagdemagus as a business owner under heavy pressure from competitors. What role would "Lance" play in that modern situation? Take time to fully imagine the episode in its modern setting. As you write, make your retelling as vivid as possible by building your sentences and paragraphs for emphasis.

**Writing a Character Sketch**

In a paper of three to four paragraphs, describe the character of Sir Launcelot. How does he respond to temptation? to the challenge of deadly combat? to a young woman in distress? In your final paragraph, give your opinion of Launcelot as the "supreme" knight of the Round Table.

 **BIOGRAPHY**

## T. H. White
## 1906–1964

His early career as a schoolteacher may have given Terence Hanbury White his rare gift for writing books that in their simplicity and charm appeal equally to adults and children. Born in Bombay, India, White won first-class honors at Cambridge University and taught school in England until, at thirty, he became a full-time writer. White began his reworking of Malory's Arthurian stories with *The Sword in the Stone* (1939). Other installments appeared over the years until *The Once and Future King* was published as a complete work in 1958. White's novel was the basis for *Camelot,* a Broadway musical in 1960 and a film in 1967. An animated Disney film was made of *The Sword in the Stone* in 1963.

## *Comment*

### Malory and Middle English

Although T. H. White wrote in modern English, Sir Thomas Malory wrote *Morte d'Arthur* in a dialect of Middle English. The passage at the right describes—in Malory's original language—a scene you will encounter in the next selection. The passage concerns Sir Bedivere's casting the sword Excalibur back into the lake from which Arthur once got it. You may wish to try reading this passage aloud and then modernizing it before comparing it to Keith Baines's version on page 366.

Than sir Bedwere departed and wente to the swerde and lyghtly toke hit up, and so he wente unto the watirs syde. And there he bounde the gyrdyll aboute the hyltis, and threw the swerde as farre into the watir as he myght. And there cam an arme and an honde above the watir, and toke hit and cleyght hit, and shoke hit thryse and braundysshed, and than vanysshed with the swerde into the watir.

**HZ** Review ALLUSION in the Handbook of Literary Terms, page 789.

# The Death of King Arthur

**Sir Thomas Malory**   Great Britain

*Translated by* Keith Baines

**The beginning of the end of Arthur's reign comes with the discovery by knights of the Round Table of the love between Launcelot and Gwynevere. Arthur feels forced by law to burn his wife at the stake. Launcelot saves Gwynevere at the last moment, but in the process kills two brothers of Gawain, Arthur's favorite nephew. Arthur leads an attack on Launcelot in France, but Launcelot seriously wounds Gawain. While Arthur is away in France, Modred, Arthur's mean-spirited illegitimate son, seizes the throne. Arthur hastens back to England.**

uring the absence of King Arthur from Britain, Sir Modred, already vested with sovereign powers, had decided to usurp the throne. Accordingly, he had false letters written—announcing the death of King Arthur in battle—and delivered to himself. Then, calling a parliament, he ordered the letters to be read and persuaded the nobility to elect him king. The coronation took place at Canterbury and was celebrated with a fifteen-day feast.

Sir Modred then settled in Camelot and made overtures to Queen Gwynevere to marry him. The queen seemingly acquiesced, but as soon as she had won his confidence, begged leave to make a journey to London in order to prepare her trousseau.[1] Sir Modred consented, and the queen rode straight to the Tower[2] which, with the aid of her loyal nobles, she manned and provisioned for her defense.

Sir Modred, outraged, at once marched against her, and laid siege to the Tower, but despite his large army, siege engines, and guns, was unable to effect a breach. He then tried to entice the queen

---

1. *trousseau* (trü sō′), a bride's outfit of linen, clothes, and jewelry.
2. *Tower*, Tower of London, a stronghold.

James Archer, *La Morte D'Arthur*, 1861, City Art Galleries, Manchester, England

from the Tower, first by guile and then by threats, but she would listen to neither. Finally the Archbishop of Canterbury came forward to protest:

"Sir Modred, do you not fear God's displeasure? . . . If you do not revoke your evil deeds I shall curse you with bell, book, and candle."[3]

"Fie on you! Do your worst!" Sir Modred replied.

"Sir Modred, I warn you take heed! or the wrath of the Lord will descend upon you."

"Away, false priest, or I shall behead you!"

The Archbishop withdrew, and after excommunicating[4] Sir Modred, abandoned his office and fled to Glastonbury. There he took up his abode as a simple hermit, and by fasting and prayer sought divine intercession in the troubled affairs of his country.

Sir Modred tried to assassinate the Archbishop, but was too late. He continued to assail the queen with entreaties and threats, both of which failed, and then the news reached him that King Arthur was returning with his army from France in order to seek revenge.

Sir Modred now appealed to the barony[5] to support him, and it has to be told that they came forward in large numbers to do so. Why? it will be asked. Was not King Arthur, the noblest sov-

---

**3.** *curse you with bell, book, and candle*, expel you from the church by ritualistic use of these items.
**4.** *excommunicating*, severing from membership in the church.
**5.** *barony*, lower ranks of nobles.

ereign Christendom had seen, now leading his armies in a righteous cause? The answer lies in the people of Britain, who, then as now, were fickle. Those who so readily transferred their allegiance to Sir Modred did so with the excuse that whereas King Arthur's reign had led them into war and strife, Sir Modred promised them peace and festivity.

Hence it was with an army of a hundred thousand that Sir Modred marched to Dover[6] to battle against his own father, and to withhold from him his rightful crown.

As King Arthur with his fleet drew into the harbor, Sir Modred and his army launched forth in every available craft, and a bloody battle ensued in the ships and on the beach. If King Arthur's army were the smaller, their courage was the higher, confident as they were of the righteousness of their cause. Without stint they battled through the burning ships, the screaming wounded, and the corpses floating on the blood-stained waters. Once ashore they put Sir Modred's entire army to flight.

The battle over, King Arthur began a search for his casualties, and on peering into one the of ships found Sir Gawain, mortally wounded. Sir Gawain fainted when King Arthur lifted him in his arms; and when he came to, the king spoke:

"Alas! dear nephew, that you lie here thus, mortally wounded! What joy is now left to me on this earth? You must know it was you and Sir Launcelot I loved above all others, and it seems that I have lost you both."

"My good uncle, it was my pride and my stubbornness that brought all this about, for had I not urged you to war with Sir Launcelot your subjects would not now be in revolt. Alas, that Sir Launcelot is not here, for he would soon drive them out! And it is at Sir Launcelot's hands that I suffer my own death: the wound which he dealt me has reopened. I would not wish it otherwise, because is he not the greatest and gentlest of knights?

"I know that by noon I shall be dead, and I repent bitterly that I may not be reconciled to Sir Launcelot; therefore I pray you, good uncle, give me pen, paper, and ink so that I may write to him."

A priest was summoned and Sir Gawain confessed;[7] then a clerk brought ink, pen, and paper, and Sir Gawain wrote to Sir Launcelot as follows:

"Sir Launcelot, flower of the knighthood: I, Sir Gawain, son of King Lot of Orkney and of King Arthur's sister, send you my greetings!

"I am about to die; the cause of my death is the wound I received from you outside the city of Benwick; and I would make it known that my death was of my own seeking, that I was moved by the spirit of revenge and spite to provoke you to battle.

"Therefore, Sir Launcelot, I beseech you to visit my tomb and offer what prayers you will on my behalf; and for myself, I am content to die at the hands of the noblest knight living.

"One more request: that you hasten with your armies across the sea and give succor[8] to our noble king. Sir Modred, his bastard son, has usurped the throne and now holds against him with an army of a hundred thousand. He would have won the queen, too, but she fled to the Tower of London and there charged her loyal supporters with her defense.

"Today is the tenth of May, and at noon I shall give up the ghost; this letter is written partly with my blood. This morning we fought our way ashore, against the armies of Sir Modred, and that is how my wound came to be reopened. We won the day, but my lord King Arthur needs you, and I too, that on my tomb you may bestow your blessing."

---

6. **Dover**, port city on southern English coast, across from France.
7. **confessed**, made his confession, a religious practice to ask God's forgiveness for sins, here in preparation for death.
8. **succor**, help and aid.

Sir Gawain fainted when he had finished, and the king wept. When he came to he was given extreme unction,[9] and died, as he had anticipated, at the hour of noon. The king buried him in the chapel at Dover Castle, and there many came to see him, and all noticed the wound on his head which he had received from Sir Launcelot.

Then the news reached Arthur that Sir Modred offered him battle on the field at Baron Down. Arthur hastened there with his army, they fought, and Sir Modred fled once more, this time to Canterbury.

When King Arthur had begun the search for his wounded and dead, many volunteers from all parts of the country came to fight under his flag, convinced now of the rightness of his cause. Arthur marched westward, and Sir Modred once more offered him battle. It was assigned for the Monday following Trinity Sunday,[10] on Salisbury Down.

Sir Modred levied fresh troops from East Anglia and the places about London, and fresh volunteers came forward to help Arthur. Then, on the night of Trinity Sunday, Arthur was vouchsafed[11] a strange dream:

He was appareled in gold cloth and seated in a chair which stood on a pivoted scaffold. Below him, many fathoms deep, was a dark well, and in the water swam serpents, dragons, and wild beasts. Suddenly the scaffold tilted and Arthur was flung into the water, where all the creatures struggled toward him and began tearing him limb from limb.

Arthur cried out in his sleep and his squires hastened to waken him. Later, as he lay between waking and sleeping, he thought he saw Sir Gawain, and with him a host of beautiful noblewomen. Arthur spoke:

"My sister's son! I thought you had died; but now I see you live, and I thank the lord Jesu! I pray you, tell me, who are these ladies?"

"My lord, these are the ladies I championed in righteous quarrels when I was on earth. Our lord God has vouchsafed that we visit you and plead with you not to give battle to Sir Modred tomorrow, for if you do, not only will you yourself be killed, but all your noble followers too. We beg you to be warned, and to make a treaty with Sir Modred, calling a truce for a month, and granting him whatever terms he may demand. In a month Sir Launcelot will be here, and he will defeat Sir Modred."

Thereupon Sir Gawain and the ladies vanished, and King Arthur once more summoned his squires and his counselors and told them his vision. Sir Lucas and Sir Bedivere were commissioned to make a treaty with Sir Modred. They were to be accompanied by two bishops and to grant, within reason, whatever terms he demanded.

The ambassadors found Sir Modred in command of an army of a hundred thousand and unwilling to listen to overtures of peace. However, the ambassadors eventually prevailed on him, and in return for the truce granted him suzerainty of Cornwall and Kent,[12] and succession to the British throne when King Arthur died. The treaty was to be signed by King Arthur and Sir Modred the next day. They were to meet between the two armies, and each was to be accompanied by no more than fourteen knights.

Both King Arthur and Sir Modred suspected the other of treachery, and gave orders for their armies to attack at the sight of a naked sword. When they met at the appointed place the treaty was signed and both drank a glass of wine.

Then, by chance, one of the soldiers was bitten

---

9. *extreme unction,* sacrament in the Roman Catholic Church in which a priest anoints the dying person with consecrated oil.
10. **Trinity Sunday,** feast day honoring the Holy Trinity, observed the eighth Sunday after Easter.
11. *vouchsafed,* granted.
12. **suzerainty of Cornwall and Kent,** dominion or power over two southern counties of England.

in the foot by an adder[13] which had lain concealed in the brush. The soldier unthinkingly drew his sword to kill it, and at once, as the sword flashed in the light, the alarums were given, trumpets sounded, and both armies galloped into the attack.

"Alas for this fateful day!" exclaimed King Arthur, as both he and Sir Modred hastily mounted and galloped back to their armies. There followed one of those rare and heartless battles in which both armies fought until they were destroyed. King Arthur, with his customary valor, led squadron after squadron of cavalry into the attack, and Sir Modred encountered him unflinchingly. As the number of dead and wounded mounted on both sides, the active combatants continued dauntless until nightfall, when four men alone survived.

King Arthur wept with dismay to see his beloved followers fallen; then, struggling toward him, unhorsed and badly wounded, he saw Sir Lucas the Butler and his brother, Sir Bedivere.

"Alas!" said the king, "that the day should come when I see all my noble knights destroyed! I would prefer that I myself had fallen. But what has become of the traitor Sir Modred, whose evil ambition was responsible for this carnage?"

Looking about him King Arthur then noticed Sir Modred leaning with his sword on a heap of the dead.

"Sir Lucas, I pray you give me my spear, for I have seen Sir Modred."

"Sire, I entreat you, remember your vision—how Sir Gawain appeared with a heaven-sent message to dissuade you from fighting Sir Modred. Allow this fateful day to pass; it is ours, for we three hold the field, while the enemy is broken."

"My lords, I care nothing for my life now! And while Sir Modred is at large I must kill him: there may not be another chance."

"God speed you, then!" said Sir Bedivere.

When Sir Modred saw King Arthur advance with his spear, he rushed to meet him with drawn sword. Arthur caught Sir Modred below the shield and drove his spear through his body; Sir Modred, knowing that the wound was mortal, thrust himself up to the handle of the spear, and then, brandishing his sword in both hands, struck Arthur on the side of the helmet, cutting through it and into the skull beneath; then he crashed to the ground, gruesome and dead.

King Arthur fainted many times as Sir Lucas and Sir Bedivere struggled with him to a small chapel nearby, where they managed to ease his wounds a little. When Arthur came to, he thought he heard cries coming from the battlefield.

"Sir Lucas, I pray you, find out who cries on the battlefield," he said.

Wounded as he was, Sir Lucas hobbled painfully to the field, and there in the moonlight saw the camp followers[14] stealing gold and jewels from the dead, and murdering the wounded. He returned to the king and reported to him what he had seen, and then added:

"My lord, it surely would be better to move you to the nearest town?"

"My wounds forbid it. But alas for the good Sir Launcelot! How sadly I have missed him today! And now I must die—as Sir Gawain warned me I would—repenting our quarrel with my last breath."

Sir Lucas and Sir Bedivere made one further attempt to lift the king. He fainted as they did so. Then Sir Lucas fainted as part of his intestines broke through a wound in the stomach. When the king came to, he saw Sir Lucas lying dead with foam at his mouth.

"Sweet Jesu, give him succor!" he said. "This noble knight has died trying to save my life—alas that this was so!"

Sir Bedivere wept for his brother.

---

13. *adder*, small poisonous snake or viper.
14. *camp followers*, civilians who follow troops and sell their services as they can.

"Sir Bedivere, weep no more," said King Arthur, "for you can save neither your brother nor me; and I would ask you to take my sword Excalibur to the shore of the lake and throw it in the water. The return to me and tell me what you have seen."

"My lord, as you command, it shall be done."

Sir Bedivere took the sword, but when he came to the water's edge, it appeared so beautiful that he could not bring himself to throw it in, so instead he hid it by a tree, and then returned to the king.

"Sir Bedivere, what did you see?"

"My lord, I saw nothing but the wind upon the waves."

"Then you did not obey me; I pray you, go swiftly again, and this time fulfill my command."

Sir Bedivere went and returned again, but this time too he had failed to fulfil the king's command.

"Sir Bedivere, what did you see?"

"My lord, nothing but the lapping of the waves."

"Sir Bedivere, twice you have betrayed me! And for the sake only of my sword: it is unworthy of you! Now I pray you, do as I command, for I have not long to live."

This time Sir Bedivere wrapped the girdle[15] around the sheath and hurled it as far as he could into the water. A hand appeared from below the surface, took the sword, waved it thrice, and disappeared again. Sir Bedivere returned to the king and told him what he had seen.

"Sir Bedivere, I pray you now help me hence, or I fear it will be too late."

Sir Bedivere carried the king to the water's edge, and there found a barge in which sat many beautiful ladies with their queen. All were wearing black hoods, and when they saw the king, they raised their voices in a piteous lament.

"I pray you, set me in the barge," said the king.

Sir Bedivere did so, and one of the ladies laid the king's head in her lap; then the queen spoke to him:

"My dear brother, you have stayed too long: I fear that the wound on your head is already cold."

Thereupon they rowed away from the land and Sir Bedivere wept to see them go.

"My lord King Arthur, you have deserted me! I am alone now, and among enemies."

"Sir Bedivere, take what comfort you may, for my time is passed, and now I must be taken to Avalon for my wound to be healed. If you hear of me no more, I beg you pray for my soul."

The barge slowly crossed the water and out of sight while the ladies wept. Sir Bedivere walked alone into the forest and there remained for the night.

In the morning he saw beyond the trees of a copse a small hermitage. He entered and found a hermit kneeling down by a fresh tomb. The hermit was weeping as he prayed, and then Sir Bedivere recognized him as the Archbishop of Canterbury, who had been banished by Sir Modred.

"Father, I pray you, tell me, whose tomb is this?"

"My son, I do not know. At midnight the body was brought here by a company of ladies. We buried it, they lit a hundred candles for the service, and rewarded me with a thousand bezants."[16]

"Father, King Arthur lies buried in this tomb."

Sir Bedivere fainted when he had spoken, and when he came to he begged the Archbishop to allow him to remain at the hermitage and end his days in fasting and prayer.

"Father, I wish only to be near to my true liege."

"My son, you are welcome; and do I not recog-

---

15. *girdle*, a band encircling the waist, wider than a belt.
16. *bezants*, gold coins.

Aubrey Beardsley, Drawing for a 1909 edition of *Le Morte d'Arthur* (detail), The British Library, London

nize you as Sir Bedivere the Bold, brother to Sir Lucas the Butler?"

Thus the Archbishop and Sir Bedivere remained at the hermitage, wearing the habits of hermits and devoting themselves to the tomb with fasting and prayers of contrition.[17]

Such was the death of King Arthur as written down by Sir Bedivere. By some it is told that there were three queens on the barge: Queen Morgan le Fay, the Queen of North Galys, and the Queen of the Waste Lands; and others include the name of Nyneve, the Lady of the Lake who had served King Arthur well in the past, and had married the good knight Sir Pelleas.

In many parts of Britain it is believed that King Arthur did not die and that he will return to us and win fresh glory and the Holy Cross of our Lord Jesu Christ; but for myself I do not believe this, and would leave him buried peacefully in his tomb at Glastonbury, where the Archbishop of Canterbury and Sir Bedivere humbled themselves, and with prayers and fasting honored his memory. And inscribed on his tomb, men say, is this legend:

HIC IACET ARTHURUS,
REX QUONDAM REXQUE FUTURUS.[18]

---

17. *contrition*, repentance.
18. *HIC . . . FUTURUS*, "Here lies Arthur, the once and future king."

# *from* Idylls of the King

**Alfred, Lord Tennyson**   Great Britain

---

An idyll (ī′dl) is a poem, sometimes narrative and epic in scope.
Tennyson spent sixty years writing his idylls recounting the Arthurian
legends. Here he presents a scene from "The Passing of Arthur," in
which Arthur and Bedivere talk just before the dying king departs on
the barge for the mythical island of Avalon, here spelled Avilion.

---

Then loudly cried the bold Sir Bedivere:
"Ah! my Lord Arthur, whither shall I go?
Where shall I hide my forehead and my eyes?
For now I see the true old times are dead,
When every morning brought a noble chance,
And every chance brought out a noble knight.
400  Such times have been not since the light that led
The holy Elders with the gift of myrrh.[1]
But now the whole Round Table is dissolved
Which was an image of the mighty world,
And I, the last, go forth companionless,
And the days darken round me, and the years,
Among new men, strange faces, other minds."

And slowly answer'd Arthur from the barge:
"The old order changeth, yielding place to new,
And God fulfils himself in many ways,
410  Lest one good custom should corrupt the world.
Comfort thyself: what comfort is in me?
I have lived my life, and that which I have done
May He within himself make pure! but thou,
If thou shouldst never see my face again,
Pray for my soul. More things are wrought by
      prayer
Than this world dreams of. Wherefore, let thy voice
Rise like a fountain for me night and day.
For what are men better than sheep or goats
That nourish a blind life within the brain,
420  If, knowing God, they lift not hands of prayer

Both for themselves and those who call them friend?
For so the whole round earth is every way
Bound by gold chains about the feet of God.
But now farewell. I am going a long way
With these thou seest—if indeed I go—
For all my mind is clouded with a doubt—
To the island-valley of Avilion;
Where falls not hail, or rain, or any snow,
Nor ever wind blows loudly; but it lies
430  Deep-meadow'd, happy, fair with orchard lawns
And bowery hollows crown'd with summer sea,
Where I will heal me of my grievous wound."

So said he, and the barge with oar and sail
Moved from the brink, like some full-breasted
      swan
That, fluting a wild carol ere her death,
Ruffles her pure cold plume, and takes the flood
With swarthy webs. Long stood Sir Bedivere
Revolving many memories, till the hull
Look'd one black dot against the verge of dawn,
440  And on the mere[2] the wailing died away.

---

1. *holy Elders with the gift of myrrh,* the wise men in the
Gospel of Matthew who follow the star to Bethlehem to
offer the infant Jesus gifts of gold, frankincense, and myrrh
(a fragrant gum resin from the myrrh shrub used for
making incense, perfume, and medicine).
2. *mere,* sea.

"The Passing of Arthur" from *Idylls of the King* by Alfred, Lord
Tennyson, 1859.

## THINK AND DISCUSS

### THE DEATH OF KING ARTHUR

#### Understanding

1. Who is Modred and how does he begin his revolt against Arthur?
2. How does Sir Gawain make peace with Launcelot before he dies?
3. Both Arthur and Modred agree to avoid a final conflict. How then does the battle break out?
4. An enemy had stolen Excalibur's magic scabbard long before, leaving Arthur vulnerable to injury. How is he wounded?

#### Analyzing

5. How do Arthur's two dreams warn him of the future?
6. Why does Arthur engage in personal combat against Modred despite the warnings of dreams and friends?
7. With what details does Malory emphasize the grimness and savagery of the last battle?
8. Summarize how Bedivere returns Excalibur to its rightful place.
9. What details at the end of the passage suggest that Arthur is dead and buried?
10. What details suggest that Arthur might still be alive?
11. Explain the **paradox** in the words inscribed on Arthur's tomb, calling him "the once and future king."

#### Extending

12. In your opinion, could the tragic conclusion of Arthur's life have been avoided? Explain.
13. Why do you suppose the narrator records the legend that Arthur still lives, even though he himself does not believe it?

### FROM IDYLLS OF THE KING

#### Understanding

1. At what point in the story does this scene take place?

#### Analyzing

2. What emotions seem to dominate Bedivere in this scene?
3. What attitude toward his own fate is revealed in Arthur's speech to Bedivere?
4. What last request does Arthur make?

#### Extending

5. Like Malory, Tennyson leaves a glimmer of hope that Arthur might be healed and restored. Do you think this hope is a sentimental distraction or an essential part of the legend of Arthur? Explain.

### REVIEWING: Allusion  H✍
### See Handbook of Literary Terms, p. 789

As allusions call to mind persons, places, events, or works of literature or art, they may clarify meaning or enrich our appreciation of a work.

1. What allusion do you find in Bedivere's speech in the Tennyson excerpt?
2. What does Bedivere emphasize by this allusion?

### VOCABULARY
#### Synonyms

Replace each italicized word in the sentences below with a synonym from the list. You may have to change the form of the synonym to fit the sentence. You will not use all the words.

| | | |
|---|---|---|
| banish | levy | righteous |
| fickle | helm | pivot |

1. *Uncertain* weather postponed the battle.
2. Arthur *expelled* Launcelot from England.
3. Gawain *turned* to attack a new foe.
4. Modred *collected* fresh troops for a new battle against Arthur.
5. Arthur remains a model of a *just* leader.

## COMPOSITION

### Writing Arthur's Last Letter

Imagine that Arthur, like Gawain, had time to write one letter before he died. To whom do you think he would write? Gwynevere? Launcelot? his subjects? Would he be forgiving? accusing? consoling? encouraging? Choose a recipient for the letter; then write Arthur's last message.

### Analyzing a Poem

Read Tennyson's biography below. Considering that the poet probably wrote a version of "The Passing of Arthur" shortly after the death of Arthur Hallam, what similarities do you find between Hallam and the king? What similarities do you find between Tennyson's situation and Bedivere's? In a paper of several paragraphs, show how this scene from "The Passing of Arthur" reveals Tennyson's personal struggle to find consolation and meaning in life after the death of his friend.

## BIOGRAPHY

### Alfred, Lord Tennyson
### 1809–1892

Alfred Tennyson wrote poetry from childhood, training himself for the vocation of poet as another boy might train himself to be a doctor or an engineer. At nineteen Tennyson entered Cambridge University, where he became the friend of Arthur Hallam. Hallam, more than anyone else, believed in Tennyson's future as a poet and constantly encouraged his efforts. The sudden death of Hallam due to a brain injury in 1833 was a severe shock to Tennyson and the eventual source of some of his greatest poetry. In the years he took to recover, Tennyson wrote a series of poems meditating on the death; he also began a version of "The Passing of Arthur" during this time. Recognition came gradually, and it was not until he published *In Memoriam*, the Hallam elegies, in 1850 that he won great distinction. He was soon named Poet Laureate of England, a title he would hold for nearly half a century.

The first four poems of *Idylls of the King* were published in 1859. For most of the remainder of his long life Tennyson worked on the *Idylls*, gradually rounding out the epic of the Round Table in its days of glory and in its fall. The *Idylls* had much to do with making Tennyson the most popular poet England has ever known.

# Comment

## Was Arthur Buried at Glastonbury?

Is it fact or fiction? Did Arthur really live, and if so, how closely did he resemble the King Arthur of legend? We know that the legend tells how Arthur was taken to the Isle of Avalon for treatment of mortal wounds or to die. Some people say that Avalon really exists at a place in the south of England known as Glastonbury. Tourists can visit the gravesite, they say, and a few historians consider the claim possible.

Centuries ago Glastonbury was surrounded by marshes that made it seem to be a sort of island. Ancient Welsh legends tell of a British general who fought in the area of Glastonbury around the year 500. Later, in the twelfth century, a writer named Geoffrey of Monmouth wrote a history of the kings of Britain. He mixed folk tales and outright fiction into his historical chronicles, but the monks at Glastonbury Abbey believed Geoffrey's account of Arthur's reign. They came upon graves just south of the great chapel at the Abbey, and the exhumed bodies were judged to be those of Arthur and Gwynevere. The monks built a shrine that was visited by later English kings and queens before it was eventually destroyed and the bones scattered. When Sir Thomas Malory wrote his account of Arthur's adventures, he named Glastonbury as the legendary king's burial place. The site of the graves now bears a commemorative plaque.

The supposed gravesite of Arthur and Gwynevere at Glastonbury (left), and a statue of Arthur by Peter Vischer, from a design by Albrecht Dürer, at Innsbruck, Austria.

# THINKING CRITICALLY
# ABOUT LITERATURE

## UNIT 4   LEGENDS OF ARTHUR

### ■ CONCEPT REVIEW

The following passage contains some of the important ideas and literary elements found in this unit. The notes in the right-hand margin highlight some of these concepts and will help you think critically about your reading. Page numbers in the notes refer to applications of literary terms. These terms are discussed in depth in the Handbook of Literary Terms.

As related earlier, the uproar resulting from the betrayal of King Arthur by Launcelot and Gwynevere leads to the banishment of Launcelot. He returns to his father's home in Benwick, France. King Arthur and his armies pursue him there, with Sir Gawain determined to avenge the deaths of his two brothers, killed by Launcelot when he rescued Gwynevere. Gawain challenges Launcelot to personal combat.

# Gawain and Launcelot in Combat

**Sir Thomas Malory**   Great Britain

*Translated by* Keith Baines

"My lord Sir Launcelot: traitor to the king and to me, come forth if you dare and meet your mortal foe, instead of lurking like a coward in your castle!"

Sir Launcelot heard the challenge, and one of his kinsmen spoke to him:

"My lord, you must accept the challenge, or be shamed forever."

"Alas, that I should have to fight Sir Gawain!" said Sir Launcelot. "But now I am obliged to."

Sir Launcelot gave orders for his most powerful courser to be harnessed,

■ "Traitor" and "coward" are deadly insults to a knight's honor.

and when he had armed, rode to the tower and addressed King Arthur:

"My lord King Arthur, it is with a heavy heart that I set forth to do battle with one of your own blood; but now it is incumbent upon my honor to do so. For six months I have suffered your majesty to lay my lands waste and to besiege me in my own city. My courtesy is repaid with insults, so deadly and shameful that now I must by force of arms seek redress."

■ Launcelot sees himself as the injured party in his conflict with Arthur.

"Have done, Sir Launcelot, and let us to battle!" shouted Sir Gawain.

Sir Launcelot rode from the city at the head of his entire army. King Arthur was astonished at his strength and realized that Sir Launcelot had not been boasting when he claimed to have acted with forbearance. "Alas, that I should ever have come to war with him!" he said to himself.

■ Arthur's reaction is just what Launcelot intended by displaying his army.

It was agreed that the two combatants should fight to the death, with interference from none. Sir Launcelot and Sir Gawain then drew apart and galloped furiously together, and so great was their strength that their horses crashed to the ground and both riders were overthrown.

A terrible sword fight commenced, and each felt the might of the other as fresh wounds were inflicted with every blow. For three hours they fought with scarely a pause, and the blood seeped out from their armor and trickled to the ground. Sir Launcelot found to his dismay that Sir Gawain, instead of weakening, seemed to increase in strength as they proceeded, and he began to fear that he was battling not with a knight but with a fiend incarnate. He decided to fight defensively and to conserve his strength.

■ **Paradox** (page 336): Sir Gawain gains strength even as he fights a wearying battle.

■ **Allusion** (page 359): A fiend incarnate would be a demon in human form.

It was a secret known only to King Arthur and to Sir Gawain himself that his strength increased for three hours in the morning, reaching its zenith at noon, and waning again. This was due to an enchantment that had been cast over him by a hermit when he was still a youth. Often in the past, as now, he had taken advantage of this.

Thus when the hour of noon had passed, Sir Launcelot felt Sir Gawain's strength return to normal, and knew that he could defeat him.

"Sir Gawain, I have endured many hard blows from you these last three hours, but now beware, for I see that you have weakened, and it is I who am the stronger."

Thereupon Sir Launcelot redoubled his blows, and with one, catching Sir Gawain sidelong on the helmet, sent him reeling to the ground. Then he courteously stood back.

"Sir Launcelot, I still defy you!" said Sir Gawain from the ground. "Why do you not kill me now? for I warn you that if ever I recover I shall challenge you again."

■ Both knights reveal chivalrous qualities: Gawain, courage; Launcelot, mercy.

"Sir Gawain, by the grace of God I shall endure you again," Sir Launcelot replied, and then turned to the king:

"My liege, your expedition can find no honorable conclusion at these walls, so I pray you withdraw and spare your noble knights. Remember me

■ Launcelot's tone seems almost arrogant toward his liege.

with kindness and be guided, as ever, by the love of God."

"Alas!" said the king, "Sir Launcelot scruples to fight against me or those of my blood, and once more I am beholden to him."

Sir Launcelot withdrew to the city and Sir Gawain was taken to his pavilion, where his wounds were dressed. King Arthur was doubly grieved, by his quarrel with Sir Launcelot and by the seriousness of Sir Gawain's wounds.

■ Note that Arthur's only role in this passage is to express surprise and regret.

## THINK AND DISCUSS
### Understanding
1. How long has Launcelot been under siege in his castle?
2. How does Gawain provoke Launcelot to fight?
3. What does Arthur realize when he sees Launcelot's army?
4. Describe the fight between Gawain and Launcelot.
5. Why is Arthur "doubly grieved" at the end of this episode?

### Analyzing
6. In what ways is the fight between Gawain and Launcelot typical of the combats you have read about in this unit?
7. What knightly virtues does Launcelot display in this episode?
8. Much is made of Launcelot's honor in this passage. What dishonor concerning Launcelot, Arthur, and Gwynevere is curiously unmentioned by anyone in this episode?

### Extending
9. Considering the cause of the quarrel between them, do you think Launcelot's attitude toward Arthur is appropriate? Explain.

### REVIEWING LITERARY TERMS
#### Paradox
1. What paradox does Launcelot discover about Gawain's strength during the fight?

2. After Gawain's life is spared, Arthur feels obligated to Launcelot. In what sense is this a paradoxical situation?

#### Allusion
3. At one point in the fight, Launcelot fears he is "battling a fiend incarnate." Explain this allusion.

## ■ CONTENT REVIEW
### THINKING SKILLS
#### Classifying
1. This unit includes retellings of Arthurian stories by Stewart, White, and Tennyson. Based on these passages, which writer seems closest in detail and spirit to Malory's versions? Which writers make the greatest changes to Malory's materials?
2. Classify the following characters based on their contribution to the greatness of Arthur's reign, or to its downfall: Merlin, Sir Ector, Gwynevere, Launcelot, Modred. If you place any character in both categories, write a brief explanation of the paradox.

#### Generalizing
3. What is Merlin's role in Arthur's life from infancy to kingship? At what point does his role seem to lessen?
4. At several points in his life Arthur has knowledge of the future. What effect do these predictions generally have on Arthur's actions?

## Synthesizing

5. The novelist John Steinbeck was deeply influenced as a boy by reading the legend of King Arthur: "I think my sense of right and wrong . . . and any thought I may have against the oppressor and for the oppressed, came from this secret book." Do you think Steinbeck's experience was a typical one for readers first encountering the Arthurian legend? Was your first response to the Arthur stories similar to or different from Steinbeck's? Explain.

6. Imagine that a new film has been made based on Malory's stories and that the producers are concerned that no one will want to see a movie entitled *The Death of Arthur*. Write a new title for the movie based on Arthur's life. (Do *not* use the word *Camelot*.)

## Evaluating

7. Based on your readings in this unit, to what extent is Arthur an ideal or model leader? Would his qualities be valuable in a national leader today? Explain.

8. Identify three causes of Arthur's downfall. Then rank them, listing the most significant cause first. Be prepared to explain your choices.

## ■ COMPOSITION REVIEW

Choose one of the following assignments and write the composition.

### Writing a Letter to the Editor

Write a three- or four-paragraph letter to your local newspaper in which you compare a national leader now in the news with King Arthur. Begin by describing Arthur's leadership traits, then make a comparison to the abilities of the present leader. You might include your opinion of how Arthur might have handled some current problem.

### Explaining an Opinion

Consider the roles women and men play in the stories in this unit. Would you want to have been a woman in medieval times? Why or why not? (Choose the alternative question if you wish: Would you want to have been a man in medieval times?) Before writing a four-paragraph paper, review the stories and develop at least three reasons to support your opinion.

### Analyzing the Code of Chivalry

According to their code of chivalry, knights promise to be faithful to God and their liege lord, to be brave and fair in battle, and to protect women and children. How well do the knights you have read about live up to this code? Choose one knight from this unit and demonstrate in three or four paragraphs how well—or how poorly—he follows the code of chivalry.

### Writing a Summary

Write a three- to five-paragraph summary of Arthur's life from birth to Avalon. Remember to be brief and accurate, and to focus on the main events of his life. Write a title for this summary that expresses your overall impression of Arthur's life.

### Reviewing Writer's Craft: Build Sentences for Emphasis and Interest

Imagine that you are Sir Bedivere and are writing a letter to your wife describing Arthur's last fight with Modred. Take care to construct your sentences to achieve variety, emphasis, and power. Your letter should be at least four paragraphs long and should include details of the battlefield after the conflict is ended.

# EXPERIENCE IN SHORT FICTION

Mort Künstler, *Ellis Island* (detail), 1985, Private Collection

# PREVIEW

## UNIT 5    EXPERIENCE IN SHORT FICTION

**Features**
Reading for Realism, Fantasy, Satire
Writer's Craft: Use Language That
    Appeals to the Senses
Comment: An Artist Shares His Family Life
Comment: The Nobel Prize in Literature
Comment: A Gruesome Tale of
    Edgar Allan Poe

**Application of Literary Terms**
irony
symbol
stereotype
satire
mood

**Reading Literature Skillfully**
comparison/contrast

**Vocabulary Skills**
context
etymology
antonyms

**Thinking Skills**
classifying
generalizing
synthesizing
evaluating

**Composition Assignments Include**
Describing by Comparison
Writing a Persuasive Letter
Predicting Outcomes
Writing an Alternate Ending
Writing to Describe a Setting
Anticipating Reactions
Reading/Writing Log
Explaining a Character's Nature
Analyzing a Story's Ending
Judging a Character's Method
Making Analogies
Writing a Diary Entry
Writing Satire
Writing About Imagery
Writing About Theme
Offering Alternate Explanations
Writing About Mood

**Enrichment**
Reading with Musical Accompaniment
Researching Attitudes on Luck
Making a Speech
Drawing and Discussing Art
Creating a Portrait

**Thinking Critically About Literature**
Concept Review
Content Review
Composition Review

# *Reading* FOR REALISM, FANTASY, AND SATIRE

Realism, fantasy, and satire are styles used by authors to portray characters, events, and settings. Recognizing differences in these styles will help you understand fiction.

## Realism

*Realism* in literature is the attempt to describe the world and life without idealizing them. While another literary style called *Romanticism* shows an ideal world in which good people and ideas always prevail over evil, authors who prefer realism hold that virtue doesn't always triumph in life or in their art. Whereas in Romantic fiction the underdog regularly wins, picnics are never rained out, and stories have happy endings, realistic writers reject descriptions and outcomes that they judge too sentimental to be true. Realistic stories include objective descriptions that reflect the nasty and trivial details of life as well as the beautiful and the heroic.

Realistic writers may emphasize familiar actions and character traits that readers find consistent with their personal experience and observation. In "The Sentimentality of William Tavener," for example, readers can easily relate to the quiet conversations, daily struggles, and affectionate reminiscences of characters in an American farm family. Realistic characters have flaws; they are neither faultlessly heroic nor simply wicked.

Most critics and readers tend to judge realistic and Romantic stories individually, rather than considering either style itself to be superior.

## Fantasy

Writers of *fantasy* do not limit themselves to verifiable human experiences. They deliberately break from reality; their characters are not restricted to the bounds of human abilities and scientific laws. Like writers of science fiction, authors of fantastical literature try to stretch the reader's imagination beyond the familiar. In this unit you will read "The Rocking-Horse Winner" and "The Masque of the Red Death," two stories that transcend reality and take readers into the realm of fantasy.

## Satire

Writers of *satire* present a humorously critical view of the world or part of it. Their intentions generally are to improve social institutions, point out weaknesses in human nature, or just poke fun at behavior. "Action Will Be Taken," a story in this unit, provides a clear example of **satire** by exaggerating the attitudes and manners of some modern business people.

As you read the stories in Unit Five, you will notice that some stories may combine realistic elements with aspects of fantasy or satire. You also will notice that authors who write in any of these styles use **comparisons and contrasts** to make the stories more vivid and compelling. Characters, various settings, or events in a story can parallel one another or can differ markedly. Often the comparisons and contrasts support a realistic style. Sometimes they make fantasy or satire even more striking.

See IRONY in the Handbook of Literary Terms, page 804.

# The Necklace

**Guy de Maupassant**   France

---

**It was dazzlingly beautiful—and more costly than anyone could have imagined.**

She was one of those pretty, charming young ladies, born, as if through an error of destiny, into a family of clerks. She had no dowry, no hopes, no means of becoming known, appreciated, loved, and married by a man either rich or distinguished; and she allowed herself to marry a petty clerk in the office of the Board of Education.

She was simple, not being able to adorn herself, but she was unhappy, as one out of her class; for women belong to no caste, no race; their grace, their beauty, and their charm serving them in the place of birth and family. Their inborn finesse, their instinctive elegance, their suppleness of wit are their only aristocracy, making some daughters of the people the equal of great ladies.

She suffered incessantly, feeling herself born for all delicacies and luxuries. She suffered from the poverty of her apartment, the shabby walls, the worn chairs, and the faded stuffs. All these things, which another woman of her station would not have noticed, tortured and angered her. The sight of the little Breton,[1] who made this humble home, awoke in her sad regrets and desperate dreams. She thought of quiet antechambers with their Oriental hangings lighted by high bronze torches, and of the two great footmen in short trousers who sleep in the large armchairs, made sleepy by the heavy air from the heating apparatus. She thought of large drawing rooms hung in old silks, of graceful pieces of furniture carrying bric-a-brac of inestimable value, and of the little perfumed coquettish apartments made for five o'clock chats with most intimate friends, men known and sought after, whose attention all women envied and desired.

When she seated herself for dinner before the round table, where the tablecloth had been used three days, opposite her husband who uncovered the tureen with a delighted air, saying: "Oh! the

---

*Guy de Maupassant* (gē də mō pȧ säN′).

**1. Breton** (bret′n), a native of Brittany, a coastal region in western France.

William McGregor Paxton, *The Breakfast* (detail), 1911, Private Collection.

good potpie! I know nothing better than that," she would think of the elegant dinners, of the shining silver, of the tapestries peopling the walls with ancient personages and rare birds in the midst of fairy forests; she thought of the exquisite food served on marvelous dishes, of the whispered gallantries, listened to with the smile of the Sphinx while eating the rose-colored flesh of the trout or a chicken's wing.

She had neither frocks nor jewels, nothing. And she loved only those things. She felt that she was made for them. She had such a desire to please, to be sought after, to be clever and courted.

She had a rich friend, a schoolmate at the convent, whom she did not like to visit; she suffered so much when she returned. And she wept for whole days from chagrin, from regret, from despair and disappointment.

One evening her husband returned, elated, bearing in his hand a large envelope.

"Here," he said, "here is something for you."

She quickly tore open the wrapper and drew out a printed card on which were inscribed these words:

*The Minister of Public Instruction and Madame George Ramponneau ask the honor of M. and Mme. Loisel's[2] company Monday evening, January 18, at the Minister's residence.*

---

2. *Ramponneau* (ràm pə nō′) . . . *M. and Mme. Loisel's* (lwä zelz′). *M.* and *Mme.* are the abbreviations for *Monsieur* and *Madame*, respectively.

Instead of being delighted, as her husband had hoped, she threw the invitation spitefully upon the table, murmuring:

"What do you suppose I want with that?"

"But, my dearie, I thought it would make you happy. You never go out, and this is an occasion, and a fine one! I had a great deal of trouble to get it. Everybody wishes one, and it is very select; not many are given to employees. You will see the whole official world there."

She looked at him with an irritated eye and declared impatiently:

"What do you suppose I have to wear to such a thing as that?"

He had not thought of that; he stammered:

"Why, the dress you wear when we go to the theater. It seems very pretty to me."

He was silent, stupefied, in dismay, at the sight of his wife weeping. Two great tears fell slowly from the corners of her eyes toward the corners of her mouth; he stammered:

"What is the matter? What is the matter?"

By a violent effort she had controlled her vexation and responded in a calm voice, wiping her moist cheeks:

"Nothing. Only I have no dress and consequently I cannot go to this affair. Give your card to some colleague whose wife is better fitted out than I."

He was grieved but answered:

"Let us see, Matilda. How much would a suitable costume cost, something that would serve for other occasions, something very simple?"

She reflected for some seconds, making estimates and thinking of a sum that she could ask for without bringing with it an immediate refusal and a frightened exclamation from the economical clerk.

Finally she said in a hesitating voice:

"I cannot tell exactly, but it seems to me that four hundred francs[3] ought to cover it."

He turned a little pale, for he had saved just this sum to buy a gun that he might be able to join some hunting parties the next summer, on the plains at Nanterre,[4] with some friends who went to shoot larks up there on Sunday. Nevertheless, he answered:

"Very well. I will give you four hundred francs. But try to have a pretty dress."

The day of the ball approached, and *Mme.* Loisel seemed sad, disturbed, anxious. Nevertheless, her dress was nearly ready. Her husband said to her one evening:

"What is the matter with you? You have acted strangely for two or three days."

And she responded: "I am vexed not to have a jewel, not one stone, nothing to adorn myself with. I shall have such a poverty-laden look. I would prefer not to go to this party."

He replied: "You can wear some natural flowers. At this season they look very chic. For ten francs you can have two or three magnificent roses."

She was not convinced. "No," she replied, "there is nothing more humiliating than to have a shabby air in the midst of rich women."

Then her husband cried out: "How stupid we are! Go and find your friend *Madame* Forestier[5] and ask her to lend you her jewels. You are well enough acquainted with her to do this."

She uttered a cry of joy. "It is true!" she said. "I had not thought of that."

The next day she took herself to her friend's house and related her story of distress. *Mme.* Forestier went to her closet with the glass doors, took out a large jewel case, brought it, opened it, and said: "Choose, my dear."

She saw at first some bracelets, then a collar of

---

3. **four hundred francs,** about $240 in United States currency at the time of the story. The franc itself was worth about sixty cents.
4. *Nanterre* (näɴ ter′).
5. *Forestier* (fôr es tyā′).

pearls, then a Venetian cross of gold and jewels and of admirable workmanship. She tried the jewels before the glass, hesitated, but could neither decide to take them nor leave them. Then she asked:

"Have you nothing more?"

"Why, yes. Look for yourself. I do not know what will please you."

Suddenly she discovered in a black satin box a superb necklace of diamonds, and her heart beat fast with an immoderate desire. Her hands trembled as she took them up. She placed them about her throat, against her dress, and remained in ecstasy before them. Then she asked in a hesitating voice full of anxiety:

"Could you lend me this? Only this?"

"Why, yes, certainly."

She fell upon the neck of her friend, embraced her with passion, then went away with her treasure.

The day of the ball arrived. *Mme.* Loisel was a great success. She was the prettiest of all, elegant, gracious, smiling, and full of joy. All the men noticed her, asked her name, and wanted to be presented. All the members of the Cabinet wished to waltz with her. The Minister of Education paid her some attention.

She danced with enthusiasm, with passion, intoxicated with pleasure, thinking of nothing, in the triumph of her beauty, in the glory of her success, in a kind of cloud of happiness that came of all this homage and all this admiration, of all these awakened desires and this victory so complete and sweet to the heart of woman.

She went home toward four o'clock in the morning. Her husband had been half asleep in one of the little salons since midnight with three other gentlemen whose wives were enjoying themselves very much.

He threw around her shoulders the wraps they had carried for the coming home, modest garments of everyday wear, whose poverty clashed with the elegance of the ball costume. She felt this and wished to hurry away in order not to be noticed by the other women who were wrapping themselves in rich furs.

Loisel detained her. "Wait," said he. "You will catch cold out there. I am going to call a cab."

But she would not listen and descended the steps rapidly. When they were in the street they found no carriage, and they began to seek for one, hailing the coachmen whom they saw at a distance.

They walked along toward the Seine,[6] hopeless and shivering. Finally they found on the dock one of those old nocturnal coupés that one sees in Paris after nightfall, as if they were ashamed of their misery by day.

It took them as far as their door in Martyr Street, and they went wearily up to their apartment. It was all over for her. And on his part he remembered that he would have to be at the office by ten o'clock.

She removed the wraps from her shoulders before the glass for a final view of herself in her glory. Suddenly she uttered a cry. Her necklace was not around her neck.

Her husband, already half undressed, asked: "What is the matter?"

She turned toward him excitedly:

"I have—I have—I no longer have *Madame Forestier's* necklace."

He arose in dismay: "What! How is that? It is not possible."

And they looked in the folds of the dress, in the folds of the mantle, in the pockets, everywhere. They could not find it.

He asked: "You are sure you still had it when we left the house?"

"Yes, I felt it in the vestibule as we came out."

---

6. *Seine* (sān), river that flows through the center of Paris.

"But if you had lost it in the street we should have heard it fall. It must be in the cab."

"Yes. It is probable. Did you take the number?"

"No. And you, did you notice what it was?"

"No."

They looked at each other, utterly cast down. Finally Loisel dressed himself again.

"I am going," said he, "over the track where we went on foot, to see if I can find it."

And he went. She remained in her evening gown, not having the force to go to bed, stretched upon a chair, without ambition or thoughts.

Toward seven o'clock her husband returned. He had found nothing.

He went to the police and to the cab offices and put an advertisement in the newspapers, offering a reward; he did everything that afforded them a suspicion of hope.

She waited all day in a state of bewilderment before this frightful disaster. Loisel returned at evening, with his face harrowed and pale, and had discovered nothing.

"It will be necessary," said he, "to write to your friend that you have broken the clasp of the necklace and that you will have it repaired. That will give us time to turn around."

She wrote as he dictated.

At the end of a week they had lost all hope. And Loisel, older by five years, declared:

"We must take measures to replace this jewel."

The next day they took the box which had enclosed it to the jeweler whose name was on the inside. He consulted his books.

"It is not I, *Madame*," said he, "who sold this necklace; I only furnished the casket."

Then they went from jeweler to jeweler, seeking a necklace like the other one, consulting their memories, and ill, both of them, with chagrin and anxiety.

In a shop of the Palais-Royal[7] they found a chaplet of diamonds which seemed to them exactly like the one they had lost. It was valued at forty thousand francs. They could get it for thirty-six thousand.

They begged the jeweler not to sell it for three days. And they made an arrangement by which they might return it for thirty-four thousand francs if they found the other one before the end of February.

Loisel possessed eighteen thousand francs which his father had left him. He borrowed the rest.

He borrowed it, asking for a thousand francs of one, five hundred of another, five louis[8] of this one, and three louis of that one. He gave notes, made ruinous promises, took money of usurers and the whole race of lenders. He compromised his whole existence, in fact, risked his signature without even knowing whether he could make it good or not, and, harrassed by anxiety for the future, by the black misery which surrounded him, and by the prospect of all physical privations and moral torture, he went to get the new necklace, depositing on the merchant's counter thirty-six thousand francs.

When *Mme.* Loisel took back the jewels to *Mme.* Forestier the latter said to her in a frigid tone:

"You should have returned them to me sooner, for I might have needed them."

She did open the jewel box as her friend feared she would. If she should perceive the substitution what would she think? What should she say? Would she take her for a robber?

*Mme.* Loisel now knew the horrible life of necessity. She did her part, however, completely, heroically. It was necessary to pay this frightful

---

7. *Palais-Royal* (pà lā′ rwä yal′), a Parisian shopping district.

8. *louis* (lü′ē), a French gold coin equal in value to twenty francs. At the time of the story, five louis were worth about sixty dollars.

debt. She would pay it. They sent away the maid; they changed their lodgings; they rented some rooms under a mansard roof.

She learned the heavy cares of a household, the odious work of a kitchen. She washed the dishes, using her rosy nails upon the greasy pots and the bottoms of the stew pan. She washed the soiled linen, the chemises and dishcloths, which she hung on the line to dry; she took down the refuse to the street each morning and brought up the water, stopping at each landing to breathe. And, clothed like a woman of the people, she went to the grocer's, the butcher's, and the fruiterer's with her basket on her arm, shopping, haggling to the last sou[9] her miserable money.

Every month it was necessary to renew some notes, thus obtaining time, and to pay others.

The husband worked evenings, putting the books of some merchants in order, and nights he often did copying at five sous a page.

And this life lasted for ten years.

At the end of ten years they had restored all, all, with interest of the usurer, and accumulated interest, besides.

*Mme.* Loisel seemed old now. She had become a strong, hard woman, the crude woman of the poor household. Her hair badly dressed, her skirts awry, her hands red, she spoke in a loud tone and washed the floors in large pails of water. But sometimes, when her husband was at the office, she would seat herself before the window and think of that evening party of former times, of that ball where she was so beautiful and so flattered.

How would it have been if she had not lost that necklace? Who knows? Who knows? How singular is life and how full of changes! How small a thing will ruin or save one!

One Sunday, as she was taking a walk in the Champs Élysées[10] to rid herself of the cares of the week, she suddenly perceived a woman walking with a child. It was *Mme.* Forestier, still young, still pretty, still attractive. *Mme.* Loisel was affected. Should she speak to her? Yes, certainly. And now that she had paid, she would tell her all. Why not?

She approached her. "Good morning, Jeanne."

Her friend did not recognize her and was astonished to be so familiarly addressed by this common personage. She stammered:

"But, *Madame*—I do not know—You must be mistaken."

"No, I am Matilda Loisel."

Her friend uttered a cry of astonishment: "Oh! My poor Matilda! How you have changed."

"Yes, I have had some hard days since I saw you, and some miserable ones—and all because of you."

"Because of me? How is that?"

"You recall the diamond necklace that you loaned me to wear to the Minister's ball?"

"Yes, very well."

"Well, I lost it."

"How is that, since you returned it to me?"

"I returned another to you exactly like it. And it has taken us ten years to pay for it. You can understand that it was not easy for us who have nothing. But it is finished, and I am decently content."

*Mme.* Forestier stopped short. She said:

"You say that you bought a diamond necklace to replace mine?"

"Yes. You did not perceive it then? They were just alike?"

And she smiled with a proud and simple joy. *Mme.* Forestier was touched and took both her hands as she replied:

"Oh, my poor Matilda! Mine were false. They were not worth over five hundred francs!"

---

9. *sou* (sü), a former French coin that was worth one-twentieth of a franc, or about a penny.
10. *Champs Élysées* (shäṅ zä lē zā′), a famous avenue in Paris.

## THINK AND DISCUSS

### Understanding

1. Describe Matilda's feelings about her life as the story opens.
2. What two "problems" make Matilda unwilling to go to the party? How are they resolved?
3. What extra work do Matilda and her husband do to repay the debt? How long does it take?

### Analyzing

4. When using a surprise ending, a careful author provides clues preparing the reader to accept that ending. Name some clues that hint at the story's surprise ending.
5. How does the story's **point of view** help to keep the outcome secret?
6. In your opinion, are the things that happen to Matilda the result of fate or coincidence, or are they caused by her own character? Give reasons for your answer.
7. At the end of the story, the narrator asks, "How would it have been if she had not lost the necklace? . . . How small a thing will ruin or save one!" Explain in what way Matilda was both ruined and saved.

### Extending

8. In your opinion, is the ending of the story happy or unhappy? Discuss.

### APPLYING: Irony H𝕫

**See Handbook of Literary Terms, p. 804**

The ending of this story, as with many surprise endings, results in **irony** of situation: after working all those years to replace the necklace, Matilda finds out it was not worth so much. There are many small ironies throughout the story that make this ending even more poignant. Discuss the irony in each of the following incidents in "The Necklace."

1. Matilda's friend Mme. Forestier, whom she admires for her wealth, lends her a paste necklace.
2. Matilda is ecstatic at the party because it is her first glimpse of a lifestyle she earnestly desires for herself.
3. Matilda tells the story of replacing the lost necklace with dignity and pride.

## VOCABULARY

### Context

Using context clues, choose the correct meaning of the italicized word in each of the following sentences.

1. There is rarely a moment of silence in that house; everyone in the family seems to talk *incessantly*.
   (**a**) calmly; (**b**) continually; (**c**) argumentatively; (**d**) persuasively.
2. There is practically no sign of raccoons in our neighborhood during the day; however, their *nocturnal* activities—which often awaken us—never let us forget them.
   (**a**) unnoticeable; (**b**) mid-morning; (**c**) remarkably quiet; (**d**) nighttime.
3. Benedict hated to shovel snow, so this blizzard and the snowdrifts on the sidewalk seemed to him particularly *odious*.
   (**a**) hateful; (**b**) easy; (**c**) entertaining; (**d**) fair.
4. The *harrowed* look on her face showed that the incident had bothered her more than she had admitted.
   (**a**) delighted; (**b**) distressed; (**c**) confused; (**d**) confident.
5. By polishing her boots regularly, Lu had preserved the *suppleness* of the leather even after years of wear.
   (**a**) ability to bend easily; (**b**) ability to keep out cold; (**c**) color; (**d**) up-to-date style.

## COMPOSITION
### Describing by Comparison

In the opening paragraphs of "The Necklace," the author conveys Matilda's frustration and bitterness with descriptions that contrast her ordinary existence with the better life she dreams about. In a two-paragraph composition, describe first a real-life setting, situation, or lifestyle to which you are accustomed. In the second paragraph, write an idealized version of the same situation or setting. Describe it the way you would like it to be. Be sure to use specific contrasting details. Remember that each paragraph should reveal contrasting emotions as well as detailed descriptions.

### Writing a Persuasive Letter

While describing Matilda's success at the ball, Guy de Maupassant uses words that imply a great deal about how women feel in such circumstances. He describes Matilda as "intoxicated with pleasure . . . in a kind of cloud of happiness that came of all this homage and all this admiration . . . of this . . . victory so complete and sweet to the heart of woman." Decide whether you agree or disagree with the author's implication. Write a letter to Guy de Maupassant in which you comment about this aspect of his characterization of Matilda. You may want to suggest that he clarify whether the statement above is about all women or just Matilda. Support whatever opinion you express with convincing arguments and evidence from the story. Because the author died in 1893, you may deliver the letter to your teacher.

## ENRICHMENT
### Reading with Musical Accompaniment

Select an episode from "The Necklace" and then select appropriate background music which contributes to the desired mood. Read the selection to your classmates while the music plays. You might select several different musical backgrounds and have the class decide which one works best.

## BIOGRAPHY

### Guy de Maupassant
### 1850–1893

Called one of the most productive writers of all time, de Maupassant is best known as a master of short fiction. He is credited with the invention of the "whiplash ending," which he cunningly employs in "The Necklace."

Born in Normandy, France, de Maupassant was raised by a cultivated mother who knew the novelist Gustave Flaubert (flō ber′). At seventeen, the young man began what was to be a ten-year apprenticeship with the noted author, learning the craft of writing. His hundreds of short stories became examples of the form to readers worldwide. Often portraying the conflicts of average people, they are characterized by the author's detached tone, irony, and pessimism.

**Review IRONY in the Handbook of Literary Terms, page 804.**

# The Interlopers

**Saki**   Great Britain

"Each had a rifle in his hand; each had hate in his heart and murder uppermost in his mind."

In a forest of mixed growth somewhere on the eastern spurs of the Carpathians,[1] a man stood one winter night watching and listening, as though he waited for some beast of the woods to come within the range of his vision, and later, of his rifle. But the game for whose presence he kept so keen an outlook was none that figured in the sportsman's calendar as lawful and proper for the chase; Ulrich von Gradwitz[2] patrolled the dark forest in quest of a human enemy.

The forest lands of Gradwitz were of wide extent and well stocked with game; the narrow strip of precipitous woodland that lay on its outskirts was not remarkable for the game it harbored or the shooting it afforded, but it was the most jealously guarded of all its owner's territorial possessions. A famous lawsuit, in the days of his grandfather, had wrested it from the illegal possession of a neighboring family of petty landowners; the dispossessed party had never acquiesced in the judgment of the courts, and a long series of poaching affrays and similar scandals had embittered the relationships between the families for three generations. The neighbors' feud had grown into a personal one since Ulrich had come to be head of his family; if there was a man in the world whom he detested and wished ill to, it was Georg Znaeym,[3] the inheritor of the quarrel and the tireless game snatcher and raider of the disputed border forest.

The feud might, perhaps, have died down or been compromised if the personal ill will of the two men had not stood in the way; as boys they had thirsted for one another's blood; as men each prayed that misfortune might fall on the other; and this wind-scourged winter night Ulrich had banded together his foresters to watch the dark forest, not in quest of four-footed quarry but to keep a lookout for the prowling thieves whom he

---

1. *Carpathians* (kär pā′thē ənz), mountain chain extending from northern Romania to Czechoslovakia.
2. *Ulrich von Gradwitz* (ül′rik fən gräd′vits).
3. *Georg Znaeym* (gā′ôrg znä′im).

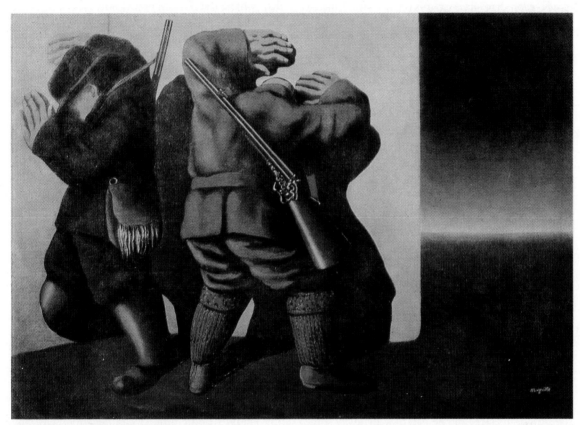

René Magritte, *Huntsmen on the Edge of Night*,
1928, Private Collection

suspected of being afoot from across the land boundary. The roebuck, which usually kept in the sheltered hollows during a storm-wind, were running like driven things tonight; and there was movement and unrest among the creatures that were wont to sleep through the dark hours. Assuredly there was a disturbing element in the forest, and Ulrich could guess the quarter from whence it came.

He strayed away by himself from the watchers whom he had placed in ambush on the crest of the hill, and wandered far down the steep slopes amid the wild tangle of undergrowth, peering through the tree trunks and listening through the whistling and skirling of the wind and the restless beating of the branches for sight or sound of the marauders. If only on this wild night, in this dark, lone spot, he might come across Georg Znaeym, man to man, with none to witness—that was the wish that was uppermost in his thoughts. And as he stepped round the trunk of a huge beech, he came face to face with the man he sought.

The two enemies stood glaring at one another for a long, silent moment. Each had a rifle in his hand; each had hate in his heart and murder uppermost in his mind. The chance had come to give full play to the passions of a lifetime. But a man who has been brought up under the code of a restraining civilization cannot easily nerve himself to shoot down his neighbor in cold blood and without a word spoken, except for an offense against his hearth and honor. And before the moment of hesitation had given way to action, a deed of nature's own violence overwhelmed them both. A fierce shriek of the storm had been answered by a splitting crash over their heads; and ere they could leap aside, a mass of falling beech tree had thundered down on them. Ulrich von Gradwitz found himself stretched on the ground, one arm numb beneath him and the other held almost as helpless in a tight tangle of forked branches, while both legs were pinned beneath the fallen mass. His heavy shooting boots had saved his feet from being crushed to pieces; but if his fractures were not so serious as they might have been, at least it was evident that he could not move from his present position till someone came to release him. The descending twigs had slashed the skin of his face, and he had to wink away some drops of blood from his eyelashes before he could take in a general view of the disaster. At his side, so near that under ordinary circumstances he could almost have touched him, lay Georg Znaeym, alive and struggling, but obviously as helplessly pinioned down as himself. All round them lay a thick-strewn wreckage of splintered branches and broken twigs.

Relief at being alive and exasperation at his captive plight brought a strange medley of pious thank offerings and sharp curses to Ulrich's lips. Georg, who was nearly blinded with the blood which trickled across his eyes, stopped his strug-

gling for a moment to listen and then gave a short, snarling laugh.

"So you're not killed, as you ought to be; but you're caught, anyway," he cried; "caught fast. Ho, what a jest, Ulrich von Gradwitz snared in his stolen forest. There's real justice for you!"

And he laughed again, mockingly and savagely.

"I'm caught in my own forest land," retorted Ulrich. "When my men come to release us, you will wish, perhaps, that you were in a better plight than caught poaching on a neighbor's land. Shame on you!"

Georg was silent for a moment; then he answered quietly:

"Are you sure that your men will find much to release? I have men, too, in the forest tonight, close behind me; and *they* will be here first and do the releasing. When they drag me out from under these branches, it won't need much clumsiness on their part to roll this mass of trunk right over on the top of you. Your men will find you dead under a fallen tree. For form's sake I shall send my condolences to your family."

"It is a useful hint," said Ulrich fiercely. "My men had orders to follow in ten minutes' time, seven of which must have gone by already; and when they get me out—I will remember the hint. Only as you will have met your death poaching on my lands, I don't think I can decently send any message of condolence to your family."

"Good," snarled Georg, "good. We'll fight this quarrel out to the death—you and I and our foresters, with no cursed interlopers to come between us. Death to you, Ulrich von Gradwitz!"

"The same to you, Georg Znaeym, forest thief, game snatcher!"

Both men spoke with the bitterness of possible defeat before them, for each knew that it might be long before his men would seek him out or find him; it was a bare matter of chance which party would arrive first on the scene.

Both had now given up the useless struggle to

free themselves from the mass of wood that held them down; Ulrich limited his endeavors to an effort to bring his one partially free arm near enough to his outer coat pocket to draw out his wine flask. Even when he had accomplished that operation, it was long before he could manage the unscrewing of the stopper or get any of the liquid down his throat. But what a Heaven-sent draft it seemed! It was an open winter, and little snow had fallen as yet, hence the captives suffered less from the cold than might have been the case at that season of the year; nevertheless, the wine was warming and reviving to the wounded man, and he looked across with something like a throb of pity to where his enemy lay, barely keeping the groans of pain and weariness from crossing his lips.

"Could you reach this flask if I threw it over to you?" asked Ulrich suddenly. "There is good wine in it, and one may as well be as comfortable as one can. Let us drink, even if tonight one of us dies."

"No. I can scarcely see anything, there is so much blood caked round my eyes," said Georg; "and in any case I don't drink wine with an enemy."

Ulrich was silent for a few minutes and lay listening to the weary screeching of the wind. An idea was slowly forming and growing in his brain, an idea that gained strength every time that he looked across at the man who was fighting so grimly against pain and exhaustion. In the pain and languor that Ulrich himself was feeling, the old fierce hatred seemed to be dying down.

"Neighbor," he said presently, "do as you please if your men come first. It was a fair compact. But as for me, I've changed my mind. If my men are the first to come, you shall be the first to be helped, as though you were my guest. We have quarreled like devils all our lives over this stupid strip of forest where the trees can't even stand upright in a breath of wind. Lying here tonight, thinking, I've come to think that we've been rather fools; there are better things in life than getting the better of a boundary dispute. Neighbor, if you will help me to bury the old quarrel I—I will ask you to be my friend."

Georg Znaeym was silent for so long that Ulrich thought, perhaps, he had fainted with the pain of his injuries. Then he spoke slowly and in jerks:

"How the whole region would stare and gabble if we rode into the market square together. No one living can remember seeing a Znaeym and a Von Gradwitz talking to one another in friendship. And what peace there would be among the forester folk if we ended our feud tonight. And if we choose to make peace among our people, there is none other to interfere, no interlopers from outside. . . . You would come and keep the Sylvester night[4] beneath my roof, and I would come and feast on some high day at your castle. . . . I would never fire a shot on your land, save when you invited me as a guest; and you should come and shoot with me down in the marshes where the wild fowl are. In all the countryside there are none that could hinder if we willed to make peace. I never thought to have wanted to do other than hate you all my life; but I think I have changed my mind about things, too, this last half-hour. And you offered me your wine flask. . . . Ulrich von Gradwitz, I will be your friend."

For a space both men were silent, turning over in their minds the wonderful changes that this dramatic reconciliation would bring about. In the cold, gloomy forest, with the wind tearing in fitful gusts through the naked branches and whistling around the tree trunks, they lay and waited for the help that would now bring release and succor to both parties. And each prayed a private prayer that his men might be the first to arrive, so that he might be the first to show honorable attention to

---

4. *Sylvester night*, New Year's Eve. Festivities honor St. Sylvester.

the enemy that had become a friend.

Presently, as the wind dropped for a moment, Ulrich broke silence.

"Let's shout for help," he said; "in this lull our voices may carry a little way."

"They won't carry far through the trees and undergrowth," said Georg; "but we can try. Together, then."

The two raised their voices in a prolonged hunting call.

"Together again," said Ulrich a few minutes later, after listening in vain for an answering halloo.

"I heard something that time, I think," said Ulrich.

"I heard nothing but the pestilential wind," said Georg hoarsely.

There was silence again for some minutes, and then Georg gave a joyful cry.

"I can see figures coming through the wood. They are following in the way I came down the hillside."

Both men raised their voices in as loud a shout as they could muster.

"They hear us! They've stopped. Now they see us. They're running down the hill toward us," cried Ulrich.

"How many of them are there?" asked Georg.

"I can't see distinctly," said Ulrich; "nine or ten."

"Then they are yours," said Georg; "I had only seven out with me."

"They are making all the speed they can, brave lads," said Ulrich gladly.

"Are they your men?" asked Georg. "Are they your men?" he repeated impatiently as Ulrich did not answer.

"No," said Ulrich with a laugh, the idiotic chattering laugh of a man unstrung with hideous fear.

"Who are they?" asked Georg quickly, straining his eyes to see what the other would gladly not have seen.

"*Wolves!*"

---

**THINK AND DISCUSS**

**Understanding**

1. What was the original cause of the feud between Ulrich's and Georg's families?

2. Who makes the first gesture of friendship and what is it?

**Analyzing**

3. Cite words or phrases from the story that describe the setting and convey a **mood** of menace and wildness.

4. Find wording early in the story that foreshadows the ending.

5. Identify three different conflicts in the story. Which one ultimately proves to be the most important? Explain.

**Extending**

6. Critics often mention this story as an example of Saki's biting humor. Do you find the ending humorous? Why or why not?

**See Handbook of Literary Terms, p. 804**

The author of "The Interlopers" uses irony of situation and dramatic irony throughout the story, but the reader is not fully aware of these ironies until the end.

1. What is ironic about the end of the story?
2. Explain the irony of the story's title.

## COMPOSITION ◄━━●

### Predicting Outcomes

Like "The Necklace," this story has a surprising and cruel ending. Perhaps you were not surprised because you noticed hints provided through foreshadowing. If so, you were able to predict the outcome of the story through textual clues. Write a three-paragraph composition which analyzes the details in the story which predict the ending.

### Writing an Alternate Ending

Write a new ending to the story that maintains the element of surprise but is not as cruel as the original ending. Keep in mind that your ending should not contradict the details provided throughout the story. The same details must predict your ending.

## BIOGRAPHY

### Saki
### 1870–1916

British writer H. H. Munro adopted the pen name "Saki" while writing political sketches for the *Westminster Gazette*. However, the name became widely known through his short stories. *Reginald* (1904), *The Chronicles of Clovis* (1911), and *Beasts and Super Beasts* (1914), all successful collections, displayed Munro's satirical humor as well as his fascination with the unusual.

Munro was born in Akyab (now Sittwe), Burma, where his father was a colonel in the Bengal Staff Corps. He was sent home to England to the care of relatives at the age of two, after the death of his mother. In 1893 he returned to Burma, but poor health led him back to England and a career as both a journalist and short story writer. He joined the army at the beginning of World War I and went to France in 1915. Within a year he was killed in battle.

# The Man from Kabul[1]

**Rabindranath Tagore**   India

---

**A friendship becomes a faded memory; however, the bond of affection somehow endures.**

---

My five-year-old daughter, Mini, cannot live without chattering. I really believe that in all her life she has not wasted a minute in silence. Her mother is often vexed at this, and would like to stop her prattle, but I would not. For Mini to be quiet is unnatural, and I cannot bear it long. And so my own talk with her is always lively.

One morning, for instance, when I was in the midst of the seventeenth chapter of my new novel, my little Mini stole into the room, and putting her hand into mine, said, "Father! Ramdayal,[2] the doorkeeper, calls a crow a crew! He doesn't know anything, does he?"

Before I could explain to her the difference between one language and another in this world, she had embarked on the full tide of another subject. "What do you think, Father? Bhola says there is an elephant in the clouds, blowing water out of his trunk, and that is why it rains!"

And then, darting off anew, while I sat still, trying to think of some reply to this: "Father, what relation is Mother to you?"

With a grave face I contrived to say, "Go and play with Bhola, Mini! I am busy!"

The window of my room overlooks the road. The child had seated herself at my feet near my table, and was playing softly, drumming on her knees. I was hard at work on my seventeenth chapter, in which Pratap Singh, the hero, has just caught Kanchanlata,[3] the heroine, in his arms, and is about to escape with her by the third-story window of the castle, when suddenly Mini left her play and ran to the window, crying, "A Kabuliwallah! A Kabuliwallah!"[4] And indeed, in the street below, there was a man from Kabul, walking slowly along. He wore the loose, soiled clothing of his people, and a tall turban; he carried a bag on his back and boxes of grapes in his hands.

I cannot tell what my daughter's feelings were when she saw this man, but she began to call him loudly. "Ah!" thought I. "He will come in, and my seventeenth chapter will never be finished!" At that very moment the Kabuliwallah turned and looked up at the child. When she saw this, she

---

*Rabindranath Tagore* (rä bēn′drä nät′ tə gôr′).

**1.** *Kabul* (kä′bùl), capital of Afghanistan, a country bordering on Pakistan to the northwest of India.
**2.** *Ramdayal* (räm′dä yäl).
**3.** *Pratap Singh* (prə täp′ sin′hə) . . . *Kanchanlata* (kun′chən lä′tə).
**4.** *Kabuliwallah* (kä′bùl ē wä′lə).

Slight abridgement of "The Man from Kabul" by Rabindranath Tagore. Reprinted by permission of Macmillan, London and Basingstoke.

was overcome by terror, and running to her mother's protection, disappeared. She had a blind belief that inside the bag which the big man carried there were perhaps two or three other children like herself. The peddler meanwhile entered my doorway and greeted me with a smile.

So precarious was the position of my hero and my heroine that my first impulse was to stop and buy something, since Mini had called the man to the house. I made some small purchases, and we began to talk about Abdur Rahman, the Russians, the English, and the Frontier Policy.[5]

As he was about to leave, he asked, "And where is the little girl, sir?"

And then, thinking that Mini must get rid of her false fear, I had her brought out.

She stood by my chair and looked at the Kabuliwallah and his bag. He offered her nuts and raisins, but she would not be tempted, and only clung the closer to me, with all her doubts increased.

This was their first meeting.

A few mornings later, however, as I was leaving the house, I was startled to find Mini seated on a bench near the door, laughing and talking, with the great Kabuliwallah at her feet. In all her life, it appeared, my small daughter had never found so patient a listener, save her father. And already the corner of her little sari was stuffed with almonds and raisins, the gift of her visitor. "Why did you give her those?" I said, and taking out an eight-anna piece,[6] I handed it to him. The man accepted the money without demur and put it into his pocket.

Alas, on my return, an hour later, I found the unfortunate coin had made twice its own worth of trouble! For the Kabuliwallah had given it to Mini; and her mother, catching sight of the bright round object, had pounced on the child with: "Where did you get that eight-anna piece?"

"The Kabuliwallah gave it to me," said Mini cheerfully.

George Stubbs, *Two Indian Servants with Cheetah and Stag* (detail), Manchester City Art Gallery, Manchester, England

"The Kabuliwallah gave it to you!" cried her mother, greatly shocked. "Oh, Mini! How could you take it from him?"

I entered at that moment, and saving her from impending disaster, proceeded to make my own inquiries.

It was not the first or the second time, I found, that the two had met. The Kabuliwallah had overcome the child's first terror by a judicious bribe of nuts and almonds, and the two were now great friends.

They had many quaint jokes, which amused

---

**5. Abdur Rahman** (ǝb dür′ ra män′) . . . **Frontier Policy,** a political figure and issues of the time. Abdur Rahman became ruler of Afghanistan in 1880, a period when England and Russia were rivals for its control. Afghanistan's attempts to avoid the influence of the two powers and England's foreign-policy aim to expand into Kabul resulted in a war between England and Afghanistan.
**6. eight-anna piece.** An anna was a coin once used in India and Pakistan that at the time of the story was worth approximately one penny. An eight-anna piece was worth eight cents; this had more purchasing power than the same amount today.

them greatly. Mini would seat herself before him, look down on his gigantic frame in all her tiny dignity, and with her face rippling with laughter, would begin: "O Kabuliwallah! Kabuliwallah! What have you got in your bag?"

And he would reply, in the nasal accents of the mountaineer, "An elephant!" Not much cause for merriment, perhaps; but how they both enjoyed the fun! And for me, this child's talk with a grown-up man had always in it something strangely fascinating.

Then the Kabuliwallah, not to be behindhand, would take his turn: "Well, little one, and when are you going to your father-in-law's house?"

Now, nearly every small Bengali maiden had heard long ago about her father-in-law's house; but we were a little newfangled,[7] and had kept these things from our child, so that Mini at this question must have been a trifle bewildered. But she would not show it, and with ready fact replied, "Are *you* going there?"

Amongst men of the Kabuliwallah's class, however, it is well-known that the words "father-in-law's house" have a double meaning. It is a euphemism for jail, the place where we are well cared for, at no expense to ourselves. In this sense would the sturdy peddler take my daughter's question. "Oh," he would say, shaking his fist at an invisible policeman, "I will thrash my father-in-law!" Hearing this, and picturing the poor discomfited relative, Mini would go off into peals of laughter in which her formidable friend would join.

These were autumn mornings, the very time of year when kings of old went forth to conquest; and I, without stirring from my little corner in Calcutta,[8] would let my mind wander over the whole world. At the very name of another country, my heart would go out to it, and at the sight of a foreigner in the streets, I would fall to weaving a network of dreams—the mountains, the glens, and the forests of his distant land, with his

cottage in their midst, and the free and independent life, or faraway wilds. Perhaps scenes of travel are conjured up before me and pass and repass in my imagination all the more vividly because I lead an existence so like a vegetable that a call to travel would fall upon me like a thunderbolt. In the presence of this Kabuliwallah, I was immediately transported to the foot of arid mountain peaks, with narrow little defiles twisting in and out amongst their towering heights. I could see the string of camels bearing the merchandise, and the company of turbaned merchants, some carrying their queer old firearms, and some their spears, journeying downward toward the plains. I could see— But at some such point, Mini's mother would intervene, and implore me to "Beware of that man."

Mini's mother is unfortunately very timid. Whenever she hears a noise in the street, or sees people coming toward the house, she always jumps to the conclusion that they are either thieves, or drunkards, or snakes, or tigers, or malaria, or cockroaches, or caterpillars. Even after all these years of experience, she is not able to overcome her terror. So she was full of doubts about the Kabuliwallah, and used to beg me to keep a watchful eye on him.

If I tried to laugh her fear gently away, she would turn around seriously, and ask me solemn questions:

Were children never kidnapped?

Was it not true that there was slavery in Kabul?

Was it so very absurd that this big man should be able to carry off a tiny child?

---

7. *Bengali maiden . . . newfangled.* A Bengali was a native of Bengal, a former province of India; traditionally, the joining of an Indian woman to her husband's family through marriage meant that she was no longer considered part of her own family. This view was less rigidly held, however, as Indian society became influenced by "newfangled" Western culture.

8. *Calcutta.* The story takes place in this seaport city in eastern India that at that time was the country's capital.

I urged that though not impossible, it was very improbable. But this was not enough, and her dread persisted. But as it was a very vague dread, it did not seem right to forbid the man the house, and the intimacy went on unchecked.

Once a year, in the middle of January, Rahman the Kabuliwallah used to return to his own country, and as the time approached, he would be very busy, going from house to house collecting his debts. This year, however, he could always find time to come and see Mini. It might have seemed to a stranger that there was some conspiracy between the two, for when he could not come in the morning, he would appear in the evening.

Even to me it was a little startling, now and then, suddenly to surprise this tall, loose-garmented man, laden with his bags, in the corner of a dark room; but when Mini ran in, smiling, with her "O Kabuliwallah! Kabuliwallah!" and the two friends, so far apart in age, subsided into their old laughter and their old jokes, I felt reassured.

One morning, a few days before he had made up his mind to go, I was correcting proof sheets in my study. The weather was chilly. Through the window the rays of the sun touched my feet, and the slight warmth was very welcome. It was nearly eight o'clock, and early pedestrians were returning home with their heads covered. Suddenly I heard an uproar in the street, and looking out, saw Rahman being led away bound between two policemen, and behind them a crowd of inquisitive boys. There were bloodstains on his clothes, and one of the policemen carried a knife. I hurried out, and stopping them, inquired what it all meant. Partly from one, partly from another, I gathered that a certain neighbor had owed the peddler something for a Rampuri shawl,[9] but had denied buying it, and that in the course of the quarrel, Rahman had struck him. Now, in his excitement, the prisoner began calling his enemy all sorts of names, when suddenly in a veranda of my house appeared my little Mini, with her usual exclamation: "O Kabuliwallah! Kabuliwallah!" Rahman's face lighted up as he turned to her. He had no bag under his arm today, so that she could not talk about the elephant with him. She therefore at once proceeded to the next question: "Are you going to your father-in-law's house?" Rahman laughed and said, "That is just where I am going, little one!" Then, seeing that the reply did not amuse the child, he held up his fettered hands. "Ah!" he said, "I would have thrashed that old father-in-law, but my hands are bound!"

On a charge of murderous assault, Rahman was sentenced to several years' imprisonment.

Time passed, and he was forgotten. Our accustomed work in the accustomed place went on, and the thought of the once-free mountaineer spending his years in prison seldom or never occurred to us. Even my lighthearted Mini, I am ashamed to say, forgot her old friend. New companions filled her life. As she grew older, she spent more of her time with girls. So much, indeed, did she spend with them that she came no more, as she used to do, to her father's room, so that I rarely had any opportunity of speaking to her.

Years had passed away. It was once more autumn, and we had made arrangements for our Mini's marriage. It was to take place during the Puja holidays.[10] The light of our home would depart to her husband's house, and leave her father's in shadow.

The morning was bright. After the rains, it seemed as though the air had been washed clean and the rays of the sun looked like pure gold. So bright were they that they made even the sordid brick walls of our Calcutta lanes radiant. Since early dawn the wedding pipes had been sounding, and at each burst of sound my own heart throbbed. The wail of the tune, "Bhairavi," seemed to intensify the pain I felt at the approaching separation.[11] My Mini was to be married that night.

From early morning, noise and bustle had pervaded the house. In the courtyard there was the canopy to be slung on its bamboo poles; there were chandeliers with their tinkling sound to be hung in each room and veranda. There was endless hurry and excitement. I was sitting in my

---

9. *Rampuri shawl,* an item from Rampur, an Indian town.
10. *Puja holidays,* a religious festival observed by Hindus.
11. *"Bhairavi"* (bī rä′vē) . . . *approaching separation.* The tune appropriately underscores Mini's departure; its title is the name of an Indian goddess believed to assist souls in departing to heaven.

study, looking through the accounts, when someone entered, saluting respectfully, and stood before me. It was Rahman the Kabuliwallah. At first I did not recognize him. He carried no bag, his long hair was cut short, and his old vigor seemed to have gone. But he smiled, and I knew him again.

"When did you come, Rahman?" I asked him.

"Last evening," he said, "I was released from jail."

The words struck harshly upon my ears. I had never before talked with one who had wounded his fellow man, and my heart shrank within itself when I realized this; for I felt that the day would have been better omened had he not appeared.

"There are ceremonies going on," I said, "and I am busy. Perhaps you could come another day?"

He immediately turned to go; but as he reached the door, he hesitated, and said, "May I not see the little one, sir, for a moment?" It was his belief that Mini was still the same. He had pictured her running to him as she used to do, calling, "O Kabuliwallah! Kabuliwallah!" He had imagined, too, that they would laugh and talk together, just as of old. Indeed, in memory of former days, he had brought, carefully wrapped up in a paper, a few almonds and raisins and grapes, obtained somehow or other from a countryman; for what little money he had, had gone.

I repeated, "There is a ceremony in the house, and you will not be able to see anyone today."

The man's face fell. He looked wistfully at me for a moment, then said, "Good morning," and went out.

I felt a little sorry, and would have called him back, but I found he was returning of his own accord. He came close up to me and held out his offerings with the words: "I have brought these few things, sir, for the little one. Will you give them to her?"

I took them, and was going to pay him, but he caught my hand and said, "You are very kind, sir! Keep me in your memory. Do not offer me money! You have a little girl; I, too, have one like her in my own home. I think of her, and bring this fruit to your child—not to make a profit for myself."

Saying this, he put his hand inside his big loose robe and brought out a small and dirty piece of paper. Unfolding it with great care, he smoothed it out with both hands on my table. It bore the impression of a little hand. Not a photograph. Not a drawing. Merely the impression of an ink-smeared hand laid flat on the paper. This touch of the hand of his own little daughter he had carried always next to his heart, as he had come year after year to Calcutta to sell his wares in the streets.

Tears came to my eyes. I forgot that he was a poor Kabuli fruit-seller, while I was— But no, what was I more than he? He also was a father.

That impression of the hand of his little Parvati in her distant mountain home reminded me of my own little Mini.

I sent for Mini immediately from the inner apartment. Many difficulties were raised, but I swept them aside. Clad in the red silk of her wedding day, with the sandal paste on her forehead, and adorned as a young bride, Mini came and stood modestly before me.

The Kabuliwallah seemed amazed at the apparition. He could not revive their old friendship. At last he smiled and said, "Little one, are you going to your father-in-law's house?"

But Mini now understood the meaning of the word "father-in-law," and she could not answer him as of old. She blushed at the question and stood before him with her bridelike face bowed down.

I remembered the day when the Kabuliwallah and my Mini had first met, and I felt sad. When she had gone, Rahman sighed deeply and sat down on the floor. The idea had suddenly come to him that his daughter, too, must have grown up while he had been away so long, and that he would have to make friends anew with her, also. Assuredly he would not find her as she was when he left her. And besides, what might not have happened to her in these eight years?

The marriage pipes sounded, and the mild autumn sunlight streamed around us. But Rahman sat in the little Calcutta lane and saw before him the barren mountains of Afghanistan.

I took out a currency note, gave it to him, and said, "Go back to your daughter, Rahman, in your own country, and may the happiness of your meeting bring good fortune to my child!"

Having made this present, I had to curtail some of the festivities. I could not have the electric lights I had intended, nor the military band, and the ladies of the house were despondent about it. But to me the wedding feast was all the brighter for the thought that in a distant land a long-lost father had met again his only child.

## THINK AND DISCUSS
### Understanding
1. What characteristics of Mini can be seen in the opening paragraphs of the story?
2. What reminder of his own daughter did the Kabuliwallah, Rahman, carry next to his heart?
3. How does the Kabuliwallah get himself into trouble?

### Analyzing
4. Why is the Kabuliwallah drawn to Mini?
5. Explain the double meaning of the phrase "going to your father-in-law's house." In what way does it **foreshadow** the action of the story?
6. Does Rahman's "murderous assault" with a knife fit in with what you otherwise know about his character? Discuss.
7. Identify and explain the following examples of **irony**: Mini asking Rahman if he were "going to his father-in-law's house"; Rahman telling Mini that "I will thrash my father-in-law"; and the irony of Rahman's return on the wedding day.

### Extending
8. Explain how this story is about the way love relationships change due to time, nature, and circumstances.

## READING LITERATURE SKILLFULLY
### Comparing and Contrasting
When writing fiction, authors often use similarities and differences between characters and their situations to produce conflict in their stories. As you read, you will find it helpful to compare these similarities and contrast these differences. Doing this will better enable you to understand each character and conflict. In "The Man from Kabul" there is a great difference between the way Mini treats Rahman when she is a child and the way she treats him as an adult. Recognizing this difference helps you to realize that, through time, relationships can change drastically. Think about the characters in this story and answer the following questions.

1. Compare and contrast the mother's and the father's attitudes toward Mini's chattering.

2. How is the Kabuliwallah at the beginning of the story the same as the Kabuliwallah at the end of the story? How is he different?

## COMPOSITION
### Writing About an Uncomfortable Experience
"The Man from Kabul" has elements of setting, custom, and speech that are particular to India. When people travel to other countries or find themselves in strange surroundings, they often experience "culture shock"—a feeling of disorientation, or losing one's bearings, in a particular environment. Write a three-paragraph composition describing an experience in which a setting made you feel ill at ease. You may write about experiencing "culture shock" in a foreign country or in a setting closer to home.

### Writing About a Cultural Misunderstanding
The man from Kabul, an outsider in the story's Indian setting, does not succeed in living there peacefully and happily. Failure to adapt to any country's social customs may cause one to act in a way that causes unexpected results, which may be serious or at least embarrassing. Write three to four paragraphs to explain how irony results from the interaction of this story's setting and characterization. See "Writing About Irony" in the Writer's Handbook.

## BIOGRAPHY

### Rabindranath Tagore
### 1861–1941

Tagore was the eldest of seven sons of an extremely wealthy family in Calcutta, India. (His surname actually is a title of nobility.) Educated by tutors and private schools, he showed early promise as a poet. In 1890 he was put in charge of the family's rural estates, where he came to know the sufferings of the poor. The experience prompted Tagore to work for social reform in his homeland.

Already acclaimed in India for his poems, he attracted a following in England by publishing translations of his works. In 1913 Tagore became the first non-Westerner to win the Nobel Prize for Literature. In an action characteristic of his devotion to India's improvement, he donated the prize money to a school he had founded there.

Among Tagore's best-known works are a novel, *The Home and the World* (1916), and the short story collections *The Hungry Stones* (1916) and *The Supreme Right* (1919). Much of his writing contains elements of humor, satire, and mysticism.

# A Letter to God

**Gregorio López y Fuentes**   Mexico

---

**How strange to find a letter addressed to God! Never in all his days as
a mailman had he come upon that house.**

---

he house—the only one in the whole valley—stood at the top of a low hill that looked like one of those primitive, truncated pyramids some wandering tribes abandoned when they moved on. From there you could see the meadows, the river, the stubble pasture, and next to the corral the field of ripe corn with beans blossoming purple among the stalks—the unmistakable sign of a good crop. The only thing the earth needed was a good rain, or at least one of those heavy showers that form puddles between the rows. To doubt that it would rain would have been the same as mistrusting the experience of veteran farmers who believed in planting on a certain day of the year.

Lencho, who knew the country well, had spent the morning scanning the sky to the northeast.

"Now at last the rain is really coming, old girl."

And his wife, who was cooking dinner, replied: "May God grant it."

The older children worked in the field while the younger ones played near the house until their mother called to them all: "Come for dinner—!"

It was during the meal that great drops of rain began to fall, as Lencho had predicted. Mountainous masses of clouds could be seen coming from the northeast, and the air was fresh and cool. The man went out to fetch some implements that had been left on a stone fence, just to feel the pleasurable sensation of the rain on his body. When he came in, he exclaimed:

"These are not drops of water falling from the sky, they are bright coins: the big drops are ten-centavo coins, and the little drops are the fives—"

And he gazed with contented eyes at the field of ripe corn and beans in blossom, all veiled in the filmy curtain of rain. But suddenly a strong wind began to blow, and hailstones as big as acorns started to come down with the raindrops. These indeed looked like new silver coins. The children dashed out into the rain to pick up the largest of the icy pearls.

"This is really very bad," the man exclaimed with chagrin. "Let's hope it stops soon."

But it did not stop soon. For an hour the hail came down upon the house, the garden, the mountain, the corn, and the whole valley. The field was white, as if covered with salt; the trees were left leafless, the corn destroyed, the beans left without a blossom. And Lencho's heart was filled with grief.

After the storm had passed, Lencho told his

---

***Gregorio López y Fuentes*** (lō′pez ē fü en′tez).

Eduardo Kingman, *The Indian and the Land*, Permanent Collection of the International Business Machines Corporation

children as he stood in the middle of the field: "A cloud of locusts would have left more than this; the hailstorm left nothing. This year we'll have no corn or beans—"

The night was one of weeping.

"All our work for nothing!"

"And no one to help us!"

"This year we shall be hungry!"

But in the hearts of all who lived in that solitary house in the middle of the valley, there was one hope—the help of God.

"Don't be so upset, even though it's a hard blow. Remember that being hungry never kills anybody!"

"That's what they say—being hungry never kills anybody."

And during the night Lencho thought a great deal about what he had seen in the village church on Sundays: a triangle, and inside the triangle an eye. An eye that seemed very big, an eye—as they had explained it to him—which sees everything, even what is in the depths of one's conscience.

Lencho was an uncouth peasant who worked hard in the fields, but he knew how to write. At daybreak the following Sunday, having strengthened himself in the conviction that there is Someone who watches over us, he began to write a letter that he would carry personally into town and drop in the mail. It was nothing less than a letter to God!

"Dear God," he wrote, "if You do not help me, I and my whole family will be hungry this year. I need a hundred pesos[1] to sow again, and to live on while the new crop is growing, because the hailstorm—"

He wrote "To God" on the envelope, put the

---

1. *a hundred pesos* (pā′sōz), Mexican money worth about fifty dollars in United States currency at the time of the story. The peso is the basic monetary unit of Mexico.

letter inside, and went into town, still worried. At the post office he put a stamp on the letter and dropped it into the mailbox.

An employee who was a mailman and also an assistant at the post office came over to his boss and, laughing heartily, showed him the letter addressed to God. Never in all his days as a mailman had he come upon that house. The postmaster, fat and jolly, began to laugh, too, but suddenly became serious; and as he tapped the table with the letter, he observed, "What faith! Oh, that I had the faith of the man who wrote this letter! To believe as he believes; to wait with the confidence he feels as he waits; to start corresponding with God!"

And in order not to disillusion that abundant faith, revealed by a letter that could not be delivered, the postmaster had an idea: to answer the letter. But when he opened it, he found that in order to do something more would be needed than good will, paper, and ink. He kept on with his plan, however. He asked his helper for some money, he himself gave part of his salary, and several friends of his were induced to give something "for a charitable cause."

It was impossible for him to accumulate the hundred pesos requested by Lencho, and he could send the peasant only a little over half. He put the bills into an envelope addressed to Lencho, and with them a letter that had only one word as a signature: God.

The following Sunday Lencho came in, a little earlier than usual, to ask if there was a letter for him. It was the mailman himself who handed him the letter while the postmaster, with the happy glow of a man who has done a good deed, watched through the door from his office. Lencho showed not the slightest surprise when he saw the bills— so very sure was he—but became angry when he counted the money. God could not have made a mistake, or have denied what Lencho had requested!

He went at once to the window and asked for paper and ink. At the public desk he began to write, wrinkling his brow because of the effort it cost him to express his thoughts. When he had finished, he went up and bought a stamp, licked it with his tongue, and then stuck it on with a bang of his fist.

As soon as the letter fell into the drop, the postmaster got it and opened it up. It said:

"Dear God: You know that money I asked you for? Only sixty pesos reached me. Please send me the rest; I need it badly. But don't send it through the post office because the employees are very dishonest. Lencho."

## THINK AND DISCUSS
### Understanding
1. What happens to Lencho's crops?
2. According to Lencho, what is his only hope?
3. What motivates the postmaster to collect money for Lencho?

### Analyzing
4. Explain the **irony** of the rainstorm at the beginning of the story.
5. When Lencho receives only sixty pesos instead of the one hundred he has requested, is his faith in God affected in any way? Explain.

6. Explain the **dramatic irony** of Lencho's second letter to God.

### Extending

7. Faith may be defined as a belief in something for which there is no objective proof. Explain the importance and value of Lencho's faith in this story.

## THINKING SKILLS
### Classifying

To **classify** is to arrange things into categories or groups according to some system. In "A Letter to God," much of the action can be classified as either good or bad. For instance, the fact that it rains is good for Lencho and his crops. But the ensuing hailstorm and its effects are devastating. Review the story, paying particular attention to things that Lencho anticipates, things he does, and things that actually happen to him. Then make a list, classifying each as either good or bad.

## COMPOSITION
### Writing a Letter

Assume you are the postmaster and have just received Lencho's second letter to God. You decide to answer the letter. Write a brief letter to Lencho, reprimanding him and detailing reasons for your displeasure. Or, if you prefer, write a brief letter of apology for not supplying the missing forty pesos, detailing reasons for your not doing so.

### Writing to Describe a Setting

Go back to the beginning of "A Letter to God" and reread the first paragraph. You will notice that the author uses precise and vivid words when describing the setting of his story. Think about a setting that is familiar to you—your neighborhood, a park, or perhaps a commercial street—and write a descriptive paragraph similar to that in the story. Be sure to use the most precise and vivid words you can find to describe your setting.

## BIOGRAPHY

### Gregorio López y Fuentes
### 1895–1966

Born in Veracruz, Mexico, López y Fuentes was raised on a ranch where he saw, at close hand, the problems of desperately poor Mexicans. Later he taught in rural elementary schools in the area where he was born. His students were Indians. In 1910 he fought beside these people in the revolution that overthrew the repressive government of President Porfirio Díaz. His novel *El indio (The Indian)* portrays in detail the desperation of poor Mexicans and Indians during the revolutionary period. He continued in his concern for these people whose lives frequently ended in tragedy. *The Indian* won the first Mexican National Prize for Literature. "A Letter to God" appears in his collection of stories entitled *Mexican Country Tales*, written to be used as a textbook in rural schools.

## Writer's Craft

**Use Language That Appeals to the Senses**

Good writing includes vivid details that appeal to the reader's senses. Such imagery transports the reader into the world the writer has created and makes that world not only imaginable but tangible—something you can see and touch.

In "The Interlopers" Saki describes the sound of the tree falling atop the two rivals. Notice how the words appeal to the sense of sound in the passage below.

> A fierce shriek of the storm had been answered by a splitting crash over their heads; and ere they could leap aside, a mass of falling beech tree had thundered down on them.

As Saki uses sensory-laden language to capture action, Guy de Maupassant uses such language to bring the personalities of his characters into relief. In "The Necklace," the reader becomes acquainted with Matilda's longing for a luxurious setting and a sumptuous meal as she sits down to dinner. Notice how effectively the words describe the sight she imagines:

> . . . she would think of the elegant dinners, of the shining silver, of the tapestries peopling the walls with ancient personages and rare birds in the midst of fairy forests; she thought of the exquisite food served on marvelous dishes, of the whispered gallantries, listened to with the smile of the Sphinx while eating the rose-colored flesh of the trout or a chicken's wing.

Rabindranath Tagore also relies on language that appeals to the senses to make "The Man from Kabul" come alive for the reader. Notice the fresh imagery Tagore uses in painting a picture of Mini's wedding day.

> The morning was bright. After the rains, it seemed as though the air had been washed clean and the rays of the sun looked like pure gold. So bright were they that they made even the sordid brick walls of our Calcutta lanes radiant. Since early dawn the wedding pipes had been sounding. . . .

When you read a short story, take particular note of the way the author uses descriptions that appeal to your senses. Such passages help you visualize scenes, experience events, and better understand the writer's message.

Just as writers appeal to your senses, you can appeal to others' senses as you write.

When writing, ask yourself how the object, setting, or action you are describing appeals to your senses. What vivid details will help make your composition more vivid? What do you smell? hear? taste? feel? By being in touch with your senses, you will succeed in helping the reader experience what you are describing.

---

When you read, notice descriptions that appeal to your five senses.

When you write, use precise and vivid words that will enable your readers to experience what you are describing.

---

**See SYMBOL in the Handbook of Literary Terms, page 828.**

# The Sentimentality of William Tavener

**Willa Cather   USA**

---

**"The strategic contest had gone on so long that it had almost crowded out the memory of a closer relationship."**

---

t takes a strong woman to make any sort of success of living in the West, and Hester undoubtedly was that. When people spoke of William Tavener as the most prosperous farmer in McPherson County, they usually added that his wife was a "good manager." She was an executive woman, quick of tongue and something of an imperatrix.[1] The only reason her husband did not consult her about his business was that she did not wait to be consulted.

It would have been quite impossible for one man, within the limited sphere of human action, to follow all Hester's advice, but in the end William usually acted upon some of her suggestions. When she incessantly denounced the "shiftlessness" of letting a new threshing machine stand unprotected in the open, he eventually built a shed for it. When she sniffed contemptuously at his notion of fencing a hog corral with sod walls, he made a spiritless beginning on the structure—merely to "show his temper," as she put it—but in the end he went off quietly to town and bought enough barbed wire to complete the fence. When the first heavy rains came on, and the pigs rooted down the sod wall and made little paths all over it to facilitate their ascent, he heard his wife relate with relish the story of the little pig that built a mud house, to the minister at the dinner table, and William's gravity never relaxed for an instant. Silence, indeed, was William's refuge and his strength.

William set his boys a wholesome example to respect their mother. People who knew him very well suspected that he even admired her. He was a hard man towards his neighbors, and even to-

---

1. *imperatrix* (im′pə rā′trix), an empress or woman who rules.

John Steuart Curry, *Father and Mother*, collection IBM Corporation, Armonk, New York

wards his sons; grasping, determined, and ambitious.

There was an occasional blue day about the house when William went over the store bills, but he never objected to items relating to his wife's gowns or bonnets. So it came about that many of the foolish, unnecessary little things that Hester bought for her boys she had charged to her personal account.

One spring night Hester sat in a rocking chair by the sitting-room window, darning socks. She rocked violently and sent her long needle vigorously back and forth over her gourd,[2] and it took only a very casual glance to see that she was wrought up over something. William sat on the other side of the table reading his farm paper. If he had noticed his wife's agitation, his calm, clean-shaven face betrayed no sign of concern. He must have noticed the sarcastic turn of her remarks at the supper table, and he must have noticed the moody silence of the older boys as they ate. When supper was but half over little Billy, the youngest, had suddenly pushed back his plate and slipped away from the table, manfully trying to swallow a sob. But William Tavener

---

2. *sent her long needle . . . gourd.* Because a small gourd easily conforms to the inside of small articles of clothing, it is a handy tool for darning.

never heeded ominous forecasts in the domestic horizon, and he never looked for a storm until it broke.

After supper the boys had gone to the pond under the willows in the big cattle corral to get rid of the dust of plowing. Hester could hear an occasional splash and a laugh ringing clear through the stillness of the night as she sat by the open window. She sat silent for almost an hour reviewing in her mind many plans of attack. But she was too vigorous a woman to be much of a strategist, and she usually came to her point with directness. At last she cut her thread and suddenly put her darning down, saying emphatically:

"William, I don't think it would hurt you to let the boys go to that circus in town tomorrow."

William continued to read his farm paper, but it was not Hester's custom to wait for an answer. She usually divined his arguments and assailed them one by one before he uttered them.

"You've been short of hands all summer, and you've worked the boys hard, and a man ought use his own flesh and blood as well as he does his hired hands. We're plenty able to afford it, and it's little enough our boys ever spend. I don't see how you can expect 'em to be steady and hard workin', unless you encourage 'em a little. I never could see much harm in circuses, and our boys have never been to one. Oh, I know Jim Howley's boys get drunk an' carry on when they go, but our boys ain't that sort, an' you know it, William. The animals are real instructive, an' our boys don't get to see much out here on the prairie. It was different where we were raised, but the boys have got no advantages here, an' if you don't take care, they'll grow up to be greenhorns."

Hester paused a moment, and William folded up his paper, but vouchsafed no remark. His sisters in Virginia had often said that only a quiet man like William could ever have lived with Hester Perkins. Secretly, William was rather proud of his wife's "gift of speech," and of the fact that she could talk in prayer meeting as fluently as a man. He confined his own efforts in that line to a brief prayer at Covenant meetings.

Hester shook out another sock and went on.

"Nobody was ever hurt by goin' to a circus. Why, law me! I remember I went to one myself once, when I was little. I had most forgot about it. It was over at Pewtown, an' I remember how I had set my heart on going. I don't think I'd ever forgiven my father if he hadn't taken me, though that red-clay road was in a frightful way after the rain. I mind they had an elephant and six poll parrots, an' a Rocky Mountain lion, an' a cage of monkeys, an' two camels. My! but they were a sight to me then!"

Hester dropped the black sock and shook her head and smiled at the recollection. She was not expecting anything from William yet, and she was fairly startled when he said gravely, in much the same tone in which he announced the hymns in prayer meeting:

"No, there was only one camel. The other was a dromedary."

She peered around the lamp and looked at him keenly.

"Why, William, how come you to know?"

William folded his paper and answered with some hesitation, "I was there, too."

Hester's interest flashed up. "Well, I never, William! To think of my finding it out after all these years! Why, you couldn't have been much bigger'n our Billy then. It seems queer I never saw you when you was little, to remember about you. But then you Back Creek folks never have anything to do with us Gap people. But how come you to go? Your father was stricter with you than you are with your boys."

"I reckon I shouldn't 'a gone," he said slowly, "but boys will do foolish things. I had done a good deal of fox hunting the winter before, and Father let me keep the bounty money. I hired Tom Smith's Tap to weed the corn for me, an' I slipped off unbeknownst to Father an' went to the show.''

Hester spoke up warmly: "Nonsense, William! It didn't do you no harm, I guess. You was always worked hard enough. It must have been a big sight for a little fellow. That clown must have just tickled you to death.''

William crossed his knees and leaned back in his chair.

"I reckon I could tell all that fool's jokes now. Sometimes I can't help thinkin' about 'em in meetin' when the sermon's long. I mind I had on a pair of new boots that hurt me like the mischief, but I forgot all about 'em when that fellow rode the donkey. I recall I had to take them boots off as soon as I got out of sight o' town, and walked home in the mud barefoot.''

"O poor little fellow!" Hester ejaculated, drawing her chair nearer and leaning her elbows on the table. "What cruel shoes they did use to make for children. I remember I went up to Back Creek to see the circus wagons go by. They came down from Romney, you know. The circus men stopped at the creek to water the animals, an' the elephant got stubborn an' broke a big limb off the yellow willow tree that grew there by the toll-house porch,[3] an' the Scribners were 'fraid as death he'd pull the house down. But this much I saw him do; he waded in the creek an' filled his trunk with water and squirted it in at the window and nearly ruined Ellen Scribner's pink lawn dress that she had just ironed an' laid out on the bed ready to wear to the circus.''

"I reckon that must have been a trial to Ellen," chuckled William, "for she was mighty prim in them days.''

Hester drew her chair still nearer William's. Since the children had begun growing up, her conversation with her husband had been almost wholly confined to questions of economy and expense. Their relationship had become purely a business one, like that between landlord and ten-

ant. In her desire to indulge her boys she had unconsciously assumed a defensive and almost hostile attitude towards her husband. No debtor ever haggled with his usurer more doggedly than did Hester with her husband in behalf of her sons. The strategic contest had gone on so long that it had almost crowded out the memory of a closer relationship. This exchange of confidences to-night, when common recollections took them unawares and opened their hearts, had all the miracle of romance. They talked on and on; of old neighbors, of old familiar faces in the valley where they had grown up, of long-forgotten incidents of their youth—weddings, picnics, sleighing parties, and baptizings. For years they had talked of nothing else but butter and eggs and the prices of things, and now they had as much to say to each other as people who meet after a long separation.

When the clock struck ten, William rose and went over to his walnut secretary and unlocked it. From his red leather wallet he took out a ten-dollar bill and laid it on the table beside Hester.

"Tell the boys not to stay late, an' not to drive the horses hard," he said quietly, and went off to bed.

Hester blew out the lamp and sat still in the dark a long time. She left the bill lying on the table where William had placed it. She had a painful sense of having missed something, or lost something; she felt that somehow the years had cheated her.

The little locust trees that grew by the fence were white with blossoms. Their heavy odor floated in to her on the night wind and recalled a night long ago, when the first whippoorwill of the spring was heard, and the rough, buxom girls of Hawkins Gap had held her laughing and struggling under the locust trees, and searched in her bosom for a lock of her sweetheart's hair, which is

---

3. *toll-house porch.* It was once customary for tollgate operators to live in houses situated near the gate.

supposed to be on every girl's breast when the first whippoorwill sings. Two of those same girls had been her bridesmaids. Hester had been a very happy bride. She rose and went softly into the room where William lay. He was sleeping heavily, but occasionally moved his hand before his face to ward off the flies. Hester went into the parlor and took the piece of mosquito net from the basket of wax apples and pears that her sister had made before she died. One of the boys had brought it all the way from Virginia, packed in a tin pail, since Hester would not risk shipping so precious an ornament by freight. She went back to the bed-room and spread the net over William's head. Then she sat down by the bed and listened to his deep, regular breathing until she heard the boys returning. She went out to meet them and warn them not to waken their father.

"I'll be up early to get your breakfast, boys. Your father says you can go to the show." As she handed the money to the eldest, she felt a sudden throb of allegiance to her husband and said sharply, "And you be careful of that, an' don't waste it. Your father works hard for his money."

The boys looked at each other in astonishment and felt that they had lost a powerful ally.

## THINK AND DISCUSS
### Understanding
1. Why did William Tavener never consult his wife about business?
2. List five arguments Hester raises for the boys being allowed to attend the circus.
3. How did the boys feel when their mother gave them the ten dollars?

### Analyzing
4. Compare and contrast the personalities of Hester and William.
5. What evidence is there early in the story of the soft side of Hester's and William's nature?
6. When and how do William and Hester show their "sentimentality"?
7. Identify and explain the irony in the final sentence in the story.

### Extending
8. In describing William and Hester's new relationship, the author refers to the "miracle of romance." Do you think the use of the word *miracle* is appropriate in this sense? Explain.

### APPLYING: Symbol HⓉ
See Handbook of Literary Terms, p. 828
Some literary **symbols**—concrete things that represent something abstract—are complicated and make the reader look beyond the immediate context of a selection for their meaning. Others seem to grow naturally out of the context and thus are not difficult to notice or understand.

1. As Hester and William reminisce, what does the circus come to stand for in their minds?
2. Do you think the circus will symbolize anything more when they remember the conversation of this night four or five years later? Discuss.

*The Sentimentality of William Tavener* 411

**3.** What is symbolic about Hester's removing the netting from the wax fruit and putting it over William's head?

## COMPOSITION
### Writing About Rural Life Then and Now

Details of the setting presented in the story, as well as comments made in their discussion, give a fairly clear idea of the lives of William and Hester. From these details, decide in what ways their lives were similar to or different from those of people living in rural areas today. Write a three- or four-paragraph composition comparing and contrasting rural life then and now. See "Writing to Compare and Contrast" in the Writer's Handbook.

**Anticipating Reactions**

After reading about William and Hester Tavener, you have a good idea about how they might react to a given situation. Imagine that you are their son or daughter. Write a two- or three-paragraph composition describing how you would expect your parents to react to one of the following situations. If you like, you may invent your own situation. You tell them you want to move to a city; you tell them that you don't want to follow in their footsteps and be a farmer; after seeing the circus, you tell them that you want to join it; or you tell them you think they are too old to run the farm and you want to take over.

## BIOGRAPHY

### Willa Cather
### 1873–1947

Willa Cather's cherished memories of the prairie frontier determined her literary direction. In her first writings she attempted to follow the sophisticated trends popular with Eastern writers, but she finally found her best material at home, out of her own youthful experiences and observations. Born in Gore, Virginia, Cather moved with her family to Red Cloud, Nebraska, in 1883. She grew up there among immigrant farmers from Scandinavia and Bohemia. In a style that was noted for its accuracy and simplicity, she portrayed their struggle to adapt to the frontier in her first story collection, *The Troll Garden* (1905), and in her novels *O Pioneers!* (1913) and *My Ántonia* (1918). The optimism behind these works began fading during World War I, when Cather started having doubts about the future of the human race. Her Pulitzer Prize-winning novel, *One of Ours* (1922), reflected this disillusionment. However, she captured the spirit of the pioneer in *Death Comes for the Archbishop* (1927), a historical novel regarded as an American masterpiece.

Review SYMBOL in the Handbook of Literary Terms, page 828.

# The Rocking-Horse Winner

**D. H. Lawrence**   Great Britain

**To meet the ceaseless demands of a troubled household, Paul turned in desperation to his wooden rocking horse.**

here was a woman who was beautiful, who started with all the advantages, yet she had no luck. She married for love, and the love turned to dust. She had bonny children, yet she felt they had been thrust upon her, and she could not love them. They looked at her coldly, as if they were finding fault with her. And hurriedly she felt she must cover up some fault in herself. Yet what it was that she must cover up she never knew. Nevertheless, when her children were present, she always felt the center of her heart go hard. This troubled her, and in her manner she was all the more gentle and anxious for her children, as if she loved them very much. Only she herself knew that at the center of her heart was a hard little place that could not feel love, no, not for anybody. Everybody else said of her: "She is such a good mother. She adores her children." Only she herself, and her children themselves, knew it was not so. They read it in each other's eyes.

There was a boy and two little girls. They lived in a pleasant house, with a garden, and they had discreet servants, and felt themselves superior to anyone in the neighborhood.

Although they lived in style, they felt always an anxiety in the house. There was never enough money. The mother had a small income, and the father had a small income, but not nearly enough for the social position which they had to keep up. The father went into town to some office. But though he had good prospects, these prospects never materialized. There was always the grinding sense of the shortage of money, though the style was always kept up.

At last the mother said: "I will see if *I* can't make something." But she did not know where to begin. She racked her brains and tried this thing and the other, but could not find anything successful. The failure made deep lines come into her face. Her children were growing up, they would have to go to school. There must be more money, there must be more money. The father, who was always very handsome and expensive in his tastes, seemed as if he never *would* be able to do anything worth doing. And the mother, who had a great belief in herself, did not succeed any better, and her tastes were just as expensive.

And so the house came to be haunted by the unspoken phrase: There *must* be more money! There *must* be more money! The children could hear it all the time, though nobody said it aloud. They heard it at Christmas, when the expensive and splendid toys filled the nursery. Behind the shining modern rocking horse, behind the smart doll's house, a voice would start whispering: "There *must* be more money! There *must* be more money!" And the children would stop playing, to listen for a moment. They would look into each other's eyes, to see if they had all heard. And each one saw in the eyes of the other two that they, too, had heard. "There *must* be more money! There *must* be more money!"

It came whispering from the springs of the still-swaying rocking horse, and even the horse, bending his wooden, champing head, heard it. The big doll, sitting so pink and smirking in her new pram, could hear it quite plainly, and seemed to be smirking all the more self-consciously because of it. The foolish puppy, too, that took the place of the teddy bear, he was looking so extraordinarily foolish for no other reason but that he heard the secret whisper all over the house: "There *must* be more money!"

Yet nobody ever said it aloud. The whisper was everywhere, and therefore no one spoke it. Just as no one ever says: "We are breathing!" in spite of the fact that breath is coming and going all the time.

"Mother," said the boy Paul one day, "why don't we keep a car of our own? Why do we always use Uncle's, or else a taxi?"

"Because we're the poor members of the family," said the mother.

"But why *are* we, Mother?"

"Well—I suppose," she said slowly and bitterly, "it's because your father has no luck."

The boy was silent for some time.

"Is luck money, Mother?" he asked, rather timidly.

"No, Paul. Not quite. It's what causes you to have money."

"Oh!" said Paul vaguely. "I thought when Uncle Oscar said *filthy lucker*, it meant money."

"*Filthy lucre*[1] does mean money," said the mother. "But it's lucre, not luck."

"Oh!" said the boy. "Then what is luck, Mother?"

"It's what causes you to have money. If you're lucky you have money. That's why it's better to be born lucky than rich. If you're rich, you may lose your money. But if you're lucky, you will always get more money."

"Oh! Will you? And is Father not lucky?"

"Very unlucky, I should say," she said bitterly.

The boy watched her with unsure eyes.

"Why?" he asked.

"I don't know. Nobody ever knows why one person is lucky and another unlucky."

"Don't they? Nobody at all? Does nobody know?"

"Perhaps God. But He never tells."

"He ought to, then. And aren't you lucky either, Mother?"

"I can't be, if I married an unlucky husband."

"But by yourself, aren't you?"

"I used to think I was, before I married. Now I think I am very unlucky indeed."

"Why?"

"Well—never mind! Perhaps I'm not really," she said.

The child looked at her, to see if she meant it. But he saw, by the lines of her mouth, that she

---

1. *lucre* (lü′kər), money considered bad or degrading.

was only trying to hide something from him.

"Well, anyhow," he said stoutly, "I'm a lucky person."

"Why?" said his mother, with a sudden laugh.

He stared at her. He didn't even know why he had said it. "God told me," he asserted, brazening it out.

"I hope He did, dear!" she said, again with a laugh, but rather bitter.

"He did, Mother!"

"Excellent!" said the mother, using one of her husband's exclamations.

The boy saw she did not believe him; or, rather, that she paid no attention to his assertion. This angered him somewhat, and made him want to compel her attention.

He went off by himself, vaguely, in a childish way, seeking for the clue to "luck." Absorbed, taking no need of other people, he went about with a sort of stealth, seeking inwardly for luck. He wanted luck, he wanted it, he wanted it. When the two girls were playing dolls in the nursery, he would sit on his big rocking horse, charging madly into space, with a frenzy that made the little girls peer at him uneasily. Wildly the horse careered, the waving dark hair of the boy tossed, his eyes had a strange glare in them. The little girls dared not speak to him.

When he had ridden to the end of his mad little journey, he climbed down and stood in front of his rocking horse, staring fixedly into its lowered face. Its red mouth was slightly open, its big eye was wide and glassy bright.

"Now!" he would silently command the snorting steed. "Now, take me to where there is luck! Now take me."

And he would slash the horse on the neck with the little whip he had asked Uncle Oscar for. He *knew* the horse could take him to where there was luck, if only he forced it. So he would mount again, and start on his furious ride, hoping at last to get there. He knew he could get there.

"You'll break your horse, Paul!" said the nurse.

"He's always riding like that! I wish he'd leave off!" said his elder sister Joan.

But he only glared down on them in silence. Nurse gave him up. She could make nothing of him. Anyhow he was growing beyond her.

One day his mother and his Uncle Oscar came in when he was on one of his furious rides. He did not speak to them.

"Hallo, you young jockey! Riding a winner?" said his uncle.

"Aren't you growing too big for a rocking horse? You're not a very little boy any longer, you know," said his mother.

But Paul only gave a blue glare from his big, rather close-set eyes. He would speak to nobody when he was in full tilt. His mother watched him with an anxious expression on her face.

At last he suddenly stopped forcing his horse into the mechanical gallop, and slid down. "Well, I got there!" he announced fiercely, his blue eyes still flaring, and his sturdy long legs straddling apart.

"Where did you get to?" asked his mother.

"Where I wanted to go," he flared back at her.

"That's right, son!" said Uncle Oscar. "Don't you stop till you get there. What's the horse's name?"

"He doesn't have a name," said the boy.

"Gets on without all right?" asked the uncle.

"Well, he has different names. He was called Sansovino last week."

"Sansovino, eh? Won the Ascot.[2] How did you know his name?"

"He always talks about horse races with Bassett," said Joan.

The uncle was delighted to find that his small

---

2. *Ascot,* a horse race. Other races mentioned are Lincoln (the shortened name for Lincolnshire), Leger, Grand National, and Derby (där′bē).

George Stubbs, *Duke of Richmond Racehorses Exercising at Goodwood* (detail), 1760, Goodwood House, Sussex

nephew was posted with all the racing news. Bassett, the young gardener, who had been wounded in the left foot in the war and had got his present job through Oscar Cresswell, whose batman[3] he had been, was a perfect blade of the "turf." He lived in the racing events, and the small boy lived with him.

Oscar Cresswell got it all from Bassett.

"Master Paul comes and asks me, so I can't do more than tell him, sir," said Bassett, his face terribly serious, as if he were speaking of religious matters.

"And does he ever put anything on a horse he fancies?"

"Well—I don't want to give him away—he's a young sport, a fine sport, sir. Would you mind asking him himself? He sort of takes a pleasure in it, and perhaps he'd feel I was giving him away, sir, if you don't mind."

Bassett was serious as a church.

---

3. *batman.* Bassett had been Cresswell's servant while the latter served in the army.

The uncle went back to his nephew, and took him off for a ride in the car.

"Say, Paul, old man, do you ever put anything on a horse?" the uncle asked.

The boy watched the handsome man closely.

"Why, do you think I oughtn't to?" he parried.

"Not a bit of it! I thought perhaps you might give me a tip for the Lincoln."

The car sped on into the country, going down to Uncle Oscar's place in Hampshire.

"Honor bright?" said the nephew.

"Honor bright, son!" said the uncle.

"Well, then, Daffodil."

"Daffodil! I doubt it, sonny. What about Mirza?"

"I only know the winner," said the boy. "That's Daffodil."

"Daffodil, eh?"

There was a pause. Daffodil was an obscure horse comparatively.

"Uncle!"

"Yes, son?"

"You won't let it go any further, will you? I promised Bassett."

"Bassett be . . . , old man! What's he got to do with it?"

"We're partners. We've been partners from the first. Uncle, he lent me my first five shillings,[4] which I lost. I promised him, honor bright, it was only between me and him; only you gave me that ten-shilling note I started winning with, so I thought you were lucky. You won't let it go any further, will you?"

The boy gazed at his uncle from those big, hot, blue eyes, set rather close together. The uncle stirred and laughed uneasily.

"Right you are, son! I'll keep your tip private. Daffodil, eh! How much are you putting on him?"

"All except twenty pounds,"[5] said the boy. "I keep that in reserve."

The uncle thought it a good joke.

"You keep twenty pounds in reserve, do you, you young romancer? What are you betting, then?"

"I'm betting three hundred," said the boy gravely. "But it's between you and me, Uncle Oscar! Honor bright?"

The uncle burst into a roar of laughter.

"It's between you and me all right, you young Nat Gould,"[6] he said, laughing. "But where's your three hundred?"

"Bassett keeps it for me. We're partners."

"You are, are you! And what is Bassett putting on Daffodil?"

"He won't go quite as high as I do, I expect. Perhaps he'll go a hundred and fifty."

"What, pennies?" laughed the uncle.

"Pounds," said the child, with a surprised look at his uncle. "Bassett keeps a bigger reserve than I do."

Between wonder and amusement Uncle Oscar was silent. He pursued the matter no further, but he determined to take his nephew with him to the Lincoln races.

"Now son," he said, "I'm putting twenty on Mirza, and I'll put five for you on any horse you fancy. What's your pick?"

"Daffodil, Uncle."

"No, not the fiver on Daffodil!"

"I should if it was my own fiver," said the child.

"Good! Good! Right you are! A fiver for me and a fiver for you on Daffodil."

The child had never been to a race meeting before, and his eyes were blue fire. He pursed his mouth tight, and watched. A Frenchman just in front had put his money on Lancelot. Wild with

---

4. *five shillings.* At the time of this story, this amount in English money was worth about $1.25.
5. *twenty pounds.* The English pound was worth nearly five dollars in United States currency; thus, twenty pounds was worth almost one hundred dollars.
6. *Nat Gould,* journalist, author, and highly respected racing authority.

excitement, he flayed his arms up and down, yelling *Lancelot! Lancelot!* in his French accent.

Daffodil came in first, Lancelot second, Mirza third. The child, flushed and with eyes blazing, was curiously serene. His uncle brought him four five-pound notes, four to one.

"What am I to do with these?" he cried, waving them before the boy's eyes.

"I suppose we'll talk to Bassett," said the boy. "I expect I have fifteen hundred now; and twenty in reserve; and this twenty."

His uncle studied him for some moments.

"Look here, son!" he said. "You're not serious about Bassett and that fifteen hundred, are you?"

"Yes, I am. But it's between you and me, Uncle. Honor bright!"

"Honor bright all right, son! But I must talk to Bassett."

"If you'd like to be a partner, Uncle, with Bassett and me, we could all be partners. Only, you'd have to promise, honor bright, Uncle, not to let it go beyond us three. Bassett and I are lucky, and you must be lucky, because it was your ten shillings I started winning with. . . ."

Uncle Oscar took both Bassett and Paul into Richmond Park[7] for an afternoon, and there they talked.

"It's like this, you see, sir," Bassett said. "Master Paul would get me talking about racing events, spinning yarns, you know, sir. And he was always keen on knowing if I'd made or if I'd lost. It's about a year since, now, that I put five shillings on Blush of Dawn for him—and we lost. Then the luck turned, with that ten shillings he had from you, that we put on Singhalese. And since that time it's been pretty steady, all things considering. What do you say, Master Paul?"

"We're all right when we're sure," said Paul. "It's when we're not quite sure that we go down."

"Oh, but we're careful then," said Bassett.

"But when you are *sure?*" smiled Uncle Oscar.

"It's Master Paul, sir," said Bassett, in a secret, religious voice. "It's as if he had it from heaven. Like Daffodil, now, for the Lincoln. That was as sure as eggs."

"Did you put anything on Daffodil?" asked Oscar Cresswell.

"Yes, sir. I made my bit."

"And my nephew?"

Bassett was obstinately silent, looking at Paul.

"I made twelve hundred, didn't I, Bassett? I told Uncle I was putting three hundred on Daffodil."

"That's right," said Bassett, nodding.

"But where's the money?" asked the uncle.

"I keep it safe locked up, sir. Master Paul he can have it any minute he likes to ask for it."

"What, fifteen hundred pounds?"

"And twenty! And *forty*, that is, with the twenty he made on the course."

"It's amazing!" said the uncle.

"If Master Paul offers you to be partners, sir, I would if I were you; if you'll excuse me," said Bassett.

Oscar Cresswell thought about it.

"I'll see the money," he said.

They drove home again, and sure enough, Bassett came round to the garden house with fifteen hundred pounds in notes. The twenty pounds reserve was left with Joe Glee, in the Turf Commission deposit.[8]

"You see, it's all right, Uncle, when I'm *sure!* Then we go strong, for all we're worth. Don't we, Bassett?"

"We do that, Master Paul."

"And when are you sure?" said the uncle, laughing.

"Oh, well, sometimes I'm *absolutely* sure, like about Daffodil," said the boy; "and sometimes I

---

7. *Richmond Park*, a deer park just outside of London.
8. *Turf Commission deposit*, a type of bank in which English bettors deposit betting funds.

have an idea; and sometimes I haven't even an idea, have I, Bassett? Then we're careful, because we mostly go down."

"You do, do you! And when you're sure, like about Daffodil, what makes you sure, sonny?"

"Oh, well, I don't know," said the boy uneasily. "I'm sure, you know, Uncle; that's all."

"It's as if he had it from heaven, sir," Bassett reiterated.

"I should say so!" said the uncle.

But he became a partner. And when the Leger was coming on, Paul was "sure" about Lively Spark, which was a quite inconsiderable horse. The boy insisted on putting a thousand on the horse, Bassett went for five hundred, and Oscar Cresswell two hundred. Lively Spark came in first, and the betting had been ten to one against him. Paul had made ten thousand.

"You see," he said, "I was absolutely sure of him."

Even Oscar Cresswell had cleared two thousand.

"Look here, son," he said, "this sort of thing makes me nervous."

"It needn't, Uncle! Perhaps I shan't be sure again for a long time."

"But what are you going to do with your money?" asked the uncle.

"Of course," said the boy, "I started it for Mother. She said she had no luck, because Father is unlucky, so I thought if *I* was lucky, it might stop whispering."

"What might stop whispering?"

"Our house. I *hate* our house for whispering."

"What does it whisper?"

"Why—why"—the boy fidgeted—"why, I don't know. But it's always short of money, you know, Uncle."

"I know it, son, I know it."

"You know people send Mother writs,[9] don't you, Uncle?"

"I'm afraid I do," said the uncle.

"And then the house whispers, like people laughing at you behind your back. It's awful, that is! I thought if I was lucky . . ."

"You might stop it," added the uncle.

The boy watched him with big blue eyes that had an uncanny cold fire in them, and he said never a word.

"Well, then!" said the uncle. "What are we doing?"

"I shouldn't like Mother to know I was lucky," said the boy.

"Why not, son?"

"She'd stop me."

"I don't think she would."

"Oh!"—and the boy writhed in an odd way— "I *don't* want her to know, Uncle."

"All right, son! We'll manage it without her knowing."

They managed it very easily. Paul, at the other's suggestion, handed over five thousand pounds to his uncle, who deposited it with the family lawyer, who was then to inform Paul's mother that a relative had put five thousand pounds into his hands, which sum was to be paid out a thousand pounds at a time, on the mother's birthday, for the next five years.

"So she'll have a birthday present of a thousand pounds for five successive years," said Uncle Oscar. "I hope it won't make it all the harder for her later."

Paul's mother had her birthday in November. The house had been "whispering" worse than ever lately, and, even in spite of his luck, Paul could not bear up against it. He was very anxious to see the effect of the birthday letter, telling his mother about the thousand pounds.

When there were no visitors, Paul now took his meals with his parents, as he was beyond the nursery control. His mother went into town

---

**9. writs,** legal documents. Here the term is used to mean that legal action is about to be taken to collect unpaid bills.

nearly every day. She had discovered that she had an odd knack of sketching furs and dress materials, so she worked secretly in the studio of a friend who was the chief "artist" for the leading drapers.[10] She drew the figures of ladies in furs and ladies in silk and sequins for the newspaper advertisements. This young woman artist earned several thousand pounds a year, but Paul's mother only made several hundred, and she was again dissatisfied. She so wanted to be first in something, and she did not succeed, even in making sketches for drapery advertisements.

She was down to breakfast on the morning of her birthday. Paul watched her face as she read her letters. He knew the lawyer's letter. As his mother read it, her face hardened and became more expressionless. Then a cold, determined look came on her mouth. She hid the letter under the pile of others, and said not a word about it.

"Didn't you have anything nice in the post for your birthday, Mother?" said Paul.

"Quite moderately nice," she said, her voice cold and absent.

She went away to town without saying more.

But in the afternoon Uncle Oscar appeared. He said Paul's mother had had a long interview with her lawyer, asking if the whole five thousand could not be advanced at once, as she was in debt.

"What do you think, Uncle?" said the boy.

"I leave it to you, son."

"Oh, let her have it, then! We can get some more with the other," said the boy.

"A bird in the hand is worth two in the bush, laddie!" said Uncle Oscar.

"But I'm sure to *know* for the Grand National; or the Lincolnshire; or else the Derby. I'm sure to know for *one* of them," said Paul.

So Uncle Oscar signed the agreement, and Paul's mother touched the whole five thousand. Then something very curious happened. The voices in the house suddenly went mad, like a chorus of frogs on a spring evening. There were certain new furnishings, and Paul had a tutor. He was *really* going to Eton, his father's school, in the following autumn. There were flowers in the winter, and a blossoming of the luxury Paul's mother had been used to. And yet the voices in the house, behind the sprays of mimosa and almond blossom, and from under the piles of iridescent cushions, simply trilled and screamed in a sort of ecstasy. "There *must* be more money! Oh-h-h; there *must* be more money! Oh, now, now-w! Now-w-w—there *must* be more money!—more than ever! More than ever!"

It frightened Paul terribly. He studied away at his Latin and Greek with his tutors. But his intense hours were spent with Bassett. The Grand National had gone by: he had not "known," and had lost a hundred pounds. Summer was at hand. He was in agony for the Lincoln. But even for the Lincoln he didn't "know," and he lost fifty pounds. He became wild-eyed and strange, as if something were going to explode in him.

"Let it alone, son! Don't you bother about it!" urged Uncle Oscar. But it was as if the boy couldn't really hear what his uncle was saying.

"I've got to know for the Derby! I've got to know for the Derby!" the child reiterated, his big blue eyes blazing with a sort of madness.

His mother noticed how overwrought he was.

"You'd better go the seaside. Wouldn't you like to go now to the seaside, instead of waiting? I think you'd better," she said, looking down at him anxiously, her heart curiously heavy because of him.

But the child lifted his uncanny blue eyes.

"I couldn't possibly go before the Derby, Mother!" he said. "I couldn't possibly!"

"Why not?" she said, her voice becoming heavy when she was opposed. "Why not? You can still go from the seaside to see the Derby with your Uncle Oscar, if that's what you wish. No

---

10. *drapers*, a dealer in cloth or dry goods. [*British*]

need for you to wait here. Besides, I think you care too much about these races. It's a bad sign. My family has been a gambling family, and you won't know till you grow up how much damage it has done. But it has done damage. I shall have to send Bassett away, and ask Uncle Oscar not to talk racing to you, unless you promise to be reasonable about it; go away to the seaside and forget it. You're all nerves!"

"I'll do what you like, Mother, so long as you don't send me away till after the Derby," the boy said.

"Send you away from where? Just from this house?"

"Yes," he said, gazing at her.

"Why, you curious child, what makes you care about this house so much, suddenly? I never knew you loved it."

He gazed at her without speaking. He had a secret within a secret, something he had not divulged, even to Bassett or to his Uncle Oscar.

But his mother, after standing undecided and a little bit sullen for some moments, said:

"Very well, then! Don't go to the seaside till after the Derby, if you don't wish it. But promise me you won't let your nerves go to pieces. Promise you won't think so much about horse racing and *events* as you call them!"

"Oh, no," said the boy casually. "I won't think much about them, Mother. You needn't worry. I wouldn't worry, Mother, if I were you."

"If you were me and I were you," said his mother, "I wonder what we *should* do!"

"But you know you needn't worry, Mother, don't you?" the boy repeated.

"I should be awfully glad to know it," she said wearily.

"Oh, well, you *can*, you know. I mean, you *ought* to know you needn't worry," he insisted.

"Ought I? Then I'll see about it," she said.

Paul's secret of secrets was his wooden horse, that which had no name. Since he was emanci-

pated from a nurse and a nursery-governess, he had had his rocking horse removed to his own bedroom at the top of the house.

"Surely, you're too big for a rocking horse!" his mother had remonstrated.

"Well, you see, Mother, till I can have a *real* horse, I like to have *some* sort of animal about," had been his quaint answer.

"Do you feel he keeps you company?" she laughed.

"Oh, yes! He's very good, he always keeps me company, when I'm there," said Paul.

So the horse, rather shabby, stood in an arrested prance in the boy's bedroom.

The Derby was drawing near, and the boy grew more and more tense. He hardly heard what was spoken to him, he was very frail, and his eyes were really uncanny. His mother had sudden strange seizures of uneasiness about him. Sometimes, for half an hour, she would feel a sudden anxiety about him that was almost anguish. She wanted to rush to him at once, and know he was safe.

Two nights before the Derby, she was at a big party in town, when one of her rushes of anxiety about her boy, her first-born, gripped her heart till she could hardly speak. She fought with the feeling, might and main, for she believed in common sense. But it was too strong. She had to leave the dance and go upstairs to telephone to the country. The children's nursery-governess was terribly surprised and startled at being rung up in the night.

"Are the children all right, Miss Wilmot?"

"Oh, yes, they are quite all right."

"Master Paul? Is he all right?"

"He went to bed as right as a trivet. Shall I run up and look at him?"

"No," said Paul's mother reluctantly. "No! Don't trouble. It's all right. Don't sit up. We shall be home fairly soon." She did not want her son's privacy intruded upon.

William Merritt Chase, *Portrait of Lady in Pink*, circa 1888–1889, Museum of Art, Rhode Island School of Design, Providence, Rhode Island

"Very good," said the governess.

It was about one o'clock when Paul's mother and father drove up to their house. All was still. Paul's mother went to her room and slipped off her white fur cloak. She had told her maid not to wait up for her. She heard her husband downstairs, mixing a whiskey-and-soda.

And then, because of the strange anxiety at her heart, she stole upstairs to her son's room. Noiselessly she went along the upper corridor. Was there a faint noise? What was it?

She stood, with arrested muscles, outside his door, listening. There was a strange, heavy, and yet not loud noise. Her heart stood still. It was a soundless noise, yet rushing and powerful. Something huge, in violent, hushed motion. What was it? What in God's name was it? She ought to know. She felt that she knew the noise. She knew what it was.

Yet she could not place it. She couldn't say what it was. And on and on it went, like a madness.

Softly, frozen with anxiety and fear, she turned the door handle.

The room was dark. Yet in the space near the window, she heard and saw something plunging to and fro. She gazed in fear and amazement.

Then suddenly she switched on the light, and saw her son, in his green pajamas, madly surging on the rocking horse. The blaze of light suddenly lit him up, as he urged the wooden horse, and lit her up, as she stood, blonde, in her dress of pale green and crystal, in the doorway.

"Paul!" she cried. "Whatever are you doing?"

"It's Malabar!" he screamed, in a powerful, strange voice. "It's Malabar!"

His eyes blazed at her for one strange and senseless second, as he ceased urging his wooden horse. Then he fell with a crash to the ground, and she, all her tormented motherhood flooding upon her, rushed to gather him up.

But he was unconscious, and unconscious he remained with some brain fever. He talked and tossed, and his mother sat stonily by his side.

"Malabar! It's Malabar! Bassett, Bassett, I *know!* It's Malabar!"

So the child cried, trying to get up and urge the rocking horse that gave him his inspiration.

"What does he mean by Malabar?" asked the heart-frozen mother.

"I don't know," said the father stonily.

"What does he mean by Malabar?" she asked her brother Oscar.

"It's one of the horses running for the Derby," was the answer.

And, in spite of himself, Oscar Cresswell spoke to Bassett, and himself put a thousand on Malabar: at fourteen to one.

The third day of the illness was critical: they were waiting for a change. The boy, with his rather long, curly hair, was tossing ceaselessly on the pillow. He neither slept nor regained consciousness, and his eyes were like blue stones. His mother sat, feeling her heart had gone, turned actually into a stone.

In the evening, Oscar Cresswell did not come, but Bassett sent a message, saying could he come up for one moment, just one moment? Paul's mother was very angry at the intrusion, but on second thought she agreed. The boy was the same. Perhaps Bassett might bring him to consciousness.

The gardener, a shortish fellow with a little brown mustache, and sharp little brown eyes, tiptoed into the room, touched his imaginary cap to Paul's mother, and stole to the bedside, staring with glittering, smallish eyes, at the tossing, dying child.

"Master Paul!" he whispered. "Master Paul! Malabar came in first all right, a clean win. I did as you told me. You've made over seventy thousand pounds, you have; you've got over eighty thousand. Malabar came in all right, Master Paul."

"Malabar! Malabar! Did I say Malabar, Mother? Did I say Malabar? Do you think I'm lucky, Mother? I knew Malabar, didn't I? Over eighty thousand pounds! I call that lucky, don't you, Mother? Over eighty thousand pounds! I knew, didn't I know I knew? Malabar came in all right. If I ride my horse till I'm sure, then I tell you, Bassett, you can go as high as you like. Did you go for all you were worth, Bassett?"

"I went a thousand on it, Master Paul."

"I never told you, Mother, that if I can ride my horse, and *get* there, then I'm absolutely sure—oh, absolutely! Mother, did I ever tell you? I *am* lucky!"

"No, you never did," said the mother.

But the boy died in the night.

And even as he lay dead, his mother heard her brother's voice saying to her: "My God, Hester, you're eighty-odd thousand to the good, and a poor devil of a son to the bad. But, poor devil, poor devil, he's best gone out of a life where he rides his rocking horse to find a winner."

## THINK AND DISCUSS

### Understanding

1. How is Paul's mother characterized in the opening lines of the story?
2. What anxiety did the family have in the house? How did it haunt them?
3. According to the mother, why is it better to be born lucky than rich?
4. When Paul's uncle asks what he intends to do with the winnings, what is Paul's answer?

### Analyzing

5. Though seemingly a minor **character,** what important role does the father play in the plot?
6. How does Paul go about becoming lucky?
7. Explain why the whispering grows louder after Paul's mother receives five thousand pounds. How does this affect Paul?

### Extending

8. Defend or criticize this statement: "Money is the root of all evil" is a good expression of the **theme** of "The Rocking-Horse Winner."
9. Which elements and incidents in the story do you consider most fantastic or unbelievable? Can you find some psychological explanation for any of these fantasy elements? Explain.

### REVIEWING: Symbol H$\cancel{Z}$
#### See Handbook of Literary Terms, p. 828

Many stories contain a single symbol that stands for one object or idea and reappears periodically throughout the story. Other stories may contain several symbols. Think about "The Rocking-Horse Winner" and explain the symbolic meaning of the following: the whispering, the money, the rocking horse, Paul's rocking on the horse, and what happens to Paul at the end.

## COMPOSITION ◄━━●

### Reading/Writing Log

In "The Rocking-Horse Winner" D. H. Lawrence uses imagery that borders on the fantastic. Review the story, paying close attention to the adjectives that describe Paul's eyes. You will notice that words like *uncanny, strange,* and *flaring* suggest either the supernatural or madness. In your reading/ writing log or another notebook, write the descriptions and what you think they suggest about Paul. Is he portrayed as a character capable of some supernatural action, or is he presented as a character who is going or has gone mad?

### Explaining a Character's Nature

After reviewing the descriptions of Paul's eyes, read other descriptions of Paul throughout the story. Then write a two-paragraph composition explaining whether you think the narrator is portraying a boy who has somehow acquired supernatural powers or if Paul has simply gone mad. Be sure to use examples from the story to support your viewpoint.

### Analyzing a Story's Ending

When you reached the end of "The Rocking-Horse Winner," you may have been surprised by Paul's abrupt death. Do you think this is an effective way to end the story? If so, write a three-paragraph composition explaining why you think it is effective. If you do not think it is an effective ending, write what you think would have been a more appropriate ending, and explain why.

**Researching Attitudes on Luck**

While luck is important to Paul's mother and in the minds of racetrack bettors, many influential people consider the idea of luck to be nothing more than nonsense. You and a few classmates—or your class—may find out how people in your community think about luck either by interviewing community leaders and everyday people or by conducting a survey of fellow students or citizens and then reporting the results. Interviews with labor and business directors, religious leaders, politicians, educators, athletes, and other residents may focus on whether they believe in luck, how they respond to people who count on luck (or fear bad luck), and how they might teach young people about the concept of luck if they had a chance. A school newspaper or club can help you conduct a survey of student opinion about similar questions. After your research, report the results to your class.

# BIOGRAPHY

## D. H. Lawrence
## 1885–1930

The son of a coal miner, David Herbert Lawrence was born in the small provincial town of Eastwood, England, where he endured a miserable childhood. His strong-willed mother urged him to become a teacher, a profession he took up at the age of twenty and followed for a number of years. During this period, he also wrote and, with the publication of his first work and the death of his mother, left teaching to write full-time. In almost twenty years of writing, he produced nearly forty volumes of fiction, poetry, drama, literary description, and travel description. His novels and short stories came to be regarded as early examples of modern psychological fiction.

Long threatened by tuberculosis, Lawrence traveled widely in search of healthful environments. He and his wife resided briefly at many European locations and at a retreat in Taos, New Mexico, that became famous for his presence. Lawrence was only forty-four when he died of the disease.

# The Needle

**Isaac Bashevis Singer**   Poland/USA

**Some might take extreme measures in choosing the right mate, but according to the teller of this tale, "Everything depends on luck."**

y good people, nowadays all marriages are arranged by Mr. Love. Young folks fall in love and begin to date. They go out together until they start to quarrel and hate each other. In my time we relied on father and mother and the matchmaker. I myself did not see my Todie until the wedding ceremony, when he lifted the veil from my face. There he stood with his red beard and disheveled sidelocks. It was after Pentecost,[1] but he wore a fur coat as if it were winter. That I didn't faint dead away was a miracle from heaven. I had fasted through the long summer day. Still, I wish my best friends no worse life than I had with my husband, he should intercede for me in the next world. Perhaps I shouldn't say this, but I can't wait until our souls are together again.

"Yes, love-shmuv. What does a young boy or girl know about what is good for them? Mothers used to know the signs. In Krasnostaw[2] there lived a woman called Reitze Leah,[3] and when she was looking for brides for her sons she made sure to drop in on her prospective in-laws early in the morning. If she found that the bed linens were dirty and the girl in question came to the door with uncombed hair, wearing a sloppy dressing gown, that was it. Before long everybody in the neighboring villages was on to her, and when she

was seen in the marketplace early in the morning, all the young girls made sure their doors were bolted. She had six able sons. None of the matches she made for them was any good, but that is another story. A girl may be clean and neat before the wedding, but afterwards she becomes a slattern. Everything depends on luck.

"But let me tell you a story. In Hrubyeshow there lived a rich man, Reb Lemel Wagmeister.[4] In those days we didn't use surnames, but Reb Lemel was so rich that he was always called Wagmeister. His wife's name was Esther Rosa, and she came from the other side of the Vistula.[5] I see

---

*Isaac Bashevis Singer* (bə shev′is).

1. *sidelocks . . . Pentecost.* Sidelocks, locks of hair worn long on the side of the head, are worn by Jewish male Hasidim (has′i dim), members of a religious movement founded in the 1700s in Poland. Pentecost is a religious festival observed during the spring.
2. *Krasnostaw* (krus′nů stäf), a village in Poland. Other places mentioned are Hrubyeshow (hrü byesh′üf), Zamosc (zä′mosh), Lublin (lü′blēn), and Warsaw, all cities in Poland; and Vienna, the capital of Austria.
3. *Reitze Leah* (rī′tzə lä′ə).
4. *Reb Lemel Wagmeister* (reb′ lä′məl väg′mī′stər). *Reb* is a title of respect meaning "rabbi" or "mister."
5. *Vistula* (vis′chə lə), the longest river in Poland.

"The Needle" from *The Seance and Other Stories* by Isaac Bashevis Singer. Copyright © 1964, 1965, 1966, 1967, 1968 by Isaac Bashevis Singer. Reprinted by permission of Farrar, Straus and Giroux, Inc., and Laurence Pollinger Ltd. Slightly abridged.

Mane Katz (män kats), *Jewish Wedding*, Private Collection.

her with my own eyes: a beautiful woman, with a big-city air. She always wore a black-lace mantilla over her wig. Her face was as white and smooth as a girl's. Her eyes were dark. She spoke Russian, Polish, German, and maybe even French. She played the piano. Even when the streets were muddy, she wore high-heeled patent-leather shoes. One autumn I saw her hopping from stone to stone like a bird, lifting her skirt with both hands, a real lady. They had an only son, Ben Zion. He was as like his mother as two drops of water. We were distant relatives, not on her side but on her husband's. Ben Zion—Benze, he was called—had every virtue: he was handsome, clever, learned. He studied the Torah[6] with the rabbi in the daytime and in the evening a teacher of secular subjects took over. Benze had black hair and a fair complexion, like his mother. When he took a walk in the summertime wearing his elegant gaberdine with a fashionable slit in the back, and his smart kid boots, all the girls mooned over him through the windows. Although it is the custom to give dowries only to daughters, Benze's father set aside for his son a sum of ten thousand rubles.[7] What difference did it make to him? Benze was his only heir. They tried to match him with the richest girls in the province, but Esther Rosa was very choosy. She had nothing to do, what with three maids, a manservant, and a coachman in addition. So she spent her time looking for brides for Benze. She had already inspected the best-looking girls in half of Poland, but not one had she found without some defect. One wasn't beautiful enough; another, not sufficiently clever. But what she was looking for most was nobility of character. 'Because,' she said, 'if a woman is coarse, it is the husband who suffers. I don't want any woman to vent her spleen on my Benze.' I was already married at the time. I married when I was fifteen. Esther Rosa had no real friend in Hrubyeshow and I became a frequent visitor to her house. She taught me how to knit and embroider and do needlepoint. She had golden hands. When the fancy took her, she could make herself a dress or even a cape. She once made me a dress, just for the fun of it. She had a good head for business as well. Her husband hardly took a step without consulting her. Whenever she told him to buy or sell a property, Reb Lemel Wagmeister immediately sent for Lippe the agent and said: 'My wife wants to buy or sell such-and-such.' She never made a mistake.

"Well, Benze was already nineteen, and not even engaged. In those days nineteen was considered an old bachelor. Reb Lemel Wagmeister complained that the boy was being disgraced by his mother's choosiness. Benze developed pimples on his forehead.

"One day I came to see Esther Rosa to borrow a ball of yarn. And she said to me: 'Zeldele,[8] would you like to ride to Zamosc with me?'

" 'What will I do in Zamosc?' I asked.

" 'What difference does it make?' she replied. 'You'll be my guest.'

"Esther Rosa had her own carriage, but this time she went along with someone else who was going to Zamosc. I guessed that the journey had something to do with looking over a bride, but Esther Rosa's nature was such that one didn't ask questions. If she were willing to talk, well and good. If not, you just waited. To make it short, I went to tell my mother about the trip. No need to ask my husband. He sat in the study house all day long. When he came home in the evening, my mother served him his supper. In those days a young Talmud scholar[9] barely knew he had a wife. I don't believe that he would have recognized me if he met me on the street. I packed a dress and a pair of bloomers—I beg your pardon—and I was ready for the trip. We were traveling in a nobleman's carriage and he did the driving himself. Two horses like lions. The road was dry and smooth as a table. When we arrived in Zamosc, he let us off not at the marketplace but on a side street where the Gentiles live. Esther Rosa thanked him and he tipped his hat and waved his whip at us good-naturedly. It all looked arranged.

---

6. *Benze* (ben′tsə) . . . *studied the Torah.* The young man was studying the first five books of the Old Testament.
7. *ten thousand rubles.* At the time of the story, this amount in Russian money was worth about five thousand dollars in United States currency.
8. *Zeldele* (zel′də lə).
9. *Talmud scholar.* It was once customary for all young Jewish men to study the Talmud, a collection of sixty-three volumes containing Jewish law in the form of interpretation and expansion of Old Testament teachings.

"As a rule, when Esther Rosa traveled anyplace she dressed as elegantly as a countess. This time she wore a simple cotton dress, and a kerchief over her wig. It was summer and the days were long. We walked to the marketplace and she inquired for Berish Lubliner's dry-goods store. A large store was pointed out to us. Nowadays in a dry-goods store you can only buy yard goods, but in those days they sold everything: thread, wool for knitting, and odds and ends. What didn't they sell? It was a store as big as a forest, filled with merchandise to the ceiling. At a high desk-stand a man sat writing in a ledger, as they do in the big cities. I don't know what he was, the cashier or a bookkeeper. Behind a counter stood a girl with black eyes that burned like fire. We happened to be the only customers in the store, and we approached her. 'What can I do for you?' she asked. 'You seem to be strangers.'

" 'Yes, we are strangers,' said Esther Rosa.

" 'What would you like to see?' the girl asked.

" 'A needle,' said Esther Rosa.

"The moment she heard the word 'needle,' the girl's face changed. Her eyes became angry. 'Two women for one needle,' she said.

"Merchants believe that a needle is unlucky. Nobody ever dared to buy a needle at the beginning of the week, because they knew it meant the whole week would be unlucky. Even in the middle of the week the storekeepers did not like to sell needles. One usually bought a spool of thread, some buttons, and the needle was thrown in without even being mentioned. A needle costs only half a groshen and it was a nuisance to make such small change.

" 'Yes,' said Esther Rosa. 'All I need is a needle.'

"The girl frowned but took out a box of needles. Esther Rosa searched through the box and said: 'Perhaps you have some other needles?'

" 'What's wrong with these?' the girl asked impatiently.

" 'Their eyes are too small,' Esther Rosa said. 'It will be difficult to thread them.'

" 'These are all I have,' the girl said angrily. 'If you can't see well, why don't you buy yourself a pair of eyeglasses.'

"Esther Rosa insisted. 'Are you sure you have no others? I must have a needle with a larger eye.'

"The girl reluctantly pulled out another box and slammed it down on the counter. Esther Rosa examined several needles and said: 'These too have small eyes.'

"The girl snatched away the box and screamed: 'Why don't you go to Lublin and order yourself a special needle with a big eye.'

"The man at the stand began to laugh. 'Perhaps you need a sackcloth needle,' he suggested. 'Some nerve,' the girl chimed in, 'to bother people over a half-groshen sale.'

"Esther Rosa replied: 'I have no use for sackcloth or for girls who are as coarse as sackcloth.' Then she turned to me and said: 'Come, Zeldele, they are not our kind.'

"The girl turned red in the face and said loudly, 'What yokels! Good riddance!'

"We went out. The whole business had left a bad taste in my mouth. A woman passed by and Esther Rosa asked her the way to Reb Zelig Izbitzer's dry-goods store. 'Right across the street,' she said, pointing. We crossed the marketplace and entered a store that was only a third of the size of the first one. Here too there was a young saleswoman. This one wasn't dark; she had red hair. She was not ugly but she had freckles. Her eyes were as green as gooseberries. Esther Rosa asked if she sold needles. And the girl replied, 'Why not? We sell everything.'

" 'I'm looking for a needle with a large eye, because I have trouble threading needles,' Esther Rosa said.

" 'I'll show you every size we have and you can pick the one that suits you best,' the girl replied.

"I had already guessed what was going on and

my heart began to beat like a thief's. The girl brought out about ten boxes of needles. 'Why should you stand?' she said. 'Here is a stool. Please be seated.' She also brought a stool for me. It was perfectly clear to me that Esther Rosa was going to test her too.

" 'Why are the needles all mixed together?' Esther Rosa complained. 'Each size should be in a different box.'

" 'When they come from the factory, they are all sorted out,' the girl said apologetically. 'But they get mixed up.' I saw Esther Rosa was doing her best to make the girl lose her temper. 'I don't see too well,' Esther Rosa said. 'It's dark here.'

" 'Just one moment and I'll move the stools to the door. There is more light there,' the girl replied.

" 'Does it pay you to make all this effort just to sell a half-penny needle?' Esther Rosa asked. And the girl answered: 'First of all, a needle costs only a quarter of a penny, and then as the Talmud says, the same law applies to a penny as it does to a hundred guilders.[10] Besides, today you buy a needle and tomorrow you may be buying satins for a trousseau.'

" 'Is that so? Then how come the store is empty?' Esther Rosa wanted to know. 'Across the street, Berish Lubliner's store is so full of customers you can't find room for a pin between them. I bought my materials there but I decided to come here for the needle.'

"The girl became serious. I was afraid that Esther Rosa had overdone it. Even an angel can lose patience. But the girl said, 'Everything according to God's will.' Esther Rosa made a move to carry her stool to the door, but the girl stopped her. 'Please don't trouble yourself. I'll do it.' Esther Rosa interrupted. 'Just a moment, I want to tell you something.'

" 'What do you want to tell me?' the girl said, setting down the stool.

" 'My daughter, *Mazel Tov!*'[11] Esther Rosa called out.

"The girl turned as white as chalk. 'I don't understand,' she said.

" 'You will be my daughter-in-law,' Esther Rosa announced. 'I am the wife of Reb Lemel Wagmeister of Hrubyeshow. I have come here to look for a bride for my son. Not to buy a needle. Reb Berish's daughter is like a straw mat and you are like silk. You will be my Benze's wife, God willing.'

"That the girl didn't faint dead away was a miracle from heaven. Everybody in Zamosc had heard of Reb Lemel Wagmeister. Zamosc is not Lublin. Customers came in and saw what was happening. Esther Rosa took a string of amber beads out of her basket. 'Here is your engagement gift. Bend your head.' The girl lowered her head submissively and Esther Rosa placed the beads around her neck. Her father and mother came running into the store. There was kissing, embracing, crying. Someone immediately rushed to tell the story to Reb Berish's daughter. When she heard what had happened, she burst into tears. Her name was Itte.[12] She had a large dowry and was known as a shrew saleswoman. Zelig Izbitzer barely made a living.

"My good people, it was a match. Esther Rosa wore the pants in the family. Whatever she said went. And as I said, in those days young people were never asked. An engagement party was held and the wedding soon after. Zelig Izbitzer could not afford a big wedding. He barely could give his daughter a dowry, for he also had two other daughters and two sons who were studying in the yeshiva.[13] But, as you know, Reb Lemel Wagmeister had little need for her dowry. I went to

---

10. *a hundred guilders,* about twenty dollars.
11. *Mazel Tov* (ma′zəl tôv), congratulations. [*Hebrew*]
12. *Itte* (ē′tə).
13. *yeshiva* (yə shē′və), a Jewish school for higher studies, often a rabbinical seminary.

the engagement party and I danced at the wedding. Esther Rosa dressed the girl like a princess. She became really beautiful. When good luck shines, it shows on the face. Whoever did not see that couple standing under the wedding canopy and later dancing the virtue dance will never know what it means to have joy in children. Afterwards they lived like doves. Exactly to the year, she bore a son.

"From the day Itte discovered that Esther Rosa had come to test her, she began to ail. She spoke about the visit constantly. She stopped attending customers. Day and night she cried. The matchmakers showered her with offers, but first she wouldn't have anyone else and second what had happened had given her a bad name. You know how people exaggerate. All kinds of lies were invented about her. She had insulted Esther Rosa in the worst way, had spat in her face, had even beaten her up. Itte's father was stuffed with money and in a small town everybody is envious of his neighbor's crust of bread. Now his enemies had their revenge. Itte had been the real merchant and without her the store went to pieces. After a while she married a man from Lublin. He wasn't even a bachelor. He was divorced. He came to Zamosc and took over his father-in-law's store. But he was as much a businessman as I am a musician.

"That is how things are. If luck is with you, it serves you well. And when it stops serving you, everything goes topsy-turvy. Itte's mother became so upset she developed gallstones, or maybe it was jaundice. Her face became as yellow as saffron. Itte no longer entered the store. She became a stay-at-home. It was hoped that when she became pregnant and had a child, she would forget. But twice she miscarried. She became half crazy, went on cursing Frieda Gittel—that is what Benze's wife was called—and insisted that the other had connived against her. Who knows what goes on in a madwoman's head? Itte also foretold that Frieda Gittel would die and that she, Itte, would take her place. When Itte became pregnant for the third time, her father took her to a miracle-worker. I've forgotten to mention that by this time her mother was already dead. The miracle-worker gave her potions and talismans, but she miscarried again. She began to run to doctors and to imagine all kinds of illnesses.

"Now listen to this. One evening Itte was sitting in her room sewing. She had finished her length of thread and wanted to rethread her needle. While getting the spool she placed the needle between her lips. Suddenly she felt a stab in her throat and the needle vanished. She searched all over for it, but—what is the saying—'Who can find a needle in a haystack?' My dear people, Itte began to imagine that she had swallowed the needle. She felt a pricking in her stomach, in her breast, her legs. There is a saying 'A needle wanders.' She visited the leech,[14] but what does a leech know? She went to doctors in Lublin and even in Warsaw. One doctor said one thing; another, something different. They poked her stomach but could find no needle. God preserve us. Itte lay in bed and screamed that the needle was pricking her. The town was in a turmoil. Some said that she had swallowed the needle on purpose to commit suicide. Others, that it was a punishment from God. But why should she have been punished? She had already suffered enough for her rudeness. Finally she went to Vienna to a great doctor. And he found the way out. He put her to sleep and made a cut in her belly. When she woke up he showed her the needle that he was supposed to have removed from her insides. I wasn't there. Perhaps he really found a needle, but that's not what people said. When she returned from Vienna, she was her former self again. The store had gone to ruin. Her father was

---

14. *the leech,* one who applies leeches—bloodsucking worms—to draw blood from wounds.

already in the other world. Itte, however, opened a new store. In the new store she succeeded again, but she never had any children.

"I've forgotten to mention that after what happened between Esther Rosa and the two girls, the salesgirls of Zamosc became the souls of politeness, not only to strangers, but even to their own townspeople. For how could one know whether a customer had come to buy or to test? The book peddler did a fine trade in books on etiquette, and when a woman came to buy a ball of yarn, she was offered a chair.

"I can't tell you what happened later, because I moved away from Zamosc. In the big cities one forgets about everything, even about God. Reb Lemel Wagmeister and Esther Rosa have long since passed away. I haven't heard from Benze or his wife for a long time. Yes, a needle. Because of a rooster and a chicken a whole town was de-stroyed in the Holy Land,[15] and because of a needle a match was spoiled. The truth is that everything is fated from heaven. You can love someone until you burst, but if it's not destined, it will come to naught. A boy and a girl can be keeping company for seven years, and a stranger comes along and breaks everything up. I could tell you a story of a boy who married his girl's best friend out of spite, and she, to spite him, kept to her bed for twenty years. Tell it? It's too late. If I were to tell you all the stories I know, we'd be sitting here for seven days and seven nights."

---

15. *Because . . . Holy Land.* It was an ancient Jewish custom to carry a chicken and rooster before the bride and groom in a wedding procession to symbolize a fruitful union. According to the Talmud, when a contingent of Roman soldiers once happened upon such a scene in a town near Jerusalem, a skirmish took place that was reported to Roman authorities as a rebellion. As a result, Roman forces destroyed the town.

## THINK AND DISCUSS
### Understanding
1. What complaint does Zedele, the narrator of the story, make about marriages nowadays as compared with the old days?
2. Does the narrator's story about Reitze Leah support her point? Discuss.
3. How does Esther Rosa use a needle to test the natures of Itte and Frieda Gittel? What qualities is she looking for?

### Analyzing
4. What makes Zedele think Esther Rosa's trip to Zamosc has a hidden purpose?
5. What is the cause of Itte's many problems after she fails the test?
6. Does the needle test work? Explain.
7. What might the needle **symbolize** to each of the following characters? Esther Rosa, Itte, Frieda Gittel, the narrator?

### Extending
8. Do you think the "needle test" is a fair and accurate measure of character? Explain.

## VOCABULARY
### Etymology

| | | |
|---|---|---|
| dowry | mantilla | talisman |
| Gentile | naught | trousseau |

Refer to the Glossary for the etymologies of the words listed above. Then write the number of each of the following statements and, next to each number, the word from the list that it best fits. You will not use all the words. Be prepared to pronounce each word and explain its meaning.

1. Comes from a French word that originally meant "bundle."
2. Comes from a Latin word that has meant "foreign" and, earlier, "of a people."
3. Comes from a Spanish word.
4. Has a history that includes French, Arabic, and a similarly spelled Greek word.
5. Comes from Old English.

## COMPOSITION
### Judging a Character's Method

In "The Needle," Esther Rosa seems to have found an effective way of screening the worthiness of two young women to become her daughter-in-law. Do you think this method, or one similar to it, could be applied effectively today? If so, explain why in a two-paragraph composition. If not, write a two-paragraph composition suggesting a different method or methods that you think would be more effective today.

### Writing a Letter

In "The Needle," Itte blames her many problems in life on her having failed the needle test. Write a letter to Itte explaining that her problems have other causes, and offer suggestions as to how she can improve her attitude toward life.

## BIOGRAPHY

### Isaac Bashevis Singer
### 1904–

Isaac Bashevis Singer's writings are rooted in his Polish-Jewish background. Born in Radzymin (räd zi'mēn), Poland, he came from a family of rabbis and received an intensely religious education; however, he came to share his older brother's strong interest in nonreligious writings. Following his brother to Warsaw in the 1920s, Singer became an editor and short story contributor to a literary magazine. In 1935 he settled in the United States, producing fiction in Yiddish for a newspaper. He gained a wider audience and much critical praise when these works were translated into English. In 1978 his writing won him the Nobel Prize.

An old-fashioned storyteller in a modern age, Singer is best known for his short stories. A few of his collections are *Gimpel the Fool* (1957), *The Spinoza of Market Street* (1961), *A Crown of Feathers* (1973), and *Old Love* (1979). A book for young people, *A Day of Pleasure: Stories of a Boy Growing Up in Warsaw* (1969), won the 1970 National Book Award.

# The Rat Trap

**Selma Lagerlöf**  Sweden

**The peddler's outlook on life had been shaped by his experiences.
Then there came a chance to take on the experiences of someone else.**

nce upon a time there was a man who went around selling small rat traps of wire. He made them himself at odd moments, from material he got by begging in the stores or at the big farms. But even so, the business was not especially profitable, so he had to resort to both begging and petty thievery to keep body and soul together. Even so, his clothes were in rags, his cheeks were sunken, and hunger gleamed in his eyes.

No one can imagine how sad and monotonous life can appear to such a vagabond, who plods along the road, left to his own meditations. But one day this man had fallen into a line of thought which really seemed to him entertaining. He had naturally been thinking of his rat traps when suddenly he was struck by the idea that the whole world about him—the whole world with its lands and seas, its cities and villages—was nothing but a big rat trap. It had never existed for any other purpose than to set baits for people. It offered riches and joys, shelter and food, heat and clothing, exactly as the rat trap offered cheese and pork, and as soon as anyone let himself be tempted to touch the bait, it closed in on him, and then everything came to an end.

The world had, of course, never been very kind to him, so it gave him unwonted joy to think ill of it in this way. It became a cherished pastime of his, during many dreary ploddings, to think of people he knew who had let themselves be caught in the dangerous snare, and of others who were still circling around the bait.

One dark evening as he was trudging along the road he caught sight of a little gray cottage by the roadside, and he knocked on the door to ask shelter for the night. Nor was he refused. Instead of the sour faces which ordinarily met him, the owner, who was an old man without wife or child, was happy to get someone to talk to in his loneliness. Immediately he put the porridge pot on the fire and gave him supper; then he carved off such a big slice from his tobacco roll that it was enough for both the stranger's pipe and his own. Finally he got out an old pack of cards and played *mjölis*[1] with his guest until bedtime.

The old man was just as generous with his

---

*Selma Lagerlöf* (lä′gər ləv).

1. *mjölis* (myu′lis), a Swedish card game.

confidences as with his porridge and tobacco. The guest was informed at once that in his days of prosperity his host had been a crofter at the Ramsjö Ironworks[2] and had worked on the land. Now that he was no longer able to do day labor, it was his cow which supported him. Yes, that bossy was extraordinary. She could give milk for the creamery every day, and last month he had received all of thirty kronor[3] in payment.

The stranger must have seemed incredulous, for the old man got up and went to the window, took down a leather pouch which hung on a nail in the very window frame, and picked out three wrinkled ten-kronor bills. These he held up before the eyes of his guest, nodding knowingly, and then stuffed them back into the pouch.

The next day both men got up in good season. The crofter was in a hurry to milk his cow, and the other man probably thought he should not stay in bed when the head of the house had gotten up. They left the cottage at the same time. The crofter locked the door and put the key in his pocket. The man with the rat traps said good-by and thank you, and thereupon each went his own way.

But half an hour later the rat-trap peddler stood again before the door. He did not try to get in, however. He only went up to the window, smashed a pane, stuck in his hand, and got hold of the pouch with their thirty kronor. He took the money and thrust it into his own pocket. Then he hung the leather pouch very carefully back in its place and went away.

As he walked along with the money in his pocket he felt quite pleased with his smartness. He realized, of course, that at first he dared not continue on the public highway, but must turn off the road, into the woods. During the first few hours this caused him no difficulty. Later in the day it became worse, for it was a big and confusing forest which he had gotten into. He tried, to be sure, to walk in a definite direction, but the paths twisted back and forth so strangely! He walked and walked, without coming to the end of the wood, and finally he realized that he had only been walking around in the same part of the forest. All at once he recalled his thoughts about the world and the rat trap. Now his own turn had come. He had let himself be fooled by a bait and had been caught. The whole forest, with its trunks and branches, its thickets and fallen logs, closed in upon him like an impenetrable prison from which he could never escape.

It was late in December. Darkness was already descending over the forest. This increased the danger, and increased also his gloom and despair. Finally he saw no way out, and he sank down on the ground, tired to death, thinking that his last moment had come. But just as he laid his head on the ground, he heard a sound—a hard, regular thumping. There was no doubt as to what that was. He raised himself. "Those are the hammer strokes from an iron mill," he thought. "There must be people nearby." He summoned all his strength, got up, and staggered in the direction of the sound.

The Ramsjö Ironworks, which are now closed down, was, not so long ago, a large plant, with smelter, rolling mill, and forge. In the summertime long lines of heavily loaded barges and scows slid down the canal, which led to a large inland lake, and in the wintertime the roads near the mill were black from all the coal dust which sifted down from the big charcoal crates.

During one of the long dark evenings just before Christmas, the master smith and his helper sat in the dark forge near the furnace waiting for the pig iron, which had been put in the fire, to be

---

**2. crofter at the Ramsjö** (räm′shu) **Ironworks.** A crofter is a person who cultivates a very small farm (croft), usually as a tenant of someone else—in this case, of the Ramsjö Ironworks.

**3. thirty kronor.** A krona is a silver and copper coin that is the Swedish monetary unit; thirty kronor at the time amounted to six dollars in United States currency.

ready to put on the anvil. Every now and then one of them got up to stir the glowing mass with a long iron bar, returning in a few moments, dripping with perspiration, though, as was the custom, he wore nothing but a long shirt and a pair of wooden shoes.

All the time there were many sounds to be heard in the forge. The big bellows groaned and the burning coal cracked. The fire boy shoveled charcoal into the maw of the furnace with a great deal of clatter. Outside roared the waterfall, and a sharp north wind whipped the rain against the brick-tiled roof.

It was probably on account of all this noise that the blacksmith did not notice that a man had opened the gate and entered the forge, until he stood close up to the furnace.

Surely it was nothing unusual for poor vagabonds without any better shelter for the night to be attracted to the forge by the glow of light which escaped through the sooty panes, and to come in to warm themselves in front of the fire. The blacksmiths glanced only casually and indifferently at the intruder. He looked the way people of his type usually did, with a long beard, dirty, ragged, and with a bunch of rat traps dangling on his chest.

He asked permission to stay, and the master blacksmith nodded a haughty consent without honoring him with a single word.

The tramp did not say anything, either. He had not come there to talk but only to warm himself and sleep.

In those days the Ramsjö iron mill was owned by a very prominent ironmaster, whose greatest ambition was to ship out good iron to the market. He watched both night and day to see that the work was done as well as possible, and at this very moment he came into the forge on one of his nightly rounds of inspection.

Naturally the first thing he saw was the tall ragamuffin who had eased his way so close to the furnace that steam rose from his wet rags. The ironmaster did not follow the example of the blacksmiths, who had hardly deigned to look at the stranger. He walked close up to him, looked him over very carefully, then tore off his slouch hat to get a better view of his face.

"But of course it is you, Nils Olof?" he said. "How do you look!"

The man with the rat traps had never before seen the ironmaster of Ramsjö and did not even know what his name was. But it occurred to him that if the fine gentleman thought he was an old acquaintance, he might perhaps throw him a couple of kronor. Therefore he did not want to undeceive him all at once.

"Yes, God knows things have gone downhill with me," he said.

"You should not have resigned from the regiment," said the ironmaster. "That was the mistake. If only I had still been in the service at the time, it never would have happened. Well, now of course you will come home with me."

To go along up to the manor house and be received by the owner like an old regimental comrade—that, however, did not please the tramp.

"No, I couldn't think of it!" he said, looking quite alarmed.

He thought of the thirty kronor. To go up to the manor house would be like throwing himself voluntarily into the lions' den. He only wanted a chance to sleep here in the forge and then sneak away as inconspicuously as possible.

The ironmaster assumed that he felt embarrassed because of his miserable clothing.

"Please don't think that I have such a fine home that you cannot show yourself there," he said. "Elizabeth is dead, as you may already have heard. My boys are abroad, and there is no one at home except my oldest daughter and myself. We were just saying that it was too bad we didn't have any company for Christmas. Now come along with me and help us make the Christmas food disappear a little faster."

But the stranger said no, and no, and again no, and the ironmaster saw that he must give in.

"It looks as though Captain von Ståhle prefers to stay with you tonight, Stjernström,"[4] he said to the master blacksmith, and turned on his heel.

But he laughed to himself as he went away, and the blacksmith, who knew him, understood very well that he had not said his last word.

It was not more than half an hour before they heard the sound of carriage wheels outside the forge, and a new guest came in, but this time it was not the ironmaster. He had sent his daughter, apparently hoping that she would have better powers of persuasion than he himself.

She entered, followed by a valet, carrying on his arm a big fur coat. She was not at all pretty, but seemed modest and quite shy. In the forge everything was just as it had been earlier in the evening. The master blacksmith and his apprentice still sat on their bench, and iron and charcoal still glowed in the furnace. The stranger had stretched himself out on the floor and lay with a piece of pig iron under his head and his hat pulled down over his eyes. As soon as the young girl caught sight of him she went up and lifted his hat. The man was evidently used to sleeping with one eye open. He jumped up abruptly and seemed to be quite frightened.

"My name is Edla Willmansson," said the young girl. "My father came home and said that you wanted to sleep here in the forge tonight, and then I asked permission to come and bring you home to us. I am so sorry, Captain, that you are having such a hard time."

She looked at him compassionately, with her heavy eyes, and then she noticed that the man was afraid. "Either he has stolen something or else he has escaped from jail," she thought, and added quickly, "You may be sure, Captain, that you will be allowed to leave us just as freely as you came. Only please stay with us over Christmas Eve."

She said this in such a friendly manner that the rat-trap peddler must have felt confidence in her.

"It would never have occurred to me that you would bother with me yourself, miss," he said. "I will come at once."

He accepted the fur coat, which the valet handed him with a deep bow, threw it over his rags, and followed the young lady out to the carriage, without granting the astonished blacksmiths so much as a glance.

But while he was riding up to the manor house he had evil forebodings.

"Why the devil did I take that fellow's money?" he thought. "Now I am sitting in the trap and will never get out of it."

The next day was Christmas Eve, and when the ironmaster came into the dining room for breakfast he probably thought with satisfaction of his old regimental comrade whom he had run across so unexpectedly.

"First of all we must see to it that he gets a little flesh on his bones," he said to his daughter, who was busy at the table. "And then we must see that he gets something else to do than to run around the country selling rat traps."

"It is queer that things have gone downhill with him as badly as that," said the daughter. "Last night I did not think there was anything about him to show that he had once been an educated man."

"You must have patience, my little girl," said the father. "As soon as he gets clean and dressed up, you will see something different. Last night he was naturally embarrassed. The tramp manners will fall away from him with the tramp clothes."

---

4. *von Ståhle* (fôn stô′lə) . . . *Stjernström* (styern′strum).

Just as he said this the door opened and the stranger entered. Yes, now he was truly clean and well dressed. The valet had bathed him, cut his hair, and shaved him. Moreover, he was dressed in a good-looking suit of clothes which belonged to the ironmaster. He wore a white shirt and a starched collar and whole shoes.

But although his guest was now so well-groomed, the ironmaster did not seem pleased. He looked at him with puckered brow, and it was easy enough to understand that when he had seen the strange fellow in the uncertain reflection from the furnace he might have made a mistake, but that now, when he stood there in broad daylight, it was impossible to mistake him for an old acquaintance.

"What does this mean?" he thundered.

The stranger made no attempt to dissimulate. He saw at once that all the splendor had come to an end.

"It is not my fault, sir," he said. "I never pretended to be anything but a poor trader, and I pleaded and begged to be allowed to stay in the forge. But no harm has been done. At worst I can put on my rags again and go away."

"Well," said the ironmaster, hesitating a little, "it was not quite honest, either. You must admit that, and I should not be surprised if the sheriff would like to have something to say in the matter."

The tramp took a step forward and struck the table with his fist.

"Now I am going to tell you, Mr. Ironmaster, how things are," he said. "This whole world is nothing but a big rat trap. All the good things that are offered you are nothing but cheese rinds and bits of pork, set out to drag a poor fellow into trouble. And if the sheriff comes now and locks me up for this, then you, Mr. Ironmaster, must remember that a day may come when you yourself may want to get a big piece of pork, and then you will get caught in the trap."

The ironmaster began to laugh.

"That was not so badly said, my good fellow. Perhaps we should let the sheriff alone on Christmas Eve. But now get out of here as fast as you can."

But just as the man was opening the door, the daughter said, "I think he ought to stay with us today. I don't want him to go." And with that she went and closed the door.

"What in the world are you doing?" said the father.

The daughter stood there quite embarrassed and hardly knew what to answer. That morning she had felt so happy when she thought how homelike and Christmassy she was going to make things for the poor hungry wretch. She could not get away from the idea all at once, and that was why she had interceded for the vagabond.

"I am thinking of this stranger here," said the young girl. "He walks and walks the whole year long, and there is probably not a single place in the whole country where he is welcome and can feel at home. Wherever he turns he is chased away. Always he is afraid of being arrested and cross-examined. I should like to have him enjoy a day of peace with us here—just one in the whole year."

The ironmaster mumbled something in his beard. He could not bring himself to oppose her.

"It was all a mistake, of course," she continued. "But anyway I don't think we ought to chase away a human being whom we have asked to come here, and to whom we have promised Christmas cheer."

"You do preach worse than a parson," said the ironmaster. "I only hope you won't have to regret this."

The young girl took the stranger by the hand and led him up to the table.

"Now sit down and eat," she said, for she could see that her father had given in.

The man with the rat traps said not a word; he

Carl Larsson, *Now It Is Christmas Again* (detail), Private Collection

only sat down and helped himself to the food. Time after time he looked at the young girl who had interceded for him. Why had she done it? What could the crazy idea be?

After that, Christmas Eve at Ramsjö passed just as it always had. The stranger did not cause any trouble because he did nothing but sleep. The whole forenoon he lay on the sofa in one of the guest rooms and slept at one stretch. At noon they woke him up so that he could have his share of the good Christmas fare but after that he slept again. It seemed as though for many years he had not been able to sleep as quietly and safely as here at Ramsjö.

In the evening, when the Christmas tree was lighted, they woke him up again, and he stood for a while in the drawing room, blinking as though the candlelight hurt him, but after that he disappeared again. Two hours later he was aroused once more. He then had to go down into the dining room and eat the Christmas fish[5] and porridge.

As soon as they got up from the table he went around to each one present and said thank you and good night, but when he came to the young girl she gave him to understand that it was her father's intention that the suit which he wore was to be a Christmas present—he did not have to return it; and if he wanted to spend next Christmas Eve in a place where he could rest in peace, and be sure that no evil would befall him, he would be welcomed back again.

The man with the rat traps did not answer anything to this. He only stared at the young girl in boundless amazement.

---

5. *Christmas fish,* probably lutefisk (lüd′ə fisk), which is served in Sweden traditionally on the eve of Christmas.

The next morning the ironmaster and his daughter got up in good season to go to the early Christmas service. Their guest was still asleep, and they did not disturb him.

When, at about ten o'clock, they drove back from church, the young girl sat and hung her head even more dejectedly than usual. At church she had learned that one of the old crofters of the ironworks had been robbed by a man who went around selling rat traps.

"Yes, that was a fine fellow you let into the house," said her father. "I only wonder how many silver spoons are left in the cupboard by this time."

The wagon had hardly stopped at the front steps when the ironmaster asked the valet whether the stranger was still there. He added that he had heard at church that the man was a thief. The valet answered that the fellow had gone and that he had not taken anything with him at all. On the contrary, he had left behind a little package which Miss Willmansson was to be kind enough to accept as a Christmas present.

The young girl opened the package, which was so badly done up that the contents came into view at once. She gave a little cry of joy. She found a small rat trap, and in it lay three wrinkled ten-kronor notes. But that was not all. In the rat trap lay also a letter written in large, jagged characters:

*Honored and noble Miss:*

*Since you have been so nice to me all day long, as if I was a captain, I want to be nice to you, in return, as if I was a real captain: for I do not want you to be embarrassed at this Christmas season by a thief; but you can give back the money to the old man on the roadside, who has the money pouch hanging on the window frame as a bait for poor wanderers.*

*The rat trap is a Christmas present from a rat who would have been caught in this world's rat trap if he had not been raised to captain, because in that way he got power to clear himself.*

*Written with friendship and high regard,*

*Captain von Ståhle.*

## THINK AND DISCUSS
### Understanding
1. As the story opens, what reasons does the vagabond have for feeling so pessimistic about the world?
2. Why does the vagabond leave the highway and enter the forest?
3. What mistake does the ironmaster make when he meets the vagabond?

### Analyzing
4. Do you get the impression that the vagabond desires material possessions? Explain.

5. Is the crofter in any way to blame for the theft of his money? Discuss.
6. What do the invitations of Willmansson and his daughter reveal about their characters?
7. What significant change in the vagabond's philosophy is suggested by his letter to the "Honored and Noble Miss"?

### Extending
8. Selma Lagerlöf's writings frequently contain themes of goodness triumphing over the forces of low-mindedness and cruelty. Explain how this story illustrates such a **theme.**

## THINKING SKILLS
### Generalizing

To **generalize** is to draw a general conclusion from particular information. Cheerful circumstances in life might cause someone to generalize that "life is a bowl of cherries." In contrast, the poverty and struggle of the peddler has led him to generalize that the world is a rat trap. By the end of the story, he might be prepared to reverse this idea. Write a generalization that could describe his new view. Read it to a small discussion group in your class and explain why you think he would feel that way.

## COMPOSITION
### Making Analogies

As you may know, an *analogy* is a comparison drawn between two different things that have some points in common. Many analogies have been made to express attitudes about life and the world. (For example, "The world is a space station on which we live and work.") In "The Rat Trap," the peddler compares the world to a rat trap. Think of other analogies of life and the world that you have heard. Select one and write a two-paragraph composition explaining whether you agree or disagree with it. If you like, you may make up your own analogy and explain it.

### Writing an Imaginative Letter

Imagine that you are the tramp five years after the events in the story. What is your situation in life? How are you making a living? What is your attitude toward the world around you? Answer these questions in a three-paragraph letter to Edla Willmansson. Try to express the tramp's mood in the letter and to write in a style that he might use.

## BIOGRAPHY

### Selma Lagerlöf
### 1858–1940

Lagerlöf's sympathetic interpretation of Swedish folklore won her the 1909 Nobel Prize for Literature, making her the first woman to be so honored.

Born on the family estate in the province of Värmland, Lagerlöf grew up fascinated with the old legends of the area. She began publishing her writings during her years as a country schoolteacher, never dreaming of fame. Yet in 1891 the publication of *The Story of Gösta Berling,* her first novel, made her the best-known Scandinavian storyteller since Hans Christian Andersen. Its success allowed Lagerlöf to devote all her time to writing. Her works from this productive period include *Jerusalem* (1901–1902), an epic novel of men who travel to the Holy Land, and *The Wonderful World of Nils* (1906–1907), a two-volume young people's classic. Many of her writings have been adapted to the stage and screen.

# *Comment*

### An Artist Shares His Family Life

The inviting scene on page 439, which gives one the impression of having just walked into a story, is the work of noted Swedish artist Carl Larsson, 1853–1919. Though the painting is, in fact, a depiction of a celebration in Larsson's own living room, it perfectly captures the spirit of warmth and sharing that is such an important element in "The Rat Trap."

Larsson's dreary early life in Stockholm led him to turn to drawing as an escape. By the 1880s the diversion had become a successful career; he was one of his country's leading book illustrators and mural painters. In 1889 his wife's family gave them a rundown little house in the village of Sundborn. Now in a position to provide his seven children with the cheerful atmosphere he had not known, Larsson set out to rebuild their new residence. The result—a whimsical showplace with portraits painted on doors, unusual passages, and wood-carved dragons on the rooftops—was a structure so original in design that it remains one of Europe's most famous handcrafted homes.

The dwelling was not only a work of architectural art; it was the backdrop for many of Larsson's best-loved paintings. Acting on his wife's suggestion during one rainy and confining summer, he turned to his cozy surroundings for his subjects. From then on he devoted himself to creating delicately detailed watercolors of his family. Such images as his wife sewing, his children playing dress-up, and his dog sleeping were collected and published in *A Home* in 1899 and have been in publication ever since.

Larsson was a contemporary of Selma Lagerlöf, and each contributed greatly to Swedish cultural history. His warm depictions of home and her richly romantic tales celebrating Swedish life are regarded as national treasures.

Carl Larsson, *Now It Is Christmas Again*, Private Collection

See STEREOTYPE in the Handbook of Literary Terms, page 826.

# Enemies

**Nadine Gordimer**   South Africa

---

**What are the most effective ways of escaping an enemy?**
**Clara Hansen thought she knew them all.**

---

hen Mrs. Clara Hansen travels, she keeps herself to herself. This is usually easy, for she has money, has been a baroness and a beauty, and has survived dramatic suffering. The crushing presence of these states in her face and bearing is nearly always enough to stop the loose mouths of people who find themselves in her company. It is only the very stupid, the senile, or the self-obsessed who blunder up to assail that face, withdrawn as a castle, across the common ground of a public dining room.

Last month, when Mrs. Hansen left Cape Town for Johannesburg[1] by train, an old lady occupying the adjoining compartment tried to make of her apologies, as she pressed past in the corridor loaded with string bags and paper parcels, an excuse to open one of those pointless conversations between strangers which arise in the nervous moments of departure. Mrs. Hansen was giving last calm instructions to Alfred, her Malay[2] chauffeur and manservant, whom she was leaving behind, and she did not look up. Alfred had stowed her old calf cases from Europe firmly

and within reach in her compartment, which, of course, influence with the reservation office had ensured she would have to herself all the way. He had watched her put away in a special pocket in her handbag her train ticket, a ticket for her deluxe bed, a book of tickets for her meals. He had made sure that she had her two yellow sleeping pills and the red pills for that feeling of pressure in her head, lying in cotton wool in her silver pillbox. He himself had seen that her two pairs of spectacles, one for distance, one for reading, were in her overnight bag, and had noted that her lorgnette hung below the diamond bow on the bosom of her dress. He had taken down the folding table from its niche above the washbasin in the

---

**1.** *left Cape Town for Johannesburg* (jō han′is bȇrg′). Cape Town, sometimes referred to as "the Cape," and Johannesburg are cities in South Africa, about eight hundred miles apart.
**2.** *Malay,* person from—or whose ancestors were from—Malaysia, a country in Southeast Asia.

Adolphe Monticelli, *Portrait of a Lady,* circa 1870,
The Art Institute of Chicago

compartment, and placed on it the three magazines she had sent him to buy at the bookstall, along with the paper from Switzerland that, this week, had been kept aside unread, for the journey.

For a full fifteen minutes before the train left, he and his employer were free to ignore the to-and-fro of voices and luggage, the heat and confusion. Mrs. Hansen murmured down to him; Alfred, chauffeur's cap in hand, dusty sunlight the color of beer dimming the oil shine of his black hair, looked up from the platform and made low assent. It was hardly speech; now and then it sank away altogether into the minds of each, but the sounds of the station did not well up in its place. Alfred dangled the key of the car on his little finger. The old face beneath the toque noted it, and the lips, the infinitely weary corners of the eyes drooped in the indication of a smile. Would he really put the car away into the garage for six weeks after he'd seen that it was oiled and greased?

Unmindful of the finger, his face empty of the satisfaction of a month's wages in advance in his pocket, two friends waiting to be picked up in a house in the Malay quarter of the town, he said, "I must make a note that I mustn't send Madam's letters on after the twenty-sixth."

"No. Not later than the twenty-sixth."

Did she know? With that face that looked as if it knew everything, could she know, too, about the two friends in the house in the Malay quarter?

She said—and neither of them listened—"In case of need, you've always got Mr. Van Dam." Van Dam was her lawyer. This remark, like a stone thrown idly into a pool to pass the time, had fallen time and again between them into the widening hiatus of parting. They had never questioned or troubled to define its meaning. In ten years, what need had there ever been that Alfred couldn't deal with himself, from a burst pipe in the flat to a

jammed fastener on Mrs. Hansen's dress?

Alfred backed away from the ice-cream carton a vendor thrust under his nose; the last untidy lump of canvas luggage belonging to the woman next door thumped down like a dusty animal at Mrs. Hansen's side; the final bell rang.

As the train ground past out of the station, Alfred stood quite still with his cap between his hands, watching Mrs. Hansen. He always stood like that when he saw her off. And she remained at the window, as usual, smiling slightly, inclining her head slightly, as if in dismissal. Neither waved. Neither moved until the other was borne out of sight.

When the station was gone and Mrs. Hansen turned slowly to enter her compartment to the quickening rhythm of the train, she met the gasping face of the old woman next door. Fat overflowed not only from her jowl to her neck, but from her ankles to her shoes. She looked like a pudding that had risen too high and run down the sides of the dish. She was sprinkling cologne onto a handkerchief and hitting with it at her face as if she were trying to kill something. "Rush like that, it's no good for you," she said. "Something went wrong with my son-in-law's car, and what a job to get a taxi! *They* don't care—get you here today or tomorrow. I thought I'd never get up those steps."

Mrs. Hansen looked at her. "When one is no longer young, one must always give oneself exactly twice as much time as one needs. I have learned that. I beg your pardon." And she passed before the woman into her compartment.

The woman stopped her in the doorway. "I wonder if they're serving tea yet? Shall we go along to the dining car?"

"I always have my tea brought to me in my compartment," said Mrs. Hansen, in the low, dead voice that had been considered a pity in her day but that now made young people who could have been her grandchildren ask if she had been an actress. And she slid the door shut.

Alone, she stood a moment in the secretive privacy, where everything swayed and veered in obedience to the gait of the train. She began to look anxiously over the stacked luggage, her lips moving, but she had grown too set to adjust her balance from moment to moment, and suddenly she found herself sitting down. The train had dumped her out of the way. Good thing, too, she thought, chastising herself impatiently—counting the luggage, fussing, when in ten years Alfred's never forgotten anything. Old fool, she told herself, old fool. Her aging self often seemed to her an enemy of her real self, the self that had never changed. The enemy was a stupid one, fortunately; she merely had to keep an eye on it in order to keep it outwitted. Other selves that had arisen in her life had been much worse; how terrible had been the struggle with some of *them!*

She sat down with her back to the engine, beside the window, and put on her reading glasses and took up the newspaper from Switzerland. But for some minutes she did not read. She heard again inside herself the words *alone, alone,* just the way she had heard them fifty-nine years ago when she was twelve years old and crossing France by herself for the first time. As she had sat there, bolt upright in the corner of a carriage, her green velvet fur-trimmed cloak around her, her hamper beside her, and the locket with the picture of her grandfather hidden in her hand, she had felt a swelling terror of exhilaration, the dark, drowning swirl of cutting loose, had tasted the strength to be brewed out of self-pity and the calm to be lashed together out of panic that belonged to other times and other journeys approaching her from the distance of her future. *Alone, alone.* This that her real self had known years before it happened to her—before she had lived the journey that took her from a lover, or those others that took her from the alienated faces of madness and death—

that same self remembered years after those journeys had dropped behind into the past. Now she was alone, lonely, lone—whatever you liked to call it—all the time. There is nothing of the drama of an occasion about it, for me, she reminded herself dryly. Still, there was no denying it, *alone* was not the same as *lonely;* even the Old Fool could not blur the distinction of that. The blue silk coat quivered where Alfred had hung it, the bundle of magazines edged along the table, and somewhere above her head a loose strap tapped. She felt again aloneness as the carapace that did not shut her off but shielded her strong sense of survival—against it, and all else.

She opened the paper from Switzerland, and, with her left foot (the heat had made it a little swollen) up on the seat opposite, she began to read. She felt lulled and comfortable and was not even irritated by the thuds and dragging noises coming from the partition behind her head; it was clear that that was the woman next door—*she* must be fussing with her luggage. Presently a steward brought a tea tray, which Alfred had ordered before the train left. Mrs. Hansen drew in her mouth with pleasure at the taste of the strong tea, as connoisseurs do when they drink old brandy, and read the afternoon away.

She took her dinner in the dining car because she had established in a long experience that it was not a meal that could be expected to travel train corridors and remain hot, and also because there was something shabby, something *petit bourgeois,*[3] about taking meals in the stuffy cubicle in which you were also to sleep. She tidied her hair around the sides of her toque—it was a beautiful hat, one of four, always the same shape, that she had made for herself every second year in Vienna—took off her rings and washed her

---

3. *petit bourgeois* (pet′ē bùr zhwä′), lower middle class [*French*].

hands, and powdered her nose, pulling a critical, amused face at herself in the compact mirror. Then she put on her silk coat, picked up her handbag, and went with upright dignity, despite the twitchings and lurchings of the train, along the corridors to the dining car. She seated herself at an empty table for two beside a window, and, of course, although it was early and there were many other seats vacant, the old woman from the compartment next door, entering five minutes later, came straight over and sat down opposite her.

Now it was impossible not to speak to the woman, and Mrs. Hansen listened to her with the distant patience of an adult giving half an ear to a child, and answered her when necessary, with a dry simplicity calculated to be far above her head. Of course, Old Fool was tempted to unbend, to lapse into the small boastings and rivalries usual between two old ladies. But Mrs. Hansen would not allow it and certainly not with this woman— this acquaintance thrust upon her in a train. It was bad enough that, only the week before, Old Fool had led her into one of these pathetic pieces of senile nonsense, cleverly disguised—Old Fool could be wily enough—but, just the same, unmistakably the kind of thing that people found boring. It was about her teeth. At seventy-one they were still her own, which was a self-evident miracle. Yet she had allowed herself, at a dinner party given by some young friends who were obviously impressed by her, to tell a funny story (not quite true, either) about how, when she was a weekend guest in a house with an oversolicitous hostess, the jovial host had hoaxed his wife by impressing upon her the importance of providing a suitable receptacle for their guest's teeth when she took them out overnight. There was a glass beside the jug of water on the bedside table; the hostess appeared, embarrassedly, with another. "But, my dear, what is the other glass for?" The denouement, laughter, etc. Disgusting. Good teeth as well as bad aches and pains must be kept

to oneself; when one is young, one takes the first for granted, and does not know the existence of the others.

So it was that when the menu was held before the two women Mrs. Hansen ignored the consternation into which it seemed to plunge her companion, forestalled the temptation to enter, by contributing her doctor's views, into age's passionate preoccupation with diet, and ordered fish.

"D'you think the fish'll be all right? I always wonder, on a train, you know. . . ." said the woman from the next compartment.

Mrs. Hansen merely confirmed her order to the waiter by lowering her eyes and settling her chin slightly. The woman decided to begin at the beginning, with soup. "Can't go far wrong with soup, can you?"

"Don't wait, please," said Mrs. Hansen when the soup came.

The soup was watery, the woman said. Mrs. Hansen smiled her tragic smile, indulgently. The woman decided that she'd keep Mrs. Hansen company, and risk the fish, too. The fish lay beneath a pasty blanket of white sauce, and while Mrs. Hansen calmly pushed aside the sauce and ate, the woman said, "There's nothing like the good, clean food cooked in your own kitchen."

Mrs. Hansen put a forkful of fish to her mouth and, when she had finished it, spoke at last. "I'm afraid it's many years since I had my own kitchen for more than a month or two a year."

"Well, of course, if you go about a lot, you get used to strange food, I suppose. I find I can't eat half the stuff they put in front of you in hotels. Last time I was away, there were some days I didn't know what to have at all for lunch. I was in one of the best hotels in Durban and all there was was this endless curry—curry this, curry that— and a lot of dried-up cold meats."

Mrs. Hansen shrugged. "I always find enough for my needs. It does not matter much."

"What can you do? I suppose this sauce is the

wrong thing for me, but you've got to take what you get when you're traveling," said the woman. She broke off a piece of bread and passed it swiftly around her plate to scoop up what was left of the sauce. "Starchy," she added.

Mrs. Hansen ordered a cutlet, and, after a solemn study of the menu, the other woman asked for the item listed immediately below the fish—oxtail stew. While they were waiting she ate bread and butter and, shifting her mouthful comfortably from one side of her mouth to the other, accomplished a shift of her attention, too, as if her jaw and her brain had some simple mechanical connection. "You're not from here, I suppose?" she asked, looking at Mrs. Hansen with the appraisal reserved for foreigners and the license granted by the tacit acceptance of old age on both sides.

"I have lived in the Cape, on and off, for some years," said Mrs. Hansen. "My second husband was Danish, but settled here."

"I could have married again. I'm not boasting, I mean, but I did have the chance, if I'd've wanted to," said the woman. "Somehow, I couldn't face it, after losing my first—fifty-two, that's all, and you'd have taken a lease on his life. Ah, those doctors. No wonder I feel I can't trust them a minute."

Mrs. Hansen parted the jaws of her large, elegant black bag to take out a handkerchief; the stack of letters that she always had with her—new ones arriving to take the place of old with every airmail—lay exposed. Thin letters, fat letters, big envelopes, small ones; the torn edges of foreign stamps, the large, sloping, and small, crabbed hands of foreigners writing foreign tongues. The other woman looked down upon them like a tourist, curious, impersonally insolent, envious. "Of course, if I'd been the sort to run about a lot, I suppose it might have been different. I might have met someone really *congenial*. But there's my daughters. A mother's responsibility is never

over—that's what I say. When they're little, it's little troubles. When they're grown up, it's big ones. They're all nicely married, thank God, but you know, it's always something—one of them sick, or one of the grandchildren, bless them. . . . I don't suppose you've got any children. Not even from your first, I mean?"

"No," said Mrs. Hansen. "No." And the lie, as always, came to her as a triumph against that arrogant boy (Old Fool persisted in thinking of him as a gentle-browed youth bent over a dachshund puppy, though he was a man of forty-five by now) whom truly she had made, as she had warned she would, no son of hers. When the lie was said it had the effect of leaving her breathless, as if she had just crowned a steep rise. Firmly and calmly, she leaned forward and poured herself a glass of water, as one who has deserved it.

"My, it does look fatty," the other woman was saying over the oxtail, which had just been placed before her. "My doctor'd have a fit if he knew I was eating this." But eat it she did, and cutlet and roast turkey to follow. Mrs. Hansen never knew whether or not her companion rounded off the meal with rhubarb pie (the woman had remarked, as she saw it carried past, that it looked soggy), because she herself had gone straight from cutlet to coffee, and, her meal finished, excused herself before the other was through the turkey course. Back in her compartment, she took off her toque at last and tied a gray chiffon scarf around her head. Then she waited for the man to come and convert her seat into the deluxe bed Alfred had paid for in advance.

It seemed to Mrs. Hansen that she did not sleep very well during the early part of the night, though she did not quite know what it was that made her restless. She was awakened, time and again, apparently by some noise that had ceased by the time she was conscious enough to identify it. The third or fourth time this happened, she woke to silence and a sense of absolute cessation, as if the world had stopped turning. But it was only the train that had stopped. Mrs. Hansen lay and listened. They must be at some deserted siding in the small hours; there were no lights shining in through the shuttered window, no footsteps, no talk. The voice of a cricket, like a fingernail screeching over glass, sounded, providing, beyond the old woman's closed eyes, beyond the dark compartment and the shutters, a landscape of grass, dark, and telephone poles.

Suddenly the train gave a terrific reverberating jerk, as if it had been given a violent push. All was still again. And in the stillness, Mrs. Hansen became aware of groans coming from the other side of the partition against which she lay. The groans came, bumbling and nasal, through the wood and leather; they sounded like a dog with its head buried in a cushion, worrying at the feathers. Mrs. Hansen breathed out once, hard, in annoyance, and turned over; the greedy old pig, now she was suffering agonies of indigestion from that oxtail, of course. The groans continued at intervals. Once there was a muffled tinkling sound, as if a spoon had been dropped. Mrs. Hansen lay tense with irritation, waiting for the train to move on and drown the woman's noise. At last, with a shake that quickly settled into a fast clip, they were off again, lickety-lack, lickety-lack, past (Mrs. Hansen could imagine) the endless telephone poles, the dark grass, the black-coated cricket. Under the dialogue of the train, she was an unwilling eavesdropper to the vulgar intimacies next door; then either the groans stopped or she fell asleep in spite of them, for she heard nothing till the steward woke her with the arrival of early-morning coffee.

Mrs. Hansen sponged herself, dressed, and had a quiet breakfast, undisturbed by anyone, in the dining car. The man sitting opposite her did not even ask her so much as to pass the salt. She was back in her compartment, reading, when the ticket examiner came in to take her ticket away (they would be in Johannesburg soon), and of course, she knew just where to lay her hand on it, in her bag. He leaned against the doorway while she got it out. "Hear what happened?" he said.

"What happened?" she said uncertainly, screwing up her face because he spoke indistinctly, like most young South Africans.

"Next door," he said. "The lady next door, elderly lady. She died last night."

"She died? That woman died?" She stood up and questioned him closely, as if he were irresponsible.

"Yes," he said, checking the ticket on his list. "The bed boy found her this morning, dead in her bed. She never answered when the steward came round with coffee, you see."

"My God," said Mrs. Hansen. "My God. So she died, eh?"

"Yes, lady." He held out his hand for her ticket; he had the tale to tell all up and down the train.

With a gesture of futility, she gave it to him.

After he had gone, she sank down on the seat, beside the window, and watched the veld go by, the grasses streaming past in the sun like the long black tails of the widow birds blowing where they swung upon the fences. She had finished her paper and magazines. There was no sound but the sound of the hurrying train.

When they reached Johannesburg she had all her luggage trimly closed and ready for the porter from the hotel at which she was going to stay. She left the station with him within five minutes of the train's arrival, and was gone before the doctor, officials, and, she supposed, newspaper reporters came to see the woman taken away from the compartment next door. What could I have said to them? she thought, pleased with her sensible escape. Could I tell them she died of greed? Better not to be mixed up in it.

And then she thought of something. Newspaper reporters. No doubt there would be a piece in the Cape papers tomorrow. ELDERLY WOMAN FOUND DEAD IN CAPE-JOHANNESBURG TRAIN.

As soon as she had signed the register at the hotel she asked for a telegram form. She paused a moment, leaning on the marble-topped reception desk, looking out over the heads of the clerks.

Her eyes, which were still handsome, crinkled at the corners; her nostrils lifted; her mouth, which was still so shapely because of her teeth, turned its sad corners lower in her reluctant, calculating smile. She printed Alfred's name and the address of the flat in Cape Town, and then wrote quickly, in the fine hand she had mastered more than sixty years ago: "It was not me. Clara Hansen."

## THINK AND DISCUSS
### Understanding
1. What details in the opening paragraphs help establish Mrs. Hansen's social background?
2. During the fifteen minutes before the train leaves, Mrs. Hansen and her chauffeur Alfred engage in small talk. What is each of them thinking about?
3. How does Mrs. Hansen get rid of the old woman the first time? the second time?

### Analyzing
4. Mrs. Hansen sometimes thinks of her "Old Fool" self as opposed to her "real" self. Under what circumstances did her real self learn to find strength and pleasure in being alone?
5. Would the Old Fool self be likely to feel lonely? Explain.
6. What do Mrs. Hansen's actions after she learns of the woman's death reveal about her character?
7. Does the author intend for you to pity Mrs. Hansen, to criticize her, or both? Justify your answer.

### Extending
8. The other woman, who dies on the train, is a character foil—a character who helps the reader to better judge the central character, in this case Mrs. Hansen. How does she help the reader to better understand Mrs. Hansen?
9. Who are the "enemies" indicated in the title of the story? Explain.

### APPLYING: Stereotype H⅄
**See Handbook of Literary Terms, p. 826**

By definition, a **stereotyped** character is one-dimensional and therefore unlikely to arouse much interest or sympathy. In this story, however, the author lulls the reader into regarding the woman in the next compartment as a stereotype, then dramatically forces a reconsideration of that view.

1. Discuss which of the following characteristics of the old woman are stereotypical: carrying "string bags and paper parcels"; overeating; discussing her doctor's views on diet and health; worrying about her children and grandchildren; talking to strangers.
2. When and how does the woman become a three-dimensional character?

## COMPOSITION
### Writing About Character Foils

Originally a foil was a piece of bright metal placed under a precious stone to increase its brilliance. In literature the word applies to a character who by contrast highlights the distinctive characteristics of another, usually the central character. For example, in "Enemies" the fat woman who dies is a foil to Mrs. Hansen. Write a three-paragraph composition in which you contrast specific characteristics of the unnamed woman to highlight opposite traits in Mrs. Hansen. Refer to specific details to support your proof that she is a character foil.

### Writing a Diary Entry

Imagine that you are Mrs. Hansen. Write a three-paragraph entry in your diary describing your train journey. Be sure your account accurately summarizes the events and reflects Mrs. Hansen's attitudes.

## ENRICHMENT
### Making a Speech

Imagine that your class has been asked to help plan a movie or videotape production of "Enemies." You have been asked to select two famous actresses who could play the parts of Mrs. Hansen and the other woman on the train. Prepare and give a speech presenting your choices, naming the performers and telling your class why they should be cast in the roles. You may want to find pictures of the actresses to use in your presentation.

## BIOGRAPHY

### Nadine Gordimer
### 1923–

Believing that a writer should try to "make sense of life," Gordimer has used her writings to explore the complexity of human relationships. In her many novels and stories she describes the private, social, and political sides of modern life in ways that provide insights rather than judgments. Gordimer's birthplace is a small town near Johannesburg, South Africa. She lives in Johannesburg and lends her voice to those who oppose the policies of racial separation in her country. Her writings are not published there, but they have earned her wide recognition in many other parts of the world. Her fiction, in books such as *Livingstone's Companions* (1971) and *A Sport of Nature* (1987), reflects themes of exile and aloneness and frequently presents characters who are strangers in their own land. She often lectures in the United States and abroad, and she has adapted her stories for film.

**See SATIRE in the Handbook of Literary Terms, page 822.**

# Action Will Be Taken

**Heinrich Böll**   Germany

**Is action the same thing as productivity? It all depends. . . .**

robably one of the strangest interludes in my life was the time I spent as an employee in Alfred Wunsiedel's[1] factory. By nature I am inclined more to pensiveness and inactivity than to work, but now and again prolonged financial difficulties compel me—for pensiveness is no more profitable than inactivity—to take on a so-called job. Finding myself once again at a low ebb of this kind, I put myself in the hands of the employment office and was sent with seven other fellow-sufferers to Wunsiedel's factory, where we were to undergo an aptitude test.

The exterior of the factory was enough to arouse my suspicions: the factory was built entirely of glass brick, and my aversion to well-lit buildings and well-lit rooms is as strong as my aversion to work. I became even more suspicious when we were immediately served breakfast in the well-lit, cheerful coffee shop: pretty waitresses brought us eggs, coffee, and toast; orange juice was served in tastefully designed jugs; goldfish pressed their bored faces against the sides of pale-green aquariums. The waitresses were so cheerful that they appeared to be bursting with good cheer. Only a strong effort of will—so it seemed to me—restrained them from singing away all day long. They were as crammed with unsung songs as chickens with unlaid eggs.

Right away I realized something that my fellow-sufferers evidently failed to realize: that this breakfast was already part of the test; so I chewed away reverently, with the full appreciation of a person who knows he is supplying his body with valuable elements. I did something which normally no power on earth can make me do: I drank orange juice on an empty stomach, left the coffee and egg untouched, as well as most of the toast, got up, and paced up and down the coffee shop, pregnant with action.

As a result I was the first to be ushered into the

---

**Heinrich Böll** (hīn′rik bœl).

1. *Wunsiedel's* (vün′zē′dlz).

room where the questionnaires were spread out on attractive tables. The walls were done in a shade of green that would have summoned the word "delightful" to the lips of interior-decoration enthusiasts. The room appeared to be empty, and yet I was so sure of being observed that I behaved as someone pregnant with action behaves when he believes himself unobserved: I ripped my pen impatiently from my pocket, unscrewed the top, sat down at the nearest table and pulled the questionnaire toward me, the way irritable customers snatch at the bill in a restaurant.

*Question No. 1: Do you consider it right for a human being to possess only two arms, two legs, eyes, and ears?*

Here for the first time I reaped the harvest of my pensive nature and wrote without hesitation: "Even four arms, legs, and ears would not be adequate for my driving energy. Human beings are very poorly equipped."

*Question No. 2: How many telephones can you handle at one time?*

Here again the answer was as easy as simple arithmetic: "When there are only seven telephones," I wrote, "I get impatient; there have to be nine before I feel I am working to capacity."

*Question No. 3: How do you spend your free time?*

My answer: "I no longer acknowledge the term free time—on my fifteenth birthday I eliminated it from my vocabulary, for in the beginning was the act."

I got the job. Even with nine telephones I really didn't feel I was working to capacity. I shouted into the mouthpieces: "Take immediate action!" or: "Do something!—We must have some action—Action will be taken—Action has been taken—Action should be taken." But as a rule—for I felt this was in keeping with the tone of the place—I used the imperative.

Of considerable interest were the noon-hour breaks, when we consumed nutritious foods in an atmosphere of silent good cheer. Wunsiedel's factory was swarming with people who were obsessed with telling you the story of their lives, as indeed vigorous personalities are fond of doing. The story of their lives is more important to them than their lives; you have only to press a button, and immediately it is covered with spewed-out exploits.

Wunsiedel had a right-hand man called Broschek,[2] who had in turn made a name for himself by supporting seven children and a paralyzed wife by working night shifts in his student days, and successfully carrying on four business agencies, besides which he had passed two examinations with honors in two years. When asked by reporters: "When do you sleep, Mr. Broschek?" he had replied: "It's a crime to sleep!"

Wunsiedel's secretary had supported a paralyzed husband and four children by knitting, at the same time graduating in psychology and German history as well as breeding shepherd dogs, and she had become famous as a night-club singer where she was known as *Vamp Number Seven.*

Wunsiedel himself was one of those people who every morning, as they open their eyes, make up their minds to act. "I must act," they think as they briskly tie their bathrobe belts around them. "I must act," they think as they shave, triumphantly watching their beard hairs being washed away with the lather: these hirsute vestiges are the first daily sacrifices to their driving energy. Action has been taken. Bread gets eaten, eggs are decapitated.

With Wunsiedel, the most trivial activity looked like action: the way he put on his hat, the way—quivering with energy—he buttoned up his overcoat, the kiss he gave his wife, everything was action.

When he arrived at his office he greeted his secretary with a cry of "Let's have some action!" And in ringing tones she would call back: "Action

---

2. *Broschek* (brō′shek).

will be taken!" Wunsiedel then went from department to department, calling out his cheerful: "Let's have some action!" Everyone would answer: "Action will be taken!" And I would call back to him too, with a radiant smile, when he looked into my office: "Action will be taken!"

Within a week I had increased the number of telephones on my desk to eleven, within two weeks to thirteen, and every morning on the streetcar I enjoyed thinking up new imperatives, or chasing the words *take action* through various tenses and modulations: for two whole days I kept saying the same sentence over and over again because I thought it sounded so marvelous: "Action ought to have been taken"; for another two days it was: "Such action ought not to have been taken."

So I was really beginning to feel I was working to capacity when there actually was some action. One Tuesday morning—I had hardly settled down at my desk—Wunsiedel rushed into my office crying his "Let's have some action!" But an inexplicable something in his face made me hesitate to reply, in a cheerful gay voice as the rules dictated: "Action will be taken!" I must have paused too long, for Wunsiedel, who seldom raised his voice, shouted at me: "Answer! Answer, you know the rules!" And I answered, under my breath, reluctantly, like a child who is forced to say: I am a naughty child. It was only by a great effort that I managed to bring out the sentence: "Action will be taken," and hardly had I uttered it when there really was some action: Wunsiedel dropped to the floor. As he fell he rolled over onto his side and lay right across the open doorway. I knew at once, and I confirmed it when I went slowly around my desk and approached the body on the floor: he was dead.

Shaking my head I stepped over Wunsiedel, walked slowly along the corridor to Broschek's office, and entered without knocking. Broschek was sitting at his desk, a telephone receiver in each hand; between his teeth a ballpoint pen with which he was making notes on a writing pad, while with his bare feet he was operating a knitting machine under the desk. In this way he helps to clothe his family. "We've had some action," I said in a low voice.

Broschek spat out the ballpoint pen, put down the two receivers, reluctantly detached his toes from the knitting machine.

"What action?" he asked.

"Wunsiedel is dead," I said.

"No," said Broschek.

"Yes," I said, "come and have a look!"

"No," said Broschek, "that's impossible," but he put on his slippers and followed me along the corridor.

"No," he said, when we stood beside Wunsiedel's corpse, "no, no!" I did not contradict him. I carefully turned Wunsiedel over onto his back, closed his eyes, and looked at him pensively.

I felt something like tenderness for him, and realized for the first time that I had never hated him. On his face was that expression which one sees on children who obstinately refuse to give up their faith in Santa Claus, even though the arguments of their playmates sound so convincing.

"No," said Broschek, "no."

"We must take action," I said quietly to Broschek.

"Yes," said Broschek, "we must take action."

Action was taken: Wunsiedel was buried, and I was delegated to carry a wreath of artificial roses behind his coffin, for I am equipped with not only a penchant for pensiveness and inactivity but also a face and figure that go extremely well with dark suits. Apparently as I walked along behind Wunsiedel's coffin carrying the wreath of artificial roses I looked superb. I received an offer from a fashionable firm of funeral directors to join their staff as a professional mourner. "You are a born mourner," said the manager, "your outfit would

Ralph Helmick, *Natures*, 1983, Stux Gallery, Boston.

be provided by the firm. Your face—simply superb!"

I handed in my notice to Broschek, explaining that I had never really felt I was working to capacity there; that, in spite of the thirteen telephones, some of my talents were going to waste. As soon as my first professional appearance as a mourner was over I knew: This is where I belong, this is what I am cut out for.

Pensively I stand behind the coffin in the funeral chapel, holding a simple bouquet, while the organ plays Handel's *Largo*,[3] a piece that does not receive nearly the respect it deserves. The cemetery café is my regular haunt; there I spend the intervals between my professional engagements,

3. *Handel's Largo,* a musical composition by German-born English composer George Handel that is often played on solemn occasions.

although sometimes I walk behind coffins which I have not been engaged to follow, I pay for flowers out of my own pocket and join the welfare worker who walks behind the coffin of some homeless person. From time to time I also visit Wunsiedel's grave, for after all I owe it to him that I discovered my true vocation, a vocation in which pensiveness is essential and inactivity my duty.

It was not till much later that I realized I had never bothered to find out what was being produced in Wunsiedel's factory. I expect it was soap.

## THINK AND DISCUSS
### Understanding
1. What details about the factory suggest that effort has been made to make working there pleasant?
2. What seems to be the main activity the narrator engages in?
3. To what action is the narrator referring when he says, "There actually was some action"?

### Analyzing
4. According to the narrator, two qualities are part of his nature: pensiveness and inactivity. What is the difference between these traits?
5. What **stereotypical** person is the author criticizing through the incredible industry of Broschek and Wunsiedel's secretary?

### Extending
6. What other objects besides telephones might work equally well as symbols of business or industry?

## APPLYING: Satire  H⅄
**See Handbook of Literary Terms, p. 822**

In order to successfully satirize something so broad and general as modern industry, a writer must choose and subject various distinct aspects of it to effective **satire.** Thus, he or she may use irony to present one aspect, gentle exaggeration to describe another, and burlesque to ridicule others. Explain the satire in each of the following, and decide what satiric device has been used to communicate it.

1. the narrator's interest in variations of "Action will be taken"
2. Wunsiedel's early-morning activities
3. the industriousness of Broschek and of Wunsiedel's secretary
4. the factory's modern, cheery cafeteria
5. the narrator's success as a quiet mourner

## Writing Satire

Select an event or activity familiar to you and your classmates that you think could be satirized in an amusing way. (Possibilities include such things as a parade, television show, school dance, pep rally, or the hype that precedes a big sports event like the World Series or the Super Bowl.) Then select details related to the event that should be included in the description and decide how you can satirize them most effectively—through exaggeration, humor, irony, understatement, burlesque, or other techniques.

## Satirizing Character Types

Character types can also provide opportunities for satire. Select a character type familiar to you and your classmates that you think could be satirized in an amusing rather than cruel way. (Possibilities include such types as the social snob, the athlete, the brain, or the music groupie.) Remember, you are satirizing a type, not an individual. Then select details related to the type that should be included in the description and decide how you can satirize the type most effectively—through exaggeration, humor, irony, understatement, or other techniques.

# BIOGRAPHY

## Heinrich Böll
## 1917–1985

Böll spent most of his life in his native city of Cologne, Germany, where he witnessed the shattering effects of two World Wars. In 1939 he was drafted into the infantry, fighting but wanting the Nazi government to lose in World War II. At its end he returned to Cologne to attend the university there and to begin his writing career.

Through his writings, Böll did much to revive interest in German literature, which prior to the war had been reduced to a tool of the Nazi regime. Such works as *The Train Was on Time* (1949) and *Traveller, If You Come to the Spa* (1950) describe soldiers' wartime experiences. He later shifted his focus to satiric portraits—of which "Action Will Be Taken" is an example—of the generations of Germans who have survived World War II.

Böll's contribution to the rebirth of German literature won him the Nobel Prize in 1972. An active defender of freedom of literature, he donated part of his prize money to aid writers imprisoned for their political beliefs. He died near Bonn at the age of 67.

## Comment

### The Nobel Prize in Literature

Heinrich Böll and many other authors represented in *Traditions in Literature* have been awarded the prestigious Nobel Prize. The origin of this prize forms an intriguing story in itself.

In 1888 an obituary in a French newspaper reported the death of Alfred Nobel, Swedish inventor of dynamite. The report was a mistake; the newspaper had confused Alfred Nobel with his brother Ludwig, who had died. Reading it, however, Alfred must have been shocked at the disdainful portrayal of himself as a man who had created his fortune from weapons of war. Perhaps he hoped to be remembered as a promoter of peace, not as the "dynamite king" described in the obituary. Whatever his reason, during the next eight years he formulated a plan that altered his image. When Nobel finally died in 1896, his will established a fund of nine million dollars for the promotion of a peaceful and better world. He designated income from the fund to be awarded annually in prizes in five categories—literature, physics, chemistry, physiology or medicine, and international peace.

The Nobel Prize in Literature is awarded, according to Nobel's will, to "the person who shall have produced in the field of literature the most distinguished work of an idealistic tendency." Since 1901 a committee of the

The Nobel Prize medallion

Swedish Academy has annually reviewed the work of recommended authors, regardless of their nationality. The award is made to living authors for their entire body of work; the Academy may withhold it if no living author is considered worthy of the prize that year.

**Review STEREOTYPE in the Handbook of Literary Terms, page 826.**

# Miss Brill

**Katherine Mansfield**  New Zealand

"How she loved sitting here, watching it all! It was like a play. It was exactly like a play."

lthough it was so brilliantly fine— the blue sky powdered with gold and great spots of light like white wine splashed over the Jardins Publiques[1]—Miss Brill was glad that she had decided on her fur. The air was motionless, but when you opened your mouth there was just a faint chill, like a chill from a glass of iced water before you sip, and now and again a leaf came drifting—from nowhere, from the sky. Miss Brill put up her hand and touched her fur. Dear little thing! It was nice to feel it again. She had taken it out of its box that afternoon, shaken out the moth powder, given it a good brush, and rubbed the life back into the dim little eyes.[2] "What has been happening to me?" said the sad little eyes. Oh, how sweet it was to see them snap at her again from the red eiderdown! . . . But the nose, which was of some black composition, wasn't at all firm. It must have had a knock, somehow. Never mind—a little dab of black sealing-wax when the time came—when it was absolutely necessary . . . Little rogue! Yes, she really felt like that about it. Little rogue biting its tail just by her left ear. She could have taken it off and laid it on her lap and stroked it. She felt a tingling in her hands and arms, but that came from walking, she supposed. And when she breathed, something light and sad—no, not sad, exactly—something gentle seemed to move in her bosom.

There were a number of people out this afternoon, far more than last Sunday. And the band sounded louder and gayer. That was because the Season had begun. For although the band played all the year round on Sundays, out of season it was never the same. It was like some one playing with only the family to listen; it didn't care how it played if there weren't any strangers present.

---

1. *Jardins Publiques* (zhär daN′ py blēk′), public gardens, or park [*French*].
2. *dim little eyes*. The fur necklet, or collar piece, had decorative eye pieces at the head end, which also had a jaw-shaped latch. The fur clasped around the wearer's neck when the "jaw" closed around the furry tail.

Wasn't the conductor wearing a new coat, too? She was sure it was new. He scraped with his foot and flapped his arms like a rooster about to crow, and the bandsmen sitting in the green rotunda blew out their cheeks and glared at the music. Now there came a little "flutey" bit—very pretty!—a little chain of bright drops. She was sure it would be repeated. It was; she lifted her head and smiled.

Only two people shared her "special" seat; a fine old man in a velvet coat, his hands clasped over a huge carved walking-stick, and a big old woman, sitting upright, with a roll of knitting on her embroidered apron. They did not speak. This was disappointing, for Miss Brill always looked forward to the conversation. She had become really quite expert, she thought, at listening as though she didn't listen, at sitting in other people's lives just for a minute while they talked round her.

She glanced, sideways, at the old couple. Perhaps they would go soon. Last Sunday, too, hadn't been as interesting as usual. An Englishman and his wife, he wearing a dreadful Panama hat and she button boots. And she'd gone on the whole time about how she ought to wear spectacles; she knew she needed them; but that it was no good getting any; they'd be sure to break and they'd never keep on. And he'd been so patient. He'd suggested everything—gold rims, the kind that curved round your ears, little pads inside the bridge. No, nothing would please her. "They'll always be sliding down my nose!" Miss Brill had wanted to shake her.

The old people sat on the bench, still as statues. Never mind, there was always the crowd to watch. To and fro, in front of the flower beds and the band rotunda, the couples and groups paraded, stopped to talk, to greet, to buy a handful of flowers from the old beggar who had his tray fixed to the railings. Little children ran among them, swooping and laughing; little boys with big white silk bows under their chins, little girls, little French dolls, dressed up in velvet and lace. And sometimes a tiny staggerer came suddenly rocking into the open from under the trees, stopped, stared, as suddenly sat down "flop," until its small high-stepping mother, like a young hen, rushed scolding to its rescue. Other people sat on the benches and green chairs, but they were nearly always the same, Sunday after Sunday, and—Miss Brill had often noticed—there was something funny about nearly all of them. They were odd, silent, nearly all old, and from the way they stared they looked as though they'd just come from dark little rooms or even—even cupboards!

Behind the rotunda the slender trees with yellow leaves down drooping, and through them just a line of sea, and beyond the blue sky with gold-veined clouds.

Tum-tum-tum tiddle-um! tiddle-um! tum tiddley-um tum ta! blew the band.

Two young girls in red came by and two young soldiers in blue met them, and they laughed and paired and went off arm-in-arm. Two peasant women with funny straw hats passed, gravely, leading beautiful smoke-colored donkeys. A cold, pale nun hurried by. A beautiful woman came along and dropped her bunch of violets, and a little boy ran after to hand them to her, and she took them and threw them away as if they'd been poisoned. Dear me! Miss Brill didn't know whether to admire that or not! And now an ermine toque and a gentleman in gray met just in front of her. He was tall, stiff, dignified, and she was wearing the ermine toque she'd bought when her hair was yellow. Now everything, her hair, her face, even her eyes, was the same color as the shabby ermine, and her hand, in its cleaned glove, lifted to dab her lips, was a tiny yellowish paw. Oh, she was so pleased to see him—delighted! She rather thought they were going to meet that afternoon. She described where she'd been—

Georges Seurat, *Sunday Afternoon on the Island of La Grande Jatte*, 1884–1886, The Art Institute of Chicago

everywhere, here, there, along by the sea. The day was so charming—didn't he agree? And wouldn't he, perhaps? . . . But he shook his head, lighted a cigarette, slowly breathed a great deep puff into her face, and, even while she was still talking and laughing, flicked the match away and walked on. The ermine toque was alone; she smiled more brightly than ever. But even the band seemed to know what she was feeling and played more softly, played tenderly, and the drum beat, "The Brute! The Brute!" over and over. What would she do? What was going to happen now? But as Miss Brill wondered, the ermine toque turned, raised her hand as though she'd seen some one else, much nicer, just over there, and pattered away. And the band changed again

and played more quickly, more gayly than ever, and the old couple on Miss Brill's seat got up and marched away, and such a funny old man with long whiskers hobbled along in time to the music and was nearly knocked over by four girls walking abreast.

Oh, how fascinating it was! How she enjoyed it! How she loved sitting here, watching it all! It was like a play. It was exactly like a play. Who could believe the sky at the back wasn't painted? But it wasn't till a little brown dog trotted on solemn and then slowly trotted off, like a little "theater" dog, a little dog that had been drugged, that Miss Brill discovered what it was that made it so exciting. They were all on the stage. They weren't only the audience, not only looking on; they were acting. Even she had a part and came every Sunday. No doubt somebody would have noticed if she hadn't been there; she was part of the performance after all. How strange she'd never thought of it like that before! And yet it explained why she made such a point of starting from home at just the same time each week—so as not to be late for the performance—and it also explained why she had quite a queer, shy feeling at telling her English pupils how she spent her Sunday afternoons. No wonder! Miss Brill nearly laughed out loud. She was on the stage. She thought of the old invalid gentleman to whom she read the newspaper four afternoons a week while he slept in the garden. She had got quite used to the frail head on the cotton pillow, the hollowed eyes, the open mouth and the high pinched nose. If he'd been dead she mightn't have noticed for weeks; she wouldn't have minded. But suddenly he knew he was having the paper read to him by an actress! "An actress!" The old head lifted; two points of light quivered in the old eyes. "An actress—are ye?" And Miss Brill smoothed the newspaper as though it were the manuscript of her part and said gently: "Yes, I have been an actress for a long time."

The band had been having a rest. Now they started again. And what they played was warm, sunny, yet there was just a faint chill—a something, what was it?—not sadness—no, not sadness—a something that made you want to sing. The tune lifted, lifted, the light shone; and it seemed to Miss Brill that in another moment all of them, all the whole company, would begin singing. The young ones, the laughing ones who were moving together, they would begin, and the men's voices, very resolute and brave, would join them. And then she too, she too, and the others on the benches—they would come in with a kind of accompaniment—something low, that scarcely rose or fell, something so beautiful—moving . . . And Miss Brill's eyes filled with tears and

she looked smiling at all the other members of the company. Yes, we understand, we understand, she thought—though what they understood she didn't know.

Just at that moment a boy and a girl came and sat down where the old couple had been. They were beautifully dressed; they were in love. The hero and heroine, of course, just arrived from his father's yacht. And still soundlessly singing, still with that trembling smile, Miss Brill prepared to listen.

"No, not now," said the girl. "Not here, I can't."

"But why? Because of that stupid old thing at the end there?" asked the boy. "Why does she come here at all—who wants her? Why doesn't she keep her silly old mug at home?"

"It's her fu-fur which is so funny," giggled the girl. "It's exactly like a fried whiting."

"Ah, be off with you!" said the boy in an angry whisper. Then: "Tell me, *ma petite chère*[3]—"

"No, not here," said the girl. "Not *yet*."

On her way home she usually bought a slice of honeycake at the baker's. It was her Sunday treat. Sometimes there was an almond in her slice, sometimes not. It made a great difference. If there was an almond it was like carrying home a tiny present—a surprise—something that might very well not have been there. She hurried on the almond Sundays and struck the match for the kettle in quite a dashing way.

But today she passed the baker's by, climbed the stairs, went into the little dark room—her room like a cupboard—and sat down on the red eiderdown. She sat there for a long time. The box that the fur came out of was on the bed. She unclasped the necklet quickly; quickly, without looking, laid it inside. But when she put the lid on she thought she heard something crying.

---

3. *ma petite chère* (mà pə tēt′ sher), my little dear [*French*].

## THINK AND DISCUSS

### Understanding

1. To what does Miss Brill compare the chill in the air?
2. Where is the story set?
3. Why does Miss Brill love sitting in her "special" seat and watching everything?

### Analyzing

4. What makes Miss Brill's usual seat in the park "special"?
5. What does Miss Brill's being so annoyed with the English woman who talked about "how she ought to wear spectacles" reveal about Miss Brill?
6. Explain the **dramatic irony** of Miss Brill's thinking, "They were odd, silent, nearly all old, and from the way they stared they looked as though they'd just come from dark little rooms or even—even cupboards!"

### Extending

7. One young reader has said she found the character Miss Brill somewhat funny at a few points in the story but that she felt sympathy for her at the end. Did your feelings about Miss Brill change during the story? Explain.

### REVIEWING: Stereotype  HT
See Handbook of Literary Terms, p. 826

Authors frequently use stereotyped characters, settings, and even situations to achieve and heighten a desired effect. In "Miss Brill" Katherine Mansfield creates an easily recognizable, typical character who might be called an old maid.

1. What makes Miss Brill resemble a stereotypical old maid?
2. Explain how Miss Brill sees the world in stereotypical terms.

## THINKING SKILLS

### Evaluating

To **evaluate** is to make a judgment based on a standard. For example, a teacher may judge a student's writing on the basis of how well it completes an assignment or whether it expresses ideas with originality. Similarly, readers evaluate the writing of short story authors. How would you evaluate Katherine Mansfield's characterization? You may have noticed that Mansfield describes Miss Brill in terms of her clothing and personal effects. The character wears a fur collar. Do the descriptions of the fur and Miss Brill's thoughts about it suggest that she is old-fashioned, prim, or set in her ways? What does the condition of the fur tell you about her economic status?

Review the story to note details of clothing and personal effects of other characters. List details that you judge most effective in helping you picture the characters. Then imagine a character of your own and think about how he or she would dress. Your class might identify characters who are individualistic or stereotypical. Name the articles of clothing that would characterize your character, and listen as your classmates describe theirs. In light of your attempts to characterize people by describing clothing and personal effects, evaluate Mansfield's use of such detail in "Miss Brill." Explain your opinion in the class discussion.

### COMPOSITION
### Writing a Sensory Description

Miss Brill is sensitive to what she sees and hears, mentally recording sensory impressions in great detail, to which she responds emotionally.

Imagine yourself to be a person in the park who notices Miss Brill. Write a paragraph describing this old woman and her behavior so that your reader can see and feel about her as you do. Appeal to your reader's senses with sensory details. Remember, she can't hear you so feel free to be perfectly frank.

**Writing About Theme**

In a three-paragraph essay, state what you believe to be the theme of "Miss Brill." Then analyze how three of the following literary elements work to convey that theme: character, plot, conflict, climax, symbol, or irony.

**ENRICHMENT**
**Creating a Portrait**

Make a portrait of Miss Brill in the artistic medium of your choice—a sketch, a painting or watercolor, a clay figure, or another form of art or craft. Review the story and picture the character in detail. Draw a rough sketch and then make your final image or collage of images. You may want to display your work in class and compare it to the artwork of others.

# BIOGRAPHY

## Katherine Mansfield

### 1888–1923

Kathleen Mansfield Beauchamp was born in Wellington, New Zealand, where her father was a banker and industrialist. She had her first story published when she was nine. Six years later she was sent to London where she attended Queen's College. Mansfield achieved literary success with *Bliss and Other Stories*, published in 1920. She went to Paris for special medical treatment in 1922, the same year *The Garden Party* was published. She died and was buried in Avon, France. Her last work, *The Little Girl*, was published posthumously in 1924.

**See MOOD in the Handbook of Literary Terms, page 808.**

# Tuesday Siesta

**Gabriel García Márquez**   Colombia

"Two big rusty keys hung on the inside of the door; the girl imagined . . . that they were Saint Peter's keys."

he train emerged from the quivering tunnel of sandy rocks, began to cross the symmetrical, interminable banana plantations, and the air became humid and they couldn't feel the sea breeze anymore. A stifling blast of smoke came in the car window. On the narrow road parallel to the railway there were oxcarts loaded with green bunches of bananas. Beyond the road, in uncultivated spaces set at odd intervals there were offices with electric fans, red-brick buildings, and residences with chairs and little white tables on the terraces among dusty palm trees and rosebushes. It was eleven in the morning, and the heat had not yet begun.

"You'd better close the window," the woman said. "Your hair will get full of soot."

The girl tried to, but the shade wouldn't move because of the rust.

They were the only passengers in the lone third-class car. Since the smoke of the locomotive kept coming through the window, the girl left her seat and put down the only things they had with them: a plastic sack with some things to eat and a bouquet of flowers wrapped in newspaper. She sat on the opposite seat, away from the window, facing her mother. They were both in severe and poor mourning clothes.

The girl was twelve years old, and it was the first time she'd ever been on a train. The woman seemed too old to be her mother, because of the blue veins on her eyelids and her small, soft, and shapeless body, in a dress cut like a cassock. She was riding with her spinal column braced firmly against the back of the seat, and held a peeling patent-leather handbag in her lap with both hands. She bore the conscientious serenity of someone accustomed to poverty.

By twelve the heat had begun. The train stopped for ten minutes to take on water at a station where there was no town. Outside, in the mysterious silence of the plantations, the shadows

*Gabriel García Márquez* (gä bryel′ gär sē′ä mär′käs).

"Tuesday Siesta" from *No One Writes to the Colonel* by Gabriel García Márquez, translated by J. S. Bernstein. Copyright © 1968 in the English translation by Harper & Row, Publishers, Inc. Reprinted by permission of the publisher.

Mariano Miguel, *La Popa*, 1923, The Cuban Foundation Collection of the Museum of Arts and Sciences, Daytona Beach, Florida.

seemed clean. But the still air inside the car smelled like untanned leather. The train did not pick up speed. It stopped at two identical towns with wooden houses painted bright colors. The woman's head nodded and she sank into sleep. The girl took off her shoes. Then she went to the washroom to put the bouquet of flowers in some water.

When she came back to her seat, her mother was waiting to eat. She gave her a piece of cheese, half a cornmeal pancake, and a cookie, and took an equal portion out of the plastic sack for herself. While they ate, the train crossed an iron bridge very slowly and passed a town just like the ones before, except that in this one there was a crowd in the plaza. A band was playing a lively tune under the oppressive sun. At the other side of town the plantations ended in a plain which was cracked from the drought.

The woman stopped eating.

"Put on your shoes," she said.

The girl looked outside. She saw nothing but the deserted plain, where the train began to pick up speed again, but she put the last piece of cookie into the sack and quickly put on her shoes. The woman gave her a comb.

"Comb your hair," she said.

The train whistle began to blow while the girl was combing her hair. The woman dried the sweat from her neck and wiped the oil from her face with her fingers. When the girl stopped combing, the train was passing the outlying houses of a town larger but sadder than the earlier ones.

"If you feel like doing anything, do it now," said the woman. "Later, don't take a drink anywhere even if you're dying of thirst. Above all, no crying."

The girl nodded her head. A dry, burning wind came in the window, together with the locomotive's whistle and the clatter of the old cars. The woman folded the plastic bag with the rest of the food and put it in the handbag. For a moment a complete picture of the town, on that bright August Tuesday, shone in the window. The girl wrapped the flowers in the soaking-wet newspapers, moved a little farther away from the window, and stared at her mother. She received a pleasant expression in return. The train began to whistle and slowed down. A moment later it stopped.

There was no one at the station. On the other side of the street, on the sidewalk shaded by the almond trees, only the pool hall was open. The town was floating in the heat. The woman and the girl got off the train and crossed the abandoned station—the tiles split apart by the grass growing up between—and over to the shady side of the street.

It was almost two. At that hour, weighted down by drowsiness, the town was taking a siesta. The stores, the town offices, the public school were closed at eleven, and didn't reopen until a little before four, when the train went back. Only the hotel across from the station, with its bar and pool hall, and the telegraph office at one side of the plaza stayed open. The houses, most of them built on the banana company's model, had their doors locked from inside and their blinds drawn. In some of them it was so hot that the residents ate lunch in the patio. Others leaned a chair against the wall, in the shade of the almond trees, and took their siesta right out in the street.

Keeping to the protective shade of the almond trees, the woman and the girl entered the town without disturbing the siesta. They went directly to the parish house. The woman scratched the metal grating on the door with her fingernail, waiting a moment, and scratched again. An electric fan was humming inside. They did not hear the steps. They hardly heard the slight creaking of a door, and immediately a cautious voice, right next to the metal grating: "Who is it?" The woman tried to see through the grating.

"I need the priest," she said.

"He's sleeping now."

"It's an emergency," the woman insisted.

Her voice showed a calm determination.

The door was opened a little way, noiselessly, and a plump, older woman appeared, with very pale skin and hair the color of iron. Her eyes seemed too small behind her thick eyeglasses.

"Come in," she said, and opened the door all the way.

They entered a room permeated with an old smell of flowers. The woman of the house led them to a wooden bench and signaled them to sit down. The girl did so, but her mother remained standing, absent-mindedly, with both hands clutching the handbag. No noise could be heard above the electric fan.

The woman of the house reappeared at the door at the far end of the room. "He says you should come back after three," she said in a very low voice. "He just lay down five minutes ago."

"The train leaves at three-thirty," said the woman.

It was a brief and self-assured reply, but her voice remained pleasant, full of undertones. The woman of the house smiled for the first time.

"All right," she said.

When the far door closed again, the woman sat down next to her daughter. The narrow waiting room was poor, neat, and clean. On the other side of the wooden railing which divided the room, there was a worktable, a plain one with an oilcloth cover, and on top of the table a primitive typewriter next to a vase of flowers. The parish records were beyond. You could see that it was an office kept in order by a spinster.

The far door opened and this time the priest appeared, cleaning his glasses with a handkerchief. Only when he put them on was it evident that he was the brother of the woman who had opened the door.

"How can I help you?" he asked.

"The keys to the cemetery," said the woman.

The girl was seated with the flowers in her lap and her feet crossed under the bench. The priest looked at her, then looked at the woman, and then through the wire mesh of the window at the bright, cloudless sky.

"In this heat," he said. "You could have waited until the sun went down."

The woman moved her head silently. The priest crossed to the other side of the railing, took out of the cabinet a notebook covered in oilcloth, a wooden penholder, and an inkwell, and sat down at the table. There was more than enough hair on his hands to account for what was missing on his head.

"Which grave are you going to visit?" he asked.

"Carlos Centeno's," said the woman.

"Who?"

"Carlos Centeno," the woman repeated.

The priest still did not understand.

"He's the thief who was killed here last week," said the woman in the same tone of voice. "I am his mother."

The priest scrutinized her. She stared at him with quiet self-control, and the Father blushed. He lowered his head and began to write. As he filled the page, he asked the woman to identify herself, and she replied unhesitatingly, with precise details, as if she were reading them. The Father began to sweat. The girl unhooked the buckle of her left shoe, slipped her heel out of it, and rested it on the bench rail. She did the same with the right one.

It had all started the Monday of the previous week, at three in the morning, a few blocks from there. Rebecca, a lonely widow who lived in a house full of odds and ends, heard above the sound of the drizzling rain someone trying to force the front door from outside. She got up, rummaged around in her closet for an ancient revolver that no one had fired since the days of Colonel Aureliano Buendía,[1] and went into the living room without turning on the lights. Orienting herself not so much by the noise at the lock as by a terror developed in her by twenty-eight years of loneliness, she fixed in her imagination not only the spot where the door was but also the exact height of the lock. She clutched the weapon with both hands, closed her eyes, and squeezed the trigger. It was the first time in her life that she had fired a gun. Immediately after the explosion, she could hear nothing except the murmur of the drizzle on the galvanized roof. Then she heard a little metallic bump on the cement porch, and a very low voice, pleasant but terribly exhausted: "Ah, Mother." The man they found dead in front of the house in the morning, his nose blown to bits, wore a flannel shirt with colored stripes, everyday pants with a rope for a belt, and was barefoot. No one in town knew him.

"So his name was Carlos Centeno," murmured the Father when he finished writing.

"Centeno Ayala,"[2] said the woman. "He was my only boy."

The priest went back to the cabinet. Two big rusty keys hung on the inside of the door; the girl imagined, as her mother had when she was a girl and as the priest himself must have imagined at some time, that they were Saint Peter's keys. He took them down, put them on the open notebook on the railing, and pointed with his forefinger to a place on the page he had just written, looking at the woman.

"Sign here."

The woman scribbled her name, holding the handbag under her arm. The girl picked up the flowers, came to the railing shuffling her feet, and watched her mother attentively.

The priest sighed.

"Didn't you ever try to get him on the right track?"

The woman answered when she finished signing.

"He was a very good man."

The priest looked first at the woman and then at the girl, and realized with a kind of pious amazement that they were not about to cry. The woman continued in the same tone:

"I told him never to steal anything that anyone needed to eat, and he minded me. On the other hand, before, when he used to box, he used to spend three days in bed, exhausted from being punched."

"All his teeth had to be pulled out," interrupted the girl.

"That's right," the woman agreed. "Every mouthful I ate those days tasted of the beatings my son got on Saturday nights."

"God's will is inscrutable," said the Father.

But he said it without much conviction, partly because experience had made him a little skeptical and partly because of the heat. He suggested that they cover their heads to guard against sunstroke. Yawning, and now almost completely asleep, he gave them instructions about how to find Carlos Centeno's grave. When they came back, they didn't have to knock. They should put the key under the door; and in the same place, if they could, they should put an offering for the Church. The woman listened to his directions with great attention, but thanked him without smiling.

The Father had noticed that there was someone looking inside, his nose pressed against the metal grating, even before he opened the door to the street. Outside was a group of children. When the door was opened wide, the children scattered. Ordinarily, at that hour there was no one in the

---

1. *Aureliano Buendía* (ou′rā lyä′nō bwän dē′ä).
2. *Centeno Ayala* (ä yä′lä). In Spanish-speaking countries a person's first name and surname are customarily followed by his or her mother's maiden name. Thus, the young man's full name was Carlos Centeno Ayala.

street. Now there were not only children. There were groups of people under the almond trees. The Father scanned the street swimming in the heat and then he understood. Softly, he closed the door again.

"Wait a moment," he said without looking at the woman.

His sister appeared at the far door with a black jacket over her nightshirt and her hair down over her shoulders. She looked silently at the Father.

"What was it?" he asked.

"The people have noticed," murmured his sister.

"You'd better go out by the door to the patio," said the Father.

"It's the same there," said his sister. "Everybody is at the windows."

The woman seemed not to have understood until then. She tried to look into the street through the metal grating. Then she took the bouquet of flowers from the girl and began to move toward the door. The girl followed her.

"Wait until the sun goes down," said the Father.

"You'll melt," said his sister, motionless at the back of the room. "Wait and I'll lend you a parasol."

"Thank you," replied the woman. "We're all right this way."

She took the girl by the hand and went into the street.

---

## THINK AND DISCUSS
### Understanding
1. What details during the train ride help the reader to visualize a rural, twentieth-century, South American setting?
2. What details convey the poverty of the mother and daughter?
3. How do the priest and his housekeeper show consideration for the woman?

### Analyzing
4. What does the description of the mother "riding with her spinal column braced firmly against the back of the seat" suggest about her character?
5. Explain what qualities you infer she possesses as you read about the following: her warning to her daughter as they get off the train; her statements when the priest's housekeeper opens the door; and her actions at the end of the story.
6. What opinion does the priest seem to have of the dead son?
7. What effect on the reader does the author seek by making the setting, circumstances, and people so oppressive?

### Extending
8. Who or what do you consider to be the mother's **antagonist** in this story?

## APPLYING: Mood
### See Handbook of Literary Terms, p. 808

By definition, **mood** is the feeling the author conveys to the reader through the setting, imagery, details, descriptions, and other evocative words. In "Tuesday Siesta" the author seeks to evoke feelings of pity toward the characters and anger toward the social conditions that create such human suffering. Describe the mood and explain how the writer creates it through the setting and imagery.

## COMPOSITION
### Writing About Imagery

The use of imagery contributes to the mood of a written work by helping the reader to experience what he or she is reading. Review the story for words and phrases that appeal to the senses. Does such imagery help you to identify with the feelings of the characters? Does the imagery convey a pleasant or unpleasant atmosphere? Write a three-paragraph essay that analyzes the author's use of imagery and its effectiveness.

### Writing About Theme

Write a three-paragraph essay, beginning by stating what you believe to be the central idea of this story. Then analyze how three of the following literary elements, present in the story, help to reveal your theme statement: character, setting, mood, allusion, conflict, foreshadowing, and resolution. See "Writing About Theme" in the Writer's Handbook.

## BIOGRAPHY
### Gabriel García Márquez
### 1928–

The sweltering setting of "Tuesday Siesta" may be based on the small Caribbean town of Aracataca (ä′rä kä tä′kä), Colombia, the birthplace of Gabriel García Márquez. To mold his fictional views of Latin American life and conflicts, García Márquez has drawn material from actual locations and history. In doing so, he has advanced—and revived interest in—his continent's literary tradition. In 1982 he was awarded the Nobel Prize in Literature.

García Márquez began his career as a reporter for a newspaper. Encouraged by his well-received short stories, which appeared in the paper's literary section, he published his first novel, *Leaf Storm*, in 1955. His major work is *One Hundred Years of Solitude* (1967). His writings often feature a blend of reality and fantasy.

**Review MOOD in the Handbook of Literary Terms, page 808.**

# The Demon Lover

**Elizabeth Bowen**   Ireland

---

**"She took the letter rapidly upstairs with her, without a stop to look at the writing till she reached what had been her bedroom, where she let in light."**

---

oward the end of her day in London Mrs. Drover went round to her shut-up house to look for several things she wanted to take away. Some belonged to herself, some to her family, who were by now used to their country life. It was late August; it had been a steamy, showery day; at the moment the trees down the pavement glittered in an escape of humid yellow afternoon sun. Against the next batch of clouds, already piling up ink-dark, broken chimneys and parapets stood out. In her once familiar street, as in any unused channel, an unfamiliar queerness had silted up; a cat wove itself in and out of railings but no human eye watched Mrs. Drover's return. Shifting some parcels under her arm, she slowly forced round her latchkey in an unwilling lock, then gave the door, which had warped, a push with her knee. Dead air came out to meet her as she went in.

The staircase window having been boarded up, no light came down into the hall. But one door, she could just see, stood ajar, so she went quickly through into the room and unshuttered the big window in there. Now the prosaic woman, looking about her, was more perplexed than she knew by everything that she saw, by traces of her long former habit of life—the yellow smoke stain up the white marble mantelpiece, the ring left by a vase on the top of the escritoire; the bruise in the wallpaper where, on the door being thrown open widely, the china handle had always hit the wall. The piano, having gone away to be stored, had left what looked like claw marks on its part of the parquet. Though not much dust had seeped in, each object wore a film of another kind; and, the only ventilation being the chimney, the whole drawing room smelled of the cold hearth. Mrs. Drover put down her parcels on the escritoire and left the room to proceed upstairs; the things she wanted were in a bedroom chest.

---

She had been anxious to see how the house was—the part-time caretaker she shared with some neighbors was away this week on his holiday, known to be not yet back. At the best of times he did not look in often, and she was never sure that she trusted him. There were some cracks in the structure, left by the last bombing,[1] on which she was anxious to keep an eye. Not that one could do anything—

A shaft of refracted daylight now lay across the hall. She stopped dead and stared at the hall table—on this lay a letter addressed to her.

She thought first—then the caretaker *must* be back. All the same, who, seeing the house shuttered, would have dropped a letter in the box? It was not a circular, it was not a bill. And the post office redirected, to the address in the country, everything for her that came through the post. The caretaker (even if he *were* back) did not know she was due in London today—her call here had been planned to be a surprise—so his negligence in the manner of this letter, leaving it to wait in the dusk and the dust, annoyed her. Annoyed, she picked up the letter which bore no stamp. But it cannot be important, or they would know. . . . She took the letter rapidly upstairs with her, without a stop to look at the writing till she reached what had been her bedroom, where she let in light. The room looked over the garden and other gardens; the sun had gone in; as the clouds sharpened and lowered, the trees and rank lawns seemed already to smoke with dark. Her reluctance to look again at the letter came from the fact that she felt intruded upon—and by someone contemptuous of her ways. However, in the tenseness preceding the fall of rain she read it; it was a few lines.

*Dear Kathleen,*

*You will not have forgotten that today is our anniversary, and the day we said. The years have gone by at once slowly and fast. In view of the fact that* nothing *has changed, I shall rely upon you to keep your promise. I was sorry to see you leave London, but was satisfied that you would be back in time. You may expect me, therefore, at the hour arranged.*

*Until then . . .*

*K.*

Mrs. Drover looked for the date; it was today's. She dropped the letter onto the bedsprings, then picked it up to see the writing again—her lips, beneath the remains of lipstick, beginning to go white. She felt so much the change in her own face that she went to the mirror, polished a clear patch in it and looked at once urgently and stealthily in. She was confronted by a woman of forty-four, with eyes staring out under a hat brim that had been rather carelessly pulled down. She had not put on any more powder since she left the shop where she ate her solitary tea. The pearls her husband had given her on their marriage hung loose round her now rather thinner throat, slipping into the V of the pink wool jumper her sister knitted last autumn as they sat round the fire. Mrs. Drover's most normal expression was one of controlled worry, but of assent. Since the birth of the third of her little boys, attended by a quite serious illness, she had had an intermittent muscular flicker to the left of her mouth, but in spite of this she could always sustain a manner that was at once energetic and calm.

Turning from her own face as precipitately as she had gone to meet it, she went to the chest where the things were, unlocked it, threw up the lid, and knelt to search. But as rain began to come crashing down she could not keep from looking over her shoulder at the stripped bed on which the letter lay. Behind the blanket of rain the clock of the church that still stood struck six—with

---

1. *the last bombing.* The city of London was subjected to aerial bombardment many times during World War II, the time setting of the story.

rapidly heightening apprehension she counted each of the slow strokes, "The hour arranged . . . My God," she said, "*what* hour? How should I . . . ? After twenty-five years, . . ."

The young girl talking to the soldier in the garden had not ever completely seen his face. It was dark; they were saying good-by under a tree. Now and then—for it felt, from not seeing him at this intense moment, as though she had never seen him at all—she verified his presence for these few moments longer by putting out a hand, which he each time pressed, without very much kindness, and painfully, onto one of the breast buttons of his uniform. That cut of the button on the palm of her hand was, principally, what she was to carry away. This was so near the end of a leave from France that she could only wish him already gone. It was August, 1916.[2] Being not kissed, being drawn away from and looked at intimidated Kathleen till she imagined spectral glitters in the place of his eyes. Turning away, and looking back up the lawn she saw, through branches of trees, the drawing-room window alight; she caught a breath for the moment when she could go running back there into the safe arms of her mother and sister, and cry: "What shall I do, what shall I do? He has gone."

Hearing her catch her breath, her fiancé said, without feeling, "Cold?"

"You're going away such a long way."

"Not so far as you think."

"I don't understand?"

"You don't have to," he said. "You will. You know what we said."

"But that was—suppose you—I mean, suppose."

"I shall be with you," he said, "sooner or later. You won't forget that. You need do nothing but wait."

Only a little more than a minute later she was free to run up the silent lawn. Looking in through the window at her mother and sister, who did not for the moment perceive her, she already felt that unnatural promise drive down between her and the rest of all humankind. No other way of having given herself could have made her feel so apart, lost and foresworn. She could not have plighted a more sinister troth.

Kathleen behaved well when, some months later, her fiancé was reported missing, presumed killed. Her family not only supported her but were able to praise her courage without stint because they could not regret, as a husband for her, the man they knew almost nothing about. They hoped she would, in a year or two, console herself—and had it been only a question of consolation things might have gone much straighter ahead. But her trouble, behind just a little grief, was a complete dislocation from everything. She did not reject other lovers, for these failed to appear; for years she failed to attract men—and with the approach of her thirties she became natural enough to share her family's anxiousness on this score. She began to put herself out, to wonder; and at thirty-two she was very greatly relieved to find herself being courted by William Drover. She married him, and the two of them settled down in this quiet, arboreal part of Kensington;[3] in this house the years piled up, her children were born and they all lived till they were driven out by the bombs of the next war. Her movements as Mrs. Drover were circumscribed, and she dismissed any idea that they were still watched.

As things were—dead or living, the letter writer sent her only a threat. Unable, for some minutes, to go on kneeling with her back exposed

---

2. *August, 1916,* a month during the time of World War I, fought in Europe from 1914 to 1918.
3. *Kensington,* a residential district in London.

Rodolfo Amoêdo, *Bad News*, 1895, Museu Nacional de Belas Artes, Rio de Janeiro, Brazil

to the empty room, Mrs. Drover rose from the chest to sit on an upright chair whose back was firmly against the wall. The desuetude of her former bedroom, her married London home's whole air of being a cracked cup from which memory, with its reassuring power, had either evaporated or leaked away, made a crisis—and at just this crisis the letter writer had, knowledgeably, struck. The hollowness of the house this evening canceled years on years of voices, habits, and steps. Through the shut windows she only heard rain fall on the roofs around. To rally herself, she said she was in a mood—and, for two or three seconds shutting her eyes, told herself that she had imagined the letter. But she opened them—there it lay on the bed.

On the supernatural side of the letter's entrance she was not permitting her mind to dwell. Who, in London, knew she meant to call at the house today? Evidently, however, this had been known. The caretaker, *had* he come back, had had no cause to expect her: he would have taken the letter in his pocket, to forward it, at his own time, through the post. There was no other sign that the caretaker had been in—but, if not? Letters dropped in at doors of deserted houses do not fly or walk to tables in halls. They do not sit on the dust of empty tables with the air of certainty that they will be found. There is needed some human hand—but nobody but the caretaker had a key. Under circumstances she did not care to consider, a house can be entered without a key. It was possible that she was not alone now. She might be waited for, downstairs. Waited for—until when? Until "the hour arranged." At least that was not six o'clock; six had struck.

She rose from the chair and went over and locked the door.

The thing was, to get out. To fly? No, not that: she had to catch her train. As a woman whose utter dependability was the keystone of her family life, she was not willing to return to the country, to her husband, her little boys and her sister, without the objects she had come to fetch.

Resuming work at the chest she set about making up a number of parcels in a rapid, fumbling-decisive way. These, with her shopping parcels, would be too much to carry; these meant a taxi—

at the thought of the taxi her heart went up and her normal breathing resumed. I will ring up the taxi now; the taxi cannot come too soon: I shall hear the taxi out there running its engine, till I walk calmly down to it through the hall. I'll ring up—But no: the telephone is cut off. . . . She tugged at a knot she had tied wrong.

The idea of flight . . . He was never kind to me, not really. I don't remember him kind at all. Mother said he never considered me. He was set on me, that was what it was—not love. Not love, not meaning a person well. What did he do, to make me promise like that? I can't remember— But she found that she could.

She remembered with such dreadful acuteness that the twenty-five years since then dissolved like smoke and she instinctively looked for the weal left by the button on the palm of her hand. She remembered not only all that he said and did, but the complete suspension of *her* existence during that August week. I was not myself—they all told me so at the time. She remembered—but with one white burning blank as where acid has been dropped on a photograph; *under no conditions* could she remember his face.

So, wherever he may be waiting I shall not know him. You have no time to run from a face you do not expect.

The thing was to get to the taxi before any clock struck what could be the hour. She would slip down the street and round the side of the square to where the square gave on the main road. She would return in the taxi, safe, to her own door, and bring the solid driver into the house with her to pick up the parcels from room to room. The idea of the taxi driver made her decisive, bold; she unlocked the door, went to the top of the staircase, and listened down.

She heard nothing—but while she was hearing nothing the *passé*[4] air of the staircase was dis-

---

4. *passé* (pa sā′), old, stale [*French*].

turbed by a draft that traveled up to her face. It emanated from the basement; down there a door or window was being opened by someone who chose this moment to leave the house.

The rain had stopped; the pavements steamily shone as Mrs. Drover let herself out by inches from her own front door into the empty street. The unoccupied houses opposite continued to meet her look with their damaged stare. Making toward the thoroughfare and the taxi, she tried not to keep looking behind. Indeed, the silence was so intense—one of those creeks of London silence exaggerated this summer by the damage of war—that no tread could have gained on hers unheard. Where her street debouched on the square where people went on living she grew conscious of and checked her unnatural pace. Across the open end of the square two buses impassively passed each other; women, a perambulator, cyclists, a man wheeling a barrow signaled, once again, the ordinary flow of life.

At the square's most populous corner should be—and was—the short taxi rank.[5] This evening, only one taxi—but this, although it presented its blank rump, appeared already to be alertly waiting for her. Indeed, without looking round the driver started his engine as she panted up from behind and put her hand on the door. As she did so, the clock struck seven. The taxi faced the main road; to make the trip back to her house it would have to turn—and she settled back on the seat and the taxi *had* turned before she, surprised by its knowing movement, recollected that she had not "said where." She leaned forward to scratch at the glass panel that divided the driver's seat from her own.

The driver braked to what was almost a stop, turned round, and slid the glass panel back; the jolt of this flung Mrs. Drover forward till her face was almost into the glass. Through the aperture driver and passenger, not six inches between them, remained for an eternity eye to eye. Mrs. Drover's mouth hung open for some seconds before she could issue her first scream. After that she continued to scream freely and to beat with her gloved hands on the glass all round as the taxi, accelerating without mercy, made off with her into the hinterland of deserted streets.

---

5. *taxi rank,* row or line of taxicabs waiting to pick up fares; here, a place for taxis to line up.

## THINK AND DISCUSS
### Understanding
1. Why is Mrs. Drover reluctant to really examine the letter?
2. How many years have passed since Mrs. Drover parted from the young soldier?
3. What idea occurs to Mrs. Drover that gives her courage?
4. What is her first clue that there is something strange about the taxi?

### Analyzing
5. What details of the **setting** make it understandable that Mrs. Drover might develop an uncomfortable or stressful frame of mind?
6. How do Mrs. Drover's first reactions to the letter reveal her character?
7. What details in the **flashback** to 1916 suggest she was uncomfortable in her relationship with the young soldier?

**Extending**

8. What single detail in the story is most convincing that this is a tale of the supernatural, not to be explained away in psychological terms?

**REVIEWING: Mood**

**See Handbook of Literary Terms, p. 808**

An author may use what is revealed about the setting and a character's thoughts, as well as information withheld from the reader, to create a mood of mystery and suspense in a story. Think about the place and atmosphere, the title, the character's thoughts, and the missing details of "The Demon Lover."

1. What imagery, character's experiences and character traits, and other details might help a reader feel the same uneasiness that Mrs. Drover feels?

2. How does the mood of the story make the strange, fantasy-like outcome more convincing?

**COMPOSITION**

**Offering Alternate Explanations**

Write a two-paragraph composition in which you present two different but reasonable explanations for what happens in the story. The first paragraph should state that the story is one of the supernatural; the second, that it is the story of a disturbed mind. Be sure to support what you write with specific details from the story.

**Writing About Mood**

"The Demon Lover" begins in a very low-key, calm mood. Everything is familiar and calming. Then it moves through various stages of mystery, growing suspense and anxiety, reduced tension, and finally hysteria. Write a three-paragraph essay in which you trace these four stages using specific details from the story. See "Writing About Mood or Tone" in the Writer's Handbook.

**BIOGRAPHY**

**Elizabeth Bowen**

**1899–1973**

Born in Dublin, Ireland, Bowen was a member of an upper-class Anglo-Irish family. At seven she was taken to live in the south of England, but at nineteen she left home and lived in London and on the Continent, particularly in Italy. She married in 1923 and continued to write stories. With publication of the novel *The Heat of the Day* (1949), she gained recognition as a major modern novelist. She spent the World War II years working days for the Ministry of Information and at night as an air-raid warden. She traveled extensively, spending considerable time writing and lecturing in the United States.

# The Masque of the Red Death

**Edgar Allan Poe**   USA

---

**Prince Prospero and his thousand guests might entertain themselves at a masque—a masquerade ball—within the sealed castle walls. But shut outside was the dreaded plague, the "Red Death."**

---

he Red Death had long devastated the country. No pestilence had ever been so fatal, or so hideous. Blood was its Avatar[1] and its seal—the redness and the horror of blood. There were sharp pains, and sudden dizziness, and then profuse bleeding at the pores, with dissolution. The scarlet stains upon the body and especially upon the face of the victim were the pest ban which shut him out from the aid and from the sympathy of his fellow men. And the whole seizure, progress, and termination of the disease were the incidents of half an hour.

But the Prince Prospero was happy and dauntless and sagacious. When his dominions were half depopulated, he summoned to his presence a thousand hale and light-hearted friends from among the knights and dames of his court, and with these retired to the deep seclusion of one of his castellated abbeys. This was an extensive and magnificent structure, the creation of the Prince's own eccentric yet august taste. A strong and lofty wall girdled it in. This wall had gates of iron. The courtiers, having entered, brought furnaces and massy hammers and welded the bolts. They resolved to leave means neither of ingress nor egress to the sudden impulses of despair or of frenzy from within. The abbey was amply provisioned. With such precautions the courtiers might bid defiance to contagion. The external world could take care of itself. In the meantime it was folly to grieve, or to think. The Prince had provided all the appliances of pleasure. There were buffoons, there were *improvisatori*,[2] there were ballet dancers, there were musicians, there was Beauty, there was wine. All these and security were within. Without was the Red Death.

It was toward the close of the fifth or sixth month of his seclusion, and while the pestilence raged most furiously abroad, that the Prince Prospero entertained his thousand friends at a masked ball of the most unusual magnificence.

It was a voluptuous scene, that masquerade. But first let me tell of the rooms in which it was held. There were seven—an imperial suite. In many palaces, however, such suites form a long and straight vista, while the folding doors slide back nearly to the walls on either hand, so that the view of the whole extent is scarcely impeded.

---

1. *Avatar* (av'ə tär'), a sign or manifestation in bodily form; (in Hindu mythology) incarnation.
2. *improvisatori* (im'prō vē'zä tō'rē), poets and singers of improvised verses, performers who sing without rehearsal [*Italian*].

"The Masque of the Red Death" by Edgar Allan Poe, 1842, from *Tales*, 1845.

Here the case was very different, as might have been expected from the Prince's love of the bizarre. The apartments were so irregularly disposed that the vision embraced but little more than one at a time. There was a sharp turn at every twenty or thirty yards, and at each turn a novel effect. To the right and left, in the middle of each wall, a tall and narrow Gothic window looked out upon a closed corridor which pursued the windings of the suite. These windows were of stained glass whose color varied in accordance with the prevailing hue of the decorations of the chamber into which it opened. That at the eastern extremity was hung, for example, in blue—and vividly blue were its windows. The second chamber was purple in its ornaments and tapestries, and here the panes were purple. The third was green throughout, and so were the casements. The fourth was furnished and lighted with orange, the fifth with white, the sixth with violet. The seventh apartment was closely shrouded in black velvet tapestries that hung all over the ceiling and down the walls, falling in heavy folds upon a carpet of the same material and hue. But in this chamber only, the color of the windows failed to correspond with the decorations. The panes here were scarlet—a deep blood-color. Now in no one of the seven apartments was there any lamp or candelabrum, amid the profusion of golden ornaments that lay scattered to and fro or depended from the roof. There was no light of any kind emanating from lamp or candle within the suite of chambers. But in the corridors that followed the suite there stood, opposite to each window, a heavy tripod, bearing a brazier of fire, that projected its rays through the tinted glass and so glaringly illuminated the room. And thus were produced a multitude of gaudy and fantastic appearances. But in the western or black chamber the effect of the firelight that streamed upon the dark hangings through the blood-tinted panes was ghastly in the extreme, and produced so wild a look upon the countenances of those who entered that there were few of the company bold enough to set foot within its precincts at all.

It was in this apartment, also, that there stood against the western wall a gigantic clock of ebony. Its pendulum swung to and fro with a dull, heavy, monotonous clang; and when the minute hand made the circuit of the face, and the hour was to be stricken, there came from the brazen lungs of the clock a sound which was clear and loud and deep and exceedingly musical, but of so peculiar a note and emphasis that, at each lapse of an hour, the musicians of the orchestra were constrained to pause, momentarily, in their performance, to hearken to the sound; and thus the waltzers perforce ceased their evolutions; and there was a brief disconcert of the whole gay company; and, while the chimes of the clock yet rang, it was observed that the giddiest grew pale, and the more aged and sedate passed their hands over their brows as if in confused revery or meditation. But when the echoes had fully ceased, a light laughter at once pervaded the assembly; the musicians looked at each other and smiled as if at their own nervousness and folly, and made whispering vows, each to the other, that the next chiming of the clock should produce in them no similar emotion; and then, after the lapse of sixty minutes (which embrace three thousand and six hundred seconds of the Time that flies) there came yet another chiming of the clock, and then were the same disconcert and tremulousness and meditation as before.

But, in spite of these things, it was a gay and magnificent revel. The tastes of the Prince were peculiar. He had a fine eye for colors and effects. He disregarded the *decora*[3] of mere fashion. His plans were bold and fiery, and his conceptions glowed with barbaric luster. There are some who would have thought him mad. His followers felt

---

3. *decora* (dā kô′rä), plural of *decorum*, thing that is proper in behavior or tasteful in dress [*Latin*].

Francisco Goya, *The Burial of the Sardine* (detail), Real Academia de San Fernando, Madrid.

that he was not. It was necessary to hear and see and touch him to be *sure* that he was not.

He had directed, in great part, the movable embellishments of the seven chambers, upon occasion of this great *fête;*[4] and it was his own guiding taste which had given character to the masqueraders. Be sure they were grotesque. There were much glare and glitter and piquancy and phantasm—much of what has been since seen in *Hernani.*[5] There were arabesque figures with unsuited limbs and appointments. There were delirious fancies such as the madman fashions. There was much of the beautiful, much of the wanton, much of the bizarre, something of the terrible, and not a little of that which might have excited disgust. To and fro in the seven chambers there stalked, in fact, a multitude of dreams. And these—the dreams—writhed in and about, taking hue from the rooms, and causing the wild music of the orchestra to seem as the echo of their steps. And, anon, there strikes the ebony clock which stands in the hall of the velvet. And then, for a moment, all is still, and all is silent save the voice of the clock. The dreams are stiff frozen as they stand. But the echoes of the chime die away— they have endured but an instant—and a light, half-subdued laughter floats after them as they depart. And now again the music swells, and the dreams live, and writhe to and fro more merrily than ever, taking hue from the many tinted windows through which stream the rays from the tripods. But to the chamber which lies most westwardly of the seven, there are now none of the maskers who venture; for the night is waning away, and there flows a ruddier light through the blood-colored panes; and the blackness of the sable drapery appalls; and to him whose foot falls upon the sable carpet, there comes from the near clock of ebony a muffled peal more solemnly emphatic than any which reaches *their* ears who indulge in the more remote gaieties of the other apartments.

But these other apartments were densely crowded, and in them beat feverishly the heart of life. And the revel went whirlingly on, until at length there commenced the sounding of midnight upon the clock. And then the music ceased, as I have told; and the evolutions of the waltzers were quieted; and there was an uneasy cessation of all things as before. But now there were twelve strokes to be sounded by the bell of the clock; and thus it happened, perhaps, that more of thought crept, with more of time, into the meditations of the thoughtful among those who reveled. And thus, too, it happened, perhaps, that before the last echoes of the last chime had utterly sunk into silence, there were many individuals in the crowd who had found leisure to become aware of the presence of a masked figure which had arrested the attention of no single individual before. And the rumor of this new presence having spread itself whisperingly around, there arose at length from the whole company a buzz, or murmur, expressive of disapprobation and surprise—then, finally, of terror, of horror, and of disgust.

In an assembly of phantasms such as I have painted, it may well be supposed that no ordinary appearance could have excited such sensation. In truth the masquerade license of the night was nearly unlimited; but the figure in question had out-Heroded Herod,[6] and gone beyond the bounds of even the Prince's indefinite decorum. There are chords in the hearts of the most reckless which cannot be touched without emotion. Even with the utterly lost, to whom life and death are equally jests, there are matters of which no jest can be made. The whole company, indeed,

---

4. *fête* (fet), feast or festival [*French*].
5. *Hernani* (er nä′nē), a romantic play by the French author Victor Hugo (1802–1885).
6. *Herod* (her′əd), a king of ancient Judea, noted for the massacre of innocent children. To "out-Herod" him would be to commit an even more shocking outrage.

seemed now deeply to feel that in the costume and bearing of the stranger neither wit nor propriety existed. The figure was tall and gaunt, and shrouded from head to foot in the habiliments of the grave. The mask which concealed the visage was made so nearly to resemble the countenance of a stiffened corpse that the closest scrutiny must have had difficulty in detecting the cheat. And yet all this might have been endured, if not approved, by the mad revelers around. But the mummer had gone so far as to assume the type of the Red Death. His vesture was dabbled in *blood*—and his broad brow, with all the features of the face, was besprinkled with the scarlet horror.

When the eyes of Prince Prospero fell upon this spectral image (which, with a slow and solemn movement, as if more fully to sustain its role, stalked to and fro among the waltzers) he was seen to be convulsed, in the first moment with a strong shudder either of terror or distaste; but, in the next, his brow reddened with rage.

"Who dares?" he demanded hoarsely of the courtiers who stood near him—"who dares insult us with this blasphemous mockery? Seize him and unmask him—that we may know whom we have to hang at sunrise, from the battlements!"

It was in the eastern or blue chamber in which stood the Prince Prospero as he uttered these words. They rang throughout the seven rooms loudly and clearly—for the Prince was a bold and robust man, and the music had become hushed at the waving of his hand.

It was in the blue room where stood the Prince, with a group of pale courtiers by his side. At first, as he spoke, there was a slight rushing movement of this group in the direction of the intruder, who at the moment was also near at hand, and now, with deliberate and stately step, made closer approach to the speaker. But from a certain nameless awe with which the mad assumptions of the mummer had inspired the whole party, there were found none who put forth hand to seize him; so

that, unimpeded, he passed within a yard of the Prince's person; and while the vast assembly, as if with one impulse, shrank from the centers of the rooms to the walls, he made his way uninterruptedly, but with the same solemn and measured step which had distinguished him from the first, through the blue chamber to the purple—through the purple to the green—through the green to the orange—through this again to the white—and even thence to the violet, ere a decided movement had been made to arrest him. It was then, however, that the Prince Prospero, maddening with rage and the shame of his own momentary cowardice, rushed hurriedly through the six chambers, while none followed him on account of a deadly terror that had seized upon all. He bore aloft a drawn dagger, and had approached, in rapid impetuosity, to within three or four feet of the retreating figure, when the latter, having attained the extremity of the velvet apartment, turned suddenly and confronted his pursuer. There was a sharp cry—and the dagger dropped gleaming upon the sable carpet, upon which, instantly afterward, fell prostrate in death the Prince Prospero. Then, summoning the wild courage of despair, a throng of the revelers at once threw themselves into the black apartment, and, seizing the mummer, whose tall figure stood erect and motionless within the shadow of the ebony clock, gasped in unutterable horror at finding the grave cerements and corpselike mask, which they handled with so violent a rudeness, untenanted by any tangible form.

And now was acknowledged the presence of the Red Death. He had come like a thief in the night. And one by one dropped the revelers in the blood-bedewed halls of their revel, and died each in the despairing posture of his fall. And the life of the ebony clock went out with that of the last of the gay. And the flames of the tripods expired. And Darkness and Decay and the Red Death held illimitable dominion over all.

*Comment*

## A Gruesome Tale of Edgar Allan Poe

Edgar Allan Poe's works often have a somber, almost grotesque mood that, to many readers, seems shrouded in mystery. If you read his works carefully, paying strict attention to the detailed descriptions and vivid imagery for which Poe is famous, the stories become less difficult and more enlightening.

In "The Masque of the Red Death," Poe presents a common theme—humanity's futile struggle with time and mortality. As in many of his stories, Poe hurls his characters into the clutch of mysterious, fatal forces, and portrays their anguish as they struggle against an inevitably ugly death. As the story opens, the reader learns about the "Red Death," which Prince Prospero and his court try to avoid by heartlessly secluding themselves in his palace. In describing the plague and its effects, Poe sets the brooding, somber mood that pervades the entire story.

It is in the description of the seven rooms in the palace that Poe's descriptive genius comes alive. The reader learns not only the exact setting of the masquerade, but also the strange tastes of Prince Prospero. It is important to note that the westernmost room—the black room—is the only exception to the color pattern. This detail foreshadows the tragedy that ends the story.

Central to the theme of the story is the great clock of ebony that stands against the western wall—symbolic of the passing of mortal time or the approaching limit of human mortality. When it chimes, its sound is so peculiar that all activity ceases. Even "the giddiest grew pale, and the more aged and sedate passed their hands over their brows as if in confused revery or meditation." Everyone stops to contemplate something unpleasant—perhaps death or the brevity of life.

At midnight a strange, masked guest

Poe's stories sometimes mix incidents of horror with occasions of festivity such as masquerades or carnivals. A similar mixture is suggested by one hideous costume in Francisco Goya's painting *The Burial of the Sardine* at Real Academia de San Fernando, Madrid.

provokes feelings of terror, horror, and disgust in the other guests. His mask resembles the face of a stiffened corpse dabbled in the bloody signs of the plague itself. Prince Prospero, outraged at the intrusion of the uninvited guest, is insulted at this "blasphemous mockery." Not realizing that he is pursuing the Red Death, he chases the guest through all seven rooms. When they reach the west room, Prince Prospero meets his death. Afterwards, it is only a matter of time before all the guests meet the same end in the final paragraph.

## THINK AND DISCUSS

### Understanding

1. How long does the "Red Death" take to kill?
2. What is the attitude of those courtiers inside the abbey toward those outside?
3. What pleasures had the prince provided for his courtiers?
4. What prevented the courtiers from stopping the intruder from his progress from room to room?

### Analyzing

5. Explain the irony of the prince's name.
6. What does the ebony clock symbolize?
7. Give examples of Poe's techniques for creating **mood** through setting, imagery, and vivid words.
8. What is the central conflict in this story, and who are the **protagonist** and **antagonist?**
9. What is ironic about the way Prince Prospero meets death?

## VOCABULARY

### Antonyms, Context

Antonyms are words that mean the opposite of other words. Match the numbered words with their antonyms in the following list. You will not use all the choices. You may refer to the Glossary.

1. arabesque
2. dauntless
3. impetuous
4. prostrate
5. wane

a. restrained
b. unnecessary
c. increase
d. unadorned
e. stupid
f. cowardly
g. standing

Each of the following words has more than one meaning. The meaning in context depends on the word's part of speech as it is used in context. Look up these multiple-meaning words in your Glossary and read each definition. Then match the definitions listed on the right to the word and use on the left.

1. brazen (adjective)
2. brazen (verb)
3. countenance (noun)
4. countenance (verb)
5. hale (adjective)
6. hale (verb)
7. peal (noun)
8. peal (verb)
9. shroud (noun)
10. shroud (verb)

a. strong, healthy
b. sound out, ring
c. loud, long sound
d. make shameless
e. shameless; harsh
f. burial garment
g. compel to go
h. facial expression
i. conceal
j. approve; encourage

## THINKING SKILLS

### Synthesizing

To **synthesize** is to put together parts and elements so as to form a whole, a new pattern or structure not evident before. In "The Masque of the Red Death," the narrator provides a detailed description of the seven rooms in which the masquerade ball takes place. Review these descriptions carefully. As you read, consider the following questions: How are the rooms distributed? Where are the corridors located in relation to each room? How many windows are in each room, and on what walls are they located? What is the only source of light for each room? Where is the ebony clock? Draw a map of these seven rooms, showing the position of each of the items listed above. Be sure to provide a direction indicator, and mark the color of each room.

## COMPOSITION ◁━◉

### Writing About Dreams

This story has a nightmarish quality in its bizarre setting, characters, and action. Most of us have dreams or nightmares, easily recalled in detail soon after they occur. Write a descriptive paragraph of such an experience, emphasizing or changing the bizarre elements, which may seem to make little sense. Be willing to intrigue your reader, as long as your images are clear. If you prefer, make up a nightmare to tell.

**Analyzing Poe's Writing Style**

Edgar Allan Poe felt that a writer of fiction should create a single impression in the reader, such as the impact of horror often felt by readers of "The Masque of the Red Death." Review the story to see whether all elements lead to that impression, in your opinion. Then write a four-paragraph essay analyzing how well the plot, setting, characters, point of view, and other literary devices lend the story the impact or quality that you have found.

**ENRICHMENT**
**Drawing and Discussing Art**

In this story, the narrator describes the Red Death as a costumed character. Work with classmates to prepare drawings of this figure to be discussed and displayed in class. Refer to the details provided by the narrator.

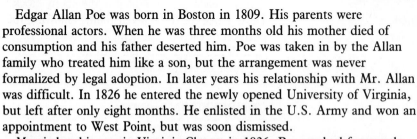

## BIOGRAPHY

### Edgar Allan Poe
### 1809–1849

Edgar Allan Poe was born in Boston in 1809. His parents were professional actors. When he was three months old his mother died of consumption and his father deserted him. Poe was taken in by the Allan family who treated him like a son, but the arrangement was never formalized by legal adoption. In later years his relationship with Mr. Allan was difficult. In 1826 he entered the newly opened University of Virginia, but left after only eight months. He enlisted in the U.S. Army and won an appointment to West Point, but was soon dismissed.

Married to his cousin Virginia Clemm in 1836, Poe worked frequently as an editor for various literary magazines, in which he published his own work. Though he is best known for his haunting poems and stories, Poe also contributed important ideas to literary theory.

# THINKING CRITICALLY
# ABOUT LITERATURE

## UNIT 5   EXPERIENCE IN SHORT FICTION

### ■ CONCEPT REVIEW

This story about a fictional dauphin (dô′fən)—the oldest son of the king of France and heir to the throne when France was a kingdom—illustrates literary elements and ideas about short stories that you have studied. It is accompanied by notes designed to help you think critically about your reading. Page numbers in the notes refer to applications of literary terms. These terms are also discussed in the Handbook of Literary Terms. Read the story and then answer the questions that follow.

# The Death of the Dauphin

**Alphonse Daudet**   France

The little Dauphin is ill; the little Dauphin is dying. In all the churches of the kingdom the Holy Sacrament remains exposed night and day, and great tapers burn, for the recovery of the royal child. The streets of the old capital are sad and silent, the bells ring no more, the carriages slacken their pace. In the neighborhood of the palace the curious townspeople gaze through the railings upon the beadles with gilded paunches, who converse in the courts and put on important airs.

All the castle is in a flutter. Chamberlains and major-domos run up and down the marble stairways. The galleries are full of pages and of courtiers in silken apparel, who hurry from one group to another, begging in low tones for news. Upon the wide perrons the maids of honor, in tears, exchange low courtesies and wipe their eyes with daintily embroidered handkerchiefs.

A large assemblage of robed physicians has gathered in Orangery. They

**■ Holy Sacrament:** the consecrated bread of Holy Communion, kept for devotion in churches.

**■ beadles:** parish officers.

**■ perrons:** broad steps or platforms.

**■ Stereotype** (page 450): The number and behavior of the beadles, chamberlains, maids of honor, scullions, and other attendants present a stereotypical picture of a royal palace.

---

*Alphonse Daudet* (dō dā′).

"The Death of the Dauphin" by Alphonse Daudet, 1869, from *Treasury of World Literature*, edited by Dagobert D. Runes, Philosophical Library, Publishers.

can be seen through the panes waving their long black sleeves and inclining their periwigs with professional gestures. The governor and the equerry of the little Dauphin walk up and down before the door awaiting the decision of the Faculty. Scullions pass by without saluting them. The equerry swears like a pagan; the governor quotes verses from Horace.

And meanwhile, over there, in the direction of the stables, is heard a long and plaintive neighing; it is the little Dauphin's sorrel, forgotten by the hostlers, and calling sadly before his empty manger.

And the King? Where is his highness the King? The King has locked himself up in a room at the other end of the castle. Majesties do not like to be seen weeping. For the Queen it is different. Sitting by the bedside of the little Dauphin, she bows her fair face, bathed in tears, and sobs very loudly before everybody, like a mere draper's wife.

On the bed embroidered with lace the little Dauphin, whiter than the pillows on which he is extended, lies with closed eyes. They think that he is asleep; but no, the little Dauphin is not asleep. He turns towards his mother, and seeing her tears, he asks:

"*Madame la Reine,* why do you weep? Do you really believe that I am going to die?"

The Queen tries to answer. Sobs prevent her from speaking.

■ **Madame la Reine** (mà dàm′ là ren): Madame Queen [*French*].

"Do not weep, *Madame la Reine.* You forget that I am the Dauphin, and that Dauphins cannot die thus."

The Queen sobs more violently, and the little Dauphin begins to feel frightened.

"Holloa!" says he, "I do not want Death to come and take me away, and I know how to prevent him from coming here. Order up on the spot forty of the strongest lansquenets to keep guard around our bed! Have a hundred big cannons watch day and night, with lighted fuses, under our windows! And woe to Death if he dares to come near us!"

■ **lansquenet** (lǝns′ke net′): a hired foot soldier.

■ **Irony** (page 386): We know a key fact that the Dauphin has yet to learn: his troops cannot kill Death.

In order to humor the royal child, the Queen makes a sign. On the spot the great cannons are heard rolling in the courts, and forty tall lansquenets, with halberds in their fists, draw up around the room. They are all veterans, with grizzly mustaches. The little Dauphin claps his hands on seeing them. He recognizes one, and calls,

"Lorrain! Lorrain!"

The veteran makes a step towards the bed.

"I love you well, my old Lorrain. Let me see your big sword. If Death wants to fetch me, you will kill him, won't you?"

Lorrain answers:

"Yes, *Monseigneur.*"

And two great tears roll down his tanned cheeks.

At that moment the chaplain approaches the little Dauphin and, pointing

■ **Monseigneur** (môn se-nyœr′): French title of honor.

to the crucifix, talks to him in low tones. The little Dauphin listens with astonished air; then, suddenly interrupting him,

"I understand well what you are saying, *Monsieur l'Abbé;* but still, couldn't my little friend Beppo die in my place, if I gave him plenty of money?"

The chaplain continues to talk to him in low tones, and the little Dauphin looks more and more astonished.

When the chaplain has finished, the little Dauphin resumes, with a heavy sigh:

"What you have said is all very sad, *Monsieur l'Abbé;* but one thing consoles me, and that is that up there, in the Paradise of the stars, I shall still be the Dauphin. I know that the good God is my cousin, and cannot fail to treat me according to my rank."

Then he adds, turning towards his mother:

"Bring me my fairest clothes, my doublet of white ermine, and my pumps of velvet! I wish to look brave to the angels, and to enter Paradise in the dress of a Dauphin."

A third time the chaplain bends over the little Dauphin, and talks to him in low tones. In the midst of his discourse the royal child interrupts him angrily.

"Why, then," he cries, "to be Dauphin is nothing at all!"

And refusing to listen to anything more, the little Dauphin turns towards the wall and weeps bitterly.

■ **Monsieur l'Abbé** (mə syœ′ là bā′): Sir Abbot, or Priest [*French*].

■ A stereotyped royal character might expect to find someone to stand in for him in any unpleasant duty.

■ **Mood** (page 471): The atmosphere of the story may become sadder in spite of the Dauphin's hope.

■ **Symbol** (page 411): The Dauphin looks on fur clothes and velvet shoes (pumps) as signs of his glory, but his plan to wear them to Paradise has another meaning to us.

*September* from The *Trés Riches Heures du Duc du Berry* (detail), Musée Condé, Chantilly, France

## THINK AND DISCUSS
### Understanding
1. What is the first reason the Dauphin gives for believing that he will not die?
2. Why does the Dauphin ask for forty lansquenets and a hundred cannons?
3. Who does the Dauphin suggest die in his place?

### Analyzing
4. The author doesn't tell the reader what the chaplain says when he first speaks to the Dauphin. What do you infer he says?
5. What illusion does the Dauphin cling to when he accepts the fact that he is dying?
6. What do you infer the Chaplain says to the Dauphin the third time he speaks?

### Extending
7. Do you feel pity for the Dauphin at the end of the story? Why or why not?

## REVIEWING LITERARY TERMS
### Mood
1. What descriptions at the beginning establish the mood of mourning, and what evocative phrase at the end deepens the mood? What is this new mood?

### Symbol
2. When the Dauphin realizes that he is going to die, he requests that his mother bring him his finest clothes. What do you think they symbolize for him? What might this symbolize for the reader?

### Irony
3. What irony of life does the Dauphin finally see?

### Satire
4. What absurd and dangerous social attitude does the author expose to our scrutiny?

## ■ CONTENT REVIEW
### THINKING SKILLS
#### Classifying
1. Many of the characters in the stories in Unit Five undergo a transformation during the course of their stories. Other characters seem to change little or not at all. For example, Ulrich and Georg become friends after having been enemies for years, while Lencho changes relatively little. Think about the other characters you have read about in this unit. Make two lists, classifying those characters who have changed a great deal and those who have changed little or not at all.

#### Generalizing
2. To what extent are the main characters in "The Necklace," "The Interlopers," "The Rat Trap," and "The Masque of the Red Death" to blame for the predicaments they find themselves in? To what extent are their problems caused by fate or coincidence? Write a generalization about the role that fate or coincidence plays in each story.

#### Synthesizing
3. Think about the stories in which the climax is brought about by a decisive happening—such as the tree falling upon Ulrich and Georg. Then decide what you think might have happened if that occurrence had been avoided, and write how one such story would change. Here are some questions you may want to consider: What if the man from Kabul had never gone to jail? What if Frieda Gittel had also failed the needle test? What if the ironmaster never found out the rat-trap peddler's true identity?

**4.** Many of the stories in Unit Five include key characters who rarely appear, such as Paul's father in "The Rocking-Horse Winner," or characters that are less developed than the main characters. Choose one of the following characters and describe what you think he or she would be like. What does he or she look like? How might the character get along with other characters? What conflicts might he or she encounter? Characters you may write about include Paul's father, Mini as an adult, the taxi driver in "The Demon Lover," the woman's son in "Tuesday Siesta," Lencho's wife, Esther Rosa's son, or another that interests you.

### Evaluating

**5.** Unit Five contains several realistic stories: "The Necklace," "The Interlopers," "The Sentimentality of William Tavener," and so on. As you read these stories, you find yourself drawn into the characters' lives and worlds by the authors' realistic, detailed descriptions and use of language. Choose one of the realistic stories in this unit and evaluate how well the author draws the reader into the story. Discuss his or her use of language in describing the characters and the action, as well as his or her use of imagery.

## ■ COMPOSITION REVIEW

Choose one of the following assignments and write the composition.

### Resolving a Story's Ending

Neither "The Interlopers" nor "Tuesday Siesta" has an absolutely clear ending; we think we know what happened to the characters, but we cannot be sure. Likewise, we may wonder what "Miss Brill" will do next. Choose one of the stories and decide what you would say if you could add three more paragraphs to the end of it. Make sure your ending fits the context.

Write the three paragraphs, making them sound as much like the author's style as possible.

### Comparing Long and Short Stories

Can a very short story be as effective as a longer one? Think about what the authors of "The Rocking-Horse Winner" (the longest story in the unit) and "The Death of the Dauphin" or "A Letter to God" (among the shortest) were trying to accomplish and how well each met his goals. Then decide which story you think is more successful. Write a three-paragraph composition beginning "A very short (or *long*) story can be just as effective as a very long (or *short*) one." Back up that statement with specifics from the story you've chosen.

### Describing and Explaining Contrasts

Both "Action Will Be Taken" and "The Rat Trap" involve factories, but those factories are presented quite differently. Review the stories, noting differences between the factories and determining reasons for the differences, such as the time, the location, or the purpose of the story. Write a three- or four-paragraph composition contrasting the two factories and explaining why you think they are so different.

### Reviewing Writer's Craft: Use Language That Appeals to the Senses

Imagine a character, an incident involving characters, or a setting that you could feature in a short story. Decide what the character, group of characters, or setting looks and sounds like, how the action would appear to an observer, and what details would make you recall the sights, sounds, feelings, and smells of the scene. Then write a character sketch, story scene, or description of setting that appeals strongly to the reader's senses. Your composition should be three or four paragraphs long.

# SHAKESPEAREAN DRAMA

Jean-Léon Gérome, *The Death of Caesar* (detail), 1859, Walters Art Gallery, Baltimore

# JULIUS CAESAR

# PREVIEW

## UNIT 6  SHAKESPEAREAN DRAMA

**Julius Caesar** / William Shakespeare
from **Antony and Cleopatra** / William Shakespeare

**Features**
Reading a Shakespearean Tragedy
Background
Writer's Craft: Use Precise,
   Active Verbs
Comment: Putting the Plays on Stage
Comment: *Julius Caesar* and the Tragic Hero

**Application of Literary Terms**
blank verse
foreshadowing

**Reading Literature Skillfully**
graphic aids

**Vocabulary Skills**
context
etymology
dictionary and glossary
word structure:
   prefixes and root words

**Thinking Skills**
generalizing
synthesizing

**Composition**
Writing a Newspaper Story
Analyzing the Commoners' Role
Reading/Writing Log
Writing as a Character
Examining Dramatic Structure
Giving Testimony as a Character
Analyzing the Commoners' Changing Role
Comparing the Public and Private Caesars
Writing About Portia's Role
Discussing Brutus' Character
Analyzing Falling Action in a Tragedy
Writing Persuasively

**Enrichment**
Speaking and Listening
Researching Shakespeare's Sources
Readers Theater
Group Activity: Mass Media
Producing a Newspaper or Magazine

**Thinking Critically About Literature**
Concept Review
Content Review
Composition Review

# Reading A SHAKESPEAREAN TRAGEDY

A tragedy is a drama in which the main character suffers disaster after a serious struggle but faces his or her downfall in a heroic way. Like most tragedies by William Shakespeare, *Julius Caesar* is based on actual historical occurrences, in this case the events leading to, including, and following the political assassination of Julius Caesar in 44 B.C. Since the play depicts occurrences in the lives of real people, it is in a sense biographical rather than fictional. As you read it, be aware that Shakespeare did not distort its biographical elements, but he did supplement them to build suspense, to clarify the motivation of the characters, and to provide comic relief.

## The Play's Structure

The plot of a Shakespearean tragedy follows a pattern: the fortunes of the leading character (called the tragic hero or **protagonist**) improve until the third act, in which the play reaches its structural **climax** or high point. Then the fortunes of the hero decline until, in Act Five, the leading character dies, the tragedy is complete, and the play ends. Technically the components of this structure are called the rising action, the climax, and the falling action.

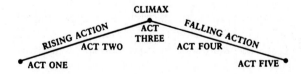

## Soliloquies and Asides

To help his audience understand what a character is thinking or to provide information other characters are not to know, Shakespeare uses *soliloquies* and *asides*. In a soliloquy the character speaks alone, and the audience "overhears" his or her inner thoughts. According to a convention of the Elizabethan theater, characters speak truthfully in soliloquies. In an aside, a character is onstage with others but speaks to himself or herself, "overheard" by the audience, or to one other person.

## The Globe Theater

The theater in which *Julius Caesar* was first produced was located across the Thames (temz) River from London during the reign of Queen Elizabeth I. The Globe Theater was octagonal in shape, three stories high, and constructed of oak timbers and white plaster walls. Rising above the thatched roof were three attached "huts" and a tower from which a flag flew on days when a play was to be presented. Consult the diagram of the Globe Theater on the next page.

Within the theater were three *galleries*, or audience areas, each projecting beyond the one beneath. The galleries and the area behind the stage were roofed, as was the stage, but the rest of the interior was open to the elements. This unprotected area, used to allow light and air into the crowded theater, was where the groundlings—apprentices and others who could afford only a penny to see the play—stood.

At one end of the unroofed area, or *yard*, was the performing area. This consisted of a *platform stage* that projected into the audience area. Two pillars, one at either end of the front of the stage, supported a canopy, on which rested the huts and the playhouse turret. On the under part of the canopy, which was painted blue, were pictures of the sun, the moon, and signs of the zodiac. This area was called the *Heavens*.

Under the platform stage, and sometimes used for acting, was an area known as *Hell*, where stage props were stored. In the center of the platform stage was a large trap door that provided access from this lower area.

Behind the platform stage, serving as a background, was a three-story structure called the *tiring house*. On its first level it contained a curtained *inner stage*, also called the *study*, which was flanked at right and left by doors. The second level held the *balcony stage* and, behind it, a second curtained area known as the *chamber*. The balcony stage projected slightly over the platform and was flanked by *bay-window stages*. The curtained *music gallery*, on the third level, could also function as a stage.

The performing areas of the Globe Theater included the platform stage (1) and other acting levels beneath the canopy (2), huts (3), and playhouse turret (4); the cellar-like Hell (5), offering entrances and exits through the trap door (6); the curtained inner stage (7), flanked by doors (8); the balcony stage (9) and behind it the chamber; the bay-window stages (10); and the music gallery (11).

The platform-level inner stage and the balcony-level chamber were almost identical. When the front curtains of either stage were drawn apart, the inner area suggested the interior of a room. The side walls were made of tapestry hangings that could be changed between scenes, and each rear wall had a door and a window with similar tapestry hangings in between. The doors were connected by a backstage stairway allowing access from one level to the next, but both they and the windows could be covered with tapestries.

### Reading *Julius Caesar*

Reading and visualizing the action in *Julius Caesar* will be easier if you keep the stages of the Globe Theater in mind. The diagram here can serve as a **graphic aid** that you can refer to as you read each scene. A note at the beginning of each scene tells the main part of the area on which it was acted, and some stage directions identify places where parts of scenes were performed. Photographs of a modern production also help you picture the characters, as well as the costumes, props, and action.

Shakespeare wrote *Julius Caesar* in 1599, and it was one of the first plays to be acted at the new Globe Theater. Nearly all parts of the Globe's performing area were used in the production. Most outdoor scenes took place on the platform and most indoor scenes on the inner stage or balcony. In one scene the trapdoor was used, and in some the platform and inner stage were used simultaneously.

The cast includes many characters, and the dialogue is not written in the casual style of twentieth-century conversation. Use the notes and numbered questions in the margins of the pages to fully understand words, ancient Roman customs, and developments in *Julius Caesar*. Like Shakespeare's audiences, who knew the history of Caesar, you may find yourself caught up in the story as you notice the ways characters explain their motives, take bold actions, and make tragic mistakes.

# BACKGROUND

*Julius Caesar* is a play of political intrigue, assassination, and revenge set against the backdrop of the Roman Empire. It features not one but two possible heroes out of its four major characters and ultimately depicts the downfall of both.

Shakespeare drew on Plutarch's *Lives of the Noble Greeks and Romans*, translated from Latin by Sir Thomas North, for most of the material in the play. "The Life of Caesar" gave him much of the basic plot; "The Life of Brutus" provided characterization, especially of Brutus and Cassius; and "The Life of Mark Antony" gave him information about Antony, as well as the idea for another tragedy, *Antony and Cleopatra*, written in 1606.

## Major Characters

**Julius Caesar** (100 B.C.–44 B.C.) was a great conqueror and politician. He gained territory for Rome and frequently sent money back to the city to be used for public works or to help the common people. Although he was given the honor of ruling Rome as long as he lived, many suspected that he wanted to set up a monarchy so that power would pass to his heirs. Caesar was married to Calpurnia, but thus far she had borne him no children.

**Marcus Brutus** (85 B.C.–42 B.C.) was a descendant of Lucius Junius Brutus, who had driven out the Tarquin kings and made Rome a republic. Marcus Brutus was a quiet idealist who enjoyed reading and study. At one time he had supported Pompey, one of Caesar's chief rivals for power, and had fought with him against Caesar. After Pompey's defeat Caesar pardoned Brutus, and the two resumed their friendship. Though Brutus liked Caesar, he feared Caesar's ambition. Brutus was married to

Portia, whose father had killed himself rather than submit to Caesar's rule.

**Caius Cassius** (? B.C.–42 B.C.) was a thin, quick-tempered, practical man with a grudge against Caesar. He had supported Pompey in the war against Caesar. After Brutus was pardoned, Caesar also pardoned Cassius, who was Brutus' brother-in-law.

**Mark Antony** (83 B.C.–30 B.C.) was a young man notorious for his wild living. He had fought under Caesar and supported Caesar's ambitious schemes. A holder of various public offices including that of tribune, Antony understood the instability of the commoners and how a speaker could sway their emotions.

## As the Play Opens

For many years Caesar had been struggling with Pompey, once his ally, for control of Rome and its territories. Eventually war broke out between them. In 48 B.C. Caesar, a superb military leader, defeated Pompey. Fleeing to Egypt for safety, Pompey was killed there by a servant of the ruler, but his two sons took up the war. They, however, were also defeated by Caesar, and one died.

Returning to Rome, Caesar became dictator and then dictator for life. Many Romans became suspicious of Caesar's growing power and feared that he would put an end to their republic. Rome had had a republican form of government since 509 B.C. Still other Romans were angry that Caesar wished to celebrate a public triumph over Pompey's sons, who were not foreigners but Romans like themselves.

The action of the play begins on February 15, 44 B.C., the feast of Lupercalia (lü pər kā′lē ə) and the day Caesar has selected to celebrate his triumph.

**See BLANK VERSE in the Handbook of Literary Terms, page 790.**

# Julius Caesar

**William Shakespeare**   Great Britain

## CHARACTERS

**JULIUS CAESAR**

**OCTAVIUS CAESAR**

**MARK ANTONY** } *triumvirs° after the death of Julius Caesar*

**M. AEMILIUS LEPIDUS**

**CICERO**

**PUBLIUS** } *senators*

**POPILIUS LENA**

**MARCUS BRUTUS**

**CASSIUS**

**CASCA**

**TREBONIUS** } *conspirators against Julius Caesar*

**CAIUS LIGARIUS**

**DECIUS BRUTUS**

**METELLUS CIMBER**

**CINNA**

**FLAVIUS** *and* **MARULLUS,** *tribunes°*

**ARTEMIDORUS OF CNIDOS,** *a teacher of rhetoric*

**SOOTHSAYER**

**CINNA,** *a poet*

*Another* **POET**

**LUCILIUS**

**TITINIUS**

**MESSALA**

**YOUNG CATO** } *officers under Brutus and Cassius*

**VOLUMNIUS**

**FLAVIUS**

**VARRO**

**CLITUS**

**CLAUDIUS** } *soldiers in Brutus' army*

**DARDANIUS**

*triumvirs* (trī um′vərz), three officials who jointly ruled Rome, from the Latin *trium virorum*, "of three men."

*tribunes*, elected officials who serve as spokesmen for the commoners and protect them from the government if necessary.

STRATO  
LUCIUS  } *servants and slaves to Brutus*

**PINDARUS**, *servant and slave to Cassius*

**CALPURNIA**, *wife to Caesar*
**PORTIA**, *wife to Brutus*

**SENATORS, CITIZENS, GUARDS, ATTENDANTS**, *etc.*

# ACT ONE

## SCENE 1

Rome. A street. [Played on the Platform.]

*It is February fifteenth, the festival of Lupercalia. The* COMMONERS *are in a holiday mood, eager to celebrate* CAESAR's *victory over* POMPEY's *sons.*

*A crowd of excited* COMMONERS, *dressed in holiday garments, rushes onto the platform at left door. All talk at once and look expectantly toward the right, the direction from which* CAESAR's *procession will appear. Offstage shouts and cheers, indications that* CAESAR *draws closer, send the* COMMONERS *scurrying for vantage points.*

*Meanwhile, the tribunes* FLAVIUS *and* MARULLUS *have entered at inner-stage curtains. As they stride briskly forward, it is apparent that they disapprove of the general holiday mood.* FLAVIUS *addresses the* COMMONERS *angrily.*

**FLAVIUS.** Hence! Home, you idle creatures, get you home!
  Is this a holiday? What, know you not,
  Being mechanical,° you ought not walk
  Upon a laboring day without the sign

5 Of your profession?° (*Singing one out*) Speak, what trade art
    thou?
**CARPENTER.** Why, sir, a carpenter.
**MARULLUS.** Where is thy leather apron and thy rule?
  What dost thou with thy best apparel on?
  (*To another*) You, sir, what trade are you?

10 **COBBLER.** Truly, sir, in respect of a fine workman, I am but, as
    you would say, a cobbler.°
**MARULLUS** (*impatiently*). But what trade art thou? Answer me
    directly.
**COBBLER.** A trade, sir, that I hope I may use with a safe

> **1** How are the opening lines of the play effective in getting audience attention?
> ***mechanical**, workingmen.*
>
> ***you ought not ... profession**, a reference to a law of Shakespeare's own time requiring workers to wear their laboring clothes and carry the tools of their profession.*
>
> ***cobbler**. In Shakespeare's time this word meant not only a shoe mender but also a clumsy worker. This explains Marullus' question.*

15  conscience, which is indeed, sir, a mender of bad soles.

(*The* COMMONERS *laugh at the pun.*)

FLAVIUS. What trade, thou knave? Thou naughty knave, what
    trade?

COBBLER. Nay, I beseech you, sir, be not out with me.° Yet if you
    be out, sir, I can mend you.

FLAVIUS. What mean'st thou by that? Mend me, thou saucy fellow?

20  COBBLER. Why, sir, cobble you.

FLAVIUS (*scowling*). Thou art a cobbler, art thou?

COBBLER. Truly, sir, all that I live by is with the awl. I meddle
    with no trademan's matters, nor women's matters; but withal° I
    am indeed, sir, a surgeon to old shoes. When they are in great

25  danger, I recover them. As proper men as ever trod upon neat's
    leather° have gone upon my handiwork.

FLAVIUS. But wherefore art not in thy shop today?
    Why dost thou lead these men about the streets?

COBBLER (*grinning*). Truly, sir, to wear out their shoes, to get

30  myself into more work. But indeed, sir, we make holiday
    to see Caesar and rejoice in his triumph.

(*The mob shouts its agreement.*)

MARULLUS (*addressing the mob*). Wherefore rejoice? What
    conquest brings he home?
    What tributaries° follow him to Rome,
    To grace in captive bonds his chariot-wheels?

(*The shouting of the mob grows louder.*)

35  You blocks, you stones, you worse than senseless things!
    O you hard hearts, you cruel men of Rome,
    Knew you not Pompey?° Many a time and oft
    Have you climbed up to walls and battlements,
    To towers and windows, yea, to chimney-tops,°

40  Your infants in your arms, and there have sat
    The livelong day, with patient expectation,
    To see great Pompey pass the streets of Rome.
    And when you saw his chariot but appear,
    Have you not made an universal shout,

45  That Tiber° trembled underneath her banks
    To hear the replication° of your sounds
    Made in her concave shores?
    And do you now put on your best attire?
    And do you now cull out a holiday?

50  And do you now strew flowers in his way
    That comes in triumph over Pompey's blood?°

500  *Julius Caesar*

---

**be not . . . me,** a pun. *To be out* means "out of temper" and also "having worn-out soles."

**withal,** yet. This is also a pun on "with awl" (a shoemaker's tool).

**as ever . . . leather,** as ever wore shoes of cowhide.

2  Shakespeare usually has characters from upper social levels, like Marullus and Flavius, speak in blank verse; commoners speak prose. What other indication is there that Marullus and Flavius outrank the commoners?

**tributaries,** captives who must pay tribute to Rome for their freedom.

**Knew . . . Pompey?** The fickle mob had cheered this enemy of Caesar. **chimney-tops.** Ancient Rome had no chimney-tops. An error such as this, deliberate or otherwise, is called an anachronism (ə nak′rə niz′əm). Look for others as you read.

**Tiber** (tī′bər), a river. **replication,** echo.

**Pompey's blood,** Pompey's sons.

*(The mob, subdued by* MARULLUS' *words, is silent now.)*
    Be gone!
    Run to your houses, fall upon your knees,
    Pray to the gods to intermit° the plague
55  That needs must light on this ingratitude.
    FLAVIUS. Go, go, good countrymen, and, for this fault,
    Assemble all the poor men of your sort;
    Draw them to Tiber banks, and weep your tears
    Into the channel, till the lowest stream
60  Do kiss the most exalted shores of all.°
*(The* COMMONERS, *singly or in pairs, file off the platform at left.)*
    *(To* MARULLUS*)* See whether their basest metal be not moved.
    They vanish tongue-tied in their guiltiness.
*(There is a loud flourish of trumpets offstage.)*
    Go you down that way towards the Capitol;
    This way will I. Disrobe the images°
65  If you do find them decked with ceremonies.
    MARULLUS *(cautiously).* May we do so?
    You know it is the feast of Lupercal.°
    FLAVIUS. It is no matter. Let no images
    Be hung with Caesar's trophies. I'll about,
70  And drive away the vulgar° from the streets.
    So do you too, where you perceive them thick.
    These growing feathers° plucked from Caesar's wing
    Will make him fly an ordinary pitch,
    Who else would soar above the view of men
75  And keep us all in servile fearfulness.
*(The* TRIBUNES *exit, going in different directions.)*


# SCENE 2

Rome. A public place. [Played on the Platform.]
*Groups of* COMMONERS *run onto the platform, looking offstage at* CAESAR'S
*approaching procession.*° SOLDIERS *march on at right door and force people
back so the procession can pass. There is a loud flourish of trumpets; and*
CAESAR *appears at right, accompanied by* ANTONY, CALPURNIA, PORTIA,
DECIUS, CICERO, BRUTUS, CASSIUS, *and* CASCA. *More* COMMONERS *follow,
among them a* SOOTHSAYER. *Last come* FLAVIUS *and* MARULLUS, *watching
but saying nothing. Amid cheers,* CAESAR *leads the procession well onto the
platform, then stops. All bow, rendering* CAESAR *homage.*

*intermit,* withhold.

3 | Why does Marullus
    want the commoners
to stop their celebrating?

*weep your tears . . . of all,*
weep enough tears to bring
the lowest waterline up to
the highest.

*Disrobe the images,* take
down the decorations that
have been placed on
Caesar's statues.

*the feast of Lupercal,*
celebrated in honor of
Lupercus, god of fertility.

*the vulgar,* the commoners.

*These growing feathers,*
Caesar's new followers.
Falconers sometimes clip
their birds' wings to keep
them from flying too great a
height, or pitch. So Caesar,
without the help of the
commoners, would be
checked in his ambition to
rise.

4 | What conflict has
    already been set up in
this first scene?

*Caesar's . . . procession.*
On Lupercalia in Rome,
groups watched priest-
celebrants who ran a
specified course, striking
people in their way with
goatskin thongs. Women
desiring children purposely
sought to be struck as a
cure for barrenness.

CAESAR. Calpurnia!

CASCA.                     Peace, ho! Caesar speaks.

CAESAR.                                   Calpurnia!

CALPURNIA (*stepping forward*). Here, my lord.

CAESAR. Stand you directly in Antonius' way,
    When he doth run his course.° Antonius!

(ANTONY *hurries forward and stands before* CAESAR.)

5 ANTONY. Caesar, my lord?

CAESAR. Forget not, in your speed, Antonius,
    To touch Calpurnia; for our elders say,
    The barren, touchèd in this holy chase,
    Shake off their sterile curse.

ANTONY.                     I shall remember.

10  When Caesar says, "Do this," it is performed. (*He steps back.*)

CAESAR. Set on, and leave no ceremony out.

**When he doth run his course.** Antony, as one of the priests of Lupercus, is one of the young nobles making the run through the streets.

5 *Lines 6–10.* Why does Caesar want Antony to touch Calpurnia? How will those Romans who think Caesar wants to be king react to his words to Antony?

JULIUS CAESAR receives the homage of a kneeling MARK ANTONY and others as CALPURNIA looks on, in an American Shakespeare Theatre production.

*(The trumpets flourish; the procession starts forward.)*

SOOTHSAYER *(in awesome tones).* Caesar!

CAESAR *(stopping).* Ha? Who calls?

*(The crowd murmurs, wondering who thus has accosted* CAESAR.*)*

CASCA. Bid every noise be still. Peace yet again!

15 CAESAR. Who is it in the press that calls on me?

I hear a tongue, shriller than all the music,

Cry "Caesar!" Speak. Caesar is turned to hear.

SOOTHSAYER *(ominously).* Beware the ides of March.°

CAESAR *(looking to right and left).*                What man is

that?

BRUTUS. A soothsayer bids you beware the ides of March.

20 CAESAR. Set him before me; let me see his face.

CASSIUS *(stepping forward).* Fellow, come from the throng. Look

upon Caesar.

*(*SOLDIERS *drag the* SOOTHSAYER *before* CAESAR.*)*

CAESAR. What sayest thou to me now? Speak once again.

SOOTHSAYER. Beware the ides of March.

*(For a moment* CAESAR, *looking disturbed, stares at the* SOOTH-

SAYER; *then he turns to* ANTONY, *who begins to laugh. When oth-

ers join in,* CAESAR *with a gesture dismisses the* SOOTHSAYER.*)*

CAESAR. He is a dreamer. Let us leave him. Pass.

*(The trumpets flourish; the procession and the crowd go out at

left,* BRUTUS *and* CASSIUS *remaining behind.* BRUTUS *stands at

one side, lost in thought.* CASSIUS *approaches him.)*

25 CASSIUS. Will you go see the order of the course?

BRUTUS. Not I.

CASSIUS. I pray you, do.

BRUTUS. I am not gamesome. I do lack some part

Of that quick spirit° that is in Antony.

30 Let me not hinder, Cassius, your desires;

I'll leave you.

CASSIUS. Brutus, I do observe you now of late.

I have not from your eyes that gentleness

And show of love as I was wont to have.°

35 You bear too stubborn and too strange a hand

Over your friend that loves you.

BRUTUS.                Cassius,

Be not deceived. If I have veiled my look,

I turn the trouble of my countenance

Merely upon myself.° Vexed I am

40 Of late with passions of some difference,

**6** This is the first hint of Caesar's deafness, something not mentioned in Shakespeare's source, Plutarch. Why might Shakespeare have included it as part of his characterization of Caesar?

**the ides** (īdz) **of March,** March 15, noted by the Romans as the midpoint of the month. It fell one month after the feast of Lupercal.

**7** How does Caesar respond to the Soothsayer's warning? Do you think the presence of the crowd influenced his response? Explain.

**quick spirit,** lively disposition.

**as I was wont to have,** that I customarily had.

**I turn . . . upon myself.** Brutus is troubled by his thoughts, not by Cassius.

Conceptions only proper to myself,
Which give some soil, perhaps, to my behaviors.
But let not therefore my good friends be grieved—
Among which number, Cassius, be you one—
45 Nor construe any further my neglect,
Than that poor Brutus, with himself at war,
Forgets the shows of love to other men.
    CASSIUS. Then, Brutus, I have much mistook your passion,
    By means whereof this breast of mine hath buried
50 Thoughts of great value, worthy cogitations.°
    Tell me, good Brutus, can you see your face?
    BRUTUS. No, Cassius, for the eye sees not itself
    But by reflection, by some other things.
(He moves toward front platform; CASSIUS follows.)
    CASSIUS. 'Tis just.
55 And it is very much lamented, Brutus,
    That you have no such mirrors as will turn
    Your hidden worthiness into your eye,
    That you might see your shadow. I have heard
    Where many of the best respect in Rome,
60 Except immortal Caesar, speaking of Brutus
    And groaning underneath this age's yoke,
    Have wished that noble Brutus had his eyes.
    BRUTUS (facing CASSIUS). Into what dangers would you lead me,
        Cassius,
    That you would have me seek into myself
65 For that which is not in me?
    CASSIUS. Therefore, good Brutus, be prepared to hear;
    And since you know you cannot see yourself
    So well as by reflection, I, your glass,
    Will modestly discover to yourself
70 That of yourself which you yet know not of.
    And be not jealous on me, gentle Brutus.
    Were I a common laughter,° or did use
    To stale with ordinary oaths my love
    To every new protester; if you know
75 That I do fawn on men and hug them hard
    And after scandal them, or if you know
    That I profess myself in banqueting
    To all the rout,° then hold me dangerous.
(There is a flourish of trumpets offstage, then loud cheers.
    BRUTUS and CASSIUS look up.)

504 *Julius Caesar*

8 | *Lines 32–47.* Cassius complains of Brutus' unusual behavior. How does he describe it? What is Brutus' response?

***Then . . . worthy cogitations.*** Here Cassius hints at the thoughts (cogitations) locked in his own breast and begins sounding out Brutus to see whether he has the same thoughts and will join with the conspirators.

***a common laughter,*** a buffoon laughed at or scorned by everyone.

***the rout,*** the rabble; worthless people.

**BRUTUS.** What means this shouting? I do fear the people
80     Choose Caesar for their king.

**CASSIUS.**                    Ay, do you fear it?
    Then must I think you would not have it so.

**BRUTUS.** I would not, Cassius, yet I love him well.
    But wherefore do you hold me here so long?
    What is it that you would impart to me?
85     If it be aught toward the general good,
    Set honor in one eye and death in the other,
    And I will look on both indifferently;°
    For let the gods so speed me as I love
    The name of honor more than I fear death.

90 **CASSIUS.** I know that virtue to be in you, Brutus,
    As well as I do know your outward favor.
    Well, honor is the subject of my story.
    I cannot tell what you and other men
    Think of this life; but, for my single self,
95     I had as lief not be as live to be
    In awe of such a thing as I myself.
    I was born free as Caesar; so were you.
    We both have fed as well, and we can both
    Endure the winter's cold as well as he.
100     For once, upon a raw and gusty day,
    The troubled Tiber chafing with her shores,
    Caesar said to me, "Darest thou, Cassius, now
    Leap in with me into this angry flood,
    And swim to yonder point?" Upon the word,
105     Accoutered° as I was, I plungèd in
    And bade him follow; so indeed he did.
    The torrent roared, and we did buffet it,
    With lusty sinews throwing it aside
    And stemming it with hearts of controversy;
110     But ere we could arrive the point proposed,
    Caesar cried, "Help me, Cassius, or I sink!"
    Ay, as Aeneas, our great ancestor,
    Did from the flames of Troy upon his shoulder
    The old Anchises bear,° so from the waves of Tiber
115     Did I the tired Caesar. (*Angrily*) And this man
    Is now become a god, and Cassius is
    A wretched creature and must bend his body
    If Caesar carelessly but nod on him. (*He pauses.*)
    He had a fever when he was in Spain.

**9** Upon what statement of Brutus' does Cassius pounce? What does this suggest about Cassius' feelings toward Caesar?

***If it be . . . indifferently.*** If what Cassius has in mind is for the public welfare and is honorable, Brutus will do it even if it means death.

***Accoutered*** (ə kü′tərd) ***as I was.*** Cassius was fully dressed.

***as Aeneas*** (i nē′əs) . . . ***Anchises*** (an kī′sēz) ***bear.*** Aeneas, carrying his aged father Anchises and leading his little son, escaped from burning Troy and wandered for years. Finally he reached the banks of the Tiber, where his descendants founded Rome.

120 And when the fit was on him, I did mark
How he did shake. 'Tis true, this god did shake.
His coward lips did from their color fly,°
And that same eye whose bend doth awe the world
Did lose his° luster. I did hear him groan.
125 Ay, and that tongue of his that bade the Romans
Mark him and write his speeches in their books,
"Alas," it cried, "Give me some drink, Titinius,"
As a sick girl. Ye gods, it doth amaze me
A man of such a feeble temper° should
130 So get the start of the majestic world
And bear the palm° alone.
  (*Loud shouts and the flourish of trumpets heard offstage*)
BRUTUS (*crossing to right pillar*). Another general shout?
  I do believe that these applauses are
  For some new honors that are heaped on Caesar.
135 CASSIUS (*following*). Why, man, he doth bestride the narrow world
Like a Colossus,° and we petty men
Walk under his huge legs and peep about
To find ourselves dishonorable graves.
Men at some time are masters of their fates.
140 The fault, dear Brutus, is not in our stars,
But in ourselves, that we are underlings.
Brutus and Caesar. What should be in that "Caesar"?
Why should that name be sounded more than yours?
Write them together, yours is as fair a name;
145 Sound them, it doth become the mouth as well;
Weigh them, it is as heavy; conjure with 'em,
"Brutus" will start a spirit° as soon as "Caesar."
Now, in the names of all the gods at once,
Upon what meat doth this our Caesar feed
150 That he is grown so great? Age, thou art shamed!
Rome, thou hast lost the breed of noble bloods!
When went there by an age, since the great flood,
But it was famed with more than with one man?
When could they say, till now, that talked of Rome,
155 That her wide walks encompassed but one man?
Now is it Rome indeed and room enough,
When there is in it but one only man.
O, you and I have heard our fathers say
There was a Brutus once that would have brooked
160 The eternal devil to keep his state in Rome

*His coward lips . . . fly.*
His lips became white.

*his, its* in modern usage.

*A man . . . feeble temper.*
The Romans worshiped
strength, and here Cassius
paints Caesar as a weakling.
*the palm,* symbol of victory.

10 *Lines 100–131.* What
physical weaknesses
does Cassius say Caesar has?
How suitable are these to a
great public hero and
conqueror?

*Like a Colossus* (kə los′əs).
The Colossus was a huge
statue of Apollo at Rhodes.
According to legend, it was
so enormous that it bestrode
the entrance to the harbor,
and ships passed between its
legs.

11 *Lines 140–141.* These
lines are often quoted.
Explain in your own words
what they mean.

*start a spirit,* call forth a
ghost from the spirit world.

As easily as a king.

(*Loud shouts and the flourish of trumpets offstage*)

**BRUTUS.** That you do love me, I am nothing jealous.
What you would work me to, I have some aim.
How I have thought of this, and of these times,
I shall recount hereafter. For this present,
I would not, so with love I might entreat you,
Be any further moved. What you have said
I will consider; what you have to say
I will with patience hear, and find a time
Both meet to hear and answer such high things.
Till then, my noble friend, chew upon this:
Brutus had rather be a villager
Than to repute himself a son of Rome
Under these hard conditions as this time
Is like to lay upon us.

**CASSIUS.** I am glad that my weak words
Have struck but thus much show of fire from Brutus.

(*The sounds of approaching people are heard from offstage.*)

**BRUTUS.** The games are done and Caesar is returning.

**CASSIUS.** As they pass by, pluck Casca by the sleeve,
And he will, after his sour fashion, tell you
What hath proceeded worthy note today.

(CAESAR *and his followers reenter at left and start across the*
*platform,* ANTONY *on* CAESAR'*s left,* CASCA *following at rear.*)

**BRUTUS.** I will do so. But, look you, Cassius,
The angry spot doth glow on Caesar's brow,
And all the rest look like a chidden train.°
Calpurnia's cheek is pale, and Cicero
Looks with such ferret and such fiery eyes°
As we have seen him in the Capitol,
Being crossed in conference by some senators.

**CASSIUS.** Casca will tell us what the matter is.

(CAESAR *stops before he reaches center platform and looks*
*speculatively at* CASSIUS.)

**CAESAR.** Antonius!

**ANTONY.** Caesar?

**CAESAR.** Let me have men about me that are fat,
Sleek-headed men, and such as sleep o' nights.
Yond Cassius has a lean and hungry look.
He thinks too much. Such men are dangerous.

**ANTONY.** Fear him not, Caesar; he's not dangerous.

165

170

175

180

185

190

195

---

**12** *Lines 159–161.* Cassius suggests that Brutus' ancestor Lucius Junius Brutus, the founder of the republic, would no more have allowed the devil to set up his throne in Rome than he would have allowed a king to. Why might Cassius be reminding his friend of this earlier Brutus?

**13** How does Brutus indicate that Cassius' words have had some effect on him? How does he indicate that Cassius' idea does not come as a surprise to him? Why might Brutus want time to consider Cassius' suggestions?

*like a chidden train,* like a group of people who were harshly scolded.
*such ferret . . . eyes,* red and angry-looking eyes, like a weasel's.

**14** By their appearance, Caesar and his followers have undergone a radical change of mood. How do they now feel?

**15** What reason does Caesar give for calling Cassius dangerous? Do you agree with Caesar's opinion? Why might Cassius be so opposed to Caesar?

*Act One, Scene 2* **507**

He is a noble Roman, and well given.

CAESAR. Would he were fatter! But I fear him not.

Yet if my name were liable to fear,

200 I do not know the man I should avoid

So soon as that spare Cassius. He reads much,

He is a great observer, and he looks

Quite through the deeds of men. He loves no plays,

As thou dost, Antony; he hears no music.

205 Seldom he smiles, and smiles in such a sort

As if he mocked himself and scorned his spirit

That could be moved to smile at anything.

Such men as he be never at heart's ease

Whiles they behold a greater than themselves,

210 And therefore are they very dangerous.

I rather tell thee what is to be feared

Than what I fear; for always I am Caesar.

Come on my right hand, for this ear is deaf,

And tell me truly what thou think'st of him.

(ANTONY *steps to* CAESAR's *right. The trumpets sound and the procession, with* CASCA *still at rear, moves slowly out at right. When* CASCA *reaches center platform he is detained by* BRUTUS *and* CASSIUS.)

215 CASCA. You pulled me by the cloak. Would you speak with me?

BRUTUS. Ay, Casca. Tell us what hath chanced today,

That Caesar looks so sad.

CASCA. Why, you were with him, were you not?

BRUTUS. I should not then ask Casca what had chanced.

220 CASCA. Why, there was a crown offered him, and being offered him, he put it by with the back of his hand, thus; and then the people fell a-shouting.

BRUTUS. What was the second noise for?

CASCA. Why, for that too.

225 CASSIUS. They shouted thrice. What was the last cry for?

CASCA. Why, for that too.

BRUTUS (*incredulously*). Was the crown offered him thrice?

CASCA. Ay, marry,° was't, and he put it by thrice, every time gentler than other, and at every putting-by mine honest

230 neighbors shouted.

CASSIUS. Who offered him the crown?

CASCA. Why, Antony.

BRUTUS. Tell us the manner of it, gentle Casca.

CASCA. I can as well be hanged as tell the manner of it. It was

**16** *Lines 211–212.* What insight into Caesar's character do these lines give? Note the two lines that follow; how do they contradict Caesar's opinion of himself?

**17** Note that Casca speaks here in prose, not blank verse. How might what Cassius says in lines 179–181 about Casca's manner of speaking account for this?

*marry,* a mild oath.

235 mere foolery; I did not mark it. I saw Mark Antony offer him a
crown—yet 'twas not a crown neither, 'twas one of these
coronets—and, as I told you, he put it by once; but, for all
that, to my thinking, he would fain have had it. Then he offered
it to him again; then he put it by again; but, to my thinking, he
240 was very loath to lay his fingers off it. And then he offered it
the third time. He put it the third time by, and still as he
refused it, the rabblement hooted and clapped their chapped
hands, and threw up their sweaty nightcaps,° and uttered such a
deal of stinking breath because Caesar refused the crown that it
245 had almost choked Caesar, for he swounded and fell down at it.
And for mine own part I durst not laugh, for fear of opening my
lips and receiving the bad air.

nightcaps, an anachronism.

CASSIUS. But, soft, I pray you. What, did Caesar swoon?

CASCA. He fell down in the market-place, and foamed at mouth,
250 and was speechless.

18 Based on Casca's description, how do you think the commoners felt about Caesar being given a crown?

BRUTUS. 'Tis very like. He hath the falling sickness.

CASSIUS. No, Caesar hath it not, but you and I,
And honest Casca, we have the falling sickness.°

falling sickness, epilepsy. Note how Cassius, in the next few lines, uses the words figuratively, suggesting a similarity between "falling" and failing to take action.

CASCA. I know not what you mean by that, but I am sure Caesar
255 fell down. If the tag-rag people did not clap him and hiss him,
according as he pleased and displeased them, as they use to do
the players in the theater, I am no true man.

BRUTUS. What said he when he came unto himself?

CASCA. Marry, before he fell down, when he perceived the common
260 herd was glad he refused the crown, he plucked me ope his
doublet° and offered them his throat to cut. An° I had been a
man of any occupation, if I would not have taken him at a
word, I would I might go to hell among the rogues. And so he
fell. When he came to himself again, he said, If he had done or
265 said anything amiss, he desired their worships to think it was
his infirmity. Three or four wenches, where I stood, cried,
"Alas, good soul!" and forgave him with all their hearts. But
there's no heed to be taken of them. If Caesar had stabbed their
mothers, they would have done no less.

doublet, a man's close-fitting jacket. Doublets were not worn until about the 1400s; hence, another anachronism. An, if.

270 BRUTUS. And after that, he came thus sad away?

CASCA. Ay.

CASSIUS. Did Cicero say anything?

CASCA. Ay, he spoke Greek.

CASSIUS. To what effect?

275 CASCA. Nay, an I tell you that, I'll ne'er look you i' th' face again.
But those that understood him smiled at one another and shook

their heads; but, for mine own part, it was Greek to me.°
I could tell you more news too. Marullus and Flavius, for
pulling scarfs off Caesar's images, are put to silence.° Fare you
280 well. There was more foolery yet, if I could remember it.

CASSIUS. Will you sup with me tonight, Casca?

CASCA. No, I am promised forth.

CASSIUS. Will you dine with me tomorrow?

CASCA. Ay, if I be alive, and your mind hold, and your dinner
285 worth the eating.

CASSIUS. Good. I will expect you.

CASCA. Do so. Farewell, both. (*He exits at inner-stage curtains.*)

BRUTUS. What a blunt fellow is this grown to be!
He was quick mettle° when he went to school.

290 CASSIUS. So is he now in execution
Of any bold or noble enterprise,
However he puts on this tardy form.
This rudeness is a sauce to his good wit,
Which gives men stomach to digest his words
295 With better appetite.

BRUTUS. And so it is. For this time I will leave you.
Tomorrow, if you please to speak with me,
I will come home to you; or, if you will,
Come home to me, and I will wait for you.

300 CASSIUS. I will do so. Till then, think of the world.
(BRUTUS *exits at left.*)
Well, Brutus, thou art noble. Yet I see
Thy honorable metal may be wrought
From that it is disposed.° Therefore it is meet°
That noble minds keep ever with their likes;
305 For who so firm that cannot be seduced?
Caesar doth bear me hard,° but he loves Brutus.
If I were Brutus now and he were Cassius,
He should not humor me,° I will this night,
In several hands,° in at his windows, throw,
310 As if they came from several citizens,
Writings, all tending to the great opinion
That Rome holds of his name, wherein obscurely
Caesar's ambition shall be glancèd at.°
And after this let Caesar seat him sure,
315 For we will shake him, or worse days endure.
(*He exits at inner-stage curtains.*)

*it was Greek to me,* a saying popular even today when a person is unable to understand something.

*put to silence,* deprived of their rank as tribunes, which permitted them to speak for the people.

*quick mettle,* easily stirred to action, and quick-witted.

*Thy honorable . . . disposed,* your spirit can be turned from its natural inclination.
*meet,* fitting; appropriate.
*Caesar . . . hard,* Caesar hates me.

*humor me,* win me over to his opinions.

*In several hands,* in different handwritings.

*glancèd at,* hinted at.

**19** *Lines 301–315.* This is the play's first soliloquy. Explain in your own words what Cassius is saying.

# SCENE 3

Rome. A street. [Played on the Platform.]

*It is the night before the ides of March. A month has gone by since* CASSIUS
*first spoke to* BRUTUS *about* CAESAR. *Unperturbed by this wild night,* CICERO
*enters at left. There is lightning and thunder as* CASCA, *his sword drawn, enters
at right.*

CICERO (*calmly*). Good even,° Casca. Brought you Caesar home?

    Why are you breathless? And why stare you so?

CASCA. Are not you moved, when all the sway of earth

    Shakes like a thing unfirm? O Cicero,

5    I have seen tempests when the scolding winds

    Have rived the knotty oaks, and I have seen

    The ambitious ocean swell and rage and foam

    To be exalted with the threatening clouds;

    But never till tonight, never till now,

10    Did I go through a tempest dropping fire.

    (*More thunder, then a scream,* CASCA *darts to left pillar.*)

    Either there is a civil strife in heaven,

    Or else the world, too saucy with the gods,

*even,* evening

CICERO and CASCA encounter the eerie atmosphere and alarming events of the night, in the
American Shakespeare Theatre production.

Incenses them to send destruction.

CICERO (*drawing closer*). Why, saw you anything more wonderful?

15 CASCA. A common slave—you know him well by sight—
Held up his left hand, which did flame and burn
Like twenty torches joined, and yet his hand,
Not sensible of fire,° remained unscorched.
Besides—I had not since put up my sword—

20 Against° the Capitol I met a lion,
Who glazed° upon me, and went surly by
Without annoying me. And there were drawn
Upon a heap a hundred ghastly women,
Transformèd with their fear, who swore they saw

25 Men, all in fire, walk up and down the streets.
And yesterday the bird of night did sit
Even at noon-day upon the market-place,
Hooting and shrieking. When these prodigies
Do so conjointly meet, let not men say

30 "These are their reasons, they are natural,"
For I believe they are portentous things
Unto the climate that they point upon.°

CICERO. Indeed, it is a strange-disposèd time.
But men may construe things after their fashion,

35 Clean from the purpose of the things themselves.°
Comes Caesar to the Capitol tomorrow?

CASCA. He doth; for he did bid Antonius
Send word to you he would be there tomorrow.

CICERO. Good night then, Casca. This disturbèd sky

40 Is not to walk in.

CASCA.                    Farewell, Cicero.

(CICERO *exits at right. There is another flash of lightning and*
CASCA *retreats to rear platform, where he takes shelter under the*
*projecting balcony.* CASSIUS *enters at left.*)

CASSIUS. Who's there?

CASCA.                    A Roman.

CASSIUS.                                        Casca, by your voice.

(*He joins* CASCA *under the balcony.*)

CASCA. Your ear is good. Cassius, what night° is this!

CASSIUS. A very pleasing night to honest men.

CASCA. Who ever knew the heavens menace so?

45 CASSIUS. Those that have known the earth so full of faults.
For my part, I have walked about the streets,
Submitting me unto the perilous night,

*Not sensible of fire,* not feeling the fire.

*Against,* opposite; nearby.

*glazed,* peered; stared.

20 What unusual sights has Casca seen?

*When these prodigies . . . upon.* Though some may try to explain these marvels (prodigies) as natural, Casca regards them as omens foretelling disaster for Rome.

*But men . . . themselves.* Cicero thinks men who are inclined that way will often read undue significance into happenings such as these.

*what night,* what a night.

And, thus unbracèd,° Casca, as you see,
Have bared my bosom to the thunder-stone;
50 And when the cross blue lightning seemed to open
The breast of heaven, I did present myself
Even in the aim and very flash of it.

CASCA. But wherefore did you so much tempt the heavens?
It is the part of men to fear and tremble,
55 When the most mighty gods by tokens send
Such dreadful heralds to astonish us.

CASSIUS. You are dull, Casca, and those sparks of life
That should be in a Roman you do want,
Or else you use not. You look pale, and gaze,
60 And put on fear, and cast yourself in wonder,
To see the strange impatience of the heavens.
But if you would consider the true cause
Why all these fires, why all these gliding ghosts,
Why birds and beasts from quality and kind,
65 Why old men, fools, and children calculate,°
Why all these things change from their ordinance,°
Their natures, and preformed faculties,
To monstrous quality—why, you shall find
That heaven hath infused them with these spirits
70 To make them instruments of fear and warning
Unto some monstrous state.
Now could I, Casca, name to thee a man
Most like this dreadful night,
That thunders, lightens, opens graves, and roars
75 As doth the lion in the Capitol—
A man no mightier than thyself or me
In personal action, yet prodigious grown
And fearful, as these strange eruptions are.

CASCA. 'Tis Caesar that you mean, is it not, Cassius?
80 CASSIUS. Let it be who it is. For Romans now
Have thews and limbs like to their ancestors;
But, woe the while, our fathers' minds are dead,
And we are governed with our mothers' spirits.
Our yoke and sufferance show us womanish.
85 CASCA. Indeed, they say the senators tomorrow
Mean to establish Caesar as a king,
And he shall wear his crown by sea and land,
In every place, save here in Italy.

CASSIUS. I know where I will wear this dagger then;

*thus unbracèd.* Cassius opens his garment at the neck, exposing his chest to the thunderbolts.

*calculate,* prophesy.

*ordinance,* accustomed ways.

21 How do you know whom Cassius is referring to?

90  Cassius from bondage will deliver Cassius.
    Therein, ye gods, you make the weak most strong;
    Therein, ye gods, you tyrants do defeat.
    Nor stony tower, nor walls of beaten brass,
    Nor airless dungeon, nor strong links of iron,
95  Can be retentive to the strength of spirit;
    But life, being weary of these worldly bars,
    Never lacks power to dismiss itself.
    If I know this, know all the world besides,
    That part of tyranny that I do bear
100 I can shake off at pleasure.
    (*The thunder rumbles; the two men gradually move forward.*)
    CASCA.                    So can I.
    So every bondman in his own hand bears
    The power to cancel his captivity.
    CASSIUS. And why should Caesar be a tyrant then?
    Poor man, I know he would not be a wolf,
105 But that he sees the Romans are but sheep;
    He were no lion, were not Romans hinds.°
    Those that with haste will make a mighty fire
    Begin it with weak straws. What trash is Rome,
    What rubbish and what offal, when it serves
110 For the base matter to illuminate
    So vile a thing as Caesar! But, O grief,
    Where hast thou led me? I perhaps speak this
    Before a willing bondman; then I know
    My answer must be made. But I am armed,
115 And dangers are to me indifferent.
    CASCA. You speak to Casca, and to such a man
    That is no fleering° tell-tale. (*Offering his hand*) Hold, my hand.
    Be factious for redress of all these griefs,°
    And I will set this foot of mine as far
120 As who goes farthest.
    CASSIUS.                There's a bargain made.
    Now know you, Casca, I have moved already
    Some certain of the noblest-minded Romans
    To undergo with me an enterprise
    Of honorable-dangerous consequence;
125 And I do know, by this, they stay for me
    In Pompey's porch.° For now, this fearful night,
    There is no stir or walking in the streets,
    And the complexion of the element

22 What does Cassius say he will do if Caesar becomes king?

*He were . . . hinds.* He would be no lion, if Romans were not submissive like deer. (A hind is a female deer.)

*fleering*, deceitful.

*Be factious . . . griefs,* be ready to join Casca to right the grievances Romans have suffered at Caesar's hands.

23 How does Casca react to Cassius' dangerous words about Caesar?

*stay . . . porch,* wait for me on the porch of Pompey's theater.

In favor's° like the work we have in hand,
130    Most bloody, fiery, and most terrible.
(*Hurrying footsteps are heard offstage at right.*)
CASCA. Stand close awhile, for here comes one in haste.
CASSIUS. 'Tis Cinna; I do know him by his gait.
    He is a friend.
(CINNA *enters in haste.*)
            Cinna, where haste you so?
CINNA. To find out you. (*Moving forward*) Who's that? Metellus
    Cimber?
135  CASSIUS. No, it is Casca; one incorporate
    To our attempts.° Am I not stayed for, Cinna?
CINNA. I am glad on't. What a fearful night is this!
    There's two or three of us have seen strange sights.
CASSIUS. Am I not stayed for? Tell me.
140  CINNA. Yes, you are. O Cassius, if you could
    But win the noble Brutus to our party—
CASSIUS. Be you content. Good Cinna, take this paper,
    And look you lay it in the praetor's chair,°
    Where Brutus may but find it. And throw this
145  In at his window. Set this up with wax
    Upon old Brutus'° statue. All this done,
    Repair to Pompey's porch, where you shall find us.
    Is Decius Brutus and Trebonius there?
CINNA (*stopping*). All but Metellus Cimber; and he's gone
150    To seek you at your house. Well, I will hie,
    And so bestow these papers as you bade me.
CASSIUS. That done, repair to Pompey's theater.
(CINNA *runs off at right as* CASSIUS *turns to* CASCA.)
    Come, Casca, you and I will yet ere day
    See Brutus at his house. Three parts of him
155  Is ours already, and the man entire
    Upon the next encounter yields him ours.°
CASCA. O, he sits high in all the people's hearts;
    And that which would appear offense in us,
    His countenance, like richest alchemy,
160    Will change to virtue and to worthiness.
CASSIUS. Him and his worth, and our great need of him.
    You have right well conceited.° Let us go,
    For it is after midnight, and ere day
    We will awake him and be sure of him.
(*He and* CASCA *exit at right.*)

*the element . . . favor's*, the sky is in appearance.

*one incorporate . . . attempts*, one who knows our plans and is in sympathy with them.

*in the praetor's chair.* Brutus at this time was a praetor (prē′tər), a Roman judge or magistrate.

*old Brutus'*, Lucius Junius Brutus'.

24   What are these papers that Cassius wants positioned for Brutus to find?

*Three parts . . . ours.* Brutus is almost persuaded to join the conspirators; when they next meet with him, they will undoubtedly win him over completely.

*conceited*, estimated.

25   Why are the conspirators so eager to have Brutus join them?

## THINK AND DISCUSS
### SCENE 1
**Understanding**

1. What feelings do the commoners express for Caesar as the play opens?
2. What does Marullus ask them to recall?

**Analyzing**

3. What two contrasting opinions of Caesar are expressed in this scene?
4. The first act of a Shakespearean drama includes reports of the antecedent action, events before the opening of the play that will affect its outcome. What antecedent action is reported in this scene?

### SCENE 2
**Understanding**

1. What does Caesar ask Antony to do during his run? Why does Caesar ask this?
2. As Brutus and Cassius talk, how does Cassius make the point that Caesar is no more fit to lead Rome than he or Brutus?
3. Casca informs Cassius about what happens offstage. What does Caesar do three times?

**Analyzing**

4. Characterize Caesar as he appears in the opening lines of the scene.
5. How might Casca's description of the offstage encounter between Caesar and Antony add to the fear Brutus has voiced?
6. How does this scene present the main conflict in the play? Which side do you think Brutus will join?

**Extending**

7. Do you think that a modern crowd would be as emotional and as swayed by speeches as the Roman commoners seem to be? Explain.

### SCENE 3
**Understanding**

1. What are two examples of unusual incidents that Casca has witnessed during the night?
2. Do Cassius and Casca react to the strange events and conditions of the night in the same manner? Explain.

**Analyzing**

3. How does the conspiracy against Caesar become more solidified in this scene?

**Extending**

4. Today we would explain some of the strange events seen by Cassius and Casca as natural phenomena. Which of them can you account for in this way?

### APPLYING: Blank Verse Hʒ
**See Handbook of Literary Terms, p. 790**

Most of the characters in *Julius Caesar* speak in **blank verse,** a form of poetry in iambic pentameter. Each line has ten syllables—five unstressed alternating with five stressed. Blank verse has no regular rhyme. Writers of blank verse occasionally insert short lines for dramatic effect, and there are other ways to make blank verse more flexible. A few of them are explained here.

1. A grave accent above a normally silent vowel can be used to add a syllable to a line. In "Indeed, it is a strange-disposèd time," *disposèd* is pronounced in three syllables, thus giving the line the correct meter. Find another line using a grave accent in Act One and read it aloud.
2. Lines of verse sound less choppy if they have little or no punctuation to make a reader pause at the end of each line. In Act One, Scene 2, lines 135 to 138 make up a sentence that runs four lines without a stop. Locate

these lines spoken by Cassius and read them aloud. Then find another similar example in Act One.

3. A line of blank verse can be divided among two or more characters. Often this is done to speed the dialogue and increase the dramatic tension. Examples occur in Scene 3, lines 40 and 41. Casca's "Farewell, Cicero" is the second half of line 40. It can be called line 40*b*. Line 41 has three parts. Identify 41a, 41b, and 41c. Then find another divided line in Scene 2 or 3.

## READING LITERATURE SKILLFULLY
### Graphic Aids

Use the diagram of the Globe Theater on page 496 and the stage directions in Act One to answer the following questions.

1. In Scene 1 the commoners enter from the left and, after the tribunes berate them, exit to the left. How would the meaning change if they were to exit to the right?
2. In Scene 3 Cicero enters at the left and exits at the right. Immediately afterward Cassius enters at left. Why would it be impractical at the Globe Theater to have Cassius enter at the right?

## VOCABULARY
### Context

Read the following listed words within their context in the play to determine their meanings. Then rewrite the sentences below to include the appropriate words. You will not use every word.

servile (Scene 1, line 75)
countenance (Scene 2, line 38)
repute (Scene 2, line 173)
loath (Scene 2, line 240)
portentous (Scene 3, line 31)
prodigious (Scene 3, line 77)

1. Trying to set a new record, the student swallowed an amazing number of goldfish.
2. We were all very reluctant to ford the river, but there was no other way across.

3. Michael and Toni are considered to be the leaders of the gang, detectives have said.
4. Lu interpreted the two hawks circling over the campfire as indicating evil to come.
5. Gus refuses to put himself in such a slavelike position.

## COMPOSITION
### Writing a Newspaper Story

Imagine that you are a reporter in ancient Rome, and your assignment is to write a story describing Caesar's rejection of the crown. Reread Scene 2, lines 6-24, 182-188, and 215-277. Note the details concerning who offered the crown, how Caesar acted, and how the commoners reacted. Write a five- to seven-paragraph account, using such details. If you wish, use your imagination to add new details such as Calpurnia's reaction, Casca's opinions, and so forth.

### Analyzing the Commoners' Role

The commoners play a major part in Act One, since Caesar needs their support if he hopes to found a dynasty. Consider what is shown of their nature in Scene 1 and reported about them in Scene 2; take notes as you reread the scenes. Use your notes to write a three- to five-paragraph composition discussing the commoners' emotionalism and the ways they are affected by the speeches and actions of leaders. Save a copy of your composition and notes for possible reference later as part of a further study of the commoners following Act Three.

## ENRICHMENT
### Speaking and Listening

Act One contains two speeches that offer chances for excellent oral presentation. The first is Marullus' oration to the commoners (Scene 1, lines 32-55); the second is Cassius' soliloquy about getting Brutus to join the conspiracy (Scene 2, lines 301-315). Choose one and, after rehearsing it, present it to the class.

# Writer's Craft

## Use Precise, Active Verbs

The use of precise, active verbs invigorates writing. Precise verbs describe specific actions and convey definite images. For example, the verbs *stroll, saunter, stride,* and *stumble* each help readers to picture a certain style of locomotion in a way that makes the verb *walk* seem vague and nondescript.

Active rather than passive verbs distinguish forceful writing. Compare the verb forms in the following pair of sentences. "Shakespeare packed the speeches in his plays with active verbs." "Active verbs are found in Shakespeare's plays." The active verb in the first sentence creates a stronger statement.

Note how the active verbs in the following speech of Marullus bring particular actions to mind and add to his accusatory tone. To *cull out* is to pick out or to select.

And do you now cull out a holiday?
And do you now strew flowers in his way
That comes in triumph over Pompey's blood?

Precise verbs may have great persuasive power, as illustrated in the following excerpt from a speech by Cassius. In this speech he hurls a direct challenge at anyone who might think he is an opportunist.

            . . . if you know
That I do fawn on men and hug them hard
And after scandal them, or if you know
That I profess myself in banqueting
To all the rout, then hold me dangerous.

Besides highlighting action, strong verbs also sharpen descriptive passages. In Brutus' description of his mood, he uses a few passive verbs (*be deceived* and *am vexed*) when he cannot trace the action to a source, but what active voice verbs does he use to describe his own actions?

Be not deceived. If I have veiled my look,
I turn the trouble of my countenance
Merely upon myself. Vexed I am. . . .

Notice how Shakespeare gives life to the following speech by loading it with precise, active verbs. They enrich the descriptions and intensify the action in Cassius' account of his adventure with Caesar.

For once, upon a raw and gusty day,
The troubled Tiber chafing with her shores,
Caesar said to me, "Darest thou, Cassius, now
Leap in with me into this angry flood,
And swim to yonder point?" Upon the word,
Accoutered as I was, I plunged in
And bade him follow; so indeed he did.
The torrent roared, and we did buffet it,
With lusty sinews throwing it aside
And stemming it with hearts of controversy;
But ere we could arrive the point proposed,
Caesar cried, "Help me, Cassius, or I sink!"

As you read the rest of *Julius Caesar*, notice the precise, active verbs that provide vigorous descriptions of action.

---

When you read, note precise and active verbs.
When you write, use precise and active verbs to convey a sense of action and to enliven descriptions.

---

# ACT TWO

## SCENE 1

Rome. Brutus' orchard.° [Played on the Platform, Inner Stage, and Bay-Window Stage.]

*It is a few hours later. The scene opens as the curtains of the inner stage are drawn apart to reveal* BRUTUS *in a secluded corner of his garden. He is seated, deep in thought, on a small bench which is flanked by a pair of trees.* BRUTUS *has spent a wakeful night, and now begins to walk restlessly back and forth. Suddenly he strides forward, onto the platform, and calls to his* SERVING BOY, *who is asleep just inside the upper-right window.*

**BRUTUS** (*at the window*). What, Lucius, ho!
  (*To himself*) I cannot, by the progress of the stars,
  Give guess how near to day. (*Calling*) Lucius, I say!
  I would it were my fault to sleep so soundly.
5  When, Lucius, when? Awake, I say! What, Lucius!
(LUCIUS *appears at the window, opens the casement, and leans out.*)
**LUCIUS** (*sleepily*). Called you, my lord?
**BRUTUS.** Get me a taper in my study, Lucius.
  When it is lighted, come and call me here.
**LUCIUS.** I will, my lord.
(*As* LUCIUS *withdraws,* BRUTUS *resumes his restless pacing. He is alone with his thoughts, which he now speaks.*)
10 **BRUTUS.** It must be by his° death. And, for my part,
  I know no personal cause to spurn at him,
  But for the general.° He would be crowned.
  How that might change his nature, there's the question.
  It is the bright day that brings forth the adder,
15  And that craves wary walking. Crown him that,
  And then I grant we put a sting in him
  That at his will he may do danger with.
  The abuse of greatness is when it disjoins
  Remorse° from power. And, to speak truth of Caesar,
20  I have not known when his affections swayed

*orchard,* garden.

*his,* Caesar's.

***I know no personal . . . general.*** Though Brutus has no personal reason for striking at Caesar, he nevertheless feels he should do so for the public (general) good.

***Remorse,*** pity.

*Act Two, Scene 1* **519**

More than his reason. But 'tis a common proof
That lowliness is young ambition's ladder,
Whereto the climber-upward turns his face;
But when he once attains the upmost round,
25 He then unto the ladder turns his back,
Looks in the clouds, scorning the base degrees
By which he did ascend. So Caesar may.
Then, lest he may, prevent.° And, since the quarrel
Will bear no color for the thing he is,
30 Fashion it thus: that what he is, augmented,
Would run to these and these extremities.
And therefore think him as a serpent's egg
Which, hatched, would, as his kind, grow mischievous,
And kill him in the shell.

(LUCIUS, *yawning, enters the platform at right door. He carries*
*a letter—a small scroll.*)

35 LUCIUS. The taper burneth in your closet,° sir.
Searching the window for a flint, I found
This paper, thus sealed up, and I am sure
It did not lie there when I went to bed.
(*He gives* BRUTUS *the letter.*)
BRUTUS. Get you to bed again. It is not day.
(LUCIUS *starts to leave.*)
40 Is not tomorrow, boy, the ides of March?
LUCIUS. I know not, sir.
BRUTUS. Look in the calendar, and bring me word.
LUCIUS. I will, sir. (*He exits at right.*)
BRUTUS. The exhalations whizzing in the air°
45 Give so much light that I may read by them.
(*He opens the letter and reads.*)
"Brutus, thou sleepest; awake, and see thyself!
Shall Rome, etc. Speak, strike, redress!
Brutus, thou sleepest; awake!"
Such instigations have been often dropped
50 Where I have took them up.
"Shall Rome, etc." Thus must I piece it out:
Shall Rome stand under one man's awe? What, Rome?
My ancestors did from the streets of Rome
The Tarquin° drive, when he was called a king.
55 "Speak, strike, redress!" Am I entreated
To speak and strike? (*He raises a clenched fist.*) O Rome, I
   make thee promise,

26 *Lines 10–34.* What
reasons does Brutus
consider for assassinating
Caesar? [Note that this is
the first of four, fairly short,
related soliloquies; to keep
his audience's—including
the groundlings'—attention,
Shakespeare usually avoided
very long speeches.]

**prevent,** he must be
prevented.

**closet,** study; room.

*The exhalations . . . air,*
the falling stars.

*The Tarquin,* Tarquinius
Superbus, the last Roman
king.

If the redress will follow, thou receivest
Thy full petition at the hand of Brutus!
(LUCIUS *reenters*.)
LUCIUS. Sir, March is wasted fifteen days.
(*There is a knock at left.*)
60 BRUTUS. 'Tis good. Go to the gate; somebody knocks.
(LUCIUS *hurries to open the door at left.*)
Since Cassius first did whet me against Caesar,
I have not slept.
Between the acting of a dreadful thing
And the first motion, all the interim is
65 Like a phantasma, or a hideous dream.
The Genius and the mortal instruments°
Are then in council; and the state of man,
Like to a little kingdom, suffers then
The nature of an insurrection.
70 LUCIUS (*rejoining* BRUTUS). Sir, 'tis your brother° Cassius at the
door,
Who doth desire to see you.
BRUTUS.                    Is he alone?
LUCIUS. No, sir, there are moe° with him.
BRUTUS.                         Do you know them?
LUCIUS. No, sir; their hats are plucked about their ears,
And half their faces buried in their cloaks,°
75 That by no means I may discover them
By any mark of favor.°
BRUTUS.            Let 'em enter.
(LUCIUS *hurries to open the door at left.*)
They are the faction. O conspiracy,
Sham'st thou to show thy dangerous brow by night,
When evils are most free? O, then by day
80 Where wilt thou find a cavern dark enough
To mask thy monstrous visage? Seek none, conspiracy!
Hide it in smiles and affability;
For if thou path, thy native semblance on,
Not Erebus itself were dim enough
85 To hide thee from prevention.°
(LUCIUS *ushers in the* CONSPIRATORS—CASSIUS, CASCA, DECIUS,
CINNA, METELLUS CIMBER, *and* TREBONIUS. *While the*
CONSPIRATORS *are approaching* BRUTUS, LUCIUS *exits at right.*)
CASSIUS (*stepping forward*). I think we are too bold upon your rest.
Good morrow, Brutus. Do we trouble you?

27 How does Brutus react to Cassius' carefully placed letter?

28 *Lines 61–69.* What do these lines show about Brutus' conscience? What figure of speech is used in lines 67–69? Explain its meaning.

*The Genius . . . instruments,* the soul and the body.

*brother,* that is, brother-in-law. Cassius was married to Brutus' sister.

*moe,* more.

*hats . . . cloaks.* Both are anachronisms.

*any mark of favor,* any features by which they can be recognized.

29 What do these lines reveal of Brutus' feelings about the conspiracy?

*For if thou . . . prevention.* If the conspirators walk about (path) wearing their natural appearance (not assuming false smiles), not even Erebus (er'ə bəs) would be dark enough to keep them from detection. Erebus, according to Greek and Roman mythology, was a dark, gloomy place through which the dead passed en route to Hades.

**BRUTUS.** I have been up this hour, awake all night.

Know I these men that come along with you?

90 **CASSIUS.** Yes, every man of them, and no man here

But honors you; and every one doth wish

You had but that opinion of yourself

Which every noble Roman bears of you.

This is Trebonius.

**BRUTUS** (*extending his hand*). He is welcome hither.

**CASSIUS.** This, Decius Brutus.

95 **BRUTUS.** He is welcome too.

**CASSIUS.** This, Casca; this, Cinna; and this, Metellus Cimber.

**BRUTUS.** They are all welcome.

What watchful cares do interpose themselves

Betwixt your eyes and night?

100 **CASSIUS.** Shall I entreat a word?

(**BRUTUS** *and* **CASSIUS** *step back to speak privately. The other*
**CONSPIRATORS** *talk idly.*)

**DECIUS.** Here lies the east. Doth not the day break here?

**CASCA.** No.

**30** Does Brutus' courteous behavior toward the conspirators agree with what he said in lines 81–85? Explain.

Several CONSPIRATORS visit the troubled BRUTUS in a scene from *Julius Caesar*, as performed by the American Shakespeare Theatre.

CINNA. O, pardon, sir, it doth; and yon gray lines
    That fret the clouds are messengers of day.
105 CASCA. You shall confess that you are both deceived.
    Here, as I point my sword, the sun arises,
    Which is a great way growing on° the south,
    Weighing the youthful season of the year.
    Some two months hence, up higher toward the north
110 He first presents his fire; and the high east
    Stands, as the Capitol, directly here.
    (BRUTUS *and* CASSIUS *rejoin the group*.)
    BRUTUS. Give me your hands all over, one by one.
    CASSIUS. And let us swear our resolution.
    BRUTUS. No, not an oath. If not the face of men,
115 The sufferance of our souls, the time's abuse—
    If these be motives weak, break off betimes,
    And every man hence to his idle bed;
    So let high-sighted tyranny range on,
    Till each man drop by lottery.° But if these,
120 As I am sure they do, bear fire enough
    To kindle cowards and to steel with valor
    The melting spirits of women, then, countrymen,
    What need we any spur but our own cause
    To prick us to redress? What other bond
125 Than secret Romans, that have spoke the word,
    And will not palter?° And what other oath
    Than honesty to honesty engaged
    That this shall be, or we will fall for it?
    Swear priests and cowards, and men cautelous,°
130 Old feeble carrions, and such suffering souls
    That welcome wrongs; unto bad causes swear
    Such creatures as men doubt; but do not stain
    The even virtue of our enterprise,
    Nor the insuppressive mettle of our spirits,
135 To think that or our cause or° our performance
    Did need an oath; when every drop of blood
    That every Roman bears, and nobly bears,
    Is guilty of a several bastardy,
    If he do break the smallest particle
140 Of any promise that hath pass'd from him.
    CASSIUS. But what of Cicero? Shall we sound him?
    I think he will stand very strong with us.
    CASCA. Let us not leave him out.

*growing on*, toward.

*If not the face . . . by lottery.* If the wrongs the conspirators see about them are not sufficient to bind them to firm purpose, then let each man go his own way, become a weakling, and die when it suits a tyrant's whims.

*palter*, talk insincerely.

*cautelous*, deceitful.

*or . . . or*, either . . . or.

**31** What are Brutus' reasons for not wanting the conspirators to swear loyalty oaths? How practical is his viewpoint?

CINNA. No, by no means.

METELLUS. O, let us have him, for his silver hairs

145 Will purchase us a good opinion
And buy men's voices to commend our deeds.
It shall be said his judgment ruled our hands;
Our youths and wildness shall no whit appear,
But all be buried in his gravity.

150 BRUTUS. O, name him not. Let us not break with him;°
For he will never follow anything
That other men begin.

CASSIUS. Then leave him out.

CASCA. Indeed he is not fit.

DECIUS. Shall no man else be touched but only Caesar?

155 CASSIUS. Decius, well urged. I think it is not meet
Mark Antony, so well beloved of Caesar,
Should outlive Caesar. We shall find of him
A shrewd contriver; and you know, his means,
If he improve° them, may well stretch so far

160 As to annoy° us all. Which to prevent,
Let Antony and Caesar fall together.

BRUTUS. Our course will seem too bloody, Caius Cassius,
To cut the head off and then hack the limbs,
Like wrath in death and envy afterwards;

165 For Antony is but a limb of Caesar.
Let's be sacrificers, but not butchers, Caius.
We all stand up against the spirit of Caesar,
And in the spirit of men there is no blood.
O, that we then could come by Caesar's spirit,

170 And not dismember Caesar! But, alas,
Caesar must bleed for it. And, gentle friends,
Let's kill him boldly, but not wrathfully;
Let's carve him as a dish fit for the gods,
Not hew him as a carcass fit for hounds.

175 And let our hearts, as subtle masters do,
Stir up their servants° to an act of rage,
And after seem to chide them. This shall make
Our purpose necessary, and not envious;
Which so appearing to the common eyes,

180 We shall be called purgers, not murderers.
And for Mark Antony, think not of him;
For he can do no more than Caesar's arm
When Caesar's head is off.

---

**break with him**, break the news of the conspiracy to him.

32 *Lines 141–152.* Note the practical reasons the conspirators mention for having Cicero, a well-known statesman, join them; and how Brutus, always an idealist, goes against their advice. What reasons does Brutus give for his decision?

**improve**, exploit; make good use of.
**annoy**, harm.

33 Subsequent events will prove that this is Brutus' second error in judgment. What are his reasons for not wanting to kill Antony?

**their servants**, our hands.

34 Do you think the commoners will understand the distinction Brutus is making? Discuss.

---

524 *Julius Caesar*

CASSIUS (*still unconvinced*). Yet I fear him,
  For in the ingrafted love he bears to Caesar—
185 BRUTUS. Alas, good Cassius, do not think of him.
  If he love Caesar, all that he can do
  Is to himself—take thought and die for Caesar.
  And that were much he should, for he is given
  To sports, to wildness, and much company.
190 TREBONIUS. There is no fear in him.° Let him not die,
  For he will live, and laugh at this hereafter.
(*A clock offstage begins to strike.*)
BRUTUS. Peace! Count the clock°
CASSIUS.                              The clock hath stricken three.
TREBONIUS. 'Tis time to part.
CASSIUS.                              But it is doubtful yet
  Whether Caesar will come forth today, or no;
195 For he is superstitious grown of late,
  Quite from the main opinion he held once
  Of fantasy, of dreams, and ceremonies.
  It may be these apparent prodigies,
  The unaccustomed terror of this night,
200 And the persuasion of his augurers°
  May hold him from the Capitol today.
DECIUS. Never fear that. If he be so resolved,
  I can o'ersway him; for he loves to hear
  That unicorns may be betrayed with trees,
205 And bears with glasses, elephants with holes,
  Lions with toils,° and men with flatterers;
  But when I tell him he hates flatterers,
  He says he does, being then most flattered.
  Let me work;
210 For I can give his humor the true bent,
  And I will bring him to the Capitol.
CASSIUS. Nay, we will all of us be there to fetch him.
BRUTUS. By the eighth hour. Is that the uttermost?
CINNA. Be that the uttermost, and fail not then.
215 METELLUS. Caius Ligarius doth bear Caesar hard,
  Who rated° him for speaking well of Pompey.
  I wonder none of you have thought of him.
BRUTUS. Now, good Metellus, go along by him.
  He loves me well, and I have given him reasons;
220 Send him but hither, and I'll fashion him.
CASSIUS. The morning comes upon's. We'll leave you, Brutus.

**There is no fear in him,** there is no reason to fear Antony.

**Count the clock,** one of the most famous anachronisms in the play. Yet Shakespeare had to have some way of conveying to his audience what time it was.

**augurers** (ô′gər ərz), priests who predicted the future by reading signs. Also called *augurs*.

35 What reasons does Cassius give for the possibility of Caesar's not going to the Capitol?

**That unicorns . . . toils,** methods thought effective for capturing animals. The mythological unicorn was incited to charge; the hunter stepped behind a nearby tree, and the unicorn, unable to stop, drove his horn into the trunk. A bear could supposedly be distracted by putting a mirror in its paws; fascinated by its reflection, it was easy prey for a hunter. Elephants were captured in pits, and lions were sometimes rendered helpless by nets (toils).

**rated,** berated; angrily rebuked.

And, friends, disperse yourselves; but all remember
What you have said, and show yourselves true Romans.
**BRUTUS.** Good gentlemen, look fresh and merrily;
225   Let not our looks put on° our purposes,
But bear it as our Roman actors do,
With untired spirits and formal constancy.
And so good morrow to you every one.

(*The* CONSPIRATORS *exit at left. For a moment* BRUTUS *stands lost in thought; then he crosses to window at upper right and calls.*)
Boy! Lucius! Fast asleep? It is no matter.
230   Enjoy the honey-heavy dew of slumber.
Thou hast no figures nor no fantasies
Which busy care draws in the brains of men;
Therefore thou sleepest so sound.

(PORTIA, *wearing a night robe, enters at right. Her face is pale and worried as she follows* BRUTUS *to the inner stage.*)
**PORTIA.**                    Brutus, my lord!
**BRUTUS.** Portia, what mean you? Wherefore rise you now?
235   It is not for your health thus to commit
Your weak condition to the raw cold morning.
**PORTIA.** Nor for yours neither. You've ungently, Brutus,
Stole from my bed. And yesternight, at supper,
You suddenly arose, and walked about,
240   Musing and sighing, with your arms across,
And when I asked you what the matter was,
You stared upon me with ungentle looks.
I urged you further; then you scratched your head,
And too impatiently stamped with your foot.
245   Yet I insisted, yet you answered not,
But, with an angry wafture of your hand,
Gave sign for me to leave you. So I did,
Fearing to strengthen that impatience
Which seemed too much enkindled, and withal°
250   Hoping it was but an effect of humor,°
Which sometime hath his hour with every man.
It will not let you eat, nor talk, nor sleep,
And could it work so much upon your shape
As it hath much prevailed on your condition,
255   I should not know you, Brutus. (*Pleadingly*) Dear my lord,
Make me acquainted with your cause of grief.
**BRUTUS.** I am not well in health, and that is all.
**PORTIA.** Brutus is wise, and, were he not in health,

*put on,* betray.

*withal,* in addition to this.
*an effect of humor,* a whim.

**36** What does Portia's thumbnail description of Brutus indicate about his state of mind?

526   *Julius Caesar*

PORTIA expresses concern for BRUTUS in the American Shakespeare Theatre production of *Julius Caesar.*

He would embrace the means to come by it.
260 **BRUTUS.** Why, so I do. (*He seats himself wearily on the nearby bench.*) Good Portia, go to bed.
**PORTIA** (*drawing closer*). Is Brutus sick? And is it physical
To walk unbracèd and suck up the humors
Of the dank morning? What, is Brutus sick,
And will he steal out of his wholesome bed
265 To dare the vile contagion of the night,
And tempt the rheumy and unpurgèd air°
To add unto his sickness? No, my Brutus,
You have some sick offense within your mind,
Which by the right and virtue of my place
270 I ought to know of. And, upon my knees (*Kneeling*)
I charm you, by my once-commended beauty,
By all your vows of love, and that great vow
Which did incorporate and make us one,
That you unfold to me, your self, your half,
275 Why you are heavy, and what men tonight
Have had resort to you; for here have been
Some six or seven, who did hide their faces
Even from darkness.

*the rheumy* (rü′mē) . . . *air,* air that causes colds because it has not yet been purified (purged) by the sun.

BRUTUS. Kneel not, gentle Portia. (*He raises her.*)

PORTIA. I should not need, if you were gentle Brutus.

280 Within the bond of marriage, tell me, Brutus,
Is it excepted I should know no secrets
That appertain to you?° Am I yourself
But, as it were, in sort or limitation,
To keep with you at meals, comfort your bed,

285 And talk to you sometimes? Dwell I but in the suburbs
Of your good pleasure? If it be no more,
Portia is Brutus' harlot, not his wife.

BRUTUS. You are my true and honorable wife,
As dear to me as are the ruddy drops

290 That visit my sad heart.

PORTIA. If this were true, then should I know this secret.
I grant I am a woman, but withal
A woman that Lord Brutus took to wife.
I grant I am a woman, but withal

295 A woman well-reputed, Cato's daughter.
Think you I am no stronger than my sex,
Being so fathered° and so husbanded?
Tell me your counsels, I will not disclose 'em.
I have made strong proof of my constancy,

300 Giving myself a voluntary wound
Here, in the thigh. Can I bear that with patience,
And not my husband's secrets?

BRUTUS (*to the heavens*). O ye gods,
Render me worthy of this noble wife! (*There is a knock at left.*)
Hark, hark! One knocks. Portia, go in awhile,

305 And by and by thy bosom shall partake
The secrets of my heart.
All my engagements I will construe° to thee,
All the charactery° of my sad brows.
Leave me with haste.

(PORTIA *hastens to right door and exits.*)
Lucius, who's that knocks?

(LUCIUS *goes to open door at left and admits* CAIUS LIGARIUS,
*who is wearing a kerchief.*)

310 LUCIUS. Here is a sick man that would speak with you.

BRUTUS. Caius Ligarius, that Metellus spake of.
Boy, stand aside. (LUCIUS *exits.*) Caius Ligarius, how?°

LIGARIUS. Vouchsafe good morrow from a feeble tongue.

BRUTUS. Oh, what a time have you chose out, brave Caius,

*Is it excepted . . . you?*
Portia is asking if an
exception was made in the
marriage vows so that she
would have no legal right
to inquire into Brutus'
affairs.

*Being so fathered.* Portia's
father, Cato, had killed
himself rather than submit
to Caesar's tyranny. He
was Brutus' uncle as well
as his father-in-law.

*construe,* explain.
*charactery,* lines of worry.

*how?* how are you?

315     To wear a kerchief! Would you were not sick!

LIGARIUS. I am not sick, if Brutus have in hand
    Any exploit worthy the name of honor.

BRUTUS. Such an exploit have I in hand, Ligarius,
    Had you a healthful ear to hear of it.

320 LIGARIUS. By all the gods that Romans bow before,
    I here discard my sickness! Soul of Rome! (*He removes kerchief.*)
    Brave son, derived from honorable loins!
    Thou, like an exorcist, hast conjured up
    My mortified spirit.° Now bid me run,

325     And I will strive with things impossible,
    Yea, get the better of them. What's to do?

BRUTUS. A piece of work that will make sick men whole.

LIGARIUS. But are not some whole that we must make sick?

BRUTUS. That must we also. What it is, my Caius,

330     I shall unfold to thee as we are going
    To whom it must be done.

LIGARIUS.           Set on your foot,
    And with a heart new-fired I follow you,
    To do I know not what; but it sufficeth
    That Brutus leads me on. (*A clap of thunder sounds.*)

BRUTUS.          Follow me, then. (*They exit.*)

# SCENE 2

Rome. Caesar's house. [Played in the Balcony-Stage Chamber.]
*It is early morning on the ides of March. Several hours have elapsed since the*
CONSPIRATORS *met in* BRUTUS' *garden. The curtains of the balcony stage*
*(above) are drawn open just as* CAESAR *enters at right. Speaking to himself, he*
*crosses to the left, where his street robe is draped across a high-backed chair.*

CAESAR. Nor heaven nor° earth have been at peace tonight.
    Thrice hath Calpurnia in her sleep cried out,
    "Help, ho, they murder Caesar!" Who's within? (*He claps.*)
(*A* SERVANT *enters at left.*)

SERVANT. My lord?

5 CAESAR. Go bid the priests do present sacrifice
    And bring me their opinions of success.°

SERVANT. I will, my lord.
(*He exits at the door in the rear wall of the balcony stage as* CALPURNIA,
    *who is clad in her night robe, enters at right.*)

CALPURNIA. What mean you, Caesar? Think you to walk forth?

37 Caius Ligarius' illness is taken directly from Shakespeare's source, Plutarch. What dramatic effect might Shakespeare have been trying to achieve by including it? Note that wearing a kerchief to combat a cold is another anachronism.

*conjured . . . spirit,* brought to life my deadened spirit.

*Nor . . . nor,* neither . . . nor.

*Go bid the priests . . . success.* Caesar wishes to consult the augurers. By killing a bird and examining its entrails, augurers felt they could predict the future.

You shall not stir out of your house today.

10 **CAESAR.** Caesar shall forth. The things that threatened me
Ne'er looked but on my back. When they shall see
The face of Caesar, they are vanishèd.

**CALPURNIA.** Caesar, I never stood on ceremonies,°
Yet now they fright me. There is one within,°
15 Besides the things that we have heard and seen,
Recounts most horrid sights seen by the watch.
A lioness hath whelpèd in the streets,
And graves have yawned and yielded up their dead;
Fierce fiery warriors fight upon the clouds,
20 In ranks and squadrons and right form of war,
Which drizzled blood upon the Capitol;
The noise of battle hurtled in the air,
Horses did neigh, and dying men did groan,
And ghosts did shriek and squeal about the streets.
25 O Caesar, these things are beyond all use,°
And I do fear them.

**CAESAR.** What can be avoided
Whose end is purposed by the mighty gods?°
Yet Caesar shall go forth; for these predictions
Are to the world in general as to Caesar.

30 **CALPURNIA.** When beggars die, there are no comets seen;
The heavens themselves blaze forth the death of princes.

**CAESAR.** Cowards die many times before their deaths;
The valiant never taste of death but once.
Of all the wonders that I yet have heard,
35 It seems to me most strange that men should fear,
Seeing that death, a necessary end,
Will come when it will come.

(*The* SERVANT *reenters.*)

What say the augurers?

**SERVANT.** They would not have you to stir forth today.
Plucking the entrails of an offering forth,
40 They could not find a heart within the beast.°

**CAESAR.** The gods do this in shame of cowardice.
Caesar should be a beast without a heart,
If he should stay at home today for fear.
No, Caesar shall not. Danger knows full well
45 That Caesar is more dangerous than he.
We° are two lions littered in one day,
And I the elder and more terrible;

---

38 How do these lines show Caesar's egotism?

*never stood on ceremonies,* never believed greatly in signs and portents.

*one within,* a servant.

*beyond all use,* not customary; supernatural.

*What can be . . . gods?* Note Caesar's belief in fatalism, the idea that fate controls everything that happens.

39 What does Calpurnia mean by this statement?

40 *Lines 32–33.* These are often-quoted lines. Explain their meaning.

*Plucking . . . the beast.* The arrangement of the inner parts (entrails) of a bird was considered significant in foretelling the future.

*We,* Caesar and danger.

And Caesar shall go forth.

CALPURNIA (*going to him*). Alas, my lord,
Your wisdom is consumed in confidence.
50 Do not go forth today! Call it my fear
That keeps you in the house, and not your own.
We'll send Mark Antony to the Senate-house,
And he shall say you are not well today.
Let me, upon my knee, prevail in this. (*She kneels.*)
55 CAESAR (*raising her*). Mark Antony shall say I am not well,
And for thy humor I will stay at home.

(DECIUS *enters at rear door.*)

Here's Decius Brutus. He shall tell them so.

DECIUS (*bowing*). Caesar, all hail! Good morrow, worthy Caesar.
I come to fetch you to the Senate-house.
60 CAESAR. And you are come in very happy time
To bear my greeting to the senators
And tell them that I will not come today.
Cannot, is false, and that I dare not, falser;
I will not come today. Tell them so, Decius.
65 CALPURNIA. Say he is sick.

CAESAR (*loudly*).                    Shall Caesar send a lie?
Have I in conquest stretched mine arm so far,
To be afeard to tell graybeards the truth?
Decius, go tell them Caesar will not come.

DECIUS. Most mighty Caesar, let me know some cause,
70 Lest I be laughed at when I tell them so.

CAESAR. The cause is in my will. I will not come;
That is enough to satisfy the Senate.
But for your private satisfaction,
Because I love you, I will let you know.
75 Calpurnia here, my wife, stays me at home.
She dreamt tonight she saw my statuë,°
Which, like a fountain with an hundred spouts,
Did run pure blood; and many lusty Romans
Came smiling, and did bathe their hands in it.°
80 And these does she apply for warnings and portents
And evils imminent, and on her knee
Hath begged that I will stay at home today.

DECIUS. This dream is all amiss interpreted;
It was a vision fair and fortunate.
85 Your statue spouting blood in many pipes,
In which so many smiling Romans bathed,

**statuë** (stach′ü ə),
pronounced in three
syllables for the sake of the
meter.

**She dreamt . . . hands in
it.** These lines foreshadow
future events. Keep them
in mind as you read
further.

*Act Two, Scene 2* **531**

Signifies that from you great Rome shall suck
Reviving blood, and that great men shall press
For tinctures, stains, relics, and cognizance.
90 This by Calpurnia's dream is signified.
CAESAR. And this way have you well expounded it.
DECIUS. I have, when you have heard what I can say;
And know it now. The Senate have concluded
To give this day a crown to mighty Caesar.
95 If you shall send them word you will not come,
Their minds may change. Besides, it were a mock
Apt to be rendered,° for some one to say,
"Break up the Senate till another time
When Caesar's wife shall meet with better dreams."
100 If Caesar hide himself, shall they not whisper
"Lo, Caesar is afraid"?
Pardon me, Caesar, for my dear dear love
To your proceeding bids me tell you this;
And reason to my love is liable.
105 CAESAR. How foolish do your fears seem now, Calpurnia!
I am ashamèd I did yield to them.
Give me my robe, for I will go.
(*While* DECIUS *is assisting* CAESAR *with his robe,* PUBLIUS,
BRUTUS, LIGARIUS, METELLUS, CASCA, TREBONIUS, *and* CINNA
*enter at rear door. Each man, in turn, bows to* CAESAR.)
And look where Publius is come to fetch me.
PUBLIUS. Good morrow, Caesar.
CAESAR (*in a dignified manner*). Welcome, Publius.
110 What, Brutus, are you stirred so early too?
Good morrow, Casca. Caius Ligarius,
Caesar was ne'er so much your enemy
As that same ague° which hath made you lean.
What is 't o'clock?
BRUTUS.                    Caesar, 'tis strucken eight.
115 CAESAR. I thank you for your pains and courtesy.
(ANTONY *enters at rear door.*)
See, Antony, that revels long o' nights,
Is notwithstanding up. Good morrow, Antony.
ANTONY (*bowing*). So to most noble Caesar.
CAESAR. Bid them prepare within.°
120 I am to blame to be thus waited for.
Now, Cinna. Now, Metellus. What, Trebonius!
I have an hour's talk in store for you;

*it were a mock . . .
rendered,* people would
likely sneer at Caesar's
excuse.

41 Decius said in the
previous scene (lines
203–212) that he knew how
to handle Caesar. How
does he interpret
Calpurnia's dream? What
other incentives does he
give Caesar to go to the
Capitol?

*ague* (ā′gyü), fever.

*prepare within,* set out
refreshments in another
room.

Remember that you call on me today.
Be near me, that I may remember you.

125 **TREBONIUS.** Caesar, I will. (*Aside*) And so near will I be
That your best friends shall wish I had been further.

**CAESAR.** Good friends, go in, and taste some wine with me,
And we, like friends, will straightway go together.

**BRUTUS** (*aside*). That every like is not the same, O Caesar,

130 The heart of Brutus earns to think upon!°
(CAESAR, *followed by the others, exits at rear door.* CALPURNIA
*waits a moment, then exits as balcony-stage curtains are closed.*)

*That every . . . think upon.* Brutus' heart grieves that everyone who appears to be a friend is not a friend.

# SCENE 3

Rome. A street near the Capitol. [Played on the Platform.]
ARTEMIDORUS, *a teacher of rhetoric, enters at left. In his hands he
carries a paper which he intends to present to* CAESAR. *Moving slowly
across the platform, he reads to himself in a low tone.*

**ARTEMIDORUS.** "Caesar, beware of Brutus; take heed of Cassius;
come not near Casca; have an eye to Cinna; trust not Trebonius;
mark well Metellus Cimber; Decius Brutus loves thee not; thou
hast wronged Caius Ligarius. There is but one mind in all these

5 men, and it is bent against Caesar. If thou beest not immortal,
look about you. Security gives way to conspiracy.° The mighty
gods defend thee! Thy lover,° Artemidorus."
Here will I stand till Caesar pass along,
And as a suitor will I give him this.

10 My heart laments that virtue cannot live
Out of the teeth of emulation.
If thou read this, O Caesar, thou mayest live;
If not, the Fates with traitors do contrive. (*He exits at right.*)

*Security . . . conspiracy,* overconfidence eases the way for conspirators. *lover,* Shakespeare often used this word to mean "friend."

42 How much does Artemidorus know about the conspiracy?

# SCENE 4

Rome. Another part of the same street, before the house of Brutus.
[Played on the Platform.]
*It is now nearly nine o'clock on the morning of the ides of March. Though*
BRUTUS *left for the Capitol only a short time ago,* PORTIA'S *anxiety has
become almost unbearable. She enters the platform at inner-stage curtains,
followed by* LUCIUS.

**PORTIA.** I prithee,° boy, run to the Senate-house.
(LUCIUS *starts to speak, but* PORTIA *continues.*)

*prithee,* pray thee; request of you.

Stay not to answer me, but get thee gone.
Why dost thou stay?

LUCIUS (*in bewilderment*). To know my errand, madam.

PORTIA. I would have had thee there and here again

5   Ere I can tell thee what thou shouldst do there.—

(*Aside*) O constancy,° be strong upon my side,

Set a huge mountain 'tween my heart and tongue!

I have a man's mind, but a woman's might.

How hard it is for women to keep counsel!°—

10   Art thou here yet?

LUCIUS.           Madam, what should I do?

Run to the Capitol, and nothing else?

And so return to you, and nothing else?

PORTIA. Yes, bring me word, boy, if thy lord look well,

For he went sickly forth; and take good note

15   What Caesar doth, what suitors press to him.

Hark, boy, what noise is that?

LUCIUS. I hear none, madam.

PORTIA.               Prithee, listen well.

I heard a bustling rumor, like a fray,°

And the wind brings it from the Capitol.

20 LUCIUS. Sooth,° madam, I hear nothing.

(*The* SOOTHSAYER *enters at left.*)

PORTIA (*eagerly*). Come hither, fellow; which way hast thou been?

SOOTHSAYER. At mine own house, good lady.

PORTIA. What is 't o'clock?

SOOTHSAYER.         About the ninth hour, lady.

PORTIA. Is Caesar yet gone to the Capitol?

25 SOOTHSAYER. Madam, not yet. I go to take my stand,

To see him pass on to the Capitol.

PORTIA. Thou hast some suit to Caesar, hast thou not?

SOOTHSAYER. That I have, lady, if it will please Caesar

To be so good to Caesar as to hear me:

30   I shall beseech him to befriend himself.

PORTIA. Why, know'st thou any harm's intended towards him?

SOOTHSAYER. None that I know will be, much that I fear may

     chance.

Good morrow to you. Here the street is narrow.

The throng that follows Caesar at the heels,

35   Of senators, of praetors, common suitors,

Will crowd a feeble man almost to death.

I'll get me to a place more void,° and there

---

**constancy,** self-control.

**to keep counsel,** to keep a secret.

**43** Lines 1–19. What is Portia's state of mind? What might account for it?

**like a fray,** like fighting.

**Sooth,** in truth.

**44** Why might Portia ask the Soothsayer this question?

**more void,** more empty; less crowded.

---

Speak to great Caesar as he comes along. *(He exits at right.)*

PORTIA. I must go in. Ay me, how weak a thing

40  The heart of a woman is! O Brutus,
The heavens speed thee in thine enterprise!
*(Aside)* Sure, the boy heard me.
*(Speaking breathlessly to* LUCIUS*)*—Brutus hath a suit
That Caesar will not grant.—O, I grow faint.—

45  Run, Lucius, and commend me to my lord;
Say I am merry. Come to me again,
And bring me word what he doth say to thee.

*(*LUCIUS *runs off at right;* PORTIA *exits at inner-stage curtains.)*

**45** What would modern women think of Portia's comments about the weakness of a woman (lines 8–9 and 39–40)? Does Shakespeare intend to emphasize Portia's weakness, or might he have another purpose in mind?

**46** Line 42 seems to prove that Brutus has told Portia of his plans. Why is she immediately afraid that Lucius has heard her? How does the rest of the speech show her agitation?

## THINK AND DISCUSS
### SCENE 1
#### Understanding
1. What decisions does Brutus make about Cicero and Mark Antony after assuming the leadership of the conspiracy?
2. Which decision troubles Cassius more?
3. Portia is concerned about Brutus' welfare. What request does she make of him?
4. Who else joins the conspiracy in this scene? Explain the circumstances.

#### Analyzing
5. Review Brutus' four short soliloquies at the beginning of the scene. Why does he decide to join the conspirators?
6. From the discussion between Brutus and Portia, describe their relationship.

### SCENE 2
#### Understanding
1. Why is Decius the first conspirator to arrive at Caesar's house?

#### Analyzing
2. Compare Calpurnia's request of Caesar with Portia's request of Brutus in the previous scene. How do the men's responses differ?

3. How does Decius show his understanding of Caesar's personality during Scene 2?
4. In what way is this scene significant in furthering the action of the play?

#### Extending
5. Cassius does not escort Caesar to the capitol. In your judgment, is this an oversight on Shakespeare's part or is it intentional? Explain your choice.

### SCENES 3 AND 4
#### Understanding
1. How does Artemidorus' letter differ from the warnings in earlier scenes?
2. Who else intends to warn Caesar?

#### Analyzing
3. What purpose is served in having these warning episodes placed where they are?
4. Why can you infer that Portia has learned Brutus' secret?

#### Extending
5. Do you think that Portia approves of the assassination plot? Discuss.
6. One student has criticized the portrayal of Portia in Scene 4, especially her comments

about "how hard it is for women to keep counsel" and "how weak a thing the heart of woman is!" Do you suppose these lines would have been different if *Julius Caesar* had been written by a woman? If so, how? If not, why not?

## APPLYING: Foreshadowing H𝒯
### See Handbook of Literary Terms, p. 800

Just as dark clouds foreshadow a storm, actions and descriptions in literary works may **foreshadow,** or hint at and indicate beforehand, events yet to come in the plot. Shakespeare's theater audience lived in a kingdom, and the portrayal of a violent attack on a leader like Caesar might have shocked such an audience. But Shakespeare prepared the audience for the assassination scene by having Cassius and Brutus talk about it and by filling the early scenes with hints such as the Soothsayer's warning about the ides of March.

1. In Act Two Calpurnia says to Caesar:
   When beggars die, there are no comets seen;
   The heavens themselves blaze forth the death
      of princes.
   What does she mean, and how does her speech call attention to strange events that foreshadow the action yet to come?
2. What do Caesar's augurers do that further hints at the outcome of Caesar's day?

## COMPOSITION ✒
### Reading/Writing Log

Just as a great author such as Shakespeare enriches his plays with precise verbs used in the active voice, so you can give your writing power and vividness by choosing strong verbs. You can even use Shakespeare as a model by reviewing Act Two to find dialogue in which the verbs strike you as effective. If you are keeping a reading/writing log, record five sentences from *Julius Caesar* with vigorous, precise verbs in your log; if not, write them on another paper. Write your own powerful sentences of description, narration, or

persuasion using the same verbs or others.

### Writing as a Character

Retell the events in the orchard through the eyes of Lucius. Write a diary or journal entry, as Lucius might write it, beginning as he is awakened by Brutus (Act Two, Scene 1, line 5) and ending with his final exit (line 312). Remember that he is not onstage at all times, so check his entrances and exits. You may limit your three- to five-paragraph paper to what he sees while onstage or extend it to cover conversations he overhears or witnesses from his window. Write your diary entry in first person as a young page would write it. Choose precise, active verbs to make it interesting.

### Examining Dramatic Structure

Act One of a Shakespearean tragedy introduces the main characters and the conflict; in Act Two one or more characters make a no-turning-back decision. Choose either act to analyze; then review it with these functions in mind, taking notes as you read. Use these notes as the basis for a three- to five-paragraph essay explaining what the act you've chosen should accomplish and showing how well Shakespeare has fulfilled that goal. Choose precise verbs to make your writing clear. See "Writing About Drama" in the Writer's Handbook.

## ENRICHMENT
### Researching Shakespeare's Sources

As the basis for facts in *Julius Caesar*, Shakespeare used three selections from the Greek biographer Plutarch's *Lives of the Noble Greeks and Romans:* "The Life of Caesar," "The Life of Brutus," and "The Life of Antony." You may want to volunteer to read one of the *Lives* and to report orally to the class on the portions Shakespeare used and, perhaps, some interesting portions that he did not use. If two volunteers read each selection, you may divide the task between the pair. Since the reports will cover the entire play, start work now and deliver the reports after Act Five is read.

## Putting the Plays on Stage

You have already seen how the stage of a playhouse like the Globe was designed to accommodate a variety of settings and actions. You should also know something about by whom and under what general circumstances Shakespeare's plays were originally presented.

Under Queen Elizabeth I the acting profession in England was just beginning to become respectable. Since laws still existed for the imprisonment of "rogues, vagabonds, and strolling players," acting companies were taken under the protection of the country's great lords, who issued warrants permitting them to travel throughout England. Shakespeare's own acting company was first known as the Lord Chamberlain's Men ("Men" because all women's roles were played by young male apprentices). Then, when James I became king in 1603, the company was taken under his royal protection and became the King's Men.

The acting companies of the day were more similar to business partnerships than to today's acting groups. Major actors owned shares in their companies and often belonged to them for life; most of the members of Shakespeare's company, for instance, were already with the group when he joined it and stayed on after he retired. Such an arrangement gave Shakespeare the advantage of being able to write parts for specific actors, tailoring roles to their particular strengths and weaknesses. Thus the role of Brutus was probably designed for Richard Burbage, the "star" of the company; to John Heminges, who usually portrayed older men, most likely went the part of Julius Caesar; thin and sallow Richard Cowley may have played Cassius, he of the "lean and hungry look." Shakespeare himself generally played minor roles in his plays; in *Julius Caesar* he probably took the part of Cinna the poet, who appears in Act Three.

Another difference between acting groups then and now is the number of plays they performed. Whereas currently the general practice is for one play to be presented daily until the end of its run, in Shakespeare's time acting companies performed in repertory—that is, a different play was produced each day. Records from the period indicate that an acting company might present eleven different plays on eleven consecutive days, a feat that does not seem too remarkable until you realize that the same actors were probably in all the performances.

Interestingly, modern groups devoted to staging Shakespeare's plays follow many of the practices of that earlier period. Contemporary Shakespearean playhouses, for example, are nearly always modeled on the Globe. In Shakespearean acting companies it is not uncommon for an actor to stay with the group for several years. And the plays usually are presented in repertory, though five or six plays per season tends to be the limit. These practices are followed not simply to slavishly imitate Shakespeare's era, but because they have been judged effective in their own right. In our time audiences rarely accept realistic portrayals of women by young men. Today leading actresses play the female roles.

# ACT THREE

## SCENE 1

Rome. Before the Capitol. [Played on the Platform and Inner Stage.]
*Today—the ides of March—*CAESAR *is to meet with the* SENATORS.
ARTEMIDORUS *and the* SOOTHSAYER *enter at left among a crowd of
well-wishers. The crowd bursts into cheers as* CAESAR *enters at right,
followed by* ANTONY, POPILIUS, PUBLIUS, *and the* CONSPIRATORS.
CAESAR *approaches the* SOOTHSAYER, *and speaks defiantly.*

**CAESAR.** The ides of March are come.

**SOOTHSAYER.** Ay, Caesar, but not gone.

(CAESAR, *waving the* SOOTHSAYER *aside, is approached by*
ARTEMIDORUS, *who presents his paper.*)

**ARTEMIDORUS.** Hail, Caesar! Read this schedule.°

(DECIUS, *waving another paper, pushes* ARTEMIDORUS *aside.*)

**DECIUS.** Trebonius doth desire you to o'er-read,

5    At your best leisure, this his humble suit.

**ARTEMIDORUS.** O Caesar, read mine first, for mine's a suit
That touches Caesar nearer. Read it, great Caesar.

**CAESAR.** What touches us ourself shall be last served.

**ARTEMIDORUS.** Delay not, Caesar. (*He thrusts his paper in*
CAESAR's *face.*) Read it instantly.

10 **CAESAR.** What, is the fellow mad?

(PUBLIUS *and* CASSIUS *force* ARTEMIDORUS *aside.*)

**PUBLIUS.**                    Sirrah, give place.

**CASSIUS.** What, urge you your petitions in the street?
Come to the Capitol.

(CASSIUS *points toward inner stage, where curtains are slowly
being drawn apart to reveal the interior of the Senate-house. Some*
SENATORS *are already seated on the stage; a statue of* POMPEY
*stands forward at left.* CAESAR *moves onto inner stage, followed by*
ANTONY, PUBLIUS, METELLUS, TREBONIUS, *and* CAIUS LIGARIUS.)

**POPILIUS** (*passing* CASSIUS). I wish your enterprise today may thrive.

**CASSIUS** (*innocently*). What enterprise, Popilius?

**POPILIUS.**                    Fare you well.

(*He joins* CAESAR.)

15 **BRUTUS.** (*fearfully*). What said Popilius Lena?

**47** What might Shakespeare's purpose be in opening the scene with this exchange between Caesar and the Soothsayer?

*schedule,* document.

**48** What is the content of the paper Artemidorus wants Caesar to read?

**49** Why do you think both Cassius and, in lines 4–5, Decius try to interrupt Artemidorus?

**50** Cassius answers the senator Popilius "innocently." How would an actor playing Cassius show that Popilius' words have meaning for him?

CASSIUS. He wished today our enterprise might thrive.
 I fear our purpose is discovered.
BRUTUS. Look, how he makes to Caesar.° Mark him.
CASSIUS. Casca, be sudden, for we fear prevention.
20 Brutus, what shall be done? If this be known,
 Cassius or Caesar never shall turn back,
 For I will slay myself.
BRUTUS *(with relief)*.  Cassius, be constant.
 Popilius Lena speaks not of our purposes;
 For, look, he smiles, and Caesar doth not change.
*(ANTONY and TREBONIUS leave the inner stage and move off the platform at right.)*
25 CASSIUS. Trebonius knows his time; for, look you, Brutus,
 He draws Mark Antony out of the way.
DECIUS. Where is Metellus Cimber? Let him go
 And presently prefer his suit° to Caesar.
BRUTUS. He is addressed.° Press near and second him.
30 CINNA. Casca, you are the first that rears your hand.
*(BRUTUS, CASSIUS, CASCA, DECIUS, and CINNA cross to the inner stage, where CAESAR is calling the group to order.)*
CAESAR. Are we all ready? What is now amiss
 That Caesar and his Senate must redress?
METELLUS. Most high, most mighty, and most puissant Caesar,
 Metellus Cimber throws before thy seat
35 An humble heart—*(He falls on his knees.)*
CAESAR.          I must prevent thee, Cimber.
 These couchings° and these lowly courtesies
 Might fire the blood of ordinary men,
 And turn preordinance and first decree
 Into the law of children.° Be not fond°
40 To think that Caesar bears such rebel blood
 That will be thawed from the true quality
 With that which melteth fools—I mean, sweet words,
 Low-crooked curtsies, and base spaniel fawning.
 Thy brother° by decree is banishèd.
45 If thou dost bend and pray and fawn for him,
 I spurn thee like a cur out of my way.
*(He pushes METELLUS aside.)*
 Know, Caesar doth not wrong, nor without cause
 Will he be satisfied.
METELLUS. Is there no voice more worthy than my own,
50 To sound more sweetly in great Caesar's ear
 For the repealing of my banished brother?

*makes to Caesar*, presses toward Caesar.

51 By this point, how many people besides the conspirators know or suspect something is about to happen to Caesar? Name them, and explain (if possible) where they got their information.

52 Why does Trebonius draw Antony aside?

*presently . . . his suit*, immediately present his petition.
*addressed*, ready.

*couchings*, kneelings.

*And turn . . . children*, and turn established laws and procedures into the whims of children.
*fond*, here meaning "foolish enough."

*Thy brother*. Publius Cimber, who had incurred Caesar's wrath.

BRUTUS (*kneeling*). I kiss thy hand, but not in flattery, Caesar,
    Desiring thee that Publius Cimber may
    Have an immediate freedom of repeal.
55 CAESAR (*in surprise*). What, Brutus!
    CASSIUS (*kneeling also*).        Pardon, Caesar! Caesar, pardon!
    As low as to thy foot doth Cassius fall,
    To beg enfranchisement for Publius Cimber.°
(*One by one, the other* CONSPIRATORS *kneel.*)
    CAESAR. I could be well moved, if I were as you.
    If I could pray to move, prayers would move me.
60 But I am constant as the northern star,
    Of whose true-fixed and resting quality
    There is no fellow in the firmament.
    The skies are painted with unnumbered sparks,
    They are all fire and every one doth shine,
65 But there's but one in all doth hold his place.
    So in the world: 'tis furnished well with men,
    And men are flesh and blood, and apprehensive;°
    Yet in the number I do know but one
    That unassailable holds on his rank,
70 Unshaked of motion. And that I am he,
    Let me a little show it, even in this—
    That I was constant Cimber should be banished,
    And constant do remain to keep him so.
    CINNA. O Caesar—
    CAESAR.        Hence! Wilt thou lift up Olympus?
75 DECIUS. Great Caesar—
    CAESAR.        Doth not Brutus bootless° kneel?
    CASCA (*leaping up*). Speak, hands, for me! (*He stabs* CAESAR.)
(*The other* CONSPIRATORS, *daggers in hand, spring to their feet. They surge
forward, and all but* BRUTUS *stab* CAESAR. CAESAR, *crying out, tries to ward
off the blows until he sees* BRUTUS' *uplifted dagger, then covers his face with
his cloak and submits.* BRUTUS *stabs* CAESAR.)
    CAESAR. Et tu, Brutè!° Then fall, Caesar!
(CAESAR *staggers forward and dies at the foot of* POMPEY'S *statue.*)
    CINNA (*shouting*). Liberty! Freedom! Tyranny is dead!
    Run hence, proclaim, cry it about the streets.
80 CASSIUS. Some to the common pulpits,° and cry out
    "Liberty, freedom, and enfranchisement."
(*The* CONSPIRATORS *move onto the platform, where the people stand as if
stunned by the sudden attack on* CAESAR. *Then the crowd, including*
ARTEMIDORUS *and the* SOOTHSAYER, *begin to flee in panic.*)
    BRUTUS (*calling out*). People and senators, be not affrighted.

*To beg enfranchisement* (en fran′chīz mənt) . . . *Cimber,* to ask that Publius Cimber be allowed to return to Rome and be given again his full rights as a citizen.

*apprehensive,* aware of what is going on.

53 Olympus was a high mountain in Greece considered the home of the gods. How does this allusion, as well as the content of his speeches in lines 35–48 and 58–73, show Caesar's egotism? Why might Shakespeare have placed these speeches right before the murder?

*bootless,* in vain.

*Et tu, Brutè* (brü′tā) "And you, Brutus!" [Latin] The betrayal completely overwhelms Caesar.

*common pulpits,* elevated areas where public debates were held.

54 What is ironic about where Caesar dies?

CAESAR is assassinated. The American Shakespeare Theatre.

Fly not; stand still. Ambition's debt is paid.

CASCA. Go to the pulpit, Brutus.

85 DECIUS. And Cassius too.

BRUTUS.                     Where's Publius?°

CINNA. Here, quite confounded with this mutiny.

METELLUS. Stand fast together, lest some friend of Caesar's
  Should chance—

BRUTUS. Talk not of standing. (*Extending his hand*) Publius, good
    cheer.

90   There is no harm intended to your person.
    Nor to no Roman else. So tell them, Publius.

CASSIUS. And leave us, Publius, lest that the people,
  Rushing on us, should do your age some mischief.

BRUTUS. Do so, and let no man abide this deed°

95   But we the doers.

(PUBLIUS, *accompanied by* POPILIUS, *moves off at left just as* TREBONIUS
*reenters at right.*)

*Publius,* an elderly senator
who is stunned by what has
just occurred.

*abide this deed,* answer for
this deed.

CASSIUS. Where is Antony?

TREBONIUS.                          Fled to his house amazed.
    Men, wives, and children stare, cry out, and run
    As it were doomsday.

BRUTUS *(resignedly)*.     Fates,° we will know your pleasures.
    That we shall die, we know; 'tis but the time,
100    And drawing days out, that men stand upon.°

CASSIUS. Why, he that cuts off twenty years of life
    Cuts off so many years of fearing death.

BRUTUS. Grant that, and then is death a benefit.
    So are we Caesar's friends, that have abridged
105    His time of fearing death. Stoop, Romans, stoop,
    And let us bathe our hands in Caesar's blood
    Up to the elbows, and besmear our swords.
    Then walk we forth, even to the market-place,
    And, waving our red weapons o'er our heads,
110    Let's all cry, "Peace, freedom, and liberty!"

CASSIUS. Stoop, then, and wash. (*The* CONSPIRATORS *kneel and
    begin to dip their hands and weapons in* CAESAR's *blood.*)
                                    How many ages hence
    Shall this our lofty scene be acted over
    In states unborn and accents yet unknown!

BRUTUS. How many times shall Caesar bleed in sport,
115    That now on Pompey's basis° lies along
    No worthier than the dust!

CASSIUS. So oft as that shall be,
    So often shall the knot of us be called
    The men that gave their country liberty.

    (*They rise.*)

120 DECIUS. What, shall we forth?

CASSIUS.                          Aye, every man away;
    Brutus shall lead; and we will grace his heels
    With the most boldest and best hearts of Rome.

    (*A* SERVANT *of* ANTONY *enters at right.*)

BRUTUS. Soft! Who comes here? A friend of Antony's?

SERVANT *(kneeling)*. Thus, Brutus, did my master bid me kneel.
125    Thus did Mark Antony bid me fall down;
    And, being prostrate, thus he bade me say:
    Brutus is noble, wise, valiant, and honest;
    Caesar was mighty, bold, royal, and loving.
    Say I love Brutus, and I honor him;
130    Say I feared Caesar, honored him, and loved him,

---

*Fates,* the three goddesses who were thought to control human destinies.
*stand upon,* are concerned with.

55 | How do you think the commoners will react to this display?

56 | How accurate is Cassius' prophecy? What is ironic about it and the two short speeches following it?

*on Pompey's basis,* at the foot of Pompey's statue.

---

If Brutus will vouchsafe that Antony
May safely come to him, and be resolved°
How Caesar hath deserved to lie in death,
Mark Antony shall not love Caesar dead

135 So well as Brutus living, but will follow
The fortunes and affairs of noble Brutus
Through the hazards of this untrod state°
With all true faith. So says my master Antony.

**BRUTUS.** Thy master is a wise and valiant Roman;

140 I never thought him worse.
Tell him, so please him come unto this place,
He shall be satisfied and, by my honor,
Depart untouched.°

**SERVANT.**        I'll fetch him presently. (SERVANT *exits.*)

**BRUTUS.** I know that we shall have him well to friend.

145 **CASSIUS.** I wish we may. But yet have I a mind
That fears him much; and my misgiving still
Falls shrewdly to the purpose.

(ANTONY, *reentering at right, strides toward* CAESAR'S *body.*)

**BRUTUS.** But here comes Antony.—Welcome, Mark Antony.

**ANTONY** (*ignoring* BRUTUS). O mighty Caesar! Dost thou lie so low?

150 Are all thy conquests, glories, triumphs, spoils,
Shrunk to this little measure? Fare thee well.—
(*To the* CONSPIRATORS) I know not, gentlemen, what you intend,
Who else must be let blood, who else is rank;°
If I myself, there is no hour so fit

155 As Caesar's death hour, nor no instrument
Of half that worth as those your swords, made rich
With the most noble blood of all this world.
I do beseech ye, if you bear me hard,
Now, whilst your purpled hands do reek and smoke,

160 Fulfill your pleasure. Live a thousand years,
I shall not find myself so apt° to die;
No place will please me so, no mean° of death,
As here by Caesar, and by you cut off,
The choice and master spirits of this age.

165 **BRUTUS** (*disturbed*). O Antony, beg not your death of us.
Though now we must appear bloody and cruel,
As, by our hands and this our present act
You see we do, yet see you but our hands
And this the bleeding business they have done.

170 Our hearts you see not. They are pitiful;

---

**be resolved,** have it explained to him.

**untrod state,** new and unfamiliar state of affairs; the image can be compared to a field unmarked by footsteps (untrod).

***Thy master . . . untouched.*** In tragedies of Shakespeare's day the fortunes of the hero reach their height, and then occurs a scene where they begin to fall. Critics who see Brutus as the hero of the play (see Comment on page 559 for a discussion of this) often claim that the dramatic reverse occurs when Brutus agrees to see Antony and explain Caesar's assassination to him. Note, by contrast, Cassius' "misgiving" in lines 145–147.

***Who else must . . . rank,*** who else must be destroyed.

**apt,** ready.
**mean,** method.

And pity to the general wrong of Rome—
As fire drives out fire, so pity pity°—
Hath done this deed on Caesar. For your part,
To you our swords have leaden points, Mark Antony.
175 Our arms in strength of malice, and our hearts
Of brothers' temper, do receive you in
With all kind love, good thoughts, and reverence.
 CASSIUS. Your voice shall be as strong as any man's
In the disposing of new dignities.
180 BRUTUS. Only be patient till we have appeased
The multitude, beside themselves with fear,
And then we will deliver you the cause
Why I, that did love Caesar when I struck him,
Have thus proceeded.
 ANTONY (extending his hand). I doubt not of your wisdom.
185 Let each man render me his bloody hand.
First, Marcus Brutus, will I shake with you;
Next, Caius Cassius, do I take your hand;
Now, Decius Brutus, yours; now yours, Metellus;
Yours, Cinna; and, my valiant Casca, yours;
190 Though last, not least in love, yours, good Trebonius.
Gentlemen all—alas, what shall I say?
My credit now stands on such slippery ground
That one of two bad ways you must conceit° me,
Either a coward or a flatterer.
195 (Addressing CAESAR's body) That I did love thee, Caesar, O,
  'tis true!°
If then thy spirit look upon us now,
Shall it not grieve thee dearer than thy death
To see thy Antony making his peace,
Shaking the bloody fingers of thy foes—
200 Most noble!—in the presence of thy corse?°
Had I as many eyes as thou hast wounds,
Weeping as fast as they stream forth thy blood,
It would become me better than to close
In terms of friendship with thine enemies.
205 Pardon me, Julius! Here wast thou bayed, brave hart,°
Here didst thou fall, and here thy hunters stand,
Signed in thy spoil, crimsoned in thy lethe.°
O world, thou wast the forest to this hart,
And this, indeed, O world, the heart of thee!
210 How like a deer, strucken by many princes,

**so pity pity,** so pity for the wrongs Rome has endured from Caesar overshadows pity for his death.

57 In offering Antony a say in handing out new government positions (dignities), Cassius is offering him power. What has Brutus offered him? Contrast the two men's approaches.

*conceit,* consider.

**That I did love . . . true.** In this speech, as in his preceding one, Antony cleverly alternates between placating the conspirators and revealing his feelings about Caesar's death.
*corse,* corpse.

**hart,** Antony here puns on *hart* ("stag") and *heart.*

*lethe* (lē′thē), death.

Dost thou here lie!

CASSIUS (*sharply*). Mark Antony—

ANTONY.              Pardon me, Caius Cassius.
  The enemies of Caesar shall say this;
  Then, in a friend, it is cold modesty.

215 CASSIUS. I blame you not for praising Caesar so,
  But what compact mean you to have with us?
  Will you be pricked in number of our friends,°
  Or shall we on, and not depend on you?

ANTONY. Therefore I took your hands, but was indeed
220 Swayed from the point, by looking down on Caesar.
  Friends am I with you all and love you all,
  Upon this hope, that you shall give me reasons
  Why and wherein Caesar was dangerous.

BRUTUS. Or else were this a savage spectacle.
225 Our reasons are so full of good regard°
  That were you, Antony, the son of Caesar,
  You should be satisfied.

ANTONY.            That's all I seek,
  And am moreover suitor that I may
  Produce his body to the market-place,
230 And in the pulpit, as becomes a friend,
  Speak in the order° of his funeral.

BRUTUS. You shall, Mark Antony.

CASSIUS (*very much disturbed*).     Brutus, a word with you.
  (*Taking* BRUTUS *aside*) You know not what you do. Do not
    consent
  That Antony speak in his funeral.
235 Know you how much the people may be moved
  By that which he will utter?

BRUTUS.            By your pardon;
  I will myself into the pulpit first,
  And show the reason of our Caesar's death.
  What Antony shall speak, I will protest°
240 He speaks by leave and by permission,
  And that we are contented Caesar shall
  Have all true rites and lawful ceremonies.
  It shall advantage more than do us wrong.

CASSIUS (*dubiously*). I know not what may fall; I like it not.
  (BRUTUS *and* CASSIUS *rejoin* ANTONY *and the others.*)
245 BRUTUS. Mark Antony, here, take you Caesar's body.
  You shall not in your funeral speech blame us,

*pricked . . . friends,* numbered among our friends.

*good regard,* merit.

*order,* ceremony.

58 *Lines 227–244.* Here Brutus has made another error in judgment. What is it? What is Cassius' reaction?

But speak all good you can devise of Caesar,
And say you do 't by our permission.°
Else shall you not have any hand at all
250 About his funeral. And you shall speak
In the same pulpit whereto I am going,
After my speech is ended.

**ANTONY.**                    Be it so.
I do desire no more.

**BRUTUS.** Prepare the body then, and follow us.

(*The* CONSPIRATORS *follow* BRUTUS *out at right.* ANTONY *gazes at*
CAESAR, *then prepares to cover the body with the dead man's cloak.*)

255 **ANTONY.** Oh, pardon me, thou bleeding piece of earth,
That I am meek and gentle with these butchers!
Thou are the ruins of the noblest man
That ever livèd in the tide of times.
Woe to the hand that shed this costly blood!
260 Over thy wounds now do I prophesy—
Which, like dumb mouths, do ope their ruby lips
To beg the voice and utterance of my tongue—
A curse shall light upon the limbs of men;
Domestic fury and fierce civil strife
265 Shall cumber all the parts of Italy;
Blood and destruction shall be so in use
And dreadful objects° so familiar
That mothers shall but smile when they behold
Their infants quartered° with the hands of war,
270 All pity choked with custom of fell deeds;°
And Caesar's spirit, ranging for revenge,
With Ate° by his side come hot from hell,
Shall in these confines with a monarch's voice
Cry "Havoc"° and let slip the dogs of war,°
275 That this foul deed shall smell above the earth
With carrion men, groaning for burial.

(*A* SERVANT *enters at left.*)
You serve Octavius Caesar, do you not?

**SERVANT.** I do, Mark Antony.

**ANTONY.** Caesar did write for him to come to Rome.

280 **SERVANT.** He did receive his letters, and is coming,
And bid me say to you by word of mouth—(*He sees the body.*)
O Caesar!

**ANTONY.** Thy heart is big. Get thee apart and weep.
Passion, I see, is catching, for mine eyes,

*You shall not . . .*
*permission.* Keep these
lines in mind as you read
Scene 2, to see whether
Antony obeys Brutus'
directions when speaking to
the commoners.

*objects*, sights.

*quartered*, torn to pieces.

*with custom of fell deeds,*
with savage deeds that have
become customary.

*Ate* (ā′tē), Greek goddess
of vengeance.

*"Havoc,"* a command,
which could be given only
by a king, which meant
"Kill all! Take no
prisoners."

*let slip the dogs of war,* let
loose fire, sword, and
famine.

285 Seeing those beads of sorrow stand in thine,
    Began to water. Is thy master coming?
  SERVANT. He lies tonight within seven leagues of Rome.°
  ANTONY. Post back with speed, and tell him what hath chanced.
    Here is a mourning Rome, a dangerous Rome,
290 No Rome of safety for Octavius yet;
    Hie hence, and tell him so. (*The* SERVANT *starts to leave.*) Yet,
       stay awhile.
    Thou shalt not back till I have borne this corse
    Into the market-place. There shall I try,
    In my oration, how the people take
295 The cruel issue of these bloody men.
    According to the which thou shalt discourse
    To young Octavius of the state of things.
    Lend me your hand.
  (ANTONY *and the* SERVANT *pick up* CAESAR's *body and proceed to carry it
  off at right door. At the same time the curtains of the inner stage are drawn
  closed.*)

*He lies . . . Rome.* With the news that Caesar's grandnephew Octavius is within seven leagues (twenty-one miles) of Rome, Antony's side is strengthened, for Caesar had recently made Octavius his adopted son and heir. He would thus attract Caesar's supporters.

# SCENE 2

Rome. The Forum. [Played on the Platform and Balcony Stage.]
BRUTUS *and* CASSIUS, *with groups of indignant* CITIZENS *at their heels, enter
at left. The* CITIZENS *are clamoring for an explanation of* CAESAR's
*assassination. It is apparent from their threatening gestures and shouts that the
people will become violent unless* BRUTUS *speaks to them. He does so from the
balcony, which represents a raised pulpit in this scene.*

  CITIZENS (*angrily*). We will be satisfied! Let us be satisfied!°
  BRUTUS. Then follow me, and give me audience, friends.
    Cassius, go you into the other street,
    And part the numbers.°
5   (*Loudly*) Those that will hear me speak, let 'em stay here;
    Those that will follow Cassius, go with him;
    And public reasons shall be rendered
    Of Caesar's death.
  (BRUTUS *exits at inner-stage curtains to ascend the pulpit.*)
  FIRST CITIZEN.        I will hear Brutus speak.
  SECOND CITIZEN. I will hear Cassius; and compare their reasons,
10   When severally° we hear them rendered.
  (CASSIUS *moves off at right, accompanied by various* CITIZENS
  *who clamor loudly.* BRUTUS *appears above at the balcony railing.*)

*We . . . satisfied.* Note how throughout this scene the commoners are easily swayed to support either side.
*part the numbers,* divide the crowd.

*severally,* separately.

*Act Three, Scene 2* **547**

**THIRD CITIZEN.** The noble Brutus is ascended. Silence!

**BRUTUS** (*speaking earnestly*). Be patient till the last. (*Pause*)
Romans, countrymen, and lovers!

(*There are shouts from the mob.*)

Hear me for my cause, and be silent, that you may hear.

15   Believe me for mine honor, and have respect to mine honor,
that you may believe. Censure me in your wisdom, and awake
your senses, that you may the better judge. If there be any in
this assembly, any dear friend of Caesar's, to him I say, that
Brutus' love to Caesar was no less than his. If then that friend

20   demand why Brutus rose against Caesar, this is my answer:
Not that I loved Caesar less, but that I loved Rome more. Had
you rather Caesar were living and die all slaves, than that
Caesar were dead, to live all free men? As Caesar loved me, I
weep for him; as he was fortunate, I rejoice at it; as he was

25   valiant, I honor him; but, as he was ambitious, I slew him.
There is tears for his love; joy for his fortune; honor for his
valor; and death for his ambition. Who is here so base that
would be a bondman? If any, speak, for him have I offended.
Who is here so rude that would not be Roman? If any, speak,

30   for him have I offended. Who is here so vile that will not love
his country? If any, speak, for him have I offended. I pause for
a reply.

**ALL** (*shouting*). None, Brutus, none.

**BRUTUS.** Then none have I offended. I have done no more to

35   Caesar than you shall do to Brutus. The question of his death
is enrolled° in the Capitol; his glory not extenuated,° wherein he
was worthy, nor his offenses enforced, for which he suffered
death.

(ANTONY *enters at left. Behind him come* ATTENDANTS *carrying*
CAESAR's *bier.*)

Here comes his body, mourned by Mark Antony, who, though

40   he had no hand in his death, shall receive the benefit of his
dying, a place in the commonwealth, as which of you shall not?
With this I depart, that, as I slew my best lover for the good of
Rome, I have the same dagger for myself, when it shall please
my country to need my death.

45   **ALL** (*shouting*). Live, Brutus, live, live!

(BRUTUS *exits at balcony curtains to descend from the pulpit.*)

**FIRST CITIZEN.** Bring him with triumph home unto his house.

**SECOND CITIZEN.** Give him a statue with his ancestors.

**THIRD CITIZEN.** Let him be Caesar.

**59** Note that Brutus'
speech is in prose—
brief, unadorned, and to
the point. Throughout, he
gives logical reasons for the
assassination, appealing to
his audience's minds rather
than the mob's passion.
What does he mean by
"Not that I loved Caesar
less, but that I loved Rome
more" (line 21)?

*The question . . . is
enrolled,* the reason for
Caesar's death is recorded.

*his glory not extenuated*
(ek sten′yü āt əd), his
fame has not been
detracted from because of
the manner of his dying.

FOURTH CITIZEN.                    Caesar's better parts
    Shall be crowned in Brutus.
50 FIRST CITIZEN. We'll bring him to his house with shouts and clamors.
    (*The mob greets* BRUTUS *with cheers as he reenters the platform
    at inner-stage curtains.*)
    BRUTUS. My countrymen—
    (*The crowd cheers wildly.*)
    SECOND CITIZEN (*shouting*). Peace, silence! Brutus speaks.
    FIRST CITIZEN. Peace, ho!
    BRUTUS. Good countrymen, let me depart alone,
55     And, for my sake, stay here with Antony.
    Do grace to Caesar's corpse, and grace his speech
    Tending to Caesar's glories, which Mark Antony,
    By our permission, is allowed to make.
    I do entreat you, not a man depart,
60     Save I alone, till Antony have spoke. (*He exits alone at right.*)
    FIRST CITIZEN. Stay, ho, and let us hear Mark Antony.
    THIRD CITIZEN. Let him go up into the public chair.
    We'll hear him. Noble Antony, go up.
    (*There are murmurs from the mob.*)
    ANTONY. For Brutus' sake, I am beholding to you.
    (ANTONY *exits at inner-stage curtains to ascend the pulpit. His*
    ATTENDANTS *place* CAESAR's *body well forward on platform.*)
65 FOURTH CITIZEN. What does he say of Brutus?
    THIRD CITIZEN. He says, for Brutus' sake
    He finds himself beholding to us all.
    FOURTH CITIZEN. 'Twere best he speak no harm of Brutus here.
    FIRST CITIZEN. This Caesar was a tyrant.
    THIRD CITIZEN.                    Nay, that's certain.
70     We are blest that Rome is rid of him.
    (ANTONY *appears above at the balcony railing.*)
    SECOND CITIZEN. Peace! Let us hear what Antony can say.
    ANTONY. You gentle Romans—
    (*The crowd is not yet quiet.*)
    CITIZENS.                    Peace, ho! Let us hear him.
    ANTONY. Friends, Romans, countrymen, lend me your ears.
    I come to bury Caesar, not to praise him.
75     The evil that men do lives after them;
    The good is oft interrèd with their bones.
    So let it be with Caesar. The noble Brutus
    Hath told you Caesar was ambitious.
    If it were so, it was a grievous fault,

60 | What do these lines—
especially the
comment, "Let him be
Caesar"—tell about how
well the commoners have
understood Brutus' speech?

80 And grievously hath Caesar answered it.
Here, under leave of Brutus and the rest—
*(The mob murmurs angrily.)*
    For Brutus is an honorable man;°
    So are they all, all honorable men—
    Come I to speak in Caesar's funeral.
85 He was my friend, faithful and just to me;
    But Brutus says he was ambitious,
    And Brutus is an honorable man.
    He° hath brought many captives home to Rome,
    Whose ransoms did the general coffers fill.°
90 Did this in Caesar seem ambitious?
    When that the poor have cried, Caesar hath wept;
    Ambition should be made of sterner stuff.
    Yet Brutus said he was ambitious,
    And Brutus is an honorable man.°
95 You all did see that on the Lupercal
    I thrice presented him a kingly crown,
    Which he did thrice refuse. Was this ambition?°
    Yet Brutus says he was ambitious,
    And, sure, he is an honorable man.
100 I speak not to disprove what Brutus spoke,
    But here I am to speak what I do know.
    You all did love him once, not without cause.
    What cause withholds you then, to mourn for him?
    O judgment! Thou art fled to brutish beasts,
105 And men have lost their reason. *(He pauses.)* Bear with me;
    My heart is in the coffin there with Caesar,
    And I must pause till it come back to me. *(He weeps openly.)*
    **FIRST CITIZEN** *(soberly)*. Methinks there is much reason in his
        sayings.
    **SECOND CITIZEN.** If thou consider rightly of the matter,
110 Caesar has had great wrong.
    **THIRD CITIZEN.**                Has he, masters?
    I fear there will a worse come in his place.
    **FOURTH CITIZEN.** Marked ye his words? He would not take the crown;
        Therefore 'tis certain he was not ambitious.
    **FIRST CITIZEN.** If it be found so, some will dear abide° it.
115 **SECOND CITIZEN.** Poor soul! His eyes are red as fire with weeping.
    **THIRD CITIZEN.** There's not a nobler man in Rome than Antony.
    **FOURTH CITIZEN** *(pointing)*. Now mark him, he begins again to
        speak.

**Brutus is an honorable man.** The crowd's anger at words against Brutus makes Antony quick to express his admiration for the man—and for the other conspirators.

**He,** Caesar.

**the general coffers fill,** Caesar hadn't kept the ransom money for himself.

**Brutus is an honorable man.** Note the tinge of irony beginning to creep in.

**Lupercal . . . ambition.** Compare this explanation of Caesar's reaction with Casca's view in Act One, Scene 2.

61 Here Antony is overcome with grief and finds himself unable to go on. Do you think he realizes the effectiveness of this pause? Are his tears genuine?

**abide,** pay for.

ANTONY. But yesterday the word of Caesar might
Have stood against the world. Now lies he there,
120 And none so poor to do him reverence.°
O masters! If I were disposed to stir
Your hearts and minds to mutiny and rage,
I should do Brutus wrong, and Cassius wrong,
Who, you all know, are honorable men.
*(There is derisive laughter from the mob.)*
125 I will not do them wrong; I rather choose
To wrong the dead, to wrong myself and you,
Than I will wrong such honorable men. *(He pulls a scroll from
his garment.)*
But here's a parchment with the seal of Caesar;
I found it in his closet,° 'tis his will.
130 Let but the commons hear this testament—
Which, pardon me, I do not mean to read—
And they would go and kiss dead Caesar's wounds
And dip their napkins° in his sacred blood,
Yea, beg a hair of him for memory,
135 And, dying, mention it within their wills,
Bequeathing it as a rich legacy
Unto their issue.
FOURTH CITIZEN. We'll hear the will! Read it, Mark Antony.
ALL *(shouting).* The will, the will! We will hear Caesar's will.
140 ANTONY. Have patience, gentle friends, I must not read it.
It is not meet you know how Caesar loved you.
*(He puts the will away.)*
You are not wood, you are not stones, but men;
And, being men, hearing the will of Caesar,
It will inflame you, it will make you mad.
*(There are cries of "No! No!")*
145 'Tis good you know not that you are his heirs,
For, if you should, O, what would come of it!
FOURTH CITIZEN. Read the will! We'll hear it, Antony.
*(There are cries of "Yes! Yes!")*
You shall read us the will, Caesar's will.
ANTONY. Will you be patient? Will you stay awhile?
150 I have o'ershot myself° to tell you of it.
I fear I wrong the honorable men
Whose daggers have stabbed Caesar; I do fear it.
*(There are angry shouts from the mob.)*
FOURTH CITIZEN. They were traitors. *(Sarcastically)* Honorable men!

*And none . . . reverence,*
the dead Caesar is now
poorer (lower in estate)
than the poorest Roman.

62 By this point, what
tone of voice is
Antony using when he
repeats this phrase?

*closet,* study; private
chamber.

*napkins,* handkerchiefs.

63 What might be
behind Antony's
refusing to read the will?

*I have . . . myself.* Antony
has said more than he
intended, or pretends so.

**ALL** (*clamoring*). The will! The testament!

155 **SECOND CITIZEN.** They were villains, murderers. The will! Read
     the will!

(*There are cries of "Read! Read!"*)

**ANTONY.** You will compel me then to read the will?
    Then make a ring about the corpse of Caesar,
    And let me show you him that made the will.
    Shall I descend? And will you give me leave?

160 **SEVERAL CITIZENS.** Come down.

**SECOND CITIZEN.** Descend.

**THIRD CITIZEN.** You shall have leave.

(ANTONY *exits at balcony curtains in order to descend from the
pulpit; the crowd circles* CAESAR's *body.*)

**FOURTH CITIZEN.**                    A ring; stand round.

**FIRST CITIZEN.** Stand from the hearse,° stand from the body.

(*The crowd moves back when* ANTONY *reenters the platform.*)

**SECOND CITIZEN.** Room for Antony, most noble Antony.

165 **ANTONY.** Nay, press not so upon me. Stand far off.

**SEVERAL CITIZENS.** Stand back! Room! Bear back!

**ANTONY.** If you have tears, prepare to shed them now.
    You all do know this mantle. (*Pointing to* CAESAR's *cloak*) I
     remember
    The first time ever Caesar put it on;

170     'Twas on a summer's evening, in his tent,
    That day he overcame the Nervii.°
    Look, in this place ran Cassius' dagger through.
    See what a rent the envious Casca made.
    Through this the well-beloved Brutus stabbed,

175     And, as he plucked his cursèd steel away,
    Mark how the blood of Caesar followed it;
    As rushing out of doors, to be resolved
    If Brutus so unkindly knocked or no;
    For Brutus, as you know, was Caesar's angel.

180     Judge, O you gods, how dearly Caesar loved him!
    This was the most unkindest cut of all;
    For when the noble Caesar saw him stab,
    Ingratitude, more strong than traitors' arms,
    Quite vanquished him. Then burst his mighty heart,

185     And, in his mantle muffling up his face,
    E'en at the base of Pompey's statuë,
    Which all the while ran blood, great Caesar fell.
    O, what a fall was there, my countrymen!

---

*hearse,* bier.

*Nervii* (nèr'vē ī), a warlike
tribe against whom Caesar
led the decisive charge.

64  There is no way
Antony could have
known which conspirator
was responsible for which
wound. What is his
purpose in identifying the
cuts in Caesar's cloak with
individual conspirators?

ANTONY mourns the death of CAESAR and speaks passionately to the crowd of citizens. The American Shakespeare Theatre.

Then I, and you, and all of us fell down,
190　Whilst bloody treason flourished over us.
O, now you weep, and I perceive you feel
The dint° of pity. These are gracious drops.
Kind souls, what weep you when you but behold
Our Caesar's vesture wounded?° (*He flings* CAESAR'*s cloak aside*.) Look you here,
195　Here is himself, marred, as you see, with traitors.
(*The* CITIZENS *cry out in horror*.)
**FIRST CITIZEN.** O piteous spectacle!
**SECOND CITIZEN.** O noble Caesar!
**THIRD CITIZEN.** O woeful day!
**FOURTH CITIZEN.** O traitors, villains!
200　**FIRST CITIZEN.** O most bloody sight!
**SECOND CITIZEN.** We will be revenged.
**ALL** (*shouting*). Revenge! About! Seek! Burn! Fire! Kill! Slay!
Let not a traitor live! (*They start to leave*.)
**ANTONY** (*commandingly*). Stay, countrymen.

*dint*, effect.

*Caesar's vesture wounded*, the cuts in Caesar's clothing.

65 What effect is Antony trying to achieve by showing the body? How have his previous words led up to it?

205   **FIRST CITIZEN.** Peace there! Hear the noble Antony.

      **SECOND CITIZEN.** We'll hear him, we'll follow him, we'll die with
           him!

      *(The mob returns to* ANTONY.*)*

      **ANTONY.** Good friends, sweet friends, let me not stir you up
         To such a sudden flood of mutiny.
         They that have done this deed are honorable.

210       What private griefs° they have, alas, I know not,
         That made them do it. They are wise and honorable,
         And will no doubt with reasons answer you.
         I come not, friends, to steal away your hearts.
         I am no orator, as Brutus is,

215       But, as you know me all, a plain, blunt man,
         That love my friend; and that they know full well
         That gave me public leave to speak of him.
         For I have neither wit, nor words, nor worth,
         Action, nor utterance, nor the power of speech

220       To stir men's blood. I only speak right on.
         I tell you that which you yourselves do know,
         Show you sweet Caesar's wounds, poor poor dumb mouths,
         And bid them speak for me. But were I Brutus,
         And Brutus Antony, there were an Antony

225       Would ruffle up your spirits, and put a tongue
         In every wound of Caesar that should move
         The stones of Rome to rise and mutiny.

      *(The mob are now nearly uncontrollable and shout wildly.)*

      **ALL.** We'll mutiny!

      **FIRST CITIZEN.** We'll burn the house of Brutus.

230   **THIRD CITIZEN.** Away, then! Come, seek the conspirators.

      *(Again the mob starts to leave.)*

      **ANTONY.** Yet hear me, countrymen. Yet hear me speak.

      **ALL.** *(turning).* Peace, ho! Hear Antony. Most noble Antony!

      **ANTONY.** Why, friends, you go to do you know not what.
         Wherein hath Caesar thus deserved your loves?

235       Alas, you know not! I must tell you, then,
         You have forgot the will I told you of.

      *(He takes the will from his garment.)*

      **ALL** *(returning to him).* Most true. The will! Let's stay and hear
         the will.

      **ANTONY** *(showing it).* Here is the will, and under Caesar's seal.

      *(He breaks the seal, unrolls the scroll, and reads.)*
         To every Roman citizen he gives,

*private griefs,* personal reasons.

66 *Lines 213–220.* Is what Antony says in these lines true?

240      To every several° man, seventy-five drachmas.°

*(The mob murmurs its approval.)*

**SECOND CITIZEN.** Most noble Caesar! We'll revenge his death.

**THIRD CITIZEN.** O royal Caesar!

**ANTONY.**                  Hear me with patience.

**ALL.** Peace, ho!

**ANTONY.** Moreover, he hath left you all his walks,

245      His private arbors and new-planted orchards,

On this side Tiber;° he hath left them you,

And to your heirs forever—common pleasures,

To walk abroad and recreate yourselves.

Here was a Caesar! When comes such another?

250 **FIRST CITIZEN.** Never, never! Come, away, away!

We'll burn his body in the holy place,

And with the brands fire the traitors' houses.

Take up the body.

*(A group of* CITIZENS *take up* CAESAR's *bier.)*

**SECOND CITIZEN.** Go fetch fire!

255 **THIRD CITIZEN.** Pluck down benches!

**FOURTH CITIZEN.** Pluck down forms,° windows, anything!

*(The* CITIZENS, *bearing* CAESAR's *body aloft, exit at right door.)*

**ANTONY.** Now let it work. Mischief, thou art afoot,

Take thou what course thou wilt!

*(A* SERVANT *of* OCTAVIUS CAESAR *enters at left.)*

                       How now, fellow?

**SERVANT.** Sir, Octavius is already come to Rome.

260 **ANTONY.** Where is he?

**SERVANT.** He and Lepidus are at Caesar's house.

**ANTONY.** And thither will I straight to visit him.

He comes upon a wish. Fortune is merry,

And in this mood will give us anything.

265 **SERVANT.** I heard him say, Brutus and Cassius

Are rid° like madmen through the gates of Rome.

**ANTONY.** Belike they had some notice of the people,

How I had moved them. Bring me to Octavius.

*(*ANTONY *leads his* ATTENDANTS *and the* SERVANT *out at left door.)*

# SCENE 3

Rome. A street near the Forum. [Played on the Platform.]

CINNA *the poet enters through right door.* CITIZENS *follow, gesturing and looking at him suspiciously.*

---

**several,** individual.
**seventy-five drachmas** (drak′məz). Authorities disagree in estimating this amount; the figures vary from $10 to $100. Regardless, the purchasing power of any money was far greater then than it is now.

**On this side Tiber,** on this side of the Tiber, a river. Shakespeare shortened the phrase to maintain the rhythm of this speech.

**forms,** public benches.

**Are rid,** have ridden. Brutus and Cassius are fleeing from the wrath of the mob.

CINNA (*thoughtfully*). I dreamt tonight° that I did feast with Caesar,
    And things unluckily charge my fantasy.
    I have no will to wander forth of doors,
    Yet something leads me forth.

tonight, last night.

5 **FIRST CITIZEN** (*to* CINNA). What is your name?

**SECOND CITIZEN.** Whither are you going?

**THIRD CITIZEN.** Where do you dwell?

**FOURTH CITIZEN.** Are you a married man or a bachelor?

**SECOND CITIZEN.** Answer every man directly.

10 **FIRST CITIZEN.** Ay, and briefly.

**FOURTH CITIZEN.** Ay, and wisely.

**THIRD CITIZEN.** Ay, and truly, you were best.

(*The* CITIZENS *surround* CINNA *threateningly.*)

CINNA (*surprised*). What is my name? Whither am I going? Where
    do I dwell? Am I a married man or a bachelor? Then, to
15     answer every man directly and briefly, wisely and truly: wisely
    I say, I am a bachelor.

**SECOND CITIZEN.** That's as much as to say, they are fools that
    marry. You'll bear me a bang for that, I fear. Proceed directly.

CINNA. Directly, I am going to Caesar's funeral.

20 **FIRST CITIZEN.** As a friend or an enemy?

CINNA. As a friend.

**SECOND CITIZEN.** That matter is answered directly.

**FOURTH CITIZEN.** For your dwelling—briefly.

CINNA. Briefly, I dwell by the Capitol.

25 **THIRD CITIZEN.** Your name, sir, truly.

CINNA. Truly, my name is Cinna.

(CITIZENS *start back in anger, then take hold of* CINNA's *arms
and begin shaking him.*)

**FIRST CITIZEN.** Tear him to pieces! He's a conspirator!

CINNA (*desperately*). I am Cinna the poet, I am Cinna the poet!

**FOURTH CITIZEN.** Tear him for his bad verses, tear him for his bad
30     verses!

CINNA (*pleadingly*). I am not Cinna the conspirator.

**FOURTH CITIZEN.** It is no matter, his name's Cinna. Pluck but his
    name out of his heart, and turn him going.

**THIRD CITIZEN.** Tear him, tear him! Come, brands, ho!
35     Firebrands! To Brutus', to Cassius'; burn all! Some to Decius'
    house, and some to Casca's; some to Ligarius'. Away, go!

(CITIZENS *exit to the left, dragging off the struggling* CINNA.)

**67** What does this scene show about the nature of the commoners?

## THINK AND DISCUSS
### SCENE 1
#### Understanding
1. Describe the conspirators' mood before Caesar begins the Senate proceedings. Use specific details to support your answer.
2. Describe the events leading up to Caesar's assassination.

#### Analyzing
3. How do Antony's speeches to the conspirators show they should hesitate to trust him?
4. How does Brutus think he can overcome the danger of Antony's speaking to the people?
5. When and how does Antony reveal his true motives? What are they?

#### Extending
6. Would you say that Shakespeare's overall portrayal of Caesar, including his death, is favorable or unfavorable? Discuss.

### SCENES 2 AND 3
#### Understanding
1. Summarize in your own words the reasons Brutus gives the crowd for the assassination of Caesar.
2. How do the people react to Brutus' speech?

#### Analyzing
3. Give examples from Antony's speech that appeal to the following feelings of the crowd: their emotions about honor and ambition; their greed; their compassion; their capacity for hatred and revenge.
4. How does Scene 3 offer evidence of the success of Antony's speech?

#### Extending
5. One purpose of Scene 3 is to provide comic relief. Yet it shows a murderous mob setting upon an innocent man. In your judgment, what about it makes it humorous?

## REVIEWING: Foreshadowing  H𝕏
### See Handbook of Literary Terms, p. 800
Actions in plays often foreshadow events yet to come in the plot. For example, early in Act One the Soothsayer warns of Caesar's impending murder.

1. What hints can you find in Act Three that point to Antony's real plans for his speech at Caesar's funeral?
2. What does Antony's speech beginning, "Oh, pardon me, thou bleeding piece of earth . . ." foreshadow?

## VOCABULARY
### Etymology, Dictionary, and Glossary
In the Glossary, find the etymology—the origin or history—of each listed word. Then for each numbered statement that follows the list, write the word that the statement describes. You will not use all the words.

| | |
|---|---|
| parchment | sirrah |
| inter | discourse |
| prostrate | bequeath |

1. This word is derived from a Latin word meaning "a running about."
2. This word, now archaic, probably originated as a compound.
3. This word comes from a place name.
4. This word is derived from Latin words meaning "in earth."
5. This word comes from two Old English words.

## THINKING SKILLS
### Generalizing
Many readers recognize lines from speeches in *Julius Caesar* that have become famous

quotations used by public speakers in the modern world. For example, Antony's statement, "The evil that men do lives after them; / The good is oft interrèd with their bones," expresses one common belief about the fragile reputations of people who have died. To apply the statement to people other than Caesar involves **generalizing,** drawing a wider conclusion from a particular statement.

Other often-quoted lines from the play are shown here. They may be used to express ideas about people and issues that transcend the play. As a volunteer in your class reads each line aloud, you and your classmates can offer examples of circumstances in which a person might apply the idea or sentiment to a situation today. The class may then decide whether the line fits each proposed use.

1. Beware the ides of March. (deadly warning)
2. He thinks too much. Such men are dangerous.
3. It was Greek to me. (lack of understanding)
4. The fault . . . is not in our stars, but in ourselves.
5. *Et tu, Brutè!* (expression of surprise upon receiving an insult from a friend)

## COMPOSITION

### Giving Testimony as a Character

Publius, an elderly senator, accompanies the conspirators to Caesar's house (Act Two, Scene 4) and is with Caesar when Artemidorus tries to warn him (Act Three, Scene 1). Then Publius is stunned when he witnesses the assassination (Scene 2). Imagine that you are Publius and you have been asked by the Roman authorities to provide them with a deposition, a written account of what occurred that day. Review the scenes in which Publius appears and take notes as to what he saw. Then write a three- to five-paragraph paper beginning, "I, Publius, Roman Senator, hereby certify that what follows is an accurate account of what occurred on the ides of March."

### Analyzing the Commoners' Changing Role

The commoners have a major role in Act Three, appearing at the beginning of Scene 1 and in Scenes 2 and 3. In a three- to five-paragraph essay, discuss their emotions and how easily they are swayed by orators. If you wrote on this topic after Act One, you may wish to use that paper and your notes as you prepare to write this one. Decide whether you want to make a judgment about the commoners or to analyze how they are portrayed before you write your thesis or main idea. Then write and revise the essay to support that idea.

### Comparing the Public and Private Caesars

Julius Caesar is often said to have a private character that makes him behave naturally and a public character concerned only with projecting an image of greatness. Write a four- or five-paragraph essay for an audience of your classmates in which you analyze Caesar's public and private characters. Support your ideas with specific examples from the play. See "Writing to Compare and Contrast" in the Writer's Handbook.

## ENRICHMENT

### Readers Theater

Act Three is the high point of the play, with much activity and many speaking parts. The class as a whole can do a Readers Theater presentation of the act. One student should serve as director to coordinate the speaking parts. The number of students for each scene is: Scene 1, fourteen roles, including two servants; Scene 2, seven roles, including four citizens and a servant; Scene 3, five roles, including four citizens and Cinna.

# Comment

## *Julius Caesar* and the Tragic Hero

According to Aristotle's *Poetics*, an influential book on the nature of poetry and tragedy, a tragic hero is a man of high rank or station in life who possesses a tragic flaw that leads to his downfall. Though we have no hard evidence that Shakespeare ever read Aristotle, we do know that his tragic heroes tend to fit snugly into this definition.

A major problem arises, however, in dealing with *Julius Caesar:* who is the tragic hero, Caesar or Brutus? Since both characters can be seen to have tragic flaws—Caesar his arrogant ambition and Brutus his idealistic, impractical nature—each man has supporters who can advance convincing arguments in favor of their candidate.

Proponents of Caesar argue that since the play is named for him, he therefore must be its hero. They refute the argument that a character killed in Act Three cannot be a tragic hero by pointing out that Caesar's ghost or spirit pervades Acts Four and Five. Both Brutus and Cassius invoke his name at their hour of greatest travail, making clear that even though he is dead, his influence is still strong.

Those who maintain that Brutus is the tragic hero point out that audience interest centers on his inner conflict as Cassius seeks to draw him into the conspiracy; that it is to him Caesar speaks his final dying words; that his subsequent actions remain the almost constant focus of audience attention; and that it is his corpse over which the final eulogy is said—an honor traditionally reserved for the tragic hero. To these arguments may be added another: Shakespeare uses the soliloquy to help his audience understand the mental state of his major characters, and in *Julius Caesar* Brutus has several soliloquies while Caesar has none at all. This is a clear indication that Shakespeare at least wished to focus the attention and sympathy of his audience on Brutus.

By the time you finish the play, you should have your own definite ideas as to whom Shakespeare intended to be his tragic hero, Caesar or Brutus.

Brutus salutes Caesar in the 1953 M-G-M film *Julius Caesar*.

# ACT FOUR

## SCENE 1

A house in Rome. [Played in the Balcony-Stage Chamber.]

*For many months after* CAESAR's *death in March, 44* B.C., *chaos has reigned in Rome. The leading* CONSPIRATORS *have fled east to Greece and Asia Minor.* MARK ANTONY *has attempted to make himself virtual dictator of Rome, but has been opposed by young* OCTAVIUS CAESAR, *grandnephew and political heir of* JULIUS CAESAR; *and a devastating civil war has broken out. In October, 43* B.C., ANTONY *and* OCTAVIUS *agree to combine forces, and invite* M. AEMILIUS LEPIDUS, *one of* JULIUS CAESAR's *former lieutenants, to join them. Together they will control Rome—and rule the world.*

*The scene begins as the curtains of the balcony stage are drawn apart to reveal* ANTONY, OCTAVIUS, *and* LEPIDUS *seated around a table. They are scrutinizing a wax tablet which lists the names of those Romans who might oppose them. The three men are making plans to crush all opposition to their scheme.*

ANTONY. These many, then, shall die. Their names are pricked.°

OCTAVIUS. Your brother too must die. Consent you, Lepidus?

LEPIDUS. I do consent—

OCTAVIUS. Prick him down, Antony.

LEPIDUS. Upon condition Publius shall not live,
5 Who is your sister's son, Mark Antony.

ANTONY (*picking up the stylus°*). He shall not live. Look, with a
spot I damn him.°
But, Lepidus, go you to Caesar's house.
Fetch the will hither, and we shall determine
How to cut off some charge in legacies.°

10 LEPIDUS. What, shall I find you here?

OCTAVIUS. Or here, or at the Capitol.

(LEPIDUS *leaves at the door in the rear wall of the balcony stage.*)

ANTONY. This is a slight unmeritable man,
Meet to be sent on errands. Is it fit,
The threefold world divided, he should stand
15 One of the three to share it?

OCTAVIUS. So you thought him,
And took his voice who should be pricked to die
In our black sentence and proscription.°

ANTONY. Octavius, I have seen more days than you;
And though we lay these honors on this man,

---

*These many . . . pricked,*
the names of many men on
the list are marked for
death.

*stylus* (stī′ləs), a pointed
instrument for writing.

*with a spot I damn him,*
my mark condemns him to
death.

*we shall determine . . .
legacies.* Antony wishes to
find a way to reduce the
amount Caesar has
bequeathed each Roman.

**68** By this point in the
scene, Antony has
been involved in three
questionable activities.
What are they? What, if
anything, in earlier acts has
foreshadowed this
behavior?

*took his voice . . .
proscription,* accepted his
statements about who
should be marked for death
by our condemnation.

OCTAVIUS and ANTONY reach agreement.
The American Shakespeare Theatre.

20　To ease ourselves of divers sland'rous loads,°
　　He shall but bear them as the ass bears gold,
　　To groan and sweat under the business,
　　Either led or driven, as we point the way;
　　And having brought our treasure where we will,
25　Then take we down his load, and turn him off,
　　Like to the empty ass, to shake his ears
　　And graze in commons.°

**OCTAVIUS.**　　　　　　You may do your will;
　　But he's a tried and valiant soldier.

**ANTONY.** So is my horse, Octavius, and for that
30　I do appoint him store of provender.°
　　It is a creature that I teach to fight,
　　To wind, to stop, to run directly on,
　　His corporal motion governed by my spirit.
　　And, in some taste, is Lepidus but so.
35　He must be taught, and trained, and bid go forth—
　　A barren-spirited fellow, one that feeds
　　On objects, arts, and imitations,
　　Which, out of use and staled by other men,
　　Begin his fashion. Do not talk of him

*divers* (dī′vərz) *sland'rous loads,* various slanderous, or false, charges that may be leveled against us.

*commons,* public pastures.

*appoint . . . provender,* provide him with food.

**69** What do you expect will ultimately happen to Lepidus?

*Act Four, Scene 1* **561**

40 But as a property. And now, Octavius,
Listen great things. Brutus and Cassius
Are levying powers. We must straight make head.°
Therefore let our alliance be combined,
Our best friends made, our means stretched;
45 And let us presently go sit in council°
How covert matters may be best disclosed,
And open perils surest answered.°
OCTAVIUS. Let us do so, for we are at the stake,
And bayed about with many enemies;°
50 And some that smile have in their hearts, I fear,
Millions of mischiefs.
(*As* ANTONY *and* OCTAVIUS *exit, the curtains of the balcony stage are drawn closed.*)

# SCENE 2

Brutus' camp at Sardis, a city in Asia Minor. In front of Brutus' tent.
[Played on the Platform and the Inner Stage.]
*Several months have passed since* ANTONY *and* OCTAVIUS *made their plans.
Far from Rome,* BRUTUS *awaits the arrival of* CASSIUS, *whose actions have so troubled* BRUTUS *that he has asked him here for a conference.*

*The scene begins as* LUCIUS *enters the platform at inner-stage curtains. He then draws the curtains aside, revealing the interior of* BRUTUS' *tent. The interior is sparsely furnished with a table, some low stools, and a few cushions.*

*While* LUCIUS *busies himself within the tent,* BRUTUS *and a group of his* SOLDIERS *enter the platform at left door.* LUCILIUS *and* TITINIUS, *friends of* BRUTUS, *enter the platform at right. They have just returned from* CASSIUS' *camp and are accompanied by his servant* PINDARUS.

BRUTUS (*raising his arm in salute*). Stand, ho!°
LUCILIUS. Give the word, ho!° And stand.
BRUTUS. What now, Lucilius. Is Cassius near?
LUCILIUS. He is at hand, and Pindarus is come
5   To do you salutation° from his master.
BRUTUS. He greets me well. Your master, Pindarus,
In his own change, or by ill officers,°
Hath given me some worthy cause to wish
Things done, undone; but if he be at hand,
10   I shall be satisfied.°
PINDARUS.                I do not doubt

---

**Brutus and Cassius . . . head.** Brutus and Cassius were in Greece and Asia Minor, gathering forces; so must Antony and his associates.

**sit in council,** discuss.

**How covert . . . answered,** how hidden (covert) dangers may be discovered, and dangers already known be met most securely.

**we are at the stake . . . enemies,** we are tied to a stake, or post, while enemies bark like dogs about to attack us.

**Stand, ho!** Halt!
**Give the word, ho!** Tell the soldiers to halt.

**To do you salutation,** to bring you greeting.

**In his own . . . officers,** by his own change of heart or by bad advice from troublemakers.

**be satisfied,** find out.

But that my noble master will appear
Such as he is, full of regard and honor.
**BRUTUS.** He is not doubted. (*Motioning* LUCILIUS *aside*) A word,
    Lucilius,
How he received you; let me be resolved.°
15 **LUCILIUS.** With courtesy and with respect enough,
But not with such familiar instances,°
Nor with such free and friendly conference,
As he hath used of old.
**BRUTUS.**              Thou hast described
A hot friend cooling. Ever note, Lucilius,
20 When love begins to sicken and decay,
It useth an enforcèd ceremony.°
There are no tricks in plain and simple faith,
But hollow men, like horses hot at hand,
Make gallant show and promise of their mettle;
25 But when they should endure the bloody spur,
They fall their crests, and, like deceitful jades,
Sink in the trial. Comes his army on?
**LUCILIUS.** They mean this night in Sardis to be quartered.
The greater part, the horse in general,°
30 Are come with Cassius.
(*Martial music is heard offstage, followed by a* SENTRY's *ringing challenge and
the murmured answer.*)
**BRUTUS.**           Hark, he is arrived.
March gently on to meet him.
(CASSIUS, *with a group of his* SOLDIERS, *enters at right.*)
**CASSIUS** (*saluting*). Stand, ho!
**BRUTUS** (*returning the salute*). Stand, ho! Speak the word along.
**FIRST SOLDIER.** Stand!
35 **SECOND SOLDIER.** Stand!
**THIRD SOLDIER.** Stand!
**CASSIUS.** Most noble brother, you have done me wrong.
**BRUTUS.** Judge me, you gods! Wrong I mine enemies?
And, if not so, how should I wrong a brother?
40 **CASSIUS.** Brutus, this sober form of yours hides wrongs;
And when you do them—
**BRUTUS** (*interrupting*).      Cassius, be content;
Speak your griefs softly. I do know you well.
Before the eyes of both our armies here,
Which should perceive nothing but love from us,
45 Let us not wrangle. Bid them move away.

*A word . . . resolved.* Not content with Pindarus' assurance of Cassius' loyalty, Brutus wishes further report from Lucilius, his own man.
*familiar instances,* signs of friendship.

*enforcèd ceremony,* forced politeness.

70   What has happened to the relationship between Brutus and Cassius?

*the horse in general,* the regular cavalry.

Then in my tent, Cassius, enlarge your griefs,
And I will give you audience.

CASSIUS (*to his servant*).        Pindarus,
    Bid our commanders lead their charges off
    A little from this ground.

(PINDARUS, *followed by* CASSIUS' SOLDIERS, *departs at right.*)

50 BRUTUS. Lucilius, do you the like, and let no man
    Come to our tent till we have done our conference.
    Let Lucius and Titinius guard our door.

(BRUTUS *watches as his* SOLDIERS *follow* LUCILIUS *off at left.*
*Then he and* CASSIUS *move to the inner stage.*)

71 Why does Brutus take Cassius into his tent and have the door guarded? How is this scene similar to what occurred between Antony and Octavius in the preceding scene?

# SCENE 3

Sardis. Within Brutus' tent. [Played in the Inner Stage and on the Platform.]

*Only a few seconds have elapsed since the preceding scene.* LUCIUS *and* TITINIUS *guard the entrance to* BRUTUS' *tent.* BRUTUS *and* CASSIUS *stand facing each other on the inner stage.* CASSIUS *is very angry.*

CASSIUS. That you have wronged me doth appear in this:
    You have condemned and noted° Lucius Pella
    For taking bribes here of the Sardians,°
    Wherein my letters, praying on his side,
5    Because I knew the man, were slighted off.
BRUTUS. You wronged yourself to write in such a case.
CASSIUS. In such a time as this it is not meet
    That every offense should bear his comment.°
BRUTUS. Let me tell you, Cassius, you yourself
10    Are much condemned to have an itching palm,°
    To sell and mart° your offices for gold
    To undeservers.
CASSIUS (*hotly*).    I an itching palm?
    You know that you are Brutus that speaks this,
    Or, by the gods, this speech were else your last!
15 BRUTUS. The name of Cassius honors this corruption,
    And chastisement doth therefore hide his head.°
CASSIUS. Chastisement!
BRUTUS. Remember March, the ides of March remember.
    Did not great Julius bleed for justice' sake?
20    What villain touched his body that did stab

**noted**, disgraced.

**For taking . . . Sardians** (sär′dē ənz). Brutus had, on the Sardians' complaints, publicly accused Lucius Pella of embezzling public money and, finding him guilty, had condemned him.

**That every . . . comment**, that every minor offense should be criticized.

**to have an itching palm**, to be greedy for money.

**mart**, market.

72 *Lines 9–12.* Of what is Brutus accusing Cassius?

**The name of Cassius . . . head.** Because Cassius approves of these dishonest practices, no one can be punished.

And not for justice? What, shall one of us,
That struck the foremost man of all this world
But for supporting robbers,° shall we now
Contaminate our fingers with base bribes,
25 And sell the mighty space of our large honors
For so much trash as may be graspèd thus?
I had rather be a dog, and bay the moon,
Than such a Roman.

CASSIUS.                     Brutus, bait not me!
I'll not endure it. You forget yourself
30 To hedge me in.° I am a soldier, I,
Older in practice, abler than yourself
To make conditions.°

BRUTUS.                     Go to! You are not, Cassius.

CASSIUS. I am.

BRUTUS (firmly). I say you are not.

35 CASSIUS. Urge me no more, I shall forget myself.
Have mind upon your health. Tempt me no further.

BRUTUS (unconcernedly). Away, slight man!

CASSIUS (in amazement). Is't possible?

BRUTUS.                     Hear me, for I will speak.
Must I give way and room to your rash choler?°
40 Shall I be frighted when a madman stares?

CASSIUS. O ye gods, ye gods! Must I endure all this?

BRUTUS. All this! Ay, more. Fret till your proud heart break.
Go show your slaves how choleric you are,
And make your bondmen tremble. Must I budge?
45 Must I observe you? Must I stand and crouch
Under your testy humor? By the gods,
You shall digest the venom of your spleen
Though it do split you; for, from this day forth,
I'll use you for my mirth, yea, for my laughter,
50 When you are waspish.

CASSIUS (in disbelief).     Is it come to this?

BRUTUS. You say you are a better soldier.
Let it appear so; make your vaunting true,
And it shall please me well. For mine own part,
I shall be glad to learn of noble men.

55 CASSIUS (pleading). You wrong me every way! You wrong me,
     Brutus.
I said, an elder soldier, not a better.
Did I say "better"?

*That struck . . . robbers,*
who killed Caesar for
protecting dishonest public
figures.

*hedge me in,* interfere with
me.

*To make conditions,* to
plan the campaign and tend
to its details.

73 | Note that here and in
the next few lines
Brutus and Cassius resort
to childish argument and
name-calling. How should
the actors playing their
parts deliver the lines?

*rash choler* (kol′ ər),
violent temper.

74 | *Lines 42–50.* Of what
is Brutus accusing
Cassius? Is it only Cassius
who is displaying the
qualities mentioned in the
lines? Discuss.

BRUTUS (*indifferently*). If you did, I care not.

CASSIUS. When Caesar lived, he durst not thus have moved me.

BRUTUS. Peace, peace! You durst not so have tempted him.

60 CASSIUS. I durst not!

BRUTUS. No.

CASSIUS. What, durst not tempt him?

BRUTUS.                                        For your life you durst not.

CASSIUS (*hand on dagger*). Do not presume too much upon my
        love.
    I may do that I shall be sorry for.

65 BRUTUS. You have done that you should be sorry for.
    There is no terror, Cassius, in your threats,
    For I am armed so strong in honesty
    That they pass by me as the idle wind,
    Which I respect not. I did send to you
70  For certain sums of gold—which you denied me—
    For I can raise no money by vile means.
    By heaven, I had rather coin my heart
    And drop my blood for drachmas than to wring
    From the hard hands of peasants their vile trash
75  By any indirection.° I did send
    To you for gold to pay my legions,
    Which you denied me. Was that done like Cassius?
    Should I have answered Caius Cassius so?
    When Marcus Brutus grows so covetous
80  To lock such rascal counters° from his friends,
    Be ready, gods, with all your thunderbolts;
    Dash him to pieces!

CASSIUS.                        I denied you not.

BRUTUS. You did.

CASSIUS. I did not; he was but a fool that brought
85  My answer back. Brutus hath rived° my heart.
    A friend should bear his friend's infirmities,
    But Brutus makes mine greater than they are.

BRUTUS. I do not, till you practice them on me.

CASSIUS. You love me not.

BRUTUS (*coldly*).            I do not like your faults.

90 CASSIUS. A friendly eye could never see such faults.

BRUTUS. A flatterer's would not, though they do appear
    As huge as high Olympus.

CASSIUS (*tragically*). Come, Antony, and young Octavius, come,
    Revenge yourselves alone on Cassius,

*indirection*, devious or
hidden means.

*rascal counters*, worthless
coins.

75  *Lines 65–82.* Brutus
    here displays another
side of his character. Of
what does he boast? Why
does he need Cassius' aid?
Where do you suppose
Cassius might get the gold?

*rived*, split; broken.

95 For Cassius is aweary of the world;
Hated by one he loves, braved by his brother,
Checked like a bondman, all his faults observed,
Set in a notebook, learned, and conned by rote,°
To cast into my teeth. Oh, I could weep
100 My spirit from mine eyes! (*He unsheathes his dagger.*) There is
   my dagger,
And here my naked breast; within, a heart
Dearer than Pluto's mine,° richer than gold.
If that thou be'st a Roman, take it forth.
I, that denied thee gold, will give my heart.
105 Strike, as thou didst at Caesar; for I know,
When thou didst hate him worst, thou lovedst him better
Than ever thou lovedst Cassius.
BRUTUS (*his good humor returning*). Sheathe your dagger.
Be angry when you will, it shall have scope;
Do what you will, dishonor shall be humor.°
110 O Cassius, you are yokèd with a lamb
That carries anger as the flint bear fire,
Who, much enforcèd, shows a hasty spark,
And straight is cold again.
CASSIUS (*misunderstanding*). Hath Cassius lived
To be but mirth and laughter to his Brutus,
115 When grief and blood ill-tempered vexeth him?
BRUTUS. When I spoke that, I was ill-tempered too.
CASSIUS. Do you confess so much? Give me your hand.
BRUTUS. And my heart too.
CASSIUS (*with emotion*).        O Brutus!
BRUTUS.                          What's the matter?
CASSIUS. Have not you love enough to bear with me,
120 When that rash humor which my mother gave me
Makes me forgetful?
BRUTUS.            Yes, Cassius; and, from henceforth,
When you are over-earnest with your Brutus,
He'll think your mother chides, and leave you so.
(POET *enters through front of inner stage, followed by* LUCIUS,
TITINIUS, *and* LUCILIUS.)
POET (*pleadingly*). Let me go in to see the generals.°
125 There is some grudge between 'em, 'tis not meet
They be alone.
LUCILIUS (*firmly*). You shall not come to them.
POET. Nothing but death shall stay me.

*conned by rote*, memorized until letter-perfect.

*Pluto's mine*. Pluto, the god of the underworld, is here confused with Plutus, the Greek god of riches.

76 *Lines 93–107*. Cassius here gives up the argument. What does he ask Brutus to do, and why?

*dishonor shall be humor*, when you dishonor me by insults, I shall consider it merely your whim.

77 How does Cassius manage to sidestep the responsibility for his behavior?

*Let me . . . generals*. Some readers claim there is no reason for this episode, which ends on line 137, being in the play. However, Shakespeare may have included it as comic relief between the tension caused by Brutus and Cassius' argument and the emotion brought forth by the news that Brutus will reveal shortly after the poet leaves.

CASSIUS. How now? What's the matter?

POET (chidingly). For shame, you generals! What do you mean?

130 Love and be friends, as two such men should be;
For I have seen more years, I'm sure, than ye.

CASSIUS (amused). Ha, ha, how vilely doth this cynic rhyme!

BRUTUS (impatiently). Get you hence, sirrah. Saucy fellow, hence!

CASSIUS. Bear with him, Brutus. 'Tis his fashion.

135 BRUTUS. I'll know his humor, when he knows his time.
What should the wars do with these jigging fools?
Companion, hence! (He turns away.)

CASSIUS.                   Away, away, be gone!

(POET exits hastily through front of inner stage.)

BRUTUS. Lucilius and Titinius, bid the commanders
Prepare to lodge their companies tonight.

140 CASSIUS. And come yourselves, and bring Messala with you
Immediately to us.

(LUCILIUS and TITINIUS exit at left.)

BRUTUS.                   Lucius, a bowl of wine!

(LUCIUS crosses to the table, where he lights a taper° and pours a
bowl of wine for BRUTUS.)

CASSIUS (wryly). I did not think you could have been so angry.

BRUTUS. O Cassius, I am sick of many griefs.

CASSIUS. Of your philosophy you make no use,°

145 If you give place to accidental evils.

BRUTUS. No man bears sorrow better. Portia is dead.

CASSIUS. Ha! Portia?

BRUTUS. She is dead.

CASSIUS. How 'scaped I killing when I crossed you so?

150 O insupportable and touching loss!
Upon what sickness?

BRUTUS.                   Impatient of my absence,
And grief that young Octavius with Mark Antony
Have made themselves so strong—for with her death
That tidings came—with this she fell distract,

155 And, her attendants absent, swallowed fire.°

CASSIUS. And died so?

BRUTUS (nodding).     Even so.

CASSIUS.                   O ye immortal gods!

BRUTUS. Speak no more of her. Give me a bowl of wine.
In this I bury all unkindness, Cassius. (He drinks.)

CASSIUS. My heart is thirsty for that noble pledge.

160 Fill, Lucius, till the wine o'erswell the cup;

taper, candle.

*Of your philosophy . . .
use.* Brutus was a Stoic
(stō′ik). Believers in this
philosophy thought that
people should rise above
emotional upsets and be
unmoved by any of life's
happenings.

*swallowed fire.* Portia
reportedly snatched some
burning charcoal from a
fire and, holding it in her
closed mouth, stifled
herself and thus died.

78 Is Brutus as unfeeling
   as these words
suggest? Explain.

I cannot drink too much of Brutus' love.

(LUCIUS *pours a bowl of wine for* CASSIUS. *As he does so,* BRUTUS *greets* TITINIUS, *who has reentered the platform at left.* TITINIUS *is accompanied by* MESSALA, *a friend of* BRUTUS.)

BRUTUS. Come in, Titinius! Welcome, good Messala.
  Now sit we close about this taper here,
  And call in question our necessities.° (*They all sit at the table.*)

165 CASSIUS (*aside*). Portia, art thou gone?

BRUTUS (*aside, to* CASSIUS). No more, I pray you.
  (*To* MESSALA) Messala, I have here receivèd letters,
  That young Octavius and Mark Antony
  Come down upon us with a mighty power,
  Bending their expedition toward Philippi.° (*He unrolls a scroll.*)

170 MESSALA. Myself have letters of the selfsame tenor.°

BRUTUS. With what addition?

MESSALA. That by proscription and bills of outlawry°
  Octavius, Antony, and Lepidus
  Have put to death an hundred senators.

175 BRUTUS. Therein our letters do not well agree;
  Mine speak of seventy senators that died
  By their proscriptions, Cicero being one.

CASSIUS (*in disbelief*). Cicero one!

MESSALA. Cicero is dead,
  And by that order of proscription.

180 Had you your letters from your wife, my lord?

BRUTUS (*flatly*). No, Messala.

MESSALA. Nor nothing in your letters writ of her?

BRUTUS. Nothing, Messala.

MESSALA. That, methinks, is strange.

BRUTUS. Why ask you? Hear you aught of her in yours?

185 MESSALA. No, my lord.

BRUTUS (*showing interest*). Now, as you are a Roman, tell me
    true.

MESSALA. Then like a Roman bear the truth I tell:
  For certain she is dead, and by strange manner.

BRUTUS (*stoically*). Why, farewell, Portia. We must die, Messala.
190 With meditating that she must die once,
  I have the patience to endure it now.

MESSALA. Even so great men great losses should endure.

CASSIUS (*emotionally*). I have as much of this in art as you,
  But yet my nature could not bear it so.

195 BRUTUS. Well, to our work alive. What do you think

**call in question our necessities**, discuss our problems.

***Philippi*** (fə lip′ī), a city in ancient Macedonia, now part of Greece.

**of the selfsame tenor,** bearing the same tidings.

**bills of outlawry,** public notices declaring certain persons no longer protected by Roman law. As enemies of the state they may be killed.

79 Why might Cassius be surprised at Cicero's death?

80 Some scholars think this retelling of the news of Portia's death was the episode Shakespeare actually wanted to use in the play, but that he forgot to take out the earlier episode dealing with it. Others argue that the earlier episode provides a perfect reason for Brutus' uncharacteristic emotional tirade and that he shows his stoicism as he listens to Messala bring up the subject again. Do you think Shakespeare intended to keep one or both episodes?

Of marching to Philippi presently?°

CASSIUS. I do not think it good.

BRUTUS.                 Your reason?

CASSIUS.                       This it is:

'Tis better that the enemy seek us.

So shall he waste his means, weary his soldiers,

200    Doing himself offense; whilst we, lying still,

Are full of rest, defense, and nimbleness.

BRUTUS. Good reasons must of force give place to better.

The people 'twixt Philippi and this ground

Do stand but in a forced affection,

205    For they have grudged us contribution.

The enemy, marching along by them,

By them shall make a fuller number up,

Come on refreshed, new-added, and encouraged;

From which advantage shall we cut him off

210    If at Philippi we do face him there,

These people at our back.

CASSIUS (pleading).        Hear me, good brother.

BRUTUS. Under your pardon. You must note beside

That we have tried the utmost of our friends,

Our legions are brimfull, our cause is ripe.

215    The enemy increaseth every day;

We, at the height, are ready to decline.

There is a tide in the affairs of men,

Which, taken at the flood, leads on to fortune;

Omitted, all the voyage of their life

220    Is bound in shallows and in miseries.

On such a full sea are we now afloat,

And we must take the current when it serves,

Or lose our ventures.

CASSIUS (resignedly).    Then, with your will, go on.

We'll along ourselves, and meet them at Philippi.

225 BRUTUS. The deep of night is crept upon our talk,

And nature must obey necessity,

Which we will niggard° with a little rest.

There is no more to say?

CASSIUS.               No more. Good night.

Early tomorrow will we rise, and hence.

230 BRUTUS (standing). Lucius! My gown. (To the three others)

    Farewell, good Messala.

Good night, Titinius. Noble, noble Cassius,

*presently,* immediately.

**81** *Lines 195–223.* Here again Brutus makes an error in judgment, but Cassius lets him have his way. Why does Brutus think they should go to Philippi? Why does Cassius disagree?

*we will niggard,* we will satisfy somewhat.

Good night, and good repose.

CASSIUS.                               O my dear brother!

This was an ill beginning of the night.

Never come such division 'tween our souls!

235   Let it not, Brutus.

BRUTUS.                   Everything is well.

CASSIUS. Good night, my lord.

BRUTUS. Good night, good brother.

TITINIUS *and* MESSALA. Good night, Lord Brutus.

BRUTUS.                                   Farewell,
    everyone.

(CASSIUS, TITINIUS, *and* MESSALA *move from the inner stage to
the platform and exit at right.* LUCIUS *unfolds his master's night
robe.*)

Give me the gown. Where is thy instrument?°

240   LUCIUS. Here in the tent.

BRUTUS.                     What, thou speak'st drowsily?

Poor knave,° I blame thee not; thou art o'erwatched.°

Call Claudius and some other of my men;

I'll have them sleep on cushions in my tent.

LUCIUS (*moving onto platform*). Varro and Claudius!

(VARRO *and* CLAUDIUS, *entering at left, cross to inner stage.*)

245   VARRO. Calls my lord?

BRUTUS. I pray you, sirs, lie in my tent and sleep.

It may be I shall raise you by and by

On business to my brother Cassius.

VARRO. So please you, we will stand and watch your pleasure.

250   BRUTUS. I will not have it so. Lie down, good sirs.

It may be I shall otherwise bethink me.

(VARRO *and* CLAUDIUS *lie down.*)

Look, Lucius, here's the book I sought for so;

I put it in the pocket of my gown.

LUCIUS. I was sure your lordship did not give it me.

255   BRUTUS. Bear with me, good boy, I am much forgetful.

Canst thou hold up thy heavy eyes awhile,

And touch thy instrument a strain or two?

LUCIUS. Ay, my lord, an't° please you.

BRUTUS.                               It does, my boy.

I trouble thee too much, but thou art willing.

260   LUCIUS. It is my duty, sir.

BRUTUS. I should not urge thy duty past thy might;

I know young bloods look for a time of rest. (*He seats himself.*)

---

**thy instrument,** your lute.

**knave,** lad.

**thou art o'erwatched.**
Lucius has been up too
long and is exhausted.

**an't,** if it.

LUCIUS. I have slept, my lord, already.

BRUTUS. It was well done; and thou shalt sleep again;

265     I will not hold thee long. If I do live,

    I will be good to thee.

(LUCIUS *sits on some cushions near the table and plays and sings, gradually falling asleep.*)

BRUTUS. This is a sleepy tune. O murderous slumber,

    Layest thou thy leaden mace° upon my boy,

    That plays thee music? Gentle knave, good night;

270     I will not do thee so much wrong to wake thee.

    If thou dost nod, thou break'st thy instrument;

    I'll take it from thee. And, good boy, good night.

(*He removes* LUCIUS' *instrument.*)

    Let me see, let me see; is not the leaf turned down°

    Where I left reading? Here it is, I think. (*He begins to read.*)

(*The* GHOST OF CAESAR *slowly ascends through the trap door in the floor of the inner stage.*)

275     How ill this taper burns! Ha! Who comes here?

    I think it is the weakness of mine eyes

    That shapes this monstrous apparition.

    It comes upon me. Art thou any thing?

    Art thou some god, some angel, or some devil,

280     That mak'st my blood cold and my hair to stare?

    Speak to me what thou art.

GHOST (*in sepulchral tones*). Thy evil spirit, Brutus.

BRUTUS.                                 Why com'st

    thou?

GHOST. To tell thee thou shalt see me at Philippi.

BRUTUS. Well; then I shall see thee again?

285 GHOST. Ay, at Philippi.

BRUTUS. Why, I will see thee at Philippi, then.

(*The* GHOST *descends.*)

    Now I have taken heart thou vanishest.

    Ill spirit, I would hold more talk with thee.

    Boy, Lucius! Varro! Claudius! Sirs, awake!

290     Claudius!

LUCIUS (*still half-asleep*). The strings, my lord, are false.

BRUTUS. He thinks he still is at his instrument.

    Lucius, awake!

LUCIUS. My lord?

BRUTUS. Didst thou dream, Lucius, that thou so criedst out?

295 LUCIUS. My lord, I do not know that I did cry.

**thy leaden mace.** Morpheus (môr′fē əs), the Greek god of dreams, carried a leaden club with which he cast the spell of slumber.

**the leaf turned down,** an anachronism. Roman books were in the form of scrolls; there were no pages to turn down.

**82** In Shakespeare's source, Plutarch, what appeared to Brutus was a ghost calling itself Brutus' "evil genius." How has Shakespeare heightened the dramatic effect by changing this to the ghost of Caesar?

**BRUTUS.** Yes, that thou didst. Didst thou see anything?

**LUCIUS.** Nothing, my lord.

**BRUTUS.** Sleep again, Lucius. Sirrah Claudius!

(*To* VARRO) Fellow thou, awake!

**VARRO.**                    My lord?

**CLAUDIUS.**                              My lord?

300 **BRUTUS.** Why did you so cry out, sirs, in your sleep?

**VARRO** *and* **CLAUDIUS.** Did we, my lord?

**BRUTUS.**                              Ay. Saw you anything?

**VARRO.** No, my lord, I saw nothing.

**CLAUDIUS.**                    Nor I, my lord.

**BRUTUS.** Go and commend me to my brother Cassius.

Bid him set on his powers betimes before,°

305 And we will follow.

**VARRO** *and* **CLAUDIUS.** It shall be done, my lord.

(VARRO *and* CLAUDIUS *move from the inner stage to the platform and exit at right.* BRUTUS *and* LUCIUS *remain on the inner stage as the curtains are drawn closed.*)

**83** Why might Brutus have awakened these others to ask if they had seen anything?

***set on . . . before,*** start his forces moving ahead.

---

## THINK AND DISCUSS
### SCENE 1
**Understanding**

1. What is the reason for the disagreement between Antony and Octavius?
2. What points does Antony make in winning the argument?

**Analyzing**

3. What significant decision do the two men make at the end of the scene?
4. Does Antony's general ruthlessness surprise you? Why or why not?

**Extending**

5. Do you think this scene in any way suggests the way military or political leaders in our modern world behave? Explain.

### SCENES 2 AND 3
**Understanding**

1. What has caused the quarrel between Brutus and Cassius?
2. What unfavorable qualities of Brutus are revealed during his argument with Cassius?
3. What does he finally say is the reason for his ill temper?
4. What plan of action do Brutus and Cassius adopt after their quarrel?

**Analyzing**

5. Review the episode where Cassius first arrives outside Brutus' tent. Is the conduct of each man consistent with what you have learned of their personalities to this point? Discuss.
6. How does the report about Portia affect your

feelings about Brutus, concerning his treatment of Cassius in this scene?

7. Considering Cassius' and Brutus' opposing opinions of their plan of action for carrying out the war, do you think they make the right decision? Discuss.

8. Things seem to be looking up for Brutus after his meeting with Cassius. What then happens during the night, and how does it change his mood?

**Extending**

9. Do you think that Shakespeare uses good showmanship in having the poet break into Brutus' tent? Why or why not?

## VOCABULARY
### Word Structure: Prefixes and Root Words

The Latin prefix *en-* means "to cause to be," as in *enfeeble*, or "to put on or in," as in *enthrone*. Form new words by adding *en-* to the words listed here. Then choose the correct new words to complete the sentences that follow, changing tenses or endings as necessary. You will not use all the words.

circle   rich   noble
large   shrine   venom

1. The student council's treasury was _____ from the profits of the car wash.

2. This photograph is so vivid that we want to _____ it to hang it on the wall.

3. The swimming pool at the club is completely _____ with flowers and shrubs.

4. The local headhunters used to _____ their darts with the juice of a native plant.

5. Roberto's show of courage, saving the baby from the fire, _____ him in our view.

## COMPOSITION ✑
### Writing About Portia's Role

In order to discuss Portia, consider the scenes in which she appears or is mentioned: Act Two, Scenes 1 and 4, and Act Four, Scene 2. Take notes that will help you describe her character and discuss her importance to the play in an essay at least three paragraphs long. Support your thesis statement with evidence from those scenes and, if you wish, other scenes. See "Writing About Characters" in the Writer's Handbook for help with prewriting, writing, and revising.

### Discussing Brutus' Character

Discuss the changes that have taken place in Brutus' character since the death of Caesar. Pay particular attention to the way he greets Cassius in Scene 2 and their ensuing argument in Scene 3. Take notes that will help you support your statements with evidence. Use your last paragraph to explain the reasons for as many of these changes as you can. Your paper should be at least three paragraphs long. See "Writing About Characters" in the Writer's Handbook.

## ENRICHMENT
### Group Activity: Mass Media

Your class can prepare a television-style special report on the aftermath of the assassination of Caesar. The special "broadcast"—to be performed in class or videotaped—is to take place on the eve of the final battle between the two sides in the play.

The following roles are needed: a news "anchor" can write and deliver the introduction, set up the order of interviews and commentaries, and introduce interviewers, interviewees, and commentators. Interviewees may include Antony, Brutus, Cassius, Lucius, Calpurnia, Octavius, the Soothsayer, and others, including commoners. Students playing these characters will review their roles in the play to be able to respond to questions; they may prepare by answering some questions in writing. Two to four interviewers, depending on class size, will divide the interviews equally and prepare questions. Two commentators, one pro-Caesar, one pro-Brutus, will each write and deliver a commentary. There should be a role for everyone in the class, if possible. Students not "on-camera" may constitute the audience.

# ACT FIVE

## SCENE 1

The Plains of Philippi. [Played on the Platform.]
*The combined armies of* BRUTUS *and* CASSIUS *are about to engage the combined
forces of* ANTONY *and* OCTAVIUS. *Offstage can be heard occasional battle
sounds. There is a brief silence; then* OCTAVIUS *enters at right, followed by*
ANTONY *and a few* OFFICERS.

OCTAVIUS. Now, Antony, our hopes are answered.
   You said the enemy would not come down,
   But keep the hills and upper regions.
   It proves not so. Their battles° are at hand;

 5   They mean to warn° us at Philippi here,
   Answering before we do demand of them.
ANTONY. Tut, I am in their bosoms,° and I know
   Wherefore they do it. They could be content
   To visit other places,° and come down

10   With fearful bravery, thinking by this face
   To fasten in our thoughts that they have courage;
   But 'tis not so.
*(A* MESSENGER *enters from left.)*
MESSENGER.    Prepare you, generals.
   The enemy comes on in gallant show;
   Their bloody sign° of battle is hung out,

15   And something to be done immediately.
ANTONY. Octavius, lead your battle softly on
   Upon the left hand of the even field.
OCTAVIUS. Upon the right hand I; keep thou the left.
ANTONY *(angrily)*. Why do you cross me in this exigent?

20 OCTAVIUS *(stubbornly)*. I do not cross you; but I will do so.
*(Drum beat.* BRUTUS, CASSIUS, LUCILIUS, TITINIUS, MESSALA, *and
certain troops enter at left. The two armies stand facing.)*
BRUTUS *(to* CASSIUS*)*. They stand, and would have parley.
CASSIUS *(to* TITINIUS*)*. Stand fast, Titinius. We must out and talk.
*(*BRUTUS *and* CASSIUS *move toward* ANTONY *and* OCTAVIUS.*)*
OCTAVIUS *(nervously)*. Mark Antony, shall we give sign of battle?
ANTONY. No, Caesar, we will answer on their charge.°

25   Make forth.° The generals would have some words.
*(He goes to* BRUTUS *and* CASSIUS.*)*
OCTAVIUS *(to his men)*. Stir not until the signal. *(He joins* ANTONY.*)*

*battles,* armies.
*warn,* challenge.

*bosoms,* secret councils.

*They could . . . places,*
they would prefer to be
elsewhere.

*bloody sign,* red flag.

84 | Has the relationship
between Antony and
Octavius changed much
since they last appeared?
Discuss.

*answer . . . charge,* fight
when they attack us.
*Make forth,* step out ahead
of the troops.

**BRUTUS.** Words before blows. Is it so, countrymen?

**OCTAVIUS** (*jeeringly*). Not that we love words better, as you do.

**BRUTUS.** Good words are better than bad strokes, Octavius.

30 **ANTONY.** In your bad strokes, Brutus, you give good words.
    Witness the hole you made in Caesar's heart,
    Crying "Long live! Hail! Caesar!"

**CASSIUS.**                              Antony,
    The posture of your blows are yet unknown;
    But for your words, they rob the Hybla bees,°
35  And leave them honeyless.

**ANTONY.** Not stingless too?

**BRUTUS.**                    O, yes, and soundless too.
    For you have stolen their buzzing, Antony,
    And very wisely threat before you sting.

**ANTONY** (*furious*). Villains! You did not so, when your vile daggers
40  Hacked one another in the sides of Caesar.
    You showed your teeth like apes, and fawned like hounds,
    And bowed like bondmen, kissing Caesar's feet,
    Whilst damnèd Casca, like a cur, behind
    Struck Caesar on the neck. O you flatterers!

45 **CASSIUS** (*to* BRUTUS, *angrily*). Flatterers? Now, Brutus, thank
        yourself!
    This tongue had not offended so today
    If Cassius might have ruled.

**OCTAVIUS.** Come, come, the cause. If arguing make us sweat,
    The proof of it will turn to redder drops.
50  Look, (*He draws.*)
    I draw a sword against conspirators.
    When think you that the sword goes up again?
    Never, till Caesar's three and thirty wounds
    Be well avenged, or till another Caesar
55  Have added slaughter to the sword of traitors.

**BRUTUS.** Caesar, thou canst not die by traitors' hands,
    Unless thou bring'st them with thee.

**OCTAVIUS** (*smugly*).                 So I hope.
    I was not born to die on Brutus' sword.

**BRUTUS** (*angrily*). O, if thou wert the noblest of thy strain,°
60  Young man, thou couldst not die more honorable.

**CASSIUS** (*jeeringly*). A peevish schoolboy, worthless of such honor,
    Joined with a masker and a reveler!

**ANTONY.** Old Cassius still.

**OCTAVIUS.**              Come, Antony, away!

*Hybla* (hī′ blə) *bees,* bees from Hybla, an area in ancient Sicily famous for its honey.

85 | What is Cassius referring to?

*strain,* lineage.

Defiance, traitors, hurl we in your teeth.

65 If you dare fight today, come to the field;

If not, when you have stomachs.

(ANTONY, OCTAVIUS, *and the armies turn and leave at right.*)

CASSIUS. Why, now, blow wind, swell billow, and swim bark!

The storm is up, and all is on the hazard.

BRUTUS. Ho, Lucilius! Hark, a word with you.

LUCILIUS (*comes up to* BRUTUS).          My lord?

(*They converse apart.*)

70 CASSIUS. Messala!

MESSALA (*comes up to* CASSIUS). What says my general?

CASSIUS.                           Messala,

This is my birthday; as this very day

Was Cassius born. Give me thy hand, Messala.

Be thou my witness that against my will,

As Pompey was, am I compelled to set

75 Upon one battle all our liberties.

You know that I held Epicurus° strong

And his opinion. Now I change my mind,

And partly credit things that do presage.

Coming from Sardis, on our former ensign°

80 Two mighty eagles fell, and there they perched,

Gorging and feeding from our soldiers' hands,

Who to Philippi here consorted us.

This morning are they fled away and gone,

And in their steads do ravens, crows, and kites

85 Fly o'er our heads, and downward look on us,

As we were sickly prey. Their shadows seem

A canopy most fatal, under which

Our army lies, ready to give up the ghost.

MESSALA. Believe not so.

CASSIUS.                I but believe it partly,

90 For I am fresh of spirit, and resolved

To meet all perils very constantly.

BRUTUS (*ending the conversation*). Even so, Lucilius.

CASSIUS.                     Now, most

noble Brutus,

The gods today stand friendly, that we may,

Lovers in peace, lead on our days to age!°

95 But since the affairs of men rest still incertain,

Let's reason with the worst that may befall.

If we do lose this battle, then is this

*Epicurus* (ep′ə kyür′əs), Greek philosopher who did not believe in omens or superstitions.

*former ensign,* foremost or forwardmost standard bearer.

**86** What reasons is Cassius giving for being pessimistic about the outcome of the battle?

*Now . . . days to age.* Cassius hopes that the gods will be on their side so the two will end their days as friends in peaceful times.

The very last time we shall speak together.
What are you then determinèd to do?

100 **BRUTUS.** Even by the rule of that philosophy
By which I did blame Cato for the death
Which he did give himself°—I know not how,
But I do find it cowardly and vile,
For fear of what might fall, so to prevent
105 The time of life°—arming myself with patience
To stay the providence of some high powers
That govern us below.°

**CASSIUS** (*unbelievingly*). Then, if we lose this battle,
You are contented to be led in triumph
Through the streets of Rome?

110 **BRUTUS.** No, Cassius, no; think not, thou noble Roman,
That ever Brutus will go bound to Rome;
He bears too great a mind. But this same day
Must end that work the ides of March begun;
And whether we shall meet again I know not.
115 Therefore, our everlasting farewell take.
Forever, and forever, farewell, Cassius!
If we do meet again, why, we shall smile;
If not, why then this parting was well made.

**CASSIUS.** Forever, and forever, farewell, Brutus!
120 If we do meet again, we'll smile indeed;
If not, 'tis true this parting was well made.

**BRUTUS.** Why, then, lead on. O, that a man might know
The end of this day's business ere it come!
But if sufficeth that the day will end,
125 And then the end is known. Come, ho! Away!
(**BRUTUS** *and* **CASSIUS** *move off at right.*)


# SCENE 2

The field of battle. [Played on the Platform.]

*The battle is well under way.* **BRUTUS** *and his followers form the left flank of the combined army and face the forces of* **OCTAVIUS;** **CASSIUS** *and his men form the right flank and are opposed to* **ANTONY.** **BRUTUS,** *with* **MESSALA** *following, enters at left. He has prepared various dispatches which he must send to* **CASSIUS.**

**BRUTUS.** Ride, ride, Messala, ride, and give these bills
Unto the legions on the other side.

*Even by . . . give himself.* Stoicism, the philosophy Brutus followed, did not favor suicide; thus Brutus blamed his father-in-law Cato for killing himself.

*prevent the time of life,* cut short one's own life by suicide.

*To stay . . . below,* to await (stay) a normal death to be sent when the gods so decree.

**87** *Lines 92–125.* These lines show that Brutus and Cassius have set aside their earlier quarrel. Why might they now be so friendly? What do the lines reveal about their characters in the face of danger?

*(Loud alarums° are heard offstage.)*

Let them set on at once; for I perceive

But cold demeanor in Octavius' wing,

5 And sudden push gives them the overthrow.

Ride, ride, Messala. Let them all come down.

*(BRUTUS and MESSALA exit, going in different directions.)*

**alarums,** trumpet blasts, drum beats, and other calls to arms, or battle alarms.

88 Brutus sees signs of faltering (cold demeanor) in Octavius' men and thinks one strong attack will overcome them. What is in the message he sends to Cassius?

# SCENE 3

A hill in another part of the battlefield. [Played on the Platform and the Balcony.]

*It is now late afternoon. Several* SOLDIERS, *weary from the fighting, enter at right and group themselves near the left pillar. As offstage alarums sound,* CASSIUS *and* TITINIUS *enter at right.* CASSIUS, *carrying a broken standard, speaks angrily.*

CASSIUS *(pointing to right).* Oh, look, Titinius, look, the villains fly!°

Myself have to mine own turned enemy;°

This ensign here of mine was turning back;

I slew the coward, and did take it° from him.

5 TITINIUS. O Cassius, Brutus gave the word too early,

Who, having some advantage on Octavius,

Took it too eagerly. His soldiers fell to spoil,°

Whilst we by Antony are all enclosed.

*(CASSIUS tosses the broken standard to the* SOLDIERS. *As they move off at left,* PINDARUS, CASSIUS' *servant, runs on at right.)*

PINDARUS. Fly further off, my lord, fly further off!

10 Mark Antony is in your tents, my lord.

Fly, therefore, noble Cassius, fly far off.

CASSIUS. This hill is far enough. Look, look, Titinius!

Are those my tents where I perceive the fire?

TITINIUS. They are, my lord.

CASSIUS.                              Titinius, if thou lovest me,

15 Mount thou my horse, and hide thy spurs in him,

Till he have brought thee up to yonder troops

And here again, that I may rest assured

Whether yond troops are friend or enemy.°

TITINIUS. I will be here again, even with a thought.°

*(He exits at right.)*

20 CASSIUS *(pointing to balcony).* Go, Pindarus, get higher on that hill.

My sight was ever thick.° Regard Titinius,

And tell me what thou not'st about the field.

*fly,* flee.

*Myself . . . enemy.* Cassius has had to turn on some of his own men who were deserting. Even an ensign was in headlong flight.

*it,* the ensign's standard.

*fell to spoil,* began plundering Octavius' camp.

89 How is it Brutus' fault that Cassius' men have been encircled (enclosed) by Antony's forces?

*that I may . . . enemy.* Cassius wonders if the horsemen approaching are from his or Brutus' army, or are Antony's men.

*even . . . thought,* quick as a thought.

*My sight . . . thick.* I've always been nearsighted.

*Act Five, Scene 3* **579**

(PINDARUS *exits at inner-stage curtains to ascend the hill.*)
    This day I breathèd first. Time is come round,
    And where I did begin, there shall I end.°
25  My life is run his compass. Sirrah, what news?
  PINDARUS (*appearing above*). O my lord!
  CASSIUS. What news?
  PINDARUS. Titinius is enclosèd round about
    With horsemen, that make to him on the spur;
30  Yet he spurs on. Now they are almost on him.
    Now, Titinius! Now some light.° Oh, he
    Lights too. He's ta'en.
(*There are shouts offstage.*)
              And, hark! They shout for joy.
  CASSIUS. Come down, behold no more.
    Oh, coward that I am, to live so long,
35  To see my best friend ta'en before my face!
(PINDARUS *exits at balcony curtains in order to descend from the hill. In a moment he rejoins* CASSIUS.)
    Come hither, sirrah.
    In Parthia° did I take thee prisoner;
    And then I swore thee, saving of thy life,
    That whatsoever I did bid thee do,
40  Thou shouldst attempt it. Come now, keep thine oath.
    Now be a freeman, and with this good sword,
    That ran through Caesar's bowels, search this bosom.°
    Stand not to answer. Here, take thou the hilts;
    And, when my face is covered, as 'tis now,
45  Guide thou the sword.
(PINDARUS *obeys and stabs* CASSIUS.)
              Caesar, thou art revenged.
    Even with the sword that killèd thee. (CASSIUS *dies.*)
  PINDARUS. So, I am free; yet would not so have been,
    Durst I have done my will. O Cassius!
    Far from this country Pindarus shall run,
50  Where never Roman shall take note of him.
(PINDARUS, *leaving* CASSIUS' *sword behind, hastens to left door and exits. Then* TITINIUS, *with* MESSALA, *reenters at right. On his head* TITINIUS *wears a garland signifying victory.*)
  MESSALA. It is but change,° Titinius; for Octavius
    Is overthrown by noble Brutus' power,
    As Cassius' legions are by Antony.
  TITINIUS. These tidings will well comfort Cassius.

**This day . . . end,** I shall die on the same day I was born.

**light,** dismount.

**90** What does Cassius think has happened to his friend Titinius?

**Parthia** (pär′thē ə), an ancient country in Asia.

**Now be . . . bosom,** Cassius will give Pindarus his freedom if Pindarus will kill Cassius. It was a custom in ancient warfare to avoid the shame of captivity at all costs, even death, to preserve military honor.

**91** What is ironic about Cassius' manner of death?

**but change,** a fair exchange.

55 MESSALA. Where did you leave him?

TITINIUS.                    All disconsolate,
  With Pindarus his bondman, on this hill.

MESSALA. Is not that he that lies upon the ground?

TITINIUS (running forward). He lies not like the living. O my heart!

MESSALA. Is not that he?

TITINIUS (sadly).          No, this was he, Messala,
60  But Cassius is no more. O setting sun,
  As in thy red rays thou dost sink tonight,
  So in his red blood Cassius' day is set!
  The sun of Rome is set. Our day is gone;
  Clouds, dews, and dangers come; our deeds are done!
65  Mistrust of my success hath done this deed.

MESSALA. Mistrust of good success hath done this deed.
  O hateful error, melancholy's child,
  Why dost thou show to the apt thoughts of men
  The things that are not?° O error, soon conceived,
70  Thou never com'st unto a happy birth,
  But kill'st the mother that engendered thee!

TITINIUS (calling). What, Pindarus? Where art thou, Pindarus?

MESSALA. Seek him, Titinius, whilst I go to meet
  The noble Brutus, thrusting his report
75  Into his ears. I may say "thrusting" it;
  For piercing steel and darts envenomèd
  Shall be as welcome to the ears of Brutus
  As tidings of this sight.

TITINIUS.              Hie, you, Messala,
  And I will seek for Pindarus the while.

(As MESSALA exits at left, TITINIUS kneels beside CASSIUS.)
80  Why didst thou send me forth, brave Cassius?
  Did I not meet thy friends?° And did not they
  Put on my brows this wreath of victory,
  And bid me give it thee? Didst thou not hear their shouts?
  Alas, thou hast misconstrued everything!
85  But, hold thee, take this garland on thy brow.

(He places the wreath on CASSIUS' head.)
  Thy Brutus bid me give it thee, and I
  Will do his bidding. (He rises.) Brutus, come apace,
  And see how I regarded Caius Cassius. (He takes CASSIUS' sword.)
  By your leave, gods!—This is a Roman's part.°
90  Come, Cassius' sword, and find Titinius' heart. (Kills himself.)

(Alarums offstage. MESSALA reenters at left with BRUTUS, YOUNG

*Why dost thou . . . not?*
Why do men so readily
accept things as true when
they are really not?

*thy friends,* that is, Brutus'
man Messala and his army.

92 | What really happened
   | to Titinius?

*This is a Roman's part.*
The Romans prided
themselves on being
freemen. Titinius decides
to avoid capture, according
to the ancient Roman
custom.

CATO, STRATO, VOLUMNIUS, LUCILIUS, *and several* SOLDIERS.)

**BRUTUS.** Where, where, Messala, doth his body lie?

**MESSALA.** Lo, yonder, and Titinius mourning it.

**BRUTUS.** Titinius' face is upward.

**CATO** (*going to* TITINIUS).                He is slain.

**BRUTUS.** O Julius Caesar, thou art mighty yet!

95      Thy spirit walks abroad, and turns our swords
        In our own proper entrails.

(*There are low alarums offstage.*)

**CATO.**                             Brave Titinius!
        Look whether he have not crowned dead Cassius!

**BRUTUS.** Are yet two Romans living such as these?
        The last of all the Romans, fare thee well!

100     It is impossible that ever Rome
        Should breed thy fellow. Friends, I owe moe tears
        To this dead man than you shall see me pay.
        I shall find time, Cassius, I shall find time.

(*He motions to the* SOLDIERS, *who pick up the bodies of* CASSIUS
*and* TITINIUS.)

        Come, therefore, and to Thasos° send his body.

105     His funerals shall not be in our camp,
        Lest it discomfort us. Lucilius, come,
        And come, young Cato, let us to the field.
        Labeo and Flavius, set our battles on:
        'Tis three o'clock; and, Romans, yet ere night

110     We shall try fortune in a second fight. (*All exit at left.*)


# SCENE 4

Another part of the battlefield. [Played on the Platform.]

*Alarum.* BRUTUS, *exhausted, runs on from right, sword in hand, followed by*
MESSALA, YOUNG CATO, LUCILIUS, *and* FLAVIUS.


**BRUTUS** (*encouragingly*). Yet, countrymen, O, yet hold up your
        heads! (*He,* MESSALA, *and* FLAVIUS *run off left.*)

**CATO.** Who will go with me?
        I will proclaim my name about the field:
        I am the son of Marcus Cato, ho!

5       A foe to tyrants, and my country's friend.
        I am the son of Marcus Cato, ho!

(ANTONY'S SOLDIERS *run on from right, fight with* LUCILIUS *and*
YOUNG CATO.)


**93** What does Brutus mean in these lines?

*Thasos* (thä′sôs), an island in the Aegean Sea.

LUCILIUS (*hitting his chest*). And I am Brutus, Marcus Brutus I!
  Brutus, my country's friend! Know me for Brutus!
(YOUNG CATO *is slain by* ANTONY'S SOLDIERS.)
  O young and noble Cato, art thou down?
10  Why, now thou diest as bravely as Titinius,
  And mayst be honored, being Cato's son. (*He stands mourning.*)
FIRST SOLDIER. Yield, or thou diest.
LUCILIUS.                    Only I yield to die.°

Only I . . . die, I yield
only to die immediately.

(*Handing over his sword*)
There is so much that thou wilt kill me straight;
  Kill Brutus, and be honor'd in his death.
15  FIRST SOLDIER. We must not. A noble prisoner!
  SECOND SOLDIER. Room, ho! Tell Antony, Brutus is ta'en.
(ANTONY *enters from left.*)
  FIRST SOLDIER. I'll tell the news. Here comes the general.
  Brutus is ta'en, Brutus is ta'en, my lord.
  ANTONY. Where is he?
20  LUCILIUS (*pleased with his ruse*). Safe, Antony; Brutus is safe
    enough.
  I dare assure thee that no enemy
  Shall ever take alive the noble Brutus.
  The gods defend him from so great a shame!
  When you do find him, or alive or dead,
25  He will be found like Brutus, like himself.
  ANTONY. This is not Brutus, friend, but, I assure you,
  A prize no less in worth. Keep this man safe;
  Give him all kindness. I had rather have
  Such men my friends than enemies. Go on,
30  And see whe'er Brutus be alive or dead;
  And bring us word unto Octavius' tent
  How every thing is chanced.
(SOLDIERS *lead* LUCILIUS *through inner-stage curtains;* ANTONY
*exits right.*)

**94** Why might Lucilius
be claiming to be
Brutus?

# SCENE 5

Another part of the battlefield. [Played on the Platform.]
*As the scene begins, a large rock is raised through the trap door in the center of
the platform. Then* VOLUMNIUS, *carrying a lighted torch, enters at left. He is
followed by* BRUTUS, CLITUS, DARDANIUS, *and* STRATO. *All are overcome
with fatigue and a sense of defeat.*

**BRUTUS.** Come, poor remains of friends, rest on this rock.

**CLITUS.** Statilius showed the torchlight, but, my lord,
  He came not back. He is or ta'en or slain.°

**BRUTUS.** Sit thee down, Clitus. Slaying is the word.

5  It is a deed in fashion. Hark thee, Clitus. (*Whispers to* CLITUS.)

**CLITUS.** What, I, my lord? No, not for all the world.

**BRUTUS.** Peace then. No words.

**CLITUS** (*with fervor*).        I'll rather kill myself.

**BRUTUS.** Hark thee, Dardanius. (*Again he whispers his request.*)

**DARDANIUS** (*aghast*).        Shall I do such a deed?

(BRUTUS *walks away from the men.*)

**CLITUS.** O Dardanius!

10 **DARDANIUS.** O Clitus!

**CLITUS.** What ill request did Brutus make to thee?

**DARDANIUS.** To kill him, Clitus. Look, he meditates.

**CLITUS.** Now is that noble vessel full of grief,
  That it runs over even at his eyes.

15 **BRUTUS.** Come hither, good Volumnius; list a word.

**VOLUMNIUS** (*bowing*). What says my lord?

**BRUTUS.**                    Why this, Volumnius:
  The ghost of Caesar hath appeared to me
  Two several times by night; at Sardis once,
  And, this last night, here in Philippi fields.

20  I know my hour has come.

**VOLUMNIUS.**            Not so, my lord.

**BRUTUS.** Nay, I am sure it is, Volumnius.
  Thou seest the world, Volumnius, how it goes;
  Our enemies have beat us to the pit.°

(*Low alarums signal the approach of* ANTONY *and* OCTAVIUS.)
  It is more worthy to leap in ourselves,

25  Than tarry till they push us. Good Volumnius,
  Thou know'st that we two went to school together.
  Even for that our love of old, I prithee,
  Hold thou my sword-hilts, whilst I run on it.

**VOLUMNIUS.** That's not an office for a friend, my lord.

(*More alarums are sounded, this time louder.*)

30 **CLITUS.** Fly, fly, my lord! There is no tarrying here.

**BRUTUS** (*going to each in turn*). Farewell to you; and you; and
  you, Volumnius.
  Strato, thou hast been all this while asleep;
  Farewell to thee too, Strato. Countrymen,
  My heart doth joy that yet in all my life

*Statilius* (stə til′ē əs)
. . . *slain.* Statilius had
volunteered to slip through
the enemy's lines and
observe their camp; later, if
all was well with him, he
would signal with a torch.
He did signal, but never
returned. It was thought he
was killed shortly after he
flashed the signal.

**95** What new information
does Brutus reveal?
Why might Shakespeare
have chosen to reveal it in
this way?

*pit,* a trap for wild animals.
Brutus is speaking
figuratively.

**96** What is Brutus asking
of Volumnius? How
does this apparently differ
from what he asked Clitus
and Dardanius? Why might
he have changed his mind?
What is Volumnius'
response?

BRUTUS reflects on his life.
The American Shakespeare Theatre.

35 I found no man but he was true to me.
I shall have glory by this losing day
More than Octavius and Mark Antony
By this vile conquest shall attain unto.
So fare you well at once; for Brutus' tongue
40 Hath almost ended his life's history.
Night hangs upon mine eyes; my bones would rest.
That hath but labored to attain this hour.
(*The alarum grows urgent, accompanied by cries of "Fly, fly!"*)
CLITUS. Fly, my lord, fly!
BRUTUS.                Hence! I will follow.
(CLITUS, DARDANIUS, *and* VOLUMNIUS *hurry off at right.* STRATO,
*awake now, starts to follow them.*)
I prithee, Strato, stay thou by thy lord.
45 Thou art a fellow of a good respect;
Thy life hath had some smatch° of honor in it.
Hold then my sword, and turn away thy face,
While I do run upon it. Wilt thou, Strato?
STRATO. Give me your hand first. Fare you well, my lord.
50 BRUTUS. Farewell, good Strato.
(STRATO *takes the sword and holds it with the blade exposed.*

**smatch,** taste; touch.

*As* STRATO *averts his face,* BRUTUS *runs upon the naked blade.)*

  Caesar, now be still.
I killed not thee with half so good a will. (BRUTUS *dies.)*
*(Offstage trumpets sound retreat as two* SOLDIERS *with torches enter at left. They light the way for* ANTONY *and* OCTAVIUS. *More* SOLDIERS *follow, among them* MESSALA *and* LUCILIUS, *now prisoners. All see* STRATO *standing over the dead* BRUTUS.)*

OCTAVIUS. What man is that?

MESSALA. My master's man. Strato, where is thy master?

STRATO. Free from the bondage you are in, Messala.

55  The conquerors can but make a fire of him,°
    For Brutus only overcame himself,
    And no man else hath honor by his death.°

LUCILIUS. So Brutus should be found. I thank thee, Brutus,
    That thou has proved Lucilius' saying true.°

60 OCTAVIUS. All that served Brutus, I will entertain them.°
    Fellow, wilt thou bestow thy time with me?

STRATO. Ay, if Messala will prefer° me to you.

OCTAVIUS. Do so, good Messala.

MESSALA. How died my master, Strato?

65 STRATO. I held the sword, and he did run on it.

MESSALA. Octavius, then take him to follow thee,
    That did the latest service to my master.

ANTONY (*looking at the body*). This was the noblest Roman of
    them all.
    All the conspirators save only he

70  Did that they did in envy of great Caesar;
    He, only in a general honest thought
    And common good to all, made one of them.°
    His life was gentle, and the elements°
    So mixed in him that Nature might stand up

75  And say to all the world, "This was a man!"
*(ANTONY removes his cloak and covers BRUTUS with it. He then signals to the* SOLDIERS, *who lift* BRUTUS' *body onto their shields.)*

OCTAVIUS. According to his virtue let us use him,
    With all respect and rites of burial.
    Within my tent his bones tonight shall lie,
    Most like a soldier, ordered honorably.

80  So call the field to rest; and let's away,
    To part the glories° of this happy day.
*(All exit at right to the solemn accompaniment of offstage drums beating a death march.)*

---

**97** In what respect do Brutus' last words resemble those of Cassius?

*The conquerors . . . him,* a reference to the Roman custom of burning the dead.
*no man . . . death,* no one can claim the honor of defeating him in combat.
*Lucilius' . . . true.* Lucilius had said that Brutus' enemies would never take him alive.
*I will . . . them,* I will take all of Brutus' servants and soldiers and make them my own.
*prefer,* recommend.

**98** This is a new tone in Antony's comments about Brutus. How has his attitude changed? Why do you think it has changed?

*made one of them,* joined them.

*elements,* the four basic elements—earth, air, fire, and water. According to Antony, they were mixed in Brutus in ideal proportions.

**99** Do you agree with Antony's assessment of Brutus? Discuss.

*part the glories,* divide the honors.

## THINK AND DISCUSS
### SCENES 1 AND 2
#### Understanding
1. In Scene 1 Cassius tells Messala, "against my will . . . am I compelled to set/Upon one battle all our liberties." What worry is he expressing about the battle?
2. What omens does he think may forecast defeat for him?
3. What plan of attack does Brutus want to put into action in Scene 2?

#### Analyzing
4. What is the mood of Brutus' farewell to Cassius? Is this understandable? Explain.
5. Contrast Antony's and Octavius' relationship in Scene 1 with that of Brutus and Cassius.
6. What might account for the difference in how the pairs are getting along?
7. What might be the dramatic purposes of Scene 2, which is only six lines long?

### SCENE 3
#### Understanding
1. As the scene opens, Cassius tells how he has retrieved his army's standard, or flag. How has he done so, and how does he feel about it?
2. What does Pindarus see that causes him to misjudge what has happened to Titinius?
3. How does Cassius identify the day he dies?

#### Analyzing
4. How are Cassius' decision and manner of death in keeping with his character?
5. How does his death affect Titinius?
6. How do these events affect Brutus?

#### Extending
7. How much that occurs in this scene do you think a Shakespearean audience might charge to Julius Caesar's influence?

### SCENES 4 AND 5
#### Understanding
1. What does Lucilius do to protect Brutus in Scene 4?
2. What decision by Brutus in Scene 5 shows that he knows the battle is lost?

#### Analyzing
3. What qualities do his soldiers show in their refusal to kill Brutus?
4. Bidding his friends farewell, Brutus says he has found "no man but was true to me." Who did take unfair advantage of Brutus' trust? Under what circumstances?
5. What does Brutus' remark show about him?
6. How sincere do you think Antony is in making his remarks over Brutus' body?

#### Extending
7. What role would you expect Antony and Octavius to play in Rome's future?

## THINKING SKILLS
### Synthesizing
To **synthesize** is to put together parts and elements so as to form a whole, a new pattern or structure. Practice the thinking skills involved in synthesizing by casting an imaginary theater or movie production of *Julius Caesar*. Put together your knowledge of what each of the major characters is like with your thoughts and opinions about performers of today who might portray each one. Write a cast list, with each Shakespearean role on the left and on the right the name of an actor, actress, singer, politician, or other person who will play the role. Be sure to cast Caesar, Brutus, Cassius, Antony, Portia, Casca, Calpurnia, Lepidus, the Soothsayer, Cinna the poet, and at least five other parts. You may also cast the parts of as many other conspirators, senators, officers, soldiers, tribunes, servants, commoners, and

others as you wish. Be ready to explain your reasons for each casting decision to your classmates.

## COMPOSITION
### Analyzing Falling Action in a Tragedy

After reaching their highest point in Act Three, the fortunes of the protagonist of a Shakespearean tragedy go steadily downhill through Act Five, where the character finally dies. Review Acts Three to Five to see how this pattern is followed in *Julius Caesar*. As you read, take notes to use in writing about Brutus as a central character. Write a three- to five-paragraph composition describing the decline in Brutus' fortunes. Include his own mistakes as well as things done to him by others. Your audience will be your teacher and classmates. See "Writing About Plot and Plot Devices" in the Writer's Handbook.

### Writing Persuasively

Some critics claim that it is really Julius Caesar (or his spirit) that defeats Brutus and Cassius at Philippi. Do you agree with this view? Go through Act Five and pertinent parts of Act Four for evidence to help you first form and then support your opinion. Take notes as you read. Write a three- to five-paragraph essay in which you state your view on this question and support it with reasons and evidence. Your audience will be your teacher and classmates. See "Writing About Drama" in the Writer's Handbook.

## ENRICHMENT
### Producing a Newspaper or Magazine

You and your classmates can cooperate to produce a newspaper or news magazine to be dated the day after the battle at Philippi. One student should serve as editor-in-chief to coordinate activities; others should serve as reporters (covering such stories as the reason for the battle, the deaths of famed military leaders Brutus and Cassius, the future of Rome, the way the battle was won by Antony and Octavius, and other topics of interest). Other students may serve as columnists (advice to the lovelorn, gossip, arts, and the like), cartoonists, artists (since there were no photographers in 42 B.C.), and typists. The publication might also include editorials, letters to the editor, classified ads, and display advertisements. Each student should be able to find an area of interest in which to work. One copy could be displayed in class, or the edition could be copied or printed for distribution, if possible.

## BIOGRAPHY

### William Shakespeare
### 1564–1616

The first reference to William Shakespeare in documents of his era is a baptismal record for April 26, 1564, at Holy Trinity Church in Stratford-on-Avon, England. Since at the time it was customary for infants to be baptized when three days old, it is generally assumed that Shakespeare was born on April 23. His father was John Shakespeare, a glovemaker and farm-product dealer who during William's boyhood was elected to various offices, becoming in time high bailiff or mayor. Once William could read and write English, a requirement then for going to school, he undoubtedly was enrolled in Stratford's excellent grammar school, taught by an Oxford University graduate. There he learned Latin and a little Greek.

In 1577 John Shakespeare suffered financial reverses, and it is assumed that William dropped out of school. He is next heard of in 1582, when he married Anne Hathaway from the neighboring hamlet of Shottery. Their first child was born in 1583, followed two years later by twins.

Historians have found few records of Shakespeare's life before 1592, but by then he was in London, where there was a performance of *Harry the Sixth* (apparently Shakespeare's *Henry VI, Part I*) on March 3. Later that year he is mentioned as a playwright in a pamphlet by Robert Greene. From at least 1592 to 1610 Shakespeare lived primarily in London, writing two or more plays a year for his acting company. By 1597 he was wealthy enough to buy New Place, one of the largest houses in Stratford, which he made his principal residence in 1610, traveling to London only when necessary.

When Shakespeare died on April 23, 1616, he left the world thirty-seven plays, a number of long poems, and a collection of sonnets. Recognizing the importance of his plays, his fellow actors John Heminges and Henry Condell arranged to have them collected and published in 1623 in a large volume known today as the First Folio.

In Wenceslaus Hollar's drawing of London's Thames River, 1647, the labels of the bear-baiting arena and the Globe Theater are mistakenly reversed.

# THINKING CRITICALLY
# ABOUT LITERATURE

## UNIT 6   SHAKESPEAREAN DRAMA

### ■ CONCEPT REVIEW

At the end of each unit in *Traditions in Literature* is a selection that illustrates many of the literary elements and ideas that you have studied. It is accompanied by notes designed to help you think critically about your reading. Page numbers in the notes refer to applications of literary terms. A more extensive discussion of these terms appears in the Handbook of Literary Terms.

Read this scene from Shakespeare's *Antony and Cleopatra*, a tragedy featuring certain characters that appeared in *Julius Caesar*. Then answer the questions that follow.

# *from* Antony and Cleopatra

**William Shakespeare**   Great Britain

*Antony and Cleopatra* is a late Shakespearean tragedy, written in 1606 or 1607, seven or eight years after *Julius Caesar*. It picks up the fortunes of Mark Antony two years after his victory at the end of the earlier play. Antony has continued as the "masker and reveler" described in *Julius Caesar,* but he is known as an excellent soldier. He, Octavius Caesar, and Lepidus rule as a triumvirate, or three-man council of leaders, over all of the Roman Empire. Octavius is now called *Caesar,* a name destined to become almost an emperor's title.

Antony, who controls Egypt, Greece, and the East, has been carrying on a romance with the Egyptian queen Cleopatra, but he returns to Rome after learning that his wife, Fulvia, has died. There is still feuding between Antony and Octavius Caesar. In an attempt to strengthen their alliance, Caesar arranges the marriage of his sister Octavia to Antony in a state ceremony. The scene that follows depicts the departure of Antony and Octavia to Athens, the Greek city from which Antony will rule his third of the empire.

# ACT THREE SCENE 2

## CHARACTERS

MARK ANTONY ⎫
OCTAVIUS CAESAR ⎬ *triumvirs*
M. AEMILIUS LEPIDUS ⎭
AGRIPPA, *friend to Caesar*
DOMITIUS ENOBARBUS, *friend to Antony*
OCTAVIA, *sister to Caesar and wife to Antony*

---

Caesar's house in Rome. [Played on the Platform stage.]
AGRIPPA *enters at one door,* ENOBARBUS *at another.*

AGRIPPA. What, are the brothers° parted?

ENOBARBUS. They have dispatch'd with Pompey,° he is gone;
    The other three are sealing. Octavia weeps
    To part from Rome; Caesar is sad; and Lepidus,

5     Since Pompey's feast, as Menas says, is troubled
    With the green sickness.

AGRIPPA.            'Tis a noble Lepidus.

ENOBARBUS. A very fine one. O, how he loves Caesar!

AGRIPPA. Nay, but how dearly he adores Mark Antony!

ENOBARBUS. Caesar? Why, he's the Jupiter of men.

10 AGRIPPA. What's Antony? The god of Jupiter.

ENOBARBUS. Spake you of Caesar? How, the nonpareil!

AGRIPPA. O Antony! O thou Arabian bird!

ENOBARBUS. Would you praise Caesar, say "Caesar," go no further.

AGRIPPA. Indeed, he plied them both with excellent praises.

15 ENOBARBUS. But he loves Caesar best; yet he loves Antony.
    Hoo! Hearts, tongues, figures, scribes, bards, poets cannot
    Think, speak, cast,° write, sing, number, hoo!
    His love to Antony. But as for Caesar,
    Kneel down, kneel down, and wonder.

AGRIPPA.            Both he loves.

20 ENOBARBUS. They are his shards,° and he their beetle. (*Trumpets within.*) So;
    This is to horse. Adieu,° noble Agrippa.

AGRIPPA. Good fortune, worthy soldier, and farewell.

(CAESAR, ANTONY, LEPIDUS, *and* OCTAVIA *enter.*)

ANTONY. No further, sir.

---

- **brothers**: brothers-in-law.

- **Pompey**: Pompey's son.

- **Blank verse** (page 516): Characters speak in verse.

- Agrippa and Enobarbus are satirizing Lepidus' attempts to flatter both Caesar and Antony.

- **cast**: calculate.

- **shards**: hard casings around beetle wings.

- **Adieu** (ə dü′): good-by [French].

**CAESAR.** You take from me a great part of myself;

25   Use me well in 't. Sister, prove such a wife
As my thoughts make thee, and as my farthest band°
Shall pass on thy approof. Most noble Antony,
Let not the piece° of virtue, which is set
Betwixt us as the cement of our love,

30   To keep it builded, be the ram to batter
The fortress of it; for better might we
Have loved without this mean, if on both parts
This be not cherished.

**ANTONY.**                    Make me not offended
In your distrust.

**CAESAR.**          I have said.

**ANTONY.**                    You shall not find,

35   Though you be therein curious, the least cause
For what you seem to fear. So the gods keep you,
And make the hearts of Romans serve your ends!
We will here part.

**CAESAR.** Farewell, my dearest sister, fare thee well.

40   The elements be kind to thee, and make
Thy spirits all of comfort! Fare thee well.

**OCTAVIA.** My noble brother! *(She weeps.)*

**ANTONY.** The April's in her eyes; it is love's spring,
And these the showers to bring it on. Be cheerful.

45 **OCTAVIA.** Sir, look well to my husband's house;° and—

**CAESAR.** What, Octavia?

**OCTAVIA.**               I'll tell you in your ear. *(She whispers*
*to* CAESAR.*)*

**ANTONY.** Her tongue will not obey her heart, nor can
Her heart inform her tongue—the swan's downfeather,
That stands upon the swell at full of tide,

50   And neither way inclines.

**ENOBARBUS** *(aside to* AGRIPPA*).* Will Caesar weep?

**AGRIPPA** *(aside to* ENOBARBUS*).*               He has a cloud in 's
face.

**ENOBARBUS** *(aside to* AGRIPPA*).* He were the worse for that, were he a
horse;
So is he being a man.

**AGRIPPA** *(aside to* ENOBARBUS*).* Why, Enobarbus,
When Antony found Julius Caesar dead,

55   He cried almost to roaring; and he wept
When at Philippi he found Brutus slain.

- **band:** bond, or promise.

- **piece:** masterpiece.

- Note Caesar's warning to Antony. His intensity is indicated by the pacing of his speech.

- **Foreshadowing** (page 536): Caesar's concern and Antony's edgy assurances hint at the division between the two men that will result when Antony is unfaithful later in the play.

- **my husband's house:** Octavia, a widow, refers here to her former husband.

- In a metaphor, Octavia's mixed emotions are compared to a feather floating on the crest of a wave; no one knows which way it will go.

- **aside:** Enobarbus and Agrippa speak privately, under their breath, to one another.

ENOBARBUS (*aside to* AGRIPPA). That year, indeed, he was troubled with a
    rheum:°

  What willingly he did confound he wailed,

  Believe 't, till I wept too.

CAESAR.           No, sweet Octavia,

60   You shall hear from me still;° the time shall not

  Outgo my thinking on you.

ANTONY.           Come, sir, come,

  I'll wrestle with you in my strength of love.

  Look, (*embracing him*) here I have you; thus I let you go,

  And give you to the gods.

CAESAR.           Adieu; be happy!

65 LEPIDUS. Let all the numbers of the stars give light

  To thy fair way!

CAESAR.        Farewell, farewell! (*He kisses* OCTAVIA.)

ANTONY.           Farewell!

(*Trumpets sound, as all exit.*)

- **rheum** (rüm): head cold.

- **still:** constantly.

- Antony's statement is a hyperbole; he will not wrestle Caesar, but embrace him in a hearty farewell.

- Note that the heightened emotions of saying good-by are conveyed by the rush of speeches in divided lines. Octavia, overcome by sadness, doesn't speak.

## THINK AND DISCUSS
### Understanding
1. What event is taking place in this scene?
2. How does Octavia feel about leaving Rome?
3. How does Caesar feel about her departure?

### Analyzing
4. What do Agrippa and Enobarbus imply in their conversation about Lepidus?
5. Why do Enobarbus and Agrippa carry on one conversation in **asides**?
6. Does this scene indicate that Caesar completely trusts Antony? Explain.
7. When Enobarbus criticizes Caesar for weeping, how does Agrippa respond?
8. Octavia speaks to Caesar but not to her husband. What does this imply about her relationship to Antony?

### Extending
9. Lepidus has only one speech in this scene. How is this similar to or different from the way he was portrayed in *Julius Caesar*?

## REVIEWING LITERARY TERMS
### Blank Verse
1. This scene contains many small exchanges of conversation between pairs of characters. How do you think the divided lines of blank verse affect the pace and unity of the scene when the lines are spoken on stage?

### Foreshadowing
2. Agrippa and Enobarbus, friends of Caesar and Antony, make fun of Lepidus, who is one of the three most powerful men in the Roman world. Does this suggest that Lepidus will remain equal to Caesar and Antony in power? Explain.
3. Does the conversation between Caesar and Antony assure you that their alliance will remain undisturbed throughout the play?

## ■ CONTENT REVIEW
### THINKING SKILLS
#### Classifying
In addition to a tragic hero and a major conflict, many Shakespearean tragedies also

feature the following elements. Give one example of each in *Julius Caesar*, and explain its effect on the plot. Have a class list compiled.

1. Desire for revenge
2. Use of humor to relieve a somber mood
3. Supernatural occurrence
4. Chance happening that causes catastrophe

### Generalizing

5. Shakespeare makes each conspirator's name memorable by having Ligarius join last, Decius convince Caesar to go to the capitol, Trebonius draw Antony away, Metellus plead for his brother, Casca strike first, and so forth. Yet only two conspirators—Brutus and Cassius—can be considered leaders throughout the play. How does Shakespeare make it clear that the rest of the conspirators do not remain important after the climax of the play?

6. Portia and Calpurnia are both the wives of influential Romans and main characters. In your opinion, do the similarities of these women allow you to draw any general conclusion about how Shakespeare depicted honorable wives? Or has Shakespeare drawn very different characters that make such generalizing difficult? Explain and support your answer.

### Evaluating

Judge the four listed figures in the play in two ways. For each character, first cite a detail that makes you feel that Shakespeare portrayed the person realistically. Then tell whether you think the character bears notable responsibility for his final fate in the play. Explain your judgment.

7. Julius Caesar
8. Cassius
9. Brutus
10. Mark Antony

11. An informed voter may evaluate political candidates in terms of a standard of capable leadership and cast a vote based on that evaluation. You have read Shakespeare's portrayal of three triumvirs of the Roman empire—Mark Antony, Octavius Caesar, and Lepidus—in scenes from two plays. Keeping in mind what you know of their behavior, military experience, sense of honor, intelligence, and honesty, think about how well each measures up to your idea of what a great leader should be. Remember that they control an empire stretching across parts of ancient Europe, Asia, and Africa. (Look at maps of the Mediterranean Sea area to see the extent of their rule.) On a slip of paper write the name of the triumvir—or any other character from either play—that you would support as a leader, if you were a citizen of the empire. Join your class in voting by dropping your ballot into a box in class. Give reasons for your vote and one statement of advice you would give the winner of the mock election.

### Synthesizing

12. When *Julius Caesar* was performed at the Globe, Shakespeare is thought to have played the parts of Cinna the poet and the unnamed poet in Act Four. His audiences probably recognized him as the playwright—and a well-known poet—as well as an actor. Review the dialogue in each scene; then explain how Shakespeare's presence would have added to the humor.

# ■ COMPOSITION REVIEW

From the assignments that follow choose one and write a three- to five-paragraph composition on the topic.

## Writing an Introduction

Plan and write an introduction to *Julius Caesar* for students who will read the play next year. Tell them how to go about reading it, what they might find difficult, what they might enjoy, and the like. First jot down your ideas as they come to you; then organize your notes before you begin writing. Be as sincere and objective as you can. See "Writing About Drama" in the Writer's Handbook.

## Writing Persuasively

There are those who say Cassius is a better person than his role as a conspirator suggests; there are also those who call Brutus a stuffed shirt and a windbag. Choose either view and decide whether you agree with it by analyzing what you have seen of the character in the play. Write an essay for an audience of your classmates giving specific reasons and evidence why you accept or reject the view you've chosen.

## Discussing a Famous Saying

According to a famous quotation from Sir J.E.E. Dalberg, known as Lord Acton, "Power tends to corrupt and absolute power corrupts absolutely." Apply this statement to *Julius Caesar*, considering how power affects the major characters. Write an essay showing how Lord Acton's view seems to be one Shakespeare could accept.

## Writing Literary Criticism

Discuss the effectiveness of Shakespeare's use of blank verse in *Julius Caesar*. Consider the difference in emotional impact of Brutus' funeral oration in prose and Antony's in blank verse; the devices Shakespeare uses to keep his verse from becoming monotonous or singsong; and short, memorable expressions in blank verse, such as Cassius' oft-quoted "The fault, dear Brutus, is not in our stars,/But in ourselves, that we are underlings." See "Writing About Poetry and Poetic Devices" in the Writer's Handbook.

## Reviewing Writer's Craft: Use Precise, Active Verbs

Study Antony's funeral oration to see how Shakespeare shows the power of "loaded" language to sway a crowd. Consider how the crowd would be unable to check any doubtful statements; how he arouses emotions against popular figures; how he turns around Brutus' claim that Caesar was ambitious; and how he teases his audience by mentioning the will. Write an essay analyzing Antony's oratory, commenting on words or points he repeats, questions he asks, claims that he is no orator, and physical gestures he uses. Make sure you understand how truthful and accurate he is being at each point, and choose the points you want to emphasize rather than trying to discuss every aspect of the scene. Use precise, active verbs to describe what Antony does.

# NONFICTION

Boris Koustodieff, *Village Festival* (detail), 1910, Russian Museum, Leningrad

# PREVIEW

## UNIT 7   NONFICTION

**The Secret Room** / Corrie ten Boom
**I Escape from the Boers** / Winston Churchill
**By Any Other Name** / Santha Rama Rau
**First Lady Under Fire** / Margaret Truman
**Four Letters** / Dolley Madison, Bartolomeo Vanzetti, Anne M. Lindbergh, Harry S. Truman
**Three Days to See!** / Helen Keller
**Grandmother Zabielska** / Zofia Starowieyska Morstin
**The Day We Flew the Kites** / Frances Fowler
**My Store of Grievances** / John Welter
**Biographies Bring New Companions** / Marchette Chute
**A Kiowa Grandmother** / N. Scott Momaday

**Features**
Reading Nonfiction: Biographies and
   Autobiographies
Writer's Craft: Write Good Beginnings
Reading Nonfiction: Letters
Comment: The Art of Writing Letters
Reading Nonfiction: Essays
Comment: Structure and Formality in the Essay

**Applications of Literary Terms**
connotation/denotation
style

**Reading Literature Skillfully**
fact/opinion
main idea/supporting details

**Vocabulary Skills**
context
dictionary/glossary

**Thinking Skills**
classifying
generalizing
synthesizing
evaluating

**Composition Assignments Include**
Describing Character Traits
Reporting a News Event
Evaluating an Autobiographical Account
Commenting on Dolley Madison's Courage
Reading/Writing Log
Writing a Letter to the Editor
Describing Helen Keller
Writing a Tribute
Writing a Character Study
Describing a Memorable Experience
Analyzing an Essay
Writing Satire
Voicing a Complaint

**Enrichment**
Researching a World War II Topic
Comparing an Author's Works
Presenting Television Interviews
Reading Letters of Great Writers
Presenting a Thematic Report
Dramatizing an Essay
Gathering Facts Through Research

**Thinking Critically About Literature**
Concept Review
Content Review
Composition Review

## Biographies and Autobiographies

A well-written biography, an account of a person's life, presents the life and times of the subject—perhaps a famous living person or historical figure—in depth. If the person writes the story of his or her own life, the work is called an autobiography.

Biographies and autobiographies of eminent people fascinate many readers by providing pictures of the circumstances surrounding historical events, great discoveries, and well-known relationships. You may enjoy intriguing biographical writing the same way you appreciate finely crafted fiction or drama. Yet biographies and autobiographies are nonfiction. They are based on facts and on authors' opinions about real people.

## The Author's Perspective

A biographer may admire his or her subject and write a laudatory work, one that expresses praise. On the other hand, a biographer may write a critical work that reveals a negative portrayal of the subject. Most readers prefer biographies by writers who seek to explore and tell the story of a life as it really unfolded. Such writers do not shy away from making positive or negative judgments, but they do not let their own perspective get in the way of fairly presenting the subject's life and its significance.

The writer of an autobiography, naturally, begins with a very personal perspective. An autobiography cannot be presented in a disinterested fashion, nor would most readers want it to be. Yet it can be written truthfully and accurately.

You can judge a biography or autobiography not only by how entertaining it is but also by how well it agrees with what you know about people, places, and events involved in the story.

## The Biographical Work

A biography or autobiography may cover an entire lifetime or isolate a significant period in a person's life. In this unit, for example, you will read an autobiographical account of an early period in Winston Churchill's life. Although it does not list or describe more famous events in this statesman's life, "I Escape from the Boers" does provide insight into Churchill's determination, intelligence, and courage.

## Reading Nonfiction

Nonfiction is prose literature that deals with real people and events rather than imaginary ones. As you read biographies, autobiographies, and other nonfiction, you will depend on authors for careful, truthful presentations. Biographers, for example, should give complete accounts without unfairly eliminating important information simply because it runs counter to the impression the biographer wants to make. To determine how reliable a biography is, you can read to determine the author's purpose and perspective. Is the author writing to inform, persuade, or entertain the reader? Does the author present the subject objectively or subjectively?

Readers must be willing to question and, if necessary, investigate the author's facts, use of facts to develop opinions, and completeness. If you read with this attitude, you can judge the quality, validity, and relevance of nonfiction.

The autobiographical and biographical selections on the following pages tell about significant events in the lives of noteworthy people. In such short selections, whole lives cannot be told, but the selections offer good examples of these types of writing. The narratives also reveal character traits and strengths that become most evident in times of challenge or crisis.

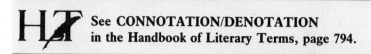

See CONNOTATION/DENOTATION
in the Handbook of Literary Terms, page 794.

# The Secret Room

**Corrie ten Boom**   The Netherlands
(with John and Elizabeth Sherrill)

**Corrie ten Boom's predicament called for desperate but careful steps:
more and more Jews were turning to her to escape the Nazis, whose
eyes and ears were everywhere.**

*When Nazi armies invaded Corrie ten Boom's homeland in 1940, she and
her fellow citizens observed many dreadful changes. Living in the Holland
province city of Haarlem (här′ ləm) with her sister, Betsie, and elderly father,
she tried to maintain the appearance of an ordinary life, working as a watch-
maker at the Beje (bā′ yā), their combined home and shop. But as the following
excerpt makes clear, there was also an unseen side to her life.*

*Other family members introduced in Corrie's story are Peter, her nephew;
Willem (vil′ əm), her minister brother (who ran a home for the aged at
Hilversum that he used as an escape route for fleeing Jews); Tine and Kik,
Willem's wife and son; and Nollie, Peter's mother and another sister
of Corrie's.*

It was Sunday, May 10, 1942, exactly two years after the fall of
Holland. The sunny spring skies,
the flowers in the lamppost boxes,
did not at all reflect the city's mood. German
soldiers wandered aimlessly through the streets,
some looking as if they had not yet recovered from
a hard Saturday night.

Each month the occupation seemed to grow
harsher, restrictions more numerous. The latest
heartache for Dutchmen was an edict making it a
crime to sing the "Wilhelmus,"[1] our national anthem.

---

1. *"Wilhelmus"* (vil′ helm əs).

This building, called the
Beje (bā'yā), contained the
ten Boom family home, the
watch shop, and eventually
the secret room.

Father, Betsie, and I were on our way to the Dutch Reformed church in Velsen,[2] a small town not far from Haarlem, where Peter had won the post of organist in competition against forty older and more experienced musicians. The organ at Velsen was one of the finest in the country; though the train seemed slower each time, we went frequently.

Peter was already playing, invisible in the tall organ loft, when we squeezed into the crowded pew. That was one thing the occupation had done for Holland: churches were packed.

After hymns and prayers came the sermon, a good one today, I thought. The closing prayers were said. And then, electrically, the whole church sat at attention. Without preamble, every stop pulled out to full volume, Peter was playing the "Wilhelmus"!

Father, at eighty-two, was the first one on his feet. Now everyone was standing. From somewhere in back of us a voice sang out the words. Another joined in, and another. Then we were all singing together, the full voice of Holland singing her forbidden anthem. We sang at the top of our lungs, sang our oneness, our hope, our love for Queen and country. On this anniversary of defeat it seemed almost for a moment that we were victors.

Afterward we waited for Peter at the small side door of the church. It was a long time before he was free to come away with us, so many people wanted to embrace him, to shake his hand and thump his back. Clearly he was enormously pleased with himself.

But now that the moment had passed I was, as usual, angry with him. The Gestapo[3] was certain to hear about it, perhaps already had: their eyes and ears were everywhere. For what had Peter risked so much? Not for people's lives but for a gesture. For a moment's meaningless defiance.

At Bos en Hoven Straat,[4] however, Peter was a hero as one by one his family made us describe again what had happened. The only members of the household who felt as I did were the two Jewish women staying at Nollie's. One of these was an elderly Austrian lady whom Willem had sent into hiding here.

The other woman was a young, blonde, blue-eyed Dutch Jew with flawless false identity papers supplied by the Dutch national underground itself. The papers were so good and Annaliese looked so unlike the Nazi stereotype of a Jew that she went freely in and out of the house, shopping and helping out at the school, giving herself out to be a friend of the family whose husband had died in the bombing of Rotterdam.

I spent an anxious afternoon, tensing at the sound of every motor, for only the police, Germans, and NSBers[5] had automobiles nowadays. But the time came to go home to the Beje and still nothing had happened.

I worried two more days, then decided either Peter had not been reported or that the Gestapo had more important things to occupy them. It was Wednesday morning just as Father and I were unlocking our workbenches that Peter's little sister Cocky burst into the shop.

"Opa! Tante Corrie![6] They came for Peter! They took him away!"

"Who? Where?"

But she didn't know and it was three days before the family learned that he had been taken to the federal prison in Amsterdam.

---

2. **Velsen** (vel′zən). Other Netherlands locations mentioned in the selection are Rotterdam, Amsterdam, Utrecht (yü′trekt), and Aerdenhout (er′dən hout′).

3. **Gestapo** (gə stä′pō), an official group of secret police created during the Nazi regime, known for its brutality.

4. **Straat** (strät), street. [*Dutch*]

5. **NSBers.** The letters stand for the Dutch name of the National Socialist Movement. The members of this Dutch political party collaborated with the Nazis.

6. **Opa** (ō′pä), **Tante** (tän′tə) **Corrie.** Grandfather, Auntie Corrie.

It was 7:55 in the evening, just a few minutes before the new curfew hour of 8:00. Peter had been in prison for two weeks. Father and Betsie and I were seated around the dining-room table, Father replacing watches in their pockets and Betsie doing needlework, our big, black, slightly Persian cat curled contentedly in her lap. A knock on the alley door made me glance in the window mirror. There in the bright spring twilight stood a woman. She carried a small suitcase and—odd for the time of year—wore a fur coat, gloves, and a heavy veil.

I ran down and opened the door. "Can I come in?" she asked. Her voice was high-pitched in fear.

"Of course." I stepped back. The woman looked over her shoulder before moving into the little hallway.

"My name is Kleermaker. I'm a Jew."

"How do you do?" I reached out to take her bag, but she held on to it. "Won't you come upstairs?"

Father and Betsie stood up as we entered the dining room. "Mrs. Kleermaker, my father and my sister."

"I was about to make some tea!" cried Betsie. "You're just in time to join us!"

Father drew out a chair from the table and Mrs. Kleermaker sat down, still gripping the suitcase. The "tea" consisted of old leaves which had been crushed and reused so often they did little more than color the water. But Mrs. Kleermaker accepted it gratefully, plunging into the story of how her husband had been arrested some months before, her son gone into hiding. Yesterday the S.D.—the political police who worked under the Gestapo—had ordered her to close the family clothing store. She was afraid now to go back to the apartment above it. She had heard that we had befriended a man on this street. . . .

"In this household," Father said, "God's people are always welcome."

"We have four empty beds upstairs," said Betsie. "Your problem will be choosing which one to sleep in!"

Just two nights later the same scene was repeated. The time was again just before 8:00 on another bright May evening. Again there was a furtive knock at the side door. This time an elderly couple was standing outside.

"Come in!"

It was the same story: the same tight-clutched possessions, the same fearful glance and tentative tread. The story of neighbors arrested, the fear that tomorrow their turn would come.

That night after prayer time the six of us faced our dilemma. "This location is too dangerous," I told our three guests. "We're half a block from the main police headquarters. And yet I don't know where else to suggest."

Clearly it was time to visit Willem again. So the next day I repeated the difficult trip to Hilversum. "Willem," I said, "we have three Jews staying right at the Beje. Can you get places for them in the country?"

Willem pressed his fingers to his eyes and I noticed suddenly how much white was in his beard. "It's getting harder," he said. "Harder every month. They're feeling the food shortage now even on the farms. I still have addresses, yes, a few. But they won't take anyone without a ration card."

"Without a ration card! But Jews aren't issued ration cards!"

"I know." Willem turned to stare out the window. For the first time I wondered how he and Tine were feeding the elderly men and women in their care.

"I know," he repeated. "And ration cards can't be counterfeited. They're changed too often and they're too easy to spot. Identity cards are different. I know several printers who do them. Of course you need a photographer."

A photographer? Printers? What was Willem

talking about? "Willem, if people need ration cards and there aren't any counterfeit ones, what do they do?"

Willem turned slowly from the window. He seemed to have forgotten me and my particular problem. "Ration cards?" He gestured vaguely. "You steal them."

I stared at this Dutch Reformed clergyman. "Then, Willem, could you steal . . . I mean . . . could you get three stolen cards?"

"No, Corrie! I'm watched! Don't you understand that? Every move I make is watched!"

He put an arm around my shoulder and went on more kindly. "Even if I can continue working for a while, it will be far better for you to develop your own sources. The less connection with me—the less connection with anyone else—the better."

Joggling home on the crowded train, I turned Willem's words over and over in my mind. "Your own sources." That sounded so—so professional. How was I going to find a source of stolen ration cards? Who in the world did I know? . . .

And at that moment a name appeared in my mind.

Fred Koornstra.

Fred was the man who used to read the electric meter at the Beje. The Koornstras had a retarded daughter, now a grown woman, who attended the "church" I had been conducting for the feeble-minded for some twenty years. And now Fred had a new job working for the Food Office. Wasn't it in the department where ration books were issued?

That evening after supper I bumped over the brick streets to the Koornstra house. The tires on my faithful old bicycle had finally given out and I joined the hundreds clattering about town on metal wheel rims. Each bump reminded me jarringly of my fifty years.

Fred, a bald man with a military bearing, came to the door and stared at me blankly when I said I wanted to talk to him about the Sunday service. He invited me in, closed the door, and said "Now Corrie, what is it you really came to see me about?"

("Lord," I prayed silently, "if it is not safe to confide in Fred, stop this conversation now before it is too late.") "I must first tell you that we've had some unexpected company at the Beje. First it was a single woman, then a couple, when I got back this afternoon, another couple." I paused for just an instant. "They are Jews."

Fred's expression did not change.

"We can provide safe places for these people but they must provide something too. Ration cards."

Fred's eyes smiled. "So. Now I know why you came here."

"Fred, is there any way you can give out extra cards? More than you report?"

"None at all, Corrie. Those cards have to be accounted for a dozen ways. They're checked and double-checked."

The hope that had begun to mount in me tumbled. But Fred was frowning.

"Unless—" he began.

"Unless?"

"Unless there should be a holdup. The Food Office in Utrecht was robbed last month—but the men were caught."

He was silent a while. "If it happened at noon," he said slowly, "when just the record clerk and I are there . . . and if they found us tied and gagged . . ." He snapped his fingers. "And I know just the man who might do it! Do you remember the—"

"Don't!" I said, remembering Willem's warning. "Don't tell me who. And don't tell me how. Just get the cards if you possibly can."

Fred stared at me a moment. "How many do you need?"

I opened my mouth to say, "Five." But the number that unexpectedly and astonishingly came out instead was, "One hundred."

When Fred opened the door to me just a week later, I gasped at the sight of him. Both eyes were a greenish purple, his lower lip cut and swollen.

"My friend took very naturally to the part," was all he would say.

But he had the cards. On the table in a brown envelope were one hundred passports to safety. Fred had already torn the "continuing coupon" from each one. This final coupon was presented at the Food Office the last day of each month in exchange for the next month's card. With these coupons Fred could "legally" continue to issue us one hundred cards.

We agreed that it would be risky for me to keep coming to his house each month. What if he were to come to the Beje instead, dressed in his old meterman uniform?

The meter in the Beje was in the back hall at the foot of the stairs. When I got home that afternoon I pried up the tread of the bottom step, as Peter had done higher to hide a radio, and found a hollow space inside. Peter would be proud of me, I thought as I worked—and was flooded by a wave of lonesomeness for that brave and cocksure boy. The hinge was hidden deep in the wood, the ancient riser undisturbed. I was ridiculously pleased with it.

We had our first test of the system on July 1. Fred was to come in through the shop as he always had, carrying the cards beneath his shirt. He would come at 5:30, when Betsie would have the back hall free of callers. To my horror at 5:25 the shop door opened and in stepped a policeman.

He was a tall man with close-cropped orange-red hair whom I knew by name—Rolf van Vliet—but little else. Rolf had brought in a watch that needed cleaning, and he seemed in a mood to talk.

My throat had gone dry, but Father chatted cheerfully as he took off the back of Rolf's watch and examined it. What were we going to do? There was no way to warn Fred Koornstra. Promptly at 5:30 the door of the shop opened and in he walked, dressed in his blue workclothes. It seemed to me that his chest was too thick by a foot at least.

With magnificent aplomb Fred nodded to Father, the policeman, and me. "Good evening." Courteous but a little bored.

He strode through the door at the rear of the shop and shut it behind him. My ears strained to hear him lift the secret lid. There! Surely Rolf must have heard it too.

The door behind us opened again. So great was Fred's control that he had not ducked out the alleyway exit, but came strolling back through the shop.

"Good evening," he said again.

"Evening."

He reached the street door and was gone. We had got away with it this time, but somehow, some way, we were going to have to work out a warning system.

For meanwhile, in the weeks since Mrs. Kleermaker's unexpected visit, a great deal had happened at the Beje. Supplied with ration cards, Mrs. Kleermaker and the elderly couple and the next arrivals and the next had found homes in safer locations. But still the hunted people kept coming, and the needs were often more complicated than ration cards and addresses. If a Jewish woman became pregnant, where could she go to have her baby? If a Jew in hiding died, how could he be buried?

"Develop your own sources," Willem had said. And from the moment Fred Koornstra's name had popped into my mind, an uncanny realization had been growing in me. We were friends with half of Haarlem! We knew nurses in the maternity hospital. We knew clerks in the Records Office. We knew someone in every business and service in the city.

We didn't know, of course, the political views of all these people. But—and here I felt a strange leaping of my heart—God did! I knew I was not clever or subtle or sophisticated; if the Beje was becoming a meeting place for need and supply, it was through some strategy far higher than mine.

A few nights after Fred's first "meterman" visit the alley bell rang long after curfew. I sped downstairs, expecting another sad and stammering refugee. Betsie and I had already made up beds for four new overnight guests that evening: a Jewish woman and her three small children.

But to my surprise, close against the wall of the dark alley, stood Kik. "Get your bicycle," he ordered with his usual young abruptness. "And put on a sweater. I have some people I want you to meet."

"Now? After curfew?" But I knew it was useless to ask questions. Kik's bicycle was tireless too, the wheel rims swathed in cloth. He wrapped mine also to keep down the clatter, and soon we were pedaling through the blacked-out streets of Haarlem at a speed that would have scared me even in daylight.

"Put a hand on my shoulder," Kik whispered. "I know the way."

We crossed dark side streets, crested bridges, wheeled round invisible corners. At last we crossed a broad canal and I knew we had reached the fashionable suburb of Aerdenhout.

We turned into a driveway beneath shadowy trees. To my astonishment Kik picked up my bicycle and carried both his and mine up the front steps. A serving girl with starched white apron and ruffled cap opened the door. The entrance hall was jammed with bicycles.

Then I saw him. One eye smiling at me, the other at the door, his vast stomach hastening ahead of him. Pickwick![7]

He led Kik and me into the drawing room where, sipping coffee and chatting in small groups, was the most distinguished-looking group of men and women I had ever seen. But all my attention, that first moment, was on the inexpressibly fragrant aroma in that room. Surely, was it possible, they were drinking real coffee?

Pickwick drew me a cup from the silver urn on the sideboard. It was coffee. After two years, rich, black, pungent Dutch coffee. He poured himself a cup too, dropping in his usual five lumps of sugar as though rationing had never been invented. Another starched and ruffled maid was passing a tray heaped high with cakes.

Gobbling and gulping I trailed about the room after Pickwick, shaking the hands of the people he singled out. They were strange introductions for no names were mentioned, only, occasionally, an address, and "Ask for Mrs. Smit." When I had met my fourth Smit, Kik explained with a grin, "It's the only last name in the underground."

So this was really and truly the underground! But—where were these people from? I had never laid eyes on any of them. A second later I realized with a shiver down my spine that I was meeting the national group.

Their chief work, I gleaned from bits of conversation, was liaison with England and the Free Dutch forces fighting elsewhere on the continent. They also maintained the underground route through which downed Allied plane crews reached the North Sea coast.

But they were instantly sympathetic with my efforts to help Haarlem's Jews. I blushed to my hair roots to hear Pickwick describe me as "the head of an operation here in this city." A hollow space under the stairs and some haphazard friendships were not an operation. The others here were

---

7. *Pickwick.* The author recognizes one of her wealthy Dutch customers who looks like Pickwick, the Dickens character.

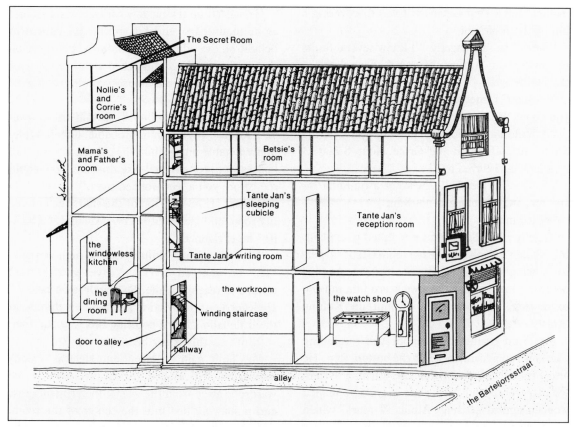

The rooms of the building offered many spaces and a great distance between the street and the hiding place.

obviously competent, disciplined, and professional.

But they greeted me with grave courtesy, murmuring what they had to offer as we shook hands. False identity papers. The use of a car with official government plates. Signature forgery.

In a far corner of the room Pickwick introduced me to a frail-appearing little man with a wispy goatee. "Our host informs me," the little man began formally, "that your headquarters building lacks a secret room. This is a danger for all, those you are helping as well as yourselves and those who work with you. With your permission I will pay you a visit in the coming week. . . ."

Years later I learned that he was one of the most famous architects in Europe. I knew him only as Mr. Smit.

Just before Kik and I started our dash back to the Beje, Pickwick slipped an arm through mine. "My dear, I have good news. I understand that Peter is about to be released." . . .

So he was, three days later, thinner, paler, and not a whit daunted by his two months in a concrete cell. Nollie, Tine, and Betsie used up a month's sugar ration baking cakes for his welcome-home party.

And one morning soon afterward the first customer in the shop was a small thin-bearded man named Smit. Father took his jeweler's glass from his eye. If there was one thing he loved better than making a new acquaintance, it was discovering a link with an old one.

"Smit," he said eagerly. "I know several Smits in Amsterdam. Are you by any chance related to the family who—"

"Father," I interrupted, "this is the man I told you about. He's come to, ah, inspect the house."

"A building inspector? Then you must be the Smit with offices in the Grote Hout Straat. I wonder that I haven't—"

"Father!" I pleaded, "he's not a building inspector, and his name is not Smit."

"Not Smit?"

Together Mr. Smit and I attempted to explain, but Father simply could not understand a person's being called by a name not his own. As I led Mr. Smit into the back hall we heard him musing to himself, "I once knew a Smit on Koning Straat. . . ."

Mr. Smit examined and approved the hiding place for ration cards beneath the bottom step. He also pronounced acceptable the warning system we had worked out. This was a triangle-shaped wooden sign advertising "Alpina Watches" which I had placed in the dining-room window. As long as the sign was in place, it was safe to enter.

But when I showed him a cubbyhole behind the corner cupboard in the dining room, he shook his head. Some ancient redesigning of the house had left a crawl space in that corner and we'd been secreting jewelry, silver coins, and other valuables there since the start of the occupation. Not only the rabbi had brought us his library but other Jewish families had brought their treasures to the Beje for safekeeping. The space was large enough that we had believed a person could crawl in there if necessary, but Mr. Smit dismissed it without a second glance.

"First place they'd look. Don't bother to change it though. It's only silver. We're interested in saving people, not things."

He started up the narrow corkscrew stairs, and as he mounted so did his spirits. He paused in delight at the odd-placed landings, pounded on the crooked walls, and laughed aloud as the floor levels of the two old houses continued out of phase.

"What an impossibility!" he said in an awe-struck voice. "What an improbable, unbelievable, unpredictable impossibility! Miss ten Boom, if all houses were constructed like this one, you would see before you a less worried man."

At last, at the very top of the stairs, he entered my room and gave a little cry of delight. "This is it!" he exclaimed.

"You want your hiding place as high as possible," he went on eagerly. "Gives you the best chance to reach it while the search is on below." He leaned out the window, craning his thin neck, the little faun's beard pointing this way and that.

"But . . . this is my bedroom. . . ."

Mr. Smit paid no attention. He was already measuring. He moved the heavy, wobbly old wardrobe away from the wall with surprising ease and pulled my bed into the center of the room. "This is where the false wall will go!" Excitedly he drew out a pencil and drew a line along the floor thirty inches from the back wall. He stood up and gazed at it moodily.

"That's as big as I dare," he said. "It will take a cot mattress, though. Oh, yes. Easily!"

I tried again to protest, but Mr. Smit had forgotten I existed. Over the next few days he and his workmen were in and out of our house constantly. They never knocked. At each visit each man carried in something. Tools in a folded newspaper. A few bricks in a briefcase. "Wood!" he exclaimed when I ventured to wonder if a wooden wall would not be easier to build. "Wood sounds hollow. Hear it in a minute. No, no. Brick's the only thing for false walls."

After the wall was up, the plasterer came, then

the carpenter, finally the painter. Six days after he had begun, Mr. Smit called Father, Betsie, and me to see.

We stood in the doorway and gaped. The smell of fresh paint was everywhere. But surely nothing in this room was newly painted! All four walls had that streaked and grimy look that old rooms got in coal-burning Haarlem. The ancient molding ran unbroken around the ceiling, chipped and peeling here and there, obviously undisturbed for a hundred and fifty years. Old water stains streaked the back wall, a wall that even I, who had lived half a century in this room, could scarcely believe was not the original, but set back a precious two-and-a-half feet from the true wall of the building.

Built-in bookshelves ran along this false wall, old, sagging shelves whose blistered wood bore the same water stains as the wall behind them. Down in the far lefthand corner, beneath the bottom shelf, a sliding panel, two feet high and two wide, opened into the secret room.

Mr. Smit stooped and silently pulled this panel up. On hands and knees Betsie and I crawled into the narrow room behind it. Once inside we could stand up, sit or even stretch out one at a time on the single mattress. A concealed vent, cunningly let into the real wall, allowed air to enter from outside.

"Keep a water jug there," said Mr. Smit, crawling in behind us. "Change the water once a week. Hardtack and vitamins keep indefinitely. Anytime there is anyone in the house whose presence is unofficial, all possessions except the clothes actually on his back must be stored in here."

Dropping to our knees again, we crawled single file out into my bedroom. "Move back into this room," he told me. "Everything exactly as before."

With his fist he struck the wall above the bookshelves.

"The Gestapo could search for a year," he said. "They'll never find this one."

## THINK AND DISCUSS
### Understanding
1. Describe the hiding place. (You may want to look at the diagram on page 607.)
2. Which details of the construction of the secret room most surprise Corrie ten Boom?
3. Why is the architect Smit so sure the Gestapo will never discover it?

### Analyzing
4. Why does Peter's playing the "Wilhelmus" arouse such intense feelings in the audience?
5. How does this episode in the church help set the **mood** for what follows?
6. How does ten Boom's ongoing volunteer work provide her with a contact, a source of help in her secret work?
7. How does Fred Koornstra's method of covering up the fake robbery illustrate the wisdom of Willem's advice?
8. Explain ten Boom's reactions and those of the national underground leaders when she finally meets them.

### Extending
9. After the war, Corrie ten Boom set up a home in the Netherlands for other victims of Nazi purges, as well as for some of the Nazi tormentors. Why do you think she was willing to help the tormentors after the war?

**APPLYING: Connotation/Denotation** H𝒯
**See Handbook of Literary Terms, p. 794**

**Connotations** are the associations and added meanings surrounding a word that are not part of its literal dictionary definition, or **denotation.** The connotations of certain words may call to a reader's mind emotions—favorable or unfavorable—that add significance and impact beyond the denotations alone.

1. When Corrie ten Boom mentions older people, she refers to them as *elderly* rather than *old.* How does this word choice express her feeling about the people?
2. She discusses the connotation of a word when she comments about how she felt upon being told to "develop her own sources." How does the term *sources* sound to her? How does it affect her work?

## COMPOSITION ◄━━
### Retelling an Episode

This selection contains several instances of Corrie and her family's welcoming Jewish refugees into their home. Write a three-paragraph account for your classmates in which you describe what she does to protect one or more of the refugees. If you wish, you may invent an imaginary episode and narrate it.

### Describing Character Traits

Obviously, the risks ten Boom and her associates take show courage. However, her narrative reveals that other qualities such as coolheadedness, cooperation, and ingenuity were just as important in the defense against the Nazis. Review the selection for evidence of these character traits, take notes, and write a three-paragraph composition in which you show how ten Boom has demonstrated all of these traits. If you prefer, select a single quality and describe how characters demonstrate it.

## ENRICHMENT
### Researching a World War II Topic

"The Secret Room" provides information about events in Europe that led to World War II. To learn more about the time and place in which the ten Boom family lived, go to your school library for reference books and conduct research on the Netherlands or other European countries greatly affected by the war, such as Germany, France, Russia, or Poland. Take notes on the way of life before, during, and after the war. If possible, interview someone who lived in Europe during the war or fought in the war. When you finish your research, report your findings to the rest of the class.

## BIOGRAPHY

### Corrie ten Boom
### 1892–1983

Corrie ten Boom was fifty-two years old when the Nazis, suspecting the family of hiding Jews, arrested them. Imprisoned, her father was the first to die; then Betsie, who along with Corrie had endured unspeakable torments in the concentration camp at Ravensbruck, died.

As the result of a clerical error, ten Boom was released close to the end of World War II instead of being sent to the gas chambers. She returned to her home, regained health, and went on to establish a home for other victims of Nazi purges. Details of her remarkable experiences are recorded in her autobiography, *The Hiding Place.*

# I Escape from the Boers

**Winston Churchill**   Great Britain

**Fleeing across the vast South African territory, young Churchill finds that his own basic qualities and the stars overhead are all he can rely on.**

*The year was 1899. A longstanding land- and political-rights dispute flared into war between British immigrants in South Africa, who had been pouring in since the early 1800s, and the Boers (bôrz), the descendants of Dutch farmers who had settled in South Africa in the mid-1600s. Battle lines of the Boer War were drawn quickly: Great Britain backed the cause of its former subjects by sending troops to British-controlled Cape Colony; the South African Republic, based in the Transvaal (trans väl') province, was joined by the neighboring Orange Free State in protecting its borders from the British.*

*Twenty-five-year-old Winston Churchill, known only as the son of an English lord, set out eagerly for South Africa as a soldier and war correspondent for the* Morning Post. *This dual role enabled him to participate in and report on the action. Within a month after Churchill's arrival, he took part in the daring rescue of an armored train that had been ambushed by the Boers. Although he aided in the escape of several wounded soldiers, he was captured by the enemy and taken to a prison camp in Pretoria, the capital city. The following is Churchill's descriptive account of his escape from the prison, a feat that catapulted him into public life.*

he State Model Schools[1] stood in the midst of a quadrangle, and were surrounded on two sides by an iron grille and on two by a corrugated-iron fence about ten feet high. These boundaries offered little obstacle to anyone who possessed the activity of youth, but the fact that they were guarded on the inside by sentries, fifty yards apart, armed with rifle and revolver, made them a well-nigh insuperable barrier. No walls are so hard to pierce as living walls.

After anxious reflection and continual watching, it was discovered by several of the prisoners that when the sentries along the eastern side walked about on their beats they were at certain

---

1. ***State Model Schools,*** Churchill's place of confinement.

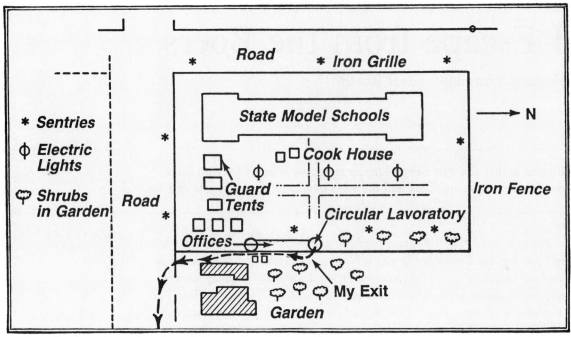

The grounds of the State Model Schools, from which Churchill escaped.

moments unable to see the top of a few yards of the wall near a small circular lavatory office. The electric lights in the middle of the quadrangle brilliantly lighted the whole place, but the eastern wall was in shadow. The first thing was therefore to pass the two sentries near the office. It was necessary to hit off the exact moment when both their backs should be turned together. After the wall was scaled we should be in the garden of the villa next door. There the plan came to an end. Everything after this was vague and uncertain. How to get out of the garden, how to pass unnoticed through the streets, how to evade the patrols that surrounded the town, and above all how to cover the two hundred and eighty miles to the Portuguese frontier,[2] were questions which would arise at a later stage.

Together with two British officers I made an abortive attempt, not pushed with any decision, on December 11. There was no difficulty in get-

ting into the circular office. But to climb out of it over the wall was a hazard of the sharpest character. Anyone doing so must at the moment he was on the top of the wall be plainly visible to the sentries fifteen yards away, if they were in the right place and happened to look! Whether the sentries would challenge or fire depended entirely upon their individual dispositions, and no one could tell what they would do. Nevertheless I was determined that nothing should stop my taking the plunge the next day. As the twelfth wore away my fears crystallized more and more into desperation. In the evening, after my two friends had made an attempt but had not found the moment propitious, I strolled across the quandrangle and secreted myself in the circular office. Through an aperture in the metal casing of which it was built I

2. *Portuguese frontier,* the border of Portuguese East Africa (now Mozambique), northeast of South Africa and a place of safety.

watched the sentries. For some time they remained stolid and obstructive. Then all of a sudden one turned and walked up to his comrade, and they began to talk. Their backs were turned.

Now or never! I stood on a ledge, seized the top of the wall with my hands, and drew myself up. Twice I let myself down again in sickly hesitation, and then with a third resolve scrambled up and over. My waistcoat got entangled with the ornamental metalwork on the top. I had to pause for an appreciable moment to extricate myself. In this posture I had one parting glimpse of the sentries still talking with their backs turned fifteen yards away. One of them was lighting his cigarette, and I remember the glow on the inside of his hands as a distinct impression which my mind recorded. Then I lowered myself lightly down into the adjoining garden and crouched among the shrubs. I was free! The first step had been taken, and it was irrevocable. It now remained to await the arrival of my comrades. The bushes in the garden gave a good deal of cover, and in the moonlight their shadows fell dark on the ground. I lay there for an hour in great impatience and anxiety. People were continually moving about in the garden, and once a man came and apparently looked straight at me only a few yards away. Where were the others? Why did they not make the attempt?

Suddenly I heard a voice from within the quadrangle say, quite loud, "All up." I crawled back to the wall. Two British officers were walking up and down inside, laughing and talking all manner of nonsense—amid which I caught my name. I risked a cough. One of the officers immediately began to chatter alone. The other said, slowly and clearly, "They cannot get out. The sentry suspects. It's all up. Can you get back again?" But now all my fears fell from me at once. I said to the officers, "I shall go on alone."

Now I was in the right mood for these undertakings—failure being almost certain, no odds against success affected me. The gate which led into the road was only a few yards from another sentry. I said to myself, "Toujours de l'audace,"[3] put my hat on my head, strode into the middle of the garden, walked past the windows of the house without any attempt at concealment, and so went through the gate and turned to the left. I passed the sentry at less than five yards. Most of them knew me by sight. Whether he looked at me or not I do not know, for I never turned my head. I restrained with the utmost difficulty an impulse to run. But after walking a hundred yards and hearing no challenge, I knew that the second obstacle had been surmounted. I was at large in Pretoria.

I walked on leisurely through the night, humming a tune and choosing the middle of the road. The streets were full of burghers,[4] but they paid no attention to me. Gradually I reached the suburbs, and on a little bridge I sat down to reflect and consider. I was in the heart of the enemy's country. I knew no one to whom I could apply for succor. Nearly three hundred miles stretched between me and Delagoa Bay.[5] My escape must be known at dawn. Pursuit would be immediate. Yet all exits were barred. The town was picketed, the country was patrolled, the trains were searched, the line was guarded. I wore a civilian brown flannel suit. I had seventy-five pounds[6] in my pocket and four slabs of chocolate, but the compass and the map which might have guided me, the meat lozenges which should have sustained me, were in my friends' pockets in the State Model Schools. Worst of all, I could not speak a word of Dutch or Kaffir,[7] and how was I to get food or direction?

---

3. *"Toujours de l'audace"* (tü zhur′ də lō dàs′), boldness always pays. [*French*]
4. *burghers* (bèr′gərz), Dutch settlers in South Africa and their descendants.
5. *Delagoa Bay,* bay just inside the Portuguese East Africa border.
6. *seventy-five pounds.* At that time, this amount in English money was worth about three hundred dollars.
7. *Kaffir* (kaf′ər), the language of the Kaffirs, a Bantu native group in South Africa.

But when hope had departed, fear had gone as well. I formed a plan, I would find the Delagoa Bay Railway. Without map or compass, I must follow that in spite of the pickets. I looked at the stars. Orion shone brightly. Scarcely a year before he had guided me when lost in the desert to the banks of the Nile. He had given me water. Now he should lead to freedom. I could not endure the want of either.

After walking south for half a mile I struck the railroad. Was it the line to Delagoa Bay or the Pietersburg[8] branch? If it were the former, it should run east. But, so far as I could see, this line ran northwards. Still, it might be only winding its way out among the hills. I resolved to follow it. The night was delicious. A cool breeze fanned my face, and a wild feeling of exhilaration took hold of me. At any rate, I was free, if only for an hour. That was something. The fascination of the adventure grew. Unless the stars in their courses fought for me, I could not escape. Where, then, was the need of caution? I marched briskly along the line. Here and there the lights of a picket fire gleamed. Every bridge had its watchers. But I passed them all, making very short detours at the dangerous places, and really taking scarcely any precautions. Perhaps that was the reason I succeeded.

As I walked I extended my plan. I could not march three hundred miles to the frontier. I would board a train in motion and hide under the seats, on the roof, on the couplings—anywhere. What train should I take? The first, of course. After walking for two hours I perceived the signal lights of a station. I left the line, and circling round it, hid in the ditch by the track about two hundred yards beyond the platform. I argued that the train would stop at the station and that it would not have got up too much speed by the time it reached me. An hour passed. I began to grow impatient. Suddenly I heard the whistle and the approaching rattle. Then the great yellow head-lights of the engine flashed into view. The train waited five minutes at the station, and started again with much noise and steaming. I crouched by the track. I rehearsed the act in my mind. I must wait until the engine has passed, otherwise I should be seen. Then I must make a dash for the carriages.

The train started slowly, but gathered speed sooner than I had expected. The flaring lights drew swiftly near. The rattle became a roar. The dark mass hung for a second above me. Then I hurled myself on the trucks, clutched at something, missed, clutched again, missed again, grasped some sort of handhold, was swung off my feet—my toes bumping on the line, and with a struggle seated myself on the couplings of the fifth truck from the front of the train. It was a goods train, and the trucks were full of sacks, soft sacks covered with coal dust. They were in fact bags filled with empty coal bags going back to their colliery.[9] I crawled on top and burrowed in among them. In five minutes I was completely buried. The sacks were warm and comfortable. Perhaps the engine driver had seen me rush up to the train and would give the alarm at the next station; on the other hand, perhaps not. Where was the train going to? Where would it be unloaded? Would it be searched? Was it on the Delagoa Bay line? What should I do in the morning? Ah, never mind that. Sufficient for the night was the luck thereof. Fresh plans for fresh contingencies. I resolved to sleep, nor can I imagine a more pleasing lullaby than the clatter of the train that carries an escaping prisoner at twenty miles an hour away from the enemy's capital.

How long I slept I do not know, but I woke up suddenly with all feelings of exhilaration gone, and only the consciousness of oppressive difficulties heavy on me. I must leave the train before

---

8. *Pietersburg* (pē′tərz bèrg′), a South African city about two hundred miles north of Pretoria.

9. *colliery* (kol′yər ē), a coal-mining complex.

daybreak, so that I could drink at a pool and find some hiding place while it was still dark. I would not run the risk of being unloaded with the coal bags. Another night I would board another train. I crawled from my cozy hiding place among the sacks and sat again on the couplings. The train was running at a fair speed, but I felt it was time to leave it. I took hold of the iron handle at the back of the truck, pulled strongly with my left hand, and sprang. My feet struck the ground in two gigantic strides, and the next instant I was sprawling in the ditch, considerably shaken but unhurt. The train, my faithful ally of the night, hurried on its journey.

It was still dark. I was in the middle of a wide valley, surrounded by low hills, and carpeted with high grass drenched in dew. I searched for water in the nearest gully, and soon found a clear pool. I was very thirsty, but long after I had quenched my thirst I continued to drink, that I might have sufficient for the whole day.

Presently the dawn began to break, and the sky to the east grew yellow and red, slashed across with heavy black clouds. I saw with relief that the railway ran steadily towards the sunrise. I had taken the right line, after all.

Having drunk my fill, I set out for the hills, among which I hoped to find some hiding place, and as it became broad daylight I entered a small grove of trees which grew on the side of a deep ravine. Here I resolved to wait till dusk. I had one consolation: no one in the world knew where I was—I did not know myself. It was now four o'clock. Fourteen hours lay between me and the night. My impatience to proceed while I was still strong doubled their length. At first it was terribly cold, but by degrees the sun gained power, and by ten o'clock the heat was oppressive. My sole companion was a gigantic vulture, who manifested an extravagant interest in my condition, and made hideous and ominous gurglings from time to time. From my lofty position I commanded a view of the whole valley. A little tin-roofed town lay three miles to the westward. Scattered farmsteads, each with a clump of trees, relieved the monotony of the undulating ground. At the foot of a hill stood a Kaffir kraal,[10] and the figures of its inhabitants dotted the patches of cultivation or surrounded the droves of goats and cows which fed on the pasture. . . . During the day I ate one slab of chocolate, which, with the heat, produced a violent thirst. The pool was hardly half a mile away, but I dared not leave the shelter of the little wood, for I could see the figures of white men riding or walking occasionally across the valley, and once a Boer came and fired two shots at birds close to my hiding place. But no one discovered me.

The elation and the excitement of the previous night had burned away, and a chilling reaction followed. I was very hungry, for I had had no dinner before starting, and chocolate, though it sustains, does not satisfy. I had scarcely slept, but yet my heart beat so fiercely and I was so nervous and perplexed about the future that I could not rest. I thought of all the chances that lay against me; I dreaded and detested more than words can express the prospect of being caught and dragged back to Pretoria. I realized with awful force that no exercise of my own feeble wit and strength could save me from my enemies, and I prayed long and earnestly for help and guidance. My prayer, as it seems to me, was swiftly and wonderfully answered.

During the day I had watched the railway with attention. I saw two or three trains pass along it each way. I argued that the same number would pass at night. I resolved to board one of these. I thought I could improve on my procedure of the previous evening. I had observed how slowly the trains, particularly long goods-trains, climbed some of the steep gradients. Sometimes they were

---

10. *kraal* (kräl), an enclosed village of South African natives.

hardly going at a foot's pace. It would probably be easy to choose a point where the line was not only on an upgrade but also on a curve. Thus I could board some truck on the convex side of the train when both the engine and the guard's van were bent away, and when consequently neither the engine driver nor the guard would see me. This plan seemed to me in every respect sound. I saw myself leaving the train again before dawn, having been carried forward another sixty or seventy miles during the night. That would be scarcely one hundred and fifty miles from the frontier. And why should not the process be repeated? Where was the flaw? I could not see it. With three long bounds on three successive nights I could be in Portuguese territory. Meanwhile I still had two or three slabs of chocolate and a pocketful of crumbled biscuit—enough, that is to say, to keep body and soul together at a pinch without running the awful risk of recapture entailed by accosting a single human being. In this mood I watched with increasing impatience the arrival of darkness.

The long day reached its close at last. The western clouds flushed into fire; the shadows of the hills stretched out across the valley; a ponderous Boer wagon with its long team crawled slowly along the tracks towards the township; the Kaffirs collected their herds and drew them round their kraal; the daylight died, and soon it was quite dark. Then, and not until then, I set forth. I hurried to the railway line, scrambling along through the boulders and high grass and pausing on my way to drink at a stream of sweet cold water. I made my way to the place where I had seen the trains crawling so slowly up the slope, and soon found a point where the curve of the track fulfilled all the conditions of my plan. Here, behind a little bush, I sat down and waited hopefully. An hour passed; two hours passed; three hours—and yet no train. Six hours had now elapsed since the last, whose time I had carefully noted, had gone by. Surely one was due.

Another hour slipped away. Still no train! My plan began to crumble and my hopes to ooze out of me. After all, was it not quite possible that no trains ran on this part of the line during the dark hours? This was in fact the case, and I might well have continued to wait in vain till daylight. However, between twelve and one in the morning, I lost patience and started along the track, resolved to cover at any rate ten or fifteen miles of my journey. I did not make much progress. Every bridge was guarded by armed men; every few miles were huts. At intervals there were stations with tin-roofed villages clustering around them. All the veldt was bathed in the bright rays of the full moon, and to avoid these dangerous places I had to make wide circuits and even to creep along the ground. Leaving the railroad I fell into bogs and swamps, brushed through high grass dripping with dew, and waded across the streams over which the bridges carried the railway. I was soon drenched to the waist. I had been able to take very little exercise during my month's imprisonment, and I was quickly tired with walking and with want of food and sleep. Presently I approached a station. It was a mere platform in the veldt, with two or three buildings and huts around it. But laid up on the sidings, obviously for the night, were three long goods-trains. Evidently the flow of traffic over the railway was uneven. These three trains, motionless in the moonlight, confirmed my fears that traffic was not maintained by night on this part of the line. Where, then, was my plan which in the afternoon had looked so fine and sure?

It now occurred to me that I might board one of these stationary trains immediately, and hiding amid its freight be carried forward during the next day—and night too if all were well. On the other hand, where were they going to? Where would they stop? Where would they be unloaded? Once I entered a wagon my lot would be cast. It was necessary at all costs before taking such a step to find out where these trains were going. To do this I must penetrate the station, examine the labels on the trucks or on the merchandise, and see if I could extract any certain guidance from them. I crept up to the platform and got between two of the long trains on the siding. I was proceeding to examine the markings on the trucks when loud voices rapidly approaching on the outside of the trains filled me with fear. Several Kaffirs were laughing and shouting in their unmodulated tones, and I heard, as I thought, a European voice arguing or ordering. At any rate, it was enough for me. I retreated between the two trains to the extreme end of the siding, and slipped stealthily but rapidly into the grass of the illimitable plain.

There was nothing for it but to plod on—but in an increasingly purposeless and hopeless manner. I felt very miserable when I looked around and saw here and there the lights of houses and thought of the warmth and comfort within them, but knew that they meant only danger to me. Far off on the moonlit horizon there presently began to shine the row of six or eight big lights which marked either Witbank or Middleburg station. Out in the darkness to my left gleamed two or three fires. I was sure they were not the lights of houses, but how far off they were or what they were I could not be certain. The idea formed in my mind that they were the fires of a Kaffir kraal. Then I began to think that the best use I could make of my remaining strength would be to go to these Kaffirs. I had heard that they hated the Boers and were friendly to the British. At any rate, they would probably not arrest me. They might give me food and a dry corner to sleep in. Although I could not speak a word of their language, yet I thought perhaps they might understand the value of a British bank note. They might even be induced to help me. A guide, a pony—but, above all, rest, warmth, and food—such were the promptings which dominated my mind. So I set out towards the fires.

I must have walked a mile or so in this resolve before a realization of its weakness and imprudence took possession of me. Then I turned back again to the railway line and retraced my steps perhaps half the distance. Then I stopped and sat down, completely baffled, destitute of any idea what to do or where to turn. Suddenly without the slightest reason all my doubts disappeared. It was certainly by no process of logic that they were dispelled. I just felt quite clear that I would go to the Kaffir kraal.

I walked on rapidly towards the fires, which I had in the first instance thought were not more than a couple of miles away from the railway line. I soon found they were much farther away than that. After about an hour or an hour and a half they still seemed almost as far off as ever. But I persevered, and presently between two and three o'clock in the morning I perceived that they were not the fires of a Kaffir kraal. The angular outline of buildings began to draw out against them, and soon I saw that I was approaching a group of houses around the mouth of a coal mine. The wheel which worked the winding gear was plainly visible, and I could see that the fires which had led me so far were from the furnaces of the engines. Hard by, surrounded by one or two slighter structures, stood a small but substantial stone house two stories high.

I halted in the wilderness to survey this scene and to resolve my action. It was still possible to turn back. But in that direction I saw nothing but the prospect of further futile wanderings terminated by hunger, fever, discovery, or surrender. On the other hand, here in front was a chance. I had heard it said before I escaped that in the mining district of Witbank and Middleburg there were a certain number of English residents who had been suffered to remain in the country in order to keep the mines working. Had I been led to one of these? What did this house which frowned dark and inscrutable upon me contain? A

Briton or a Boer; a friend or a foe?

The odds were heavy against me, and it was with faltering and reluctant steps that I walked out of the shimmering gloom of the veldt into the light of the furnace fires, advanced towards the silent house, and struck with my fist upon the door.

There was a pause. Then I knocked again. And almost immediately a light sprang up above and an upper window opened.

"*Wer ist da?*"[11] cried a man's voice.

I felt the shock of disappointment and consternation to my fingers.

"I want help; I have had an accident," I replied.

Some muttering followed. Then I heard steps descending the stairs, the bolt of the door was drawn, the lock was turned. It was opened abruptly, and in the darkness of the passage a tall man hastily attired, with a pale face and dark mustache, stood before me.

"What do you want?" he said, this time in English.

I had now to think of something to say. I wanted above all to get into parley with this man, to get matters in such a state that instead of raising an alarm and summoning others he would discuss things quietly.

"I am a burgher," I began. "I have had an accident. I was going to join my commando at Komati Poort.[12] I have fallen off the train. We were skylarking. I have been unconscious for hours. I think I have dislocated my shoulder."

It was astonishing how one thinks of these things. This story leaped out as if I had learned it by heart. Yet I had not the slightest idea what I was going to say or what the next sentence would be.

The stranger regarded me intently, and after some hesitation said at length, "Well, come in." He retreated a little into the darkness of the passage, threw open a door on one side of it, and

pointed with his left hand into a dark room. I walked past him and entered, wondering if it was to be my prison. He followed, struck a light, lit a lamp, and set it on the table at the far side of which I stood. I was in a small room, evidently a dining room and office in one. I noticed, besides the large table, a roll desk, two or three chairs, and one of those machines for making soda-water. On his end of the table my host had laid a revolver, which he had hitherto presumably been holding in his right hand.

"I think I'd like to know a little more about this railway accident of yours," he said, after a considerable pause.

"I think," I replied, "I had better tell you the truth."

"I think you had," he said, slowly.

So I took the plunge and threw all I had upon the board.

"I am Winston Churchill, War Correspondent of the *Morning Post*. I escaped last night from Pretoria. I am making my way to the frontier." (Making my way!) "I have plenty of money. Will you help me?"

There was another long pause. My companion rose from the table slowly and locked the door. After this act, which struck me as unpromising, and was certainly ambiguous, he advanced upon me and suddenly held out his hand.

"Thank God you have come here! It is the only house for twenty miles where you would not have been handed over. But we are all British here, and we will see you through."

It is easier to recall across the gulf of years the spasm of relief which swept over me than it is to describe it. A moment before I had thought myself trapped; and now friends, food, resources, aid

---

11. *"Wer ist da?"* "Who is there?"; a phrase in Afrikaans (af'rə käns'), the language related to Dutch and spoken by the Boers.
12. *Komati Poort* (kō mä'tē pôrt'), a South African city on the border of Portuguese East Africa.

were all at my disposal. I felt like a drowning man pulled out of the water and informed he has won the Derby!

My host now introduced himself as Mr. John Howard, manager of the Transvaal Collieries. He had become a naturalized burgher of the Transvaal some years before the war. But out of consideration for his British race and some inducements which he had offered to the local Field Cornet, he had not been called up to fight against the British. Instead he had been allowed to remain with one or two others on the mine, keeping it pumped out and in good order until coal cutting could be resumed. He had with him at the mine-head, besides his secretary, who was British, an engineman from Lancashire and two Scottish miners. All these four were British subjects and had been allowed to remain only upon giving their parole to observe strict neutrality. He himself as burgher of the Transvaal Republic would be guilty of treason in harboring me, and liable to be shot if caught at the time or found out later on.

"Never mind," he said, "we will fix it up somehow." And added, "The Field Cornet was round here this afternoon asking about you. They have got the hue and cry out all along the line and all over the district."

I said that I did not wish to compromise him. Let him give me food, a pistol, a guide, and if possible a pony, and I would make my own way to the sea, marching by night across country far away from the railway line or any habitation.

He would not hear of it. He would fix up something. But he enjoined the utmost caution. Spies were everywhere. He had two Dutch servant-maids actually sleeping in the house. There were many Kaffirs employed about the mine premises and on the pumping machinery of the mine. Surveying these dangers he became very thoughtful.

Then: "But you are famishing."

I did not contradict him. In a moment he had bustled off into the kitchen. He returned after an interval with the best part of a cold leg of mutton and various other delectable commodities, and, leaving me to do full justice to these, quitted the room and let himself out of the house by a back door.

Nearly an hour passed before Mr. Howard returned. In this period my physical well-being had been brought into harmony with the improvement in my prospects. I felt confident of success and equal to anything.

"It's all right," said Mr. Howard. "I have seen the men, and they are all for it. We must put you down the pit tonight, and there you will have to stay till we can see how to get you out of the country. One difficulty," he said, "will be the *skoff* (food). The Dutch girl sees every mouthful I eat. The cook will want to know what has happened to her leg of mutton. I shall have to think it all out during the night. You must get down the pit at once. We'll make you comfortable enough."

Accordingly, just as the dawn was breaking, I followed my host across a little yard into the enclosure in which stood the winding-wheel of the mine. Here a stout man, introduced as Mr. Dewsnap, of Oldham, locked my hand in a grip of crushing vigor.

A door was opened and I entered the cage. Down we shot into the bowels of the earth. At the bottom of the mine were the two Scottish miners with lanterns and a big bundle which afterwards proved to be a mattress and blankets. We walked for some time through the pitchy labyrinth, with frequent turns, twists, and alterations of level, and finally stopped in a sort of chamber where the air was cool and fresh. Here my guide set down his bundle, and Mr. Howard handed me a couple of candles, a bottle of whiskey, and a box of cigars.

"There's no difficulty about these," he said. "I keep them under lock and key. Now we must plan how to feed you tomorrow."

"Don't you move from here, whatever happens," was the parting injunction. "There will be Kaffirs about the mine after daylight, but we shall be on the lookout that none of them wanders this way. None of them has seen anything so far."

My four friends trooped off with their lanterns, and I was left alone. Viewed from the velvety darkness of the pit, life seemed bathed in rosy light. After the perplexity and even despair through which I had passed I counted upon freedom as certain. Speeded by intense fatigue, I soon slept the sleep of the weary—but of the triumphant.

I do not know how many hours I slept, but the following afternoon must have been far advanced when I found myself thoroughly awake. I put out my hand for the candle, but could feel it nowhere. I did not know what pitfalls these mining galleries might contain, so I thought it better to lie quiet on my mattress and await developments. Several hours passed before the faint gleam of a lantern showed that someone was coming. It proved to be Mr. Howard himself, armed with a chicken and other good things. He also brought several books. He asked me why I had not lighted my candle. I said I couldn't find it.

"Didn't you put it under the mattress?" he asked.

"No."

"Then the rats must have got it."

He told me there were swarms of rats in the mine, that some years ago he had introduced a particular kind of white rat, which was an excellent scavenger, and that these had multiplied and thriven exceedingly. He told me he had been to the house of an English doctor twenty miles away to get the chicken. He was worried at the attitude of the two Dutch servants, who were very inquisitive about the depredations upon the leg of mutton for which I had been responsible. If he could not get another chicken cooked for the next day, he would have to take double helpings on his own plate and slip the surplus into a parcel for me while the servant was out of the room. He said that inquiries were being made for me all over the district by the Boers, and that the Pretoria Government was making a tremendous fuss about my escape. The fact that there were a number of English remaining in the Middleburg mining region indicated it as a likely place for me to have turned to, and all persons of English origin were more or less suspect.

I again expressed my willingness to go on alone with a Kaffir guide and a pony, but this he utterly refused to entertain. It would take a lot of planning, he said, to get me out of the country, and I might have to stay in the mine for quite a long time.

"Here," he said "you are absolutely safe. Mac" (by which he meant one of the Scottish miners) "knows all the disused workings and places that no one else would dream of. There is one place here where the water actually touches the roof for a foot or two. If they searched the mine, Mac would dive under that with you into the workings cut off beyond the water. No one would ever think of looking there."

He stayed with me while I dined, and then departed, leaving me, among other things, half-a-dozen candles which, duly warned, I tucked under my pillow and mattress.

I slept again for a long time, and woke suddenly with a feeling of movement about me. Something seemed to be pulling at my pillow. I put out my hand quickly. There was a perfect scurry. The rats were at the candles. I rescued the candles in time, and lighted one. Luckily for me, I have no horror of rats as such, and being reassured by their evident timidity, I was not particularly uneasy. All the same, the three days I passed in the mine were not among the most pleasant which my memory reillumines. The patter of little feet and a perceptible sense of stir and scurry were continuous. Once I was waked up from a doze by one actually galloping across me. On the candle being lighted these beings became invisible.

The next day—if you can call it day—arrived in due course. This was December 14, and the third day since I had escaped from the State Model Schools. It was relieved by a visit from the two Scottish miners, with whom I had a long confabulation. I then learned, to my surprise, that the mine was only about two hundred feet deep.

On the fifteenth Mr. Howard announced that the hue and cry seemed to be dying away. No trace of the fugitive had been discovered throughout the mining district. The talk among the Boer officials was now that I must be hiding at the house of some British sympathizer in Pretoria. They did not believe that it was possible I could have got out of the town. In these circumstances he thought that I might come up and have a walk on the veldt that night, and that if all was quiet the next morning I might shift my quarters to the back room of the office. On the one hand he seemed reassured, and on the other increasingly excited by the adventure. Accordingly, I had a fine stroll in the glorious fresh air and moonlight, and thereafter, anticipating slightly our program, I took up my quarters behind packing cases in the inner room of the office. Here I remained for three more days, walking each night on the endless plain with Mr. Howard or his assistant.

On the sixteenth, the fifth day of escape, Mr. Howard informed me he had made a plan to get me out of the country. The mine was connected with the railway by a branch line. In the neighborhood of the mine there lived a Dutchman, Burgener by name, who was sending a consignment of wool to Delagoa Bay on the nineteenth. This gentleman was well disposed to the British. He had been approached by Mr. Howard, had been made a party to our secret, and was willing to assist. Mr. Burgener's wool was packed in great bales and would fill two or three large trucks. These trucks were to be loaded at the mine's siding. The bales could be so packed as to leave a small place in the center of the truck in which I could be concealed. A tarpaulin would be fastened over each truck after it had been loaded, and it was very unlikely indeed that, if the fastenings were found intact, it would be removed at the frontier. Did I agree to take this chance?

I was more worried about this than almost anything that had happened to me so far in my adventure. When by extraordinary chance one has gained some great advantage or prize and actually had it in one's possession and been enjoying it for several days, the idea of losing it becomes almost insupportable. I had really come to count upon freedom as a certainty, and the idea of having to put myself in a position in which I should be perfectly helpless, without a move of any kind, absolutely at the caprice of a searching party at the frontier, was profoundly harassing. Rather than face this ordeal I would much have preferred to start off on the veldt with a pony and a guide, and far from the haunts of man to make my way march by march beyond the wide territories of the Boer Republic. However, in the end I accepted the proposal of my generous rescuer, and arrangements were made accordingly.

I should have been still more anxious if I could have read some of the telegrams which were reaching English newspapers. For instance:

Pretoria, December 13.—Though Mr. Churchill's escape was cleverly executed there is little chance of his being able to cross the border.

Pretoria, December 14.—It is reported that Mr. Winston Churchill has been captured at the border railway station of Komati Poort.

Lourenço Marques,[13] December 16.—It is reported that Mr. Churchill has been captured at Waterval Boven.

---

13. *Lourenço Marques* (lô ren'sō mär'kes), a city near the head of Delagoa Bay.

London, December 16.—With reference to the escape from Pretoria of Mr. Winston Churchill, fears are expressed that he may be captured again before long and if so may probably be shot;

or if I had read the description of myself and the reward for my recapture which were now widely distributed or posted along the railway line. I am glad I knew nothing of all this.

The afternoon of the eighteenth dragged slowly away. To be a fugitive, to be a hunted man, to be "wanted," is a mental experience by itself. The risks of the battlefield, the hazards of the bullet or the shell are one thing. Having the police after you is another. The need for concealment and deception breeds an actual sense of guilt very undermining to morale. Feeling that at any moment the officers of the law may present themselves or any stranger may ask the questions, "Who are you?" "Where do you come from?" "Where are you going?"—to which questions no satisfactory answer could be given—gnawed the structure of self-confidence. I dreaded in every fiber the ordeal which awaited me at Komati Poort and which I must impotently and passively endure if I was to make good my escape from the enemy.

In this mood I was startled by the sound of rifle shots close at hand, one after another at irregular intervals. A sinister explanation flashed through my mind. The Boers had come! Howard and his handful of Englishmen were in open rebellion in the heart of the enemy's country! I had been strictly enjoined upon no account to leave my hiding place behind the packing cases in any circumstances whatever, and I accordingly remained there in great anxiety. Presently it became clear that the worst had not happened. The sounds of voices and presently of laughter came from the office. Evidently a conversation amicable, sociable in its character was in progress. At last the

voices died away, and then after an interval my door opened and Mr. Howard's pale, somber face appeared, suffused by a broad grin. He relocked the door behind him and walked delicately towards me, evidently in high glee.

"The Field Cornet has been here," he said. "No, he was not looking for you. He says they caught you at Waterval Boven yesterday. But I didn't want him messing about, so I challenged him to a rifle match at bottles. He won two pounds off me and has gone away delighted.

"It is all fixed up for tonight," he added.

"What do I do?" I asked.

"Nothing. You simply follow me when I come for you."

At two o'clock on the morning of the nineteenth I awaited, fully dressed, the signal. The door opened. My host appeared. He beckoned. Not a word was spoken on either side. He led the way through the front office to the siding where three large bogie trucks[14] stood. Three figures, evidently Dewsnap and the miners, were strolling about in different directions in the moonlight. A gang of Kaffirs were busy lifting an enormous bale into the rearmost truck. Howard strolled along to the first truck and walked across the line past the end of it. As he did so he pointed with his left hand. I nipped on to the buffers and saw before me a hole between the wool bales and the end of the truck, just wide enough to squeeze into. From this there led a narrow tunnel formed of wool bales into the center of the truck. Here was a space wide enough to lie in, high enough to sit up in. In this I took up my abode.

Three or four hours later, when gleams of daylight had reached me through the interstices of my shelter and through chinks in the boards of the floorings of the truck, the noise of an ap-

---

14. **bogie trucks,** low, strong, four-wheeled trucks or carts, in this case built as railroad cars. [*British*]

proaching engine was heard. Then came the bumping and banging of coupling up. And again, after a further pause, we started rumbling off on our journey into the unknown.

I now took stock of my new abode and of the resources in munitions and supplies with which it was furnished. First there was a revolver. This was a moral support, though it was not easy to see in what way it could helpfully be applied to any problem I was likely to have to solve. Secondly, there were two roast chickens, some slices of meat, a loaf of bread, a melon, and three bottles of cold tea. The journey to the sea was not expected to take more than sixteen hours, but no one could tell what delay might occur to ordinary commercial traffic in time of war.

There was plenty of light now in the recess in which I was confined. There were many crevices in the boards composing the sides and floor of the truck, and through these the light found its way between the wool bales. Working along the tunnel to the end of the truck, I found a chink which must have been nearly an eighth of an inch in width, and through which it was possible to gain a partial view of the outer world. To check the progress of the journey I had learned by heart beforehand the names of all the stations on the route. I can remember any of them today: Witbank, Middleburg, Bergendal, Belfast, Dalmanutha, Machadodorp, Waterval Boven, Waterval Onder, Elands, Nooidgedacht,[15] and so on to Komati Poort. We had by now reached the first of these. At this point the branch line from the mine joined the railway. Here, after two or three hours' delay and shunting, we were evidently coupled up to a regular train, and soon started off at a superior and very satisfactory pace.

All day long we traveled eastward through the Transvaal, and when darkness fell we were laid up for the night at a station which, according to my reckoning, was Waterval Boven. We had accomplished nearly half of our journey. But how long should we wait on this siding? It might be for days; it would certainly be until the next morning. During all the dragging hours of the day I had lain on the floor of the truck occupying my mind as best I could, painting bright pictures of the pleasures of freedom, of the excitement of rejoining the army, of the triumph of a successful escape—but haunted also perpetually by anxieties about the search at the frontier, an ordeal inevitable and constantly approaching. Now another apprehension laid hold upon me. I wanted to go to sleep. Indeed, I did not think I could possibly keep awake. But if I slept I might snore! And if I snored while the train was at rest in the silent siding, I might be heard. And if I were heard! I decided in principle that it was only prudent to abstain from sleep, and shortly afterwards fell into a blissful slumber from which I was awakened the next morning by the banging and jerking of the train as the engine was again coupled to it.

All this day, we rattled through the enemy's country, and late in the afternoon we reached the dreaded Komati Poort. Peeping through my chink, I could see this was a considerable place, with numerous tracks of rails and several trains standing on them. Numbers of people were moving about. There were many voices and much shouting and whistling. After a preliminary inspection of the scene I retreated, as the train pulled up, into the very center of my fastness, and covering myself up with a piece of sacking lay flat on the floor of the truck and awaited developments with a beating heart.

Three or four hours passed, and I did not know whether we had been searched or not. Several times people had passed up and down the train talking in Dutch. But the tarpaulins had not been removed, and no special examination seemed to have been made of the truck. Meanwhile darkness

---

15. *Machadodorp* (mä′chä do′dôrp) . . . *Nooidgedacht* (nü′it kú däkt′).

had come on, and I had to resign myself to an indefinite continuance of my uncertainties. It was tantalizing to be held so long in jeopardy after all these hundreds of miles had been accomplished, and I was now within a few hundred yards of the frontier. Again I wondered about the dangers of snoring. But in the end I slept without mishap.

We were still stationary when I awoke. Perhaps they were searching the train so thoroughly that there was consequently a great delay! Alternatively, perhaps we were forgotten on the siding and would be left there for days or weeks. I was greatly tempted to peer out, but I resisted. At last, at eleven o'clock, we were coupled up, and almost immediately started. If I had been right in thinking that the station in which we had passed the night was Komati Poort, I was already in Portuguese territory. But perhaps I had made a mistake. Perhaps I had miscounted. Perhaps there was still another station before the frontier. Perhaps the search still impended. But all these doubts were dispelled when the train arrived at the next station. I peered through my chink and saw the uniform caps of the Portuguese officials on the platform and the name Resana Garcia[16] painted on a board. I restrained all expression of my joy until we moved on again. Then, as we rumbled and banged along, I pushed my head out of the tarpaulin and sang and shouted and crowed at the top of my voice. Indeed, I was so carried away by thankfulness and delight that I fired my revolver two or three times in the air as a *feu de joie*.[17] None of these follies led to any evil results.

It was late in the afternoon when we reached Lourenço Marques. My train ran into a goods yard, and a crowd of Kaffirs advanced to unload it. I thought the moment had now come for me to quit my hiding place, in which I had passed nearly three anxious and uncomfortable days. I had already thrown out every vestige of food and had removed all traces of my occupation. I now slipped out at the end of the truck between the couplings, and mingling unnoticed with the Kaffirs and loafers in the yard—which my slovenly and unkempt appearance well fitted me to do—I strolled my way towards the gates and found myself in the streets of Lourenço Marques.

Burgener was waiting outside the gates. We exchanged glances. He turned and walked off into the town, and I followed twenty yards behind. We walked through several streets and turned a number of corners. Presently he stopped and stood for a moment gazing up at the roof of the opposite house. I looked in the same direction, and there—blessed vision!—I saw floating the gay colors of the Union Jack. It was the British Consulate.

The secretary of the British Consul evidently did not expect my arrival.

"Be off," he said. "The Consul cannot see you today. Come to his office at nine tomorrow, if you want anything."

At this I became so angry, and repeated so loudly that I insisted on seeing the Consul personally at once, that that gentleman himself looked out of the window and finally came down to the door and asked me my name. From that moment every resource of hospitality and welcome was at my disposal. A hot bath, clean clothing, an excellent dinner, means of telegraphing—all I could want.

I devoured the file of newspapers which was placed before me. Great battles had taken place since I had climbed the wall of the States Model Schools, and casualties on a scale unknown to England since the Crimean War. All this made me eager to rejoin the army, and the Consul himself was no less anxious to get me out of Lourenço Marques, which was full of Boers and Boer sympathizers. Happily the weekly steamer was leav-

---

16. **Resana Garcia,** a border town within Portuguese East Africa.
17. *feu de joie* (fœ də zhwä′), a rapid-fire rifle salute on an occasion of rejoicing. [*French*]

ing for Durban[18] that very evening; in fact, it might almost be said it ran in connection with my train. On this steamer I decided to embark.

The news of my arrival had spread like wildfire through the town, and while we were at dinner the Consul was at first disturbed to see a group of strange figures in the garden. These, however, turned out to be Englishmen, fully armed, who had hurried up to the Consulate determined to resist any attempt at my recapture. Under the escort of these patriotic gentlemen I marched safely through the streets to the quay, and at about ten o'clock was on salt water in steamship *Induna*.

I reached Durban to find myself a popular hero. I was received as if I had won a great victory. The harbor was decorated with flags. Bands and crowds thronged the quays. The Admiral, the General, the Mayor pressed on board to grasp my hand. I was nearly torn to pieces by enthusiastic kindness. Whirled along on the shoulders of the crowd, I was carried to the steps of the town hall, where nothing would content them but a speech, which after a becoming reluctance I was induced to deliver. Sheaves of telegrams from all parts of the world poured in upon me, and I started that night for the army in a blaze of triumph.

---

18. **Durban,** an east-coast South African city founded by the British.

## THINK AND DISCUSS
### Understanding
1. How does Churchill escape from the State Model Schools?
2. During the escape, how does he cope with the long hours in hiding, the lack of water, and the rats in the coal mine?

### Analyzing
3. Early in his account Churchill states, "No walls are so hard to pierce as living walls." How does this **figurative expression** relate to his situation at the opening of the selection?
4. Churchill's spirits are high at the outset of his escape. What are his feelings at the point he decides to go toward the fires of the Kaffir kraal?
5. What does the series of telegrams included in the account reveal about the danger he has faced?
6. Churchill is not totally comfortable with the escape method provided by the British sympathizer. Point out aspects of it that are at odds with his take-charge nature.

### Extending
7. Winston Churchill wrote this account in a very subjective, personal style. In the first-person **point of view,** he records his thoughts and feelings. How do you think the account would differ if it had been written by an objective, uninvolved observer?

## VOCABULARY
### Context
Find the meaning of the words below in the Glossary. Then read each sentence that follows and, on a sheet of paper, write the number of the sentence and the word that fits the blank. You will not use every word.

| | | |
|---|---|---|
| accost | undulating | stolid |
| futile | ominous | insupportable |
| succor | elation | parley |

1. The hunters sought shelter after seeing the _____ clouds.
2. The small boat bobbed up and down on the _____ waves.

3. After several _____ attempts, he realized that his efforts were in vain.

4. As the explorers made their way through the jungle, they felt completely oppressed by the _____ heat of the sun.

5. Judging by his _____ character, we knew that he would not be easily swayed.

## THINKING SKILLS

### Synthesizing

To **synthesize** is to put together parts or elements so as to form a whole, a new pattern or structure not evident before. Review "I Escape from the Boers" and take careful notes of the places Churchill stopped after escaping from the State Model Schools. Using a map of South Africa as a guide, draw your own map of Churchill's escape route, showing various stops he made on the way.

## COMPOSITION

### Reporting a News Event

Assume that you are a reporter for a British newspaper, and you are sent to cover Churchill's appearance at Lourenço Marques. Review Churchill's account for details, and then write a four-paragraph news story in your own words. Include what he looks like, how he announces his arrival, and how the English citizens in the city react to his escape.

### Evaluating an Autobiographical Account

In writing this account, Churchill had to decide how to portray himself. He knew that he could either handle his subject in a completely factual and unemotional manner or personalize it by including his motives and feelings. Review the selection to judge the extent to which he personalized it. Then write a three-paragraph composition to be read by your teacher in which you evaluate his use of facts and his inclusion of personal feelings. See "Writing About Nonfiction" in the Writer's Handbook.

## ENRICHMENT

### Comparing an Author's Works

"I Escape from the Boers" is one of Winston Churchill's more interesting and inspiring works, but it is by no means his only one. He wrote many books and essays, the best-known being his six-volume history, *The Second World War.* Go to your school or local library and find other books, articles, or essays by Winston Churchill. After reading one book or several short selections, compare it or them with the selection in this book. Then prepare a brief presentation to tell the class what you read, how it compares with "I Escape from the Boers," and why you did or did not like it.

## BIOGRAPHY

### Winston Churchill
### 1874–1965

A member of one of England's most distinguished families, Churchill showed no intellectual promise as a youth. To compensate for this, his father, Lord Randolph, sent him to Sandhurst, the British military school. His studies improved there, and he later became a maker of history. In the bleakest days of World War II, he became England's prime minister. His stubborn courage and stirring speeches helped to restore British faith and pride. *The Second World War* (1948–1954), his six-volume history, is regarded as a great literary achievement. In 1953 he won the Nobel Prize in Literature.

# By Any Other Name

**Santha Rama Rau**   India

"The English children in the front of the class—there were about eight or ten of them—giggled and twisted around in their chairs to look at me."

t the Anglo-Indian[1] day school in Zorinabad to which my sister and I were sent when she was eight and I was five and a half, they changed our names. On the first day of school, a hot, windless morning of a north Indian September, we stood in the headmistress's study and she said, "Now you're the *new* girls. What are your names?"

My sister answered for us. "I am Premila, and she"—nodding in my direction—"is Santha."

The headmistress had been in India, I suppose, fifteen years or so, but she still smiled her helpless inability to cope with Indian names. Her rimless half-glasses glittered, and the precarious bun on the top of her head trembled as she shook her head. "Oh, my dears, those are much too hard for me. Suppose we give you pretty English names. Wouldn't that be more jolly? Let's see, now— Pamela for you, I think." She shrugged in a baffled way at my sister. "That's as close as I can get. And for *you*," she said to me, "how about Cynthia? Isn't that nice?"

My sister was always less easily intimidated than I was, and while she kept a stubborn silence, I said, "Thank you," in a very tiny voice.

We had been sent to that school because my father, among his responsibilities as an officer of the civil service, had a tour of duty to perform in the villages around that steamy little provincial town, where he had his headquarters at that time. He used to make his shorter inspection tours on horseback, and a week before, in the stale heat of a typically postmonsoon day, we had waved good-by to him and a little procession—an assistant, a secretary, two bearers, and the man to look after the bedding rolls and luggage. They rode away through our large garden, still bright green from the rains, and we turned back into the twilight of the house and the sound of fans whispering in every room.

Up to then, my mother had refused to send Premila to school in the British-run establishments of that time, because, she used to say, "you can bury a dog's tail for seven years and it still comes out curly, and you can take a Britisher away from his home for a lifetime and he still remains insular." The examinations and degrees from entirely Indian schools were not, in those days, considered valid. In my case, the question

*Santha Rama Rau* (sän′thä rä′mä rou).

1. *Anglo-Indian,* having to do with people of English descent living in India. From the mid-1700s until 1947 most of India was under British rule.

had never come up, and probably never would have come up if Mother's extraordinary good health had not broken down. For the first time in my life, she was not able to continue the lessons she had been giving us every morning. So our Hindi books were put away, the stories of the Lord Krishna[2] as a little boy were left in midair, and we were sent to the Anglo-Indian school.

That first day of school is still, when I think of it, a remarkable one. At that age, if one's name is changed, one develops a curious form of dual personality. I remember having a certain detached and disbelieving concern in the actions of "Cynthia," but certainly no responsibility. Accordingly, I followed the thin, erect back of the headmistress down the veranda to my classroom feeling, at most, a passing interest in what was going to happen to me in this strange, new atmosphere of School.

The building was Indian in design, with wide verandas opening onto a central courtyard, but Indian verandas are usually whitewashed, with stone floors. These, in the tradition of British schools, were painted dark brown and had matting on the floors. It gave a feeling of extra intensity to the heat.

I suppose there were about a dozen Indian children in the school—which contained perhaps forty children in all—and four of them were in my class. They were all sitting at the back of the room, and I went to join them. I sat next to a small, solemn girl who didn't smile at me. She had long, glossy-black braids and wore a cotton dress, but she still kept on her Indian jewelry—a gold chain around her neck, thin gold bracelets, and tiny ruby studs in her ears. Like most Indian children, she had a rim of black kohl[3] around her eyes. The cotton dress should have looked strange, but all I could think of was that I should ask my mother if I couldn't wear a dress to school, too, instead of my Indian clothes.

I can't remember too much about the proceedings in class that day, except for the beginning. The teacher pointed to me and asked me to stand up. "Now, dear, tell the class your name."

I said nothing.

"Come along," she said, frowning slightly. "What's your name, dear?"

"I don't know," I said finally.

The English children in the front of the class—there were about eight or ten of them—giggled and twisted around in their chairs to look at me. I sat down quickly and opened my eyes very wide, hoping in that way to dry them off. The little girl with the braids put out her hand and very lightly touched my arm. She still didn't smile.

Most of that morning I was rather bored. I looked briefly at the children's drawings pinned to the wall, and then concentrated on a lizard clinging to the ledge of the high, barred window behind the teacher's head. Occasionally it would shoot out its long yellow tongue for a fly, and then it would rest, with its eyes closed and its belly palpitating, as though it were swallowing several times quickly. The lessons were mostly concerned with reading and writing and simple numbers—things that my mother had already taught me—and I paid very little attention. The teacher wrote on the easel blackboard words like *bat* and *cat*, which seemed babyish to me; only *apple* was new and incomprehensible.

When it was time for the lunch recess, I followed the girl with the braids out onto the veranda. There the children from the other classes were assembled. I saw Premila at once and ran over to her, as she had charge of our lunchbox. The children were all opening packages and sitting down to eat sandwiches. Premila and I were the only ones who had Indian food—thin wheat

---

2. **Lord Krishna**, one of the most widely worshiped of the Hindu deities.

3. **kohl** (kōl), a metallic powder used in the Orient to darken the eyelids and lashes.

chapatties,[4] some vegetable curry, and a bottle of buttermilk. Premila thrust half of it into my hand and whispered fiercely that I should go and sit with my class, because that was what the others seemed to be doing.

The enormous black eyes of the little Indian girl from my class looked at my food longingly, so I offered her some. But she only shook her head and plowed her way solemnly through her sandwiches.

I was very sleepy after lunch, because at home we always took a siesta. It was usually a pleasant time of day, with the bedroom darkened against the harsh afternoon sun, the drifting off into sleep with the sound of Mother's voice reading a story in one's mind, and, finally, the shrill, fussy voice of the ayah[5] waking one for tea.

At school, we rested for a short time on low, folding cots on the veranda, and then we were expected to play games. During the hot part of the afternoon we played indoors, and after the shadows had begun to lengthen and the slight breeze of the evening had come up we moved outside to the wide courtyard.

I had never really grasped the system of competitive games. At home, whenever we played tag or guessing games, I was always allowed to "win"—"because," Mother used to tell Premila, "she is the youngest, and we have to allow for that." I had often heard her say it, and it seemed

---

4. *chapatties* (chə pat′ēz), thin griddle-cakes of unleavened bread, eaten in northern India.
5. *ayah* (ä′yə), a native maid or nurse in India.

quite reasonable to me, but the result was that I had no clear idea of what "winning" meant.

When we played twos-and-threes that afternoon at school, in accordance with my training, I let one of the small English boys catch me, but was naturally rather puzzled when the other children did not return the courtesy. I ran about for what seemed like hours without ever catching anyone, until it was time for school to close. Much later I learned that my attitude was called "not being a good sport," and I stopped allowing myself to be caught, but it was not for years that I really learned the spirit of the thing.

When I saw our car come up to the school gate, I broke away from my classmates and rushed toward it yelling, "Ayah! Ayah!" It seemed like an eternity since I had seen her that morning—a wizened, affectionate figure in her white cotton sari, giving me dozens of urgent and useless instructions on how to to be good girl at school. Premila followed more sedately, and she told me on the way home never to do that again in front of the other children.

When we got home we went straight to Mother's high, white room to have tea with her, and I immediately climbed onto the bed and bounced gently up and down on the springs. Mother asked how we had liked our first day in school. I was so pleased to be home and to have left that peculiar Cynthia behind that I had nothing whatever to say about school, except to ask what *apple* meant. But Premila told Mother about the classes, and added that in her class they had weekly tests to see if they had learned their lessons well.

I asked, "What's a test?"

Premila said, "You're too small to have them. You won't have them in your class for donkey's years." She had learned the expression that day and was using it for the first time. We all laughed enormously at her wit. She also told Mother, in an aside, that we should take sandwiches to school

the next day. Not, she said, that *she* minded. But they would be simpler for me to handle.

That whole lovely evening I didn't think about school at all. I sprinted barefoot across the lawns with my favorite playmate, the cook's son, to the stream at the end of the garden. We quarreled in our usual way, waded in the tepid water under the lime trees, and waited for the night to bring out the smell of the jasmine. I listened with fascination to his stories of ghosts and demons, until I was too frightened to cross the garden alone in the semi-darkness. The ayah found me, shouted at the cook's son, scolded me, hurried me in to supper—it was an entirely usual, wonderful evening.

It was a week later, the day of Premila's first test, that our lives changed rather abruptly. I was sitting at the back of my class, in my usual inattentive way, only half listening to the teacher. I had started a rather guarded friendship with the girl with the braids, whose name turned out to be Nalini (Nancy, in school). The three other Indian children were already fast friends. Even at that age it was apparent to all of us that friendship with the English or Anglo-Indian children was out of the question. Occasionally, during the class, my new friend and I would draw pictures and show them to each other secretly.

The door opened sharply and Premila marched in. At first, the teacher smiled at her in a kindly and encouraging way and said, "Now, you're little Cynthia's sister?"

Premila didn't even look at her. She stood with her feet planted firmly apart and her shoulders rigid, and addressed herself directly to me. "Get up," she said. "We're going home."

I didn't know what had happened, but I was aware that it was a crisis of some sort. I rose obediently and started to walk toward my sister.

"Bring your pencils and your notebook," she said.

I went back for them, and together we left the

room. The teacher started to say something just as Premila closed the door, but we didn't wait to hear what it was.

In complete silence we left the school grounds and started to walk home. Then I asked Premila what the matter was. All she would say was "We're going home for good."

It was a very tiring walk for a child of five and a half, and I dragged along behind Premila with my pencils growing sticky in my hand. I can still remember looking at the dusty hedges, and the tangles of thorns in the ditches by the side of the road, smelling the faint fragrance from the eucalyptus trees and wondering whether we would ever reach home. Occasionally a horse-drawn tonga[6] passed us, and the women, in their pink or green silks, stared at Premila and me trudging along on the side of the road. A few coolies[7] and a line of women carrying baskets of vegetables on their heads smiled at us. But it was nearing the hottest time of day, and the road was almost deserted. I walked more and more slowly, and shouted to Premila, from time to time, "Wait for me!" with increasing peevishness. She spoke to me only once, and that was to tell me to carry my notebook on my head, because of the sun.

When we got to our house the ayah was just taking a tray of lunch into Mother's room. She immediately started a long, worried questioning about what are you children doing back here at this hour of the day.

Mother looked very startled and very concerned, and asked Premila what had happened.

Premila said, "We had our test today, and She made me and the other Indians sit at the back of the room, with a desk between each one."

Mother said, "Why was that, darling?"

"She said it was because Indians cheat," Premila added. "So I don't think we should go back to that school."

Mother looked very distant, and was silent a long time. At last she said, "Of course not, darling." She sounded displeased.

We all shared the curry she was having for lunch, and afterward I was sent off to the beautifully familiar bedroom for my siesta. I could hear Mother and Premila talking through the open door.

Mother said, "Do you suppose she understood all that?"

Premila said, "I shouldn't think so. She's a baby."

Mother said, "Well, I hope it won't bother her."

Of course, they were both wrong. I understood it perfectly, and I remember it all very clearly. But I put it happily away, because it had all happened to a girl called Cynthia, and I never was really particularly interested in her.

---

6. *tonga* (ton′gə), a horse-drawn vehicle with two wheels, commonly used in India.
7. *coolies* (kü′lēz), formerly, unskilled laborers in India hired for very low wages.

## THINK AND DISCUSS
### Understanding
1. Before they are sent to the Anglo-Indian school, where do Santha and Premila receive their education?

2. Why does the headmistress change the sisters' names on the first day of school?
3. Santha experiences "culture shock," a reaction to abrupt contact with another

culture, at the Anglo-Indian school. In what ways is she different from her classmates?

**Analyzing**

4. For the Indian children, what are the advantages and disadvantages of attending a British-run school?
5. The headmistress virtually represents a **stereotype** of an old-fashioned schoolmarm. What details create this stereotype?
6. Why does Santha tell the teacher she does not know her name? What are the reactions of most other students and of the little Indian girl?
7. Premila is more mature than Santha. How does she show her greater sensitivity and adaptability to the school? How does she show that she cares for her sister?

**Extending**

8. Why does Premila think the girls should not go back to school? Do you think she is right? What would you do in the same situation? Explain.

## COMPOSITION

**Writing About an Experience**

From the beginning, Santha and Premila are made to feel like outsiders in the Anglo-Indian school. Think about an experience you have had that made you feel like an outsider. Try to remember all the details you can, and list them as answers to the following questions: What was the occasion? Who or what made you feel like an outsider? What was your reaction? How did the experience end? How do you feel about it now? Use your answers as the basis for a three- to five-paragraph composition to be shared with close friends. Try your best to use realistic details that will help your audience "see" what is happening and to share your experience with you.

**Writing a Character Sketch**

In "By Any Other Name," you have seen Santha and Premila in their relationships with each other at school, at home, with their mother, and with their nurse. Jot down notes about these relationships and use them as the basis for a three- to five-paragraph composition in which you characterize either Santha or Premila. Be sure to use details from the selection as evidence for your characterization.

## BIOGRAPHY

### Santha Rama Rau
### 1923–

Born in Madras, India, Santha Rama Rau left her homeland when she was six years old and did not return for ten years. Her father was a career diplomat, posted to many different locations. Later she traveled to the United States to attend college. After graduation, she returned to India and began writing, publishing *Home to India* (1945).

She has written biographies, novels, and travel books. Her books have an unusual viewpoint, that of a person equally at home in the East and the West. Several magazine articles about her life have been collected in her book *Gifts of Passage* (1961). American cooks have enjoyed her writing about Indian cuisine in *The Cooking of India* (1969).

632 *Nonfiction*

# First Lady Under Fire

**Margaret Truman   USA**

**As the panic of war spread and people began to flee Washington, D.C., Dolley Madison was determined to remain at home. She assured her husband that she was not afraid to stay in the White House without him.**

Dolley was the daughter of Virginia parents who moved to Philadelphia when she was fourteen. Perhaps in defiance of snobbish city folk, she persisted in spelling her name with an "e" because that was the way the clerk of the country parish had written it in the register when she was baptized. It was a small sign of her personal resistance to the life her parents had chosen for themselves and their family. A Quaker[1] convert, Dolley's father practiced his faith with fervor. He joined the wing of the Quaker movement which banned all worldly show in clothes, jewelry, or household furnishings. Other Quakers (called "wet" because their principles were supposedly limp) were more inclined to enjoy life.

Dolley's normal, Virginia-bred high spirits were frowned on by the elders of her meeting as flirtations with Satan. She secretly defied them by wearing a brooch on her dress, concealed by a kerchief. But she did not dare attend the dances and plays that other girls her age enjoyed in booming Philadelphia. That might have brought her a public denunciation at the Sunday meeting.

Quakers made significant contributions to the tradition of feminine courage in America by treating men and women as equals and encouraging their members to oppose moral complacency and inhumanity wherever they saw it. But the version of the faith Dolley encountered apparently undid these positive influences by a fiercely negative approach to almost everything else.

The meeting's control of its members extended to the choice of a marriage partner. It was strictly forbidden to marry outside the faith. Here, too, Dolley showed signs of rebellion. She put off, delayed, evaded John Todd, a well-to-do Quaker lawyer, for over two years. Only the pleas of her father on his deathbed persuaded her to say yes.

Two years after Dolley's marriage, her younger sister Lucy eloped with George Steptoe Washington, a nephew of President Washington. She was promptly read out of the Quaker meeting—a grim experience similar to excommunication. Dolley heard her sister condemned for "the ac-

---

1. *Quaker* (kwā′kər), member of a Christian group called the Society of Friends.

Gilbert Stuart's portraits, *Mrs. James Madison*, Pennsylvania Academy of the Fine Arts, and *George Washington*, 1797, National Gallery of Art, Washington, D.C.

complishment of her marriage with a person not in membership with us, before a hireling priest." In spite of this fire-and-brimstone beginning, Lucy's marriage proved to be a happy one.

A year later, John Todd died in the yellow fever epidemic of 1793. His lively twenty-five-year-old widow was soon being wooed by a number of important politicians who were spending much of their time in Philadelphia, which was then the nation's capital. Among the suitors were Senator Aaron Burr of New York and Congressman James Madison of Virginia. Dolley was drawn to the shy, spare little Virginian in spite of the seventeen-year difference in their ages. Madison's twinkling blue eyes intimated—and his conversation soon confirmed—a sense of humor which he carefully concealed from the public. But he was not a

Quaker, and it took all Dolley's courage to accept his offer of marriage. Years later, she revealed in a letter how "our Society used to control me entirely" and spoke of her "ancient terror of them." On her wedding night she wrote an emotional letter to a friend, lamenting her Philadelphia "enemies" who were smearing her reputation for marrying "the man who of all others I most admire."

It is never easy to break with a childhood faith and modify it according to one's adult understanding. When the decision is made by a woman as part of a personal commitment to a man, it becomes a form of courage. For Dolley, it intensified her dedication to her husband—and his devotion to her. But Dolley did not entirely turn her back on her Quaker past. She abandoned the austere prohibitions against stylish clothes and balls and parties but she retained the Quaker virtues of honesty and charity.

By charity I mean generosity of spirit. It was, I believe, the secret of Dolley's charisma. Long before anyone used this word, Dolley personified it. But to work for a lifetime, this kind of personal power has to be based on genuine feelings. When the feelings are false, the charisma very quickly disintegrates into mere charm. Dolley's charisma was rooted in her Quaker belief in the goodness of most people, even when they were behaving atrociously for political reasons. She also possessed several talents that any politician would envy—a gift for remembering names and faces, and a knack for saying the right thing at the right time.

Dolley's banquets, balls, and Wednesday "levees" were among the liveliest parties in Washington. Only the staunchest President-haters had the willpower to boycott them. Washington Irving,[2] a diehard Federalist,[3] attended one White House reception and came away charmed. He described the First Lady as "a fine, portly, buxom dame, who has a smile and a pleasant word for everybody." But even Dolley's delightful personality could not induce him to say a good word about her husband. The author dismissed the President as "a withered Apple-john."

Soon after the Madisons moved into the White House, Congress appropriated funds to decorate the mansion. The building had been little more than half finished when its first occupants, John and Abigail Adams, arrived in 1800. The walls lacked plaster, temporary wooden steps stood at all the doors, and the now magnificent East Room was fit only for hanging the wash. The "President's Palace" was finally completed during Thomas Jefferson's second term. By the time Dolley Madison became First Lady, it was time to start worrying about its furnishings.

Dolley began decorating two rooms on the main floor—the Ladies' Drawing Room (the present Red Room) and the Oval Drawing Room (the present Blue Room). Working with architect Benjamin Latrobe, she selected furnishings in the "very latest Sheraton style."[4]

The Ladies' Drawing Room was done in yellow, with high-backed sofas and chairs upholstered in bright yellow satin and a yellow damask fireboard in front of the mantel. The Oval Room was even more splendid. Latrobe and Dolley furnished it with a Brussels carpet, bronze lamps, and thirty-six specially designed Grecian chairs. The predominant color was red, and the long graceful windows, one of the most striking features of the room, were handsomely draped in crimson velvet.

Dolley used part of the congressional appropriation to purchase new silver and crystal and a set of blue and gold Lowestoft china for the State Dining Room. At Latrobe's suggestion, she hung a large gold-framed portrait of George Washington on the main wall. The painting had been started by Gilbert Stuart and completed by a later painter named Winstanley.

Dolley Madison's interior decorating came to a halt in 1811. She had already spent about $12,000 on the mansion, and there was no hope of getting additional funds because the nation was by now perilously close to war. The congressional elections of 1810 had brought a new coalition of young Republicans to power. Predominantly southerners and westerners, they were more fervently anti-British than the rest of their party—mainly because they and their constituents hoped to make a quick fortune in real estate from British-held Canada and West Florida.

Under the leadership of Henry Clay of Ken-

---

2. *Washington Irving,* American writer (1783–1859).
3. *Federalist,* member of a U.S. political party (1791–1816). Most Federalists were pro-British and anti-French during the War of 1812.
4. *Sheraton style,* refers to Thomas Sheraton (1751–1806), an English cabinetmaker and furniture designer.

tucky and John C. Calhoun of South Carolina, the War Hawks[5] began pushing for a showdown with the British over the impressment of American seamen. The congressional vote was extremely close—79 to 49 in the House and 19 to 13 in the Senate—but the War Hawks prevailed. On June 19, 1812, President Madison signed a declaration of war against Great Britain.

The first year of the conflict brought a series of shattering American defeats. The Federalists were livid. "Mr. Madison's War" was denounced in highly inflammatory terms. Worse, there was a woeful decline of public confidence in the presidency. New England, a Federalist stronghold, was in a virtual state of secession. In Vermont, the Governor ordered the state militia to resign from national service. In Massachusetts there was talk of negotiating a separate peace with the enemy.

"That little man in the palace," his enemies called the five-foot-six-inch Madison, who was savagely roasted in Federalist newspapers. "The white house" became a term of opprobrium and was regularly spelled with small letters to indicate disapproval of its occupant.

The Madisons' private life became the subject of venomous rumors and gossip. Dolley was criticized for using snuff in public and was suspected of wearing rouge. She was also accused of being unfaithful to her husband; he in turn was whispered to be impotent.

A Federalist clergyman, the Reverend Mr. Breckinridge, tongue-lashed Dolley when she showed up in his congregation on Sunday. His chief complaint was that she had given dinner parties on the Sabbath, but he was also incensed at Congress, which had recently passed a law allowing the mail to be moved on Sunday. The minister insisted that vengeance would be exacted for these sins.

"It is the government that will be punished," he roared, "and, as the Nineveh[6] of old, it will not be the habitations of the people, but your temples and your palaces that will be burned to the ground."

Even the Reverend Mr. Breckinridge must have been stunned when, not long after his sermon, his dire prediction came true.

In the fall of 1813, it became apparent that the British intended to strike a blow at the nation's capital. Their ships moved freely up and down Chesapeake Bay, and British officers in disguise visited Washington with impunity. The Admiral in command of the fleet, George Cockburn, boldly announced that he would soon make his bow in Mrs. Madison's drawing room. But for the better part of the year, the British did not attack. They waged a war of nerves, obviously hoping that the mere threat of an assault might incite the local citizens against the President.

The Washington state of mind was ample justification for such a shrewd policy. Even then, in its infancy, the capital was an emotional, gossip-ridden city, and the distraught citizens were soon taking out their tensions on President Madison. The slanders against him became more and more vicious, and there were rumors of an assassination plot, which would make a British invasion superfluous.

When worried friends urged Dolley to leave the city, she came close to losing her temper for perhaps the first time in her life. "I am determined to stay with my husband," she said. She began sleeping with a Tunisian saber, a souvenir of the war with the Barbary pirates, beside her bed. The President revealed some steel of his own beneath his shy, introverted personality. He ordered a troop of militia stationed on the White House grounds. Panic-prone Washington got the Madison message. No one was running the Presi-

---

5. *War Hawks*, a group of U.S. congressmen who favored the war with Britain known as the War of 1812.
6. *Nineveh* (nin′ə vəh), the last capital of the ancient Assyrian Empire. In 612 B.C. the city was captured and destroyed by Babylon and the ancient country of Media.

dent of the United States out of the White House without a fight.

On August 19, 1814, the British finally decided to strike. A fleet carrying a raiding force of 4,500 veteran infantrymen dropped anchor at the mouth of the Patuxent River in Maryland, less than a day's march from Washington. Madison's Secretary of War, John Armstrong, insisted that they had no intention of attacking the capital and refused to enforce the President's orders to defend the city. Only when the British debarked at Benedict, Maryland, a few days later, and began marching toward the capital, did Armstrong frantically start collecting the various regiments and brigades which he had scattered up and down the coastline.

By then it was too late. The six thousand amateur militiamen and the few hundred sailors and marines Armstrong assembled were an army in name only. They had neither discipline, organization, nor *esprit de corps*.[7] With the British attack a virtual certainty, President Madison decided to ride out to the battlefield. There was a chance that his presence might give the untrained soldiers an extra measure of confidence.

The President expected to be gone only overnight, but he hesitated to leave Dolley behind in the White House. A timid woman would have retreated to safer quarters in Virginia. But Dolley cheerfully assured her harassed husband that she was not in the least afraid to stay in the White House without him, no matter what everyone else in Washington decided to do. I have the feeling that she was trying to encourage the President, who was anything but sure of himself on military matters.

The following day, August 23, Madison sent Dolley a report that the American troops were in good spirits, and he was optimistic that they could hold off the British invaders. Before the day was over, however, the President was forced to change his mind. Two British deserters had been brought before him, and he asked the enemy soldiers if the British Army was as strong as the American force they could see all around them. With a grim smile, the two redcoats replied, "We think it is."

Soon a report of what the British soldiers had told the President was circulating throughout Washington, creating instant panic. A mass exodus began. Horses and wagons became as scarce as competent generals. Dolley watched the frantic excitement from the White House but remained untouched by it. She had seen a similar panic in the yellow fever epidemic of 1793, which had turned Philadelphia into a ghost town. Perhaps she remembered that Quakers were among the few who stayed to nurse the writhing victims of that plague. Perhaps simply surviving one panic is the best recipe for dealing with the next one. At any rate, Dolley stood her ground.

Then came word from her husband which made her wonder if even the President was succumbing to the general fright. He told her to be ready to leave the White House at a moment's notice and begged her to make sure his presidential papers were not left behind.

Even in 1814, when Presidents did not accumulate enough papers to fill a library, this was no small order. Mr. Madison had been in office five years. Dolley instantly summoned the White House chief steward, Jean Pierre Sioussat. Called French John, he had been Thomas Jefferson's doorman. Dolley had promoted him to his present post. She told him to find a horse and carriage, even if he had to beg, borrow, or steal them. French John proved Dolley was a good judge of character. Resourcefulness, the ability to deal with the unexpected, is a must in a White House steward. He was back within the hour with a horse and wagon. Dolley did not ask him where he got them. She personally packed the Presi-

---

7. *esprit de corps* (e sprē′ də kôr′), group spirit; comradeship. [*French*]

dent's papers into a big leatherbound trunk and ordered them to be taken immediately to a hiding place in the country.

I shudder to think of what the British could have done with those papers if they had captured them. They would have used selective quotations from them to make the President look like a crook, a fool, a coward, a liar—just about anything that would help to drive him from office. Once they accomplished that feat, America might have been theirs for dismembering.

With her husband's papers safe, there was no vital reason for Dolley to remain in the White House. But she stayed anyway. She was hoping her presence would persuade some Washingtonians to ignore the pervasive panic and organize a defense for the city. Like most First Ladies, she felt an intense personal responsibility for the mansion. She encouraged the servants by telling them that the President would return at any moment with good news from the battlefield. Then they would have the laugh on all those brave residents of the capital who were running for Virginia.

Alas, on the battlefield, Madison's worst military fears were coming true. Secretary of War Armstrong still kept saying that the British had no intention of marching on Washington. He did allow Captain Joshua Barney to place a battery of guns across the road to the capital. But Barney and his sailors received no support from the ragtag army Armstrong had assembled. The battle of Bladensburg was little more than a skirmish. After a few rounds, the militia broke and galloped for the horizon. All hope of defending Washington vanished with them.

On the morning of the battle of Bladensburg, August 24, Dolley was up at dawn. She stationed herself on the White House roof, spyglass in hand, hoping to catch sight of her husband in the distance. But there was no sign of the President. All she saw were swarms of people and wagons piled high with trunks and household goods streaming steadily toward the bridge that led across the Potomac to Virginia.

As the morning wore on, Dolley could hear the boom of cannons echoing in the distance. It soon became obvious that the battle was turning into a rout. Groups of frightened and dispirited militiamen began straggling into the city. Many of them had turned tail and run when a new British weapon, low-flying Congreve rockets, came tearing into their ranks.

As the news of the American defeat and the imminent British arrival spread through the capital, the rush to escape became even more frantic. The militia assigned to protect the White House deserted their posts and disappeared among the masses of people hurrying toward the Potomac.

Still Dolley refused to budge. She ordered the servants to prepare dinner for the President and his Cabinet and told them to set out some wine on the sideboard in the dining room. By now, she must have been seriously worried about her husband's safety, but the orders helped steady the morale of the White House staff and kept them from joining the general flight from the city. She was demonstrating better leadership in the crisis than any American male, including her husband, showed on this dismal day.

The preparations for dinner were well underway when a pair of horsemen covered with dust appeared at the White House door. They brought a message from President Madison urging Dolley to leave Washington at once. But Dolley was still loath to abandon the White House. If she only had a cannon to station at every window, she vowed that she would stay and defend the mansion herself. French John had a better idea. He suggested a gunpowder booby trap that would blow up the British if they opened the front gate.

Dolley vetoed this plan. Her cool head now conceded the necessity of retreating from the White House. But she still declined to panic. She would take as much as she could carry with her.

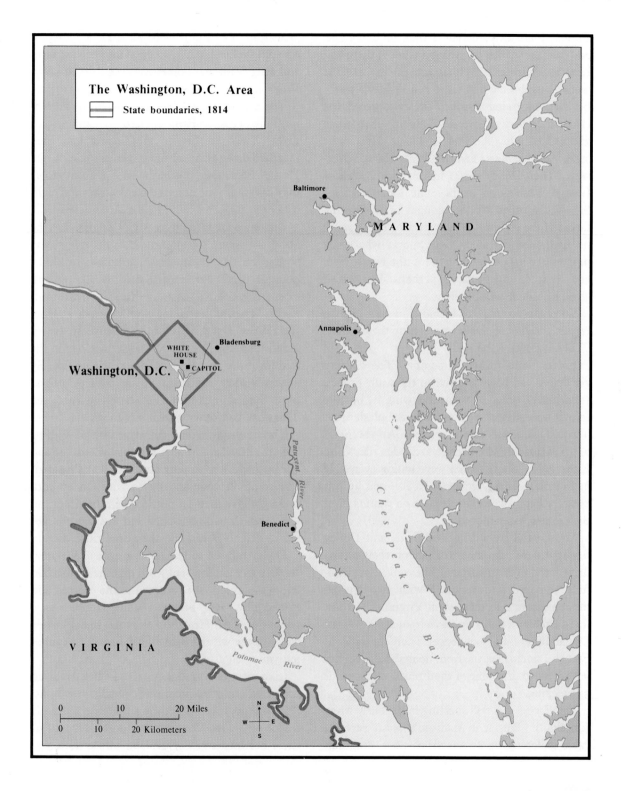

The Washington, D.C. Area

State boundaries, 1814

Baltimore

M A R Y L A N D

Annapolis

Bladensburg

WHITE
HOUSE

Washington, D.C.

CAPITOL

Patuxent River

Benedict

Chesapeake Bay

VIRGINIA

Potomac River

0        10        20 Miles
0    10      20 Kilometers

N
W    E
S

French John was ordered to find another horse and carriage, which he promptly did. If there had been an Avis-Rent-A-Horse around in 1814, he would have been a natural to run it. He certainly believed in trying harder. Dolley ordered the crimson draperies in the Oval Room taken down and packed into John's latest vehicle. Next came some valuable books and the White House silverware. Then Dolley's eyes fell on the portrait of George Washington in the State Dining Room. She was appalled by the thought of leaving the father of the country to the mercy of the enemies he had once defeated. God knows what they might do to it—set it up on the White House lawn and use it for target practice perhaps. The British sense of humor was peculiar.

With the coolness of a soldier determined to retreat with honor, Dolley pointed to the portrait. "Take it down," she said.

French John rushed to comply. The massive gilt frame had been screwed to the wall. French John put two men to work removing it, but the screws were driven so deeply into the plaster that it would take hours to get them out. An old friend of the Madisons, Mr. Carroll, arrived at the White House while the two men were toiling away. He had come to escort Dolley to safety, and he was not very happy when she insisted on waiting until the picture was removed.

Mr. Carroll fretted and fidgeted, and Dolley finally ordered the men to abandon their screwdrivers and break the frame. The canvas was carefully removed and sent off with two trusted messengers to a farmhouse in Virginia. The last thing Dolley swooped up was a framed copy of the Declaration of Independence. Then she ordered French John to lock the front door and deliver her pet parrot to the home of the French minister for safekeeping.

Mr. Carroll was still snorting impatiently when Jim Smith, President Madison's black servant, came galloping up to the front door shouting,

"Clear out! Clear out!" This time Dolley obeyed. She put on her bonnet, stepped into her carriage, and set off for the home of a friend in Rokeby, Virginia, a mile away.

The British, led by Admiral Cockburn and Major General Robert Ross, entered Washington that night. They set fire to the Capitol and then marched down Pennsylvania Avenue to the White House. Smashing the locks on the front door, they burst into the deserted mansion around eight o'clock.

The spits of meat were still sizzling over the coals; the wine, in handsome glass decanters, was sitting on the sideboard. Admiral Cockburn poured a glass for himself and his officers and drank a mocking toast to President Madison's health. Then, after taking a yellow cushion from the Ladies' Drawing Room as a souvenir, he ordered his troops to pile all the furnishings in the middle of the East Room and set them on fire. By eleven o'clock, the mansion was a huge, blazing pyre. Similar fires burned at the Navy Yard, the Treasury, and other public buildings.

The next day Dolley journeyed on to Wiley's Tavern, near Little Falls, Virginia, where she and her husband were finally reunited. The President arrived about noon and stayed with Dolley until midnight. He then set out to rejoin the American army, which had regrouped and was now marching to defend Baltimore, the next British target.

Dolley refused to remain a refugee in Virginia. As soon as Madison sent word that the British had left Washington, she returned to the charred and ruined city. Her beloved White House was a burnt-out shell. Heartbroken at the sight, Dolley wrote to the wife of Benjamin Latrobe, "I cannot tell you what I felt."

Like most courageous people, Dolley Madison had acted out of an inner sense of what was right. She had no way of knowing that her dramatic rescue of George Washington's portrait would silence her husband's critics and infuse the once-divided nation with a new spirit. The day after the news of the British burning of the White House reached New York, huge numbers of volunteers, including many women, rushed to complete the construction of Fort Greene in Brooklyn. In Baltimore, a local orator declared, "The spirit of the nation is aroused." The furious defense of that city by the men manning Fort McHenry made the British think twice about further forays ashore. The battle prompted one former opponent of "Mr. Madison's War" to change his mind rather dramatically. Inspired by the American flag defiantly waving in the midst of the rockets' red glare, Francis Scott Key wrote our national anthem.

Key was not the only defector from the Federalist ranks. All along the Atlantic seaboard, people who had been denouncing the war and talking surrender abruptly changed their minds. In less than a month came news of a shattering American victory over the British invasion fleet on Lake Champlain. Confronted by a united, determined people, the British were more than willing to sign a peace treaty six months later.

With the White House uninhabitable, the Madisons moved into nearby Octagon House. (Why it was given this name is a mystery, since it is partly triangular and partly circular in shape.) In this elegant brick mansion Dolley soon resumed her popular Wednesday evening receptions. Now she was everyone's favorite. Criticism dwindled to the vanishing point—and so did the President's political opposition. For talking treason and secession, the Federalist party practically went out of business—and President Madison's successor, James Monroe, ushered in eight years of what came to be called "the era of good feeling." I like to believe that a lot of these good feelings flowered from the genius—and above all, the courage—of Dolley Madison.

## THINK AND DISCUSS

### Understanding

1. Which of James Madison's qualities attract Dolley most?
2. To what personal attacks are President Madison and Dolley subjected after he signs the declaration of war against Great Britain?

### Analyzing

3. In what ways does Dolley assert her independence before her first marriage? How does she conform to her parents' wishes?
4. She dislikes some aspects of her upbringing, but how does it help her later in life?
5. Describe the items Dolley saves from the White House, how she saves them, and what, if anything, her actions mean to the country.

6. What is it that helps "infuse the once divided nation with a new spirit"? How is this spirit shown in New York? in Baltimore?
7. How does the title of this biography apply to aspects of Dolley's life other than the burning of the White House?

### Extending

8. In what respects do you think Dolley Madison was more like a modern woman than like a woman of the early 1800s?
9. As the daughter of a president, Margaret Truman once lived in the White House. Several times in this biography she obviously is speaking from her own experience. List several examples of this.

## THINKING SKILLS
### Generalizing

To **generalize** is to draw general conclusions from particular information. From the descriptions of the impact the War of 1812 had on Washington, various states, and U. S. citizens, you can generalize about hardships and demands that war imposes on a country where battles are fought. Describe four possible effects of war in the 1800s on a land.

## COMPOSITION ◆━━
### Writing a Front-Page Story

Imagine that you are a reporter assigned to write a front-page story about the burning of Washington in 1814. Begin your story with an opening paragraph that includes the five *w*'s of journalism: who, what, where, when, and why. Then go on to include such details as the President's whereabouts; Dolley's rescue of various items from the White House; and the burning of the Capitol, the White House, and other government buildings. End your article by commenting on the state of the country and what you think may happen next.

### Commenting on Dolley Madison's Courage

Reread this selection, noting specific instances of Dolley's courage in the years before she married Madison, as well as after. Organize your notes and use them to write a three- to five-paragraph composition in which you analyze and discuss Dolley's courage and explain the heritage of that courage to those of us living in America today.

## ENRICHMENT
### Presenting Television Interviews

Assume that television existed in Madison's day and that you were there. Pretend there is to be a presentation investigating Dolley's bravery before the White House is burned. Your class will interview President Madison, the Reverend Mr. Breckinridge, Admiral Cockburn, Secretary of War Armstrong, "French John" Sioussat, Mr. Carroll, Jim Smith, and perhaps one or two other servants, American soldiers, Washingtonians, and the French ambassador. Decide whether or not to interview Dolley herself. The class should select a moderator responsible for organizing the presentation, including a brief introduction and a summary, and introducing the interviewers. Each interviewer will write the questions, and students playing the interviewed people will answer. If a video camera is available, the presentation can be taped.

# BIOGRAPHY

# Margaret Truman
# 1924–

A native of Independence, Missouri, and the daughter of President Harry S. Truman, Margaret Truman has been close to much of modern history in the making, especially during the seven years she lived in the White House. After graduating from George Washington University, she tried several careers—concert singer, summer stock actress, and broadcaster—before becoming a successful author. Besides *Women of Courage*, from which "First Lady Under Fire" is taken, she has written a number of books, including biographies of her parents and a series of murder mysteries set in Washington, D.C.

## Write Good Beginnings

A good beginning commands attention and draws a reader into a piece of writing. Skillful writers strive to start each piece of writing with bold statements, intriguing facts, humorous anecdotes, or riveting details that cause the reader to stop and take notice.

In the nonfiction you have just read, each author focuses the beginning of his or her autobiographical piece on the setting or circumstances central to the theme. In the first paragraph of "I Escape from the Boers," Winston Churchill maps out the State Model Schools where he had been held prisoner. His opening introduces his theme that human rather than physical barriers were the toughest challenges he faced in trying to escape and rejoin the British army. Churchill's statement and following details help orient the reader, arouse curiosity, and create suspense.

The opening of "The Secret Room" by Corrie ten Boom contrasts the outward appearance of the Dutch city of Haarlem with the underlying mood of its citizens:

> It was Sunday, May 10, 1942, exactly two years after the fall of Holland. The sunny spring skies, the flowers in the lamppost boxes, did not at all reflect the city's mood. German soldiers wandered aimlessly through the streets, some looking as if they had not yet recovered from a hard Saturday night.

This contrast attracts the reader's attention. The anecdote about Peter's closing hymn then highlights the indomitable spirit of the occupied country and introduces the theme of resistance against the Nazis.

Like Churchill and ten Boom, Santha Rama Rau begins "By Any Other Name" with a description of the setting and circumstances central to her story.

> At the Anglo-Indian day school in Zorinabad to which my sister and I were sent when she was eight and I was five and a half, they changed our names.

Rama Rau's introduction illustrates the British attitude toward the Indian students in the Anglo-Indian school. She then hints at Premila's pride in her identity and heritage. Both of these themes are key to the essay. By establishing these themes early in the story, Rama Rau gives her essay strength and cohesion.

---

When you read, notice the way good writers use strong beginnings to grab the reader's attention and to establish themes.

When you write, open each piece of writing with a beginning that commands attention, arouses curiosity, or helps establish your theme.

---

## Letters

One of the most interesting ways to learn about a person is to read a collection of that person's letters. Although letters are written as private communications, many prominent people allow their letters to be published later as historical documents and literary works. The personal quality of letters provides readers with a glimpse into the family relationships, friendships, and private thoughts of world leaders, entertainers, and other illustrious figures.

There are built-in advantages to reading letters. The reader knows who both the writer and the audience are. The audience is the person or group to whom the letter was written. Whether a letter appeals to your interests or not often depends on the writer's style as well as the letter's topic and contents. The letters in this unit represent a variety of writing styles, from Anne Morrow Lindbergh's unconsciously polished prose to Bartolomeo Vanzetti's occasional struggles with the fine points of English, which was not his native language.

## Fact and Opinion

As you read letters, you will find it important to distinguish between statements of **fact,** statements of **opinion,** and mixed statements— those that contain both fact and opinion. Statements of fact can be shown to be true or false. A writer's opinions, on the other hand, are judged either valid or unconvincing on the basis of how reasonably he or she supports them.

In letters, as in biographies and other nonfiction, writers often state opinions as if they are facts. Readers may appreciate the confidence of a writer who states opinions forcefully, while

they still recognize that opinions are neither proven nor provable. Yet thoughtful readers can accept, respect, or believe opinions that seem solid and persuasive. Even critical readers realize that it is not necessary to painstakingly analyze most statements in a letter or another nonfiction work for facts and opinions.

## Letters That Enliven History

Letters that deal with historical events usually contain facts about the occasions and the people concerned, along with opinions about the events. Writers of nonfiction often mix fact and opinion, as when Margaret Truman comments on the army gathered by Secretary of War John Armstrong, in "First Lady Under Fire": "The six thousand amateur militiamen and the few hundred sailors and marines Armstrong assembled were an army in name only." From this sentence we learn facts about how many troops were assembled, and we encounter a compelling opinion about how ineffective this army could be.

Some of the most entertaining statements in letters are the descriptions of behind-the-scenes activities in famous places and circumstances, such as the White House and the meetings of world leaders. You will find this to be the case in Dolley Madison's letter to her sister as British troops bore down on the President's home and in Harry Truman's letter about heads of state meeting at the end of World War II.

Before you read a letter, take note of who wrote it, to whom it was written, and the relationship of that addressee to the writer. As you read, take note of the author's purpose. Enjoy the style and the glimpses of the writer's personality and the "inside" historical information the letter contains.

See STYLE in the Handbook of Literary Terms, page 827.

# Four Letters

### Dolley Madison (1768–1849)  USA

**This letter describes the same tense days in the life of Dolley Madison recounted in "First Lady Under Fire." During the War of 1812, while President Madison was with his troops, Mrs. Madison was forced to flee the White House to escape a British attack on Washington.**

Tuesday, August 23rd, 1814

My dear Sister:

    My husband left me yesterday morning to join General Winder. He inquired anxiously whether I had courage or firmness to remain in the

From *Our First Ladies*, 5th edition, by Jane and Burt McConnell. Thomas Y. Crowell Company, 1969. Abridged.

President's house until his return on the morrow, or succeeding day, and on my assurance that I had no fear but for him and the success of our army, he left, beseeching me to take care of myself, and of the Cabinet papers, public and private. I have since received two dispatches from him, written with a pencil. The last is alarming, because he desires that I should be ready at a moment's warning to enter my carriage and leave the city; that the enemy seemed stronger than had at first been reported, and it might happen that they would reach the city with the intention of destroying it.

I am accordingly ready; I have pressed as many Cabinet papers into trunks as to fill one carriage; our private property must be sacrificed, as it is impossible to procure wagons for its transportation. I am determined not to go myself until I see Mr. Madison safe, so that he can accompany me, as I hear of much hostility toward him. Disaffection stalks around us.

My friends and acquaintances are all gone—even Colonel C. with his hundred, who were stationed as a guard in this enclosure. French John,[1] with his usual activity and resolution, offers to spike the cannon at the gate, and lay a train of powder which would blow up the British should they enter the house. To the last proposition I positively object, without being able to make him understand why all advantages in war may not be taken.

*Wednesday Morning, twelve o'clock.*—Since sunrise I have been turning my spy-glass in every direction and watching with unwearied anxiety, hoping to discover the approach of my dear husband and his friends, but alas! I can descry only groups of military, wandering in all directions, as if there was a lack of arms, or of spirit to fight for their own fireside.

*Three o'clock.*—Will you believe it, my sister? We have had a battle, or skirmish, near Bladensburg,[2] and here I am still, within the sound of the cannon! Mr. Madison comes not. May God protect us! Two messengers, covered with dust, come to bid me fly; but here I mean to wait for him. . . . At this late hour a wagon has been procured, and I have had it filled with plate and the most valuable portable articles belonging to the house. Whether it will reach its destination, the Bank of Maryland, or fall into the hands of the British soldiery, events must determine.

Our kind friend, Mr. Carroll, has come to hasten my departure, and in a very bad humor with me, because I insist on waiting until the large picture of General Washington[3] is secured, and it requires to be

---

1. *French John,* John Sioussat (syü sä′), a loyal servant.
2. *Bladensburg,* a town in Maryland.
3. *picture of General Washington,* the famous Gilbert Stuart portrait, shown on page 634, that is still displayed at the White House.

unscrewed from the wall. This process was found too tedious for these perilous moments; I have ordered the frame to be broken, and the canvas taken out. It is done! and the precious portrait placed in the hands of two gentlemen of New York for safe keeping.

And now, dear sister, I must leave this house, or the retreating army will make me a prisoner in it by filling up the road I am directed to take. When I shall again write to you, or where I shall be tomorrow, I cannot tell!

Dolley

## THINK AND DISCUSS
### Understanding
1. What is the last thing to delay Dolley's departure from the White House?

### Analyzing
2. Dolley Madison makes no mention of her own patriotism and bravery, but they are nevertheless conveyed in her letter. Give examples of them.

### Extending
3. Would Dolley's letter be as interesting if she had written it after her escape? Explain.

## APPLYING: Style  H🗡
### See Handbook of Literary Terms, p. 827

**Style** is the manner in which writers use words and sentences to fit their ideas. Style involves many choices on the part of the writer: types of words, placement of words in a sentence, the purpose of the written work, tone, mood, imagery, figurative language, sound devices, and rhythm. Though the style of a letter arises naturally from an individual's unique thoughts and feelings, it can be shaped by the circumstances in which it is created.

1. What is Dolley's purpose in writing to her sister?
2. Most of Dolley's letter is written hastily and under pressure, as she expects to have to flee Washington, D.C., at any moment. What in its style gives evidence of that haste and pressure?
3. At times, the letter reads almost like a journal entry, recording something the writer wishes to remember later. What about its style creates that impression?

## Bartolomeo Vanzetti (1888–1927)

**Writing this letter on the eve of his execution, Italian immigrant Vanzetti directed his statements to the young son of his co-defendant, protesting his own innocence and that of the boy's father, Nicola Sacco. Considered radicals at an anti-radical time, the two were convicted of robbing and murdering two shoe-factory employees in the Boston area in 1920. Their trial and deaths led to international debate over their guilt or innocence, a question that to this date has not been settled.**

August 21, 1927

My dear Dante:

I still hope, and we will fight until the last moment, to revindicate our right to live and to be free, but all the forces of the State and of the money and reaction are deadly against us because we are libertarians or anarchists.

I write little of this because you are now and yet too young to understand these things and other things of which I would like to reason with you.

But, if you do well, you will grow and understand your father's and my case and your father's and my principles, for which we will soon be put to death.

I tell you now that all that I know of your father, he is not a criminal, but one of the bravest men I ever knew. Some day you will understand what I am about to tell you. That your father has sacrificed everything

Ben Shahn, *Bartolomeo Vanzetti and Nicola Sacco*, 1931–32, Collection, The Museum of Modern Art, New York

dear and sacred to the human heart and soul for his fate in liberty and justice for all. That day you will be proud of your father, and if you come brave enough, you will take his place in the struggle between tyranny and liberty and you will vindicate his (our) names and our blood.

If we have to die now, you shall know, when you will be able to understand this tragedy in its fullest, how good and brave your father has been with you, your father and I, during these eight years of struggle, sorrow, passion, anguish and agony. . . .

I would like you to remember me as a comrade and friend to your father, your mother and Ines, Susie and you, and I assure you that neither have I been a criminal, that I have committed no robbery and no murder, but only fought modestly to abolish crimes from among mankind and for the liberty of all.

Remember Dante, each one who will say otherwise of your father and I, is a liar, insulting innocent dead men who have been brave in their life. Remember and know also, Dante, that if your father and I would have been cowards and hypocrites and renegades of our faith, we would not have been put to death. They would not even have convicted a leprous dog; not even executed a deadly poisoned scorpion on such evidence as that they framed against us. They would have given a new trial to a matricide and habitual felon on the evidence we presented for a new trial.

Remember, Dante, remember always these things; we are not criminals; they convicted us on a frame-up; they denied us a new trial; and if we will be executed after seven years, four months and seventeen days of unspeakable tortures and wrong, it is for what I have already told you; because we were for the poor and against the exploitation and oppression of the man by the man.

The documents of our case, which you and other ones will collect and preserve, will prove to you that your father, your mother, Ines, my family, and I have been sacrificed by and to a State Reason of the American Plutocratic reaction.

The day will come when you will understand the atrocious cause of the above written words, in all its fullness. Then you will honor us.

Now Dante, be brave and good always. I embrace you. . . .

Bartolomeo

## THINK AND DISCUSS

### Understanding

1. How does Bartolomeo Vanzetti want Dante Sacco to remember him? Of what does he assure him in the letter?
2. At one point Vanzetti says he was fighting for two causes. What are they?

### Analyzing

3. In writing to young Dante Sacco, what major point is Vanzetti trying to make?
4. Based on Vanzetti's letter, who do you infer were his enemies?
5. Vanzetti writes that his and Sacco's ordeal has lasted for seven years, four months, and seventeen days. What does this careful account of the time imply about his feelings?

### Extending

6. Had television existed at the time of the Sacco and Vanzetti trial, might the outcome have been different? Explain.

# Anne Morrow Lindbergh (1906–    )

**In 1929 the bride of world-famous aviator Charles Lindbergh wrote this letter to her mother during a stopover on her flying honeymoon.**

Hotel Chase, Saint Louis, June 28th

Mother darling—

I tried to write you from Indianapolis, but it has been very hurried. We haven't slept twice at one place, flying every day so far. But we are staying here today and tomorrow because something in the plane is being looked over. . . .

Yesterday was the most thrilling day. Flying from Indianapolis, about sunset we started to climb. There was a rainbow behind us, a glorious bow that was much bigger and brighter than those on the ground. We saw more than a half circle. It was so real and yet so vanishing—about to vanish—that it reminded me of the visions one reads about. Do you remember the poor monk who had a vision of an angel and then heard the monastery doorbell ring and was torn between his duty and the vision, finally went to the door, and came back to find it still there? It was so beautiful with great piled-up golden clouds behind, and I thought of your saying to me in Mexico that first morning, "Anne, you'll have the sky— the sky!" It was glorious of you.

Then we went up, up above the clouds, at dusk, fifteen thousand feet. At about eight thousand, looking down, there was a blue mist over the flat

---

land so that a new horizon was made. It looked as though we were on a sea and the land, patchworked below the mist, looked sunk in many depths of blue water. Then up further through mist, it was very cold and suddenly out on a plateau of blue-gray clouds, as far as one could see, and the sky bright blue above us. It is an indescribable feeling—those cold blue motionless stretches of cotton wool. Like ice in their motionless stillness, but soft and piled up like feathers. I think it is more like a mammoth bed of gray feathers than anything else. Then we dove down out of this bright cold blue into sudden warmth and *dark*. The earth was dark and lights of towns peppered the ground. We came into Saint Louis at night but you could still see those two great rivers[1] and where they joined, broad, peaceful, and gleaming between the dark shores. It was thrilling.

---

1. *two great rivers,* the Missouri and the Mississippi.

## THINK AND DISCUSS
### Understanding
1. According to Anne Lindbergh, what made the flight from Indianapolis to St. Louis so thrilling?

### Analyzing
2. To draw an analogy to something she experienced, Lindbergh refers to a story about a monk who sees a vision. Describe what she experienced and the effect created by the comparison.

### Extending
3. How does the **tone** of Lindbergh's letter compare with that of Dolley Madison's?

## READING LITERATURE SKILLFULLY
### Fact and Opinion
When you read nonfiction, you will want to distinguish statements of fact from opinions in order to understand the author's comments more clearly. A statement of fact can be proven true or false. An opinion, even a well-supported opinion with which you agree, is a personal view not subject to factual proof. Mixed statements express both fact and opinion. For example, Lindbergh's comment about a rainbow, "There was a rainbow behind us, a glorious bow that was much bigger and brighter than those on the ground," begins with a verifiable description of the rainbow's location. Yet the word *glorious* conveys her impression of the rainbow's grandeur, an opinion.

In the last two sentences of the letter she tells about seeing two rivers at St. Louis. Which points are statements of fact and which are opinions?

## The Art of Writing Letters

Letter writing, public and personal, goes back as far as history itself. Ancient Romans composed verse epistles (letters) to their friends, discussing philosophical or literary matters or satirizing people and government institutions. St. Paul's epistles, contained in the New Testament, provided spiritual guidance for the early Christians.

In the eighteenth century, letter writing rose to the status of fine art. Noted authors like British poet Alexander Pope followed the custom of the ancient Romans in directing verse epistles to friends, but most of these were, in fact, intended for public consumption. Rather than speaking directly to the person they were addressed to, such letters generally were essays satirizing some aspect of society, and many caused a great furor when they were published. The art of writing personal letters also flourished at this time. Originally written to family members and close friends, those that have survived exist now as historical documents, often providing unexpected insights into the world in which the correspondents lived.

Surprisingly, the modern novel owes much to letter writing. In eighteenth-century England Samuel Richardson, who had earlier published a book containing samples of the proper letters for various occasions, conceived the idea of telling a story through a series of letters written by and to the heroine. The result was *Pamela* (1740), sometimes called the first real English novel.

Perhaps the greatest influence on the decline of letter writing from the late nineteenth century to the present has been the telephone, admittedly a more direct form of communication. Nowadays public letters are no more exotic than letters to newspaper or magazine editors or to a columnist like "Dear Abby." Of these and the personal letters presently being written, it can be said with certainty that few display the grand style of the previous ages. In turning more to phone than pen, have people lost a valuable skill? An answer might be found in reviewing the letters in the unit, three of which were written by twentieth-century figures.

# Harry S. Truman (1884–1972)

**President Truman wrote faithfully to his wife from Berlin, even though he was heavily involved in the Potsdam Conference, a meeting of world leaders following Germany's defeat in World War II.**

Berlin
July 20, 1945

Dear Bess:

It was an experience to talk to you from my desk here in Berlin night before last. It sure made me homesick. . . .[1] You never saw as completely ruined a city. But they did it. I am most comfortably fixed and the palace where we meet is one of two intact palaces left standing. . . .

We had a tough meeting yesterday. I reared up on my hind legs and told 'em where to get off and they got off. I have to make it perfectly plain to them at least once a day that so far as this President is concerned Santa Claus is dead and that my first interest is U.S.A., then I want the . . . War won[2] and I want 'em both[3] in it. Then I want peace—world peace and will do what can be done by us to get it. But certainly am not going to set up another [illegible] here in Europe, pay reparations, feed the world, and get nothing for it but a nose thumbing. They are beginning to awake to the fact that I mean business.

It was my turn to feed 'em at a formal dinner last night. Had Churchill on my right, Stalin[4] on my left. We toasted the British King, the Soviet President, the U.S. President, the two honor guests, the foreign ministers, one at a time, etc. etc. ad lib. Stalin felt so friendly that he toasted the pianist when he played a Tskowsky (you spell it) piece[5] especially for him. The old man loves music. He told me he'd import the greatest Russian pianist for me tomorrow. Our boy was good. His name is List and he

---

1. **homesick.** . . . The series of periods indicates an editorial deletion.
2. *I want the . . . War won,* another editorial deletion. The reference is to the yet-unsettled war with Japan.
3. *'em both,* England and the Soviet Union.
4. **Churchill . . . Stalin.** Churchill is Winston Churchill, the prime minister of Great Britain and the author of "I Escape from the Boers" in this unit. Joseph Stalin, 1879–1953, was dictator of the Soviet Union from 1929 to 1953.
5. *a Tskowsky . . . piece,* a misspelled reference to Russian composer Peter Ilich Tchaikovsky, 1840–1893.

Greta Hampton, *Harry S. Truman*, 1947, The White House, Washington, D.C.

played Chopin, Von Weber, Schubert, and all of them.

The ambassadors and Jim Byrnes said the party was a success. Anyway they left in a happy frame of mind. I gave each of them a fine clock, specially made for them, and a set of that good navy luggage. Well I'm hoping to get done in a week. I'm sick of the whole business—but we'll bring home the bacon.

Kiss Margie,[6] lots and lots of love,
Harry

6. *Margie,* Margaret Truman, the President's daughter and the author of "First Lady Under Fire" in this unit.

## THINK AND DISCUSS
### Understanding
1. What makes Harry Truman homesick?
2. What two heads of state does Truman meet with in Berlin?

### Analyzing
3. What do you infer Truman means when, after writing "You never saw such a ruined city," he adds, "But they did it"?
4. Which comments in Truman's letter show him as a loving husband and father and a down-to-earth observer of a formal event?

## Extending

5. How does Truman's behind-the-scenes glimpse of a meeting of the world's great leaders affect your opinion of them and their responsibilities? Does it diminish their importance, make them seem more important, or have another effect? Explain.

## REVIEWING: Style H/T
**See Handbook of Literary Terms, p. 827**

Style, the manner in which a writer makes words and sentences fit ideas, is a combination of the techniques and devices of writing used to express the writer's thoughts.

1. What words or phrases in Harry Truman's letter show his down-to-earth attitude toward his meeting with other world leaders?
2. How do you suppose the letter's tone would differ if it had been directed to another government official rather than to Mrs. Truman?

## COMPOSITION
### Reading/Writing Log

As you read the four letters in this section, you probably noticed the great difference in style and tone of each letter. In each case, the tone and style depend not only upon who is writing the letter, but also on who will read it. Dolley Madison's letter to her sister gets right to the point at the very beginning of the letter, in a very hurried, almost frantic tone. Bartolomeo Vanzetti carefully states the purpose of his letter to the young Dante Sacco in the first paragraph. Anne Lindbergh's and Harry Truman's letters have a more relaxed, familiar tone. Review each letter and decide which one you think has the most intriguing beginning that makes you want to read on. Then copy the first paragraph in your Reading/Writing Log.

### Writing an Open Letter

When reading a newspaper, perhaps you have seen an "open letter." This is a letter directed to a prominent person or group of people, but it is published instead of being sent so that others may read the message. It may be congratulatory, inquiring, critical, or sympathetic. Prepare an open letter to a prominent person in today's world—a politician, a sports figure, an entertainer, or another public figure. Make sure the beginning of your letter makes clear to readers in the general public why you are writing the letter and what you are saying in it.

### Writing a Letter to the Editor

Write a letter to the editor of a local newspaper expressing your concern about some topic of local, national, or international interest. The first paragraph should explain what you are writing about and why. Then go on to amplify your position. Although you are not required to mail your letter, you can do so if you wish.

## ENRICHMENT
### Reading Letters of Great Writers

Many libraries contain volumes of letters written by great writers, historical figures, and other prominent persons. Using the card catalog in a school or community library, find and read a collection of letters by someone who interests you. If you prefer, read letters from another source, such as the epistles of Paul in the New Testament, other letters by religious leaders of the past or present, or letters from your own relatives that may be kept as keepsakes known to your family.

## Essays

An essay is a literary work of nonfiction written about a certain topic, or subject. Essays are written to express ideas, to inform, or to persuade the audience. Formal essays discuss ideas in scholarly language and structure. Informal essays are more personal. They generally use conversational language. Some informal essays may be humorous or satirical.

At times, informal essays that include information about the writer's or other people's experiences resemble biography or autobiography. To some readers, the line between these types of nonfiction is almost invisible. However, if the piece of writing is concerned more with ideas than with what happens to the people for its own sake, the work is considered an informal essay.

## Understanding Essays

When you read essays like those in this unit, you must become aware of how ideas are used and how they are related to one another in importance. This will not be difficult, because you already know how to recognize a selection's **main idea**—the main point the essay communicates—and how the author develops the idea by using **supporting details.** Often a *thesis,* a proposition or statement set forth to be supported, or a main idea is stated at or near the beginning of the essay. In some cases, however, the central idea does not become clear until the end of the essay. An author may want to lay the groundwork for a main idea, so that

the point strikes readers as fully established by the time they encounter it. Some writers imply a main idea so strongly that they need not state it explicitly. If you were to describe the many fine works of art in a museum, for example, you may not need to mention that it is a treasure house of fine art. Some formal essays may require rereading before the ideas are fully understood, and most readers find the effort to do so rewarding.

Of equal importance to understanding an essay's ideas is the need to recognize the author's purpose. For example, a satirical essay's tone may convince readers to face a problem about which the author cares. Readers of "My Store of Grievances" by John Welter can infer the author's purpose—to call attention to a topic about which he has a clear opinion. Understanding what an author's purpose is does not require an endorsement of that purpose or agreement with the author's judgments.

## The Power of Well-Written Essays

Informal essays may provide insights into the lives of their authors. Helen Keller's "Three Days to See!" effectively conveys its message while it reveals a great deal about the inner beauty and observant nature of the woman who wrote it.

Read the modern essays that follow. They illustrate the range and variety that essays can present in structure, topic, and tone. They also indicate how clearly and powerfully some writers can communicate ideas.

# Three Days to See!

**Helen Keller**   USA

> **"I who am blind can give one hint to those who see: Use your eyes as if tomorrow you would be stricken blind."**

have often thought it would be a blessing if each human being were stricken blind and deaf for a few days at some time during his early adult life. Darkness would make him more appreciative of sight; silence would teach him the joys of sound.

Now and then I have tested my seeing friends to discover what they see. Recently I asked a friend, who had just returned from a long walk in the woods, what she had observed. "Nothing in particular," she replied. I was astonished.

How was it possible, I asked myself, to walk for an hour through the woods and see nothing worthy of note? I who cannot see find hundreds of things to interest me through mere touch. I feel the delicate symmetry of a leaf. I pass my hands lovingly about the smooth skin of a silver birch, or the rough, shaggy bark of a pine. In spring I touch the branches of trees hopefully in search of a bud, the first sign of awakening nature after her winter's sleep. Occasionally, if I am very fortunate, I place my hand gently on a small tree and feel the happy quiver of a bird in full song.

At times my heart cries out with longing to see all these things. If I can get so much pleasure from mere touch, how much more beauty must be revealed by sight. And I have imagined, selecting carefully, what I should most like to see if I were given the use of my eyes, say, for just a three-day period.

I should divide the period into three parts. On the first day, I should want to see the people whose kindness and companionship have made my life worth living. I do not know what it is to see into the heart of a friend through that "window of the soul," the eye. I can only "see" through my fingertips the outline of a face. I can detect laughter, sorrow, and many other obvious emotions. I know my many friends, not by sight, but only from the feel of their faces.

How much easier, how much more satisfying it is for you who can see to grasp quickly the essential qualities of another person by watching the subtleties of expression, the quiver of a muscle, the flutter of a hand. But does it ever occur to you to use your sight to see into the inner nature of a friend? Do not most of you seeing people grasp only casually the outward features of a familiar face and let it go at that?

For instance, can you describe accurately the faces of five good friends? As an experiment, I have questioned husbands about the color of their

Claude Monet, *The Beach at Sainte-Adresse*, 1867, The Metropolitan Museum of Art, New York.

wives' eyes, and often they express embarrassed confusion and admit that they do not know.

Oh, the things that I should see if I had the power of sight for just three days!

The first day would be a busy one. I should call to me all my dear friends and look long into their faces, imprinting upon my mind the outward evidences of the beauty that is within them. I should let my eyes rest, too, on the face of a baby, so that I could catch a vision of the eager, innocent beauty which precedes the individual's consciousness of the conflicts which life develops. I should like to see the books which have been read to me, and which have revealed to me the deepest channels of human life. And I should like to look into the loyal, trusting eyes of my dogs, the little Scottie and the stalwart Great Dane.

In the afternoon I should take a long walk in the woods and intoxicate my eyes on the beauties of the world of nature. And I should pray for the glory of a colorful sunset. That night, I think, I should not be able to sleep.

The next day I should arise with the dawn and see the thrilling miracle by which night is transformed into day. I should behold with awe the magnificent panorama of light with which the sun awakens the sleeping earth.

This day I should devote to a hasty glimpse of the world, past and present. I should want to see the pageant of man's progress and so I should go to the museums. There my eyes would see the condensed history of the earth—animals and the races of men pictured in their native environment; gigantic carcasses of dinosaurs and mastodons which roamed the earth before man appeared, with his tiny stature and powerful brain, to conquer the animal kingdom.

My next stop would be the museum of art. I know well through my hands the sculptured gods and goddesses of the ancient Nile land. I have felt copies of Parthenon friezes and I have sensed the rhythmic beauty of charging Athenian warriors. The gnarled, bearded features of Homer[1] are dear to me, for he, too, knew blindness.

So on this, my second day, I should try to probe into the soul of man through his art. The things I knew through touch I should now see. More splendid still, the whole magnificent world of painting would be opened to me. I should be able to get only a superficial impression. Artists tell me that for a deep and true appreciation of art one must educate the eye. One must learn through experience to weigh the merits of line, of composition, of form, and color. If I had eyes, how happily would I embark on so fascinating a study!

The evening of my second day I should spend at a theater or at the movies. How I should like to see the fascinating figure of Hamlet, or the gusty Falstaff[2] amid colorful Elizabethan trappings!

I cannot enjoy the beauty of rhythmic movement except in a sphere restricted to the touch of my hands. I can vision only dimly the grace of a Pavlova,[3] although I know something of the delight of rhythm for often I can sense the beat of music as it vibrates through the floor. I can well imagine that cadenced motion must be one of the most pleasing sights in the world. I have been able to gather something of this by tracing with my fingers the lines in sculptured marble; if this static grace can be so lovely, how much more acute must be the thrill of seeing grace in motion.

The following morning I should again greet the dawn, anxious to discover new delights, new revelations of beauty. Today, this third day, I shall spend in the workaday world, amid the haunts of men going about the business of life. The city becomes my destination. There I must go at once!

First, I stand at a busy corner merely looking at people, trying by sight of them to understand something of their daily lives. I see smiles and I am happy. I see serious determination and I am proud. I see suffering and I am compassionate.

I stroll down Fifth Avenue. I throw my eyes out of focus, so that I see no particular object but only a seething kaleidoscope of color. I am certain that the colors of women's dresses moving in a throng must be a gorgeous spectacle of which I should never tire. But perhaps if I had sight I should be like most other women—too interested in styles to give much attention to the splendor of color in the mass.

From Fifth Avenue I make a tour of the city—to the slums, to factories, to parks where children play. I take a stay-at-home trip abroad by visiting the foreign quarters. Always my eyes are open wide to all the sights of both happiness and misery so that I may probe deep and add to my understanding of how people work and live.

My third day of sight is drawing to an end. Perhaps there are many serious pursuits to which

---

1. **Parthenon friezes** (frēz′əz) . . . **Homer.** The friezes, sculptures depicting historical and mythological figures, once decorated the Parthenon, an ancient Greek temple. They are now found in various museums. Homer, the great epic poet of Greece who lived during the ninth century B.C., overcame blindness to compose the *Illiad* and the *Odyssey*.
2. **Hamlet . . . Falstaff,** well-known characters from Shakespeare's plays.
3. **Pavlova,** Anna Pavlova, 1885–1931, famed Russian ballerina.

I should devote the few remaining hours, but I am afraid that on the evening of that last day I should again run away to the theater, to a hilariously funny play, so that I might appreciate the overtones of comedy in the human spirit.

At midnight permanent night would close in on me again. Naturally in those three short days I should not have seen all I wanted to see. Only when darkness had again descended upon me should I realize how much I had left unseen.

Perhaps this short outline does not agree with the program you might set for yourself if you knew that you were about to be stricken blind. I am, however, sure that if you faced that fate, you would use your eyes as never before. Everything you saw would become dear to you. Your eyes would touch and embrace every object that came within your range of vision. Then, at last, you would really see, and a new world of beauty would open itself before you.

I who am blind can give one hint to those who see: Use your eyes as if tomorrow you would be stricken blind. And the same method can be applied to the other senses.

Hear the music of voices, the song of a bird, the mighty strains of an orchestra, as if you would be stricken deaf tomorrow. Touch each object as if tomorrow your tactile sense would fail. Smell the perfume of flowers, taste with relish each morsel, as if tomorrow you could never smell and taste again. Make the most of every sense; glory in all the facets of pleasure and beauty which the world reveals to you through the several means of contact which nature provides. But of all the senses, I am sure that sight must be far and away the most delightful.

---

## THINK AND DISCUSS
### Understanding
1. What does Helen Keller say she would do on her first day with sight? the second day? the third day?
2. What does Helen think the sense of sight might convey to her on the second day that her sense of touch could not?
3. What does Helen think she would learn from her activities on the third day?

### Analyzing
4. What statement about the condition of blindness does Helen Keller make in the opening paragraph of the essay? On what personal experiences does she base this view?

### Extending
5. Reread Helen's closing message to the sighted. What do you think is her purpose in writing this essay?

## READING LITERATURE SKILLFULLY
### Main Idea and Supporting Details
As you read works of nonfiction, it is important to identify the main idea of the essay or article you are reading. The main idea can be stated directly in the essay or it can be implied. In addition, you should take careful note of the supporting details in an essay. These details help clarify the main idea and make the essay more interesting and vivid.

1. Where at the beginning of her essay does Helen Keller state the main idea? What is it?
2. How does she organize the details to support the main idea?
3. Where in the essay does she restate the main idea?

## COMPOSITION

### Writing a Personal Account

Think about all the activities you do in a normal day: eating meals, going to school, playing sports or music, and so on. Then think about doing one of these things without being able to see. Choose one activity and write a three- to five-paragraph composition describing how you would accomplish it without sight. You may base your account on personal experience or imagination. You might find it helpful to review the structure and style of Helen Keller's essay, particularly her use of imagery. Before writing, see "Developing Your Style" in the Writer's Handbook.

### Describing Helen Keller

From the information provided in this essay and the biographical sketch of Helen Keller, write a three-paragraph composition in which you characterize her for someone who knows nothing about her life. Consider the things that she wants to see and why she wants to see them. Before writing, take notes and organize them in an outline. See "Developing Your Style" in the Writer's Handbook.

## ENRICHMENT

### Presenting a Thematic Report

Helen Keller's life serves as an example of the courage, patience, and enthusiasm needed to overcome physical difficulties. Many other people's lives illustrate this theme. Go to the library and find information about someone else who has overcome a severe physical disability. It could be an athlete, an entertainer, a writer, or another figure. Then prepare a brief report of your findings and tell the class whom you learned about, what difficulties he or she overcame, and how.

## BIOGRAPHY

## Helen Keller
## 1880–1968

Born in Tuscumbia, Alabama, Helen Keller contracted a disease as an infant that left her blind and deaf. Because of her disabilities, she was unable to learn to speak. Through the efforts of her gifted and determined teacher, Anne Sullivan, Helen learned sign language and Braille, and, when she eventually earned a college degree, set about helping others.

When she was sixteen, Keller learned to speak and then became active in the American Foundation for the Blind. She lectured extensively to educate the general public about the problems of the disabled. She also produced *The Story of My Life* (1903), the first of several accounts of her fascinating experiences. The story of Helen's early triumph is best known through William Gibson's play *The Miracle Worker* (1957). "Three Days to See!" has long been recognized for its literary value as well as its inspirational message.

# Grandmother Zabielska[1]

**Zofia Starowieyska Morstin**   Poland

---

**Even the final days of life can provide important lessons.**

---

he death of Grandmother Zabielska was the first one experienced by the children. Both their grandfathers had died long before. None of the children remembered them. She was the first person whom they knew, whom they lived with, to leave this familiar life. For that reason her end became for them a kind of model death. It also explains how the seventy-second year, the age at which she died, came to mark for them the close of human life, just as the red line on a thermometer points to the normal temperature. They always believed that whoever died before that age died too young, while every additional year was a gift.

In the same way, through her death, their attitude towards that special moment of life was determined—and determined properly; although sad, the fact was simple and natural. There was nothing dramatic about it. It was, like Grandmother's life, well balanced, Christian, conducted intelligently and generously.

As soon as her condition was diagnosed as pneumonia, her bed was moved from the northern bedroom to the sunny living room. Treatment with oxygen was then unknown, and the disease was not accompanied, as it is now, by the threatening hiss of the oxygen tank. As much fresh air as possible was supplied for the congested lungs, but of course only natural sources were available.

Here, in the red living room, air was plentiful. Also, there was enough space for an altar, in front of which Father Wojciech,[2] one of Grandmother's sons, said Mass every morning so she could share in the service and receive Holy Communion.

The sick woman, like everyone around her, fully realized that the end was near, for at that time there was no recovery from pneumonia for an old person. Grandmother Zabielska was not in the habit of deceiving herself; even this awesome fact she met as reasonably as she had always met all unavoidable events.

She did not complain, nor was she ever restive. On the contrary, she was gracious and grateful for the gentle care with which Emilia, her daughter-in-law, nursed her so efficiently. Nobody could please the sick woman as well as she did, for Pani Emilia,[3] though she had no natural leanings toward good Samaritanism, wanted to do everything well for those she loved.

Meanwhile, Grandmother Zabielska set about

---

1. *Zabielska* (zä byel′skə).
2. *Wojciech* (voi′cheн).
3. *Pani* (pä′nyi) *Emilia. Pani* is a complimentary title meaning "lady." [*Polish*]

*Zofia Starowieyska Morstin* (zô′fyä stär′ō vyä′skä môr′stĕn).

"Grandmother Zabielska" by Zofia Starowieyska Morstin, translated by Wanda Jaeckel, from *The Modern Polish Mind*, edited by Maria Kuncewiz, 1962. Reprinted by permission of Maxwell Aley Associates.

preparing for death in her orderly way. As Wojciech did not leave his mother's side, he would be on hand at the appropriate moment to administer the last rites.[4] In the Zabielski family it was not the custom when someone was dying to tell that person a white lie about recovering, but for Emilia's people, who loved talk, ornaments, and gentle ironies, these straightforward manners seemed brutal. They used to say that the Zabielskis died like peasants.

The sacrament of Extreme Unction was received by the patient in all the severity of truth. The business of the will was clear and decided ahead of time; it needed no explanation. The last instructions by Grandmother Zabielska, however, concerned matters so trivial that everyone was astonished that they were recalled at such a moment. But she, always tidy to the point of perfection, did not believe that small things should be forgotten on the doorstep of eternity. And so one day she called the eighteen-year-old sister of her daughter-in-law, and rather harshly ordered her to put the last stitches on the embroidery of a gray tablecloth. She herself would not have time, and she hated to leave a piece of work unfinished.

"But make sure that all the cross-stitches go in the same direction," she said.

And when Basia[5] began to reply that she could finish it herself upon recovering, Grandmother Zabielska interrupted. "I know what I'm talking about; you will finish the tablecloth. But you are messy and always mix up the stitches, and this time I want you to work carefully."

Basia kept her promise. Those were the only straight stitches she ever made.

A frequent guest at the sickbed was Emilia's mother, Pani Liza. The two old friends talked about the approaching parting. Pani Liza was very sorry to see her companion go, and with all her warm heart she tried to anticipate and understand the dejection and sorrow of her relative. The tearing-off process of death frightened her

because—although reaching longingly for God—she had her roots deeply in life. Letting her thoughts out, she would say, more frankly than diplomatically, "How hard it must be to leave this world! To leave everything and everyone."

"Oh, no," the answer came. "When the dessert is to be passed, we don't want to go back to the soup."

But Pani Liza was not convinced that one could leave this world without regret. Not only was she more passionately attached to life, but also—being more pious—she was continuously stirred by feelings of doubt and guilt, never sure whether she had not committed a grave sin. That was why she could not understand her friend's composure. (Her own death, when it came, was very different: although she died in a nun's habit, and in a state of grace, her end was full of anguish, dreadful fears, and heart-rending sorrow. And perhaps in forewarning of these tortures she did not hesitate to say things which, presumably, would upset her friend.)

"It is so horrifying," she would say, "to know that soon one will face God's Judgment."

This prospect did not disturb Grandmother Zabielska either.

"But why?" she said soberly and reasonably. "When we knew that something was bad, we simply tried not to do it."

People are apt to judge themselves tolerantly; nevertheless in decisive moments panic seizes them. Then from the peaks of self-confidence, they fall into the depths of doubt. Not so Grandmother Zabielska; she never lost her balance. What she thought of herself no one knew, for she never talked about herself. Her one bit of self-praise in that last hour was a modest one. She simply stated that she did no wrong, or rather,

---

4. *last rites.* Known also as Extreme Unction, these are religious rites performed for a dying person.
5. *Basia* (bä′shə).

tried to do no wrong. She was sure of it. Her moral standard was minimal: to avoid wrong. It was realized in full.

She imposed this peace-in-death on everyone around her. Everyone was sad—no one despaired.

Once a day the children were called to Grandmother's bedside. They would stand there a while, silent, suddenly hushed, and then they would go back to their rooms. Mrs. Zabielska looked at the children seriously—strictly, they thought. But this was entirely on the surface. She loved them very much and was proud of them. She was proud of their robust health, their tallness, their gaiety and brightness.

One afternoon Pani Emilia entered the nursery where they sat at the low table having their afternoon snack, and told them that Helenka and Maciej[6] were to come with her, because their grandmother was dying. She waited, leaning down on the little table. From her neck hung a long, heavy chain the end of which, together with the watch, was tucked under the belt. Tears rolled down her face. The children got up quietly and went with her down to the living room, where everyone—family and servants—was kneeling in a circle around the bed, reciting the litany for the dying. The children knelt and prayed with the others—for the first time participating in the grave matter of death.

No shadow of terror fell on their lives. This "good death" they remembered many, many years later, when—quite grown-up—they followed the coffin of Grandmother Zabielska's son, Uncle Kazimierz.[7] Around them the Second World War was blazing and the terror of the German occupation raged. It was a time rife with death—dreadful, cruel, and unnatural. But Uncle Kazimierz escaped this fate. He died a ripe old age in his own home, among his children and grandchildren. He died a sudden death, but not unexpected. His coffin was carried by his neighbors out of the place in which he had spent his life. According to ancient custom, the casket was lowered three times on every threshold: the dead man had to say good-by to his house.

Later on that sunny summer day, among the murmur of trees and flutter of flags, with ringing bells and wailing funeral chants, he was taken to the cemetery by his family, neighbors, and friends. And everyone felt, in spite of their sorrow at bidding farewell to this good and cheerful man, that they were taking part in something proper—not frightening at all. This was how a man should die, in his house, among his own people—by God's, not man's hand.

---

6. **Helenka** (hä län′kə) . . . **Maciej** (mä′chä).
7. **Kazimierz** (kä zē′myesh).

## THINK AND DISCUSS
### Understanding
1. Why does the narrator say that Grandmother Zabielska's death became a kind of "model death" for the children?

2. At the beginning of the story, why is everyone so sure that Grandmother will die soon?

## Analyzing

3. What attitudes toward death and dying were held by Pani Emilia and Pani Liza?
4. Grandmother Zabielska commented to Pani Liza, "When the dessert is to be passed, we don't want to go back to the soup." How does this statement express her ideas about death?
5. What can you infer about Basia's feelings for Grandmother from the way in which Basia completes the embroidery on the tablecloth?
6. The author indicates at the beginning of the essay that sharing Grandmother Zabielska's experience would have long-range effects. How does her description of Uncle Kazimierz's death support this assertion?
7. Do you think the mention of the period in which Uncle Kazimierz's death occurred in any way affects the essay's **theme**? Discuss.

## Extending

8. One student has commented that this essay is more about how to live than about dying. Explain why you agree or disagree.

## COMPOSITION
### Writing a Character Study

In "Grandmother Zabielska," the reader is not told about Grandmother's early life. But through her conversations and what the narrator says, you can determine the sort of woman she was. In a three- to five-paragraph composition to be shared with your classmates, write a character sketch of Grandmother Zabielska. Be sure that your description of her is consistent with what you have learned about her in the story. See "Writing About Nonfiction" in the Writer's Handbook.

### Writing a Tribute

It is obvious that this essay was written many years after Grandmother Zabielska died, when the sorrow of her loss was in the past. Think about a well-known person from the past whom you greatly admire—a world leader, an author, an entertainer, a sports figure—and write a three- to five-paragraph tribute in honor of that person. You may be asked to read your tribute to the class.

## BIOGRAPHY

## Zofia Starowieyska Morstin
## 1895–1966

A product of a well-to-do, land-owning family, Morstin was educated both in her homeland and abroad. Upon her return to Poland, she joined the staff of a newspaper and also produced several works of fiction. During World War II, when Germany occupied Poland, she devoted her time to writing a series of essays on the Italian Renaissance—a safe subject. After the war, she became a book reviewer and columnist for a popular Catholic weekly. "Grandmother Zabielska" is taken from *Our Home,* a collection of memoirs of her early years.

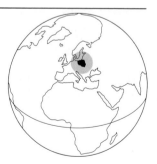

# The Day We Flew the Kites

Frances Fowler   USA

**"We never knew where the hours went on that hilltop day. There were no hours, just a golden, breezy Now."**

S tring!" shouted Brother, bursting into the kitchen. "We need lots more string."

It was Saturday. As always, it was a busy one, for "Six days shalt thou labor and do all thy work" was taken seriously in those days. My father and Mr. Patrick next door were doing chores about their large yards. March was a busy time.

Indoors, Mother and Mrs. Patrick were running around in their usual Saturday marathon, complicated by spring cleaning. Such a windy day was ideal for "turning out" clothes closets. Already woolens flapped on clotheslines which snaked across the adjoining back yards.

Somehow the boys had slipped away to the back lot with their kites. Now, even at the risk of having Brother impounded for beating carpets or washing windows, they had sent him to the house for more string. All theirs had played out—heaven knows how many yards! Apparently there was no limit to the heights to which kites would soar today.

My mother looked out the window. The sky was piercingly blue; the breeze fresh and infinitely exciting. Up in all that blueness sailed great puffy billows of clouds. It had been a long, hard winter, but today was Spring.

My mother looked from the pie-baking clutter on the kitchen table to the disordered sitting room, its furniture all moved out of line for a really Spartan[1] sweeping. Again her eyes wavered toward the window. "Come on, girls!" She fumbled in the kitchen-table drawer for a new roll of twine. "Let's take string to the boys and watch them fly the kites a minute."

On the way we met our neighbor, Mrs. Patrick, laughing guiltily, escorted by her girls.

There never was such a day for flying kites! God doesn't make two such days in a century. We played all our fresh twine into the boys' kites, and still they soared. We could hardly distinguish the tiny, orange-colored specks. Now and then we slowly reeled one in, finally bringing it, dipping and tugging, to earth, for the sheer joy of sending it up again, feeling its vibrant tug against the twine as it sought the sky. What a thrill to run with them, to the right, to the left, and see our poor, earth-bound movements reflected minutes

---

1. *Spartan* (spärt′n), severe, stern, and simple, like the lives of the people of Sparta, a city in ancient Greece known for its strict discipline.

later, in the majestic sky-dance of the kites! We wrote "wishes" on slips of paper, punched holes in them, and slipped them over the string. Slowly, irresistibly, they climbed up until they reached the kites. Surely all such wishes would be granted!

Even our fathers dropped hoe and hammer and joined us. Our mothers took their turn, laughing like schoolgirls. Their hair blew out of their decorous pompadours and curled loose about their cheeks, their gingham aprons whipped about their legs. Mingled with our puppyish delight was a feeling akin to awe. These adults were playing with us, really playing! The gulf between parent and child was greater then than now. Once I looked at Mother and thought she looked actually pretty! And her over forty!

We never knew where the hours went on that hilltop day. There were no hours, just a golden, breezy Now. I think we were all a little beyond

John Falter, *Boys and Kites*, Low Illustration Collection, New Britain Museum of American Art, New Britain, Connecticut

ourselves. Parents forgot their duty and their dignity; children forgot the combativeness and small spites. "Perhaps it's like this in the Kingdom of Heaven," I thought confusedly. All our personalities stood out clearer, more individual than ever, and yet there was no sense of separateness.

It was growing dark before, drunk with sun and air, we all stumbled sleepily back to the houses. Things were just as we had left them, but Mother looked as if she hardly saw the half-rolled pastry, the stripped sitting room. I suppose we had some sort of supper. I suppose there must have been a surface tidying-up, for the house on Sunday looked decorous enough, or do I remember?

The strange thing was, we didn't mention that day, afterward. I felt a little embarrassed. Surely none of those other sensible, balanced people had thrilled to it as deeply as I; none had had ridiculous, sacrilegious thoughts about comparing flying kites with the Kingdom of Heaven. I locked the memory up in that deepest part of me where we keep "the things that cannot be and yet are" . . . and the years went on.

A good many years had passed, and one day I was flying about a kitchen of my own in a city apartment. I was trying to get some work out of the way while my three-year-old insistently whined her desire to "go park and see ducks."

"I can't go!" (My reasonableness was wearing thin.) "I have this and this and this to do first, and when I'm through I'll be too tired to walk that far."

My mother, who was visiting us, looked up from the peas she was shelling. "It's a wonderful day," she offered, "really warm, yet there's a fine, fresh breeze. It reminds me of that day we flew the kites." I stopped in my dash between stove and sink. So she remembered! The locked door flew open, and with it a gush of memories, and the application of her little parable. There had been much to do on that long-ago Saturday.

I pulled off my apron. "Come on," I told my little girl. "You're right, it's too good a day to miss."

Another decade passed. We were in the uneasy aftermath of a great war. All evening we had been asking our returned soldier, the youngest Patrick boy, about his experiences as a prisoner of war. He had talked freely, but now for a long time he had been silent, watching his cigarette smoke curl upward into the summer darkness. The silence seemed suddenly to throb. What was he thinking of . . . what dark and dreadful things? What was he going to tell?

"Say!" A smile twitched his lips. He looked like the little boy he used to be, the very little boy always tagging behind us others. "Say, do you remember . . . no, of course you wouldn't. It probably didn't make the impression on you it did on me. It was the first time I'd seen them."

I hardly dared speak. "Remember what?"

"I used to think of that day a lot in P.W. camp, when things weren't too good. Do you remember the day we flew the kites?"

Winter came, and the sad duty of a call of condolence on Mrs. Patrick, recently widowed. Her family had moved away many years before, but she had brought back her husband's body to our town for burial. I dreaded the call. I couldn't imagine how Mrs. Patrick would face life alone.

I found her quite gray, a little stooped, much thinner than in her vigorous, maternal middle years. But she still had those warm, brown eyes, that low, caressing voice. We talked a little of my family and her grandchildren and the changes in our town. Then she was silent, looking down at her lap. I cleared my throat. Now I must say something about her loss, and she would begin to cry.

When I looked up, I was dumbfounded. Mrs. Patrick was smiling. "I was just sitting here thinking," she said. "Henry had such fun that day. Frances, do you remember the day we flew the kites?"

## THINK AND DISCUSS

### Understanding

1. What was there about the day that caused everyone to put aside responsibilities and join in the kite flying?
2. This essay can be divided into four parts, each with a different **setting**. What are they?

### Analyzing

3. What does the narrator mean when she says, "God doesn't make two such days in a century"?
4. How does the kite-flying day affect the later day in the city?
5. How had the kite-flying day affected the Patrick boy?
6. How had it affected Mr. and Mrs. Patrick?

### Extending

7. Do you think Fowler's statement that the gulf between parent and child was greater in the past than now is true? Explain.

## VOCABULARY

### Dictionary/Glossary, Context

Definitions in dictionary and glossary entries tell you the meaning or meanings of words, but often you must interpret the meaning as it applies to a word's context. On a separate sheet of paper, write the number of each question below and the letter that identifies the correct answer. If necessary, look up each italicized word in the Glossary.

1. If someone told you to wait in the *adjoining* room, where would you go?
   (**a**) to the room downstairs; (**b**) to the room next-door; (**c**) to the kitchen; (**d**) to the attic.
2. If your pet dog is *impounded*, what happens to it?
   (**a**) it is given its vaccine shots; (**b**) it is registered by the city; (**c**) it is locked up; (**d**) it is bitten by another dog.
3. If a worker becomes *dumbfounded*, he or she is which of the following?
   (**a**) ready to retire; (**b**) bewildered; (**c**) stupid; (**d**) furious.
4. If your art teacher told you to draw a picture of a woman with a *pompadour* hairdo, you would draw a woman with which style?
   (**a**) hair cropped short; (**b**) very curly hair; (**c**) almost no hair; (**d**) a high, puffy hairdo.
5. If someone is said to be *sacrilegious*, which description applies to the person?
   (**a**) holy to the point of sainthood; (**b**) generous; (**c**) guilty of violating something sacred; (**d**) an innocent victim.

## COMPOSITION

### Describing a Memorable Experience

Fowler's essay deals with an everyday event that left a permanent impression on everyone who participated. Think about such an experience that you have shared with family or friends. Describe what it was, how you felt at the time, and why you remember it now. Write three to five paragraphs to be shared with your friends or classmates.

### Analyzing an Essay

Reread Fowler's essay and take notes on the four episodes it describes. The most space is devoted to the first episode, for it is the most important. Note the people involved, then go on to the next three, considering the intervening time and the seriousness of each occasion. Write a three- to five-paragraph composition for your teacher, analyzing the structure of the essay and explaining how each subsequent recollection grows in emotional intensity. See "Writing to Analyze Author's Style" in the Writer's Handbook.

**Review SATIRE in the Handbook of Literary Terms, page 822.**

# My Store of Grievances

**John Welter** USA

---

**"This is a convenience store. Do you know what that means?"**

---

What I'm going to call my new chain of convenience stores that will make me rich is Get It and Get Out.

I asked Dr. Joyce Brothers[1] about the name and she said, "If you want to make your customers feel unwelcome and drive them away, you should use that name." I do, and so I will. Once I start my new chain of Get It and Get Out stores, I'll pledge to the customers, "Poor service and high prices." I'll have a big neon sign in blue and orange letters and artsy glass that says WE'RE OPEN 24 HOURS A DAY AND WE HATE IT.

Psychology like that is essential in a convenience store, and I'll probably put up a sign that says, OUR PRICES ARE HIGH AND WE DON'T CARE. I think the customers will find that irresistible, and if they don't, it just doesn't matter. Almost certainly I'll put up a huge neon sign in blue and yellow that says, WE'RE GOING TO CHEAT YOU, AND SO WHAT? I like neon. Whether the customers do doesn't interest me.

Here's what might happen in my store. A woman (I could use a man, but I thought of a woman first, all right?) would walk up to the checkout counter with a small box of noodles and say, "Isn't this pretty high, a dollar ten for a small box of noodles?"

I'd say, "That's not so bad. Our prices change without notice, and *uh-oh*—now those noodles cost two dollars."

The woman would be furious and say, "This is outrageous."

"Ma'am," I'd say, "I'm not responsible for your mood swings. This is a convenience store. Do you know what that means? It means we can cheat you however we feel like it." Then I'd point behind me to the purple-and-red neon sign on the wall that says OUTRAGED CUSTOMERS WILL BE ASKED TO LEAVE.

As for my staff, I'll hire people who don't know arithmetic, so that if a question ever arises about a customer's being charged the wrong price, the clerks will say, "I don't know arithmetic. It's store policy." I will make sure that most of my clerks have never operated a cash register before, so my store will have long lines of irritated customers watching my clerks stare blankly at the cash register as if they had been told never to understand why they were hired.

If that doesn't sufficiently interfere with progress, I'll insist that my clerks talk on the phone

---

1. **Dr. Joyce Brothers,** psychologist and author.

"My Store of Grievances" by John Welter, from *The Atlantic*, August, 1987. Reprinted by permission of the author.

with their boyfriends or girlfriends and regard customers as intruders. Instead of hiring good-natured, conscientious people who know you have to work for a living, I'll carefully screen the applicants in search of people who will behave as if they think their job is demeaning and not worth taking seriously and who will let you know it.

When a customer gets angry and demands to speak to the manager, my clerks will be trained to say, "He ain't here. Never is."

If a customer then says, "I insist on seeing the manager. Where is he?" the standard answer from my clerks will be, "He's out somewhere gettin' a new neon sign that says EVERYTHING WE SELL COSTS TOO MUCH."

My stores will sell soft drinks in wax-paper cups that don't have lids to fit them. "Do you have any lids to fit these cups?" a customer will ask.

"No," my clerks will reply. "Manager says it's cheaper to buy lids that don't fit."

As a strict store policy, we will always be out of drinking straws. When a customer says, "Do you have any more straws?" the clerks will say, "I'll go back in the back and look." Then the clerks will disappear into the back of the store for at least two minutes, where they'll maybe look at magazines or make calls to their girlfriends. After that they'll return sluggishly to the checkout counter and say, "Couldn't find 'em."

From time to time a customer might feel neglected or unappreciated, and he or she will say angrily, "Doesn't this store's management *care* about its customers?"

"Of course we do," I'll say, and I'll point to the big neon sign in red and lavender letters that says WE FEEL THAT THE CUSTOMER IS A CONDUIT OF MONEY.

And here's an important emotional touch that will be featured in all of my Get It and Get Out stores. Once a customer has paid for all of his items and the goods are placed in a sack that's too small and rips open, the clerks will say, "Now get lost."

## THINK AND DISCUSS
### Understanding
1. What are the requirements for being a clerk in the author's imaginary store?
2. What does the narrator insist that the clerks do while at work?
3. What is the problem with the soft drink cups? with the straws? with the paper sacks?

### Analyzing
4. Explain the double meaning of the title.
5. Just as a poet's use of **hyperbole**—figurative exaggeration—is not taken literally, we do not seriously accept the narrator's plans to run a store such as Get It and Get Out. What part of the plan do you find most exaggerated or ridiculous?

### Extending
6. As a customer, have you experienced any of the problems the author suggests or any similar grievances? Explain.

### REVIEWING: Satire HT
See Handbook of Literary Terms, p. 822
Writers use satire not only to entertain, often with biting humor, but also to draw attention to

problems in society caused by the weaknesses of institutions and people who manage them. To ridicule stores that he feels offer rude service, John Welter uses exaggeration and the surprising portrayal of an imaginary merchant—the narrator—who doesn't pretend to serve anyone but himself.

1. Explain the satire in the store's name.
2. How do the signs the narrator describes differ from the signs in real stores?

## THINKING SKILLS
### Classifying

To **classify** things is to arrange them into categories or groups according to some system. For example, nonfiction works can be classified as biography, letters, essays, and articles. In "My Store of Grievances," many different complaints can be found. Review the essay and take note of the various implied complaints about convenience stores. Then write five lists in which you classify these complaints under the following categories: management, sales clerks, goods, prices, and store appearance.

## COMPOSITION
### Writing Satire

Welter's essay is an excellent example of a satiric treatment of an everyday annoyance. Using his essay as a model, write a three- to five-paragraph essay to be shared with your classmates in which you give an exaggerated treatment to something that annoys you. You may write about long lines at the supermarket or other stores, the food in a restaurant or cafeteria, neighborhood nuisances, the behavior of people in crowds, or another target.

### Voicing a Complaint

You may agree with John Welter about store service, or you may feel that his criticisms are unfounded or excessive. Determine how you feel and then prepare to write either a letter to an imaginary store owner or corporate president or a response to this satirical essay. If you plan to take Welter's side, review the selection or your own experience to focus on a few specific complaints. If you plan to defend the stores, write an essay to your class describing the typical circumstances in stores, as you see them. Make your three- or four-paragraph paper persuasive by employing evidence and a tone that will convince your audience.

## ENRICHMENT
### Dramatizing an Essay

This essay is an excellent vehicle for dramatization. As a class, write dialogue for the situations described in the essay, and then use the dialogue to put on a skit. You will need to include the roles of one or two customers, one or two sales clerks, and the manager. To capture the effect of the neon signs—and to add a touch of humor—make signs that a student with a flashlight can illuminate at the appropriate moments. If your class has access to a video camera, record your production and show it to other classes.

## BIOGRAPHY

### John Welter
### 1951–

John Welter was born in Monohans, Texas, and grew up in various states and regions of the United States, as his father worked in industries that served the federal government. Welter lived in Texas, Oklahoma, Colorado, Kansas, Missouri, and North Carolina, with the longest period spent in Kansas City. His background gave him a sense of our national culture as well as the richness of regional life. He works as a feature writer for *The News and Observer* in Chapel Hill, North Carolina, and as an editorial-page writer for the *Kansas City Star*. An admirer of humorists such as S. J. Perelman and Mark Twain, he feels that it is important for readers to recognize irony when they encounter it. "Many people," he says, "are too literal-minded. They accept everything they read as either true or not true." He believes that satire and ironic writing may convey an underlying truth not measured in how factually provable they may be. Welter, who now lives in Carrboro, North Carolina, writes humorous pieces for publications such as *The Atlantic*, where "My Store of Grievances" first appeared.

## Structure and Formality in the Essay

Essays generally fall into two broad categories, the formal and the informal. A formal essay concentrates on the explication of ideas, is rigidly structured, is almost always written in the third person, and uses language and syntax intended for thoughtful, educated readers. An informal essay is concerned with the author's personality as well as ideas, is loosely structured and usually written in the first person, and uses the language and syntax of everyday educated speech.

What often determines the formality or informality of an essay is the degree to which these basic elements are utilized or combined. Of the essays in this unit, "Three Days to See!" is the most rigidly structured, proceeding in chronological order, yet its first-person narration and emotional quality keep it from being a formal essay. Another essay rendered informal by its point of view and appeal to emotions is "The Day We Flew the Kites." Less formal

still is the personal memoir "Grandmother Zabielska." It makes a point, then illustrates it by recounting the family's experience, and finally applies it to a future event. Though told in third person, the essay's loose time order keeps it informal.

The essay form also can be used for lighter prose, as exemplified by "My Store of Grievances." Although this essay is not rigidly structured, its idea is clearly and humorously expressed through the use of exaggeration and satire. Its satirical tone unifies the essay.

The final essay in this section, "Biographies Bring New Companions," gains its coherence from a unifying main idea, which is explicitly expressed by the author. Its formal structure and thesis may be apparent to perceptive readers, but its tone of enthusiasm and appreciation make some readers overlook structure. Often the best structure is the least apparent.

# Biographies Bring New Companions

Marchette Chute   USA

"**Biography brings the times to life again, just as it brings the people. . . .**"

There are many ways of enjoying ourselves, and one of the pleasantest is to meet interesting people.

The world is full of remarkable men and women, but even if we had time to go all over the earth to visit them and carried a suitcase stuffed with letters of introduction, we should still not be able to encounter more than a small fraction of the people we admire. Soldiers, statesmen, writers, scientists, inventors, actors, painters—most of them we shall never meet. But there is one easy way to get to know them all, and that is in the biographies that are written about them.

A biography is the life story of a real person. If it is a good biography it brings its hero as vividly to life as if he were standing in the same room. If you met him in person you would probably not get more than a polite handshake and a "How do you do?"; but in a biography you can find out all about him—what he did when he was a small boy, the way he went about his work, the friends he made, even his taste in neckties. It is not surprising that so many people like to read biographies, for they are a kind of window into a man's life; the better the biography the larger and clearer the window.

Moreover, anyone who reads biographies meets not only the people who are alive today but those who lived in all the past centuries. The men and women whose lives are worth remembering stretch over the whole of history, like a great, lighted procession, and we could never make their acquaintance if it were not for biographies.

It is true that a biographer has an easier time of it if the man he is writing about is still alive. James Boswell, for instance, could sit in the same room with Dr. Johnson,[1] with his eyes and ears open like a good reporter's, listening delightedly and remembering what he heard, so that when he came to write his book he could transfer Johnson's bossy, magnificent self to paper and catch the very sound of his voice. If the hero is no longer living and his life has to be reconstructed from documents, the biographer has a more difficult time of it. But everyone leaves records of

---

1. *James Boswell . . . Dr. Johnson.* Boswell (1740–1795) was a Scottish writer famous for his biography of Samuel Johnson (1709–1784), an English author and lexicographer.

himself, and it is the biographer's task to put them together and bring back a living man.

This sense of reality, of showing great people as they really were, is one of the best things about biography. A non-reader, for instance, might think of George Washington as being the way he is shown on dollar bills. He looks strong-minded and dignified in a stuffed kind of way, what with his unyielding mouth and glassy eyes, but he does not look as if he had ever really been alive. But a good biography shows the real man, the Washington who took such enormous risks and who knew that he would be hanged for treason if he failed in what he was trying to do. Washington was not a great man because he somehow soared above the troubles of ordinary people—confusion and discouragement and a sense of defeat; he was a great man because he never gave in to them.

A good portrait can sometimes bring a man back to life, but even then it fixes him at just one moment of time. The pictures of Longfellow,[2] for instance, show him with a beard, and it is hard to remember that he was once a small boy going to school, or a young man trying to work out his first rhymes. Cicero[3] is a marble figure in a toga, and no one would guess what a complex, sensitive, brilliant, and irritating man he was in real life. A biography of Cicero brings him back as his friends in politics knew him, and a schoolroom bust turns into an interesting person to know.

A good biography takes away the sense of "costume" that often blocks our imagination when we think about the past. Because Napoleon wore a cocked hat and Queen Elizabeth a starched ruff and Richard the Lion-Hearted armor instead of khaki, we forget that these were just their ordinary clothes, and we think of them as being remote, unfamiliar, and just a little odd. This is hardly fair, because if you look at old photographs of your friends, the clothes of ten or twenty years ago will look just as odd. It is time that turns clothes into costume, and a good biography can

destroy time. What happened to Abraham Lincoln or Joan of Arc becomes "now" as long as you are reading about them, and no one who reads a good biography of Leonardo da Vinci could ever again think that Renaissance Italy was peopled by remote figures in improbable costumes. Biography brings the times to life again, just as it brings the people; and it makes the world a more spacious and interesting place to live in.

Another advantage of reading biography is that it widens your sense of enjoyment over things that have nothing to do with books. Even the pasteurizing of milk is more interesting if you know something about that stubborn man, Louis Pasteur. Brooklyn Bridge is twice as impressive if you know about the father and son[4] who gave their lives to bring it into being, and traveling in the Far West becomes a special adventure to anyone who has read about Lewis and Clark. Radium becomes an even more awe-inspiring discovery if you know how a small woman in black named Madam Curie struggled with fierce patience to find it; and even a new type of wheat becomes more important if you know about the man who brought it into being.

So many things that now seem like fixed stars were born of fierce struggle and apparent defeat. Lincoln believed that he had done a poor job after he delivered the Gettysburg Address, and Keats died believing that his name would not be remembered. Beethoven wrote his greatest music after he became deaf, and Milton his greatest poetry after he became blind. The people who are worth knowing are the people who never gave up, and a good biography illuminates the springs of their

---

**2. Longfellow,** Henry Wadsworth Longfellow (1807–1882), American poet.
**3. Cicero,** Marcus Tullius Cicero (106–43 B.C.), Roman orator, writer, and statesman. He appears as a character in the play *Julius Caesar*.
**4. father and son,** John A. Roebling, who designed the bridge, and his son Washington A. Roebling, who directed its construction after his father's death.

heroism. From the outside, to their own friends, many of them seemed ordinary enough people; but each of them held a kind of special light inside himself, and a good biography shows why.

Even in the case of Shakespeare, whose life has nothing to do with the delight that any reader can get from his plays, it gives an added interest to know something about him as a man. It is interesting to know he worked in the theater all his adult life; he himself was an actor. Other playwrights of the time usually entered the theater only for conferences. He helped build the finest theater in London and owned part of it, and a little of the greatness of his plays comes from his thorough understanding of stagecraft and the needs of an audience. Many people in his own day did not think Shakespeare's plays were very good, since they pleased ordinary people and it was felt that really good work ought to please only a chosen few; but everyone liked him as a man, and two of his fellow actors loved him so much that they saved all his plays in the special collection that is now known as the First Folio.

Good biography brings the past near and makes it real. It gives us a more spacious world to live in and heroes for our companions, and it pushes back the horizon so that we can make friends not only with the people around us but with all the people in history who have made the world a place worth living in.

## THINK AND DISCUSS
### Understanding
1. According to Chute, what are some of the advantages of reading biographies?
2. What does she say a biography teaches about history?

### Analyzing
3. Explain how biographies bring new companions.
4. How can what we read in biographies encourage us when we feel we are failing or not doing well in some endeavor?
5. Explain the meaning of Chute's **metaphor**, "Biographies . . . are a kind of window into a man's life; the better the biography the larger and clearer the window."

### Extending
6. One student has commented that a biography releases its readers from the prison of their own time and place. How is this so?

7. In what ways can this essay prepare you to get more out of reading a biography?

## THINKING SKILLS
### Evaluating
To **evaluate** is to make a judgment based on some sort of standard. A book reviewer evaluates a book according to certain standards of writing skill, worthwhile content, and level of interest. You can evaluate literature if you have a standard in mind. Review the essay "Biographies Bring New Companions" to determine a standard you can use to judge the quality of biographical or autobiographical writing. Write a standard of judgment that you have drawn from this essay, and compare your standard to those of your classmates. Then choose the selection from the Biographies and Autobiographies section at the beginning of this unit that best meets your standard of quality.

## COMPOSITION

### Recording Your Current Interests

Imagine that, years from now, someone were to ask you what you were like when you were in high school. Make a list of the things you think will be important parts of your answer—your interests, current events in your life and the world, your plans for the future, and so on. Then write three to five paragraphs describing those aspects of your life today that you think will be the most interesting ten years from now. If you like, save the letter and read it some time in the future.

### Writing a Biographical Sketch

Select a student to be your partner and ask him or her questions that will enable you to write a three- to five-paragraph biography of his or her life. Then reverse roles. When you are finished, students who are willing can have their biographies read aloud anonymously, and the rest of the class can guess whose biography it is.

## ENRICHMENT

### Gathering Facts Through Research

Marchette Chute's short essay names several famous people. Each person in the class can select one of the names mentioned and find three to five interesting facts about that person's life. Use the books, magazines, and encyclopedias in the school or community library as your sources of information. When you finish, share your information with the rest of the class. If you like, read your facts without telling the name of the person they describe; let the class guess who it is.

## BIOGRAPHY

## Marchette Chute

## 1909–

Marchette Chute is well qualified to write about biography, for she is famous for the biographies she has written, among them *Chaucer of England, Shakespeare of London,* and *Ben Jonson of Westminster*. She was born in Minnesota and graduated from the University of Minnesota, but now lives in New York City. In her writing she has specialized in literary biographies, especially those of Medieval and Renaissance authors. When she was honored by election to the American Academy of Arts and Letters, it was on the basis of the "scrupulous scholarship" and "rare imaginative understanding" of her biographies.

# THINKING CRITICALLY
# ABOUT LITERATURE

## UNIT 7  NONFICTION

### ■ CONCEPT REVIEW

The following selection illustrates many of the important ideas and literary terms you have studied in this unit of Nonfiction. The selection is accompanied by notes and questions designed to help you think critically about your reading. The page numbers in the marginal notes refer to the applications of literary terms in the unit. A more extensive discussion of these terms can be found in the Handbook of Literary Terms.

In "A Kiowa Grandmother," N. Scott Momaday pays tribute not only to a special relative but also to his people. He tells of his own journey to trace the migration of the tribe, and he richly describes and explains the culture that produced the woman who provides his focus in the selection. Read it and then answer the questions that follow.

# A Kiowa Grandmother

**N. Scott Momaday**  USA

A single knoll rises out of the plain in Oklahoma, north and west of the Wichita Range. For my people, the Kiowas, it is an old landmark, and they gave it the name Rainy Mountain. The hardest weather in the world is there. Winter brings blizzards, hot tornadic winds arise in the spring, and in summer the prairie is an anvil's edge. The grass turns brittle and brown, and it cracks beneath your feet. There are green belts along the rivers and creeks, linear groves of hickory and pecan, willow and witch hazel. At a distance in

■ **Kiowas** (kī′ə wəz): members of a Native American tribe of the western United States.

■ **Style** (page 647): Note the details the author uses to help you see, hear, and feel the landscape.

From *The Way to Rainy Mountain* by N. Scott Momaday. Copyright © 1969 by The University of New Mexico Press. Reprinted by permission. Slightly abridged.

July or August the steaming foliage seems almost to writhe in fire. Great green and yellow grasshoppers are everywhere in the tall grass, popping up like corn to sting the flesh, and tortoises crawl about on the red earth, going nowhere in the plenty of time. Loneliness is an aspect of the land. All things in the plain are isolate; there is no confusion of objects in the eye, but *one* hill or *one* tree or *one* man. To look upon that landscape in the early morning, with the sun at your back, is to lose the sense of proportion. Your imagination comes to life, and this, you think, is where Creation was begun.

I returned to Rainy Mountain in July. My grandmother had died in the spring, and I wanted to be at her grave. She had lived to be very old and at last infirm. Her only living daughter was with her when she died, and I was told that in death her face was that of a child.

I like to think of her as a child. When she was born, the Kiowas were living the last great moment of their history. For more than a hundred years they had controlled the open range from the Smoky Hill River to the Red, from the headwaters of the Canadian to the fork of the Arkansas and Cimarron. In alliance with the Comanches, they had ruled the whole of the southern Plains. War was their sacred business, and they were among the finest horsemen the world has ever known. But warfare for the Kiowas was preeminently a matter of disposition rather than of survival, and they never understood the grim, unrelenting advance of the U. S. Cavalry. When at last, divided and ill-provisioned, they were driven onto the Staked Plains in the cold rains of autumn, they fell into panic. In Palo Duro Canyon they abandoned their crucial stores to pillage and had nothing then but their lives. In order to save themselves, they surrendered to the soldiers at Fort Sill and were imprisoned in the old stone corral that now stands as a military museum. My grandmother was spared the humiliation of those high gray walls by eight or ten years, but she must have known from birth the affliction of defeat, the dark brooding of old warriors.

Her name was Aho, and she belonged to the last culture to evolve in North America. Her forebears came down from the high country in western Montana nearly three centuries ago. They were a mountain people, a mysterious tribe of hunters whose language has never been positively classified in any major group. In the late seventeenth century they began a long migration to the south and east. It was a journey toward the dawn, and it led to a golden age. Along the way the Kiowas were befriended by the Crows, who gave them the culture and religion of the Plains. They acquired horses, and their ancient nomadic spirit was suddenly free of the ground. They acquired Tai-me, the sacred Sun Dance doll, from that moment the object and symbol of their worship, and so shared in the divinity of the sun. Not least, they acquired the sense of destiny, therefore courage and pride. When they entered upon the southern Plains they had been transformed. No longer were

■ **Red . . . Canadian . . . Arkansas . . . Cimarron:** rivers in Oklahoma.

■ **Comanches** (kə-man′chēz): members of another tribe. Kiowas and Comanches once fought as allies in territorial wars.

■ **Staked Plains:** region of the southern Great Plains, in Texas and New Mexico.

■ The author uses his account of his grandmother's life as a literary vehicle to explore and tell about the Kiowa migration and culture.

■ **Crows:** members of a Native American tribe of Montana.

■ Note the importance of Tai-me (tī mā) to Kiowa religion and culture.

Stephen Mopope, *The Procession*, 1958, Philbrook Art Center, Tulsa, Oklahoma

they slaves to the simple necessity of survival; they were a lordly and dangerous society of fighters and thieves, hunters and priests of the sun. According to their origin myth, they entered the world through a hollow log. From one point of view, their migration was the fruit of an old prophecy, for indeed they emerged from a sunless world.

Although my grandmother lived out her long life in the shadow of Rainy Mountain, the immense landscape of the continental interior lay like memory in her blood. She could tell of the Crows, whom she had never seen, and of the Black Hills, where she had never been. I wanted to see in reality what she had seen more perfectly in the mind's eye, and traveled fifteen hundred miles to begin my pilgrimage.

■ Momaday's long journey retraces his tribal ancestors' footsteps.

Yellowstone, it seemed to me, was the top of the world, a region of deep lakes and dark timber, canyons and waterfalls. But, beautiful as it is, one might have the sense of confinement there. The skyline in all directions is close at hand, the high wall of the woods and deep cleavages of shade. There is a perfect freedom in the mountains, but it belongs to the eagle and the elk, the badger and the bear. The Kiowas reckoned their stature by the distance they could see, and they were bent and blind in the wilderness.

Descending eastward, the highland meadows are a stairway to the plain. In July the inland slope of the Rockies is luxuriant with flax and buckwheat, stonecrop and larkspur. The earth unfolds and the limit of the land recedes. Clusters of trees, and animals grazing far in the distance, cause the vision to reach away and wonder to build upon the mind. The sun follows a longer course in the day, and the sky is immense beyond all comparison. The great billowing clouds that sail upon it are shadows that move upon the grain like water, dividing light. Farther down, in the land of the Crows and Blackfeet, the plain is yellow. Sweet clover takes hold of the hills and bends upon itself to cover and seal the soil. There the Kiowas paused on their way; they had come to the place where they must change their lives. The sun is at home on the plains. Precisely there does it have the certain character of a god. When the Kiowas came to the land of the Crows, they could see the dark lees of the hills at dawn across the Bighorn River, the profusion of light on the grain shelves, the oldest deity ranging after the solstices. Not yet would they veer southward to the caldron of the land that lay below; they must wean their blood from the northern winter and hold the mountains a while longer in their view. They bore Tai-me in procession to the east.

A dark mist lay over the Black Hills, and the land was like iron. At the top of a ridge I caught sight of Devil's Tower upthrust against the gray sky as if in the birth of time the core of the earth had broken through its crust and the motion of the world was begun. There are things in nature that engender an awful quiet in the heart of man; Devil's Tower is one of them. Two centuries ago, because they could not do otherwise, the Kiowas made a legend at the base of the rock. My grandmother said:

*Eight children were there at play, seven sisters and their brother. Suddenly the boy was struck dumb; he trembled and began to run upon his hands and feet. His fingers became claws, and his body was covered with fur. Directly there was a bear where the boy had been. The sisters were terrified; they ran, and the bear after them. They came to the stump of a great tree, and the tree spoke to them. It bade them climb upon it, and as they did so it began to rise into the air. The bear came to kill them, but they were just beyond its reach. It reared against the tree and scored the bark all around with its claws. The seven sisters were borne into the sky, and they became the stars of the Big Dipper.*

■ **Connotation/Denotation** (page 610): Powerful words such as *luxuriant, immense,* and *profusion* reflect the vast, awesome landscape.

■ **Devil's Tower:** a volcanic rock tower in northeast Wyoming that rises over twelve hundred feet above the Belle Fourche River; now a national monument.

From that moment, and so long as the legend lives, the Kiowas have kinsmen in the night sky. Whatever they were in the mountains, they could be no more. However tenuous their well-being, however much they had suffered and would suffer again, they had found a way out of the wilderness.

My grandmother had a reverence for the sun, a holy regard that now is all but gone out of mankind. There was a wariness in her, and an ancient awe. She was a Christian in her later years, but she had come a long way about, and she never forgot her birthright. As a child she had been to the Sun Dances; she had taken part in those annual rites, and by then she had learned the restoration of her people in the presence of Tai-me. She was about seven when the last Kiowa Sun Dance was held in 1887 on the Washita River above Rainy Mountain Creek. The buffalo were gone. In order to consummate the ancient sacrifice—to impale the head of the buffalo bull upon the medicine tree—a delegation of old men journeyed into Texas, there to beg and barter for an animal from the Goodnight herd. She was ten when the Kiowas came together for the last time as a living Sun Dance culture. They could find no buffalo; they had to hang an old hide from the sacred tree. Before the dance could begin, a company of soldiers rode out from Fort Sill under orders to disperse the tribe. Forbidden without cause the essential act of their faith, having seen the wild herds slaughtered and left to rot upon the ground, the Kiowas backed away forever from the medicine tree. That was July 20, 1890, at the great bend of the Washita. My grandmother was there. Without bitterness, and for as long as she lived, she bore a vision of deicide.

■ **Goodnight herd:** the herd of Charles Goodnight, a well-known cattle rancher.

■ Momaday chooses the connotative word *slaughtered* rather than a synonym such as *killed*.

■ **deicide** (dē′ə sīd): the killing of a god; in effect, the death of a religion.

■ Note how the author establishes the idea that her image occupies his memory and then uses supporting details to illustrate the many ways he remembers her.

Now that I can have her only in memory, I see my grandmother in the several postures that were peculiar to her: standing at the wood stove on a winter morning and turning meat in a great iron skillet; sitting at the south window, bent above her beadwork, and afterwards, when her vision failed, looking down for a long time into the fold of her hands; going out upon a cane, very slowly as she did when the weight of age came upon her; praying. I remember her most often at prayer. She made long, rambling prayers out of suffering and hope, having seen many things. I was never sure that I had the right to hear, so exclusive were they of all mere custom and company. The last time I saw her she prayed standing by the side of her bed at night, the light of a kerosene lamp moving upon her dark skin. Her long, black hair, always drawn and braided in the day, lay upon her shoulders like a shawl. I do not speak Kiowa, and I never understood her prayers, but there was something inherently sad in the sound, some merest hesitation upon the syllables of sorrow. She began in a high and descending pitch, exhausting her breath to silence; then again and again—and always the same intensity of effort, of something that is, and is not, like urgency in the human voice.

Transported so in the dancing light among the shadows of her room, she seemed beyond the reach of time. But that was illusion; I think I knew then that I should not see her again.

Houses are like sentinels in the plain, old keepers of the weather watch. There, in a very little while, wood takes on the appearance of great age. All colors wear soon away in the wind and rain, and then the wood is burned gray and the grain appears and the nails turn red with rust. The windowpanes are black and opaque; you imagine there is nothing within, and indeed there are many ghosts, bones given up to the land. They stand here and there against the sky, and you approach them for a longer time than you expect. They belong in the distance; it is their domain.

Once there was a lot of sound in my grandmother's house, a lot of coming and going, feasting and talk. The summers there were full of excitement and reunion. The Kiowas are a summer people; they abide the cold and keep to themselves, but when the season turns and the land becomes warm and vital they cannot hold still; an old love of going returns upon them. The aged visitors who came to my grandmother's house when I was a child were made of lean and leather, and they bore themselves upright. They wore great black hats and bright ample shirts that shook in the wind. They rubbed fat upon their hair and wound their braids with strips of colored cloth. Some of them painted their faces and carried the scars of old and cherished enmities. They were an old council of warlords, come to remind and be reminded of who they were. Their wives and daughters served them well. The women might indulge themselves; gossip was at once the mark and compensation of their servitude. They made loud and elaborate talk among themselves, full of jest and gesture, fright and false alarm. They went abroad in fringed and flowered shawls, bright beadwork and German silver. They were at home in the kitchen, and they prepared meals that were banquets.

There were frequent prayer meetings, and great nocturnal feasts. When I was a child I played with my cousins outside, where the lamplight fell upon the ground and the singing of the old people rose up around us and carried away into the darkness. There were a lot of good things to eat, a lot of laughter and surprise. And afterwards, when the quiet returned, I lay down with my grandmother and could hear the frogs away by the river and feel the motion of the air.

Now there is a funeral silence in the rooms, the endless wake of some final word. The walls have closed in upon my grandmother's house. When I

■ Here Momaday returns to the present but relates his emotions to the experiences of the earlier part of the article.

returned to it in mourning, I saw for the first time in my life how small it was. It was late at night, and there was a white moon; nearly full. I sat for a long time on the stone steps by the kitchen door. From there I could see out across the land; I could see the long row of trees by the creek, the low light upon the rolling plains, and the stars of the Big Dipper. Once I looked at the moon and caught sight of a strange thing. A cricket had perched upon the handrail, only a few inches away from me. My line of vision was such that the creature filled the moon like a fossil. It had gone there, I thought, to live and die, for there, of all places, was its small definition made whole and eternal. A warm wind rose up and purled like the longing within me.

■ In characteristic style the author notices images of nature and ties them to his theme.

The next morning I awoke at dawn and went out on the dirt road to Rainy Mountain. It was already hot, and the grasshoppers began to fill the air. Still, it was early in the morning, and the birds sang out of the shadows. The long yellow grass on the mountain shone in the bright light, and a scissortail hied above the land. There, where it ought to be, at the end of a long and legendary way, was my grandmother's grave. Here and there on the dark stones were ancestral names. Looking back once, I saw the mountain and came away.

■ Note the impact of the rather abrupt ending.

Stephen Mopope, *The Procession* (detail), Philbrook Art Center

## THINK AND DISCUSS

### Understanding

1. From what source do the Kiowa people acquire the Sun Dance religion? How does it affect their self-image?
2. What becomes the object and symbol of their worship?
3. What incident stops the Kiowa from holding their Sun Dances?

### Analyzing

4. Explain the Kiowa legend about Devil's Tower.
5. What do Momaday's grandmother's life and death symbolize to Momaday?
6. Why do you suppose Momaday retraces the ancestral route of his people before he visits his grandmother's grave?
7. Although Yellowstone represents "the top of the world" to Momaday, he understands why the Kiowas did not settle there permanently. Explain.

### Extending

8. Do you think Momaday was happier before or after he retraced the ancestral route of his people? Explain.
9. What do you find most impressive about this selection—the mood of loneliness and melancholy, the personality of Aho, the feeling that an age and a culture have come to an end, or some other impression? Explain.

## REVIEWING LITERARY TERMS

### Connotation/Denotation

1. What is the denotation of the word *slaughtered* as applied to the wild herds of buffalo? What is its connotation? Why did Momaday choose the word?

### Style

2. What would you say is Momaday's purpose in writing this selection?
3. What is its tone?
4. How does the imagery demonstrate his love of nature?
5. How do his descriptions of Aho show his love and respect for her?

## ■ CONTENT REVIEW

### THINKING SKILLS

#### Classifying

1. In her article on biography, Marchette Chute mentions nineteen different men and women whom we can learn about from biographies. List their names down the left-hand column of a piece of paper. Divide the rest of the paper into eight more columns and head them as follows: *Artist, Author, Explorer, Composer, Orator, President or Ruler, Saint and Soldier,* and *Scientist.* Put a check in the column that represents the occupation of each person on your list, and analyze it to see which occupations are represented most frequently.

#### Generalizing

2. Consider the following qualities: courage, ingenuity, independence, coolheadedness. Then think about the people you have read

about in the autobiographical and biographical selections in this unit. Choose one quality and show how that quality was exhibited by three or more individuals in the selections. Give reasons for your choices. If you think of a different quality you would like to write about, do so.

3. Dolley Madison said that she acted out of an "inner sense of what is right." Can you generalize that any other person you have read about in this unit might have acted out of a similar personal sense of right and wrong? What makes you think as you do?

## Synthesizing

4. Consider the content and theme of each of the five essays in this unit. Considering these essays, develop your own description of how essays often relate to the theme of discovery.

5. Create a title for each of the four letters in the unit, based on the topic and content of each.

## Evaluating

6. Do you think personal letters can be effective historical documents? Why or why not? Use the letters in this unit to support your answer.

# ■ COMPOSITION REVIEW

Choose one of the following assignments and write the composition.

## Writing About Nonfiction

Most of the selections in this unit describe events that actually happened to the writers. Select three of these and write a five-paragraph composition in which you discuss the stories you feel best fit the title "Truth Is Stranger Than Fiction." Use the first paragraph to introduce your idea to the reader. Then devote one paragraph to each of the three selections you have chosen, and use the fifth paragraph to briefly state your conclusion.

## Writing a Letter

Write a five-paragraph letter to your teacher in which you evaluate the contents of this unit. Before you write, consider the following questions: Which type of nonfiction would you like to read more? Why? Which selection did you find the most interesting? the least interesting? Why? Which selections do you think should be skipped? Are there any types of nonfiction selections you would like to add? What are they?

## Writing About Influential Persons and Events

Three of the nonfiction selections deal with an important influence on the writer. In the selections by Morstin and Momaday, the influence is wielded by a grandmother. In "The Day We Flew the Kites" it is an event. Write a five-paragraph composition in which you analyze these influences.

## Reviewing Writer's Craft: Write Good Beginnings

Write a three- to five-paragraph composition in which you analyze in depth one of the selections in this unit. Consider how well it accomplishes its purpose; its tone; its style; and its interest to the general reader. Introduce your ideas with a paragraph spelling out how and why the selection impressed you in a positive (or a negative) way. Use your introduction to interest your audience—your classmates—in your main idea and the supporting details that you will include.

# T HE NOVEL

Diego Rivera, *The Grinder*, 1924, Museo de Arte Moderno, Mexico City

# MASTER AND MAN

by Leo Tolstoy

Mariamna Davydoff, *Deeds of Years Gone By*, 1986, Private Collection

# PREVIEW

## UNIT 8   THE NOVEL

**The Pearl** / John Steinbeck
**Master and Man** / Leo Tolstoy
from **Ethan Frome** / Edith Wharton

**Features**
Reading a Novel
Introduction to *The Pearl*
Comment: Steinbeck Finds a Pearl
Writer's Craft: Write Good Endings
Introduction to *Master and Man*
Comment: The Russian Peasant

**Review of Literary Terms**
setting *(The Pearl)*
foreshadowing *(The Pearl)*
theme *(Master and Man)*

**Reading Literature Skillfully**
making judgments *(The Pearl)*

**Vocabulary Skills**
word structure: Latin word parts *(The Pearl)*
synonyms *(The Pearl)*
word analogies *(Master and Man)*

**Thinking Skills**
generalizing *(Master and Man)*
synthesizing *(The Pearl)*
evaluating *(The Pearl)*

**Composition**
Writing About a Special Object
Writing a Summary
Writing About Setting
Writing About Theme
Reading/Writing Log
Comparing and Contrasting Characters
Predicting Possible Outcomes
Analyzing Dreams
Describing a Reformed Character

**Enrichment**
Conducting Literary Research *(The Pearl)*
Making an Oral Report *(Master and Man)*

**Thinking Critically About Literature**
Concept Review
Content Review
Composition Review

# *Reading* A NOVEL

A novel is a long work of prose fiction dealing with characters, situations, and scenes that resemble those of real life. The two main selections in this unit are novels that, on the surface, seem to be adventure stories. Adventure *is* one of their primary elements. Against a background of chilling danger, frustration, or violence, each author tells a story of moral dilemma, and each offers a tribute to basic human goodness. Due to their brevity, both *The Pearl* by John Steinbeck and *Master and Man* by Leo Tolstoy can best be classified as novelettes, or short novels.

As you read them, pay close attention to characters, plot, setting, and theme.

## Characters

Both *The Pearl* and *Master and Man* have two main characters. As you read, think about the relationship between the characters. Is one character dominant? How does the relationship change? Is the narrator sympathetic to the characters? Are the characters admirable? Are their backgrounds and aspirations similar? How likely is it that they will find themselves at odds with one another?

## Plot

Both novels in this unit have strong plots. Because they are novelettes, very little subplot, or subordinate minor plot, is evident. In both novels, there are internal and external conflicts. In *The Pearl*, note how the main characters must struggle against threats from others and must test their own impulses to protect themselves and their baby. In *Master and Man* the dominant conflict pits characters against nature. One character also reveals a greater internal dilemma as the plot unfolds.

## Setting

*The Pearl* is set on the warm coast of Baja California in Mexico, while *Master and Man* takes place in the intense cold of a Russian December. Take note of how the settings change and help determine the choices faced by the characters at crucial points in the stories.

## Theme

The authors of both novels, separated by time and place as they wrote, took up strikingly similar themes. Both works concern the effects of greed on people, but each handles its underlying meaning in its own way. As you read a novel, you will gradually become aware of theme if the author has skillfully and artistically conveyed ideas. An author usually devotes his or her primary interest to the story and its power to interest, inspire, entertain, and even involve readers. As readers, we can take note of the forces that triumph, the best choices characters make, and the meaning these prevailing elements suggest.

As you read a novel, be prepared to **make judgments** about its action and its fiction elements. You may have strong feelings of approval or disagreement with a character's actions or motives. Be willing to ask yourself about the wisdom, practical nature, and moral qualities of characters' behavior. Consider also the author's skills. How clear are the novel's purpose, mood, and tone? How effective is the use of imagery and figurative language? Your awareness—asking these and other questions—will give you a clearer picture of the writer's craft and help you understand and evaluate novels.

# INTRODUCTION to *The Pearl*

## BIOGRAPHY of John Steinbeck   1902–1968

Born in California, John Steinbeck intermittently attended Stanford University between 1919 and 1925. His first collection of short stories, *The Pastures of Heaven* (1930), portrayed people of a farm community in Salinas Valley. A series of novels—*Tortilla Flat* (1935), *In Dubious Battle* (1936), and *Of Mice and Men* (1937)—described the lives of ordinary farmers and migratory workers. In 1940 he won a Pulitzer Prize for *Grapes of Wrath* (1939), an account of the migration of Oklahoma farmers to California. In *The Wayward Bus* (1947) he condemned the greed he saw in modern civilization. In 1950 Steinbeck wrote *East of Eden*, which expressed his faith in the human ability to triumph over evil. *Travels with Charley* (1962) is a view of American life as seen by Steinbeck on a trip through the U.S. with his dog Charley.

In 1962, Steinbeck became the seventh American-born writer to win the Nobel Prize in Literature. He died in New York City.

The setting of *The Pearl* is rural Mexico, and the main characters, Kino and Juana, are ordinary, poor, and struggling, like many of the characters that populate Steinbeck's novels. A few people in the town of La Paz (lä päs′) are well-to-do. The people outside La Paz who dive for pearls in the waters of the Gulf of California, however, live humble lives. Despite the severe social and economic disparities that surround them, Kino and Juana are happy living close to nature. But the evil forces of human greed and social inequity destroy their contentment. *The Pearl* contains elements of the lyrical, mystical, realistic, and sociological, all reflected in the imaginative "songs" Kino hears throughout the story.

Some readers regard *The Pearl* as a parable, a story that embodies a moral or ethical principle. As you read the novel, try to determine the message the author conveys through his depiction of the internal and external conflicts facing Kino and Juana.

**HT** Review SETTING and FORESHADOWING in the Handbook of Literary Terms, pages 824 and 800.

# The Pearl

**John Steinbeck**  USA

n the town they tell the story of the great pearl—how it was found and how it was lost again. They tell of Kino, the fisherman, and of his wife, Juana, and of the baby, Coyotito.[1] And because the story has been told so often, it has taken root in every man's mind. And, as with all retold tales that are in people's hearts, there are only good and bad things and black and white things and good and evil things and no in-between anywhere.

"If this story is a parable, perhaps everyone takes his own meaning from it and reads his own life into it. In any case, they say in the town that . . ."

## I

Kino awakened in the near dark. The stars still shone and the day had drawn only a pale wash of light in the lower sky to the east. The roosters had been crowing for some time, and the early pigs were already beginning their ceaseless turning of twigs and bits of wood to see whether anything to eat had been overlooked. Outside the brush house in the tuna clump, a covey of little birds chittered and flurried with their wings.

Kino's eyes opened, and he looked first at the lightening square which was the door and then he looked at the hanging box where Coyotito slept.

And last he turned his head to Juana, his wife, who lay beside him on the mat, her blue head shawl over her nose and over her breasts and around the small of her back. Juana's eyes were open too. Kino could never remember seeing them closed when he awakened. Her dark eyes made little reflected stars. She was looking at him as she was always looking at him when he awakened.

Kino heard the little splash of morning waves on the beach. It was very good—Kino closed his eyes again to listen to his music. Perhaps he alone did this and perhaps all of his people did it. His people had once been great makers of songs so that everything they saw or thought or did or heard became a song. That was very long ago. The songs remained; Kino knew them, but no new songs were added. That does not mean that there were no personal songs. In Kino's head there was a song now, clear and soft, and if he had been able to speak it, he would have called it the Song of the Family.

His blanket was over his nose to protect him from the dank air. His eyes flicked to a rustle

---

1. *Kino* (kē′nō) . . . *Juana* (wä′nä) . . . *Coyotito* (kō yō-tē′ tō), Spanish for *Little Coyote*, a nickname for the baby.

beside him. It was Juana arising, almost sound-lessly. On her hard bare feet she went to the hanging box where Coyotito slept, and she leaned over and said a little reassuring word. Coyotito looked up for a moment and closed his eyes and slept again.

Juana went to the fire pit and uncovered a coal and fanned it alive while she broke little pieces of brush over it.

Now Kino got up and wrapped his blanket about his head and nose and shoulders. He slipped his feet into his sandals and went outside to watch the dawn.

Outside the door he squatted down and gathered the blanket ends about his knees. He saw the specks of Gulf[2] clouds flame high in the air. And a goat came near and sniffed at him and stared with its cold yellow eyes. Behind him Juana's fire leaped into flame and threw spears of light through the chinks of the brush-house wall and threw a wavering square of light out the door. A late moth blustered in to find the fire. The Song of the Family came now from behind Kino. And the rhythm of the family song was the grinding stone where Juana worked the corn for the morn-ing cakes.

The dawn came quickly now, a wash, a glow, a lightness, and then an explosion of fire as the sun arose out of the Gulf. Kino looked down to cover his eyes from the glare. He could hear the pat of the corncakes in the house and the rich smell of them on the cooking plate. The ants were busy on the ground, big black ones with shiny bodies, and little dusty quick ants. Kino watched with the detachment of God while a dusty ant frantically tried to escape the sand trap an ant lion had dug for him. A thin, timid dog came close and, at a soft word from Kino, curled up, arranged its tail neatly over its feet, and laid its chin delicately on the pile. It was a black dog with yellow-gold spots where its eyebrows should have been. It was a morning like other mornings and yet perfect among mornings.

Kino heard the creak of the rope when Juana took Coyotito out of his hanging box and cleaned him and hammocked him in her shawl in a loop that placed him close to her breast. Kino could see these things without looking at them. Juana sang softly an ancient song that had only three notes and yet endless variety of interval. And this was part of the family song too. It was all part. Some-times it rose to an aching chord that caught the throat, saying this is safety, this is warmth, this is the *Whole*.

Across the brush fence were other brush houses, and the smoke came from them too, and the sound of breakfast, but those were other songs, their pigs were other pigs, their wives were not Juana. Kino was young and strong and his black hair hung over his brown forehead. His eyes were warm and fierce and bright and his mustache was thin and coarse. He lowered his blanket from his nose now, for the dark poisonous air was gone and the yellow sunlight fell on the house. Near the brush fence two roosters bowed and feinted at each other with squared wings and neck feathers ruffed out. It would be a clumsy fight. They were not game chickens. Kino watched them for a moment, and then his eyes went up to a flight of wild doves twinkling inland to the hills. The world was awake now, and Kino arose and went into his brush house.

As he came through the door Juana stood up from the glowing fire pit. She put Coyotito back in his hanging box and then she combed her black hair and braided it in two braids and tied the ends with thin green ribbon. Kino squatted by the fire pit and rolled a hot corncake and dipped it in sauce and ate it. And he drank a little pulque[3] and that was breakfast. That was the only breakfast he had ever known outside of feast days and one incredible fiesta on cookies that had nearly killed

---

2. **Gulf,** the Gulf of California, an arm of the Pacific Ocean between the Mexican peninsula of Baja California and the mainland of Mexico.
3. **pulque** (pül′ kā), a fermented drink of Mexico, made from the juice of the maguey cactus.

him. When Kino had finished, Juana came back to the fire and ate her breakfast. They had spoken once, but there is not need for speech if it is only a habit anyway. Kino sighed with satisfaction—and that was conversation.

The sun was warming the brush house, breaking through its crevices in long streaks. And one of the streaks fell on the hanging box where Coyotito lay, and on the ropes that held it.

It was a tiny movement that drew their eyes to the hanging box. Kino and Juana froze in their positions. Down the rope that hung the baby's box from the roof support a scorpion moved slowly. His stinging tail was straight out behind him, but he could whip it up in a flash of time.

Kino's breath whistled in his nostrils and he opened his mouth to stop it. And then the startled look was gone from him and the rigidity from his body. In his mind a new song had come, the Song of Evil, the music of the enemy, of any foe of the family, a savage, secret, dangerous melody, and underneath, the Song of the Family cried plaintively.

The scorpion moved delicately down the rope toward the box. Under her breath Juana repeated an ancient magic to guard against such evil, and on top of that she muttered a Hail Mary between clenched teeth. But Kino was in motion. His body glided quietly across the room, noiselessly and smoothly. His hands were in front of him, palms down, and his eyes were on the scorpion. Beneath it in the hanging box Coyotito laughed and reached up his hand toward it. It sensed danger when Kino was almost within reach of it. It stopped, and its tail rose up over its back in little jerks and the curved thorn on the tail's end glistened.

Kino stood perfectly still. He could hear Juana whispering the old magic again, and he could hear the evil music of the enemy. He could not move until the scorpion moved, and it felt for the source of the death that was coming to it. Kino's hand went forward very slowly, very smoothly. The

thorned tail jerked upright. And at that moment the laughing Coyotito shook the rope and the scorpion fell.

Kino's hand leaped to catch it, but it fell past his fingers, fell on the baby's shoulder, landed and struck. Then, snarling, Kino had it, had it in his fingers, rubbing it to a paste in his hands. He threw it down and beat it into the earth floor with his fist, and Coyotito screamed with pain in his box. But Kino beat and stamped the enemy until it was only a fragment and moist place in the dirt. His teeth were bared and fury flared in his eyes and the Song of the Enemy roared in his ears.

But Juana had the baby in her arms now. She found the puncture with redness starting from it already. She put her lips down over the puncture and sucked hard and spat and sucked again while Coyotito screamed.

Kino hovered; he was helpless, he was in the way.

The screams of the baby brought the neighbors. Out of their brush houses they poured— Kino's brother Juan Tomás and his fat wife Apolonia[4] and their four children crowded in the door and blocked the entrance, while behind them others tried to look in, and one small boy crawled among legs to have a look. And those in front passed the word back to those behind— "Scorpion. The baby has been stung."

Juana stopped sucking the puncture for a moment. The little hole was slightly enlarged and its edges whitened from the sucking, but the red swelling extended farther around it in a hard lymphatic mound. And all of these people knew about the scorpion. An adult might be very ill from the sting, but a baby could easily die from the poison. First, they knew, would come swelling and fever and tightened throat, and then cramps in the stomach, and then Coyotito might die if enough of the poison had gone in. But the stinging pain of the bite was going away.

---

4. *Juan Tomás* (wän tō mäs′) . . . *Apolonia* (ä pō lō′nyä).

Coyotito's screams turned to moans.

Kino had wondered often at the iron in his patient, fragile wife. She, who was obedient and respectful and cheerful and patient, she could arch her back in child pain with hardly a cry. She could stand fatigue and hunger almost better than Kino himself. In the canoe she was like a strong man. And now she did a most surprising thing.

"The doctor," she said. "Go to get the doctor."

The word was passed out among the neighbors where they stood close packed in the little yard behind the brush fence. And they repeated among themselves, "Juana wants the doctor." A wonderful thing, a memorable thing, to want the doctor. To get him would be a remarkable thing. The doctor never came to the cluster of brush houses. Why should he, when he had more than he could do to take care of the rich people who lived in the stone and plaster houses of the town.

"He would not come," the people in the yard said.

"He would not come," the people in the door said, and the thought got into Kino.

"The doctor would not come," Kino said to Juana.

She looked up at him, her eyes as cold as the eyes of a lioness. This was Juana's first baby—this was nearly everything there was in Juana's world. And Kino saw her determination and the music of the family sounded in his head with a steely tone.

"Then we will go to him," Juana said, and with one hand she arranged her dark blue shawl over her head and made of one end of it a sling to hold the moaning baby and made of the other end of it a shade over his eyes to protect him from the light. The people in the door pushed against those behind to let her through. Kino followed her. They went out of the gate to the rutted path and the neighbors followed them.

The thing had become a neighborhood affair. They made a quick soft-footed procession into the center of the town, first Juana and Kino, and behind them Juan Tomás and Apolonia, her big stomach jiggling with the strenuous pace, then all the neighbors with the children trotting on the flanks. And the yellow sun threw their black shadows ahead of them so that they walked on their own shadows.

They came to the place where the brush houses stopped and the city of stone and plaster began, the city of harsh outer walls and inner cool gardens where a little water played and the bougainvillaea crusted the walls with purple and brick-red and white. They heard from the secret gardens the singing of caged birds and heard the splash of cooling water on hot flagstones. The procession crossed the blinding plaza and passed in front of the church. It had grown now, and on the outskirts the hurrying newcomers were being softly informed how the baby had been stung by a scorpion, how the father and mother were taking it to the doctor.

And the newcomers, particularly the beggars from the front of the church who were great experts in financial analysis, looked quickly at Juana's old blue skirt, saw the tears in her shawl, appraised the green ribbon on her braids, read the age of Kino's blanket and the thousand washings of his clothes, and set them down as poverty people and went along to see what kind of drama might develop. The four beggars in front of the church knew everything in the town. They were students of the expressions of young women as they went into confession, and they saw them as they came out and read the nature of the sin. They knew every little scandal and some very big crimes. They slept at their posts in the shadow of the church so that no one crept in for consolation without their knowledge. And they knew the doctor. They knew his ignorance, his cruelty, his avarice, his appetites, his sins. They knew his clumsy abortions and the little brown pennies he gave sparingly for alms. They had seen his corpses go into the church. And, since early Mass was over and business was slow, they followed the procession, these endless searchers after perfect knowledge of their fellow men, to see what the fat lazy doctor would do about an indigent baby with a scorpion bite.

The scurrying procession came at last to the big gate in the wall of the doctor's house. They could hear the splashing water and the singing of caged birds and the sweep of the long brooms on the flagstones. And they could smell the frying of good bacon from the doctor's house.

Kino hesitated a moment. This doctor was not of his people. This doctor was of a race which for nearly four hundred years had beaten and starved and robbed and despised Kino's race, and frightened it too, so that the indigene[5] came humbly to the door. And as always when he came near to one of this race, Kino felt weak and afraid and angry at the same time. Rage and terror went together. He could kill the doctor more easily than he could talk to him, for all of the doctor's race spoke to all

---

5. *indigene*, native. Historically, in Latin America there existed a great class distinction and hostility between the descendants of the conquering Spaniards and those of the native Indians.

Diego Rivera, *The Peasant*, 1943, Harry Ransom Humanities Research Center, The University of Texas at Austin

of Kino's race as though they were simple animals. And as Kino raised his right hand to the iron ring knocker in the gate, rage swelled in him, and the pounding music of the enemy beat in his ears, and his lips drew tight against his teeth—but with his left hand he reached to take off his hat. The iron ring pounded against the gate. Kino took off his hat and stood waiting. Coyotito moaned a little in Juana's arms and she spoke softly to him. The procession crowded close the better to see and hear.

After a moment the big gate opened a few inches. Kino could see the green coolness of the garden and little splashing fountain through the opening. The man who looked out at him was one of his own race. Kino spoke to him in the old language. "The little one—the first born—has been poisoned by the scorpion," Kino said. "He requires the skill of the healer."

The gate closed a little, and the servant refused to speak in the old language. "A little moment," he said. "I go to inform myself," and he closed the gate and slid the bolt home. The glaring sun threw the bunched shadows of the people blackly on the white wall.

In his chamber the doctor sat up in his high bed. He had on his dressing gown of red watered silk that had come from Paris, a little tight over the chest now if it was buttoned. On his lap was a silver tray with a silver chocolate pot and a tiny cup of eggshell china, so delicate that it looked silly when he lifted it with his big hand, lifted it with the tips of thumb and forefinger and spread the other three fingers wide to get them out of the way. His eyes rested in puffy little hammocks of flesh and his mouth drooped with discontent. He was growing very stout, and his voice was hoarse with the fat that pressed on his throat. Beside him on a table was a small Oriental gong and a bowl of cigarettes. The furnishings of the room were heavy and dark and gloomy. The pictures were religious, even the large tinted photograph of his dead wife, who, if Masses willed and paid for out of her own estate could do it, was in Heaven. The doctor had once for a short time been a part of the great world and his whole subsequent life was memory and longing for France. "That," he said, "was civilized living"—by which he meant that on a small income he had been able to keep a mistress and eat in restaurants. He poured his second cup of chocolate and crumbled a sweet biscuit in his fingers. The servant from the gate came to the open door and stood waiting to be noticed.

"Yes?" the doctor asked.

"It is a little Indian with a baby. He says a scorpion stung it."

The doctor put his cup down gently before he let his anger rise.

"Have I nothing better to do than cure insect bites for 'little Indians'? I am a doctor, not a veterinary."

"Yes, Patron," said the servant.

"Has he any money?" the doctor demanded. "No, they never have any money. I, I alone in the world am supposed to work for nothing—and I am tired of it. See if he has any money!"

At the gate the servant opened the door a trifle and looked out at the waiting people. And this time he spoke in the old language.

"Have you money to pay for the treatment?"

Now Kino reached into a secret place somewhere under his blanket. He brought out a paper folded many times. Crease by crease he unfolded it, until at last there came to view eight small misshapen seed pearls, as ugly and gray as little ulcers, flattened and almost valueless. The servant took the paper and closed the gate again, but this time he was not gone long. He opened the gate just wide enough to pass the paper back.

"The doctor has gone out," he said. "He was called to a serious case." And he shut the gate quickly out of shame.

And now a wave of shame went over the whole

procession. They melted away. The beggars went back to the church steps, the stragglers moved off, and the neighbors departed so that the public shaming of Kino would not be in their eyes.

For a long time Kino stood in front of the gate with Juana beside him. Slowly he put his suppliant hat on his head. Then, without warning, he struck the gate a crushing blow with his fist. He looked down in wonder at his split knuckles and at the blood that flowed down between his fingers.

# II

The town lay on a broad estuary, its old yellow plastered buildings hugging the beach. And on the beach the white and blue canoes that came from Nayarit[6] were drawn up, canoes preserved for generations by a hard shell-like waterproof plaster whose making was a secret of the fishing people. They were high and graceful canoes with curving bow and stern and a braced section midships where a mast could be stepped to carry a small lateen sail.

The beach was yellow sand, but at the water's edge a rubble of shell and algae took its place. Fiddler crabs bubbled and sputtered in their holes in the sand, and in the shallows little lobsters popped in and out of their tiny homes in the rubble and sand. The sea bottom was rich with crawling and swimming and growing things. The brown algae waved in the gentle currents and the green eel grass swayed and little sea horses clung to its stems. Spotted botete, the poison fish, lay on the bottom in the eel-grass beds, and the bright-colored swimming crabs scampered over them.

On the beach the hungry dogs and the hungry pigs of the town searched endlessly for any dead fish or sea bird that might have floated in on a rising tide.

Although the morning was young, the hazy mirage was up. The uncertain air that magnified some things and blotted out others hung over the whole Gulf so that all sights were unreal and vision could not be trusted; so that sea and land had the sharp clarities and the vagueness of a dream. Thus it might be that the people of the Gulf trust things of the spirit and things of the imagination, but they do not trust their eyes to show them distance or clear outline or any optical exactness. Across the estuary from the town one section of mangroves stood clear and telescopically defined, while another mangrove clump was a hazy black-green blob. Part of the far shore disappeared into a shimmer that looked like water. There was no certainty in seeing, no proof that what you saw was there or was not there. And the people of the Gulf expected all places were that way, and it was not strange to them. A copper haze hung over the water, and the hot morning sun beat on it and made it vibrate blindingly.

The brush houses of the fishing people were back from the beach on the right-hand side of the town, and the canoes were drawn up in front of this area.

Kino and Juana came slowly down to the beach and to Kino's canoe, which was the one thing of value he owned in the world. It was very old. Kino's grandfather had brought it from Nayarit, and he had given it to Kino's father, and so it had come to Kino. It was at once property and source of food, for a man with a boat can guarantee a woman that she will eat something. It is the bulwark against starvation. And every year Kino refinished his canoe with the hard shell-like plaster by the secret method that had also come to him from his father. Now he came to the canoe and touched the bow tenderly as he always did. He laid his diving rock and his basket and the two

---

6. *Nayarit* (nī yä rēt′), a Mexican state situated on the Pacific coast of the mainland.

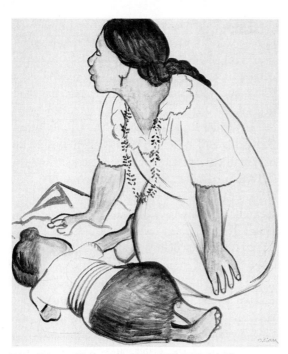

Diego Rivera, *Mother and Child*, 1926, Philadelphia Museum of Art

ropes in the sand by the canoe. And he folded his blanket and laid it in the bow.

Juana laid Coyotito on the blanket, and she placed her shawl over him so that the hot sun could not shine on him. He was quiet now, but the swelling on his shoulder had continued up his neck and under his ear and his face was puffed and feverish. Juana went to the water and waded in. She gathered some brown seaweed and made a flat damp poultice of it, and this she applied to the baby's swollen shoulder, which was as good a remedy as any and probably better than the doctor could have done. But the remedy lacked his authority because it was simple and didn't cost anything. The stomach cramps had not come to Coyotito. Perhaps Juana had sucked out the poison in time, but she had not sucked out her worry over her first-born. She had not prayed directly for the recovery of the baby—she had prayed that they might find a pearl with which to hire the doctor to cure the baby, for the minds of people are as unsubstantial as the mirage of the Gulf.

Now Kino and Juana slid the canoe down the beach to the water, and when the bow floated, Juana climbed in, while Kino pushed the stern in and waded beside it until it floated lightly and trembled on the little breaking waves. Then in co-ordination Juana and Kino drove their double-bladed paddles into the sea, and the canoe creased the water and hissed with speed. The other pearlers were gone out long since. In a few moments Kino could see them clustered in the haze, riding over the oyster bed.

Light filtered down through the water to the bed where the frilly pearl oysters lay fastened to the rubbly bottom, a bottom strewn with shells of broken, opened oysters. This was the bed that had raised the King of Spain to be a great power in Europe in past years, had helped to pay for his wars, and had decorated the churches for his soul's sake. The gray oysters with ruffles like skirts on the shells, the barnacle-crusted oysters with little bits of weed clinging to the skirts and small crabs climbing over them. An accident could happen to these oysters, a grain of sand could lie in the folds of muscle and irritate the flesh until in self-protection the flesh coated the grain with a layer of smooth cement. But once started, the flesh continued to coat the foreign body until it fell free in some tidal flurry or until the oyster was destroyed. For centuries men had dived down and torn the oysters from the beds and ripped them open, looking for the coated grains of sand. Swarms of fish lived near the bed to live near the oysters thrown back by the searching men and to nibble at the shining inner shells. But the pearls were accidents, and the finding of one was luck, a little pat on the back by God or the gods or both.

Kino had two ropes, one tied to a heavy stone and one to a basket. He stripped off his shirt and trousers and laid his hat in the bottom of the canoe. The water was oily smooth. He took his rock in one hand and his basket in the other, and he slipped feet first over the side and the rock carried him to the bottom. The bubbles rose behind him until the water cleared and he could see. Above, the surface of the water was an undulating mirror of brightness, and he could see the bottoms of the canoes sticking through it.

Kino moved cautiously so that the water would not be obscured with mud or sand. He hooked his foot in the loop on his rock and his hands worked quickly, tearing the oysters loose, some singly, others in clusters. He laid them in his basket. In some places the oysters clung to one another so that they came free in lumps.

Now, Kino's people had sung of everything that happened or existed. They had made songs to the fishes, to the sea in anger and to the sea in calm, to the light and the dark and the sun and the moon, and the songs were all in Kino and in his people—every song that had ever been made, even the ones forgotten. And as he filled his basket the song was in Kino, and the beat of the song was his pounding heart as it ate the oxygen from his held breath, and the melody of the song was the gray-green water and the little scuttling animals and the clouds of fish that flitted by and were gone. But in the song there was a secret little inner song, hardly perceptible, but always there, sweet and secret and clinging, almost hiding in the counter-melody and this was the Song of the Pearl That Might Be, for every shell thrown in the basket might contain a pearl. Chance was against it, but luck and the gods might be for it. And in the canoe above him Kino knew that Juana was making the magic of prayer, her face set rigid and her muscles hard to force the luck, to tear the luck out of the god's hands, for she needed the luck for the swollen shoulder of Coyotito. And because the need was great and the desire was great, the little secret melody of the pearl that might be was stronger this morning. Whole phrases of it came

clearly and softly into the Song of the Undersea.

Kino, in his pride and youth and strength, could remain down over two minutes without strain, so that he worked deliberately, selecting the largest shells. Because they were disturbed, the oyster shells were tightly closed. A little to his right a hummock of rubbly rock stuck up, covered with young oysters not ready to take. Kino moved next to the hummock, and then, beside it, under a little overhang, he saw a very large oyster lying by itself, not covered with its clinging brothers. The shell was partly open, for the overhang protected this ancient oyster, and in the lip-like muscle Kino saw a ghostly gleam, and then the shell closed down. His heart beat out a heavy rhythm and the melody of the maybe pearl shrilled in his ears. Slowly he forced the oyster loose and held it tightly against his breast. He kicked his foot free from the rock loop, and his body rose to the surface and his black hair gleamed in the sunlight. He reached over the side of the canoe and laid the oyster in the bottom.

Then Juana steadied the boat while he climbed in. His eyes were shining with excitement, but in decency he pulled up his rock, and then he pulled up his basket of oysters and lifted them in. Juana sensed his excitement, and she pretended to look away. It is not good to want a thing too much. It sometimes drives the luck away. You must want it just enough, and you must be very tactful with God or the gods. But Juana stopped breathing. Very deliberately Kino opened his short strong knife. He looked speculatively at the basket. Perhaps it would be better to open *the* oyster last. He took a small oyster from the basket, cut the muscle, searched the folds of flesh, and threw it in the water. Then he seemed to see the great oyster for the first time. He squatted in the bottom of the canoe, picked up the shell and examined it. The flutes were shining black to brown, and only a few small barnacles adhered to the shell. Now Kino was reluctant to open it. What he had seen, he knew, might be a reflection, a piece of flat shell accidentally drifted in or a complete illusion. In this Gulf of uncertain light there were more illusions than realities.

But Juana's eyes were on him and she could not wait. She put her hand on Coyotito's covered head. "Open it," she said softly.

Kino deftly slipped his knife into the edge of the shell. Through the knife he could feel the muscle tighten hard. He worked the blade lever-wise and the closing muscle parted and the shell fell apart. The lip-like flesh writhed up and then subsided. Kino lifted the flesh, and there it lay, the great pearl, perfect as the moon. It captured the light and refined it and gave it back in silver incandescence. It was as large as a sea-gull's egg. It was the greatest pearl in the world.

Juana caught her breath and moaned a little. And to Kino the secret melody of the maybe pearl broke clear and beautiful, rich and warm and lovely, glowing and gloating and triumphant. In the surface of the great pearl he could see dream forms. He picked the pearl from the dying flesh and held it in his palm, and he turned it over and saw that its curve was perfect. Juana came near to stare at it in his hand, and it was the hand he had smashed against the doctor's gate, and the torn flesh of the knuckles was turned grayish white by the sea water.

Instinctively Juana went to Coyotito where he lay on his father's blanket. She lifted the poultice of seaweed and looked at the shoulder. "Kino," she cried shrilly.

He looked past his pearl, and he saw that the swelling was going out of the baby's shoulder, the poison was receding from its body. Then Kino's fist closed over the pearl and his emotion broke over him. He put back his head and howled. His eyes rolled up and he screamed and his body was rigid. The men in the other canoes looked up, startled, and then they dug their paddles into the sea and raced toward Kino's canoe.

# III

A town is a thing like a colonial animal. A town has a nervous system and a head and shoulders and feet. A town is a thing separate from all other towns, so that there are no two towns alike. And a town has a whole emotion. How news travels through a town is a mystery not easily to be solved. News seems to move faster than small boys can scramble and dart to tell it, faster than women can call it over the fences.

Before Kino and Juana and the other fishers had come to Kino's brush house, the nerves of the town were pulsing and vibrating with the news— Kino had found the Pearl of the World. Before panting little boys could strangle out the words, their mothers knew it. The news swept on past the brush houses, and it washed in a foaming wave into the town of stone and plaster. It came to the priest walking in his garden, and it put a thoughtful look in his eyes and a memory of certain repairs necessary to the church. He wondered what the pearl would be worth. And he wondered whether he had baptized Kino's baby, or married him for that matter. The news came to the shop-keepers, and they looked at men's clothes that had not sold so well.

The news came to the doctor where he sat with a woman whose illness was age, though neither she nor the doctor would admit it. And when it was made plain who Kino was, the doctor grew stern and judicious at the same time. "He is a client of mine," the doctor said. "I'm treating his child for a scorpion sting." And the doctor's eyes rolled up a little in their fat hammocks and he thought of Paris. He remembered the room he had lived in there as a great and luxurious place, and he remembered the hard-faced woman who had lived with him as a beautiful and kind girl, although she had been none of these three. The doctor looked past his aged patient and saw himself sitting in a restaurant in Paris and a waiter was just opening a bottle of wine.

The news came early to the beggars in front of the church, and it made them giggle a little with pleasure, for they knew that there is no almsgiver in the world like a poor man who is suddenly lucky.

Kino has found the Pearl of the World. In the town, in little offices, sat the men who bought pearls from the fishers. They waited in their chairs until the pearls came in, and then they cackled and fought and shouted and threatened until they reached the lowest price the fisherman would stand. But there was a price below which they dared not go, for it had happened that a fisherman in despair had given his pearls to the church. And when the buying was over, these buyers sat alone and their fingers played restlessly with the pearls, and they wished they owned the pearls. For there were not many buyers really— there was only one, and he kept these agents in separate offices to give a semblance of competition. The news came to these men, and their eyes squinted and their fingertips burned a little, and each one thought how the patron could not live forever and someone had to take his place. And each one thought how with some capital he could get a new start.

All manner of people grew interested in Kino— people with things to sell and people with favors to ask. Kino had found the Pearl of the World. The essence of pearl mixed with essence of men and a curious dark residue was precipitated. Every man suddenly became related to Kino's pearl, and Kino's pearl went into the dreams, the speculations, the schemes, the plans, the futures, the wishes, the needs, the lusts, the hungers, of everyone, and only one person stood in the way and that was Kino, so that he became curiously every man's enemy. The news stirred up something infinitely black and evil in the town; the black distillate was like the scorpion, or like hun-ger in the smell of food, or like loneliness when love is withheld. The poison sacs of the town began to manufacture venom, and the town swelled and puffed with the pressure of it.

But Kino and Juana did not know these things. Because they were happy and excited they thought everyone shared their joy. Juan Tomás and Apolonia did, and they were the world too. In the afternoon, when the sun had gone over the mountains of the Peninsula to sink in the outward sea, Kino squatted in his house with Juana beside him. And the brush house was crowded with neighbors. Kino held the great pearl in his hand, and it was warm and alive in his hand. And the music of the pearl had merged with the music of the family so that one beautified the other. The neighbors looked at the pearl in Kino's hand and they wondered how such luck could come to any man.

And Juan Tomás, who squatted on Kino's right hand because he was his brother, asked, "What will you do now that you have become a rich man?"

Kino looked into his pearl, and Juana cast her eyelashes down and arranged her shawl to cover her face so that her excitement could not be seen. And in the incandescence of the pearl the pictures formed of the things Kino's mind had considered in the past and had given up as impossible. In the pearl he saw Juana and Coyotito and himself standing and kneeling at the high altar, and they were being married now that they could pay. He spoke softly, "We will be married—in the church."

In the pearl he saw how they were dressed— Juana in a shawl stiff with newness and a new skirt, and from under the long skirt Kino could see that she wore shoes. It was in the pearl—the picture glowing there. He himself was dressed in new white clothes, and he carried a new hat—not of straw but of fine black felt—and he too wore shoes—not sandals but shoes that laced. But

Coyotito—he was the one—he wore a blue sailor suit from the United States and a little yachting cap such as Kino had seen once when a pleasure boat put into the estuary. All of these things Kino saw in the lucent pearl and he said, "We will have new clothes."

And the music of the pearl rose like a chorus of trumpets in his ears.

Then to the lovely gray surface of the pearl came the little things Kino wanted: a harpoon to take the place of one lost a year ago, a new harpoon of iron with a ring in the end of the shaft; and—his mind could hardly make the leap—a rifle—but why not, since he was so rich. And Kino saw Kino in the pearl, Kino holding a Winchester carbine. It was the wildest daydreaming and very pleasant. His lips moved hesitantly over this— "A rifle," he said. "Perhaps a rifle."

It was the rifle that broke down the barriers. This was an impossibility, and if he could think of having a rifle whole horizons were burst and he could rush on. For it is said that humans are never satisfied, that you give them one thing and they want something more. And this is said in disparagement, whereas it is one of the greatest talents the species has and one that has made it superior to animals that are satisfied with what they have.

The neighbors, close pressed and silent in the house, nodded their heads at his wild imaginings. And a man in the rear murmured, "A rifle. He will have a rifle."

But the music of the pearl was shrilling with triumph in Kino. Juana looked up, and her eyes were wide at Kino's courage and at his imagination. And electric strength had come to him now the horizons were kicked out. In the pearl he saw Coyotito sitting at a little desk in a school, just as Kino had once seen it through an open door. And Coyotito was dressed in a jacket, and he had on a white collar and a broad silken tie. Moreover, Coyotito was writing on a big piece of paper. Kino

looked at his neighbors fiercely. "My son will go to school," he said, and the neighbors were hushed. Juana caught her breath sharply. Her eyes were bright as she watched him, and she looked quickly down at Coyotito in her arms to see whether this might be possible.

But Kino's face shone with prophecy. "My son will read and open the books, and my son will write and will know writing. And my son will make numbers, and these things will make us free because he will know—he will know and through him we will know." And in the pearl Kino saw himself and Juana squatting by the little fire in the brush hut while Coyotito read from a great book. "This is what the pearl will do," said Kino. And he had never said so many words together in his life. And suddenly he was afraid of his talking. His hand closed down over the pearl and cut the light away from it. Kino was afraid as a man is afraid who says, "I will," without knowing.

Now the neighbors knew they had witnessed a great marvel. They knew that time would now date from Kino's pearl, and that they would discuss this moment for many years to come. If these things came to pass, they would recount how Kino looked and what he said and how his eyes shone, and they would say, "He was a man transfigured. Some power was given to him, and there it started. You see what a great man he has become, starting from that moment. And I myself saw it."

And if Kino's planning came to nothing, those same neighbors would say, "There it started. A foolish madness came over him so that he spoke foolish words. God keep us from such things. Yes, God punished Kino because he rebelled against the way things are. You see what has become of him. And I myself saw the moment when his reason left him."

Kino looked down at his closed hand and the knuckles were scabbed over and tight where he had struck the gate.

Diego Rivera, *Nocturnal Landscape*, 1947, Museo de Arte Moderno, Mexico City

Now the dusk was coming. And Juana looped her shawl under the baby so that he hung against her hip, and she went to the fire hole and dug a coal from the ashes and broke a few twigs over it and fanned a flame alive. The little flames danced on the faces of the neighbors. They knew they should go to their own dinners, but they were reluctant to leave.

The dark was almost in, and Juana's fire threw shadows on the brush walls when the whisper came in, passed from mouth to mouth. "The Father is coming—the priest is coming." The men uncovered their heads and stepped back from the door, and the women gathered their shawls about their faces and cast down their eyes. Kino and Juan Tomás, his brother, stood up. The priest came in—a graying, aging man with an old skin and a young sharp eye. Children, he considered these people, and he treated them like children.

"Kino," he said softly, "thou art named after a great man—and a great Father of the Church." He made it sound like a benediction. "Thy namesake tamed the desert and sweetened the minds of thy people, didst thou know that? It is in the books."

Kino looked quickly down at Coyotito's head, where he hung on Juana's hip. Some day, his mind said, that boy would know what things were in the books and what things were not. The music had gone out of Kino's head, but now, thinly, slowly, the melody of the morning, the music of evil, of the enemy sounded, but it was faint and weak. And Kino looked at his neighbors to see who might have brought this song in.

But the priest was speaking again. "It has come to me that thou hast found a great fortune, a great pearl."

Kino opened his hand and held it out, and the priest gasped a little at the size and beauty of the pearl. And then he said, "I hope thou wilt remember to give thanks, my son, to Him who has given thee this treasure, and to pray for guidance in the future."

Kino nodded dumbly, and it was Juana who spoke softly. "We will, Father. And we will be married now. Kino has said so." She looked at the neighbors for confirmation, and they nodded their heads solemnly.

The priest said, "It is pleasant to see that your first thoughts are good thoughts. God bless you, my children." He turned and left quietly, and the people let him through.

But Kino's hand had closed tightly on the pearl again, and he was glancing about suspiciously, for the evil song was in his ears, shrilling against the music of the pearl.

The neighbors slipped away to go to their houses, and Juana squatted by the fire and set her clay pot of boiled beans over the little flame. Kino stepped to the doorway and looked out. As always, he could smell the smoke from many fires, and he could see the hazy stars and feel the damp of the night air so that he covered his nose from it. The thin dog came to him and threshed itself in greeting like a wind-blown flag, and Kino looked down at it and didn't see it. He had broken through the horizons into a cold and lonely outside. He felt alone and unprotected, and scraping crickets and shrilling tree frogs and croaking toads seemed to be carrying the melody of evil. Kino shivered a little and drew his blanket more tightly against his nose. He carried the pearl still in his hands, tightly closed in his palm, and it was warm and smooth against his skin.

Behind him he heard Juana patting the cakes before she put them down on the clay cooking sheet. Kino felt all the warmth and security of his family behind him, and the Song of the Family came from behind him like the purring of a kitten. But now, by saying what his future was going to be like, he had created it. A plan is a real thing, and things projected are experienced. A plan once made and visualized becomes a reality along with other realities—never to be destroyed but easily to be attacked. Thus Kino's future was real, but having set it up, other forces were set up to destroy it, and this he knew, so that he had to prepare to meet the attack. And this Kino knew also—that the gods do not love men's plans, and the gods do not love success unless it comes by accident. He knew that the gods take their revenge on a man if he be successful through his own efforts. Consequently Kino was afraid of plans, but having made one, he could never destroy it. And to meet the attack, Kino was already making a hard skin for himself against the world. His eyes and his mind probed for danger before it appeared.

Standing in the door, he saw two men approach; and one of them carried a lantern which lighted the ground and the legs of the men. They turned in through the opening of Kino's brush fence and came to his door. And Kino saw that one was the doctor and the other the servant who had opened the gate in the morning. The split knuckles on Kino's right hand burned when he saw who they were.

The doctor said, "I was not in when you came this morning. But now, at the first chance, I have come to see the baby."

Kino stood in the door, filling it, and hatred raged and flamed in back of his eyes, and fear too, for the hundreds of years of subjugation were cut deep in him.

"The baby is nearly well now," he said curtly.

The doctor smiled, but his eyes in their little lymph-lined hammocks did not smile.

He said, "Sometimes, my friend, the scorpion sting has a curious effect. There will be apparent improvement, and then without warning—pouf!" He pursed his lips and made a little explosion to show how quick it could be, and he shifted his small black doctor's bag about so that the light of the lamp fell upon it, for he knew that Kino's race love the tools of any craft and trust them. "Sometimes," the doctor went on in a liquid tone, "sometimes there will be a withered leg or a blind eye or a crumpled back. Oh, I know the sting of the scorpion, my friend, and I can cure it."

Kino felt the rage and hatred melting toward fear. He did not know, and perhaps this doctor did. And he could not take the chance of putting his certain ignorance against this man's possible knowledge. He was trapped as his people were always trapped, and would be until, as he had said, they could be sure that the things in the books were really in the books. He could not take a chance—not with the life or with the straightness of Coyotito. He stood aside and let the doctor and his man enter the brush hut.

Juana stood up from the fire and backed away as he entered, and she covered the baby's face with the fringe of her shawl. And when the doctor went to her and held out his hand, she clutched the baby tight and looked at Kino where he stood with the fire shadows leaping on his face.

Kino nodded, and only then did she let the doctor take the baby.

"Hold the light," the doctor said, and when the servant held the lantern high, the doctor looked for a moment at the wound on the baby's shoulder. He was thoughtful for a moment and then he rolled back the baby's eyelid and looked at the eyeball. He nodded his head while Coyotito struggled against him.

"It is as I thought," he said. "The poison has gone inward and it will strike soon. Come look!" He held the eyelid down. "See—it is blue." And Kino, looking anxiously, saw that indeed it was a little blue. And he didn't know whether or not it was always a little blue. But the trap was set. He couldn't take the chance.

The doctor's eyes watered in their little hammocks. "I will give him something to try to turn the poison aside," he said. And he handed the baby to Kino.

Then from his bag he took a little bottle of white powder and a capsule of gelatine. He filled the capsule with the powder and closed it, and then around the first capsule he fitted a second capsule and closed it. Then he worked very deftly. He took the baby and pinched its lower lip until it opened its mouth. His fat fingers placed the capsule far back on the baby's tongue, back of the point where he could spit it out, and then from the floor he picked up the little pitcher of pulque and gave Coyotito a drink, and it was done. He looked again at the baby's eyeball and he pursed his lips and seemed to think.

At last he handed the baby back to Juana, and he turned to Kino. "I think the poison will attack within the hour," he said. "The medicine may save the baby from hurt, but I will come back in an hour. Perhaps I am in time to save him." He took a deep breath and went out of the hut, and his servant followed him with the lantern.

Now Juana had the baby under her shawl, and she stared at it with anxiety and fear. Kino came to her, and he lifted the shawl and stared at the baby. He moved his hand to look under the eyelid, and only then saw that the pearl was still in his hand. Then he went to a box by the wall, and from it he brought a piece of rag. He wrapped the pearl in the rag, then went to the corner of the brush house and dug a little hole with his fingers in the dirt floor, and he put the pearl in the hole and covered it up and concealed the place. And then he went to the fire where Juana was squatting, watching the baby's face.

The doctor, back in his house, settled into his chair and looked at his watch. His people brought him a little supper of chocolate and sweet cakes and fruit, and he stared at the food discontentedly.

In the houses of the neighbors the subject that would lead all conversations for a long time to come was aired for the first time to see how it would go. The neighbors showed one another with their thumbs how big the pearl was, and they made little caressing gestures to show how lovely it was. From now on they would watch Kino and Juana very closely to see whether riches turned their heads, as riches turn all people's heads. Everyone knew why the doctor had come. He was not good at dissembling and he was very well understood.

Out in the estuary a tight woven school of small fishes glittered and broke water to escape a school of great fishes that drove in to eat them. And in the houses the people could hear the swish of the small ones and the bouncing splash of the great ones as the slaughter went on. The dampness arose out of the Gulf and was deposited on bushes and cacti and on little trees in salty drops. And the night mice crept about on the ground and the little night hawks hunted them silently.

The skinny black puppy with flame spots over his eyes came to Kino's door and looked in. He nearly shook his hind quarters loose when Kino glanced up at him, and he subsided when Kino looked away. The puppy did not enter the house, but he watched with frantic interest while Kino ate his beans from the little pottery dish and wiped it clean with a corncake and ate the cake and washed the whole down with a drink of pulque.

Kino was finished and was rolling a cigarette when Juana spoke sharply. "Kino." He glanced at her and then got up and went quickly to her for he saw fright in her eyes. He stood over her, looking down, but the light was very dim. He kicked a pile of twigs into the fire hole to make a blaze, and then he could see the face of Coyotito. The baby's face was flushed and his throat was working and a little thick drool of saliva issued from his lips. The spasm of the stomach muscles began, and the baby was very sick.

Kino knelt beside his wife. "So the doctor knew," he said, but he said it for himself as well as for his wife, for his mind was hard and suspicious and he was remembering the white powder. Juana rocked from side to side and moaned out the little Song of the Family as though it could ward off the danger, and the baby vomited and writhed in her arms. Now uncertainty was in Kino, and the music of evil throbbed in his head and nearly drove out Juana's song.

The doctor finished his chocolate and nibbled the little fallen pieces of sweet cake. He brushed his fingers on a napkin, looked at his watch, arose, and took up his little bag.

The news of the baby's illness traveled quickly among the brush houses, for sickness is second only to hunger as the enemy of poor people. And some said softly, "Luck, you see, brings bitter friends." And they nodded and got up to go to Kino's house. The neighbors scuttled with covered noses through the dark until they crowded into Kino's house again. They stood and gazed, and they made little comments on the sadness that this should happen at a time of joy, and they said,

"All things are in God's hands." The old women squatted down beside Juana to try to give her aid if they could and comfort if they could not.

Then the doctor hurried in, followed by his man. He scattered the old women like chickens. He took the baby and examined it and felt its head. "The poison it has worked," he said. "I think I can defeat it. I will try my best." He asked for water, and in the cup of it he put three drops of ammonia, and he pried open the baby's mouth and poured it down. The baby spluttered and screeched under the treatment, and Juana watched him with haunted eyes. The doctor spoke a little as he worked. "It is lucky that I know about the poison of the scorpion, otherwise—" and he shrugged to show what could have happened.

But Kino was suspicious, and he could not take his eyes from the doctor's open bag, and from the bottle of white powder there. Gradually the spasms subsided and the baby relaxed under the doctor's hands. And then Coyotito sighed deeply and went to sleep, for he was very tired with vomiting.

The doctor put the baby in Juana's arms. "He will get well now," he said. "I have won the fight." And Juana looked at him with adoration.

The doctor was closing his bag now. He said, "When do you think you can pay this bill?" He said it even kindly.

"When I have sold my pearl I will pay you," Kino said.

"You have a pearl? A good pearl?" the doctor asked with interest.

And then the chorus of the neighbors broke in. "He has found the Pearl of the World," they cried, and they joined forefinger with thumb to show how great the pearl was.

"Kino will be a rich man," they clamored. "It is a pearl such as one has never seen."

The doctor looked surprised. "I had not heard of it. Do you keep this pearl in a safe place?

Perhaps you would like me to put it in my safe?"

Kino's eyes were hooded now, his cheeks were drawn taut. "I have it secure," he said. "Tomorrow I will sell it and then I will pay you."

The doctor shrugged, and his wet eyes never left Kino's eyes. He knew the pearl would be buried in the house, and he thought Kino might look toward the place where it was buried. "It would be a shame to have it stolen before you could sell it," the doctor said, and he saw Kino's eyes flick involuntarily to the floor near the side post of the brush house.

When the doctor had gone and all the neighbors had reluctantly returned to their houses, Kino squatted beside the little glowing coals in the fire hole and listened to the night sound, the soft sweep of the little waves on the shore and the distant barking of dogs, the creeping of the breeze through the brush house roof and the soft speech of his neighbors in their houses in the village. For these people do not sleep soundly all night; they awaken at intervals and talk a little and then go to sleep again. And after a while Kino got up and went to the door of his house.

He smelled the breeze and he listened for any foreign sound of secrecy or creeping, and his eyes searched the darkness, for the music of evil was sounding in his head and he was fierce and afraid. After he had probed the night with his senses he went to the place by the side post where the pearl was buried, and he dug it up and brought it to his sleeping mat, and under his sleeping mat he dug another little hole in the dirt floor and buried his pearl and covered it up again.

And Juana, sitting by the fire hole, watched him with questioning eyes, and when he had buried his pearl she asked, "Who do you fear?"

Kino searched for a true answer, and at last he said, "Everyone." And he could feel a shell of hardness drawing over him.

After a while they lay down together on the sleeping mat, and Juana did not put the baby in his box tonight, but cradled him on her arms and covered his face with her head shawl. And the last light went out of the embers in the fire hole.

But Kino's brain burned, even during his sleep, and he dreamed that Coyotito could read, that one of his own people could tell him the truth of things. And in his dream, Coyotito was reading from a book as large as a house, with letters as big as dogs, and the words galloped and played on the book. And then darkness spread over the page, and with the darkness came the music of evil again, and Kino stirred in his sleep; and when he stirred, Juana's eyes opened in the darkness. And then Kino awakened, with the evil music pulsing in him, and he lay in the darkness with his ears alert.

Then from the corner of the house came a sound so soft that it might have been simply a thought, a little furtive movement, a touch of a foot on earth, the almost inaudible purr of controlled breathing. Kino held his breath to listen, and he knew that whatever dark thing was in his house was holding its breath too, to listen. For a time no sound at all came from the corner of the brush house. Then Kino might have thought he had imagined the sound. But Juana's hand came creeping over to him in warning, and then the sound came again! the whisper of a foot on dry earth and the scratch of fingers in the soil.

And now a wild fear surged in Kino's breast, and on the fear came rage, as it always did. Kino's hand crept into his breast where his knife hung on a string, and then he sprang like an angry cat, leaped striking and spitting for the dark thing he knew was in the corner of the house. He felt cloth, struck at it with his knife and missed, and struck again and felt his knife go through cloth, and then his head crashed with lightning and exploded with pain. There was a soft scurry in the doorway, and running steps for a moment, and then silence.

Kino could feel warm blood running down from his forehead, and he could hear Juana calling to him. "Kino! Kino!" And there was terror in her voice. Then coldness came over him as quickly as the rage had, and he said, "I am all right. The thing has gone."

He groped his way back to the sleeping mat. Already Juana was working at the fire. She uncovered an ember from the ashes and shredded little pieces of cornhusk over it and blew a little flame into the cornhusks so that a tiny light danced through the hut. And then from a secret place Juana brought a little piece of consecrated candle and lighted it at the flame and set it upright on a fireplace stone. She worked quickly, crooning as she moved about. She dipped the end of her head shawl in water and swabbed the blood from Kino's bruised forehead. "It is nothing," Kino said, but his eyes and his voice were hard and cold and a brooding hate was growing in him.

Now the tension which had been growing in Juana boiled up to the surface and her lips were thin. "This thing is evil," she cried harshly. "This pearl is like a sin! It will destroy us," and her voice rose shrilly. "Throw it away, Kino. Let us break it between stones. Let us bury it and forget the place. Let us throw it back into the sea. It has brought evil. Kino, my husband, it will destroy us." And in the firelight her lips and her eyes were alive with her fear.

But Kino's face was set, and his mind and his will were set. "This is our one chance," he said. "Our son must go to school. He must break out of the pot that holds us in."

"It will destroy us all," Juana cried. "Even our son."

"Hush," said Kino. "Do not speak any more. In the morning we will sell the pearl, and then the evil will be gone, and only the good remain. Now hush, my wife." His dark eyes scowled into the little fire, and for the first time he knew that his knife was still in his hands, and he raised the blade and looked at it and saw a little line of blood on the steel. For a moment he seemed about to wipe the blade on his trousers but then he plunged the knife into the earth and so cleansed it.

The distant roosters began to crow and the air changed and the dawn was coming. The wind of the morning ruffled the water of the estuary and whispered through the mangroves, and the little waves beat on the rubbly beach with an increased tempo. Kino raised the sleeping mat and dug up his pearl and put it front of him and stared at it.

And the beauty of the pearl, winking and glimmering in the light of the little candle, cozened his brain with its beauty. So lovely it was, so soft, and its own music came from it—its music of promise and delight, its guarantee of the future, of comfort, of security. Its warm lucence promised a poultice against illness and a wall against insult. It closed a door on hunger. And as he stared at it Kino's eyes softened and his face relaxed. He could see the little image of the consecrated candle reflected in the soft surface of the pearl, and he heard again in his ears the lovely music of the undersea, the tone of the diffused green light of the sea bottom. Juana, glancing secretly at him, saw him smile. And because they were in some way one thing and one purpose, she smiled with him.

And they began this day with hope.

## THINK AND DISCUSS
### Understanding
1. List the events that lead up to the visit to the doctor.
2. Why does Kino hate or distrust the doctor and his race?
3. How big is the pearl Kino finds, and what does he hope to acquire when he sells it?
4. How do Kino's neighbors and the townspeople react to the pearl?
5. When the doctor finally arrives to see the baby, what excuse does he give for not having attended to him earlier?

### Analyzing
6. The opening chapter describes several contrasts. What is the contrast between the village and the town? between Kino and the doctor?
7. Kino hears the Song of the Family, as well as other songs, very strongly in Chapter I. What purposes do such songs serve in Kino's life and in the novel?
8. At this point midway through the novel's **plot,** Kino and his family are involved in some serious conflicts. Describe the internal and external conflicts they face.
9. What **symbolic** meaning does the pearl begin to have in Chapter III?

### Extending
10. At the beginning of Chapter II, the author describes the formation process of a pearl. How do you think this process can be compared to the formation of human character?
11. To the villagers, Kino had found "the Pearl of the World." Explain in what sense the narrator suggests this is true.

## REVIEWING: Setting  H↗
See Handbook of Literary Terms, p. 824

The **setting** is the time and place in which the action of a narrative occurs. In a novel, each scene may present a new setting. Often, the setting does more than simply provide a background for the action. In *The Pearl*, for instance, the setting helps create the atmosphere from which the story evolves.

1. Describe, in your own words, two of the settings in *The Pearl* and explain how they affect the story's action.
2. The setting of Chapter III is the town, which the narrator compares to a "colonial animal," that has "a nervous system and a head and shoulders and feet." The narrator also says that the town "has a whole emotion." By **personifying** the setting in this way, what kind of atmosphere does the narrator create? How does the setting relate to the action of the story?
3. Would the story be believable or effective if it were to take place in a modern city? Explain.

## READING LITERATURE SKILLFULLY
### Making Judgments

When reading fiction, you should be able to make reasonable judgments about what you read. Some readers are misled when they fail to recognize what they read as an author's subjective description or interpretation of events. It is up to the reader, then, to determine the author's purpose and to judge the effectiveness of the writing and react to it accordingly. For example, if you were to read an article and know that the author's purpose is to persuade you, then you would know that it is not necessary to accept (or reject) everything the author says.

Besides recognizing the author's purpose in a novel, it can be important for you to judge the narrator's attitude toward the characters in the story. How does the narrator feel toward the characters? Is he compassionate? cynical? objective? You will find that the narrator's attitude and perspective greatly affect the tone of the story you are reading. Making sound judgments about the point of view will greatly help you to understand the story and its theme.

1. Do you think Steinbeck's purpose in writing *The Pearl* is merely to entertain the reader, or is he commenting on problems facing society? Explain.
2. What is the **point of view?** Do you think the narrator feels compassion for Kino or simply narrates the events in an objective manner? Give evidence to support your answer.
3. Based on what you have read so far, do you think Steinbeck's portrayal of society is believable or unbelievable? Explain.

## VOCABULARY
### Word Structure: Latin Word Parts

The words *incandescence* and *lucence* are both used in descriptions of the pearl. Their Latin roots *candere* and *lucere* both mean "to shine." A related Latin word, *lumen*, means "light." The words listed below all come from these roots. Arrange the words in two lists, according to the root they come from. Then select the word that best completes each of the following sentences. Check your work in the Glossary.

| | |
|---|---|
| candelabrum | candle |
| illuminate | candor |
| translucent | lucid |
| luminary | candid |

1. Hazy light shone through a _____ window.
2. The _____ held a dozen candles.
3. In spite of her fatigue, the doctor's mind was as _____ as those of the well-rested nurses.
4. The politician clearly had nothing to hide;

his answers to the questions were quite _____.
5. The red spotlights _____ the stage in a fiery glow.

## THINKING SKILLS
### Synthesizing

To **synthesize** is to put together parts and elements so as to form a whole, a new pattern not evident before. Refer back to the Introduction to *The Pearl* to find out where the action takes place. Locate the setting on the map. Then locate other places mentioned in the novel, such as the Gulf and Nayarit.

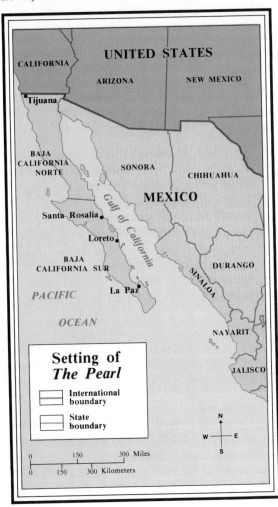

Setting of *The Pearl*

International boundary

State boundary

1. Using the scale of miles, determine how far from the U.S. border the action takes place.
2. What is the nearest U.S. state that can be reached by land?
3. If you were to travel from where you live to Kino's village, in what direction would you have to travel?

## COMPOSITION

### Writing About a Special Object

Most of us have owned something that represents special hopes and dreams in our lives, even if it is less costly than the pearl in Steinbeck's novel. Such an object may or may not be as significant as, for example, an engagement ring that signifies the hopes and dreams of a happy marriage. Think about something you own, have owned, or would like to own. In a three-paragraph composition, describe the object in detail and explain why it is (or would be) special to you. If the item, however humble it may be, symbolizes a wish or dream, explain what it represents for you.

### Writing a Summary

In three paragraphs, summarize the action in Chapters I, II, and III of *The Pearl*. Review the chapters and jot down the significant events of the plot. Be sure you focus your summary on the main conflicts between the protagonist(s) and antagonist(s). Before writing, refer to "Writing to Summarize" in the Writer's Handbook.

# IV

It is wonderful the way a little town keeps track of itself and of all its units. If every single man and woman, child and baby, acts and conducts itself in a known pattern and breaks no walls and differs with no one and experiments in no way and is not sick and does not endanger the ease and peace of mind or steady unbroken flow of the town, then that unit can disappear and never be heard of. But let one man step out of the regular thought or the known and trusted pattern, and the nerves of the townspeople ring with nervousness and communication travels over the nerve lines of the town. Then every unit communicates to the whole.

Thus, in La Paz, it was known in the early morning through the whole town that Kino was going to sell his pearl that day. It was known among the neighbors in the brush huts, among the pearl fishermen; it was known among the Chinese grocery-store owners; it was known in the church, for the altar boys whispered about it. Word of it crept in among the nuns; the beggars in front of the church spoke of it, for they would be there to take the tithe of the first fruits of the luck. The little boys knew about it with excitement, but most of all the pearl buyers knew about it, and when the day had come, in the offices of the pearl buyers, each man sat alone with his little black velvet tray, and each man rolled the pearls about with his fingertips and considered his part in the picture.

It was supposed that the pearl buyers were individuals acting alone, bidding against one another for the pearls the fishermen brought in. And once it had been so. But this was a wasteful method, for often, in the excitement of bidding for a fine pearl, too great a price had been paid to the fishermen. This was extravagant and not to be countenanced. Now there was only one pearl buyer with many hands, and the men who sat in their offices and waited for Kino knew what price they would offer, how high they would bid, and what method each one would use. And although these men would not profit beyond their salaries, there was excitement among the pearl buyers, for there was excitement in the hunt, and if it be a man's function to break down a price, then he must take joy and satisfaction in breaking it as far down as possible. For every man in the world functions to the best of his ability, and no one does less than his best, no matter what he may think about it. Quite apart from any reward they might get, from any word of praise, from any promotion, a pearl buyer was a pearl buyer, and the best and happiest pearl buyer was he who bought for the lowest prices.

The sun was hot yellow that morning, and it drew the moisture from the estuary and from the Gulf and hung it in shimmering scarves in the air so that the air vibrated and vision was insubstantial. A vision hung in the air to the north of the city—the vision of a mountain that was over two hundred miles away, and the high slopes of this mountain were swaddled with pines and a great stone peak arose above the timber line.

And the morning of this day the canoes lay lined up on the beach; the fishermen did not go out to dive for pearls, for there would be too much happening, too many things to see when Kino went to sell the great pearl.

In the brush houses by the shore Kino's neighbors sat long over their breakfasts, and they spoke of what they would do if they had found the pearl. And one man said that he would give it as a present to the Holy Father in Rome. Another said that he would buy Masses for the souls of his family for a thousand years. Another thought he might take the money and distribute it among the poor of La Paz; and a fourth thought of all the good things one could do with the money from the pearl, of all the charities, benefits, of all the rescues one could perform if one had money. All of the neighbors hoped that sudden wealth would not turn Kino's head, would not make a rich man of him, would not graft onto him the evil limbs of greed and hatred and coldness. For Kino was a well-liked man; it would be a shame if the pearl destroyed him. "That good wife Juana," they said, "and the beautiful baby Coyotito, and the others to come. What a pity it would be if the pearl should destroy them all."

For Kino and Juana this was the morning of mornings of their lives, comparable only to the day when the baby was born. This was to be the day from which all other days would take their arrangement. Thus they would say, "It was two years before we sold the pearl," or, "It was six weeks after we sold the pearl." Juana, considering the matter, threw caution to the winds, and she dressed Coyotito in the clothes she had prepared for his baptism, when there would be money for his baptism. And Juana combed and braided her hair and tied the ends with two little bows of red ribbon, and she put on her marriage skirt and waist. The sun was quarter high when they were ready. Kino's ragged white clothes were clean at least, and this was the last day of his raggedness. For tomorrow, or even this afternoon, he would have new clothes.

The neighbors, watching Kino's door through the crevices in their brush houses, were dressed and ready too. There was no self-conciousness about their joining Kino and Juana to go pearl selling. It was expected, it was an historic moment, they would be crazy if they didn't go. It would be almost a sign of unfriendship.

Juana put on her head shawl carefully, and she draped one end under her right elbow and gathered it with her right hand so that a hammock hung under her arm, and in this little hammock she placed Coyotito, propped up against the head shawl so that he could see everything and perhaps remember. Kino put on his large straw hat and felt it with his hand to see that it was properly placed, not on the back or side of his head, like a rash, unmarried, irresponsible man, and not flat as an elder would wear it, but tilted a little forward to show aggressiveness and seriousness and vigor. There is a great deal to be seen in the tilt of a hat on a man. Kino slipped his feet into his sandals and pulled the thongs up over his heels. The great pearl was wrapped in an old soft piece of deerskin and placed in a little leather bag, and the leather bag was in a pocket in Kino's shirt. He folded his blanket carefully and draped it in a narrow strip over his left shoulder, and now they were ready.

Kino stepped with dignity out of the house, and Juana followed him, carrying Coyotito. And as they marched up the freshet-washed alley toward the town, the neighbors joined them. The houses belched people; the doorways spewed out children. But because of the seriousness of the occasion, only one man walked with Kino, and that was his brother, Juan Tomás.

Juan Tomás cautioned his brother. "You must be careful to see they do not cheat you," he said.

And, "Very careful," Kino agreed.

"We do not know what prices are paid in other places," said Juan Tomás. "How can we know what is a fair price, if we do not know what the pearl buyer gets for the pearl in another place?"

"That is true," said Kino, "but how can we know? We are here, we are not there."

As they walked up toward the city the crowd grew behind them, and Juan Tomás, in pure nervousness, went on speaking.

"Before you were born, Kino," he said, "the old ones thought of a way to get more money for their pearls. They thought it would be better if they had an agent who took all the pearls to the capital and sold them there and kept only his share of the profit."

Kino nodded his head. "I know," he said. "It was a good thought."

"And so they got such a man," said Juan Tomás, "and they pooled the pearls, and they

started him off. And he was never heard of again and the pearls were lost. Then they got another man, and they started him off, and he was never heard of again. And so they gave the whole thing up and went back to the old way."

"I know," said Kino. "I have heard our father tell of it. It was a good idea, but it was against religion, and the Father made that very clear. The loss of the pearl was a punishment visited on those who tried to leave their station. And the Father made it clear that each man and woman is like a soldier sent by God to guard some part of the castle of the Universe. And some are in the ramparts and some far deep in the darkness of the walls. But each one must remain faithful to his post and must not go running about, else the castle is in danger from the assaults of Hell."

"I have heard him make that sermon," said Juan Tomás. "He makes it every year."

The brothers, as they walked along, squinted their eyes a little, as they and their grandfathers and their great-grandfathers and done for four hundred years, since first the strangers came with arguments and authority and gunpowder to back up both. And in the four hundred years Kino's people had learned only one defense—a slight slitting of the eyes and a slight tightening of the lips and a retirement. Nothing could break down this wall, and they could remain whole within the wall.

The gathering procession was solemn, for they sensed the importance of this day, and any children who showed a tendency to scuffle, to scream, to cry out, to steal hats and rumple hair, were hissed to silence by their elders. So important was this day that an old man came to see, riding on the stalwart shoulders of his nephew. The procession left the brush huts and entered the stone and plaster city where the streets were a little wider and there were narrow pavements beside the buildings. And as before, the beggars joined them as they passed the church; the grocers looked out at them as they went by; the little saloons lost their customers and the owners closed up shop and went along. And the sun beat down on the streets of the city and even tiny stones threw shadows on the ground.

The news of the approach of the procession ran ahead of it, and in their little dark offices the pearl buyers stiffened and grew alert. They got out papers so that they could be at work when Kino appeared, and they put their pearls in the desks, for it is not good to let an inferior pearl be seen beside a beauty. And word of the loveliness of Kino's pearl had come to them. The pearl buyers' offices were clustered together in one narrow street, and they were barred at the windows, and wooden slats cut out the light so that only a soft gloom entered the offices.

A stout slow man sat in an office waiting. His face was fatherly and benign, and his eyes twinkled with friendship. He was a caller of good mornings, a ceremonious shaker of hands, a jolly man who knew all jokes and yet who hovered close to sadness, for in the midst of a laugh he could remember the death of your aunt, and his eyes could become wet with sorrow for your loss. This morning he had placed a flower in a vase on his desk, a single scarlet hibiscus, and the vase sat beside the black velvet-lined pearl tray in front of him. He was shaved close to the blue roots of his beard, and his hands were clean and his nails polished. His door stood open to the morning, and he hummed under his breath while his right hand practiced legerdemain. He rolled a coin back and forth over his knuckles and made it appear and disappear, made it spin and sparkle. The coin winked into sight and as quickly slipped out of sight, and the man did not even watch his own performance. The fingers did it all mechanically, precisely, while the man hummed to himself and peered out the door. Then he heard the tramp of feet of the approaching crowd, and the fingers of his right hand worked faster and faster until, as the figure of Kino filled the doorway, the coin flashed and disappeared.

"Good morning, my friend," the stout man said. "What can I do for you?"

Kino stared into the dimness of the little office, for his eyes were squeezed from the outside glare. But the buyer's eyes had become as steady and cruel and unwinking as a hawk's eyes, while the rest of his face smiled in greeting. And secretly, behind his desk, his right hand practiced with the coin.

"I have a pearl," said Kino. And Juan Tomás stood beside him and snorted a little at the understatement. The neighbors peered around the doorway, and a line of little boys clambered on the window bars and looked through. Several little boys, on their hands and knees, watched the scene around Kino's legs.

"You have a pearl," the dealer said. "Sometimes a man brings in a dozen. Well, let us see your pearl. We will value it and give you the best price." And his fingers worked furiously with the coin.

Now Kino instinctively knew his own dramatic effects. Slowly he brought out the leather bag, slowly took from it the soft and dirty piece of deerskin, and then he let the great pearl roll into the black velvet tray, and instantly his eyes went to the buyer's face. But there was no sign, no movement, the face did not change, but the secret hand behind the desk missed in its precision. The coin stumbled over a knuckle and slipped silently into the dealer's lap. And the fingers behind the desk curled into a fist. When the right hand came out of hiding, the forefinger touched the great pearl, rolled it on the black velvet; thumb and forefinger picked it up and brought it near to the dealer's eyes and twirled it in the air.

Kino held his breath, and the neighbors held their breath, and the whispering went back

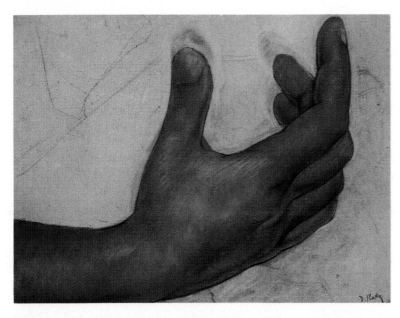

Diego Rivera, *Untitled (Hand)*, circa 1921–1922, San Francisco Museum of Modern Art

through the crowd. "He is inspecting it—No price has been mentioned yet—They have not come to a price."

Now the dealer's hand had become a personality. The hand tossed the great pearl back to the tray, the forefinger poked and insulted it, and on the dealer's face there came a sad and contemptuous smile.

"I am sorry, my friend," he said, and his shoulders rose a little to indicate that the misfortune was no fault of his.

"It is a pearl of great value," Kino said.

The dealer's fingers spurned the pearl so that it bounced and rebounded softly from the sides of the velvet tray.

"You have heard of fool's gold," the dealer said. "This pearl is like fool's gold. It is too large. Who would buy it? There is no market for such things. It is a curiosity only. I am sorry. You thought it was a thing of value, and it is only a curiosity."

Now Kino's face was perplexed and worried. "It is the Pearl of the World," he cried. "No one has ever seen such a pearl."

"On the contrary," said the dealer, "it is large and clumsy. As a curiosity it has interest; some museum might perhaps take it to place in a collection of seashells. I can give you say, a thousand pesos."

Kino's face grew dark and dangerous. "It is worth fifty thousand," he said. "You know it. You want to cheat me."

And the dealer heard a little grumble go through the crowd as they heard his price. And the dealer felt a little tremor of fear.

"Do not blame me," he said quickly. "I am only an appraiser. Ask the others. Go to their offices and show your pearl—or better let them come here, so that you can see there is no collusion. Boy," he called. And when his servant looked through the rear door, "Boy, go to such a one, and such another one and such a third one. Ask them to step in here and do not tell them why. Just say that I will be pleased to see them." And his right hand went behind the desk and pulled another coin from his pocket, and the coin rolled back and forth over his knuckles.

Kino's neighbors whispered together. They had been afraid of something like this. The pearl was large, but it had a strange color. They had been suspicious of it from the first. And after all, a thousand pesos was not to be thrown away. It was comparative wealth to a man who was not wealthy. And suppose Kino took a thousand pesos. Only yesterday he had nothing.

But Kino had grown tight and hard. He felt the creeping of fate, the circling of wolves, the hover of vultures. He felt the evil coagulating about him, and he was helpless to protect himself. He heard in his ears the evil music. And on the black velvet the great pearl glistened, so that the dealer could not keep his eyes from it.

The crowd in the doorway wavered and broke and let the three pearl dealers through. The crowd was silent now, fearing to miss a word, to fail to see a gesture or an expression. Kino was silent and watchful. He felt a little tugging at his back, and he turned and looked in Juana's eyes, and when he looked away he had renewed strength.

The dealers did not glance at one another nor at the pearl. The man behind the desk said, "I have put a value on this pearl. The owner here does not think it fair. I will ask you to examine this—this thing and make an offer. Notice," he said to Kino, "I have not mentioned what I have offered."

The first dealer, dry and stringy, seemed now to see the pearl for the first time. He took it up, rolled it quickly between thumb and forefinger, and then cast it contemptuously back into the tray.

"Do not include me in the discussion," he said dryly. "I will make no offer at all. I do not want it. This is not a pearl—it is a monstrosity." His thin lips curled.

Now the second dealer, a little man with a shy soft voice, took up the pearl, and he examined it carefully. He took a glass from his pocket and inspected it under magnification. Then he laughed softly.

"Better pearls are made of paste," he said. "I know these things. This is soft and chalky, it will lose its color and die in a few months. Look—." He offered the glass to Kino, showed him how to use it, and Kino, who had never seen a pearl's surface magnified, was shocked at the strange-looking surface.

The third dealer took the pearl from Kino's hands. "One of my clients likes such things," he said. "I will offer five hundred pesos, and perhaps I can sell it to my client for six hundred."

Kino reached quickly and snatched the pearl from his hand. He wrapped it in the deerskin and thrust it inside his shirt.

The man behind the desk said, "I'm a fool, I know, but my first offer stands. I still offer one thousand. What are you doing?" he asked, as Kino thrust the pearl out of sight.

"I am cheated," Kino cried fiercely. "My pearl is not for sale here. I will go, perhaps even to the capital."

Now the dealers glanced quickly at one another. They knew they had played too hard; they knew they would be disciplined for their failure, and the man at the desk said quickly, "I might go to fifteen hundred."

But Kino was pushing his way through the crowd. The hum of talk came to him dimly, his rage blood pounded in his ears, and he burst through and strode away. Juana followed, trotting after him.

When the evening came, the neighbors in the brush houses sat eating their corncakes and beans, and they discussed the great theme of the morning. They did not know, it seemed a fine pearl to them, but they had never seen such a pearl before, and surely the dealers knew more about the value of pearls than they. "And mark this," they said.

"Those dealers did not discuss these things. Each of the three knew the pearl was valueless."

"But suppose they had arranged it before?"

"If that is so, then all of us have been cheated all of our lives."

Perhaps, some argued, perhaps it would have been better if Kino took the one thousand five hundred pesos. That is a great deal of money, more than he has ever seen. Maybe Kino is being a pigheaded fool. Suppose he should really go to the capital and find no buyer for his pearl. He would never live that down.

And now, said other fearful ones, now that he had defied them, those buyers will not want to deal with him at all. Maybe Kino has cut off his own head and destroyed himself.

And others said, Kino is a brave man, and a fierce man; he is right. From his courage we may all profit. These were proud of Kino.

In his house Kino squatted on his sleeping mat, brooding. He had buried his pearl under a stone of the fire hole in his house, and he stared at the woven tules of his sleeping mat until the crossed design danced in his head. He had lost one world and had not gained another. And Kino was afraid. Never in his life had he been far from home. He was afraid of strangers and of strange places. He was terrified of that monster of strangeness they called the capital. It lay over the water and through the mountains, over a thousand miles, and every strange terrible mile was frightening. But Kino had lost his old world and he must clamber on to a new one. For his dream of the future was real and never to be destroyed, and he had said "I will go," and that made a real thing too. To determine to go and to say it was to be halfway there.

Juana watched him while he buried his pearl, and she watched him while she cleaned Coyotito and nursed him, and Juana made the corncakes for supper.

Juan Tomás came in and squatted down beside Kino and remained silent for a long time, until at last Kino demanded, "What else could I do? They are cheats."

Juan Tomás nodded gravely. He was the elder, and Kino looked to him for wisdom. "It is hard to know," he said. "We do know that we are cheated from birth to the overcharge on our coffins. But we survive. You have defied not the pearl buyers, but the whole structure, the whole way of life, and I am afraid for you."

"What have I to fear but starvation?" Kino asked.

But Juan Tomás shook his head slowly. "That we must all fear. But suppose you are correct—suppose your pearl is of great value—do you think then the game is over?"

"What do you mean?"

"I don't know," said Juan Tomás, "but I am afraid for you. It is new ground you are walking on, you do not know the way."

"I will go. I will go soon," said Kino.

"Yes," Juan Tomás agreed. "That you must do. But I wonder if you will find it any different in the capital. Here, you have friends and me, your brother. There, you will have no one."

"What can I do?" Kino cried. "Some deep outrage is here. My son must have a chance. That is what they are striking at. My friends will protect me."

"Only so long as they are not in danger or discomfort from it," said Juan Tomás. He arose, saying, "Go with God."

And Kino said, "Go with God," and did not even look up, for the words had a strange chill in them.

Long after Juan Tomás had gone Kino sat brooding on his sleeping mat. A lethargy had settled on him, and a little gray hopelessness. Every road seemed blocked against him. In his head he heard only the dark music of the enemy.

His senses were burningly alive, but his mind went back to the deep participation with all things, the gift he had from his people. He heard every little sound of the gathering night, the sleepy complaint of settling birds, the love agony of cats, the strike and withdrawal of little waves on the beach, and the simple hiss of distance. And he could smell the sharp odor of exposed kelp from the receding tide. The little flare of the twig fire made the design on his sleeping mat jump before his entranced eyes.

Juana watched him with worry, but she knew him and she knew she could help him best by being silent and by being near. And as though she too could hear the Song of Evil, she fought it, singing softly the melody of the family, of the safety and warmth and wholeness of the family. She held Coyotito in her arms and sang the song to him, to keep the evil out, and her voice was brave against the threat of the dark music.

Kino did not move nor ask for his supper. She knew he would ask when he wanted it. His eyes were entranced, and he could sense the wary, watchful evil outside the brush house; he could feel the dark creeping things waiting for him to go out into the night. It was shadowy and dreadful, and yet it called to him and threatened him and challenged him. His right hand went into his shirt and felt his knife; his eyes were wide; he stood up and walked to the doorway.

Juana willed to stop him; she raised her hand to stop him, and her mouth opened with terror. For a long moment Kino looked out into the darkness and then he stepped outside. Juana heard the little rush, the grunting struggle, the blow. She froze with terror for a moment, and then her lips drew back from her teeth like a cat's lips. She set Coyotito down on the ground. She seized a stone from the fireplace and rushed outside, but it was over by then. Kino lay on the ground, struggling to rise, and there was no one near him. Only the shadows and the strike and rush of waves and the hiss of distance. But the evil was all about, hidden behind the brush fence, crouched beside the house in the shadow, hovering in the air.

Juana dropped her stone, and she put her arms around Kino and helped him to his feet and supported him into the house. Blood oozed down from his scalp and there was a long deep cut in his cheek from ear to chin, a deep, bleeding slash. And Kino was only half conscious. He shook his head from side to side. His shirt was torn open and his clothes half pulled off. Juana sat him down on his sleeping mat and she wiped the thickening blood from his face with her skirt. She brought him pulque to drink in a little pitcher, and still he shook his head to clear out the darkness.

"Who?" Juana asked.

"I don't know," Kino said. "I didn't see."

Now Juana brought her clay plot of water and she washed the cut on his face while he stared dazed ahead of him.

"Kino, my husband," she cried, and his eyes stared past her. "Kino, can you hear me?"

"I hear you," he said dully.

"Kino, this pearl is evil. Let us destroy it before it destroys us. Let us crush it between two stones. Let us—let us throw it back in the sea where it belongs. Kino, it is evil, it is evil!"

And as she spoke the light came back in Kino's eyes so that they glowed fiercely and his muscles hardened and his will hardened.

"No," he said. "I will fight this thing. I will win over it. We will have our chance." His fist pounded the sleeping mat. "No one shall take our good fortune from us," he said. His eyes softened then and he raised a gentle hand to Juana's shoulder. "Believe me," he said. "I am a man." And his face grew crafty.

"In the morning we will take our canoe and we will go over the sea and over the mountains to the capital, you and I. We will not be cheated. I am a man."

"Kino," she said huskily, "I am afraid. A man can be killed. Let us throw the pearl back into the sea."

"Hush," he said fiercely. "I am a man. Hush." And she was silent, for his voice was command. "Let us sleep a little," he said. "In the first light we will start. You are not afraid to go with me?"

"No, my husband."

His eyes were soft and warm on her then, his hand touched her cheek. "Let us sleep a little," he said.

# V

The late moon arose before the first rooster crowed. Kino opened his eyes in the darkness, for he sensed movement near him, but he did not move. Only his eyes searched the darkness, and in the pale light of the moon that crept through the holes in the brush house Kino saw Juana arise silently from beside him. He saw her move toward the fireplace. So carefully did she work that he heard only the lightest sound when she moved the fireplace stone. And then like a shadow she glided toward the door. She paused for a moment beside the hanging box where Coyotito lay, then for a second she was back in the doorway, and then she was gone.

And rage surged in Kino. He rolled up to his feet and followed her as silently as she had gone, and he could hear her quick footsteps going toward the shore. Quietly he tracked her, and his brain was red with anger. She burst clear of the brush line and stumbled over the little boulders toward the water, and then she heard him coming and she broke into a run. Her arm was up to throw when he leaped at her and caught her arm and wrenched the pearl from her. He struck her in the face with his clenched fist and she fell among the boulders, and he kicked her in the side. In the pale light he could see the little waves break over her, and her skirt floated about and clung to her legs as the water receded.

Kino looked down at her and his teeth were bared. He hissed at her like a snake, and Juana stared at him with wide unfrightened eyes, like a sheep before the butcher. She knew there was murder in him, and it was all right; she had accepted it, and she would not resist or even protest. And then the rage left him and a sick disgust took its place. He turned away from her and walked up the beach and through the brush line. His senses were dulled by his emotion.

He heard the rush, got his knife out and lunged at one dark figure and felt his knife go home, and then he was swept to his knees and swept again to the ground. Greedy fingers went through his clothes, frantic fingers searched him, and the pearl, knocked from his hand, lay winking behind a little stone in the pathway. It glinted in the soft moonlight.

Juana dragged herself up from the rocks on the edge of the water. Her face was a dull pain and her side ached. She steadied herself on her knees for a while and her wet skirt clung to her. There was no anger in her for Kino. He had said, "I am a man," and that meant certain things to Juana. It meant that he was half insane and half god. It meant that Kino would drive his strength against the sea. Juana, in her woman's soul, knew that the mountain would stand while the man broke himself; that the sea would surge while the man drowned in it. And yet it was this thing that made him a man, half insane and half god, and Juana had need of a man; she could not live without a man. Although she might be puzzled by these differences between man and woman, she knew them and accepted them and needed them. Of course she would follow him, there was no question of that. Sometimes the quality of woman, the reason, the caution, the sense of preservation, could cut through Kino's manness and save them all. She climbed painfully to her feet, and she dipped her cupped palms in the little waves and washed her bruised face with the stinging salt water, and then she went creeping up the beach after Kino.

A flight of herring clouds had moved over the sky from the south. The pale moon dipped in and out of the strands of clouds so that Juana walked in darkness for a moment and in light the next. Her back was bent with pain and her head was low. She went through the line of brush when the moon was covered, and when it looked through she saw the glimmer of the great pearl in the path behind the rock. She sank to her knees and picked it up, and the moon went into the darkness of the clouds again. Juana remained on her knees while she considered whether to go back to the sea and finish her job, and as she considered, the light came again, and she saw two dark figures lying in the path ahead of her. She leaped forward and saw that one was Kino and the other a stranger with dark shiny fluid leaking from his throat.

Kino moved sluggishly, arms and legs stirred like those of a crushed bug, and a thick muttering came from his mouth. Now, in an instant, Juana knew that the old life was gone forever. A dead man in the path and Kino's knife, dark bladed beside him, convinced her. All of the time Juana had been trying to rescue something of the old peace, of the time before the pearl. But now it was gone, and there was no retrieving it. And knowing this, she abandoned the past instantly. There was nothing to do but to save themselves.

Her pain was gone now, her slowness. Quickly she dragged the dead man from the pathway into the shelter of the brush. She went to Kino and sponged his face with her wet skirt. His senses were coming back and he moaned.

"They have taken the pearl. I have lost it. Now it is over," he said. "The pearl is gone."

Juana quieted him as she would quiet a sick child. "Hush," she said. "Here is your pearl. I found it in the path. Can you hear me now? Here is your pearl. Can you understand? You have killed a man. We must go away. They will come for us, can you understand? We must be gone before the daylight comes."

"I was attacked," Kino said uneasily. "I struck to save my life."

"Do you remember yesterday?" Juana asked. "Do you think that will matter? Do you remember the men of the city? Do you think your explanation will help?"

Kino drew a great breath and fought off his weakness. "No," he said. "You are right." And his will hardened and he was a man again.

"Go to our house and bring Coyotito," he said, "and bring all the corn we have. I will drag the canoe into the water and we will go."

He took his knife and left her. He stumbled toward the beach and he came to his canoe. And when the light broke through again he saw that a great hole had been knocked in the bottom. And a searing rage came to him and gave him strength. Now the darkness was closing in on his family; now the evil music filled the night, hung over the mangroves, skirled in the wave beat. The canoe of his grandfather, plastered over and over, and a splintered hole broken in it. This was an evil beyond thinking. The killing of a man was not so evil as the killing of a boat. For a boat does not have sons, and a boat cannot protect itself, and a wounded boat does not heal. There was sorrow in Kino's rage, but this last thing had tightened him beyond breaking. He was an animal now, for hiding, for attacking, and he lived only to preserve himself and his family. He was not conscious of the pain in his head. He leaped up the beach, through the brush line toward his brush house, and it did not occur to him to take one of the canoes of his neighbors. Never once did the thought enter his head, any more than he could have conceived breaking a boat.

The roosters were crowing and the dawn was not far off. Smoke of the first fires seeped out through the walls of the brush houses, and the first smell of cooking corncakes was in the air. Already the dawn birds were scampering in the bushes. The weak moon was losing its light and the clouds thickened and curdled to the southward. The wind blew freshly into the estuary, a nervous, restless wind with the smell of storm on its breath, and there was change and uneasiness in the air.

Kino, hurrying toward his house, felt a surge of exhilaration. Now he was not confused, for there was only one thing to do, and Kino's hand went first to the great pearl in his shirt and then to his knife hanging under his shirt.

He saw a little glow ahead of him, and then without interval a tall flame leaped up in the dark with a crackling roar, and a tall edifice of fire lighted the pathway. Kino broke into a run; it was his brush house, he knew. And he knew that these houses could burn down in a very few moments. And as he ran a scuttling figure ran toward him— Juana, with Coyotito in her arms and Kino's shoulder blanket clutched in her hand. The baby moaned with fright, and Juana's eyes were wide and terrified. Kino could see the house was gone, and he did not question Juana. He knew, but she said, "It was torn up and the floor dug—even the baby's box turned out, and as I looked they put the fire to the outside."

The fierce light of the burning house lighted Kino's face strongly. "Who?" he demanded.

"I don't know," she said. "The dark ones."

The neighbors were tumbling from their houses now, and they watched the falling sparks and stamped them out to save their own houses. Suddenly Kino was afraid. The light made him afraid. He remembered the man lying dead in the brush beside the path, and he took Juana by the arm and drew her into the shadow of a house away from the light, for light was danger to him. For a moment he considered and then he worked among the shadows until he came to the house of Juan Tomás, his brother, and he slipped into the

Diego Rivera, *Mexican Woman with Basket*, 1935, San Francisco Museum of Modern Art

doorway and drew Juana after him. Outside, he could hear the squeal of children and the shouts of the neighbors, for his friends thought he might be inside the burning house.

The house of Juan Tomás was almost exactly like Kino's house; nearly all the brush houses were alike, and all leaked light and air, so that Juana and Kino, sitting in the corner of the brother's house, could see the leaping flames through the wall. They saw the flames tall and furious, they saw the roof fall and watched the fire die down as quickly as a twig fire dies. They heard the cries of warning of their friends, and the shrill, keening cry of Apolonia, wife of Juan Tomás. She, being the nearest woman relative, raised a formal lament for the dead of the family.

Apolonia realized that she was wearing her second-best head shawl and she rushed to her house to get her fine new one. As she rummaged in a box by the wall, Kino's voice said quietly, "Apolonia, do not cry out. We are not hurt."

"How do you come here?" she demanded.

"Do not question," he said. "Go now to Juan Tomás and bring him here and tell no one else. This is important to us, Apolonia."

She paused, her hands helpless in front of her, and then, "Yes, my brother-in-law," she said.

In a few moments Juan Tomás came back with her. He lighted a candle and came to them where they crouched in a corner and he said, "Apolonia, see to the door, and do not let anyone enter." He was older, Juan Tomás, and he assumed the authority. "Now, my brother," he said.

"I was attacked in the dark," said Kino. "And in the fight I have killed a man."

"Who?" asked Juan Tomás quickly.

"I do not know. It is all darkness—all darkness and shape of darkness."

"It is the pearl," said Juan Tomás. "There is a devil in this pearl. You should have sold it and passed on the devil. Perhaps you can still sell it and buy peace for yourself."

And Kino said, "Oh, my brother, an insult has been put on me that is deeper than my life. For on the beach my canoe is broken, my house is burned, and in the brush a dead man lies. Every escape is cut off. You must hide us, my brother."

And Kino, looking closely, saw deep worry come into his brother's eyes and he forestalled him in a possible refusal. "Not for long," he said quickly. "Only until a day has passed and the new night has come. Then we will go."

"I will hide you," said Juan Tomás.

"I do not want to bring danger to you," Kino said. "I know I am like a leprosy. I will go tonight and then you will be safe."

"I will protect you," said Juan Tomás, and he called, "Apolonia, close up the door. Do not even whisper that Kino is here."

They sat silently all day in the darkness of the house, and they could hear the neighbors speaking of them. Through the walls of the house they could watch their neighbors raking the ashes to find the bones. Crouching in the house of Juan Tomás, they heard the shock go into their neighbors' minds at the news of the broken boat. Juan Tomás went out among the neighbors to divert their suspicions, and he gave them theories and ideas of what had happened to Kino and to Juana and to the baby. To one he said, "I think they have gone south along the coast to escape the evil that was on them." And to another, "Kino would never leave the sea. Perhaps he found another boat." And he said, "Apolonia is ill with grief."

And in that day the wind rose up to beat the Gulf and tore the kelps and weeds that lined the shore, and the wind cried through the brush houses and no boat was safe on the water. Then Juan Tomás told among the neighbors, "Kino is gone. If he went to the sea, he is drowned by now." And after each trip among the neighbors Juan Tomás came back with something borrowed. He brought a little woven straw bag of red beans and a gourd full of rice. He borrowed a cup of dried peppers and a block of salt, and he brought in a long working knife, eighteen inches long and heavy, as a small ax, a tool and a weapon. And when Kino saw this knife his eyes lighted up, and he fondled the blade and his thumb tested the edge.

The wind screamed over the Gulf and turned the water white, and the mangroves plunged like frightened cattle, and a fine sandy dust arose from the land and hung in a stifling cloud over the sea. The wind drove off the clouds and skimmed the sky clean and drifted the sand of the country like snow.

Then Juan Tomás, when the evening approached, talked long with his brother. "Where will you go?"

"To the north," said Kino. "I have heard that there are cities in the north."

"Avoid the shore," said Juan Tomás. "They

are making a party to search the shore. The men in the city will look for you. Do you still have the pearl?"

"I have it," said Kino. "And I will keep it. I might have given it as a gift, but now it is my misfortune and my life and I will keep it." His eyes were hard and cruel and bitter.

Coyotito whimpered and Juana muttered little magics over him to make him silent.

"The wind is good," said Juan Tomás. "There will be no tracks."

They left quietly in the dark before the moon had risen. The family stood formally in the house of Juan Tomás. Juana carried Coyotito on her back, covered and held in by her head shawl, and the baby slept, cheek turned sideways against her shoulder. The head shawl covered the baby, and one end of it came across Juana's nose to protect her from the evil night air. Juan Tomás embraced his brother with the double embrace and kissed him on both cheeks. "Go with God," he said, and it was like a death. "You will not give up the pearl?"

"This pearl has become my soul," said Kino. "If I give it up I shall lose my soul. Go thou also with God."

# VI

The wind blew fierce and strong, and it pelted them with bits of sticks, sand, and little rocks. Juana and Kino gathered their clothing tighter about them and covered their noses and went out into the world. The sky was brushed clean by the wind and the stars were cold in a black sky. The two walked carefully, and they avoided the center of town where some sleeper in a doorway might see them pass. For the town closed itself in against the night, and anyone who moved about in the darkness would be noticeable. Kino threaded his way around the edge of the city and turned

north, north by the stars, and found the rutted sandy road that led through the brushy country toward Loreto where the miraculous Virgin[7] has her station.

Kino could feel the blown sand against his ankles and he was glad, for he knew there would be no tracks. The little light from the stars made out for him the narrow road through the brushy country. And Kino could hear the pad of Juana's feet behind him. He went quickly and quietly, and Juana trotted behind him to keep up.

Some ancient thing stirred in Kino. Through his fear of dark and the devils that haunt the night, there came a rush of exhilaration; some animal thing was moving in him so that he was cautious and wary and dangerous; some ancient thing out of the past of his people was alive in him. The wind was at his back and the stars guided him. The wind cried and whisked in the brush, and the family went on monotonously, hour after hour. They passed no one and saw no one. At last, to their right, the waning moon arose, and when it came up the wind died down, and the land was still.

Now they could see the little road ahead of them, deep cut with sand-drifted wheel tracks. With the wind gone there would be footprints, but they were a good distance from the town and perhaps their tracks might not be noticed. Kino walked carefully in a wheel rut, and Juana followed in his path. One big cart, going to the town in the morning, could wipe out every trace of their passage.

All night they walked and never changed their pace. Once Coyotito awakened, and Juana shifted him in front of her and soothed him until he went to sleep again. And the evils of the night were about them. The coyotes cried and laughed in the

---

7. **Virgin,** Mary, the mother of Jesus. In Latin America, most towns have stations, or shrines, in their churches honoring Mary. Although many of the shrines have different names, they all contain representations of the revered saint.

brush, and the owls screeched and hissed over their heads. And once some large animal lumbered away, crackling the undergrowth as it went. And Kino gripped the handle of the big working knife and took a sense of protection from it.

The music of the pearl was triumphant in Kino's head, and the quiet melody of the family underlay it, and they wore themselves into the soft padding of sandaled feet in the dusk. All night they walked, and in the first dawn Kino searched the roadside for a covert to lie in during the day. He found his place near to the road, a little clearing where deer might have lain, and it was curtained thickly with the dry brittle trees that lined the road. And when Juana had seated herself and had settled to nurse the baby, Kino went back to the road. He broke a branch and carefully swept the footprints where they had turned from the roadway. And then, in the first light, he heard the creak of a wagon, and he crouched beside the road and watched a heavy two-wheeled cart go by, drawn by slouching oxen. And when it had passed out of sight, he went back to the roadway and looked at the rut and found that the footprints were gone. And again he swept out his traces and went back to Juana.

She gave him the soft corncakes Apolonia had packed for them, and after a while she slept a little. But Kino sat on the ground and stared at the earth in front of him. He watched the ants moving, a little column of them near to his foot, and he put his foot in their path. Then the column climbed over his instep and continued on its way, and Kino left his foot there and watched them move over it.

The sun arose hotly. They were not near the Gulf now, and the air was dry and hot so that the brush cricked with heat and a good resinous smell came from it. And when Juana awakened, when the sun was high, Kino told her things she knew already.

"Beware of that kind of tree there," he said, pointing. "Do not touch it, for if you do and then touch your eyes, it will blind you. And beware of the tree that bleeds. See, that one over there. For if you break it the red blood will flow from it, and it is evil luck." And she nodded and smiled a little at him, for she knew these things.

"Will they follow us?" she asked. "Do you think they will try to find us?"

"They will try," said Kino. "Whoever finds us will take the pearl. Oh, they will try."

And Juana said, "Perhaps the dealers were right and the pearl has no value. Perhaps this has all been an illusion."

Kino reached into his clothes and brought out the pearl. He let the sun play on it until it burned in his eyes. "No," he said, "they would not have tried to steal it if it had been valueless."

"Do you know who attacked you? Was it the dealers?"

"I do not know," he said. "I didn't see them."

He looked into his pearl to find his vision. "When we sell it at last, I will have a rifle," he said, and he looked into the shining surface for his rifle, but he saw only a huddled dark body on the ground with shining blood dripping from its throat. And he said quickly, "We will be married in a great church." And in the pearl he saw Juana with her beaten face crawling home through the night. "Our son must learn to read," he said frantically. And there in the pearl Coyotito's face, thick and feverish from the medicine.

And Kino thrust the pearl back into his clothing, and the music of the pearl had become sinister in his ears and it was interwoven with the music of evil.

The hot sun beat on the earth so that Kino and Juana moved into the lacy shade of the brush, and small gray birds scampered on the ground in the shade. In the heat of the day Kino relaxed and covered his eyes with his hat and wrapped his blanket about his face to keep the flies off, and he slept.

Diego Rivera, *The Mixcoac
Ravine*, 1906, Property of
the State of Veracruz

But Juana did not sleep. She sat quiet as a stone and her face was quiet. Her mouth was still swollen where Kino had struck her, and big flies buzzed around the cut on her chin. But she sat as still as a sentinel, and when Coyotito awakened she placed him on the ground in front of her and watched him wave his arms and kick his feet, and he smiled and gurgled at her until she smiled too. She picked up a little twig from the ground and tickled him, and she gave him water from the gourd she carried in her bundle.

Kino stirred in a dream, and he cried out in a guttural voice, and his hand moved in symbolic fighting. And then he moaned and sat up suddenly, his eyes wide and his nostrils flaring. He listened and heard only the cricking heat and the hiss of distance.

"What is it?" Juana asked.

"Hush," he said.

"You were dreaming."

"Perhaps." But he was restless, and when she gave him a corncake from her store he paused in his chewing to listen. He was uneasy and nervous; he glanced over his shoulder; he lifted the big

knife and felt its edge. When Coyotito gurgled on the ground Kino said, "Keep him quiet."

"What is the matter?" Juana asked.

"I don't know."

He listened again, an animal light in his eyes. He stood up then, silently; and crouched low, he threaded his way through the brush toward the road. But he did not step into the road; he crept into the cover of a thorny tree and peered out along the way he had come.

And then he saw them moving along. His body stiffened and he drew down his head and peeked out from under a fallen branch. In the distance he could see three figures, two on foot and one on horseback. But he knew what they were, and a chill of fear went through him. Even in the distance he could see the two on foot moving slowly along, bent low to the ground. Here, one would pause and look at the earth, while the other joined him. They were trackers, they could follow the trail of a bighorn sheep in the stone mountains. They were as sensitive as hounds. Here, he and Juana might have stepped out of the wheel rut, and these people from the inland, these hunters, could follow, could read a broken straw or a little tumbled pile of dust. Behind them, on a horse, was a dark man, his nose covered with a blanket, and across his saddle a rifle gleamed in the sun.

Kino lay as rigid as the tree limb. He barely breathed, and his eyes went to the place where he had swept out the track. Even the sweeping might be a message to the trackers. He knew these inland hunters. In a country where there is little game they managed to live because of their ability to hunt, and they were hunting him. They scuttled over the ground like animals and found a sign and crouched over it while the horseman waited.

The trackers whined a little, like excited dogs on a warming trail. Kino slowly drew his big knife to his hand and made it ready. He knew what he must do. If the trackers found the swept place, he must leap for the horseman, kill him quickly and take the rifle. That was his only chance in the world. And as the three drew nearer on the road, Kino dug little pits with his sandaled toes so that he could leap without warning, so that his feet would not slip. He had only a little vision under the fallen limb.

Now Juana, back in her hidden place, heard the pad of the horse's hoofs, and Coyotito gurgled. She took him up quickly and put him under her shawl and gave him her breast and he was silent.

When the trackers came near, Kino could see only their legs and only the legs of the horse from under the fallen branch. He saw the dark horny feet of the men and their ragged white clothes, and he heard the creak of leather of the saddle and the clink of spurs. The trackers stopped at the swept place and studied it, and the horseman stopped. The horse flung his head up against the bit and the bit-roller clicked under his tongue and the horse snorted. Then the dark trackers turned and studied the horse and watched his ears.

Kino was not breathing, but his back arched a little and the muscles of his arms and legs stood out with tension and a line of sweat formed on his upper lip. For a long moment the trackers bent over the road, and then they moved on slowly, studying the ground ahead of them, and the horseman moved after them. The trackers scuttled along, stopping, looking, and hurrying on. They would be back, Kino knew. They would be circling and searching, peeping, stooping, and they would come back sooner or later to his covered track.

He slid backward and did not bother to cover his tracks. He could not; too many little signs were there, too many broken twigs and scuffed places and displaced stones. And there was a panic in Kino now, a panic of flight. The trackers would find his trail, he knew it. There was no escape, except in flight. He edged away from the road and went quickly and silently to the hidden place where Juana was. She looked up at him in question.

"Trackers," he said. "Come!"

And then a helplessness and a hopelessness swept over him, and his face went black and his eyes were sad. "Perhaps I should let them take me."

Instantly Juana was on her feet and her hand lay on his arm. "You have the pearl," she cried hoarsely. "Do you think they would take you back alive to say they had stolen it?"

His hand strayed limply to the place where the pearl was hidden under his clothes. "They will find it," he said weakly.

"Come," she said. "Come!"

And when he did not respond, "Do you think they would let me live? Do you think they would let the little one here live?"

Her goading struck into his brain; his lips snarled and his eyes were fierce again. "Come," he said. "We will go into the mountains. Maybe we can lose them in the mountains."

Frantically he gathered the gourds and the little

bags that were their property. Kino carried a bundle in his left hand, but the big knife swung free in his right hand. He parted the brush for Juana and they hurried to the west, toward the high stone mountains. They trotted quickly through the tangle of the undergrowth. This was panic flight. Kino did not try to conceal his passages; he trotted, kicking the stones, knocking the telltale leaves from the little trees. The high sun streamed down on the dry creaking earth so that even vegetation ticked in protest. But ahead were the naked granite mountains, rising out of erosion rubble and standing monolithic against the sky. And Kino ran for the high place, as nearly all animals do when they are pursued.

This land was waterless, furred with the cacti which could store water and with the great-rooted brush which could reach deep into the earth for a little moisture and get along on very little. And underfoot was not soil but broken rock, split into small cubes, great slabs, but none of it water-rounded. Little tufts of sad dry grass grew between the stones, grass that had sprouted with one single rain and headed, dropped its seed, and died. Horned toads watched the family go by and turned their little pivoting dragon heads. And now and then a great jackrabbit, disturbed in his shade, bumped away and hid behind the nearest rock. The singing heat lay over this desert country, and ahead the stone mountains looked cool and welcoming.

And Kino fled. He knew what would happen. A little way along the road the trackers would become aware that they had missed the path, and they would come back, searching and judging, and in a little while they would find the place where Kino and Juana had rested. From there it would be easy for them—these little stones, the fallen leaves and the whipped branches, the scuffed places where a foot had slipped. Kino could see them in his mind, slipping along the

track, whining a little with eagerness, and behind them, dark and half disinterested, the horseman with the rifle. His work would come last, for he would not take them back. Oh, the music of evil sang loud in Kino's head now, it sang with the whine of heat and with the dry ringing of snake rattles. It was not large and overwhelming now, but secret and poisonous, and the pounding of his heart gave it undertone and rhythm.

The way began to rise, and as it did the rocks grew larger. But now Kino had put a little distance between his family and the trackers. Now, on the first rise, he rested. He climbed a great boulder and looked back over the shimmering country, but he could not see his enemies, not even the tall horseman riding through the brush. Juana had squatted in the shade of the boulder. She raised her bottle of water to Coyotito's lips; his little dried tongue sucked greedily at it. She looked up at Kino when he came back; she saw him examine her ankles, cut and scratched from the stones and brush, and she covered them quickly with her skirt. Then she handed the bottle to him, but he shook his head. Her eyes were bright in her tired face. Kino moistened his cracked lips with his tongue.

"Juana," he said, "I will go on and you will hide. I will lead them into the mountains, and when they have gone past, you will go north to Loreto or to Santa Rosalia. Then, if I can escape them, I will come to you. It is the only safe way."

She looked full into his eyes for a moment. "No," she said. "We go with you."

"I can go faster alone," he said harshly. "You will put the little one in more danger if you go with me."

"No," said Juana.

"You must. It is the wise thing and it is my wish," he said.

"No," said Juana.

He looked then for weakness in her face, for

fear or irresolution, and there was none. Her eyes were very bright. He shrugged his shoulders helplessly then, but he had taken strength from her. When they moved on it was no longer panic flight.

The country, as it rose toward the mountains, changed rapidly. Now there were long outcroppings of granite with deep crevices between, and Kino walked on bare unmarkable stone when he could and leaped from ledge to ledge. He knew that wherever the trackers lost his patch they must circle and lose time before they found it again. And so he did not go straight for the mountains any more; he moved in zigzags, and sometimes he cut back to the south and left a sign and then went toward the mountains over bare stone again. And the path rose steeply now, so that he panted a little as he went.

The sun moved downward toward the bare stone teeth of the mountains, and Kino set his direction for a dark and shadowy cleft in the range. If there were any water at all, it would be there where he could see, even in the distance, a hint of foliage. And if there were any passage through the smooth stone range, it would be by this same deep cleft. It had its danger, for the trackers would think of it too, but the empty water bottle did not let that consideration enter. And as the sun lowered, Kino and Juana struggled wearily up the steep slope toward the cleft.

High in the gray stone mountains, under a frowning peak, a little spring bubbled out of a rupture in the stone. It was fed by shade-preserved snow in the summer, and now and then it died completely and bare rocks and dry algae were on its bottom. But nearly always it gushed out, cold and clean and lovely. In the times when the quick rains fell, it might become a freshet and send its column of white water crashing down the mountain cleft, but nearly always it was a lean little spring. It bubbled out into a pool and then fell a hundred feet to another pool, and this one,

overflowing, dropped again, so that it continued, down and down, until it came to the rubble of the upland, and there it disappeared altogether. There wasn't much left of it then anyway, for every time it fell over an escarpment the thirsty air drank it, and it splashed from the pools to the dry vegetation. The animals from miles around came to drink from the little pools, and the wild sheep and the deer, the pumas and raccoons, and the mice—all came to drink. And the birds which spent the day in the brushland came at night to the little pools that were like steps in the mountain cleft. Beside this tiny stream, wherever enough earth collected for root-hold, colonies of plants grew, wild grape and little palms, maidenhair fern, hibiscus, and tall pampas grass with feathery rods raised above the spike leaves. And in the pool lived frogs and water-skaters, and water-worms crawled on the bottom of the pool. Everything that loved water came to these few shallow places. The cats took their prey there, and strewed feathers and lapped water through their bloody teeth. The little pools were places of life because of the water, and places of killing because of the water, too.

The lowest step, where the stream collected before it tumbled down a hundred feet and disappeared into the rubbly desert, was a little platform of stone and sand. Only a pencil of water fell into the pool, but it was enough to keep the pool full and to keep the ferns green in the underhang of the cliff, and wild grape climbed the stone mountain and all manner of little plants found comfort here. The freshets had made a small sandy beach through which the pool flowed, and bright green watercress grew in the damp sand. The beach was cut and scarred and padded by the feet of animals that had come to drink and to hunt.

The sun had passed over the stone mountains when Kino and Juana struggled up the steep broken slope and came at last to the water. From this step they could look out over the sunbeaten desert to the blue Gulf in the distance. They came utterly weary to the pool, and Juana slumped to her knees and first washed Coyotito's face and then filled her bottle and gave him a drink. And the baby was weary and petulant, and he cried softly until Juana gave him her breast, and then he gurgled and clucked against her. Kino drank long and thirstily at the pool. For a moment, then, he stretched out beside the water and relaxed all his muscles and watched Juana feeding the baby, and then he got to his feet and went to the edge of the step where the water slipped over, and he searched the distance carefully. His eyes set on a point and he became rigid. Far down the slope he could see the two trackers; they were little more than dots or scurrying ants and behind them a larger ant.

Juana had turned to look at him and she saw his back stiffen.

"How far?" she asked quietly.

"They will be here by evening," said Kino. He looked up the long steep chimney of the cleft where the water came down. "We must go west," he said, and his eyes searched the stone shoulder behind the cleft. And thirty feet up on the gray shoulder he saw a series of little erosion caves. He slipped off his sandals and clambered up to them, gripping the bare stone with his toes, and he looked into the shallow caves. They were only a few feet deep, wind-hollowed scoops, but they sloped slighty downward and back. Kino crawled into the largest one and lay down and knew that he could not be seen from the outside. Quickly he went back to Juana.

"You must go up there. Perhaps they will not find us there," he said.

Without question she filled her water bottle to the top, and then Kino helped her up to the shallow cave and brought up the packages of food and passed them to her. And Juana sat in the cave entrance and watched him. She saw that he did not try to erase their tracks in the sand. Instead,

he climbed up the brush cliff beside the water, clawing and tearing at the ferns and wild grape as he went. And when he had climbed a hundred feet to the next bench, he came down again. He looked carefully at the smooth rock shoulder toward the cave to see that there was no trace of passage, and last he climbed up and crept into the cave beside Juana.

"When they go up," he said, "we will slip away, down to the lowlands again. I am afraid only that the baby may cry. You must see that he does not cry."

"He will not cry," she said, and she raised the baby's face to her own and looked into his eyes and he stared solemnly back at her.

"He knows," said Juana.

Now Kino lay in the cave entrance, his chin braced on his crossed arms, and he watched the blue shadow of the mountain move out across the brushy desert below until it reached the Gulf, and the long twilight of the shadow was over the land.

The trackers were long in coming, as though they had trouble with the trail Kino had left. It was dusk when they came at last to the little pool. And all three were on foot now, for a horse could not climb the last steep slope. From above they were thin figures in the evening. The two trackers scurried about on the little beach, and they saw Kino's progress up the cliff before they drank. The man with the rifle sat down and rested himself, and the trackers squatted near him, and in the evening the points of their cigarettes glowed and receded. And then Kino could see that they were eating, and the soft murmur of their voices came to him.

Then darkness fell, deep and black in the mountain cleft. The animals that used the pool came near and smelled men there and drifted away again into the darkness.

He heard a murmur behind him. Juana was whispering, "Coyotito." She was begging him to be quiet. Kino heard the baby whimper, and he knew from the muffled sounds that Juana had covered his head with her shawl.

Down on the beach a match flared, and in its momentary light Kino saw that two of the men were sleeping, curled up like dogs, while the third watched, and he saw the glint of the rifle in the match light. And then the match died, but it left a picture on Kino's eyes. He could see it, just how each man was, two sleeping curled and the third squatting in the sand with the rifle between his knees.

Kino moved silently back into the cave. Juana's eyes were two sparks reflecting a low star. Kino crawled quietly close to her and he put his lips near to her cheek.

"There is a way," he said.

"But they will kill you."

"If I get first to the one with the rifle," Kino said, "I must get to him first, then I will be all right. Two are sleeping."

Her hand crept out from under her shawl and gripped his arm. "They will see your white clothes in the starlight."

"No," he said. "And I must go before moonrise."

He searched for a soft word and then gave it up. "If they kill me," he said, "lie quietly. And when they are gone away, go to Loreto."

Her hand shook a little, holding his wrist.

"There is no choice," he said. "It is the only way. They will find us in the morning."

Her voice trembled a little. "Go with God," she said.

He peered closely at her and he could see her large eyes. His hand fumbled out and found the baby, and for a moment his palm lay on Coyotito's head. And then Kino raised his hand and touched Juana's cheek, and she held her breath.

Against the sky in the cave entrance Juana could see that Kino was taking off his white clothes, for dirty and ragged though they were they would show up against the dark night. His own brown skin was a better protection for him. And then she saw how he hooked his amulet neck-string about the horn handle of his great knife, so that it hung down in front of him and left both hands free. He did not come back to her. For a moment his body was black in the cave entrance, crouched and silent, and then he was gone.

Juana moved to the entrance and looked out. She peered like an owl from the hole in the mountain, and the baby slept under the blanket on her back, his face turned sideways against her neck and shoulder. She could feel his warm breath against her skin, and Juana whispered her combination of prayer and magic, her Hail Marys and her ancient intercession, against the black unhuman things.

The night seemed a little less dark when she looked out, and to the east there was a lightning in the sky, down near the horizon where the moon would show. And, looking down, she could see the cigarette of the man on watch.

Kino edged like a slow lizard down the smooth rock shoulder. He had turned his neck-string so that the great knife hung down from his back and could not clash against the stone. His spread fingers gripped the mountain, and his bare toes found support through contact, and even his chest lay against the stone so that he would not slip. For any sound, a rolling pebble or a sigh, a little slip of flesh on rock, would rouse the watchers below. Any sound that was not germane to the night would make them alert. But the night was not silent; the little tree frogs that lived near the stream twittered like birds, and the high metallic ringing of the cicadas filled the mountain cleft. And Kino's own music was in his head, the music of the enemy, low and pulsing, nearly asleep. But the Song of the Family had become as fierce and sharp and feline as the snarl of a female puma. The family song was alive now and driving him down on the dark enemy. The harsh cicada seemed to take up its melody, and the twittering

Diego Rivera, *Copalli*, 1937, The Brooklyn Museum

tree frogs called little phrases of it.

And Kino crept silently as a shadow down the smooth mountain face. One bare foot moved a few inches and the toes touched the stone and gripped, and the other foot a few inches, and then the palm of one hand a little downward, and then the other hand, until the whole body, without seeming to move, had moved. Kino's mouth was open so that even his breath would make no sound, for he knew that he was not invisible. If the watcher, sensing movement, looked at the dark place against the stone which was his body, he could see him. Kino must move so slowly he would not draw the watcher's eyes. It took him a long time to reach the bottom and to crouch behind a little dwarf palm. His heart thundered in his chest and his hands and face were wet with sweat. He crouched and took slow long breaths to calm himself.

Only twenty feet separated him from the enemy now, and he tried to remember the ground between. Was there any stone which might trip him in his rush? He kneaded his legs against cramp and found that his muscles were jerking after their long tension. And then he looked apprehensively to the east. The moon would rise in a few mo-

ments now, and he must attack before it rose. He could see the outline of the watcher, but the sleeping men were below his vision. It was the watcher Kino must find—must find quickly and without hesitation. Silently he drew the amulet string over his shoulder and loosened the loop from the horn handle of his great knife.

He was too late, for as he rose from his crouch the silver edge of the moon slipped above the eastern horizon, and Kino sank back behind his bush.

It was an old and ragged moon, but it threw hard light and hard shadow into the mountain cleft, and now Kino could see the seated figure of the watcher on the little beach beside the pool. The watcher gazed full at the moon, and then he lighted another cigarette, and the match illumined his dark face for a moment. There could be no waiting now; when the watcher turned his head, Kino must leap. His legs were as tight as wound springs.

And then from above came a little murmuring cry. The watcher turned his head to listen and then he stood up, and one of the sleepers stirred on the ground and awakened and asked quietly, "What is it?"

"I don't know," said the watcher. "It sounded like a cry, almost like a human—like a baby."

The man who had been sleeping said, "You can't tell. Some coyote bitch with a litter. I've heard a coyote pup cry like a baby."

The sweat rolled in drops down Kino's forehead and fell into his eyes and burned them. The little cry came again and the watcher looked up the side of the hill to the dark cave.

"Coyote maybe," he said, and Kino heard the harsh click as he cocked the rifle.

"If it's a coyote, this will stop it," the watcher said as he raised the gun.

Kino was in mid-leap when the gun crashed and the barrel-flash made a picture on his eyes. The great knife swung and crunched hollowly. It bit through neck and deep into chest, and Kino was a terrible machine now. He grasped the rifle even as he wrenched free his knife. His strength and his movement and his speed were a machine. He whirled and struck the head of the seated man like a melon. The third man scrabbled away like a crab, slipped into the pool, and then he began to climb frantically, to climb up the cliff where the water penciled down. His hands and feet threshed in the tangle of the wild grapevine, and he whimpered and gibbered as he tried to get up. But Kino had become as cold and deadly as steel. Deliberately he threw the lever of the rifle, and then he raised the gun and aimed deliberately and fired. He saw his enemy tumble backward into the pool, and Kino strode to the water. In the moonlight he could see the frantic frightened eyes, and Kino aimed and fired between the eyes.

And then Kino stood uncertainly. Something was wrong, some signal was trying to get through to his brain. Tree frogs and cicadas were silent now. And then Kino's brain cleared from its red concentration and he knew the sound—the keening, moaning, rising hysterical cry from the little cave in the side of the stone mountain, the cry of death.

Everyone in La Paz remembers the return of the family; there may be some old ones who saw it, but those whose fathers and whose grandfathers told it to them remember it nevertheless. It is an event that happened to everyone.

It was late in the golden afternoon when the first little boys ran hysterically in the town and spread the word that Kino and Juana were coming back. And everyone hurried to see them. The sun was settling toward the western mountains and the shadows on the ground were long. And perhaps that was what left the deep impression on those who saw them.

The two came from the rutted country road into the city, and they were not walking in single file, Kino ahead and Juana behind, as usual, but side by side. The sun was behind them and their long shadows stalked ahead, and they seemed to carry two towers of darkness with them. Kino had a rifle across his arm and Juana carried her shawl like a sack over her shoulder. And in it was a small limp heavy bundle. The shawl was crusted with dried blood, and the bundle swayed a little as she walked. Her face was hard and lined and leathery with fatigue and with the tightness with which she fought fatigue. And her wide eyes stared inward on herself. She was as remote and as removed as Heaven. Kino's lips were thin and his jaws tight, and the people say that he carried fear with him, that he was as dangerous as a rising storm. The people say that the two seemed to be removed from human experience; that they had gone through pain and had come out on the other side; that there was almost a magical protection about them. And those people who had rushed to see them crowded back and let them pass and did not speak to them.

Kino and Juana walked through the city as though it were not there. Their eyes glanced neither right nor left nor up nor down, but stared only straight ahead. Their legs moved a little jerkily, like well-made wooden dolls, and they carried pillars of black fear about them. And as they walked through the stone and plaster city brokers peered at them from barred windows and servants put one eye to a slitted gate and mothers turned the faces of their youngest children inward against their skirts. Kino and Juana strode side by side through the stone and plaster city and down among the brush houses, and the neighbors stood back and let them pass. Juan Tomás raised his hand in greeting and did not say the greeting and left his hand in the air for a moment uncertainly.

In Kino's ears the Song of the Family was as fierce as a cry. He was immune and terrible, and his song had become a battle cry. They trudged past the burned square where their house had been without even looking at it. They cleared the brush that edged the beach and picked their way down the shore toward the water. And they did not look toward Kino's broken canoe.

And when they came to the water's edge they stopped and stared out over the Gulf. And then Kino laid the rifle down, and he dug among his clothes, and then he held the great pearl in his hand. He looked into its surface and it was gray and ulcerous. Evil faces peered from it into his eyes, and he saw the light of burning. And in the surface of the pearl he saw the frantic eyes of the man in the pool. And in the surface of the pearl he saw Coyotito lying in the little cave with the top of his head shot way. And the pearl was ugly; it was gray, like a malignant growth. And Kino heard the music of the pearl, distorted and insane. Kino's hand shook a little, and he turned slowly to Juana and held the pearl out to her. She stood beside him, still holding her dead bundle over her shoulder. She looked at the pearl in his hand for a moment and then she looked into Kino's eyes and said softly, "No, you."

And Kino drew back his arm and flung the pearl with all his might. Kino and Juana watched it go, winking and glimmering under the setting sun. They saw the little splash in the distance, and they stood side by side watching the place for a long time.

And the pearl settled into the lovely green water and dropped toward the bottom. The waving branches of the algae called to it and beckoned to it. The lights on its surface were green and lovely. It settled down to the sand bottom among the fern-like plants. Above, the surface of the water was a green mirror. And the pearl lay on the floor of the sea. A crab scampering over the bottom raised a little cloud of sand, and when it settled the pearl was gone.

And the music of the pearl drifted to a whisper and disappeared.

## THINK AND DISCUSS
### Understanding
1. According to Juan Tomás, why can't the average man know what is a fair price for the pearls?
2. What happens when Juana attempts to throw the pearl back into the sea?
3. What defense for his killing a man does Kino explain to Juana?
4. What steps does Kino take to make sure he and Juana won't be followed on their journey?

### Analyzing
5. In what ways are the business practices of the pearl buyers unfair and dishonest?
6. The pearl buyer likens Kino's pearl to fool's gold. Literally he means the pearl only looks to be of value. In what larger sense are his words true?
7. When she realizes Kino has killed a man, Juana realizes that "the old life was gone forever." What is implied by the words *old life?*
8. Describe the character-versus-character conflict that dominates the **plot** in the final chapter.
9. What do you think is the climax of the entire novel: the struggle between Kino and the trackers, resulting in Coyotito's death, or the return of Kino and Juana to their village?

### Extending
10. In view of the outcome, what is **ironic** about Kino's wish for the discovery of a pearl?
11. Is the pearl a **symbol** of both good and evil or of only one of these? Explain.
12. Do you think this parable of the pearl presents a primarily pessimistic or optimistic view of life? Explain.

## REVIEWING: Foreshadowing H✏

**See Handbook of Literary Terms, p. 800**

Foreshadowing is the use of hints made by the author to prepare readers for events that come later in the story. In *The Pearl* the author hints at future events on several occasions.

1. Early in the story, the narrator describes Kino's interest in watching an ant escaping a trap dug by an ant lion. Explain the symbolism in this description, and tell how it foreshadows events to come.
2. What does the brief description of the big fish eating the small fish (page 707) foreshadow?
3. What is foreshadowed by the description on page 726 of an ant crawling over Kino's shoe when he places his foot in the insect's path?

## THINKING SKILLS
### Evaluating

To **evaluate** is to make a judgment based on some sort of standard. For example, a jeweler will evaluate the qualities of a precious stone in order to determine its worth. You can evaluate aspects of John Steinbeck's writing.

1. Why do you think Steinbeck gave names only to his major characters?
2. Is this decision to name only a few characters an effective device, or should the author have given names to the doctor, the priest, and the pearl broker?
3. Does the absence of names relate in any way to the idea of *The Pearl* being a parable, a story that carries a moral or ethical principle?

## VOCABULARY
### Synonyms

A synonym is a word that has the same or nearly the same meaning as another word. On a separate sheet of paper, rewrite each of the sentences below, replacing the word in italics

with its synonym from the list below.

| | | |
|---|---|---|
| benign | puma | precipitated |
| semblance | countenance | transfigured |
| judicious | monolithic | avarice |
| disparagement | freshet | resinous |

1. Corruption is often the result of uncontrolled *greed*.
2. Although the queen had absolute control, she was generally considered a *kind* ruler.
3. After a lively debate, the city council may *approve* the proposal.
4. The hostile actions are believed to have *started* the war.
5. While in the mountains, the hunters encountered several *wildcats*.
6. The thief's story was an obvious lie; it had no *appearance* of truth whatsoever.
7. When Barb put on the strong glasses, everything before her suddenly became *transformed* into a grotesque figure.
8. They erected a *monumental* statue in their leader's honor.
9. The chairman was known for his thoughtful, *wise* decisions.
10. The children couldn't wait to wade in the cool *stream*.

## COMPOSITION ✎
### Writing About Setting

In three to five paragraphs analyze the setting of *The Pearl*. Is it of major or minor importance to the plot? What effects does it have on the characters? First jot down major events. Beside these events, jot down the setting in which each takes place. Then consider these questions about setting before writing your composition. See "Writing About Setting" in the Writer's Handbook. Assume you are writing for your teacher.

### Writing About Theme

Write a three-paragraph paper in which you state the theme of *The Pearl* and analyze how characterization, conflict, and symbolism contribute to this theme. Assume you are writing for a literary magazine. See "Writing About Theme" in the Writer's Handbook.

## ENRICHMENT
### Conducting Literary Research

Authors often make allusions, or references to people, events, and ideas, in novels. Investigating such references is one way of broadening the reader's knowledge. Select one of the following assignments and make an oral report to your class.

1. When the priest says "Kino, thou art named after a great man—and a father of the Church," he is referring to Saint Thomas Aquinas. Find out about Thomas Aquinas, a famous historical figure, and present an oral report to the class. You may want to use library reference works such as encyclopedias, biographical dictionaries, and history books in your research.

2. The following quotation describes in part the colonial relationship between Mexico and Spain: "This was the [pearl] bed that had raised the King of Spain to be a great power in Europe in past years, had helped to pay for his wars, and had decorated the churches for his soul's sake." Research some facts about Mexico's colonial history and present a brief oral report. Use history books and encyclopedias in your research.

### Steinbeck Finds a Pearl

Although John Steinbeck is not considered simply a regional writer, a number of his novels do reflect life in twentieth-century California and nearby Baja California, Mexico. His novels *The Grapes of Wrath, Tortilla Flat, Of Mice and Men,* and others deal with laborers in rural California. *The Pearl,* which is set in the coastal region of Mexico, was inspired by a Mexican legend that Steinbeck learned while conducting research in the area.

According to the tale, an Indian boy from La Paz, Mexico, found a giant pearl in the Gulf of California. After visiting several appraisers, the boy became angry and discouraged because each of them had offered him a ridiculously small amount of money in exchange for the pearl. When he realized that he would never get a fair price for his pearl, the boy hid the pearl beneath a stone on the beach. After being attacked and almost killed by thieves in search of the pearl, he cursed it and threw it back into the ocean, thus freeing himself from the pain and suffering that it had inflicted upon him.

Nobody knows whether the incident ever really happened, although many people in the region held it to be true. In his book *The Log from the Sea of Cortez,* Steinbeck says it is "so much like a parable that it almost can't be [true]. The Indian boy is too heroic, too wise." In writing *The Pearl,* Steinbeck has expounded upon this tale, emphasizing his admiration for the poor and his belief in the basic goodness of people and the struggle against injustice.

## Write Good Endings

Good writers put a great deal of thought into the final chapters and words of their books. They know that a reader's ultimate feeling about a piece of writing may depend on the work's conclusion. Providing a good ending is an unrepeatable opportunity for the writer.

Some poor endings just fizzle out, weakening what might have been forceful writing. Some endings fail to tie together loose ends, leaving the reader confused. A good ending clearly establishes the author's intent. The ending may challenge the reader to further reflect on ideas posed by the author.

Of equal importance to the final pages of a novel are the endings of each chapter. The ending of a chapter can add a new twist to a story. At the end of the first chapter of *The Pearl*, when Juana and Kino are turned away from the doctor's gate without receiving treatment for their baby, Kino loses his temper, strikes the gate with a crushing blow, and splits open his knuckles. This moment reveals a new side of Kino. Until this point, Kino has held inside himself any rage he feels against the doctor. He has shown only humility in the face of power and authority. Kino's outburst hints at his deep frustration and his readiness to fight for himself and for his family.

The end of the second chapter surprises the reader. It is difficult to tell if Kino's shout is a shout of joy or of terror, of hope or of fear. Steinbeck creates this ambiguity to cause the reader to question whether the pearl bodes good or evil.

> Then Kino's fist closed over the pearl and his emotion broke over him. He put back his head and howled. His eyes rolled up and he screamed and his body was rigid. The men in the other canoes looked up, startled, and then

they dug their paddles into the sea and raced toward Kino's canoe.

The fourth chapter ends on a note that contrasts sharply with the violent action that precedes it. Steinbeck uses the ending to remind the reader of Kino's tender side. The ending also breaks the mounting tension of the novel.

The conclusion of *The Pearl* portrays Juana and Kino's ultimate rejection of the pearl and of the life that accompanied their sea-drawn gem. Steinbeck paints a vivid scene of the pearl's return to the sea floor.

> And the pearl settled into the lovely green water and dropped toward the bottom. The waving branches of the algae called to it and beckoned to it. The lights on its surface were green and lovely. It settled down to the sand bottom among the fern-like plants. Above, the surface of the water was a green mirror. And the pearl lay on the floor of the sea. A crab scampering over the bottom raised a little cloud of sand, and when it settled the pearl was gone.
>
> And the music of the pearl drifted to a whisper and disappeared.

Steinbeck's novel concludes gently. Yet it raises questions in the reader's mind. Are Juana and Kino resigned to a life of poverty or will they find new ways to challenge the bonds that hold them in submission? Will their lives be better or worse after disposing of the pearl?

---

As you read, notice how good endings challenge you to think beyond the story.

As you write, use endings that challenge the reader to think beyond the story or piece of writing.

---

## INTRODUCTION to *Master and Man*

## BIOGRAPHY of Leo Tolstoy   1828–1910

Born in czarist Russia, Tolstoy enjoyed the privileges of an aristocratic family. For forty years he took advantage of his wealth and social position, but then he turned against his class, feeling that wealth corrupted people. Turning over his fortune to his family, he spent his remaining years in poverty. Tolstoy's early writings are about people with money and title, complex characters who reveal the subtle virtues and vices of humanity. During this period he completed *War and Peace* and began writing *Anna Karenina*, both recognized as masterpieces of literary realism. In these novels Tolstoy criticized the social shams of the aristocracy and their rampant material values. Searching for a way to draw closer to God, Tolstoy lived and worked with the peasants. His religious readings led him to believe in a doctrine of nonresistance, upon which he based the latter part of his life. He condemned his earlier writings and turned from the realistic to the idealistic. He chose to inspire mankind, not to dwell on its imperfections. *Master and Man*, written in 1895, reveals this philosophy.

Tolstoy wrote *Master and Man* when Russia was under the control of a czar, or emperor. It is set decades before the 1917 revolution that led to the formation of the Soviet Union. Thus it is set in a time when the opulent wealth of the aristocratic minority contrasted sharply with the poverty of the peasant masses.

### The Russian Peasant

Prior to emancipation in 1861, Russian peasants were divided into four groups. Serfs were owned by the landowners. "Possessionary" peasants worked in factories and were the property of factory owners. Instead of wages, they were given small plots of farmland. They went with the factory upon its sale. State peasants and those owned by the crown lived in communes and could choose their own village government. They could not be sold without the land that they farmed.

Tolstoy favored emancipation; but such ideas were met with hostility by the majority of the nobility, and few attempts at land reform were successful. Only when the peasants began to show signs of revolt did the nobility agree to set them free. Thus, the peasants that Tolstoy writes about in *Master and Man* are free agents. Like their ancestors, however, they remain at the bottom of the social scale.

# Master and Man

**Leo Tolstoy**   Russia

# I

It was in the seventies, the day after the feast of Saint Nicholas[1] in the winter. There had been a festival in the parish, and the church sexton, Vassili Andreitch Brekhunoff,[2] (who was also a merchant of the second guild), had been forced to remain at home, since not only was his presence necessary at the church, but he had been receiving and entertaining some of his friends and relations. Now, however, the last of his guests had departed, and he was able to get himself ready to visit a neighboring landowner, for the purpose of buying some timber for which he had long been in treaty. He was in a hurry to be off, lest rival buyers from the town should deprive him of this eligible bargain. The only reason why the young landowner had asked ten thousand rubles[3] for the timber was that Vassili Andreitch had offered him seven—and seven represented about a third of its value. Perhaps Vassili might have gone on haggling still further (for the wood was in his own district, and there was a recognized agreement between the local merchants and himself that one merchant should not bid against another in the same district), were it not that he had heard that the Government forest contractors were also thinking of coming to treat for the Goviatchkinsky timber, and therefore he had better make up his mind to go at once and clinch the matter. So, as soon as ever the festival was over, he took seven hundred rubles of his own out of the strong-box, added to them two thousand three hundred more out of the church funds which he had by him (making three thousand in all), and counted them carefully. Then he placed them in his pocketbook and got ready to go.

Nikita—the only one of Vassili's workmen who was not drunk that day—ran to put the horse in. Nikita was not drunk that day for the reason that he had formerly been a toper, but, after pawning his jacket and leather boots for drink during the meat-eating days,[4] had suddenly foresworn liquor altogether, and drunk nothing during the second month. Even on the present occasion he had kept

---

1. *seventies . . . Saint Nicholas.* The setting is December 7 during the 1870s. The feast of Nicholas, patron saint of Russia, is December 6. On that day, gifts were exchanged, inspired by the legend of St. Nicholas, who is said to have given gifts to the poor. Santa Claus has his origin in St. Nicholas.
2. *Vassili Andreitch Brekhunoff* (vä′sē lē än drā′yich bri kü′nyôf). The middle name in Russia is a patronymic, a name based on one's father's name and a suffix. *Andreitch* comes from a form of Andrew.
3. *rubles,* units of money in the Soviet Union and formerly in the Russian empire. At the time of this story the ruble was worth about fifty cents.
4. *meat-eating days,* the final days before a fast, a period when church members abstain from meat or follow other religious dietary restrictions.

Leo Tolstoy, *Master and Man,* J. M. Dent & Sons Ltd., 1910.

Ivan Kramskoy, *Study for
"Peasant with a Bridle,"*
1882, The Russian
Museum, Leningrad

his vow, in spite of the temptation of the liquor which had flowed in all directions during the first two days of the festival.

He was a *muzhik*[5] of about fifty, and hailed from a neighboring village—where, however, it was said that he was not a householder, but had lived most of his life among strangers. Everywhere he was valued for his handiness, industry and strength, as well as, still more, for his kindly, cheerful disposition. Yet he had never remained long in any one place, since twice a year, or more,

he had been accustomed to get drunk, and at those times would not only pawn everything he possessed, but grow uproarious and quarrelsome as well. Vassili himself had dismissed him more than once, yet had always taken him on again because of the store which he set by his honesty, care for animals, and (most important of all) cheapness. In fact, Vassili allowed Nikita a wage,

---

**5. *muzhik*** (mü zhik′), a Russian peasant, or working-class farmer [< Russian].

not of eighty rubles a year—the true market value of such a workman—but of forty only. Moreover, this wage was doled out irregularly and in driblets, as well as, for the most part, not in cash at all, but in the form of goods purchased at a high price from Vassili's own store.

Nikita's wife, Martha—a rugged dame who had once been good-looking—lived at home with their little lad and two girls, but never invited her husband to come and see her; since, in the first place, she had lived for the last twenty years with a cooper (originally a *muzhik* from a distant village who had come to lodge in the hut), and, in the second, because, although she could do what she liked with her husband when he was sober, she dreaded him like fire when he was drunk. Once, for instance, when drunk at home he had seized the occasion to avenge himself upon his wife for all his submissiveness to her when sober by breaking into her private box, possessing himself of her best clothes, laying all the gowns and other gewgaws upon the wood-block, and chopping them into shreds with an axe. Yet all his earnings were handed over to Martha. Never once had he disputed this arrangement. In fact, only a couple of days before the festival she had driven over to Vassili's store, and been supplied by him with white meal, tea, sugar, and a pint of vodka, to the value of three rubles, as well as with five rubles in cash—for all of which she had thanked Vassili as for a particular favor, although, as a matter of fact, Vassili was in Nikita's debt to the extent of at least twenty rubles.

"What agreement need you and I make together?" Vassili had said to Nikita. "Take what you need as you earn it. I don't do business as other folks do—keep my creditors waiting, and go in for detailed accounts and deductions and so on. You and I can trust one another. Only serve me well, and I shall never fail you."

In saying this, Vassili really had believed that he was being good to Nikita, for he could speak so persuasively and had always been so entirely sup-

ported in his decisions by his dependents, from Nikita upwards, that even he himself had come to feel comfortably persuaded that he was not cheating them, but actually benefiting them.

"Yes, yes, I understand you, Vassili Andreitch," Nikita had replied. "I understand you perfectly well, and will serve and work for you as for my own father."

Nevertheless Nikita had not been ignorant that Vassili was cheating him. He had only felt that it would be no use his trying to get a detailed account out of his master, and that, in default of another place to go to, he had better grin and bear it and take what he could get.

So, when ordered to harness the horse, Nikita proceeded to the stable in his usual cheerful, good-natured manner, and with the usual easy stride of his rather waddling legs. There he took down from a peg the heavy headstall, with its straps and tassels, and, rattling the bit against the side-pieces, proceeded to the stall where the horse was standing which he was to get ready.

"Oh ho, so you find time long, do you, my little beauty?" he said in reply to the low whinny of welcome which greeted him from the shapely, middle-sized, low-rumped, dark-brown stallion cob which was the sole occupant of the loose-box.

"Nay, nay," he went on. "You are in a hurry to be off, I daresay, but I must water you first," (he always spoke to the animal as one might speak to a being capable of understanding human speech). Then, having wiped the sleek, though dusty and harness-galled, back of the cob with a cloth, he adjusted the headstall to the handsome young head, pulled the ears and forehead-tuft through, let down the halter, and led the animal out to drink. As soon as Brownie had picked his way gingerly out of the dung-heaped stall he grew lively and threw up his heels, pretending that he wanted to kick Nikita as the latter trotted beside him to the water-trough.

"Quiet then, quiet then, you little rascal!" exclaimed Nikita, though well aware that Brownie was taking good care to throw out his hind leg in such a manner as only to graze Nikita's greasy fur coat, not strike it direct—a trick which Nikita always admired. Having drunk his fill of cold water, the animal snorted as he stood twitching his strong, wet lips, from the hairs of which the bright, transparent drops kept dripping back into the trough. Then he stood motionless for an instant or two, as though engaged in thought, and then suddenly gave a loud neigh.

"You don't want any more. You wouldn't get it even if you did, so you needn't ask for it," said Nikita, explaining his conduct to Brownie with absolute gravity and precision. Then he set off running back to the stable, holding the spirited young cob by the halter as the animal kicked and snorted all across the yard. None of the other workmen were about—only the cook's husband, who had come over for the festival from another village.

"Go in, will you, my boy," said Nikita to this man, "and ask which sledge I am to get ready— the big one or the little one?"

The man disappeared into the house (which was iron-roofed and stood upon a raised foundation), and returned in a moment with a message that it was the little sledge which was to be used. Meanwhile Nikita had slipped the collar over the cob's head and adjusted the brass-studded saddle-piece, and was now walking, with the light-painted *douga*[6] in one hand and the end of the cob's halter in the other, towards the two sledges standing beneath the shed.

"If the little sledge, then the little sledge," he remarked, and proceeded to back the clever little animal into the shafts (it pretending meanwhile to bite him) and, with the other man's assistance, to harness it to the vehicle. When all was ready and there remained only the reins to be put on, Nikita sent his assistant to the stable for some straw, and then to the storehouse for a sack.

"There now, that will do," said Nikita as he stuffed into the sledge the freshly-cut oaten straw which the man had brought. "But nay, nay" (to Brownie). "You need not prick your ears like that!—Well, suppose we put the straw so, and the sack on the top of it. Then it will be comfortable to sit upon,"—and he suited the action to the words by tucking the edges of the sack under the straw disposed around the seat.

"Thank you, my boy," he added to the cook's husband. "Two pairs of hands work quicker than one." After that he buckled the loose ends of the reins together, mounted the splashboard, and drove the good little steed, all impatient to be off, across the frozen dung of the yard to the entrance-gates.

"Uncle Mikit, Uncle Mikit[7]!" came the shrill little voice of a seven-year-old boy from behind him, as the youngster ran hastily out of the porch into the yard—a youngster who was dressed in a short jacket of black fur, new white bast shoes, and a cozy cap. "Let *me* get up too," he implored, fastening his jacket as he ran.

"Well, well! Come here then, my dear," said Nikita, pulling up. Then, seating his master's pale, thin little son behind him, he drove the boy, beaming with pleasure, out into the street.

It was now three o'clock in the afternoon and freezing hard, the thermometer registering only ten degrees; yet the weather was dull and gusty, and fully half the sky was covered by a low, dark bank of cloud. In the courtyard the air was still, but directly one stepped into the street outside the wind became more noticeable and the snow could be seen twirling itself about in wreaths as it was swept from the roof of a neighboring outbuilding into the corner near the bath-house. Hardly had Nikita returned through the gates and turned the cob's head towards the steps when Vassili Andreitch—a cigarette between his lips, and a sheepskin coat upon his shoulders, fastened

---

6. *douga* (dü′gä), curved harness frame [< Russian].

7. **Uncle Mikit.** *Uncle, aunt, grandfather,* and other titles are used in Russia as terms of affection applied to any older person. *Mikit* is a diminutive, or shortened form, of *Nikita*.

Ivan Bilibin, *Illustration to Pushkin's "Tale of Tsar Saltan"* (detail), 1905

tightly and low down with a belt—came out of the house-door upon the high, snow-trampled flight of steps, making them creak loudly under his felt boots as he did so.

Drawing the last whiff from his cigarette, he threw down the end and stamped it out. Then, puffing the smoke out of his moustache, he glanced at the cob as it re-entered the gates, and began to turn out the corners of his coat-collar in such a way that the fur should be next his face on either side (his face was clean-shaven, except for a moustache), and yet not liable to be fouled with his breath.

"So you have managed it, you little monkey?" he exclaimed as he caught sight of his little boy seated in the sledge. Vassili was a little animated with the wine which he had been drinking with his guests, and therefore the more ready to approve of all that belonged to him and all that he had done in life. The aspect of his little son at that moment—of the little boy whom he intended to be his heir—afforded him the greatest satisfaction as he stood blinking at him and grinning with his long teeth. In the porch behind Vassili stood his pale, thin wife, Vassilia Andreitcha. She was with child, and had her head and shoulders muffled up in a woollen shawl, so that only her eyes were visible.

"Had not you better take Nikita with you?" she said, stepping timidly forward from the porch. Vassili returned her no answer, but merely frowned angrily as though somehow displeased at her words, and spat upon the ground.

"You see, you will be traveling with money on you," she continued in the same anxious tone. "Besides, the weather might grow worse."

"Don't I know the road, then, that I must needs have a guide with me?" burst out Vassili with that unnatural stiffening of his lips which marked his conversations with buyers and sellers when he was particularly desirous of enunciating each syllable distinctly.

"Yes, do take him, for heaven's sake, I implore you," repeated his wife as she shifted her shawl to protect the other side of her face.

"Goodness! Why, you stick to me like a bathing-towel!" cried Vassili. "Where can I find room for him on the sledge?"

"I am quite ready to go," put in Nikita, cheerfully. "Only, someone else must feed the other horses while I am away" (this last to his mistress).

"Yes, yes, I will see to that, Nikita," she replied. "I will tell Simon to do it."

"Then I am to go with you, Vassili Andreitch?" said Nikita, expectantly.

"Well, I suppose I must humor the good lady," answered Vassili. "Only, if you go, you had better put on a rather better, not to say warmer, diplomatist's uniform than that,"—and he smiled and winked one eye at Nikita's fur jacket, which, truth to tell, had holes under its two arms, down the back, and round the sides, besides being greasy, matted, shorn of hooks, and torn into strips round the edges.

"Here, my good fellow! Come and hold the cob, will you?" shouted Nikita across the yard to the cook's husband.

"No, no, let *me* do it," cried the little boy, drawing his small, red, frozen hands out of his pockets and catching hold of the chilly reins.

"Don't be too long over your new uniform, please," said Vassili to Nikita with a grin.

"No, no, Vassili Andreitch—I shan't be a moment," protested Nikita as he went shuffling hurriedly off in his old felt boots towards the servants' quarters across the yard.

"Now then, my good Arininshka, give me my *khalat*[8] from the stove! I am going with master!" shouted Nikita as he burst into the hut and seized his belt from a peg. The cook, who had been enjoying a good sleep after dinner and was now getting tea ready for her husband, greeted Nikita cheerfully, and, catching the infection of his haste, began to bustle about as briskly as himself. First she took from near the stove a shabby, but well-aired, cloth *khalat*, and set about shaking and smoothing it out with all possible speed.

"*You* are far more fit to go with the master than I am," he said to the cook, in accordance with his usual habit of saying something civil to everyone with whom he came in contact. Then, twisting about him the shabby, well-worn belt, he succeeded first in compressing his not over-prominent stomach, and then in drawing the belt with a great effort over his fur coat.

"There you are!" he said (not to the cook but to the belt) as he tucked its ends in. "You can't very well burst apart like that." Then, with a hoist and much heaving of the shoulders, he drew the cloth *khalat* over all (stretching its back well, to give looseness in the arms), and patted it into place under the armpits. Finally he took his mittens from a shelf.

"Now," said he, "I am all right."

"But you have forgotten about your feet," cried the cook. "Those boots are awful."

Nikita stopped as if struck by this.

"Yes, perhaps I ought to ch—" he began, but

---

8. *Arininshka* (ä′rē nin′shka) . . . *khalat* (kə lät′). *Arininshka* is the name of the cook. A *khalat* is a man's knee-length frock coat, not much warmer than a housecoat or robe.

changed his mind, and exclaiming, "No, he might go without me if I did—I have not far to walk," bolted off into the yard.

"But won't you be cold in that *khalat* only, Nikita?" said his mistress when he reached the sledge.

"No indeed! How should I? It is *very* warm," answered Nikita as he disposed the straw over the forepart of the sledge in such a manner as would conceal his feet after he had mounted, and thrust the whip (not needed for so willing a steed) under the straw.

Vassili had already taken his seat, his broad back, with its double covering of furs, filling almost the entire rear part of the sledge. Then, taking up the reins, he flicked the cob with them, while Nikita jumped into the forepart of the sledge just as it started, and sat leaning forward to the left and sticking out one leg.

# II

The good little cob moved the sledge rapidly along with a light creaking of the runners as he trotted at a round pace over the well-beaten, frozen piece of road leading to the village.

"Hullo! What have *you* jumped up for?" cried Vassili, suddenly, clearly enjoying the fact that an unauthorized passenger was trying to perch himself upon the runners behind. ("Give me the whip, Nikita!" he interjected). "*I'll* thrash you, you young rascal! Run along home to your mother!"

The boy jumped off. Brownie broke into a gallop, but soon changed to a trot again.

Kresti, where Vassili lived, was a hamlet of six houses only, and when they had got beyond the blacksmith's hut at the end they at once perceived that the wind was much stronger than they had thought it to be, and that the road ahead was almost invisible. The track of the sledge became snowed over almost as fast as made, and only the fact that the road was a little higher than the ground on either side of it rendered it at all distinguishable. The snow was whirling over the whole countryside and blotting out the horizon, while the Teliatinsky forest—generally clearly visible—now showed only as a dark mass looming at intervals through the snow-dust. The wind was blowing from the left, and kept turning Brownie's mane over his thick, fat neck and blowing his feathery tail—bound at the top in a plain knot—across his flank. Owing to the wind, too, Nikita's tall coat-collar, where he sat on the weather side of the sledge, kept pressing itself tightly against his cheeks and nose.

"The cob can't get up much of a pace today; there's too much snow on the ground," said Vassili, who prided himself on the excellence of his steed. "Once I drove him to Pashutino in half an hour."

"What did you say?" asked Nikita, whose tall coat-collar had prevented him from hearing what was said.

"I said that I have driven to Pashutino in half an hour," bawled Vassili.

"That's something to boast of indeed! He's a good animal if ever there was one!" commented Nikita, after which they kept silence for a while. Vassili, however, was inclined to be talkative.

"What do you think? I told your wife the other day not to let her cooper drink all the tea," he bawled once more, in the firm conviction that Nikita must be feeling flattered at being talked to by such an important and highly-educated man as himself, as well as so greatly taken with his own joke about the cooper that it never entered into his head that the topic might be distasteful to Nikita. However, the latter had once more failed to catch his master's words for the violence of the wind, so Vassili repeated his pleasantry at the very top of his "educated" voice.

"God be with her, Vassili Andreitch!" returned Nikita when he understood. "I never interfere with their affairs. She has given me little cause for blame, and, so long as she treats the lad well, I merely say, 'God be with her!' "

"Well, well," said Vassili, and changed the subject. "Are you going to buy a horse in the spring?" he continued.

"I only wish I could," replied Nikita as he turned his coat-collar back a little and leant over towards his master. The new topic interested him, and he wanted to catch every word. "My little lad is fast growing up and ought to learn to plow, but I have squandered all my money."

"Well, if you'll take the low-rumped nag off my hands I won't ask you much for it," said Vassili, whose spirits were rising, and who therefore recurred instinctively to his ruling passion—the passion which absorbed his whole faculties—namely, the pursuit of bargains.

"I would rather you lent me fifteen rubles and let me go and buy one in the horse-market," answered Nikita, knowing full well that the low-rumped nag which Vassili was asking him to buy was worth no more than seven rubles at the outside, but that as soon as ever Vassili had handed him over the animal he would swear that it was worth at least twenty-five, and therefore retain about half a year's wages to cover the amount.

"The horse is a splendid one," went on Vassili in his precise, businesslike tones. "I want to do you a service as well as myself. Honestly, now. Brekhunoff would never do *any* man a bad turn. I would rather be out of pocket myself than see others so. Yes, on my honor. The horse is a magnificent one."

"I am sure of it," said Nikita with a sigh. Then, finding it useless to try and listen further, he turned up his coat-collar again, and his face and ear became covered in a twinkling. For about half an hour they drove in silence. The wind kept getting down Nikita's legs and through a hole in his mitten, but he hunched his shoulders and breathed into the coat-collar muffled over his mouth, so that he did not feel the cold very much after all.

"What do you think? Shall we go round by Karamishevo or straight on?" asked Vassili presently. The road by way of Karamishevo was the longer and the rougher one, yet, on the other hand, it was clearly defined by posts on either side. The road straight on was a good deal nearer, but used by few travelers, as well as either altogether devoid of posts or marked only by small ones which would now be almost drifted over. Nikita debated matters for a moment.

"The road by Karamishevo is longer than the other one, but a good deal the easier to drive over," he decided at length.

"Yet, if we go straight on," pursued Vassili, who was inclined towards the route he named, "we have only to get into the hollow, and then we can't possibly lose our way. It will be splendid going through the forest."

"As you wish," said Nikita, and turned up his coat-collar again.

Accordingly Vassili had his way, and after driving about half a verst[9] further on, turned to the left where a tall young oak tree stood. Its branches and the few dead leaves which still clung to them were being madly dashed about by the wind, which, after the turning, met the travelers almost full in the face. Light snow began to fall, and Vassili tightened the reins, puffed out his cheeks, and let the breath escape slowly from under his moustache, while Nikita dozed. They had driven like this in silence for about ten minutes when Vassili gave an exclamation.

"What is it?" asked Nikita, opening his eyes.

Vassili returned no answer, but twisted himself round to look back. Then he gazed ahead. The cob was still trotting along, his flanks steaming with sweat.

"What is it?" asked Nikita again.

"What is it, do you say?" cried Vassili in angry mimicry of the question. "Why, only that I

---

9. *verst,* a Russian unit of distance equal to about 3,500 feet (1,067 meters) or two thirds of a mile.

can't see any posts now. We must be off the road."

"Wait a minute, then, while I go and look for it," said Nikita as he leapt lightly from the sledge and, taking the whip from beneath the straw, went ahead and towards the left—the side on which he had been sitting. The snow had not been very deep that year, so that, as yet, the road had been easily passable the whole way along; but here there were patches where it reached knee-high and smothered Nikita's boot-tops. He kept on trying the ground, both with his feet and the whip, as he walked along; yet the road had vanished.

"Well?" said Vassili when Nikita returned to the sledge.

"No road on this side," answered Nikita. "I must try the other."

"There seems to be something dark showing ahead," remarked Vassili. "Go and see what it is."

Nikita did so, and found it to be only a spot where the naked sprouts of some winter corn sown on a piece of black earth were making a dark patch on the snow as they waved before the wind. Nikita circled round to the right, and then returned to the sledge again, beat the snow from his *khalat* and boots, and remounted.

"We must go to the right," he said with decision. "The wind was on our left a moment ago, but now it is straight in our faces. Yes, to the right," he concluded with an air of conviction.

Vassili just managed to catch what he said, and turned the cob in the direction indicated; yet no road revealed itself there, although they went on for a considerable time. Meanwhile the wind showed no signs of dropping, and the snow continued.

"Well, we are altogether lost now, Vassili Andreitch," observed Nikita, suddenly, and half as though he were pleased at the fact. "What is this, though?" he went on, pointing to a blackened potato-top[10] which was projecting above the snow. Vassili at once stopped the cob, which was now sweating heavily and moving its stout flanks with difficulty.

"Yes, what is it?" he echoed.

"It means that we are on the Zakharovek estate. That is where we have got to."

"Surely not?" exclaimed Vassili.

"Yes, it is as I say," insisted Nikita. "You can tell, too, by the sound of the sledge-runners that we are driving over a potato-field. Look at the bits of potato-tops which they have dragged off. Yes, these are the Zakharovek market-gardens."

"A fine place to get landed in!" said Vassili. "Well, what is to be done now?"

"We must keep on going to the right, and we shall be sure to come out somewhere or other," answered Nikita. "If we don't actually strike Zakharovek we shall at all events come across some tenant's farm."

Vassili assented, and drove the cob forward in the direction Nikita had advised. They proceeded thus for a considerable time, now coming upon bare grass, now upon rough patches of frozen ground, over which the sledge went grating loudly. Then, again, they would find themselves passing over stubble of winter or spring corn, with the dead straw or sticks of weeds projecting above the snow and waving madly before the wind. More than once they found themselves laboring through deep, level, pure-white drifts, with nothing whatever showing above the top. All the while the snow-fall continued and the snow-dust whirled about the ground. The cob was evidently failing now, for his flanks were white and steaming with sweat, and he proceeded only at a foot's pace. Suddenly he stumbled, and then plunged forward into some ditch or gully. Vassili was for pulling up, but Nikita shouted to him:

"Why stop? Go on, go on! We must get him out of this. Now then, my beauty! Now then, my

---

10. *potato-top*, the top of a potato plant.

pet!" he went on to the cob encouragingly as he leapt from the sledge—only to stick fast in the ditch himself. However, the cob extricated himself presently, and scrambled back onto the frozen ridge which lined the bank. Evidently it was a ditch dug out by hand.

"Where are we now?" queried Vassili.

"We must find that out," answered Nikita. "Let us push on a bit, and we shall arrive somewhere."

"Isn't that the Goviatchkinsky forest, surely?" said his master presently, pointing to something black looming through the snow ahead.

"It may be. We had better push on and find out," rejoined Nikita. As a matter of fact, he had already distinguished the oblong patches of some withered vine-leaves showing against the blackness of the object in question, and knew, therefore, that is was more likely to be a habitation of some kind than a forest; yet he hesitated to speak before he knew for certain. Sure enough, they had not proceeded more than twenty yards beyond the ditch when trees showed up clearly before them and some melancholy sound became audible. Nikita had guessed rightly. It was not a forest they had come to, but a row of tall vines, with a few withered leaves still quivering upon them. Evidently they marked the trench of a threshing-floor. Just as the travelers had almost reached these vines and could tell that the melancholy sound arose from the wind sweeping through their rustling leaves, the cob took a sudden plunge upwards with his fore hoofs, pulled up his hindquarters after them, turned to the left, and went on with the snow no longer reaching to his knees. It was the road again!

"Now we have reached it!" exclaimed Nikita, "but the Lord only knows where!"

The cob, however, never faltered, but went straight ahead along the snow-swept road; until, just as they had covered about a hundred yards, there uprose before them the rectangular outlines of a wattled barn, with its roof piled with snow and the snow-dust blowing from it in clouds. Passing the barn, the road wound back into the wind a little, and they found themselves in a snowdrift. A short way further on could be seen an opening between two buildings, so that it was clear that the road lay through the snowdrift, and that the latter must be surmounted. Sure enough, they had no sooner accomplished this than they found themselves in a village street, in the nearest courtyard of which some frozen linen was hanging from a line and rustling distractedly in the wind. It comprised two shirts (one of them white and the other one red), a pair of drawers, some leggings, and a petticoat, of which the white shirt was particularly abandoned in its antics as it waved its sleeves before the wind.

"Ugh, the lazy woman—though I am sorry to have to say it of her!" said Nikita with a glance at the waving shirts. "To think of not getting one's linen ready for the festival!"

# III

The wind was as strong at the entrance to the street as it had been in the open country, and the roadway piled with snow, but in the middle of the hamlet everything seemed warm and quiet and cheerful. A dog came barking out of a yard, while in another yard an old woman came running from somewhere, with her head swathed in a handkerchief, but stopped as she was making for the door of the hut and stood for a moment on the threshold to gaze at the new arrivals. From the middle of the village came the sound of girls singing, and altogether there seemed to be less wind and cold and snow here than outside.

"Why, this must be Grishkino,[11]" said Vassili.

"It is," replied Nikita: and Grishkino it was.

---

11. *Grishkino* (gri'shkin ə), the name of a village.

It turned out afterwards that they had left the road upon their right, and traveled some eight versts at a tangent to their former direction—though still more or less in the direction of their proper goal. Yet Goviatchkina[12] was fully five versts from Grishkino.

Halfway up the street they encountered a tall man walking in the center of the roadway.

"Who are you?" he cried as he stopped. Then, recognizing Vassili, he caught hold of one of the shafts, rested his hands upon it, and climbed to the seat of the sledge. It was a friend of Vassili's named Isai,[13] known as the worst horse-thief in the district.

"Well, and whither is God taking you now?" said Isai, suffusing Nikita with the smell of the vodka which he had been drinking.

"We have been trying to get to Goviatchkina."

"What a way to take, then! You should have gone by Malakhovo."

"It's no good saying what we *should* have done when we didn't do it," retorted Vassili as he pulled up the cob.

"That is a good animal," remarked Isai, looking the cob over, and passing his hand under the now drooping stump of its stout, knotted tail in his usual horsey manner. "Are you going to stay the night here?"

"No, my friend. We have further to go yet."

"You had much better stay. But who is this? Why, if it isn't Nikita Stepanitch![14]"

"Yes, no one else," replied Nikita. "But pray tell us, brother, how to avoid losing our way again."

"How to avoid losing your way again? Why, turn back, go right along the street, and the road is straight in front of you. Don't turn to the left, but keep on until you come nearly to a large village, and then—to the right."

"But whereabouts is the turning near that village?" asked Nikita again. "Is it on the summer or the winter road?"

"The winter. You will come to a copse there, and exactly opposite the copse there stands a tall, ragged oaken post. That is where you are to turn off."

Accordingly Vassili turned the cob's head round, and drove off down the street again.

"You had better have stayed the night here," shouted Isai after them, but Vassili shook up the cob and returned no answer. To cover five versts of level road, of which two would run through forest, seemed an easy enough prospect, especially in view of the fact that the snow now seemed to them to have ceased and the wind to have dropped.

Passing from the street again, with its roadway trampled hard and showing black here and there with patches of fresh dung, they drove past the yard where the linen was hanging out to dry, (the white shirt had now partly torn away from the line and was dangling by one frozen sleeve only), and went on until they came to the vine-stocks with their quaintly murmuring leaves. Here they were in the open country again—only to discover that the blizzard had in no way abated, but rather, on the contrary, increased. The road was drifted over ahead, and nothing but the posts alongside could keep them from leaving it. These posts, too, were difficult to distinguish, since the wind was head on.

Vassili knit his brows as he bent forward to watch for the posts, but gave the cob more rein than before, and trusted to its sagacity. Sure enough, the cob never faltered, but went on turning to the left or right, according to the windings of the road, and feeling for it with his hoofs; so that, despite the fact that the wind kept rising and the snow falling ever thicker and thicker, the

---

12. *Goviatchkina* (gô vyäch′kǝ nä), the name of the hamlet at the Goviatchkinsky forest, Vassili's destination.
13. *Isai* (ē sä′ē).
14. *Stepanitch* (ste pän′yich), Nikita's patronymic name, which might be rendered in English as *Stephen's son.*

posts remained plainly visible on either side.

They had been driving like this for about ten minutes when there suddenly loomed up something black in front of the cob—something which was moving along in a tangled whirl of wind-driven snow. It was a party of fellow-travelers whom Brownie had outpaced, and the back of whose sledge he had actually struck into with his fore-hoofs.

"Pull out! Hi! Look out in front of you!" came in a chorus of shouts from this vehicle, and Vassili pulled out accordingly. In the sledge were seated three *muzhiks* and an old woman. Evidently they were guests returning from the village festival. One of the men was lashing the snow-covered flanks of their pony with a dry branch, his two comrades were shouting and gesticulating at one another in the forepart of the sledge, and the old woman—muffled up and white over with snow—was seated motionless at the back.

"Whose men are you?" shouted Vassili.

"A-a-a-skie!" was all that could be heard in answer.

"Eh?"

"A-a-a-skie!" repeated one of the *muzhiks* at the top of his voice, but it was impossible to distinguish precisely what he said.

"Lay on! Don't give way to them!" shouted another to the one belaboring the pony with the branch.

"You are returning from the festival, I suppose?"

"They are gaining, they are gaining! Lay on, Semka! Pull out, you! Lay on!"

The sledges kept bumping against each other, almost interlocking, and then parting again, until finally the *muzhik's* sledge began to be overhauled. Their shaggy, fat-bellied, snow-covered pony, blowing heavily under its low *douga*, and evidently frantic (though in vain) to escape from the flagellation of the dry branch, kept shuffling along on its stumpy legs through the deep snow, although at times they almost gave way beneath it. Its muzzle—that, apparently, of a young animal, with its lower lip projecting like a fish's, the nostrils distended, and the ears laid back in terror—kept level with Nikita's shoulder for a few seconds, and then began to drop behind.

"That's what drink will make men do," observed Nikita. "The pony will be ruined by treatment like that. What Asiatic brutes the fellows are!"

For several minutes the sobbing of the distressed pony's nostrils could be heard behind them, as well as the drunken shouts of the *muzhiks*. Then the first sound died away, and presently the second also. Nothing whatever was to be heard now except the whistling of the wind in the travelers' ears and an occasional faint scrape of the runners over patches which the wind had swept bare.

This contest with the rival sledge had cheered and enlivened Vassili, so that he drove the cob with greater assurance than ever, and without watching for the posts at all—leaving matters, in fact, to the cob entirely. Nikita also had nothing to do, so that, as usual with him when thus situated, he fell into a doze, in order to make up for arrears of sleep at other times. Suddenly the cob stopped short, almost pitching Nikita forward out of the sledge.

"We have gone wrong again," said Vassili.

"How do you know?"

"Because there are no posts to be seen. We must have left the road."

"Well, if we have, I must look for it again," remarked Nikita abruptly as he got out and began to trudge about the snow, stepping as lightly as possible on the balls of his splayed-out feet. He kept this up for a long time—now disappearing from view, now reappearing, now vanishing again—and then returned.

"No road there," he remarked as he mounted the sledge. "It must be somewhere ahead."

The dusk was now coming on, and although the blizzard had not increased it also had not lessened.

"If only we could hear those *muzhiks!*" sighed Vassili.

"They won't overtake us now," replied Nikita, "for we must have left the road a long way back. Perhaps they have done the same," he added, as an afterthought.

"Well, which way now?" inquired Vassili.

"Give the cob his head," advised Nikita, "and perhaps he will take us right. Here, give me the reins."

Vassili relinquished them none the less readily because his hands were half frozen in their warm mittens. Nikita took the reins, but let them lie quite passively in his fingers, endeavoring not to give them the slightest twitch. In fact, he took keen pleasure in thus trying the intelligence of his favorite. Sure enough, after pricking his ears first to the one side and then to the other, the clever animal started to turn around.

"He can almost speak!" cried Nikita. "My word, how well he knows what to do! On you go, then! On with you! Tchk, tchk!"

The wind was now at their backs again, and it seemed warmer.

"Ah, what a knowing fellow he is!" went on Nikita, delighted with his pet. "A Kirghizenok[15] is strong enough, of course, but an absolute fool; whereas this fellow—well, see what he found out with his ears alone! No need of telegraphs for him, when he can smell out a road a verst away!"

And, indeed, less than half an hour later a black object—either a wood or a village—began to loom ahead, while the posts reappeared on their right, placing it beyond doubt that the travelers had hit the road once more.

"If this isn't Grishkino again!" exclaimed Nikita suddenly.

And Grishkino it was. On their left showed the barn with the snow-dust blowing from its roof, while further on could be seen the clothes-line, with its burden of shirts and drawers still fluttering in the wind. Once again they drove up the street and found everything grow suddenly quiet and warm and cheerful. Once again the miry roadway appeared, voices and singing became audible, and the dog barked as before. The dusk, however, was now so far advanced that lights could be seen gleaming in some of the windows.

Halfway up the street Vassili turned the cob's head towards a large hut with a double coping of bricks, and pulled up at the steps. Nikita approached the gleaming, snow-encrusted window, in the light of which the dancing snowflakes glittered brightly, and knocked at a pane with the butt-end of his whip.

"Who is there?" cried a voice in answer to Nikita's summons.

"The Brekhunoffs from Kresti, brother," replied Nikita. "Please let us in."

Someone could be heard moving away from the window, and in another two minutes the sound of the inner door opening with a wrench. Then the latch of the outer door rattled, and there came out a tall old white-bearded *muzhik*, holding the door half-closed behind him to keep the wind from blowing into the hut. He was clad in a fur coat, hastily thrown over a white holiday shirt, while behind him stood a young fellow in a red shirt and tall boots.

"How is it with you, Andreitch?" inquired the old man.

"We have lost our way, my friend," replied Vassili. "We tried to get to Goviatchkina, but landed here. Then we set off again, and have just missed the road for the second time."

"But how came you to go wrong?" asked the old man. "Here, Petrushka"—and he turned to

---

15. *Kirghizenok* (kir gēz′ə nôk), a kind of horse bred by the Kirghiz people of Mongolia in Asia.

the young fellow in the red shirt—"go and open the yard-gates.

"Certainly," responded the youngster cheerfully, and ran forward out of the porch.

"No, no. We must not stop the night," interposed Vassili.

"But where can you be going now? It is nearly dark. You had much better stay here."

"I should have been only too glad to do so, but I simply cannot. Business, you see, my friend—and business won't wait."

"Then at least come in and warm yourselves with some tea," said the old man.

"Yes, we might do that," replied Vassili. "The night won't grow any darker than it is now, for the moon will soon be rising. Shall we go in and warm ourselves, Nikita?"

"Yes, I could do with something to warm me," replied Nikita, who was desperately cold, and only too eager to thaw his frozen limbs before a stove.

Vassili thereupon entered the hut with the old man, while Nikita drove the sledge through the yard-gates, duly opened for him by Petrushka. Under the latter's guidance he then led the cob under the roof of a shed. The shed was heaped high with dung, so that the cob's lofty *douga* caught upon a beam; whereupon the cock and hens which were roosting there were moved to uneasy flutterings and scratchings of their claws, some sheep darted away in terror, with much pattering of their hoofs over the frozen dung, and a dog whined loudly, then growled in angry alarm, and finally barked at the intruder in puppy fashion.

Nikita had a word for them all. He begged the hens' pardon, and quieted them by saying that he would not disturb them further; chided the sheep for their unreasoning nervousness; and never ceased to make overtures to the dog as he tied up his steed.

"We shall be all right now," he said as he beat the snow from his clothes. "Hush, then, how he growls!" he added to the dog. "It is all right now. Quiet, then, stupid! Be quiet! You are only disturbing yourself for nothing. We are not thieves."

"They are what we might call our three domestic councilors," remarked Petrushka as he drew the sledge under the shed with his powerful hands.

"Why 'councilors'?" asked Nikita.

"Because," said Petrushka, with a smile, "you will find it written in Paulson's[16] book: 'When a thief is sneaking up to a house the dog barks out in his own language—Wake up! the cock sings out—Get up! and the cat starts washing herself—meaning thereby to say: A guest is at hand, so let us be ready to receive him!' "

Petrushka, it seemed, was of a literary turn, and knew by heart the only book which he possessed—some book or other by Paulson. He was particularly fond of it when he had had a little to drink—as now—and would quote such extracts from it as might seem to him to fit the occasion.

"That is just right," observed Nikita.

"Yes, isn't it?" answered Petrushka. "But you are simply frozen. Shall I take you in to tea now, my boy?"

"Yes, by all means," replied Nikita, and they crossed the yard to the hut door.

# IV

The homestead where Vassili had pulled up was one of the richest in the village, for the family held no less than five lots of land, as well as rented some, while in the stables stood six horses, three cows, two draft-bullocks, and a flock of twenty sheep. In all, there lived around the courtyard of the homestead twenty-two souls—namely, four

---

16. *Paulson's,* a reference to the author of a primer, or beginner's book, in which Petrushka had read a story called "The Three Domestic Councilors."

married sons, six grandchildren (of whom one—Petrushka—was married), two great-grand-children, three orphans, and four daughters-in-law, with their children. In addition to these there were two sons employed as water-carriers in Moscow, while a third was in the army. At the present moment there were at home only the old man, his wife, the second of the married sons, the elder of the two sons who worked at Moscow (come over for the festival), the various wives and children, and a neighboring gossip.

It was one of those rare households which are still to be found undivided, yet one in which there were already at work those deep-rooted internal dissensions which generally originate among the women of a family, and which would break up this family also in time.

Over the table in the hut there hung a shaded lamp, throwing a clear light upon the crockery below, upon a bottle of vodka, and upon sundry viands, as well as over the clay walls of the room. In one corner—the "corner beautiful"—there hung some ikons,[17] with pictures on either side of them. In the place of honor at the table sat Vassili, stripped now to his black under-jacket, and chewing his frozen moustache as he gazed round the hut and at those about him with his prominent, hawklike eyes. Next to him sat the bald, white-bearded head of the family (dressed in a white shirt of home manufacture), while, further on, were the son who had come over from Moscow for the festival (straight-backed, square-shouldered, and wearing a similar shirt to his father's, but of finer material), a second square-shouldered son (the eldest of those living at home), and, lastly, the neighbor—a red-haired, lanky *muzhik*.

These *muzhiks* had had their supper and vodka, and were just about to drink tea when the travelers arrived. Consequently, the samovar on the floor by the stove was already boiling. Near the stove, also, and in shelf-bunks could be seen various children, while the old woman—her face cov-ered in every direction with fine wrinkles, furrowing even her lips—bustled about behind Vassili. As Nikita entered the hut she was just taking her guest some vodka, which she had poured out into a tumbler of thick glass.

"You must not refuse it, Vassili Andreitch," she said. "No, you really must not. You need something to refresh you. Drink it down, my dear sir."

Nikita found himself greatly excited by the smell of the vodka—especially now that he was so cold and hungry. He knit his brows and, shaking the snow from his hat and *khalat*, halted for a moment before the ikons, with his eyes turned away from the company. He crossed himself three times and made a genuflection, after which he turned first to his host and saluted him, then to those present at the table, and then to the women standing by the stove. Finally, with a general greeting of "A merry festival to you all!" he started to take off his *khalat*—though still without looking at the table.

"But you are frozen all over, my brother!" cried the eldest brother as he stared at Nikita's snow-caked eyes, beard, and face. For answer, Nikita divested himself of his *khalat*, shook it out, and hung it over the stove; after which he at length approached the table. Offered vodka, he had almost taken the glass and tilted the fragrant, shining liquor into his mouth, when he glanced at Vassili and remembered the pawned boots, as well as the cooper and the young son for whom he had promised to buy a horse in the spring. So he ended by declining the vodka with a sigh.

"I would rather not drink it, I thank you humbly," he said with knitted brows, and seated himself on a bench by the window.

---

17. *"corner beautiful"* . . . *ikons* (ī'konz). One corner of a peasant's hut was decorated. An ikon, or icon, is a picture of Christ or a saint, painted on wood and considered sacred in the Eastern Church.

"But why?" asked the eldest brother.

"Because I would rather not, I would rather not," Nikita replied without raising his eyes as he squinted down at his short beard and moustache and thawed the icicles out of them.

"It does not suit him," put in Vassili, smacking his lips over a cracknel washed down with vodka.

"Well, give me the teapot, then," said the kindly old woman. "I will get you some tea, for you must be frozen. Why are you so long with the samovar, my good women?"

"It is quite ready," retorted one of the younger ones as she wiped the covered samovar with a napkin. Then, raising it with some difficulty, she came and plumped it down on the table.

Meanwhile, Vassili had been relating how he and his companion had missed their way, wandered about, fallen in with the drunken *muzhiks*, and twice returned to the village. His hosts marveled at the story, and then went on to explain how and where they had gone wrong, who the drunken *muzhiks* had been, and the route which Vassili and Nikita must take when they set off again.

"Why, even a child could find the way as far as Moltchanovka," said the neighbor; "and, once there, you only have to hit the turning near the village. You will see a copse there. To think that you never got so far!"

"But hadn't you better stay the night here?" put in the old woman, persuasively. "The women shall get you a bed ready."

"Yes, do so, for if you were to get lost again it might be a terrible business," added her husband.

"No, no, I really cannot, my good friend," replied Vassili. "Business is business. Delay an hour, and you lose a year," he added, remembering the timber and the rival buyers who might forestall him. "Shall we go now?" (this last to Nikita).

Nikita returned no answer for a moment, and seemed absorbed in the task of thawing out his beard and moustache. At length he muttered gruffly:

"It would hardly do to get lost again, would it?"

As a matter of fact, he was gruff because he wanted the vodka so badly, and the only thing which would assuage that yearning of his was tea—which he had not yet been offered.

"But we need only to reach that turning," protested Vassili, "and we simply *can't* lose our way afterwards. From there onwards it will be all forest road."

"Well, it is for you to say, Vassili Andreitch," said Nikita as he took the tumbler of tea now proffered him. "If we must go, we must, that's all."

"Drink up the tea, then, and quick march."

Nikita said no more (although he shook his head disapprovingly), but poured the tea out carefully into the saucer and began to warm his work-swollen fingers in the steam. Then, having bitten off a crumb from his lump of sugar, he bowed to his hosts, said "A good health to you all!" and poured the grateful liquid down his throat.

"If only we had someone to guide us to the turning!" sighed Vassili.

"That could be managed," said the eldest brother. "Petrushka could harness a horse and go with you as far as that."

"Harness up, then, brother, and my best thanks to you," exclaimed Vassili.

"And to you also, good sir," said the hospitable old woman. "We have been only too pleased to see you."

"Petrushka, off you go and harness the mare," ordered the eldest brother.

"Very well," replied Petrushka smilingly as he seized his cap from a peg and departed.

Whilst the horses were being got ready the conversation passed to the subject which had been interrupted when Vassili drove up to the window. It seemed that the old man had been complaining to the neighbor (who was also the local elder[18]) about his third son, who had sent him no gift for the festival, but had given his wife a French shawl.

"The young people are getting out of hand nowadays," said the old man.

"Indeed they are!" agreed the neighbor. "There is no living with them. They are growing much too clever. Look at Demotchkin, who broke his father's arm the other day—all through his being too clever, of course!"

Nikita kept listening and looking from one to the other of the speakers' faces with an evident desire to join in the conversation, but he was too full of tea to do so, and therefore merely nodded his head approvingly at intervals. He had drunk tumbler after tumbler of tea, until he had grown warmer and warmer and more and more good-humored. The conversation lasted for quite a long time on this subject—on the evil of dividing up families—and proved too absorbing to be success-fully diverted, so that in time it passed to the dissensions in this particular household—to the separation which the second son (who had been sitting by meanwhile and maintaining a sullen silence) was demanding. Evidently it was a moot point, and the question above all others which was exercising the household, yet politeness had hith-erto prevented the family from discussing such a private affair before strangers. At length, how-ever, the old man could not forbear, and with tears in his voice went on to say that, so long as he lived, he would never permit the separation; that he maintained his household to the glory of God; and that, once it were divided, it would become scattered all over the world.

"Yes, that is what happened to the Matvieffs," observed the neighbor. "They were a comfortable household once, but separated—and now not a single one of them has anything left."

"That is what you desire for *us*, I suppose?" said the old man, turning to his son.

The son returned no answer, and an awkward silence ensued until interrupted by Petrushka, who had duly harnessed his horse and been back in the hut for some minutes past, smiling the whole time.

"It reminds me of a fable in Paulson," he said. "A father gave his son a broom to tear across. None of them could tear it: but, twig by twig—well, that was easy enough. So also it will be in our case," he added with a broad smile. "But I am quite ready to start now."

"Then, if you are ready, let us be off," said Vassili. "About that separation, good grand-father—do not give in. It is *you* who have made the household, and therefore it should be *you* who are master of it. If necessary, refer the matter to the magistrate. He would settle it for you."

"But to behave like this, to behave like this!" cried the old man, with unrestrained grief. "There is no living with them. It is the Devil's doing entirely."

Meanwhile Nikita, his fifth tumbler of tea swal-lowed, had placed the empty glass by his side instead of returning it, in the hope that he would be given a sixth. But there was no more water left in the samovar, and so the hostess brewed no more tea, while Vassili was already putting his fur coat on. Accordingly, there being nothing else for it, Nikita rose, replaced his lump of sugar (which he had nibbled on every side) in the sugar-basin, wiped his perspiring face with the lappet of his jacket, and went to put on his *khalat*. This done, he sighed heavily. Then he thanked and took leave of his hosts, and left the warm, bright living room for the cold, dark porch, which was rattling with the wind which hurtled through it and which had drifted the snow through the chinks of the quaking outer door until it lay in heaps upon the

---

18. *elder,* an older man of the village who is considered a leader or wise adviser.

floor. Thence he passed into the dark courtyard.

Petrushka, clad in a sheepskin jacket, was standing by his horse in the middle of the yard and smilingly quoting some verses from Paulson:

"The lowering tempest hides the sky,
    The whirlwind brings the driving snow;
Now like a wild beast it doth cry,
    Now like a child it whimpers low."

Nikita nodded his head approvingly and unhooked the reins, while the old man brought a lantern into the porch to guide Vassili to the sledge. He tried to light him with it, but it was blown out in a twinkling. Even in the yard it was easy to tell that the storm was worse than ever.

"What fearful weather!" thought Vassili to himself. "Perhaps we shall never get there. However, there is business to be thought of. Besides, I have got myself ready now, and my host's horse has been put in. God send we get there, though!"

The old man likewise was thinking that it would be better for them not to set out, but he had already tried to dissuade them, and they had not listened to him. It would be no use asking them again.

"Perhaps, too, it is only old age which makes me so nervous, and they will arrive safely," he thought. "Let us ourselves at least go to bed in the meanwhile. Enough of talking for tonight."

Petrushka, at all events, had no thought of danger. He knew the road and the whole neighborhood too well for that. Moreover, he had been greatly put upon his mettle by the couplet about the whirlwind and the snow, which seemed to him to describe with extraordinary exactness what was to be seen in the yard. As for Nikita, he had no wish to go at all, but he had been too long accustomed not to have his own way and to serve others; so that in the end there was no one to prevent them from setting out.

# V

Vassili walked through the porch, peered about in the darkness till he discerned where the sledge was, took the reins, and climbed in.

"All right in front!" he cried. Petrushka, kneeling in his own sledge, started his horse, and Brownie, with a loud neigh as he scented the mare in front of him, dashed away after her. They issued thus into the village street, passed the outskirts, and took the same road as before—the road which ran past the yard with the frozen linen (although the linen was quite invisible now), past the barn heaped with snow, and from the gables of which a cloud of snow-dust kept blowing, and past the bending vines with their mysterious murmurings and pipings. Then once more the travelers were launched upon a sea of snow, which raged both above and below them. The wind was so strong that when it was upon their flank and their wrappings filled before it, it actually careened the sledge to one side and threw the cob out of his stride. Petrushka kept shouting encouragement as he drove his stout mare ahead of them, while the cob followed her closely.

After about ten minutes' driving, Petrushka turned aside and shouted something, but neither Vassili nor Nikita could tell what he said for the sound of the wind. They guessed, however, that they had reached the turning. Sure enough, Petrushka had wheeled to the right, and the wind, which had hitherto been chiefly on their flank, now met them full in the face, whilst something could be seen showing black through the snow on their right hand. It was the copse which marked the turning.

"God go with you!" cried Petrushka.

"Thank you, thank you, Petrushka!"

"The lowering tempest hides the sky," shouted the lad once more, and vanished.

"Goodness, what a poetry-spouter!" remarked Vassili as he started the cob again.

I. J. Alex, *The Coach* (detail), Private Collection

"Yes, he is a fine young fellow, a real honest *muzhik*," returned Nikita, and they went on. In order not to squander the warmth engendered by the tea which he had drunk in the hut, Nikita wrapped himself up well, hunched his shoulders until his short beard covered his throat, and sat perfectly silent. In front of him he could see the two dark lines of the shafts forever cheating his eye, and looking to him like the ruts of a beaten road; the cob's tossing flank and knotted, wind-blown tail; and, further ahead, the animal's lofty *douga*, nodding head and neck, and disheveled mane. At intervals posts would leap into sight, and he would know that the sledge was still keeping the road and that there was nothing for him to do. Vassili held the reins loosely, leaving it to the cob to guide himself. Nevertheless, although Brownie had had a long rest in the village, he went unwillingly, and as though he would like to turn aside at any moment, so that Vassili frequently had to straighten him again.

"There goes a post on the right—two—three," counted Vassili. "And there is the forest in front," he went on to himself as he gazed at something showing dark ahead of them. However, what had seemed to him a forest proved to be only a bush. This they passed, and had covered another fifty yards or so—when, behold! there was neither forest nor a fourth post to be seen!

"Never mind; we shall be at the forest in a moment," thought Vassili as, excited by the vodka and tea, he jerked the reins again instead of pulling up. The willing, docile animal obeyed and, now at an amble and now at a moderate trot, went whither he was driven, although he knew that it was in the wrong direction. Another ten minutes passed, and still there was no forest.

"We have missed the road again!" exclaimed Vassili, at last pulling up. Without speaking, Nikita descended from the sledge, and, after tucking up his *khalat*, which sometimes clung to

him and sometimes flapped up and down, according to the strength of the gusts of wind, began to flounder about over the snow. First he tried the one side, and then the other, and thrice vanished altogether. At last, however, he returned, and took the reins from Vassili's hands.

"We must go towards the right," he said brusquely and decisively as he turned the cob in that direction.

"Very well; if to the right, to the right," agreed Vassili as he surrendered the reins and thrust his numbed hands up his sleeves. Nikita said nothing more beyond crying, "Now do your best, my pet!" to the cob. Nevertheless, the animal moved forward only at a foot's pace, in spite of all Nikita's shaking of the reins. The snow was knee-deep in places, and the sledge moved through it in jerks with each stride of the animal. Presently Nikita took up the whip, which had been hanging over the splash-board, and used it once; whereupon the good cob, unused to its lash, plunged forward and broke into a trot—only, however, to subside again into an alternative amble and walk. They proceeded thus for about five minutes. It was so dark, and there was such a swirl of snow both around them and on the ground, that it was scarely possible for them even to see the cob's *douga*. Sometimes, indeed, it was almost as though the sledge were standing still and the ground gliding backwards from it.

Suddenly the cob stopped short, as though he had scented something in front of him. Nikita threw down the reins and leapt lightly out, in order to go to the cob's head and see what he was jibbing at; but hardly had he taken a single stride ahead of the animal when his legs shot up and he rolled down some steep declivity.

"Phew, phew, phew!" he kept exclaiming all the time he was descending and trying in vain to stop himself, but his course was only arrested when his legs plowed their way into a deep snow-drift at the bottom, while, shaken by his struggles, the drift overhanging the bank above him descended upon his head and crammed a large portion of its mass down the back of his neck.

"What a one you are, then!" said Nikita, reproachfully, both to the snowdrift and to the ravine, as he attempted to shake the snow out of his coat-collar.

"Nikita, Nikita!" came in a shout from Vassili above, but Nikita sent no answering call. He was too busy for that, for he was employing all his energies in shaking himself and searching for the whip, which had rolled away somewhere while he was shooting down the declivity. Having found it at last, he tried to reascend at the spot where he had come down, but found it impossible to do so, since he merely slid back with each successive attempt; so that finally he was forced to proceed along the bottom to find a way out. Nevertheless, only a few yards from the point where he had descended he found a place where he managed to creep up on all fours, after which he began to walk along the edge towards the spot where he judged the cob to be. Both cob and sledge were wholly invisible, but inasmuch as he was walking against the wind, he could hear Vassili's shouts and Brownie's welcoming neigh some moments before he actually caught sight of them.

"I am coming, I am coming," he exclaimed. "Why make such a fuss about it?"

It was not until he was almost upon the sledge that he was able to distinguish the cob, with Vassili standing beside it—the latter looming very large in the obscurity.

"How the devil did you manage to lose yourself?" began his master, angrily. "We must turn back and at least try to return to Grishkino."

"I should be only too glad," retorted Nikita. "But which way are we to go? If we fall into this ravine we might never get out of it again. I myself have just found it pretty hard to do so."

"Yet we cannot stay here, can we? We *must* go *some*where," retorted Vassili.

Nikita said nothing, but sat down on the rim of the sledge, pulled off his boots, and shook out the snow which had collected in them. That done, he gathered up a handful of straw and carefully plugged a hole in the left one.

Vassili also said nothing, as though he meant now to leave everything to Nikita. When the latter had finished pulling on his boots again, he tucked his legs onto the sledge, put on his mittens, took up the reins, and turned the cob parallel to the ravine. They had not gone more than a hundred yards, however, before the animal pulled up short. In front of them lay the ravine again!

Once more Nikita got out and went probing about over the snow. He was absent for some time, but at length reappeared on the opposite side of the sledge to that which he had started from.

"Are you there, Andreitch?" he shouted.

"Yes," replied Vassili. "Well, what now?"

"There is no getting out this way; it is too dark, and there are too many ravines about. We must try driving back against the wind."

After doing so for a little while they stopped, and Nikita once more alighted and went creeping about over the snow. Then he remounted, but only to alight again almost immediately; until at length he came to a halt by the sledge in a perfectly breathless condition.

"Well, what?" inquired Vassili.

"Only that I am fairly done, and the cob nearly so too."

"What are we to do, then?"

"Wait a minute." Nikita departed again, but returned in a moment or two.

"Keep close behind me," he cried as he walked on before the cob. Vassili had now ceased to give orders, but humbly obeyed Nikita's directions.

"This way—after me," cried the latter again as he turned sharply to the right and, taking Brownie by the head, led him downwards towards a snowdrift. The cob held back at first, and then made a plunge forward as though to leap the snowdrift. Failing in the attempt, he sank in up to the collar.

"Get out of the sledge," cried Nikita to Vassili, who had retained his seat meanwhile. Then, grasping one of the shafts, he exerted all his strength to help the cob to drag the sledge out of the drift.

"Pull, my pet!" he cried to Brownie. "One good pull and the thing is done. Now, now! Just one good pull!"

The cob made a brave effort, and yet another, but, failing to extricate himself, settled down as though to reflect upon the situation.

"Come, come, my pet; this won't do," Nikita adjured Brownie. "Now then, once again!" and he tugged at the shaft on his side, while Vassili tugged at the other. The cob shook his head for a moment, and then plunged forward suddenly in another attempt.

"That's it! You're not going to be buried this time, eh?" cried Nikita, encouragingly.

Another plunge—a second—a third—and the cob had cleared the drift and stopped short, shaking himself all over and breathing heavily. Nikita was for dragging the sledge a little further yet, but Vassili was so exhausted with the weight of his two heavy coats that he gave up and climbed in again.

"Let me rest a minute," he said, as he loosened the handkerchief which he had wound round his coat-collar before leaving the village.

"Very well; there is no great hurry," returned Nikita. "Sit still, and I will lead the cob."

Accordingly Vassili remained in the sledge, while Nikita led the animal forward for about ten yards, down a slope, then up again a little way, and finally came to a halt.

The spot where he had done so was not actually in the ravine itself, where the snow blowing off the hillocks and accumulating might have buried them entirely, but in a spot partly sheltered by the lee side of the ravine. Occasionally the wind seemed to drop a little, but it was not for long; whilst, as if to make up for such lulls, the blizzard would increase tenfold after they were over, and tear and swirl around the travelers more cruelly than ever. One of these violent gusts struck the sledge just as Vassili was descending from it to go and take counsel with Nikita as to what they should do next, with the result that they could only cower down without speaking until the fury of the squall was spent. As for Brownie, he flattened his ears and shook his head in disgust. When the squall had abated a little, Nikita took off his mittens, tucked them into his belt, blew upon his hands, and set to work to unfasten the bow-rein from the *douga*.

"Why are you doing that?" asked Vassili.

"Because there is nothing else to be done," replied Nikita, though half-apologetically. "I am absolutely tired out now."

"Then aren't we going to try and get any further?"

"No, for we are only exhausting the cob for nothing," said Nikita, pointing to the animal where it stood patiently waiting for what might be required of it, yet scarcely able to hold itself upright on its stout, sweat-belathered flanks. "Brownie is willing enough, but he can hardly stand on his legs. There is nothing for it but to spend the night here."

Nikita said this as if he were proposing to put up in an inn-yard, and went on unfastening the collar-thong until the two clasps of the collar fell apart.

"But we shall freeze to death here!" cried Vassili.

"Well? What if we do? It cannot be helped," was all that Nikita vouchsafed to reply.

## THINK AND DISCUSS
### Understanding
1. For what reasons does Vassili value Nikita as an employee?
2. What is Vassili's "ruling passion"?
3. When Vassili and Nikita arrive in Grishkino for the second time, why is Nikita anxious to accept the old man's invitation to rest inside the house?
4. What thoughts prevent Nikita from drinking the vodka offered to him in the home of the old man?
5. At the end of Chapter IV, why does Nikita passively accept his master's wish to continue their journey?

### Analyzing
6. In Chapter III what effect does the contest between Vassili's sledge and that of the three *muzhiks* have on his spirits?
7. In Chapter I, Vassili ponders the idea of his son being the heir to his riches. Based on this passage, what can the reader infer about Vassili's attitude toward life and possessions?
8. Throughout these opening chapters, Vassili ignores the warning signals of nature and the advice of men. What does his response reveal about his **character**?
9. Four times the narrator refers to the frozen clothes on a line in the hamlet of Grishkino. Explain the different reasons for each reference.
10. In Chapter IV, the old man asks one son if he wants to see their family end the same way the Matvieff family ended. The son gives no answer. But Petrushka, another son, answers with a fable. Does the fable support the father's view? Explain.
11. Describe the central conflict in the **plot** of the novel so far.

### Extending
12. Explain how the horse Brownie can be viewed as a symbol of the Russian peasant. Reviewing the Comment article "The Russian Peasant" may provide some ideas.
13. Although Tolstoy's fiction is rich in detail, he gives only limited details about the hospitable old man and his large family. What purpose is served by such omission?
14. Explain how Nikita's character reflects Tolstoy's belief in nonresistance.

## THINKING SKILLS
### Generalizing
To **generalize** is to draw a general conclusion from particular information. For example, a geographer will study the physical characteristics of a particular area and then make generalizations about how the people who live there adapt to their environment. Reading *Master and Man* enables you to make generalizations about human survival in the most adverse conditions imaginable.

List five or six other settings in the United States or around the world and, for each, imagine and describe circumstances in which two characters might face an equivalent danger due to a harsh climate. For example, you might list two people battling an ocean storm in a boat near the Hawaiian Islands or a couple of pioneer settlers lost in a desert. You may want to look at a map or atlas to help you find possible settings. When you finish, compare your lists with those of your classmates.

## COMPOSITION

### Reading/Writing Log

Review the chapter endings in the first half of *Master and Man* to recall which ones most strongly interested you or compelled you to read on. In your reading/writing log or another notebook, write the heading *Good Endings* and under it identify two chapter endings you liked best. Explain why your choices are examples of good endings.

### Comparing and Contrasting Characters

Write a two- or three-paragraph composition that compares and contrasts character traits of Vassili and Nikita. Use details from the text to support your ideas. Remember, the clearest comparisons and contrasts use precise and descriptive words. Give your composition a good ending by expressing a clear conclusion about the similarity or difference you find most significant.

### Predicting Possible Outcomes

Throughout *Master and Man*, Tolstoy gives emphasis to the details of the increasing severity of the snow, wind, and darkness. Do you think that he uses these details to foreshadow a possibly dangerous situation ahead? Write a three-paragraph composition in which you explain what these details of setting foreshadow. Is it danger for Vassili and Nikita? possible tragedy? As you write, be sure to use vivid language, and use details from the story to support your ideas. Write a good ending, predicting whether or not the two characters will face life-threatening danger from the storm, in your opinion.

# VI

Vassili was warm enough in his two heavy coats, especially after his exertions in the snowdrift. Yet, for all that, the frost seemed to breathe down his back when he understood that they had to spend the night there. To calm his apprehensions, he sat down in the sledge and pulled out his matches and cigarettes.

Meanwhile Nikita unharnessed the cob. He undid the belly-band and saddle-piece, ran the reins out, unfastened the traces, and took off the *douga*, talking cheerily to the animal the while.

"Out you come, out you come," he said as he led it out of the shafts. "Let me take off your bit and tie you up here, and then you shall have some straw." He suited the action to the word. "Eat away, and you will feel all the better for it."

Nevertheless, Brownie did not seem to grow easier under Nikita's touch, but kept fidgeting about as he stood tail onwards to the wind. Every moment he would shift his legs, press up to the sledge, and rub his head against Nikita's sleeve. However, as if unwilling to seem churlish about the meal of straw which Nikita had strewn before his nose, he took an occasional straw from the sledge, but appeared at once to come to the conclusion that straw did not meet the case, and threw it down again; whereupon the wind caught it in a twinkling, whirled it away, and buried it in the snow.

"Suppose we make a signal of distress," said Nikita, presently. He turned the sledge a little towards the wind, tied the shafts together with the belly-band, turned them up, and rested them against the splashboard.

"Now, if anyone passes this way they will be able to see us by the shafts, and come and dig us out. I learnt that trick from the old people," and he clapped his mittens together and put them on.

Meanwhile Vassili had unhooked his fur coat and made a shelter of its skirts. Then he struck match after match against the steel match-box, but his hands were shaking so violently with the cold that each successive match either failed to light at all or was blown out by the wind as he was in the act of lifting it to his cigarette. At length a match did flare up properly, illuminating for a brief second the pelt of his fur coat, his hand with the gold ring on its curved index finger, and the snow-covered straw which projected from under the sacking. The cigarette lighted, he drew a couple of greedy whiffs, swallowed the smoke, and puffed it out again through his moustache. Then he was about to take a third whiff, when the wind caught the lighted end of the cigarette and carried it away to join the wisps of straw!

Nevertheless, even these meager mouthfuls of smoke had exercised a cheering effect upon him. "If we *must* spend the night here, well, we must, that's all," he said undauntedly. "Wait a moment and I will rig up a flag."

Picking up the handkerchief which he had unwound from his neck and thrown down upon the floor of the sledge, he took off his mittens, climbed onto the splashboard, stretched himself on tiptoe to reach the belly-band, and tied the handkerchief round one end of it and of the shaft in a stout knot. The handkerchief at once began to wave wildly—now clinging to the shaft, now suddenly filling out again and straining at the knot as its folds cracked in the wind.

"Is not that clever of me?" said Vassili as he stepped down again, much pleased with his handiwork. "Now, if we could lie together, that would be the warmest way, but I'm afraid that there isn't room for both of us."

"Never mind; I will find a place for myself," answered Nikita. "Only, I must cover the cob over first, for he has been sweating a lot and is tired out. Wait a minute"—and, diving into the sledge, he dragged the sacking from under Vassili. Possessed of this, he folded it double, and, removing the saddlepiece and crupper from Brownie's back, covered him over.

"You will be warmer like this, little fool," he said as he replaced the saddle-piece and crupper. "And now," he added to Vassili, "I will take the apron if you don't want it tonight. Give you some straw, too," and, thus taking one thing and another from beneath Vassili, he went to the back of the sledge, dug a hole in the snow there, and lined it with straw. Then he pulled his cap over his eyes, wrapped his *khalat* about him, with the apron over all, and squatted down upon the straw with his back resting against the bark tail-board of the sledge, that it might protect him from the wind and snow.

Vassili shook his head in disapproval of Nikita's proceedings (it was contrary to his habit to encourage the peasantry in their rude, uncouth ways), and then set about making his own preparations for the night. First of all, he smoothed out what straw was left in the sledge, padding it a little thicker where his thigh-bone was to rest. Then he pulled on his mittens and lay down with his head in one of the corners near the splashboard, that the latter might protect him from the wind.

Somehow he did not feel sleepy, but lay thinking. He thought chiefly of the one thing which constituted his whole pride, ideal, aim and joy in life—namely, the making of money, and yet more money. He thought of the means by which certain acquaintances of his had made their money, how they were using it, and the means by which he, like they, might make a great deal more than he already possessed. The purchase of the Goviatchkinsky forest seemed to him a matter of vast importance, since out of this forest he hoped to make, at one stroke, a sum, possibly, of ten thousand rubles. He mentally reckoned up the value of timber which he had viewed in the autumn, and on the basis of the two *dessiatins*[19] he

19. *dessiatins* (des′yə tēnz), Russian units of land measure, each equal to about 2.7 acres.

had then inspected went on to calculate the whole.

"The oakwood will do for sledge runners if cut up, and for beams as they stand," he said to himself. "And after they are felled there should be left about 30 *sazhens*[20] of firewood to the *dessiatin*." Thus calculating, he could see that the total value of the forest worked out at about 12,000 rubles, but could not reckon to an exact figure in the absence of tables. "All the same," he went on, "I am not going to give even so much as 10,000 for it—only 8,000—and that subject to deductions for open spaces. I will grease the surveyor's palm with a hundred rubles, or perhaps a hundred and fifty, and he will measure me off the clearings at at least five *dessiatins*. Yes, the owner will be glad to let the forest go at 8,000 rubles. I have 3,000 ready for him here," thought Vassili as he felt for his pocketbook with the inside of his forearm; "and that should melt him. How on earth we came to miss that turning God only knows. There must be a forest and a forest-keeper somewhere about there. His dog ought to have heard us. The cursed brutes never bark when they're wanted to."

He turned back his coat-collar from his ear and listened. Nothing was to be heard but the whistling of the wind, the rustling and cracking of the handkerchief on the shafts, and the swish of the snow as it lashed the bark sides of the sledge. He covered his ear over again.

"If only I had known that we should have to spend the night here!" he thought. "Well, we shall get there tomorrow, all the same. It will only mean one day lost. Besides, those other fellows wouldn't come either—not in such weather."

Suddenly he remembered that on the 9th of the month he was to be paid some money for wethers by the butcher.

"I ought to be back by then to receive it. He couldn't take me in over the price, whereas my wife doesn't in the least know how to bargain. In fact, she doesn't understand how to talk to any-one," he went on as he remembered her failure to make conversation to the commissary[21] of police, who had been one of their guests of yesterday for the festival. "She is a *woman*—that is the long and the short of it. Moreover, what had she ever seen before I married her? Her father was only a well-to-do *muzhik*. A shabby little farm—that was all his property. But what have I not acquired in fifteen years? A store, two taverns, a mill, a granary, two rented holdings, and an iron-roofed villa and warehouse combined." He swelled with pride. "Rather different to her father, I think! In fact, who is the chief man in the district today? Why, Vassili Brekhunoff, of course!"

"And why so?" he continued presently. "Because I devote my whole attention to business and work hard—not like some people who lie abed and play the fool. *I* don't sleep whole nights away. No. Blizzard or no blizzard, out I go if necessary, and my business gets done. They think me a fool, and laugh at my money-making; but never mind, Vassili—go on working hard, even if it makes your head ache. If necessary, spend a night in the open like this rather than lose time. Never mind if you cannot sleep, either. To be able to think such thought is a pillow in itself," he concluded proudly.

"Some people seem to think that riches come to one by chance. Pooh! There is only one Mironoff in a million. No. Work hard, and God will give you the rest. If only He give you health and strength, that alone should be sufficient."

And the mere thought that he might one day become such a millionaire as Mironoff, who had risen from nothing, so fired Vassili with ecstasy that he yearned to have someone to speak to. Yet there was no one. Ah, but, once he could win to Goviatchkina, he would have a landowner to speak to—and to bamboozle as well!

---

20. *sazhens* (sä′zhənz), Russian units of measure equal to seven feet.

21. *commissary*, deputy or representative.

Charles Burchfield, *Winter Moonlight*,
1951, Wichita Art Museum

"Good heavens, how it blows!" he continued as he listened to a squall of wind which was beating against the splashboard and bending it inwards as it lashed the bark planking with snow. "It is drifting the snow so much that perhaps we shall never get out in the morning."

Nothing could be seen in the white swirl of obscurity but Brownie's dark head and tail and the sack covering his back. At intervals the wind would toss the corners of the sack aloft, while in front and behind and on either side of the sledge whirled the same uniform mass of whiteness—now lightening a little, now suddenly becoming denser.

"I was a fool ever to have listened to Nikita," he thought. "We ought to have done on again, and we should have landed somewhere. We might have reached Grishkino again, and been able to put up at Tarass's place after all. Yet here we have to stick all night! What is the good of that? God gives to those who help themselves, but not to loafers, sluggards, and fools. I must try smoking again."

He sat up, got out a cigarette, and then rolled over on his stomach to shield the flame of the match from the wind with the flap of his coat. Yet the wind found an entry somehow, and blew out the matches, one by one. At length he contrived to keep one alight, and started smoking. He felt greatly pleased with his success, and although the wind got more of the smoke than he did, he managed to draw three whiffs, and was much cheered by them. He rolled himself back into a sitting posture, wrapped himself up again, and started once more to think over and consider matters; until suddenly, and without warning, he lost consciousness and went off into a doze.

All at once something seems to jostle him, and he awoke. It might have been Brownie pulling away straw from beneath him, or it might have been the result of some internal disturbance, but at all events he awoke—and with his heart beating so fast and so furiously that the very sledge seemed to be shaking under him. He opened his eyes. The scene around him appeared exactly the same, except that it seemed lighter.

"It must be the dawn," he thought to himself. "It will soon be morning now."

Then all at once he remembered that the fact of its getting lighter could only mean that the moon was rising. He raised himself again, and looked at the cob. Brownie was standing with his hindquarters to the wind, and shaking all over. The snow-heaped sacking was turned up over his back on the windward side, and the crupper was slipping down over his flank, while his snow-powdered head and wind-tossed mane and forehead-tuft were more clearly visible than before. As for Nikita, he was still squatting in the same position as when he had first sat down, with his feet and the apron with which he had covered his head all piled with snow.

"A *muzhik* never freezes," thought Vassili as he bent over the back of the sledge and looked at him. "No, not for all his poor clothes. He can be trusted for that. Yet the *muzhiks* are a stupid lot— a mere welter of ignorance."

For a moment he thought of taking the sacking off the cob's back and covering Nikita over with it, but it was too cold to get up and make the effort. Moreover, he was afraid of the cob starving if he did.

"What on earth did I take Nikita for?" he reflected. "I have *her* stupidity to thank for it all" (he was thinking of his wife). Then he rolled back into his former position by the splashboard. "My uncle spent a night in the snow like this," he went on, "yet he took no harm. Sebastian, too, once had to be dug out," he continued as another instance occurred to him. "Sebastian died, though, for he was frozen stiff as a carcass. If only we had stayed at Grishkino!"

Wrapping his coat more carefully about him, so that the protection of the fur should not be wasted at any point, but keep him warm from head to heels, he closed his eyes and tried to sleep again. Yet, for all his efforts, he could not succeed, but, on the contrary, continued absolutely alert and wakeful. Once more be began to make business calculations and to run over his outstanding debts. Once more, too, he began to appraise himself and to congratulate himself on his position in the world.

Nonetheless, his every thought seemed to be broken in upon by a sort of haunting fear, as well as by a feeling of vexation that they had not stayed at Grishkino.

"To think of it!" he murmured. "Why, at this moment I might have been lying in a warm bed!"

More than once he turned himself over and resettled himself, in a vain endeavor to find an easier position and one more protected from the wind, but each new posture proved more uncomfortable than the last. At length he raised himself again, changed his position altogether, wrapped his legs up carefully, closed his eyes, and tried to lie perfectly still. Yet, either his feet, squeezed into their stiff top-boots, had begun to ache, or the wind was catching him somewhere, but at all events he had not been lying long in this position before he found himself angrily remembering that at this very moment he might have been lying in a warm hut at Grishkino. Again he raised himself, again he wrapped his coat about him, and resettled himself. Once he thought he heard the far-off sound of cocks crowing, whereupon he turned down the collar of his coat in a tremor of joy and listened attentively; yet, for all his straining of his ears, he could hear nothing but the whistling of the wind through the shafts, the flapping of the handkerchief, and the lashing of the snow against the bark sides of the sledge.

As for Nikita, he remained squatting as he had done since the previous evening. Never once had he stirred, nor returned any answer to Vassili's shouts, although the latter had called to him more than once.

"*He* seems to have no difficulty in sleeping," thought Vassili with irritation as he leant over the back of the sledge and looked at the snow-covered Nikita.

In all, Vassili must have got up and lain down again at least twenty times. It seemed to him as if the night would never end.

"Surely it must be nearly morning now?" he thought once as he raised himself and glanced about him. "How would it be to look at my watch? But no; I might get frozen if I unhooked my coat. Yet, once I knew that it was drawing towards morning, things would seem better, and we would set about harnessing the cob."

In the depths of his soul, however, Vassili knew quite well that it could not be near morning yet. The truth was that his nervous panic was increasing to such an extent that he wished both to verify his supposition and to deceive himself. In the end he finished by carefully unhooking his fur coat, thrusting his hand in, and groping about till he dug down to his waistcoat. A further series of efforts enabled him to draw out his silver watch, with its enameled chasing of flowers. Then he tried to look at it, but nothing could be seen without a light. Once more he lay down upon his elbows and stomach (as he had done when getting ready to smoke), pulled out his matches, and set about striking one. By this time he had grown more expert at the business, and, feeling for the match with the largest head of sulphur, he contrived to light it at the first attempt. Then, thrusting the dial of the watch under the light, he looked at it, and could hardly believe his eyes! It was only ten minutes past one! The whole night lay before him!

"Oh, the long, long night!" he groaned, feeling as though the frost were striking down his back already. Then, hooking his coat up again and wrapping it about him, he sat back in the corner of the sledge, and prepared to wait with what patience he might.

Suddenly, above the monotonous wail of the wind he heard a new sound—a sound made by some living creature. It grew steadily louder, attained its maximum, and began as steadily to die away again. There could be no doubt what it was. It was a wolf. Nor was the beast so far off that the wind could drown the gradations of tone in its howl as it moved its jaws from side to side. Vassili put back his coat-collar from his ear and listened strainedly. Brownie was doing the same, his ears sharply pricked, and when the howl ceased he changed his legs and snorted uneasily. After this Vassili found it more than ever impossible to sleep—found it impossible to steady his nerves for a moment. The more he tried to think of his business affairs and accounts, his reputation, dignity, and wealth, the more did terror begin to master him; while, above all other thoughts, and yet mixed up with them, floated the persistent question—"Why did we not stop the night at Grishkino?"

"God be with that landowner and his forest," he thought to himself, "yet I wish I had never come across either of them. To have to spend the night here! They say that men who have been drinking always freeze readily, and *I* have been drinking tonight."

Listening thus to his own suggestions, he could feel himself beginning to tremble, though he hardly knew why—whether from cold, that is to say, or from fear. He tried to cover himself up and lie down as before but found this impossible. He could not remain still, even for a second, but felt as if he must be up and doing something to stifle the terror which was rising in him, and against which he felt himself powerless. He got out his matches and cigarettes once more, but of the former there remained but three, and they of the sorriest kind. Indeed, all of them fizzled out without lighting when struck.

"The devil take you, you cursed bit of rubbish! Go and be hanged to you!" he burst out (though hardly knowing what it was he was swearing at) as he hurled the battered cigarette away. The match-box was about to follow it, when he stayed his hand, and thrust the box into his pocket. Such a fit of restlessness now seized upon him that he could stay no longer where he was. Leaping from the sledge, and standing with his back to the wind, he began lowering and tightening up his belt again.

"Why should we lie here, waiting for death to come?" he exclaimed as a new idea suddenly struck him. "Why not mount the cob and ride away? With only a man on his back he would never stick fast." Then he thought of Nikita. "Oh, but it would be nothing to him to die," he went on. "What can his life matter to him? He has nothing much to lose with it, whereas I have much to gain with mine."

So he untied the cob, threw the halter over its neck, and tried to mount, but his fur coat and boots weighed him down, and he slipped back every time. Then he climbed onto the sledge and tried to mount from there, but the sledge kept rocking under his weight, and he failed again. At length, and for the third time, he drew the cob close to the sledge, balanced himself cautiously on the rim, and succeeded so far as to find himself stretched face downwards athwart the animal's back. Lying thus, he wriggled himself forward

once or twice until he had got his leg over and seated himself, his toes resting in the trace-loops of the saddle-piece. But the jolting of the sledge as it shook under Vassili's weight had awakened Nikita, who now raised himself and seemed to Vassili to be saying something.

"Look here, you fool," shouted Vassili. "It's all through you that we have got into this plight—got into it for nothing, too," and, tucking the flapping skirts of his greatcoat beneath his knees, he turned the cob round, and rode away from the sledge in the direction where he thought the forest and the forest-keeper's lodge must be.

# VII

Up to this moment Nikita had never once stirred since he first squatted down behind the sledge and covered himself over with the apron. Like all people who live in close contact with nature and are familiar with hardship, he was patient and could sit waiting for hours, or even for days, without growing restless or losing his temper. He had heard his master call out to him twice, yet had returned no answer, for the sole reason that he did not feel inclined to stir or to go to the trouble of raising his voice. Although he was warm enough at the time he had sat down, both with the tea which he had drunk and with the exertion of plunging through snowdrifts, he knew that that would not last long, and that he would be powerless to restore the warmth by exercising himself, since he felt as utterly worn out as a horse feels when it stops and can go no further, despite the severest whipping, and his master sees that no further work can be got out of him until he has been rested and fed. Moreover, one of his feet had got frostbitten through its ragged boot, so that the big toe had lost all sensation and his whole body was becoming steadily colder and colder. Consequently, in time, the thought began to enter his head that he might have to die that night. Yet the thought was neither particularly unwelcome nor particularly awe-inspiring. It was not particularly unwelcome, for the reason that his life had not been exactly an uninterrupted holiday, but, on the contrary, a life of ceaseless servitude, of which he was beginning to grow weary. Nor did the thought seem to him particularly awe-inspiring, for the reason that, over and above the masters whom he had served on earth—masters such as Vassili Andreitch—he had always felt himself dependent upon the Great Master who had sent him into this life, and knew that, in dying, he would still remain that Master's servant, and that that Master would be good to him.

"Should I be sorry to leave the life in which I am settled and which I accustomed to?" he thought. "Well, even if I have to go, I cannot help myself, and it were best to prepare for the new one."

"My sins?" he went on presently as he remembered his drunken orgies, the money squandered on drink, his insults to his wife, his frequent oaths, his neglect of church-going, his non-observance of fast-days, and all the many things for which the priest had reproved him at confession time. "Well, of course they were sins—I have never denied that; but it was God who made me what I am. Yet, what terrible sins they have been! What will become of me for such sins?"

Then, from thinking of what might be in store for him that night he passed, without recurring to that thought, to memories which came into his head at random. He thought of Martha's arrival, of the workmen's carouse, of his refusal to share their liquor, of the present expedition, of Tarass's hut, of the talk about family separations, of his little lad, of Brownie (now, doubtless, growing warm under his sacking), and of the master who was making the sledge creak above him as he tossed and turned.

"Well, I had plenty of tea to drink there and was tired," he thought. "*I* had no wish to start out again. *I* had no wish to leave such good living to come and die in this hole. Yet *he* wished otherwise."

Then all these memories swam together and jumbled themselves up in his head, and he went off into a doze.

From this doze he was awakened by Vassili shaking the sledge as he mounted the cob—shaking it so violently that it slewed right round and struck Nikita in the back with one of its runners, forcing him, willy-nilly, to shift his position. Stretching out his legs with some difficulty and sweeping the snow off them; he raised himself a little, and at once felt a pang shoot through his body. Understanding at the first glance what Vassili intended to do, he begged him to leave the sacking behind, since the cob no longer needed it and it would make an additional covering for himself. He shouted to Vassili to that effect, but the latter disappeared in the snow-dust without heeding him. Left alone, Nikita considered what he had better do. He felt that he had not sufficient strength also to go off in search of a human habitation, while it was impossible for him to resume his old seat, since the snow had filled up the hole already. Even if he got into the sledge, things would not mend, for he had no extra covering, and his *khalat* and fur jacket no longer kept him warm. He could not have felt colder if he had been clad only in a shirt.

The situation was becoming one of positive agony.

"Little Father—our Little Father in Heaven!" he cried aloud; and the knowledge that he was not alone, but that there was One who could hear him and would never abandon him, brought him comfort. He drew a deep sigh and, with the apron still covering his head, crept into the sledge and lay down where his master had been. Even there, however, he could not grow warm. At first he kept shivering all over. Then the shivering fit passed away, and he began to lose consciousness. He might have been dead or asleep, for all he could tell, yet felt prepared for either eventuality.

# VIII

Meanwhile Vassili was using his heels and the spare end of the halter to urge the cob in the direction where, for some reason or another, he supposed the forest and the forest-keeper to be. The snow blinded his eyes and the wind seemed as if it were struggling to stop him, but, bending forward at times to double the skirts of his coat and tuck them between his knees and the icy saddle-piece which made his seat such an uncomfortable one, he pressed the cob onwards unceasingly. The animal moved with difficulty, yet proceeded whither it was directed in its usual docile manner.

For what seemed to him some five minutes Vassili rode straight ahead, seeing nothing in front of him but the cob's head and ears and a sea of whiteness, and hearing nothing but the whistling of the wind over the cob's ears and round the collar of his fur coat. Suddenly, however, something black showed up before him. His heart began to beat hopefully, and he rode towards the object, imagining that he already discerned in its

Frank Schoonover, *Height of Land Portage,* 1904, Private Collection

outlines the walls of the houses forming a village. The object did not keep still, however, but was forever waving from side to side. In fact, it turned out to be, not a village, but a tall piece of wormwood, which, growing out of a boundary ridge and projecting above the snow, bent violently over to one side each time that the wind struck it and went whistling through its stems. Somehow the sight of this wormwood thus tortured by the cruel wind caused Vassili to shudder, and he restarted the cob in haste, without noticing that, in turning aside to the wormwood, he had deviated from his former direction, and was now riding at a tangent to it. Nonetheless, he imagined himself still to be bearing in the fancied direction of the forest-keeper's hut, and, although the cob kept trying to swerve to the right, he as often straightened it again to the left.

For the second time a dark object loomed up before him, filling his heart with joy, since he felt certain this time that here was a village at last: yet it proved to be only another boundary ridge topped with wormwood. As in the case of the first one, the sound of the wind wailing through the dried stems seemed to fill Vassili with fear. This piece of wormwood was exactly similar to the other piece in all respects save one—namely, that beside this second piece ran the track of a horse's hoofs, slightly powdered over with snow. Vassili pulled up, leaned forward, and looked at the track carefully. It was the track of a small-sized hoof, and the covering of snow upon it was, as yet, a mere sprinkling. In short, it was the track of his own cob! He had described a complete circle, and that not a large one.

"So this is how I am to perish!" he thought. Then, lest he should yield to his terror, he started forward again, and urged on the cob even more strenuously than before. At every moment, as he strained his eyes into the swirl of whiteness before him, he seemed to see dark points stand out for a second and then vanish as soon as he looked at

them. Once he thought he heard what might have been either the barking of a dog or the howl of a wolf, but the sound was so faint and uncertain that he could not be sure whether he had really heard anything or whether it had been only his fancy. He stopped and listened attentively.

Suddenly a weird, startling cry sounded in his very ears, and everything beneath him seemed to heave and tremble. He clutched the cob's mane, yet found that that too was quivering, while the cry grew ever more and more piercing. For some seconds Vassili could not frame a thought or understand in the least what was happening. Yet all that had happened was that the cob had been seized with the idea either of inspiriting himself or of calling for help, and had neighed loudly in his raucous, guttural tones.

"How the beast frightened me, be hanged to it!" gasped Vassili to himself. Yet, although he understood now the cause of his terror, he could not shake himself free from it.

"I must consider things a moment and steady myself," he thought. Yet it was all to no purpose, for he could not master himself—could not keep from urging the cob on; taking no heed the while that he was now riding before the wind instead of against it. His body was chilled and aching all over, but especially in the lower part, next the saddle-piece, where his coat was unhooked, whilst his hands and feet were shaking violently and his breath came in gasps. He felt sure now that he was to perish in the midst of this fearful waste of snow, and that nothing could save him.

Suddenly the cob gave a groan as it stuck fast in a snowdrift, and, struggling violently, began to sink sideways onto its flank. Vassili leapt off, displacing as he did so the trace-loops in which his feet had been resting, and so also the saddle-piece on which he had been seated. Yet he had no sooner dismounted than the cob righted himself, lurched forward, took a couple of plunges, and disappeared with a loud neigh, trailing behind him the sacking and harness, and leaving Vassili stranded in the snowdrift. Vassili made a rush to catch him, but the snow was so deep, and his fur coat so heavy, that he sank knee-deep at every step, and had taken no more than twenty strides when his breath failed him, and he had to stop.

"The timber, the wethers for the butcher, the rent-hold land, the store, the taverns, the iron-roofed villa and warehouse, my little heir—am I to leave them all?" he thought. "Is it to end like this? No, no, it cannot be!"

For some reason or another there came into his mind at that moment a picture of the wormwood waving in the wind, and of himself twice riding up to it. Such terror seized upon him that he could hardly believe in the reality of what was happening. "I must be dreaming it all," he thought, and tried, as it were, to awake from his dream: yet there was no awakening for him. It was real snow that was lashing his face, heaping his form over, and chilling his right hand, which had lost its mitten. It was a real desert, too, in which he was now left lonely—as lonely as the wormwood—and in which he must await an imminent, a swift, and an unthinkable death.

"O Queen of Heaven! O Holy Father Saint Nicholas who teachest us abstinence!" he began, with a dim recollection of the thanksgiving service of yesterday, of the ikon with its blackened face and golden vestment, and of the candles for that ikon which he had sold, and which, returned to him straightway, he had replaced in his locker after lighting them for a brief moment. Again and again he besought the wonder-working Saint Nicholas to save him from his fate, promising in return a thanksgiving and many candles. Yet all the time he knew beyond the possibility of doubt that, although that blackened face and golden vestment, as well as the candles, the priest, and the thanksgivings, were all of them very impor-tant and necessary there in the church, they could do nothing for him here, and that between those candles and thanksgivings on the one hand, and his present forlorn plight on the other, there could be no real connection whatever.

"Still, I must not despair," he thought. "I have only to follow the cob's track before it gets snowed over, and it will bring me out somewhere. Only, I must not hurry too much, or I might plunge into another snowdrift and be worse off than ever."

Nevertheless, for all his determination to go quietly, he could not help quickening his pace, breaking into a run, tumbling down continually, picking himself up again, and once more falling. Moreover, the cob's track was almost invisible where the snow was not deep.

"I am done for!" he said at last. "I am not following the cob's track at all, but only losing myself."

Just as he said this, however, he happened to glance ahead, and caught sight of something dark there. It was Brownie! And not Brownie alone, but also the shafts and the handkerchief! The cob was standing beside the sledge, with the harness and sacking still dangling down his flank—but standing in a different position to before, since he was just under the shafts, and had his head (which he kept shaking at intervals) drawn close to the ground by the halter, which had caught round his pastern. It seemed that Vassili had stuck fast in the same ravine as that into which Nikita and he had previously blundered—that, as a matter of fact, the cob had been carrying him straight back to the sledge, and that, at the moment when he jumped off, he had only been fifty paces from it!

# IX

Staggering up to the sledge, Vassili grasped hold of it and stood for a long time without mov-ing as he endeavored to steady himself and regain his breath. There was nothing to be seen of Nikita in his old position, but in the sledge there lay something heaped with snow, which Vassili guessed to be his servant. Vassili's terrors had now vanished—or, if any were left, it was merely lest he should have a return of the horrible panic which he had experienced on the cob's back, and, still more, when he found himself left in the snow-drift. At all costs he must not give way to that panic again; and if he would avoid that, he must be up and doing something—must be occupying his thoughts with something. First of all he planted himself with his back to the wind, and unfastened his fur coat to cool himself. Then, when he had regained his breath a little, he shook the snow off his boots and left-hand mitten (the other one was hopelessly lost, and probably lying somewhere a couple of inches below the snow), and refastened his belt tightly—much as he was accustomed to do when he was about to step out of his store to buy cartloads of grain which the *muzhiks* had brought. This done, he set about exerting himself. The first thing which it occurred to him to do was to disentangle the cob's leg, and, the halter thus freed, he tied Brownie up to the rim of the splashboard where he had been tied before. Next, he had just gone behind the cob to straighten the crupper, sacking, and saddle-piece on his back, when he saw something stir in the sledge, and then the head of Nikita emerge from beneath the snow which covered it. The frozen man raised himself a little—though evidently with a great effort—and made a strange gesture with his hand in front of his face, as though he were brushing away a fly. As he did this he seemed to Vassili to be saying something—probably Vassili's name—so the latter left the sacking unstraightened and stepped up to the sledge.

"How is it with you now?" he asked, "and what are you trying to say?"

"Only that I—I am dying," answered Nikita with difficulty and in gasps. "Give my wages to the little lad or to the wife—it does not matter which."

"Are you frozen, then?" said Vassili.

"Yes—and dying; I know it quite well," replied Nikita in a choking voice, and still fluttering his hand before his face as through to brush away a fly. "Pardon me, for Christ's sake."

For about half a minute Vassili stood without moving and in silence. Then all at once, and with the same air of decision as marked him when he had struck hands over a good bargain, he took a step backwards, tucked up the sleeves of his coat, and began with both hands to rake the snow off Nikita and out of the sledge. This done, he unhooked his belt, opened his fur coat, pushed Nikita hastily into a straight posture, and lay down upon him in such a way that the latter should be covered, not only with the coat, but with Vassili's own warm, overheated body. With one skirt of the coat tucked between Nikita's form and the side of the sledge, and the tail of it grasped between his ankles, Vassili remained lying prone, with his head resting upon the splashboard and his ears deaf either to the movements of the cob or to the howling of the wind, but intent only on listening to Nikita's breathing. For a long time Nikita lay without moving. Then he gave a deep sigh, and stirred faintly.

"There you are, you see, and yet you talk of dying!" began Vassili. "Just you lie still and grow warm, and we—"

To his great surprise Vassili found that he could say no more, for tears were welling from his eyes and his lower jaw was working. He broke off short, and swallowed a lump in his throat.

"How absurdly weak and nervous I have made myself," he thought. Yet not only did he find this weakness far from unpleasant, but it actually gave him a sensation of joy such as he had never yet experienced.

"Yes, we shall manage it all right like this," he said to himself, conscious of a rapturous feeling of emotion. After this he lay for a long time in silence, merely wiping his eyes against the fur of the coat, and tucking back its right-hand skirt as the wind blew it up at intervals; but at length he felt as though he must communicate his joy to a fellow-creature.

"Nikita," he said.

"That is better. I am getting warm now," came from underneath him.

"Nikita, my old friend, I thought we were done for. You would have been frozen, and I—"

Once more Vassili's cheeks started quivering and his eyes filled with tears, so that he could say no more.

"No, it is no good," he said to himself. "Yet I know what I know," and he remained silent. Still he lay there. Warmth seemed to be passing into his body from Nikita below and from the fur coat above. Only the hands with which he held the skirts of the coat against Nikita's sides, and his feet, from between which the wind kept blowing the skirts away, were beginning to feel frozen. His mittenless right hand in particular felt numbed. Yet he never thought of his hands or feet—only of how he could best warm the peasant who was lying beneath him.

More than once he glanced at the cob and saw that its back was uncovered, since the sacking had now slipped off altogether and was lying on the snow. He felt as if he ought to go and cover the animal over again, yet could not make up his mind to leave Nikita, even for a moment, and thus break the spell of that rapturous joy which now possessed him. As for his terrors, they had long since fled away.

"By heavens, I am not going to be beaten!" he said to himself with reference to his efforts to warm Nikita—speaking, indeed, in just the same boastful tone in which he had been accustomed to speak of his sales or purchases.

He lay for an hour—for two—for three, but took no heed of the passing of time. At first there danced before his vision dim pictures of the storm, of the shafts, and of the cob under its high *douga*. Then these pictures became exchanged for jumbled memories of the festival, of his wife, of the commissary of police, and of the candle-locker—but beneath the picture of the candle-locker lay Nikita. Then again he saw the *muzhiks* trading with him, and the white, iron-roofed walls of his house—but beneath the picture of those walls again lay Nikita. Then everthing became confused. One thing ran into another, until at last these various scattered impressions came together as the colors of a rainbow merge into a beam of white light, and he fell asleep. For long he slept without dreaming, but, just before the dawn came, there came also some sleep-visions. He seemed to be standing by the candle-locker, while old mother Tikhonova was asking him for a five-kopeck[22] candle for the festival. He tried to take the candle out and give it to her, but his hands remained glued in his pockets. Then he tried to walk round the locker, but his legs refused to move, and his new, clean shoes stuck fast to the stone floor, so that he could not even raise his feet to take the shoes off.

Then suddenly the locker was not a locker at all, but a bed, and on that bed Vassili could see himself lying, face downwards—lying on his own bed at home. He was lying on the bed, and could not rise, although it was necessary for him to do so, seeing that Ivan Matveitch,[23] the commissary of police, was coming to see him presently, and he must go with Ivan either to buy some timber or to put the crupper straight on the cob's back—he could not be sure which. He kept asking his wife, "Has he not come yet, Mikolovna?" and she kept answering him, "No, not yet." Then he could hear someone driving up to the steps outside.

---

22. *kopeck* (kō′ pek), Russian unit of money worth $\frac{1}{100}$ of a ruble.
23. *Matveitch* (mät vā′ yich).

Surely it must be he? But no—the vehicle had driven past. "Is he not come yet, Mikolovna?" he asked his wife once more, and once more she replied, "No, not yet." Thus he lay and lay upon the bed, unable to rise, and ever waiting—waiting: and the waiting was at once painful and joyous. Suddenly the joy of it was filled to the full! He for whose coming he had been waiting, was now at hand and it was not Ivan Matveitch nor anyone else. Yet still it was the Man for whom he had been waiting. He entered—did that Man—and called him: and this Man who had called him cried out to him again and bade him go and lie down upon Nikita. And Vassili was glad that this Someone had come. "Yes, I will go!" he cried in his joy, and with that cry Vassili awoke.

Yes, he awoke—but awoke a very different man to what he had been when he fell asleep. He tried to rise, and could not. He tried to move his hand, and could not. He tried to move his leg, and could not. Then he tried to turn his head, but that also he could not do. This surprised him, yet in no way troubled him. Then he remembered that Nikita was lying beneath him, and that Nikita was growing warm and was coming back to life. It seemed to him that he was Nikita, and Nikita was he, and that his life was no longer within himself, but within Nikita. He strained his ears till he caught the sound of breathing—yes, the faint, deep breathing of Nikita. "Nikita is alive!" he cried to himself in triumph, "and therefore so also am I!"

Then he began to think about his money, his store, his house, his sales and purchases, and Mironoff's millions. He could not understand how that man whom men called Vassili Brekhunoff could bear to interest himself in such things as he did. "That man can never have known what is the greatest thing of all," he thought of this Vassili Brekhunoff. "He can never have known what I know. Yes, I know it for certain now. At last—I KNOW!"

Once again he heard the Man calling him who had called to him before, and his whole being seemed to respond in joy and loving-kindness as he replied: "I am coming, I am coming!" For he felt that he was free at last, and that nothing could hold him further.

And, indeed, nothing further than that did Vassili Andreitch see or hear or feel in this world.

Around him the tempest still kept on. The same swirls of snow kept circling in eddies and covering the coats of the dead Vassili Andreitch and the trembling Brownie, the sledge (now almost invisible) and, stretched out upon its floor, the now reviving Nikita as he lay prone beneath the body of his dead master.

# X

Just before morning Nikita awoke. It was the frost making its way down his back which aroused him. He had just been dreaming that he was driving from the mill with a load of his master's flour, and that, instead of taking the bridge over the stream, he went by the ford, and stuck fast. He could see himself getting under the load and trying to lift it as he straightened his back. Yet, strange to say, the load would not move, but clung always to his back, so that he could neither move the cart nor withdraw himself from beneath it. It seemed to be breaking his very loins. And how cold it felt! At all costs he must get away from beneath it. "Hold on," he found himself saying to the someone who was causing the load to break his back. "Take off some of the sacks." Yet the load kept growing colder and colder, and pressing more and more heavily upon him. Then suddenly something gave a loud bang, and he became fully awake and remembered all that had happened. That chilly load—it was his dead frozen master. That loud bang—it had been caused by Brownie striking his hoofs against the sledge.

"Andreitch, Andreitch!" he cried cautiously to his master (though he half guessed the truth already) as he raised his back stiffly. But Andreitch returned no answer, while his body and legs were cold and stiff and heavy as weights.

"There is no doubt that he is dead," thought Nikita. He turned his head round, pushed the snow away from in front of his face, and opened his eyes. It was quite light now. The wind was still humming through the shafts and the snow streaming down—but with this difference, that the snow was no longer dashing itself against the sides of the sledge, but piling itself up in silence over sledge and cob—from the latter of which not even the sound of breathing was now to be heard.

"Brownie too must be frozen," thought Nikita. And, indeed, those two loud hoof-strokes upon the sledge which had awakened him had been the last efforts of the now dead and frozen animal to keep upon his legs.

"O God, Little Father of ours, surely thou wilt call me also?" said Nikita. "If so, Thy will be done. It would be hard that two of us should be taken and the other left. Let death come when it will," and he drew his hand in again, closed his eyes and fell asleep, firmly convinced that this time he was really and truly dead.

It was about the time of the midday meal next day when some *muzhiks* dug out Vassili and Nikita—seventy yards only from the road, and half a verst from the village.

The snow had drifted completely over the sledge, but the shafts, with the handkerchief on them, were still visible. Brownie, belly-deep in the snow, stood a white frozen mass, his dead muzzle pressed tightly inwards against his rigid neck, his nostrils fringed with icicles, and his eyes coated over and glazed with ice as with frozen tears. Moreover, he had so wasted away in that one night that there remained of him but skin and bones. As for Vassili, he too was as stiff as a frozen

I. J. Alex, *Slavic Peasant*, Private Collection

carcass, and when his legs were pulled aside the corpse rolled off Nikita in a solid lump. His prominent, hawk-like eyes were frozen hard, and his mouth (open a little under his cropped moustache) filled with snow. Nikita only was alive, though frostbitten all over. Yet, when brought to himself, he could not be persuaded that he was not dead, and that all that was now happening to him was not taking place in the next world instead of in this. Indeed, his first feeling when he heard the *muzhiks* shouting above him as they dug out the sledge and then rolled the stiffened Vassili off him was one of surprise that *muzhiks* shouted in the next world even as they had shouted in this, and had similar bodies! When at length he understood that he was really here—here in this present world—he felt vexed rather than pleased, especially as he could feel that the fingers of both his hands were frostbitten.

For about two months he lay in hospital. Three of his fingers had to be amputated, but the others healed, so that he was able to go to work again and to live twenty years longer—first as a laborer, and then, in his old age, as a watchman. Indeed, he died only this year[24]—at home and under the ikons, with a lighted wax candle in his hands, just as he had always wished. Before his death he took leave of his old wife, and pardoned her for the cooper. He took leave also of his son and grandchildren, and died thoroughly happy to think that his death left his son and daughter-in-law freed from the burden of having a supernumerary mouth to feed, and that this time he himself would really pass from a life which had grown wearisome to him to that other life which had been growing more and more familiar and alluring to him each year and hour. Is he better or worse off now where he has awakened after his death—the death which really came that time? Is he disillusioned, or has he really found what he expected? Soon we shall all know.

24. *this year*, probably 1895, the year Tolstoy wrote this novel.

## THINK AND DISCUSS
### Understanding
1. Why is the thought of death not particularly unwelcome to Nikita?
2. Why doesn't Nikita seek help after Vassili abandons him?
3. What promises does Vassili make when he pleads to St. Nicholas to save him?
4. What does the heavy load that Nikita dreams is on his back turn out to be?
5. Where are Vassili and Nikita when they are "dug out" by some *muzhiks?*

### Analyzing
6. Chapter VI gives a focus to Vassili's response to their plight; Chapter VII to Nikita's response. Contrast their responses.
7. Identify the two major **conflicts** in the story and explain why one is more important than the other.
8. Why does Vassili abandon Nikita? Is this action consistent with his **character** as Tolstoy has portrayed him? Explain.
9. Explain the **irony** involved in Vassili's death.
10. In what sense is Vassili "saved" even in death?

### Extending
11. What characteristics of Vassili and Nikita reveal Tolstoy's philosophy of life? Review the biography of Tolstoy that precedes the novel for helpful ideas.
12. Who do you think is happier at the time of his death, Vassili or Nikita? Explain.

### REVIEWING: Theme  HT
**See Handbook of Literary Terms, p. 829**
The **theme** of a story is the underlying main idea, which may be stated directly or implied. At the end of Chapter IX in *Master and Man,* Vassili has a revelation which leads him to understand a central truth about life. From this revelation, the reader can infer the novel's theme.

1. What does the "new" Vassili know at the time of his death that the "old" Vassili did not? Your answer will be a statement of Tolstoy's theme.
2. Explain the double meaning of the title and how it relates to the story's theme.

## VOCABULARY
### Word Analogies

Word analogy tests require that you understand the relationship between a pair of words and then choose another pair of words that represent the same relationship. For example, *nose* is to *nasal* as *throat* is to *guttural*. Such word analogies usually are expressed in a formula, as follows.

nose : nasal :: throat : guttural

Study the relationship of the following pairs of words in capital letters; then look at the third word and decide which of the three ensuing choices can be paired with it to form a relationship similar to that of the first word pair. If necessary, you may use Glossary.

1. UPSIDE-DOWN : UPRIGHT :: gentlest : _____
   (a) mildest; (b) severest; (c) inferior
2. HORSESHOE : BLACKSMITH :: barrel : _____
   (a) sexton; (b) cooper; (c) tracker
3. BUS : STAGECOACH :: snowmobile : _____
   (a) buggy; (b) yacht; (c) sledge
4. FLOWERS : BED :: trees : _____
   (a) copse; (b) branch; (c) timber
5. SPEECH : TALK :: wisdom : _____
   (a) honesty; (b) lunacy; (c) sagacity
6. BORROWER : LENDER :: debtor : _____
   (a) creditor; (b) employee; (c) toper
7. MIRY : FIRM :: moot : _____
   (a) controversial; (b) unsettled; (c) certain
8. NOVEL : SHORT STORY :: city : _____
   (a) hovel; (b) metropolis; (c) hamlet
9. JUICE : PITCHER :: tea : _____
   (a) samovar; (b) bag; (c) leaf
10. FOOD : VIANDS :: whipping : _____
    (a) gesticulation; (b) soothing;
    (c) flagellation

## COMPOSITION
### Analyzing Dreams

Many people believe that the strange details of some dreams are based on real details in the dreamer's experience and may be helpful to better understand human psychology—that is, to better understand how people truly think and feel. Write three or four paragraphs in which you explain how various details in Vassili's "sleep-visions" relate to his real experience and to the way he truly thinks and feels.

### Describing a Reformed Character

Imagine that, instead of dying, Vassili survives the snowstorm and lives on. Write three or four paragraphs describing how you think he would or would not change as a result of the revelation he experiences when he is near death. Ask yourself how his relationship with Nikita would change or remain the same. Would his relationship with his family change? How would his attitudes toward business and the poor change? When writing, be sure to use descriptive, precise words, and, whenever possible, support your ideas with examples from the story.

## ENRICHMENT
### Making an Oral Report

After reading *Master and Man*, you have learned a great deal about life and travel in Russia during the nineteenth century. In order to learn more about the way people lived one hundred years ago, go to your school library to conduct research on a country of your choice. Using sources such as history books, encyclopedias, maps, and magazines, look for information on such topics as the way people dressed, the way they traveled, what they ate, what they did for fun, and so on. When you are through, give a brief oral report to your class, using pictures, maps, and other graphic aids or artifacts that help make your report more interesting.

# THINKING CRITICALLY
# ABOUT LITERATURE

## UNIT 8   THE NOVEL

### ■ CONCEPT REVIEW

This selection is one chapter of an American novel that depicts a life of confinement faced by some New Englanders in the past. It illustrates some of the literary elements and ideas you have studied in this unit and throughout this book. The selection is accompanied by notes designed to help you think critically about your reading. A discussion of certain literary terms in the notes appears in the Handbook of Literary Terms.

In the novel, Ethan Frome farms land that is only marginally productive. He and his wife Zenobia do not get along well, since she is preoccupied with her chronic illnesses and he feels trapped in his loveless marriage, on a farm he cannot sell. Mattie Silver, Zenobia's cousin, comes to live with the Fromes and work as a servant and companion to Zenobia; Ethan becomes fascinated with the young woman. When his wife goes away to visit a new doctor, Ethan faces a winter night at home with Mattie.

# *from* Ethan Frome

## Edith Wharton   USA

They finished supper, and while Mattie cleared the table Ethan went to look at the cows and then took a last turn about the house. The earth lay dark under a muffled sky and the air was so still that now and then he heard a lump of snow come thumping down from a tree far off on the edge of the wood-lot.

When he returned to the kitchen Mattie had pushed up his chair to the stove and seated herself near the lamp with a bit of sewing. The scene was just as he had dreamed of it that morning. He sat down, drew his pipe from his pocket and stretched his feet to the glow. His hard day's work in the keen air made him feel at once lazy and light of mood, and he had a confused sense of being in another world, where all was warmth and harmony and time could

■ Note the still, tranquil mood that is set at the beginning of the chapter.

Edith Wharton, *Ethan Frome*, Charles Scribner's Sons, 1911.

bring no change. The only drawback to his complete well-being was the fact that he could not see Mattie from where he sat; but he was too indolent to move and after a moment he said: "Come over here and sit by the stove."

Zeena's empty rocking-chair stood facing him. Mattie rose obediently, and seated herself in it. As her young brown head detached itself against the patch-work cushion that habitually framed his wife's gaunt countenance, Ethan had a momentary shock. It was almost as if the other face, the face of the superseded woman, had obliterated that of the intruder. After a moment Mattie seemed to be affected by the same sense of constraint. She changed her position, leaning forward to bend her head above her work, so that he saw only the foreshortened tip of her nose and the streak of red in her hair; then she slipped to her feet, saying "I can't see to sew," and went back to her chair by the lamp.

■ Zeena: Ethan's wife, who is away at the time.

Ethan made a pretext of getting up to replenish the stove, and when he returned to his seat he pushed it sideways that he might get a view of her profile and of the lamplight falling on her hands. The cat, who had been a puzzled observer of these unusual movements, jumped up into Zeena's chair, rolled itself into a ball, and lay watching them with narrowed eyes.

■ The cat is occupying Zeena's chair, symbolically suggesting her presence.

Deep quiet sank on the room. The clock ticked above the dresser, a piece of charred wood fell now and then in the stove, and the faint sharp scent of the geraniums mingled with the odour of Ethan's smoke, which began to throw a blue haze about the lamp and to hang its greyish cobwebs in the shadowy corners of the room.

■ Note how the author's use of imagery to describe the scene appeals to the senses.

All constraint had vanished between the two, and they began to talk easily and simply. They spoke of every-day things, of the prospect of snow, of the next church sociable, of the loves and quarrels of Starkfield. The commonplace nature of what they said produced in Ethan an illlusion of long-established intimacy which no outburst of emotion could have given, and he set his imagination adrift on the fiction that they had always spent their evenings thus and would always go on doing so . . .

"This is the night we were to have gone coasting. Matt," he said at length, with the rich sense, as he spoke, that they could go on any other night they chose, since they had all time before them.

■ coasting: sledding.

She smiled back at him. "I guess you forgot!"

"No, I didn't forget; but it's as dark as Egypt outdoors. We might go to-morrow if there's a moon."

She laughed with pleasure, her head tilted back, the lamplight sparkling on her lips and teeth. "That would be lovely, Ethan!"

He kept his eyes fixed on her, marvelling at the way her face changed with each turn of their talk, like a wheat-field under a summer breeze. It was intoxicating to find such magic in his clumsy words, and he longed to try new ways of using it.

■ Note the comparison made between Mattie's face and a field of wheat.

"Would you be scared to go down the Corbury road with me on a night like this?" he asked.

Her cheeks burned redder. "I ain't any more scared than you are!"

"Well, *I'd* be scared, then; I wouldn't do it. That's an ugly corner down by the big elm. If a fellow didn't keep his eyes open he'd go plumb into it." He luxuriated in the sense of protection and authority which his words conveyed. To prolong and intensify the feeling he added: "I guess we're well enough here."

■ Ethan's comment about crashing into a tree fore-shadows an event that occurs later in the novel.

She let her lids sink slowly, in the way he loved. "Yes, we're well enough here," she sighed.

Her tone was so sweet that he took the pipe from his mouth and drew his chair up to the table. Leaning forward, he touched the farther end of the strip of brown stuff that she was hemming. "Say, Matt," he began with a smile, "what do you think I saw under the Varnum spruces, coming along home just now? I saw a friend of yours getting kissed."

The words had been on his tongue all the evening, but now that he had spoken them they struck him as inexpressibly vulgar and out of place.

Mattie blushed to the roots of her hair and pulled her needle rapidly twice or thrice through her work, insensibly drawing the end of it away from him. "I suppose it was Ruth and Ned," she said in a low voice, as though he had suddenly touched on something grave.

■ Note how the mood changes from one of quiet tranquility to one of tension.

Ethan had imagined that his allusion might open the way to the accepted pleasantries, and these perhaps in turn to a harmless caress, if only a mere touch on her hand. But now he felt as if her blush had set a flaming guard about her. He supposed it was his natural awkwardness that made him feel so. He knew that most young men made nothing at all of giving a pretty girl a kiss, and he remembered that the night before, when he had put his arm about Mattie, she had not resisted. But that had been out-of-doors, under the open irresponsible night. Now, in the warm lamplit room, with all its ancient implications of conformity and order, she seemed infinitely farther away from him and more unapproachable.

■ Ethan characterizes himself as having a "natural awkwardness" which inhibits his actions.

To ease his constraint he said: "I suppose they'll be setting a date before long."

"Yes. I shouldn't wonder if they got married some time along in the summer." She pronounced the word *married* as if her voice caressed it. It seemed a rustling covert leading to enchanted glades. A pang shot through Ethan, and he said, twisting away from her in his chair: "It'll be your turn next, I wouldn't wonder."

She laughed a little uncertainly. "Why do you keep on saying that?"

He echoed her laugh. "I guess I do it to get used to the idea."

He drew up to the table again and she sewed on in silence, with dropped lashes, while he sat in fascinated contemplation of the way in which her hands went up and down above the strip of stuff, just as he had seen a pair of birds make short perpendicular flights over a nest they were building. At length, without turning her head or lifting her lids, she said in a low tone: "It's not because you think Zeena's got anything against me, is it?"

His former dread started up full-armed at the suggestion. "Why, what do you mean?" he stammered.

She raised distressed eyes to his, her work dropping on the table between them. "I don't know. I thought last night she seemed to have."

"I'd like to know what," he growled.

"Nobody can tell with Zeena." It was the first time they had ever spoken so openly of her attitude toward Mattie, and the repetition of the name seemed to carry it to the farther corners of the room and send it back to them in long repercussions of sound. Mattie waited, as if to give the echo time to drop, and then went on: "She hasn't said anything to *you?*"

He shook his head. "No, not a word."

She tossed the hair back from her forehead with a laugh. "I guess I'm just nervous, then. I'm not going to think about it any more."

"Oh, no—don't let's think about it, Matt!"

The sudden heat of his tone made her colour mount again, not with a rush, but gradually, delicately, like the reflection of a thought stealing slowly across her heart. She sat silent, her hands clasped on her work, and it seemed to him that a warm current flowed toward him along the strip of stuff that still lay unrolled between them. Cautiously he slid his hand palm-downward along the table till his finger-tips touched the end of the stuff. A faint vibration of her lashes seemed to show that she was aware of his gesture, and that it had sent a counter-current back to her; and she let her hands lie motionless on the other end of the strip.

As they sat thus he heard a sound behind him and turned his head. The cat had jumped from Zeena's chair to dart at a mouse in the wainscot, and as a result of the sudden movement the empty chair had set up a spectral rocking.

The cat's sudden move startles Ethan and Mattie and brings them back to reality.

"She'll be rocking in it herself this time to-morrow," Ethan thought. "I've been in a dream, and this is the only evening we'll ever have together." The return to reality was as painful as the return to consciousness after taking an anaesthetic. His body and brain ached with indescribable weariness, and he could think of nothing to say or to do that should arrest the mad flight of the moments.

His alteration of mood seemed to have communicated itself to Mattie. She looked up at him languidly, as though her lids were weighted with sleep and it cost her an effort to raise them. Her glance fell on his hand, which now completely covered the end of her work and grasped it as if it were a part of herself. He saw a scarcely perceptible tremor cross her face, and without knowing what he did he stooped his head and kissed the bit of stuff in his hold. As his lips rested on it he felt it glide slowly from beneath them, and saw that Mattie had risen and was silently rolling up her work. She fastened it with a pin, and then, finding her thimble and scissors, put them with the roll of stuff into the box covered with fancy paper which he had once brought to her from Bettsbridge.

He stood up also, looking vaguely about the room. The clock above the dresser struck eleven.

"Is the fire all right?" she asked in a low voice.

He opened the door of the stove and poked aimlessly at the embers. When he raised himself again he saw that she was dragging toward the stove the old soap-box lined with carpet in which the cat made its bed. Then she recrossed the floor and lifted two of the geranium pots in her arms, moving them away from the cold window. He followed her and brought the other geraniums, the hyacinth bulbs in a cracked custard bowl and the German ivy trained over an old croquet hoop.

When these nightly duties were performed there was nothing left to do but to bring in the tin candlestick from the passage, light the candle and blow out the lamp. Ethan put the candlestick in Mattie's hand and she went out of the kitchen ahead of him, the light that she carried before her making her dark hair look like a drift of mist on the moon.

"Good night, Matt," he said as she put her foot on the first step of the stairs.

She turned and looked at him a moment. "Good night, Ethan," she answered, and went up.

When the door of her room had closed on her he remembered that he had not even touched her hand.

■ The characters have expressed their feelings only indirectly due to their circumstances. The theme of the novel concerns such limits on people's choices.

## THINK AND DISCUSS
### Understanding
1. From Ethan's point of view, what is the drawback to his complete well-being?
2. On what does Ethan set his imagination?
3. What had once been Ethan's and Mattie's scheduled plan for this night?
4. What words spoken by Ethan does he soon feel are vulgar and out of place?
5. What does Ethan remember after Mattie has retired to her room?

### Analyzing
6. Explain how the cat may be seen as representative of Zeena (Ethan's absent wife).
7. Identify two or three comparisons Ethan creates in reference to Mattie. What do these comparisons suggest about their relationship?
8. What occurs that brings Ethan and Mattie back suddenly to the reality of their hopeless situation?

## REVIEWING LITERARY TERMS

### Setting

1. Describe, in your own words, the setting of this passage. What feelings in the reader does the setting provoke?
2. Although Zeena is not physically present in this scene, what elements in the setting remind the reader (and the characters) of her presence?

### Foreshadowing

3. Although it is not mentioned in the chapter you just read, Ethan and Mattie do, indeed, go sledding. However, their excursion meets some tragic results. Find a passage that foreshadows a disaster.
4. Another important event in the novel, after Zeena's return, is that she decides Mattie must leave the house. Find elements in this chapter that foreshadow this event.

### Theme

5. Ethan feels happiest when he imagines that every evening would be as pleasant as this one. Why does he know that his image will be short-lived?
6. Typical stories about married characters portray marriage as a warm, happy, or exciting relationship. What aspects of the Fromes' marriage make it support a theme about bleak and limited lives?

## ■ CONTENT REVIEW

### THINKING SKILLS

#### Classifying

1. In the three novels in this unit, there are definite relationships that separate the characters. That is, some of the characters are served by others. List the characters you read about in this unit and classify them as either those who are served or those who serve.

### Generalizing

After reading *The Pearl* and/or *Master and Man,* you have learned quite a bit about the times and countries these novels are set in, and how the climate affects the characters' ways of life. Review one of the stories to help you answer the following questions.

2. How does the climate affect the way the characters dress?
3. How does the climate or setting affect the way the characters travel?
4. What effect does the setting have on where the characters sleep?
5. Does the setting affect the way the characters earn their living? How?

### Synthesizing

6. In *Master and Man,* Vassili and Nikita can be considered victims of their environment. However, it could be argued that they are victims of their own lack of good judgment and that they create their own problems. Think about their struggle against the elements, and consider ways they could have made their journey safer. What could they have done to avoid getting lost, freezing, and risking death?
7. In *The Pearl,* Kino and Juana are also victims of their environment, but they do not seem as directly responsible for their problems as Vassili and Nikita. As a result, they suffer a tremendously tragic loss at the end of the story. Think about how you would have liked the story to end and write a summary of what you think should have happened. Be sure the characters' actions in your ending are believable or consistent with their actions in the rest of the story.

### Evaluating

8. At the beginning of *The Pearl* and *Master and Man*, the relationships between the main characters seem clearly defined as those who are in charge (Kino and Vassili) and those who follow (Juana and Nikita). However, as each story develops, it becomes apparent that there exists a mutual dependence between the main characters. Think about one of the novels and explain how the actions of each character involved demonstrate mutual dependence, in your judgment. If you disagree, explain how you evaluate the relationship.

## ■ COMPOSITION REVIEW

Choose one of the following assignments and write the composition.

### Identifying Prejudice in Fiction

Both *The Pearl* and *Master and Man* contain elements of prejudice between social classes. Review one of the stories to identify such prejudice, and write a two- or three-paragraph composition detailing the prejudice and explaining its use in the story. Be sure to use details from the story to support your ideas.

### Writing from an Alternate Point of View

In Chapter V of *Ethan Frome*, the narrator describes the scene essentially from Ethan's perspective, not revealing Mattie's thoughts and emotions, but only her reactions. Write a three-paragraph account of the scene from Mattie's viewpoint which reveals her thoughts and feelings.

### Writing About Inanimate Objects

Inanimate objects can be used by authors to motivate characters. In *The Pearl*, the pearl itself is such an object. In *Master and Man* it is the money carried by Vassili, and in *Ethan Frome*, it is Zeena's rocking chair. Choose one of these objects and write three paragraphs explaining how it affects the characters.

### Challenging a Social Evil

The novels in this unit illustrate how novelists can depict social conditions and problems in their fiction. Write a composition of at least four paragraphs in which you identify one current social evil which, in your opinion, should be challenged. Cite your reasons for believing as you do, as well as the methods by which you believe reform can be achieved.

### Reviewing Writer's Craft: Write Good Endings

Think about the lessons that can be learned from *The Pearl* and *Master and Man*. Then consider a moral that you may use in a story. Write an original parable—a short tale that embodies a moral or ethical principle—in modern terms. When you write, be sure to use an ending and moral that will challenge the reader to think beyond your story.

Berthe Morisot, *The Mother and Sister of the Artist* (detail), 1869–1870, National Gallery of Art, Washington, D.C.

# HANDBOOK OF LITERARY TERMS

# ■ ALLITERATION

An Austrian army, awfully array'd,
Boldly by battery besieged Belgrade;

What is the recurring initial sound in each line above? These lines contain extreme examples of *alliteration*, the repetition of identical or similar sounds at the beginnings of words or within the words themselves, particularly at the beginning of accented syllables. You are probably already familiar with alliteration as it is used in advertising: "Quick Clean Car Care" or "Buy Big Broiled Burgers." Many ordinary expressions contain alliteration: *wild west; through thick and through thin; merry month of May; rough and ready.*

Alliteration can draw attention to certain words in a poem:

*S*afe upon the *s*olid rock the
ugly house*s* *s*tand:
Come and *s*ee my *s*hining pala*c*e
built upon the *s*and!

Edna St. Vincent Millay
**Figs from Thistles**

It can link together words that are similar in thought or feeling:

*C*old are the *c*rabs that *c*rawl on yonder hills,
*C*older the *c*ucumbers that grow beneath. . . .

Edward Lear
**"Cold Are the Crabs"**

It can point up contrasts:

The *H*art loves the *h*igh wood,
the *H*are loves the *h*ill. . . .

Alliteration in poetry gives pleasure, but a good poet also may make the sound reflect the meaning of a poem, as shown in the examples that follow:

When he saw *Gr*endel's *gr*uesome footprints,
that *gr*eat man *gr*ieved for his retainers.

**Beowulf** (translated by
*Kevin Crossley-Holland*)

Does the repeated *gr* sound help to make this line seem light or heavy?

**Sea-Weed**

Sea-weed sways and sways and swirls
as if swaying were its form of stillness;
and if it flushes against fierce rock
it slips over as shadows do, without hurting itself.

D. H. Lawrence

What effect does the repeated *s* sound have?

---

# ■ ALLITERATION (ə lit′ə rā′shən)

**The repetition of similar or identical sounds at the beginnings of words or in accented syllables. It is used to create melody, establish mood, emphasize certain words, and point up similarities and contrasts.**

---

From "Alliteration, or The Siege of Belgrade," *The Cherry Tree*, A Collection of Poems chosen by Geoffrey Grigson. Published by The Vanguard Press, Inc. Copyright, © mcmlix, by Geoffrey Grigson. Reprinted by permission of the author.

From *Collected Poems*, Harper & Row. Copyright 1922, 1950 by Edna St. Vincent Millay. Reprinted by permission of Norma Millay Ellis.

From "The Hart Loves the High Wood," *The Gambit Book of Popular Verse*, Edited with an introduction by Geoffrey Grigson. Published by Gambit, Inc., 1971. Reprinted by permission of the author.

Excerpt from *Beowulf*, by Kevin Crossley-Holland. Translation copyright © 1968 by Kevin Crossley-Holland. Reprinted by permission of Farrar, Straus & Giroux, Inc. and Deborah Rogers Ltd.

"Sea-Weed" from *The Complete Poems of D. H. Lawrence*, Collected and Edited by Vivian de Sola Pinto and F. Warren Roberts. Copyright © 1964, 1971 by Angelo Ravagli and C. M. Weekley, Executors of The Estate of Frieda Lawrence Ravagli. All Rights Reserved. Reprinted by permission of Viking Penguin Inc. and Laurence Pollinger Ltd.

■ Apply to "**Sonnet 65**" on page 281.

# ■ ALLUSION

March 15 hit hard this year—gray, rainy, and a chill wind that bit right through my jacket. By the time I reached school, my shoes were soaked, my socks damp and itchy, and my homework soggy. As I sat down in my first-period class, world history, Mr. Brutto told us to take out a clean sheet of paper and clear our desks. It meant only one thing: a pop quiz. I guess that old bird was right when he said to beware the ides of March. I should've stayed in bed.

Who is the "old bird" referred to in the above paragraph? What does the writer of the paragraph mean by referring to the "ides of March"? How does the reference relate to the events in the paragraph? (For the source of the *allusion,* see *Julius Caesar,* Act One, Scene 2.)

An allusion is a reference to any historical, cultural, mythical, or literary event or any other aspect of ancient or modern culture. Some allusions are so familiar that you may not think of them as such. For example, the Biblical figures David and Goliath often are alluded to in any kind of match that involves opponents of apparently unequal size or strength. A fantastic young hitter on a baseball team may be called "a new Hank Aaron" by sportswriters.

Allusions in literature may be used to increase meaning, beauty, or mood, or to add depth to a work. They provide a concise means of strengthening atmosphere or clarifying tone. Allusions may be incidental to a work, or they may be crucial to its understanding. Sometimes they require research on the part of the reader.

In order to understand the cartoon, the reader must be familiar with a certain Mother Goose nursery rhyme. The reference to "Humpty" in the cartoon should prompt a recollection of Humpty Dumpty, the character in the rhyme who was hurt beyond repair in a fall from a wall. Recalling that Humpty Dumpty was an egg should enhance the allusion the cartoon makes to the nursery rhyme. The reader can conclude that the hen is the object of the sympathetic message probably because Humpty Dumpty was her egg.

The requirements for allusions are that they be accurate and appropriate to the subject at hand. Unless one were being sarcastic, one would not call the last racehorse to cross the finish line "Pegasus," the winged horse of Greek mythology; nor, when speaking of a quick errand, would one allude to the quest of King Arthur's knights for the Holy Grail. No one reads simply to fill his or her head with sources of allusion, but the ability to recognize allusions is a satisfying result of wide reading.

## ■ ALLUSION (ə lü′zhən)

**A reference to a historical or literary figure or event. It may allude to myth, religion, or to any other aspect of ancient or modern culture.**

■ Apply to **"The Tale of Sir Launcelot"** on page 349.

**Frank and Ernest**

WE WERE ALL SORRY TO HEAR ABOUT HUMPTY.

3-5 THAVES

# ■ ASSONANCE

While in the wild wood I did lie,
A child—with a most knowing eye.

*Edgar Allan Poe*
**"Romance"**

What words are accented in the above lines? What vowel sound is often repeated in those accented words? The recurring *i* sound is an example of *assonance:* identical or similar vowel sounds followed by different consonant sounds, and occurring generally in accented words or syllables. Assonance differs from rhyme in that rhyme is a similarity of both vowel and consonant sounds. *Wild* and *child* or *lie* and *eye* are rhyming words; *while* and *wild* illustrate assonance.

Point out the examples of assonance in the following lines.

Then a mile of warm sea-scented beach;
Three fields to cross till a farm appears . . .

*Robert Browning*
**"Meeting at Night"**

Not only are assonant words stressed rhythmically, but also assonance emphasizes words whose meanings are already associated: *sea, beach, fields.* Assonance can thus contribute not only to the sound or musical quality of a poem, but also to its meaning.

## ■ ASSONANCE (as′n əns)

**The repetition of similar or identical vowel sounds followed by different consonant sounds in stressed words or syllables. Assonance can contribute to the meaning of a work, to its musical quality, and to its unity.**

■ Apply to **"On the Grasshopper and Cricket"** on page 282.

# ■ BLANK VERSE

And at the threshold of her chamber door
The Carthage lords did there the queen await;
The trampling steed, with gold and purple decked,
Chawing the foamy bit, there fiercely stood.

*Henry Howard, Earl of Surrey*
*from* **The Fourth Book of Virgil**

1. Do the above lines rhyme?
2. How many feet are there in each line?
3. What is the meter? (See **RHYTHM** for a discussion of meter and scansion.)

In the sixteenth century, English lyric poets discovered that the English language has a natural iambic beat. They also found that combinations of English words fall naturally into lines of five feet. Once the lyricists had recognized iambic pentameter as a natural English line, they used it extensively (though not exclusively) for rhymed verse.

Dramatists and narrative poets, however, aware that comparatively few English words end with the same sound, found it difficult to sustain rhymed iambic pentameter lines for five acts of a play or for several hundred lines of narrative poetry. Consequently, they began to write unrhymed iambic pentameter lines, or *blank verse*. Blank verse was later used in LYRIC poetry as well.

Read the following passages; explain whether or not each of them is in blank verse.

Come live with me and be my Love,
And we will all the pleasures prove
That hills and valleys, dales and fields,
Or woods or steepy mountain yields.

*Christopher Marlowe*
**"The Passionate Shepherd
to His Love"**

That time of year thou mayst in me behold
When yellow leaves, or none, or few, do hang
Upon those boughs which shake against the cold,
Bare ruined choirs where late the sweet birds sang.

*William Shakespeare*
**"Sonnet 73"**

Alas! for this gray shadow, once a man—
So glorious in his beauty and thy choice,
Who madest him thy chosen, that he seemed
To his great heart none other than a god!

*Alfred, Lord Tennyson*
**"Tithonus"**

William Shakespeare was a master of both rhymed verse and blank verse. He cast his dramas in blank-verse lines.

O, he sits high in all the people's hearts;
And that which would appear offense in us,
His countenance, like richest alchemy,
Will change to virtue and to worthiness.

*William Shakespeare,*
***Julius Caesar*, Act One, Scene 3**

Occasionally a line or lines of a blank-verse passage may depart from a regular iambic pattern. The following lines are spoken by one of the conspirators against Caesar. What line deviates strongly from the iambic pentameter pattern?

Their minds may change. Besides, it were a mock
Apt to be rendered, for some one to say,
"Break up the Senate till another time,
When Caesar's wife shall meet with better dreams."
If Caesar hide himself, shall they not whisper
"Lo, Caesar is afraid"?

***Julius Caesar*, Act Two, Scene 2**

Such shifts enabled Shakespeare to use blank verse to achieve a great variety of dramatic effects. Note how the last line of the passage above stands out because of its different line length. This dramatic line is the one which finally convinces Caesar to go to the Senate on the fateful ides of March, and so it is crucial to the play.

## ■ BLANK VERSE

**Unrhymed poetry in iambic pentameter—ten-syllable lines with five unstressed syllables alternating with five stressed syllables. An unstressed syllable begins the line. Poets who write in blank verse may vary the beat within this basic structure.**

■ Apply to *Julius Caesar* on page 498.

HANDBOOK OF LITERARY TERMS

# ■ CHARACTERIZATION

People are interested in other people: how they act, where they go, what they think about in any number of situations. That interest is one of the reasons many people enjoy reading stories about imaginary people who seem real.

*Characterization* is the technique a writer uses to create lifelike characters. A writer may use any of various methods of characterization, but the most thorough depiction of a character will probably include all of the following.

(The examples are from the novel *Emma* by Jane Austen, 1816.)

An author may simply describe a character:

Emma Woodhouse, handsome, clever, and rich, with a comfortable home and happy disposition, seemed to unite some of the best blessings of existence; and had lived nearly twenty-one years in the world with very little to distress or vex her.

With this method an author can tell the reader exactly what he or she wants the reader to know about a character's age, appearance, situation in life, or personality traits.

An author may choose to reveal a character's speech and behavior:

"And you have forgotten one matter of joy to me," said Emma, "and a very considerable one—that I made the match myself. I made the match, you know, four years ago; and to have it take place, and be proved in the right, when so many people said Mr. Weston would never marry again, may comfort me for anything."

This method makes demands on the reader's ability to make INFERENCES or conclusions about a character. On another occasion with two other friends, Harriet Smith and Mr. Elton, Emma again reveals her taste for matchmaking:

They now walked on together quietly, till within view of the vicarage pales, when a sudden resolution, of at least getting Harriet into the house, made her [Emma] again find something very much amiss about her boot, and fall behind to arrange it once more. She then broke the lace off short, and dexterously throwing it into a ditch, was presently obliged to entreat them to stop, and acknowledge her inability to put herself to rights so as to be able to walk home in tolerable comfort.

"Part of my lace is gone," said she, "and I do not know how I am to contrive. I really am a most troublesome companion to you both, but I hope I am not often ill-equipped. Mr. Elton, I must beg leave to stop at your house, and ask your housekeeper for a bit of ribband or string, or anything just to keep my boot on."

A writer may also describe opinions and reactions of some characters to another character. In the next passage two of Emma's close acquaintances, Mrs. Weston and Mr. Knightley, speak together about Emma and her friendship with someone of whom they faintly disapprove, Harriet Smith:

". . . One hears sometimes of a child being 'the picture of health'; now Emma always gives me the idea of being the complete picture of grown-up health. She is loveliness itself. Mr. Knightley, is not she?"

"I have not a fault to find with her person," he replied. "I think her all you describe. I love to look at her; and I will add this praise, that I do not think her personally vain. Considering how very handsome she is, she appears to be little occupied with it; her vanity lies another way. Mrs. Weston, I am not to be talked out of my dislike of her intimacy with Harriet Smith, or my dread of its doing them both harm."

"And I, Mr. Knightley, am equally stout in my confidence of its not doing them any harm. With all dear Emma's little faults, she is an excellent creature. Where shall we see a better daughter, or a kinder sister, or a truer friend? No, no; she has qualities which may be trusted; she will never lead any one really wrong; she will make no lasting blunder; where Emma errs once, she is in the right a hundred times."

Again, the readers must draw their own conclusions about the personality of Emma by noting what is said about her.

Finally, a writer can reveal a character's personality by disclosing his or her thoughts and feelings. The following excerpt finds Emma contemplating her relationship with a young man, Frank Churchill, who has been visiting his relatives, the Westons, at their estate, Randalls, and who has now left for his own home.

Emma continued to entertain no doubt of her being in love. Her ideas only varied as to the how much. At first, she thought it was a good deal; and afterwards, but little. She had great pleasure in hearing Frank Churchill talked of; and, for his sake, greater pleasure than ever in seeing Mr. and Mrs. Weston; she was very often thinking of him, and quite impatient for a letter, that she might know how he was, how were his spirits, how was his aunt, and what was the chance of his coming to Randalls again this spring. But, on the other hand, she could not admit herself to be unhappy, nor, after the first morning, to be less disposed for employment than usual; she was still busy and cheerful; and, pleasing as he was, she could yet imagine him to have faults; and farther, though thinking of him so much, and, as she sat drawing or working, forming a thousand amusing schemes for the progress and close of their attachment, fancying interesting dialogues, and inventing elegant letters; the conclusion of every imaginary declaration on his side was that she *refused him.* Their affection was always to subside into friendship. Everything tender and charming was to mark their parting; but still they were to part. When she became sensible of this, it struck her that she could not be very much in love; for in spite of her previous and fixed determination never to quit her father, never to marry, a strong attachment certainly must produce more of a struggle than she could foresee in her own feelings.

These selections represent but a small part of Jane Austen's characterization of Emma, but having read them, you have an idea of the sort of person Emma is.

1. Is Emma unattractive?
2. Has she had a difficult life?
3. What is something she prides herself on doing?

4. Is Emma self-confident or hesitant in making decisions?
5. What is her relationship with her father?
6. Will she stoop to deception to bring about something she desires? Support your opinion.
7. Is she honest with herself?

Not all written works emphasize characterization. When plot or setting is emphasized over character the characters are apt to be stereotypes. (See **STEREOTYPE**.)

## ■ CHARACTERIZATION

**The technique a writer uses to create and reveal the personalities of the characters in a written work. A writer may describe a character's physical appearance and situation, reveal a character's thoughts, or show the reactions of other characters.**

■ Apply to "**The Secret Life of Walter Mitty**" on page 40.

# ■ CONNOTATION/ DENOTATION

If you look up the word *father* in the dictionary, the first definition you find is "male parent." For most people, however, the same word has additional meanings and carries other implications, such as love, protection, security, and sympathy. Thus, we talk about the *father*land, the *father* of our country, and a *father*ly attitude.

Many words in everyday use do double duty. On the one hand they have one or more dictionary meanings, or *denotations*. On the other, they have *connotations*, or meanings and associations beyond the dictionary meaning. A connotative word gathers its associations from people's experiences, both personal and universal. For instance, look at the word pairs below. Both words in each pair have similar denotations, but different connotations. Think of a context in which you would use each word.

poor—needy   rich—wealthy
foreigner—alien   secret agent—spy
close—intimate   questioning—interrogation

Now read the following lines of poetry by Edgar Allen Poe and think about the connotation and denotation of the adjectives.

The skies they were ashen and sober;
   The leaves they were crisped and sere.

The word *ashen* literally means "like ash," but used in this poem, the poet wishes to convey a dreary, dingy, gray sky. One denotation of *sober* is "quiet in color." But, as used in this verse, *sober* reinforces the image of a calm, gray sky. How do you think the meaning of the second line would change if the poet had chosen the words *hard* and *dried* instead of *crisped* and *sere?*

What does the word *night* mean to you? Is it a time to go to sleep? a fearful time? a retreat from the day's work? Read the following poem to find the various ways the poet sees night.

What different connotations does the word *night* take in each stanza?

## Four Glimpses of Night

### I.
Eagerly
Like a woman hurrying to her lover
Night comes to the room of the world
And lies, yielding and content
5 Against the cool round face
Of the moon.

### II.
Night is a curious child, wandering
Between earth and sky, creeping
In windows and doors, daubing
10 The entire neighborhood
With purple paint.
Day
Is an apologetic mother
Cloth in hand
15 Following after.

### III.
Peddling
From door to door
Night sells
Black bags of peppermint stars
20 Heaping cones of vanilla moon
Until
His wares are gone
Then shuffles homeward
Jingling the grey coins
25 Of daybreak.

### IV.
Night's brittle song, sliver-thin
Shatters into a billion fragments
Of quiet shadows
At the blaring jazz
30 Of a morning sun.

*Frank Marshall Davis*

## ■ CONNOTATION

**The interpretations of a word beyond its literal definition.**

## ■ DENOTATION

**The literal meaning of a word.**

■ Apply to "**The Secret Room**" on page 600.

# ■ CONSONANCE

The moan of doves in immemorial elms,
And murmuring of innumerable bees.

*Alfred, Lord Tennyson*
**"The Princess"**

Read the lines above softly to yourself. What consonant sound is repeated several times? What effect does the repeated sound have on your reading of the lines?

The repeated *m* sound within the words is an example of *consonance:* the repetition of the same consonant sound preceded by a different vowel sound. In the above lines the repeated *m* sound has the effect of emphasizing the words in which it is found.

Consonance at the end of two or more lines of poetry is called *half rhyme* or *slant rhyme* because only the final consonant sounds are alike. (See **RHYME**.) Read the following stanza.

Nothing lovelier than that lonely call,
Bare and singular, like a gull,
And three notes or four, then that was all.
It drew up from the quiet like a well,
Waited, sang, and vanishing, was still.

*Jon Swan*
**"In Her Song She Is Alone"**

Consonance is also used to suggest associations between words. Note how the *l* sound effectively unites the key words of the stanza: *call* with *gull* and *well* with *still*. The *l* sound has a lingering, almost echoing effect. How is that appropriate to the stanza's **TONE**?

Dove

# ■ CONSONANCE (kon′sə nəns)

**The repetition of similar or identical consonant sounds preceded by different vowel sounds. It is often used instead of rhyme at the end of lines of poetry. Consonance can stress important words and strengthen meaning through word association. It may add to the unity of sound and sense in a poem.**

"Four Glimpses of Night" by Frank Marshall Davis, from *The Poetry of the Negro 1746–1970*. Published by Doubleday & Company, Inc. Reprinted by permission of the author.

From "In Her Song She Is Alone" by Jon Swan, *The New Yorker*, August 10, 1957. Copyright © 1957, 1984 The New Yorker Magazine, Inc. Reprinted by permission.

■ Apply to **"A Round Shape Water Takes Inside the Gourd"** on page 285.

# ■ FIGURATIVE LANGUAGE

Read each set of lines.

**A.** She has a pink-and-white complexion.
   There is a garden in her face,
      Where roses and lilies grow;

> *Thomas Campion*
> **"Cherry-Ripe"**

**B.** When I am old, wrinkled, chilly, and white-
      haired . . .
   When age hath made me what I am not now;
   And every wrinkle tells me where the plough
   Of time hath furrowed; when an ice shall flow
   Through every vein, and all my head wear snow;

> *Thomas Randolph*
> **"Upon His Picture"**

In example A, what two things are being compared? How does the literal description in the first line differ from the images created in the second and third lines? In example B, what images does the poet create to describe the passage of time? Which images are literal descriptions and which are more figurative suggestions of an aging man? In both examples, the poets have made use of *figurative language*.

*Figurative language* is the use of words outside their usual, or literal, meanings. By suggesting new associations or comparisons, they can add beauty to and increase the impact or vitality of the lines and works in which they are found. Sometimes figurative language may seem even more direct than literal language because it enables the reader to grasp the idea quickly. The various elements of figurative language are called *figures of speech*. The most commonly used figures of speech are SIMILE, METAPHOR, and PERSONIFICATION.

To be successful, figurative language must be appropriate. Although figurative language may compare basically different things, there must be a point of similarity between the objects for the figure of speech to be effective. For example, if a person said, "I've been shoveling snow for an hour, and my hands are like blocks of ice," most listeners would understand the connection—ice is cold and hard and hands can feel cold and hard. If, however, the person compared his or her hands to daisies or cameras, the listener would very probably have no idea what was meant. There must be some recognizable point of similarity for the figure of speech to be appropriate. Read the following lines and decide (1) what things are being compared and (2) whether the figurative language is effective and appropriate.

**A.** The lion's roar rolled like thunder.

**B.** The frightened lost child cowered in the aisle like a golden eagle.

**C.** O my luve is like a red, red rose
   That's newly sprung in June:
   O my luve is like the melodie
   That's sweetly played in tune.

> *Robert Burns*
> **"A Red, Red Rose"**

**D.** The tears on her checks were glistening rocks.

A figure of speech need not be limited to one phrase, line, sentence, or paragraph. It may often be extended to include any of these, or even the entire work. If a figure of speech extends through a paragraph, for instance, it should be consistent. That is, if many different comparisons or associations are used to describe the same thing, they should create the same general image. For example, a lantern in the

window may seem to a weary traveler to beam "a finger of light" that "points the way home," "beckons him in welcome," and "warmly strokes his cheek as he nears the house." It would be inconsistent then to change the image to compare the lantern to the sun or the moon.

Read the following lines. The main character, Macbeth, has just murdered his sleeping king.

Methought I heard a voice cry, "Sleep no more!
Macbeth does murder sleep," the innocent sleep,
Sleep that knits up the raveled sleave of care,
The death of each day's life, sore labor's bath,
Balm of hurt minds, great nature's second course,
Chief nourisher in life's feast—

*William Shakespeare*
***Macbeth***, Act Two, Scene 2

To what various things is sleep compared? What is Macbeth saying literally? How does the use of figurative language give the reader a clear idea about Macbeth's state of mind?

## ■ FIGURATIVE LANGUAGE

**The use of words outside their literal, or usual, meanings. Figurative language is used to add beauty, increase vitality and impact, suggest associations and comparisons, and develop conciseness.**

■ Apply to "**Those Winter Sundays**" on page 266.

# ■ FLASHBACK

The following is from a novel about the experiences of an English schoolmaster. At the book's opening, the main character, Mr. Chips, is very old, under the care of his landlady, Mrs. Wickett, and long retired from teaching at Brookfield, a boys' school. Read the passage, paying close attention to the order of events.

*from* **Goodbye, Mr. Chips**

He was getting on in years (but not ill, of course); indeed, as Doctor Merivale said, there was really nothing the matter with him. "My dear fellow, you're fitter than I am," Merivale would say, sipping a glass of sherry when he called every fortnight or so. "You're past the age when people get those horrible diseases; you're one of the few lucky ones who're going to die a really natural death. That is, of course, if you die at all. You're such a remarkable old boy that one never knows." But when Chips had a cold or when east winds roared over the fenlands, Merivale would sometimes take Mrs. Wickett aside in the lobby and whisper: "Look after him, you know. His chest . . . it puts a strain on his heart. Nothing really wrong with him—only anno Domini,[1] but that's the most fatal complaint of all, in the end."

Anno Domini . . . by Jove, yes. Born in 1848, and taken to the Great Exhibition as a toddling child—not many people still alive could boast a thing like that. Besides, Chips could even remember Brookfield in Wetherby's time. A phenomenon, that was. Wetherby had been an old man in those days—1870—easy to remember because of the Franco-Prussian War. Chips had put in for Brookfield after a year at Melbury, which he hadn't liked, because he had been ragged there a good deal. But Brookfield he *had* liked, almost from the beginning. He remembered that day of his preliminary interview—sunny June, with the air full of flower scents and the plick-plock of cricket on the pitch. Brookfield was playing Barnhurst, and one of the Barnhurst boys, a chubby little fellow, made a brilliant century.[2] Queer that a thing like that should stay in the memory so clearly. Wetherby himself was very fatherly and courteous: he must have been ill then, poor chap, for he died during the summer vacation, before Chips began his first term. But the two had seen and spoken to each other, anyway.

Chips often thought, as he sat by the fire at Mrs. Wickett's: I am probably the only man in the world who has a vivid recollection of old Wetherby. . . . Vivid, yes; it was a frequent picture in his mind, that summer day with the sunlight filtering through the dust in Wetherby's study. "You are a young man, Mr. Chipping, and Brookfield is an old foundation. Youth and age often combine well. Give your enthusiasm to Brookfield, and Brookfield will give you something in return. And don't let anyone play tricks with you. I—er—gather that discipline was not always your strong point at Melbury?"

"Well, no, perhaps not, sir."

"Never mind; you're full young; it's largely a matter of experience. You have another chance here. Take up a firm attitude from the beginning—that's the secret of it."

Perhaps it was. He remembered that first tremendous ordeal of taking prep; a September sunset more than half a century ago; Big Hall full of lusty barbarians ready to pounce on him as their legitimate prey. His youth, fresh-complexioned, high-collared, and side-whiskered (odd fashions people followed in those days), at the mercy of five hundred unprincipled ruffians to whom the baiting of new masters was a fine art, an exciting sport, and something of a tradition. Decent little beggars individually, but, as a mob, just pitiless and implacable. The sudden hush as he took his place at the desk on the dais; the scowl he assumed to cover his inward nervousness; the tall clock ticking behind him, and the smells of ink and varnish; the last blood-red rays slanting in slabs through the stained-glass windows. Someone dropped a desk lid. Quickly, he must take everyone by surprise; he must show that there was no nonsense about him. "You there in the fifth row—you with the red hair—what's your name?" "Colley,

---

**1.** *anno Domini* (an′ō dom′ə nī), in the (specified) year since the birth of Christ. Used in the above context to suggest old age.
**2.** *century*, (in cricket) a score of one hundred or more points in one period of play.

sir." "Very well, Colley, you have a hundred lines." No trouble at all after that. He had won his first round.

And years later, when Colley was an alderman of the City of London and a baronet and various other things, he sent his son (also redhaired) to Brookfield, and Chips would say: "Colley, your father was the first boy I ever punished when I came here twenty-five years ago. He deserved it then, and you deserve it now." How they all laughed; and how Sir Richard laughed when his son wrote home the story in next Sunday's letter!

And again, years after that, many years after that, there was an even better joke. For another Colley had just arrived—son of the Colley who was a son of the first Colley. And Chips would say, punctuating his remarks with that little "umph-um" that had by then become a habit with him: "Colley, you are—umph—a splendid example of—umph—inherited traditions. I remember your grandfather—umph—he could never grasp the Ablative Absolute.[3] A stupid fellow, your grandfather. And your father, too—umph—I remember him—he used to sit at that far desk by the wall—he wasn't much better, either. But I do believe—my dear Colley—that you are—umph—the biggest fool of the lot!" Roars of laughter.

A great joke, this growing old—but a sad joke, too, in a way. And as Chips sat by his fire with autumn gales rattling the windows, the waves of humor and sadness swept over him very often until tears fell, so that when Mrs. Wickett came in with his cup of tea she did not know whether he had been laughing or crying. And neither did Chips himself.

*James Hilton*

Arrange the following events of Mr. Chips's life in the order they actually occurred.

1. He assigns his very first punishment to red-haired Richard Colley.
2. He attends the Great Exhibition.
3. He meets Mr. Wetherby at Brookfield.
4. He teaches one year at Melbury.
5. He teases the grandson of the first student he ever punished.

You may know that you have arranged the events in *chronological order*, the order in which

they happened in Mr. Chips's lifetime. Yet, did you notice that Mr. Chips is presented as very old at both the beginning and end of the passage? Did you realize that these events are not happening to Mr. Chips as you read them, but are incidents from his earlier life that he recalls while sitting by his fire? The author accomplishes these shifts in time through the use of *flashback*, an interruption in the narrative to show a scene or scenes that happened before that particular point.

A flashback can easily cover years of chronological time and give information that helps the reader better understand the characters and events of a story's present action. For example, you learned through a sequence of flashbacks that Mr. Chips's teaching career spanned at least three generations and provided years of memories that he continues to cherish.

This device also helps the reader anticipate what will occur when the major action is resumed. Mr. Chips's flashbacks at the beginning of the novel provide only a brief glimpse of his long career. Based on your knowledge of these flashbacks, what do you think will be the subject of the rest of the novel?

## ■ FLASHBACK

**An interruption in the major action of a story, play, or nonfiction work to show an episode that happened at an earlier time. A flashback can shed light on characters and events of the present by providing background information.**

3. *ablative* (ab′lə tiv) *absolute,* a grammatical construction in Latin.

From *Goodbye, Mr. Chips* by James Hilton. Copyright 1934 by James Hilton. Copyright © renewed 1962 by Alice Hilton. Reprinted by permission of Little, Brown and Company in association with the Atlantic Monthly Press.

■ Apply to *Our Town* on page 172.

# ■ FORESHADOWING

Shortly after the opening of the story "The Monkey's Paw," the White family questions their guest, Sergeant-Major Morris, about the mummified monkey's paw he acquired in India. After telling them of the spell put on the paw that allows three men three wishes each, Morris is asked if he has had his three wishes.

"I have," he said quietly, and his blotchy face whitened.

At this point the reader does not know what the monkey's paw can or cannot do, but does learn that the very thought of it frightens a professional soldier. This hint, clue, or indication of what is to come is called *foreshadowing.*

Foreshadowing serves two purposes: (1) it stimulates interest on the part of the reader, listener, or viewer to learn what happens next; and (2) it prepares the reader, listener, or viewer, in part at least, for the direction the plot will take, thus making it seem more real.

In "Life is Sweet at Kumansenu," there are several clues foreshadowing the revelation that Meji is actually dead: he wears a scarf around his neck, apparently to hide the wound which caused his death; he is pale and cold; and he casts no shadow. When his daughter Asi asks him why he wears a scarf, he replies, "Because my head would fall off if I didn't." It is not until the end of the story that the reader is certain that it was Meji's ghost that returned to thank his mother and bid her goodbye.

# ■ FORESHADOWING

**The technique of giving the reader, listener, or viewer of a story or play hints of what is to come in that work.**

■ Apply to *Julius Caesar* on page 519.

# ■ FREE VERSE

I don't bother with rhymes. It is seldom
That there are two trees equal, side by side.

*Alberto Caeiro*
**"XIV"** (translated by *Jonathan Griffin*)

*Free verse*, a form of unrhymed English poetry, has become a favorite form of many modern poets. (See also **BLANK VERSE**.) Free verse is called "free" because the poet does not follow set patterns of rhyme, meter, or line length.

Free-verse poets believe rhyme is an inadequate poetic device. They point out that rhyme may restrict, even dictate, the meaning of a poem. For example, imagine a poet who is composing a serious tercet, a stanza of three rhyming lines, about a dove he once held in his hand and touched gently. The word *dove* suggests that his three lines will rhyme the *-ove* sound. He begins:

A gray, white-throated dove
Lay quivering in my glove;

In the next line, he wants to say, "I gave it a gentle touch." *Touch* does not rhyme with *dove* or *glove* so he casts about for a word that does, with this result.

A gray, white-throated dove
Lay quivering in my glove;
I gave it a gentle shove.

The rhyme has drastically changed the poet's meaning. To avoid such a predicament, free-verse poets dispense with regular rhyme. If they regulate sound at all it is mainly through **ALLITERATION** and **ASSONANCE**.

Free-verse poets, unlike blank-verse poets, believe meter is an unnecessary poetic device

From "XIV" by Alberto Caeiro (Fernando Pessoa), translated by Jonathan Griffin, from Volume 1 of *The Selected Poems of Fernando Pessoa*. Carcanet Press. Reprinted by permission of Jonathan Griffin.

since every word we use has a natural rhythm of its own. Depending upon the natural stress (or lack of stress) in words, free-verse lines such as these:

Beautiful evening
Calm, free

are just as rhythmical in their way as is this metrical version.

It is / a beau / teous eve / ning, calm / and free.

*William Wordsworth*
**"It Is a Beauteous Evening"**

Often the free-verse poet gives his reader a clue to the movement of his poem by beginning each rhythmical unit on a new line. Listen as this poem is read aloud, noticing how a new rhythmical unit begins with each capitalized word that begins a line.

### When I Heard the Learn'd Astronomer

When I heard the learn'd astronomer,
When the proofs, the figures, were ranged in
  columns before me,
When I was shown the charts and diagrams, to add,
  divide, and measure them,
When I sitting heard the astronomer where he
  lectured with much applause in the lecture-
  room,
5 How soon unaccountable I became tired and sick,
Till rising and gliding out I wander'd off by myself,
In the mystical moist night air, and from time to
  time,
Look'd up in perfect silence at the stars.

*Walt Whitman*

## ■ FREE VERSE

**Poetry that follows no set patterns of rhyme, meter, or line length.**

■ Apply to **"By the Bivouac's Fitful Flame"** on page 287.

## ■ HYPERBOLE

When people use such expressions as "It's raining cats and dogs" or "He is as big as a house," they are exaggerating the truth and do not expect to be taken literally. The use of exaggeration for effect is called *hyperbole*.

Authors use hyperbole to give emphasis to their point. For example, the following lines by Gwendolyn Brooks show the power of the language used by Martin Luther King, Jr., and its effect on his listeners:

His word still burns the center of the sun,
  above the thousands and the
  hundred thousands.

A promise of undying love is emphasized in the lines from "A Red, Red Rose" by Robert Burns.

Till a' the seas gang dry, my dear,
  And the rocks melt wi' the sun!
I will luve thee still, my dear,
  While the sands o' life shall run.

What feeling about poetry do you think the speaker wishes to emphasize through hyperbole in the following poem?

Two girls discover
the secret of life
in a sudden line of
poetry.

*Denise Levertov*
*from* **The Secret**

## ■ HYPERBOLE

**A figure of speech using great exaggeration to emphasize strong feeling and to create a satiric, comic, or sentimental effect.**

From "Martin Luther King Jr." by Gwendolyn Brooks. Reprinted by permission of Broadside Press and the author.

Denise Levertov, *O Taste and See.* Copyright © 1964 by Denise Levertov Goodman. Reprinted by permission of New Directions Publishing Corporation.

■ Apply to **"For Anne Gregory"** on page 272.

# ■ IMAGERY

**The Pond**

Cold, wet leaves
Floating on moss-coloured water,

And the croaking of frogs—
  Cracked bell-notes in the twilight.

*Amy Lowell*

Which words or phrases in this poem appeal to your senses of sight, sound, and touch? Sensory appeals made through descriptions and details are called *images*. Now look for images as you read the passage below from Charles Dickens's *A Christmas Carol*.

It was his own room. There was no doubt about that. But it had undergone a surprising transformation. The walls and ceiling were so hung with living green, that it looked a perfect grove; from every part of which, bright gleaming berries glistened. The crisp leaves of holly, mistletoe, and ivy reflected back the light, as if so many little mirrors had been scattered there; and such a mighty blaze went roaring up the chimney, as that dull petrification of a hearth had never known in Scrooge's time, or Marley's, or for many and many a winter season gone. Heaped up on the floor, to form a kind of throne, were turkeys, geese, game, poultry, brawn, great joints of meat, suckling-pigs, long wreaths of sausages, mince-pies, plum-puddings, barrels of oysters, red-hot chestnuts, cherry-cheeked apples, juicy oranges, luscious pears, immense twelfth-cakes, and seething bowls of punch, that made the chamber dim with their delicious steam.

To which senses does the passage appeal? What details does Dickens add to the recital of food that make it more than a holiday grocery list? Which images appeal particularly to your sense of taste? of smell?

A skilled writer can use imagery to convey to readers a sense of experiencing what they are

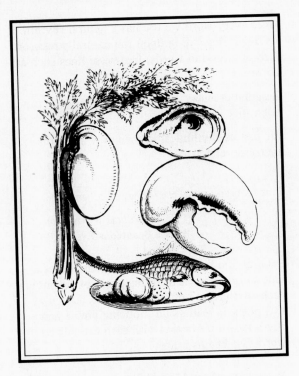

reading about, and so involving them in the world of the written selection.

Read the following passage about Tayo, a young Indian home from the Korean War, and try to imagine the scene as you read.

Tayo stood near the horses, looking down the path over the way they had come. The plateaus and canyons spread out below him like clouds falling into each other past the horizon. The world below was distant and small; it was dwarfed by a sky so blue and vast the clouds were lost in it. Far into the south there were smoky blue ridges of the mountain haze at Zuni. He smoothed his hand over the top of his head and felt the sun. The mountain wind was cool; it smelled like springs hidden deep in mossy black stone. He could see no signs of what had been set loose upon the earth: the highways, the towns, even the fences were gone.

What images of sight, touch, and smell are depicted? In what part of the country would you say the story takes place? How is the sense of the vastness of the place communicated? What emotions or feelings are evoked?

In the following passage, Tayo is hurt and losing consciousness:

Black pebbles and the ancient gray cinders the mountain had thrown poked into his backbone. He closed his eyes but did not sleep. He felt cold gusts of wind scattering dry oak leaves in the grass. He listened to the cowboy collect tobacco juice in his mouth and the squirting liquid sound when he spat. He was aware of the center beneath him; it soaked into his body from the ground through the torn skin on his hands, covered with powdery black dirt. The magnetism of the center spread over him smoothly like rainwater down his neck and shoulders: the vacant cool sensation glided over the pain like feather-down wings. It was pulling him back, close to the earth, where the core was cool and silent as mountain stone . . .

What do you think is the most vivid image in this passage? How is the sensation of losing consciousness communicated?

# IMAGERY

**The use of concrete details that appeal to the five senses. By appealing to a reader's senses, a writer can more easily communicate an experience.**

■ Apply to **"Improved Farm Land"** on page 258.

# INFERENCE

"Very well, Your Honor. I shall rephrase the question."

What kind of question could have had such an effect on the witness? Do you think he was prepared for the question? In considering the clues in the cartoon and drawing a conclusion from them, you are making an *inference*.

Writers often give their readers only limited or indirect information and expect them to make their own inferences about time, setting, characters, and actions. Note the clues for making inferences in the passage below, from Sherwood Anderson's "I'm a Fool."

And so, there not being any work in our town any more than when I left there to go to the races, I went off to Sandusky and got a pretty good place taking care of horses for a man who owned a teaming and delivery and storage and coal and real-estate business there. It was a pretty good place with good eats, and a day off each week, and sleeping on a cot in a big barn, and mostly just shoveling in hay and oats to a lot of big good-enough skates of horses that couldn't have trotted a race with a toad. I wasn't dissatisfied and I could send money home.

And then, as I started to tell you, the fall races come to Sandusky and I got the day off and I went. I left the job at noon and had on my good clothes and my new brown derby hat I'd bought the Saturday before, and a stand-up collar.

First of all I went downtown and walked about with the dudes. I've always thought to myself, "Put up a good front," and so I did it. I had forty dollars in my pockets and so I went into the West House, a big hotel, and walked up to the cigar stand. "Give me three twenty-five-cent cigars," I said. There was a lot of horsemen and strangers and dressed-up people from other towns standing around in the lobby and in the bar, and I mingled amongst them. In the bar there was a fellow with a cane and a Windsor tie on, that it made me sick to look at him. I like a man to be a man and dressed up, but not to go put on that kind of airs. So I pushed him aside, kind of rough, and had me a drink of whiskey. And then he looked at me, but he changed his mind and didn't say anything. And then I had another drink of whiskey, just to show him something, and went out and had a hack[1] out to the races, all to myself, and when I got there I bought myself the best seat I could get up in the grandstand, but didn't go in for any of these boxes. That's putting on too many airs.

1. What evidence is there that the coming of the fall races to Sandusky is a special occasion to the narrator?
2. When the narrator roughly pushes aside the fellow in the Windsor tie, the man does nothing but look at him. The speaker infers that the man is a coward. What other inference can you make?
3. The narrator does not like people "putting on . . . airs." What actions does the narrator take that reveal him to be the same as those he criticizes?

Notice that the author does not directly describe the narrator; he relies on the readers to read between the lines.

## ■ INFERENCE

**A reasonable conclusion about the behavior of a character or the meaning of an event drawn from limited details supplied by the author.**

1. *hack,* horse-drawn carriage for hire.
From "I'm a Fool" by Sherwood Anderson. Copyright 1922 by Dial Publishing Co., Inc. Copyright renewed 1949 by Eleanor Copenhaver Anderson. Reprinted by permission of Harold Ober Associates Incorporated.

■ Apply to **"The Romancers"** on page 159.

## ■ IRONY

In the following excerpt from *The Sketch Book,* Washington Irving, an early nineteenth-century American author, explains his reasons for wanting to visit Europe and England: to see great men.

. . . for I had read in the works of various philosophers, that all animals degenerated in America, and man among the number. A great man of Europe, thought I, must therefore be as superior to a great man of America as a peak of the Alps to a highland of the Hudson; and in this idea I was confirmed by observing the comparative importance and swelling magnitude of many English travellers among us, who, I was assured, were very little people in their own country. I will visit this land of wonders, thought I, and see the gigantic race from which I am degenerated.

Does Irving really think the English are superior to Americans? What clues lead to your conclusions? Irving says one thing in this passage, but he means just the opposite. This is an example of *verbal irony*—the surface meaning of what one writes or says being the opposite of the intended meaning.

Verbal irony in everyday speech is easily recognized because the listener has the speaker's tone of voice and facial expression to aid him. For example, if you and a friend have planned a day picnicking and hiking, and when you step out the door it begins to rain, one of you might say, "Oh, good! I was hoping it would rain." This is actually just the opposite of what you were hoping and is an example of verbal irony. When reading, one must be alert to a writer's use of irony or the point may be missed entirely. Verbal irony is frequently used as a device of SATIRE.

*Irony of situation* occurs when events turn out contrary to what is expected or what seems appropriate. "The Gift of the Magi," a short story by O. Henry, turns on irony of situation. In it a penniless young couple want to buy each

*"I think something's coming now."*

Drawing by Lorenz; © 1983 The New Yorker Magazine, Inc.

other special holiday presents. The wife has her beautiful long hair cut off, sells it, and buys a chain worthy of her husband's prized gold pocket watch. The husband sells his watch to buy tortoise-shell combs for his wife's beautiful hair. What is the double irony of the story?

Irony may be gentle, sad, bitter, or, as in "The Gift of the Magi," bittersweet. The general TONE of the piece will indicate the author's intention.

The subway rider in the cartoon above is making a reasonable assumption. What do you know that she does not that makes her comment particularly humorous?

*Dramatic irony* occurs when the reader or viewer knows more about the actual situation than the characters do. It is often found in drama; for example, an offhand remark is made or a seemingly unimportant action occurs which has significance hidden from the character involved, but revealed to the audience. Dramatic irony may be humorous, as in the cartoon above; poignant, as in *Our Town* (page 172); or ominous, as in *Julius Caesar*, when the audience knows Brutus is plotting Caesar's death but Caesar does not.

# ■ IRONY

A contrast between what is said and what is actually meant is called *verbal irony*. *Irony of situation* occurs when things turn out contrary to what is expected. *Dramatic irony* occurs when the reader or viewer is aware of something about which the character involved knows nothing. Irony is a common device in satire.

■ Apply to **"The Necklace"** on page 380.

# ■ LYRIC

### Together

Because we do
All things together
All things improve
Even weather.
5 Our daily meat
And bread taste better,
Trees greener,
Rain is wetter.

*Paul Engle*

What emotion is expressed in the poem? Do
you think the poet is concerned primarily with
telling a story or expressing a feeling?

The poem above belongs to a category of
poetry called *lyric* poetry. Instead of telling a
story, as a narrative poem does, a lyric is a short
poem expressing a personal, basic emotion—
love, sorrow, joy, patriotism, religious feeling,
or any other sentiment sincerely felt by the
poet.

### The Rustling of Grass

I cannot tell why,
But the rustling of grass,
As the summer winds pass
Through the field where I lie,
5 Brings to life a lost day,
Long ago, far away,
When in childhood I lay
Looking up at the sky
And the white clouds that pass,
10 Trailing isles of grey shadow
Across the gold grass . . .
O, the dreams that drift by
With the slow flowing years,
Hopes, Memories, tears,
15 In the rustling grass.

*Alfred Noyes*

What emotion is expressed in this poem?

# ■ LYRIC

**A short poem expressing a basic, personal
emotion such as grief, happiness, love, or
melancholy.**

"Together" from *Embrace: Selected Love Poems* by Paul Engle.
Copyright © 1969 by Paul Engle. Reprinted by permission of
Random House, Inc.

"The Rustling of Grass" from *Collected Poems* by Alfred Noyes (J.B.
Lippincott). Copyright 1913, 1941 by Alfred Noyes. Reprinted by
permission of Harper & Row, Publishers, Inc. and Hugh Noyes.

■ Apply to **"I Wandered Lonely As a Cloud"** on page 235.

# ■ METAPHOR

Life's but a walking shadow, a poor player
That struts and frets his hour upon the stage. . . .

*William Shakespeare*
*Macbeth*, Act Five, Scene 5

What two things is life compared with in the above lines? Are the comparisons appropriate? The lines contain examples of *metaphor*, a figure of speech that implies comparison between two basically dissimilar things. The comparison is implied because no connective word such as *like* or *as* is used. (See **FIGURATIVE LANGUAGE**.)

We all use metaphors daily without giving them much thought. A student who is finally understanding chemistry might say he is beginning to see the light, or a teacher who is explaining the basics of trigonometry might say that the explanation is just the tip of the iceberg. In each case, qualities of one thing are being assigned to completely different things.

Writers use metaphors to expand meanings through surprising associations. A metaphor need not be limited to a single line or sentence. Sometimes a writer will continue a metaphor throughout a paragraph, stanza, or entire work. This is called an *extended metaphor*.

**Forgotten Dreams**

The soft gray hands of sleep
Toiled all night long
To spin a beautiful garment
Of dreams;
5 At dawn
The little task was done.
Awakening,
The garb so deftly spun
Was only a heap
10 Of raveled thread—
A vague remembrance
In my head.

*Edward Silvera*

What things are being compared in the poem? Is the metaphor extended throughout the poem? Do you think the comparisons are appropriate? Are the metaphors effective in describing dreams? For a metaphor to be effective, it must reveal or suggest a common quality between the things compared. For example, what if the poet had begun the poem with "The rough red hands of sleep"? Why would that not be as effective as "soft gray"?

Not only must a metaphor be appropriate, it must also be consistent. A metaphor that is not consistent is called a *mixed metaphor*. The commentator Edwin Newman calls a mixed metaphor "a figure of speech that is out of control." For example: "With feline grace, Alice stretched and strolled across the room, a great golden canary ready to pounce." What is inconsistent about this metaphor?

The following quote is from a newspaper article. As you read it, think about whether or not the metaphors used in this context are appropriate.

"I personally resent it: this commission being asked to draw a budget for a plan we had no part in developing," Frank said. "The rug was pulled out from under us, leaving us to hang in limbo and at the end of a primrose path," he said.

*St. Louis Globe-Democrat*

What mixed metaphors do you find in this statement? What is Frank trying to say?

Now read the following poem and note the precise images created by the metaphors.

"Forgotten Dreams" from *The Poetry of the Negro 1746–1970*, Edited by Langston Hughes and Arna Bontemps. Published by Doubleday & Company, Inc.

HANDBOOK OF LITERARY TERMS

### Egg

In this kingdom
the sun never sets;
under the pale oval
of the sky
5 there seems no way in
or out,
and though there is a sea here
there is no tide.

For the egg itself
10 is a moon
glowing faintly
in the galaxy of the barn,
safe but for the spoon's
ominous thunder,
15 the first delicate crack
of lightning.

*Linda Pastan*

What is the "sun"? the "pale oval of the sky"? the "sea"? What is meant by lines 15 and 16? Do you think the metaphors are appropriate? consistent?

## ■ METAPHOR

**A figure of speech that implies comparison between two fundamentally different things. The qualities of one are ascribed to the other. An *extended metaphor* is a metaphor continued throughout a stanza, paragraph, or entire work. A *mixed metaphor* is an inconsistent comparison.**

Reprinted from *The Five Stages of Grief*, Poems by Linda Pastan, by permission of W. W. Norton & Company, Inc., and Jean V. Naggar Literary Agency. Copyright © 1978 by Linda Pastan.

■ Apply to "**Afterglow**" on page 268.

## ■ MOOD

### Dawn

Ecstatic bird songs pound
the hollow vastness of the sky
with metallic clinkings—
beating color up into it
5 at a far edge,—beating it, beating it
with rising, triumphant ardor,—
stirring it into warmth,
quickening in it a spreading change,—
bursting wildly against it as
10 dividing the horizon, a heavy sun
lifts himself—is lifted—
bit by bit above the edge
of things,—runs free at last
out into the open—! lumbering
15 glorified in full release upward—
                    songs cease.

*William Carlos Williams*

Does the poem describe an indoor or outdoor scene? Which words create an atmosphere of intensifying activity? To what senses does the author appeal? Would you characterize the poem as sad? joyous? mysterious?

Though the reader knows from the title that the poem describes a sunrise, the reader does note the additional detail—"the hollow vastness of the sky"—that sets the scene for some sort of happening. The sense of intensifying activity is communicated through such words as "rising," "stirring," "quickening," and "spreading." Various details produce the IMAGERY that appeals to the reader's senses: the changing

"Dawn" from *Collected Poems, Volume I: 1909–1939*. Copyright 1938 by New Directions Publishing Corporation. Reprinted by permission of New Directions Publishing Corporation and Carcanet Press Limited.

color of the sky, the pound of ecstatic bird songs, the warmth of the sky. Such references create images that appeal to sight, sound, and touch.

All of the details, the descriptions, the imagery, the SETTING, and evocative words come together to create the *mood* of surging triumph that surrounds the poem.

## ■ MOOD

The atmosphere and feeling that a writer creates in a work through the choice of setting, imagery, details, descriptions, and other evocative words.

■ Apply to "**Tuesday Siesta**" on page 465.

# ■ ONOMATOPOEIA

Read the following lines from the poem, "The Cataract of Lodore," in which the poet, Robert Southey, describes a waterfall.

And rushing and flushing and brushing and gushing,
And flapping and rapping and clapping and slapping,
And curling and whirling and purling and twirling,
And thumping and plumping and bumping and
    jumping,
And dashing and flashing and splashing and clashing;

What words does the poet use to suggest the sounds of falling water? Words such as *gushing, clapping, slapping, thumping,* and *splashing* are examples of *onomatopoeia,* the use of words whose sounds suggest the sounds made by objects or activities.

Read the following lines. Decide which words are examples of onomatopoeia.

When blood is nipp'd and ways be foul,
Then nightly sings the staring owl,
            Tu-whit;
Tu-who, a merry note . . .

*William Shakespeare*
**"Winter,"** from ***Love's Labours Lost***

The wind blew east: we heard the roar
Of Ocean on his wintry shore,
And felt the strong pulse throbbing there
Beat with a low rhythm our inland air.

*John Greenleaf Whittier*
**"Snowbound"**

Which words above strongly suggest their sense? Which more subtly suggest their sense?

Words such as *bam, pow,* and *clang,* and animal sounds such as *miaow, woof,* and *quack* are examples of onomatopoetic words used mainly when sound is the effect desired. Other words suggest their sense more subtly and may be used to create atmosphere, set the scene, or heighten **IMAGERY.** Examples of such words might be *slushing* through the melting snow, the *whistle* of the ball in the air, the *clatter* of horses' hooves on city streets.

Sometimes authors invent onomatopoetic words to convey unusual sound imagery in stories or poems. James Thurber uses a "sound effect"—written *pocketa-pocketa*—to represent the sounds of machinery in "The Secret Life of Walter Mitty." Thurber adds humor to the story by using this same example of onomatopoeia in different scenes, suggesting that Walter Mitty imagines a similar sound again and again, for any purpose.

More often, authors draw upon real words for onomatopoeia.

There was clearly nothing to do but flop down on the shabby little couch and howl. So Della did it. Which instigates the moral reflection that life is made up of sobs, sniffles, and smiles, with sniffles predominating.

*O. Henry*
*from* **"The Gift of the Magi"**

What words in this paragraph imitate the sounds a sad character might make? How do these words suggest that the narrator, while sympathizing with Della, may feel that her sadness is not overwhelming or endless? Note that a word such as *sniffles* evokes a less troubled response from most readers than a more serious word such as *weeping* would.

# ■ ONOMATOPOEIA
(on′ə mat′ə pē′ə)

**The use of words whose sounds suggest the sounds made by objects or activities.**

■ Apply to **"In an Iridescent Time"** on page 286.

# ■ PARADOX

What is meant by the saying, "The more we learn, the less we know"? It is a seemingly self-contradictory statement, and yet there is sense to be made of it. Such a statement that seems to say two opposite things is called a *paradox*. Writers employ paradoxical statements to concentrate the readers' attention or to emphasize a point.

The term *paradox* also applies to people or situations that seem to have two contradictory elements: a wealthy person who chooses to live in the conditions of severest poverty might be considered a paradox. Something extremely out of the ordinary such as a silent city street on a weekday noon or springlike temperatures occurring within a wintry season might be called paradoxes. The English author G. K. Chesterton wrote a collection of stories, *Tales of the Long Bow,* each of which unfolds from a paradoxical situation. In this book and in others where paradoxes are found, their use is to make readers stop and think about what they are reading and about any possible symbolism developed or emphasized by the use of apparent opposites.

"Good families are generally worse than any others," she said.

*Anthony Hope*
**The Prisoner of Zenda**

This paradoxical statement refers to noble ("good") families, whose wealth and social position allow family members to be more idle and less industrious than other families, according to the character who is speaking.

The following poem is also based on a paradox. As you read it, use the context to help you understand the meaning of *darkness* and *light.*

**To See**

To see that the
darkness is
darkness is
already light.

*Cid Corman*

# ■ PARADOX

**A seemingly self-contradictory statement that still is true. The term is also used for a person or situation that seems to incorporate two opposite elements.**

"To See" by Cid Corman, *Origin,* Third Series, No. 7, 1967. Reprinted by permission of the author.

■ Apply to **"The Coronation of Arthur"** on page 330.

# ■ PERSONIFICATION

**Sunday Rain**

The window screen
is trying to do
its crossword puzzle
but appears to know
5 only vertical words.

*John Updike*

Is the window screen in the poem really doing a crossword puzzle? Does having the screen described in human terms make it easier for you to understand the image the poet is trying to communicate?

We often give human characteristics to nonhuman objects, animals, or ideas. If your car has a flat tire, you may say it "limped" into the nearest garage. Or you may hear someone say that the TV sat staring across the room. These figures of speech are called *personification*. Personification lets the reader see inanimate objects and abstract ideas in terms of familiar human qualities.

What is being personified in the lines below? Point out the word or words the poet uses to personify the subject in each example.

A. Winter sat tight on
   our shoulder blades,

*Ann Darr*
**"The Stone Under the Skin"**

B. Leaves don't fall. They descend.
   Longing for earth, they come winging.

*Malka Heifetz Tussman*
**"Leaves"**

A poet may use personification throughout a poem as in "Sunday Rain," or there may be personification in only one stanza within a poem.

But vainly the fierce frost
Interns poor fish, ranks trees in an armed host,
Hangs daggers from house eaves
And on the windows ferny ambush weaves;
5 In the long war grown warmer
The sun will strike him dead and strip his armor.

*Andrew Young*
**"Hard Frost"**

1. How are the frost and the sun made to seem human?
2. To what human events does the poet compare the actions described here?

Writers of prose use personification too. Here are two examples from Charles Dickens's "The Holly Tree," a short story.

As we got into the country, everything seemed to have grown old and gray. The roads, the trees, the thatched roofs of cottages and homesteads, the ricks in farmers' yards . . .

. . . the midnight wind that rattled at my lattice windows came moaning at me from Stonehenge.

---

# ■ PERSONIFICATION
(pər son′ə fə kā′shən)

**A figure of speech in which human characteristics are attributed to nonhuman animals, objects, or ideas.**

---

■ Apply to **"The Naming of Cats"** on page 270.

# ■ PLOT

## Grand Inquisitor

"Haunted, sir? No, not what you'd call haunted. Of course, one of the gentlemen who lived here last was murdered but still . . . Haunted's a nasty thing to say about nice rooms like these, isn't it, sir? And so you're two brothers, as well as the Mr. Farmiloes. Funny how things do repeat themselves."

The resident housekeeper of No. 82, Regency Chambers, paused and eyed the prospective owners with a certain pleasant relish oozing through her habitual melancholy. It would be her task to cook for them and look after them. She was a crooked wisp of a woman, fading into the late sixties, with eyes like a jugged hare; narrow in the shoulders, she was yet broad in the beam, like an old ship; and her movements, too, were clumsy like those of an old-fashioned ship, of which her face, startled yet wooden, might have been the figurehead.

As the two gentlemen had already signed the contract for No. 82, she felt that they might be admitted at once to its privileges; so she told them the story of the bachelor brothers Farmiloe:

The elder, Roger, was big and handsome in a beefy sort of way. He had a self-confident chest and a beaming red face; and nearly everything he did, he did well. "Bet you can't do this!" he was often heard boasting to his pathetic little junior, and always he was right: Leslie couldn't do "this."

Leslie Farmiloe was not at all handsome. He was timid and had a sort of impediment in his speech, which sounded like the ghost of a chuckle. He was partially bald, too, though he was not yet forty, whereas Roger's hair was thick as a doormat.

Roger, retired from the army, worked in the City; and Leslie studied geology at home. He was supposed to be writing a tome on various minerals, their strata and sub-strata, and was always surrounded by encyclopedias and dictionaries and maps. Endless notes he made on scraps of paper; but he never left these about, because Roger, his patron and hero, must not be annoyed by litter. At least, not by Leslie's litter; his own was different.

In the mornings, when they breakfasted together, Roger usually bullied him; but in the evenings he chaffed him. The two processes were very much alike. The legend stood that Leslie adored his bluff, genial brother, and would endure any amount of good-natured torment from him.

Sundays Roger spent in a knotted agony, sweating at every pore, over the *Weekly Scrutiny;* Leslie watching him with large mild blue eyes, the while thinking no doubt what a wonderful fellow this was, and what a shame that on every seventh day he should be so humiliated by the "Grand Inquisitor."

For this was Roger's one great weakness, and his only intellectual amusement—crossword puzzles. And of all crossword puzzles, the only ones he could not master with his usual swaggering facility were those set by Grand Inquisitor of the *Weekly Scrutiny.* They were devils, those Grand Inquisitor puzzles! Roger Farmiloe nearly burst his veins trying to solve them, but he had never yet succeeded in filling in the spaces of any one of them right up to the very end.

Occasionally he managed to wring out a quarter or even a third of the answers, and then he would sit for hours, staring and baffled; or else, in a boiling temper, flinging his dictionaries about; or resting his head helplessly against the cool varnished spaces of the Pacific Ocean on the old-fashioned globe of the world. Leslie was no help. Leslie would not even know that "yen" was a Japanese coin, or "emu" an Australian bird. Even the elementary mysteries of "eft" and "eli" were blank to Leslie. "To think," groaned Roger, "that my brother—my brother—should be a fool!"

Laboriously he set to work again, writhing a little in the ingenious web of clues, allusions, double meanings, anagrams, quotations, and beheaded syllables.

Leslie watched him with large mild blue eyes.

One Sunday afternoon Leslie Farmiloe was discovered lying dead on the carpet, his bald head and the globe of the world having come into too violent contact. The globe had hardly suffered at all.

"Grand Inquisitor" by G. B. Stern, *The Ladies' Home Journal,* March 1931. Reprinted by permission of The Society of Authors as the literary representative of the Estate of G. B. Stern.

HANDBOOK OF LITERARY TERMS

There were three extraordinary things about the case. One was the expression on the face of the dead little man—sneering and triumphant. It was so unlike any that had ever been seen on him. The second thing that excited comment was the bits of paper strewn about the room, scrawled over and over—even the blotting paper; some crumpled up and hurled about, scribbled with amazing and incomprehensible messages, as though the unknown murderer had been surprised in the working out of some esoteric code: "Yolc" . . . "Cramoisy" . . . "Sckats" . . . "Ecaroh" . . . "Pachisi" . . . "Wolliw" . . .

And Roger Farmiloe had disappeared.

Eventually he was found and brought back, still apparently struggling under a terrific sense of grievance and anxious to tell the whole English-speaking world, his judge and his jury, the spectators at the trial, and the journalists who visited him eager for a good story, exactly what had led him to slay poor harmless Leslie.

For there the little brother had sat, Sunday after Sunday, meekly in his corner, his feet resting on the crossbar of the chair, so that his knees were almost level with his chin. Outwardly meek, but inwardly gloating,

gloating with ruthless revengeful ferocity, remembering the humiliations he had suffered from Roger all through the past week; gloating over the full-blooded successful big brother helplessly caught in the toils of Grand Inquisitor's wheel and rack and thumbscrew. For instance: "In opposition to jug-jug." . . . "More than one eight gives the ear the second half of this cheers, two-thirds of eleven are the first half." . . . "The oat is heard above me in Calydon." . . . "The forge of the flea." . . . Until Roger, glancing up too suddenly, on that fatal afternoon when the tragedy had occurred, had surprised on little Leslie's face a fleeting grin of mockery. This week's was a particularly malevolent example of the Grand Inquisitor's most fiendish art, and Roger was fractious. Immediately two dictionaries sped through the room and hit the wall, one on either side of the younger of the Farmiloe brothers.

"I suppose," bellowed Roger, "that you, being a half-wit and an imbecile and an idiot, imagine you can do this better than me?" and expected Leslie to shrink and cower, and to whisper his usual apologies after the usual challenge of "bet you can't do this."

But Leslie replied tranquilly, with that ghost of a chuckle bubbling through his speech: "Do you know—ch-ch—I rather think—ch-ch—I rather think I could.

"Come on, then," shouted Roger, marveling at the half-wit's effrontery. So little Leslie climbed down from his chair and tripped across the room, seized a pencil, bent over the folded page, the ruled squares of the crossword blurred already and indented by poor Roger's attempts and crossings out.

And with swift neatness, still smiling in that odd triumphant way, he filled in the whole solution, first across and then down.

It was Roger's turn to watch, which he did in dumb, fishlike bewilderment.

This was outrageous! This was incredible! It couldn't be true, and yet—it was true. Three more words—two—one—and Leslie had finished. "You see," he said, kindly explaining, but not bothering to hide the fact that he was patronizing that poor burly oaf, Roger Farmiloe, "you see: 'Seat renowned for its association with Arachnida' must be 'tuffet.' Of course you know that Arachnida is the class name of spiders, scorpions, and mites."

Either this was magic, or—

Suddenly Roger Farmiloe guessed.

With a roar like a bull, he flung down his accusation. "You! You're Grand Inquisitor!"

"Dear me, yes," replied little Leslie Farmiloe, sweetly and gently. "Fancy you only discovering that now! It's been such fun every Sunday, sitting here and watching you."

"Haunted, sir? No, not what you'd call haunted. Of course one of the gentlemen who lived here last was hanged. . . ."

*Gladys Bronwyn Stern*

The *plot* of a story is the series of related events that present a problem or *conflict*, lead to the *climax* or point at which the conflict must be resolved, and finally result in a *conclusion* of the conflict.

Who are the main characters of "Grand Inquisitor"? List some of the ways in which

they differ. How have these differences affected their relationship?

In most stories there is a conflict of opposing forces that must be resolved. In "Grand Inquisitor" the conflict is between the two Farmiloe brothers: Roger, the bully, and Leslie, the bullied. Conflicts that pit character against character, character against nature (weather, animals), or character against the forces of society (opinion, convention) are called *external* conflicts.

Conflicts within the character such as between duty and desire, between opposing emotions, or between character and conscience are called *internal* conflicts. Conflict in a story is rarely entirely one or the other. Describe the internal and external conflicts in "Grand Inquisitor."

What is the conclusion of the conflict between Roger and Leslie? What brings it about? The climax of the story occurs when Roger realizes that Leslie is the author of the puzzles with which Roger wrestles each Sunday. At this point something has to happen. The conflict must be resolved. Why is Roger unable to accept his discovery about Leslie?

If, at the climax of the story, Roger had expressed his amazement and then gone on to admire Leslie's talent, how might the conclusion of the story have been different?

Roger cannot accept the knowledge that the brother he despises and bullies can best him at something and gloat over his victory. He murders Leslie. Given what you know of Roger, is this a logical conclusion to the story?

# ■ PLOT

**A series of related events that present and resolve a conflict. The usual pattern of plot is conflict, climax, and conclusion.**

■ Apply to **"The Monkey's Paw"** on page 7.

# ■ POINT OF VIEW

Every literary work is told to the reader by a *speaker* or *voice*, commonly called the *narrator*. The author, in choosing a narrator for fiction, does much more than select someone to tell the story; he or she determines what the reader will see through the narrator's eyes.

The relationship between the narrator of a story and the story he or she relates is called the *point of view*. There are basically two main points of view: *first person* and *third person*.

The following passage is from "The Secret Sharer" by Joseph Conrad.

And I told him a little about myself. I had been appointed to take charge while I least expected anything of the sort, not quite a fortnight ago. I didn't know either the ship or the people. Hadn't had the time in port to look about me or size anybody up. And as to the crew, all they knew was that I was appointed to take the ship home. For the rest, I was almost as much of a stranger on board as himself, I said. And at the moment I felt it most acutely.

The "I" in the passage refers to a young ship's captain, a major character who is telling the story of his dreamlike encounter with a mysterious stranger. The "I" indicates that the story is told from a *first-person point of view*.

First-person narrators are always characters in the story. If they are major characters, they tend to report mainly what happens to them; if they are minor characters, they generally tell what they see happening to others. The information they communicate may be limited by what they observe, but in many cases readers can draw INFERENCES from the information. (For another example of the first-person point of view see "The Boar Hunt.")

In the following passage from *Hans Brinker* by Mary Mapes Dodge, two major characters think about their injured father.

Gretel could not remember him otherwise than as the strange, silent man, whose eyes followed her vacantly whichever way she turned. But Hans had recollections of a hearty, cheerful-voiced father who was never tired of bearing him upon his shoulder, and whose careless song still seemed echoing near when Hans lay awake at night and listened.

What is recorded in this passage is what is going on inside the characters' minds. It could only be told by an all-knowing or *omniscient* (om nish′ənt) narrator. An omniscient narrator is not a character in the story, but is capable of relating what characters say, do, and think. Now read this passage about the main character in Audrey M. Lee's "Waiting for Her Train."

. . . She is giving the menu a respectable glance, demonstrating her discriminating taste with proper deliberation. Then with the same deliberating eye, she looks at the long line of people waiting to take advantage of the early morning special breakfasts. A glass of water will do until the line is shorter. That is her reasoning. . . .

Sometimes, as in "Waiting for Her Train," the narrator knows and relates the thoughts of only one character. This is called the *third-person limited* point of view.

Another kind of third-person point of view occurs when the narrator acts as an anonymous reporter, relating only what he or she sees and hears and drawing no conclusions. This is called the *third-person objective* point of view because the reader learns from the narrator only what he or she would learn from observing the characters; that is, what they say and do, but not what they think (unless they say aloud what they are thinking).

Joseph Conrad, *'Twixt Land and Sea*. New York: Doubleday & Company, Inc., 1912.

Mary Mapes Dodge, *Hans Brinker, or The Silver Skates*. New York: James O'Kane, 1866.

From "Waiting for Her Train" by Audrey Lee. Copyright © 1971 by Audrey Lee. Reprinted by permission of the author.

The following passage is from "The Death of Ivan Ilych" by Leo Tolstoy.

Ivan Ilych had been a colleague of the gentlemen present and was liked by them all. He had been ill for some weeks with an illness said to be incurable. His post had been kept open for him, but there had been conjectures that in case of his death Alexeev might receive his appointment, and that either Vinnikov or Shtabel would succeed Alexeev. So on receiving the news of Ivan Ilych's death the first thought of each of the gentlemen in that private room was of the changes and promotions it might occasion among themselves or their acquaintances.

Is the above passage in the first or third person? Does the narrator relate only what is happening or also what any character is thinking? What point of view is represented in the passage?

# ■ POINT OF VIEW

**The relationship between the narrator of a story and the characters and action in it. The two most common points of view are *first person* and *third person*. The first-person narrator might offer a personal account of his or her own experiences, past or present, or may focus on what happens to other characters. The third-person narrator stands anonymously outside a story's action, presenting an all-knowing or omniscient point of view, a limited point of view that centers on the thoughts and actions of only one character, or an objective point of view that describes only what can be seen.**

Leo Tolstoy, *The Death of Ivan Ilych*, 1884, translated by Aylmer Maude, Oxford University Press.

■ Apply to **"Forgiveness in Families"** on page 77

# ■ PROTAGONIST/ ANTAGONIST

The leading character of a short story, play, or novel is called the *protagonist*. The work mainly concerns or is about the protagonist. Thus, the protagonist of the story "The Conjurer's Revenge" is the Conjurer; the protagonist in "The Adventure of the Blue Carbuncle" is Sherlock Holmes.

In most stories the protagonist is opposed by an adversary called the *antagonist*. The antagonist may be a villainous character or may simply be the source of conflict in the story. The loud-mouthed Quick Man in "The Conjurer's Revenge" is the antagonist in that story. The antagonist need not be a character, however; in "The Adventure of the Blue Carbuncle," for example, the antagonist is the mysterious "puzzle" that Holmes tries to solve. The character Ryder has committed the crime, but he is only one part of the mystery Holmes grapples with.

In a well-known story by Jack London, "To Build a Fire," the sole character is the protagonist; the antagonist is the weather that surrounds him. Fate, chance, a set of events, a character, or any combination of these may be the antagonist of a work.

# ■ PROTAGONIST/ ANTAGONIST

(prō tag′ə nist); (an tag′ə nist)

**The protagonist is the main character in a short story, play, or novel.**
**The adversary who opposes the protagonist is called the antagonist. The antagonist may be another character in the work, the forces of nature, fate, chance, or any combination of these.**

■ Apply to *Twelve Angry Men* on page 131.

HANDBOOK OF LITERARY TERMS

# ■ RHYME

### The Swan and Goose

| | |
|---|---|
| A rich man bought a Swan and Goose— | *a* |
| That for song and this for use. | *a* |
| It chanced his simple-minded cook | *b* |
| One night the Swan for Goose mistook. | *b* |
| 5 But in the dark about to chop | *c* |
| The Swan in two above the crop, | *c* |
| He heard the lyric note, and stayed | *d* |
| The action of the fatal blade. | *d* |
| And thus we see a proper tune | *e* |
| 10 Is sometimes very opportune. | *e* |

*Aesop*
*(translated by William Ellery Leonard)*

*Rhyme* is the repetition of similar or identical sounds in the stressed syllables of words. Where are the rhyming words in the lines above? How many different rhyming sounds are there in the poem? Which words that rhyme are not spelled similarly?

Rhyme is among the sound devices poets use. One of its chief uses is the pleasure it gives the reader. This fable might have been written in prose, but the rhyme adds to its amusing tone.

Rhyme found at the ends of lines is called *end rhyme*. When there is a definite pattern to the end rhyme, it is called *rhyme scheme*.

If one were to chart the rhyme scheme of a poem, one would represent the first rhyming sound as *a* and the second rhyming sound as *b*. Thus the rhyme scheme for "The Swan and Goose" would be *a a b b c c d d, e e*. More intricate rhyme schemes are possible. Read the following poem. Chart the rhyme scheme.

### The Craftsman

I ply with all the cunning of my art
This little thing, and with consummate care
I fashion it—so that when I depart,
Those who come after me shall find it fair
5 And beautiful. It must be free of flaws—
Pointing no laborings of weary hands;
And there must be no flouting of the laws

Of beauty—as the artist understands.
Through passion, yearnings infinite—yet dumb—
10 I lift you from the depths of my own mind
And gild you with my soul's white heat to plumb
The souls of future men. I leave behind
This thing that in return this solace gives:
"He who creates true beauty ever lives."

*Marcus B. Christian*

How does the rhyme scheme of the last two lines differ from that of the previous lines? Note how this difference emphasizes the last two lines and sets them apart from the rest of the poem. Notice also how the rhyme scheme divides the poem into four distinct parts. How many lines are there in the poem? The form of this poem and its rhyme is that of a Shakespearean sonnet.

### Midsummer Jingle

I've an ingle, shady ingle, near a dusky bosky dingle
Where the sighing zephyrs mingle with the purling of
    the stream.
There I linger in the jungle, and it makes me thrill
    and tingle,
Far from city's strident jangle as I angle, smoke and
    dream.

5 Through the trees I'll hear a single ringing sound, a
    cowbell's jingle,
And its ting-a-ling'll mingle with the whispers of the
    breeze;
So, although I've not a single sou, no potentate or
    king'll
Make me jealous while I angle in my ingle 'neath the
    trees.

*Newman Levy*

From *Aesop and Hyssop*, translated by William Ellery Leonard. Reprinted by permission of Open Court Publishing Company, La Salle, Ill.

From *The Poetry of the Negro 1746–1970*, Edited by Langston Hughes and Arna Bontemps. Published by Doubleday & Company, Inc.

"Midsummer Jingle" from *Gay But Wistful* by Newman Levy. Published by Alfred A. Knopf, Inc. Reprinted by permission of the estate of Newman Levy.

Which words within the lines rhyme with the words at the ends of the lines? Rhyming sounds within lines are called *internal rhyme*. In this poem, the poet has chosen real words with similar sounds to create an almost musical internal rhyme.

Do *jingle, jangle,* and *jungle* rhyme? Words that sound similar but are not identical are called *half rhymes* or *slant rhymes*. (See also CONSONANCE.)

Half rhyme adds variety to the sound of poems and is much used by more recent poets. Poets who use half rhyme have a much wider selection of words from which to choose since the number of identically rhyming words is actually rather limited.

> "And now there came both mist and snow,
> And it grew wondrous cold;
> And ice, mast-high, came floating by
> As green as emerald
>
> 5 "And through the drifts the snowy cliffs
> Did send a dismal sheen;
> Nor shapes of men nor beasts we ken—
> The ice was all between."

*Samuel Taylor Coleridge*
**"The Rime of the Ancient Mariner"**

Point out examples of internal rhyme. What example of half rhyme is in the first stanza?

# ■ RHYME

**Words having the same sound in their stressed syllables. Its use may give pleasure to the ear, emphasize important words or lines, and unify parts of the poem or the whole poem.**

■ Apply to **"The Fool and the Poet"** on page 280.

# ■ RHYTHM

Language has *rhythm* because we give words a certain stress, or accent, in pronouncing them. We say *beGIN* and *MERcy, interRUPT* and *BEAUtiful*. Both prose and poetry have rhythm, but in poetry the rhythm is regulated. What we call rhythm, or *meter*, in English poetry is the pattern of accented and unaccented syllables.

Rhythm alone does not make a poem, as these lines show:

Birds GO rePAST the Ego YOU,
DULL ROLLer SKATE sinCERE we DO.

Meter must echo sense. Poets who write solemnly of death do not want their lines to bounce along like a nursery jingle. They will use meter (in combination with other devices) to create a slow, solemn movement. The pace of a poem must be appropriate to the emotion.

The most common meter in English is *iambic*, an unaccented syllable followed by an accented syllable (⌣ ′). The English language has many words that consist of two syllables. Because most of these two-syllable words, like *beGIN*, are accented on the final syllable, English speech has a natural iambic beat. As a result, the rhythm of an iambic line moves smoothly:

⌣ ′ ⌣ ′ ⌣ ′ ⌣ ′
Beneath / it rung / the bat-/tle shout. . . .

*Oliver Wendell Holmes*
**"Old Ironsides"**

*Trochaic* meter, an accented syllable followed by an unaccented syllable, (′ ⌣), as in *MERcy*, reverses the natural iambic beat. As such, a trochaic line seems to move roughly:

′ ⌣ ′ ⌣ ′ ⌣ ′ ⌣
Thou, when / thou re- / turnst, wilt / tell me.

*John Donne*
**"Song"**

*Anapestic* meter (˘ ˘ ′), as in *interRUPT*, tends to move in leaps:

˘ ˘ ′ ˘ ˘ ′ ˘ ˘ ′ ˘ ˘ ′
The As syr / ian came down / like the wolf / on the fold.

*Lord Byron*
**"The Destruction of Sennacherib"**

*Dactylic* meter (′ ˘ ˘), as in *BEAUtiful*, moves in thrusts:

′ ˘ ˘ ′ ˘ ˘
O the wild / charge they made!

*Alfred, Lord Tennyson*
**"The Charge of the Light Brigade"**

*Spondaic* meter (′′) consists of two accented syllables.

Poets can manipulate any one of the basic meters so that it moves quickly or slowly. They adjust the motion of a poem by occasionally substituting a different meter in a line. Identify the substitute meter in each example.

˘ ˘ ′ ˘ ˘ ′ ˘ ˘ ′ ˘ ˘ ′
**1.** The ship / was cheered, / the har / bor cleared,

′ ˘ ˘ ′ ˘ ˘ ′
Mer ri / ly did / we drop

*Samuel Taylor Coleridge*
**"The Rime of the Ancient Mariner"**

′ ˘ ˘ ′ ˘ ˘
**2.** Can non to / right of them,

′ ˘ ˘ ′ ˘ ˘
Can non to / left of them,

′ ˘ ˘ ′ ˘
Can non be / hind them

′ ˘ ˘ ′ ˘
Vol leyed and / thun dered;

*Alfred, Lord Tennyson*
**"The Charge of the Light Brigade"**

In the example from Coleridge, the pace quickens when the poet reverses the *accented* syllables. In the example from Tennyson the pace slows when the poet decreases the number of *unaccented* syllables. This is *how* the movement changes, but it is even more important to recognize *why* it changes. Tennyson, for example, slows the line so that it echoes (and emphasizes) the mournful tone of the stanza. Rhythm is part of a poem's meaning.

Much modern poetry frequently departs from a regular meter or rhythm, but all poems have rhythm; that is, there are always some words or syllables that are stressed more than others.

*Scansion* (skan′shən)

When we scan a line of poetry, we determine the kind of meter it contains and then count the

number of metrical units, or *feet*, in a line. A *foot* is a group of syllables constituting a metrical unit of a verse.

˘　/
Thus I

˘　/
Pass by

˘　/
And die

˘　/
As one

˘　/
Un known

˘　/
And gone.

Robert Herrick
**"Upon His Departure Hence"**

Because each line of Herrick's poem is written in the *iambic* meter, and because each line contains *one* iambic foot, we say the lines of the poem are basically *iambic monometer*.

The English word *monometer* (mə nom′ə tər) is derived from the Greek prefix *mono-* ("one") and the Greek word *metron* ("measure"). Other words that indicate the length of lines are:

*dimeter* (dim′ə tər) (two feet)
*trimeter* (trim′ə tər) (three feet)
*tetrameter* (te tram′ə tər) (four feet)
*pentameter* (pen tam′ə tər) (five feet)

Scan the following examples. On a separate sheet of paper, copy the defining sentence. Then fill in the name of the meter (*iambic, trochaic, anapestic,* or *dactylic*), number of feet in the lines (*1, 2, 3, 4,* or *5*), and the scansion pattern (the name of the meter plus *monometer, dimeter, trimeter, tetrameter,* or *pentameter*).

　/　˘　　/　˘　　/　˘
1. Mor tal / man and / wo man,

　/　˘　　/　˘　　/　˘
Go up / on your / tra vel!

Elizabeth Barrett Browning
**"A Drama of Exile"**

Each of Browning's lines is written in the _____ meter. Because each line contains _____ feet, the lines are _____ _____.

　˘　/　˘　/　˘　/　˘　/　˘　/
2. How like / a win / ter hath / my ab / sence been

　˘　/　˘　/　˘　/　˘　/　˘　/
From thee, / the plea / sure of / the fleet / ing year!

William Shakespeare
**"Sonnet 97"**

Each of Shakespeare's lines is written in the _____ meter. Because each line contains _____ feet, the lines are _____ _____.

　/　˘　˘　/　˘　˘
3. Cold in hu / man i ty,

　/　˘　˘　/　˘　˘
Burn ing in / san i ty.

Thomas Hood
**"The Bridge of Sighs"**

Each of Hood's lines is written in the _____ meter. Because each line contains _____ feet, the lines are _____ _____.

## ■ RHYTHM

**The arrangement of stressed and unstressed syllables in speech and writing.**

■ Apply to **"The Traveler's Curse After Misdirection"** on page 278.

Drawing by Lorenz; © 1977 The New Yorker Magazine, Inc.

THIS STRUCTURE WILL BE TORN DOWN AND REPLACED BY A NEW 44-STORY COOKIE

## ■ SATIRE

1. Of what situation is the cartoonist making fun?
2. Do you think the cartoonist is trying to correct the situation, or is he simply commenting on it?
3. Is the general tone of the cartoon humorous or critical? (See **TONE**.)

*Satire* is a device used by writers (and cartoonists) to ridicule people and their institutions, whether social, political, religious, or commercial, in order to reveal their foolishness or vice. The aim of satire is to comment on the situation, often with an eye toward correcting it by making society more aware of the problem.

Satire is frequently a more successful means of bringing a situation to the public's notice than plain criticism. While the subject and the writer's intent may well be serious, satire itself is entertaining, whether gently humorous or savagely witty. Irony, humor, sarcasm, and exaggeration are common devices of satire. (See **IRONY**.)

Characters, plot devices, and settings in satirical literary works often are based on **STEREOTYPES**. Authors may present standardized, conventional characters, places, or events in order to poke fun at types of people, institutions, and circumstances that seem recognizable to many readers.

Read the following poem. Try to determine whether the poet is gently, or bitterly, humorous.

### We Are Going to See the Rabbit

We are going to see the rabbit.
We are going to see the rabbit.
Which rabbit, people say?
Which rabbit, ask the children?
5 Which rabbit?
The only rabbit,
The only rabbit in England,
Sitting behind a barbed-wire fence
Under the floodlights, neon lights,

---

"We are going to see the rabbit. . . ." from *Collected Poems 1952–83* by Alan Brownjohn, published by Martin Secker & Warburg Limited. Reprinted by permission of the author.

10 Sodium lights,
Nibbling grass
On the only patch of grass
In England, in England
(Except the grass by the hoardings[1]
15 Which doesn't count.)
We are going to see the rabbit
And we must be there on time.

First we shall go by escalator,
Then we shall go by underground,
20 And then we shall go by motorway
And then by helicopterway,
And the last ten yards we shall have to go
On foot.
And now we are going
25 All the way to see the rabbit.
We are nearly there,
We are longing to see it,
And so is the crowd
Which is here in thousands
30 With mounted policemen
And big loudspeakers
And bands and banners,
And everyone has come a long way.
But soon we shall see it
35 Sitting and nibbling
The blades of grass
On the only patch of grass
In—but something has gone wrong!
Why is everyone so angry,
40 Why is everyone jostling
And slanging and complaining?

The rabbit has gone,
Yes, the rabbit has gone.
He has actually burrowed down into the earth
45 And made himself a warren,[2] under the earth,
Despite all these people.
And what shall we do?
What *can* we do?

It is all a pity, you must be disappointed.
50 Go home and do something else for today,
Go home again, go home for today.
For you cannot hear the rabbit, under the earth,
Remarking rather sadly to himself, by himself,
As he rests in his warren, under the earth:
55 "It won't be long, they are bound to come,
They are bound to come and find me, even here."

*Alan Brownjohn*

Why is the rabbit so special? What do you suppose has happened to the other rabbits? the grass? What is the poet commenting on in the second stanza? Is the poet optimistic or pessimistic about the future of wildlife? Do you think the poem is meant solely to entertain the reader or to stir a feeling that "something must be done"?

When people, actions, or literary works are satirized by ridiculous exaggeration, it is called *burlesque*. Comedians on television often perform burlesques of old movies and soap operas. In writing, burlesque may be characterized by an inconsistency between the subject matter and the style: the struggle between a spider and a fly, for example, written in epic form.

Mimicking aimed at a particular writer or work is called *parody* (par′ə dē). In parody the outstanding characteristics of a work or writer are so exaggerated that anyone in the least familiar with the original will recognize the parodied style. Before you read the following parody, turn to page 549 and read lines 73–76. Then you will recognize the famous lines which are parodied below.

Wits, comics, funnymen, spare me your jeers;
I've come to help your humor, not to pan it.
Your skits are long, your repartee is dull;
Your jokes were old when Noah was a lad.

---

1. **hoardings,** billboards. [*British*]
2. **warren,** place underground where rabbits live.

Now try writing a parody of a well-known nursery rhyme. Be sure that the rhythm and rhyme of your parody are close to the original.

## ■ SATIRE

**A technique that ridicules people and their institutions in an effort to expose their weaknesses and evils. The purpose of satire often is to bring about a change. Exaggeration and irony are frequent devices of satire.** *Burlesque* **is a means of making people, actions, or literary forms ridiculous through extreme exaggeration.** *Parody* **is mimicking aimed at making fun of a particular writer's style or work.**

■ Apply to **"Action Will Be Taken"** on page 452.

FAT AND LEAN.

From *Rebecca* by Daphne du Maurier. Copyright 1938 by Daphne du Maurier Browning. Reprinted by permission of *Doubleday Publishing*, a division of Bantam, Doubleday, Dell Publishing Group, Inc. and Curtis Brown Group Ltd.

## ■ SETTING

The following passage is from the opening pages of *Rebecca* by Daphne du Maurier.

There was Manderley, our Manderley, secretive and silent as it had always been, the grey stone shining in the moonlight of my dream, the mullioned windows reflecting the green lawns and the terrace. Time could not wreck the perfect symmetry of those walls, nor the site itself, a jewel in the hollow of a hand.

. . . When I thought of Manderley in my waking hours I would not be bitter. I should think of it as it might have been, could I have lived there without fear. I should remember the rose garden in summer, and the birds that sang at dawn. Tea under the chestnut tree, and the murmur of the sea coming up to us from the lawns below.

What is Manderley? Is the narrator still at Manderley? Is Manderley inland or on the coast? What do these lines tell the reader about the narrator?

The two paragraphs tell the observant reader a good deal about Manderley, the English country estate where most of *Rebecca* takes place. They describe the *setting* of the novel: an old, grand, stone house in the midst of fine green lawns situated above the sea. The time is not specified, but the reader can make an **INFERENCE** that the narrator has lived at Manderley in the past, and that the memories of having lived there are not all happy ones.

The setting is the time and place in which the action of a narrative occurs. Setting helps in the understanding of character and action. Later in the story, which is told in **FLASHBACK,** the narrator meets the owner of Manderley, Maximilian de Winter.

. . . I thought how unreal he would look against a Florida background. He belonged to a walled city of the fifteenth century, a city of narrow, cobbled streets, and thin spires, . . . a past of narrow stairways and dim dungeons, a past of whispers in the dark, of shimmering rapier blades, of silent, exquisite courtesy.

What does the narrator's imagined setting for Mr. de Winter tell you about him? Setting can help the reader understand character through association with familiar backgrounds.

A third function of setting is to help create the atmosphere and mood of the narrative. Consider the following paragraph from *Rebecca*, which describes the narrator's first ride up the drive to the great house.

This drive twisted and turned as a serpent, scarce wider in places than a path, and above our heads was a great colonnade of trees, whose branches nodded and intermingled with one another, making an archway for us, like the roof of a church. Even the midday sun would not penetrate the interlacing of those green leaves, they were too thickly entwined, one with another, and only little flickering patches of warm light would come in intermittent waves to dapple the drive with gold. It was very silent, very still. On the highroad there had been a gay west wind blowing in my face, making the grass on the hedges dance in unison, but here there was no wind. Even the engine of the car had taken a new note, throbbing low, quieter than before. As the drive descended to the valley so the trees came in upon us, great beeches with lovely smooth white stems, lifting their myriad branches to one another, and other trees, trees I could not name, coming close, so close that I could touch them with my hands. On we went, over a little bridge that spanned a narrow stream, and still this drive that was no drive twisted and turned like an enchanted ribbon through the dark and silent woods, penetrating even deeper to the very heart surely of the forest itself, and still there was no clearing, no space to hold a house.

Is the atmosphere created cheerful or subdued? What are the elements that add a sinister quality to the description? How does the setting affect what you expect of the story?

Finally, setting may aid the development of the plot. When the narrator goes to Manderley, she goes as the second Mrs. de Winter. The reader is told that the first Mrs. de Winter, a beautiful and vivacious woman, was drowned in the bay below the grounds. Mrs. Danvers, the housekeeper, shows the narrator to her rooms in the east wing of the house overlooking the rose garden.

"You can't see the sea from here then," I said, turning to Mrs. Danvers.

"No, not from this wing," she answered, "you can't even hear it, either. You would not know the sea was anywhere near, not from this wing.

". . . the rooms in the west wing are very old. The bedroom in the big suite is twice as large as this, a very beautiful room too, with a scrolled ceiling."

. . . I did not know why she must speak with such an undercurrent of resentment, implying as she did at the same time that this room, where I found myself to be installed, was something inferior, not up to Manderley standard, a second-rate room, as it were, for a second-rate person.

. . . [Mrs. Danvers] paused an instant, feeling me with her eyes. "They used to live in the west wing and use those rooms when Mrs. de Winter was alive. That big room I was telling you about, that looked down to the sea, was Mrs. de Winter's bedroom."

The plot of *Rebecca* concerns the two wives, one dead and one the narrator. Do you see how the above passage foreshadows a rivalry between the women? Do you expect the sea to play an important role in the plot? One woman's room looks out over the sea and the rose garden; the other's room, only the rose garden. How do you think this might influence the plot?

## ■ SETTING

**The time and place in which the action of a narrative occurs. The setting may serve simply as a background for characters and events or it may help create the atmosphere from which the story evolves. It may directly affect the plot's development, and it may help in the understanding of character, or even be vital to that understanding.**

■ Apply to "**The Boar Hunt**" on page 59.

# ■ SIMILE

My heart is like a singing bird
  Whose nest is in a water'd shoot

*Christina Rossetti*
**"A Birthday"**

A maid whom there were none to praise
  And very few to love . . .
—Fair as a star, when only one
  Is shining in the sky.
*William Wordsworth*
**"She Dwelt Among the
Untrodden Ways"**

In both examples above, comparisons are made. What is being compared in each? What word in each example tells you that a comparison is being made?

A *simile* is a stated comparison between two things that are literally unlike but share some quality or qualities that the writer wishes to emphasize. A simile is expressed by the use of the word *like* or *as*. In the first simile, the speaker's heart is like a singing bird. What feeling does this comparison suggest? The second simile compares the fairness of a beloved woman to the shining of a single star. What qualities do the two elements of the comparison share?

Be careful not to confuse similes with literal comparisons. When we express such comparisons as "She looks like her mother" or "He writes as well as a professional writer," we are being literal.

# ■ SIMILE

**A figure of speech involving a direct comparison between two unlike things and using words such as *like* or *as*.**

■ Apply to "**Harlem**" on page 267.

# ■ STEREOTYPE

Read the following passages about characters. Decide which person each passage is describing.

**A.** Jeffrey Lombard was tall and dark with just a tinge of silver at his temples. Always impeccably dressed, he wore his tailored suits with a kind of lazy grace that belied his athletic prowess. Well-read and witty, he enjoyed the respect and influence that always assured him the best tables when dining out. Lombard was a sought-after escort, but, as yet, no woman had managed to hold him for long.

Lombard probably is a (**a**) coal miner; (**b**) truck driver; (**c**) secret agent; (**d**) jockey.

**B.** Grace Meadowes was smart, no doubt about that. When George had died, she'd invested wisely and was now nicely set up for life. If only her darling Billy hadn't married that silly Florence. What on earth had he seen in her anyway? Adjusting her best rose-trimmed hat, she resolutely set her shoulders as she glanced in the mirror. A plain face with a determined jaw gazed back at her.

Meadowes probably is a (**a**) domineering mother-in-law; (**b**) timid, retiring woman; (**c**) heroine of a historical novel; (**d**) schoolgirl.

**C.** Herbie sweated profusely and seemed to shrink as he sagged against the wall. He was a weasel-faced little man with scanty hair and a pasty complexion. He was scared, but too out of breath to keep running. He hadn't worked these streets for all those years for nothing, so as they hovered close he blubbered out a deal.

Herbie is probably a (**a**) hardware salesman; (**b**) chef; (**c**) small-time crook; (**d**) veterinarian.

The above characters are examples of *stereotypes*. Stereotyped characters are those that embody a conventional idea about whatever character is being portrayed. Make a list of some other stereotyped characters.

Stereotypes in written works need to be recognized as stereotypes rather than as fully developed characters. Stereotypes are useful when the author wants to compare and contrast different reactions in a limited space or time as in the play *Twelve Angry Men*.

Secondary characters, too, are often presented as stereotypes; they are better foils if they remain one-dimensional.

Reading about stereotyped characters in popular fiction is often pleasurable because such characters are predictable, and the reader knows what to expect. Usually, however, a writer will try to develop characters more fully. (See **CHARACTERIZATION**.)

**PLOTS** and **SETTINGS** may be stereotyped also. Very likely as you have watched a program on television or read a book, you have suddenly realized that it is similar to something you have seen or read before. An example of a stereotyped plot might be one in which a doctor, a lawyer, or a policeman discovers that his best friend is taking drugs or bribes or kickbacks. Make a list of other stereotyped plots you have seen on television or read.

Settings that for one reason or another are continually depicted in the same manner are stereotyped. Examples might be a wholesome farm, a "wicked" city, or the glamorous French Riviera. Anyone who lives in any of these places knows that such views are one-sided.

Stereotypes can be harmful if they lead a reader to accept certain standardized views about people, situations, or places. In real life they are all more complex.

---

## ■ STEREOTYPE (ster′ē ə tīp′)

**Standardized, conventional ideas about characters, plots, and settings. An example of a stereotyped character might be an absent-minded professor; a stereotyped plot might be a story about a brave dog saving a small child; a stereotyped setting might be a ghost town in the old west.**

■ Apply to **"Enemies"** on page 443.

---

## ■ STYLE

As you read the following paragraphs, try to determine what makes them different.

**A.** At any time of year the view from the Paris bridges is very nice, especially in the evening. It is just like a picture-postcard scene with the buildings on both sides of the river, and the big trees that come right down to the water. Behind them, in the west, you can see the large Louvre, the famous museum. It sort of glows when the sun goes down. Toward the other direction you can see the outline of the also-famous Cathedral of Notre Dame.

**B.** At any season, and all year long, in the evening the view of the city from the bridges was always exquisitely pictorial. One's eyes became the eyes of a painter, because the sight itself approximated art, with the narrow, pallid façades of the buildings lining the river; with the tall trees growing down by the water's edge; with, behind them, the vast chiaroscuro[1] of the palatial Louvre, lightened by the luminous lemon color of the Paris sunset off toward the west; with the great square, pale stone silhouette of Notre Dame to the east.

*Janet Flanner*
*from* **"That Was Paris"**

What do you think is the purpose of the paragraphs? To entertain? to inform? to create a scene? All of these things?

Which paragraph has more difficult words? Longer sentences? Which paragraph is more conversational? Does one paragraph give you a clearer picture of the scene than the other? If so, which? Are **IMAGERY** and **FIGURATIVE LANGUAGE** employed?

Two elements are necessary when writing: ideas (or a subject) and the words to express those ideas. The manner in which writers make words fit their ideas is called *style*. Style is a combination of the many techniques and devices

---

1. *chiaroscuro* (kē är′ə skyūr′ō), pattern of light and shade.

Janet Flanner, "That Was Paris." *The New Yorker*, March 11, 1972.

of writing and the way they are used to express the writer's ideas.

Both paragraphs are about the view from the bridges of Paris, but the styles are vastly different. The first paragraph mainly informs the reader about the view. The writer uses simple, informal language. The TONE might be described as conversational, much like what one might write in a letter home. No particular MOOD is established, though it is plain the writer is enjoying the view.

In the second paragraph the style is much more complex. The writer attempts to make the scene as real for the reader as it is for the viewer. There is a faintly reminiscent TONE, as though the writer were remembering how things looked rather than describing them as she now sees them. The language is more formal and ornate than that of the first paragraph, and the IMAGERY and FIGURATIVE LANGUAGE are more concrete: "narrow, pallid façades," "the palatial Louvre," "the luminous lemon color of the Paris sunset," and "the great square, pale stone silhouette of Notre Dame." A METAPHOR is found in the sentence "One's eyes became the eyes of a painter." There is ALLITERATION: "the palatial Louvre, lightened by the luminous lemon color. . . ." The MOOD created is quiet, almost dreamy.

All people who write have their own individual ideas and use the language that they think best expresses those ideas. Thus, everyone has his or her own style of writing.

## ■ STYLE

**The manner in which writers use words and sentences to fit their ideas. Style involves many choices on the part of the writer: types of words, placement of words in a sentence, the purpose of the written work, tone, mood, imagery, figurative language, sound devices, and rhythm.**

■ Apply to "**Four Letters**" on page 645.

## ■ SYMBOL

Judge not the play before the play be done.

The line above is literal advice that might be offered to any theatergoer. There is no reason to suppose "play" means or stands for anything except itself. Now read the line in the context of the poem.

My soul, sit thou a patient looker on;
Judge not the play before the play be done:
Her plot has many changes; every day
Speaks a new scene; the last act crowns the play.

*Francis Quarles*
*from* **Epigram**

1. What is the first indication that "play" now may mean more than just a theater production?
2. What might "play" refer to in this context?
3. What might the "plot" be?
4. What is the "last act"?

When read in context, "play" becomes a *symbol*, something that, in addition to its own meaning, suggests or represents something else: in this case, a person's life.

Not all works employ symbolism. Readers should not try to force meaning that is not there, nor should they try to make symbols of things that have only literal meaning.

Consider the symbols in the following poem.

**A White Rose**

The red rose whispers of passion,
    And the white rose breathes of love;
Oh, the red rose is a falcon,
    And the white rose is a dove.

5 But I send you a cream-white rosebud,
    With a flush on its petal tips;
For the love that is purest and sweetest
    Has a kiss of desire on the lips.

*John Boyle O'Reilly*

1. What do the red and white roses symbolize for the speaker?
2. Why does the speaker compare the red rose with a falcon and the white rose with a dove?
3. In the second stanza, what symbol is used to describe the speaker's love? How is it described?

## ■ SYMBOL

**Something concrete, such as an object, person, place, or happening, that stands for or represents something abstract such as an idea, a quality, a concept, or a condition.**

■ Apply to "The Sentimentality of William Tavener" on page 407.

## ■ THEME

**One Hard Look**

Small gnats that fly
In hot July
And lodge in sleeping ears
Can rouse therein
5 A trumpet's din
With Day of Judgment fears.

Small mice at night
Can wake more fright
Than lions at midday;
10 A straw will crack
The camel's back—
There is no easier way.

One smile relieves
A heart that grieves
15 Though deadly sad it be,
And one hard look
Can close the book
That lovers love to see.

*Robert Graves*

How can small gnats create more noise than a trumpet, according to the first stanza of the poem above? How might mice rustling at night be more frightening than lions during the day? How might a sad person's smiling or being smiled at help lessen his or her grief? What is the poet saying in the last three lines of the third stanza? (Keep in mind the expression "a face like an open book.")

Which of the following statements best reveals the meaning of the poem? (a) Small sounds at night seem noisier than loud ones during the day; (b) Things seem different by the light of day; (c) Small things in general can make big differences in the way one feels; (d) Don't despise the little things.

"One Hard Look" from *Country Sentiment* by Robert Graves. Published by Alfred A. Knopf, Inc. Copyright 1920 by Robert Graves. Reprinted by permission of AP Watt Ltd.

The meaning underlying a literary work is called the *theme*. The theme of the above poem is revealed in statement (**c**).

Statement (**d**) presents a moral: it tells the reader how to act. It is not the theme, because the poet does not tell the reader how to think or behave. He simply states various examples and leaves it up to the reader to make an INFERENCE about the theme: seemingly insignificant things can make all the difference to the way one feels.

Statement (**a**) relates what plot there is in stanzas one and two. A PLOT is a pattern of events, things that happen in a narrative or poem. The theme is the central idea, what the work is about.

It is important to recognize the difference between the theme and the *subject* of a literary work. The subject is the topic about which the author has chosen to write. The theme, however, makes a statement about that topic or expresses an opinion about it. The subject of the above poem is suggested by the title, "One Hard Look"; the theme is the great effect small things can have.

**Soup**

I saw a famous man eating soup.
I say he was lifting a fat broth
Into his mouth with a spoon.
His name was in the newspapers that day
5 Spelled out in tall black headlines
And thousands of people were talking about him.

When I saw him,
He sat bending his head over a plate
Putting soup in his mouth with a spoon.

*Carl Sandburg*

1. What sets the man in the poem apart from most other people?
2. What impression of him do you have from this poem?
3. What do you think is the theme of this poem?

Not every work has a theme. Works with no theme are most likely to be those written entirely for the entertainment of the reader. Examples might be mystery or adventure stories. Some literary works—*Julius Caesar*, for example—have more than one theme.

---

## ■ THEME

**The underlying meaning of a literary work. The theme may be stated or implied. Theme differs from the subject of a literary work in that it involves a statement or opinion about that subject. Not every literary work has a theme. Some literary works have more than one theme.**

---

"Soup" from *Smoke and Steel* by Carl Sandburg, copyright 1920 by Harcourt Brace Jovanovich, Inc.; renewed 1948 by Carl Sandburg. Reprinted by permission of the publisher.

■ Apply to "**Through the Tunnel**" on page 95.

HANDBOOK OF LITERARY TERMS

# ■ TONE

The following passage is from the novel *Oliver Twist* by Charles Dickens. It concerns the members of the board who administer the affairs of the local workhouse where the paupers, or poor people of the area, may find employment, food, and lodging.

As you read, try to determine Dickens's attitude toward his subject.

The members of this board were very sage, deep, philosophical men; and when they came to turn their attention to the workhouse, they found out at once, what ordinary folks would never have discovered—the poor people liked it! It was a regular place of public entertainment for the poorer classes; a tavern where there was nothing to pay; a public breakfast, dinner, tea, and supper all the year round; a brick and mortar elysium,[1] where it was all play and no work. "Oho!" said the board, looking very knowing; "we are the fellows to set this to rights; we'll stop it all, in no time." So, they established the rule, that all poor people should have the alternative (for they would compel nobody, not they), of being starved by a gradual process in the house, or by a quick one out of it. With this view, they contracted with the water-works to lay on an unlimited supply of water; and with a corn-factor to supply periodically small quantities of oatmeal; and issued three meals of thin gruel a day, with an onion twice a week, and half a roll on Sundays. They made a great many other wise and humane regulations, having reference to the ladies, which it is not necessary to repeat; kindly undertook to divorce poor married people, in consequence of the great expense of a suit in Doctors' Commons; and, instead of compelling a man to support his family, as they had theretofore done, took his family away from him, and made him a bachelor! There is no saying how many applicants for relief, under these last two heads, might have started up in all classes of society, if it had not been coupled with the workhouse; but the board were long-headed men, and had provided for this difficulty. The relief was inseparable from the workhouse and the gruel; and that frightened people.

---

1. *elysium* (i lizh′əm, i liz′ē əm), paradise.

Further on, Dickens explains parenthetically that the board would "compel" no one to adopt one manner of starvation over the other. What is the **INFERENCE** the reader may draw from this statement?

When relating the arrangements for food, Dickens points out that the board contracted for an "unlimited supply of water," and "small quantities of oatmeal" with an onion "twice a week" and "half a roll on Sundays." He then notes that the board made "a great many other wise and humane regulations," implying that the aforementioned are wise and humane also. Is that the actual case?

Noting that relief from family responsibilities might have proved too popular with "all classes of society," Dickens refers to the board members as "long-headed" men who had foreseen and provided for that event; that is, "The relief was inseparable from the workhouse and the gruel; and that frightened people." What is the tone here?

Through his choice of words and the juxtaposition of the cruelties inflicted on poor people with the wisdom of the board in inflicting them, Dickens has created a passage that is ironic in tone with both humorous and serious overtones to it.

Determine the tone of this poem:

### Daniel at Breakfast

His paper propped against the electric toaster
    (Nicely adjusted to his morning use),
Daniel at breakfast studies world disaster
    And sips his orange juice.

5 The words dismay him. Headlines shrilly chatter
    Of famine, storm, death, pestilence, decay.
Daniel is gloomy, reaching for the butter.
    He shudders at the way

War stalks the planet still, and men know hunger,
10     Go shelterless, betrayed, may perish soon.
The coffee's weak again. In sudden anger
    Daniel throws down his spoon

And broods a moment on the kitchen faucet
    The plumber mended, but has mended ill;
15 Recalls tomorrow means a dental visit,
    Laments the grocery bill.

Then, having shifted from his human shoulder
    The universal woe, he drains his cup,
Rebukes the weather (surely turning colder),
20     Crumples his napkin up
And, kissing his wife abruptly at the door,
Stamps fiercely off to catch the 8:04.

*Phyllis McGinley*

1. What terrible things does this poem portray happening in the world?
2. What "terrible" things are happening at home to Daniel?
3. Which do you think upsets him more? Do you think the narrator is sympathetic to Daniel's trials?
4. What are some clues in the poem as to the way the narrator views Daniel's situation?

## ■ TONE

**The attitude of the writer toward his or her subject. Tone may be stated or implied. Tone may be revealed by the author's word choice and arrangement of ideas, events, and descriptions.**

■ Apply to **"One Perfect Rose"** on page 247.

Jacques-Louis David, *Portrait of Alexandre Lenoir*, 1817, The Louvre, Paris, France

# WRITER'S HANDBOOK

# The Writing Process

Writing an essay on a literary topic is similar to many other kinds of writing you are asked to do. You need to make sure you understand the assignment, if a specific one is given, and then to plan your answer carefully in order to include all necessary information. This article will give some specific tips on how to apply three steps of the writing process—prewriting, writing, and revising—to literature assignments.

## PREWRITING

### 1. Identify Purpose and Audience

When you are asked to write about a piece of literature, your first task is to determine exactly what you are being asked to do. When you read an assignment, look for words like the following and be sure you know what they mean.

**analyze:** examine critically so as to bring out the essential elements of a piece of writing

**compare/contrast:** point out how two or more things are alike and how they are different

**illustrate:** make clear by examples, comparisons, quotations, and so forth

**describe:** create a word picture or an account of something

**explain:** make clear something not evident or understood

**discuss:** consider all sides of a question

**interpret:** bring out more than the obvious meaning by using special knowledge or imagination

**convince:** persuade by argument or proof

**create:** produce from your own thought or imagination

**imagine:** form an image or idea; put yourself in a new situation

**defend:** write in favor of an opinion

**support:** prove ideas, claims, or opinions

In addition, look for key words that clarify the scope of the assignment and identify the intended audience. Underline them or jot them down. Your intended audience determines the amount of background you need to give, as well as your choice of words. In the following example, based on a poem by Robert Frost, note that you are to focus on how three specific aspects of the poem contribute to its sounding like prose. Note also that your audience will be your classmates.

"The Exposed Nest" is typical of much of Frost's poetry in that it reads as easily as prose, yet is composed in precise poetic form. Write a four- or five-paragraph essay in which you analyze for your classmates how the poem's subject matter, rhyme, and meter contribute to its prose sound. Support your statements with specific examples from the poem.

### 2. Form a Thesis Statement

Assignments requiring only a one-paragraph response can be developed around a topic sentence, a sentence stating the paragraph's main point or idea. Longer compositions, however, are nearly always built around a thesis statement. A thesis statement, generally placed in the opening paragraph of a composition, indicates what your topic is and what aspects of it you will be covering. It may also express your attitude about the topic. One or several sentences in length, the thesis statement is a kind of preview of what the other paragraphs in the composition will cover.

Often the wording of the assignment will give you a clue as to what your thesis statement

WRITER'S HANDBOOK

should say. Notice how the following thesis statement about "The Exposed Nest" echoes the wording of the assignment above.

In reading Robert Frost's "The Exposed Nest," one cannot help noticing that despite its precise poetic form, the poem reads as easily as prose. Three aspects of the poem that help create this effect are its language, rhyme, and meter.

### 3. Take Effective Notes

A well-worded thesis statement can help you decide what kind of information you will need to make your point. Here, for example, you should begin by reviewing or rereading "The Exposed Nest" to form some opinions of how its subject matter, rhyme, and meter make the poem seem like prose. Then jot down some general notes on these opinions.

A strong literary essay contains many clear, precise examples and pieces of evidence. While examining "The Exposed Nest," you should also copy down specific examples of the three aspects under consideration—language, rhyme, and meter—using one of the following two methods.

*Direct quotation.* In a direct quotation, you would copy exact words from the selection, in the exact order in which they are presented. The quote is enclosed in quotation marks, and ellipses (. . .) are used to show where words have been left out. When poetry is quoted, a slash is placed at the end of a line.

"I haven't any memory . . ./Of ever coming to the place again."

*Paraphrase.* In a paraphrase, you express the sense of a passage in your own words. Usually the source is indicated right with the paraphrase.

In the first five lines of "The Exposed Nest," the speaker informs his companion that because she frequently sought new forms of amusement, he went to the meadow to

help her, as he thought, stand a bunch of hay on end.

### 4. Organize Your Notes

The best way to organize your notes often can be determined by what you have said in your thesis statement. Because this essay is to discuss three specific aspects of "The Exposed Nest," your notes can be organized into a rough outline using the three heads: language, rhyme, and meter. Begin by jotting down the purpose of the essay, and include some notes for the introductory and closing paragraphs.

Forms such as charts and cluster diagrams also can be used to organize notes, as you will see in subsequent lessons.

## WRITING

### 5. Write Your First Draft

Concentrate on getting your ideas on paper quickly, without paying much attention to correct form. Complete and well-organized notes should help make the writing easy. Compare the essay on the next page with the notes that were prepared for it, and notice how each part of the composition—the introduction, the body, and the conclusion—fulfills certain functions.

*Introductory paragraph.* The purpose of the introductory paragraph is to present the thesis statement. Sometimes you will have to sketch in background material for the thesis statement to make sense, but if your audience is your teacher or classmates, you can usually get to the point quickly.

*Body paragraphs.* The paragraphs in the body of the essay present the substance of your explanation or argument. As a general rule, each main point you want to discuss should be treated in a separate paragraph.

*Concluding paragraph.* The concluding paragraph can simply restate the thesis statement, or it can briefly summarize the essay or make a final

WRITER'S HANDBOOK

comment. The method you choose will depend on what came before.

*Title.* Titles should be simple, and descriptive of what your paper is about. Most writers worry too much about titles. Use the title of the literary work you are writing about, and expand the title to say what you are discussing, if you wish.

## REVISING

If possible, set aside your completed first draft for a few days. Do your ideas still make sense when you analyze them with a fresh eye? It often is useful to read your draft first to a partner or group to let others help you see your essay's strong and weak points. Use the following checklist to get a general idea of what should be improved in your essay.

### Content and Organization Checklist
- Is the main point of the essay expressed in a strong thesis statement? Will the introduction catch the reader's interest?
- Do the paragraphs in the body focus on specific aspects of the thesis statement?
- Is the topic of each body paragraph developed fully through specific examples or arguments?
- Does each sentence in a paragraph relate to its topic sentence?
- Are ideas presented in a logical order?
- Are transitional words used within and between paragraphs?
- Should more information be added? Should some information be moved to a different place?
- Does the concluding paragraph provide a suitable ending to the essay?

### Style Checklist
- Have you used simple, direct language rather than wordy expressions?
- Are the point of view and tone consistent?
- Does the composition contain a variety of sentence types?

- Have you combined sentences where appropriate? Do the combining words you've used show how ideas are related?
- Have you avoided joining too many ideas with *and*?
- Have you avoided repeating yourself unnecessarily?
- Have you used active rather than passive verbs? Are the tenses of verbs consistent?
- Have you used clear, interesting modifiers?
- Have you avoided overused words like *nice* and *good*?
- Are all pronoun references clear?

### Mechanical Checklist
- Is each paragraph indented?
- Have you used correct spelling, capitalization, and punctuation?
- Have you avoided sentence fragments and run-ons?

---

Outline
1. Introduction (include thesis statement)
2. Language
   —poem like a friendly recollection
   —informal language: "chomping"
   —conversational phrases: "I thought" (li. 4), "if you asked me" (li. 7), "—have you—" (li. 33)
3. Rhyme
   —rhymes vary
   —alternate—abaca (li. 1-5)
   —triples in li. 16-18 and 22-24
   —some rhymes widely separated
   —not predictably at conclusions of thoughts
4. Meter
   —iambic pentameter used throughout
   —many sentences that "run on" beyond the ends of lines
   —long sentences spread over several lines (such as li. 2-8, li. 20-25)
5. Conclusion (recap of essay content)

---

The Exposed Nest

1. In reading Robert Frost's "The Exposed Nest," one cannot help noticing that despite its precise poetic language, the poem reads as easily as prose. Three aspects that help create this effect are its language, rhyme, and meter.

2. The poem opens like a conversation between friends: "You were forever finding some new play." This casualness is enhanced by ordinary language ("The cutter bar had just gone chomping over") and conversational phrases ("I haven't any memory—have you?—" line 23).

3. Frost uses a variety of rhyme patterns. The first five lines use an alternating pattern (abaca), but more frequently the rhymes are separated by two or more lines. Twice Frost offers triple rhymes ("light/right/sight"; "shirred/bird/deferred"). Also, Frost seldom uses rhymes at the conclusion of thoughts. As a result, the rhymes in "The Exposed Nest" occur, not with thudding predictability, but with a pleasant sense of coincidence.

4. Frost's use of iambic rhythm helps the poem flow like ordinary speech. Frost adds to this natural effect by using many run-on lines, such as "Why is there then/No more to tell?" Long sentences run over several metrical lines, such as lines 2-8 and 20-25.

5. "The Exposed Nest" is a good example of a gifted poet using the classic elements of poetry—language, rhyme, and meter—to capture the sound of ordinary human talk and make it live for generations to come.

WRITER'S HANDBOOK

## ASSIGNMENT

Complete either of the essay assignments on page 15. Follow the steps of the writing process as outlined in this lesson.

# Developing Your Style

Ideally, **style** expresses your uniqueness in writing as your voice expresses your uniqueness in speech. As your voice changes depending on whether you're giving a warning, soothing a child, or asking a question, so your style alters with your audience and your purpose.

Some elements of style are beyond your conscious control. Style is partly an expression of the way you see things, the way your mind works, the way you respond to words. But other elements of style result from deliberate decisions you make before you write, as you write, and as you revise.

How can you improve your style? Read as much and as widely as you can. Write often. And keep the following suggestions in mind.

## 1. Be Yourself

Use words and images that are natural to you. When you write about literature, you may find it appropriate to use a slightly more formal style. Nevertheless, your purpose is to share ideas, not to prostrate your reader by the capaciousness of your verbal arsenal nor by the baroque felicities, or, as it were, the architectural symmetries of your sentential configurations. Fancy language that distracts the reader from meaning (as in the previous sentence) is poor style.

Being a good reader can complicate the matter of "being yourself." You may find yourself unconsciously imitating the style of your favorite writer or, like a chameleon, adopting the style of whatever book you read last. This is not so much a problem as it is a phase that almost all writers go through. The trick is not to avoid such influence, but to absorb it. Keep reading, widely and often, and keep writing.

## 2. Be Honest

Write what you believe. You cannot concentrate on developing your style if you are preoccupied with trying to guess what your teacher wants. A writing assignment is not an algebra problem; it's seldom a question of giving a correct or incorrect solution. What is wanted is a clear expression of *your* ideas.

You won't always have your choice of topics, nor will every assignment spontaneously ignite your interest and emotions. In those cases, light your own match; scratch at the assignment until you find some issue, some angle that you can discuss with conviction.

## 3. Be Direct

Say what you mean clearly and in the fewest possible words.

Use direct words. Some synonyms are understood more quickly than others. *Lie* is more direct than *untruth* or *falsehood; home* is more direct than *dwelling* or *abode; book* more direct than *volume.*

Rely on verbs and nouns to carry your meaning. Be sparing in your use of adjectives and adverbs.

Use passive verbs only for special reasons: when you want to emphasize the receiver of an action—"Todd was struck by a foul ball"—or when the doer of the action is unimportant or unknown—"the cake was left by an anonymous caller."

"Chop deadwood" in your writing.

*Not:* It was during the month of July
*But:* In July
*Not:* Due to the fact that
*But:* Because
*Not:* true facts, join together, red in color
*But:* facts, join, red

## 4. Be Fresh

Your goal here is not primarily to be original (hard to do), but to avoid laziness. Mistrust words and phrases that come too easily to mind. Clichés such as "white as a sheet" or "clean as a whistle" contribute only a tired predictability to your style. When you revise, don't tolerate a sentence like "His heart broke with grief." Try "His heart shattered . . ." or "He wilted with grief."

What about "His heart was freeze-dried with grief"? No, this will only puzzle your reader. Be fresh but not bizarre.

## 5. Be Emphatic

Emphasis involves more than scattering exclamation marks and underlines. These devices are overused. Consider the following options.

*Emphatic words.* A well-chosen, forceful word is worth a half-dozen exclamation marks.

*Emphatic position.* The beginning and the end are positions of stress within a sentence, a paragraph, or an entire composition. Arrange your ideas and phrase your sentences accordingly. In revising, give particular polish to your first and last sentences.

*Emphatic rhythms.* Skilled writers control the rhythms of their words to stress their ideas. A short, terse sentence amid longer sentences rivets a reader's attention, as does a short paragraph amid longer paragraphs. Occasionally inverting the usual grammatical order of a sentence also can create emphasis. "Lying in the mud was Jane's mitten" has a stronger, fresher effect than if it were written in usual subject-verb order.

*Emphatic repetition.* Stylistic repetition (as opposed to unnecessary, accidental, or boring repetition) can effectively emphasize ideas. A classic example is Lincoln's "government of the people, by the people, and for the people . . . ." Emphasis can be achieved by repeating words, phrases, or grammatical patterns.

Overuse can weaken the impact of any of these techniques. Practice them, but use them carefully.

## 6. Review for Style

Whenever you review and evaluate a draft of your work, keep matters of style in mind. The following questions may help you.

• Do the sentences and paragraphs express your own voice?
• Do the opinions expressed in the paper represent your true convictions?
• Is your language strong, direct, and concise?
• Have you avoided clichés?
• Are important points made forcefully?

You will find this article helpful in completing the assignments on pages 117, 170, 264, and 662.

WRITER'S HANDBOOK

# Writing to Summarize

The ability to write brief, accurate summaries of material (books, stories, speeches, films) is essential to many types of writing assignments; you may also find summarizing personally valuable as a study skill. By definition, summarizing cannot be a lengthy chore, but it requires several skills: the abilities to recognize the key details of a work, to see the relationships between details, and to express your understanding in as few of your own words as possible.

## PREWRITING
### Sample Assignment

In one paragraph, summarize Act Three, Scene 1 of *Julius Caesar*.

### 1. Think It Through
The following guidelines will help you in preparing any summary.

*Be brief.* Sometimes, as in the sample, your assignment will give a target length. Most stories, acts, or scenes can be summarized in a paragraph. An entire book may require three or four paragraphs. Your purpose may influence the length of your summary as well. If you are to focus on only one incident in a story, you might devote an entire paragraph to the summary of that incident.

*Be concise.* Avoid the "play-by-play" mistake: "First Caesar speaks with a soothsayer, then Artemidorus approaches him and says . . ." You cannot tell everything that happened or mention every character; nor is there room for direct quotation. Use your own words.

*Use the present tense.* It is customary to use the present tense in writing summaries of literary works: "Caesar refuses the request." You will find that this practice will solve some tricky problems with time sequence.

### 2. Make Notes
Though your paper may be only one paragraph, you still will find it helpful to "think on paper." To complete the sample assignment, review Act Three, Scene 1, listing important incidents and characters. As you go over your list, try to eliminate every unnecessary item. Your final list can serve as a rough outline for your summary.

In summarizing a book, you might write a one-sentence summary as you complete each chapter. Combined with transitional words and phrases, these sentences would form a useful first-draft summary of the whole work.

## WRITING
Two summaries of Act Three, Scene 1 of Julius Caesar are shown on the next page. The first-draft version is too long. Notice how the writer then omitted irrelevant details, combined sentences, and summarized events to produce the final version.

# REVISING

In addition to reviewing the checklists on page 836, ask yourself these questions:
• Have I included all important events?
• Are there any irrelevant points?
• Have I combined sentences by subordinating some ideas?

• Would the author of the work, or any other reader, recognize the plot?

You will find this article helpful in completing the assignments on pages 141, 345, 375, and 713.

**WRITER'S HANDBOOK**

---

**First Draft**

As Caesar approaches the Senate-house, Artemidorus attempts to hand him a warning note, but the old man is brushed aside. Seated on the rostrum, Caesar hears a petition for the return of Metellus Cimber's exiled brother. When Caesar refuses the petition, he is attacked by the conspirators. First stabbed by Casca, Caesar fends off the attackers until he sees Brutus' upraised dagger; then, overcome by his friend's treachery, he submits and falls dead at the foot of Pompey's statue. Led by Brutus and Cassius, the conspirators bathe their hands in Caesar's blood to show their mutual responsibility. Antony's servant arrives, asking safe conduct for his master, who wishes to come to the Senate-house to hear the conspirators' explanation for their deed. Cassius warns Brutus not to trust the wily Antony, but Brutus disregards the warning and plans to give Antony permission to speak at the funeral after he himself has explained the reason for the assassination. After Brutus leaves, Antony addresses Caesar's corpse, pouring out his desire for revenge; he is interrupted by a servant announcing the arrival in Rome of Caesar's grandnephew, Octavius.

---

**Final Version**

Approaching the Senate-house Caesar spurns the warning note of Artemidorus and enters to hear Metellus Cimber's pleas for the return of his exiled brother. When Caesar refuses the request, the conspirators encircle and stab him; seeing that Brutus is among them, Caesar gives up the fight and dies. Amid the general tumult Antony's servant enters, requesting safe conduct for his master so that he may come to hear the conspirators' explanation for their act. Brutus not only agrees; he also, against Cassius' advice, gives Antony permission to speak at Caesar's funeral. After Brutus leaves, Antony addresses Caesar's corpse, pouring out his desire for revenge.

# Writing to Compare and Contrast

A writing assignment that asks you to compare or to compare and contrast requires examination and discussion of two or more characters, events, objects, or ideas. **Compare** suggests a focus on similarities or likeness; **contrast,** a focus on differences. Comparison/contrast is a basic mental process, a useful everyday skill, and the basis for a great many literary discussions and writing assignments.

## PREWRITING

**Sample Assignment**

Comparison/contrast assignments can be general or specific.

> Compare and contrast Brutus and Mark Antony.
> Compare Brutus and Mark Antony as public speakers.

Whether stated or not, comparison/contrast assignments require you to come to a judgment or conclusion about the elements you compare.

### 1. Identify Points of Comparison

Begin by listing points of comparison—issues or categories that apply to each subject. For example, if you're comparing two characters as speakers, your initial points of comparison might be:

> purpose of speech
> attitude toward audience
> technique
> effect on audience

As you study your material you probably will drop some points of comparison and add others. But having these in mind will get you organized. Try not to jump to conclusions at this stage. Wait until you've carefully examined your subject before making judgments.

### 2. Make Lists or Charts

As you study your subjects, jot down your notes in separate columns for each. Group these notes by points of comparison, and try to keep equivalent details on the same line in both lists. As the example on the next page shows, your lists won't always be equal line-for-line, but trying for parallelism will help you produce a complete and balanced file of information.

### 3. Form an Opinion

Write your opinion on the comparison of your subjects in one or two sentences. This might become your thesis statement, or you might not use it at all. But establishing your opinion at this point will help you sift through your details and shape the paper.

## WRITING

### 4. Pick a Pattern

As you begin to write, you will find that there are a number of ways to organize a comparison/contrast paper.

*Item-by-item.* Basically, this is your chart written in sentence form. "Brutus wanted to reassure the angry and excited Romans. Mark Antony, on the other hand, wanted to prod them into a vengeful rage. Brutus wanted to explain . . ."

| Points of Comparison | Brutus | Mark Antony |
|---|---|---|
| Purpose of Speech | to calm mob<br><br>to justify the killing of Caesar | to stir up mob<br><br>to remind listeners of Caesar's goodness<br><br>to "sneak" the speech past conspirators |
| Attitude Toward Audience | more formal and distant<br><br>begins with commands: "Hear me . . . be silent" | more emotional<br><br>begins with request: "lend me your ears" |

and so on. This method can be effective in one- or two-paragraph compositions. In longer papers, the pattern tends to create a monotonous, ping-pong effect. It's also difficult to steer your reader to an overall conclusion.

*Whole-to-whole.* You may choose to discuss completely one of your subjects first, then turn to the second subject for similar scope and treatment. (You'll find that your second discussion will almost always be easier to write and take fewer words than the first.)

*Part-to-part.* Here you discuss all the similarities of your subjects in one section and all the differences in another. Follow this simple rule: *The more important discussion goes last.* If you wish to emphasize the differences between your subjects, discuss differences last.

Comparison/contrast papers tend naturally to have a balanced, parallel style, but watch out for wordy repetition or a boring sameness of sentence pattern and length.

## REVISING

Evaluate your first draft with the checklists on page 836. Also check for these points:
- Is the flow of ideas made clear by transitions such as *similarly, likewise, but, on the other hand, in contrast?*
- Have you avoided overuse of the same transitions?
- Does your paper simply run out of ideas or does it come to a conclusion?

You will find this article helpful in completing the assignments on pages 76, 274, 337, 451, and 763, and others.

WRITER'S HANDBOOK

# Writing to Persuade

You are frequently asked to express and defend a viewpoint about a work of literature. You have two jobs here: first to reach a conclusion about the selection and second, to convince your reader to share that conclusion. Be careful not to reach a conclusion until you've reread and carefully considered the story, poem, or play in question.

## PREWRITING

### Sample Assignment

Is Mr. White an innocent victim of the curse of "The Monkey's Paw," or is he in some way responsible for the catastrophe that occurs? Support your opinion with details from the story.

### 1. State Your Position

After reviewing the story, jot down your conclusion. Write it like a challenge, as clearly and as forcefully as you can. Such a tone will help persuade others.

> Mr. White is *not* innocent; it is his greedy curiosity that starts the fatal chain of events.

This statement may eventually be refined into your thesis statement, but for now it functions as a magnet to help you pick out evidence from the selection.

### 2. List Your Evidence

Brainstorm. Quickly list everything you can think of—facts, reasons, inferences, opinions—that can possibly support your statement. Then skim through the selection for additional details you may have forgotten. Your purpose at this stage is just to get this material down on paper.

### 3. Select Your Evidence

Evidence can be evaluated in the following ways.

*Factual evidence.* Your most solid evidence will be factual details about which there can be no disagreement.

> Mr. White literally reaches into the fire to save the paw.

That is true; readers can look it up.

*Inferential evidence.* Few issues in literature are settled by merely listing facts. Inferential evidence is based on inferences, generalizations, logic, and common sense. Handling such evidence skillfully is the best test of your abilities as a careful reader and a persuasive writer.

> Though no details are given, the sergeant-major's "whitened" face and shakiness clearly show that his experiences with the paw were disastrous.

*Weak evidence.* Your poorest evidence will be your own unsupported opinions. Such "evidence" often pulls you and your reader away from, rather than into, the story. The effect of one opinion followed by another is usually unpersuasive:

> Mr. White seems uneducated. Of course, he lives in a rural area, far from the mental stimulus of city life.

Some writers instinctively insert sweeping language ("of course," "it's true," "always") to make their opinions seem more convincing.

When you spot *always, every, never, none, everybody knows, nobody believes,* or other sweeping generalizations in your first draft, you may suspect that your argument is on thin ice.

### 4. Consider Opposing Evidence

Before going further ask: "What's the best evidence against my position? Why doesn't this evidence change my mind?" It's possible you *will* change your mind. If so, better now than later. Go back to the evidence and reshape your position.

If your position survives those two questions, plan on including a discussion of opposing evidence early in your own argument.

It is true that the White family is portrayed as charming, loving, contented. White even says " . . . I've got all I want." But if he is content, why does he ask so many questions about the paw? Why does he literally reach into the fire to save it? Why does he insist on paying for it? Why does he wish for more money? White's greedy actions speak louder than his statement about contentment.

By discussing opposing evidence, you're demonstrating that you are smart enough to see other sides to an issue, fair enough to consider them, and confident enough to overcome them.

### 5. Use Evidence Fairly

Misreading or careless analysis of a text can lead to a poor selection of evidence:

Herbert believes that they are going to be "rich, and famous, and happy."

By missing or ignoring Herbert's joking tone, mentioned earlier in the story, this writer has distorted the evidence.

## WRITING

### 6. Arrange Your Evidence Effectively

As you begin your first draft, remember that the positions of emphasis are first and last. If you have only a few items of evidence, you might begin with the most important. The danger of leading off with your best evidence is that your argument loses force as it goes on, like a singer running out of breath. Try saving the best evidence for last. This virtually guarantees a strong conclusion.

### 7. Finish Strong and Fast

Once you've made your final (and best) point, quickly bring your paper to a close. Summarize your evidence and state your conclusion. Do not repeat or weakly echo your first paragraph. Leave your reader with a sense of completeness and finality.

Even the next morning, White wants to believe that fortune will come his way, for he repeats the sergeant-major's statement that one might attribute a happening to coincidence. Mr. White is clearly to blame for the tragedy; ignoring repeated warnings to destroy the paw, he, and only he, makes the fatal wish.

## REVISING

Test your first draft. Stop being a writer; become a skeptic. Ask yourself "Who says?" and "So what?" after every supporting detail.

- Read the first sentences of each of your paragraphs. Do these clearly express the points of your argument? Do you get a sense of flow and direction? Does the argument build or fade, or does it wander in a circle?
- Are there any short paragraphs? This often is a sign of scanty support for a point. Back up any unsupported opinions or cross them out.

You will find this article helpful in completing the assignments on pages 156, 255, 387, and 656, and others.

WRITER'S HANDBOOK

# Writing About Plot and Plot Devices

The **plot** of a story consists of exposition, a series of related events that presents a problem or conflict, leads to a climax, and results in a resolution of the conflict. Writing assignments about plot may ask you to identify the conflict, evaluate the entire sequence of events, or discuss the relationship of the plot to other aspects of the story, such as character or theme.

## PREWRITING

### Sample Assignment

Several things contribute to an effective plot. The sequence of events must be arranged in order and linked together in a chain of natural cause and effect; the characters' actions must be consistent with their personalities as the author has drawn them; events must lead naturally to a climax which in turn has a satisfactory resolution. In addition, there should be some suspense. We should care what happens in the story. Does "The Monkey's Paw" have an effective plot? In a four- to five-paragraph essay, analyze the plot of the story, pointing out strengths and weaknesses as you see them.

### 1. Think It Through

The following questions may help you consider any assignment on plot.

*Are the events linked together in a chain of natural cause and effect? Are some events too coincidental to be believed, or too incidental to be interesting?* In a well-plotted story, each event has a purpose: to move the story forward, to reveal character, establish mood, suggest theme, and so on.

*Do the characters act consistently and believably?* Characters may develop and change, but they should not do so simply to create convenient solutions to plot problems.

*Does the climax follow events naturally, or does it seem forced or contrived?* The climax should

"make sense" in terms of the action that leads up to it and the characters involved in it.

*Is the resolution satisfactory?* Some endings leave the reader feeling tricked by a surprise outcome; even surprise or "twist" endings should be believable. Other endings disappoint by being too predictable; readers guess the resolution long before they finish reading.

*How does the writer develop suspense?* Writers can intensify reader interest in a narrative with foreshadowing, conflict, characterization, and other techniques.

### 2. Trace the Structure of the Plot

Whether you are asked to analyze an entire narrative or a single episode, reserve judgment about meaning, author's purpose, and so on until you have studied the work thoroughly. Many students find it helpful to diagram the plot structure. Study the plot diagram on the next page.

### 3. Develop Your Thesis Statement

Is the plot of "The Monkey's Paw" effective? Even if the story does not seem satisfactory in all respects, you may still decide that the plot is basically a good one. It is not necessary to wholly praise or wholly condemn a work. Below is a possible thesis statement on "The Monkey's Paw."

"The Monkey's Paw" has an effective, suspenseful plot that uses a series of wishes and their grim fulfillment to create suspense.

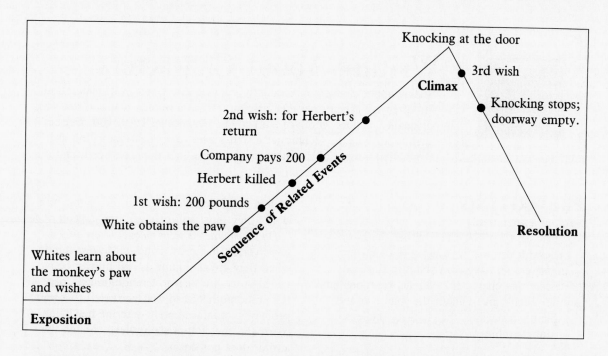

Knocking at the door

Climax

3rd wish

Knocking stops;
doorway empty.

2nd wish: for Herbert's
return

Company pays 200

Herbert killed

Sequence of Related Events

1st wish: 200 pounds

White obtains the paw

Resolution

Whites learn about
the monkey's paw
and wishes

**Exposition**

#### 4. Order Your Points of Discussion

Your assignment may suggest or imply a possible outline for your paper. After rereading the sample assignment, you might establish the following order for your discussion.

1. Introduction, thesis statement
2. Sequence of events
3. Characters' actions
4. Climax
5. Resolution

## WRITING

### Model

Each of your body paragraphs should discuss one major point. The following paragraph evaluates the consistency of characterization in the story.

Some readers may question whether Mr. White acts consistently in his pursuit of the paw. As a retired, seemingly contented man, why is White so greedily insistent on possessing the paw? The answer may be found in two almost unnoticeable details of

characterization early in the story. White's style of playing chess shows him to be an impulsive risk-taker. His sudden and excessive anger about where he lives ("this is the worst") reveals his discontent. In view of these details, his grab for the paw becomes more understandable.

## REVISING

In addition to reviewing the checklists on page 836, ask yourself these questions:
- Does the introductory paragraph mention the title and author of the work?
- Does the paper make clear the links between the major events or episodes in the plot?
- Is the conflict of the story correctly identified?
- Is the climax of the story correctly identified?
- Are the elements of plot related both to characters and to the author's purpose or theme?

You will find this article helpful in completing the assignments on pages 32, 157, and 588.

# Writing About Characters

Writing about characters frequently involves two levels of consideration. You often are asked to evaluate a character as a human being, discussing personality, actions, motives, and so on. On another level, you may be asked to analyze the techniques a writer uses to create—out of ink and imagination—some of the memorable figures that populate our literature.

## PREWRITING

**Sample Assignment**

Choose what you feel is either the most believable or most unbelievable short-story character you have read about in this text. Review that character's actions, reactions, and other details given about the character and explain what makes the character believable or unbelievable.

### 1. Think It Through

Whenever you are asked to examine characters for a writing assignment, think about the following questions.

*What methods does the author use to create a character?* Consider physical description; characters' thoughts, statements, and actions; opinions expressed by other characters; and contrast with other characters.

*Who are the major characters and who are the minor ones?* Main characters usually are central to the action of a story. Minor characters, though not fully portrayed, may make a crucial difference in what happens.

*Do the characters have clear motivations for their actions?* Well-developed characters do not act or react without some motivation, whether internal or external. When analyzing a work, try to determine what motivates each character. (What, for example, motivates Walter Mitty?) Characters' actions and reactions must be consistent with the personalities that the author has created for them. Although characters may

undergo significant changes in the course of a work, they must still behave "in character."

*Do the characters seem unique, or are they stereotypes?* Characters stand out in our minds when they are as unique as real human beings. In the story "A Visit to Grandmother," page 47, the grandmother is so well portrayed that you probably could accurately describe her living room and the clothes she prefers, though the author does not do so.

### 2. Analyze the Character

Having considered the basic issues, you're now prepared to focus specifically on the assignment. How is the character revealed? What adjectives and adverbs are used? What is the character wearing? What objects or belongings are mentioned? How does what the character says reveal (or not reveal) what he or she is thinking?

### 3. Develop Your Thesis Statement

Your thesis statement will help you establish the scope of your paper.

The most believable character is Mrs. Hansen in "Enemies" by Nadine Gordimer (page 443) because she is so completely described.

### 4. Take Notes

As you review the selection to gather evidence in support of your thesis, you may find it helpful to create a chart for your notes, as

| Author's Description | Character's Statements | Character's Inner Thoughts | Character's Attitude Toward Other Characters |
|---|---|---|---|
| Mrs. Hansen has been a beauty; has a blue silk coat and a toque. Wealthy; has been a baroness; has a chauffeur and manservant; "keeps herself to herself;" "withdrawn as a castle." | "I always have my tea brought to me in my compartment."<br><br>"I always find enough for my needs. It does not matter much."<br><br>Lies when she says she had no children. Why? | Feels her aging self an enemy of her real self; "alone, lonely, lone;" refers to Old Fool—a part of herself she is ashamed of? Is she self-centered? Why does she send the telegram? | Matter-of-fact; condescending toward the fat lady; Hansen is in sharp contrast to the other woman who is talkative and greedy. |

shown in the example. You may wish to add other columns to your own chart (Character's Actions, Character's Motivations) or to delete columns that do not apply.

# WRITING

The model below shows the first two and final paragraphs of a paper based on the sample assignment. Notice that the first sentence forthrightly states the paper's thesis. Do you think the statements in the second paragraph need to be supported with details?

## Model

The most believable character is Mrs. Hansen in "Enemies" by Nadine Gordimer, because she is so completely described. We learn about Mrs. Hansen chiefly through her inner thoughts, but the author provides physical description and creates a strong contrast between Mrs. Hansen and the fat lady on the train, thus further adding to the characterization.

We know that Mrs. Hansen is a rich widow. She has once been a great beauty and a baroness. She seems able to afford any luxury she will permit herself. . . .

Reading about Mrs. Hansen makes one wish to know more about her. What are the details of her past life? What happened to her son? Perhaps one test of whether a character is believable is whether the character is described so that the reader would like to meet her.

# REVISING

Evaluate your first draft with the checklists on page 836. Also consider these points:
• Is the character accurately presented as he or she appears in the story?
• Are examples from the story included to support the character traits discussed?

You will find this article helpful in completing the assignments on pages 46, 200, 574, and 779, and others.

# Writing About Setting

**Setting,** the time and place of a narrative, can vary in importance. In some stories, setting is incidental; events might have taken place "anywhere, anytime." In other works, setting plays a vital role: contributing to mood, affecting the course of action, shaping the lives of characters. A carefully detailed setting makes a story more believable and real to the reader.

## PREWRITING

### Sample Assignment

Assignments about setting frequently ask you to examine the effect of setting on plot or characters (or the reader), to evaluate the appropriateness of setting to a particular story or poem, or to tell how setting contributes to mood or meaning.

In a paper of three or four paragraphs, explain the importance of setting in "Through the Tunnel" to one of your classmates. Focus your discussion on the influence of setting on the plot and theme of the story.

### 1. Think It Through

In writing about setting you usually will have to consider the following questions.

*Where does the action take place?* Place setting can include the geographical region (Europe, for example), a specific locale (a village in Switzerland), or a particular room (a cottage attic). Climate and weather can be important features of setting. A fog can create a mood of mystery and dread; a blizzard can be a factor in the plot.

*When does the action take place?* Time setting can include the general period (the present time, for example) or a specific year. Season and time of day also can be key features of time setting.

*How does the writer establish the setting?* Sometimes a writer will directly state the time and place of the narrative. Other times you must infer the setting from details. Descriptions

of scenery or rooms, the clothing and equipment of characters, the way characters speak and their possible references to actual events can be important clues to setting.

*What details of setting are essential to the narrative?* The relative importance of various elements of setting will change from story to story. In one story, time of year may be unimportant, but time of day may be vital. A good way to test details for importance is to imagine the events occurring in a different time or place. If you apply this test to "Through the Tunnel," you might conclude that the seaside location is one absolutely essential detail of setting.

### 2. Review the Selection

As you review the selection with the above questions in mind, you may find it helpful to create a chart for your notes. This will help you organize aspects of setting, their supporting details, and their effects on the story. The chart shown on the next page is designed to develop the effect of setting on plot and theme.

### 3. Develop Your Thesis

Remember as you examine your notes that your purpose is not simply to identify the setting, but to discuss the associations, implications, and effect of those details as well. The sample assignment asks for a focus on the effect of setting on plot and theme. This dual

| Setting | Supporting Details | Effect |
|---------|--------------------|--------|
| beach | crowded, safe, big<br>"a place for small children" | links beach to childhood |
| bay | wild, rocky, rough<br>cold currents, deep water<br>rocks like "monsters"<br><br>Swimmers are "like men"<br>to Jerry. | links bay to challenge,<br>threat, and danger<br><br>links bay to growing up,<br>maturity |

purpose should be reflected in your thesis statement.

Setting is essential to the plot of "Through the Tunnel." Jerry's desire to swim through an underwater tunnel is the basic conflict of the story. But the seaside setting also emphasizes the story's theme that growing up means facing challenges independently. Doris Lessing's descriptions of the beach and the bay reflect Jerry's choices between safety and danger, childhood and maturity.

## WRITING
### Model
The thesis statement above is complete and polished enough to serve as an introductory paragraph. Notice that the following body paragraph not only provides details of setting but explains their effects.

In contrast to the safe beach, the bay is "wild" and "rocky." Jerry sees submerged rocks as "discolored monsters" and is shocked by cold currents from "the real sea." In contrast to the bright hues of the beach, the colors here are darker, "purple and darker blue." Here too are "big boys—men, to Jerry." These details create a setting that is

challenging and even dangerous. It is also a place linked in Jerry's mind with "men"— with being grown up.

The final paragraph brings the paper to an emphatic conclusion. Note that the thesis is not merely repeated, but stated in a more forceful way.

The seaside setting provides the external conflict of "Through the Tunnel." Lessing has also used setting to reflect her theme—so clearly and definitely that it is possible to express that theme in terms of setting. In going "through the tunnel" to adulthood, young people must leave the safe beach of childhood and swim independently in the "real sea" of life.

## REVISING
Evaluate your first draft with the checklists on page 836. Also check for these points.
• Have you identified the setting as completely and accurately as possible?
• Have you explained the effect of setting on the selection—or on characters, plot, or mood as specified in the assignment?

You will find this article helpful in completing the assignments on pages 72, 405, and 736.

WRITER'S HANDBOOK

# Writing About Theme

**Theme** is the underlying meaning in a work. It is something apart from the events in a narrative, though those events contribute to our understanding of theme. Setting, dialogue, point of view, characterization, and other elements may contribute as well. Writing assignments about theme may ask you to identify the theme of a work or to show how the writer expressed his or her theme through various literary techniques.

## PREWRITING
### Sample Assignment

Thornton Wilder has said that his play *Our Town* is not "a picture of life in a New Hampshire village" nor an explanation of the "conditions of life after death," but rather an "attempt to find a value above all price for the smallest events in our daily life." Review the entire play. Does Wilder's statement conform to your sense of the play and its theme? Explain your opinion to your classmates in a paper of five or six paragraphs.

### 1. Think It Through

Occasionally you will encounter a selection that includes a direct statement of theme; see the last paragraph of "The Story of the Widow's Son" (page 104) for an example. More often, however, you will have to infer the theme by considering several elements of the work.

Remember that a theme is a statement and that a statement is a sentence. When you use one word or a simple phrase ("simplicity" or "life in a small town") you may be identifying the subject of the work, but certainly not its theme. Also make sure not to mistake a summary ("A young man loves, marries, and loses the girl next door") for a statement of theme.

### 2. Review the Work

Use the following questions to develop supporting evidence for a selection's theme.

*Does the title suggest the theme?* Titles always name a work; frequently they state the subject; sometimes they suggest the theme. Wilder's title implies the importance of Grover's Corners by suggesting that it is "everybody's town."

*Does the setting reinforce the theme?* Wilder invests "our town" with importance by supplying various technical details of location, geology ("it lies on some of the oldest land in the world"), and population. Within the setting of Grover's Corners we are to see the whole human experience in miniature.

*Do the events of the plot further the theme?* A key plot event of the play is Emily's visit, after she dies, to an ordinary day earlier in her life. She finds it unbearable that human beings never "realize life while they live it."

*Does the point of view affect the theme?* One of several unusual features of the play is that it has a narrator who creates an omniscient viewpoint. Carefully review the Stage Manager's words for thematic meaning.

When narrators in stories or novels make thematic statements, they often do so at the beginning or end of the narrative.

*Do the statements of any character indicate the theme?* Thematic statements can be made by any character in a story or play, but you should carefully "consider the source." For example, Simon Stimson's bitter remarks on what it means to be human in the last scene of the play are "not the whole truth," as Mrs. Gibbs tartly reminds him.

*Are any statements, words, or events repeated?* Repetition creates emphasis and may signal a thematic meaning. In *Our Town* consider the repetition of the hymn "Blessed Be the Tie That Binds," the word *million,* and the kitchen scenes of breakfast preparation.

### 3. Organize Your Material

In dealing with longer works such as a novel or play, you will find it helpful to write summaries of each section of the work and determine the thematic contribution of that part. Long works may deal with several themes and you may need more than a single sentence to express them.

In arranging your material, you might choose to follow the sequence of events in the play. A rough outline of your five paragraphs might look like this:

1. Intro, thesis statement
2. Act One—daily life
3. Act Two—love and marriage
4. Act Three—death
5. Conclusion

Alternatively, you could organize your paper on three or four major points or details.

1. Intro, thesis statement
2. Placing the town in the universe
3. Focus on the basic events of life
4. Emphasizing time
5. Conclusion

Whatever plan you develop, remember that the assignment asks you to be comprehensive ("Review the entire play").

## WRITING

The introduction and one body paragraph of a paper based on the sample assignment are shown. Can you tell by tone and style that the paper was written for a "classmate" audience?

### Model

I believe Thornton Wilder's assessment of his play is accurate. *Our Town* is "an attempt to find a value above all price for the smallest events of our daily life." From beginning to end, the play explores this paradox of "priceless triviality."

For example, in his presentation of Grover's Corners, Wilder insists on the town's ordinariness, yet demonstrates that it has a unique place in the universe. We may smile when the Stage Manager cites lattitude and longitude; we may laugh outright at Professor Willard's lectures on geology and anthropology. But these details locate "our town" in a definite time and place. For me, the clinching evidence is the story of Jane Crofut's letter at the end of Act One. Here the playwright puts into practice his belief in the value of "the smallest detail," for he uses this little anecdote—a joke, really—to make one of the profoundest points in the play. Jane Crofut, "our town," and each of us have a place in "the Solar System, the Universe, the Mind of God."

## REVISING

Use the checklists on page 836 to evaluate your first draft. Also check these points:
- Have you accurately stated the theme in sentence form?
- Have you convincingly shown how the title, setting, characters, dialogue, or other elements relate to the theme?

You will find this article helpful in completing the assignments on pages 103, 210, 471, and 736.

WRITER'S HANDBOOK

# Writing About Point of View

**Point of view** refers to the relationship between the narrator of a story (or the speaker in a poem) and the characters and action. The author's choice of point of view affects every aspect of the work. Writing assignments about point of view frequently will ask you to show how a choice of narrator influences characterization, plot, or theme.

## PREWRITING
### Sample Assignment

In a paper of three or four paragraphs, tell how Conan Doyle's choice of narrator in "The Adventure of the Blue Carbuncle" affects the characterization of Holmes.

### 1. Think It Through

Review what you know about point of view. Stories told in the **third person** have an unnamed narrator who does not participate in the story. Such narrators can be **objective,** reporting what characters do and say, but never revealing the thoughts or feelings experienced by any character. "The Conjurer's Revenge" (page 3) is an example of the objective viewpoint. Third-person narrators also can be **limited,** revealing the thoughts and feelings of one character and telling the story from that character's viewpoint. "Lamb to the Slaughter" is told from a limited point of view. In other stories the narrator can be **omniscient,** able to reveal the thoughts and feelings of any character and to describe events through the eyes of any character. Though "Through the Tunnel" (page 95) concentrates on Jerry's experiences, the point of view is omniscient because the mother's thoughts and feelings are also revealed.

In **first-person** narratives, the "I" who tells the story may be a major or minor character. "The Adventure of the Blue Carbuncle" is told in the first person by Dr. Watson.

### 2. Study the Viewpoint Character

First-person and third-person limited stories feature a viewpoint or focal character. Readers experience the story through that character's eyes, ears, and thoughts. The choice of a viewpoint character is critically important, since it controls what the reader knows and influences how the reader responds to the story. Ask the following questions as you review the story.

*From whose viewpoint is the story told?* This character may be major or minor, participant or onlooker. Though viewpoint characters may be protagonists, that is not always the case. Dr. Watson is not the protagonist of "The Adventure of the Blue Carbuncle."

*What is the viewpoint character like?* A character's personality may affect your interest in the story; his or her intelligence and perceptiveness will determine how much you learn about events.

*How does the choice of viewpoint affect plot and suspense?* The effectiveness of many plots depends on when the reader learns certain details. Choice of viewpoint can help a writer control the flow of information. Suspense depends on what the reader does not know. Consider how the suspense of "The Adventure of the Blue Carbuncle" would be affected if Holmes, rather than Watson, were the viewpoint character of the story.

*What other elements of the story are affected by the viewpoint character?* Consider characterization, mood, theme, and so on.

*Does the viewpoint ever change? If so, why?* Writers usually have specific reasons for shifting to another viewpoint character.

# WRITING

When you write about point of view, don't assume that the opinions and attitudes expressed in the story or poem belong to the author. Attribute such ideas to "the narrator" or "the speaker" (in poems) rather than to "the author" or "the poet." Also, when writing about third-person stories, be careful not to confuse "narrator" with "viewpoint character"; these are the same only in first-person stories.

A model based on the sample assignment is shown below.

# REVISING

Use the checklists on page 836 to evaluate your first draft. Also check for these points:

- Have you correctly identified the point of view and viewpoint character?
- Have you accurately described the viewpoint character?
- Have you clearly stated the ways in which the point of view affects the story?
- Have you used the terms "narrator" and "viewpoint character" correctly?

You will find this article helpful in completing the assignments on pages 86, 94, and 786.

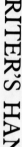

---

"The Adventure of the Blue Carbuncle"

The choice of the well-meaning, eager, but somewhat dull-witted Dr. Watson as narrator enables Conan Doyle to show off Holmes's brilliant deductive powers. Watson, for example, sees nothing remarkable about the hat Commissionaire Peterson brings to Holmes. "On the contrary, Watson," says Holmes, "you can see everything. You fail, however, to reason from what you see." Watson even thinks Holmes is joking and says, "I have no doubt that I am very stupid, but I must confess that I am unable to follow you." Holmes continues with his deductions, now seeming more brilliant than ever.

Watson is allowed a moment of insight here and there. He is able to state that the blue carbuncle must belong to the Countess of Morcar, and he does remember that it was lost at the Hotel Cosmopolitan. But the author severely limits Watson's observations. It is Holmes who acts, Holmes who makes inferences and directs the show. Watson's role is to scratch his head, ask questions, follow Holmes around, report on his ruses to obtain information, and describe the setting.

Watson, however, is essential to the story. He asks the questions the reader wants to ask. He is always a step or two behind Holmes, just as the reader is. His point of view is the reader's point of view, and it enables Holmes to emerge as the great detective—rational, logical, thoughtful, clever, adventurous—who believes that the solution to a problem is its own reward.

# Writing About Mood or Tone

**Mood** is the atmosphere or feeling created within a literary work by the writer's choice of setting, imagery, and other details. **Tone** is the attitude of the writer toward his subject. Tone and mood may be described in similar terms. For example, you may say that a poem by Poe is gloomy (mood), or that the speaker has a gloomy attitude toward life (tone). To write effectively about mood or tone, you must be able to clearly distinguish between them.

Individual sample assignments are given for mood and tone. They are discussed separately in this article.

## PREWRITING

### Sample Assignment—Mood

What is the mood of "Afterglow" by Jorge Luis Borges (page 268)? In one or two paragraphs, describe that mood for your classmates, identifying the words and images that create it.

### 1. Review the Selection

Reread the poem several times, aloud if possible. What words specifically refer to emotion? What other words seem to have a particular emotional effect as you read them? What images strike you as especially vivid? You might list your details as shown below.

*"Emotion" words*
"disturbing" (lines 1, 3)
"desperate" (4)
"fear" (9)

*Other key words or phrases*
"nothing is left" (6)
"tautly drawn and different" (8)
"hallucination" (9)
"falsity" (12)
"broken" (13)

*Key images*
"turns the plain to rust" (5)
"holding on to that light" (8)

### 2. Develop Your Thesis Statement

After studying your notes, you might come to the following conclusion.

The mood of "Afterglow" is one of tension, strain, and dread.

You might note, incidentally, that the tone of this poem is quite different from the mood. Though the mood might be edgy and fearful, the speaker's attitude is calm, detached, and assertive.

## WRITING

The first paragraph of a paper based on the sample assignment is shown.

### Model

In "Afterglow" Jorge Luis Borges reverses the expectations of his title. Where we might expect in "Afterglow" a mellow, sunset calmness, Borges instead creates a mood of tension, strain, and dread. His first sentence announces "Sunset is always distributing," and Borges sustains that sense of disturbance throughout the poem. Such words and phrases as "desperate glow," "tautly drawn and different," "hallucination," "fear," and "falsity" contribute to the edgy, fearful mood.

# PREWRITING

## Sample Assignment—Tone

In a paper of three or four paragraphs, compare and contrast any two letters in the Nonfiction unit in terms of their tone. In each case, show how the tone is appropriate (or inappropriate), given the writer's subject, audience, and purpose.

## 1. Review the Selections

After reviewing all four letters and making a selection, carefully study the two letters you have chosen. You may find it helpful to write your notes in the form of a chart. If you have chosen to compare the letters of Anne Lindbergh and Bartolomeo Vanzetti, your chart might resemble the one shown below.

## 2. Develop Your Thesis Statement

Your thesis statement should clearly identify the tone of each letter. You might choose to discuss one letter at a time in subsequent body paragraphs, or use audience, subject, and purpose as the focus. Rough outlines of the two alternatives are shown.

| | |
|---|---|
| 1. Introduction | 1. Introduction |
| 2. Lindbergh letter | 2. Audience |
| 3. Vanzetti letter | 3. Subject |
| 4. Conclusion | 4. Purpose |
| | 5. Conclusion |

## WRITING

A model based on the sample assignment is shown on the next page.

| Points of comparison | Lindbergh letter | Vanzetti letter |
|---|---|---|
| tone | informal<br>friendly<br>cheerful | formal<br>somber<br>instructive |
| audience | mother | Sacco's son |
| subject | honeymoon flight | reasons for impending execution |
| purpose | to describe her experiences | to defend his principles<br><br>to comfort Sacco's son |

# REVISING

Use the checklists on page 836 to evaluate your first draft. Also consider the following points.
- Have you correctly inferred the mood or the tone of the work as required?
- Have you supported your inference with evidence (including quotations) from the work?

You will find this article helpful in completing assignments on pages 255, 323, and 478.

WRITER'S HANDBOOK

---

Tone in the Letters of Lindbergh and Vanzetti

A bride flies through the glories of a sunset. A man waits to be executed. It is difficult to imagine a sharper contrast of situation. For Anne Morrow Lindbergh and Bartolomeo Vanzetti, their radically different situations result in the radically different tones of their letters.

Anne Morrow Lindbergh's letter is written to her mother, which both explains her informal, affectionate tone and excuses her somewhat terse and hasty beginning. Her sky-high spirits have their source in the literal heights of fifteen thousand feet, and Lindbergh uses a repetitive abundance of happy adjectives to describe the joys of honeymoon aviation: "thrilling" (twice), "glorious" (twice), and "indescribable."

Writing from the very shadows of death, Vanzetti adopts a sober, dignified tone that only occasionally spills into bitterness. His purpose is to comfort his comrade's son and to defend, one final time, his principles. Aware that Dante may be "too young to understand," Vanzetti avoids the complexities of his trial and his cause and asks Dante to "remember." The word—remember—tolls through the letter like a mournful bell: "remember me as a comrade and friend," "Remember, Dante, remember always these things." Vanzetti has written a letter that is difficult to forget.

Though they have quite different audiences and purposes, Lindbergh and Vanzetti have each effectively and appropriately communicated the emotions of their situations.

---

# Writing About Irony

The ability to recognize and discuss **irony** in a literary work is a significant measure of your insight as a reader and writer. Writing assignments dealing with irony may ask you to identify and explain an ironic statement or situation, to discuss the irony of a writer's tone, or to point out how irony contributes to the overall meaning of a work.

## PREWRITING

### Sample Assignment

In a paper of three to five paragraphs, discuss the irony of "The Interlopers" by Saki. How does irony contribute to the theme of the story?

### 1. Think It Through

The following points may help you as you consider an assignment on irony.

Remember that irony has several forms. **Verbal irony** occurs when a speaker says one thing but means the opposite. **Irony of situation** occurs when something happens that is opposite to what is expected. **Dramatic irony** occurs when the reader or audience knows more about a situation than characters in the story or play.

Irony can be amusing and surprising, but not every clever remark or unexpected outcome is ironic. When in doubt, look for an element of reversal, of contrast, of "oppositeness" that characterizes irony.

Irony may not always be evident on a first reading. Some statements or actions become ironic in light of later events. In "The Interlopers," for example, Ulrich von Gradwitz stands "as though he waited for some beast of the woods to come within range of his vision." On first reading this is a simple descriptive detail. In view of the end of the story, however, it becomes ironic.

Finally, remember that an ironic work frequently has an ironic title. In analyzing any selection for irony, consider whether its title has more than one level of meaning.

### 2. Review the Selection

As you go over the story in light of your assignment, jot down details of irony. You may need to organize these notes according to category, but in "The Interlopers" irony of situation predominates. A partial list of ironic details would include:

Ulrich wishes to confront his enemy, and he does, too suddenly to be ready.

Before the men can take violent action, they are stopped by the violence of nature (the tree falls on them).

The men call for rescuers, but attract wolves.

Be sure to consider the possible irony of the title of the story. Since the assignment asks you to discuss irony in relation to theme, you should come to a conclusion about the story's theme:

Fate has the power to cancel human efforts, both good and bad.

## WRITING

A writing model is shown on the next page. Notice that in this model, the most important point is discussed in the last paragraph.

# REVISING

In addition to reviewing the revision checklists on page 836, check your work for the following points.

- Have you identified the type of irony used in the selection?
- In discussing the story, have you resisted the temptation to retell the whole plot in detail?
- Have you concluded with your most important point?
- Does your paper have a suitable title?

You will find this article helpful in completing the composition assignments on pages 393 and 401.

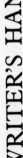

---

### Irony in "The Interlopers"

The power of fate to cancel human efforts—both bad and good—is the theme of Saki's "The Interlopers." The writer makes abundant use of irony in crafting his story and emphasizing his theme.

At the beginning of the story, Ulrich von Gradwitz, hunting in a disputed forest, wishes he could confront his enemy, Georg Znaeym, "man to man." This wish is instantly fulfilled as he passes a tree. Before either man can make a violent response, the violence of nature traps both men under a falling tree. Alone at last with his mortal enemy, each man is ironically unable to do any harm.

Irony of situation occurs as well in the story's conclusion. Now friends, the two men "wait for the help that would now bring release." Their first act of cooperation—joining their voices to call for help—is also their last. In the grimmest irony of all, Ulrich and Georg have attracted not a rescue party, but a pack of wolves.

The story's title points to the most significant irony. Both Georg and Ulrich assert their right to quarrel and later to make peace with "none to witness," "no cursed interlopers," "no interlopers from outside." But despite their wishes, fate ironically interferes. A falling tree ends their feud. At the end, a pack of wolves races in to end their reconciliation and their lives. Saki's ironic use of "interlopers" helps emphasize his theme of the intervening power of fate over human intentions.

---

# Writing About Poetry and Poetic Devices

To understand the meaning of a poem you must be especially aware of its language and sound. This requires a grasp of the poem's words, figurative language, and imagery; its rhythm; and its use of sound devices such as rhyme, alliteration, or onomatopoeia. Assignments about poetry frequently will ask you not only to identify these elements, but to show how they contribute to the poem's meaning and effect.

## PREWRITING

### Sample Assignment

Compare and contrast the emotional effects of "Sonnet 65" by Shakespeare and "On the Grasshopper and Cricket" by John Keats.

### 1. Read the Poem Carefully

In at least one of your readings, read the poem aloud. Poetry is meant to be heard. Use footnotes or the dictionary to clarify unfamiliar expressions. You may need to untangle some phrases by trying to express them in your own words. Once you are familiar with the content, ask the following questions:

*What kind of poem is it?* Not all poems are easily classified, but it's useful to recognize types of poetry. You would evaluate a narrative poem (which tells a story) differently from a lyric poem (which expresses an emotion or impression). As you know from the Comment article on page 284, both poems in the sample assignment are sonnets, lyric poems of fourteen pentameter lines.

*Who is the speaker?* The poet is not necessarily the speaker in the poem. Even with the first-person reference ("my love"), you can't be certain that Shakespeare is the speaker in "Sonnet 65." All you can be sure of is that the speaker is one who is worried about the permanence of his love in a world in which nothing endures. Whenever you write about

ideas or feelings expressed in a poem, attribute them to "the speaker" rather than to "the poet."

*What is the subject?* Sometimes the subject is announced by the title or directly stated in the poem. Keats's subject is given twice (lines 1 and 9). In other poems you must infer the subject. The subject of "Sonnet 65" is mortality, the destroying power of time.

*What emotional effect does the poem create?* You might agree that "On the Grasshopper and Cricket" creates a feeling of warmth, cheerfulness, and optimism. By contrast, "Sonnet 65" jangles with anxiety and despair that is only slightly diminished by the hope of the closing couplet.

*What devices of language and sound create that effect?* While you will want to be complete in your analysis, don't simply check off the "grocery list" of poetic devices. You might note, for example, that rhyme knits together the ideas of "Sonnet 65." That's true, but it's a generic truth, applicable to any well-written sonnet. Concentrate instead on the techniques that create the specific effects of the poem: the harsh-sounding, harsh-meaning words ("wrackful siege," "batt'ring days"), alliteration and other sound devices (the poem virtually hisses with the sound of "s"), the powerfully contrasted images (brass, rock, and steel images against "flower," "honey breath," and "best jewel").

| Points of Comparison | Sonnet 65 | On the Grasshopper and Cricket |
|---|---|---|
| Type of poem | Shakespearean sonnet | Petrarchan sonnet |
| Speaker | one who is in love? (line 14) | one who drowses? (line 13) |
| Speaker's tone | fretful, fearful | reassuring |
| Mood | dark, despairing hopeful in last two lines | warm, cheerful, optimistic |
| Poetic devices | harsh sounds ("wrackful," "batt'ring") | positive words: "delights," "pleasant," "warmth" |

### 2. Organize Your Material

Take notes as you consider these questions. Since the sample assignment asks that you compare and contrast the emotional effects of the poems, you will find it helpful to create a chart for your notes. The sample above shows how you might begin.

## WRITING

The paragraphs of a paper are shown on the next page. Note that the writer starts with a thesis statement and has chosen to completely discuss each poem in turn. Note also that the writer attributes thoughts and feelings to "the speaker" in the poem, not "the poet" or "Shakespeare."

## REVISING

Use the checklists on page 836 to evaluate your first draft. Also check for these points:
- Were you able to identify the form of the poem?
- Does your paper state the subject of the poem?
- Have you accurately described the devices of language and sound used in the poem?
- Have you shown how the poetic devices reveal the meaning or create the emotional effects of the poem?

You will find this article helpful in completing assignments on pages 232, 288, 323, and 595.

## Comparison of Two Sonnets

The effects achieved in "Sonnet 65" by William Shakespeare and "On the Grasshopper and Cricket" by John Keats are different because the subjects and authors' purposes are different, but the poems are equally successful because both poets have mastered the particular sonnet form they chose to use.

The three quatrains in the Shakespearean sonnet contain a series of related questions. How shall beauty withstand mortality when brass, stone, earth, and sea cannot? How can "summer's honey breath" withstand death when rocks and steel are decayed by Time? How can "Time's best jewel" (a metaphor for love) escape Time?

The tone of the first twelve lines is wondering, sorrowful, and even agitated. The speaker's agitation is most evident in the first part of line 9: "O fearful meditation!" The lines that speak of the ravages of time have a harsh sound, conveyed by the words "brass," "stone," "rage," "wrackful siege," "batt'ring days," "rocks impregnable," and "gates of steel." The lines that speak of love have a softer effect: "beauty held a plea," "summer's honey breath," "Time's best jewel."

The Petrarchan structure of the Keats sonnet neatly reflects seasonal divisions: "summer" in the octet, "winter" in the sestet. But where we might expect a study in contrast, the speaker rather insists on similarities. Each part of the sonnet begins with a similar statement: "The poetry of earth is never dead" (line 1) and "The poetry of earth is ceasing never" (line 9).

The parallelism of those lines is matched by other similarities in the octet and sestet. Both parts pulse with warmth (from "sun" and "stove"). Both parts feature musical insects that carry connotations of happiness and cheer. The grasshopper is linked to "summer luxury," "delights," and "fun." The cricket is associated with "song" and "warmth," and its music becomes indistinguishable—to our drowsy speaker, at least—with the grasshopper's. In this Petrarchan sonnet, octet and sestet reinforce each other and emphasize the speaker's assertion about the vitality of "the poetry of earth."

WRITER'S HANDBOOK

# Writing About Drama

A play exists to be performed. Reading the text of a play is always a substitute experience for seeing and hearing the play. To write effectively about drama, it is vital not simply to master the "story" elements of plot, setting, character, and theme, but also to creatively visualize the play's performance.

## PREWRITING

### Sample Assignment

In the first act of a Shakespearean tragedy, the main characters and the conflict are introduced. Choose one of the three scenes in the first act of *Julius Caesar*. In a paper of three to five paragraphs, analyze the scene, discussing it in terms of its own dramatic merits and how it contributes to the purposes of the first act.

### 1. Think It Through

The following guidelines may help you in writing about any play.

*Understand the structure of the play.* Trace the key events of the plot and note how they fit into the play's formal structure of acts and scenes. In what scene does the main conflict of the play begin? Where does the climax occur? Also examine the structure of individual scenes—these may be viewed as miniature dramas in themselves, with their own conflict or problem, rising action, and climax. Pay special attention to the conclusions of scenes; often a decision is reached or an intention is revealed at these points.

*Visualize the stage directions.* Don't simply read the stage directions, *imagine* them. Consider:

*Set.* What is on the stage in each scene? Where do the actors move? You may find it helpful to make sketches or diagrams to clarify details of the set in your mind.

*Lighting.* Light (and darkness) can be used to shift attention from place to place on a set, or to emphasize certain objects or characters. In many plays lighting is used to signal the beginning and end of scenes.

*Props.* What objects are essential to the play? How do they contribute to the meaning or emotional effect of the play? How does the playwright emphasize them?

*Sound effects.* Music is perhaps the most ancient sound effect of drama; it is still commonly used today to establish mood or suggest theme. Shakespeare requires lightning and thunder in Act One, Scene 3 of *Julius Caesar*. In *Our Town*, Wilder creates an interesting effect by giving real sounds to imaginary props: milk bottles and chickens are invisible, but clinking and clucking are heard.

*Camera direction.* Plays written for film or television often are published with instructions for camera angle and movement. These directions will help you imagine what viewers would see.

*Listen to the dialogue.* Dialogue is especially important in Shakespearean drama, where the relative absence of stage direction requires readers to infer a character's emotions, expressions, and gestures from speech alone.

*Note any repetitions.* Playwrights don't repeat elements accidentally; repetition is a tool of emphasis. Watch for words or phrases that recur in dialogue, or any prop or sound effect that recurs in scenes (as, for example, Wilder's repetition of the hymn "Blessed Be the Tie That Binds").

## 2. Review the Play

As you reread the text, take notes according to the specific purpose of your assignment. If you had chosen to analyze Act One, Scene 3 of *Julius Caesar*, your notes might be as follows:

*Setting:* a Roman street during a storm
*Time:* the night before the Ides of March
*Special effects:* thunder and lightning
*Mood:* danger, dread
*Key characters:* Casca, Cassius
*Minor characters:* Cicero, Cinna
*Plot developments:* Caesar will go next day to the Capitol, perhaps to be crowned king. Cassius will meet with other conspirators. Casca joins the plot. Cassius works to draw Brutus into the conspiracy.

## 3. Plan Your Paper

There are several ways to organize your materials. You might simply work in sequence through the scene. The danger here is that your paper may lapse into mere summary rather than analysis. Perhaps a more effective plan would be to discuss the scene in terms of its principal contributions to the play. A rough outline might include the following:

1. Introduction, thesis statement
2. Plot contributions
3. Characterization
4. Mood

# WRITING

The following are the introductory paragraph and two body paragraphs from a paper based on the sample assignment. The first paragraph expresses the thesis, while the latter two paragraphs discuss what the writer regards as the scene's most significant aspect.

## Model

In the context of a "fearful night" in Act One, Scene 3 of *Julius Caesar*, Shakespeare reveals details that advance his plot and deepen our understanding of two characters. But the main contribution of this scene, I believe, is its creation of a violent and threatening mood. . . .

Scene 3 is essential not because of its details of plot or characterization. Scene 2 has already sufficiently established the characters of Casca and Cassius. The significant plot information provided here might as easily have been given in the following scene (Act Two, Scene 1). No, the essential contribution of Scene 3 is in the creation of a mood of violent strangeness.

Shakespeare takes great care in setting this mood. Four separate cues for storm effects are given. Each character in the scene, even the unfazed Cicero, alludes in some way to disturbance and strangeness. Casca's breathless descriptions of weird events provide the strongest images; his own terror provides the clearest evidence of their effect. The conspiracy thus takes form in an atmosphere of destruction and dread. The mood of Scene 3 paves the way for the violence and civil unrest of ensuing acts.

# REVISING

Use the checklists on page 836 to evaluate your first draft. Also consider these points:
• Are your conclusions based on an accurate understanding of the play's structure?
• Have you fully visualized the play (or the specific act or scene under discussion)? Is this reflected in your paper?
• Have you ordered your discussion in the most effective way?

You will find this article helpful in completing assignments on pages 170, 188, 536, and 588.

WRITER'S HANDBOOK

# Writing About Nonfiction

Nonfiction includes a wide range of prose writing: biography, autobiography, letters, diaries, essays, articles, and news stories. Whatever its form, nonfiction deals with real people, issues, and events. Writing assignments about nonfiction may ask you to determine a writer's purpose or to analyze the organization, style, and tone of a work.

## PREWRITING

### Sample Assignment

In "By Any Other Name," Santha Rama Rau writes about a childhood experience. What are her adult feelings about that early experience? Review the selection and write a paper of three to five paragraphs describing the writer's attitude and how that attitude influenced your own response as a reader.

### 1. Think It Through

In writing about nonfiction, you will find it helpful to consider the following questions.

*What is the form of the selection?* Is it a biography, an essay, an article, or a speech? As a reader you approach each of these with quite different expectations and evaluate them with different standards. Note that "By Any Other Name" is an autobiographical episode.

*What seems to be the writer's purpose?* Is the writer's intention to inform, entertain, amuse, criticize, or persuade? In "By Any Other Name," Rama Rau's purpose seems to be to share a personal childhood experience that reflects critically on relationships between English and Indian people during colonial times in India.

*Who is the writer's intended audience?* As in the case of "By Any Other Name," the audience frequently is the general reader. But don't come to that conclusion too quickly. Particularly when writing about letters and speeches, try to determine the writer's original audience.

*How has the writer organized the material?* Are events described in time-order sequence? Are ideas presented in order of importance? What other patterns (cause/effect, comparison/contrast) are evident? Does the organization effectively serve the writer's purpose? Note that Rama Rau breaks a time-order pattern by starting the passage with the moment of her "renaming'" by a teacher, then backtracking to explain why she and her sister had come to the Anglo-Indian school. Always consider a writer's purpose for breaking a pattern in such a way.

*What is the writer's tone or attitude?* Is the writer's attitude serious, angry, ironic, humorous, or something else? Is the writer striving for objectivity—reporting information as neutrally and impersonally as possible? Or is the writer subjective—expressing personal opinions and feelings along with the information? This is the key issue in terms of the sample assignment. As autobiography, "By Any Other Name" has a natural subjectivity. However, the adult writer offers little direct comment on her childhood experiences.

### 2. Develop Your Thesis

After careful review of the selection in response to the sample assignment, you might arrive at the following thesis statement.

Santha Rama Rau adopts a low-key, understated response to her childhood experiences in "By Any Other Name." By withholding her own critical feelings, Rama

Rau silently invites her readers to come to their own conclusions about the school.

# WRITING

A model based on the sample assignment is shown below.

# REVISING

Use the checklists on page 836 to evaluate your first draft. Also consider the following points:
- Have you identified the form of the selection?
- Have you accurately described the writer's attitude toward the subject?

You will find this article helpful in completing assignments on pages 626 and 666.

---

Silent Criticism in "By Any Other Name"

Santha Rama Rau adopts a low-key, understated response to her childhood experiences in "By Any Other Name." By withholding her own critical feelings, Rama Rau silently invites her readers to come to their own conclusions about the Anglo-Indian school.

As an adult narrator, Rama Rau makes only one direct—but ambiguous—statement of opinion: her first day at the school was "remarkable." The rest of her responses are given from her perspective as a five-year-old child. But here too she withholds negative feelings. We must infer that Santha is intimidated when she is given a new name. We must even infer her tears when the English students giggle at her ("I sat down quickly and opened my eyes very wide, hoping in that way to dry them off.")

But silence does not mean absence. Rama Rau's critical attitude is expressed indirectly. With the responses and remarks of her older sister and mother providing a critical context, Rama Rau lets events speak for themselves. Those events speak loudly—and negatively—to the careful reader. Despite the matter-of-fact presentation, for example, we must be appalled when an experienced headmistress casually changes a child's identity to serve her own convenience. We must be disturbed by the segregation of Indian students at the back of classrooms and the special seating arrangements during tests. We must be uncomfortable with an atmosphere that makes Indian children feel inferior in their play, their clothing, and their food. We must conclude that the Anglo-Indian school is characterized by arrogance, insensitivity, and condescension to Indian people.

By never expressing her own judgments "out loud," I believe Santha Rama Rau intensifies the critical reactions of her readers. "By Any Other Name" is a "remarkable" example of the devastating uses of understatement.

WRITER'S HANDBOOK

# Writing to Analyze Author's Style

Style refers to the way an author writes: the words chosen, their arrangement into sentences and paragraphs, the tone expressed. Ideally, style results from the blending of the writer's ideas, attitudes, personality, and purpose. Writing assignments about style frequently concern the appropriateness of a writer's style in terms of audience and purpose.

## PREWRITING

**Sample Assignment**

Choose one selection from this text and analyze the writer's style. In a paper of three to five paragraphs, explain why the writer's style is appropriate (or inappropriate) to his or her purpose and audience.

### 1. Think It Through

In the quotations below two writers talk about writing. Compare their styles.

> Writing is an adventure. To begin with it is a toy and an amusement. Then it becomes a mistress, then it becomes a master, then it becomes a tyrant. The last phase is that just as you are about to be reconciled to your servitude, you kill the monster and fling him to the public.
>
> Winston Churchill

> I think I did pretty well, considering I started out with nothing but a bunch of blank paper.
>
> Steve Martin

The writers have a similar subject and both intend to amuse, but their styles are radically different. Notice that Churchill uses formal words ("reconciled to your servitude") and a deliberate sentence structure. Note the parallelism of the third sentence and how the sentences grow longer and gather force as they roll to a dramatic—but still amusing—climax ("you kill the monster"). By contrast, Martin chooses informal words ("a bunch of blank paper"), makes personal references ("I think I did pretty well"), and constructs his sentence with seeming casualness. While each writer is expressing a viewpoint, his style is revealing something about him. It would not be difficult to guess which of the two was a prime minister, which the stand-up comedian.

As you analyze the style of any writer, a key issue is the writer's level of formality. Is the writer being informal, casual, "conversational"— or formal, dignified, and carefully structured? Levels of formality may range from a slangy chumminess to a frosty, distant abstraction; most writing falls somewhere in between. Watch for the following tendencies.

*Personal references.* Informal style often has frequent personal comments ("I think . . ."). Formal style normally avoids them ("One thinks . . .").

*Contractions.* These are common in informal writing ("can't"), but avoided in formal writing ("cannot").

*Word choice.* Some words and expressions create a more formal tone. In his Gettysburg Address, Lincoln chose to say "Fourscore and seven" rather than "Eighty-seven."

*Sentence structure.* Formal writing is marked by carefully crafted sentences, as in the Churchill quotation above. Informal writing tends to have the casual structure of ordinary speech.

## 2. Review the Selection

As you review for style, try reading the selection aloud once or twice. Listening to your own tone as you read may help you clearly establish the writer's tone.

If you had chosen to write about President Truman's letter to his wife (page 654), you might note the following details about the style.

*slang contractions:* 'em for *them*
*expressions:* "I reared up on my hind legs"
"Santa Claus is dead"
"bring home the bacon"
*reference to leader:* "the old boy"
*sentences:* short, simple, direct

## 3. Develop Your Thesis Statement

After reviewing Truman's letter and studying your notes, you might arrive at the following thesis statement.

President Truman uses a simple, homely style to describe some of the most important events and leaders of his time. Truman was always known for "plain speaking," and this letter shows the reputation was well deserved.

# WRITING

Several paragraphs of a paper based on the sample assignment are shown. Note how the thesis statement has been sharpened to a more direct evaluation of the style.

## Model

In the privacy of a letter to his wife, President Truman uses a simple, homely style to describe some of the most important events and leaders of his time. Truman was always known for "plain speaking," and this letter shows both the defects and the virtues of that style.

The key passage of the letter is Truman's description of a "tough meeting." Here he uses some colorful slang expressions ("I reared up on my hind legs and told 'em

where to get off. . . . Santa Claus is dead") to give the flavor of the meeting and his own combative attitude. Even in the context of a private letter, we might judge the style here to be a little too informal to be appropriate to the events described.

However, that same passage also shines with the virtues of Truman's style. What could be more understandable—and appealing—than Truman's policy statements: "I want the . . . War won. . . . Then I want peace—world peace." Truman's style here displays his gift for cutting to the heart of the matter.

If we are a bit uncomfortable with the image of a President rearing on his "hind legs" or referring to a world leader as "the old boy," we must remember that Truman is reporting not to the nation, but to his wife. We can appreciate that the simplicity, informality, and honesty of the style reflect the character of the man. We can also be relieved, however, that Truman didn't have to write the Gettysburg Address.

# REVISING

Use the checklists on page 836 to evaluate your first draft. Also consider the following points.
• Have you determined the writer's level of formality? tone?
• Have you established the audience and purpose of the selection?
• Have you supported your statements about the writer's style with specific quotations from and references to the selection?

You will find this article helpful in completing assignments on pages 302, 486, and 670.

# GLOSSARY OF LITERARY TERMS

Words in SMALL CAPITAL LETTERS within entries refer to other entries in the Glossary of Literary Terms. Some entries conclude with a cross-reference to the Handbook of Literary Terms, where a more detailed explanation can be found.

**alliteration** (ə lit′ə rā′shən), the REPETITION of consonant sounds at the beginnings of words or within words, particularly in accented syllables. It can be used to reinforce meaning, unify thought, or create a musical effect. "The setting sun silhouettes a sailboat" is an example of alliteration. (See the Handbook of Literary Terms.)

**allusion** (ə lü′zhən), a brief reference to a person, event, or place, real or fictitious, or to a work of art. A writer who describes any shortage with the words "The cupboard is bare" is alluding to the nursery rhyme "Old Mother Hubbard." (See the Handbook of Literary Terms.)

**analogy** (ə nal′ə jē), a literal comparison made between two items, situations, or ideas that are somewhat alike but unlike in most respects. Frequently an unfamiliar or complex object or idea will be compared to a familiar or simpler one in order to explain the first. Emily Dickinson's poem "Our Little Kinsmen," on page 234, presents an analogy.

**antagonist** (an tag′ə nist), a character in a story or play who opposes the chief character or PROTAGONIST. In *Twelve Angry Men,* page 131, Juror Three emerges as the main antagonist. (See PROTAGONIST/ANTAGONIST in the Handbook of Literary Terms.)

**assonance** (as′n əns), the REPETITION of similar vowel sounds followed by different consonant sounds in stressed syllables or words. It is used instead of RHYME. *Made* and *played* are examples of rhyme; *made* and *pale* are examples of assonance. (See the Handbook of Literary Terms.)

**autobiography** (See BIOGRAPHY.)

**ballad,** a NARRATIVE passed on in the oral tradition. It often makes use of REPETITION and DIALOGUE.

**biography,** an account of a person's life. "First Lady Under Fire," page 633, is an example of biography. AUTOBIOGRAPHY is the story of all or part of a person's life written by the person who lived it. Santha Rama Rau's "By Any Other Name," page 627, is an example of autobiography.

**blank verse,** unrhymed verse written in iambic PENTAMETER. Shakespeare's play *Julius Caesar,* page 498, is written in blank verse. (See the Handbook of Literary Terms.)

**characterization,** the methods an author uses to acquaint a reader with his or her characters. (See the Handbook of Literary Terms.)

**climax,** the decisive point in a story or play when the PLOT's central problem must be resolved in one way or another. In "The Parachutist," page 33, the problem to be resolved is whether or not the kitten will survive. The climax occurs when, given the opportunity, the kitten forces the hawk to land. Not every story or play has this kind of dramatic climax.

Sometimes a character may simply resolve a problem in his or her mind. At times there is no resolution of the plot; the climax then comes when a character realizes that a resolution is impossible.

**comedy,** a play written primarily to amuse the audience. In addition to arousing laughter, comic writing often appeals to the intellect. "The Romancers," page 159, is a comedy.

**conflict,** the struggle between two opposing forces. The four basic kinds of conflict are: (1) a person against another person ("Gawain and Launcelot in Combat," page 372); (2) a person against nature ("The Boar Hunt," page 59); (3) a person against society ("Tuesday Siesta," page 465); and (4) two elements within a person struggling for mastery ("Through the Tunnel," page 95). More than one kind of conflict can be and often is present in a work. (See also PLOT.)

**connotation,** the emotional associations surrounding a word or phrase, as opposed to its literal meaning or DENOTATION. Some connotations are fairly universal, others quite personal. (See the Handbook of Literary Terms.)

**consonance** (kon′sə nəns), the repetition of consonant sounds that are preceded by different vowel sounds. (See the Handbook of Literary Terms.)

**couplet,** a pair of rhyming lines of the same METER.

**denotation,** the strict, literal meaning of a word. (See CONNOTATION.)

**dialect,** a form of speech characteristic of a particular region or class, differing from the standard language in pronunciation, vocabulary, and grammatical form. Chig's grandmother and Aunt Rose in "A Visit to Grandmother," page 47, speak in a dialect.

**dialogue,** conversation between two or more people in a literary work. Dialogue can help to develop the CHARACTERIZATION of those speaking and those spoken about, create MOOD, advance PLOT, and develop THEME.

**dimeter** (dim′ə tər), line of VERSE having two metrical feet. (See FOOT; see also RHYTHM in

the Handbook of Literary Terms.)

**drama,** a literary work in verse or prose, written to be acted, that tells a story through the speech and actions of the characters; a play. *Our Town* in Unit 2 and *Julius Caesar* in Unit 6 are examples of drama.

**end rhyme,** the rhyming of words at the ends of lines of POETRY as in "A Poison Tree," page 231. (See also INTERNAL RHYME and RHYME.)

**essay,** a brief prose composition that presents a personal viewpoint. "Three Days to See!" on page 658 is an essay that expresses the views of Helen Keller.

**exposition,** the beginning of a work of fiction, particularly a play, in which the author sets the atmosphere and TONE, explains the SETTING, introduces the characters, and provides the reader with any other information needed in order to understand the PLOT.

**extended metaphor,** a figure of speech that is used throughout an entire work or a great part of it. It is common in poetry but often is used in prose as well. (See METAPHOR in the Handbook of Literary Terms.)

**fable,** a brief TALE, in which the characters often are animals, told to point out a MORAL truth. "The Fox and the Woodcutter," page 229, is a fable in VERSE.

**falling action,** the resolution of a dramatic PLOT, which takes place after the CLIMAX.

**fantasy/science fiction.** Both fantasy and science fiction are literary works set wholly or partly in an unreal world. Often, at least one character is unlike a human being. Frequently the PLOT concerns events that cannot be explained by current science. "The Masque of the Red Death," page 479, is a fantasy.

**fiction,** a type of literature drawn from the imagination of the author, that tells about imaginary people and events. NOVELS, SHORT STORIES, and many PLAYS are fiction.

**figurative language,** language used in a nonliteral way to express a suitable relationship between essentially unlike things. When Jorge Luis Borges describes the color of land by saying the sunset "turns the plains to rust," he is using a figure of speech, or figurative language. The more common figures of speech are SIMILE, METAPHOR, PERSONIFICATION, and HYPERBOLE. (See the Handbook of Literary Terms.)

**flashback,** interruption of a NARRATIVE to show an episode that happened before that particular point in the story. In Act Two of *Our Town* there is a flashback that begins "George has just been elected President of the Junior Class. . . ." (See the Handbook of Literary Terms.)

**folk literature,** a type of literature that has been passed orally from generation to generation and only written down after centuries. The authorship of folk literature, which includes epics, FABLES, fairy tales, LEGENDS, and MYTHS, is unknown.

**foot,** in VERSE, a group of syllables usually consisting of one accented syllable and all unaccented syllables associated with it. A foot may occasionally, for variety, have two accented syllables. (See RHYTHM in the Handbook of Literary Terms.)

**foreshadowing,** a hint given to the reader of what is to come. (See the Handbook of Literary Terms.)

**free verse,** a type of poetry written with RHYTHM and other poetic devices but without a fixed pattern of METER and RHYME. Walt Whitman, page 287, was the first recognized poet to use free verse extensively. (See the Handbook of Literary Terms.)

**haiku** (hī′kü), a brief poem of three lines, containing five syllables, seven syllables, and five syllables respectively. Six haiku poems appear on page 263.

**hero/heroine,** the central character in a NOVEL, SHORT STORY, DRAMA, or other work of FICTION. When the central character is a woman, she usually is called a *heroine* (her′ō ən). (See PROTAGONIST in the Handbook of Literary Terms.)

**hexameter** (hek sam′ə tər), line of VERSE having six metrical feet. (See FOOT; see also RHYTHM in the Handbook of Literary Terms.)

**humor,** in literature, writing whose purpose is to amuse or evoke laughter. Humorous writing can be sympathetic to human nature or satirical. "Action Will Be Taken," page 452, is an example of humorous writing.

**hyperbole** (hī pėr′bə lē), a figure of speech involving great exaggeration. The effect may be satiric, sentimental, or comic. (See the Handbook of Literary Terms.)

**imagery,** concrete words or details that appeal to the senses of sight, sound, touch, smell, taste, and to internal feelings. Imagery provides vividness in literary works and tends to arouse emotions in a reader which abstract language does not. (See the Handbook of Literary Terms.)

**inference,** a reasonable conclusion about the behavior of a character or the meaning of an event drawn from the limited information presented by the author. (See the Handbook of Literary Terms.)

**internal rhyme,** rhyming words within lines that may or may not rhyme at the end: *Into a deep sleep we wearily creep.* (See RHYME in the Handbook of Literary Terms.)

**inversion,** reversal of the usual order of the parts of a sentence, primarily for emphasis or to achieve a certain RHYTHM or RHYME. In Nguyen Trai's poem "A Round Shape Water Takes Inside the Gourd," page 285, the normal order of subject-verb-object—*Water takes a round shape inside the gourd*—is inverted. Inversion may also be called *anastrophe* (ə nas′trə fē).

**irony,** the term used to describe a contrast between what is expected, or what appears to be, and what really is. In *verbal irony,* the actual meaning of a statement is different from (often the opposite of ) what the statement literally says. *Irony of situation* refers to an occurrence that is contrary to what is expected or intended. *Dramatic irony* refers to a situation in which events or facts not known to a character on stage or in a fictional work are known to the audience or reader. (See the Handbook of Literary Terms.)

**legend,** a story handed down from the past, often associated with some period in the history of a people. A legend differs from a MYTH in having some historical truth and often less of the supernatural. Malory's *Le Morte d'Arthur* and other Arthurian tales that make up Unit 4 are based on legends of King Arthur and the Knights of the Round Table.

**light verse,** short poems written chiefly to amuse or entertain. "The Traveler's Curse After Misdirection," page 278, and "The Fool and the Poet," page 280, are examples of light verse.

**lyric,** a poem, usually short, that expresses some basic emotion or state of mind. A lyric usually creates a single impression and is highly personal. It may be rhymed or unrhymed. "I Wandered Lonely As a Cloud," page 235, fulfills the qualifications of a lyric. (See the Handbook of Literary Terms.)

**metaphor** (met′ə fôr), a figure of speech that involves an implied comparison between two different things. "His eyes are dark pools" is a metaphor. (See the Handbook of Literary Terms.)

**meter,** the pattern of stressed and unstressed syllables in POETRY. (See RHYTHM and FOOT in this Glossary or RHYTHM in the Handbook of Literary Terms.)

**mood,** the overall atmosphere or prevailing feeling within a work of art. (See the Handbook of Literary Terms.)

**moral,** the lesson or teaching in a FABLE or story. The moral of "Phoebus and Boreas," page 222, is "Clemency may be our best resource."

**motivation,** the process of presenting a convincing cause for the actions of a character in a dramatic or fictional work in order to justify those actions. Motivation usually involves a combination of external events and the character's personality traits. In "The Adventure of the Blue Carbuncle," page 17, Sherlock Holmes is motivated to investigate the movements of a stolen jewel by his love for a "puzzle" or mystery, as well as the presentation of the clues to him by Peterson.

**mystery,** a work of fiction that contains a puzzling problem or an event not explained until the end, so as to keep the reader in SUSPENSE. "The Adventure of the Blue Carbuncle," page 17, is a mystery featuring the detective Sherlock Holmes.

**myth,** a traditional story connected with the religion or beliefs of a people, usually attempting to account for something in nature. A myth has less historical background than a LEGEND. In ancient Greek myths, for example, lightning was depicted as thunderbolts cast down from Mount Olympus by the god Zeus.

**narrative,** a story or an account of an event or a series of events. A narrative may be true or fictional.

**narrator,** the teller of a story. The narrator may be a character in the story, as in "Forgiveness in Families," page 77, or someone outside the story, as in "Lamb to the Slaughter," page 87. (See POINT OF VIEW.)

**nonfiction,** literature about real people and events rather than imaginary ones. Nonfiction can be history, BIOGRAPHY, ESSAY, or article. Unit 7 is made up of nonfiction.

**novel,** a long work of NARRATIVE prose FICTION dealing with characters, situations, and SETTINGS that imitate those of real life. A *novelette* is a short novel. Unit 8 contains two novels, *The Pearl*, page 693, and *Master and Man*, page 740. Both can be considered novelettes. A similar type of work, the *novella*, is longer than a SHORT STORY but not as long as a novel.

**onomatopoeia** (on′ə mat′ə pē′ə), a word or words used in such a way that the sound imitates the sound of the thing described. An example in which sound echoes sense is found in the following lines from "William and Helen" by Sir Walter Scott:

Tramp! tramp! along the land they rode,
Splash! splash! along the sea.
(See the Handbook of Literary Terms.)

**parable,** a brief TALE that concretely illustrates an abstract idea or teaches some lesson or truth. It differs from a FABLE in that its characters generally are people rather than animals. Although *The Pearl*, page 693, and *Master and Man*, page 740, are NOVELS, both have been compared to parables.

**paradox,** a statement, often metaphorical, that seems to be self-contradictory but that has valid meaning. The Biblical expression "and the last shall be first" is a paradox. (See the Handbook of Literary Terms.)

**pentameter** (pen tam′ə tər), line of VERSE having five metrical feet. (See FOOT; see also RHYTHM in the Handbook of Literary Terms.)

**personification** (pər son′ə fə kā′shən), the representation of abstractions, ideas, animals, or inanimate objects as human beings by endowing them with human qualities. (See the Handbook of Literary Terms.)

**play** (see DRAMA.)

**plot,** in the simplest sense, a series of happenings in a literary work. The word often is used to refer to the action as it is organized around a CONFLICT and builds through complication to a CLIMAX followed by the RESOLUTION. (See the Handbook of Literary Terms.)

**poetry,** a type of literature that creates an emotional response by the imaginative use of words patterned to produce a desired effect through RHYTHM, sound, and meaning. Poetry may be rhymed or unrhymed. Among the many forms of poetry are the LYRIC, SONNET, BALLAD, BLANK VERSE, and FREE VERSE. All of the selections in Unit 3 are poetry.

**point of view,** the relationship between the teller of a story and the characters and action in it. The teller, or NARRATOR, may be a character, in which case the story is told from the *first-person* point of view, as in "The Boar Hunt," page 59. A writer who describes, in the *third person*, both the thoughts and actions of one or all of the characters is said to use the *omnis-*

*cient* (om nish′ənt) point of view, as in "Through the Tunnel," page 95. Writers who confine themselves, in the *third person*, to describing thoughts and actions of a single character are said to use the *limited* point of view, as in "The Secret Life of Walter Mitty," page 40. An author who describes only what can be seen, like a newspaper reporter, is said to use the *third-person objective* point of view. (See the Handbook of Literary Terms.)

**protagonist** (prō tag′ə nist), the leading character in a literary work. (See the Handbook of Literary Terms.)

**psalm** (säm, sälm), a song or poem in praise of God. The term is most often applied to the hymns in the Book of Psalms of the Bible. An example is "Psalm 1," page 273.

**quatrain** (kwot′rān), a verse STANZA of four lines.

**Realism,** a way of representing life as it seems to the common reader, without idealizing the world. The material selected tends to represent, with precision and detail, ordinary people in everyday speech, experiences, and settings.

**repetition,** a poetic device in which a sound, word, or phrase is repeated for emphasis or effect, as in the first and last lines of "By the Bivouac's Fitful Flame," page 287. Repetition also may appear in fictional, dramatic, or other kinds of literary works.

**resolution** (rez′ə lü′shən), the part of a PLOT following the CLIMAX in which the complications of the plot are resolved or settled. (See FALLING ACTION; see also PLOT in the Handbook of Literary Terms.)

**rhyme,** the exact repetition of sounds in at least the final accented syllables of two or more words. (See RHYME SCHEME, END RHYME, INTERNAL RHYME, and SLANT RHYME; see also RHYME in the Handbook of Literary Terms.)

**rhyme scheme** (skēm), the pattern of END RHYMES in a poem. (See RHYME in the Handbook of Literary Terms.)

**rhythm** (riTH′əm), the arrangement of stressed and unstressed sounds in speech and writing. Rhythm in POETRY may be regular or irregular. (See the Handbook of Literary Terms.)

**rising action,** the part of a dramatic PLOT that leads up to the CLIMAX. In rising action, the complication caused by the CONFLICT of opposing forces is developed.

**romance,** a long NARRATIVE in poetry or prose that originated in the medieval period. Its main elements are adventure, love, and magic. There are elements of the romance in the LEGENDS of Arthur in Unit 4.

**Romanticism,** a way of representing life that, unlike REALISM, tends to portray the uncommon. The material selected often deals with extraordinary people in unusual SETTINGS having unusual experiences. In romantic literature there often is a stress on past times and an emphasis on nature.

**satire,** the technique in writing that employs wit to ridicule a subject, usually some social institution or human weakness, with the purpose of pointing out problems in society or inspiring reform. (See the Handbook of Literary Terms.)

**scansion** (skan′shən), the marking off of lines of POETRY into FEET. (See also RHYTHM in the Handbook of Literary Terms.)

**science fiction** (see FANTASY.)

**setting,** the time (both time of day or season and period in history) and place in which the action of a NARRATIVE occurs. The setting may be suggested through DIALOGUE and action, or it may be described by the NARRATOR or one of the other characters. Setting contributes strongly to the MOOD or atmosphere and plausibility of a work. (See Handbook of Literary Terms.)

**short story,** a prose NARRATIVE that is shorter than a NOVEL and that generally describes just one event or a tightly constructed series of events. Yet a short story must have a beginning, a middle, and an end. Units 1 and 5 present a great variety of short stories.

**simile** (sim′ə lē), a figure of speech involving a comparison using a word such as *like* or *as.* (See the Handbook of Literary Terms.)

**slant rhyme,** RHYME in which the vowel sounds are not quite identical, as in these lines:
Gather friends and gather foods.
Count your blessings, share your goods.
(See RHYME in the Handbook of Literary Terms.)

**soliloquy** (sə lil′ə kwē), a dramatic convention that allows a character alone on stage to speak his or her thoughts aloud. If someone else is on stage but cannot hear the character's words, the speech becomes an *aside.* In *Julius Caesar,* page 498, there are examples of soliloquy.

**sonnet,** a LYRIC poem with a traditional form of fourteen iambic PENTAMETER lines and one of a variety of RHYME SCHEMES. Shakespeare's "Sonnet 65," page 281, and "On the Grasshopper and Cricket," page 282, are sonnets.

**speaker,** the person who is speaking in a poem, such as the "Poet" character in "The Fool and the Poet," page 280. (See Comment: The Speaker and the Poet, page 245.)

**speech,** a literary composition written to be given as a public talk. A speech may be formal or informal in STYLE, and the topic usually depends on the intended audience.

**stage directions,** directions given by the author of a PLAY to indicate the action, costumes, SETTING, arrangement of the stage, and other instructions to the actors and director of the DRAMA. For examples of stage directions, see *The Romancers,* page 159, where they are printed in italic type.

**stanza,** a group of lines that are set off and form a division in a poem. "The Crazy Woman," page 236, has three stanzas of four lines each.

**stereotype** (ster′ē ə tīp′, stir′ē ə tīp′), a conventional character, PLOT, or SETTING that possesses little or no individuality. (See the Handbook of Literary Terms.)

**style,** the distinctive handling of language by an author. It involves specific choices made with regard to the selection of words and phrases to express ideas, sentence structure and variety, FIGURATIVE LANGUAGE, and so on. (See the Handbook of Literary Terms.)

**suspense,** the methods an author uses to maintain readers' interest, and the resulting MOOD of anxious uncertainty in many interesting stories. In "Home," page 74, suspense is achieved by withholding the result of the father's attempt to make loan arrangements.

**symbol,** a person, place, event, or object that has a meaning in itself but also suggests other meanings as well. For example, a flag is a symbol of patriotism. (See the Handbook of Literary Terms.)

**tale,** a spoken or written NARRATIVE, usually less complicated than a short story. An example is "The Tale of Sir Launcelot du Lake," page 349.

**tetrameter** (te tram'ə tər), line of VERSE having four metrical feet. (See FOOT; see also RHYTHM in the Handbook of Literary Terms.)

**theme,** the underlying meaning of a literary work. A theme may be directly stated but more often is implied. (See the Handbook of Literary Terms.)

**tone,** an author's attitude toward the subject of his or her literary work and toward the reader. (See the Handbook of Literary Terms.)

**tragedy,** dramatic or NARRATIVE writing in which the main character suffers disaster after a serious and significant struggle but faces his or her downfall in such a way as to attain heroic stature. *Julius Caesar*, page 498, is a tragedy.

**trimeter** (trim'ə tər), line of VERSE having three metrical feet. (See FOOT; see also RHYTHM in the Handbook of Literary Terms.)

**verse,** in its most general sense, a synonym for POETRY. Verse also may be used to refer to poetry carefully composed as to RHYTHM and RHYME SCHEME, but of inferior literary value.

# GLOSSARY

Full
pronunciation
key

The pronunciation of each word is shown just after the word, in this way: **ab bre vi ate** (ə brē′vē āt). The letters and signs used are pronounced as in the words below. The mark ′ is placed after a syllable with primary or heavy accent, as in the example above. The mark ′ after a syllable shows a secondary or lighter accent, as in **ab bre vi a tion** (ə brē′vē ā′shən).

Some words, taken from foreign languages, are spoken with sounds that do not otherwise occur in English. Symbols for these sounds are given in the key as "foreign sounds."

| | | | | | | |
|---|---|---|---|---|---|---|
| a | hat, cap | j | jam, enjoy | u | cup, butter | **foreign sounds** |
| ā | age, face | k | kind, seek | u̇ | full, put | |
| ä | father, far | l | land, coal | ü | rule, move | Y as in French *du*. |
| | | m | me, am | | | Pronounce (ē) with the lips rounded as for (ü). |
| b | bad, rob | n | no, in | v | very, save | |
| ch | child, much | ng | long, bring | w | will, woman | a as in French *ami*. |
| d | did, red | | | y | young, yet | Pronounce (ä) with the lips spread and held tense. |
| | | o | hot, rock | z | zero, breeze | |
| e | let, best | ō | open, go | zh | measure, seizure | œ as in French *peu*. |
| ē | equal, be | ô | order, all | | | Pronounce (ā) with the lips rounded as for (ō). |
| ėr | term, learn | oi | oil, voice | ə | represents: | |
| | | ou | house, out | | a in about | N as in French *bon*. |
| f | fat, if | | | | e in taken | The N is not pronounced, but shows that the vowel before it is nasal. |
| g | go, bag | p | paper, cup | | i in pencil | |
| h | he, how | r | run, try | | o in lemon | |
| | | s | say, yes | | u in circus | H as in German *ach*. |
| i | it, pin | sh | she, rush | | | Pronounce (k) without closing the breath passage. |
| ī | ice, five | t | tell, it | | | |
| | | th | thin, both | | | |
| | | ᵺ | then, smooth | | | |

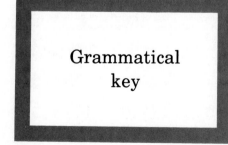

Grammatical
key

| | | | |
|---|---|---|---|
| *adj.* | adjective | *prep.* | preposition |
| *adv.* | adverb | *pron.* | pronoun |
| *conj.* | conjunction | *v.* | verb |
| *interj.* | interjection | *v.i.* | intransitive verb |
| *n.* | noun | *v.t.* | transitive verb |
| *sing.* | singular | *pl.* | plural |
| *pt.* | past tense | *pp.* | past participle |

**abash**

**a bash** (ə bash'), *v.t.* embarrass and confuse; make uneasy and somewhat ashamed; disconcert: *I was not abashed by the laughter of my classmates.* [< Old French *esbaïss-*, a form of *esbaïr* astonish] —**a bash'ment,** *n.*

**a bate** (ə bāt'), *v.*, **a bat ed, a bat ing.** —*v.t.* **1** lessen in force or intensity; reduce or decrease: *Soft words did not abate her fury.* **2** put an end to; stop: *abate a nuisance.* —*v.i.* become less in force or intensity; diminish: *The storm has abated.* [< Old French *abatre* beat down < *a-* to + *batre* to beat] —**a bat'a ble,** *adj.*

**ab bey** (ab'ē), *n., pl.* **-beys. 1** a monastery ruled by an abbot or a convent ruled by an abbess. **2** the monks or nuns living there. **3** church or building that was once an abbey or part of an abbey: *Westminster Abbey.*

**a bor tive** (ə bôr'tiv), *adj.* **1** coming to nothing; unsuccessful: *an abortive rebellion.* **2** born prematurely. **3** imperfectly formed or developed; rudimentary. —**a bor'tive ly,** *adv.*

**a byss** (ə bis'), *n.* **1** a bottomless or very great depth; chasm. **2** anything too deep or great to be measured; lowest depth.

**ac claim** (ə klām'), *v.t.* **1** welcome with shouts or other signs of approval; praise highly; applaud: *The crowd acclaimed the winning team.* **2** proclaim or announce with approval: *The newspapers acclaimed the results of the election.*

**ac cost** (ə kôst', ə kost'), *v.t.* approach and speak to first; address: *The stranger accosted me and asked for directions.* [< Middle French *accoster* < Latin *ad-* to + *costa* side, rib]

**ac qui esce** (ak'wē es'), *v.i.*, **-esced, -esc ing.** give consent by keeping silent or by not making objections; accept (the conclusions or arrangements of others); accede: *acquiesce in a decision.* [< Latin *acquiescere* < *ad-* to + *quies* rest, quiet]

**ac quit tal** (ə kwit'l), *n.* a discharge; a release after considering evidence.

**ad join ing** (ə joi'ning), *adj.* being next to or in contact with; bordering.

**ad jure** (ə jùr'), *v.t.*, **-jured, -jur ing. 1** request earnestly or solemnly; entreat. **2** command or charge (a person) on oath or the penalty of a curse (*to* do something). [< Latin *adjurare* < *ad-* to + *jurare* swear]

**a droit** (ə droit'), *adj.* **1** resourceful in reaching one's objective; ingenious; clever. **2** skillful in the use of the hands or body; dexterous. [< French < *à droit* rightly] —**a droit'ly,** *adv.* —**a droit'ness,** *n.*

**Ae o li an** (ē ō'lē ən), *adj.* **1** of Aeolus. **2 aeolian,** of, produced by, or carried by the winds.

**af fa bil i ty** (af'ə bil'ə tē), *n.* **1** condition or quality of being courteous and pleasant in responding to others. **2** graciousness. [< Latin *affabilis* easy to speak to < *affari* speak to < *ad-* to + *fari* speak] —**af'fa bly,** *adv.*

**af fray** (ə frā'), *n.* a noisy quarrel; fight in public; brawl. [< Old French *effrei*]

**af front** (ə frunt'), *n.* word or act that openly and purposely expresses disrespect; open insult: *To be called a coward is an affront.* —*v.t.* **1** insult openly; offend purposely and to one's face. **2** face courageously and defiantly; confront. [< Old French *afronter* strike on the forehead, defy, face < *a front* against the forehead]

**a ghast** (ə gast'), *adj.* struck with surprise or horror; filled with shocked amazement. [past participle of obsolete *agast* terrify < Old English *on-* on + *gæstan* frighten. Related to GHOST.]

**a kim bo** (ə kim'bō), *adj.* with the hands on the hips and the elbows bent outward. [Middle English *in kenebowe,* apparently, in keen bow, at a sharp angle]

**a kin** (ə kin'), *adj.* **1** of the same kind; alike; similar: *Your opinions are akin to mine.* **2** of the same family; related: *Your cousins are akin to you.* [for *of kin*]

**akimbo**
woman with arms akimbo

**a lack** (ə lak'), *interj.* ARCHAIC. exclamation of sorrow or regret; alas.

**a lac ri ty** (ə lak'rə tē), *n.* brisk and eager action; liveliness; *move with alacrity.* [< Latin *alacritatem* < *alacer* brisk]

**al che my** (al'kə mē), *n.* **1** the chemistry of the Middle Ages, which combined science, magic, and philosophy. Alchemy tried to find a means of transmuting cheaper metals into gold and silver. **2** any miraculous power of transformation. [< Old French *alkemie* < Medieval Latin *alchimia* < Arabic *al-kimiyā'* the art of alloying metals]

**al ien ate** (ā'lyə nāt, ā'lē ə nāt), *v.t.*, **-at ed, -at ing.** turn away the normal feelings, fondness, or devotion of anyone; make unfriendly; estrange: *The colonies were alienated from England by disputes over trade and taxation.* —**al'ien a'tor,** *n.*

**al lay** (ə lā'), *v.t.*, **-layed, -lay ing. 1** put at rest; quiet: *My fears were allayed by the news that my family was safe.* **2** relieve (pain, trouble, thirst, etc.); alleviate. [Old English *ālecgan* < *ā-* away, off + *lecgan* to lay] —**al lay'er,** *n.*

**al lu sion** (ə lü'zhən), *n.* **1** act of alluding; slight mention of something. **2** a reference to a historical or literary person, event, or place, used to heighten the significance of a poetic image or a prose passage. [< Latin *allusionem* < *alludere.*]

**alms** (ämz, älmz), *n. sing. or pl.* money or gifts given freely to help the poor; charity. [Old English *ælmysse* < Latin *eleemosyna* < Greek *eleēmosynē* pity, alms < *eleos* pity]

**a loft** (ə lôft', ə loft'), *adv.* **1** far above the earth; high up. **2** in or into the air; off from the ground. **3** high up among the sails, rigging, or masts of a ship. [< Scandinavian (Old Icelandic) *ā lopti* in the air]

**am big u ous** (am big'yü əs), *adj.* **1** having or permitting more than one interpretation or explanation; equivocal: *an ambiguous remark.* **2** of doubtful position or classification: *an ambiguous character.* [< Latin *ambiguus* < *ambigere* be uncertain, wander < *ambi-* + *agere* to drive] —**am big'u ous ly,** *adv.* —**am big'u ous ness,** *n.*

**am i ca ble** (am'ə kə bəl), *adj.* having or showing a friendly attitude; peaceable: *settle a quarral in an amicable way.* [< Late Latin *amicabilis* < Latin *amicus* friend < *amare* to love. Doublet of AMIABLE.] —**am'i ca ble ness,** *n.* —**am'i ca bly,** *adv.*

**am u let** (am'yə lit), *n.* locket, carved image, or some other small object worn as a magic charm against evil, disease, etc. [< Latin *amuletum*]

**an ar chist** (an'ər kist), *n.* **1** person who seeks to bring about the destruction of government and law; advocate of anarchism. **2** person who promotes disorder and stirs up revolt.

**an es thet ic** (an'əs thet'ik), *n.* substance that causes anesthesia, as chloroform, ether, procaine, etc. —*adj.* **1** causing anesthesia. **2** of or with anesthesia. Also, **anaesthetic.** —**an'es thet'i cal ly,** *adv.*

**an gle** (ang'gəl), *v.*, **-gled, -gling,** *n.* —*v.i.* **1** fish with a hook and line. **2** try to get something by using tricks or schemes. —*n.* INFORMAL. a special, often underhanded way of profiting. [Old English *angel* fishhook]

**a non** (ə non'), *adv.* ARCHAIC. **1** in a little while; soon. **2** at another time; again.

**an thro po log i cal** (an'thrə pə loj'ə kəl), *adj.* of anthropology, the study of humans, especially their physical characteristics, cultures, customs, and beliefs. —**an'thro po log'i cal ly,** *adv.*

**an vil** (an'vəl), *n.* an iron or steel block on which metals are hammered and shaped. [Old English *anfilt*]

**ap a thy** (ap'ə thē), *n.* **1** lack of interest in or desire for activity; indifference **2** lack of feeling. [< Greek *apatheia* < *a-* without + *pathos* feeling]

**ap er ture** (ap'ər chər, ap'ər chùr'), *n.* an opening; hole. A diaphragm regulates the size of the aperture through which light passes into a camera. [< Latin *apertura* < *aperire* to open]

**a plomb** (ə plom'), *n.* self-possession springing from perfect confidence in oneself; assurance; poise. [< French < *à plomb* according to the plummet]

**ap pall** or **ap pal** (ə pôl'), *v.t.*, **-palled, -pall ing.** fill with consternation and horror; dismay; terrify. [< Old French *apallir* make pale < *a-* to + *pale* pale]

**ap par el** (ə par'əl), *n., v.*, **-eled, -el ing** or **-elled, -el ling.**

—*n.* clothing; dress. —*v.t.* clothe; dress up. [< Old French *apareil* < *apareiller* fit out, clothe]

**ap pa ri tion** (ap′ə rish′ən), *n.* **1** a supernatural sight or thing; ghost or phantom. **2** the appearance of something strange, remarkable, or unexpected. [< Late Latin *apparitionem*]

**ap per tain** (ap′ər tān′), *v.i.* belong as a part; be connected; pertain; relate: *Forestry appertains to geography, botany, and agriculture.* [< Old French *apartenir* < Late Latin *appertinere* < Latin *ad-* to + *pertinere* pertain]

**ap prais al** (ə prā′zəl), *n.* **1** estimate of the value, amount, quality, etc.: *Their appraisal of the stock was too low.* **2** an appraising; evaluating.

**ap prais er** (ə prā′zər), *n.* **1** person authorized to fix the value of property, imported goods, etc. **2** person who appraises.

**ap pre hen sive** (ap′ri hen′siv), *adj.* afraid that some misfortune is about to occur; anxious about the future; fearful. —**ap′pre hen′sive ly,** *adv.* —**ap′pre hen′sive ness,** *n.*

**ap proof** (ə prüf′), *n.* ARCHAIC. **1** approval. **2** proof. [< Old French *aprove* < *aprover* approve < Latin *approbare*]

**ap pro pri ate** (*adj.* ə prō′prē it; *v.* ə prō′prē āt), *adj., v.,* **-at ed, -at ing.** —*adj.* especially right or proper for the occasion; suitable; fitting: *Plain, simple clothes are appropriate for school wear.* —*v.t.* **1** set apart for a special purpose: *The legislature appropriated a billion dollars for foreign aid.* **2** take for oneself; use as one's own: *You should not appropriate other people's belongings without their permission.* [< Late Latin *appropriatum* made one's own < Latin *ad-* to + *proprius* one's own] —**ap pro′pri ate ly,** *adv.* —**ap pro′pri ate ness,** *n.* —**ap pro′pri a′tor,** *n.*

**ar a besque** (ar′ə besk′), *n.* an elaborate and fanciful design of flowers, leaves, geometrical figures, etc. —*adj.* **1** carved or painted in arabesque. **2** elaborate; fanciful. [< French < Italian *arabesco* < *Arabo* Arab]

**ar bo re al** (är bôr′ē əl, är bōr′ē əl), *adj.* **1** living in or among trees. A squirrel is an arboreal animal. **2** of or like trees. —**ar bo′re al ly,** *adv.*

**ar id** (ar′id), *adj.* **1** having very little rainfall; dry: *an arid climate.* **2** unfruitful because of lack of moisture; barren: *arid soil.* [< Latin *aridus* < *arere* be dry] —**ar′id ly,** *adv.*

**ar is toc ra cy** (ar′ə stok′rə sē), *n., pl.* **-cies.** **1** class of people having a high position in society because of birth, rank, or title; nobility. **2** class of people considered superior because of intelligence, culture, or wealth; upper class. [< Late Latin *aristocratia* < Greek *aristokratia* < *aristos* best + *kratos* rule]

**ar rears** (ə rirz′), *n.pl.* **1** money due but not paid; unpaid debts. **2** unfinished work; things not done on time. **3 in arrears,** behind in payments, work, etc. [< Old French *arere* < Popular Latin *ad retro* to the rear]

**ar rest** (ə rest′), *v.t.* **1** seize (a person) and keep in custody by legal authority; apprehend: *The police arrested the woman for shoplifting.* **2** cause to stop (in a course of action); halt: *A fallen tree arrested traffic on the road.* [< Old French *arester* < Latin *ad-* + *restare* remain]

**ar ro gance** (ar′ə gəns), *n.* excessive pride with contempt of others; haughtiness.

**ar ro gant** (ar′ə gənt), *adj.* excessively proud and contemptuous of others. [< Latin *arrogantem* < *ad-* to + *rogare* ask] —**ar′ro gant ly,** *adv.*

**as cer tain** (as′ər tān′), *v.t.* find out for certain by trial and research; make sure of; determine: *ascertain the facts about a robbery.* [< Old French *ascertener* < *a-* to + *certain* certain] —**as′cer tain′a ble,** *adj.* —**as′cer tain′ment,** *n.*

**a skew** (ə skyü′), *adv., adj.* out of the proper position; turned or twisted the wrong way; awry.

**as pic** (as′pik), *n.* kind of jelly made from meat or fish stock, tomato juice, etc., used as a garnish or in salads. [< French]

**as sail** (ə sāl′), *v.t.* **1** attack repeatedly with violent blows. **2** attack with hostile words, arguments, or abuse. **3** (of a feeling) come over (a person) strongly; beset; trouble: *No doubts ever assail them.* [< Old French *asalir* < Latin *ad-* at + *salire* to leap] —**as sail′a ble,** *adj.*

**as sent** (ə sent′), *v.i.* express agreement; agree; consent: *Everyone assented to the plans for the dance.*

| a hat | i it | oi oil | ch child | ( a in about |
| ā age | ī ice | ou out | ng long | e in taken |
| ä far | o hot | u cup | sh she | ə = { i in pencil |
| e let | ō open | u̇ put | th thin | o in lemon |
| ē equal | ô order | ü rule | ᴛʜ then | ( u in circus |
| ėr term | | | zh measure | < = derived from |

**a the ist** (ā′thē ist), *n.* **1** person who does not believe in the existence of God. **2** a godless person. [< Greek *atheos* denying the gods]

**au di ble** (ô′də bəl), *adj.* that can be heard; loud enough to be heard. [< Latin *audire* hear] —**au′di bly,** *adv.*

**aught** (ôt), *pron.* ARCHAIC. anything. Also, **ought.** [Old English *āwiht* < *ā* ever + *wiht* thing]

**aug ment** (ôg ment′), *v.t., v.i.* make or become greater in size, number, amount, or degree; increase or enlarge. [< Late Latin *augmentare* < *augmentum* an increase < Latin *augere* to increase] —**aug ment′a ble,** *adj.*

**aus tere** (ô stir′), *adj.* **1** stern in manner or appearance; harsh: *a silent, austere man.* **2** severe in self-discipline; strict in morals: *The Puritans were austere.* **3** severely simple: *The tall, plain columns stood against the sky in austere beauty.* **4** grave; somber; serious. [< Greek *austēros* < *auos* dry] —**aus tere′ly,** *adv.*

**av ar ice** (av′ər is), *n.* too great a desire for money or property; greed for wealth. [< Old French < Latin *avaritia* < *avarus* greedy]

**av a ri cious** (av′ə rish′əs), *adj.* greatly desiring money or property; greedy for wealth. —**av′a ri′cious ly,** *adv.* —**av′a ri′cious ness,** *n.*

**a ver sion** (ə vėr′zhən, ə vėr′shən), *n.* **1** a strong or fixed dislike, antipathy: *an aversion to working hard.* **2** thing or person disliked.

**a vert** (ə vėrt′), *v.t.* **1** keep (a disaster, misfortune, etc.) from happening; prevent; avoid: *She averted the accident by a quick turn of her car.* **2** turn away or turn aside (the face, eyes, mind, etc.). [< Latin *avertere* < *ab-* from + *vertere* to turn] —**a vert′er,** *n.* —**a vert′i ble, a vert′a ble,** *adj.*

**a wry** (ə rī′), *adv., adj.* **1** with a twist or turn to one side: *My hat was blown awry by the wind.* **2** wrong; out of order: *Our plans have gone awry.*

**bale ful** (bāl′fəl), *adj.* **1** full of hurtful or deadly influence; destructive. **2** full of misfortune; disastrous. —**bale′ful ly,** *adv.* —**bale′ful ness,** *n.*

**balm** (bäm, bälm), *n.* **1** a fragrant, oily, sticky substance obtained from certain kinds of trees, used to heal or to relieve pain; balsam. **2** a healing or soothing influence. [< Old French *basme* < Latin *balsamum* < Greek *balsamon.*]

**bam boo zle** (bam bü′zəl), *v.,* **-zled, -zling.** INFORMAL. —*v.t.* **1** impose upon; cheat; trick. **2** puzzle; perplex. —*v.i.* use trickery. [origin uncertain] —**bam boo′zle ment,** *n.* —**bam boo′zler,** *n.*

**ban ish** (ban′ish), *v.t.* **1** compel (a person) to leave a country by order of political or judicial authority; exile. **2** drive away; dismiss; expel: *banish all cares.* [< Old French *baniss-,* a form of *banir* < Germanic. Related to BAN.]

**bard** (bärd), *n.* **1** a Celtic minstrel and poet who from earliest times to the Middle Ages sang his own poems, usually to harp accompaniment, celebrating martial exploits, etc. **2** any poet. [< Irish and Scottish Gaelic]

**bark** (bärk), *n.* **1** a three-masted ship, square-rigged on the first two masts and fore-and-aft-rigged on the other. **2** ARCHAIC. boat; ship. Also, **barque.** [< Middle French *barque* < Italian *barca* < Late Latin]

**bast** (bast), *n.* **1** the inner layer of the bark of trees that contains cells for carrying sap; phloem. **2** the tough fiber in this inner layer used in making rope, matting, etc. [Old English *bæst*]

**bea dle** (bē′dl), *n.* a minor church officer whose duties include

**bedizen**

keeping order and waiting on the clergy. [< Old French *bedel*]

**be di zen** (bi dī′zn, bi diz′n), *v.t.* dress or ornament with showy finery. [< *be-* + *dizen*] **—be di′zen ment,** *n.*

**bed lam** (bed′ləm), *n.* **1** noisy confusion; uproar. **2** ARCHAIC. insane asylum; madhouse. [< *Bedlam,* old name for the Hospital of St. Mary of *Bethlehem,* an insane asylum in London]

**be lath er** (bi laᴛʜ′ər), *v.t.* to lather thoroughly; to cover with lather or foamy liquid.

**bel lig er ent** (bə lij′ər ənt), *adj.* fond of fighting; tending or inclined to war; warlike; pugnacious. [< Latin *belligerantem* < *bellum* war + *gerere* to wage] **—bel lig′er ent ly,** *adv.*

**ben e dic tion** (ben′ə dik′shən), *n.* **1** the asking of God's blessing, as at the end of a church service or a marriage ceremony. **2** the form or ritual of this invocation. **3** blessing. [< Latin *benedictionem* < *benedicere* bless < *bene* well + *dicere* say.]

**be night ed** (bi nī′tid), *adj.* **1** not knowing right from wrong; ignorant. **2** ARCHAIC. overtaken by darkness. [< obsolete verb *benight* < *be-* + *night*]

**be nign** (bi nīn′), *adj.* **1** kindly in feeling; benevolent; gracious: *a benign old woman.* **2** showing a kindly feeling; gentle: *a benign countenance.* **3** favorable; propitious. **4** mild: *a benign climate.* **5** not dangerous to health; not malignant: *a benign tumor.* [< Latin *benignus* < *bene* well + *-gnus* born] **—be nign′ly,** *adv.*

**be queath** (bi kwēᴛʜ′, bi kwēth′), *v.t.* **1** give or leave (especially money or other personal property) by a will. **2** hand down or leave to posterity; pass along. [Old English *becwethan* < *be-* to, for + *cwethan* say] **—be queath′er,** *n.*

**be reave** (bi rēv′), *v.t.,* **-reaved** or **-reft, -reav ing.** **1** leave desolate and alone: *The family was bereaved by the death of the father.* **2** deprive ruthlessly; rob: *bereaved of hope.* [Old English *berēafian* < *be-* away + *rēafian* rob] **—be reave′ment,** *n.*

**ber lin** (bər lin′), *n.* a large, four-wheeled, closed carriage hung between two perches and having two interior seats. [< French *berline,* after Berlin, Germany, where it was first made]

**be seech** (bi sēch′), *v.t.,* **-sought** or **-seeched, -seech ing.** ask earnestly; beg; implore. [Middle English *bisechen* < *be-* thoroughly + *sechen* seek]

**be seem** (bi sēm′), *v.t.,* ARCHAIC. **—v.t.** seem proper for; befit; suit. **—v.i.** seem proper or fitting.

**be sought** (bi sôt′), *v.* a pt. and a pp. of **beseech.**

**be times** (bi tīmz′), *adv.* ARCHAIC. **1** early. **2** before it is too late. **3** in a short time; soon.

**be to ken** (bi tō′kən), *v.t.* be a sign or token of; indicate; show.

**bib u lous** (bib′yə ləs), *adj.* **1** fond of drinking alcoholic liquor. **2** showing the effects of drinking alcoholic liquor; drunk. **3** absorbent of moisture. [< Latin *bibulus* < *bibere* to drink]

**big ot** (big′ət), *n.* person who is bigoted; intolerant person. [< Middle French]

**biv ouac** (biv′wak, biv′ü ak), *n.* a temporary, outdoor camp of soldiers, mountaineers, hikers, etc., usually without tents or with very small tents.

**black guard** (blag′ärd, blag′ərd), *n.* a low, contemptible person; scoundrel.

**blade** (blād), *n.* **1** the cutting part of an edged tool or weapon, as distinguished from the handle. **2** a smart, dashing fellow. **3** leaf of grass. [Old English *blæd*] **—blade′like′,** *adj.*

**blas phe mous** (blas′fə məs), *adj.* uttering, containing, or showing blasphemy; profane. **—blas′phe mous ly,** *adv.* **—blas′phe mous ness,** *n.*

**blas phe my** (blas′fə mē), *n., pl.* **-mies.** abuse or contempt for God or sacred things; profanity.

**blight er** (blī′tər), *n.* BRITISH SLANG. **1** a contemptible, worthless person; scoundrel. **2** any person.

**bog** (bog, bôg), *n., v.,* **bogged, bog ging. —n.** piece of wet, spongy ground, consisting chiefly of decayed or decaying moss and other vegetable matter, too soft to bear the weight of any heavy body on its surface; marsh; swamp. **—v.t., v.i.** **1** sink or get stuck in a bog. **2 bog down,** sink in or get stuck so that one cannot get out without help: *She is bogged down with problems.* [< Irish or Scottish Gaelic, soft]

**bon ny** or **bon nie** (bon′ē), *adj.,* **-ni er, -ni est.** **1** fair to see; rosy and pretty: *a bonny baby.* **2** gay or cheerful. [Middle English *bonne,* apparently < Old French *bone* good < Latin *bonus*]

**bosk y** (bos′kē), *adj.,* **bosk i er, bosk i est.** **1** wooded. **2** shady. [< *busk* grove, dialectal variant of *bush*]

**bo te te** (bō tā′tā), *n.* SPANISH. a poisonous tropical fish; globefish.

**bou gain vil le a** or **bou gain vil lae a** (bü′gən vil′ē ə), *n.* any of a genus of woody tropical American vines having small flowers with large, ornamental purple or red bracts. [< New Latin < Louis Antoine de *Bougainville,* 1729–1811, French navigator]

**bow er** (bou′ər), *n.* shelter of leafy branches. [Old English *būr* dwelling]

**bow er y** (bou′ər ē), *adj.* leafy; shady.

**brach i o ce phal ic** (brak′ē ə sə fal′ik), *adj.* having a short, broad skull. Also, **brachycephalic.** [< Greek *brachys* short + *kephalē* head]

**bra vo** (brä′vō, brä′vō), *n., pl.* **-voes** or **-vos.** a hired fighter or murderer. [< Italian, literally, *wild*]

**bra zen** (brā′zn), *adj.* **1** having no shame; shameless; impudent. **2** loud and harsh; brassy. **3** made of brass. **4** like brass in color or strength. **—v.t.** **1** make shameless or impudent. **2 brazen it out** or **brazen it through,** act as if one did not feel ashamed of it: *Although he was caught lying, he tried to brazen it out by telling another lie.* [Old English *bræsen* < *bræs* brass] **—bra′zen ly,** *adv.* **—bra′zen ness,** *n.*

**bra zier** (brā′zhər), *n.* a large metal pan or tray to hold burning charcoal or coal. Braziers are used in some countries for heating rooms. [< Old French *brasier* < *breze* hot coals]

**broach** (brōch), *v.t.* **1** begin conversation or discussion about; introduce: *broach a subject.* **2** open by making a hole: *broach a barrel of cider.* [< Old French *broche* < Latin *broccus* projecting]

**brood** (brüd), *n.* the young birds hatched at one time in the nest or cared for together. **—v.i.** **1** (of birds) sit on eggs so as to hatch them; incubate. **2** think or worry a long time about some one thing. **3 brood on** or **brood over, a** keep thinking about. **b** hover over; hang close over. **—v.t.** **1** sit on (eggs) in order to hatch. **2** dwell on in thought: *For years he brooded vengeance.* **—adj.** kept for breeding: *a brood mare.* [Old English *brōd*] **—brood′ing ly,** *adv.*

**buf fet** (buf′it), *v.t.* **1** strike with the hand or fist. **2** knock about; strike repeatedly; beat back: *The waves buffeted me.* **3** fight or struggle against: *The boat buffeted the heavy waves caused by the storm.* [< Old French, diminutive of *buffe* blow]

**bull ock** (bùl′ək), *n.* **1** a castrated bull; ox; steer. **2** (originally) a young bull. [< Old English *bulluc* bull calf]

**bul wark** (bùl′wərk), *n.* **1** person, thing, or idea that is a defense or protection. **2** Usually, **bulwarks,** *pl.* side of a ship extending like a fence above the deck. **—v.t.** **1** defend; protect. **2** provide with a bulwark or bulwarks. [Middle English *bulwerk*]

**bux om** (buk′səm), *adj.* attractively and healthily plump; full-bosomed. [Middle English *buhsum* < Old English *būgan* to bend] **—bux′om ly,** *adv.* **—bux′om ness,** *n.*

**ca dence** (kād′ns), *n.* **1** the measure or beat of music, dancing, marching, or any movement regularly repeating itself; rhythm: *the cadence of a drum.* **2** fall of the voice. **3** a rising and falling sound; modulation. [< French < Italian *cadenza* < Latin *cadere* to fall]

**ca jole** (kə jōl′), *v.t.,* **-joled, -jol ing.** persuade by pleasant words, flattery, or false promises; coax. [< French *cajoler*]

**cal dron** (kôl′drən), *n.* a large kettle or boiler. Also, **cauldron.** [< Old French *caudron* < Late Latin *caldaria* < Latin *calidus* hot]

**cal i co** (kal′ə kō), *n., pl.* **-coes** or **-cos,** *adj.* **—n.** a cotton cloth that usually has colored patterns printed on one side. **—adj.** **1** made of calico: *a calico dress.* **2** spotted in colors: *We have a calico cat.* [< *Calicut,* India]

**cal lig ra phy** (kə lig′rə fē), *n.* **1** handwriting. **2** beautiful handwriting. [< Greek *kalligraphia* < *kallos* beauty + *graphein* write]

**can non ade** (kan′ə nād′), *n., v.,* **-ad ed, -ad ing. —n.** a continued firing of cannons; barrage. **—v.t.** attack with or as if with cannons.

**ca price** (kə prēs′), *n.* **1** a sudden change of mind without reason; unreasonable notion or desire; whim. **2** tendency to change suddenly and without reason. [< French < Italian *capriccio,* literally, a shiver]

**car a pace** (kär′ə pās), *n.* shell or bony covering on the back of a turtle, armadillo, lobster, crab, etc. [< French < Spanish *carapacho*]

**car bine** (kär′bīn, kär′bēn′), *n.* a short, light rifle or musket. [< French *carabine*]

**car bun cle** (kär′bung kəl), *n.* **1** a very painful, inflamed swelling under the skin caused by infection. A carbuncle discharges pus like a boil but is more serious in its effects. **2** a smooth, round garnet or other deep-red jewel. [< Latin *carbunculus* < *carbonem* coal]

**ca reer** (kə rir′), *v.i.* rush along wildly; dash: *The runaway horse careered through the streets.* [< Middle French *carrière* racecourse < Latin *carrus* wagon]

**car nage** (kär′nij), *n.* slaughter of a great number of people. [< Middle French < Italian *carnaggio,* ultimately < Latin *carnem* flesh]

**car ni vore** (kär′nə vôr, kär′nə vōr), *n.* any of an order of mammals that feed chiefly on flesh, characterized by large, sharp canine teeth and including cats, dogs, lions, tigers, bears, and seals.

**ca rouse** (kə rouz′), *v.,* **-roused, -rous ing,** *n.* —*v.i.* drink heavily; take part in noisy revels. —*n.* a noisy revel or drinking party. [< obsolete adverb, completely < German *gar aus(trinken)* (drink) all up] —**ca rous′er,** *n.* —**ca rous′ing ly,** *adv.*

**car ri on** (kar′ē ən), *n.* **1** dead and decaying flesh. **2** rottenness; filth. [< Old French *caroine* carcass < Popular Latin *caronia* < Latin *carnem* flesh]

**case ment** (kās′mənt), *n.* **1** window or part of a window which opens on hinges like a door. **2** any window.

**cas sock** (kas′ək), *n.* a long outer garment, usually black, worn by a clergyman. [< French *casaque* < Italian *casacca*]

**caste** (kast), *n.* **1** one of the social classes into which Hindus are divided. By tradition, a Hindu is born into a caste and cannot rise above it. **2** an exclusive social group; distinct class. **3** a social system having distinct classes separated by differences of birth, rank, wealth, or position. [< Portuguese *casta* race, class, animal species < Latin *castus* pure, chaste]

**cas tel lat ed** (kas′tl ā′tid), *adj.* built like a castle; having turrets and battlements.

**cat e chist** (kat′ə kist), *n.* person who catechizes.

**cat e chize** (kat′ə kīz), *v.t.,* **-chized, -chiz ing. 1** teach by questions and answers. **2** question closely.

**ca vort** (kə vôrt′), *v.* prance about; jump around: *The children cavorted about the field, racing and tumbling.*

**cen sure** (sen′shər), *n., v.,* **-sured, -sur ing.** —*n.* **1** expression of disapproval; unfavorable opinion; criticism. **2** penalty, as a public rebuke or suspension from office. —*v.t.* express disapproval of; find fault with; criticize. [< Latin *censura* < *censere* appraise]

**ces sa tion** (se sā′shən), *n.* a ceasing; a stopping. [< Latin *cessationem* < *cessare* cease]

**chaff** (chaf), *n.* **1** the tough, outer skin of wheat, oats, rye, etc., especially when separated from grain by threshing. **2** worthless stuff; rubbish. [Old English *ceaf*]

**cha grin** (shə grin′), *n.* a feeling of disappointment, failure, or humiliation. —*v.t.* cause to feel chagrin. [< French, apparently < *chat* cat + *grigner* to purse (the lips)]

**cham ber lain** (chām′bər lən), *n.* **1** person who manages the household of a sovereign or great noble. **2** a high official of a royal court. **3** treasurer: *city chamberlain.* [< Old French *chamberlenc*]

**chap lain** (chap′lən), *n.* clergyman authorized or appointed to perform religious functions for a family, court, society, public institution, or unit in the armed forces. [< Old French *chapelain* minister of a chapel < Medieval Latin *capellanus* < *cappella*]

**cha ris ma** (kə riz′mə), *n., pl.* **-ma ta** (-mə tə) a mysterious power to fascinate and attract; great personal magnetism or glamor: *the charisma of a popular leader.*

**chasm** (kaz′əm), *n.* **1** a deep opening or crack in the earth; gap. **2** a wide difference of feelings or interests between people or groups: *The chasm between England and the American colonies*

| a | hat | i | it | oi | oil | ch | child | | |
|---|---|---|---|---|---|---|---|---|---|
| ā | age | ī | ice | ou | out | ng | long | a | in about |
| ä | far | o | hot | u | cup | sh | she | e | in taken |
| e | let | ō | open | u̇ | put | th | thin | ə = i | in pencil |
| ē | equal | ô | order | ü | rule | ŦH | then | o | in lemon |
| ėr | term | | | | | zh | measure | u | in circus |
| | | | | | | | | < | = derived from |

*finally led to the Revolutionary War.* [< Latin *chasma* < Greek]

**che mise** (shə mēz′), *n.* **1** a loose, shirtlike undergarment worn by women and girls. **2** a loosely fitting dress without a belt. [< Old French < Late Latin *camisia* shirt]

**chron ic** (kron′ik), *adj.* **1** lasting a long time: *Rheumatism is often a chronic disease.* **2** suffering long from an illness: *a chronic invalid.* [< Greek *chronikos* of time < *chronos* time] —**chron′i cal ly,** *adv.*

**ci ca da** (sə kā′də, sə kä′də), *n.* a large insect, commonly called a locust, with two pairs of thin, transparent wings. The male produces a loud, shrill sound in hot, dry weather by vibrating membranes on the abdomen. [< Latin]

**cin na bar** (sin′ə bär), *n.* **1** artificial mercuric sulfide, used as a red pigment in making paints, dyes, etc. **2** a bright red color; vermilion. —*adj.* bright-red; vermilion. [< Latin *cinnabaris*]

**cir ca** (sėr′kə), *prep.* about; approximately: *Mohammed was born circa* AD*. 570.* [< Latin]

**cir cum scribe** (sėr′kəm skrīb′ sėr′kəm skrīb), *v.t.,* **-scribed, -scrib ing. 1** draw a line around; mark the boundaries of; bound. **2** surround: *the atmosphere circumscribing the earth.* **3** limit; restrict: *A prisoner's activities are circumscribed.* [< Latin *circumscribere* < *circum* around + *scribere* write]

**cite** (sīt), *v.t.,* **cit ed, cit ing. 1** quote (a passage, book, or author), especially as an authority: *I cited the encyclopedia to prove my statement.* **2** refer to; mention as an example: *The lawyer cited another case similar to the one being tried.* [< Latin *citare* summon < *ciere* set in motion]

**clam or** (klam′ər), *n.* **1** a loud noise or continual uproar; shouting. **2** a shout; outcry. **3** a noisy demand or complaint. Also, **clamour.** [< Latin < *clamare* cry out] —**clam′or er,** *n.*

**cleav age** (klē′vij), *n.* a cleaving or a being cleft; split; division.

**cleft** (kleft), —*adj.* split; divided: *a cleft stick.* —*n.* space or opening made by splitting; crack; fissure. [Old English *(ge)clyft*]

**clem en cy** (klem′ən sē), *n., pl.* **-cies. 1** gentleness in the use of power or authority; mercy or leniency: *The judge showed clemency to the prisoner.* **2** mildness: *the clemency of the weather.*

**co ag u late** (kō ag′yə lāt), *v.t., v.i.,* **-lat ed, -lat ing.** change from a liquid into a thickened mass; thicken: *Cooking coagulates the whites of egg. Blood from a cut coagulates.* [< Latin *coagulatum* curdled < *coagulum* means of curdling < *co-* together + *agere* drive] —**co ag′u la′tion,** *n.*

**co a li tion** (kō′ə lish′ən), *n.* **1** union; combination. **2** alliance of statesmen, political parties, etc., for some special purpose. In wartime several countries may form a temporary coalition against a common enemy. [< Medieval Latin *coalitionem* < Latin *coalescere.*

**cob** (kob), *n.* **1** corncob. **2** a strong horse with short legs. **3** a male swan. [Middle English *cobbe* stout man]

**cog ni zance** (kog′nə zəns, kon′ə zəns), *n.* knowledge; perception; awareness. [< Old French *conoissance* < *connoistre* know < Latin *cognoscere.*]

**com mis sion** (kə mish′ən), *v.t.* **1** give (a person) the power, right, or duty (to do something); give authority to; license; authorize; empower: *I commissioned a real estate agent to sell my house.* **2** give a commission to. **3** put into active service; make ready for use. A new warship is commissioned when it has the officers, sailors, and supplies needed for a voyage [< Latin *commissionem* < *committere* commit]

**com mod i ty** (kə mod′ə tē), *n., pl.* **-ties. 1** anything that is bought and sold: *Groceries are commodities.* **2** a useful thing.

**com mon er** (kom′ə nər), *n.* one of the common people; person who is not a noble.

**com mon wealth** (kom′ən welth′), *n.* **1** the people who make up a nation; citizens of a state. **2** a democratic state; republic.

**com pact** (kom′pakt), *n.* agreement or contract. [< Latin *compactum* < *com-* together + *pacisci* make an agreement]

**com pass** (kum′pəs), *n.* **1** instrument for showing directions, consisting of a needle or compass card that points to the North Magnetic Pole. **2** boundary; circumference. **3** space within limits; extent; range: *There have been many scientific advancements within the compass of my lifetime.* [< Old French *compas* < *compasser* divide equally < Latin *com-* with + *passus* step]

**com pla cen cy** (kəm plā′sn sē), *n.* a being pleased with oneself or what one has; self-satisfaction: *She solved the difficult puzzle easily and smiled with complacency.*

**com pla cent** (kəm plā′snt), *adj.* pleased with oneself or what one has; self-satisfied. [< Latin *complacentem* < *com-* + *placere* please] —**com pla′cent ly,** *adv.*

**com pressed** (kəm prest′), *adj.* **1** squeezed together; made smaller by pressure. **2** flattened.

**con** (kon), *v.t.,* **conned, con ning.** **1** learn well enough to remember; study. **2** examine carefully; pore over. [< Old English *cunnian* test, examine]

**con cave** (kon kav′, kon′kāv, kong′kāv), *adj.* hollow and curved like the inside of a circle or sphere; curving in. [< Latin *concavus* < *com-* + *cavus* hollow] —**con cave′ly,** *adv.*

**con cep tion** (kən sep′shən), *n.* **1** thought; idea; impression: *Your conception of the problem is different from mine.* **2** design; plan. —**con cep′tion al,** *adj.*

**con dole** (kən dōl′), *v.i.,* **-doled, -dol ing.** express sympathy; grieve; sympathize: *Their friends condoled with them at the funeral.* [< Latin *condolere* < *com-* with + *dolere* grieve, suffer]

**con du it** (kon′dü it, kon′dit), *n.* **1** channel or pipe for carrying liquids long distances. **2** pipe or underground passage for electric wires or cables. [< Old French < Medieval Latin *conductus* a leading, a pipe < Latin *conducere* to lead. Doublet of CONDUCT.]

**con fab u late** (kən fab′yə lāt), *v.i.,* **-lat ed, -lat ing.** talk together informally and intimately; chat. [ultimately < Latin < *com-* together + *fabulari* talk < *fabula* fable] —**con fab′u la′tion,** *n.*

**con fis cate** (kon′fə skāt), *v.t.,* **-cat ed, -cat ing.** **1** seize for the public treasury: *The new government confiscated the property of all the deposed leaders.* **2** seize by authority; take and keep: *The teacher confiscated my comic book.* [< Latin *confiscatum* laid away in a chest < *com-* + *fiscus* chest, public treasury]

**con gen ial** (kən jē′nyəl), *adj.* **1** having similar tastes and interests; getting on well together: *congenial companions.* **2** agreeable; suitable: *congenial work.* [< *con-* + Latin *genialis* < *genius* spirit] —**con gen′ial ly,** *adv.*

**con nois seur** (kon′ə sér′), *n.* a critical judge of art or of matters of taste; expert: *a connoisseur of antique furniture.* [< Old French < *connoistre* know < Latin *cognoscere*]

**con science** (kon′shəns), *n.* sense of right and wrong; ideas and feelings within a person that warn of what is wrong.

**con sci en tious** (kon′shē en′shəs), *adj.* **1** careful to do what one knows is right; controlled by conscience. **2** done with care to make it right; painstaking: *conscientious work.* —**con′sci en′tious ly,** *adv.* —**con′sci en′tious ness,** *n.*

**con se crate** (kon′sə krāt), *v.,* **crat ed, -crat ing,** *adj.* —*v.t.* **1** set apart as sacred; make holy; sanctify: *The new chapel in the church was consecrated by the bishop.* **2** make an object of veneration or cherished regard; hallow: *Time has consecrated these customs.* **3** devote to a purpose; dedicate: *She consecrated her life to helping the sick.* —*adj.* ARCHAIC. consecrated. [< Latin *consecratum* made sacred < *com-* + *sacer* sacred] —**con′se cra′tor,** *n.*

**con sign ment** (kən sīn′mənt), *n.* **1** act of consigning. **2** something consigned, especially a shipment sent to a person or company for safekeeping or sale.

**con so la tion** (kon′sə lā′shən), *n.* **1** a consoling. **2** a being consoled. **3** a comforting person, thing, or event. —*adj.* between losers in an earlier round of a tournament: *a consolation match.*

**con sort** (*n.* kon′sôrt; *v.* kən sôrt′), *n.* **1** husband or wife. **2** an associate. —*v.i.* **1** keep company; associate: *consorting with a rough gang.* **2** agree; accord. [< Middle French < Latin *consortem* sharer < *com-* with + *sortem* lot]

**con ster na tion** (kon′stər nā′shən), *n.* great dismay; paralyzing terror: *To our consternation the child darted out in front of the speeding car.* [< Latin *consternationem* < *consternare* terrify]

**con strain** (kən strān′), *v.t.* force; compel: *The evidence constrained me to question them further.*

**con straint** (kən strānt′), *n.* **1** a holding back of natural feelings; forced or unnatural manner; embarrassed awkwardness. **2** force; compulsion. **3** confinement. **4** restraint.

**con sum mate** (*v.* kon′sə māt; *adj.* kən sum′it), *v.,* **-mat ed, -mat ing,** *adj.* —*v.t.* bring to completion; realize; fulfill: *My ambition was consummated when I won the first prize.* —*adj.* in the highest degree; complete; perfect. [< Latin *consummatum* brought to a peak < *com-* + *summa* peak] —**con sum′mate ly,** *adv.*

**con ta gion** (kən tā′jən), *n.* **1** the spreading of disease by direct or indirect contact. **2** disease spread in this way; contagious disease. **3** the spreading of any influence from one person to another: *At the cry of "Fire!" a contagion of fear swept through the audience.* [< Latin *contagionem* a touching < *contingere*]

**con tem pla tion** (kon′təm plā′shən), *n.* **1** a looking at or thinking about something for a long time. **2** deep thought; meditation: *sunk in contemplation.* **3** expectation or intention.

**con temp tu ous** (kən temp′chü əs), *adj.* showing contempt; scornful: *a contemptuous look.* —**con temp′tu ous ly,** *adv.* —**con temp′tu ous ness,** *n.*

**con tin gen cy** (kən tin′jən sē), *n., pl.* **-cies.** **1** a happening or event depending on something that is uncertain; possibility: *The explorer carried supplies for every contingency.* **2** an accidental happening; chance.

**con tri tion** (kən trish′ən), *n.* **1** sorrow for one's sins or guilt; being contrite; penitence. **2** deep regret.

**con trive** (kən trīv′), *v.t.,* **-trived, -triv ing.** **1** plan with cleverness or skill; invent; design: *contrive a new kind of engine.* **2** plan; scheme; plot: *contrive a robbery.* **3** manage: *I will contrive to be there by ten o'clock.* **4** bring about. [< Old French *controver* < Late Latin *contropare* compare] —**con triv′er,** *n.*

**con ven ience** (kən vē′nyəns), *n.* **1** fact or quality of being convenient: *The convenience of packaged goods increases their sale.* **2** comfort; advantage; accommodation: *Many stores have a delivery service for the convenience of shoppers.* **3** anything handy or easy to use; thing that saves trouble or work: *A folding table is a convenience in a small room.*

**con vex** (kon veks′, kon′veks), *adj.* curved out like the outside of a circle or sphere; curving out: *The lens of an automobile headlight is convex.* [< Latin *convexus*] —**con vex′ly,** *adv.*

**con vic tion** (kən vik′shən), *n.* **1** act of proving or declaring guilty. **2** a being convinced. **3** firm belief; certainty.

**con vulse** (kən vuls′), *v.t.,* **-vulsed, -vuls ing.** **1** shake violently: *An earthquake convulsed the island.* **2** cause violent disturbance in; disturb violently: *His face was convulsed with rage.* **3** throw into convulsions; shake with muscular spasms: *The sick child was convulsed before the doctor came.* [< Latin *convulsum* torn away < *com-* + *vellere* to tear]

**con vul sion** (kən vul′shən), *n.* **1** Often, **convulsions,** *pl.* a violent, involuntary contracting and relaxing of the muscles; spasm; fit. **2** a fit of laughter. **3** a violent disturbance: *The country was undergoing a political convulsion.*

**con vul sive** (kən vul′siv), *adj.* **1** violently disturbing. **2** having convulsions. **3** producing convulsions. —**con vul′sive ly,** *adv.*

**coop er** (kü′pər, kup′ər), *n.* person who makes or repairs barrels, casks, etc. —*v.t.* make or repair (barrels, casks, etc.). [perhaps < Middle Dutch *kuper* < Latin *cuparius* < *cupa* cask]

**copse** (kops), *n.* thicket of small trees, bushes, shrubs, etc.; coppice. [< Old French *coupeïz* a cut-over forest < *couper* to cut]

**co quette** (kō ket′), *n.* woman who tries to attract men; flirt. [< French, feminine of *coquet*, diminutive of *coq* cock]

**co quet tish** (kō ket′ish), *adj.* **1** of a coquette, or flirt. **2** like a coquette; like a coquette's: *coquettish behavior,* —**co quet′tish ly,** *adv.*

**co ro na tion** (kôr′ə nā′shən, kor′ə nā′shən), *n.* ceremony of crowning a king, queen, emperor, etc.

**co ro ner** (kôr′ə nər, kor′ə nər), *n.* official of a local government whose principal function is to inquire in the presence of a jury into the cause of any death not clearly due to natural causes. [< Anglo-French *corouner* officer of the crown < *coroune*]

**co ro net** (kôr′ə net′, kor′ə net′), *n.* **1** a small crown, especially one indicating a rank of nobility below that of the sovereign. **2** a circle of gold, jewels, or flowers worn around the head as an ornament.

**cor por al** (kôr′pər əl), *adj.* of the body: *corporal punishment.* [< Latin *corporalem* < *corpus* body] —**cor′por al ly,** *adv.*

**cor ru gat ed** (kôr′ə gā′tid, kor′ə gā′tid), *adj.* bent or shaped into wavy ridges; wrinkled: *corrugated paper, corrugated iron.* [< Latin *corrugatum* wrinkled < *com-* + *ruga* wrinkle]

**coun te nance** (koun′tə nəns), *n., v.,* -**nanced, -nanc ing.** —*n.* **1** expression of the face: *an angry countenance.* **2** face; features: *a noble countenance.* **3** approval; encouragement: *They gave countenance to our plan, but no active help.* **4** calmness; composure: *lose countenance.* —*v.t.* approve or encourage; sanction: *I will not countenance such a plan.* [< Old French *contenance* < Medieval Latin *continentia* demeanor < Latin, self-control < *continere.*]

**coun ter cur rent** (koun′tər kėr′ənt), *n.* current running in the opposite direction; opposing current.

**coun ter pane** (koun′tər pān′), *n.* an outer covering for a bed; bedspread. [alteration of *counterpoint* quilt < Old French *cuilte-pointe* quilt stitched through]

**cou pé** (kü pā′), *n.* a four-wheeled, closed carriage with a seat for two people inside and a seat for the driver outside.

**cou pling** (kup′ling), *n.* **1** a joining together. **2** device for joining together parts of machinery. **3** a railroad coupler.

**cours er** (kôr′sər, kōr′sər), *n.* ARCHAIC. a swift horse.

**cour te sy** (kėr′tə sē), *n., pl.* -**sies.** curtsy; bow of respect or greeting by women and girls, made by bending the knees and lowering the body slightly. [< Old French *cortesie* < *cort* court < Latin *cohortem* retinue, enclosure]

**cour ti er** (kôr′tē ər, kōr′tē ər), *n.* person often present at a royal court; court attendant.

**cov et** (kuv′it), *v.t.* desire eagerly (something that belongs to another). [< Old French *coveitier* < Popular Latin *cupiditare* < Latin *cupiditatem*]

**cov et ous** (kuv′ə təs), *adj.* desiring things that belong to others.

**cov ey** (kuv′ē), *n., pl.* -**eys. 1** brood of partridge, quail, etc. **2** a small group; company. [< Old French *covee* < *cover* incubate < Latin *cubare* to lie]

**coz en** (kuz′n), *v.t., v.i.* deceive or trick; cheat; beguile. [perhaps < Italian *cozzonare* play the crafty knave] —**coz′en er,** *n.*

**cra ven** (krā′vən), *adj.* cowardly. —*n.* coward. [< Old French *cravente* overcome < Popular Latin *crepantare* < Latin *crepare* crush; burst] —**cra′ven ly,** *adv.* —**cra′ven ness,** *n.*

**cred i tor** (kred′ə tər), *n.* person to whom money or goods are due; one to whom a debt is owed.

**cre du li ty** (krə dü′lə tē, krə dyü′lə tē), *n.* a too great readiness to believe.

**crest fall en** (krest′fô′lən), *adj.* dejected; discouraged.

**cringe** (krinj), *v.,* **cringed, cring ing. 1** shrink from danger or pain; crouch in fear. **2** try to get favor or attention by servile behavior: *The courtiers cringed before the king.*

**croon** (krün), *v.i., v.t.* **1** hum, sing, or murmur in a low tone: *I crooned to the baby.* **2** sing in a low, sentimental voice. —*n.* a low humming, singing, or murmuring. [apparently < Middle Dutch *krōnen* to murmur] —**croon′er,** *n.*

**cro quet** (krō kā′), *n.* an outdoor game played by driving wooden balls through wickets with mallets. [< French, dialectal variant of *crochet.*]

**crup per** (krup′ər), *n.* **1** strap attached to the back of a harness and passed under a horse's tail to prevent the harness from slipping forward. **2** rump of a horse. [< Old French *cropiere* < *crope, croupe* croup]

| a hat | i it | oi oil | ch child | | a in about |
|---|---|---|---|---|---|
| ā age | ī ice | ou out | ng long | | e in taken |
| ä far | o hot | u cup | sh she | ə = | i in pencil |
| e let | ō open | ů put | th thin | | o in lemon |
| ē equal | ô order | ü rule | ᴛʜ then | | u in circus |
| ėr term | | | zh measure | < = derived from |

**cum ber** (kum′bər), *v.t.* **1** hold back (from running, doing, etc.); hinder. **2** block up; fill. [< Old French *combrer* impede < *combre* barrier]

**cur** (kėr), *n.* **1** a dog of mixed breed; mongrel. **2** a surly, contemptible person. [Middle English *curre,* probably < Scandinavian (Old Icelandic) *kurra* snarl]

**cur ry** (kėr′ē), *n., pl.* -**ries.** a peppery sauce or powder of spices, seeds, vegetables, etc. Curry is a popular seasoning in India. [< Tamil *kari* sauce]

**cur tail** (kėr′tāl′), *v.t.* cut short; cut off part of; reduce; lessen. [< obsolete *curtal,* adjective, cut short (especially of tails) < Old French *curtald* < *court* short < Latin *curtus* cut short]

**cyn ic** (sin′ik), *n.* **1** person inclined to believe that the motives for people's actions are insincere and selfish. **2** a sneering, sarcastic person.

**cyn i cism** (sin′ə siz′əm), *n.* **1** cynical quality of disposition. **2** a cynical remark.

**daunt** (dônt, dänt), *v.t.* **1** overcome with fear; frighten; intimidate. **2** lessen the courage of; discourage; dishearten. [< Old French *danter* < Latin *domitare* < *domare* to tame]

**daunt less** (dônt′lis, dänt′lis), *adj.* not to be frightened or discouraged; brave. —**daunt′less ly,** *adv.*

**de bouch** (di büsh′), *v.i.* **1** come out from a narrow or confined place into open country: *The crowd debouched from the theater exit into the street.* **2** come out; emerge. [< French *déboucher*] —**de bouch′ment,** *n.*

**de cliv i ty** (di kliv′ə tē), *n., pl.* -**ties.** a downward slope. [< Latin *declivitatem* < *declivis* sloping downward < *de-* + *clivus* slope]

**dec or ous** (dek′ər əs, di kôr′əs, di kōr′əs), *adj.* acting properly; in good taste; well-behaved; dignified. [< Latin *decorus* < *decor* seemliness, comeliness] —**dec′or ous ly,** *adv.* —**dec′or ous ness,** *n.*

**de fer** (di fėr′), *v.t., v.i.,* -**ferred, -fer ring.** put off to some later time; delay; postpone: *defer an exam.* [< Latin *differre*]

**de file** (di fīl′, dē′fīl), *n., v.,* -**filed, -fil ing.** —*n.* a steep and narrow valley. —*v.i.* march in single file or a narrow column. [< French *défiler*]

**deign** (dān), *v.i.* think fit; condescend. —*v.t.* condescend to give (an answer, a reply, etc.). [< Old French *deignier* < Latin *dignari* < *dignus* worthy]

**de mean** (di mēn′), *v.t.* lower in dignity or standing; humble; degrade: *Liars demean themselves.* [< *de-* down + *mean²*]

**de mean ing** (di mē′ning), *adj.* that demeans or debases: *a demeaning task.* —**de mean′ing ly,** *adv.*

**de mean or** (di mē′nər), *n.* way a person looks and acts; behavior; manner.

**de mo ni ac** (di mō′nē ak), *adj.* **1** of or like demons. **2** devilish; fiendish. **3** raging; frantic.

**de mo ni a cal** (dē′mə nī′ə kəl), *adj.* demoniac. —**de′mo ni′a cal ly,** *adv.*

**de mur** (di mėr′), *v.,* -**murred, mur ring,** *n.* —*v.i.* **1** show disapproval or dislike; take exception; object. **2** OBSOLETE. hesitate. —*n.* a demurring; objection; exception. [< Old French *demurer* < Latin *demorari* < *de-* + *morari* to delay]

**de noue ment** or **dé noue ment** (dā′nü män′, dā nü′mäN), *n.* **1** solution of a plot in a story, play, situation, etc.; end. [< French *dénouement* < *dénouer* untie]

**de nounce** (di nouns′), *v.t.,* -**nounced, -nounc ing. 1** condemn publicly; express strong disapproval of. **2** give information against; accuse. [< Old French *denoncer* < Latin *denuntiare* < *de-* + *nuntius* messenger]

**de nun ci a tion** (di nun′sē ā′shən), *n*. **1** expression of strong disapproval; public condemnation; denouncing: *the mayor's denunciation of crime.* **2** an informing against; accusation. **3** a formal notice of the intention to end a treaty, etc.

**de ploy** (di ploi′), *v.t.*, **1** spread out (troops, military units, etc.) from a column into a long battle line. **2** spread out, extend, or place, especially in a planned or strategic position: *deploy offensive missiles, deploy actors on a stage.* [< French *déployer* < *de-* de- + *ployer* to fold]

**de pose** (di pōz′), *v.*, **-posed, -pos ing.** —*v.t.* **1** put out of office or a position of authority, especially a high one like that of king. **2** declare under oath; testify: *The witness deposed that she had seen the accused on the day of the murder.* —*v.i.* testify under oath. [< Old French *deposer* < *de-* down + *poser* put] —**de pos′a ble,** *adj.* —**de pos′er,** *n*.

**dep re da tion** (dep′rə dā′shən), *n*. act of plundering; robbery; ravaging. [< Latin *depraedationem* < *de-* + *praeda* booty]

**der e lict** (der′ə likt), *adj.* abandoned, deserted, or left by its crew, owner, or guardian; forsaken: *a derelict ship.* —*n*. **1** ship abandoned and afloat at sea. **2** any useless, discarded, or forsaken thing. [< Latin *derelictum* abandoned < *de-* + *re-* behind + *linquere* leave]

**de ri sion** (di rizh′ən), *n*. **1** scornful laughter; ridicule. **2** object of ridicule. [< Latin *derisonem* < *deridere.* See DERIDE.]

**de ri sive** (di rī′siv), *adj.* that ridicules; mocking: *derisive laughter.* —**de ri′sive ly,** *adv.* —**de ri′sive ness,** *n*.

**der vish** (dėr′vish), *n*. member of a Moslem religious order that practices self-denial and devotion. Some dervishes dance and spin about violently. [< Turkish *dervis* < Persian *darvish*]

**des ue tude** (des′wə tüd, des′wə tyüd), *n*. disuse: *Many words once commonly used have fallen into desuetude.* [< Latin *desuetudo* < *de-* dis- + *suescere* accustom]

**de void** (di void′), *adj.* entirely without; empty; lacking: *A well devoid of water is useless.* [< Old French *desvoidier* < *des-* dis- + *voidier* to empty]

**dex ter i ty** (dek ster′ə tē), *n*. **1** skill in using the hands or body. **2** skill in using the mind; cleverness.

**dif fuse** (*v.* di fyüz′; *adj.* di fyüs′), *v.*, **-vused, -fus ing,** *adj.* —*v.t.* spread out so as to cover a large space or surface; scatter widely: *The sun diffuses light and heat.* —*v.i.* scatter widely; spread. —*adj.* not concentrated together at a simple point; spread out: *diffuse light.* [< Latin *diffusum* poured forth < *dis-* + *fundere* to pour] —**dif fuse′ly,** *adv.*

**di late** (dī lāt′, də lāt′), *v.*, **-lat ed, -lat ing.** —*v.t.* make larger or wider: *When you take a deep breath, you dilate your nostrils.* —*v.i.* become larger or wider: *The pupil of the eye dilates when the light gets dim.* [< Latin *dilatare* < *dis-* apart + *latus* wide]

**di lem ma** (də lem′ə), *n*. situation requiring a choice between two alternatives, which are or appear equally unfavorable; difficult choice. [< Greek *dilēmma* < *di-* two + *lēmma* premise]

**dil i gent** (dil′ə jənt), *adj.* **1** hard-working; industrious. **2** careful and steady: *a diligent search.* [< Latin *diligentem* < *dis-* apart + *legere* choose] —**dil′i gent ly,** *adv.*

**din** (din), *n., v.,* **dinned, din ning.** —*n*. a continuing loud, confused noise. —*v.i.* make a din. —*v.t.* say over and over again; repeat in a tiresome way. [< Old English *dynn*]

**din gle** (ding′gəl), *n*. a small, deep, shady valley. [origin uncertain]

**dis ap pro ba tion** (dis ap′rə bā′shən), *n*. disapproval.

**dis com fit** (dis kum′fit), *v.t.* **1** defeat the plans or hopes of; frustrate. **2** embarrass; confuse; disconcert. [< Old French *desconfit* discomfited < *des-* dis- + *confire* make, accomplish]

**dis com fi ture** (dis kum′fi chùr, dis kum′fi chər), *n*. **1** defeat of plans or hopes; frustration. **2** confusion.

**dis con tent ed** (dis′kən ten′tid), *adj.* not contented; showing discontent; dissatisfied. —**dis′con tent′ed ly,** *adv.* —**dis′con tent′ed ness,** *n*.

**dis course** (*n.* dis′kôrs, dis′kōrs; *v.* dis kôrs′, dis kōrs′), *n., v.,* **-coursed, -cours ing.** —*n*. **1** a formal or extensive speech or writing: *Lectures and sermons are discourses.* **2** talk; conversation. —*v.i.* **1** speak or write formally or at length on some subject. **2** talk; converse. [< Latin *discursus* a running about < *dis-* + *cursus* a running]

**dis creet** (dis krēt′), *adj.* very careful and sensible in speech and action; having or showing good judgment; wisely cautious. [< Old French *discret* < Late Latin *discretus* discerning < Latin *discernere* discern] —**dis creet′ly,** *adv.* —**dis creet′ness,** *n*.

**dis dain ful** (dis dān′fəl), *adj.* feeling or showing disdain; scornful. —**dis dain′ful ly,** *adv.* —**dis dain′ful ness,** *n*.

**di shev eled** or **di shev elled** (də shev′əld), *adj.* not neat; rumpled; mussed; disordered: *disheveled hair.*

**dis par age** (dis par′ij), *v.t.,* **-aged, -ag ing.** **1** speak slightingly of; belittle. **2** lower the reputation of; discredit. [< Old French *desparagier* match unequally < *des-* dis- + *parage* rank, lineage < *par* peer] —**dis par′age ment,** *n*. —**dis par′ag er,** *n*. —**dis par′ag ing ly,** *adv.*

**dis patch** (dis pach′), *v.t.* **1** send off to some place or for some purpose: *The captain dispatched a boat to bring a doctor on board ship.* **2** get done promptly or speedily; settle; conclude. **3** kill. —*n*. **1** a sending off of a letter, a messenger, etc., to a particular place or on a specified errand: *the dispatch of an embassy.* **2** a written message or communication, such as special news or government business: *a dispatch from the ambassador in France.*

**dis perse** (dis pėrs′), *v.,* **-persed, -pers ing.** —*v.t.* send or drive off in different directions; scatter. —*v.i.* spread in different directions; scatter: *The crowd dispersed when it began raining.* [< Latin *dispersum* dispersed < *dis-* apart + *spargere* to scatter]

**dis po si tion** (dis′pə zish′ən), *n*. **1** one's habitual ways of acting toward others or of thinking about things; nature: *a cheerful disposition.* **2** tendency; inclination: *a disposition to argue.* **3** a putting in a proper or desired order or position; arrangement: *the disposition of desks in a classroom.* **4** a disposing; settlement: *What disposition did the court make of the case?* **5** disposal.

**dis pos sess** (dis′pə zes′), *v.t.* **1** force to give up the possession of a house, land, etc.; oust: *The tenant was dispossessed for not paying rent.* **2** deprive. —**dis′pos ses′sor,** *n*.

**dis sem ble** (di sem′bəl), *v.,* **-bled, -bling.** —*v.t.* hide (one's real feelings, thoughts, plans, etc.); disguise: *She dissembled her anger with a smile.* [alteration (patterned after *resemble*) of obsolete *dissimule* dissimulate]

**dis sen sion** (di sen′shən), *n*. **1** disagreement in opinion that produces strife; discord. **2** a violent disagreement or quarrel.

**dis sim u late** (di sim′yə lāt), *v.,* **-lat ed, -lat ing.** —*v.t.* disguise or hide under a pretense; dissemble. —*v.t.* hide the truth; dissemble. —**dis sim′u la′tion,** *n*. —**dis sim′u la′tor,** *n*.

**dis til late** (dis′tl it, dis′tl āt), *n*. **1** a distilled liquid; something obtained by distilling. **2** anything that is concentrated or abstracted like a distillate; essence: *The book was a distillate of the author's major ideas over the years.* [< Latin *distillare* < *de-* down + *stilla* drop]

**dis tract** (dis trakt′), *v.t.* **1** turn aside or draw away (the mind, attention, etc.): *Noise distracts my attention from study.* **2** confuse; disturb. **3** make insane. —*adj.* ARCHAIC. insane; mad. [< Latin *distractum* drawn away < *dis-* + *trahere* to draw] —**dis tract′ing ly,** *adv.*

**dis traught** (dis trôt′), *adj.* **1** in a state of mental conflict and confusion; distracted. **2** crazed. [variant of obsolete *distract,* adjective, distracted]

**di verge** (də vėrj′, dī vėrj′), *v.,* **-verged, -verg ing.** —*v.i.* move or lie in different directions from the same point; branch off: *Their paths diverged at the fork in the road.* [< Late Latin *divergere* < Latin *dis-* off + *vergere* to slope]

**di verse** (də vėrs′, dī vėrs′), *adj.* **1** not alike; different: *diverse opinions.* **2** varied; diversified. [variant of *divers*] —**di verse′ly,** *adv.* —**di verse′ness,** *n*.

**di vert** (də vėrt′, dī vėrt′), *v.t.* **1** turn aside: *A ditch diverted water from the stream into the fields.* **2** amuse; entertain: *Listening to music diverted me after a hard day's work.* [< Latin *divertere* < *dis-* aside + *vertere* turn]

**di vulge** (də vulj′, dī vulj′), *v.t.,* **-vulged, -vulg ing.** make known or tell openly (something private or secret); reveal. [< Latin *divulgare* make common < *dis-* + *vulgus* common people]

**dog ged** (dô′gid, dog′id), *adj.* not giving up; stubborn: *dogged determination.* [< *dog*] —**dog′ged ly,** *adv.*

**do min ion** (də min′yən), *n.* **1** power or right of governing and controlling; rule; control. **2** territory under the control of one ruler or government.

**dou blet** (dub′lit), *n.* a man's close-fitting jacket. Men in Europe wore doublets from the 1400s to the 1600s.

**dough ty** (dou′tē), *adj.,* **-ti er, -ti est.** strong and bold; stout; brave; hearty. [Old English *dohtig* < *dugan* be of use] —**dough′-ti ly,** *adv.* —**dough′ti ness,** *n.*

**dow ry** (dou′rē), *n., pl.* **-ries. 1** money or property that a woman brings to the man she marries. **2** natural gift, talent, or quality; natural endowment: *Good health and intelligence are a precious dowry.* Also, **dower.** [< Old French *douaire* < Latin *dotare* endow]

**drap er** (drā′pər), *n.* **1** BRITISH. dealer in cloth or dry goods. **2** person who drapes. [< Old French *drap* cloth < Latin *drappus*]

**drom e dar y** (drom′ə der′ē, drum′ə der′ē), *n., pl.* **-dar ies.** a swift camel with one hump and short hair. [< Late Latin *dromedarius* < Greek *dromados (kamēlos)* running (camel) < *dromos* a running]

**du bi ous** (dü′bē əs, dyü′bē əs), *adj.* **1** filled with or being in doubt; doubtful; uncertain: *a dubious compliment.* **2** feeling doubt; wavering or hesitating. **3** of questionable character; probably bad: *a dubious scheme for making money.* [< Latin *dubiosus* < *dubius* doubtful] —**du′bi ous ly,** *adv.*

**dull ard** (dul′ərd), *n.* person who is stupid and learns very slowly.

**dumb** (dum), *adj.* **1** not able to speak. **2** silenced for the moment by fear, surprise, shyness, etc.: *She was struck dumb with astonishment.* **3** unwilling to speak; not speaking; silent.

**dum found** (dum′found′), *v.t.* amaze and make unable to speak; bewilder; confuse. Also, **dumbfound.** [< *dumb* + (*con*)*found*]

**dusk y** (dus′kē), *adj.,* **dusk i er, dusk i est. 1** somewhat dark; dark-colored. **2** dim; obscure. **3** sad; gloomy. —**dusk′i ly,** *adv.* —**dusk′i ness,** *n.*

**ear nest** (ėr′nist), *adj.* **1** strong and firm in purpose; eager and serious. **2** important: *"Life is real, life is earnest."* —*n.* **in earnest,** strong and firm in purpose; eager and serious. [Old English *eornost*] —**ear′nest ly,** *adv.* —**ear′nest ness,** *n.*

**ed dy** (ed′ē), *n., pl.* **-dies,** *v.,* **-died, -dy ing.** —*n.* **1** water, air, smoke, etc., moving against the main current, especially when having a whirling motion; small whirlpool or whirlwind. **2** any similar current of fog or dust. [perhaps < Scandinavian (Old Icelandic) *itha*]

**ef fa ble** (ef′ə bəl), *adj.* utterable; expressible. [abstracted from IN-EFFABLE]

**e gress** (ē′gres), *n.* **1** a going out: *The door was locked and no other egress was possible.* **2** a way out; exit; outlet: *The egress was plainly marked.*

**ei der down** (ī′dər doun′), *n.* **1** the soft feathers from the breasts of eiders, used to stuff pillows and bed quilts, as trimming, etc.; eider. **2** quilt stuffed with these feathers.

**e jac u late** (i jak′yə lāt), *v.t., v.i.,* **-lat ed, -lat ing.** say suddenly and briefly; exclaim. [< Latin *ejaculatum* thrown out < *ex-* out + *jacere* to throw]

**e lat ed** (i lā′tid), *adj.* in high spirits; joyful or proud. [< Latin *elatum* carried away < *ex-* out, away + *latum* carried] —**e lat′ed ly,** *adv.* —**e lat′ed ness,** *n.*

**e la tion** (i lā′shən), *n.* high spirits; joy or pride: *She was filled with elation at having won the first prize.*

**em a nate** (em′ə nāt), *v.,* **-nat ed, -nat ing.** —*v.i.* originate from a person or thing as a source; come forth; spread out: *The rumor emanated from Chicago.* —*v.t.* send out; emit. [< Latin *emanatum* flowed out < *ex-* out + *manare* to flow]

**em bel lish** (em bel′ish), *v.t.* **1** add beauty to; decorate; adorn; ornament. **2** make more interesting by adding real or imaginary details; elaborate: *embellish a story.* [< Old French *embelliss-,* a form of *embellir* embellish < *en-* in + *bel* handsome] —**em bel′lish ment,** *n.*

**em phat ic** (em fat′ik), *adj.* **1** said or done with force or stress;

---

| a hat | i it | oi oil | ch child | | ⎧ a in about |
|---|---|---|---|---|---|
| ā age | ī ice | ou out | ng long | | e in taken |
| ä far | o hot | u cup | sh she | ə = ⎨ i in pencil |
| e let | ō open | u̇ put | th thin | | o in lemon |
| ē equal | ô order | ü rule | ⱦH then | | ⎩ u in circus |
| ėr term | | | zh measure | | < = derived from |

strongly expressed: *Her answer was an emphatic "No!"* **2** attracting attention; very noticeable; striking: *The club made an emphatic success of its party.*

**em u late** (em′yə lāt), *v.t.,* **-lat ed, -lat ing. 1** copy or imitate in order to equal or excel the achievements or qualities of an admired person. **2** vie with; rival. [< Latin *aemulatum* rivaled < *aemulus* striving to equal] —**em′u la′tion,** *n.*

**en deav or** (en dev′ər), *v.i.,* *v.t.* make an effort; try hard; attempt earnestly; strive: *A runner endeavors to win a race.*

**en deav our** (en dev′ər), *v.i.,* *v.t.* BRITISH. endeavor.

**en gen der** (en jen′dər), *v.t.* bring into existence; produce; cause: *Filth engenders disease.* [< Old French *engendrer* < Latin *ingenerare* < *in-* + *generare* create]

**en ven om** (en ven′əm), *v.t.* **1** make poisonous. **2** fill with bitterness, hate, etc.

**ep i taph** (ep′ə taf), *n.* a short statement in memory of a dead person, usually put on a gravestone or tombstone. [< Greek *epitaphion* funeral oration < *epi-* upon + *taphos* tomb]

**eq uer ry** (ek′wər ē), *n., pl.* **-ries** officer of a royal or noble household who has charge of the horses. [< Old French *escuerie* stable]

**ere** (er, ar), ARCHAIC. —*prep.* before. —*conj.* **1** before. **2** sooner than; rather than. [Old English *ǣr*]

**er mine** (ėr′mən), *n., pl.* **-mines** or **mine. 1** any of several kinds of weasel of northern regions which are brown in summer but white with a black-tipped tail in winter. **2** the soft, white fur of the winter phase, used for coats, trimming, etc. [< Old French, probably < Latin *(mus) Armenius* Armenian (rat)]

**ermine** (def. 1)

**er rat ic** (ə rat′ik), *adj.* **1** not steady; uncertain; irregular: *An erratic clock is not dependable.* **2** strange; odd; eccentric: *erratic behavior.* **3** having no certain course; wandering: *an erratic star.* [< Latin *erraticus* < *errare* wander] —**er rat′i cal ly,** *adv.*

**es carp ment** (e skärp′mənt), *n.* **1** a steep slope; cliff. **2** ground made into a steep slope as part of a fortification. [< French]

**es cri toire** (es′krə twär′, es′krə twär), *n.* a writing desk. [< French]

**es sence** (es′ns), *n.* that which makes a thing what it is; necessary part or parts; important feature or features: *Being thoughtful of others is the essence of politeness.* [< Latin *essentia* < *esse* be]

**es tate** (e stāt′), *n.* **1** a large piece of land belonging to a person; landed property: *a beautiful estate with a country house and a lake on it.* **2** that which a person owns; property; possessions: *When she died, her estate was divided among her heirs.*

**es tu ar y** (es′chü er′ē), *n., pl.* **-ar ies. 1** a broad mouth of a river into which the tide flows. **2** inlet of the sea. [< Latin *aestuarium* < *aestus* tide]

**et al., 1** and others [for Latin *et alii* and other persons, or *et alia* and other things]. **2** and elsewhere [for Latin *et alibi*].

**e ther e al** (i thir′ē əl), *adj.* **1** light; airy; delicate: *the ethereal beauty of a butterfly.* **2** not of the earth; heavenly. Also, **aethereal.**

**eu phe mism** (yü′fə miz′əm), *n.* a mild or indirect expression used instead of one that is harsh or unpleasantly direct. *"Pass away"* is a common euphemism for *"die."* [< Greek *euphēmis-*

---

# evocative

*mos* < *euphēmizein* speak with fair words < *eu-* good + *phēmē* speaking < *phanai* speak]

**e voc a tive** (i vok′ə tiv, i vō′kə tiv), *adj.* tending to evoke.

**e voke** (i vōk′), *v.t.*, **e voked, e vok ing.** call forth; bring out; elicit: *A good joke evokes a laugh.* [< Latin *evocare* < *ex-* out + *vocare* to call]

**ex com mu ni ca tion** (ek′skə myü′nə kā′shən), *n.* **1** a formal cutting off from membership in the church; prohibition from participating in any of the rites of the church. **2** an official statement announcing this.

**ex e crate** (ek′sə krāt), *v.*, **-crat ed, -crat ing.** —*v.t.* **1** feel intense loathing for; abhor; detest. **2** pronounce a curse upon. —*v.i.* curse. [< Latin *exsecratum* declared accursed < *ex-* out + *sacer* sacred]

**ex ert** (eg zėrt′), *v.t.* put into use or action; bring into effect; use: *exert both strength and skill, exert authority.*

**ex er tion** (eg zėr′shən), *n.* **1** strenuous action; effort: *The exertions of the firefighters kept the fire from spreading.* **2** a putting into action; active use; use: *exertion of authority.*

**ex e unt** (ek′sē ənt), *v.i.* LATIN. they go out (a stage direction for two or more actors to leave the stage).

**ex hil a ra tion** (eg zil′ə rā′shən), *n.* **1** a being or feeling exhilarated; high spirits; lively joy. **2** an exhilarating. [ Latin *exhilaratum* made merry < *ex-* thoroughly + *hilaris* merry]

**ex i gent** (ek′sə jənt), *adj.* demanding prompt action or attention; urgent; pressing. —*n.* OBSOLETE, time of crisis or need. [< Latin *exigentem* < *ex-* out + *agere* to drive]

**ex o dus** (ek′sə dəs), *n.* a going out; departure, usually of a large number of people.

**ex ploit** (*n.* ek′sploit, ek sploit′; *v.* ek sploit′), *n.* a bold, unusual act; daring deed. —*v.t.* **1** make use of; turn to practical account: *A mine is exploited for its minerals.* **2** make unfair or selfish use of: *Nations used to exploit their colonies, taking as much wealth out of them as they could.* [< Old French *esploit* < Popular Latin *explicitum* achievement < Latin, an unfolding < *ex-* out + *plicare* to fold]

**ex ploi ta tion** (ek′sploi tā′shən), *n.* **1** use: *the exploitation of the ocean as a source for food.* **2** selfish or unfair use.

**ex pound** (ek spound′), *v.t.* **1** make clear; explain, interpret, etc. **2** set forth or state in detail. [< Old French *espondre* < Latin *exponere* < *ex-* forth + *ponere* put] —**ex pound′er,** *n.*

**ex trem i ty** (ek strem′ə tē), *n., pl.* **-ties.** **1** the very end; farthest possible place; last part or point. **2 extremities,** *pl.* the hands and feet. **3** an extreme degree: *Joy is the extremity of happiness.*

**fa cil i tate** (fə sil′ə tāt), *v.t.*, **-tat ed, -tat ing.** make easy; lessen the labor of; help bring about; assist; expedite: *A computer facilitates many tasks.* —**fa cil′i ta′tion,** *n.* —**fa cil′i ta′tor,** *n.*

**fac tion** (fak′shən), *n.* **1** group of persons in a political party, church, club, etc., acting together or having a common purpose. **2** strife or quarreling among the members of a political party, church, club, neighborhood, etc. [< Latin *factionem* party, class, originally, a doing < *facere* do. Doublet of FASHION]

**fac tious** (fak′shəs), *adj.* **1** fond of stirring up disputes; quarrelsome. **2** of or caused by faction. —**fac′tious ly,** *adv.*

**fac ul ty** (fak′əl tē), *n., pl.* **-ties.** **1** of the mind or body; capacity; capability: *the faculty of hearing, the faculty of memory.* **2** power or ability to do some special thing, especially a power of the mind: *She has a great faculty for arithmetic.* **3** the teachers of a school, college, or university. [< Latin *facultatem* < *facilis*]

**fain** (fān), *adv.* ARCHAIC, gladly; willingly. [< Old English *fægen*]

**fa kir** (fə kir′, fā′kər), *n.* **1** a Moslem holy man who lives by begging. **2** dervish. **3** a Hindu ascetic. Fakirs sometimes do extraordinary things, such as lying upon sharp knives. [< Arabic *faqīr* poor (man)]

**fal low** (fal′ō), *adj.* plowed and left unseeded for a season or more. [< Old English *fealg*] —**fal′low ness,** *n.*

**farce** (färs), *n.* **1** a play full of ridiculous happenings and unreal

situations, meant to be very funny. **2** a ridiculous mockery; absurd pretense; sham: *The trial was a mere farce.* [< French, literally, stuffing < Old French *farcir* to stuff < Latin *farcire*]

**fawn** (fôn), *v.i.* try to get favor or notice by slavish acts: *Many flattering relatives fawned on the rich old woman.* [Old English *fagnian* < *fægen* fain] —**fawn′ing ly,** *adv.*

**feint** (fānt), *n.* **1** a false appearance; pretense: *She made a feint of studying, though actually she was listening to the radio.* **2** movement intended to deceive; sham attack; pretended blow. —*v.i.* make a feint: *The fighter feinted with his right hand and struck with his left.* [< French *feinte* < *feindre* feign]

**fel on** (fel′ən), *n.* person who has committed a felony; criminal. [< Old French < Popular Latin *fellonem*]

**fer vent** (fėr′vənt), *adj.* **1** showing great warmth of feeling; very earnest; ardent: *fervent devotion.* **2** hot; glowing; intense. —**fer′vent ly,** *adv.*

**fes ter** (fes′tər), *v.i.* **1** form pus: *The neglected wound festered and became very painful.* **2** cause soreness or pain; rankle: *Resentment festered in her mind.* [< Old French *festre* < Latin *fistula* ulcer]

**fet ter** (fet′ər), *n.* **1** chain or shackle for the feet to prevent escape. **2** Usually, **fetters,** *pl.* anything that shackles or binds; restraint. —*v.t.* **1** bind with chains; chain the feet of. [Old English *feter*. Related to FOOT.]

**fick le** (fik′əl), *adj.* **1** likely to change or give up a loyalty, attachments, etc., without reason; inconstant: *a fickle friend.* **2** likely to change in nature; uncertain: *fickle weather.* [Old English *ficol* deceitful] —**fick′le ness,** *n.*

**fie** (fī), *interj.* for shame! shame! [< Old French *fi*]

**fiend** (fēnd), *n.* **1** an evil spirit; devil; demon. **2 the Fiend,** the Devil. **3** a very wicked or cruel person. [Old English *fēond* enemy, hater]

**fit ful** (fit′fəl), *adj.* going on and then stopping for a while; irregular: *a fitful sleep.* [< *fit*] —**fit′ful ly,** *adv.* —**fit′ful ness,** *n.*

**flag el la tion** (flaj′ə lā′shən), *n.* a whipping; flogging.

**flank** (flangk), *n.* **1** the fleshy or muscular part of the side of an animal or person between the ribs and the hip. **2** side of a mountain, building, etc. —*v.t.* **1** be at the side of: *A garage flanked the house.* **2** get around the far right or the far left side of. **3** attack from or on the side. —*v.i.* **1** occupy a position on a flank or side. **2** present the flank or side. [< Old French *flanc* < Germanic]

**fledg ling** or **fledge ling** (flej′ling), *n.* **1** a young bird that has just grown feathers needed for flying. **2** a young, inexperienced person.

**flot sam** (flot′səm), *n.* wreckage of a ship or its cargo found floating on the sea. [< Anglo-French *floteson* < Old French *floter* to float]

**flush** (flush), *v.i.* **1** become red suddenly; blush; glow. **2** rush suddenly; flow rapidly: *The blood flushed to her cheeks.* —*v.t.* cause to blush or glow: *Exercise flushed her face.*

**flute** (flüt), *n., v.,* **flut ed, flut ing.** —*n.* **1** a long, slender, pipe-like musical instrument, played by blowing across a hole near one end and by stopping holes along the tube with the fingers. **2** an organ stop with a flutelike tone. **3** a long, round groove, especially one of a parallel series cut in a column. **4** a decorative fine groove or crimp pressed into a fabric, as in a ruffle or pleating on a garment. —*v.i.* **1** play on a flute. **2** sing or whistle so as to sound like a flute. —*v.t.* **1** play (a melody, etc.) on a flute. **2** sing, whistle, say, etc., in flutelike tones. **3** make long, round grooves in: *flute a pillar.* [< Old French *fleüte, flaüte* < Provençal *flauta*] —**flute′like′,** *adj.*

**foal** (fōl), *n.* a young horse, donkey, etc.; colt or filly, —*v.t., v.i.* give birth to (a foal). [Old English *fola*]

**fod der** (fod′ər), *n.* coarse food for hoses, cattle, etc. Hay and cornstalks with their leaves are fodder. —*v.t.* give fodder to. [Old English *fōdor* < *fōda* food]

**fo li o** (fō′lē ō), *n., pl.* **-li os,** *adj.* —*n.* **1** a large sheet of paper folded once to make two leaves, or four pages, of a book, etc. **2** volume, usually any book more than 11 inches in height, consisting of sheets folded in this way. —*adj.* having to do with or having the form of a folio: *The encyclopedia was in twenty volumes folio.*

**GLOSSARY**

886

[< Latin, ablative of *folium* leaf]

**ford** (fôrd, fōrd), *n.* place where a river or other body of water is shallow enough to be crossed by wading or driving through the water. —*v.t.* cross (a river, etc.) at a ford. [Old English] —**ford′a ble,** *adj.*

**fore bear** (fôr′ber, fôr′bar; fōr′ber, fōr′bar), *n.* ancestor; forefather. Also, **forbear.** [< fore- + be + -er]

**fore bod ing** (fôr bō′ding, fōr bō′ding), *n.* **1** prediction; warning. **2** a feeling that something bad is going to happen; presentiment. —**fore bod′ing ly,** *adv.*

**fore short en** (fôr shôrt′n, fōr shôrt′n), *v.t.* shorten (lines, objects, etc.) in a drawing or painting in order to give the impression of depth and distance to the eye.

**fore stall** (fôr stôl′, fōr stôl′), *v.t.* prevent by acting first: *The owner forestalled a strike by starting to negotiate early with the union.* [Middle English *forstallen* < Old English *foresteall* prevention]

**for mi da ble** (fôr′mə də bəl), *adj.* hard to overcome: hard to deal with; to be dreaded: *a formidable opponent.* [< Latin *formidabilis* < *formidare* to dread < *formido* terror, dread] —**for′mi da bly,** *adv.*

**forth with** (fôrth′with′, fôrth′wiŦH′; fōrth′with′, fōrth′wiŦH′), *adv.* at once; immediately.

**free think er** (frē′thing′kər), *n.* one who forms opinions, especially on religion, independently of authority or tradition.

**fresh et** (fresh′it), *n.* **1** flood caused by heavy rains or melted snow. **2** stream or rush of fresh water flowing into the sea. [< *fresh* flood, stream, or pool of fresh water + -*et*]

**friv o lous** (friv′ə ləs), *adj.* lacking in seriousness or sense; silly: *Frivolous behavior is out of place in a courtroom.* [< Latin *frivolus*] —**friv′o lous ly,** *adv.*

**frond** (frond), *n.* the leaf of a fern, palm, or cycad. [< Latin *frondem* leaf]

**fur tive** (fėr′tiv), *adj.* **1** done quickly and with stealth to avoid being noticed; secret: *a furtive glance into the forbidden room.* **2** sly; stealthy: *a furtive manner.* [< Latin *furtivus* < *furtum* theft < *fur* thief] —**fur′tive ly,** *adv.* —**fur′tive ness,** *n.*

**fu sil lade** (fyü′zə läd′), *n.* **1** a rapid or continuous discharge of many firearms at the same time. **2** any rapid discharge or burst: *The reporters greeted the mayor with a fusillade of questions.* [< French]

**fu tile** (fyü′tl, fyü′tīl), *adj.* **1** not successful; useless; ineffectual: *He fell down after making futile attempts to keep his balance.* **2** not important; trifling. [< Latin *futilis* pouring easily, worthless < *fundere* pour] —**fu′tile ly,** *adv.*

**fu til i ty** (fyü til′ə tē), *n., pl.* -**ties.** **1** uselessness; ineffectiveness. **2** unimportance. **3** futile action, event, etc.

**gab ble** (gab′əl), *v.,* -**bled, -bling,** —*v.i.* talk rapidly with little or no meaning; jabber. —*n.* rapid talk with little or no meaning. [probably imitative] —**gab′bler,** *n.*

**gab er dine** (gab′ər dēn′, gab′ər dēn′), *n.* a man's long, loose outer garment or cloak, worn in the Middle Ages.

**gal lows** (gal′ōz), *n., pl.* -**lows es** or -**lows.** **1** a wooden structure usually consisting of a crossbar on two upright posts, used for hanging criminals. **2** punishment by hanging. [Middle English *galwes, galghes,* Old English *galga*]

**gal va nize** (gal′və nīz), *v.t.,* -**nized, -niz ing. 1** arouse suddenly; startle. **2** cover (iron or steel) with a thin coating of zinc to prevent rust. [< Luigi *Galvani*]

**gan gling** (gang′gling), *adj.* awkwardly tall and slender; lank and loosely built.

**gaunt** (gônt, gänt), *adj.* very thin and bony; with hollow eyes and a starved look: *Sickness had made him gaunt.* [origin uncertain]

**ge ne al o gist** (jē′nē al′ə jist, jē′nē ol′ə jist; jen′ē al′ə jist, jen′ē ol′ə jist), *n.* person who makes a study of or traces genealogies; that is, descents of persons or families from their ancestors.

**gen ial** (jē′nyəl), *adj.* **1** smiling and pleasant; cheerful and friendly; kindly: *a genial welcome.* **2** helping growth; pleasantly warming; comforting: *a genial climate.* [< Latin *genialis,* literally belonging to the genius < *genius* genius] —**ge′ni al′i ty** (jē′nē al′ə tē), *n.* —**gen′ial ly,** *adv.* —**gen′ial ness,** *n.*

**gen tile** or **Gen tile** (jen′tīl), *n.* person who is not a Jew. [< Late

| | | | | | |
|---|---|---|---|---|---|
| **a** hat | **i** it | **oi** oil | **ch** child | | ( a in about |
| **ā** age | **ī** ice | **ou** out | **ng** long | | e in taken |
| **ä** far | **o** hot | **u** cup | **sh** she | ə = | i in pencil |
| **e** let | **ō** open | **ù** put | **th** thin | | o in lemon |
| **ē** equal | **ô** order | **ü** rule | **ŦH** then | | u in circus |
| **ėr** term | | | **zh** measure | **<** = derived from |

Latin *gentilis* foreign < Latin, of a people, national]

**gen u flect** (jen′yə flekt), *v.i.* bend the knee as an act of reverence or worship. [< Medieval Latin *genuflectere* < Latin *genu* knee + *flectere* bend] —**gen′u flec′tion,** *n.*

**ge ra ni um** (jə rā′nē əm), *n.* **1** any of a genus of cultivated or wild plants, usually having deeply notched leaves and showy white, pink, red, or purple flowers; cranesbill. **2** the flower of any of these plants. **3** pelargonium. [< Latin < Greek *geranion* < *geranos* crane; from resemblance of seed pod to crane's bill]

**ger mane** (jər mān′), *adj.* closely connected; to the point; pertinent. [ variant of *german*]

**ges tic u late** (je stik′yə lāt), *v.i.,* -**lat ed, -lat ing.** make or use gestures to show ideas or feelings. [< Latin *gesticulatum* gesticulated, ultimately < *gestus* gesture] —**ges tic′u la′tion,** *n.*

**gew gaw** (gyü′gô), *n.* a showy trifle; gaudy, useless ornament or toy; bauble. —*adj.* showy but trifling. [Middle English *giuegoue*]

**gild** (gild), *v.t.,* **gild ed** or **gilt, gild ing. 1** cover with a thin layer of gold or similar material; make golden. **2** make (something) look bright and pleasing. [Old English -*glydan* < *gold* gold]

**ging ham** (ging′əm), *n.* a cotton cloth made from colored threads. Its patterns are usually in stripes, plaids, or checks. [< French *guingan* < Malay *ginggang* striped]

**glade** (glād), *n.* **1** a small, open space in a wood or forest. **2** everglade. [probably related to GLAD]

**gourd** (gôrd, gōrd, gůrd), *n.* **1** any of various fleshy fruits that grow on vines and are related to squash. **2** cup, bowl, etc., made from the dried shell of a gourd. [< Old French *gourde,* ultimately < Latin *cucurbita*]

**gra di ent** (grā′dē ənt), *n.* **1** rate of upward or downward slope of a road, railroad track, etc.: *steep gradients.* **2** the sloping part of a road, railroad, etc.; grade. [< Latin *gradientem* walking, going, related to *gradus* step, degree]

**grail** (grāl), *n.* (in medieval legends) the cup or dish used by Jesus at the Last Supper, and by one of His followers to catch the last drops of Jesus' blood at the Cross; Holy Grail. [< Old French *graal* < Medieval Latin *gradalis* bowl, cup]

**grate ful** (grāt′fəl), *adj.* **1** feeling kindly because of a favor received; wanting to do a favor in return; thankful. **2** pleasing; welcome: *a grateful breeze on a hot day.* [< obsolete *grate* agreeable (< Latin *gratus*) + -*ful*] —**grate′ful ly,** *adv.* —**grate′ful ness,** *n.*

**grat i fy** (grat′ə fī), *v.t.,* -**fied, -fy ing. 1** give pleasure to; please: *Flattery gratifies a vain person.* **2** give satisfaction to; satisfy; indulge: *gratify one's hunger with a large meal.* [< Latin *gratificari* < *gratus* pleasing + *facere* make, do]

**gra ting** (grā′ting), *n.* framework of parallel or crossed bars.

**grav i ty** (grav′ə tē), *n., pl.* -**ties. 1** the natural force that causes objects to move or tend to move toward the center of the earth and causes objects to have weight. **2** seriousness; earnestness. [< Latin *gravitatem* < *gravis* heavy]

**guild** (gild), *n.* **1** association or society formed by people having the same interests, work, etc., for some useful or common purpose: *the hospital guild of a church.* **2** (in the Middle Ages) an association of merchants in a town or of persons in a particular trade or craft, formed to keep standards high, promote their business interests, protect themselves, etc. Also, **gild.** [< Scandinavian (Old Icelandic) *gildi*]

**gut tur al** (gůt′ər əl), *adj.* **1** of the throat. **2** formed in the throat; harsh: *speak in a deep, guttural voice.* **3** formed between the back of the tongue and the soft palate. The g in *go* is a guttural sound. —*n.* sound formed between the back of the tongue and the soft palate. The sound *k* is a guttural in the word *cool*. [< Latin *guttur* throat] —**gut′tur al ly,** *adv.* —**gut′tur al ness,** *n.*

**gy rate** (jī′rāt, jī rāt′), *v.i.*, **-rat ed, -rat ing.** move in a circle or spiral; whirl; rotate. [< Latin *gyrus* circle < Greek *gyros*]

**ha bil i ment** (hə bil′ə mənt), *n.* **1 habiliments,** *pl.* articles of clothing; garments. **2** dress; attire. [< Old French *habillement*]

**hag gard** (hag′ərd), *adj.* looking worn from pain, fatigue, worry, hunger, etc.; careworn; gaunt. [perhaps < Old French *hagard*] —**hag′gard ly,** *adv.* —**hag′gard ness,** *n.*

**hag gle** (hag′əl), *v.*, **-gled, -gling.** —*v.i.* dispute, especially about a price or the terms of a bargain. [< Scottish *hag* to chop < Scandinavian (Old Icelandic) *höggva*]

**hal berd** (hal′bərd), *n.* weapon of the 1400s and 1500s used as a spear and as a battle-ax. [< Middle French *hallebarde* < Italian *alabarda*]

**hale**[1] (hāl), *adj.*, **hal er, hal est.** free from infirmity; strong and well. [Old English *hāl*]

**hale**[2] (hāl), *v.t.*, **haled, hal ing.** **1** compel to go. **2** drag by force. [< Old French *haler*, of Germanic origin. Doublet of HAUL.]

**ham let** (ham′lit), *n.* a small village; little group of houses in the country. [< Old French *hamelet*, diminutive of *hamel* village, of Germanic origin.]

**hard tack** (härd′tak′), *n.* a very hard, dry biscuit that resists spoiling, formerly eaten on shipboard; sea biscuit. [< *hard* + *tack* food, of unknown origin]

**halberd held by a soldier**

**har row** (har′ō), *n.* a heavy frame with iron teeth or upright disks, used by farmers to break up ground into fine pieces before planting seeds. —*v.t.* **1** pull a harrow over (land, etc.). **2** hurt; wound. **3** cause pain or torment to; distress. [Middle English *harwe*]

**hearth** (härth), *n.* **1** stone or brick floor of a fireplace, often extending into the room. **2** fireside; home: *The travelers began to long for their own hearths.* [< Old English *hearth*]

**helm** (helm), *n.* ARCHAIC. helmet. [Old English]

**hem** (hem), *n.*, *v.*, **hemmed, hem ming.** —*n.* **1** border or edge on a garment; edge made on cloth by folding it over and sewing it down. **2** border; edge. —*v.t.* **1** fold over and sew down the edge of (cloth). **2 hem in, hem around,** or **hem about, a** surround on all sides. **b** keep from getting away or moving freely. [Old English *hemm*] —**hem′mer,** *n.*

**hew** (hyü), *v.*, **hewed, hewed** or **hewn, hew ing.** —*v.t.* **1** cut with an ax, sword, etc.; chop: *He hewed down the tree.* **2** cut into shape; form by cutting with an ax, etc.: *hew stone for building, hew logs into beams.* —*v.i.* hold firmly (to); stick fast or cling (to): *hew to the rules.* [Old English *hēawan*] —**hew′er,** *n.*

**hi a tus** (hī ā′təs), *n.*, *pl.* **-tus es** or **-tus.** an empty space; space from which something necessary to completeness is missing; gap, [Latin, gap < *hiare* to gape]

**hie** (hī), *v.*, **hied, hie ing** or **hy ing.** —*v.i.* go quickly; hasten; hurry. —*v.t.* cause to hasten. [Old English *hīgian*]

**high boy** (hī′boi′), *n.* a tall chest of drawers on legs.

**hind** (hīnd), *n.*, *pl.* **hinds** or **hind.** a female deer, especially a female red deer in and after its third year. [Old English]

**hin ter land** (hin′tər land′), *n.* **1** land or district behind a coast. **2** region far from towns and cities; thinly settled country.

**hire ling** (hīr′ling), *n.* person who works only for money, without interest or pride in the work.

**hir sute** (hėr′süt), *adj.* hairy. [< Latin *hirsutus*]

**hom i cide** (hom′ə sīd, hō′mə sīd), *n.* a killing of one human being by another. Intentional homicide is murder. [< Old French, ultimately < Latin *homo* human being, man + *-cidium* act of killing or *-cida* killer]

**hos tler** (os′lər, hos′lər), *n.* person who takes care of horses at an inn or stable. Also, **ostler.** [Middle English < Old French *hostelier* < *hostel*]

**hov er** (huv′ər, hov′ər), *v.i.* **1** hang fluttering or suspended in air: *The two birds hovered over their nest.* **2** stay in or near one place; wait nearby: *The dogs hovered around the kitchen door at mealtime.* **3** be in an uncertain condition: *The patient hovered between life and death.* [Middle English *hoveren*] —**hov′er er,** *n.*

**hum mock** (hum′ək), *n.* **1** a very small, rounded hill; knoll; hillock. **2** a bump or ridge in a field of ice. **3** a raised, often fertile, area surrounded by marsh or swampland. [origin unknown]

**hus band** (huz′bənd), *n.* man who has a wife; a married man. —*v.t.* **1** manage carefully; be saving of: *husband one's strength.* **2** marry. [Old English *huūsbōnda* < Scandinavian (Old Icelandic) *hūsbōndi* < *hūs* house + *bōndi* freeholder]

**ig no ble** (ig nō′bəl), *adj.* **1** without honor; disgraceful; base: *To betray a friend is ignoble.* **2** not of noble birth or position; humble. [< Latin *ignobilis* < *in-* not + *nobilis* noble] —**ig no′bly,** *adv.*

**ig no min i ous** (ig′nə min′ē əs), *adj.* **1** shameful; disgraceful; dishonorable: *an ignominious defeat.* **2** contemptible. **3** lowering one's dignity; humiliating. —**ig′no min′i ous ly,** *adv.* —**ig′no min′i ous ness,** *n.*

**il lim it a ble** (i lim′ə tə bəl), *adj.* without limit; boundless; infinite. —**il lim′it a ble ness,** *n.* —**il lim′it a bly,** *adv.*

**il lit er ate** (i lit′ər it), *adj.* **1** unable to read and write: *People who have never gone to school are usually illiterate.* **2** showing a lack of education; not cultured: *illiterate writing.* —*n.* **1** person who is unable to read and write. **2** an uneducated person.

**il lu mi nate** (i lü′mə nāt), *v.t.*, **-nat ed, -nat ing.** **1** light up; make bright: *The room was illuminated by four large lamps.* **2** make clear; explain: *Our teacher could illuminate almost any subject we studied.* **3** decorate with lights: *The streets were illuminated for the celebration.* [< Latin *illuminatum* lit up < *in-* in + *lumen* light]

**il lus tri ous** (i lus′trē əs), *adj.* **1** very famous; great; outstanding. **2** bringing or conferring glory; glorious. [< Latin *illustris* lighted up, bright < *in-* in + *lustrum* lighting] —**il lus′tri ous ly,** *adv.* —**il lus′tri ous ness,** *n.*

**im me mo ri al** (im′ə môr′ē əl, im′ə mōr′ē əl), *adj.* extending back beyond the bounds of memory; ancient

**im mi nent** (im′ə nənt), *adj.* likely to happen soon; about to occur: *Black clouds show rain is imminent.* [< Latin *imminentem* overhanging, threatening] —**im′mi nent ly,** *adv.*

**im pale** (im pāl′), *v.t.*, **-paled, -pal ing.** pierce through with something pointed; fasten upon something pointed: *The dead butterflies were impaled on pins stuck in a sheet of cork.* [< Medieval Latin *impalare* < Latin *in-* on + *palus* stake]

**im part** (im pärt′), *v.t.* **1** give a part or share of; give: *The new furnishings imparted an air of newness to the old house.* **2** communicate; tell: *They imparted the news of their engagement to their families.* [< Latin *impartire* < *in-* in + *partem* part]

**im per a tive** (im per′ə tiv), *adj.* **1** not to be avoided; that must be done; urgent; necessary: *It is imperative that this very sick child should stay in bed.* **2** (in grammar) having to do with a verb form which expresses a command, request, or advice. "Go!" and "Stop, look, listen!" are in the imperative mood. —*n.* something imperative; command: *The dog trainer issued sharp imperatives to the dog.* [< Latin *imperativus* < *imperare* to command] —**im per′a tive ly,** *adv.*

**im per son al** (im pėr′sə nəl), *adj.* not referring to any one person in particular; not personal: *impersonal criticism.* —**im per′son al ly,** *adv.*

**im pet u os i ty** (im pech′ü os′ə tē), *n.*, *pl.* **-ties.** **1** sudden or rash energy; hastiness. **2** rushing force or violence. **3** an impetuous action.

**im pet u ous** (im pech′ü əs), *adj.* **1** acting or done with sudden or rash energy; hasty: *He was so angry that he made an impetuous decision.* **2** rushing with force and violence.

**im ple ment** (im′plə mənt), *n.* a useful article of equipment; tool; instrument; utensil. A plow, an ax, a shovel, and a broom are implements.

**im pli ca tion** (im′plə kā′shən), *n.* **1** an implying. **2** a being implied. **3** something implied; indirect suggestion; hint: *There was no implication of dishonesty in their failure in business.* **4** an implicating. **5** a being implicated.

GLOSSARY

**im plic it** (im plis′ it), *adj.* **1** meant, but not clearly expressed or distinctly stated; implied: *implicit consent.* **2** without doubting, hesitating, or asking questions; absolute. **3** involved as a necessary part or condition. [< Latin *implicitum* implied, enfolded < *in-* in + *plicare* to fold]

**im po tent** (im′pə tənt), *adj.* not having power; helpless: *We were impotent against the force of the tornado.* —**im′po tent ly,** *adv.*

**im pound** (im pound′), *v.t.* **1** shut up in a pen or pound: *impound stray animals.* **2** enclose or confine within limits: *A dam impounds water.* **3** seize and put in the custody of a court of law: *The court impounded the documents to use as evidence.* **4** seize or hold back from designated use: *to impound funds earmarked for a dam.* —**im pound′a ble,** *adj.* —**im pound′er,** *n.*

**im preg na ble** (im preg′nə bəl), *adj.* able to resist attack; not yielding to force, persuasion, etc.: *an impregnable fortress, an impregnable argument.* —**im preg′na bly,** *adv.*

**im press** (im pres′), *v.t.* **1** take or seize by authority for public use: *The police impressed our car in order to pursue the escaping robbers.* **2** force (a person) to serve in the armed forces. **3** bring in and use; press (a thing) into service by argument, etc. —*n.* impressment.

**im press ment** (im pres′mənt), *n.* an impressing of property for public use or of persons to serve in the armed forces.

**im pro vi sa to re** (im prov′ə zə tôr′e), *n., pl.* **-to ri** (-tôr′e, -tōr′e), **-tor es.** a person who improvises music or verse. [< Italian *improvvisatore*]

**im pru dence** (im prüd′ns), *n.* lack of prudence, or good judgment before acting; imprudent behavior.

**im pu ni ty** (im pyü′nə tē), *n.* freedom from punishment, injury, or other bad consequences: *If laws are not enforced, crimes are committed with impunity.* [< Latin *impunitatem*, ultimately < *in-* without + *poena* punishment]

**in can des cence** (in′kən des′ns), *n.* a being incandescent.

**in can des cent** (in′kən des′nt), *adj.* **1** heated to such a high temperature that it gives out light; glowing with heat; red-hot or white-hot. **2** shining brightly; brilliant.

**in can ta tion** (in′kan tā′shən), *n.* set of words spoken as a magic charm or to cast a magic spell. [< Latin *incantationem* < *incantare* enchant < *in-* against + *cantare* to chant]

**in car nate** (*adj.* in kär′nit, in kär′nāt; *v.* in kär′nāt), *adj., v.,* **-nat ed, -nat ing.** —*adj.* embodied in flesh, especially in human form; personified: typified: *the Devil incarnate, evil incarnate.* —*v.t.* **1** make incarnate; embody: *Lancelot incarnated the spirit of chivalry.* **2** put into or represent in concrete form; realize: *The sculptor incarnated her vision in a beautiful statue.* [< Latin *incarnatum,* < *in-* + *carnem* flesh]

**in cense** (in sens′), *v.t.,* **-censed, -cens ing.** make very angry; fill with rage. [< Latin *incensum* inflamed, enraged, set on fire < *in-* (intensive) + *candere* glow white]

**in ces sant** (in ses′nt), *adj.* never stopping; continued or repeated without interruption; continual: *the incessant noise from the factory.* [< Late Latin *incessantem* < Latin *in-* not + *cessare* cease] —**in ces′sant ly,** *adv.* —**in ces′sant ness,** *n.*

**in com pat i bil i ty** (in′kəm pat′ə bil′ə tē), *n., pl.* **-ties. 1** quality of being incompatible; lack of harmony. **2** an incompatible thing, quality, etc.

**in cred u lous** (in krej′ə ləs), *adj.* **1** not ready to believe; doubting; skeptical: *If they look incredulous show them the evidence.* **2** showing a lack of belief: *an incredulous smile.* —**in cred′u lous ly,** *adv.*

**in cum bent** (in kum′bənt), *adj.* **1** lying, leaning, or pressing on something. **2** resting on a person as a duty or obligation: *She felt it incumbent upon her to answer the letter at once.* **3** currently holding an office, position, etc.: *the incumbent governor.* —*n.* person holding an office, position, etc. [< Latin *incumbentem* < *in-* on + *-cumbere* lie down] —**in cum′bent ly,** *adv.*

**in dif fer ent** (in dif′ər ənt), *adj.* **1** having or showing no interest or attention: *indifferent to an admirer.* **2** not inclined to prefer one person or thing to another; impartial; neutral; fair: *an indifferent decision.* **3** not mattering much: unimportant. —**in dif′fer ent ly,** *adv.*

**in dis creet** (in′dis krēt′), *adj.* not discreet; not wise and judicious; imprudent. —**in′dis creet′ly,** *adv.*

| a hat | i it | oi oil | ch child | | a in about |
|---|---|---|---|---|---|
| ā age | ī ice | ou out | ng long | | e in taken |
| ä far | o hot | u cup | sh she | ə = | i in pencil |
| e let | ō open | u̇ put | th thin | | o in lemon |
| ē equal | ô order | ü rule | ŦH then | | u in circus |
| ėr term | | | zh measure | < = derived from | |

**in ef fa ble** (in ef′ə bəl), *adj.* not to be expressed in words; too great to be described in words. [< Latin *ineffabilis* < *in-* not + *effari* express in words < *ex-* out + *fari* speak] —**in ef′fa bly,** *adv.*

**in ert** (in ėrt′), *adj.* **1** having no power to move or act; lifeless: *A stone is an inert mass of matter.* **2** inactive; slow; sluggish. [< Latin *inertem* idle, unskilled < *in-* without + *artem* art, skill] —**in ert′ly,** *adv.* —**in ert′ness,** *n.*

**in ev i ta ble** (in ev′ə tə bəl), *adj.* not to be avoided; sure to happen; certain to come: *Death is inevitable.* [< Latin *inevitabilis* < *in-* not + *evitare* avoid < *ex-* out + *vitare* shun] —**in ev′i ta bly,** *adv.*

**in ex plic a ble** (in′ik splik′ə bəl, in ek′splə kə bəl), *adj.* that cannot be explained, understood, or accounted for; mysterious. —**in′ex plic′a ble ness,** *n.* —**in′ex plic′a bly,** *adv.*

**in fal li ble** (in fal′ə bəl), *adj.* **1** free from error; that cannot be mistaken: *an infallible rule.* **2** absolutely reliable; sure: *infallible obedience, an infallible remedy.* —**in fal′li bly,** *adv.*

**in fa my** (in′fə mē), *n., pl.* **-mies. 1** a very bad reputation; public disgrace: *Traitors are held in infamy.* **2** shameful badness; extreme wickedness. **3** an infamous or disgraceful act. [< Latin *infamia* < *infamis* of ill fame < *in-* without + *fama* fame, reputation]

**in firm** (in fėrm′), *adj.* lacking strength or health; physically weak or feeble, especially through age. —**in firm′ly,** *adv.*

**in flam ma to ry** (in flam′ə tôr′e, in flam′ə tōr′e), *adj.* **1** tending to excite or arouse: *an inflammatory speech.* **2** of, causing, or accompanied by inflammation: *an inflammatory condition of the tonsils.*

**in fuse** (in fyüz′), *v.t.,* **-fused, -fus ing. 1** introduce as by pouring; put in; instill: *The captain infused his own courage into his soldiers.* **2** inspire: *The soldiers were infused with his courage.* **3** steep or soak (a plant, leaves, etc.) in a liquid to get something out. [< Latin *infusum* poured in < *in-* in + *fundere* pour] —**in fus′er,** *n.*

**in gle** (ing′gəl), *n.* **1** fireplace. **2** fire burning on the hearth. [< Scottish Gaelic *aingeal* fire]

**in graft** (in graft′), *v.t.* **1** graft (a shoot, etc.) from one tree or plant into another. **2** fix in; implant. Also, **engraft.**

**in gress** (in′gres), *n.* **1** a going in or entering: *A high fence prevented ingress to the field.* **2** way of going in; entrance.

**in quis i tive** (in kwiz′ə tiv), *adj.* **1** asking many questions; curious. **2** prying into other people's affairs; too curious. —**in quis′i tive ly,** *adv.*

**in scru ta ble** (in skrü′tə bəl), *adj.* that cannot be understood; so mysterious or obscure that one cannot make out its meaning; incomprehensible. [< Late Latin *inscrutabilis* < Latin *in-* not + *scrutari* examine, ransack < *scruta* trash]

**in sig nif i cant** (in′sig nif′ə kənt), *adj.* **1** of no consequence; influence, or distinction: *an insignificant position, an insignificant person.* **2** too small to be important; unimportant; trivial; petty: *an insignificant detail, an insignificant amount of money.* —**in′sig nif′i cant ly,** *adv.*

**in so lent** (in′sə lənt), *adj.* boldly rude; intentionally disregarding the feelings of others; insulting. [< Latin *insolentem* arrogant, contrary to custom < *in-* not + *solere* be accustomed]

**in sti gate** (in′stə gāt), *v.t.,* **-gat ed, -gat ing.** urge on; stir up: *instigate a quarrel.* [< Latin *instigatum* incited, urged on] —**in′sti ga′tion,** *n.* —**in′sti ga′tor,** *n.*

**in su lar** (in′sə lər), *adj.* **1** of or having to do with islands or

GLOSSARY

889

islanders. **2** living or situated on an island. **3** standing alone like an island; isolated: *an insular position in world affairs.* **4** narrowminded; prejudiced. [< Late Latin *insularis* < Latin *insula* island] —**in′su lar ly,** *adv.*

**in su per a ble** (in sü′pər ə bəl), *adj.* that cannot be passed over or overcome; insurmountable: *an insuperable barrier.*

**in sup port a ble** (in′sə pôr′tə bəl, in′sə pōr′tə bəl), *adj.* not endurable; unbearable; intolerable.

**in ter** (in tèr′), *v.t.,* **-terred, -terring.** put (a dead body) into a grave or tomb; bury. [< Medieval Latin *interrare* < Latin *in-* in + *terra* earth]

**in ter cede** (in′tər sēd′), *v.i.,* **-ced ed, -ced ing. 1** plead for another; ask a favor from one person for another: *Friends of the condemned man interceded with the governor for a pardon.* **2** act as an intermediary in order to bring about an agreement; mediate. [< Latin *intercedere* go between < *inter-* between + *cedere* go]

**in ter ces sion** (in′tər sesh′ən), *n.* **1** act or fact of interceding. **2** prayer pleading for others. [< Latin *intercessionem* < *intercedere.*]

**in ter lop er** (in′tər lō′pər), *n.* person who interferes, unasked and unwanted; intruder.

**in ter lude** (in′tər lüd), *n.* anything thought of as filling the time between two things; interval: *an interlude of sunshine between two showers.* [< Medieval Latin *interludium* < Latin *inter-* between + *ludus* a play]

**in ter mi na ble** (in tèr′mə nə bəl), *adj.* **1** never stopping; unceasing; endless. **2** so long as to seem endless; very long and tiring. —**in ter′mi na bly,** *adv.*

**in ter mit tent** (in′tər mit′nt), *adj.* stopping for a time and beginning again; pausing at intervals. —**in′ter mit′tent ly,** *adv.*

**in ter pose** (in′tər pōz′), *v.,* **-posed, -pos ing.** —*v.t.* **1** put between; insert. **2** put forward; break in with: *She interposed an objection at this point.* —*v.i.* **1** come or be between other things. **2** interrupt. **3** interfere in order to help; intervene; intercede. [< Middle French *interposer* < *inter-* between + *poser* to place]

**in ter stice** (in tèr′stis), *n., pl.* **-sti ces** (-stə sēz′). a small or narrow space between things or parts; narrow chink, crack, or opening. [< Late Latin *interstitium* < Latin *inter-* between + *stare* to stand]

**in ter vene** (in′tər vēn′), *v.i.,* **-vened, -ven ing. 1** come between; be between: *A week intervenes between my sister's birthday and mine.* **2** come between persons or groups to help settle a dispute: *The President was asked to intervene in the coal strike.* [< Latin *intervenire* < *inter-* between + *venire* come]

**in ti mate** (in′tə māt), *v.t.,* **-mat ed, -mat ing. 1** suggest indirectly; hint. **2** make known; announce; notify. [< Latin *intimatum* made known, brought in < *intimus* inmost, superlative of *in* in] —**in′ti mat′er,** *n.*

**in tim i date** (in tim′ə dāt), *v.t.,* **-dat ed, -dat ing. 1** make afraid; frighten: *intimidate one's opponents with threats.* **2** influence or force by fear: *intimidate a witness.* [< Medieval Latin *intimidatum* frightened < Latin *in-* + *timidus* fearful] —**in tim′i da′tion,** *n.* —**in tim′i da′tor,** *n.*

**in tox i cate** (in tok′sə kāt), *v.t.,* **-cat ed, -cat ing. 1** make drunk: *Too much wine intoxicates people.* **2** excite greatly; exhilarate: *The team was intoxicated by its victory.* **3** (in medicine) to poison. [< Medieval Latin *intoxicatum* dipped in poison < Latin *in-* in + *toxicum* poison]

**in tro spec tion** (in′trə spek′shən), *n.* examination of one's own thoughts and feelings.

**in tro spec tive** (in′trə spek′tiv), *adj.* characterized by introspection. —**in′tro spec′tive ly,** *adv.*

**ir i des cent** (ir′ə des′nt), *adj.* displaying changing colors; changing color when moved or turned. [< Latin *iris, iridis* rainbow] —**ir′i des′cent ly,** *adv.*

**i ron i cal** (ī ron′ə kəl), *adj.* **1** expressing one thing and meaning the opposite: *"Speedy" was the ironical name of our turtle.* **2** contrary to what would naturally be expected: *It was ironical that the man was run over by his own automobile.* —**i ron′i cal ly,** *adv.*

**ir rel e vant** (i rel′ə vənt), *adj.* not to the point; off the subject: *an irrelevant question.* —**ir rel′e vant ly,** *adv.*

**ir res o lu tion** (i rez′ə lü′shən), *n.* a being irresolute; lack of firm decision; hesitation.

**ir rev o ca ble** (i rev′ə kə bəl), *adj.* **1** not able to be revoked; final: *an irrevocable decision.* **2** impossible to call or bring back: *the irrevocable past.* —**ir rev′o ca bly,** *adv.*

**jade** (jād), *n.* an inferior or worn-out horse. [origin uncertain]

**jan gle** (jang′gəl), *v.,* **-gled, -gling,** *n.* —*v.i.* **1** sound harshly; make a loud, clashing noise: *The pots and pans jangled in the kitchen.* **2** talk or argue in an angry or quarrelsome manner. **3** become nervous, upset, or jumpy. —*v.t.* **1** cause to make a harsh, clashing sound: *The children jangled the cowbells.* **2** have a harsh, unpleasant effect on: *All that racket jangles my nerves.* —*n.* **1** a harsh sound; clashing noise or ring. **2** a quarrel; dispute. [< Old French *jangler*] —**jan′gler,** *n.*

**jar di niere** (järd′n ir′), *n.* an ornamental pot or stand for flowers or plants. [< French *jardinière* < *jardin* garden]

**jeop ar dy** (jep′ər dē), *n.* risk; danger; peril: *Many lives were in jeopardy during the forest fire.* [< Old French *jeu parti* an even or divided game]

**jib** (jib), *v.i.,* **jibbed, jib bing.** move sideways or backward instead of forward; refuse to go ahead. [origin uncertain]

**joc und** (jok′ənd, jō′kənd), *adj.* feeling, expressing, or communicating mirth or cheer; cheerful; merry; gay. [< Latin *jocundus, jucundus* pleasant < *juvare* please]

**jol li fi ca tion** (jol′ə fə kā′shən), *n.* enjoyable entertainment; merrymaking.

**joust** (joust, just, jüst), *n.* **1** combat between two knights on horseback, armed with lances, especially as part of a tournament. **2 jousts,** *pl.* a tournament. —*v.i.* fight with lances on horseback. Also, **just.** [< Old French *jouste* < *jouster* to joust < Popular Latin *juxtare* be next to < Latin *juxta* beside] —**joust′er,** *n.*

**jowl** (joul, jōl), *n.* **1** jaw, especially the lower jaw. **2** cheek. [Old English *ceafl*]

**ju di cious** (jü dish′əs), *adj.* having, using, or showing good judgment; wise; sensible: *A judicious historian selects and weighs facts carefully and critically.* —**ju di′cious ly,** *adv.* —**ju di′cious ness,** *n.* [< Latin *judicialis* < *judicium* judgment < *judicem* judge]

**ka lei do scope** (kə lī′də skōp), *n.* **1** tube containing bits of colored glass and two mirrors. As it is turned, it reflects continually changing patterns. **2** a continually changing pattern or object: *The circus was a kaleidoscope of colors.* [< Greek *kalos* pretty + *eidos* shape + English *-scope*]

**ka pok** (kā′pok), *n.* the silky fibers around the seeds of a tropical silk-cotton tree, used for stuffing pillows, mattresses, and life preservers, for insulation, etc.; silk cotton. [< Malay]

**key stone** (kē′stōn′), *n.* **1** the middle stone at the top of an arch, holding the other stones or pieces in place. **2** part on which other related parts depend; essential principle.

**kit tle** (kit′l), *v.t.* **kit tled, kit tling.** to give birth to a litter of rabbits, kittens, etc.

**lab y rinth** (lab′ə rinth′), *n.* **1** number of connecting passages so arranged that it is hard to find one's way from point to point; maze. **2 Labyrinth** (in Greek legends) the maze built by Daedalus for King Minos of Crete to imprison the Minotaur. **3** any confusing, complicated arrangement: *a labyrinth of dark and narrow streets.*

**lack ey** (lak′ē), *n., pl.* **-eys. 1** a male servant; footman. **2** a slavish follower; toady. [< Middle French *laquais* < Spanish *lacayo* foot soldier]

**lair** (ler, lar), *n.* **1** den or resting place of a wild animal. **2** secret or secluded retreat. [< Old English *leger* < *licgan* lie down]

**la ment** (lə ment′), *v.t.* **1** express grief for; mourn for: *lament the dead.* **2** regret: *We lamented his absence.* —*v.i.* express grief; mourn; weep: *Why does he lament?* —*n.* **1** expression of grief or sorrow; wail. **2** poem, song, or tune that expresses grief. [< Latin *lamentari* < *lamentum* a wailing] —**la ment′er,** *n.* —**la ment′ing ly,** *adv.*

**lan guor** (lang′gər), *n.* **1** lack of energy; weakness; weariness: *A long illness causes languor.* **2** lack of interest or enthusiasm; indifference. **3** softness or tenderness of mood. **4** quietness; stillness: *the languor of a summer afternoon.* **5** lack of activity; sluggishness. [< Latin < *languere* be faint]

**lap pet** (lap′it), *n.* **1** a small flap or fold: *a lappet on a dress.* **2** a loose fold of flesh or membrane, such as the lobe of the ear or a bird's wattle. [< *lap*]

**las si tude** (las′ə tüd, las′ə tyüd), *n.* lack of energy; weakness; weariness; languor. [< Latin *lassitudo* < *lassus* tired]

**lateen sail,** a triangular sail held up by a long yard on a short mast. [< French *(voile) latine* Latin (sail)]

**lee** (lē), *n.* **1** shelter; protection. **2** side or part sheltered or away from the wind: *the lee of a ship.* —*adj.* sheltered or away from the wind. [Old English *hlēo*]

**leg a cy** (leg′ə sē), *n., pl.* **-cies.** money or other property left to a person by the will of someone who has died; bequest. [< Medieval Latin *legatia* < Latin *legatum* bequest < *legare* bequeath]

**lateen sails**

**leg er de main** (lej′ər də mān′), *n.* **1** sleight of hand; conjuring tricks; jugglery. **2** trickery; deception. [< French *léger de main* quick of hand]

**lep ro sy** (lep′rə sē), *n.* a chronic, infectious disease caused by certain rod-shaped bacteria that attack the skin and nerves, causing lumps or spots which may become ulcers; Hansen's disease. If not treated, the injury to the nerves results in numbness, paralysis, and deformity. [< Late Latin *leprosus* leprous < Greek *lepra* leprosy < *lepein* to peel]

**leth ar gy** (leth′ər jē), *n., pl.* **-gies.** drowsy dullness; lack of energy; sluggish inactivity. [< Greek *lēthargia* < *lēthē* forgetfulness + *argos* lazy < *a-* not + *ergon* work]

**lev ee** (lev′ē, lə vē′), *n.* **1** a formal reception: *The President held a levee on New Year's Day.* **2** reception held while rising. French kings used to hold levees in the morning while they were getting up and dressing. [< French *levé*, *lever* < *lever* to raise]

**lev y** (lev′ē), *v.,* **lev ied, lev y ing,** *n., pl.* **lev ies.** —*v.t.* **1** order to be paid: *The government levies taxes to pay its expenses.* **2** draft or enlist (citizens) for an army: *levy troops in time of war.* **3** undertake or begin; wage: *levy war against the enemy.* [< Middle French *levée* < *lever* to raise]

**lewd** (lüd), *adj.* indecent; lustful; obscene; lascivious. [Old English *lǣwede* laic, unlearned] —**lewd′ly,** *adv.* —**lewd′ness,** *n.*

**li ba tion** (lī bā′shən), *n.* **1** a pouring out of wine, water, etc., as an offering to a god. **2** the wine, water, etc., offered in this way. **3** INFORMAL. liquid poured out to be drunk; drink. [< Latin *libationem* < *libare* pour out]

**lib er tar i an** (lib′ər ter′ē ən), *n.* **1** person who advocates liberty, especially in thought or conduct. **2** person who maintains the doctrine of the freedom of the will.

**liege** (lēj), *n.* in the Middle Ages: **1** lord having a right to the homage and loyal service of his vassals. **2** vassal obliged to give homage and loyal service to his lord; liegeman. —*adj.* **1** having a right to the homage and loyal service of vassals. **2** obliged to give homage and loyal service to a lord. [< Old French, ultimately of Germanic origin]

**lim pid** (lim′pid), *adj.* **1** clear or transparent: *limpid water, limpid eyes.* **2** free from obscurity; lucid. [< Latin *limpidus*, related to *lympha* clear water]

**lin tel** (lin′tl), *n.* a horizontal beam or stone over a door, window, etc., to support the structure above it. [< Old French, threshold, ultimately < Latin *limitem* limit]

**lit a ny** (lit′n ē), *n., pl.* **-nies.** **1** prayer consisting of a series of words or requests said by a minister or priest and the congregation's responses. **2** a repeated series. [< Greek *litaneia* litany, entreaty < *litesthai* entreat]

**lithe** (līṯH), *adj.* bending easily; supple: *lithe of body, a lithe willow.* [Old English *līthe* mild] —**lithe′ly,** *adv.* —**lithe′ness,** *n.*

| a hat | i it | oi oil | ch child | { a in about |
|---|---|---|---|---|
| ā age | ī ice | ou out | ng long | e in taken |
| ä far | o hot | u cup | sh she | ə = { i in pencil |
| e let | ō open | ù put | th thin | o in lemon |
| ē equal | ô order | ü rule | ŦH then | { u in circus |
| ėr term | | | zh measure | < = derived from |

**lit ter** (lit′ər), *n.* **1** things scattered about or left in disorder; scattered rubbish. **2** the whole number of young brought forth at one birth by an animal. **3** stretcher for carrying a sick, injured, or wounded person. [< Anglo-French *litere* < Medieval Latin *lectaria* < Latin *lectus* bed]

**liv er y** (liv′ər ē), *n., pl.* **-er ies.** **1** any special uniform provided for the servants of a household, or adopted by any group or profession. **2** the feeding, stabling, and care of horses for pay. **3** the hiring out of horses and carriages. **4** the keeping of cars, boats, etc., for hire. **5** livery stable. [< Old French *livree* provisions dispensed to servants < *livrer* dispense < Latin *liberare* liberate]

**loam** (lōm), *n.* rich, fertile earth in which much humus is mixed with clay and sand. [Old English *lām*]

**loath** (lōth, lōŦH), *adj.* unwilling or reluctant; averse: *The little girl was loath to leave her mother. They were loath to admit that their son had run away.* Also, **loth.** [Old English *lāth* hostile]

**loin** (loin), *n.* **1** Usually, **loins,** *pl.* the part of the body of an animal or human being between the ribs and the hipbones. The loins are on both sides of the spinal column and nearer to it than the flanks. **2 loins,** *pl.* the genitals or the genital region. **3 gird up one's loins,** get ready for action. [< Old French *loigne*, ultimately < Latin *lumbus*]

**lor gnette** (lôr nyet′), *n.* eyeglasses or opera glasses mounted on a handle. [< French < *lorgner* look sidelong at]

**lu cent** (lü′snt), *adj.* **1** bright or shining; luminous. **2** letting light through; translucent; lucid; clear. [< Latin *lucentem*, related to *lux, lucis* light] —**lu′cent ly,** *adv.*

**lu gu bri ous** (lü gü′brē əs, lü gyü′brē əs), *adj.* too sad; overly mournful: *the lugubrious howl of a dog.* [< Latin *lugubris* < *lugere* mourn] —**lu gu′bri ous ly,** *adv.* —**lu gu′bri ous ness,** *n.*

**lum ba go** (lum bā′gō), *n.* form of rheumatism characterized by pain in the muscles of the small of the back and in the loins. [< Late Latin < Latin *lumbus* loin]

**lu mi nous** (lü′mə nəs), *adj.* **1** shining by its own light: *The sun and stars are luminous bodies.* **2** full of light; shining; bright. **3** easily understood; clear; enlightening. —**lu′mi nous ly,** *adv.*

**lux ur i ate** (lug zhùr′ē āt, luk shùr′ē āt), *v.i.,* **-at ed, -at ing.** **1** indulge in luxury. **2** take great delight; revel: *luxuriate in a hot bath.*

**mag a zine** (mag′ə zēn′, mag′ə zēn′), *n.* **1** publication issued regularly, especially weekly, semimonthly, or monthly, which contains stories, articles, etc., by various contributors. **2** room in a fort or warship for storing gunpowder and other explosives. **3** chamber for cartridges in a repeating or automatic gun. [< Old French *magazin*, ultimately < Arabic *makhzan* storehouse]

**mag is trate** (maj′ə strāt, maj′ə strit), *n.* **1** a government official who has power to apply the law and put it in force. The President is the chief magistrate of the United States. **2** judge in a minor court. A justice of the peace is a magistrate. [< Latin *magistratus*, ultimately < *magister* master < *magnus* great]

**ma jor-do mo** (mā′jər dō′mō), *n., pl.* **-mos.** **1** man in charge of a royal or noble household. **2** butler or steward. [< Spanish *mayordomo* or Italian *maggiordomo* < Medieval Latin *major domus* chief of the household]

**ma lar i a** (mə ler′ē ə, mə lar′ē ə), *n.* disease characterized by periodic chills, fever, and sweating. [< Italian < *mala aria* bad air]

**ma lign** (mə līn′), *v.t.* speak evil of; slander: *You malign an honest*

*person whom you call a liar.* —*adj.* **1** evil; injurious. **2** hateful; malicious. [< Late Latin *malignare* < Latin *malignus* disposed to evil < *malus* evil + *-gnus* born]

**man ger** (mān′jər), *n.* box or trough in which hay or other food can be placed for horses or cows to eat. [< Old French *mangeoire* < *mangier* eat < Latin *manducare* to chew]

**man grove** (mang′grōv), *n.* any of a genus of tropical trees or shrubs having branches that send down many roots which look like additional trunks. Mangroves grow in swamps and along riverbanks. [< Spanish *mangle;* spelling influenced by English *grove*]

**man i fest** (man′ə fest), *adj.* apparent to the eye or to the mind; plain; clear: *a manifest error.* —*v.t.* **1** show plainly; reveal; display. **2** put beyond doubt; prove. —*n.* list of cargo of a ship or aircraft. [< Latin *manifestus* palpable < *manus* hand + *-festus* (able to be) seized] —**man′i fest′er,** *n.* —**man′i fest′ly,** *adv.*

**man sard** (man′särd), *n.* roof with two slopes on each side. [< François *Mansard,* 1598–1666, French architect]

**mansard**

**man til la** (man til′ə, man tē′yə), *n.* veil or scarf, often of lace, covering the hair and falling down over the shoulders. [< Spanish, diminutive of *manta* cloak]

**man tle** (man′tl), *n., v.,* **-tled, -tling.** —*n.* **1** a long, loose cloak without sleeves. **2** anything that covers like a mantle: *The ground had a mantle of snow.* —*v.t.* **1** cover with a mantle. **2** cover or conceal; obscure; cloak: *Clouds mantled the moon.* [partly Old English *mentel,* partly < Old French *mantel;* both < Latin *mantellum*]

**mar a thon** (mar′ə thon), *n.* **1** a footrace of 26 miles, 385 yards (42.2 kilometers). **2** any race over a long distance. **3** any activity that calls for endurance.

**mar row** (mar′ō), *n.* **1** the soft, vascular tissue that fills the cavities of most bones and is the source of red blood cells and many white blood cells. **2** the inmost or essential part. [< Old English *mearg*]

**mass y** (mas′ē), *adj.,* **mass i er, mass i est.** bulky and heavy; massive. —**mass′i ness,** *n.*

**mas to don** (mas′tə don), *n.* any of various large extinct mammals somewhat resembling mammoths and present-day elephants. [< New Latin < Greek *mastos* breast + *odōn* tooth (from the nipple-shaped projections on its teeth)]

**ma ter i al ize** (mə tir′ē ə līz), *v.i.,* **-ized, -iz ing. 1** become an actual fact; be realized: *Our plans did not materialize.* **2** appear in material or bodily form: *A spirit materialized from the smoke of the magician's fire.* —**ma ter′i al i za′tion,** *n.*

**ma tri cide** (mā′trə sīd, mat′rə sīd), *n.* **1** act of killing one's mother. **2** person who kills his or her mother.

**maw** (mô), *n.* **1** mouth, throat, or gullet, especially of a meateating animal. **2** stomach. [< Old English *maga*]

**med ley** (med′lē), *n., pl.* **-leys. 1** mixture of things that ordinarily do not belong together. **2** piece of music made up of parts from other pieces. [< Old French *medlees, meslee* < *mesler* to mix, ultimately < Latin *miscere.*]

**me tic u lous** (mə tik′yə ləs), *adj.* extremely or excessively careful about details. [< Latin *meticulosus* fearful, timid < *metus* fear] —**me tic′u lous ly,** *adv.* —**me tic′u lous ness,** *n.*

**mim ic ry** (mim′ik rē), *n., pl.* **-ries. 1** act or practice of mimicking. **2** an instance, performance, or result of mimicking. **3** the close outward resemblance of an animal to a different one or to its environment, especially for protection or concealment.

**min gle** (ming′gəl), *v.,* **-gled, -gling.** —*v.t.* combine in a mixture; mix; blend: *Two rivers that join mingle their waters.* —*v.i.* **1** be or become mingled; mix; blend. **2** associate: *I tried to mingle with everyone at the party.* [Middle English *mengelen* < Old English *mengan* to mix] —**min′gler,** *n.*

**mir y** (mī′rē), *adj.,* **mir i er, mir i est. 1** muddy; slushy. **2** swampy; boggy; marshy. **3** dirty; filthy. —**mir′i ness,** *n.*

**mis cre ant** (mis′krē ənt), *adj.* having very bad morals; wicked; base. —*n.* a base or wicked person; villain. [< Old French *mescreant* < *mes-* wrongly, mis- + *creire* believe]

**mis shap en** (mis shā′pən), *adj.* badly shaped; deformed.

**mod u la tion** (moj′ə lā′shən), *n.* **1** a modulating. **2** an alteration in pitch, tone, or volume.

**mon o lith** (mon′l ith), *n.* **1** a single large block of stone. **2** monument, column, statue, etc., formed of a single large block of stone. [< Greek *monolithos* < *mono-* + *lithos* stone]

**mon o lith ic** (mon′l ith′ik), *adj.* of a monolith; being a monolith.

**mo nop o ly** (mə nop′ə lē), *n., pl.* **-lies. 1** the exclusive control of a commodity or service: *The only milk company in town has a monopoly on milk delivery.* **2** the exclusive possession or control of something: *a monopoly of a person's time.* [< Greek *monopōlion* < *mono-* + *pōlein* to sell]

**mon soon** (mon sün′), *n.* **1** a seasonal wind of the Indian Ocean and southern Asia, blowing from the southwest from April to October and from the northeast during the rest of the year. **2** the rainy season during which this wind blows from the southwest. [< earlier Dutch *monssoen* < Portuguese *monção* < Arabic *mausim* season]

**moot** (müt), *adj.* that can be argued; debatable; doubtful: *a moot point.* —*v.t.* **1** bring forward (a point, subject, case, etc.) for discussion. **2** discuss; debate. [Old English *mōtian* to argue, discuss < *(ge)mōt* meeting]

**mus ing** (myü′zing), *adj.* meditative. —*n.* meditation. —**mus′ing ly,** *adv.*

**mus ter** (mus′tər), *v.t.* **1** gather together; assemble; collect: *muster financial resources, muster soldiers.* **2** summon: *muster up courage.* **3** number: comprise: *The garrison musters eighty men.* [< Old French *mostrer* < Latin *monstrare* to show < *monstrum* portent]

**mute** (myüt), *adj., v.,* **mut ed, mut ing.** —*adj.* **1** not making any sound; silent: *The little girl stood mute with embarrassment.* **2** unable to speak; dumb. **3** not pronounced; silent: *The 'e' in ''mute'' is mute.* **4** without speech or sound. —*v.t.* deaden or soften the sound of (a tone, voice, a musical instrument, etc.) with or as if with a mute. [< Latin *mutus*] —**mute′ly,** *adv.*

**myr i ad** (mir′ē əd), *n.* **1** ten thousand. **2** a very great number: *There are myriads of stars.* [< Greek *myriados* ten thousand, countless]

**na ïve** or **na ive** (nä ēv′), *adj.* simple in nature; like a child; not sophisticated; artless. Aslo, **naïf.** [< French *naïve,* feminine of *naïf* < Latin *nativus*] —**na ïve′ly,** or **na ive′ly,** *adv.*

**na per y** (nā′pər ē), *n.* tablecloths, napkins, and doilies. [< Old French *naperie* < *nape* cloth]

**naught** (nôt), *n.* **1** nothing. **2** zero; 0. Also, **nought.** [Old English *nāwiht* < *nā* no + *wiht* thing]

**net tle** (net′l), *n.* any of a genus of herbs having sharp hairs on the leaves and stems that sting the skin when touched. [Old English *netele*]

**noc tur nal** (nok tėr′nl), *adj.* **1** of the night: *Stars are a nocturnal sight.* **2** active in the night: *The owl is a nocturnal bird.* [< Latin *nocturnus* of the night < *noctem* night] —**noc tur′nal ly,** *adv.*

**no mad ic** (nō mad′ik), *adj.* of nomads or their life; wandering.

**non pa reil** (non′pə rel′), *adj.* having no equal. —*n.* **1** person or thing having no equal. **2** painted bunting. **3** a small chocolate drop covered with tiny white pellets of sugar. [< Middle French < *non-* not + *pareil* equal]

**nun ner y** (nun′ər ē), *n., pl.* **-ner ies.** building or buildings where nuns live; convent.

**o blit e rate** (ə blit′ə rāt′), *v.t.,* **-rat ed, -rat ing. 1** remove all traces of; blot out; efface: *The heavy rain obliterated the footprints.* **2** blot out so as to leave no distinct traces; make unrecognizable. [< Latin *obliteratum* struck out < *ob literas (scribere)* (draw) through the letters, strike out] —**o blit′e ra′tion,** *n.* —**o blit′e ra′tor,** *n.*

892

ob sti nate (ob′stə nit), *adj.* **1** not giving in; stubborn. **2** hard to control, treat, or remove; persistent: *an obstinate cough.* [< Latin *obstinatum* determined < *ob-* by + *stare* to stand] —**ob′sti nate ly,** *adv.* —**ob′sti nate ness,** *n.*

oc clude (o klüd′), *v.,* **-clud ed, -clud ing.** —*v.t.* **1** stop up (a passage, pores, etc.); close. **2** shut in, out, or off. [< Latin *occludere* < *ob-* up + *claudere* to close]

o di ous (ō′dē əs), *adj.* very displeasing: hateful; offensive. [< Latin *odiosus* < *odium* odium] —**o′di ous ly,** *adv.*

of fal (ô′fəl, of′əl), *n.* **1** the waste parts of an animal killed for food. **2** garbage; refuse. [< *off* + *fall*]

of fice (ô′fis, of′is), *n.* **1** place in which the work of a position is done; room or rooms in which to work. **2** position, especially in the public service; post. **3** duty of one's position; task; job; work. **4** act of kindness or unkindness; attention; service: *Through the good offices of a friend, I was able to get a job.* [< Latin *officium* service < *opus* work + *facere* do]

om i nous (om′ə nəs), *adj.* unfavorable; threatening: *ominous clouds.* —**om′i nous ly,** *adv.* —**om′i nous ness,** *n.*

o paque (ō pāk′), *adj.* **1** not letting light through; not transparent or translucent. **2** not conducting heat, sound, etc. **3** not shining; dark; dull. **4** hard to understand; obscure. **5** stupid. —*n.* something opaque. [< Latin *opacus* dark, shady] —**o paque′ly,** *adv.*

op pro bri um (ə prō′brē əm), *n.* **1** disgrace or reproach caused by shameful conduct; infamy; scorn; abuse. **2** cause or object of such reproach. [< Latin < *opprobrare* to reproach < *ob-* at, against + *probrum* infamy, reproach]

o ver wrought (ō′vər rôt′), *adj.* **1** wearied or exhausted by too much work or excitement; greatly excited: *overwrought nerves.* **2** too elaborate. —*v.* a pt. and a pp. of **overwork.**

pa gan (pā′gən), *n.* **1** person who is not a Christian, Jew, or Moslem; one who worships many gods, or no gods; heathen. The ancient Greeks and Romans were pagans. **2** person who has no religion. [< Latin *paganus* rustic (at a time when Christianity was accepted by urban populations) < *pagus* village]

pal frey (pôl′frē), *n., pl.* **-freys.** ARCHAIC. a gentle riding horse, especially one used by women. [< Old French *palefrey* < Late Latin *paraveredus* horse for outlying districts]

pal lid (pal′id), *adj.* lacking normal color; wan; pale: *a pallid complexion.* [< Latin *pallidum*]

pal pi tate (pal′pə tāt), *v.i.,* **-tat ed, -tat ing. 1** beat very rapidly, as from emotion, exercise, or disease; throb: *Your heart palpitates when you are excited.* **2** quiver; tremble. [< Latin *palpitare* to throb < *palpare* to pat]

pan de mo ni um (pan′də mō′nē əm), *n.* **1** place of wild disorder or lawless confusion. **2** wild uproar or lawlessness.

pan o ram a (pan′ə ram′ə), *n.* **1** a wide, unbroken view of a surrounding region. **2** a complete survey of some subject: *a panorama of history.* **3** a continuously passing or changing scene: *the panorama of city life.* [< *pan-* + Greek *horama* view < *horan* to see]

par a mour (par′ə mùr), *n.* **1** person who takes the place of a husband or wife illegally. **2** ARCHAIC. lover. [< Old French < *par amour* by love]

par a pet (par′ə pet, par′ə pit), *n.* **1** a low wall or mound of stone, earth, etc., in front of a walk or platform at the top of a fort, trench, etc., to protect soldiers; rampart. **2** a low wall or barrier at the edge of a balcony, roof, bridge, etc. [< Italian *parapetto* < *parare* defend + *petto* chest]

par a pher nal ia (par′ə fər nā′lyə), *n., pl.* or *sing.* **1** personal belongings. **2** equipment; outfit. [< Medieval Latin < Greek *parapherna* a woman's personal property besides her dowry < *para-* beside + *phernē* dowry]

parch ment (pärch′mənt), *n.* **1** the skin of sheep, goats, etc., prepared for use as a writing material. **2** manuscript or document written on parchment. [< Old French *parchemin,* alteration of Greek *pergamēnē* of Pergamum, where it came from]

par ish (par′ish), *n.* **1** district that has its own church and clergyman. **2** people of a parish. **3** members of the congregation of a particular church. [< Old French *paroisse* < Late Latin *parochia* < Late Greek *paroikia,* ultimately < *para-* + *oikos* dwelling]

**penny**

| a | hat | i | it | oi | oil | ch | child | | a in about |
|---|-----|---|----|----|----|----|------|---|-----------|
| ā | age | ī | ice | ou | out | ng | long | | e in taken |
| ä | far | o | hot | u | cup | sh | she | ə = | i in pencil |
| e | let | ō | open | ù | put | th | thin | | o in lemon |
| ē | equal | ô | order | ü | rule | ᴙʜ | then | | u in circus |
| ėr | term | | | | | zh | measure | | < = derived from |

par ley (pär′lē), *n., pl.* **-leys. 1** conference or informal talk. **2** an informal discussion with an enemy during a truce about terms of surrender, exchange of prisoners, etc. [< Old French *parlee,* past participle of *parler* speak < Late Latin *parabolare* < *parabola* speech, story]

par lia ment (pär′lə mənt), *n.* **1** council or congress that is the highest lawmaking body in some countries. **2** the highest lawmaking body of any political unit. [< Old French *parlement* < *parler* speak. See PARLEY.]

par quet (pär kā′, pär ket′), *n., adj., v.,* **-queted** (-käd′, -ket′id), **-quet ing** (-kā′ing, -ket′ing), or **-quet ted** (-ket′id), **-quet ting** (-ket′ing). —*n.* **1** an inlaid wooden flooring. **2** the main floor of a theater; orchestra. —*adj.* made of parquet: *parquet floors.* —*v.t.* make or put down (an inlaid wooden floor). [< French, an enclosed portion, diminutive of *parc* park]

**parquet** (def. 1)

par ry (par′ē), *v.,* **-ried, -ry ing,** *n., pl.* **-ries.** —*v.t.* **1** ward off or block (a thrust, stroke, weapon, etc.) in fencing, boxing, etc. **2** meet and turn aside (an awkward question, a threat, etc.); avoid; evade. —*n.* act of parrying; avoiding. [< French *parez,* imperative of *parer* ward off < Italian *parare* < Latin, prepare]

pas teur ize (pas′chə rīz′, pas′tə rīz′), *v.t.,* **-ized, -iz ing.** heat (milk, wine, beer, etc.) to a high enough temperature and for a long enough time to destroy harmful bacteria and prevent or arrest fermentation. When milk is pasteurized, it is heated to about 145 degrees Fahrenheit (63 degrees Celsius) for not less than 30 minutes, then chilled quickly to 50 degrees Fahrenheit (10 degrees Celsius) or less. [< Louis *Pasteur*]

pa vil ion (pə vil′yən), *n.* **1** a light building, usually somewhat open, used for shelter, pleasure, etc.: *a dance pavilion, a bathing pavilion.* **2** a large tent with a floor raised on posts, and usually with a peaked top. [< Old French *pavillon* < Latin *papilionem* tent]

peal (pēl), *n.* **1** a loud, long sound: *a peal of thunder, peals of laughter.* **2** the loud ringing of bells. **3** set of bells tuned to each other, especially a set of seven tuned to the tones of the major scale for use in ringing changes. **4** a series of changes rung on a set of bells. —*v.t., v.i.* sound out in a peal; ring: *The bells pealed forth their message of joy.* [Middle English *pele,* ultimately < Latin *ad* to + *pellere* to drive]

pee vish (pē′vish), *adj.* **1** feeling cross; fretful; complaining: *a peevish child.* **2** showing annoyance or irritation. [Middle English *pevysh*] —**pee′vish ly,** *adv.* —**pee′vish ness,** *n.*

pence (pens), *n.* a pl. of **penny** (defs. 2 and 3).

pen chant (pen′chənt), *n.* a strong taste or liking; inclination: *a penchant for taking long walks.* [< French, present participle of *pencher* to incline]

pen ny (pen′ē), *n., pl.* **pen nies** (or **pence** for 2 and 3). **1** cent. 100 pennies = 1 dollar. **2** a British coin. 100 pennies = 1 pound. **3** a former British coin equal to ¹⁄₁₂ of a shilling. Until 1971, 240 pennies made one pound.

**GLOSSARY**

893

**pensive**

**pen sive** (pen′siv), *adj.* **1** thoughtful in a serious or sad way. **2** melancholy. [< Old French *pensif* < *penser* think < Latin *pensare* ponder < *pendere* weigh] —**pen′sive ly**, *adv.* —**pen′sive ness**, *n.*

**per am bu la tor** (pə ram′byə lā′tər), *n.* **1** BRITISH. a baby's carriage; pram. **2** person who perambulates.

**per cep ti ble** (pər sep′tə bəl), *adj.* that can be perceived: *a perceptible improvement.* —**per cep′ti bly**, *adv.*

**per force** (pər fôrs′, pər fōrs′), *adv.* by necessity; necessarily. [< Old French *par force* by force]

**per il ous** (per′ə ləs), *adj.* full of peril; dangerous. —**per′il ous ly**, *adv.* —**per′il ous ness**, *n.*

**per i wig** (per′ə wig), *n.* wig.

**per me ate** (pèr′mē āt), *v.t.*, **-at ed, -at ing. 1** spread through the whole of; pass through; pervade: *Smoke permeated the house.* **2** penetrate through pores or openings; soak through. [< Latin *permeatum* passed through < *per-* through + *meare* to pass]

**per pen dic u lar** (pèr′pən dik′yə lər), *adj.* **1** standing straight up; vertical; upright. **2** very steep; precipitous. **3** at right angles to a given line, plane, or surface. —*n.* **1** line or plane at right angles to another line, plane, or surface. **2** an upright or erect position. [< Latin *perpendicularis* < *perpendiculum* < *per-* thoroughly + *pendere* hang] —**per′pen dic′u lar ly**, *adv.*

**per plex** (pər pleks′), *v.t.* **1** trouble with doubt; puzzle; bewilder. **2** make difficult to understand or settle; confuse.

**per se vere** (pèr′sə vir′), *v.i.*, **-vered, -ver ing.** continue steadily in doing something hard; persist. [< Latin *perseverare* < *per-* thoroughly + *severus* strict]

**per vade** (pər vād′), *v.t.*, **-vad ed, -vad ing.** go or spread throughout; be throughout: *The odor of pines pervades the air.* [< Latin *pervadere* < *per-* through + *vadere* go] —**per vad′er**, *n.*

**pes ti lence** (pes′tl əns), *n.* **1** any infectious or contagious epidemic disease that spreads rapidly, often causing many deaths. **2** the bubonic plague.

**pes ti len tial** (pes′tl en′shəl), *adj.* **1** like a pestilence, or rapidly spreading epidemic disease; having to do with pestilences. **2** causing or likely to cause pestilence. —**pes′ti len′tial ly**, *adv.*

**pet u lant** (pech′ə lənt), *adj.* likely to have little fits of bad temper; irritable over trifles; peevish. [< Latin *petulantem*] —**pet′u lant ly**, *adv.*

**phan tasm** (fan′taz′əm), *n.* **1** thing seen only in one's imagination; unreal fancy: *the phantasms of a dream.* **2** a supposed appearance of an absent person, living or dead. **3** a deceiving likeness (of something). [< Greek *phantasma* image, ultimately < *phainein* to show]

**phan tas ma** (fan taz′mə), *n.*, *pl.* **-ma ta.** phantasm (defs. 1, 2).

**pho bi a** (fō′bē ə), *n.* a persistent, abnormal, or irrational fear of a certain thing or group of things. [< Greek *-phobia* < *phobos* fear] —**pho bic** (fō′bik), *adj.*

**phos phate** (fos′fāt), *n.* drink of carbonated water flavored with fruit syrup, and containing a little phosphoric acid.

**pil grim age** (pil′grə mij), *n.* **1** a pilgrim's journey; journey to some sacred place as an act of religious devotion. **2** a long journey.

**pil lage** (pil′ij), *v.*, **-laged, -lag ing**, *n.* —*v.t.* rob with violence; plunder: *Pirates pillaged the towns along the coast.* —*v.i.* take booty; plunder. —*n.* act of plundering or taking as spoil; plunder, especially as practiced in war. [< Old French *piller* to plunder]

**pince-nez** (pans′nā′, pins′nā′), *n.*, *pl.* **pince-nez** (pans′nāz′, pins′nāz′). eyeglasses kept in place by a spring that clips onto the bridge of the nose. [< French, pinch-nose < *pincer* to pinch + *nez* nose < Latin *nasus*]

**pin ion** (pin′yən), *v.t.* bind the arms of; bind (to something); bind: *pinion a person's arms.* [< Middle French *pignon* < Popular Latin *pinnionem* < Latin *penna* feather and *pinna* wing]

**pi ous** (pī′əs), *adj.* **1** having or showing reverence for God; righteous. **2** done under pretense of religion or of serving a good cause: *a pious fraud.* **3** sacred rather than secular. [< Latin *pius*] —**pi′ous ly**, *adv.* —**pi′ous ness**, *n.*

**pi quan cy** (pē′kən sē), *n.* piquant quality.

**pi quant** (pē′kənt), *adj.* **1** stimulating to the mind, interest, etc.: *a piquant bit of news, a piquant face.* **2** pleasantly sharp; stimulating to the taste: *a piquant sauce.* [< French, pricking, stinging]

**piv ot** (piv′ət), *n.* **1** shaft, pin, or point on which something turns. **2** a turn on or as if on a pivot. **3** that on which something turns, hinges, or depends; central point. —*v.t.* mount on, attach by, or provide with a pivot. —*v.i.* turn on or as if on a pivot. [< French]

**plac id** (plas′id), *adj.* pleasantly calm or peaceful; quiet: *a placid lake, a placid temper.* [< Latin *placidus* < *placere* to please] —**plac′id ly**, *adv.*

**plain tive** (plān′tiv), *adj.* expressive of sorrow; mournful; sad. [< Old French *plaintif* < *plaint* plaint] —**plain′tive ly**, *adv.*

**plau si ble** (plô′zə bəl), *adj.* **1** appearing true, reasonable, or fair. **2** apparently worthy of confidence but often not really so: *a plausible liar.* [< Latin *plausibilis* deserving applause, pleasing < *plaudere* applaud] —**plau′si bil′i ty**, *n.* —**plau′si bly**, *adv.*

**plight**[1] (plīt), *n.* condition or situation, usually bad: *in a sad plight.* [Middle English *plite*, originally, manner of folding < Old French *pleit* < Latin *plicare* to fold]

**plight**[2] (plīt), *v.t.* promise solemnly; pledge: *plight one's loyalty.* —*n.* a solemn promise; pledge. [Old English *plihtan* < *pliht*, originally, danger, risk]

**plum met** (plum′it), *n.* plumb. —*v.i.* plunge; drop. [< Old French *plommet* < *plomb* lead < Latin *plumbum*]

**plu to crat ic** (plü′tə krat′ik), *adj.* having power and influence because of wealth. —**plu′to crat′i cal ly**, *adv.*

**ply** (plī), *v.*, **plied, ply ing.** —*v.t.* **1** work with; use: *The dressmaker plies her needle.* **2** keep up work on; work away at or on: *ply one's trade. We plied the water with our oars.* **3** urge again and again: *She plied me with questions to make me tell the secret.* **4** supply with in a pressing manner: *ply a person with food or drink.* —*v.i.* go back and forth regularly between certain places: *A bus plies between the station and the hotel.* [variant of *apply*]

**poign ant** (poi′nyənt), *adj.* **1** very painful; piercing: *poignant suffering.* **2** stimulating to the mind, feelings, or passions; keen; intense: *a subject of poignant interest.* [< Old French, present participle of *poindre* to prick < Latin *pungere*] —**poign′ant ly**, *adv.*

**pom pa dour** (pom′pə dôr, pom′pə dōr), *n.* **1** arrangement of a woman's hair in which it is puffed high over the forehead or brushed straight up and back from the forehead. **2** hair so arranged. [< the Marquise de *Pompadour*]

**pom pos i ty** (pom pos′ə tē), *n.*, *pl.* **-ties. 1** pompous quality. **2** pompous show of self-importance.

**pom pous** (pom′pəs), *adj.* **1** trying to seem magnificent or very important; vainglorious; self-important: *a pompous manner.* **2** overly flowery or high-flown; inflated: *pompous language.* **3** characterized by pomp; splendid; magnificent. —**pom′pous ly**, *adv.* —**pom′pous ness**, *n.*

**pon der ous** (pon′dər əs), *adj.* **1** very heavy. **2** heavy and clumsy: *A hippopotamus is ponderous.* **3** dull; tiresome: *The speaker talked in a ponderous way.* —**pon′der ous ly**, *adv.*

**pop u lous** (pop′yə ləs), *adj.* full of people; having many people per square mile. —**pop′u lous ly**, *adv.* —**pop′u lous ness**, *n.*

**por ten tous** (pôr ten′təs, pōr ten′təs), *adj.* **1** indicating evil to come; ominous; threatening. **2** amazing; extraordinary. —**por ten′tous ly**, *adv.* —**por ten′tous ness**, *n.*

**post-,** *prefix.* after in time; later: *Postwar = after a war.* [< Latin]

**post chaise,** a four-wheeled carriage used for carrying passengers and mail in the 1700s and early 1800s, usually having seats for two or four people.

**poul tice** (pōl′tis), *n.* a soft, moist mass of mustard, herbs, etc., applied to the body as a medicine. [< Latin *pultes*, plural of *puls* mush]

**pram** (pram), *n.* BRITISH INFORMAL. baby carriage; perambulator.

**prat tle** (prat′l), *v.*, **-tled, -tling**, *n.* —*v.i.* **1** talk or tell freely and carelessly, as some children do. **2** talk or tell in a foolish way. —*n.* **1** childish or foolish talk. **2** babble. [< *prate*]

GLOSSARY

894

**pre am ble** (prē′am′bəl), *n.* **1** a preliminary statement; introduction to a speech or a writing. **2** a preliminary or introductory fact or circumstance, especially one showing what is to follow.

**pre car i ous** (pri ker′ē əs, pri kar′ē əs), *adj.* not safe or secure; uncertain; dangerous; risky: *Soldiers on the battlefield lead a precarious life.* [< Latin *precarius* obtainable by prayer, uncertain < *precem* prayer] —**pre car′i ous ly,** *adv.*

**prec e dence** (pres′ə dəns, pri sēd′ns), *n.* **1** act or fact of preceding. **2** higher position or rank; greater importance: *This work takes precedence over all other work.* **3** right to precede others in ceremonies or social affairs; social superiority: *A Senator takes precedence over a Representative.*

**pre cinct** (prē′singkt), *n.* **1** district within certain boundaries, for government, administrative, or other purposes: *an election precinct, a police precinct.* **2** Often, **precincts,** *pl.* **a** space within a boundary: *Do not leave the school precincts during school hours.* **b** the region immediately surrounding a place; environs: *a factory and its precincts.* **3** boundary; limit. [< Medieval Latin *praecinctum* < Latin *praecingere* enclose < *prae-* pre- + *cingere* gird]

**pre cip i tate** (*v.* pri sip′ə tāt; *adj., n.* pri sip′ə tit, pri sip′ə tāt), *v.,* **-tat ed, -tat ing,** *adj., n.* —*v.t.* **1** hasten the beginning of; bring about suddenly: *precipitate an argument.* **2** separate (a substance) out from a solution as a solid. **3** condense (water vapor) from the air in the form of rain, dew, snow, etc. —*v.i.* **1** be deposited from solution as a solid. **2** be condensed as rain, dew, snow, etc. —*adj.* **1** very hurried; sudden: *A cool breeze caused a precipitate drop in the temperature.* **2** with great haste and force; plunging or rushing headlong; hasty; rash. [< Latin *praecipitatum* thrown headlong < *praecipitem* headlong.] —**pre cip′i tate ly,** *adv.*

**pre cip i tous** (pri sip′ə təs), *adj.* **1** like a precipice; very steep: *precipitous cliffs.* **2** hasty; rash. **3** rushing headlong; very rapid. —**pre cip′i tous ly,** *adv.*

**pre em i nent** or **pre-em i nent** (prē em′ə nənt), *adj.* standing out above all others; superior to others. —**pre em′i nent ly, pre-em′i nent ly,** *adv.*

**preg nant** (preg′nənt), *adj.* **1** having an embryo or embryos developing in the uterus; being with child or young. **2** filled; full: *words pregnant with meaning.* **3** abounding with ideas; inventive: *a pregnant mind.* [< Latin *praegnantem* < *prae-* pre- + *gen-* to bear]

**pre med i tate** (prē med′ə tāt), *v.t.,* **-tat ed, -tat ing.** consider or plan beforehand: *The murder was premeditated.*

**pre rog a tive** (pri rog′ə tiv), *n.* **1** right or privilege that nobody else has: *The government has the prerogative of coining money.* **2** special superiority of right or privilege, such as may derive from an official position, office, etc. [< Latin *praerogativa* allotted to vote first < *praerogare* ask for a vote first < *prae-* pre- + *rogare* ask]

**pres age** (pres′ij; pri sāj′), *v.t.,* **pre saged, pre sag ing. 1** give warning of; predict: *Some people think that a circle around the moon presages a storm.* **2** have or give a presentiment or prophetic impression of. [< Latin *praesagium* < *prae-* pre- + *sagus* prophetic]

**pre sump tu ous** (pri zump′chü əs), *adj.* acting without permission or right; too bold; forward. —**pre sump′tu ous ly,** *adv.*

**pre text** (prē′tekst), *n.* a false reason concealing the real reason; misleading excuse; pretense: *He did not go, on the pretext of being too tired.* [< Latin *praetextum,* literally, woven in front, alleged as an excuse < *prae-* pre- + *texere* to weave]

**pri va tion** (prī vā′shən), *n.* **1** lack of the comforts or of the necessities of life: *Many children were hungry and homeless because of privation during the war.* **2** a being deprived; loss; absence. [< Latin *privationem* < *privatum* deprived]

**pro cure** (prə kyùr′), *v.t.,* **-cured, -cur ing.** obtain by care or effort; secure: *procure a job.* [< Latin *procurare* manage < *pro-* before + *cura* care]

**pro di gious** (prə dij′əs), *adj.* **1** very great; huge; vast: *The ocean contains a prodigious amount of water.* **2** wonderful; marvelous. [< Latin *prodigiosus* < *prodigium* prodigy, omen] —**pro di′gious ly,** *adv.* —**pro di′gious ness,** *n.*

| a hat | i it | oi oil | ch child | | |
|---|---|---|---|---|---|
| ā age | ī ice | ou out | ng long | | a in about |
| ä far | o hot | u cup | sh she | ə = | e in taken |
| e let | ō open | ù put | th thin | | i in pencil |
| ē equal | ô order | ü rule | ŦH then | | o in lemon |
| ėr term | | | zh measure | | u in circus |
| | | | | < = derived from | |

**prof fer** (prof′ər), *v.t.* offer for acceptance; present; tender: *We proffered regrets at having to leave so early.* [< Anglo-French *proffrir* < Old French *pro-* forth + *offrir* to offer]

**pro fuse** (prə fyüs′), *adj.* **1** very abundant: *profuse thanks.* **2** spending or giving freely; lavish; extravagant. [ < Latin *profusum* poured forth < *pro-* forth + *fundere* pour] —**pro fuse′ly,** *adv.*

**pro fu sion** (prə fyü′zhən), *n.* **1** great abundance. **2** extravagance; lavishness.

**prom on to ry** (prom′ən tôr′ē, prom′ən tōr′ē), *n., pl.* **-ries.** a high point of land extending from the coast into the water; headland. [< Latin *promonturium,* probably < *pro-* forward + *montem* mountain]

**pro pi tious** (prə pish′əs), *adj.* **1** holding well; favorable: *propitious weather for our trip.* **2** favorably inclined; gracious. [< Latin *propitius,* originally, falling forward < *pro-* forward + *petere* go toward] —**pro pi′tious ly,** *adv.* —**pro pi′tious ness,** *n.*

**pro pri e ty** (prə prī′ə tē), *n., pl.* **-ties. 1** quality or condition of being proper; fitness. **2** proper behavior: *Propriety demands good table manners.* **3** proprieties, *pl.* conventional standards or requirements of proper behavior. [ < Latin *proprietatem* appropriateness, property < *proprius* one's own, proper]

**pro sa ic** (prō zā′ik), *adj.* like prose; matter-of-fact; ordinary; not exciting. —**pro sa′i cal ly,** *adv.* —**pro sa′ic ness,** *n.*

**pro sce ni um** (prō sē′nē əm), *n., pl.* **-ni a** (-nē ə). **1** the part of the stage in front of the curtain. **2** curtain and the framework that holds it. [< Latin < Greek *proskēnion* < *pro-* in front of + *skēnē* stage, scene]

**pro scrip tion** (prō skrip′shən), *n.* a proscribing or a being proscribed; banishment; outlawry.

**pros e cu tion** (pros′ə kyü′shən), *n.* **1** the carrying on of a lawsuit: *The prosecution will be abandoned if the stolen money is returned.* **2** side that starts action against another in a court of law.

**pros trate** (pros′trāt), *adj.* **1** lying flat with face downward: *She was humbly prostrate in prayer.* **2** lying flat: *I stumbled and fell prostrate on the floor.* [< Latin *prostratum* thrown down flat < *pro-* forth + *sternere* spread out]

**prow ess** (prou′is), *n.* **1** bravery; daring. **2** brave or daring acts. **3** unusual skill or ability. [< Old French *proece* < *prod* valiant]

**prox im i ty** (prok sim′ə tē), *n.* nearness; closeness.

**pru dent** (prüd′nt), *adj.* **1** planning carefully ahead of time; sensible; discreet: *A prudent man saves part of his wages.* **2** characterized by good judgment or good management: *a prudent policy.* [< Latin *prudentem,* contraction of *providentem* provident] —**pru′dent ly,** *adv.*

**pu is sant** (pyü′ə sənt, pyü is′nt, pwis′nt), *adj.* having great power or strength; powerful; mighty. [< Old French < Popular Latin *possentem* < Latin *potentem* potent] —**pu′is sant ly,** *adv.*

**pu ma** (pyü′mə, pü′mə), *n.* a large, tawny wildcat found in many parts of North and South America; cougar; mountain lion; panther. [< Spanish < Quechua]

**pun gent** (pun′jənt), *adj.* **1** sharply affecting the organs of taste and smell: *a pungent pickle, the pungent smell of burning leaves.* **2** sharp; biting: *pungent criticism.* **3** stimulating to the mind; keen; lively: *a pungent wit.* [< Latin *pungentem* piercing, pricking < *pungere* pierce, prick]

**GLOSSARY**

**purl** (pėrl), *v.i.* **1** flow with rippling motions and a murmuring sound: *A shallow brook purls.* **2** pass with a sound like this. —*n.* **1** a purling motion or sound. **2** act of purling. [perhaps < Scandinavian (Norwegian) *purla* to ripple]

**pur vey or** (pər vā′ər), *n.* **1** person who supplies provisions. **2** person who supplies anything: *a purveyor of gossip.*

**pyre** (pīr), *n.* **1** pile of wood for burning a dead body as a funeral rite. **2** any large pile or heap of burnable material. [< Greek *pyra* < *pyr* fire]

**quad ran gle** (kwod′rang′gəl), *n.* a four-sided space or court wholly or nearly surrounded by buildings: *the quadrangle of a palace, a college quadrangle.* [< Late Latin *quadrangulum* < Latin *quadr-* four + *angulus* angle]

**quaint** (kwānt), *adj.* strange or odd in an interesting, pleasing, or amusing way: *Old photographs seem quaint to us today.* [< Old French *cointe* pretty, clever < Latin *cognitum* known] —**quaint′ly,** *adv.* —**quaint′ness,** *n.*

**quay** (kē), *n.* a solid landing place where ships load and unload, often built of stone. Also, FRENCH *quai.* [< Old French *cai*; of Celtic origin]

**quo rum** (kwôr′əm, kwōr′əm), *n.* number of members of any society or assembly that must be present if the business done is to be legal or binding. [< Latin, of whom]

**rab ble** (rab′əl), *n.* **1** a disorderly, boisterous crowd; mob. **2 the rabble,** (in contemptuous use) the lower classes. [Middle English *rabel*]

**rab ble ment** (rab′əl mənt), *n.* rabble.

**rag a muf fin** (rag′ə muf′ən), *n.* a dirty, ragged person, especially a child. [probably < *rag*]

**rak ish** (rā′kish), *adj.* **1** smart; jaunty; dashing: *a hat set at a rakish angle.* **2** suggesting dash and speed: *a rakish boat.* [< *rake*] —**rak′ish ly,** *adv.* —**rak′ish ness,** *n.*

**ram part** (ram′pärt), *n.* **1** a wide bank of earth, often with a wall on top as a fortification, built around a fort to help defend it. **2** anything that defends; defense; protection. [< Middle French *rempart* < *remparer* fortify]

**ran cid** (ran′sid), *adj.* **1** stale; spoiled: *rancid butter.* **2** tasting or smelling like stale fat or butter: *rancid odor.* [< Latin *rancidus* < *rancere* be rank] —**ran′cid ly,** *adv.* —**ran′cid ness,** *n.*

**rank** (rangk), *adj.* **1** growing in a thick, coarse way: *a rank growth of weeds.* **2** producing a dense but coarse growth: *rank swampland.* **3** having a strong, bad smell or taste: *rank meat, rank tobacco.* [Old English *ranc* proud] —**rank′ly,** *adv.* —**rank′ness,** *n.*

**ra pa cious** (rə pā′shəs), *adj.* **1** seizing by force; plundering. **2** grasping; greedy. **3** living by the capture of prey; predatory. [< Latin *rapacem* grasping < *rapere* seize] —**ra pa′cious ly,** *adv.* —**ra pa′cious ness,** *n.*

**ra pi er** (rā′pē ər), *n.* a long and light sword used for thrusting. [< Middle French *rapière*] —**ra′pi er like′,** *adj.*

**rap port** (ra pôr′, ra pōr′; ra pôrt′, ra pōrt′; French rȧ pôr′), *n.* **1** relation; connection. **2** agreement; harmony. [< French]

**rapt** (rapt), *adj.* **1** lost in delight. **2** so busy thinking of or enjoying one thing that one does not know what else is happening. [< Latin *raptum* seized] —**rapt′ly,** *adv.* —**rapt′ness,** *n.*

**rap tur ous** (rap′chər əs), *adj.* full of rapture; expressing or feeling rapture. —**rap′tur ous ly,** *adv.* —**rap′tur ous ness,** *n.*

**rash** (rash), *adj.* **1** too hasty and careless; impetuous. **2** characterized by undue haste: *a rash promise.* [Middle English *rasch* quick] —**rash′ly,** *adv.* —**rash′ness,** *n.*

**realm** (relm), *n.* **1** kingdom. **2** region or sphere in which something rules or prevails. [< Old French *realme,* ultimately < Latin *regimen* rule]

**rea son a ble** (rē′zn ə bəl), *adj.* **1** according to reason; sensible; not foolish. **2** not asking too much; fair; just. **3** able to reason. —**rea′son a ble ness,** *n.* —**rea′son a bly,** *adv.*

**re cip ro cal** (ri sip′rə kəl), *adj.* **1** in return: *Although she gave me a present, she expected no reciprocal gift from me.* **2** mutual: *reciprocal distrust.* [< Latin *reciprocus* returning] —**re cip′ro cal ly,** *adv.*

**rec on cile** (rek′ən sīl), *v.t.,* **-ciled, -cil ing. 1** make friends again. **2** settle (a disagreement or difference). **3** make agree; bring into harmony: *I could not reconcile that story with the facts.* **4** make satisfied; make no longer opposed: *It is hard to reconcile oneself to a long illness.* [< Latin *reconciliare* < *re-* back + *concilium* bond of union] —**rec′on cile′ment,** *n.* —**rec′on cil′er,** *n.*

**rec on cil i a tion** (rek′ən sil′ē ā′shən), *n.* **1** a reconciling; bringing together again in friendship. **2** a being reconciled; settlement or adjustment of disagreements or differences.

**re con struct** (rē′kən strukt′), *v.t.* construct again; rebuild; make over.

**red o lent** (red′l ənt), *adj.* having a pleasant smell; fragrant; aromatic. [< Latin *redolentem* emitting scent < *re-, red-* back + *olere* to smell] —**red′o lent ly,** *adv.*

**re dress** (*v.* ri dres′; *n.* rē′dres, ri dres′), *v.t.* set right; repair; remedy. —*n.* **1** a setting right; reparation; relief: *Anyone who has been injured deserves redress.* **2** the means of a remedy. [< Middle French *redresser* < *re-* again + *dresser* straighten, arrange]

**ref e ren dum** (ref′ə ren′dəm), *n., pl.* **-dums, -da** (-də). **1** principle or process of submitting a bill already passed by the lawmaking body to the direct vote of the citizens for approval or rejection. **2** a vote on such a bill. **3** the submitting of any matter to a direct vote. [< Latin, that which must be referred < *referre* refer]

**re fract** (ri frakt′), *v.t.* bend (a ray, waves, etc.) from a straight course. *Water refracts light.* [< Latin *refractum* broken back, refracted < *re-* back + *frangere* to break]

**re fute** (ri fyüt′), *v.t.,* **-fut ed, -fut ing.** show (a claim, opinion, or argument) to be false or incorrect; prove wrong; disprove. [< Latin *refutare* cause to fall back] —**re fut′er,** *n.*

**re it e rate** (rē it′ə rāt′), *v.t.,* **-rat ed, -rat ing.** say or do several times; repeat (an action, demand, etc.) again and again: *reiterate a command.* —**re it′e ra′tion,** *n.*

**re join** (ri join′), *v.t.* say in answer; reply. [< Old French *rejoindre* < *re-* + *joindre* join]

**re ju ve nate** (ri jü′və nāt′), *v.t.,* **-nat ed, -nat ing.** make young or vigorous again; give youthful qualities to. [< *re-* + Latin *juvenis* young] —**re ju′ve na′tion,** *n.* —**re ju′ve na′tor,** *n.*

**rel ish** (rel′ish), *n.* **1** a pleasant taste; good flavor: *Hunger gives relish to simple food.* **2** something to add flavor to food, such as olives, pickles, or a highly seasoned sauce. **3** a slight dash (of something). **4** keen enjoyment or appetite; zest: *eat with great relish.* [earlier *reles* < Old French, remainder < *relesser, relaissier* release]

**re luc tance** (ri luk′təns), *n.* **1** a reluctant feeling or action; unwillingness. **2** slowness in action because of unwillingness. [< Latin *reluctantem* struggling against < *re-* back + *luctari* to struggle]

**re mon strance** (ri mon′strəns), *n.* act of remonstrating; protest; complaint.

**re mon strate** (ri mon′strāt), *v.i.,* **-strat ed, -strat ing.** speak, reason, or plead in complaint or protest: *The teacher remonstrated with us about our unruly behavior.* [< Medieval Latin *remonstratum* pointed out, ultimately < Latin *re-* back + *monstrum* sign] —**re mon stra tion** (rē′mən strā′shən), *n.*

**ren dez vous** (rän′də vü), *n., pl.* **-vous** (-vüz). **1** an appointment or engagement to meet at a fixed place or time; meeting by agreement. **2** a meeting place; gathering place: *The family had two favorite rendezvous, the library and the garden.* [< Middle French < *rendez-vous* present yourself!]

**rent** (rent), *n.* a torn place; tear; split. —*adj.* torn; split. —*v.* pt. and pp. of **rend.**

**rep a ra tion** (rep′ə rā′shən), *n.* **1** a giving of satisfaction or compensation for wrong or injury done. **2 reparations,** *pl.* compensation for wrong or injury, especially payments made by a defeated country for the devastation of territory during war.

**re past** (ri past′), *n.* meal; food. [< Old French, ultimately < Latin *re-* again + *pascere* to feed]

**re per cus sion** (rē′pər kush′ən), *n.* **1** an indirect influence or reaction from an event: *repercussions of a scandal.* **2** sound flung back; echo. **3** a springing back; rebound; recoil.

**re plen ish** (ri plen′ish), *v.t.* fill again; provide a new supply for; renew: *replenish one's wardrobe. You had better replenish the fire.* [< Old French *repleniss-*, a form of *replenir*, fill again, ultimately < Latin *re-* again + *plenus* full] —**re plen′ish er,** *n.* —**re plen′ish ment,** *n.*

**re pute** (ri pyüt′), *n., v.,* **-put ed, -put ing.** —*n.* **1** reputation: *a generous man by repute.* **2** good reputation. —*v.t.* suppose to be; consider; suppose: *They are reputed to be quite rich.* [< Latin *reputare* consider < *re-* over + *putare* think]

**res in** (rez′n), *n.* **1** a sticky, yellow or brown, transparent or translucent substance that flows from certain plants and trees, especially the pine and fir. It does not conduct electricity and is used in medicine, varnish, plastics, inks, and adhesives. **2** rosin. **3** any of a large group of resinous substances that are made artificially and are used especially in making plastics. [< Latin *resina*] —**res′in like′,** *adj.*

**res in ous** (rez′n əs), *adj.* **1** of resin. **2** like resin. **3** containing resin; full of resin.

**re spec tive** (ri spek′tiv), *adj.* belonging to each; particular; individual: *The classes went to their respective rooms.*

**res pite** (res′pit), *n.* **1** time of relief and rest; lull: *a respite from the heat.* **2** a putting off; delay, especially in carrying out a sentence of death; reprieve. [< Old French *respit* < Late Latin *respectus* expectation < Latin, regard]

**res tive** (res′tiv), *adj.* **1** restless; uneasy. **2** hard to manage. [< Old French *restif* motionless < *rester* remain.] —**res′tive ly,** *adv.*

**re sume** (ri züm′), *v.,* **-sumed, -sum ing.** —*v.t.* **1** begin again; go on: *Resume reading where we left off.* **2** get or take again: *Those standing may resume their seats.* —*v.i.* begin again; continue. [< Latin *resumere* < *re-* again + *sumere* take up] —**re sum′a ble,** *adj.*

**re ten tive** (ri ten′tiv), *adj.* **1** able to hold or keep. **2** able to remember easily. —**re ten′tive ly,** *adv.*

**re ver be rate** (ri vėr′bə rāt′) *v.,* **-rat ed, -rat ing.** —*v.i.* **1** echo back: *His voice reverberates from the high ceiling.* **2** be cast back; be reflected a number of times, as light or heat. [< Latin *reverberatum* beaten back < *re-* back + *verber* a blow] —**re ver′be ra′tion,** *n.* —**re ver′be ra′tive,** *adj.*

**rev er y** (rev′ər ē), *n., pl.* **-er ies.** **1** dreamy thoughts; dreamy thinking of pleasant things. **2** condition of being lost in dreamy thoughts. Also, **reverie.** [< French *rêverie* < *rêver* to dream]

**re vin di cate** (rē vin′də kāt), *v.t.,* **-cat ed, -cat ing.** redefend successfully against opposition; uphold; justify: *The heir revindicated his claim to the fortune.*

**rife** (rīf), *adj.* **1** happening often; common; numerous; widespread. **2** full; abounding: *The city was rife with rumors of political corruption.* [Old English *rife*] —**rife′ly,** *adv.*

**right eous** (rī′chəs), *adj.* **1** doing right; virtuous; behaving justly: *a righteous person.* **2** proper; just; right: *righteous indignation.* [Old English *rihtwīs* < *riht* right + *wīs* way, manner] —**right′eous ly,** *adv.* —**right′eous ness,** *n.*

**rit u al** (rich′ü əl), *n.* **1** form or system of rites. The rites of baptism, marriage, and burial are parts of the ritual of most churches. **2** a prescribed order of performing a ceremony or rite. **3** any regularly followed routine.

**rit u al is tic** (rich′ü ə lis′tik), *adj.* **1** having to do with ritual or ritualism. **2** fond of ritual. —**rit′u al is′ti cal ly,** *adv.*

**roe buck** (rō′buk′), *n., pl.* **-bucks** or **-buck.** a male roe deer.

**rogue** (rōg), *n.* a mischievous person; scamp. [origin uncertain]

**rolling mill, 1** factory where metal is rolled into sheets and bars. **2** machine for doing this.

**rote** (rōt), *n.* **1** a set, mechanical way of doing things. **2** by rote, by memory without thought of the meaning: *learn a lesson by rote.* [Middle English]

**ro tun da** (rō tun′də), *n.* **1** a circular building or part of a building, especially one with a dome. **2** a large, high, circular room: *The Capitol in Washington has a large rotunda.* [< Italian *rotonda* < Latin *rotunda*, feminine, rotund]

**ru bi cund** (rü′bə kund), *adj.* reddish; ruddy. [< Latin *rubicundus* < *rubere* be red] —**ru′bi cun′di ty,** *n.*

| a hat | i it | oi oil | ch child | | ⎧ a in about |
|---|---|---|---|---|---|
| ā age | ī ice | ou out | ng long | | e in taken |
| ä far | o hot | u cup | sh she | ə = ⎨ i in pencil |
| e let | ō open | ù put | th thin | | o in lemon |
| ē equal | ô order | ü rule | ŦH then | | ⎩ u in circus |
| ėr term | | | zh measure | < = derived from |

**rud dy** (rud′ē), *adj.,* **-di er, -di est.** **1** red or reddish. **2** having a fresh, healthy, red look: *ruddy cheeks.* [Old English *rudig*] —**rud′di ly,** *adv.* —**rud′di ness,** *n.*

**rue** (rü), *v.,* **rued, ru ing,** *n.* —*v.t.* be sorry for; regret. —*n.* sorrow; regret. [Old English *hrēowan*]

**rue ful** (rü′fəl), *adj.* **1** sorrowful; unhappy; mournful: *a rueful expression.* **2** causing sorrow or pity: *a rueful sight.* —**rue′ful ly,** *adv.* —**rue′ful ness,** *n.*

**ruff** (ruf), *n.* a deep frill, stiff enough to stand out, worn around the neck by men and women in the 1500's and 1600's.

**ruf fi an** (ruf′ē ən), *n.* a rough, brutal, or cruel person; bully; hoodlum. —*adj.* rough; brutal; cruel. [< Middle French < Italian *ruffiano* pander]

ruff

**rup ture** (rup′chər), *n., v.,* **-tured, -tur ing.** —*n.* **1** a breaking. **2** a being broken. —*v.t.* **1** break off; burst; break. **2** affect with hernia. —*v.i.* suffer a break. [< Latin *ruptura* < *rumpere* to break]

**ruse** (rüz, rüs), *n.* scheme or device to mislead others; trick. [< French < *ruser* to dodge < Old French]

**sac ra ment** (sak′rə mənt), *n.* **1** any of certain religious ceremonies of the Christian church, considered especially sacred, such as baptism. **2** something especially sacred. [< Latin *sacramentum*, ultimately < *sacer* holy]

**sa cred** (sā′krid), *adj.* **1** belonging to or dedicated to God or a god; holy: *the sacred altar.* **2** that must not be violated or disregarded: *a sacred promise.*

**sac ri le gious** (sak′rə lij′əs, sak′rə lē′jəs), *adj.* injurious or insulting to sacred persons or things. —**sac′ri le′gious ly,** *adv.* —**sac′ri le′gious ness,** *n.* [< Latin *sacrilegium* temple robbery < *sacrum* sacred object + *legere* pick up, gather]

**sa dism** (sā′diz′əm, sad′iz′əm), *n.* an unnatural love of cruelty. [< French *sadisme* < Marquis de *Sade*, 1740–1814, who wrote about it]

**sa dist** (sā′dist, sad′ist), *n.* person who practices or is affected by sadism.

**sa ga cious** (sə gā′shəs), *adj.* **1** wise in a keen, practical way; shrewd.

**sa gac i ty** (sə gas′ə tē), *n.* keen, sound judgment; mental acuteness; shrewdness.

**sam o var** (sam′ə vär, sam′ə vär′), *n.* a metal urn used for heating water for tea. [< Russian, literally, self-boiler]

**sa ri** (sär′ē), *n.* the principal outer garment of Hindu women, a long piece of cotton or silk wrapped around the body, with one end falling nearly to the feet and the other end thrown over the head or shoulder. [< Hindi *sārī* < Sanskrit *śāṭī*]

**sa vant** (sə vänt′, sav′ənt), *n.* person of learning; sage; scholar. [< French, present participle of *savoir* know < Latin *sapere* be wise]

samovar

**scab bard** (skab′ərd), *n.* sheath or case for the blade of a sword, dagger, etc. [< Anglo-French *escaubers,* plural; of Germanic origin]

**scin til late** (sin′tl āt), *v.i.,* **-lat ed, -lat ing.** sparkle; flash: *The* *snow scintillates in the sun like diamonds. Brilliant wit scintillates.* —**scin′til lat′ing ly,** *adv.* —**scin′til la′tor,** *n.*

**scourge** (skèrj), *n., v.,* **scourged, scourg ing.** —*n.* **1** a whip; lash. **2** some thing or person that causes great trouble or misfortune. —*v.t.* **1** whip; flog; punish severely. **2** trouble very much; afflict; torment. [< Old French *escorge,* ultimately < Latin *ex-* out + *corium* a hide]

**scow** (skou), *n.* a large, rectangular, flat-bottomed boat used to carry freight, especially in bulk, as coal, sand, etc. [< Dutch *schouw*]

**scribe** (skrīb), *n., v.,* **scribed, scrib ing.** —*n.* **1** person who copies manuscripts. Before printing was invented, there were many scribes. **2** (in ancient times) a teacher of the Jewish law. **3** writer; author. **4** a public clerk or secretary. —*v.t.* mark or cut with something sharp. [< Latin *scriba* < *scribere* write]

**scru ple** (skrü′pəl), *v.,* **-pled, -ling.** *v.i.* **1** hesitate or be unwilling (to do something): *A dishonest person does not scruple to deceive others.* **2** have scruples. [< Latin *scrupulus* a feeling of uneasiness, originally diminutive of *scrupus* sharp stone, figuratively, uneasiness, anxiety]

**scru ti nize** (skrüt′n īz), *v.t.,* **-nized, -niz ing.** examine closely; inspect carefully: *The jeweler scrutinized the diamond for flaws.* —**scru′ti niz′er,** *n.* —**scru′ti niz′ing ly,** *adv.*

**scul lion** (skul′yən), *n.* ARCHAIC. servant who does the dirty, rough work in a kitchen. [< Old French *escouillon* swab, cloth < *escouve* broom < Latin *scopa*]

**scut tle** (skut′l), *v.,* **-tled, -tling,** *n.* —*v.i.* run with quick, hurried steps; scamper; scurry. —*n.* a short, hurried run. [variant of *scuddle,* frequentative of *scud*] —**scut′tler,** *n.*

**scythe** (sīŦH), *n., v.,* **scythed, scyth ing.** —*n.* a long, thin, slightly curved blade on a long handle, for cutting grass, etc. —*v.t.* cut or mow with a scythe. [Old English *sithe;* spelling influenced by Latin *scindere* to cut]

**se ces sion** (si sesh′ən), *n.* a formal withdrawing from an organization; a seceding.

**sec u lar** (sek′yə lər), *adj.* **1** not religious or sacred; worldly: *secular music, a secular education.* **2** living in the world; not belonging to a religious order: *the secular clergy, a secular priest.* —*n.* **1** a secular priest. **2** layperson. [< Latin *saecularis* < *saeculum* age, world] —**sec′u lar ly,** *adv.*

**sed en tar y** (sed′n ter′ē), *adj.* **1** used to sitting still much of the time: *Sedentary people get little physical exercise.* **2** that keeps one sitting still much of the time: *Bookkeeping is a sedentary occupation.* **3** not migratory: *Pigeons are sedentary birds.* **4** fixed to one spot: *a sedentary mollusk.* [< Latin *sedentarius,* ultimately < *sedere* sit] —**sed′en tar′i ly,** *adv.* —**sed′en tar′i ness,** *n.*

**sedge** (sej), *n.* any of a large family of monocotyledonous herbs growing chiefly in wet places, resembling grasses. [Old English *secg*]

**sem blance** (sem′bləns), *n.* **1** outward appearance: *Their story had the semblance of truth, but was really false.* **2** likeness: *These clouds have the semblance of a huge head.* [< Old French < *sembler* seem < Latin *similare* make similar < *similis* similar]

**ser pen tine** (*adj.* sèr′pən tēn′, sèr′pən tīn′; *n.* sèr′pən tēn′), *adj.* **1** of or like a serpent. **2** winding; twisting: *the serpentine course of a creek.* **3** cunning; sly; treacherous: *a serpentine plot.* —*n.* anything twisted or winding like a snake.

**ser vile** (sèr′vəl), *adj.* **1** like that of slaves; mean; base: *servile flattery.* **2** of or having to do with slaves: *a servile revolt, servile work.* **3** fit for a slave. **4** yielding through fear, lack of spirit, etc.: *An honest judge cannot be servile to public opinion.* [< Latin *servilis* < *servus* slave] —**ser′vile ly,** *adv.* —**ser′vile ness,** *n.*

**se vere** (sə vir′), *adj.,* **-ver er, -ver est. 1** very strict; harsh: *a severe reprimand.* **2** sharp or violent: *a severe headache, a severe storm.* **3** serious; grave: *a severe illness.* **4** very plain or simple; without ornament: *severe black clothes.* **5** difficult: *a series of severe tests.* [< Latin *severus*] —**se vere′ly,** *adv.* —**se vere′ness,** *n.*

**sex ton** (sek′stən), *n.* person who takes care of a church building. [< Old French *secrestein* < Medieval Latin *sacristanus* sacristan.]

**shrewd** (shrüd), *adj.* **1** having a sharp mind; showing a keen wit; clever. **2** keen; sharp. **3** ARCHAIC. mean; mischievous. [earlier *shrewed* bad-tempered, shrewish; wicked < *shrew*] —**shrewd′ly,** *adv.* —**shrewd′ness,** *n.*

**shroud** (shroud), *n.* **1** cloth or garment in which a dead person is wrapped or dressed for burial. **2** something that covers, conceals, or veils: *The fog was a shroud over the city.* —*v.t.* **1** wrap or dress for burial. **2** cover; conceal; veil: *Their plans are shrouded in secrecy.* [Old English *scrūd*] —**shroud′like′,** *adj.*

**siege** (sēj), *n., v.,* **sieged, sieg ing.** —*n.* **1** the surrounding of a fortified place by enemy forces trying to capture it; a besieging or a being besieged: *The Japanese laid siege to Corregidor.* **2** any long or persistent effort to overcome resistance; any long-continued attack: *a siege of illness.* **3 lay siege to, a** besiege. **b** attempt to win or gain by long and persistent effort. —*v.t.* besiege. [< Old French, seat, siege, ultimately < Latin *sedere* sit]

**sim u late** (sim′yə lāt), *v.t.,* **-lat ed, -lat ing. 1** put on a false appearance of; pretend; feign: *simulate interest.* **2** act like; look like; imitate: *Certain insects simulate flowers or leaves.* [< Latin *simulatum* simulated < *similis* like] —**sim′u la′tor,** *n.*

**sir rah** (sir′ə), *n.* ARCHAIC. fellow, used to address men and boys when speaking contemptuously, angrily, impatiently, etc. [apparently < *sir* + *ha*]

**skep ti cal** (skep′tə kəl), *adj.* **1** of or like a skeptic; inclined to doubt; not believing easily. **2** questioning the truth of theories or apparent facts. Also, **sceptical.** —**skep′ti cal ly,** *adv.*

**skirl** (skèrl), *v.t., v.i.* (of bagpipes) sound loudly and shrilly. —*n.* sound of a bagpipe. [< Scandinavian (dialectal Norwegian) *skrylla*]

**skir mish** (skèr′mish), *n.* **1** a brief fight between small groups of soldiers. **2** a slight conflict, argument, contest, etc. —*v.i.* take part in a skirmish. [< Old French *eskirmiss-,* a form of *eskirmir,* originally, ward off; < Germanic origin] —**skir′mish er,** *n.*

**slack en** (slak′ən), *v.t.* **1** make slower: *Don't slacken your efforts till the work is done.* **2** make looser: *Slacken the rope.*

**slat tern** (slat′ərn), *n.* woman or girl who is dirty, careless, or untidy in her dress, her housekeeping, etc. [origin uncertain]

**sledge** (slej), *n., v.,* **sledged, sledg ing.** —*n.* a heavy sled or sleigh, usually pulled by horses. —*v.i.* ride in a sledge. —*v.t.* carry on a sledge. [< Dutch *sleedse*]

**slouch hat,** a soft hat, usually with a broad brim that bends down easily.

**smelt er** (smel′tər), *n.* **1** person whose work or business is smelting ores or metals. **2** furnace for smelting ores.

**so lem ni ty** (sə lem′nə tē), *n., pl.* **-ties.** solemn feeling; seriousness; impressiveness.

**so lic i tous** (sə lis′ə təs), *adj.* **1** showing care or concern; anxious; concerned: *Parents are solicitous for their children's progress in school.* **2** desirous; eager: *solicitous to please.* [< Latin *sollicitus* < *sollus* all + *ciere* arouse] —**so lic′i tous ly,** *adv.*

**sol stice** (sol′stis), *n.* either of the two times in the year when the sun is at its greatest distance from the celestial equator and appears to be farthest north or south in the heavens. [< Old French < Latin *solstitium* < *sol* sun + *sistere* stand still]

**sor rel** (sôr′əl, sor′əl), *adj.* reddish-brown. —*n.* **1** a reddish brown. **2** horse having this color. [< Old French *sorel* < *sor* yellowish-brown]

**sou** (sü), *n.* **1** a former French coin, worth 5 centimes or $\frac{1}{20}$ of a franc. **2** anything of little value. [< French, ultimately < Latin *solidus* solidus (Roman coin)]

**sov er eign** (sov′rən), *n.* **1** supreme ruler; king or queen; monarch. **2** a former British gold coin, that was equal to 20 shillings or one pound. It is sometimes used as payment to countries that only accept gold. [< Old French *soverain,* ultimately < Latin *super* over]

**sov er eign ty** (sov′rən tē), *n., pl.* **-ties. 1** supreme power or authority; supremacy: *the sovereignty of the sea.* **2** complete control by a state over its own affairs independently of external interference. **3** state, territory, community, etc., that is independent or sovereign. **4** rank, power, or jurisdiction of a sovereign.

**spasm** (spaz′əm), *n.* **1** a sudden, abnormal, involuntary contraction of a muscle or muscles. **2** any sudden, brief fit or spell of unusual energy or activity. [< Greek *spasmos* < *span* draw up, tear away]

**spec tral** (spek′trəl), *adj.* **1** of or like a specter; ghostly: *the* spectral form of a ship surrounded by fog. **2** of or produced by a spectrum: *spectral colors.* **—spec′tral ly,** *adv.*

**spew** (spyü), *v.t., v.i.* throw out; cast forth; vomit. Also, **spue.** [Old English *spīwan*] **—spew′er,** *n.*

**splay** (splā), *v.t.* **1** spread out; expand; extend. **2** make slanting; bevel. *—v.i.* **1** have or lie in a slanting direction; slope. **2** spread out; flare. *—adj.* **1** wide and flat; turned outward. **2** awkward; clumsy.

**spleen** (splēn), *n.* **1** a ductless, glandlike organ at the left of the stomach in human beings that helps filter foreign substances from the blood. **2** bad temper; spite; anger. [< Greek *splēn*]

**spo rad ic** (spə rad′ik), *adj.* **1** appearing or happening at intervals in time; occasional: *sporadic outbreaks.* **2** being or occurring apart from others; isolated. **3** occurring in scattered instances; not epidemic: *sporadic cases of scarlet fever.* [< Medieval Latin *sporadicus* < Greek *sporadikos* scattered, ultimately < *spora* a sowing] **—spo rad′i cal ly,** *adv.*

**spright ly** (sprīt′lē), *adj.,* **-li er, -li est,** *adv. —adj.* lively; gay. *—adv.* in a sprightly manner. Also, **spritely.** [< *spright,* variant of *sprite*] **—spright′li ness,** *n.*

**spurn** (spėrn), *v.t.* **1** refuse with scorn; scorn: *spurn a bribe, spurn an offer of friendship.* **2** strike with the foot; kick away. *—v.i.* oppose with scorn: *spurn at restraint. —n.* **1** disdainful rejection; contemptuous treatment. **2** a kick. [Old English *spurnan*] **—spurn′er,** *n.*

**stac ca to** (stə kä′tō), *adj.* **1** (in music) with breaks between the successive tones; disconnected; detached. **2** abrupt: *a staccato manner. —adv.* in a staccato manner. [< Italian, literally, detached]

**stal wart** (stôl′wərt), *adj.* **1** strongly built; sturdy; robust. **2** strong and brave; valiant. **3** firm; steadfast. *—n.* **1** a stalwart person. **2** a loyal supporter of a political party. [Old English *stælwierthe* serviceable < *stathol* position + *wierthe* worthy] **—stal′wart ly,** *adv.* **—stal′wart ness,** *n.*

**stam mer** (stam′ər), *v.i.* hesitate in speaking; speak haltingly, as from nervousness or embarrassment. *—v.t.* utter in this way: *stammer an excuse. —n.* a stammering; stuttering. [Old English *stamerian*] **—stam′mer er,** *n.* **—stam′mer ing ly,** *adv.*

**stealth y** (stel′thē), *adj.,* **stealth i er, stealth i est.** done in a secret manner; secret; sly: *The cat crept in a stealthy way toward the bird.* **—stealth′i ly,** *adv.* **—stealth′i ness,** *n.*

**step** (step), *v.,* **stepped, step ping.** *—v.t.* **1** measure (*off*) by taking steps; pace (*off*): *Step off the distance from the door to the window.* **2** make or arrange like a flight of steps. **3** set (a mast) in place; fix or place in a support.

**stint** (stint), *v.t.* limit; restrict: *to stint expenses, to stint oneself on meals. —v.i.* be saving; get along on very little. *—n.* **1** limit; limitation: *give without stint.* **2** amount or share set aside. **3** task assigned: *Washing the breakfast dishes was her daily stint.* [Old English *styntan* to blunt] **—stint′er,** *n.* **—stint′ing ly,** *adv.*

**stol id** (stol′id), *adj.* hard to arouse; not easily excited; showing no emotion; seeming dull; impassive. [< Latin *stolidus*] **—sto lid i ty** (stə lid′ə tē), *n.* **—stol′id ly,** *adv.* **—stol′id ness,** *n.*

**strat a gem** (strat′ə jəm), *n.* scheme or trick for deceiving an enemy; trickery. [< Greek *stratēgēma* < *stratēgein* be a general < *stratēgos* general.]

**stren u ous** (stren′yü əs), *adj.* **1** very active: *We had a strenuous day moving into our new house.* **2** full of energy: *a strenuous worker.* **3** requiring much energy: *strenuous exercise.* [< Latin *strenuus*] **—stren′u ous ly,** *adv.* **—stren′u ous ness,** *n.*

**strip ling** (strip′ling), *n.* boy just coming into manhood; youth.

**stu pe fac tion** (stü′pə fak′shən, styü′pə fak′shən), *n.* **1** a dazed or senseless condition; stupor. **2** overwhelming amazement, shock, etc.

**stu pe fy** (stü′pə fī, styü′pə fī), *v.t.,* **-fied, -fy ing.** **1** make stupid, dull, or senseless. **2** overwhelm with shock or amazement; astound: *They were stupefied by the calamity.* [< Latin *stupefacere* < *stupere* be amazed + *facere* to make] **—stu′pe fi′er,** *n.* **—stu′pe fy′ing ly,** *adv.*

**suave** (swäv), *adj.* smoothly agreeable or polite. [< Latin *suavis* agreeable] **—suave′ly,** *adv.* **—suave′ness,** *n.*

**sub ju gate** (sub′jə gāt), *v.t.,* **-gat ed, -gat ing.** **1** subdue; conquer. **2** bring under complete control; make subservient or submissive. [< Latin *subjugatum* brought under the yoke < *sub-*

| a hat | i it | oi oil | ch child | | a in about |
|---|---|---|---|---|---|
| ā age | ī ice | ou out | ng long | | e in taken |
| ä far | o hot | u cup | sh she | ə = | i in pencil |
| e let | ō open | ù put | th thin | | o in lemon |
| ē equal | ô order | ü rule | ᴛʜ then | | u in circus |
| ėr term | | | zh measure | < = derived from |

under + *jugum* yoke] **—sub′ju ga′tion,** *n.* **—sub′ju ga′tor,** *n.*

**sub mis sive** (səb mis′iv), *adj.* yielding to the power, control, or authority of another; obedient; humble. **—sub mis′sive ly,** *adv.* **—sub mis′sive ness,** *n.*

**sub ser vi ent** (səb sėr′vē ənt), *adj.* **1** slavishly polite and obedient; tamely submissive; servile. **2** useful as a means to help a purpose or end; serviceable. **—sub ser′vi ent ly,** *adv.*

**sub side** (səb sīd′), *v.i.,* **-sid ed, -sid ing.** **1** grow less; die down; become less active; abate: *The storm finally subsided.* **2** sink to a lower level: *After the rain stopped, the floodwaters subsided.* [< Latin *subsidere* < *sub-* down + *sidere* settle]

**sub tle ty** (sut′l tē), *n., pl.* **-ties.** subtle—that is, delicate, faint, or discerning—quality. Also, **subtility** or **subtilty.**

**suc cor** (suk′ər), *n.* person or thing that helps or assists; help; aid. *—v.t.* help, assist, or aid (a person, etc.). [< Old French *sucurs,* ultimately < Latin *succurrere* run to help < *sub-* up to + *currere* to run] **—suc′cor er,** *n.*

**suf fuse** (sə fyüz′), *v.t.,* **-fused, -fus ing.** overspread (with a liquid, dye, etc.): *eyes suffused with tears. At twilight the sky was suffused with color.* [< Latin *suffusum* poured under < *sub-* under + *fundere* to pour]

**sum mar i ly** (sə mer′ə lē, sum′ər ə lē), *adv.* in a summary manner; briefly; without delay.

**su per fi cial** (sü′pər fish′əl), *adj.* **1** of the surface: *superficial measurement.* **2** on the surface; at the surface: *His burns were superficial and soon healed.* **3** concerned with or understanding only what is on the surface; not thorough; shallow: *superficial education, superficial knowledge.* [< Latin *superficialis* < *superficies* surface < *super-* above + *facies* form]

**su per flu ous** (sù pėr′flü əs), *adj.* **1** more than is needed: *In writing telegrams it pays to omit superfluous words.* **2** needless; unnecessary: *A raincoat is superfluous on a clear day.* [< Latin *superfluus,* ultimately < *super-* over + *fluere* to flow] **—su per′flu ous ly,** *adv.* **—su per′flu ous ness,** *n.*

**su per sede** (sü′pər sēd′), *v.t.,* **-sed ed, -sed ing.** **1** take the place of; cause to be set aside; displace: *Electric lights have superseded gaslights.* **2** succeed and supplant; replace: *A new governor superseded the old one.* [< Latin *supersedere* be superior to, refrain from < *super-* above + *sedere* sit] **—su′per sed′er,** *n.*

**sup ple** (sup′əl), *adj.,* **-pler, -plest.** **1** bending or folding easily: *a supple birch tree, supple leather.* **2** moving easily or nimbly: *a supple dancer.* **3** readily adaptable to different ideas, circumstances, people, etc.; yielding: *a supple mind.* [< Old French *souple* < Latin *supplex* submissive < *supplicare* bend down, supplicate] **—sup′ple ness,** *n.*

**sup pli ant** (sup′lē ənt), *adj.* asking humbly and earnestly: *He sent a suppliant message for help. —n.* person who asks humbly and earnestly: *She knelt as a suppliant at the altar.* [< Middle French, present participle of *supplier* supplicate]

**sup pli ca tion** (sup′lə kā′shən), *n.* **1** a supplicating, or asking humbly and earnestly. **2** Usually, **supplications,** *pl.* a humble prayer addressed to God or a deity.

**sur mount** (sər mount′), *v.t.* **1** rise above: *That mountain surmounts all the peaks near it.* **2** be above or on top of: *A statue surmounts the monument.* **3** go up and across: *surmount a hill.* **4** overcome: *surmount difficulties.* [< Old French *surmonter* < *sur-* over + *monter* to mount] **—sur mount′a ble,** *adj.*

**sur rep ti tious** (sėr′əp tish′əs), *adj.* **1** stealthy; secret: *a surreptitious glance.* **2** secret and unauthorized; clandestine: *surrep-*

*titious meetings.* [< Latin *surrepticius* < *surripere* seize secretly < *sub-* under + *rapere* to seize] —**sur′rep ti′tious ly,** *adv.*

**sym met ri cal** (si met′rə kəl), *adj.* having symmetry; well-proportioned. —**sym met′ri cal ly,** *adv.*

**sym me try** (sim′ə trē), *n., pl.* **-tries.** a regular, balanced arrangement on opposite sides of a line or plane, or around a center or axis. [< Greek *symmetria* < *syn-* together + *metron* measure]

**tab leau** (tab′lō), *n., pl.* **-leaux** (-lōz), **-leaus. 1** a striking scene; picture. **2** representation of a picture, statue, scene, etc., by a person or group posing in appropriate costume. [< French, diminutive of *table* table]

**tac it** (tas′it), *adj.* **1** implied or understood without being openly expressed; implicit: *His eating the food was a tacit confession that he liked it.* **2** unspoken; silent: *a tacit prayer.* [< Latin *tacitum* < *tacere* be silent] —**tac′it ly,** *adv.* —**tac′it ness,** *n.*

**tac tile** (tak′təl), *adj.* **1** of or having to do with touch. **2** having the sense of touch. [< Latin *tactilis* < *tangere* to touch]

**tal is man** (tal′i smən, tal′iz mən), *n., pl.* **-mans.** stone, ring, etc., engraved with figures or characters supposed to have magic power; charm. [< French < Arabic *ṭilsam* < Greek *telesma* initiation into the mysteries < *telein* perform]

**tal low** (tal′ō), *n.* the hard fat from sheep, cows, etc., after it has been melted. It is used for making candles, soap, etc. —*v.t.* grease with tallow. [Middle English *talgh*] —**tal′low like′,** *adj.*

**tan gent** (tan′jənt), *adj.* **1** in contact; touching. **2** (in geometry) touching a curve or surface at one point but not intersecting. These circles are tangent. ∞ —*n.* **1** a tangent line, curve, or surface. **2 fly off at a tangent** or **go off at a tangent,** change suddenly from one course of action or thought to another. [< Latin *tangentem*]

**ta per** (tā′pər), *n.* a slender candle.

**taut** (tôt), *adj.* tightly drawn; tense: *a taut rope.* [Middle English *tought*] —**taut′ly,** *adv.* —**taut′ness,** *n.*

**tem pest** (tem′pist), *n.* **1** a violent windstorm, usually accompanied by rain, hail, or snow. **2** a violent disturbance. [< Latin *tempestas* < *tempus* time, season]

**te na cious** (ti nā′shəs), *adj.* **1** holding fast: *the tenacious jaws of a bulldog, individuals tenacious of their rights.* **2** stubborn; persistent; obstinate: *The tenacious salesman would not take no for an answer.* **3** able to remember; retentive: *The bright child had a tenacious memory.* [< Latin *tenacem* holding fast < *tenere* to hold] —**te na′cious ly,** *adv.* —**te na′cious ness,** *n.*

**ten ta tive** (ten′tə tiv), *adj.* **1** done as a trial or experiment; experimental: *We made tentative plans to work together for six months.* **2** hesitating: *Her tentative laugh indicated that she hadn't understood the joke.* [< Medieval Latin *tentativus* < Latin *tentare* to try] —**ten′ta tive ly,** *adv.*

**ten u ous** (ten′yü əs), *adj.* **1** thin or slight; slender: *the tenuous thread of a spider's web.* **2** having slight importance; not substantial: *a tenuous claim.* [< Latin *tenuis* thin] —**ten′u ous ly,** *adv.* —**ten′u ous ness,** *n.*

**tep id** (tep′id), *adj.* moderately or slightly warm; lukewarm. [< Latin *tepidus* < *tepere* be warm] —**te pid i ty** (ti pid′ə tē), *n.* —**tep′id ly,** *adv.* —**tep′id ness,** *n.*

**tes ti mo ny** (tes′tə mō′nē), *n., pl.* **-nies. 1** statement used for evidence or proof: *A witness gave testimony that the defendant was at home all day Sunday.* **2** evidence: *The pupils presented their teacher with a watch in testimony of their respect and affection.* See synonym study below. [Old English *thanc*, originally, thought] **Syn. 1 Evidence, testimony, proof** mean that which tends to demonstrate the truth or falsity of something. **Evidence** applies to facts that indicate, without fully proving, that something is so: *Running away was evidence of his guilt.* **Testimony** applies to any speech or action which serves as evidence of something: *Her testimony contradicted that of the preceding witness.* Proof means evidence so full and convincing as to leave no doubt or little doubt: *The signed receipt is proof that the letter was delivered.*

**tes ty** (tes′tē), *adj.,* **-ti er, -ti est.** easily irritated; impatient; petulant. [< Anglo-French *testif* headstrong < Old French *teste* head.] —**tes′ti ly,** *adv.* —**tes′ti ness,** *n.*

**thence** (ᴛHens, thens), *adv.* **1** from that place; from there: *A few miles thence is a river.* **2** for that reason; therefore. **3** from that; therefrom. **4** from that time; from then: *a few years thence.* [Middle English *thannes, thennes* < Old English *thanon*]

**thews** (thüz), *n. pl.* **1** muscles. **2** sinews. **3** bodily force; might; strength. [Old English *thēaw* habit]

**thresh** (thresh), *v.t.* separate the grain or seeds from (wheat, etc.) with a flail, a machine, etc. —*v.i.* **1** thresh grain. **2** toss about; move violently; thrash. [Old English *threscan*]

**throng** (thrông, throng), *n.* **1** a crowd; multitude. **2** a pressing or crowding; crowded condition. —*v.i.* crowd; fill with a crowd: *The people thronged the theater to see the new movie.*

**tinc ture** (tingk′chər), *n., v.,* **-tured, -tur ing.** —*n.* **1** solution of medicine in alcohol: *tincture of iodine.* **2** trace; tinge. **3** color; tint. —*v.t.* **1** give a trace or tinge to. **2** color; tint. [< Latin *tinctura* < *tingere* to tinge]

**tithe** (tīᴛH), *n., v.,* **tithed, tith ing.** —*n.* **1** one tenth. **2** one tenth of one's yearly income paid as a donation or tax for the support of the church. **3** a very small part. **4** any small tax, levy, etc. —*v.t.* **1** put a tax or a levy of a tenth on. **2** pay or pledge a tithe on. —*v.i.* give or pledge one tenth of one's income to the church or to charity. [Old English *tēotha* tenth < *tēn* ten] —**tith′er,** *n.*

**to ga** (tō′gə), *n., pl.* **-gas, -gae** (-jē). **1** a loose outer garment worn in public by citizens of ancient Rome, especially in time of peace. **2** robe of office: *the toga of royalty.* [< Latin]

**tope** (tōp), *v.t., v.i.,* **toped, top ing.** drink alcoholic liquor to excess or as a habit. [origin uncertain] —**top′er,** *n.*

**toque** (tōk), *n.* hat without a brim or with a very small brim, worn by women. [< Middle French]

**tor nad ic** (tôr nad′ik), *adj.* of or like a tornado.

**tor rent** (tôr′ənt, tor′ənt), *n.* **1** a violent, rushing stream of water. **2** a heavy downpour: *The rain came down in torrents.* **3** any violent, rushing stream; flood: *a torrent of abuse.* [< Latin *torrentem* boiling, parching]

**traipse** (trāps), *v.i.,* **traipsed, traips ing.** walk about aimlessly, carelessly, or needlessly. [origin unknown]

**toque**

**trans fig ure** (tran sfig′yər), *v.t.,* **-ured, -ur ing. 1** change in form or appearance; transform: *New paint and furnishings had transfigured the old house.* **2** change so as to glorify; exalt. —**trans fig u ra′tion,** *n.* —**trans fig′ure ment,** *n.*

**trans lu cent** (tran slü′snt, tranz lü′snt), *adj.* letting light through without being transparent: *Frosted glass is translucent.* [< Latin *translucentem* < *trans-* through + *lucere* to shine] —**trans lu′cent ly,** *adv.*

**tran spire** (tran spīr′), *v.i.,* **-spired, -spir ing. 1** take place; happen; occur: *I heard later what transpired at the meeting.* **2** leak out; become known.

**trawl** (trôl), *v.i.* **1** fish with a net by dragging it along the bottom of the sea. **2** fish with a line supported by buoys and having many hooks attached. —*v.t.* catch (fish) with such a net or line. [probably < Middle Dutch *traghel* < Latin *tragula* dragnet]

**trawl er** (trô′lər), *n.* **1** boat used in trawling. **2** one who trawls.

**trel lis** (trel′is), *n.* frame of light strips of wood or metal crossing one another with open spaces in between; lattice, especially one supporting growing vines. [< Old French *trelis,* ultimately < Latin *trilix* triple-twilled < *tri-* three + *licium* thread]

**trem or** (trem′ər), *n.* **1** an involuntary shaking or trembling: *a nervous tremor in the voice.* **2** thrill of emotion or excitement. **3** state of emotion or excitement. **4** a shaking or vibrating movement. An earthquake is sometimes called an earth tremor. [< Latin] —**trem′or less,** *adj.*

**trill** (tril), *v.t., v.i.* **1** sing, play, sound, or speak with a tremulous, vibrating sound. **2** (in music) sing or play with a trill. [< Italian *trillare*]

**troth** (trôth, troth), *n.* ARCHAIC. **1** faithfulness or fidelity; loyalty. **2** promise. **3** truth. **4** betrothal. **5 plight one's troth, a** promise to marry. **b** promise to be faithful. —*v.t.* **1** promise. **2** betroth. [Old English *trēowth* < *trēow* faith]

**trous seau** (trü′sō, trü sō′), *n., pl.* **trous seaux** (trü′sōz, trü-sōz′), **trous seaus.** a bride's outfit of clothes, linen, etc. [< French, originally, bundle]

**trun cat ed** (trung′kā tid), *adj.* having or appearing to have a part cut off or missing.

**tuft ed** (tuf′tid), *adj.* **1** furnished with a tuft or tufts. **2** formed into a tuft or tufts.

**tu le** (tü′lē), *n.* either of two species of large bulrushes common in wetlands of the southwestern United States. [< Mexican Spanish < Nahuatl *tullin*]

**tu mul tu ous** (tü mul′chü əs, tyü mul′chü əs), *adj.* **1** characterized by tumult; very noisy or disorderly; violent. **2** greatly disturbed. **3** rough; stormy. **—tu mul′tu ous ly,** *adv.* **—tumul′tu ous ness,** *n.*

**tu na** (tü′nə), *n.* **1** any of several prickly pears, especially a treelike pear of tropical America with an edible fruit. **2** the fruit itself. [< Spanish < Taino]

**tu reen** (tə rēn′), *n.* a deep, covered dish for serving soup, etc. [< French *terrine* earthen vessel, ultimately < Latin *terra* earth]

**tur ret** (tėr′it), *n.* **1** a small tower, often on the corner of a building. **2** any of various low, rotating, armored structures within which guns are mounted, as in a warship or tank. **3** a plastic bubble on the fuselage of some bombers, for machine guns and a gunner.

**ty coon** (tī kün′), *n.* **1** businessman having great wealth and power. **2** title given by foreigners to the former hereditary commanders in chief of the Japanese army; shogun. [< Japanese *taikun* < Chinese *tai* great + *kiun* lord]

**ul ster** (ul′stər), *n.* a long, loose, heavy overcoat, often belted at the waist. [< *Ulster*]

**um bra geous** (um brā′jəs), *adj.* **1** likely to take offense. **2** shady.

**un a bashed** (un′ə basht′), *adj.* not embarrassed, ashamed, or awed. **—un′a bash′ed ly,** *adv.*

**u nan i mous** (yü nan′ə məs), *adj.* in complete accord or agreement; agreed: *The vote was unanimous.* [< Latin *unanimus* < *unus* one + *animus* mind] **—u nan′i mous ly,** *adv.*

**un can ny** (un kan′ē), *adj.* **1** strange and mysterious; weird: *The trees took uncanny shapes in the darkness.* **2** so far beyond what is normal or expected as to have some special power: *an uncanny knack for solving riddles.* **—un can′ni ly,** *adv.*

**un couth** (un küth′), *adj.* not refined; awkward; clumsy; crude: *uncouth manners.* [Old English *uncūth* < *un* + *cūth* known] **—un couth′ly,** *adv.* **—un couth′ness,** *n.*

**un der mine** (un′dər min′, un′dər mīn′). *v.t.,* **-mined, -mining.** **1** make a passage or hole under; dig under: *undermine a foundation.* **2** wear away the foundations of: *a cliff undermined by waves.* **3** weaken or destroy gradually: *Many severe colds have undermined her health.*

**un du late** (*v.* un′jə lāt, un′dyə lāt′; *adj.* un′jə lit, un′jə lāt; un′dyə lit, un′dyə lāt), *v.,* **-lat ed, -lat ing,** *adj.* **—v.i.** **1** move in waves: *undulating water.* **2** have a wavy form or surface: *undulating hair, an undulating prairie.* **—adj.** wavy. [< Latin *undulatus* wavy < *unda* wave]

**un gain ly** (un gān′lē), *adj.* not gainly; awkward; clumsy.

**un im peach a ble** (un′im pē′chə bəl), *adj.* free from fault, flaw, or error; not to be doubted or questioned: *an unimpeachable fact, an unimpeachable reputation.* **—un′im peach′a bly,** *adv.*

**un mod u lat ed** (un moj′ə lāt′əd), *adj.* not modulated; not adjusted so as to tone down or soften.

**un re lent ing** (un′ri len′ting), *adj.* **1** not yielding to feelings of kindness or compassion; merciless. **2** not slackening or relaxing in severity or determination. **—un′re lent′ing ly,** *adv.* **—un′re lent′ing ness,** *n.*

**un ten ant ed** (un ten′ən tid), *adj.* not having a tenant or tenants; not occupied by a tenant.

**un wit ting** (un wit′ing), *adj.* not knowing; unaware; unconscious; unintentional. **—un wit′ting ly,** *adv.*

**un wont ed** (un wun′tid, un wōn′tid, un wôn′tid), *adj.* **1** not customary; not usual: *unwonted anger.* **2** not accustomed; not used. **—un wont′ed ly,** *adv.* **—un wont′ed ness,** *n.*

**u sur er** (yü′zhər ər), *n.* person who lends money at an extremely

| a hat | i it | oi oil | ch child | | a in about |
|-------|------|--------|----------|---|------------|
| ā age | ī ice | ou out | ng long | | e in taken |
| ä far | o hot | u cup | sh she | ə = | i in pencil |
| e let | ō open | ù put | th thin | | o in lemon |
| ē equal | ô order | ü rule | ŦH then | | u in circus |
| ėr term | | | zh measure | < = derived from |

high or unlawful rate of interest.

**u surp** (yü zėrp′, yü sėrp′), *v.t.* seize and hold (power, position, authority, etc.) by force or without right: *The king's brother tried to usurp the throne.* **—v.i.** commit usurpation. [< Latin *usurpare* < *usu* through use + *rapere* seize] **—u surp′er,** *n.*

**va grant** (vā′grənt), *adj.* **1** moving in no definite direction or course; wandering: *vagrant thoughts.* **2** wandering without proper means of earning a living. [alteration of Anglo-French *vagarant*, probably < Latin *vagari* wander]

**vale** (vāl), *n.* valley. [< Old French *val* < Latin *vallis*]

**val or** (val′ər), *n.* bravery; courage. Also, BRITISH **valour.** [< Late Latin < Latin *valere* be strong]

**vamp** (vamp), *n.* an unscrupulous flirt. **—v.t.** flirt with. [short for *vampire*]

**vaunt** (vônt, vänt), *v.t.* boast of, **—v.i.** brag or boast. **—n.** a boasting assertion or speech; brag. [< Old French *vanter* < Late Latin *vanitare* be vain, boast < *vanus* vain]

**veer** (vir), *v.i.* change in direction; shift; turn: *The wind veered to the south. The talk veered to ghosts.* **—v.t.** change the direction of: *We veered our boat.* **—n.** a change of direction; shift; turn. [< Middle French *virer*] **—veer′ing ly,** *adv.*

**veld** or **veldt** (velt, felt), *n.* the open, grass-covered plains of southern Africa, often with bushes but having few trees. [< Afrikaans *veld* < Dutch, field]

**venge ance** (ven′jəns), *n.* punishment in return for a wrong; revenge: *swear vengeance against an enemy.* [< Old French < *vengier* avenge < Latin *vindicare* < *vindex* avenger]

**ves per** (ves′pər), *n.* **1** evening. **2** an evening prayer, hymn, or service. **3** vespers or Vespers, *pl.* a church service held in the late afternoon or in the evening. [< Latin]

**ves sel** (ves′əl), *n.* **1** a large boat; ship. **2** airship. **3** a hollow holder or container. Cups, bowls, pitchers, bottles, barrels, and tubs are vessels. **4** tube carrying blood or other fluid. [< Old French < Latin *vascellum*, diminutive of *vas* vessel]

**ves tige** (ves′tij), *n.* a slight remnant; trace; mark: *Ghost stories are vestiges of a former widespread belief in ghosts.* [< French < Latin *vestigium* footprint]

**ves ture** (ves′chər), *n.* **1** clothing; garments. **2** covering.

**ve to** (vē′tō), *n., pl.* **-toes,** *adj., v.* **—n.** **1** the right or power of a president, governor, etc., to reject bills passed by a lawmaking body. **2** refusal of consent; prohibition. **—adj.** having to do with a veto: *veto power.* **—v.t.** **1** reject by a veto. **2** refuse to consent to: *My parents vetoed my plan to buy a motorcycle.* [< Latin, I forbid] **—ve′to er,** *n.*

**vex** (veks), *v.t.* **1** anger by trifles; annoy; provoke. **2** worry; trouble; harass. **3** disturb by commotion; agitate: *The island was much vexed by storms.* [< Latin *vexare*] **—vex′ing ly,** *adv.*

**vex a tion** (vek sā′shən), *n.* **1** a vexing. **2** a being vexed: *His face showed his vexation at the delay.* **3** thing that vexes.

**vi and** (vī′ənd), *n.* **1** article of food. **2 viands,** *pl.* articles of choice food. [< Old French *viande* < Late Latin *vivenda* things for living < Latin, to be lived < *vivere* to live]

**vin di cate** (vin′də kāt), *v.t.,* **-cat ed, -cat ing.** **1** clear from suspicion, dishonor, a hint or charge of wrongdoing, etc.: *The verdict of "Not guilty" vindicated him.* **2** defend successfully against opposition; uphold; justify: *The heir vindicated his claim to the fortune.* **3** assert a claim to; establish possession of. [< Latin *vindicatum* defended, avenged < *vindex* defender, avenger] **—vin′di ca′tive** (vin dik′ə tiv, vin′də kā′tiv), *adj.* **—vin′di ca′tor,** *n.*

**vir ile** (vir′əl), *adj.* **1** of, belonging to, or characteristic of a man;

manly; masculine. **2** full of manly strength or masculine vigor. **3** vigorous; forceful. [< Latin *virilis* < *vir* man]

**vis age** (viz′ij), *n.* **1** face. **2** appearance or aspect. [< Old French < *vis* face < Latin *visus* sight < *videre* to see]

**vit ri ol** (vit′rē əl), *n.* **1** sulfuric acid. **2** any of certain sulfates of metals, such as **blue vitriol,** a sulfate of copper, **green vitriol,** a sulfate of iron, or **white vitriol,** a sulfate of zinc.

**viv id** (viv′id), *adj.* **1** strikingly bright; brilliant: *Dandelions are a vivid yellow.* **2** full of life; lively: *a vivid description.* **3** strong and distinct: *a vivid memory.* **4** very active or intense: *a vivid imagination.* [< Latin *vividus* < *vivere* to live] **—viv′id ly,** *adv.* **—viv′id ness,** *n.*

**vix en** (vik′sən), *n.* **1** a female fox. **2** a bad-tempered or quarrelsome woman. [Old English *fyxen* < *fox* fox]

**vo lup tu ous** (və lup′chü əs), *adj.* giving pleasure to the senses: *voluptuous music, voluptuous beauty.* [< Latin *voluptuosus* < *voluptas* pleasure]

**vo ra cious** (və rā′shəs), *adj.* **1** eating much; greedy in eating; ravenous. **2** very eager; unable to be satisfied; insatiable. [< Latin *voracis* greedy] **—vo ra′cious ly,** *adv.* **—vo ra′cious ness,** *n.*

**vouch safe** (vouch sāf′), *v.t.,* **-safed, -saf ing.** be willing to grant or give; deign (to do or give): *The proud man vouchsafed no reply when we spoke to him.*

**vul gar** (vul′gər), *adj.* **1** showing a lack of good breeding, manners, taste, etc.; not refined; coarse; low **2** of the common people. **3** current or prevalent among people; popular; general: *vulgar prejudices.* **4** in common use; common; ordinary. [< Latin *vulgaris* < *vulgus* common people] **—vul′gar ly,** *adv.* **—vul′gar ness,** *n.*

**waft** (waft, wäft), *v.t.* carry over water or through air: *The waves wafted the boat to shore.* **—***v.i.* float. **—***n.* **1** a breath or puff of air, wind, scent, etc. **2** a waving movement; wave. **3** act of wafting. [< earlier *wafter* convoy ship < Dutch and Low German *wachter* guard] **—waft′er,** *n.*

**wain scot** (wān′skŏt, wān′skət), *n., v.,* **-scot ed, -scot ing** or **-scot ted, -scot ting.** **—***n.* **1** a lining of wood, usually in panels, on the walls of a room. **2** The lower part of the wall of a room when it is decorated differently from the upper part. **—***v.t.* line (the walls of a room), especially with wood: *a room wainscoted in oak.* [< Middle Dutch *wagenschot* < *wagen* wagon + *schot* partition]

**wane** (wān), *v.,* **waned, wan ing,** *n.* **—***v.i.* **1** lose size; become smaller gradually: *The moon wanes after it has become full.* **2** decline in power, influence, or importance: *Many great empires have waned.* **3** decline in strength or intensity: *The light of day wanes in the evening.* **4** draw to a close: *Summer wanes as autumn approaches.* **—***n.* act or process of waning. [Old English *wanian*]

**wan ton** (won′tən), *adj.* **1** without reason or excuse: *a wanton attack, wanton mischief.* **2** not moral; not chaste: *a wanton woman.* **3** frolicsome; playful: *a wanton breeze, a wanton child.* **4** not restrained: *a wanton mood.* **—***n.* a wanton person. **—***v.i.* act in a wanton manner.

**wat tle** (wot′l), *n., v.,* **-tled, -tling. —***n.* **1** Also, **wattles,** *pl.* sticks interwoven with twigs or branches; framework of wicker: *a hut built of wattle.* **2** any of various acacias of Australia, used to make wattles and in tanning. **—***v.t.* **1** make (a fence, wall, roof, hut, etc.) of wattle. **2** twist or weave together (twigs, branches, etc.). **3** bind together with interwoven twigs, branches, etc. [Old English *watol*]

**weal** (wēl), *n.* streak or ridge on the skin; welt; wale; wheal. [variant of *wale*]

**wean** (wēn), *v.t.* **1** accustom (a child or young animal) to food other than its mother's milk. **2** accustom (a person) to do without something; cause to turn away: *wean someone from a bad habit.* [Old English *wenian*]

**wel ter** (wel′tər), *v.i.* **1** roll or tumble about; wallow. **2** lie soaked; be drenched. **3** be sunk or deeply involved (in). **4** (of waves, the water, or sea) surge. **—***n.* **1** a rolling or tumbling about. **2** a surging or confused mass. **3** confusion; commotion. [< Middle Dutch and Middle Low German *welteren*]

**weth er** (we̶TH′ər), *n.* a castrated ram. [Old English]

**whet** (hwet), *v.,* **whet ted, whet ting.** **1** sharpen by rubbing: *whet a knife.* **2** make keen or eager; stimulate: *The smell of food whetted my appetite.* [Old English *hwettan*]

**whit ing** (hwī′ting), *n., pl.* **-ings** or **-ing.** a common European sea fish of the same family as the cod, used for food.

**wile** (wīl), *n.* **1** a trick to deceive; cunning way: *The serpent by his wiles persuaded Eve to eat the apple.* **2** subtle trickery; slyness; craftiness. [Old English *wīgle* magic]

**wil y** (wī′lē), *adj.,* **wil i er, wil i est.** using wiles or subtle tricks to deceive; crafty; cunning; sly: *a wily thief.* **—wil′i ly,** *adv.* **—wil′i ness,** *n.*

**wont** (wunt, wōnt, wônt), *adj.* accustomed: *He was wont to read the paper at breakfast.* **—***n.* custom; habit: *She rose early, as was her wont.* [originally past participle of Old English *wunian* be accustomed]

**wrath** (rath), *n.* **1** great anger; rage. **2** vengeance or punishment caused by anger. [Old English *wrǣththu* < *wrāth* wroth]

**wrest** (rest), *v.t.* **1** twist, pull, or tear away with force; wrench away: *She wrested the knife from her attacker.* **2** take by force: *The usurper wrested the power from the king.* **3** obtain by persistence or persuasion; wring: *Wrest a secret from someone.* [Old English *wrǣstan*] **—wrest′er,** *n.*

**writhe** (rīTH), *v.,* **writhed, writh ing. —***v.i.* **1** twist and turn; twist about: *writhe in pain. The snake writhed along the branch.* **2** suffer mentally; be very uncomfortable. **—***v.t.* twist or bend (something). [Old English *writhan*]

**wrought** (rôt), *v.* ARCHAIC. a pt. and a pp. of **work. —***adj.* **1** made: *The gate was wrought with great skill.* **2** formed with care; not rough or crude. **3** manufactured or treated; not in a raw state. **4** deeply stirred; possessed of an excited state of mind.

**wrought-up** (rôt′up′), *adj.* stirred up; excited.

**yo kel** (yō′kəl), *n.* (often considered offensive) awkward or unsophisticated person from the country; rustic. [origin uncertain]

**ze nith** (zē′nith), *n.* **1** the point in the heavens directly overhead; point opposite the nadir. **2** the highest point; apex: *At the zenith of its power Rome ruled most of Europe.* [< Old French or Medieval Latin *cenith* < Arabic *samt (ar-rās)* the way (over the head)]

# INDEX OF READING AND LITERATURE TERMS

# INDEX OF VOCABULARY EXERCISES

# INDEX OF THINKING SKILLS

# INDEX OF COMPOSITION ASSIGNMENTS

# INDEX OF ENRICHMENT ACTIVITIES

# INDEX OF FEATURES

# INDEX OF AUTHORS AND TITLES

908